HANDBOOK OF
APPLIED INVESTMENT
RESEARCH

World Scientific Handbook in Financial Economics Series

(ISSN: 2010-1732)

Series Editor: William T. Ziemba
(University of British Columbia, Canada (Emeritus), London School of Economics, UK and Korea Institute of Science and Technology, South Korea)

The Handbooks in Financial Economics (HIFE) are intended to be a definitive source for comprehensive and accessible information in the field of finance. Each individual volume in the series presents an accurate self-contained survey of a sub-field of finance, suitable for use by finance, economics and financial engineering professors and lecturers, professional researchers, investments, pension fund and insurance portfolio managers, risk managers, graduate students and as a teaching supplement.

The HIFE series will broadly cover various areas of finance in a multi-handbook series. The HIFE series has its own web page that include detailed information such as the introductory chapter to each volume, an abstract of each chapter and biographies of editors. The series will be promoted by the publisher at major academic meetings and through other sources. There will be links with research articles in major journals.

The goal is to have a broad group of outstanding volumes in various areas of financial economics. The evidence is that acceptance of all the books is strengthened over time and by the presence of other strong volumes. Sales, citations, royalties and recognition tend to grow over time faster than the number of volumes published.

Published

Vol. 9 *Handbook of Applied Investment Research*
edited by John B. Guerard & William T. Ziemba

Vol. 8 *Collected Works of Marida Bertocchi*
edited by Rita L. D'Ecclesia, Stavros A. Zenios & William T. Ziemba

Vol. 7 *Handbook of Heavy-Tailed Distributions in Asset Management and Risk Management*
by Michele Leonardo Bianchi, Stoyan V. Stoyanov, Gian Luca Tassinari, Frank J. Fabozzi & Sergio M. Focardi

Vol. 6 *World Scientific Reference on Handbook of the Economics of Wine: (In 2 Volumes)*
Volume 1: Prices, Finance, and Expert Opinion
Volume 2: Reputation, Regulation, and Market Organization
edited by Orley Ashenfelter, Olivier Gergaud, Karl Storchmann & William T. Ziemba

Vol. 5 *The World Scientific Handbook of Futures Markets*
edited by Anastasios G. Malliaris & William T. Ziemba

More information on this series can also be found at http://www.worldscientific.com/series/wshfes

World Scientific Handbook in Financial Economics Series — Vol. 9

HANDBOOK OF APPLIED INVESTMENT RESEARCH

Editors

John B. Guerard

McKinley Capital Management, USA

William T. Ziemba

University of British Columbia, Canada

London School of Economics, United Kingdom

World Scientific

NEW JERSEY • LONDON • SINGAPORE • BEIJING • SHANGHAI • HONG KONG • TAIPEI • CHENNAI • TOKYO

Published by

World Scientific Publishing Co. Pte. Ltd.

5 Toh Tuck Link, Singapore 596224

USA office: 27 Warren Street, Suite 401-402, Hackensack, NJ 07601

UK office: 57 Shelton Street, Covent Garden, London WC2H 9HE

Library of Congress Cataloging-in-Publication Data

Names: Guerard, John, editor. | Ziemba, W. T., editor.

Title: Handbook of applied investment research / editors, John B. Guerard, McKinley Capital Management, USA, William T. Ziemba, University of British Columbia, Canada, London School of Economics, United Kingdom.

Description: New Jersey : World Scientific, [2021] | Series: World scientific handbook in financial economics series, 2010-1732 ; volume 9 | Includes bibliographical references and index.

Identifiers: LCCN 2020032985 | ISBN 9789811216725 (v. 9 ; hardcover) | ISBN 9789811225185 (v. 9 ; paperback) | ISBN 9789811222634 (v. 9 ; ebook for institutions) | ISBN 9789811222641 (v. 9 ; ebook for individuals)

Subjects: LCSH: Stock price forecasting--Mathematical models. | Investments. | Portfolio management.

Classification: LCC HG4637 .H34 2021 | DDC 332.63/2042--dc23

LC record available at https://lccn.loc.gov/2020032985

British Library Cataloguing-in-Publication Data

A catalogue record for this book is available from the British Library.

For any available supplementary material, please visit
https://www.worldscientific.com/worldscibooks/10.1142/11727#t=suppl

Desk Editors: Ramya Gangadharan/Lum Pui Yee

Typeset by Diacritech Technologies Pvt. Ltd.
Chennai - 600106, India

https://doi.org/10.1142/9789811222634_fmatter

About the Editors

John B. Guerard is Director of Quantitative Research at McKinley Capital Management, in Anchorage, Alaska. He earned his AB in Economics from Duke University, MA in Economics from the University of Virginia, MSIM from the Georgia Institute of Technology, and Ph.D. in Finance from the University of Texas, Austin. John taught at the McIntire School of Commerce, the University of Virginia, Lehigh University, and Rutgers University. John taught as an adjunct faculty member at the International University of Monaco, New York University, and the University of Pennsylvania. He worked with the DAIS Group at Drexel, Burnham, Lambert, Daiwa Securities Trust Company, Vantage Global Advisors, and served on the Virtual Research team at GlobeFlex Capital. John co-managed a Japanese equity portfolio with Harry Markowitz at Daiwa Securities Trust Company. While serving as Director of Quantitative Research at Vantage Global Advisors (formerly MPT Associates), Mr. Guerard was awarded the first Moskowitz Prize for research in socially responsible investing. Mr. Guerard has published several monographs, including *Corporate Financial Policy and R&D Management* (Wiley, 2006, second edition), *Quantitative Corporate Finance* (Springer, 2007, with Eli Schwartz, second edition in preparation), *The Handbook of Portfolio Construction: Contemporary Applications of Markowitz Techniques* (Springer, 2010), *Introduction to Financial Forecasting in Investment Analysis* (Springer, 2013), and *Portfolio and Investment Analysis*

using SAS (SAS Press, 2019, with Ganlin Xu). John serves as an Associate Editor of the *Journal of Investing* and The International Journal of Forecasting. Mr. Guerard has published research in The *International Journal of Forecasting, Management Science*, the *Journal of Forecasting, Journal of Investing, Research in Finance,* the *IBM Journal of Research and Development, Research Policy,* and the *Journal of the Operational Research Society.*

William T. Ziemba is the Alumni Professor (Emeritus) of Financial Modeling and Stochastic Optimization in the Sauder School of Business, University of British Columbia where he taught from 1968–2006. His PhD is from the University of California, Berkeley. He currently teaches part time and makes short research visits to various universities. At present he is the Distinguished Visiting Research Associate, Systemic Risk Centre, London School of Economics. He has been a Visiting Professor at Cambridge, Oxford, London School of Economics, University of Reading and Warwick in the UK, at Stanford, UCLA, Berkeley, MIT, University of Washington and Chicago in the US, Universities of Bergamo, Venice and Luiss in Italy, the Universities of Zurich, Cyprus,Tsukuba (Japan), KAIST (Korea), and the National University and the National Technological University of Singapore. He has been a consultant to a number of leading financial institutions including the Frank Russell Company, Morgan Stanley, Buchanan Partners, RAB Hedge Funds, Gordon Capital, Matcap, Ketchum Trading, and in the gambling area to the BC Lotto Corporation, SCA Insurance, Singapore Pools, Canadian Sports Pool, Keeneland Racetrack, and some racetrack syndicates in Hong Kong, Manila and Australia. His research is in asset-liability management, portfolio theory and practice, security market imperfections, Japanese and Asian financial markets, hedge fund strategies, risk management, sports and lottery investments, and applied stochastic programming. His co-written practitioner paper on the

Russell–Yasuda model won second prize in the 1993 Edelman Practice of Management Science Competition. He has been a futures and equity trader and hedge fund and investment manager since 1983. He has published widely in journals such as *Operations Research, Management Science, Mathematics of OR, Mathematical Programming, American Economic Review, Journal of Economic Perspectives, Journal of Finance, Journal of Economic Dynamics and Control, JFQA, Quantitative Finance, Journal of Portfolio Management* and *Journal of Banking and Finance* and in many books and special journal issues. Recent books include *Applications of Stochastic Programming* with S W Wallace, SIAMMPS (2005), *Stochastic Optimization Models in Finance*, 2nd edition with R G Vickson, World Scientific (2006) and *Handbook of Asset and Liability Modeling*, Volume 1: *Theory and Methodology* (2006) and Volume 2: *Applications and Case Studies* (2007) with S A Zenios, North Holland, *Scenarios for Risk Management and Global Investment Strategies* with Rachel Ziemba, Wiley (2007), *Handbook of Investments: Sports and Lottery Betting Markets*, with Donald Hausch, North Holland, 2008, *Optimizing the Aging, Retirement and Pensions Dilemma* with Marida Bertocchi and Sandra Schwartz (2010, 2015 (2nd edn.)) and *The Kelly Capital Growth Investment Criterion* (2010), with legendary hedge fund trader Edward Thorp and Leonard MacLean, *Calendar Anomalies and Arbitrage, The Handbook of Financial Decision Making* (with Leonard MacLean) and *Stochastic Programming* (with Horand Gassman), published by World Scientific in 2012 and 2013. Ziemba along with Orley Ashenfelter, Karl Stortzman and Olivier Gergard published a two volume handbook on the Economics of Wine in 2018, and the Handbook Futures Markets along with Tassos Mallaris was published in 2016. He is the series editor for North Holland's Handbooks in Finance, World Scientific Handbooks in Financial Economics and Books in Finance, and previously was the CORS editor of INFOR and the department of finance editor of *Management Science*, 1982–1992. He has continued his columns in *Wilmott* and his 2013 book with Rachel Ziemba have the 2007–2013 columns updated with new material published by World Scientific. Ziemba, along with Hausch, wrote the famous *Beat the Racetrack* book (1984), which was revised into *Dr Z's Beat the Racetrack* (1987), which presented their place and show betting system and the *Efficiency of Racetrack Betting Markets* (1994, 2008) — the so-called bible of racetrack syndicates. Their 1986 book *Betting at the Racetrack* extends this efficient inefficient market approach to simple exotic bets. Ziemba revised BATR into Exotic Betting at the Racetrack (World Scientific) which adds Pick 3, 4, 5, 6, etc., and the book was published in 2018. It has real bets he made across the world. Finally he has just completed *The Adventures of a Modern Renaissance Academic in Investing and Gambling*, a memoir and financial history of his investment activities over the last fifty years and *Great Investment Ideas*, which has all twelve of his applied investment papers published in the *Journal of Portfolio Management*. These hard to find papers cover many important topics including the evaluation of the greatest investors. Recent books include *Dr Z's NFL Guidebook* with Leonard Maclean, *Stock Market Crashes* with Sebastien Lleo and Mikhail Zhitlukhin, *Exotic Betting at the Racetrack, Collected Works of Marida Bertocchi* with Rita D'Ecclesia and Stavros Zenios.

https://doi.org/10.1142/9789811222634_fmatter

About the Contributors

Petra Bakosova's background is in algorithmic trading across multiple asset classes, quantitative research, and risk management. She joined Hull Investments, LLC, in 2014, and worked on projects for its proprietary trading firm Ketchum Trading, LLC, before transferring to its quantitative asset management unit HTAA, LLC, where she currently serves as the Chief Operating Officer. Ms. Bakosova holds an M.S. in Financial Mathematics and an M.B.A. from the University of Chicago. She pursued her undergraduate studies in applied mathematics at the Comenius University in Bratislava, Slovakia and Halmstad University in Halmstad, Sweden.

Bijan Beheshti, Vice President, Director of Risk and Quantitative Analytics Strategy at FactSet. Prior to his current role, he headed FactSet's Quantitative Analytics Specialist team across the Americas. He joined FactSet as a Consultant in 2010. Mr. Beheshti has published articles on global stock selection and portfolio construction in the *Journal of Investing*, *International Journal of Forecasting*, and *Frontiers in Applied Mathematics and Statistics*. Mr. Beheshti earned his B.A. in Economics at the University of California, Los Angeles and is a CFA charterholder, a U.S. CPA, and a certified Financial Risk Manager.

Brian R. Bruce is the CEO and Chief Investment Officer of Hillcrest Asset Management, an employee-owned institutional investment manager. Under Brian, Hillcrest has won numerous awards for outstanding investment performance. Before founding Hillcrest,

Brian was Chief Investment Officer at PanAgora Asset Management, a subsidiary of Putnam Investments. Previously, Brian held senior investment roles at State Street Global Advisors and the Northern Trust Co. Brian received his MBA. from the University of Chicago, M.S. from DePaul University, and B.S. from Illinois State University. He is a member of the Illinois State University College of Business Hall of Fame, is a recipient of the University of Chicago Graduate School of Business CEO Award, and was awarded the SMU Cox School of Business Media Expert of the Year Award.

Brian has published numerous scholarly articles and books including *Analysts, Lies, and Statistics,* which he co-authored with former Harvard Business School Professor Mark Bradshaw. He co-authored the only textbook for student managed portfolios, *Trading and Money Management.* He is the Editor of *Journal of Investing*, the *Journal of Index Investing* and the *Journal of Behavioral Finance.* Brian has been an adjunct professor at Baylor University and was Director of the Finance Institute and Founding Director of the Alternative Asset Management Center at the Cox School of Business at Southern Methodist University.

Constantine S. Dzhabarov is a senior research analyst in Vancouver, BC, Canada. His M.B.A with honors is from the Atkinson Graduate School of Management, Salem, Oregon. He has more than 20 years of experience in theoretical development and practical testing of intermarket financial trading models and investment strategies. He has traded futures and options for private and institutional accounts since 2001. His research is in security market imperfections and investment strategies. He has published joint papers in the *Journal of Portfolio Management*, Zack's *Handbook of Anomalies*, Ziemba's *Calendar Anomalies And Arbitrage*, and this Guerard and Ziemba's *Handbook of Equity Market Strategies.* He works with Ziemba as a researcher and analyst for the Alpha Z Futures Fund, LLC, and private accounts.

Harvey Fram, CFA, Chief Investment Officer, founded Constantia Capital in 2013, and is the Portfolio Manager for its Merger-Arbitrage, Large-Cap 130/30, and Small-Cap 130/30 strategies.

Prior to that, he was the Lead Portfolio Manager for the core equity team of Madison Square Investors, subsidiary of New York Life, for 13 years. He took over management of the Large-Cap Enhanced strategy in 2000 while developing the Mid, Small-Cap Core, and 130/30 offerings. As lead PM, he oversaw assets increasing from $15 million to over $5 billion. Before joining New York Life, Harvey was a quantitative equity research analyst at ITG, a leading technology-based equity brokerage firm. Preceding that position, he was a portfolio manager for international equity derivatives at the Palladin Group, a hedge fund. Harvey earned his M.B.A from the Wharton School at the University of Pennsylvania. He also earned degrees in Electrical Engineering from the University of the Witwatersrand and in Computer Science from the University of Cape Town in South Africa.

Sander Gerber has more than 25 years of investing experience in multiple securities classes and derivatives across a broad range of strategies. In 1991, he became a member of the American Stock Exchange, acting as an options market maker. In 1997, he founded Gerber Asset Management LLC ("GAM") to develop and engage in proprietary investment strategies, many of which are utilized by Hudson Bay today. In 2005, assisted by key employees of GAM, Mr. Gerber founded Hudson Bay, which absorbed GAM's business and 15 employees. Hudson Bay is now a multi-billion dollar hedge fund with offices in New York and London. Mr. Gerber graduated cum laude from the University of Pennsylvania, with a B.S.E in Finance from Wharton and a B.A. in Humanistic Philosophy from the College of Arts and Sciences. Mr. Gerber is a member of the Council on Foreign Relations and The Economic Club of New York. Mr. Gerber was formerly both the Vice Chair of the Board of Trustees and Chairman of the endowment investment committee of the Woodrow Wilson Center for Scholars, a public policy research center within the Smithsonian Institution.

Robert A. Gillam serves as McKinley Capital Management, LLC's Chief Executive Officer and Chief Investment Officer. Rob has been with the firm since 1994 in roles including sales, portfolio manager, and head of international investments. He is the principal strategist behind McKinley Capital innovations including Non-U.S., MEASA, Global Healthcare, the Engineering and Solutions platform, and most recently, Private Investment. As CEO/CIO, Rob is responsible for the firm's business strategy and investment process. He is supported by a robust management team and a governing Board of Directors. Rob established McKinley Capital's Scientific Advisory Board chaired by Dr. Harry Markowitz, Ph.D, winner of the Nobel Prize in Economics and founder of Modern Portfolio Theory.

Rob is an Advisory Board Member of the Jacobs Levy Equity Management Center for Quantitative Financial Research at the Wharton School. He sits on the Wharton Global Family Alliance and the Rasmuson Foundation investment committee. Rob has written numerous pieces of research including Investing in Global Equity Markets with Particular Emphasis on Chinese Stocks co-authored with Dr. Harry Markowitz, Ph.D., Dr. John B. Guerard Jr., Ph.D., and Dr. Shijie Deng. A noted speaker, Rob has been featured on the Bloomberg Invest forum, at the Milken Institute Global Conference, and the Institute for Fiduciary Education.

Rob holds a Bachelor's Degree in Finance from the Wharton School at the University of Pennsylvania, and is a CFA. Rob, his wife, and two sons reside in Anchorage, Alaska, where he enjoys fly-fishing, hiking, and wilderness adventures. A third-generation Alaskan, Rob is passionate about his home state and the unique opportunities found in the Last Frontier.

Blair Hull founded Hull Investments, LLC, in 1999 and currently serves as the firm's Chairman. Hull Investments was created to serve as a family office for three generations of the Hull family, and acts as parent company to a number of financial entities. Mr. Hull created Hull Tactical Asset Allocation, LLC, a registered investment advisor, in 2013. HTAA operates an actively managed ETF and utilizes advanced algorithms as well as macro and technical indicators to anticipate future market returns. Prior to launching Hull Tactical

Asset Allocation, LLC, Mr. Hull was the founder of Hull Trading Company and served as that firm's Chairman and Chief Executive Officer. Hull Trading Company leveraged technological innovations and quantitative models in the field of listed derivatives market-making. At its peak, the company traded on 28 exchanges in nine countries and moved nearly a quarter of the entire daily market volume on some markets, executed over 7% of the index options traded in the United States, 3% of the equity options, and 1% of all shares traded daily on the New York Stock Exchange.

Alexander Kment joined the team as a Financial Engineer at the beginning of 2016. Mr. Kment received his Master's of Science in Financial Engineering from the University of Illinois at Urbana-Champaign. He has earned his CFA chartership and holds the FRM designation as well.

Foteini Kyriazi is Managing Director at OPEKEPE, the Greek Payment Authority of Common Agricultural Policy Aid Schemes. She holds a Masters in Public Administration and a Ph.D. in Econometrics and Agricultural Economics. She is currently a post doctoral researcher at Agricultural University of Athens. Her work concentrates on the methodological aspects of forecasting, with emphasis in agricultural prices, and on the regional impact on economic growth of the Common Agricultural Policy subsidy schemes.

Tim Leung is a tenured professor of Applied Mathematics and the director of the Computational Finance & Risk Management (CFRM) program at University of Washington in Seattle. Previously, he had been an assistant professor at Johns Hopkins University and Columbia University. He obtained his B.S. from Cornell University and Ph.D. from Princeton University. His research areas are quantitative finance and stochastic optimal control, with applications to portfolio optimization, algorithmic trading, and risk management. He has published over 60 peer-reviewed articles and two books on the topics of Mean Reversion Trading and ETFs. He's the Chair for the Institute for Operations Research and Management Sciences

(INFORMS) Finance Section. In 2016, he won the Emerald Literati Network Award.

Chong Li is a Ph.D. candidate at Sichuan University. He worked on the chapter during his stay at Duke as a Visiting Scholar. His research interests include mutual funds, macro finance, and monetary policy.

Sébastien Lleo is Associate Professor of Finance at NEOMA Business School (France) and is the 2020 Bruti-Liberati Fellow at the Quantitative Finance Research Center, University of Technology Sydney (Australia). He is also a tutor on the Certificate in Quantitative Finance at Fitch Learning (UK). He joined NEOMA Business School in 2010 and served as Director of the Doctoral School for 5 years, during which he developed the Ph.D. in Management and a DBA in partnership with Shanghai Jiao Tong University. Sébastien started his career at the Bank of Canada and Canada Mortgage and Housing Corporation. Sébastien co-authored books on risk-sensitive stochastic control and stock market crashes, authored a monograph on risk management commissioned by the CFA Institute, and published more than 20 articles in academic and professional journals. He earned a Ph.D. in Mathematics from Imperial College London (UK), HDR in Social Science from Conservatoire national des arts et métiers (France), M.B.A from University of Ottawa (Canada), and M.Sc. in Management from NEOMA Business School (France). He is also a CFA Charterholder, Certified Financial Risk Manager, Professional Risk Manager, and CQF alumnus.

Harry Markowitz, President, Harry Markowitz Company. Markowitz has applied computer and mathematical techniques to various practical decision-making areas. In finance: in an article in 1952 and a book in 1959 he presented what is now referred to as MPT, "modern portfolio theory." This has become a standard topic in college courses and texts on investments, and is widely used by institutional investors and financial advisors for asset allocation, risk control, and attribution analysis. In other areas: Dr. Markowitz developed "sparse matrix" techniques for solving very large mathematical optimization problems. These techniques are now standard in production software for optimization programs. Dr. Markowitz also designed and supervised the development of the SIMSCRIPT programming language. SIMSCRIPT has been widely used for programming computer simulations of systems like factories, transportation systems, and communication networks.

In 1989, Dr. Markowitz received The John von Neumann Award from the Operations Research Society of America for his work in portfolio theory, sparse matrix techniques, and SIMSCRIPT. In 1990 he shared The Nobel Prize in Economics for his work on portfolio theory. Dr. Markowitz is the principal of Harry Markowitz Company (contact: HarryHMM@aol.com). He is also an adjunct professor at the Rady School of Management, UCSD.

Russell Read is Group Managing Partner for the C Change Group of investment funds, companies, and advisors, dedicated to materially transforming the production, distribution, and consumption of natural resources around the globe. In addition, Dr. Read serves as Senior Advisor to MSCI with respect to crafting solutions for the global asset owner community. Prior to C Change, he was Chief Investment Officer (CIO) of the Alaska Permanent Fund Corporation, the Gulf Investment Corporation (GIC), and the California Public Employees' Retirement System (CalPERS).

Dr. Read has been a resource for regulatory agencies internationally, state governments, the US Congress, and the US Senate for over two decades and served as Chairman of the Investors' Committee of the President's Working Group on Financial Markets under Treasury Secretary Henry Paulson. He was named as one of America's 30 most influential players in business and finance by SmartMoney and #35 on Institutional Investor's list of the 75 most effective chief executives.

Dr. Read received his undergraduate degree in Statistics and his MBA in Finance and International Business both from the University of Chicago and his masters in Economics and doctorate in Political Economy from Stanford University. His doctoral work The Politics and Policies of National Economic Growth focused on the particular economic roles of natural resources in economic development. He has taught graduate-level courses at the University of California at Davis, the University of Maine, and Stanford University.

Barret Pengyuan Shao is a Senior Quantitative Researcher at Evince Asset Management. He received his B.S. in automatic control from Xiamen University, B.S. in mathematical economics from Wangyanan Institute for Studies in Economics (WISE) in China, and Ph.D. in applied mathematics and statistics (quantitative finance) from Stony Brook University.

David Starer is Director of Research at Constantia Capital. He develops quantitative alpha prediction models, risk models, and optimization methods. Before joining Constantia Capital, he held senior positions at leading investment firms including Quantitative Management Associates, Jacobs Levy Equity Management, Delaware Investments, and Lend Lease Investment Management. He was a Professor of Financial Engineering at Stevens Institute of Technology where he taught portfolio theory and practice, statistics, mathematical methods, options pricing, and machine learning. David received his Ph.D. in Electrical Engineering (specializing in statistical signal processing) from Yale University, his M.Eng. (with Distinction) in Microelectronics from the University of Pretoria, and his B.Sc. (with First Class Honors) in Electrical Engineering from the University of Cape Town in South Africa.

Douglas E. Stark is a Managing Director of Hillcrest Asset Management, an employee-owned institutional investment manager. He is a portfolio manager and responsible for the quantitative modeling and research at Hillcrest. Before joining Hillcrest, Douglas was Director of Research at Martingale Asset Management. Previously, Douglas held senior investment roles at State Street Global Advisors and InterCoast Capital. Douglas Stark received his M.B.A. from Columbia University. He is a Chartered Financial Analyst.

Dimitrios Thomakos is Head of Department and Professor in Applied Econometrics at the University of Peloponnese and Senior Fellow at the Rimini Center for Economic Analysis. He holds an

M.A., M.Phil., and Ph.D. degrees in Economics from Columbia University and a Bachelor's degree in Economics from the University of Athens. His current research focuses on methodological innovations and learning in forecasting, and financial econometrics. He currently serves at the Board of Directors of Eurobank Asset Management MFMC in Athens and Luxembourg. His academic research, individual and with many collaborators, has appeared in several leading, peer-reviewed academic journals, including *the Review of Economics and Statistics, the Journal of Empirical Finance, the International Journal of Forecasting, the Journal of Forecasting,* the *Canadian Journal of Economics*, the *Journal of International Financial Markets, Institutions and Money,* the *Journal of International Money and Finance, the European Financial Management, the International Review of Financial Analysis* and many others. He is the co-author of the volume *Forecasting with the Theta Method* (Wiley, 2019) and *Financial Forecasting in the Chinese Stock Market* (Peking University Press, 2020, with John Guerard). The Theta model was the leading forecasting method in the M-forecasting competitions. Dimitrios is co-editor of the volumes *A Financial Crisis Manual* and *Taxation in Crisis.* He is the co-founder of the *quantf* ©research website and the co-director of *ForTank*, the forecasting think tank.

Edward Tower is a Professor of Economics at Duke University and a Visiting Professor at Chulalongkorn University. He has held positions at Australian National University, the University of Auckland, Claremont Graduate University, Helsinki School of Economics and Business, Nanjing University, Simon Fraser University, Tufts University, Venice International University, and the University of Zagreb. He has consulted at the Harvard Institute for International Development, the World Bank, and the U.S. Agency for International Development, and in Australia, Indonesia, Kenya, Malawi, and Sudan. He loves free trade, flexible exchange rates, and Jack Bogle. He has served on 11 editorial boards, written or coauthored 4 books & monographs, and 136 articles in journals from A to Z: the *American Economic Review* to the *Zagreb Journal of Economics*, and he has compiled 115 books on the teaching of economics. He earned his B.A. in Physics and Ph.D. in Economics at Harvard.

Hrishikesh D. Vinod is a Ph.D. in Economics from Harvard University. He has published over 150 research papers in refereed journals in Economics and Statistics. He has coedited vols. 9, 41, and 42 of the *Handbook of Statistics* with the great statistician Dr. C. R. Rao. In 2008, he published a book entitled *Hands-on Intermediate Econometrics Using R: Templates for Extending Dozens of Practical Examples.* World Scientific Publishers: Hackensack, NJ, 2008. (http://www.worldscibooks.com/economics/6895.html). A similar hands-on matrix algebra book was published in 2011. He worked in the prestigious pure research area at Bell Laboratories for many years and was an expert witness on major anti-trust cases. Since 1982 he has been a tenured full professor of Economics at the 160+-year old Fordham University in New York. Currently, he is the Director of the Institute of Ethics and Economic Policy at Fordham University. His publications are in diverse areas of statistics, econometrics, and economics. He has been cited by other researchers some 2887 times, according to ResearchGate. He is a co-author of an R package called "meboot" for maximum entropy bootstrap and "generalCor" for causality testing.

His recent awards include:

Fellow: International Institute of Public Ethics, Nathan, Queensland, Australia.

Outstanding Social Service Award, Maharashtra Foundation,

Journal of Econometrics Fellow.

Brian Ward is an execution researcher at AQR Capital Management. In this role, Brian focuses on market impact modeling, optimal trade scheduling, and conducts research on intraday price dynamics for equities, futures, and spot FX. Beyond execution research, Brian's research interests include index tracking, (L)ETFs price dynamics, as well as statistical arbitrage strategies and machine learning applied to finance. Brian holds a Ph.D. in Operations Research from Columbia University, and a B.S. and an M.S.E. in Applied Mathematics and Statistics from Johns Hopkins University.

Rhona Zhang is earning her B.A. in Economics at Northwestern University. She worked on the chapter during her senior year at the North Carolina School of Science and Mathematics. Her current research interests include mutual funds and microeconomics.

Mikhail Zhitlukhin is a senior research fellow at Steklov Mathematical Institute of the Russian Academy of Sciences in Moscow, Russia. His main research interests include stochastic calculus, optimal control, statistics of random processes, and their applications in economics and finance. He has published 25 papers in various journals and co-authored the book *Stock Market Crashes* (with W. T. Ziemba and S. Lleo). Mikhail received a Ph.D. (Candidate of Science) in Mathematics from the Russian Academy of Sciences and a Ph.D. in Economics from the University of Manchester, UK in 2013.

Alexandre Ziegler is director of the Center for Portfolio Management at the Institute of Banking and Finance of the University of Zurich. His research interests include theoretical and empirical asset pricing, information acquisition models, and applied game theory.

His research has appeared in books and in academic journals including *AEA Papers and Proceedings*, the *European Economic Review*, the *Journal of Financial Economics*, the *Journal of Financial Intermediation*, the *Journal of Mathematical Economics, Quantitative Finance*, and the *Review of Financial Studies*. In 2003, he was awarded the Latsis Prize for his work on incomplete information and heterogeneous beliefs.

He has extensive experience in quantitative asset management and software development and is the inventor or co-inventor of several patented software innovations.

He holds an M.B.A from Stanford University as well as a Ph.D. in Finance and a Habilitation in Economics from the University of St. Gallen.

Prior to joining the University of Zurich, he was Assistant Professor of Finance at the University of Lausanne.

https://doi.org/10.1142/9789811222634_fmatter

Acknowledgments

I became the Director of Quantitative Research at McKinley Capital Management, in Anchorage, Alaska in 2005. I have worked for Robert B. (Bob) and Robert A. (Rob) Gillam in the area of Applied Investment Research of equity securities. When I worked for Harry Markowitz at Daiwa Securities, we built and ran money to outperform the markets using all variables, regression techniques, and models. At McKinley Capital, we were "global growth specialists" using models containing only "growth" variables in proprietary models. We do not run monthly cross-sectional regression models using 175 independent variables, as many of our peers do. We, at McKinley Capital, were asset managers; hence, we publish research using only our "Public Model", not our proprietary model. Our public model factors are input to create a regression-based model with a global growth "footprint" and a set of exposures to growth and momentum. The reader of this volume can see my 1993 paper with Harry and Ganlin and note how modeling has changed (and yet remains very similar and statistically significant in most periods) compared to the research and modeling techniques that we used in the early 1990s. I want to acknowledge the support of Bob and Rob Gillam. Regrettably, Bob passed away several months ago. He will be greatly missed.

I appreciate the love and support of my wife, Julie, who has been extremely supportive in our 38 years of marriage, the last 30 years in a Wall Street setting. Our three children, Richard, Katherine, and Stephanie, have (more often than not) been sources of great joy. I have met many very smart, hard-working, and honorable people on the Wall Street. Many of the people I have met are exceptional and have contributed to this volume. One of the most humbling experiences on the Wall Street is regardless of how intelligent you might be, regardless of how hard you work, there are always smarter people in our community. I had great experiences with the authors of papers in this handbook, including Harry Markowitz, Ganlin Xu, Rob Gillam, Chris Mercs, Bijan Beheshti, Dimitrios Thomakos, Ed Tower, Brian Bruce, Tim Leung, Rick Vinod, Petra Bakosova, Blair Hull, David Starer, Barret Shao, and Boryana Racheva-Iotova. I have worked with several of these authors on volumes to honor Harry Markowitz and Jack Treynor, and these authors never fail to impress me with their intelligence and hard work over the past decade. Why do we publish in a Wall Street environment? It is to demonstrate expertise. I would like to acknowledge the friendship and support of Harry Markowitz, Bill Sharpe, Marty Gruber, Andrew Lo, Ganlin Xu, Bernell Stone, Ralph Steuer, Doug Martin, and Zari Rachev. I would also like to specially acknowledge the friendship and support of Bill Ziemba on this volume.

— *John B. Guerard*

This handbook of investment strategies presents a number of very good papers and ideas for successful short-term trading and long-term investing. John Guerard and I collaborate to showcase viewpoints from two important angles. Guerard has worked for many years for a major large financial institution whose goals include long-term capital growth risk adjustment. He is an expert and leading practitioner in developing and implementing factor-based fundamental anomaly models for large-scale investing. I have some experience in developing such models and his Japanese monthly factor model and its use are described in the handbook. However, my main contributions are in other areas, especially calendar anomalies, capital growth theory and practice and speculative hedge fund-type trading with short-term and long-term goals. I was hence pleased to join John Guerard to prepare this handbook. Together, we have presented useful new papers and ideas, and complemented these with reprints of major published papers that are hard to locate. They are all now in one place for easy reference. In the new and reprinted papers

I wrote or co-wrote, I had excellent co-workers, including Constantine Dzhabarov, Michael Foster, Sebastien lleo, Leonard MacLean Alex Ziegler and Mikhail Zhitlukhin. Along the way, discussions with many people were helpful, including my Japanese colleagues during my visit in 1988–1989, Ed Thorp, Sandra Schwartz and Rachel Ziemba.

—*William T. Ziemba*

https://doi.org/10.1142/9789811222634_fmatter

Contents

https://doi.org/10.1142/9789811222634_fmatter

Introduction

John B. Guerard., Jr.
McKinley Capital Management, LLC, USA

William T. Ziemba
University of British Columbia Emeritus and Distinguished Research Associate, The London School of Economics (LSE) London, United Kingdom

In this Handbook, we present both original research studies and reprints of articles addressing applied investment research, focusing on fundamental and calendar anomalies, and new investment methodologies and markets that have developed over the past 30 years. In 1991, the co-editors presented research at the Berkeley Program in Finance, in Santa Barbara. John Guerard was employed in Harry Markowitz's Daiwa Securities Global Portfolio Research Department. William (Bill) Ziemba was the Alumni Professor of Financial Modeling and Stochastic Optimization at the Sauder School of Business, University of British Columbia (where he taught from 1968–2006). John presented, with Harry Markowitz and his team, research on both U.S. and Japanese equity markets. Harry Markowitz would win the Nobel Prize in Economics within 6 months. We reprint the paper that evolved from the Berkeley Program presentation, entitled "A Comparison of Some Aspects of the U.S. and Japanese Equity Markets", *Japan & the World Economy* **5** (1993), 3–26. Professor Ziemba was presenting research that developed from his 1988–1989 term as the Yamaichi Visiting Professor of Finance, Tsukuba University, that would appear in his "Japanese

Security Market Regularities: Monthly, Turn-of-the-month and year, Holiday, and Golden Week Effects", *Japan and the World Economy* **3**, 119–146, and *Invest Japan* (his Probus 1992 monograph with Sandra Schwartz). During the next 30 years, John and Bill would publish many articles on market inefficiencies. Professor Ziemba co-edited with Professor Don Keim, *Security Market Imperfections in World Wide Equity Markets*, Cambridge University Press, 2000. Our Handbook seeks to reprint several of those articles as well as present new and updated research on inefficiencies in the U.S. and Japanese stock markets, futures markets, foreign exchange, and new investment markets.

Professor Ziemba opens the Handbook with an analysis of five investor groups seeking to beat the market. There is a very large set of financial economists who adhere to the Efficient Markets Hypothesis, EMH, set forth in 1959, and championed for well over 20 years by Professor Eugene Fama, of the University of Chicago. The EMH is the first group of investors who continually remind readers that well over 75% of active managers underperform indexes. Risk premium investors believe that risk factors, small cap, and low book-to-price firms produce higher returns, such that investors can outperform a simple single-factor risk model, such as the Capital Asset Pricing Model (CAPM). The Risk Premium Group has been dominated by Dimensional Fund Advisors and other large mutual fund companies with vast assets. The third camp is called Genius Group. These are superior investors who are brilliant or geniuses, but you cannot determine in advance who they are. Paul Samuelson has championed this argument. Samuelson felt that these investors do exist, but it is useless to try to search for them. You will find 19 duds for every star. This view is very close to the Merton–Samuelson (1974) criticism of the Kelly criterion: that is, even with an advantage, it is possible to lose a lot of your wealth. A fourth group is the Hogwash Group, whose members feel that Efficient Markets which originated in, and are perpetuated by the academic world, are a hogwash. In fact, the leading proponent of this view and one with whom it is hard to argue as he is right at the top of the list of the world's richest persons is Warren Buffett, who wants to endow university chairs in efficient markets to further improve his own very successful trading. An early member of this group, the great economist John Maynard Keynes, was an academic. We see also that although they may never have heard of the Kelly criterion, this camp, which includes George Soros, does seem to use it implicitly with large non-diversified bets on favorable investments. The last group are those who think that markets are beatable through behavioral biases, security market anomalies using computerized superior betting techniques. They construct risk-arbitrage situations with positive expectation. They research the strategy well and follow it for long periods of time repeating the advantage many times. This group believes that factor models are useful most but not all of the time and show that beta is not one of the most important variables to predict stock prices. They use very focused, disciplined, well-researched strategies with superior execution and risk control. Many of them use Kelly or fractional Kelly strategies. All of them extensively use computers for research, execution, and risk control. They focus on not losing, and they rarely have blowouts. Members include Ed Thorp (Princeton Newport and later funds), Bill Benter (the Hong Kong racing guru), Warren Buffett (Berkshire Hathaway), John Henry (trend follower and the Red Sox owner), Blair Hull (mispriced options trader), Harry McPike (trend follower), Jim Simons (Renaissance hedge fund), and David Swensen (Yale University endowment). Blowouts occur more in hedge funds that do not focus on not losing and true diversification and over-bet; when a bad scenario hits them, they get wiped out, such as LTCM, Niederhofer, and Amarant.

1. Fundamental Anomalies and Stock Selection Modeling

Fundamental Anomalies have been reported in the financial literature for the past 30 years. Dimson (1988) surveyed stock market anomalies and began the reporting of what has become a vast literature. Many financial economists reported large, and sometimes statistically significant, excess returns. The excess returns in the late-1980s tended to be dominated by the "small stock effect" in which small stocks outperformed large stocks by well over 400–500 basis points, over the period 1926–1976. Researchers tested the Value Line stock ranking system and reported the outperformance of stocks in January and various day-of-the week effects. The "low P/E" effect, earnings forecasting, and standardized unexpected earnings (SUE) effects were reported. Jacobs and Levy (1988), Ziemba and Schwartz (1992), and Bloch *et al.* (1993) reported fundamental-based and expectational data-based financial anomalies. The financial anomalies literature featured both fundamental, expectations, and calendar effects.

Our Handbook updates much of the fundamental, expectational, and momentum-based financial anomalies research during the 1988–2019 time period. The Editors and their co-authors have published peer-reviewed articles during the past 30 years that continue to report statistically significant Active Returns and Specific Returns. Guerard *et al.* (2013, 2014, 2015, 2020) have reported that fundamental-based financial anomalies have persisted using published models in the post-publication time period, 2003–2018. These studies were published in special issues of the *Japan and the World Economy, IBM Journal of Research and Development* issue on "Smarter Finance", and the *International Journal of Forecasting* issue on "International Financial Forecasting: Global Economic Linkages and Corporate Earnings". We reprint several of the Guerard, Markowitz, and Xu articles. These anomalies have produced statistically significant Active Returns in many portfolios, see Gillam and Guerard (2019).

Investing based on analysts' expectations, fundamental data, and momentum variables is a good investment strategy in the long run. Stock selection models often use momentum, analysts' expectations, and fundamental data. The authors find support for composite modeling using these sources of data, as well as evidence supporting the use of APT multi-factor models for portfolio construction and risk control. They develop and estimate three levels of testing for stock selection and portfolio construction. The use of multi-factor risk-controlled portfolio returns allows them to reject the data-mining corrections to test null hypothesis. Some readers may ask why the authors ended their analysis in 2011. The authors have updated their research through December 2018 and found similar results.

The anomalies literature can be applied in real-world global portfolio construction. Specifically, the authors find that companies generating larger corporate exports produce statistically significant positive active returns in portfolios. The corporate exports variable is the sum of dividends paid, interest paid, and net equity repurchased less net debt issued. Corporate exports result from dividend, debt, and equity decisions. The returns of the corporate exports portfolio can be increased by constraining the portfolio to include stocks identified by a stock selection model as being under-valued. In Chapter 4 by Guerard *et al.* (2014), the authors simulated portfolios during the January 2000–January 2013 period using a multi-factor risk model. They apply the Markowitz–Xu data mining corrections and find no evidence of data mining. The portfolios developed in this chapter are statistically different than the average model that could have been used to create portfolios.

The purpose of Chapter 6 by Beheshti, Guerard, and Mercs is to document the existence and effectiveness of variables reported as financial anomalies in 2003 and test whether these reported anomalies are statistically significant during the 2003–2018 time periods. One must create optimal portfolios to assess the predictive power of financial anomalies. We report results working exclusively on the FactSet Research Systems, Inc. (FactSet) platform. We report a "one-button" approach to portfolio construction and management that is consistent with the teachings of Harry Markowitz and William F. Sharpe, the creators of Modern Portfolio Theory, MPT. On the FactSet platform, we pull down FactSet Fundamentals financial data, the I/B/E/S earnings history, create fundamental ratios and data, run robust regression to implement a statistically significant stock selection model, create portfolios, and assess the portfolios over time (i.e., backtest the strategies). Beheshti, Guerard, and Mercs report that the expected returns modeling work of Ed Elton, Martin Gruber, and Mustafa Gultekin; William Ziemba and Sandra Schwartz; and John Guerard continues to drive stock returns. What do we add to an extensive anomaly literature? We test portfolio anomalies in a post-publication setting. We report three results: (1) many of the reported financial anomalies published in 1993–2003 time period maintained their statistical significance active (or excess) returns; (2) the anomalies are greater in non-U.S. markets than in the U.S.; and (3) transactions costs do not destroy the excess returns. The authors report highly statistically significant excess returns above transactions costs, and data mining corrections adjustments in U.S. and non-U.S. stocks during the 2003–2018 time period, using models published by the authors in 1993 and 1997, modeled with the FactSet Research Systems Inc., building directly upon the Guerard, Markowitz, and Xu articles reprinted in the Handbook.

In Chapter 3, MacLean, Foster, and Ziemba used a sample of Toronto and New York Stock Exchange stocks during the 1990–2002 time period to build a complex covariance model using a truncation model to eliminate smaller eigenvalues and eigenvectors based on a small number of factors. The truncation model is very similar in spirit to that mentioned in Chapter 2 by Guerard *et al.* (1993) on latent root regression estimator. The covariance complexity is used with a prior mean estimate to create a conditional mean rate of return model. The truncation estimator is a Bayes estimator with a prior mean and the complex covariance in the return model. The truncation model produces lower root mean square errors than Bayes–Stein estimators for the stocks. Moreover, and more importantly, the truncation model produces over 30% higher terminal wealth than the Bayes–Stein model of parameters. The growth optimal portfolio, the Kelly investment strategy, seeks to maximize the value of terminal wealth. The maximization of terminal wealth uses logarithmic utility with constant relative risk aversion.

Since Brian Bruce and Doug Stark built some of the earliest global earnings revision models at State Street in the early 1990s, it has become a factor in virtually all model-driven strategies. This model is the most popular method of determining investor sentiment. No new behavioral sentiment indicators were created until recently. A study done by UBS, "Online Search Frequency, Information Asymmetry, and Market Liquidity" uses a sentiment tool from a leading data vendor. According to the data vendor, their new tool analyzes news providing improved buy/hold/sell signals within milliseconds. They anticipate that users will be traders, market makers, and quant hedge funds. The big problem with news sentiment indicators is the ephemeral nature of news, which can turn from positive to negative multiple times daily. This is exemplified in the new tool mentioned above which provides signals within milliseconds. Hillcrest believes it is impractical and costly to find a way to incorporate such short-term information into a long-term strategy, such as ours, that has a holding period measured in years. Bruce and Stark (2020) and Hillcrest Research report a method of measuring the highly elusive sentiment within the company, or in other words, do the people working there have a strong belief in their products, personnel, and leadership? Without working at a company, it is difficult to ascertain the morale of the people developing, producing, and marketing the products sold. Finding a plentiful source of insight into companies led us to considering Earnings Call Transcripts. The transcripts had all of the necessary ingredients; they were produced on a consistent basis, followed a standard format (review of financials, new products, problems, and Q&A) which allowed for comparison between companies, and were not over-analyzed by the investment community. One of Bruce and Stark's favorite political axioms is "Never answer the question you are asked, answer the question you wish you were asked". Luckily, our business leaders are not as adept at obfuscation and de-clarification as our politicians, but they didn't get to the top of the business world without being able to deftly focus on those aspects that make them look good. The second phase of our research focused on determining when the managers are consciously or subconsciously hiding lingering doubts about potential problems. Whether these are problems such as an inventive new competitor, or an internal problem that they hope will find a solution by the next quarterly report, they don't want to talk about it, so they hide it by talking about something positive. To determine if we could find these situations, we developed "Deflection Phrases"; deflecting blame so that they will not be implicated. The Hillcrest Management Sentiment behavioral factor confirms our belief that analyzing earnings call transcripts is a profitable way to determine the internal sentiment within a company and that sentiment provides evidence of future returns. At Hillcrest, we continue to look for ways to exploit our unique knowledge of behavioral finance and the cognitive decision biases that affect executives, analysts, and money managers. We use this information to make constant improvements to our investment process.

2. Financial Anomalies and Calendar Effects

Chapter 9 by Dzhabarov and Ziemba updates the U.S. equity calendar work of Ziemba during the past 30 years. August, September, and October have historically had low stock market returns with many serious declines or crashes occurring in these months. The months of November–February have historically had higher than average returns; see, for example, Gultekin and Gultekin (1983) and various papers in Keim and Ziemba (2000), and Ziemba (2012). The strategy of this chapter avoids the bad months, choosing to be in cash then, and only be long the stock market in the good months. The strategy, which is called sell-in-May-and-go-away, or the Halloween Effect, is often discussed in the financial press.

For the S&P 500, a Buy-and-Hold (B&H) strategy turns \$1 on February 4, 1993 into \$6.71 on October 25, 2019; whereas, sell-in-May-and-move-into-cash had a final wealth of \$9.28, some 38.2% higher. For Sell-in-May, this counts interest (Fed funds' effective monthly rate) and for the Buy-and-Hold, this counts dividends (which for futures are capital gains). For the small cap Russell 2000, the final wealth ratios were \$6.67 and \$12.61, respectively, some 89.0% higher. The strategy using the rule sell on the first trading day in May and buy on the 6th trading day before the end of October indeed beats a Buy-and-Hold strategy relative to the S&P 500 Index and the Russell 2000 by about 1.5 and 2 times in final wealth, respectively, and in both cases with lower standard deviation risk. The strategy worked in most but not all years and in strategy design can be combined with other effects depending upon market conditions.

This advantage is greater in absolute total returns, but the percentage advantage was not as high as it was going to be in 2016. For example, the current advantage for the S&P 500 was 38.2% versus

84.2% from 1993–2016 and for the Russell 2000 the advantage was 89.0% versus 147.1%. This was caused by the huge rise of equity prices in the period 2016–2019. In this three-year period, the Sell-in-May and Buy-and-Hold strategies have essentially equivalent gains. For the Russell 2000, the Sell-in-May strategy had higher gains than Buy-and-Hold, but with just 3 years' data, it is not statistically significantly higher.

In the last 3 years, 2017–2019 with President Trump, there was a large increase in stock prices. The authors tested the equality of the mean rates of return of B&H and SIM for the S&P 500 and Russell 2000 for this period. The null hypothesis cannot be rejected for both cases and B&H and SIM were statistically equal even though the Russell 2000 SIM was higher than its Buy-and-Hold strategy.

Chapter 12 by Dzhabarov, Ziegler, and Ziemba updates the international equity calendar work of Ziemba during the past 30 years. The authors used daily equity index futures prices for 24 countries plus the Eurozone. The markets covered are the main markets followed by investors, namely those included in the "World Equity Index Futures" (WEIF) page on Bloomberg as of early November 2019 (16 countries plus the Eurozone), as well as eight others for which liquid futures are available over a relatively long period, namely India, Norway, Russia, South Africa, South Korea, Taiwan, Thailand, and Turkey. For each country, the study uses data from the first day that futures data are available in Bloomberg through October 31, 2019. All indices in the sample are large-cap indices.

Using futures data has the advantage of making the analysis of return seasonalities and the profitability of strategies exploiting them particularly simple and intuitive. Indeed, since futures are unfunded positions, their returns are by definition excess returns. Moreover, by no-arbitrage, returns on equity index futures are equal to the total return on the underlying index (including dividends) minus the return on the riskless asset. Accordingly, futures returns capture the entire equity premium. Thus, positive average returns (geometric average ordinary returns or arithmetic average log returns) during a given period mean that being invested in futures earned higher returns than being invested in cash during that period. Conversely, negative average returns imply that being invested in cash would have been the better option.

The authors find that the “Sell-in-May” effect is present in equity and equity futures markets around the globe. The November–April period exhibits not just higher average returns but also lower risk than the May–October period. Accordingly, the Sharpe ratios from investing in stock index futures between the turn of the month of November (six trading days before the end of October) and the first trading day in May are quite attractive. Strong seasonality is also apparent in average returns and Sharpe ratios computed by calendar month. Specifically, the worst month of the year in terms of average returns occurs during the summer period in all markets, and the best month occurs during the winter period in most markets. Even more strikingly, the worst month of the year lies during the August–October period in two thirds of the countries considered in the study, confirming that late summer and early autumn are the worst periods to be invested in stocks. By contrast, and contrary to conventional wisdom, in two-thirds of the countries, the largest Sharpe ratios do not accrue at year-end but rather in April, reflecting the combination of high returns and low volatility during that month. In a number of countries, being invested in the stock market during the summer months has historically generated substantial losses.

In spite of the fact that the “Sell-in-May” effect was documented in the academic literature, the authors find that cumulative returns during the summer months remain close to zero or negative in the post-publication period in most countries, and the “Buy-in-May” strategy does much worse than the “Sell-in-May” strategy in almost all markets in the sample. The authors conclude that although it may have weakened slightly in recent years, the “Sell-in-May” effect appears to have, so far, survived the publicity around it.

The Blair–Hull analysis combines seasonal anomalies, Fed announcement, and trends in a walk-forward way. Numerous papers present compelling evidence on seasonal effects of the market, with Turn of the Month and the Halloween effect being the most convincing. At the same time, there appears to be an excess return prior to Fed meetings. They combine these effects with the new trend indicator to create an effective model that beats Buy-and-Hold. This Seasonal Anomaly and Trend Model is then combined in an ensemble with other market-timing models to produce an even more powerful strategy.

Instead of forecasting market excess returns, they focus on predictability stemming from seasonal, trend, and drift anomalies. Unlike those studies, this chapter aims to discuss the use of discrete variables and deterministic models. None of these are new topics in the academic literature. To name a few existing studies, Swinkels and Van Vliet (2012) and Ziemba (2012) discuss the use of calendar anomalies, and Jensen *et al.* (1996) introduce a monetary policy indicator as a predictor for market returns. However, in addition to showing statistical significance of individual effects, they aim to build a robust model using multiple anomalies that will outperform the Buy-and-Hold strategy.

The contribution of their study to the literature is threefold. First, they propose a calibration method for individual anomalies. Most existing studies pick fixed start and end dates for calendar anomalies, but their technique offers annual calibration using Sharpe Ratio as the objective function. Second, their chapter serves as a cookbook for investors. While many papers on anomalies end with discussing their statistical significance or the lack thereof, they discuss implementation with consideration of realistic leverage available to retail clients, realistic trading costs, and problems arising from trying to allocate capital to multiple anomalies. Third, many investors might already have an allocation to more traditional macro-strategies and are curious to see whether these could be enhanced by addition of seasonal trends, pre-announcement drift, and momentum strategies. Their chapter combines these anomalies with existing market-timing strategies and some popular investment approaches to illustrate the potential of such ensembles.

They start with four robust seasonal anomalies and some of their variations, and propose a simple deterministic trading strategy for each. Then they introduce three different options of combining these four strategies. First, they look at the mean–variance optimization algorithm (Markowitz, 1952), and second, they perform a grid search on model weights to look for optimal combinations of signals rather than using portfolio optimization based on the covariance structure. Last, they consider a simple equal weight portfolio for comparison. Simultaneously, they combine all strategies on a real-time basis. Welch and Goyal (2008) demonstrate that many predictors perform poorly out-of-sample and even in the late in-sample period. By only including strategies on anomalies after they have been described, they are only looking at true out-of-sample periods and are able to demonstrate that their value for an investor's portfolio is meaningful and valuable.

But it is important to note that the real-time models still differ from the Buy-and-Hold benchmark in a statistically significant way; the equal weight real-time model at 1% significance level, and the mean–variance optimized real-time model at 5% significance level. The univariate strategies are restricted to be between 0% and 150% invested in S&P 500. The Hull Group maximize the backtested Sharpe ratio in our analysis, since this metric is rather invariant to scaling. Investors wishing to deploy these models in their portfolios can subsequently choose a level of leverage based on their risk preferences.

3. Efficient Portfolio Construction

Chapter 15 by Guerard, Rachev, and Shao reprint reports on how difficult a traditional Mean–Variance portfolio is to outperform on the bases of the Geometric Mean, Sharpe Ratio, and Information Ratio. The Mean–Variance Tracking Error at Risk (MVTar) portfolio reduces tracking error relative to the traditional Mean–Variance portfolio, allowing an asset manager to possibly increase the targeted portfolio tracking error to enhance risk-adjusted returns. Moreover, the Mean-Expected Tail Loss (M-ETL) portfolio algorithm can enhance the realized risk-return relationship.

Who is better than Harry Markowitz to discuss Mean–Variance portfolio and Mean–Semivariance optimization? Chapter 16 reports evidence as to why Mean–Variance continues to dominate asset management. In the majority of cases, it is the best method because, under widely applicable conditions, it maximizes the investor's utility, it is very easy to implement, and it is intuitively appealing. Variance, however, is a symmetric measure; meaning that mean–variance optimization disfavors large positive returns as much as it disfavors large negative returns. Generally, investors favor large positive returns, or positively skewed portfolio return distributions. Therefore, some would argue that mean–variance optimization should be augmented with methods that penalize only negative returns; i.e., with downside portfolio optimization.

For this purpose, semivariance is a particularly useful measure of downside risk because it considers returns as risky only if they are below some reference return. Despite its intuitive appeal, mean–semivariance optimization remains shrouded in mystery. This is primarily because of the difficulties raised by the apparent nonlinearity involved in the computation of semi-variance. In reality, the mean–semivariance optimization problem was solved more than 60 years ago in Markowitz (1959), which showed that if an estimate of the covariance matrix is computed using time series of security returns, the great computational benefit of the Critical Line Algorithm (CLA) could be exploited to construct mean–semivariance efficient frontiers. Niedermayer and Niedermayer (2010) have shown that the CLA can be orders of magnitude faster than other algorithms for mean–variance optimization.

It is often agreed that, intuitively, mean–semivariance portfolio optimization is more sensible than mean–variance optimization, but it is also often assumed that mean–semivariance optimization is too difficult. Even though the mean–semivariance problem was solved more than 60 years ago, portfolio managers are more familiar and comfortable with mean–variance optimization. Mean–semivariance optimization has, to a large extent, been forgotten. The purpose of this chapter is to serve as a reminder of the simplicity and intuitive appeal of mean–semivariance optimization, and to revive interest in it.

Markowitz shows how one can reduce downside exposure using mean–semivariance optimization. In general, mean–semivariance optimization is difficult to perform. However, the problem can be simplified dramatically if one uses an estimate of the covariance matrix derived from historical asset returns. In this case, one works with a particular square root of the covariance matrix from which the portfolio's semivariance is easily computed. We provide an explanation of this theory, and follow with sample R code that is extensively cross-referenced to the theory. Finally, we show how to use the historical square root of the covariance matrix to write the mean–semivariance problem in standard quadratic form, and we provide a simple R function to find the optimal mean–semivariance portfolio for any feasible expected portfolio return.

Chapter 17 by Tower examines Vanguard, Fidelity, and Dimensional Fund Advisors, three major American mutual fund companies. Ranked by assets under management, they are 2nd, 4th, and 31st , respectively (*Investment News*, 2018). The retirement plan of Duke University features nine Vanguard funds and five Fidelity funds; more than those of any other company. We suspect this is true of other retirement plans as well. Each year, the Vanguard Bogleheads meeting features experts, some of whom use DFA funds and some of whom do not.

We explore the choice of investing in the three companies. In the process, we characterize the funds. Our calculations use Fama–French factors to show the extent to which various funds out-returned their empirically determined benchmarks, and characterize the funds according to size and book-to-market value. This allows apples-to-apples comparison of funds by different families. It also allows us to evaluate passive versus active investment, and it helps investors to pick a portfolio that balances small versus big and value versus growth. Then we check our results by asking the same question, and combining Sharpe's (1992) style analysis with Ken French's 5×5 portfolios sorted by size and the ratio of book-to-market value. We also compare fund returns with their published benchmarks after style adjustment and with the whole U.S. market.

In summary, Chapter 17 reports as follows:

- The average of zero, two, and three-factor alpha for Vanguard's index portfolio minus Vanguard's managed portfolio is positive for all time spans with start dates from 2005 on through 2018, and negative from 2001 and from 2003 through 2018;

- DFA's two-factor style-adjusted returns through 2018 relative to Vanguard on average have fallen relative to the start date of 2001;
- DFA's recent excess returns over Vanguard through 2018 have fallen relative to the start date of 2001, and in comparison, to the conclusions of earlier studies;
- Fidelity's index fund portfolio has excess returns through 2018 relative to its managed funds by all three criteria in 20 out of 21 contests;
- Vanguard's two-factor style-adjusted managed portfolio out-returns Fidelity's for every start date through 2018;
- Fidelity's index portfolio out-returns Vanguard's for every start date from 2007 on through 2018 for both two-factor style-adjusted returns and unadjusted (zero-factor) returns; and
- Recently, index funds have had the edge over managed funds and DFA's style-adjusted and unadjusted returns have fallen relative to Vanguard's.

4. Asset Allocation and Non-Stock Investment Research

Chapter 18 by Racheva–Iotova studies several Behavioral Finance (BF) findings with the help of the modern methods of Rational Finance (RF) and translates the "language" of the first to the other. The chapter is based on the work of several authors approaching the problem from different perspectives and aims at ultimately providing a consistent and complete working framework. Racheva–Iotova adapts the mathematical formulation of the BF principles so that to enable the use of key methods of the RF quantitative paradigm:

1. Shapes of investors sentiments could be represented by weighting functions preserving the underlying distribution within the infinitely divisible distributions class;
2. Such chosen weighting functions further allow us to construct hedging strategies as they possess clear methods for contingent claims pricing;

3. Based on the extended notion of Stochastic Dominance, we propose reasonable approaches to optimize for Investors Value function of various shapes including the typical S-Shaped, via Rational Finance standard risk–return measures as CVaR, RVaR, and U-RVaR.

Ms. Racheva–Iotova offers a review of the most important facts on bringing together BF and RF and illuminates key theoretical facts to build a consistent and theoretically sound unified BF–RF framework where derivatives pricing, hedging, and portfolio optimization within the behavioral paradigm are quantitatively prudent. More importantly, the methods presented lay the grounds for a new generation practical framework for designing investment products for the wealth market.

Chapter 20 by Leung and Ward designs and implements a dynamic trading strategy that adjusts daily to optimally track VIX. The model is calibrated to historical data and a simulation study is performed to understand the properties exhibited by the strategy. For all long-term investors, it is very important to be able to effectively control the risk exposure of their portfolios through varying market conditions. Downside risk protection is particularly crucial. This motivates investors to consider different instruments and strategies to potentially hedge against market turbulence. One of the most widely recognized measures of expected market volatility is the CBOE Volatility Index (VIX). This is a desirable asset to hold as it has been observed empirically that volatility and market returns are anti-correlated, an effect known as asymmetric volatility. Therefore, having exposure to VIX would protect the investor by providing some gains to offset market downturns.

After compiling, our dataset and study consists of the entire closing price history from January 3, 2011 (first trading date of 2011) through December 30, 2016, which is a 6-year period from 2011 to 2016. The entire sample period from 2011 to 2016 contains 1,510 total trading days of data. Moreover, on any given day of the sample set, there are between 7 and 9 futures contracts, with 1,217 days with a full 9 months of contracts available. In other words, when there are

N futures contracts available for trading, they always consist of the N front months.

In Chapter 20, Leung and Ward presented the construction of static and dynamic portfolios of VIX futures that are optimized for VIX tracking. As discussed from both empirical and theoretical perspectives, futures prices tend not to react quickly enough to movements in the spot VIX. They also bring persistent negative returns and thus make tracking VIX difficult. The model is calibrated to historical data and a simulation study is performed to understand the properties exhibited by the strategy. In addition, comparing to the volatility ETN, we find that our dynamic strategy has a superior tracking performance.

In practice, both static and dynamic futures portfolios will involve trading costs. Nevertheless, in recent years, commission fees for futures trading have decreased significantly to around or less than \$1/contract for long and short futures positions on major brokerages. Moreover, static futures portfolios involve only 1–4 contracts and require no rebalancing once initialized, while our dynamic portfolio only needs an incremental adjustment once a day. For all Leung and Ward portfolios, the authors used futures with the shortest terms, which are typically most liquid with smaller bid–ask spreads. Hence, trading costs are unlikely to have a prohibitive impact on performance.

Chapter 19 by Kyriazi and Thomakos considers the EUR/USD and the GBP/USD exchange rates, using the Federal Reserve Bank of St. Louis FRED database, at the daily frequency, for the January 2000–August 2019 time period. Their reported foreign exchange results are as follows:

The first result refers to parsimonious modeling, as it was illustrated by the almost complete presence across rolling windows and time periods of the simple delay model. The choice of the explanatory variable in this setting is probably more important than the model itself and, furthermore, different explanatory variables and their transformations need to be tested empirically.

The second result, that relates to the first, is that there can be performance enhancements to predictability by the use of differences in the explanatory variable, much like the advantages that appear when we model and forecast a time series in differences vs its levels, like in the ARIMA framework. This result, possibly a bit surprising since the variables that are already (log-)differenced might be due to the fact that such additional differencing removes/reduces the natural outliers that occur in financial returns and is akin to some form of "acceleration" in the price series. In any event, and because we have found that such differencing is useful also when the explanatory variables are the realized volatility or the realized correlation, this is something that is of practical interest and should be further considered in modeling.

The third result refers to the use of the sequential elimination models that we have suggested. These models not only provide for considerable flexibility in specifying generic interaction effects, and thus capture linearity and some types of nonlinearity directly, they are also easy to estimate fast and ensure in-sample statistical significance by the process of sequential reduction of the levels of significance used for testing the individual coefficients. We do note that after the elimination of insignificant variables we do end up with a parsimonious model as well.

The fourth result is about the generic lack of presence of other, competing, and bench-mark models, as top performers. It is only on the sub-periods analysis that we do find the presence of some benchmark models, notably the VAR(1), and we did explain the reasons in Section 3 as to why this might be so. We also did not find any considerable presence of the "pure" nonlinear models such as the TAR model.

The fifth result is the explanations for predictability, in terms of the in-sample analysis of the top performing models. There are two issues of interest here: first, the measurement of in-sample fit in our models is via the associated R2, which is a straightforward assessor of fit in the simple delay models; it has, however, the same conceptual validity for the sequential elimination models since we ensure that insignificant variables just do not appear before computing our forecasts. The question of predictability is linked to both the size and, possibly more important, the trend of the R2 over the evaluation period. The reader would certainly ask what is the notion of discussing R2 values if these cannot be shown to be statistically significant — and that would be correct inasmuch as we consider the issue of significant improvements in predictability. But there is more to be discussed here; first, we have to obtain reductions in the statistical evaluation measures *vis-a-vis* the naive benchmark, which reductions are presented in our results; second, we have to explain where these reductions might be coming from. We then look at out-of-sample predictability, which is clearly present in terms of our statistical measures of evaluation. Kyriazi and Thomakos report in Chapter 19 that the delayed linear forecast and the adaptive learning forecast models outperformed vector autoregressive models (VAR) and threshold autoregressive models (TAR), producing statistically significant 10–15% root mean square error forecasting reductions relative to no-change forecast models. Thus, what we observe is that predictability is clearly linked with in-sample fit, that higher R2 indicated increased predictability, and that careful, parsimonious model construction is (as should be) always supportive to good forecasting performance.

In Chapter 22 by Ziemba, Ed Thorp and Bill Ziemba (with assistance from Julian Shaw) did a convergence trade based on differing Nikkei put warrant prices on the Toronto and American stock exchanges in the 1989–1990 time period. The trade was successful and Thorp won the over $1 million risk-adjusted hedge fund contest run by Barron's in 1990. There were risks involved and careful risk management was needed. This edge was based on the fact that the Japanese stock and land prices were astronomical and very intertwined. In 1988–1989, Bill was the first Yamaichi professor of Finance at the University of Tsukuba, 60 miles above Tokyo. He taught at the university from Monday to Wednesday and consulted on Thursday and Friday in Tokyo for the Yamaichi Research Institute. There he had two projects: (1) stock market anomalies and (2) stock market crashes.

Returning to Canada, Bill discovered that the Nikkei puts in Toronto, Canada, were trading 3–4 times the fair price. He called Ed Thorp and suggested that they try to do a risk arbitrage. He had wanted to do a good trade with him of the type he is well known for. He was interested in doing this but he said you have the sell but where is the buy side of the risk arbitrage?

Soon after, Bill went to the Wharton School at the University of Pennsylvania and spoke at a conference organized by Stavros Zenios, with whom he would later co-edit the *ALM Handbook* for North Holland and where Thorp would have a paper which he considered to be the best theoretical Kelly criterion paper ever written. There Bill met Julian Shaw, who was at Gordon Capital in Toronto (later Gordon Capital asked Bill to be their Japan expert and he wrote reports for their clients). Shaw wanted to meet Bill as he really liked *Beat the Racetrack*. In the conversation, Bill mentioned these Nikkei puts. Shaw replied he knew about these and had already shorted $3 million contracts, which is about a $9 million position.

Julian then told Bill that he could get the other side by calling Salomon London and they would sell them a private over-the-counter Nikkei put at fair value, but they needed to have a $500,000 investment. Bill informed Thorp and they agreed to do it. Bill established accounts in Vancouver for Thorp and himself. They then started establishing the shorts in Toronto. Then the authors had the good fortune that Nikkei puts for retail investors began trading in NY on the American Stock Exchange. They could then buy exactly the quantity they wanted and did not need to work with Salomon London.

Bill Ziemba made a nice gain for himself. Ed Thorp won the over $1 million hedge fund contest that year organized by Barron's. It was a good experience for Ziemba, Shaw, and Thorp. Shaw is now a risk manager for Barclays in London. The Ziemba Japanese experience helped Bill to better trade markets and for a large period in 2013–2018 he was the top performing trader in the U.S. futures markets in his category.

Causality modeling has been estimated for several decades. Based on The Conference Board Leading Economic Indicators (LEI) and its components, Vinod and Guerard (2020) report in Chapter 25 that the LEI time series leads weekly hours and weekly unemployment claims. The path that LEI leads the S&P 500 Index is plausible. The credit index leads LEI, suggesting that the credit index has considerable exogenous information. Moreover, oil prices lead the LEI. It appears that GDP drives LEI; hence, the quarterly index of leading indicators LEI is not exogenous but driven by changes in GDP level. On the other hand, output per hour in business sector has considerable independent influence on GDP and GNP. This suggests that output growth is driven by productivity growth. The balance of merchandise trade and corporate profits do not have independent innovations, but respond to innovations in GDP or GNP.

In the SCA replication study of the MZTT (1998) U.S. unemployment rate, weekly unemployment claims, and Leading Economic Indicator (LEI) time series, we applied traditional Granger-causality modeling substantially to reduce regression sum of squares measures relative to a traditional variation on the random walk with drift model. We replicate the seminal study and extend the analysis to 2018. The modeling process of including the LEI in forecasting the U.S. unemployment rate has been addressed before, but our results are more statistically significant. The transfer function models estimated using the SCA software system; the software used in the original MZTT analysis. We establish Granger causality between the LEI time series and the unemployment rate for 1959–2018 time period. We establish feedback between the LEI time series and the unemployment rate for 1959–1993 time period and for weekly unemployment claims and the unemployment rate for both 1959–1993 and 1959–2019 time series.

Vinod and Guerard report that the variables studied in a seminal study of the unemployment rate continue to be highly statistically significant. Increases in LEI and one of its components, the unemployment claims time series, precede a reduction in the unemployment rate. Why are these results important? The unemployment rate is at a 50-year low in the U.S. What reduces unemployment? Increasing economic activity drives down unemployment. The LEI were created by Mitchell (1913) to be a barometer of economic activity. The LEI time series and its underlying methodology have evolved through the research of Burns and Mitchell (1946), Moore (1961) and Zarnowitz (1992). The LEI time series, and one of its components, weekly employment claims, is statistically significant in forecasting the unemployment rate. The LEI time series passes the Chen–Lee test for Granger causality.

In summary, we report on the statistically significant impact of the LEI and weekly unemployment claims time series on the unemployment rate series. The MZTT variable relationships are confirmed, in-sample, and post-publication.

Chapter 26 by Gillam and Read concentrates on MEASA region, a crescent of countries beginning with Bangladesh and India in the East, continuing through the Middle East and West Africa, and terminating with the South African nations. This grouping of countries has a long history of cultural, economic, and political advantages and achievements. One need only consider the energy riches of the Middle East, the mineral, agricultural, and fishery resources of Africa, or the large and educated population of India to understand the potential of the region.

The MEASA region covers 45% of the world's population, and, with an average age of 23 years, is expected to be the most rapidly growing. The MEASA growth, combined with increased labor and resource productivity, should drive explosive economic growth. Already at 18% of global GDP, the MEASA GDP likely grew at triple the developed world economic growth rate in 2017, with 7 of the 10 fastest growing economies being in the region.

At the same time, and despite the economic potential of the region, the regional capital markets are grossly under-represented in the major MSCI world equity indexes. Out of the total 83 countries in the region, only 7 are part of the MSCI Emerging Market ("EM") Index, 15 in the MSCI Frontier Market ("FM") Index, and 5 in the MSCI Standalone Market Indexes. Despite that the MEASA markets account for 6% of total global market capitalization and 18% of global GDP, the weighting in the MSCI ACW Index is only 2%. As its countries are upgraded to frontier or emerging status, we believe that interest in the region will explode, that the index weights of its stocks will multiply, and that significant excess returns will be available.

While a breathtaking economic potential exists, institutional investors do face significant barriers to effectively purchase stock at scale and in diversity from the region. Liquidity appears limited, and registration and custody arrangements are formidable. We describe this essentially as investing on the "far side of the moon," in that despite its conceptual appeal, it has remained difficult or impossible for many institutional investors from around the world to gain effective access to this region's opportunities. Yet, savvy investment managers are now developing innovative approaches to access MEASA region stocks. As these managers introduce broad-based fund products, the riches of the region will open to those institutions with a vision for what can be. Already, the performance of stocks in the region has exceeded broad global benchmarks by hundreds of basis points over the last 15 years.

Despite the economic position and potential of the MEASA region, the index companies have yet to catch on. Though representing 18% of the world's GDP, the MEASA region companies only account for 6% of the market cap of the total for the MSCI ACWI Index constituents, and significantly, only account for 2% of the index weight. As these anomalies are corrected, we believe that investor interest in the region will explode, with subsequent positive effects on the region's equity returns. The difference in percentages (2% versus 11%) thus represents a significant 9% potential gap that is expected to narrow for the benefit of investors in these markets over time. A similar situation existed for the BRICS stocks in the early 2000s. By what mechanism was the situation rectified and index weight increased, and what was the investment result? As the BRICS countries gained in stature due to growth and economic reform, they were upgraded to "frontier and emerging" status by MSCI. Superior investment returns followed.

The rapidly growing MEASA region countries and their companies would seem to be burgeoning with attractive investment opportunities. Yet, we think of investing in this region as investing on the "far side of the moon!" This opinion is based on the perception of illiquidity and institutional barriers to investment. The situation today in the MEASA region countries seems similar to the situation in the BRICS countries in the early 2000s. As happened with the BRICS countries, the barriers to investing in the MEASA region are being removed as we write. Innovative investment advisors are set to offer mechanisms to access these markets. The rewards will go to those visionary investors who are able to first see the possibilities.

References

Bloch, M., Guerard, Jr., J. B., Markowitz, H. M., Todd, P., and Xu, G.-L. (1993). A comparison of some aspects of the U.S. and Japanese equity markets. *Japan and the World Economy* **5**, 3-26.

Burns, A. F. and Mitchell, W. C. (1946). *Measuring Business Cycles*, New York, NY: NBER.

Dimson, E. (1988). *Stock Market Anomalies.* Cambridge: Cambridge University Press.

Guerard, J.B., Jr., Deng, S., Gillam, R. A., Markowitz, H., and Xu, G. (2020). Investing in global equity markets. *Wilmott Magazine*, Volume 2020, Issue 106, 56–75.

Guerard, J. B., Jr, Rachev, S., and Shao, B. (2013). Efficient global portfolios: Big data and investment universe. *IBM Journal of Research and Development* **57** (September/October 2013), 11.1–11.11.

Guerard, J. B., Jr, Markowitz, H., and Xu, G. (2014). The role of effective corporate decisions in the creation of efficient portfolios. *IBM Journal of Research and Development* **58** (July/August 2014), 6.1–6.11.

Guerard, J. B., Jr, Markowitz, H., and Xu, G. (2015). Earnings forecasting in a global stock selection model and efficient portfolio construction and management. *International Journal of Forecasting* **31**, 550–560.

Jacobs, B. I. and Levy, K. (1988). Disentangling equity return regularities: New insights and investment opportunities. *Financial Analysts Journal* **44**, 18–43.

Markowitz, H. M. (1952). Portfolio selection. *Journal of Finance* **7**, 77–91.

Markowitz, H. M. (1959). *Portfolio Selection: Efficient Diversification of Investment.* Cowles Foundation Monograph No.16. New York, John Wiley & Sons.

Mitchell, W. C. (1913). *Business Cycles*, Berkeley, CA: University of California Press.

Moore, G. H. (1961). *Business Cycle Indicators*, Volume 1, Princeton, NJ: Princeton University Press.

Sharpe, W. F. (1964). Capital asset prices: A theory of market equilibrium under conditions of risk. *Journal of Finance* 19, 425–442.

Sharpe, W. F. (1971). Mean-absolute deviation characteristic lines for securities and portfolios. A simplified model for portfolio analysis. *Management Science* 18, B1–B13.

Ziemba, W. T. and Schwartz, S. (1992). *Invest Japan.* Chicago: Probus.

Part I

Fundamental Anomalies and Stock Selection Modeling

https://doi.org/10.1142/9789811222634_0001

Chapter 1

The Five Investor Camps that Try to Beat the Stock Market

William T. Ziemba
Sauder School of Business (Emeritus), University of British Columbia, Vancouver, Canada Distinguished Visiting Research Associate, Systemic Risk Center, London School of Economics, London, United Kingdom

This chapter categorizes investors into five groups. They are as follows: efficient markets, risk premium, genius superior traders, rejectors of efficient market theory, and those who use research to make superior risk adjusted returns. Successful investment involves estimation and optimization and these are discussed.

Keywords: Efficient and inefficient markets, risk premium, Samuelson's superior investors, Buffett's investment approach, superior investors approaches and techniques, effect of parameter errors on optimal investment choice, and Kelly and fractional Kelly optimization.

1. Introduction

In this chapter, I discuss how great investors succeed. This is an enormous topic, but the principles and results discussed here apply reasonably broadly. Winning has two parts: getting an edge and then betting well. The former simply means that investments have an advantage, so $1 invested returns on average more than $1. The latter involves not overbetting, and truly diversifying in all scenarios in a disciplined, wealth-enhancing way.

I start with a categorization of the stock market camps which discusses how various people try to get an edge. Some feel that one cannot get an edge and this then becomes a self-fulfilling prophecy. They, of course, are not in our list of great investors. By investing in index funds, they usually do reasonably well, beating about 75% of all investors.

Many great investors are Kelly or fractional Kelly bettors who focus on not losing.

2. The Various Efficient/Inefficient Market Camps: Can You Beat the Stock Market?

Market participants can be divided into five groups. There are other ways to do such a categorization, but this way is useful for our purpose of isolating and studying great investors and naturally evolves from the academic study of the efficiency of financial markets.

The five groups are as follows:

- Efficient markets (E)
- Risk premium (RP)
- Genius (G)
- Hogwash (H)
- Markets are beatable (A)

The first group are those who believe in efficient markets (E). They believe that the current prices are fair and correct except possibly for transaction costs. These transaction costs, which include commissions, bid–ask spread, and price pressures, can be very large.[1]

[1] A Barra study by Andy Rudd showed that these costs averaged 4.6% one-way for a $50,000 institutional investor sale. This is if you use a naive market order for the full transaction rather than limit orders or smaller market orders. Thorp, in a private communication, said that he traded about $60 billion in statistical arbitrage from 1992–2002 in lot sizes of 20k–100k and found that the mean transaction cost was about 1 cent per share and the market impact was about 4.5 cents per share for shares averaging about $30. So the one-way costs were about $0.18.

The leader of this school who had dominated academic journals, jobs, fame, etc., in the 1960s to the 1980s was Gene Fama of the University of Chicago. A brilliant researcher, Fama is also a tape recorder: you can turn him on or off, you can fast-forward or rewind him or change his volume, but you cannot change his views no matter what evidence you provide; he will refute it forcibly.

This group provided many useful concepts such as the capital asset pricing model of Sharpe (1964), Lintner (1965), and Mossin (1966) which provided a theoretical justification for index funds which are the efficient market camp's favored investment mode. They still beat about 75% of active managers. Since all the managers comprise the market, that's 50% of them beaten by the index. Transactions and other costs eliminate another 25%.

Over time, the hard efficient market line has softened into a risk premium (RP) camp. They feel that markets are basically efficient but one can realize extra return by bearing additional risk. They strongly argue that, if returns are above average, the risk must be there somewhere and that one simply cannot get higher returns without bearing additional risk. For example, beating the market index S&P500 is possible but is not risk adjusted by the CAPM. They measure risk by beta, which must be greater than one to receive higher than market returns on average.[2] That is, the portfolio risk is higher than the market risk. But they allow other risk factors such as small cap and low book to price. But they do not believe in full-blown 20–30 factor models. Fama and his disciples moved here in the 1990s. This camp now dominates the top U.S. academic journals and the jobs in academic finance departments at the most famous universities in the U.S. and Europe.

The third camp is called genius (G). These are superior investors who are brilliant or geniuses, but you cannot determine in advance who they are. Paul Samuelson has championed this argument. Samuelson feels that these investors do exist, but it is useless to try to find them as in the search for them you will find 19 duds for

[2]While higher beta yielding higher mean returns makes good theoretical sense, some studies show that lower beta stocks often have higher returns.

every star. This view is very close to the Merton–Samuelson (1974) criticism of the Kelly criterion: that is, even with an advantage, it is possible to lose a lot of your wealth.

Ziemba (2015), after receiving three letters from Samuelson (2006, 2007, 2008), wrote a response which discussed the four basic objections which largely focus on overbetting. I then show that while the objections are theoretically correct, well-designed Kelly applications are usually successful. Some simulations on Kelly and fractional Kelly strategies appear in MacLean *et al.* (2011). The evidence though is that you can determine them *ex ante* and to some extent they have persistent superior performance, see, for example, Fung *et al.* (1997, 2001). Soros did this with futures with superior picking of futures to bet on; this is the traders are made not born philosophy. This camp will isolate members of other camps such as those in (A) or (H).

The fourth camp is as strict in its views as camps (E) and (RP). This group feels that efficient markets which originated in and are perpetuated by the academic world are hogwash (H). In fact, the leading proponent of this view and one with whom it is hard to argue as he is right at the top of the list of the world's richest persons is Warren Buffett, who wants to give university chairs in efficient markets to further improve his own very successful trading. An early member of this group, the great economist John Maynard Keynes was an academic. We also see that although they may never have heard of the Kelly criterion, this camp, which includes George Soros, does seem to use it implicitly with large non-diversified bets on favorable investments. See Ziemba (2015) for more on this.

This group feels that by evaluating companies and buying them when their value is greater than their price, you can easily beat the market by taking a long-term view. They find these stocks and hold them forever. They find a few such stocks that they understand well and get involved in managing them, or they simply buy them and make them subsidiaries with the previous owners running the business. They forget about diversification because they try to buy only winners.

They also bet on insurance when the odds are greatly in their favor. They fully understood the concept of tail risk, which they only take at huge advantages to themselves when the bet is small relative to their wealth levels. An example of this is, as a consultant, I, with help from Sandra Schwartz and Shelby Brumelle, designed a bingo game where the top prize was $100 million, second prize was $10 million, and so on, with the smallest prize being $10. The game had a huge advantage for the house as do most lotto games, but it had huge risks in the two large top prizes. So the solution was to sell the tail to Lloyd's of London or Warren Buffett. Then the game still has a fairly high house advantage but has no risk and the buyer of the tail got an investment with a huge advantage up to 75%, which is not risky for them since this bet was small compared to their huge portfolio wealth.

The last group are those who think that markets are beatable (A) through behavioral biases and security market anomalies using computerized superior betting techniques. They construct risk arbitrage situations with a positive expectation. They thoroughly research the strategy and follow it for long periods of time repeating the advantage many times. They feel that factor models are useful most, but not all, of the time and show that beta is not one of the most important variables to predict stock prices. They use very focused, disciplined and well-researched strategies with superior execution and risk control. Many of them use Kelly or fractional Kelly strategies. All of them extensively use computers for research and execution and risk control. They focus on not losing, and they rarely have blowouts. Members of (A) include Ed Thorp (Princeton Newport and later funds), Bill Benter (the Hong Kong racing guru), Warren Buffett (Berkshire Hathaway), John Henry (trend follower and the owner of Red Sox), Blair Hull (mispriced options trader), Harry McPike (trend follower), Jim Simons (Renaissance hedge fund), Jeff Yass (Susquehanna Group), and David Swensen (Yale University endowment). Blowouts occur more in hedge funds that do not focus on not losing and true diversification and over bet; when a bad scenario hits them, they get wiped out, such as LTCM, Niederhofer, and Amaranth Advisors; see Lleo and Ziemba (2015a, 2015b).

3. How do Investors and Consultants do in All These Cases?

All investors can be multimillionaires, but the centimillionaires are in (G), (H), and (A) like those listed in (A). These people make more money for their clients than themselves, but the amount they make for themselves is a huge amount: of course, these people eat their own cooking, that is they are clients themselves with a large amount of their money in the funds they manage. An exception is someone who founded an (RP) or (E) company, kept most of the shares, and made an enormous amount of fees for themselves irrespective of the investment performance given to the clients because the sheer volume of assets they have gathered under management is so large. I was fortunate to work/consult with six of these and was also the main consultant to the Frank Russell Research Department for 9 years, which is perhaps the leading conservative RP implementor in the U.S. (A) people earn money by winning and taking a percent of the profits, Thorp returned 15.8% net with $200 million under management; fees $8 million/year (1969–1988). (E) and (RP) people earn money from fees by collecting assets through superior marketing and sticky investment decisions. My own AlphaZ Futures Fund has a net geometric mean after accounting for all fees and costs of about 40% during the period 2013–2019.

Many great investors use Kelly (1956) betting, including most in camp (A). For some theory, see Markowitz (1976, 2006), Rubinstein (1976), MacLean *et al.* (2010a, 2010b, 2011), MacLean *et al.* (2005), MacLean and Ziemba (2013a), Thorp (2011), and papers in MacLean and Ziemba (2013b). But there are critics, and chief among them are Nobel Prize winners Robert Merton and Paul Samuelson. Their argument is that successful investing requires a lot of luck and it is hard to separate luck from skill. Therefore, while many Kelly investors will make huge gains, a few will have huge losses. Indeed, they are correct. A good way to explain this is via the simulation

Donald Hausch, and I did. A simulation of 700 bets, all with a 14% edge, was performed 1000 times.[3]

In support of Kelly, 166 times out of the 1000 simulated wealth paths, the investor has more than 100 times initial wealth of $1000 with full Kelly. But this great outcome occurs only once with half Kelly. However, the probability of being ahead is higher with half Kelly, 87.0% versus 95.4%. A negative observation, and related to the Merton and Samuelson (1974) criticism, is that the minimum wealth is only 18. It is only 145 with half Kelly, namely, a 85.5% loss.[4] So you can make 700 bets, all independent, each with a 14% edge, and the result is that you still lose over 98% of your fortune with bad scenarios. Luenberger (1993) shows that, theoretically, if your utility function is based solely on the tail losses, then the optimal strategy is to tradeoff the expected log and variance of log (like a static mean–variance analysis).

4. The Importance of Getting the Mean Right

The mean dominates if the two distributions cross only once.

Theorem: Hanoch and Levy (1969) *If $X \sim F(\cdot)$ with the higher mean and $Y \sim G(\cdot)$ have cumulative distribution functions that cross only once, but are otherwise arbitrary, then F dominates G for* ***all*** *concave u. The mean of F must be at least as large as the mean of G to have dominance. Variance and other moments are unimportant. Only the means count.*

With normal distributions, X and Y will cross only once if the variance of X does not exceed that of Y. That is the basic equivalence

[3]See also the empirical paper by Bicksler and Thorp (1973) where they calculate the probability that investors will be ahead after given numbers of favorable bets and the simulations in MacLean *et al.* (2011). Their conclusions are consistent with those in the Hausch and Ziemba study which is in Ziemba (2018). A response to the Samuelson critique using Samuelson's private letters to Ziemba and Samuelson's papers, many of which are reprinted in MacLean *et al.* (2010a) is in Ziemba (2017) and Gergaud and Ziemba (2012).

[4]These fractional Kelly strategies were studied by Hausch *et al.* (1992) in a growth versus security setting. Related to this is the capital growth with a security constraint, see MacLean *et al.* (2004, 2009), and Thorp and Mizusawa (2013).

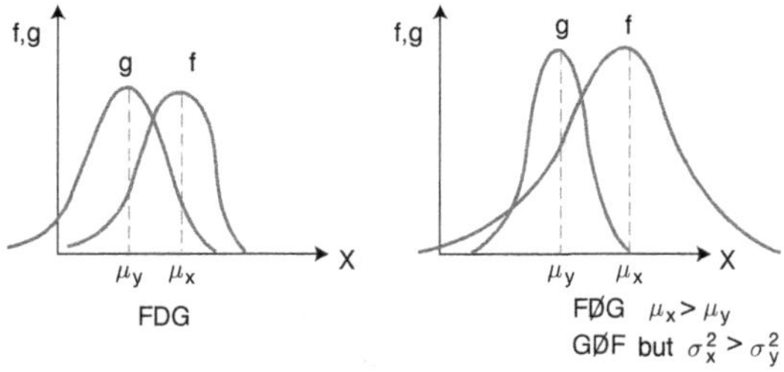

Fig. 1. The main theorem of mean–variance analysis.

of mean–variance analysis and expected utility analysis via second-order (concave, non-decreasing) stochastic dominance. See Fig. 1, where the densities are shown (the CDFs cross the same way).

5. Errors in Means, Variances, and Covariances: Empirical

Replace the true mean μ_i by the observed mean $\mu_i(1 + kZ_i)$, where Z_i is distributed $N \sim (0, 1)$ with a scale factor $k = 0.05 - 0.20$, being the size of the error. Similarly, replace the true variances and covariances by the observed variances $\sigma_i^2(1 + kZ_i)$ and covariances $\sigma_{ij}(1 + kZ_i)$. We use monthly data from 1980 to 1989 on 10 DJIA securities which include Alcoa, Boeing, Coke, Dupont, and Sears. See Chopra and Ziemba (1993) which updates and extends Kallberg and Ziemba (1984).

The certainty equivalent, CE, of a portfolio with utility function u equals u^{-1} (expected utility of a risky portfolio). This comes from the equation:

$$u(\text{CE}) = E_\xi u(\xi' x) \Rightarrow \text{CE} = u^{-1}[E_\xi u(\xi x).]$$

Assuming exponential utility and normal distributions yield exact formulas to calculate all quantities in the certainty equivalent loss, we have

$$\text{CEL} = \left\{ \frac{\text{CE}_{\text{opt}} - \text{CE}_{\text{approx}}}{\text{CE}_{\text{opt}}} \right\} 100$$

Table 1. Average ratio of CEL for errors in means, variances, and covariances.

t Risk tolerance	Errors in means vs. covariances	Errors in means vs. variances	Errors in variances vs. covariances
25	5.38	3.22	1.67
50	22.50	10.98	2.05
75	56.84	21.42	2.68
—	↓	↓	↓
—	20	10	2
—	Error Mean	Error Var	Error Covar
—	20	2	1

Observe that the mean–variance problem is

$$\text{mean}\left(\frac{\text{risk aversion}}{2}\right)\text{variance.}$$

Table 1 and Fig. 2 show that the errors in means are about 20 times the errors in covariances in terms of CEL value and the variances are twice as important as the covariances. So roughly, there is a 20:2:1 ratio in the importance of these errors. Also, this is risk aversion dependent, with $T_R = (R_A/2)100$ being the risk tolerance. So, for a high risk tolerance, that is a low risk aversion, the errors in the means are even greater. Hence, for utility functions like log of Kelly with essentially zero-risk aversion, the errors in the mean can be 100 times as important as the errors in the other parameters. So Kelly bettors should never overbet.

6. Conclusion: Spend Your Money Getting Good Mean Estimates; Use Historical Variances and Covariances

Chopra (1993) shows that the same relationship holds regarding turnover, but it is less dramatic than for the cash equivalents (see Fig. 3).

The results here apply to essentially all models. You must get the means right to win!

If the mean return for U.S. stocks is assumed to equal the long-run mean of 12% as estimated by Dimson *et al.* (2018), the model yields

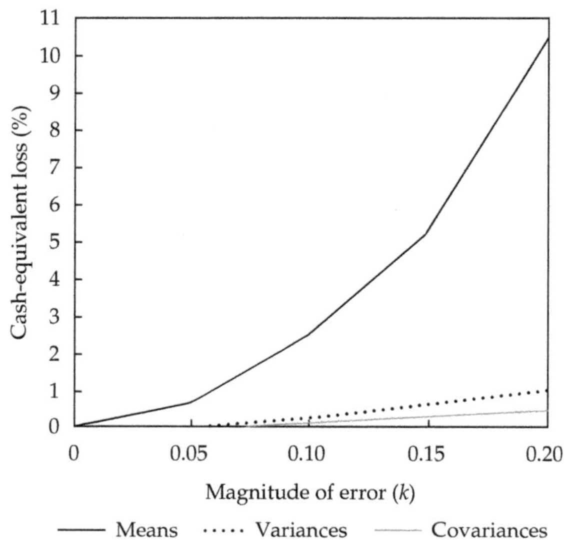

Fig. 2. Mean percentage cash equivalent loss due to errors in inputs.
Source: Chopra and Ziemba (1993).

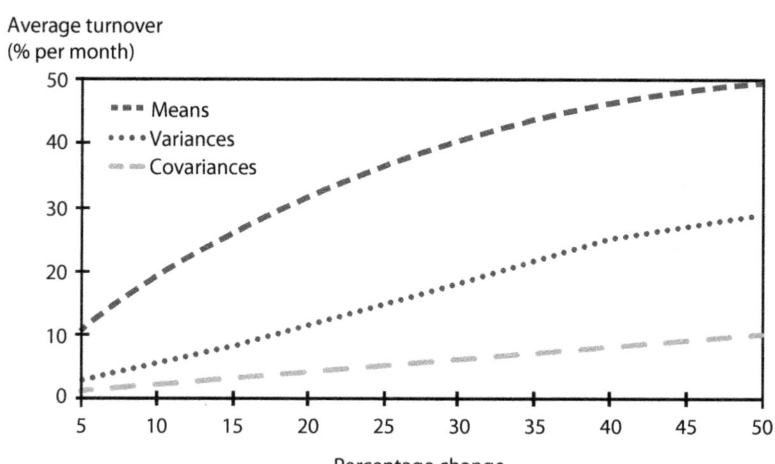

Fig. 3. Average turnover: percentage of portfolio sold (or bought) relative to preceding allocation.
Source: Chopra (1993).

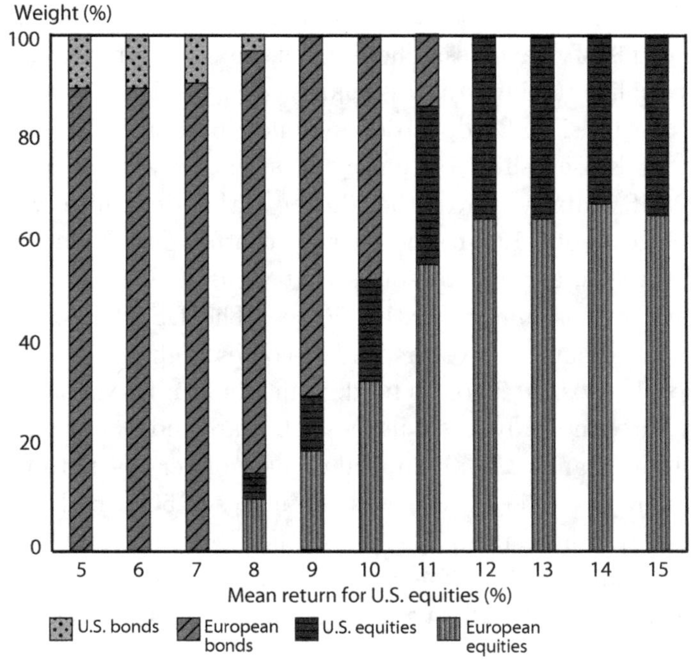

Fig. 4. Optimal asset weights at stage 1 for varying levels of U.S. equity means in a multiperiod stochastic programming pension fund model for Siemens Austria. *Source*: Geyer and Ziemba (2008).

an optimal weight for equities of 100%. A mean return for U.S. stocks of 9% implies less than 30% optimal weight for equities. This is in a five-period, 10-year stochastic programming model (see Fig. 4).

An interesting fact to note is that errors in means affect the optimal asset weights in period 1, but not so much in period 2, and hardly at all in period 5. See the graphs in Ziemba (2013). MacLean, Foster, and Ziemba (2007) show bow to use covariance to improve mean estimates.

In Ziemba (2005) and Gergaud and Ziemba (2012), a modification of the Sharpe ratio is used to evaluate great investors. The main idea is that we do not want to penalize investors for superior performance, so we will focus only on losses. But to use the Sharpe ratio, we must have a full standard deviation over the whole range of possible return outcomes and that is estimated using the downside standard deviation. That is, we artificially create gains which are mirror images of the losses. These gains are less than the real gains, so they penalize the investor less than if one uses the ordinary Sharpe ratio. Using the DSSR (downside symmetric Sharpe ratio), I found that Buffett's Berkshire Hathaway was the only fund of a group whose DSSR improves over the Sharpe ratio. Berkshire went from about 0.7 to about 1.0. I studied why the famous Buffett was not better than this, and the reason is that while he has many monthly gains, he also has many monthly losses. The DSSR is designed to measure the greatest investors and becomes higher when there are fewer monthly losses. Thorp's fund, which he ran from 1968 to 1988, had only three monthly losses in these 20 years and a very high DSSR of 13.8. Renaissance Medallion, the pioneer of very fast trading with its very high fees of 5+44, which is about fees of 50%, had a DSSR of 26.4 versus a Sharpe ratio of 2.68. So the DSSR is one way to show extreme brilliance in fund management. See Ziemba (2005) and Gergaud and Ziemba (2012), but both of these papers are reprinted in Ziemba (2017).

References

Chopra, V. K. (1993). Improving optimization. *Journal of Investing* **10**, 51–59.

Chopra, V. K. and Ziemba, W. T. (1993). The effect of errors in mean, variance and co-variance estimates on optimal portfolio choice. *Journal of Portfolio Management* **19**, 611.

Dimson, E., Marsh, P., and Staunton, M. (2019). *Global Investment Returns Yearbook, 119 Years of Financial History and Analysis*, Credit Suisse.

Fung, W. and Hsieh, D. A. (1997). Empirical characteristics of dynamic trading strategies: The case of hedge funds. *Review of Financial Studies* **10**, 275–302.

Fung, W. and Hsieh, D. A. (2001). The risk in hedge fund strategies: Theory and evidence from trend followers. *Review of Financial Studies* **14**, 313–341.

Gergaud, O. and Ziemba, W. T. (2012). Great investors: their methods, results and evaluation, *Journal of Portfolio Management* **28**(4), 128–147.

Geyer, A. and Ziemba, W. T. (2008). The Innovest Austrian Pension Fund Planning Model InnoALM. *Operations Research* **56**(4), 797–810.

Hanoch, G. and Levy, H. (1969). The efficiency analysis of choices involving risk. *Review of Economic Studies* **36**, 335–346.

Kallberg, J. G. and Ziemba, W. T. (1984). Mis-specifications in portfolio selection problems. In G. Bamberg and K. Spremann (Eds.), *Risk and Capital*, Springer Verlag, New York, pp. 74–87.

Kelly, Jr., J. R. (1956). A new interpretation of the information rate. *Bell System Technical Journal* **35**, 917–926.

Lintner, J. (1965). The valuation of risk assets and the selection of risky investment in stock portfolios and capital budgets. *Review of Economics and Statistics* **XLVII**, 13–37.

Lleo, S. and Ziemba, W. T. (2015a). Some historical perspectives on the bond-stock yield model for crash prediction around the world. *International Journal of Forecasting* **31**, 399–425.

Lleo, S. and Ziemba, W. T. (2015b). How to lose money in derivatives: Examples from hedge funds and bank trading departments, In A. Malliaris and W. T. Ziemba (Eds.), *Handbook of Futures Markets*, World Scientific, pp. 689–750.

Luenberger, D. G. (1993). A preference foundation for log mean–variance criteria in portfolio choice problems. *Journal of Economic Dynamics and Control* **17**, 887–906.

MacLean, L. C., Foster, M., and Ziemba, W. T. (2007). Empirical Bayes estimation with dynamic portfolio models. *Journal of Banking and Finance* **31**, 3503–3523.

MacLean, L. C., Sanegre, R., Zhao, Y., and Ziemba, W. T. (2004). Capital growth with security. *Journal of Economic Dynamics and Control* **28**(4), 937–954.

MacLean, L. C., Thorp, E. O., and Ziemba, W. T. (2010a). The good and bad properties of the Kelly and fractional Kelly capital growth criterion. *Quantitative Finance* (August–September), **10**, 681–687.

MacLean, L. C., Thorp, E. O., and Ziemba, W. T. (2010b). *The Kelly Capital Growth Investment Criteria*. World Scientific.

MacLean, L. C., Thorp, E. O., Zhao, Y., and Ziemba, W. T. (2011). How does the Fortune's Formula–Kelly capital growth model perform? *Journal of Portfolio Management* **37**(4), 96–111.

MacLean, L. C., Zhao, Y., and Ziemba, W. T. (2009). Optimal capital growth with convex loss penalties. Oxford, United Kingdom.

MacLean, L. C. and Ziemba, W. T. (2006). Capital growth theory and practice, In S. A. Zenios and W. T. Ziemba (Eds.), *Handbook of Asset and Liability Modeling, Volume A on theory and methodology*, North Holland, Amsterdam.

MacLean, L. C. and Ziemba, W. T. (2013a). The Kelly criterion with games of chance. In L. Vaughn Williams and D. S. Siegal (Eds.), *Oxford Handbook of Economics of Gambling*, Oxford University.

MacLean, L. C. and Ziemba, W. T. (Eds.) (2013b). *Handbook of the Fundamentals of Financial Decision Making (2 volumes)*, World Scientific.

MacLean, L. C., Ziemba, W. T., and Blazenko G. (1992). Growth versus security in dynamic investment analysis. *Management Science* **38**, 1562–1585.

MacLean, L. C., Ziemba, W. T., and Li, Y. (2005). Time to wealth goals in capital accumulation and the optimal trade-off of growth versus security. *Quantitative Finance* **5**(4), 343–357.

Mallarias, A. G. and Ziemba, W. T. (Eds.) (2015). *Handbook of Futures Markets* World Scientific.

Markowitz, H. M. (1976). Investment for the long run: New evidence for an old rule. *Journal of Finance* **31**(5), 1273–1286.

Markowitz, H. M. (2006). Samuelson and investment for the long run. In (Ed.), *Samuelsonian Economics and the Twenty-First Century*, Oxford, United Kingdom, pp. 252–261.

Merton, R. C. and Samuelson, P. A. (1974). Fallacy of the log-normal approximation to optimal portfolio decision-making over many periods. *Journal of Financial Economics* **1**, 67–94.

Mossin, J. (1966). Equilibrium in a capital asset market. *Econometrica* **34** 768–783.

Rubinstein, M. (1976). The strong case for the generalized logarithmic utility model as the premier model of financial markets. *Journal of Finance* **31**(2), 551–571.

Samuelson, P. A. (1979). Why we should not make mean log of wealth big though years to act are long. *Journal of Banking and Finance* **3**, 305–307.

Samuelson, P. A. (2006–2009). Letters to William T. Ziemba, correspondence December 13, 2006, May 7, 2008, and May 12, 2008.

Sharpe, W. F. (1964). Capital asset prices: A theory of market equilibrium under conditions of risk. *Journal of Finance* **19**, 425–442.

Thorp, E. O. (2011). The Kelly criterion in blackjack, sports betting and the stockmarket. In L. C. MacLean, E. O. Thorp, and W. T. Ziemba (Eds.), *The Kelly Capital Growth Investment Criterion*. World Scientific, pp. 789–832.

Thorp, E. O. and Mizusawa, S. (2013). Maximizing capital growth with black swan protection. In L. C. MacLean and W. T. Ziemba (Eds.), *Handbook of the Fundamentals of Financial Decision Making*. World Scientific Press, Singapore, pp. 849–873.

Ziemba, W. T. (2005). The symmetric downside-risk Sharpe ratio and the evaluation of great investors and speculators. *Journal of Portfolio Management* **32**(1), 108–122.

Ziemba, W. T. (2013). *The Stochastic Programming Approach to Asset-Liability and Asset Management*. AIMR Monograph, Charlottesville, Virginia.

Ziemba, W. T. (2015). Response to Paul A Samuelson letters and papers on the Kelly capital growth investment strategy. *Journal of Portfolio Management* **41**(1), 153–167.

Ziemba, W. T. (Ed.) (2017). *Great Investment Ideas*. World Scientific Press, Singapore.

Ziemba, W. T. (2018). *Exotic Betting at the Racetrack*. World Scientific Press, Singapore.

https://doi.org/10.1142/9789811222634_0002

Chapter 2

A comparison of some aspects of the U.S. and Japanese equity markets*

M. Bloch, J. Guerard, H. Markowitz, P. Todd and G. Xu

Daiwa Securities Trust Company, Jersey City, NJ, USA

Abstract: Comparing Japanese and U.S. securities market, the paper shows that survivor bias affecting quantitative analysis is relatively minor in Japan and substantial in the U.S. The realized average returns vs. standard derivation curve for the two countries is also quite different. But the paper suggests that the constraint levels and estimation procedures that did best in both countries in the past will do well in the future.

Keywords: Equity market; Optimized portfolios

1. Introduction

This paper describes research of the authors developed within the Global Portfolio Research Department (GPRD) of Daiwa Securities Trust Company, a subsidiary of Daiwa Securities, Japan. The principal mission of GPRD is to develop, test and apply methods of equity portfolio selection. In this study we compare certain aspects of the results of U.S. and Japanese equity portfolio analyses. An optimized portfolio using a semi-annual composite model similar to those shown in Table 1 has been used to manage the equity component of a mixed equity fund of Japanese securities, Fund Academy, since January 1991. [1]

The portfolio selection methods tested by GPRD mostly use mean-variance analysis, although some equal weighted portfolio selection procedures have also been tested for comparison purposes. Both the mean-variance analysis and the equal weighting procedures make use of "composite methods" for estimating expected returns. These methods test to see which

Correspondence to: John Guerard, Daiwa Securities Trust Co., Global Portfolio Research Department, One Evertrust Plaza, Jersey City, NJ 07302, USA.

[1] The cumulative wealth ratio of the equity component of Fund Academy was 114.20 as of 30 September 1991 (17 January 1991 = 100) whereas the corresponding wealth ratio of the Topix was 107.01.

*This article originally appeared in *Japan and the World Economy* **5**, 3–26, 1993, © 1993 by Elsevier Science Publishers.

variables out of a list of fundamental variables (such as the ratio of earnings to price, book to price, etc.) have been significant predictors of total return 'recently', and then use these variables to estimate expected return for the forthcoming period. Various methods of portfolio selection which GPRD has tested differ from each other in terms of: (a) constraints imposed on choice of portfolio, such as the level of constraints for the holding of individual securities, and constraints on turnover in changing portfolios; (b) the exact way of applying composite analysis, e.g., the definition of 'recently' in the preceding sentence, and the type of statistical inference used (OLS, latent root regression, etc.); and (c) the method of picking a point from the mean-variance frontier.

Backtests start at some date, e.g., January 1, 1975 in the case of Japanese data, select a portfolio by a prescribed method, hold the portfolio for a prescribed length of time (either a quarter or half-year, perhaps with monthly rebalancing in the interim), select a new portfolio by the method, charge the portfolio a cost for purchases and sales, and repeat this process until the end of the database. The backtest keeps track of the actual, 'out of sample', performance of the method. This performance is summarized in terms of the average, standard deviation, Sharpe ratio, semi-variance and other characteristics of the method over the period.

We attempt to make the backtests 'non-anticipating' in the sense that the method has available to it, at any point in the test, only data that was in fact available at that date. However, some runs suffer from survivor bias. That is, the database does not include all securities, then in existence at the point in time, of the class from which the method selects. Rather, it includes only those which survived until the present. This violates the requirement for a non-anticipating test in that the method is assured that all selected securities will survive until the end of the database, a piece of information which is not available in fact.

The reason that our initial backtests on Japanese data used a database without survivors was that this database was most readily available to us. Months later, when a database with non-survivors, therefore without survivor bias, was obtained and installed, we tested the effects of this bias. We also tested the effect of survivor bias for U.S. securities using annual Compustat data for fundamental variables and monthly data for prices. The principal reason for testing the effect of survivor bias in the U.S. was because quarterly Compustat data (for the top 1000 market-capitalized securities) does not contain non-survivors. We used the annual data, with and without non-survivors, to test the direction and magnitude of the survivor bias effect to help us judge how serious would be the error from this source if we used quarterly Compustat data. We were surprised, momentarily, to find that the direction of the effect of survivor bias is different for the U.S. than it is for Japan. On reflection, the difference seemed quite reasonable.

We have backtested many methods of portfolio selection, including some proprietary methods for estimating expected return not described here. Despite the fact that our composite modeling reflected regression techniques previously estimated in Guerard (1987, 1990) and Guerard and Stone (1992), all regression techniques received equal testing. Our policy in practice is based on the best method we found; that is, the method which would have done best historically. There is a question as to how to estimate the likely future performance of this policy. If we had tested only one policy, and are willing to assume that the future will be drawn from the same distribution as the past, then the best estimate of a mean would be the average of past observations. But, even assuming that the future will continue to draw from the same distributions as the past, the past average performance of the historically best policy is not a good estimate of how well it does in the future. This is because the historically best method may have been so in part because it was 'lucky'. A paper by Markowitz and Xu (1991) on 'Data Mining Corrections' presents adjustments for this effect. We will have occasion to use these data mining corrections in the present paper, but refer the reader to the Markowitz and Xu paper for their derivation.

The following two sections describe the GPRD database and its simulation of various investment strategies. The next three sections compare the differences and similarities between the U.S. and Japan with respect to the effects of survivor bias, the tradeoff between risk and return, and the optimal level of turnover permitted when reoptimizing. The next section considers whether or not a method of estimation which does well, or poorly, in one of the countries will do so in the other. A final section summarizes and suggests some broader conclusions.

2. Data

Japanese fundamental data stored in the GPRD database was collected by Nihon Keizi (Nikkei) from 1965; however, non-survivors were available only from 1970. This allowed us to begin our Japanese simulations from the beginning of 1975, since we use five years of prior returns data for the estimation of covariances. Price data was collected by the Daiwa Systems Division and was available for the period needed.

U.S. fundamental data was obtained from Compustat tapes, and price data from CRSP (Center for Research in Security Prices) tapes. Our Japanese database was set up first, and is in better shape than our U.S. data base. Specifically, our U.S. fundamental data base covers the period 1970–1990. [2]

[2] In our initial Daiwa/New York University (1991) presentation, we used 1970–1989 U.S. data. We found few data discrepancies between 1990 and 1991 Compustat databases and little simulation differences (5 basis points on average).

Non-survivors are available from Compustat for annual data only, rather than for quarterly data. Therefore our simulations use only annual U.S. fundamental data. E.g., a quarterly value for earnings to price uses the current price and the preceding annual figure for earnings, assumed known four months after the 'as of' date. A combination of considerations involving the fact that only annual fundamental data was available, the assumed four-month reporting lag and the fact that some models need five years of prior fundamental data to determine 'relatives' (e.g., the current earnings to price ratio relative to its prior five-year average) implied that some U.S. simulations could not start prior to November 1975 (denoted 7510, i.e., end of October 1975).

3. Investment methods and simulations

The underlying composite model describing total security returns is estimated using fundamental variables such as the earnings-to-price (EP), book value-to-price (BP), cash flow to price (CP), and sales-to-price-ratios (SP). We also use the current fundamental ratio relative to its five-year mean (the 'relative' variables). One may summarize the multiple regression model used to identify the determinants of U.S. equity returns in the following cross-sectional equation:

$$\begin{aligned} \mathrm{TR_T} = a_0 + a_1\mathrm{EP}_t + a_2\mathrm{BP}_t + a_3\mathrm{CP}_t + a_4\mathrm{SP}_t + a_5\mathrm{REP}_t + a_6\mathrm{RBP}_t \\ + a_7\mathrm{RCP}_t + a_8\mathrm{RSP}_t + e_t \end{aligned} \tag{1}$$

where: $\mathrm{TR_T}$ = ranked total returns (for six months (t to $t+6$) in semi-annual analysis and three months for quarterly data) following the calculation of fundamental financial variables, EP, BP, CP, SP, REP, RBP, RCP; RSP = previously defined ranked financial variables, a_0, a_1, ... a_8 = regression parameters, e_t = randomly distributed error terms.

The reader is referred to Guerard and Takano (1991) and Miller et al. (1991) for a complete description of the model. The benefits of the underlying model is that it is in keeping with the recent anomalies literature, particularly with the use of EP and BP variables (see Fama and French, 1991; and Jacobs and Levy, 1988). One can use ordinary least squares (OLS), an outlier-adjustment, or robust (ROB) regression procedure proposed by Beaton and Tukey (1974), latent root regression (LRR) for decomposing the correlation matrix into its non-predictive near-singularities (addressing multicollinearity), and using latent root regression on the robust-weighted data (referred to as weighted latent root regression, WLRR. An example of the application of the WLRR technique can be shown when one models total returns for the first quarter of 1990 using fundamental data as of December 1989.

The OLS-estimated equation (1) is:

$$\begin{aligned} \text{TR} = {} & \underset{(18.39)}{499.10} - \underset{(-4.49)}{0.219\text{EP}} - \underset{(-0.61)}{0.025\text{BP}} + \underset{(1.47)}{0.065\text{CP}} + \underset{(5.68)}{0.182\text{SP}} \quad (t) \\ & - \underset{(-0.57)}{0.023\text{REP}} + \underset{(0.55)}{0.026\text{RBP}} + \underset{(2.34)}{0.124\text{RC}} - \underset{(-2.81)}{0.141\text{RSP}}, \end{aligned}$$

$R^2 = 0.068$, $F = 8.89$.

One finds that only the sales and relative cash flow variables are statistically significant at the 10 percent level in the OLS estimation. The WLRR-estimated equation (1) for the first quarter of 1990 is:

$$\begin{aligned} \text{TR} = {} & \underset{(2.34)}{0.047\text{EP}} - \underset{(-3.83)}{0.066\text{BP}} - \underset{(-6.72)}{0.124\text{CP}} + \underset{(7.92)}{0.244\text{SP}} + \underset{(1.17)}{0.036\text{REP}} \quad (t) \\ & + \underset{(1.78)}{0.056\text{RBP}} + \underset{(0.22)}{0.007\text{RCP}} - \underset{(-2.39)}{0.061\text{RSP}}, \quad R^2 = 0.061, \ F = 12.17. \end{aligned}$$

The WLRR estimation produces a different result than the OLS estimation; earnings, sales, and relative bookvalue variables are significantly associated with total returns. The reader is referred to Gunst and Mason (1980), Guerard (1987, 1990), Guerard and Stone (1992) for a more complete discussion of regression techniques.

In our initial Japanese analysis, we estimate quarterly models using semi-annual Japanese data with quarterly prices to create quarterly ratios. The statistically significant and the coefficients having the 'correct' sign were used in the next period model. We find support for the four-quarter smoothed model described in Miller et al. (1991) using the WLRR procedure. The four-quarter smoothed composite models were used as an input to the mean-variance optimization analysis. We believed that our proposed methods of estimating expected returns might not be applicable to financial corporations. Therefore, we excluded these from all analyses performed thus far except for some Japanese analyses, not reported here, wherein we analyze the effect of indexing the financials as part of the portfolio. Specifically, the universe of securities used in the Japanese analyses reported here consist of the first section of the Tokyo Stock Exchange (TSE) less the financial firms, for a total of approximately 1000 firms. The universe for the U.S. analyses consists of the 1000 largest firms on the New York and American Stock Exchanges, again ignoring the financial firms.

Figure 1 summarizes the inputs and outputs of a mean-variance analysis. Inputs consist of estimates of expected returns for each security; estimates of variances and covariances (or the equivalent) and constraints on the choice of portfolio. The output includes the set of efficient mean and variance (or standard deviation) combinations. There is an efficient portfolio associated with any choice of efficient mean-variance combination.

Our experimentation included various combinations of expected return estimation procedure and levels of constraints on turnover and individual

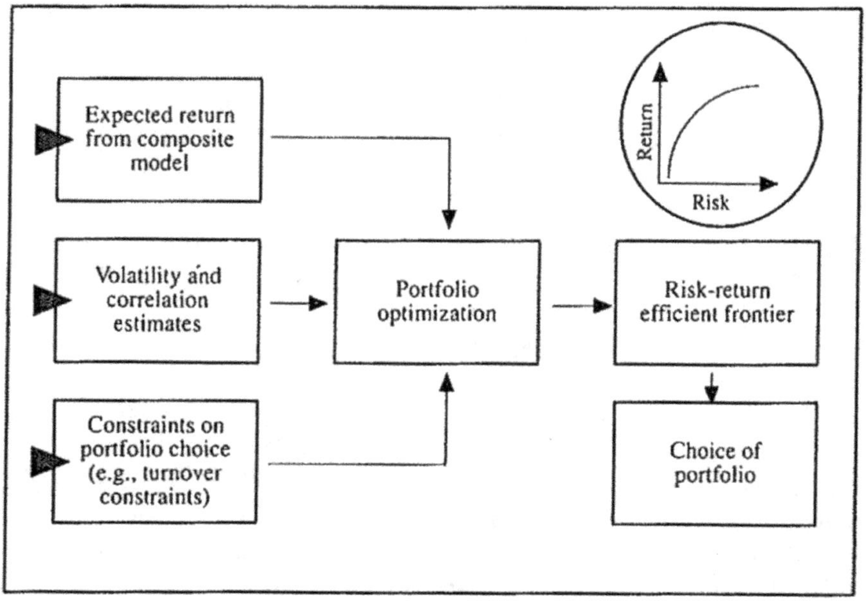

Fig. 1. Investment process.

holdings. Table 1 presents some of the simulations we have run against the Japanese database. Each line summarizes one simulation. The first column presents a simulation ID (SID); the second indicates whether the portfolio was reoptimized (OP) quarterly (3) or semiannually (6). Table 1 is sorted first by OP and then by geometric mean return (GM) in the next to last column.

After the first optimization, the optimizer is told to constrain the level of turnover in subsequent reoptimizations. For example, our first Japanese simulations used semi-annual reoptimization with a 50% turnover constraint.

Estimated future annual geometric mean (after data mining adjustment)

$$= \text{Antilog of } [(\bar{Y} + \beta^{est}(\bar{Y}_b - \bar{Y}))] - 1$$
$$= \text{Antilog of } [\,0.2899 + 0.5944\,(0.2280 - 0.1899)] - 1$$
$$= 23.68\%$$

where:

$\bar{Y}$ = the overall overage of logarithm of one plus return for all models = 0.1899

$\bar{Y}_b$ = the average of logarithm of one plus return for the Best Model = 0.2280

β^{est} = 0.5944

Fig. 2. Data mining adjustment.

We found that a 20% turnover constraint worked best for simulations with semi-annual reoptimizations, and 10% did best with quarterly reoptimizations. The turnover constraints (TOV) of various simulations is shown in the third column of Table 1. The term RP = 1 in the fourth column indicates that

Table 1
D-POS, Japan. Simulation results: sorted by geometric mean. Let UL = 2.0 TCR = 2.0 PM = −1 PPar = 0.90 Begin = 7412 End = 9012.

SID	OP	TOV	RP	Rtri	ERET	GM	Shrp
900869	3	10.00	1	25.0	PROPRIETARY	25.60	0.89
900867	3	10.00	0	0.0	PROPRIETARY	25.39	0.89
900868	3	10.00	1	20.0	PROPRIETARY	25.32	0.87
900860	3	15.00	1	25.0	PROPRIETARY	24.28	0.84
900853	3	15.00	0	0.0	PROPRIETARY	24.19	0.85
900858	3	10.00	1	25.0	PROPRIETARY	24.04	0.85
900852	3	12.50	0	0.0	PROPRIETARY	23.94	0.85
900855	3	10.00	1	20.0	PROPRIETARY	23.93	0.86
900856	3	12.50	1	20.0	PROPRIETARY	23.90	0.84
900854	3	17.50	0	0.0	PROPRIETARY	23.89	0.84
900859	3	12.50	1	25.0	PROPRIETARY	23.89	0.83
900857	3	15.00	1	20.0	PROPRIETARY	23.81	0.82
900819	3	10.00	0	0.0	REGR(WLRR,4Q,4)	22.74	0.83
900820	3	10.00	1	25.0	REGR(WLRR,4Q,4)	22.68	0.82
900944	3	10.00	0	0.0	BPR	22.43	0.78
900908	3	10.00	1	20.0	REGR(LRR,4Q,9.1)	22.23	0.75
900874	3	10.00	0	0.0	REGR(OLS,4Q,8)	22.16	0.79
900878	3	10.00	0	0.0	REGR(OLS,4Q,9.1)	22.16	0.79
900903	3	10.00	0	0.0	REGR(OLS,4Q,8)	22.16	0.79
900914	3	10.00	0	0.0	REGR(OLS,4Q,9.1)	22.16	0.79
900841	3	10.00	1	25.0	REGR(WLRR,1Q,4)	22.00	0.79
900817	3	10.00	0	0.0	REGR(LRR,4Q14)	21.99	0.76
900983	3	10.00	1	20.0	REGR(WLRR,4Q,9.1)	21.93	0.75
900984	3	10.00	1	20.0	REGR(WLRR,4Q,9.1)	21.86	0.75
900794	3	15.00	1	20.0	REGR(WLRR,1Q,4)	21.84	0.76
900818	3	10.00	1	25.0	REGR(LRR,4Q,4)	21.84	0.75
900877	3	10.00	0	0.0	REGR(WLRR,4Q,8)	21.84	0.78
900906	3	10.00	0	0.0	REGR(WLRR,4Q,8)	21.84	0.78
900985	3	12.50	1	20.0	REGR(WLRR,4Q,9.1)	21.84	0.75
900913	3	10.00	0	0.0	REGR(WLRR,4Q,9.2)	21.83	0.77
900793	3	12.50	1	20.0	REGR(WLRR,1Q,4)	21.78	0.78
900791	3	12.50	0	0.0	REGR(WLRR,1Q,4)	21.75	0.79
900792	3	15.00	0	0.0	REGR(WLRR,1Q,4)	21.68	0.77
900982	3	10.00	1	20.0	REGR(WLRR,4Q,9.1)	21.66	0.75
900842	3	10.00	1	25.0	REGR(WLRR,10,4)	21.55	0.79
900766	3	10.00	1	20.0	REGR(WLRR,1Q,4)	21.49	0.78
900810	3	15.00	0	0.0	REGR(WLRR,1Q,4)	21.47	0.76
900901	3	10.00	0	0.0	REGR(LRR,4Q,9.1)	21.45	0.72
900813	3	10.00	0	0.0	REGR(OLS,4Q,4)	21.42	0.78
900840	3	10.00	1	25.0	REGR(WLRR,1Q,4)	21.41	0.76
900838	3	10.00	1	25.0	REGR(WLRR,1Q,4)	21.40	0.76
900909	3	10.00	1	20.0	REGR(WLRR,4Q,9.1)	21.40	0.75
900910	3	10.00	0	0.0	REGR(LRR,4Q,9.2)	21.34	0.75
900816	3	10.00	1	25.0	REGR(ROB,4Q,4)	21.30	0.76
900839	3	10.00	1	25.0	REGR(WLRR,1Q,4)	21.30	0.75

Table 1 (continued)

SID	OP	TOV	RP	Rtri	ERET	GM	Shrp
900912	3	10.00	0	0.0	REGR(LRR,4Q,9.2)	21.29	0.71
900765	3	10.00	0	0.0	REGR(WLRR,1Q,4)	21.24	0.76
900815	3	10.00	0	0.0	REGR(ROB,4Q,4)	21.23	0.76
900902	3	10.00	0	0.0	REGR(WLRR,4Q,9.1)	21.16	0.74
900986	3	15.00	1	20.0	REGR(WLRR,4Q,9.1)	21.09	0.72
900954	3	10.00	0	0.0	REGR(OLS,4Q,4)	20.91	0.72
900876	3	10.00	0	0.0	REGR(LRR,4Q,8)	20.90	0.74
900905	3	10.00	0	0.0	REGR(LRR,4Q,8)	20.90	0.74
900911	3	10.00	0	0.0	REGR(ROB,4Q,9.2)	20.66	0.72
900907	3	10.00	1	20.0	REGR(ROB,4Q,9.1)	20.36	0.74
900763	3	10.00	0	0.0	REGR(LRR,1Q,4)	20.21	0.71
900875	3	10.00	0	0.0	REGR(ROB,4Q,8)	20.15	0.71
900904	3	10.00	0	0.0	REGR(ROB,4Q,8)	20.15	0.71
900787	3	12.50	0	0.0	REGR(LRR,1Q,4)	20.08	0.71
900900	3	10.00	0	0.0	REGR(ROB,4Q,9.1)	20.07	0.72
900781	3	12.50	1	20.0	REGR(OLS,1Q,4)	19.96	0.71
900788	3	15.00	0	0.0	REGR(LRR,1Q,4)	19.92	0.70
900764	3	10.00	1	20.0	REGR(LRR,1Q,4).	19.88	0.70
900790	3	15.00	1	20.0	REGR(LRR,1Q,4)	19.81	0.70
900789	3	12.50	1	20.0	REGR(LRR,1Q,4)	19.78	0.70
900779	3	12.50	0	0.0	REGR(OLS,1Q,4)	19.77	0.67
900786	3	15.00	1	20.0	REGR(ROB,1Q,4)	19.76	0.71
900780	3	15.00	0	0.0	REGR(OLS,1Q,4)	19.72	0.69
900784	3	15.00	0	0.0	REGR(ROB,1Q,4)	19.67	0.71
900782	3	15.00	1	20.0	REGR(OLS,1Q,4)	19.41	0.69
900759	3	10.00	0	0.0	REGR(OLS,1Q,4)	19.40	0.67
900785	3	12.50	1	20.0	REGR(ROB,1Q,4)	19.33	0.69
900760	3	10.00	1	20.0	REGR(OLS,1Q,4)	19.31	0.66
900783	3	12.50	0	0.0	REGR(ROB,1Q,4)	19.10	0.69
900761	3	10.00	0	0.0	REGR(ROB,1Q,4)	19.03	0.68
900931	3	10.00	0	0.0	CPR	19.01	0.68
900762	3	10.00	1	20.0	REGR(ROB,1Q,4)	19.00	0.67
900932	3	10.00	0	0.0	SPR	18.63	0.61
900716	3	10.00	1	20.0	benchmark	17.25	0.60
900927	3	10.00	0	0.0	EPR	16.82	0.57
900826	6	20.00	3	25.0	PROPRIETARY	24.63	0.84
900709	6	20.00	3	20.0	PROPRIETARY	23.61	0.81
900710	6	20.00	3	25.0	PROPRIETARY	23.44	0.82
900733	6	25.00	1	20.0	PROPRIETARY	23.34	0.80
900773	6	17.50	3	20.0	PROPRIETARY	23.26	0.78
900707	6	20.00	3	20.0	PROPRIETARY	23.08	0.79
900847	6	20.00	0	0.0	PROPRIETARY	22.62	0.81
901030	6	20.00	3	20.0	BPR	22.42	0.78
900796	6	20.00	3	20.0	REGR(OLS,2S,4)	22.33	0.79
901047	6	20.00	3	20.0	BPR	22.20	0.77
900770	6	22.50	0	0.0	REGR(OLS,1S,4)	22.17	0.77
900795	6	20.00	0	0.0	REGR(OLS,2S,4)	22.14	0.79
900749	6	20.00	3	25.0	REGR(OLS,1S,4)	22.03	0.78
900800	6	20.00	3	20.0	REGR(LRR,2S,4)	21.98	0.78
900849	6	20.00	0	0.0	REGR(LRR,3S,4)	21.98	0.77

Table 1 (continued)

SID	OP	TOV	RP	Rtri	ERET	GM	Shrp
900748	6	20.00	3	20.0	REGR(OLS,1S,4)	21.80	0.77
900754	6	20.00	3	20.0	REGR(LRR,12,4)	21.68	0.74
900747	6	20.00	0	0.0	REGR(OLS,1S,4)	21.65	0.77
900802	6	20.00	3	20.0	REGR(WLRR,2S,4)	21.60	0.79
901029	6	20.00	0	0.0	BPR	21.59	0.76
900755	6	20.00	3	25.0	REGR(LRR,1S,4)	21.52	0.74
900799	6	20.00	0	0.0	REGR(LRR,2S,4)	21.51	0.77
901046	6	20.00	0	0.0	BPR	21.49	0.76
900801	6	20.00	0	0.0	REGR(WLRR,2S,4)	21.40	0.79
900769	6	17.50	0	0.0	REGR(OLS,1S,4)	21.34	0.76
900778	6	22.50	3	20.0	REGR(WLRR,1S,4)	21.30	0.79
900772	6	22.50	0	0.0	REGR(LRR,1S,4)	21.26	0.72
900753	6	20.00	0	0.0	REGR(LRR,1S,4)	21.20	0.72
900756	6	20.00	0	0.0	REGR(WLRR,1S,4)	21.10	0.77
900757	6	20.00	3	20.0	REGR(WLRR,1S,4)	21.06	0.78
900758	6	20.00	3	25.0	REGR(WLRR,1S,4)	21.02	0.78
900777	6	17.50	3	20.0	REGR(WLRR,1S,4)	20.95	0.78
900771	6	17.50	0	0.0	REGR(LRR,1S,4)	20.93	0.71
900848	6	20.00	0	0.0	REGR(ROB,3S,4)	20.74	0.76
900776	6	22.50	3	20.0	REGR(ROB,1S,4)	20.37	0.76
900797	6	20.00	0	0.0	REGR(ROB,22,4)	20.24	0.75
900798	6	20.00	3	20.0	REGR(ROB,2S,4)	20.12	0.76
900752	6	20.00	3	25.0	REGR(ROB,1S,4)	19.56	0.73
900751	6	20.00	3	20.0	REGR(ROB,1S,4)	19.35	0.73
900750	6	20.00	0	0.0	REGR(ROB,1S,4)	19.29	0.72
900775	6	17.50	3	20.0	REGR(ROB,1S,4)	19.26	0.72
901049	6	20.00	3	20.0	CPR	18.99	0.68
901051	6	20.00	3	20.0	SPR	18.69	0.61
901048	6	20.00	0	0.0	CPR	18.65	0.67
901050	6	20.00	0	0.0	SPR	17.87	0.59
901045	6	20.00	3	20.0	EPR	17.55	0.59
901044	6	20.00	0	0.0	EPR	17.34	0.59

SID = simulation ID; OP = period of re-optimization; TOV = turnover constraint; Rtri = rebalancing trigger; ERET = model description; GM = geometric mean; Shrp = Sharpe ratio.

REGR (technique, period, equation)

Technique = OLS for ordinary least-squares regression analysis,
LRR for latent root regression,
ROB for robust regression,
WLRR for weighted latent root regression;

Period = 1S for one-period semi-annual analysis,
2S for two-period semi-annual analysis,
3S for three-period semi-annual analysis,
1Q for one-period quarterly analysis,
4Q for four-period quarterly analysis;

Equation = 4; $TRR = a_0 + a_1 EPR + a_2 BPR + a_3 CPR + a_4 SPR + a_5 REPR + a_6 RPBR + a_7 RCPR + a_8 RSPR + e_t$

8; $TRR = a_0 + a_1 EPR + a_2 BPR + a_3 CPR + a_4 SPR + e_t$

9.1; $TRR = a_0 + a_1 EPR + a_2 BPR + a_3 CPR + a_4 SPR + a_5 REPR(2) + a_6 RPBR(2) + a_7 RCPR(2) + a_8 RSPR(2) + e_t,$

where (2) denotes 2-year averages of relative variables.

9.2; $TRR = a_0 + a_1 EPR + a_2 BPR + a_3 CPR + a_4 SPR + a_5 REPR(3) + a_6 RPBR(3) + a_7 RCPR(3) + a_8 RSPR(3) + e_t,$

where (3) denotes 3-year averages of relative variables.

investment policy included monthly rebalancing between optimizations; = 3 indicates quarterly rebalancing between (semi-annual) reoptimizations; = 0 indicates no rebalancing. 'Rtri' indicates the deviation between the actual weight of a security in the portfolio, as compared to target weight, which 'triggers' the rebalancing. For example, Rtri = 0.25 indicates that if the target weight is 1.00 percent and the actual weight is 1.25 percent then some of the security will be sold to bring the weight back to one percent. (The story is slightly more complicated, as a corollary of the fact that the portfolio is kept fully invested.) At first we tried rebalancing with 5 and 10 percent trigger points, but found trigger points in the neighborhood of 25 percent worked more satisfactorily. The last two columns show the actual ('out of sample') geometric mean and Sharpe ratio (Shrp) for each run. The third from last run indicates the expected return estimation technique (ERET). For example, BPR in this column for the nineteenth simulation listed indicates that essentially each security's rank in a book to price listing was used as the estimate of its expected return. The ERET for the 17th run in Table 1 is characterized as 'REGR(WLRR,4Q,4)'. This indicates that expected return is essentially estimated by a regression of actual return ranking against several variables. WLRR indicates that a weighted latent root regression technique is used as compared to, e.g., ordinary least squares, OLS. '4Q' indicates that the coefficients used to estimate expected return are the average of four quarterly cross sectional regressions (setting to zero any coefficients in a cross sectional regression which are not significant at the 10 percent level or have the 'wrong' sign). The final '4' indicates that equation 4 of Table 1 is used in each cross sectional regression. [3] The REGR

[3] We use the 'conventional' approach to fundamental variables; that is, the earnings-to-price formulation, rather than the 'traditionally'-analyzed price-to-earnings formulation. The use of the traditional approach produces almost identical results to the conventional approach (see Table 2). For a description of the traditional approach, the 'lower P/B' or 'low P/E' model, see Guerard (1990).

Table 2
Survivor-biased-free universe, traditional modeling.

Model	GM	Sharpe
WLRR	22.51	0.83
LRR	22.30	0.80
ROB	19.87	0.71
OLS	20.90	0.73
PBR	21.65	0.77

We find no significant difference between the traditional and conventional modeling formulations. Significant excess returns are produced out-of-sample with the quarterly-based models. Furthermore, the use of the traditional modeling approach produces models that can well discriminate with respect to the average model performance, producing Markowitz and Xu, 1991) data-mining beta of 0.76 ($t = 4.25$). Thus, the best model, the REGR(WLRR,4Q), is significantly better than the average of the models.

(WLRR,4Q,4) produces the highest GM of any non-proprietary, or public, Japanese model in our analysis.

The ERET labelled PROPRIETARY, used in SID = 900869, is like REGR(WLRR,4Q,4) except that it includes two proprietary features. The only thing which we say about these two features is that they are not the result of experimentation with dozens of features. They were the results of certain theoretical considerations, and were added to John Guerard's work with composite modeling (1990, 1991). The second line in the heading of the table notes certain parameters which were the same in all the runs of Table 1. The term UL = 2.0 indicates that in all runs in this table a two percent upper limit on the holding of any one security was imposed at each optimization; TCR = 2.0 indicates that the simulation charged a two percent each way transaction cost, including estimated market impact. A pick parameter (PPar) of 1.00 would indicate that the portfolio with maximum expected return was picked from the frontier at each optimization; a zero PPar would indicate that the minimum variance portfolio was chosen each time. The indicated PPar = 0.90 means that the selected portfolio was ninety percent of the way (on the expected return axis) from the minimum variance to the maximum expected return portfolio. UNID = 150 indicates that this is the latest, unbiased Japanese database. The 'start' and 'end' parameters indicate that all these runs began at the end of 7412 and ended at the end of 9012. Also, all runs reported here used historical covariances for the preceding 60 months.

Figures 3 and 4 illustrate the value added by the REGR(WLRR,4Q,4) and proprietary model methods of expected return estimation, and by the mean-variance process. [4] Each point in the figure shows the average return and standard deviation realized ('out of sample') by an investment policy in a 7412 through 9012 Japanese simulation. (The y-axis is actually twelve times the average monthly return. This common method of 'annualizing' average monthly returns gives a lower figure than the more accurate method: annualized = exp(12 * (monthly mean − 1/2 * monthly variance)). The x-axis is the square root of 12 times monthly standard deviation. Much smoother curves are observed using these essentially monthly numbers than when the means

[4] The equally-weighted portfolio created in Figure 3 may appear somewhat strange in that there is little spread between the portfolio returns using PPar = 0.20 and PPar = 1.00. The use of a PPar of 0.20 implies that you would purchase a security if its composite score was in the highest 20 percent and sell it when it fell below the 20th percentile. One can easily imagine a security could be purchased one quarter with a composite percentile ranking of 20 and sold the next quarter with a composite percentile ranking of 21. Few managers would implement such a strategy. If one purchased securities in the upper quintile and sold when their respective composite scores fell into the lowest quintile, rebalancing every quarter to produce equally-weighted portfolios, the portfolio average annual return for REGR(WLRR,4Q,4) is 27.17 percent for the 1974–1990 period and the corresponding Sharpe ratio is 0.81. The turnover for the revised quintile strategy is 38 percent as opposed to 167 percent for the PPar strategy shown in Figure 3.

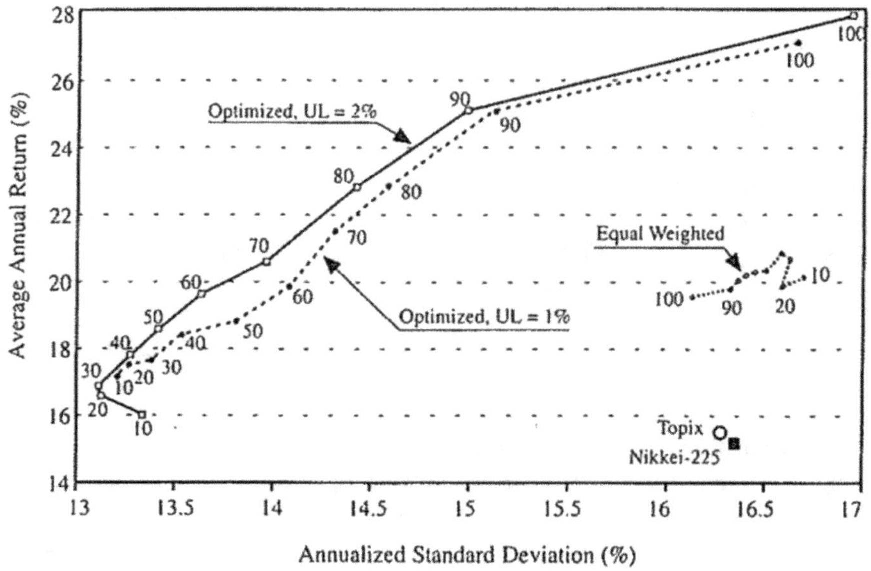

Fig. 3. Observed risk-return tradeoff, Japan. REGR(WLRR,4Q,4), TCR = 2%.

and standard deviations of (the relatively few) annual returns are plotted.) Points on the upper curve show the monthly means and standards deviation, 'annualized', for policies like that of simulation SID = 900869, except for

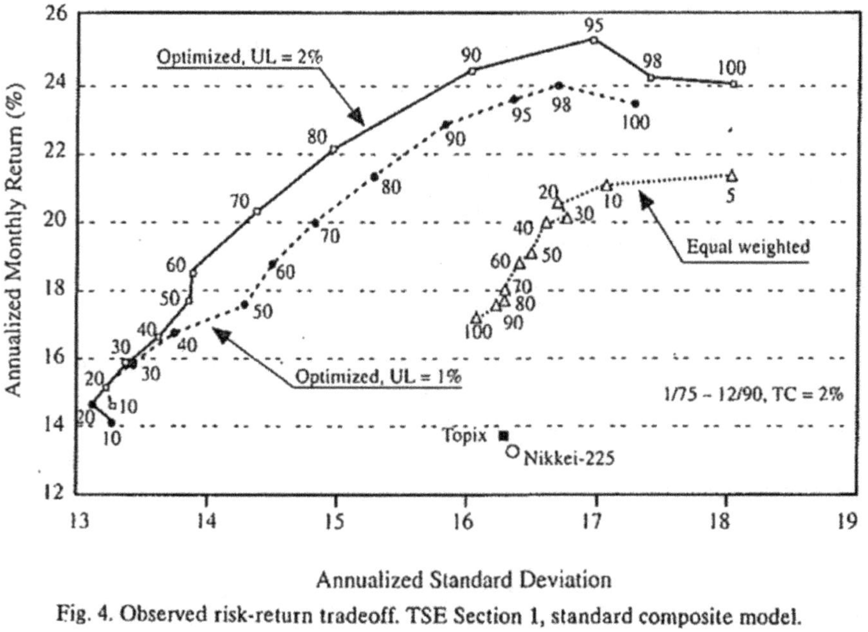

Fig. 4. Observed risk-return tradeoff. TSE Section 1, standard composite model.

choice of portfolio from the efficient frontier. The point labelled 90 represents PPar = 0.90, i.e., SID = 900869 on the first line of Table 1. We see that, by and large, the curve of actual average returns and standard deviations looks roughly like an ex ante mean-variance frontier. One difference is that the realized average return which resulted when anticipated expected return was maximized was less than the realized average return for some portfolios with lower anticipated expected return. Presumably this is due to 'sampling error' which we would expect to be greater for portfolios at the high variance end of the efficient frontier.

The second curve, labelled UL = 1%, is like the first except that an upper limit of one percent on the holdings of any one security is imposed by the optimizer in tracing out the efficient frontier. The third curve shows realized average and standard deviations of return for equal weighted portfolios. Securities are ranked according to their expected returns. For the point labelled '10', the top 10 percent are equal weighted in the portfolio; twenty percent for the point labelled '20'; etc. There is no turnover constraint associated with this method, which is one reason why the average returns for the optimized curves are much higher, for a given level of standard deviation, than those for the equal weighted portfolios. The realized average and standard deviation of returns for the Topix and the Nikkei-225, with dividends, without transaction costs, are also shown.

In Figures 5 and 6 we show the observed risk–return relationship for the REGR(WLRR,4Q,4) model in the U.S. using two and one percent transac-

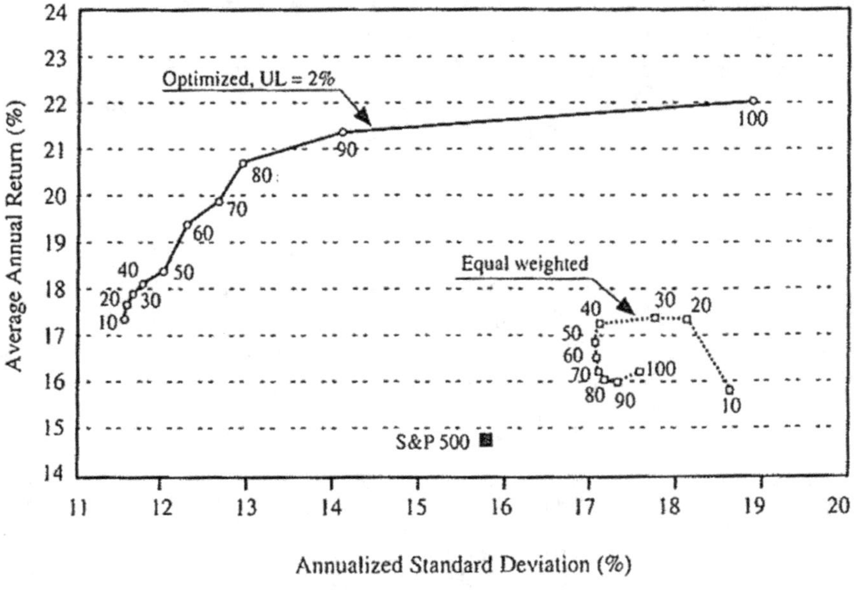

Fig. 5. Observed risk-return tradeoff, U.S. Model REGR(WLRR,4Q,4). TCR 2%.

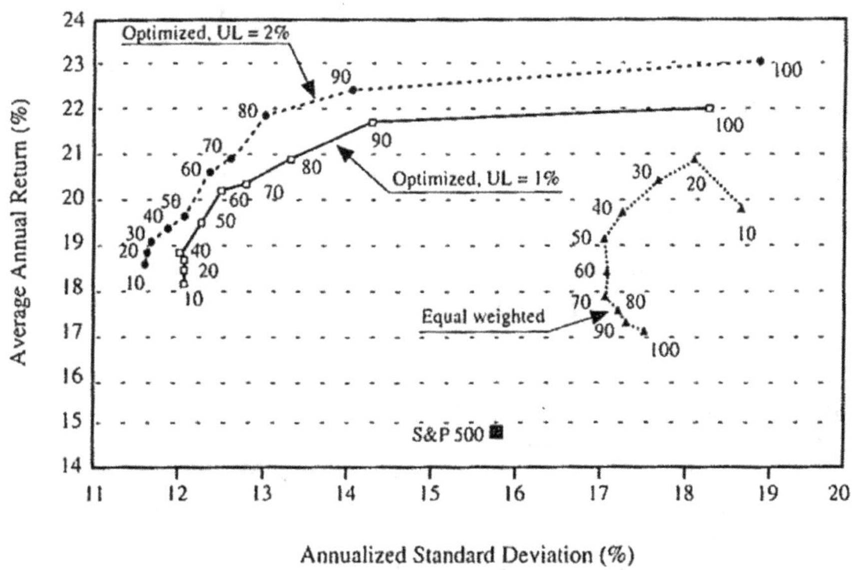

Fig. 6. Observed risk-return tradeoff, U.S. Model REGR(WLRR,4Q,4). TCR 1%.

tions costs assumptions. The REGR(WLRR,4Q,4) estimation technique produces the highest GM in the U.S. The two percent transactions cost figure is included for comparison purposes with Japan and the one percent assumption is probably more realistic. [5] The U.S. REGR(WLRR,4Q,4) with one percent transactions costs looks quite similar to the Japanese curve. Realized average returns are higher and realized standard deviations are higher in Japan than in the United States. It is very interesting to note the higher Sharpe ratios in the United States than in the Japan. We show the respective GMs and Sharpe ratios in Table 3.

4. Effects of survivor bias

For reasons noted in the introduction, we analyzed the effect of survivor bias in Japan and the U.S. The differences between the effect in the U.S. and that in Japan is illustrated in Table 4 and some following figures and table. The results in Table 4 are from the simulations in Table 1, and similar ones for the U.S., with OP = 3, TOV = 10.00, RP = Rtri = 0 and for 16 methods

[5] If one pursued the equally-weighted strategy described in footnote 4 in the United States (purchasing of the upper quintile selling of the securities once they fall into the lower quintile and quarterly rebalancing to produce equally-weighted portfolios), one finds that the equally-weighted portfolios produce average annual returns of 19.92 and 20.90 percent for the two and one percent transactions costs, respectively. The corresponding Sharpe ratios are 0.63 and 0.68, respectively, for the October 1975–December 1990 period.

Table 3
Simulation results: D-POS JP, US. Let End = 9012 TOV = 10 TCR = 2 UL = 2 NOBS = 60. UNID = 131 survivor-biased-free universe, US, Strt = 7510 UNID = 150 survivor-biased-free universe, JP, Strt = 7509.

SID	ERET	UNID	PM	PPar	GM	Shrp
901370	REGR(WLRR,4Q,4)	150	−1.0	1.00	24.55	0.81
901371	REGR(WLRR,4Q,4)	150	−1.0	0.90	22.60	0.78
901372	REGR(WLRR,4Q,4)	150	−1.0	0.80	20.75	0.71
901373	REGR(WLRR,4Q,4)	150	−1.0	0.70	19.21	0.66
901374	REGR(WLRR,4Q,4)	150	−1.0	0.60	18.12	0.62
901375	REGR(WLRR,4Q,4)	150	−1.0	0.50	16.72	0.58
901376	REGR(WLRR,4Q,4)	150	−1.0	0.40	15.89	0.55
901377	REGR(WLRR,4Q,4)	150	−1.0	0.30	15.18	0.53
901378	REGR(WLRR,4Q,4)	150	−1.0	0.20	14.92	0.51
901379	REGR(WLRR,4Q,4)	150	−1.0	0.10	14.24	0.48
50701	REGR(WLRR,4Q,4)	131	−1.0	1.00	20.61	0.89
50702	REGR(WLRR,4Q,4)	131	−1.0	0.90	20.52	1.07
50703	REGR(WLRR,4Q,4)	131	−1.0	0.80	20.03	1.11
50704	REGR(WLRR,4Q,4)	131	−1.0	0.70	19.23	1.09
50705	REGR(WLRR,4Q,4)	131	−1.0	0.60	18.80	1.09
50706	REGR(WLRR,4Q,4)	131	−1.0	0.50	17.86	1.02
50707	REGR(WLRR,4Q,4)	131	−1.0	0.40	17.60	0.98
50708	REGR(WLRR,4Q,4)	131	−1.0	0.30	17.35	0.97
50709	REGR(WLRR,4Q,4)	131	−1.0	0.20	17.11	0.95
50710	REGR(WLRR,4Q,4)	131	−1.0	0.10	16.82	0.92

SID = simulation identification number; ERET = expected return method; UL = upper limit; TCR = transactions costs percentage; TOV = turnover constraint; GM = geometric mean; Shrp = sharpe ratio.

Table 4
Differences of returns between unbiased and biased.

Models	U.S. (75.10–90.12)	Japan (75.10–90.12)
EPR	0.81	−0.47
BPR	0.33	−0.18
CPR	−0.18	−0.08
SPR	−0.21	−0.73
(OLS,4Q)	1.05	−0.29
(ROB,4Q)	0.36	0.14
(LRR,4Q)	0.60	−0.49
(WLRR,4Q)	0.72	−0.38
(OLS,2S)	1.22	0.03
(ROB,2S)	0.92	0.27
(LRR,2S)	0.86	−0.35
(WLRR,2S)	0.96	−0.23
(OLS,3S)	1.08	−0.31
(ROB,3S)	0.42	0.04
(LRR,3S)	0.00	0.33
(WLRR,3S)	0.90	−0.05
Benchmark	1.04	−0.84

U.S. average difference: 0.64; Japan average difference: −0.20; probability (that they are equal): 0.00.

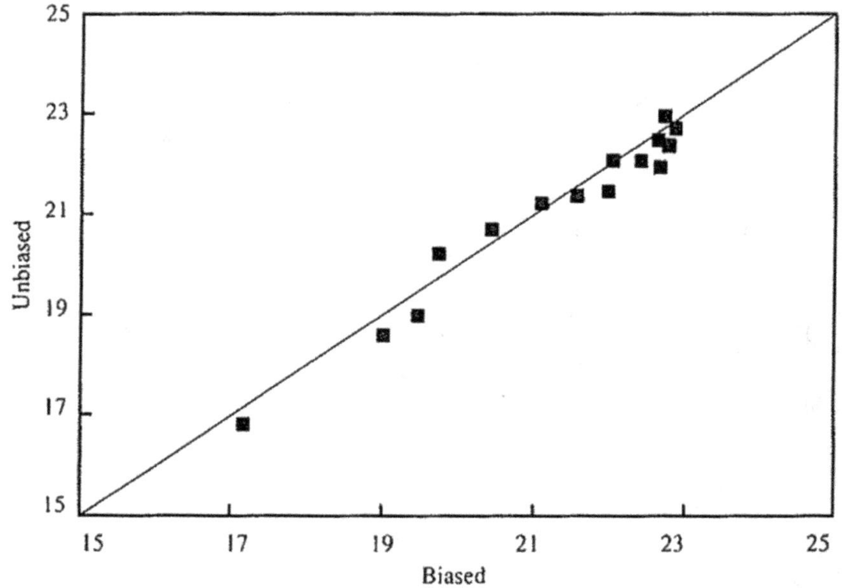

Fig. 7. Japanese survivor bias – geometric means (7412–9012).

of estimating expected return. The methods are indicated in the first column of the table. BPR, EPR, CPR and SPR are as defined in Table 1c. The others are estimation procedures denoted as REGR(x, y, z) in Table 1, with $z = 4$ and with x and y as indicated.

On the average the unbiased (including survivors) geometric means in the U.S. exceeded those of the biased (excluding survivors) GMs by 64 basis points. For the same period, the Japanese unbiased GMs were less than the biased ones by 20 basis points. The probability that the U.S and Japanese observations came from the same (normal) population is less than 0.0001. Since the U.S. unbiased average exceeds the biased average, a greater dollar's worth of non-survivors disappeared for 'profitable reasons', e.g., because of mergers and acquisitions. Since the Japanese unbiased average is less than the biased average, a greater yen's worth of non-survivors disappeared for 'unprofitable reasons', e.g., bankruptcies. It seems plausible that the difference is due to greater merger and acquisition activity in the U.S.

Figures 7 through 10, and Table 4, address the following question: if an investment policy does well (or poorly) when evaluated in terms of a biased database will it also do well (poorly) when evaluated in terms of the unbiased database. Figure 7 plots GM for the unbiased Japanese simulation, for each of the sixteen estimation techniques, against the GM for the Japanese simulation with the biased database, for the period 7412–9012. We see that in the Japanese case, at least for the 16 methods considered, if a policy did

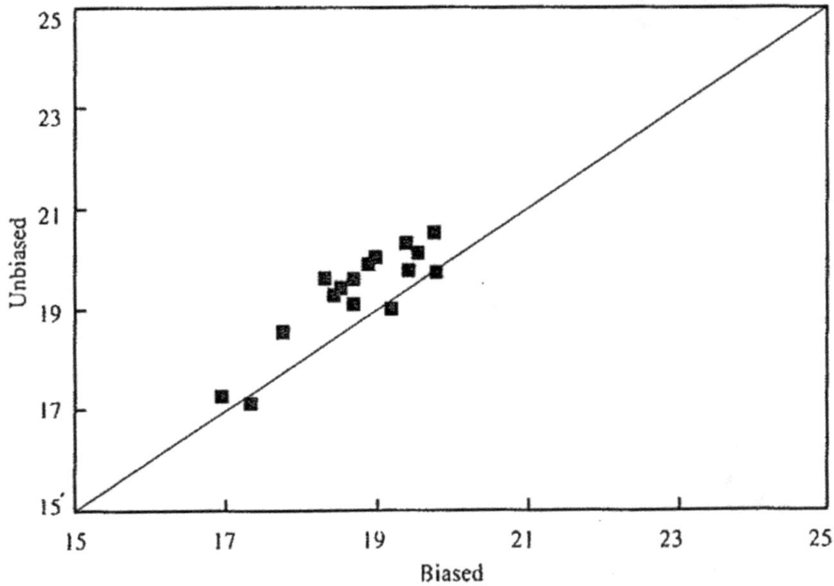

Fig. 8. U.S. survivor bias – geometric means (7510–9012).

well in a database without survivors it would do about as well with a database with survivors. The unbiased GM exceed the 45° line in the U.S., shown in Figure 8, although the correlation coefficient between the biased and unbiased GM in the U.S. is 0.885.

Figures 9 and 10, again with Japanese and U.S. biased and unbiased results, show the rankings of the 16 methods. '1' is assigned to the policy with lowest geometric mean and '16' to the policy with highest GM. We see from Figure 9, for example, that the estimation methods with the first through sixth worst GMs with the biased universe also had the first through sixth worst GMs, respectively, in the unbiased universe. In general, rank in the biased universe is highly correlated with rank in the unbiased universe. Figure 10 shows somewhat less correlation between rankings with and without survivors in the U.S. but, again, the correlation appears to be positive and substantial. [6]

5. Optimal turnover constraints and rebalancing trigger analysis

In the Japanese analysis we found that performance could be substantially improved by tightly constraining turnover when reoptimizing. Is the same

[6] There is little correlation differences between the Japanese biased and unbiased GMs when one examines the 7412–9012 period or a 7510–9012 period that would correspond to the U.S. analysis. Thus, we do not report the 'matched' figures.

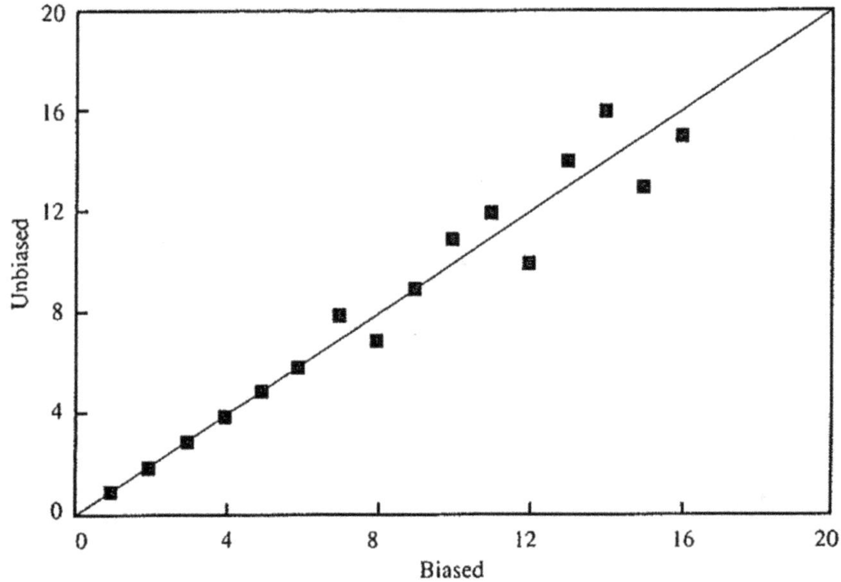

Fig. 9. Japanese survivor bias – GM ranking (7412–9012).

true in the U.S.? Is the same level of turnover constraint optimal in the U.S. as was optimal in Japan? The simulation runs reported in Table 5 indicate that, rather surprisingly to us, perhaps the answer to both questions is 'yes'. Not only does the turnover constraint make a difference in both countries,

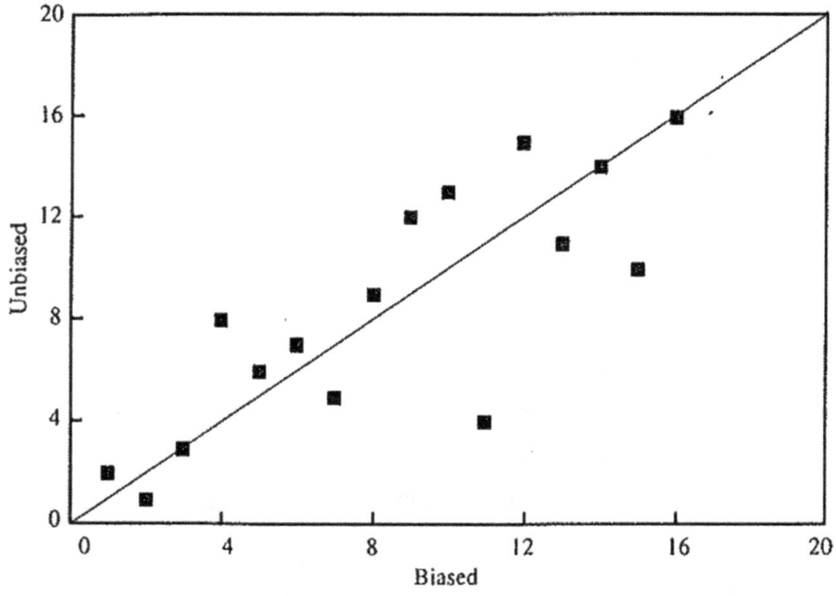

Fig. 10. U.S. survivor bias – GM ranking (7510–9012).

Table 5
Simulation results: D-POS US. Let Strt = 7510 TCR = 2 UL = 2 End = 9012. UNID = 131 survivor-biased-free universe, US.

SID	ERET	TOV	Rtri	Nobs	GM	Shrp
50539	REGR(WLRR,4Q,4)	10.0	0.0	60	20.52	1.07
50607	REGR(WLRR,4Q,4)	25.0	0.0	60	18.54	0.89
50608	REGR(WLRR,4Q,4)	20.0	0.0	60	18.99	0.96
50609	REGR(WLRR,4Q,4)	15.0	0.0	60	19.61	1.01
50610	REGR(WLRR,4Q,4)	5.0	0.0	60	20.33	1.03
50611	REGR(WLRR,4Q,4)	10.0	15.0	60	20.31	1.04
50612	REGR(WLRR,4Q,4)	10.0	20.0	60	20.52	1.05
50613	REGR(WLRR,4Q,4)	10.0	30.0	60	20.52	1.06
50614	REGR(WLRR,4Q,4)	10.0	10.0	60	20.16	1.04
50615	REGR(WLRR,4Q,4)	10.0	25.0	60	20.63	1.07
50616	REGR(WLRR,4Q,4)	10.0	0.0	48	19.93	1.05
50617	REGR(WLRR,4Q,4)	10.0	0.0	36	20.04	1.06
50618	REGR(WLRR,4Q,4)	10.0	0.0	24	19.87	1.00
50721	Benchmark	10.0	0.0	60	15.13	0.63

but the optimal level of constraint seems about the same in each, which we had not expected. We find that a 10 percent quarterly turnover constraint and 25 percent rebalancing trigger maximizes the GM in the U.S.

6. Estimation methods

Figure 11 and Table 6 consider the following question: do methods of expected return estimation which perform well (poorly) in one country

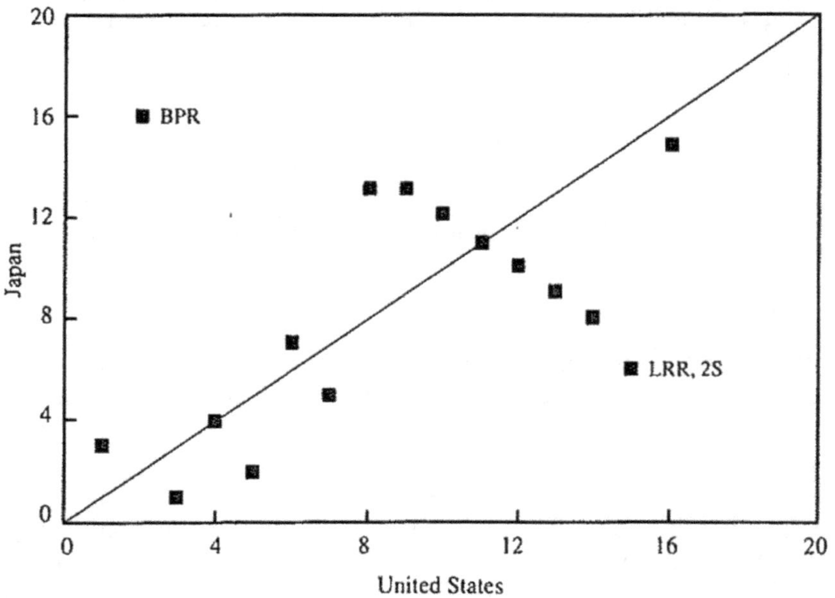

Fig. 11. U.S. vs. Japanese ER methods – unbiased GM rankings (7510–9012).

Table 6
Simulation results: D-POS JP, US. Let End = 9012 UL = 2 NOBS = 60. UNID = 131 survivor-biased-free universe, US. UNID = 150 survivor-biased-free universe, Japan.

SID	ERET	ERID	UNID	OP	TCR	TOV	GM	Shrp
50532	EPR	8260	131	3	2	10.0	18.59	0.97
50533	BPR	8270	131	3	2	10.0	17.31	0.82
50534	CPR	8280	131	3	2	10.0	19.03	1.00
50535	SPR	8290	131	3	2	10.0	17.15	0.73
50536	REGR(OLS,4Q,4)	8330	131	3	2	10.0	20.00	0.97
50537	REGR(ROB,4Q,4)	8310	131	3	2	10.0	19.81	1.03
50538	REGR(LRR,4Q,4)	8320	131	3	2	10.0	20.14	1.00
50539	REGR(WLRR,4Q,4)	8330	131	3	2	10.0	20.52	1.07
50540	benchmark	8330	131	3	2	10.0	15.13	0.63
50569	REGR(OLS,2S,4)	8380	131	6	2	20.0	19.57	0.90
50570	REGR(ROB,2S,4)	8390	131	6	2	20.0	19.45	0.98
50571	REGR(LRR,2S,4)	8400	131	6	2	20.0	20.28	0.98
50572	REGR(WLRR,2S,4)	8410	131	6	2	20.0	19.43	0.92
50573	REGR(OLS,3S,4)	8340	131	6	2	20.0	19.99	0.92
50574	REGR(ROB,3S,4)	8350	131	6	2	20.0	19.13	0.90
50575	REGR(LRR,3S,4)	8360	131	6	2	20.0	19.80	0.92
50576	REGR(WLRR,3S,4)	8370	131	6	2	20.0	19.62	0.93
901333	REGR(OLS,2S,4)	6130	150	6	2	20.0	21.15	0.73
901334	REGR(ROB,2S,4)	6140	150	6	2	20.0	19.55	0.70
901335	REGR(LRR,2S,4)	6150	150	6	2	20.0	19.77	0.66
901336	REGR(WLRR,2S,4)	6160	150	6	2	20.0	20.49	0.73
901337	REGR(OLS,3S,4)	6210	150	6	2	20.0	20.99	0.72
901338	REGR(LRR,3S,4)	6230	150	6	2	20.0	21.05	0.72
901339	REGR(ROB,3S,4)	6220	150	6	2	20.0	18.98	0.66
901340	REGR(WLRR,3S,4)	6240	150	6	2	20.0	21.15	0.73
901342	REGR(OLS,4Q,4)	6170	150	3	2	10.0	20.90	0.72
901343	REGR(ROB,4Q,4)	6180	150	3	2	10.0	21.03	0.73
901344	REGR(LRR,4Q,4)	6190	150	3	2	10.0	20.84	0.69
901345	REGR(WLRR,4Q,4)	6200	150	3	2	10.0	22.52	0.82
901346	EPR	6380	150	3	2	10.0	16.72	0.56
901347	BPR	6390	150	3	2	10.0	22.68	0.78
901348	CPR	6400	150	3	2	10.0	19.19	0.66
901349	SPR	6410	150	3	2	10.0	19.07	0.61
901341	Benchmark	6200	150	3	2	10.0	17.19	0.59

SID = simulation identification number; ERET = expected return method; TCR = transactions costs percentage; TOV = turnover constraint; GM = geometric mean; Shrp = Sharpe ratio.

perform similarly in the other? The results for this figure and table are for the same unbiased 16 cases reported in Table 4. The x-axis of Figure 11 presents the GM ranking of the method in the U.S.; the y-axis presents that in Japan. The correlation coefficient between unbiased ranked Japnese and U.S. policies is 0.396, statistically significant at the 13 percent level. In particular, the REGR(WLRR,4Q,4) is best in the U.S. and second in Japan. If you ignore two points which we have labelled, the relationship is quite close. We have no explanations for the two outliers. The point labelled BPR is especially puzzling. It reports that the Japanese simulation which estimated expected return using only book to price rankings did quite well; but the same estimation procedure did much less well in our U.S. simulation. One reason this is puzzling is that Fama and French (1992) report that BPR does well in the U.S. There is no necessary contradiction in the two results since the methodologies are different. We hope to develop a more satisfactory explanation by seeing which aspect of the differing methodology explains the differing results.

7. The possible problem of data-mining

When one attempts to identify the 'best' model building technique and strategy, one should be concerned with whether the return in excess of the benchmark could be the result of data-mining, a term normally associated with recommending the best-performing historical model without regard to the possibility that the relative performance might be continued into the future. Markowitz and Xu (1991) recently addressed the data-mining issue and present proposed data mining corrections based on three alternative models of how observations are generated. In particular, the model assumes that y_{it}, the logarithm of one plus the return for portfolio selection model i at year t, can be written as:

$$Y_{it} = \mu_i + z_t + \epsilon_{it}. \tag{2}$$

Let us assume that portfolio selection model i with expected return r_{it} equalling μ_i, is random. [7] The best linear estimate of μ_i, an unknown, given the observed r_i, is:

$$\mu_i^{\text{est}} = \bar{y} + \beta^{\text{est}}(\bar{y}_i - \bar{y}),$$

where:

$$\beta^{\text{est}} = \frac{\text{Var}(\mu)}{\text{Var}(\mu) + \text{Var}(\epsilon)/T} \tag{3}$$

and $\bar{y}$ = overall average of all portfolio selection methods.

If simulation SID = 900869 had been the only one we tried, then the historical average return would be an unbiased estimate of future expected return, assuming that the future is drawn from the same population as the past. Similarly, actual log(1 + GM) would be an unbiased estimate of its future value. This is not true in the present case, since we simulated many policies and SID = 900869 was selected as the one with maximum GM. A 'data mining correction', as discussed in Markowitz and Xu and illustrated in Figure 2, is required. According to this calculation, in the present case we should 'believe' only 59 percent of the observed difference between the best

[7] Markowitz and Xu (1991) assume $E\epsilon_{it} = 0$, and $\text{cov}(\epsilon_{is}, \epsilon_{jt}) = 0$, $\forall i = j$, $s = t$.

and the average simulated policy. Specifically, we estimate GM = 23.68 rather than 25.60 for SID = 900869, again assuming that the future is drawn from the same population as the past. Simulation results quoted below are without data mining corrections. [8]

8. The effects of shorter backtest periods

In this study, we use a 1975–1990 backtest period in Japan. If one used a subset of this period, 1985–1990 for example, one finds that the 16 basis models plus the universe benchmark, one finds that the Markowitz and Xu data-mining beta is 0.30 ($t = 1.43$) and is not statistically significant. The use of the four univariate models, the REGR(X, 4Q, 4) models, and the universe benchmark provides a data-mining beta of 0.55, which is statistically significant. Thus, the quarterly models are significantly different whereas the semi-annual models add little unique value. The benefit of the shorter period is that one can integrate earnings forecasts into the composite model. The use of the Tokyo Keizai operating income forecasts, available for the 1985–92 period, creates a Japanese trade-off curve that dominates the historical data curve (Guerard et al., 1992). Thus, one may not be as confident in modelling a subset of the period, as with the entire period, that the highest GM is not due to 'luck'. [9]

9. Summary and conjectures

The Japanese equity market has been like the U.S. market in some ways; in some ways it has been different. With respect to the quantitative analysis questions considered here we have seen, for example, that the effects of survivor bias was relatively minor in Japan and substantial in the U.S., and that the realized average return versus standard deviation curve for the period covered in Figure 11 is quite different for the two countries. On the other hand, a tight constraint on turnover produced the highest GM in both countries and, for the most part, the expected return estimation procedures which worked best in one country did best in the other. The REGR(WLRR,4Q,4) estimation procedure produced the highest GM in both

[8] The Markowitz and Xu (1991) data-mining betas were 0.476 ($t = 1.91$) for the 16 models plus the universe benchmark in Japan and 0.567($t = 2.31$) in the U.S. Thus, the 16 basis models are statistically different from the respective averages.

[9] In February 1992, GPRD re-estimated the basis sixteen backtest models (January 1975–December 1991) and found that the REGR(WLRR,4Q,4) again prevailed in the complete backtest period, producing a geometric mean of 22.72 percent (Sharpe ratio of 0.75) in an equally-weighted portfolio strategy and an optimized portfolio GM of 21.27 percent (Sharpe ratio of 0.74). The proprietary model produced an optimized portfolio GM of 24.42 percent (and a Sharpe ratio of 0.83). Thus, despite the problems of the Japanese economy in 1991, the valuation models did well in backtest and real-time (relative) performance.

countries for the complete estimation periods. In particular, the estimation procedures used in the Japanese simulation SID = 900869 outperformed all estimation procedures listed in Table 2 for the U.S. market, as it did for the Japanese.

Any attempt to extrapolate from the past is subject to the unavoidable caveat that the future may be different. This is true for intuitive investment methods as well as for quantitative ones. Despite this sobering thought, we will hazard conjectures on some subjects, and avoid them on others. We have no idea whether realized tradeoff curves will be higher or lower in the future, or whether the tradeoff curve in Japan will look like that in the U.S. But it seems like a favorable bet, if not a certain one, that the constraint levels and estimation procedures that did best in both countries in the past will do fairly well in the future.

Acknowledgements

The authors are grateful to Martin Gruber and Dale Berman for their comments on this study at the NYU/Daiwa research conference and subsequent comments during the referee process. The authors appreciate the comments of an anonymous referee. Any errors remaining are the responsibility of the authors.

References

Beaton A.E. and J.W. Tukey, 1974, The fitting of power series, meaning polynomials, illustrated on bank-spectroscopic data, Technometrics 16, 147–185.

Belsley, D.A., 1984, Collinearity and forecasting, Journal of Forecasting, 3, 183–196.

Belsley, D.A., A.E. Kuh and R.E. Welsch, 1980, Regression diagnostics – identifying influential data and sources of collinearity, (Wiley, New York).

Bloch, M., J.B. Guerard, H.M. Markowitz and P. Todd, 1991, A comparison of some aspects of U.S. and Japanese equity markets, presented at the Cross-Border Investments and Valuation Conference, New York University, September 1991.

Bunn, D., 1989, Editorial: Forecasting with more than one model, Journal of Forecasting 8, 161–166.

Chan, L., Y. Hamao and J. Lakonishok, 1991, Fundamentals and stock returns in Japan, Journal of Finance 46, 1739–1764.

Clemen, R.T., Combining forecasts: a review and annotated bibliography, International Journal of Forecasting, forthcoming.

Clemen, R.T. and R.L. Winkler, 1986, Combining economic forecasts, Journal of Business and Economic Statistics, 4, 39–46.

Dimson, E., ed., 1988, Stock market Anomalies (Cambridge University Press, Cambridge).

Elton, E.J. and M.J. Gruber, 1987, Modern portfolio theory and investment analysis (Wiley, New York).

Elton, E.J. and M.J. Gruber, 1989, Expectational data and Japanese stock prices, Japan and the World Economy 1, 391–401.

Fama, E.F. and K.R. French, 1992, Cross-sectional variation in expected stock returns Journal of Finance, 47, 427–465.

Farrell, J., 1983, Guide to Portfolio Management (McGraw-Hill, New York).

Guerard, J.B., Jr., 1987, Linear constraints, robust-weighting, and efficient composite modeling, Journal of Forecasting, 6, 193–199.

Guerard, J.B., Jr., 1990, Optimal portfolio analysis using composite model-tilting, (Drexel Burnham Lambert).

Guerard, J.B., Jr. and M. Takano, 1991, Stock selection and composite modeling in Japan, Security Analysts Journal, 29, 1–13.

Guerard, J.B., Jr. and B.K. Stone, 1992 Composite forecasting of annual corporate earnings, in: A. Chen, ed., Research in Finance, (Ct: JAI Press Greenwich) 205–230.

Gunst, R.F. and R.L. Mason, 1980, Regression analysis and its application (Marcel Dekker, New York).

Guerard, J.B., Jr., M. Takano and Y. Yamane, 1992. The development of efficient portfolios in Japan with particular emphasis on sales and earnings forecasting, presented at the I/B/E/S Quantitative Research Seminar, Tokyo. Annals of Operations Research, forthcoming.

Gunst, R.F., J.T. Webster and R.L. Mason, 1976, A comparison of least squares and latent root regression estimators, Technometrics 18, 75–83.

Jacobs, B. and K. Levy, 1988, Disentangling equity return regularities: new insights and investment opportunities, Financial Analysts Journal 00, 18–43.

Markowitz, H.M., 1956, The optimization of a quadratic function subject to linear constraints, Naval Research Logistics Quarterly 3, 111–133.

Markowitz, H.M., 1959, Portfolio selection: efficient diversification of investments (Wiley, New York).

Markowitz, H.M., 1987, Mean-variance analysis in portfolio choice and capital markets (Basil Blackwell Ltd., Oxford).

Markowitz, H.M., P. Todd, G. Xu and Y. Yamane, 1991, Fast computation of mean-variance efficient sets using historical covariance (Daiwa Securities Trust Company, Jersey City, NJ).

Markowitz, H.M. and G. Xu, Data mining corrections, submitted.

Miller, J.D., Guerard, J.B., Jr. and M. Takano, Bridging the gap between theory and practice in equity selection modeling: case studies of U.S. and Japanese models, submitted.

Rudd, A. and B. Rosenberg, 1979. Realistic portfolio optimization, in: Elton and Gruber, eds., Portfolio Theory: 25 Years Later, (North-Holland, Amsterdam).

Sharma, S. and W.L. James, 1981, Latent root regression: an alternative procedure for estimating parameters in the presence of multicollinearity, Journal of Marketing Research 18, 154–161.

Webster, J.T., R.F. Gunst and R.L. Mason, 1974, Latent root regression analysis, Technometrics 16, 513–522.

Ziemba, W.T., 1990, Fundamental factors in U.S. and Japanese stock returns, presented at the Berkeley Program in Finance, Santa Barbara, CA, September 1990.

https://doi.org/10.1142/9789811222634_0003

Chapter 3

Covariance complexity and rates of return on assets†

Leonard C. MacLean [a,*], Michael E. Foster [b], William T. Ziemba [c]

[a] *Herbert Lamb Chair in Business, School of Business Administration, Dalhousie University, Halifax, NS, Canada B3H 3J5*
[b] *School of Business Administration, Dalhousie University, Halifax, NS, Canada B3H 3J5*
[c] *Sauder School of Business, University of British Columbia, Vancouver, Canada V6T 1Z2*

Abstract

This paper considers the estimation of the expected rate of return on a set of risky assets. The approach to estimation focuses on the covariance matrix for the returns. The structure in the covariance matrix determines shared information which is useful in estimating the mean return for each asset. An empirical Bayes estimator is developed using the covariance structure of the returns distribution. The estimator is an improvement on the maximum likelihood and Bayes–Stein estimators in terms of mean squared error. The effect of reduced estimation error on accumulated wealth is analyzed for the portfolio choice model with constant relative risk aversion utility.

Keywords: Empirical Bayes estimation; Rates of return; Covariance complexity; Wealth loss

1. Introduction

The allocation of investment capital to risky and risk free opportunities is a fundamental problem in portfolio theory. A basic input to the investment decision is the distribution of future returns on securities. The prediction of future securities returns is based on price information available at the time of the decision. Prediction errors can have a large negative impact on portfolio choice and the resulting accumulation of wealth (Loffler, 2003).

* Corresponding author.
E-mail address: l.c.maclean@dal.ca (L.C. MacLean).

†This article originally appeared in *Journal of Banking and Finance* **35**, 3503–3523, 2007, © 2007 by Elsevier Science Publishers.

Errors in the prediction of mean returns are particularly damaging to wealth accumulation (Kallberg and Ziemba, 1981, 1984; Chopra and Ziemba, 1993).

A standard approach to the trading prices of securities is to consider the rate of return as a linear model (Connor and Korajczyk, 1995). The rate of return is defined over a period (Sharpe, 1964; Ross, 1976) or instantaneously (Merton, 1992). The rate depends on a variety of factors, observed and unobserved. The returns on different securities are linked through the factors. When the model is underspecified, there are unobserved factors and the prices are mis-specified (MacKinlay and Pastor, 2000). Because of the link to common factors, the mispricing is incorporated into the returns covariance matrix.

The parameters in the linear model for returns may be random variables, which requires a hierarchy of stochastic equations. The random coefficients in the stochastic equations are random parameters in the securities price distributions, and the hierarchy generates a Bayesian model for price distributions. This is an alternative approach to the missing or unobserved factors. In many Bayesian approaches, a noninformative or diffuse prior on parameters in the price distribution is postulated (Klein and Bawa, 1976; Pastor and Stambaugh, 1999). Alternatively, a conjugate prior can used so that the posterior is tractable. In the Gaussian case, this provides a framework for understanding the mechanism for sharing common information (Jones and Shanken, 2003).

In the context of the Bayes model, the optimal estimates for the expected rates of return given price information to date are the posterior means, which depend on the covariance of returns. This implies a sharing of information on asset returns to yield improved estimates. As well, the decomposition of the covariance into a prior component (common) and a conditional component (specific) isolates the mis-specification effect.

One difficulty with the Bayes approach is that the parameters in the prior distribution are unknown. There are theories which help define the prior. However, the data on returns contains information about the prior, and in the Gaussian case the prior can be filtered from the data. In that way, an empirical Bayes estimate for the posterior mean is developed (Efron and Morris, 1972; Frost and Savarino, 1986). In the dynamic model format, the observed prices are points on a trajectory and the movement of prices provides the necessary information to estimate the conditional (first order) and prior (second order) parameters in the hierarchial linear model.

The impact of modeling and estimation errors on forecasts for securities prices and the resulting effect on portfolio decisions and capital accumulation have been considered in several studies. Pastor and Stambaugh (1999) conclude that model error is less important than estimation error; see also Kallberg and Ziemba (1981) who conclude the same. With regard to estimation error, alternative estimates for the mean return have been considered in a long series of asset prices (Grauer and Hakansson, 1995), with improved results from shrinkage (Stein) estimators. MacKinlay and Pastor (2000) use a restriction, which incorporates the mean return in the covariance of returns, to calculate an estimate of expected returns which is superior to the shrinkage estimator. The results are empirical rather than theoretical, and the structure and dynamics of price distributions is not clear.

This paper further explores the connection between the expected rates of return on a set of assets and the covariance of returns on those assets. The setting is similar to MacKinlay and Pastor (2000), with unobserved factors linking the means to the covariance. The latent factors define a prior on mean returns, and Bayes theorem determines a posterior mean which depends on the covariance. Information on the relationship between asset returns is contained in the covariance, and an entropy measure called covariance complexity

(Morgerra, 1985) is used to assess the structure of relationships. The form of the posterior mean leads to an alternative empirical Bayes estimate for the expected return, where the structure/complexity in the observed covariance results in a truncation of factors. With a reduced dimension representation of covariance based on a truncation of eigenvectors, there are sufficient degrees of freedom to estimate all parameters in a Bayesian model for prices. Furthermore, the structure in the covariance affects the theoretical mean squared error of estimators and facilitates comparisons. This effect carries over to portfolio decisions and accumulated wealth.

The empirical Bayes estimator is developed from the covariance structure in Section 2. The mean squared error properties of the estimator are explored analytically and through simulation in Section 3. The estimator is compared to the Bayes–Stein (Jorion, 1986) and maximum likelihood estimators, and is shown to be superior in terms of mean squared error. In Section 4 the wealth shortfall from estimation error is considered for the expected utility maximization problem. The methods in the paper are applied to portfolios of stocks from the Toronto Stock Exchange and the New York Stock Exchange.

Appendix A contains proofs for propositions in the paper.

2. Hierarchial model for returns

Consider a competitive capital market where the trading of securities takes place in continuous time. The dynamics of prices over time will be analyzed with a hierarchial linear model. The focus is on the expected rate of return on securities.

2.1. Asset returns and covariance complexity

Let $P_i(t)$ be the trading price of security i at time t, $i = 1, \ldots, K$. The returns on assets are generated by price changes. Future trading prices and asset returns are uncertain, and characterizing the distributions for returns is the foundation for investment planning. The incremental return on asset i at time t is $R_i(t) = \frac{P_i(t+\epsilon)}{P_i(t)}$. An observation interval $[0, T]$ can be partitioned into time periods with size c and number $n = \frac{T}{c}$: $\{(0, c), \ldots, ((n-1)\epsilon, nc)\}$. The returns are presented as a sequence of incremental returns by period: $\left\{R_{it} = \frac{P_i(tc)}{P_i((t-1)c)},\right.$ $\left. t = 1, \ldots, n\right\}$. Let $Y_{it} = \ln P_i(tc)$, the log-price at the end of period t. The log-return or rate of return between times 0 and T is $\ln(R_i(T)) = \sum_{t=1}^{n} \epsilon_{it}$, where $\epsilon_{it} = \ln R_{it} = Y_{it} - Y_{i,t-1}$. The rates of return over a time interval are approximately normal. It is assumed that the rate of return in a period, ϵ_{it}, has the same distribution for $t = 1, \ldots, n$. The distribution of rates of returns, and in particular the mean $E(\epsilon_{it})$, is the quantity of interest. If there is a risk free rate of return r, then $\ln\left(\frac{R_{it}}{rc}\right) \approx \frac{R_{it}}{rc} - 1 =$ excess rate of return on asset i in period t. It is the excess return which is analyzed in MacKinlay and Pastor (2000), but the results are comparable.

Assume that the returns process in period t is defined by the hierarchy of linear equations

$$\epsilon_{it} = \theta_i + \delta_i V_i, \quad i = 1, \ldots, K, \tag{1}$$

$$\theta_i = \mu_i + \sum_{j=1}^{m} \lambda_{ij} Z_j, \quad i = 1, \ldots, K, \tag{2}$$

where V_i, $i=1,\ldots,K$, are independent standard Gaussian variables and Z_j, $j=1,\ldots,m$, $m\leqslant K$, are independent latent factors with $Z_j\propto N(0,1)$. Also V_i and Z_j are independent. This is the common factor model, with the correlation between θ_i and θ_j given as $\gamma_{ij}=\sum_{k=1}^{m}\lambda_{ik}\lambda_{jk}$. The V_i, $i=1,\ldots,K$, represent idiosyncratic variability which is specific to each asset. Let $\epsilon_t=(\epsilon_{1t},\ldots,\epsilon_{Kt})'$, $\theta=(\theta_1,\ldots,\theta_K)'$, $\Delta=\operatorname{diag}(\delta_1^2,\ldots,\delta_K^2)$, $\mu=(\mu_1,\ldots,\mu_K)'$, $\Gamma=(\gamma_{ij})$.

Given (θ,Δ), the conditional distribution of the rate of return per period is

$$(\epsilon_t|\theta,\Delta)\propto N(\theta,\Delta). \tag{3}$$

From (2) the rate has a prior distribution

$$\theta\propto N(\mu,\Gamma). \tag{4}$$

The marginal distribution of rates is

$$\epsilon_t\propto N(\mu,\Sigma), \tag{5}$$

with

$$\Sigma=\Gamma+\Delta. \tag{6}$$

If $\Lambda=(\lambda_{ij})$, then $\Gamma=\Lambda\Lambda'$ and $\Sigma=\Lambda\Lambda'+\Delta$. This form of the covariance has similarities to the structure in MacKinlay and Pastor (2000). The distinction is in the generality of Λ, where the number of factors is indeterminate and therefore the structure of Σ is general.

The covariance Σ for the rates of return is the focus for analysis. To describe the structure of the covariance, consider the eigenvalues of Σ, given by $(\phi_1,\ldots,\phi_K)$. Morgerra (1985) defines the *covariance complexity* as

Definition 1. Let $(\phi_1,\ldots,\phi_K)$ be the eigenvalues of Σ and consider the fractions $p_i=\frac{\phi_i}{\sum_{j=1}^{K}\phi_j}$. The covariance complexity is

$$C=-\frac{\sum_{i=1}^{K}p_i\log(p_i)}{\log(K)}. \tag{7}$$

This measure is a variation on the entropy from information theory. C has a minimum value of 0 (when $\phi_2=\cdots=\phi_K=0$) and maximum value of 1 (when $\phi_j=\phi, j=1,\ldots,K$). In the model, if $\delta_j=0$, $j=1,\ldots,K$, and $m=1$, so that all assets are perfectly correlated, then the minimum is achieved. If $\lambda_{ij}=0$, for all i,j and $\delta_j=\delta$ for all j, so that assets are iid, then the maximum is achieved.

Consider the conditional maximum complexity given values of $\operatorname{tr}\Sigma=$ total variance, and $m=$ the number of factors,

$$C_m=\max\{C|\operatorname{tr}\Sigma,m\}. \tag{8}$$

Proposition 1. *For given values of* $\operatorname{tr}\Sigma$ *and m, complexity is a decreasing function of the variance of* $\{\phi_1,\ldots,\phi_m\}$. *The conditional maximum complexity,* C_m, *is achieved by the eigenvalues* $\phi=\gamma+\delta$, *with multiplicity m, and* δ, *with multiplicity* $K-m$.

The situation in the proposition is where the factors are equally important. This most complex case will play an important role in the analysis of estimators.

In the analysis of the structure of $\Sigma = \Lambda\Lambda' + \Delta$, it is assumed that $\Delta = \delta^2 I$. So the specific or idiosyncratic variances of all assets are equal. This will simplify analysis by concentrating on the factors. MacKinlay and Pastor (2000) have shown that this simplification of Δ provides the best portfolios. The purpose in estimating the covariance and the rate of return on assets is to use them in portfolio construction. The reduction in the number of parameters yields smaller estimator standard errors.

At any point in time it is assumed that information is available on the history of prices and the rates of return. Consider the data on log-prices per period available at time T, $\{y_{it},\ t = 0, \ldots, n,\ i = 1, \ldots, K\}$, and the corresponding rates $\mathbb{R} = \{e_{it},\ t = 1, \ldots, n,\ i = 1, \ldots, K\}$. With $e_t = (e_{1t}, \ldots, e_{Kt})'$, the usual estimate for the mean rate of return vector, based on the data, is

$$\bar{e}_n = \frac{1}{n}\sum_{t=1}^{n} e_t. \tag{9}$$

With the prior distribution for θ in (4) and the conditional distribution for e_t in (3), the posterior distribution for θ given $\mathbb{R}$ is

$$(\theta|\mathbb{R}) \propto N(\hat{\theta}_B, \Gamma_B), \tag{10}$$

where $\hat{\theta}_B = \mu + (I - \Delta\Sigma^{-1})(\bar{e}_n - \mu)$ and $\Gamma_B = \frac{1}{n^2}(I - \Delta\Sigma^{-1})\Delta$.

The Bayes estimate for the mean rate of return at time T is the conditional expectation

$$\hat{\theta}_B = E(\theta|\mathbb{R}) = \mu + (I - \Delta\Sigma^{-1})(\bar{e}_n - \mu). \tag{11}$$

The Bayes estimate or conditional expectation plays a significant role in investment decisions. Hens and Schenk-Hoppe (2005) established the evolutionary stability of the portfolio rule which allocates wealth across assets according to the conditional expected return. So working with the Bayes estimate or a close approximation is desirable.

An important feature of the Bayes estimate is the role of the covariance between rates of return in the estimate of the mean rate of return. In essence, the return on one asset provides information about the return on related assets, and the sharing of information through common factors improves the quality of estimates (Jones and Shanken, 2003).

There are a number of points to consider about the linear pricing model.

1. The model can be presented in continuous time. If the instantaneous return is $\mathrm{d}Y_i(t)$, then for $i = 1, \ldots, K$,

   $$\mathrm{d}Y_i = \theta_i\,\mathrm{d}s + \delta_i\,\mathrm{d}V_i.$$

   This is a generalization of a single stock model in Browne and Whitt (1996), where the rate of return is a random variable. That model was also used in Rogers (2000) to study parameter estimation error. The generalization to multiple assets introduces the covariance between rates of return, and the structure of that covariance is the focal point of this paper.
2. The volatilities δ_i, $i = 1, \ldots, K$, are non-stochastic. They represent the specific or idiosyncratic variance for the return of each security. The returns are correlated, but the correlation is generated by the common factors in the rates of return. There is evidence that stochastic volatility factors are important for capturing certain aspects of returns

distributions such as heavy tails (Chernov et al., 2002). The model for returns is a vehicle for inputting information on returns into a portfolio decision. MacKinlay and Pastor (2000) show that the structure $\Delta = \delta^2 I$ is desirable.

3. An alternative approach to extreme returns involves adding independent shock terms to capture dramatic price changes. The dynamic equations become

$$\mathrm{d}Y_i = \theta_i \mathrm{d}s + \delta_i \mathrm{d}V_i + \vartheta_i \mathrm{d}N_i(\pi_i),$$

where $\mathrm{d}N_i(\pi_i)$ is a Poisson process with intensity π_i, and shock size ϑ_i, $i = 1, \ldots, K$. Between shocks, the financial market is described by the random rates model, which is sufficient to explain the mean, variance and covariance for returns. An approach to the model with shocks is to define a conditional model given the shocks. The conditional dynamics are in the form (2), and the methods of this paper are appropriate for estimating the conditional parameters. Then the shock component is iteratively determined to maximize the conditional likelihood for the observed parameters (MacLean et al., 2004).
4. The prior rates of return may be dynamic, with defining equations $\mathrm{d}\theta_i(s) = \mu_i \mathrm{d}s + \beta_i \mathrm{d}q_i$, where $\mathrm{d}q_i$, $i = 1, \ldots, K$, are correlated Brownian motions. So $\theta_i(t) = \theta_i(0) + \mu_i t + \beta_i \sqrt{t} Z_i$, $i = 1, \ldots, K$. The estimation methods discussed later are easily adapted to the estimation of parameters with dynamic stochastic rates of return.
5. The emphasis in this paper is on estimation of the mean rate of return, since it has the greatest impact on portfolio decisions. Chopra and Ziemba (1993) show that equal size errors in estimators for the means, variances, and covariances affect portfolio performance in the order of 20:2:1, respectively. Moreover, the 20 increases to 75 plus, when the risk aversion of the utility function is low as is the case with log utility. Grauer and Hakansson (1995) also report substantial improvement in investment performance using better estimates for the mean. In the fashion of MacKinlay and Pastor (2000), it is shown that the covariance is an important component in the estimation of mean rates of return. The particular aspect of interest is the covariance complexity.

2.2. Estimation of mean rates of return

The Bayes estimate in (11) depends upon the unknown covariance matrix $\Sigma = \Gamma + \Delta$. The covariance can be estimated from the data on past returns, and if it can be factored to obtain estimates of (Γ, Δ), then an empirical Bayes estimate for the mean rate of return which is consistent with the covariance structure can be generated. Assume that securities have been observed at regular intervals of width $\frac{T}{n}$ in the time period $(0, T)$. For simplicity, the interval width is assumed to be 1.

The observations on log-prices at times $t = 0, \ldots, n$ are $\{y_{it},\ i = 1, \ldots, K;\ t = 0, \ldots, n\}$, and the corresponding sample rates $e_{it} = y_{it} - y_{i,t-1}$ are $\{e_{it},\ i = 1, \ldots, K;\ t = 1, \ldots, n\}$. The parameter of interest is $E(\theta | e_{it},\ i = 1, \ldots, K;\ t = 1, \ldots, n)$.

The maximum likelihood estimate of θ is $\bar{e}_n = \frac{1}{n}\sum_{t=1}^{n} e_t$, given the sample rates e_t, $t = 1, \ldots, n$. Let the covariance matrix computed from the observed rates be S_n, the usual estimate of Σ. If the eigenvalues of Γ are $\gamma_1, \ldots, \gamma_K$, and $\Delta = \delta^2 I$, then the eigenvalues of Σ are $\gamma_1 + \delta^2, \ldots, \gamma_K + \delta^2$. When the rank of Γ is $m < K$, then $\gamma_{m+1} = \cdots = \gamma_K = 0$. Furthermore, it is possible to represent the covariance, with fewer parameters, where $\Gamma = \Lambda\Lambda'$. Consider the spectral decomposition of S_n, with the ordered eigenvalues $g_1, \ldots, g_K$ and the corresponding eigenvectors $l_1, \ldots, l_K$. To simplify the sample covariance structure analogous to $\Sigma = \Gamma + \delta^2 I$, choose a *truncation* value $m^* < K$, and define the matrices

$$H_n = \mathrm{diag}(g_1, \ldots, g_{m^*}), \tag{12}$$

$$L_n = (l_1, \ldots, l_{m^*}), \tag{13}$$

$$G_n = L_n H_n L_n', \tag{14}$$

$$d_n = [\mathrm{tr} S_n - (g_1 + \cdots + g_{m^*})]/(K - m^*), \tag{15}$$

$$D_n = d_n I. \tag{16}$$

The structured sample covariance is

$$S_n^* = G_n + D_n. \tag{17}$$

The matrices G_n, D_n, S_n^* are estimates of Γ, Δ, Σ, respectively. In the theoretical covariance, it is possible that the eigenvalues of Γ, γ_j, $j = 1, \ldots, K$, are all positive. However, it is expected that the covariance between securities prices is generated by a small number of underlying factors, and therefore the number of non-negligible eigenvalues of Γ is small relative to K. In any case m is indeterminate and an arbitrary choice introduces error. Since many of the eigenvalues and eigenvectors in the above construction are discarded, the method is referred to as *truncation*. The impact of truncation error is considered in the next section.

For the parameter μ, the prior mean, assumptions about the financial market can guide estimation. If there is a long term equilibrium value for returns on equities, then θ_i, $i = 1, \ldots, K$, have a common mean. So $\mu' = (\mu, \ldots, \mu)$ and the prior mean is estimated by $\hat{\mu}_n 1$, where 1 is a vector of ones and

$$\hat{\mu}_n = \frac{1}{nK} \sum_i \sum_t e_{it}. \tag{18}$$

The assumption of a common prior mean could be relaxed to a common mean within asset classes, or some other grouping of securities. Alternatively, the Bayes estimate can be dynamic, so that the posterior from one stage becomes the prior for the next estimation stage.

Using estimates for the parameters in the Bayes estimator, the *truncation estimator* for the conditional mean rate of return at time T is

$$\hat{\theta}_{\hat{B}} = \hat{\mu}_n 1 + (I - D_n S_n^{*-1})(\bar{e}_n - \hat{\mu}_n 1). \tag{19}$$

The truncation estimator is an empirical Bayes estimator since it is in the form of the Bayes estimator, with estimates for the prior parameters. The sample covariance carries the shared information for the set of securities. The complexity of the sample covariance is imbedded in the structure where $S_n^* = G_n + d_n I$.

3. Risk of estimator

The truncation estimator is based on a linear model for price dynamics, and incorporates into the estimates of mean rates of return structural information about the covariance between rates of return on securities. The estimator has logical appeal, but the standard assessment of an estimator is based on estimation error. This error is now considered both theoretically and numerically to establish the effect of the covariance structure on estimation of the mean. Since it is understood that estimation is based on data at time T and there are n equally spaced observations, the T and n subscripts will be dropped in all expressions.

The standard criterion for comparing estimators is the mean squared error matrix

$$E(\hat{\theta}-\theta)(\hat{\theta}-\theta)'. \tag{20}$$

(In the analysis of this section, the expectation in the MSE is with respect to the conditional and prior distributions.) The risk of an estimator is defined as the trace of the MSE matrix:

$$R(\theta,\hat{\theta}) = \mathrm{tr}E(\hat{\theta}-\theta)(\hat{\theta}-\theta)'. \tag{21}$$

In the analysis of risk, the truncation estimator is

$$\hat{\theta}_{\hat{B}} = \hat{\mu}1 + (I-\widehat{B})(\bar{e}-\hat{\mu}1), \tag{22}$$

where $\widehat{B} = DS^{*^{-1}}$. The corresponding Bayes estimate is

$$\hat{\theta}_B = \mu 1 + (I-B)(\bar{e}-\mu 1), \tag{23}$$

where $B = \Delta\Sigma^{-1}$.

3.1. Covariance complexity and theoretical risk

The risk can be written as [risk] = [Bayes risk] + [difference from Bayes risk]. These parts are considered separately. The risk of the Bayes estimator is

$$R(\theta,\hat{\theta}_B) = \frac{1}{n^2}\mathrm{tr}((I-\Delta\Sigma^{-1})\Delta) = \mathrm{tr}(\Lambda(I+\Lambda'\Delta^{-1}\Lambda)\Lambda'). \tag{24}$$

The key component of covariance is the $K\times m$ matrix Λ, m = the rank of Γ. The covariance $\Sigma = \Gamma + \delta^2 I$ has eigenvalues $\gamma_1+\delta^2 \geqslant \cdots \geqslant \gamma_m+\delta^2 > \delta^2 = \cdots = \delta^2$, which define the complexity.

Proposition 2. *Consider the Bayes risk $R(\theta,\hat{\theta}_B)$, with $\mathrm{tr}\Sigma$ and $\Delta = \delta^2 I$ fixed. For fixed m, $R(\theta,\hat{\theta}_B)$ increases as the complexity C increases. Correspondingly, $R(\theta,\hat{\theta}_B)$ increases as the variance of $(\gamma_1,\ldots,\gamma_m)$ decreases. Assuming the covariance Σ has maximum conditional complexity, C_m, then $R(\theta,\hat{\theta}_B)$ is monotone increasing in m.*

This proposition establishes the effect of covariance structure on Bayes risk. The Bayes component of risk is smaller when there is more structure (fewer factors) and the complexity of the covariance is less.

For the component identifying the difference from the Bayes estimator, a contrast is made between the truncation estimator and the maximum likelihood estimator (without structure). Consider the empirical estimator $\hat{\theta}_{\hat{B}}$, and the difference $\hat{\theta}_{\hat{B}} - \hat{\theta}_B = B(\hat{\mu}1 - \mu 1) + (B-\widehat{B})(\bar{e}-\hat{\mu}1)$. The *additional risk* for the empirical estimator is

$$R^+(\hat{\theta}_{\hat{B}}) = \mathrm{tr}EB(\hat{\mu}1-\mu 1)(\hat{\mu}1-\mu 1)'B' + \mathrm{tr}E(B-\widehat{B})(\bar{e}-\hat{\mu}1)(\bar{e}-\hat{\mu}1)'(B-\widehat{B})'.$$

This expression simplifies to

$$R^+(\hat{\theta}_{\hat{B}}) = \frac{1}{K^2 n}(1'\Sigma 1)\mathrm{tr}B11'B' + \frac{1}{n}\mathrm{tr}E(B-\widehat{B})S(B-\widehat{B}). \tag{25}$$

L.C. MacLean et al. / Journal of Banking & Finance 31 (2007) 3503–3523 3511

The mean rate of return has additional risk

$$R^{+}(\bar{e}) = \frac{1}{nK^2}(1'\Sigma 1)\text{tr}B11'B' + \frac{1}{n}\text{tr}EBS_nB. \tag{26}$$

To focus on the covariance, it is assumed that the error variance is known, and defined by $\Delta = \delta^2 I$. With the assumed structure, the additional risk for the two estimators can be compared.

The truncation estimator depends on the sample covariance in the same way the Bayes estimator depends on the true covariance, whereas the mean does not use the information in the covariance. However, the difference from the Bayes does depend on the structure. A convenient measure for comparing the additional risk for empirical estimators is the *relative savings loss* (RSL) (Efron and Morris, 1972).

Definition 2. Consider the Bayes estimator $\hat{\theta}_B$, the maximum likelihood estimator $\bar{e}$, and the truncation estimator $\hat{\theta}_{\hat{B}}$. Then the relative savings loss for the estimator $\hat{\theta}_{\hat{B}}$ is

$$\text{RSL}(\hat{\theta}_{\hat{B}}) = \frac{R^{+}(\hat{\theta}_{\hat{B}})}{R^{+}(\bar{e})}. \tag{27}$$

If the relative savings loss is less than 1, the additional risk for the truncation estimator is less than that for the mean. There are two important components in the additional risk and RSL: (i) sampling error; and (ii) truncation error. These components are considered separately: sampling error when there is no truncation error; truncation error when there is no sampling error.

If the number of factors in the random rates of return is known, then the empirical Bayes estimator $\hat{\theta}_{\hat{B}}$ is an improvement on the mean rate of return $\bar{e}$, provided there is sufficient data to identify model parameters.

Proposition 3 (Sample size). *Suppose that the number of factors $m < K$ and the volatility $\Delta = \delta^2 I$ in the random rate of return model are known. Then there is a sample size n^*, which depends on the eigenvalues, such that* $\text{RSL}(\hat{\theta}_{\hat{B}}) \leqslant 1$, *if $n \geqslant n^*$. The required sample size n^* increases as complexity increases.*

Although the proposition statement does not refer to structure, the sample size required for $\text{RSL} \leqslant 1$ does depend on structure, as is clear from the proof. This is demonstrated with an example.

Example 1. Suppose there are $K = 5$ risky assets with prices defined by Eqs. (1) and (2). Assume there is $m = 1$ factor in the random rates of return and the covariance matrix for log-prices is

$$\Sigma = \begin{bmatrix} .10 & .0395 & .0395 & .0395 & .0395 \\ .0395 & .10 & .0395 & .0395 & .0395 \\ .0395 & .0395 & .10 & .0395 & .0395 \\ .0395 & .0395 & .0395 & .10 & .0395 \\ .0395 & .0395 & .0395 & .0395 & .10 \end{bmatrix}.$$

The eigenvalues are $\phi = .250$ and $\delta^2 = .0625$ with multiplicity 4. The covariance complexity is $C = 0.65$. From the expressions for additional risk

$$R^+(\hat{\theta}_{\hat{B}}) = \frac{.078125}{n} + \frac{5.25}{n^2}$$

and

$$R^+(\bar{e}) = \frac{.343725}{n}.$$

Then the relative savings loss for the truncation estimator is $\mathrm{RSL}(\hat{\theta}_{\hat{B}}) = 0.227 + \frac{15.27}{n}$. So $\mathrm{RSL}(\hat{\theta}_{\hat{B}}) \leqslant 1$ if $n \geqslant 20$.

In practice, the number of factors in the model for asset returns is unknown. Based on the sample covariance, an estimate m^* for m is required before estimating θ. Understating the number of factors, presumably because the contribution of some factors is insignificant, is the rationale for the label truncation estimator. If the factors are equally important, so that the eigenvalues of Γ are equal and the conditional complexity is maximal, then the impact of truncation is greater. This worst case is considered since it provides a bound on the extra error from truncation. To simplify analysis, it is assumed that the sample size n is large and therefore $\Sigma = \Lambda\Lambda' + \delta^2 I$ is used in the truncation estimator. Also, $\sigma^2 = \frac{1}{K}\mathrm{tr}\Sigma$.

Proposition 4 (Truncation effect). *Suppose Σ has eigenvalues ϕ with multiplicity m and δ^2 with multiplicity $K - m$, where $\phi > \delta^2$. So the complexity of Σ is C_m. Consider $\hat{\theta}_{\hat{B}}$, the truncation estimator with number of factors $m^* < m$.* (i) *If $m < \frac{K}{2}$, then* $\mathrm{RSL}(\hat{\theta}_{\hat{B}}) \leqslant 1$. (ii) *If $m > \frac{K}{2}$, then there exists a value δ_1^2, $0 \leqslant \delta_1^2 \leqslant \sigma^2$, such that* $\mathrm{RSL}(\hat{\theta}_{\hat{B}}) \leqslant 1$ *for $\delta^2 \geqslant \delta_1^2$.*

The truncation estimator is based on a simplification of the covariance structure. When the covariance is less complex, that is, the number of latent factors is small relative to the number of assets, the effect of truncation cannot make the additional risk greater than that for the mean rate of return. This is true for maximal complexity and therefore holds in general.

If the number of factors is large, then in the most complex case the truncation estimator dominates if the idiosyncratic variance for each asset is close to the variance of the common factors. Because the maximum conditional complexity C_m is approaching the absolute maximum, the advantage of the covariance structure and the truncation estimator is small.

Example 2. To illustrate the effects of complexity and truncation, consider an example with $K = 8$ assets. The covariance structure is determined by the matrix $\Lambda_m = m^{-\frac{1}{2}}E_m$, where E_m is defined by the first m columns of the matrix

$$E = \begin{bmatrix} 1 & 1 & 1 & 1 & 1 & 1 & 1 & 1 \\ 1 & 1 & 1 & 1 & -1 & -1 & -1 & -1 \\ 1 & 1 & -1 & -1 & -1 & -1 & 1 & 1 \\ 1 & 1 & -1 & -1 & 1 & 1 & -1 & -1 \\ 1 & -1 & 1 & -1 & 1 & -1 & 1 & -1 \\ 1 & -1 & 1 & -1 & -1 & 1 & -1 & 1 \\ 1 & -1 & -1 & 1 & -1 & 1 & 1 & -1 \\ 1 & -1 & -1 & 1 & 1 & -1 & -1 & 1 \end{bmatrix}.$$

The error variance is $\delta^2 = 1$. The variance of each log-rate is 2 and $\text{tr}\Sigma = 16$. The eigenvalues of Σ are $\phi = \frac{8}{m} + 1$, with multiplicity m, and $\delta^2 = 1$, with multiplicity $K - m$. This is the situation where conditional complexity (given $(\text{tr}\Sigma, m)$) is maximal and the truncation error is greatest. In Table 1, the relative savings loss for the truncation estimator, with the range of values of m and m^*, is presented.

The cases in Table 1 present the most challenging structure. However, there is still an advantage in using the covariance in the estimation of the expected rate of return. As expected, including more factors (less truncation) improves the relative performance of the empirical Bayes (structural) estimator. The choice of a smaller number of factors (more truncation) gives results which are quite consistent across the models as m increases.

3.2. Monte Carlo study – NYSE and TSE

The analysis of theoretical risk has established the relative advantage of the truncation estimator which links the means to the covariance. To demonstrate the effect numerically, a Monte Carlo study was carried out using two data sets of actual asset returns: (i) end of month prices for 24 leading stocks from the Toronto Stock Exchange (TSE); (ii) end of month prices for 24 leading stocks from the New York Stock Exchange (NYSE). For both markets, the data covers the years 1990–2002. The correlation structure for returns is different for the stocks from the two exchanges, so a performance comparison of estimators shows the significance of structure. The percent of variance accounted for by the top five eigenvalues for each correlation matrix is shown in Table 2 as is the covariance complexity for returns on each exchange. The NYSE stocks have a much more complex covariance.

From the data on monthly closing prices for the set of 24 stocks on the Toronto Stock Exchange and the separate set of stocks on the New York Stock Exchange, the natural log of gross monthly rates of return were calculated. The mean vector and covariance matrix

Table 1
Relative savings loss with truncation: maximum complexity case

m^*	m							
	1	2	3	4	5	6	7	8
1		0.9575	0.9219	0.9007	0.8995	0.9249	0.9252	1.0
2			0.9804	0.8809	0.8769	0.9061	0.9391	1.0
3				0.8581	0.8490	0.8817	0.9214	1.0
4					0.8154	0.8419	0.8960	1.0
5						0.8055	0.8572	1.0
6							0.7921	1.0
7								1.0
C_m	0.74	0.85	0.90	0.94	0.96	0.98	0.99	1.0

Table 2
Leading eigenvalues (% of variance)

	ϕ_1	ϕ_2	ϕ_3	ϕ_4	ϕ_5	Total	Covariance complexity
NYSE	21.9	12.4	7.9	6.6	5.5	54.3	0.81
TSE	28.3	18.7	14.8	8.9	6.7	77.4	0.42

of the log-rates for each exchange was computed. The mean vector and covariance were then used as seeds for simulating monthly rates. Monthly log-return vectors were sampled from a multivariate normal distribution with the given mean and covariance from the NYSE and TSE, respectively. Vectors for 50 months were independently simulated and that provided the data for estimating the expected rates of return by the various methods: average, truncation estimator. Since the truncation estimator is an empirical Bayes estimator, it is instructive to contrast it with an alternative empirical Bayes estimator developed by Jorion (1986). In that approach the prior mean is estimated by a weighted grand mean

$$\tilde{\mu} = 1'S_n^{-1}\bar{e}/(1'S_n^{-1}1). \tag{28}$$

The Bayes–Stein (Jorion) estimate of λ is

$$\hat{\theta}_{BS} = \tilde{\mu}1 + \left(\frac{n}{\varphi + K}\right)(\bar{e} - \tilde{\mu}1) \tag{29}$$

with

$$\varphi = \frac{K+2}{(\bar{e} - \tilde{\mu}1)'S_n^{-1}(\bar{e} - \tilde{\mu}1)}. \tag{30}$$

Although they have similar forms, the concept behind the Bayes–Stein estimator is quite different from the truncation estimator. The truncation estimator adjusts the maximum likelihood estimate $\bar{e}$ based on the correlation between securities prices, or equivalently the scores on the latent market factors. The prior distribution is multivariate normal and the conditional covariance (specific variance) is diagonal. The Bayes–Stein estimator shrinks all the $\bar{e}_i$ toward the grand mean, based on variance reduction. In this case, the prior is univariate normal, and the conditional covariance is not diagonal.

For the truncation estimator in each simulated 50 month data set, the number of factors was preset at $m^* = 5$. Since the TSE data has a more compact market structure, it is expected that the truncation estimator with $m^* = 5$ will perform better in that case. This experiment was repeated 1000 times and the root mean squared error for each estimator was computed. To make the statistics comparable across stocks, the root mean squared error is reported as a percent of the actual return: PRMSE $= \frac{\{E(\hat{\theta}-\theta)^2\}^{\frac{1}{2}}}{\theta} \times 100$. The results are shown in Table 3.

There are a number of observations to be made from the Monte Carlo study.

1. The use of the covariance in the truncation estimator provides better estimates. Consistent with the theoretical results, the average of the PRMSE is smaller than for the maximum likelihood estimate (mean), and also smaller than for the Bayes–Stein estimator. This result is consistent with the simulations of MacKinlay and Pastor (2000).
2. The truncation estimator has smaller mean squared error for most stocks on the NYSE and for all stocks on the TSE. This empirical result strengthens the case for the use of covariance in the estimator. The improvement for each asset is significant since there is evidence that portfolios composed from individual assets outperform market index portfolios (Konno and Li, 1998).
3. As established in the theoretical results on covariance complexity, the performance is superior for the stocks on the TSE than the more complex NYSE. The PRMSE is much

Table 3
%Root mean squared error

NYSE stock	Estimator			TSE stock	Estimator		
	Tr	Avg	BS		Tr	Avg	BS
$S_{NYSE,1}$	1.9725	2.8432	2.1462	$S_{TSE,1}$	1.7668	4.5063	3.1027
$S_{NYSE,2}$	4.1581	4.8305	4.2945	$S_{TSE,2}$	2.7083	4.4457	3.2007
$S_{NYSE,3}$	1.8415	2.9378	2.2138	$S_{TSE,3}$	1.9782	4.3989	3.0300
$S_{NYSE,4}$	2.2514	3.0818	2.3202	$S_{TSE,4}$	1.7466	4.3747	3.0131
$S_{NYSE,5}$	2.5917	2.8565	2.2977	$S_{TSE,5}$	1.6950	4.5301	3.1046
$S_{NYSE,6}$	2.8090	2.9188	2.2270	$S_{TSE,6}$	1.8265	4.6527	3.2517
$S_{NYSE,7}$	4.9898	5.3249	5.8516	$S_{TSE,7}$	1.6682	4.2899	2.9744
$S_{NYSE,8}$	2.1711	2.9338	2.2597	$S_{TSE,8}$	1.8485	4.3125	2.9897
$S_{NYSE,9}$	2.3748	3.1987	2.5019	$S_{TSE,9}$	1.8717	4.8132	3.3046
$S_{NYSE,10}$	2.0109	3.0979	2.4649	$S_{TSE,10}$	2.0050	4.4784	3.1089
$S_{NYSE,11}$	2.5031	3.0759	2.4323	$S_{TSE,11}$	2.3007	4.5624	3.2394
$S_{NYSE,12}$	1.9821	2.9752	2.2563	$S_{TSE,12}$	2.2495	5.0386	3.4564
$S_{NYSE,13}$	2.0238	2.9266	2.2242	$S_{TSE,13}$	2.6598	4.3629	3.1579
$S_{NYSE,14}$	1.9424	3.1798	2.5272	$S_{TSE,14}$	1.9208	4.5340	3.1757
$S_{NYSE,15}$	1.9684	3.0972	2.3393	$S_{TSE,15}$	1.7682	4.4389	3.0406
$S_{NYSE,16}$	2.2664	2.6545	2.0528	$S_{TSE,16}$	1.9065	4.3880	3.0011
$S_{NYSE,17}$	2.2813	2.7824	2.1058	$S_{TSE,17}$	2.1732	4.8737	3.2946
$S_{NYSE,18}$	4.5069	5.5240	5.7066	$S_{TSE,18}$	2.1746	4.7862	3.3036
$S_{NYSE,19}$	1.8315	2.8630	2.2293	$S_{TSE,19}$	2.2255	4.4604	3.1621
$S_{NYSE,20}$	5.3000	5.6623	6.3081	$S_{TSE,20}$	1.8554	4.3601	3.0257
$S_{NYSE,21}$	2.3198	2.7973	2.1474	$S_{TSE,21}$	1.6668	4.2875	2.9623
$S_{NYSE,22}$	2.2613	3.2026	2.3916	$S_{TSE,22}$	2.0788	4.5036	3.1099
$S_{NYSE,23}$	2.7386	2.8809	2.3177	$S_{TSE,23}$	2.0384	4.4373	3.1094
$S_{NYSE,24}$	1.8536	2.9950	2.2968	$S_{TSE,24}$	1.9518	4.1811	2.8882
AVG	2.6229	3.3600	2.8297	AVG	2.0026	4.5007	3.1253

smaller because the returns for stocks on the TSE are closely related and the sharing of information has a real impact.

4. Wealth effects

The significance of quality estimates for model parameters is highlighted when those values become inputs to portfolio decisions and the accumulation of wealth over time. The dynamic process for determining a portfolio is illustrated in Fig. 1, where at discrete points in time the model parameters are re-estimated to include new information acquired for prices. The revised estimates are used in the portfolio choice model, and a new strategy is calculated. So the investment strategy depends on the estimated parameters at each stage.

This process is illustrated for the portfolio selection problem with constant relative risk aversion utility. That utility enables a closed form solution which depends on the conditional expected return. The form of the portfolio is analogous to the mean–variance portfolio used in other studies on estimation error and portfolio choice (Chopra and Ziemba, 1993; MacKinlay and Pastor, 2000). The objective is to connect the portfolio decision and accumulated wealth to the estimated return. With negative power utility, the loss in wealth resulting from estimation errors can be mitigated with the risk parameter in the utility function.

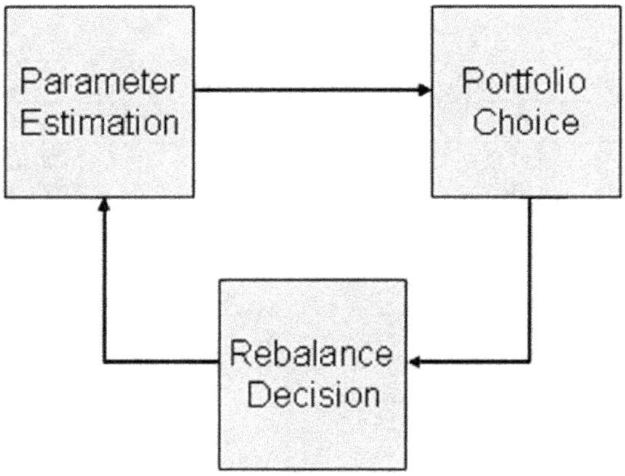

Fig. 1. Dynamic investment process.

4.1. Theoretical wealth loss

Consider an investor with wealth w_t at the start of period t who has K risky investment opportunities and one risk free opportunity with rate of return r. The investment strategy in period t is

$$X(t) = (x_1(t), \dots, x_K(t))',$$

where $x_i(t)$ is the fraction invested in risky asset i, $i = 1, \dots, K$. Short sales are permitted. From the budget constraint, the fraction in the risk free asset is $x_0(t) = 1 - \sum_{i=1}^{K} x_i(t)$. The investment decision is based on the investors knowledge of the rates of return on the assets and preferences for wealth and risk. Because the context is the effect of covariance of returns for risky assets, it is assumed that returns follow the linear model in (1) and (2), with parameters (μ, Λ, Δ), where $\Delta = \delta^2 I$.

The benchmark for estimated returns is the Bayes case, where parameter values are known. With the Bayes estimates $\hat{\theta}'_B = (\hat{\theta}_{B1}, \dots, \hat{\theta}_{BK})$, let $\hat{\alpha}'_B = (\hat{\alpha}_{B1}, \dots, \hat{\alpha}_{BK})$, where $\hat{\alpha}_{Bi}(t) = \hat{\theta}_{Bi}(t) + \frac{1}{2}\delta_i^2$, $i = 1, \dots, K$. The wealth at the beginning of period $t + 1$ with the strategy $X_B(t)$ is

$$W_B(t+1) = w_t \exp\left\{X_B(t)'(\hat{\alpha}_B(t) - re) + r - \frac{1}{2}X_B(t)'\Delta X_B(t) + X_B(t)'\Delta Z\right\}, \tag{31}$$

where $Z' = (Z_1, \dots, Z_K)$, $Z_i \propto N(0, 1)$.

The objective in selecting an investment strategy is to maximize the expected utility of wealth at time $t + 1$, with

$$Eu(W(t+1)) = E\left[\frac{W(t+1)^\beta - 1}{\beta}\right], \tag{32}$$

where $\beta < 1$ and $\beta \neq 0$. This is the constant relative risk aversion power utility function. When $\beta = 0$, $u(w) = \ln(w)$. For the linear pricing model with random rates of return, the optimal strategy is similar to the solution given by Merton (1992):

$$X_B(t) = \frac{1}{1-\beta}\Delta^{-1}(\hat{\alpha}_B(t) - re). \tag{33}$$

A derivation of the optimal solution is given in MacLean et al. (2005). When $\beta = 0$, the formula for the investment strategy is referred to as the Kelly strategy. Although it is developed from the linear pricing model, the strategy has significant properties which apply to general returns distributions (MacLean and Ziemba, 1999).

1. Of particular importance is evolutionary stability, which states that the Kelly strategy dominates any other essentially different strategy (Hens and Schenk-Hoppe, 2005).
2. The conditional covariance of log-prices, Δ, is a key component of the solution, and the simplification $\Delta = \delta^2 I$ has been justified in simulations (MacKinlay and Pastor, 2000).
3. The covariance structure for returns is embedded in the estimates $\hat{\alpha}_B$.
4. The risk aversion parameter β controls the fraction allocated to the risky assets. If $X^*(t) = \Delta^{-1}(\hat{\alpha}_B(t) - re)$, then the optimal strategy can be written as $\left(\frac{-\beta}{1-\beta}x_0^*(t), \frac{1}{1-\beta}X^*(t)\right)$, where the Kelly portfolio is blended with the risk free asset using β.

When estimates for the rates of return and idiosyncratic variance are used in calculating the investment strategy, the estimation error is a factor in the performance of the strategy. For the truncation estimator, with corresponding variance estimate, the strategy is

$$X_{\hat{B}}(t) = \frac{1}{1-\beta}\hat{\Delta}_{\hat{B}}^{-1}(\hat{\alpha}_{\hat{B}}(t) - re), \tag{34}$$

and $t+1$ period wealth is

$$W_{\hat{B}}(t+1) = w_t \exp\left\{X_{\hat{B}}(t)'(\hat{\alpha}_B(t) - re) + r - \frac{1}{2}X_{\hat{B}}(t)'\Delta X_{\hat{B}}(t) + X_{\hat{B}}(t)'\Delta Z\right\}. \tag{35}$$

The ratio

$$\mathrm{WL}(X_{\hat{B}}) = E\log\frac{W_B(t+1)}{W_{\hat{B}}(t+1)} \tag{36}$$

indicates the wealth loss from estimating the parameters in the linear model. The log of wealth defines the growth rate, so the ratio $\mathrm{WL}(X_{\hat{B}})$ is the loss in growth rate from estimating parameter values.

In the same way, the mean log rate of return (maximum likelihood estimate), with an independent estimate for covariance, can be used in the calculation of the investment strategy:

$$X_{\hat{e}}(t) = \frac{1}{1-\beta}\hat{\Delta}^{-1}(\hat{\alpha}_{\hat{e}}(t) - re). \tag{37}$$

A comparison of the empirical Bayes (truncation) strategy with the mean rate strategy is defined by the relative wealth loss.

Definition 3. Let $X_{\hat{e}}(t), X_{\hat{B}}(t)$ be the investment strategies from using the maximum likelihood, and empirical Bayes (truncation) estimates, respectively, for the expected rates of return. The one period ahead relative wealth loss is defined as

$$\mathrm{RWL}(X_{\hat{B}}) = \frac{\mathrm{WL}(X_{\hat{B}})}{\mathrm{WL}(X_{\hat{e}})}. \tag{38}$$

Following from the results on mean squared error, the wealth loss should be less for the strategy based on the truncation estimator than for the strategy based on the mean rate of return. In developing the comparison assume that $\Delta = \delta^2 I$ is given.

Proposition 5. *Assume that $\Delta = \delta^2 I$ and m are known. The wealth loss for strategies $X_{\hat{B}}$ and $X_{\bar{e}}$ is linear in the additional estimation risk. If the risk parameter is $\beta = 0$, then the strategy is loss preserving*: $\mathrm{RWL}(X_{\hat{B}}) = \mathrm{RSL}(\hat{\theta}_{\hat{B}})$. *The wealth loss can be modulated with the risk parameter*: $\mathrm{RWL}(X_{\hat{B}}) < \mathrm{RSL}(\hat{\theta}_{\hat{B}})$ *if* $\beta < 0$ *and* $\mathrm{RWL}(X_{\hat{B}}) > \mathrm{RSL}(\hat{\theta}_{\hat{B}})$ *if* $0 < \beta < 1$.

The wealth loss depends upon the risk aversion at the time of decision. In the decision rule, the risk aversion parameter β defines a fraction of capital invested in the optimal growth portfolio: $\frac{1}{1-\beta}$. When $\beta < 0$, the control of decision risk also reduces the impact of estimation error. Correspondingly, when $\beta > 0$, the overinvestment increases the effect of estimation error. In general, the improvement in parameter estimation translates into better wealth performance.

If the number of factors is unknown, then additional error from truncation will be included in the estimator and the investment decision. Consider the bias introduced by truncation

$$\Theta(\hat{\theta}_{\hat{B}}) = E(\hat{\theta}_B - \hat{\theta}_{\hat{B}})'1. \tag{39}$$

If this bias is sufficiently small, then the relationship between wealth loss and estimation error is retained.

Proposition 6. *Consider assets with price dynamics defined by* (1) *and* (2), *and investment strategy defined by* (34). *Let $\hat{\theta}_{\hat{B}}$ be the truncation estimate with number of factors $m^* < m$. If the bias for the truncation estimate satisfies*

$$\left(\frac{1}{2}\delta^2 - r\right)\Theta(\hat{\theta}_{\hat{B}}) < \mathrm{tr}EBS_nB',$$

then (i) $\mathrm{RWL}(X_{\hat{B}}) < \mathrm{RSL}(\hat{\theta}_{\hat{B}})$ *if* $\beta < 0$; (ii) $\mathrm{RWL}(X_{\hat{B}}) = \mathrm{RSL}(\hat{\theta}_{\hat{B}})$ *if* $\beta = 0$; (iii) $\mathrm{RWL}(X_{\hat{B}}) > \mathrm{RSL}(\hat{\theta}_{\hat{B}})$ *if* $0 < \beta < 1$.

For the most complex case, where the unobserved factors are equally important, the ordering on estimation loss generates an ordering on wealth loss for alternative investment strategies when the number of factors in the price dynamics is truncated.

4.2. Application to NYSE

The dynamic investment process is now implemented with the data from the New York Stock Exchange. The approach is to forecast the prices for the next month using the truncation estimator (and for comparison with the Bayes–Stein estimator), then calculate the Kelly or growth optimal investment strategy with risk index $\beta = 0$. The amount set aside for investment in each month is held at \$1000. So the strategy is constrained. The return on investment is from the actual return for the next month. The final wealth is the accumulation of returns on the monthly investments. Advantages of this methodology are: (i) the investment capital is the same for both estimation procedures; (ii) each month is the same except for the parameter estimates.

Table 4
Wealth comparison using alternative estimators

Month	Bayes–Stein	Truncation	Ratio
1	1000.00	1000.00	1.00
2	2753.84	3114.25	1.13
3	4734.16	5755.60	1.22
4	6155.03	7495.27	1.22
5	7072.46	8635.16	1.22
6	8800.46	10852.75	1.23
7	8057.76	9693.90	1.20
8	9839.54	12188.45	1.24
9	9915.73	12495.84	1.26
10	12373.73	16287.52	1.32
11	12945.05	17198.59	1.33
12	14734.91	19844.46	1.35
13	15114.73	20335.51	1.35
14	15905.18	21378.58	1.34
15	15753.94	21355.97	1.36
16	16988.85	23065.39	1.36
17	17817.41	24258.14	1.36
18	16744.71	22670.64	1.35
19	17483.44	23516.54	1.35
20	19935.02	26538.49	1.33
21	21354.56	28376.71	1.33
22	25299.94	33494.38	1.32
23	24760.45	32790.56	1.32
24	28880.96	37855.50	1.31

The segment of the data series from 1993 to 1996 is used. The forecast for rates of return for one month ahead are developed from the previous 24 months of prices, and they are used to determine the investment strategy. The return for the next month is calculated from the actual prices. This backcast is worked forward from January 1995 to December 1996, with the resulting accumulated capital shown in Table 4. The returns are very large, as is characteristic of that period, and although \$1000 is set aside for investment, the actual amount in securities is much higher, since capital is borrowed to invest in high return securities. That is a property of the capital growth strategy – very risky, and is part of the rationale for caping the seed fund at \$1000. The investment strategy is a vehicle for considering the estimation error, and the comparison of estimators rather than the size of returns is the focus. The important statistic is the relative return for the comparative estimators. The superiority of the truncation estimator, which was demonstrated in the simulations, yields superior strategies and greater wealth.

The 24 month test interval is appropriate for comparing estimators since the return dynamics are consistent over that time. The time frame does not include the market collapse following the overvaluation of securities.

5. Conclusion

The estimation of the rates of return on assets is a critical ingredient to a successful investment strategy. An effective combination of modeling and data can result in significant improvement in capital accumulation. In this paper a Bayes dynamic pricing model is the basis for a truncation estimator of the rate of return on assets. The key to the truncation estimator is the covariance between asset prices. The covariance is incorporated into the estimate of the mean. In that way, the common information in price movements contributes to improved estimation of individual estimates.

The truncation estimator is compared to well known estimators – mean and Bayes–Stein. If asset prices follow the Bayes model, then analytic results establish the superiority of the truncation estimator. From simulation results, the truncation estimator outperforms the alternatives in general.

The savings in estimation error with the proposed estimator translate into better decisions and accumulated wealth. A back test on data from the New York Stock Exchange emphasizes the gains. The analytic formulation provides an assessment of risk aversion in the face of uncertain returns. In particular, the risk aversion index can be used to offset the loss from estimation error with the truncation estimator.

Appendix A

Proof of Proposition 1. With $\gamma = \frac{\mathrm{tr}\Sigma - K\delta^2}{m}$ fixed, let $\gamma_m = m\gamma - \sum_{j=1}^{m-1}\gamma_j$. Consider $V = \sum_{j=1}^{m}(\gamma_j - \gamma)^2$, and $C = -\frac{\sum_{j=1}^{m}\left(\frac{\gamma_j+\delta^2}{\mathrm{tr}\Sigma}\right)\ln\left(\frac{\gamma_j+\delta^2}{\mathrm{tr}\Sigma}\right)}{\ln K_1}$. Substituting for γ_m and differentiating, $\frac{\partial C}{\partial \gamma_1} > 0$, and $\frac{\partial V}{\partial \gamma_1} > 0$. So $\frac{\partial C}{\partial V} = \frac{\partial C}{\partial \gamma_1} \times \left(\frac{\partial V}{\partial \gamma_1}\right)^{-1} < 0$. Since the minimum $V = 0$ occurs when $\gamma_j = \gamma$, C_m is as stated.

Proof of Proposition 2. Consider $R(\theta, \hat{\theta}_B) = \delta^2\sum_{j=1}^{m}\gamma_j(\gamma_j + \delta^2)/(\gamma_j + \delta^2)^2$. Then $\frac{\partial R}{\partial \gamma_j} > 0$, and $\frac{\partial^2 R}{\partial \gamma_j^2} < 0$, so that R is strictly concave in $(\gamma_1, \ldots, \gamma_m)$. If $R(\theta, \hat{\theta}_B) = f(\gamma_1, \ldots, \gamma_m)$, then

$$f\left(\frac{m}{m-1}\gamma, \ldots, \frac{m}{m-1}\gamma, 0\right) - f(\gamma, \ldots, \gamma) < \nabla f(\gamma, \ldots, \gamma)\begin{pmatrix} \frac{\gamma}{m-1} \\ \cdot \\ \cdot \\ \cdot \\ \frac{\gamma}{m-1} \\ -\gamma \end{pmatrix} = 0,$$

and the second statement is established.

With $\sum_{j=1}^{m}\gamma_j = m\gamma$, consider the level sets

$$A_r = \left\{(\gamma_1, \ldots, \gamma_m) \middle| \sum_{j=1}^{m}(\gamma_j - \gamma)^2 = r, \sum_{j=1}^{m}\gamma_j = m\gamma\right\}.$$

Consider $r_1 > r_2$, and $(\gamma_1^1, \ldots, \gamma_m^1) \in A_{r_1}$, $(\gamma_1^2, \ldots, \gamma_m^2) \in A_{r_2}$. Since $f(\gamma_1, \ldots, \gamma_m)$ is strictly concave, then $f(\gamma_1^1, \ldots, \gamma_m^1) < f(\gamma_1^2, \ldots, \gamma_m^2)$ and monotonicity in variance follows.

Since complexity increases as variance decreases, it follows that Bayes risk increases as complexity increases.

Proof of Proposition 3. Consider the additional risk for the truncation estimator,

$$R^+(\hat{\theta}_{\hat{B}}) = \frac{1}{nK^2}(1'\Sigma 1)\mathrm{tr}B11'B' + \frac{1}{n}\mathrm{tr}E(B - \widehat{B})S_n(B - \widehat{B})',$$

where $B = \Delta\Sigma^{-1}$ and $\widehat{B} = \Delta S^{*^{-1}}$. Also $S_n = LGL'$ for $G = \mathrm{diag}(g_1, \ldots, g_K)$. With m and $\Delta = \delta^2 I$ known, then $B = \Delta\Sigma^{-1} = \delta^2 \Lambda\Phi^{-1}\Lambda'$ and $\widehat{B} = \Delta S^{*^{-1}} = \delta^2 LG^{*^{-1}}L'$, where $\Phi = \mathrm{diag}(\phi_1, \ldots, \phi_m, \delta^2, \ldots, \delta^2)$ and $G^* = (g_1, \ldots, g_m, \delta^2, \ldots, \delta^2)$. Consider

$$\mathrm{tr}E(B - \widehat{B})S_n(B - \widehat{B})' = \mathrm{tr}EBS_nB' - 2\mathrm{tr}EBS_n\widehat{B}' + \mathrm{tr}E\widehat{B}S_n\widehat{B}'.$$

From the structure it follows that $\mathrm{tr}E\widehat{B}S_n\hat{B}' = E\left(\sum_{j=i}^{m}\frac{\delta^4}{g_j} + \sum_{j=m+1}^{K} g_j\right)$ and $\mathrm{tr}EBS_nB' = \sum_{j=1}^{m}\frac{\delta^4}{\phi_j} + \delta^2(K - m)$. From the asymptotic moments of eigenvalues (Seber, 1984) and after simplification $\mathrm{tr}EBS_n\widehat{B}' = \sum_{j=1}^{m}\frac{\delta^4}{\phi_j} + \sum_{i=1}^{m} Eg_j + \mathrm{O}(n^{-2})$.

As well

$$E\sum_{j=1}^{m}\frac{1}{g_j} = \sum_{j=1}^{m}\frac{1}{\phi_j} + \frac{1}{n}\left\{(K - m)\sum_{j=1}^{m}\frac{1}{\delta^2 - \phi_j}\right\} + \mathrm{O}(n^{-2})$$

and

$$E\sum_{j=m+1}^{I} g_j = (K - m) + \frac{1}{n}\left\{(K - m)\sum_{j=1}^{m}\frac{\gamma_j}{\delta^2 - \phi_j}\right\} + \mathrm{O}(n^{-2}).$$

Substituting expressions into the additional risk for $\hat{\theta}_{\hat{B}}$ yields

$$R^{+}(\hat{\theta}_{\hat{B}}) = \frac{1}{nK^2}(1'\Sigma 1)\mathrm{tr}B11'B' + \frac{1}{n}\left\{\frac{K - m}{n}\sum_{j=1}^{m}\frac{\delta^4 - \phi_j}{\delta^2 - \phi_j}\right\} + \mathrm{O}(n^{-2}).$$

For $\bar{e}$, it follows that

$$R^{+}(\bar{e}) = \frac{1}{nK^2}(1'\Sigma 1)\mathrm{tr}B11'B' + \frac{1}{n}\left(\sum_{j=1}^{m}\frac{\delta^4}{\phi_j} + \delta^2(K - m)\right).$$

Then $\mathrm{RSL}(\hat{\lambda}_{\hat{B}}) = \frac{R^{+}(\hat{\lambda}_{\hat{B}})}{R^{+}(\bar{e})} \leqslant 1$ if $n \geqslant \frac{1}{\delta^2}\sum_{j=1}^{m}\frac{\phi_j - \delta^4}{\phi_j - \delta^2} = n^*$.

With simple calculus, $\frac{dn^*}{dV} = \frac{dn^*}{d\gamma_1} \times \left(\frac{dV}{d\gamma_1}\right)^{-1} < 0$, and sample size is monotone decreasing in variance of eigenvalues, and increasing in complexity.

Proof of Proposition 4. With the covariance Σ having eigenvalues ϕ with multiplicity m and δ^2 with multiplicity $K - m$, let $\gamma = \phi - \delta^2$. Then the m^* truncation estimates for δ^2 and $\Lambda_{\cdot j}$ are $d^2 = \delta^2 + \frac{(m - m^*)}{(K - m^*)}\gamma$ and $l_{\cdot j} = (1 + \frac{\delta^2 - d^2}{\gamma})^{\frac{1}{2}}\Lambda_{\cdot j}$, $j = 1, \ldots, m^*$. With $\Sigma^* = L'L + D$, then $\mathrm{tr}\Sigma = \mathrm{tr}\Sigma^*$. The truncation estimator, based on Σ, has $\widehat{B} = \left[\delta^2 + \left(\frac{m - m^*}{K - m^*}\right)\gamma\right]\left(1 + \frac{\delta^2 - d^2}{\gamma}\right)\Lambda_1\Lambda_1'$, where $\Lambda = (\Lambda_1, \Lambda_2)$ and Λ_1 is $K \times m^*$ and Λ_2 is $K \times (m - m^*)$. Then the additional risk for the truncation estimator is $R(\hat{\theta}_{\hat{B}}) = \frac{1}{K^2 n}(1'\Sigma 1)\mathrm{tr}B11'B + \frac{1}{n}\frac{\gamma(m - m^*)(K^2 - 2Km^* + mm^*)}{(\gamma + \delta^2)(K - m^*)^2}$. For the mean $\bar{e}$, the additional risk is $R^{+}(\bar{e}) = \frac{1}{K^2 n}(1'\Sigma 1)\mathrm{tr}B11'B + \frac{1}{n}\frac{K\delta^2(\gamma + \delta^2) - m\gamma\delta^2}{\gamma + \delta^2}$. Without loss of generality let $\sigma^2 = 1$. Then

$\mathrm{RSL}(\hat{\theta}_{\hat{B}}) \leqslant 1$ iff $\gamma(m - m^*)(K^2 - 2Km^* + mm^*) \leqslant (K - m^*)^2\ [K\delta^2(\gamma + \delta^2) - m\gamma\delta^2]$. This becomes $a\delta^4 + b\delta^2 + c \geqslant 0$, where $a = (K - m^*)(2m - K)$, $b = (K - m^*)(K - m) + (K^2 - 2m^*K + mm^*)$, and $c = -(K^2 - 2m^*K + mm^*)$. (i) If $m < \frac{K}{2}$, $a\delta^4 + b\delta^2 + c \geqslant 0$ for

$\delta^2 \in (0,\sigma^2)$ and $\mathrm{RSL}(\hat{\theta}_{\hat{B}}) \leqslant 1$. (ii) If $m \geqslant \frac{K}{2}$, $a\delta^4 + b\delta^2 + c \geqslant 0$ and $\mathrm{RSL}(\hat{\theta}_{\hat{B}}) \leqslant 1$ for $\delta^2 \in (\delta_1^2, \sigma^2)$.

Proof of Proposition 5. Consider

$$\begin{aligned}\mathrm{WL}(X_{\hat{B}}) &= E\ln W(t+1) - E\ln W(t+1)\\ &= \frac{-\beta}{(1-\beta)^2}\delta^{-2}E(\hat{\theta}_B - \hat{\theta}_{\hat{B}})'\left(\hat{\lambda}_B + \left(\frac{1}{2}\delta^2 - r\right)1\right) + \frac{1}{2(1-\beta)^2}\delta^{-2}R^{+}(\hat{\theta}_{\hat{B}}, \hat{\theta}_B).\end{aligned}$$

Also

$$E(\hat{\theta}_B - \hat{\theta}_{\hat{B}})'\hat{\theta}_B = E(\hat{\theta}_B - \hat{\theta}_e)\hat{\theta}_B + E(\hat{\theta}_{\hat{e}} - \hat{\theta}_{\hat{B}})\hat{\theta}_B.$$

Furthermore $E(\hat{\theta}_{\hat{e}} - \hat{\theta}_{\hat{B}})'\hat{\theta}_B = -E\mathrm{tr}BS_n\widehat{B}'$ and $E(\hat{\theta}_B - \hat{\theta}_{\hat{e}})'\hat{\theta}_B = E\mathrm{tr}BS_nB - \mathrm{tr}\Delta$.

So

$$\mathrm{WL}(X_{\hat{B}}) = \frac{1}{2(1-\beta)^2}\delta^{-2}R^{+}(\hat{\theta}_{\hat{B}}, \hat{\theta}_B) + \frac{\beta}{(1-\beta)^2}\delta^{-2}\mathrm{tr}\Delta$$

and

$$\mathrm{WL}(X_{\hat{e}}) = \frac{1}{2(1-\beta)^2}\delta^{-2}R^{+}(\hat{\theta}_{\hat{e}}, \hat{\theta}_B) + \frac{\beta}{(1-\beta)^2}\delta^{-2}\mathrm{tr}\Delta - \frac{\beta}{(1-\beta)^2}\delta^{-2}\mathrm{tr}EBS_nB.$$

The statements in the proposition follows:

Proof of Proposition 6. From Proof of Proposition 5, it follows that

$$\mathrm{RWL}(X_{\hat{B}}) = \frac{R^{+}(\hat{\theta}_{\hat{B}}) + 2\beta\mathrm{tr}\Delta - 2\beta(\frac{1}{2}\delta^2 - r)\Theta(\hat{\theta}_{\hat{B}})}{R^{+}(\hat{\theta}_e) + 2\beta\mathrm{tr}\Delta - 2\beta\mathrm{tr}EBS_nB'}.$$

If the bias inequality is satisfied, then the statements relating RWL and RSL hold.

References

Browne, S., Whitt, W., 1996. Portfolio choice and the Bayesian Kelly criterion. Advances in Applied Probability 28, 1145–1176.

Chernov, M., Gallant, A.R., Ghysels, E., Tauchen, G., 2002. Alternative models for stock price dynamics working paper. CIRANO, Montreal, Canada.

Chopra, V.K., Ziemba, W.T., 1993. The effect of errors in means, variances and covariances on optimal portfolio choice. Journal of Portfolio Management 19, 6–11.

Connor, G., Korajczyk, R.A., 1995. The arbitrage pricing theory and multifactor models of asset returns. In: Jarrow, Maksimovic, Ziemba (Eds.), Finance. Elsevier Science, B.V., Amsterdam, pp. 87–144.

Efron, B., Morris, C., 1972. Empirical Bayes estimation on vector observations: An extension of Steins method. Biometrika 59, 335–347.

Frost, P.A., Savarino, J.E., 1986. An empirical Bayes approach to efficient portfolio selection. Journal of Financial and Quantitative Analysis 21 (3), 293–306.

Grauer, R.R., Hakansson, N.H., 1995. Stein and CAPM estimators of the means in asset allocation. International Review of Financial Analysis 4, 721–739.

Hens, T., Schenk-Hoppe, K.R., 2005. Evolutionary stability of portfolio rules in incomplete markets. Journal of Mathematical Economics 41, 43–66.

Jones, C.S., Shanken, J., 2003. Mutual fund performance with learning across funds. Journal of Financial Economics 78 (3), 507–552.

Jorion, P., 1986. Bayes–Stein estimation for portfolio analysis. Journal of Financial and Quantitative Analysis 21, 279–329.

Kallberg, J.G., Ziemba, W.T., 1981. Remarks on optimal portfolio selection. Methods of Operations Research 44, 507–520.

Kallberg, J.G., Ziemba, W.T., 1984. Mis-specification in portfolio selection problems. In: Bamberg, Spreemann (Eds.), Risk and Capital. Springer-Verlag, pp. 74–87.

Klein, R.W., Bawa, V.S., 1976. The effect of estimation risk on portfolio choice. Journal of Financial Economics 3, 215–231.

Konno, H., Li, J., 1998. Internationally diversified investment using an integrated portfolio model. International Journal of Theoretical and Applied Finance 1, 145–160.

Loffler, G., 2003. The effects of estimation error on measures of portfolio credit risk. Journal of Banking and Finance 27 (8), 1427–1453.

MacKinlay, A.C., Pastor, L., 2000. Asset pricing models: Implications for expected returns and portfolio selection. The Review of Financial Studies 13 (4), 883–916.

MacLean, L.C., Ziemba, W.T., 1999. Growth versus security trade-offs in dynamic investment analysis. Annals of Operations Research 85, 193–225.

MacLean, L.C., Consigli, G., Ziemba, W.T., 2004. Modelling market returns with a speculative bubble. Proceedings of the American Statistical Association. American Statistical Association, Alexandra, VA.

MacLean, L.C., Ziemba, W.T., Li, Y., 2005. Time to wealth goals in capital accumulation models. Quantitative Finance 5 (4), 343–357.

Merton, R.C., 1992. Continuous Time Finance, second ed. Blackwell Publishers, Cambridge, MA.

Morgerra, S.D., 1985. Information theoretic covariance complexity and its relation to pattern recognition. IEEE Transactions on Systems, Man and Cybernetics 15, 608–619.

Pastor, L., Stambaugh, R.F., 1999. Costs of equity capital and model mispricing. Journal of Finance 54, 67–121.

Rogers, L.C.G., 2000. The relaxed investor and parameter uncertainty. Finance and Stochastics 5, 131–154.

Ross, S.A., 1976. The arbitrage theory of capital asset pricing. Journal of Economic Theory 13 (3), 341–360.

Seber, G.C., 1984. Multivariate Observations. John Wiley, New York.

Sharpe, W.F., 1964. Capital asset prices: A theory of market equilibrium under conditions of risk. Journal of Finance 19, 425–442.

https://doi.org/10.1142/9789811222634_0004

Chapter 4

The role of effective corporate decisions in the creation of efficient portfolios*

J. B. Guerard, Jr.
H. Markowitz
G. Xu

Chief executive officers and chief financial officers seek to implement corporate financial decisions that maximize the stock price and stockholder wealth. Real assets may be tangible, such as machinery or factories, or intangible, such as technical expertise or patents. These real assets must be paid for. To finance the real assets, the financial manager makes decisions regarding the magnitude of common stock issuance and stock repurchases, long-term debt issuance, and debt repurchases. Cash flows are generated by real assets, and the stockholders receive dividend payments based on the net income generated by the corporation. Empirical evidence shows that the dividend payment decision and stock and debt repurchase decisions can increase stock prices and returns. A variable, denoted as corporate exports—which incorporates the amount of dividends, net stock issuances, and net debt repurchases—is used as an expected return to create an initial efficient frontier. A stock selection model is used as a constraint in the portfolio process in conjunction with the corporate exports variable to further increase returns. We use a data mining corrections test for establishing the statistical significance of our portfolio returns.

Introduction

Students of corporation finance are taught that management, primarily chief executive officers and chief financial officers, seek to maximize stockholder wealth. Brealey et al. [1] stated that the goal of corporate finance is to implement corporate decisions to enhance stockholder wealth by maximizing the stock price. In the world of business, real assets must be acquired for the growth of corporations and must be financed. Real assets generate cash flows that are used to pay dividends and to finance these real assets. The financial manager makes decisions regarding the magnitude of common stock issuance and stock repurchases, long-term debt issuance, and debt repurchases. Empirical evidence shows that the dividend payment decision and stock and debt repurchase decisions can increase stockholder wealth. We calculate a variable, referred to as corporate exports, composed of dividend payments, common stock issuance and stock re-purchases, long-term debt issuance, and debt re-purchases. We show that companies generating larger corporate exports increase in price relative to firms that generate lower corporate exports. Gerstner [2] stated that managers need the relevant information, make decisions based on the critical information, and communicate the information throughout the organization to enhance performance. Corporate exports are composed of variables that help maximize stockholder wealth. Gerstner reminded us that the marketplace, through demand and supply determining the company stock price, is the driving force behind all corporate activities, and corporate measures of success are ultimately customer satisfaction and shareholder value.

We show that corporate decisions with respect to dividend, stock, and debt directly affect stock prices and stockholder returns. We examine dividend payments, common stock issuance and stock re-purchases, long-term debt issuance and debt re-purchases for all publically traded United States firms for the 1971 to 2011 period. As mentioned, we create a "corporate exports" variable that incorporates the dividend, stock and debt issuance and buy-backs decisions. Schwartz and Aronson [3] stated that a balanced economic growth

*This article originally appeared in *Journal of Research and Development* **58**(4), 6:1–6:11, 2014.

model equates the income from capital and the total of aggregate savings with real investment. If the cash flow generated by operating assets exceeds the possible net real investment, then the overall corporate sector will have more funds than it can desirably re-invest in business. The corporate sector will have funds to distribute to the rest of the economy. Schwartz and Aronson called the excess of corporate funds to be distributed to the rest of the economy "corporate exports". When Schwartz and Aronson discussed corporate exports in 1966, they included dividends paid, interest paid, stock issued, and debt issued. Schwartz and Aronson reported that dividends and interest paid substantially exceeded new funds raised on the capital markets. In the United States during a fifty-year period ending in 1965, corporations raised the necessary cash primarily by issuing debt. Stock repurchases were so infrequent that the Compustat database did not include a stock repurchase variable until 1971. In 2007, Guerard and Schwartz [4] refined corporate exports to include dividends paid, interest paid, stock issuance and repurchase, and debt issuance and repurchase. Share repurchases have grown dramatically since 1971. The updated corporate exports variable can be used in conjunction with a stock selection model to identify under-valued stocks. In this paper, we calculate corporate exports for all stocks traded in the United States from 1971 to 2011 and use IBM data as an example. Companies generating larger, positive corporate exports appreciate more in price than firms with lower, or negative corporate exports.

We integrate managerial finance and investment analysis to show how corporate exports—incorporating dividend policy, debt and equity issuance and repurchase decisions, and leverage—can be used to maximize portfolio returns. We illustrate Markowitz [5, 6] portfolio optimization using the corporate exports as an expected returns variable. The corporate exports variable is statistically significant in producing positive active returns for portfolios. If one produces portfolios using the corporate exports expected returns variable and further constrains portfolios to only include stocks that are identified as attractive using a stock selection model [7, 8], then portfolio active returns increase substantially. Finally, we apply the Markowitz-Xu [9] data mining corrections test to assess the whether these returns could have been produced randomly.

Corporate financial decisions

We specifically examine dividend, debt and equity issuance and buy-back strategies, and the implied leverage decisions of firms. Miller and Modigliani [10] demonstrated that dividend policy was irrelevant to the value of the firm. In the presence of taxes, Fama and Babiack [11] reported that dividends are highly correlated with earnings. As earnings rise, there is usually some lag before former payout levels are resumed. A forecast of dividend levels can be obtained by studying past payout rates and attempting to predict future earnings levels. The amount left after common dividends are paid represents retained earnings or earnings reinvested in the firm. Buy backs are more difficult to predict than dividends. Before the prevalence of buy backs, Dividend Discount Models were more valid for companies that had a "normal," or consistent, dividend payout policy.

Equity repurchases increased substantially during the 1971 to 2012 time period, particularly since the post-crash period beginning in 1987. Grullon and Michaely [12] state that one explanation for the sudden growth in share repurchases is the Security Exchange Commission (SEC) adoption of Rule 10b-18 in 1982, which protected firms from prosecution on the basis that share repurchases manipulated their stock prices. Share repurchases increase with economic "boom" conditions and diminishes in recessions. Excess returns have been associated with share repurchases [12].

A tender offer is a general offer to stockholders to buy their stock. Equity repurchases, whether privately negotiated or via a tender offer, generally specify the number of shares the firm seeks to repurchase, the tender price at which it will repurchase shares, and the expiration date of the tender offer, which the firm may extend. Dann [13] examined 143 cash tender offers to repurchase equity during the 1962 to 1976 period, made by 122 different firms, and reported a 22.5% tender offer premium, relative to the previous day of the announcement (20.9% relative to the one month period before the announcement). Large excess returns are associated with share buybacks. Firms repurchase equity to enhance stockholder wealth. There were marginal debt effects, and approximately 95% of the enhanced value was accrued to stockholders. Lakonishok and Vermaelen [14] found excess returns to repurchases continued to 1986, but at a (slightly) diminished rate. Lakonishok and Vermaelen reported premiums of 21.8%, 24.1%, and 18.5% on tender offers during the 1962 to 1986, 1962 to 1979, and 1980 to 1986 periods, respectively. They also reported cumulative abnormal returns, or cumulative excess returns, relative to the market, of 12.5%, 14.6%, and 9.8% to non-tendering stockholders during the corresponding periods. Smaller firms produced the highest abnormal returns. The level of current and projected earnings has an impact on dividend policy and potential buy backs (Bierman [15, 16]). Firms adopt a target debt ratio by choosing between debt and equity repurchases as well as choosing between debt and equity issuances [17]. Repurchases and dividends are motivated by contracting investment opportunities [18].

Dhrymes and Kurz [19] proposed an explicit link among these dividend, investment, and debt issuance decisions and econometrically estimated a simultaneous equations system using a sample of 181 industrial and commercial firms during the period 1947 to 1960. Dhrymes and Kurz reported that debt was issued to finance capital expenditures and dividend payments. Investment and dividends were positively associated with new debt issuance. Guerard, Bean, and Andrews [20] updated the Dhrymes and Kurz analysis and reported: (1) a strong interdependence is evident between the investment and dividend decisions; and (2) a strong interdependence is evident between the investment and new debt financing decisions. Retained earnings add to the equity of the common shareholders. Retained earnings, the net income of firms not paid to stockholders in the form of dividends, represents the majority of funds that can be used to finance real assets [1, 4]. An increase in assets financed by ownership capital as opposed to debt improves the credit standing of the firm and enables it to issue debt at a relatively lower rate. Debt and internally generated funds are the primary sources of aggregate investment outlays [19].

New debt issues exceed new equity issues by a multiple exceeding eight times, a result consistent with Dhrymes and Kurz [19], Guerard et al. [20], and Myers [21]. New debt issued is identified with the financing capital expenditures in the simultaneous equation modeling. Funds represented in earnings should increase the future profits of the shareholders and eventually result in buy backs or higher dividends. It is not the increment in the book value of the shares, but a hoped-for sequence of increased earnings that makes retained earnings of value to the shareholder.

Defining and calculating corporate exports

In this paper, we calculate the net export of funds variable (CE), defined in Guerard and Schwartz [2] and Guerard [22], as:

$$CE = \textit{Dividends Paid} + \textit{Interest Paid} + \textit{Net Equity Repurchased} - \textit{Net Debt Issued}. \quad (1)$$

In 1971, the corporate sector exported over \$46 billion of funds, and by 2011, the corporate sector funds exported grew to over \$248 billion. The surplus of funds over any possible reasonable capital investment policy is the rationale behind the cash buy back of shares and the payment of dividends. In short, the corporate sector has continued to be a net exporter of funds to the rest of the economy, and has risen almost consistently throughout the 1971 to 2011 period, except when net equity re-purchases fell and new debt issues rose in the mid to late-1990s and during the financial crisis of 2007 and its aftermath. The CE variable can be criticized for ignoring cash on the balance sheet. Cash is another source of funds and may be directly distributed to stockholders as additional dividends. We find corporate exports without cash has better stock return predictive power than corporate exports including cash, although both corporate export variables are highly statistically significant. We address the predictive power of the corporate exports variable in the next section.

In **Table 1**, we show annual statistics of the components of CE as reported in the Compustat database. A second way to examine the corporate sector net export of funds is to examine the dividends paid less equity repurchased, which also is shown in Table 1. Dividends paid exceeded equity repurchased of the Compustat firms from 1971 to 2011, although equity repurchases have risen relatively to dividends since 1982. We examine the 1971 to 2011 period because Compustat does not maintain debt and equity issuance, and repurchases, prior to 1971.

An analysis of the CE components reveals that interest paid has risen faster than dividends paid during the 1971 to 2011 time period. Net debt issues have risen at an undiminished rate, with the notable exception of 2001 to 2005 and 2009, shown in **Figure 1**. As we mentioned before, we use the WRDS Compustat database of stocks in the United States in this paper. Stock repurchases rose substantially following the crash of October 1987. Net equity repurchases increased substantially in the 2002 to 2006 time period, and fell dramatically with the financial crisis.

Guerard [22] reported the ten largest and smallest corporate exporter firms in 1983 to illustrate the corporate fund generating process. The largest corporate exports firms included AT&T, IBM, and several large oil companies. These firms dominated positive corporate exports in 1983 because they paid large dividends and interest and generally re-purchased more debt than was issued (which made a great deal of sense given the level of interest rates in 1983). A similar process occurred in 2006 as Microsoft, Pfizer, and the oil companies dominated the largest corporate exporting firm (IBM fell to only the twenty-fourth largest exporter in 2006). IBM is a very interesting individual case, as it is generally a large net corporate exporter of funds, except in 1993, its near-bankruptcy year. IBM pays large dividends, repurchases huge amounts of equity, is a net issuer of debt, and issues no new equity after 1995. Indeed, IBM's repurchase of equity far exceeded its dividends paid during the 1995 to 2006 time period (see **Figure 2**). IBM's dividends exceeded its net new equity issues and net new capital issues in all years except 1993.

A stock selection model

There are many approaches to security valuation and the creation of expected returns. Fundamental data—such as earnings, book value, cash flows, and sales—have been statistically associated with stock excess returns for decades [23–28]. Chan, Hamao, and Lakonishok [25] and Lakonishok, Shleifer, and Vishny [27] are widely cited references on contrarian, or fundamentally based, investment strategies. We use a stock selection model that has evolved over the past two decades. Bloch et al. [26] used an eight-factor model to identify under-valued stocks. The eight factors are composed of current ratios of earnings, book value, cash flow, sales, and the relative variables. The relative variables are the current ratios divided by their 60-month averages. Guerard, Xu, and Gultekin [7] and Guerard,

Table 1 Corporate exports (CE), net debt issued, and net equity repurchased for all common stocks and for IBM, in the Wharton Research Data Services (WRDS) U.S. Compustat database for the 1970 to 2011 period. Data is in units of millions of dollars.

	All WRDS stocks			*IBM*		
Year	*CE*	*Net debt issued*	*Net equity repurchased*	*CE*	*Net debt issued*	*Net equity repurchased*
1970	4,610.1	0.0	0.0	59.7	0.0	0.0
1971	2,483.6	1,610.2	−708.4	35.0	20.2	9.8
1972	3,212.3	1,470.7	−656.6	33.7	39.9	30.2
1973	2,893.7	2,550.4	−982.3	54.7	15.6	27.7
1974	3,242.4	4,283.6	−946.6	92.5	5.3	37.0
1975	2,835.0	5,092.1	−1,665.6	78.8	3.0	7.0
1976	4,861.3	3,399.9	−1,838.4	113.0	2.5	4.5
1977	6,044.1	3,802.6	−1,889.5	291.0	2.3	4.2
1978	6,459.0	5,346.5	−2,009.4	226.1	7.4	4.4
1979	7,161.1	6,879.2	−2,580.0	38.0	145.0	14.6
1980	7,627.2	9,013.7	−3,407.2	188.5	60.4	9.4
1981	9,188.3	10,513.7	−4,499.7	151.0	75.1	18.1
1982	13,824.9	8,806.2	−4,212.4	177.2	48.0	29.8
1983	17,991.7	2,773.5	−6,577.6	206.9	17.4	35.1
1984	20,586.3	8,807.5	−1,285.2	229.5	136.3	76.8
1985	16,160.3	13,396.4	−3,332.5	241.6	161.4	92.8
1986	17,174.0	15,549.6	−3,565.6	455.3	105.9	84.5
1987	25,034.5	10,799.1	−3,141.2	487.4	40.8	71.9
1988	32,468.5	15,184.8	1,456.0	288.1	454.0	300.7
1989	31,902.6	19,788.2	−1,411.9	195.5	647.1	276.8
1990	39,766.7	15,402.2	−224.4	371.8	467.6	368.3
1991	33,938.1	15,167.0	−6,120.6	287.4	577.6	418.4
1992	36,927.7	8,272.9	−7,269.2	500.6	1,004.5	1,073.5
1993	28,715.1	11,544.1	−10,943.8	−199.5	1,179.4	874.1
1994	33,000.1	16,272.6	−6,399.1	571.8	533.5	944.5
1995	27,758.7	33,323.4	−3,599.7	973.2	663.6	946.0
1996	34,232.5	−95,722.6	−7,807.6	378.0	767.0	499.2
1997	31,107.1	45,005.9	−2,026.1	318.2	914.2	453.0
1998	16,294.9	73,399.7	409.9	623.3	756.7	594.2
1999	11,682.0	−138,597.8	−7,748.0	965.1	613.3	751.0
2000	2,244.9	−144,872.5	−16,381.1	569.6	960.4	756.1
2001	16,298.4	87,533.5	−5,896.0	850.6	453.5	789.8
2002	28,397.6	70,215.1	1,327.4	335.8	672.6	581.2
2003	45,555.8	56,285.1	836.0	923.8	157.3	583.1
2004	66,807.7	66,959.6	8,487.4	926.3	243.8	453.8
2005	94,585.9	73,971.1	24,002.6	767.6	436.3	352.2
2006	71,325.9	154,369.4	41,880.5	1,101.9	144.4	340.0
2007	86,392.3	181,759.3	47,005.9	1,196.8	2,174.4	1,130.6
2008	95,677.8	94,468.0	−18,798.5	728.6	1,382.9	1,024.8
2009	90,185.0	4,825.2	−45,855.1	1,517.1	668.3	1,349.5
2010	259,345.0	−109,976.5	−1,778.4	1,417.4	805.5	652.2
2011	248,780.6	−77,102.7	29,829.2	1,608.0	999.6	894.7

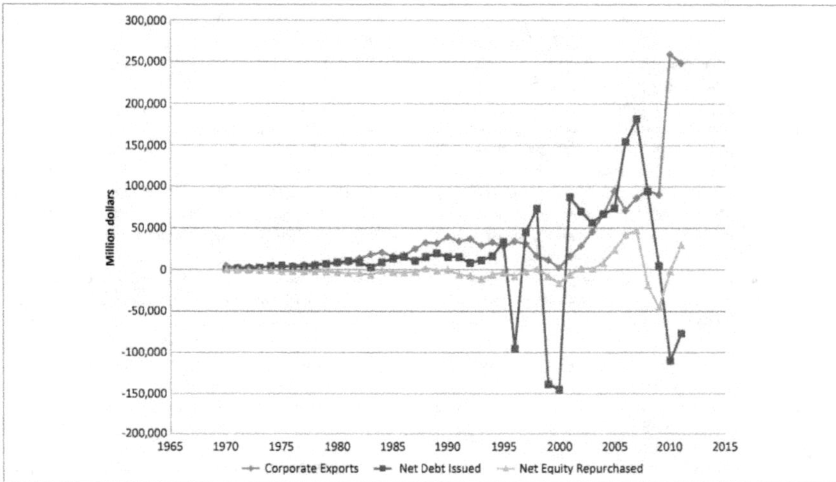

Figure 1

Corporate exports, net debt issued, and net equity repurchased of stocks in the United States in the Wharton Research Data Services (WRDS) database for 1970 to 2011.

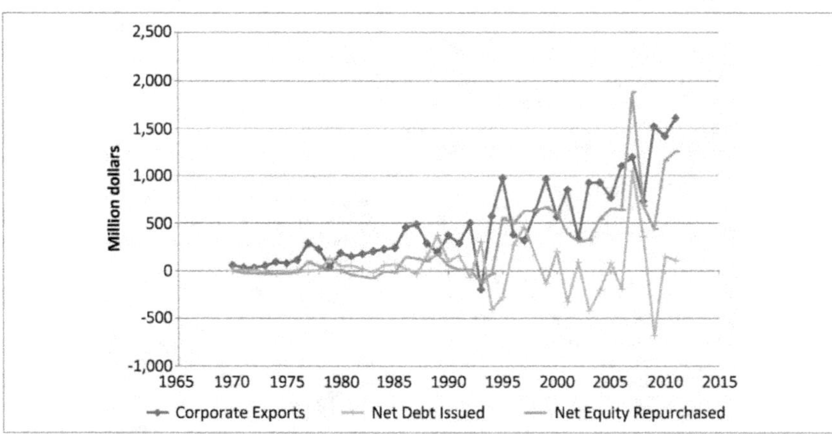

Figure 2

IBM corporate exports, net debt issued, and net equity repurchased during the 1970 to 2011 period. Data is in units of millions of dollars.

Markowitz, and Xu [8] added two variables to the Bloch et al. [26] model. Guerard et al. [8] added a price momentum (PM) variable and an earnings forecasting efficiency variable. The price momentum variable was constructed as the price one month ago divided by the price twelve months ago. The earnings forecasting variable, CTEF (Consensus Temporary Earnings Forecasting), is composed of forecasted earnings yield (FEP), earnings revisions (EREV), and EB (earnings breadth). Earnings breadth represents the net (up minus down) direction of revisions. The EP, BP, CP, SP, PM, and components of earnings forecasts and revisions are continuously examined by security analysts and quantitative specialists in the industry (see Savita Subramanian at Bank of America Merrill Lynch [29] and David Dremen [30]). We estimate a ten-factor stock selection model to use as an input to an optimization analysis. We use the (one month) total stock return, TR, as the independent variable. The monthly stock return is composed of the stock dividend yield plus the stock price appreciation. The stock selection model estimated in this study, denoted as United States Expected Returns (USER) in Guerard, Xu, and Gultekin [7], is

$$
\begin{aligned}
TR_{t+1} = {} & a_0 + a_1 EP_t + a_2 BP_t + a_3 CP_t + a_4 SP_t \\
& + a_5 REP_t + a_6 RBP_t + a_7 RCP_t + a_8 RSP_t \\
& + a_9 CTEF_t + a_{10} PM_t + e_t
\end{aligned} \tag{2}
$$

where

EP	[earnings per share]/[price per share] = earnings-price ratio;
BP	[book value per share]/[price per share] = book-price ratio;
CP	[cash flow per share]/[price per share] = cash flow-price ratio;
SP	[net sales per share]/[price per share] = sales-price ratio;
REP	[current EP ratio]/[average EP ratio over the past five years];
RBP	[current BP ratio]/[average BP ratio over the past five years];
RCP	[current CP ratio]/[average CP ratio over the past five years];
RSP	[current SP ratio]/[average SP ratio over the past five years];
CTEF	composed of consensus earnings-per-share I/B/E/S forecast, revisions, and breadth, with equally weighted components;
PM	Price Momentum;
e	randomly distributed error term.

The USER model is estimated monthly, and t is time. The cross sectional regression employ a weighted latent root regression technique to address the problems of outlier and multicollinearity issues in Equation (2). We use the normalized coefficients of the positive and statistically significant variables (10% level) as weights; and we average the variable weights over the past twelve months. Guerard, Xu, and Gultekin [7] and Guerard, Markowitz, and Xu [8] calculated information coefficients, IC, which measures the correlation between the investment strategy and subsequent performance. Higher USER values are preferred, and the IC should be positive. The IC test is referred to as a Level I test. The stock selection model, USER, the earnings efficiency model, CTEF, and the corporate exports model, CE, have positive and statistically significant ICs. The PM, CTEF and USER variable ICs are 0.035, 0.039, and 0.048, respectively, for January 2000 to January 2013 period. The CE variable has an IC of 0.045. The CE variable including cash has an IC of 0.036. An analysis of U.S. stock ICs is presented in Guerard [23]. That is, firms that are identified as being undervalued by the stock selection model, firms having higher earnings forecasting efficiency, and firms that generate higher corporate exports appreciate more than overvalued firms or firms with lesser earnings forecasted growth and firms generating lower corporate exports. Now, the question is how to combine the stock selection model and corporate exports to generate more efficient portfolios.

Constructing mean-variance efficient portfolios

Portfolio construction and management, as formulated in Markowitz [5, 6], seeks to identify the efficient frontier, the point at which the portfolio return is maximized for a given level of risk, or equivalently, portfolio risk is minimized for a given level of portfolio return. The portfolio expected return, denoted as $E(R_P)$, is calculated by taking the sum of the security weights multiplied by their respective expected returns.

$$E(R_P) = \sum_{i=1}^{N} w_i E(R_i), \tag{3}$$

where N is the number of candidate securities, and w_i is the weight for security i. A fully invested portfolio requires that $\sum_{i=1}^{N} w_i = 1$. $E(R_i)$ is the expected return for security i. The portfolio standard deviation σ_P is the square root of portfolio variance, σ_P^2, which is the sum of the weighted securities covariance:

$$\sigma_P^2 = \sum_{i=1}^{N}\sum_{j=1}^{N} w_i w_j \sigma_{ij}, \tag{4}$$

where σ_{ij} is the covariance of returns for security i and security j.

The Markowitz model holds that investors are compensated for bearing the total risk of the portfolio. Implicit in the development of the Capital Asset Pricing Model by Sharpe [31], Lintner [32], and Mossin [33] is that investors are compensated for bearing systematic or market risk, not total risk. Systematic risk is measured by a stock's beta. Beta is the slope of the market model in which the stock return is regressed as a function of the market return. Sharpe [34] proposed what he refers to as the diagonal model to simplify the computations in constructing portfolios.

Multi-Factor Risk Models hold that the total excess return for a multiple-factor model in the Rosenberg methodology for security j may be written as follows:

$$R_j = \sum_{k=1}^{K} \beta_{jk}\widetilde{f}_k + \widetilde{e}_J. \tag{5}$$

The nonfactor, or asset-specific return $\widetilde{e}_j$ on security j, is the residual risk of the security after removing the estimated impacts of the K factors. The term $\widetilde{f}_k$ is the rate of return on factor k, and β_{jk} is factor beta of security j on factor k. An extensive review of factor risk models can be found in Connor and Korajczyk [35] and Connor, Goldberg, and Korajczyk [36]. Guerard [37] demonstrated the effectiveness of the Blin and Bender APT and Sungard APT systems in portfolio construction and management. The determination of security weights, the ws, in a portfolio are the primary calculation of the Markowitz portfolio management approach.

The security weight is the proportion of the portfolio value that is invested in the individual security j. The portfolio weight of security j, is calculated as

$$w_{(\mathrm{P})j} = \frac{MV_j}{MV_{\mathrm{P}}} \tag{6}$$

where MV_j is the market value of security j, and MV_P is the market value total portfolio.

The active weight of the security j, $w_{(a)j}$, is calculated by subtracting the security weight in the (index) benchmark b, $w_{(b)j}$, from the security weight in the portfolio:

$$w_{(\mathrm{a})j} = w_{(\mathrm{P})j} - w_{(\mathrm{b})j}. \tag{7}$$

Blin and Bender created their company, named Advanced Portfolio Technologies, and its *Analytics Guide* [38]. Portfolio volatility can be decomposed into independent variance components, systematic and specific risk.

$$\sigma_{\mathrm{P}}^2 = \sigma_{\beta\mathrm{P}}^2 + \sigma_{\mathrm{SP}}^2, \tag{8}$$

where

σ_{P}^2 = total portfolio variance;
$\sigma_{\beta\mathrm{P}}^2$ = systematic portfolio volatility;
σ_{SP}^2 = specific portfolio volatility.

There are many forms of portfolio optimization and construction techniques. One could test whether the Markowitz [5] mean-variance (MV) optimization technique using the portfolio variance as the relevant risk measure dominates the risk-return trade-off curve using a variation of the mean-variance optimization model that emphasizes systematic (or market) risk, the mean-variance Tracking Error at Risk (MVTar) optimization, and mean-expected tail loss portfolio optimization (see Guerard, Rachev, and Shao [39]). There is no statistically significant difference in the two forms of Mean-Variance analysis. A measure of the trade-off between the portfolio expected return and risk (as measured by the portfolio standard deviation) is typically denoted by the Greek letter lambda (λ). Generally, the higher the lambda, the higher is the ratio of portfolio expected return to portfolio standard deviation. We assume that the portfolio manager seeks to maximize the portfolio geometric mean (GM) and Sharpe ratio as put forth in Latane [40] and Markowitz [5, 6].

Portfolio construction and management of corporate exports

We build Mean-Variance efficient portfolios using all publically traded United States stocks during the January 2000 to January 2013 period. We seek to outperform the Russell 3000 Growth benchmark. We use the Sungard APT World Risk Model composed of 20 betas estimated by principal components analysis with three years of weekly data [38]. Portfolios are created to maximize the portfolio corporate exports variable while minimizing risk with the following constraints: (1) the portfolios are fully invested; that is, security weights sum to one; (2) a 4% maximum weight can be held in any stock; (3) 8% monthly sells (turnover) is maintained; and (4) we use monthly optimization and create an efficient frontier by varying lambda. We use the same portfolio simulation conditions and the APT World 20-factor risk model, as was presented in Guerard, Rachev, and Shao [39]. The portfolio attribution analysis of the corporate exports variable for a lambda value of 500 is shown in **Table 2**. Portfolio active annual return is 9.60%, its Information Ratio is 0.71, and the active return is statistically significant, having a corresponding t value of 2.54. There are no statistically significant style or industry exposures. The corporate exports variable is statistically significant at identifying under-valued stocks. The variable used as an expected returns variable is often referred to as a portfolio tilt variable [23]. The corporate exports variable can be simulated with an additional constraint that the portfolio USER score must exceed 80 and be less than 90. The introduction of a stock selection model enhances returns such that the portfolio Geometric Mean rises from 9.5%, annually in Table 2, to 18.5%, in **Table 3**. Portfolio active annual return is 18.51%, its Information Ratio is 1.56, and the active return is statistically significant, having a corresponding t value of 5.61. The active return is driven by specific risk, 12.2% annual return with a corresponding t value of 6.33, as it should be in a well-diversified portfolio (see Table 3). There are no statistically significant style and industry exposures. Their returns, even though statistically significant, account for slightly more than 2% annual return, whereas

Table 2 Attribution of the corporate exports portfolio simulation, from 2000 to December 2012, using the Axioma World Fundamental Model. (Here, the benchmark is the Russell 3000 Growth Index, and the NoRC [or no risk control] model is used.)

Source of return	*Contribution*	*Contribution*	*Average exposure*	*Risk*	*Information ratio*	*T-statistic*
Portfolio	9.46%			20.09%		
Benchmark	−0.12			22.02		
Active	9.60%			13.57%	0.71	2.54
Factor contribution		2.06				
Style	Exchange rate stability	0.00	0.013	0.37%	0.02	0.07
	Growth	−1.33	−0.567	0.78	−1.70	−6.10
	Leverage	−1.10	0.572	0.69	−1.60	−5.76
	Liquidity	−1.49	−0.594	1.59	−0.93	−3.35
	Medium-term momentum	0.14	−0.239	1.49	0.10	0.34
	Short-term momentum	−0.13	0.011	1.34	−0.10	−0.35
	Size	−0.06	−0.483	3.22	−0.02	−0.06
	Value	2.33	0.846	1.49	1.96	7.04
	Volatility	0.39	0.166	3.52	0.11	0.39
Country	−0.01			7.19	−0.07	−0.26
Industry	2.06			3.97	0.52	1.87
Currency	1.76			4.04	0.43	1.56
Market	−0.60			2.34	−0.26	−0.93
Specific return	7.54			7.31	1.03	3.71

specific stock selection is over 12%. The Markowitz approach to portfolio construction and management is sixty years old and remains an integral tool of investment research.

A further test of data mining corrections

In the practical world of Wall Street, it is conventional wisdom to cut your historical back-tested excess returns in half; that is, if your back-tested excess return (the portfolio geometric mean return less the geometric mean of the benchmark) was 6%, or 600 basis points, an investment manager and/or a client might expect 3% excess returns in the future. Harry Markowitz and Ganlin Xu, the Daiwa Global Research Department mathematician, developed a data mining corrections (DMC) testing methodology that appeared in the *Journal of Portfolio Management* [9]. A secondary question is: could a manager have obtained a similar portfolio return using other models, rather than the model actually employed?

Let y_{it} be the logarithm of one plus the return for the ith portfolio selection model in period t. In DMC Models I and II, y_{it} is assumed to have form

$$y_{it} = \mu_i + z_t + \varepsilon_{it}, \tag{9}$$

where μ_i is the model effect, z_t is the period effect, and ε_{it} is the random deviation. These effects are all assumed to be uncorrelated. Readers are referred back to the original paper for the correlated ε_{it} case. Finally, the appropriate estimate of μ_i is not its sample average return

$$\bar{r}_i = \frac{\sum_{t=1}^{T} y_{it}}{T}, \tag{10}$$

but rather

$$\hat{\mu}_i = \bar{r} + \beta(\bar{r}_i - \bar{r}), \tag{11}$$

where $\bar{r} = \sum_{i=1}^{N} \bar{r}_i/N$ is the grand mean of methods, and $\beta = (\mathrm{Cov}(\bar{r}_i, u))/(\mathrm{Var}(\bar{r}_i))$ is the regression coefficient of μ_i as a function of $\bar{r}_i$ such that $0 < \beta < 1$. In other word, the best estimate of model effect μ_i is its sample estimate regressed back to the average estimate (the grand average). The individual variables tested in this study are as follows:

EP	earnings per share/price per share;
BP	book value per share/price per share;
CP	cash flow per share/price per share;
SP	sales per share/price per share;

Table 3 Attribution of the Corporate Exports Portfolio Simulation with an USER portfolio constraint, 2000 to December 2012, using the Axioma World Fundamental model. (Here, the benchmark is the Russell 3000 Growth Index, and the NoRC model is used.)

Source of return	*Contribution*	*Risk*	*Information ratio*	*T-statistic*
Portfolio	18.39%	18.65%		
Benchmark	-0.12	22.02		
Active	18.51%	11.86%	1.56	5.61
Factor contribution	6.29%	9.62	0.65	2.35
Style	2.07%	5.88	0.35	1.27
Country	0.66%	4.78	0.14	0.50
Industry	2.42%	3.62	0.67	2.40
Currency	1.32%	2.15	0.62	2.22
Market	-0.18%	2.35	-0.08	-0.28
Specific return	12.20%	6.94	1.76	6.33

DP dividends per share/price per share;
PM price momentum as $price_{t-1}/price_{t-12}$;
PM71 price momentum as $price_{t-1}/price_{t-7}$;
FEP1 one-year-ahead forecast earnings per share/price per share;
FEP2 two-year-ahead forecast earnings per share/price per share;
RV1 one-year-ahead forecast earnings per share monthly revision/price per share;
RV2 two-year-ahead forecast earnings per share monthly revision/price per share;
FGR1 one-year-ahead forecast earnings per share monthly breadth;
FGR2 two-year-ahead forecast earnings per share monthly breadth;
FEP1 one-year-ahead forecast earnings per share/last year's reported earnings per share;
FEP2 two-year-ahead forecast earnings per share/last year's reported earnings per share;
EWC equally-weighted EP, BP, CP, SP, REP, RBP, RCP, RSP, CTEF, and PM;
CTEF equally-weighted FEP1, FEP2, BR1, BR2, RV1, and RV2.

As a reminder, PM71 is the price momentum created by the price rising over the past 7 months, ignoring the previous month (prices mean-revert over a 1-month period). PM is the price momentum created by the price rising over the past 12 months, ignoring the previous month.

The Markowitz-Xu DMC test did not use a "holdout period," as holdout tests can be routinely data mined as well. That is, one can vary the estimation and holdout periods to generate the desired conclusion. Alternative portfolio models were created using the factors as tilt factors, such that the real question addressed is whether the model used was statistically better than the average model used to identify mispriced stocks. We use the June 2001 to January 2013 period for the Data Mining Corrections test. We test 17 models including the components of USER and the components of CTEF. The USER variable analysis passes the Data Mining Corrections test criteria for the U.S. market, indicating that the stock selection and portfolio construction methodologies produce superior returns that are not due to chance. The USER variable has a Data Mining Corrections coefficient of 0.57 and is highly statistically significant, having an F value of 2.3. Thus, one could expect 57% of the excess returns of the USER model relative to the average return to be continued. More importantly, the USER model produced a higher geometric mean than did an average model geometric mean which could have been used to manage an equity portfolio in the United States equity market during the June 2001 to December 2012 period. The USER Model passes all three Levels of hypothesis testing: 1) the model and its components have statistically significant information coefficients; 2) the strategy produces excess returns after transactions costs; and 3) the strategy produces a significantly higher geometric mean than the average model that could have been used to manage assets in the universe. The Markowitz-Xu [9] Data Mining Corrections test is a Level III test.

The Morgan Stanley Capital International (MSCI) Barra model is a multi-factor risk model developed by Rosenberg and Marathe [41] in the 1970s. We can create portfolio simulations back to 1980 using the USER model and its

Table 4 Univariate model tilts for simulated portfolios of Wharton Research Data Services (WRDS) stocks in the United States during the 1980 to 2009 period.

Portfolios	*Monthly excess return to S&P500 (%)*	*T-statistic*
USER	0.28	1.72
BR1	0.16	1.29
BR2	0.13	1.12
RV1	0.22	1.48
RV2	0.04	0.32
FEP1	0.02	0.09
FEP2	−0.19	−0.87
CTEF	0.27	2.40
EP	0.09	0.50
BP	0.07	0.33
CP	0.16	0.90
SP	0.34	1.81
DP	0.22	1.21
PM71	0.16	0.84
PM	0.16	0.70
EWC	0.14	0.80

components. The longer-run portfolio simulations are shown in **Table 4**. The 1980 to 2009 Barra-simulated portfolios allow the null hypothesis to be rejected with more than 90% confidence. The F statistic equals 1.5, and the Data Mining Corrections test is estimated to be 0.33. The USER model produces a significantly higher geometric mean than the average model that could have been used to manage assets in the WRDS U.S. stock universe during the 1980 to 2009 time period.

Conclusion

The corporate exports variable is the sum of dividends paid, interest paid, and net equity repurchased less net debt issued. Corporate exports result from dividend, debt, and equity decisions. Companies generating larger corporate exports produce higher active returns in portfolios. The corporate exports variable is statistically significant in producing positive active returns in the portfolios. The returns of the corporate exports portfolio can be increased by constraining the portfolio to include stocks identified by a stock selection model as being undervalued. In this paper, we simulated portfolios during the January 2000 to January 2013 period using a multi-factor risk model. We apply the Markowitz-Xu data mining corrections and find no evidence of data mining. The portfolios developed in this paper are statistically different than the average model that could have been used to create portfolios.

Acknowledgments

We appreciate the research suggestions of Professors Ed Elton, Richard Brealey, Mustafa Gultekin, and Bernell Stone and several anonymous referees whose comments prevented premature publication. Bernell Stone and one of the anonymous reviewers suggested that we model corporate exports to include cash on hand. We tested such a model and found virtually identical information coefficients with the corporate exports variable used in this analysis. The simulated portfolio was better with our definition of corporate exports. Any errors remaining are the responsibility of the authors.

References

1. R. Brealey, S. C. Myers, and F. Allen, *Principles of Corporate Finance*. New York, NY, USA: McGraw-Hill, 2005.
2. L. V. Gerstner, Jr., *Who Says Elephants Can't Dance?* New York, NY, USA: Harper Business, 2002.
3. E. Schwartz and R. J. Aronson, "The corporate sector: A net exporter of funds," *Southern Ecxon. J.*, vol. 33, no. 1, pp. 252–257, Jul. 1966.
4. J. B. Guerard, Jr. and E. Schwartz, *Quantitative Corporate Finance*. New York, NY, USA: Springer-Verlag, 2007.
5. H. M. Markowitz, "Portfolio selection," *J. Finance*, vol. 7, no. 1, pp. 77–91, Mar. 1952.
6. H. M. Markowitz, *Portfolio Selection: Efficient Diversification of Investment, Cowles Foundation Monograph Springer*. New York, NY, USA: Wiley, 1959.
7. J. B. Guerard, Jr., M. N. Gultekin, and G. Xu, "Investing with momentum: The past, present, and future," *J. Investing*, vol. 21, no. 1, pp. 68–80, Spring 2012.
8. J. B. Guerard, Jr., H. M. Markowitz, and G. Xu, "Earnings forecasting in a global stock selection model and efficient portfolio construction and management," *Int. J. Forecasting*, vol. 22, no. 4, pp. 121–128, Winter 2013.
9. H. M. Markowitz and G. L. Xu, "Data mining corrections," *J. Portfolio Manage.*, vol. 21, no. 1, pp. 60–69, Fall 1994.
10. M. H. Miller and F. Modigliani, "Dividend policy, growth and the valuation of shares," *J. Bus.*, vol. 34, no. 4, pp. 411–433, Oct. 1961.
11. E. F. Fama and H. Babiak, "Dividend policy: An empirical analysis," *J. Amer. Stat. Assoc.*, vol. 63, no. 324, pp. 1132–1161, Dec. 1968.
12. G. Grullon and R. Michaely, "Dividends, share repurchases, and the substitution hypothesis," *J. Finance*, vol. 57, no. 4, pp. 1649–1684, Aug. 2001.
13. L. Dann, "Common stock repurchases: An analysis of returns to bondholders and stockholders," *J. Financial Econ.*, vol. 9, no. 2, pp. 115–138, Jun. 1981.
14. J. Lakonishok and T. Vermaelen, "Anomalous price behavior around repurchase tender offers," *J. Finance*, vol. 45, no. 2, pp. 455–477, Jun. 1990.
15. H. Bierman, *Increasing Shareholder Value*. New York, NY, USA: Springer-Verlag, 2001.
16. H. Bierman, "My favorite two corporate finance puzzles," in *Variations in Economic Analysis: Essays in Honor of Eli Schwartz*, R. J. Aronson, H. L. Parmet, and R. J. Thornton, Eds. New York, NY, USA: Springer-Verlag, 2010.
17. A. Hovakimian, T. Opler, and S. Titman, "The debt-equity choice," *J. Financial Quant. Anal.*, vol. 36, no. 1, pp. 1–24, Mar. 2001.
18. G. Grullon and R. Michaely, "The information content of share repurchase programs," *J. Finance*, vol. 59, no. 2, pp. 651–680, Apr. 2004.
19. P. J. Dhrymes and M. Kurz, "Investment, dividends, and external finance behavior of firms," in *Determinants of Investment Behavior*, R. Ferber, Ed. New York, NY, USA: Columbia Univ. Press, 1967.

20. J. B. Guerard, Jr., A. S. Bean, and S. Andrews, "R&D management and corporate financial policy," *Manage. Sci.*, vol. 33, no. 11, pp. 1419–1427, Nov. 1987.
21. S. C. Myers, "The capital structure puzzle," *J. Finance*, vol. 39, no. 3, pp. 575–592, Jul. 1983.
22. J. B. Guerard, Jr., "The corporation as a net exporter of funds: Additional evidence," in *Variations in Economic Analysis: Essays in Honor of Eli Schwartz*, R. J. Aronson, H. L. Parmet, and R. J. Thornton, Eds. New York, NY, USA: Springer-Verlag, 2010.
23. J. B. Guerard, Ed., *Handbook of Portfolio Management: Contemporary Applications of Markowitz Techniques*. New York, NY, USA: Springer-Verlag, 2010.
24. G. Hawawini and D. B. Keim, "On the predictability of common stock returns: World-wide evidence," in *Handbooks in Operations Research and Management Science*, R. A. Jarrow, V. Maksimovic, and W. T. Ziemba, Eds. Amsterdam, The Netherlands: Elsevier, 1995, pp. 497–537.
25. L. K. C. Chan, Y. Hamao, and J. Lakonishok, "Fundamentals and stock returns in Japan," *J. Finance*, vol. 46, no. 5, pp. 1739–1764, Dec. 1991.
26. M. Bloch, J. B. Guerard, Jr., H. M. Markowitz, P. Todd, and G. L. Xu, "A comparison of some aspects of the U.S. and Japanese equity markets," *Jpn. World Econ.*, vol. 5, no. 1, pp. 3–26, May 1993.
27. J. Lakonishok, A. Shleifer, and R. W. Vishny, "Contrarian investment, extrapolation and risk," *J. Finance*, vol. 49, no. 5, pp. 1541–1578, Dec. 1994.
28. R. Haugen and N. Baker, "Case closed," in *The Handbook of Portfolio Construction: Contemporary Applications of Markowitz Techniques*. New York, NY, USA: Springer-Verlag, 2010.
29. S. Subramanian, D. Suzuki, A. Makedon, and J. Carey, *A PM's Guide to Stock Picking*. New York, NY, USA: Bank of America Merrill Lynch, Mar. 2013.
30. D. Dremen, *Contrarian Investment Strategies: The Next Generation*. New York, NY, USA: Simon & Schuster, 1998.
31. W. F. Sharpe, "Capital asset prices: A theory of market equilibrium under conditions of risk," *J. Finance*, vol. 19, no. 3, pp. 425–442, Sep. 1964.
32. J. Lintner, "The valuation of risk assets on the selection of risky investments in stock portfolios and capital investments," *Rev. Econ. Stat.*, vol. 47, no. 1, pp. 13–37, Feb. 1965.
33. J. Mossin, "Equilibrium in a capital asset market," *Econometrica*, vol. 34, no. 4, pp. 768–783, Oct. 1966.
34. W. F. Sharpe, "A simplified model for portfolio analysis," *Manage. Sci.*, vol. 9, no. 2, pp. 277–293, Jan. 1963.
35. G. Conner and R. A. Korajczyk, "Factor models in portfolio and asset pricing theory," in *The Handbook of Portfolio Construction: Contemporary Applications of Markowitz Techniques*, J. Guerard, Ed. New York, NY, USA: Springer-Verlag, 2010.
36. G. Connor, L. R. Goldberg, and R. A. Korajczyk, *Portfolio Risk Analysis*. Princeton, NJ, USA: Princeton Univ. Press, 2010.
37. J. B. Guerard, "Global earnings forecast efficiency," *Res. Finance*, vol. 28, pp. 19–47, 2012.
38. J. Blin, S. Bender, and J. B. Guerard, Jr., "Earnings forecasts, revisions, and momentum in the estimation of efficient market-neutral Japanese and US portfolios," *Res. Finance*, vol. 15, pp. 93–113, 1997.
39. J. B. Guerard, S. T. Rachev, and B. Shao, "Efficient global portfolios: Big data and investment universes," *IBM J. Res. & Dev.*, vol. 57, no. 5, pp. 11:1–11:11, Sep./Oct. 2013.
40. H. A. Latane, "Criteria for choice among risky ventures," *J. Pol. Econ.*, vol. 67, no. 2, pp. 144–155, Apr. 1959.
41. B. Rosenberg and V. Marathe, "Tests of capital asset pricing hypotheses," in *Res. Finance*, vol. 1, H. Levy, Ed., pp. 115–224, 1979.

John B. Guerard, Jr. *McKinley Capital Management, LLC, Anchorage, AK 99503 USA (jguerard@mckinleycapital.com).* Dr. Guerard is Director of Quantitative Research at McKinley Capital Management, in Anchorage, Alaska. He earned his Ph.D. degree in finance from the University of Texas, Austin. He has published several monographs, including *Quantitative Corporate Finance* (Springer, 2007, with Eli Schwartz) and *The Handbook of Portfolio Construction: Contemporary Applications of Markowitz Techniques* (Springer, 2010). John serves an Associate Editor of the *Journal of Investing* and *The International Journal of Forecasting*.

Harry Markowitz *GuidedChoice, San Diego, CA 92122 USA (hmarkowitz@mckinleycapital.com).* Dr. Markowitz is the Chief Architect at Guidedchoice.com in San Diego, California, and a Quantitative Research Advisor at McKinley Capital Management LLC in Anchorage, Alaska. He is a Noble Laureate, the father of Modern Portfolio Theory, and named "Man of the Century" by *Pensions and Investments* magazine. He is a recipient of the prestigious John von Neumann Theory Prize for his work in portfolio theory, sparse matrix techniques, and the SIMSCRIP programming language. Dr. Markowitz earned his Ph.D. degree from the University of Chicago. He is a quantitative research scientific advisor at McKinley Capital Management LLC in Anchorage, Alaska.

Ganlin Xu *GuidedChoice, San Diego, CA 92122 USA (gxu@mckinleycapital.com).* Dr. Xu is the Chief Technology Officer of Guidedchoice.com, where he leads a team of finance, economics, and mathematics experts to develop GuidedChoice's financial methodology, software, and systems. Dr. Xu earned his Ph.D. degree from Carnegie Mellon University. His research on portfolio theory has been published in various journals. He is a quantitative research scientific advisor McKinley Capital Management LLC in Anchorage, Alaska.

https://doi.org/10.1142/9789811222634_0005

Chapter 5

Earnings forecasting in a global stock selection model and efficient portfolio construction and management†

John B. Guerard Jr.[a,*], Harry Markowitz[a,b], GanLin Xu[a,c]

[a] McKinley Capital Management, LLC, 3301 C Street, Suite 500, Anchorage, AK 99503, United States
[b] Harry Markowitz & Company, San Diego, CA, United States
[c] Guided Choice, San Diego, CA, United States

ARTICLE INFO

Keywords:
Earnings Forecasting
I/B/E/S
Portfolio optimization
Information ratio
Efficient frontier
Active returns

ABSTRACT

Stock selection models often use analysts' expectations, momentum, and fundamental data. We find support for composite modeling using these sources of data for global stocks during the period 1997–2011. We also find evidence to support the use of SunGard APT and Axioma multi-factor models for portfolio construction and risk control. Three levels of testing for stock selection and portfolio construction models are developed and estimated. We create portfolios for January 1997–December 2011. We report three conclusions: (1) analysts' forecast information was rewarded by the global market between January 1997 and December 2011; (2) analysts' forecasts can be combined with reported fundamental data, such as earnings, book value, cash flow and sales, and also with momentum, in a stock selection model for identifying mispriced securities; and (3) the portfolio returns of the multi-factor risk-controlled portfolios allow us to reject the null hypothesis for the data mining corrections test. The earnings forecasting variable dominates our composite model in terms of its impact on stock selection.

1. Introduction

Expected returns on assets are a key input in the mean–variance portfolio selection process. One can estimate models of expected returns by using earnings expectations data, price momentum variables, and reported financial data. In this analysis, we construct and estimate a global stock selection model by using these data for the period from January 1997 to December 2011. Earnings expectations information has been being rewarded in global stocks for the past fifteen years or so, and we expect it to continue to be the primary variable driving global stocks. Despite the recent volatility of the momentum factor, momentum is still associated statistically with security returns, and can be used with other factors to rank stocks for purchase. A composite model of earnings expectations information, value, and momentum factors is estimated for global stocks in order to identify potentially mispriced stocks. In addition, the regression-weighting of factors enhanced the information coefficients relative to equally-weighted factors. Analysts' forecast and momentum variables are dominant in the regression-based composite model of expected returns. We create portfolios for the period January 1997–December 2011, and simulate portfolio returns which we compare with a set of global stock benchmark returns.

We begin with a review of the literature on stock selection models in Section 2. In Section 3, we discuss the testing of a composite model of stock selection, incorporating

* Corresponding author. Tel.: +1 907 563 4488.
E-mail addresses: jguerard@mcKinleycapital.com (J.B. Guerard Jr.), hmarkowitz@mckinleycapital.com (H. Markowitz), gxu@mckinleycapital.com (G. Xu).

†This article originally appeared in *International Journal of Forecasting* **31**(2015), 550–560 © 2014 International Institute of Forecasters.

earnings forecast information. We use an APT-based multifactor risk model to create efficient portfolios in Section 4. In Section 5, we present and estimate the data mining corrections test. In Section 6, we discuss the relevance of the "alpha alignment factor" and show its relevance. Section 7 presents our summary and conclusions.

2. A literature review of expected returns modeling and stock selection models

There are many different approaches to security valuation and the creation of expected returns. One seeks to select expected returns inputs that are associated statistically with stock returns. The correlation coefficient between the strategy and the subsequent returns is referred to as the information coefficient, IC (Grinold & Kahn, 1999). The expected returns input normally consists of variables that are denoted anomalies, which can be used as inputs to the portfolio construction process in order to produce portfolios that outperform the market. The early approaches to security analysis and stock selection involved the use of valuation techniques that used reported earnings and other financial data. Graham, Dodd, and Cottle (1934) recommended that stocks be purchased on the basis of the price-to-earnings (P/E) ratio. They suggested that no stock should be purchased if its price-to-earnings ratio exceeded 1.5 times the P/E multiple of the market. Graham and Dodd established the P/E criteria, and it was then discussed by Williams (1938), who wrote the monograph that influenced Harry Markowitz's thinking on portfolio construction. It is interesting that Graham and Dodd proposed the low P/E model at the height of the Great Depression. Basu (1977) reported evidence supporting the low P/E model. The recent literature on financial anomalies is summarized by Fama and French (2008) and Levy (1999).

There is an extensive body of literature on the impact of individual value ratios on the cross-section of stock returns. We go beyond using just one or two of the standard value ratios (EP and BP), and also include the cash-to-price ratio (CP) and/or the sales-to-price ratio (SP). The major papers on the combination of value ratios for the prediction of stock returns (including at least CP and/or SP) include those of Bloch, Guerard, Markowitz, Todd, and Xu (1993), Chan, Hamao, and Lakonishok (1991), Guerard, Rachev, and Shao (2013), Haugen and Baker (2010) and Lakonishok, Shleifer, and Vishny (1994).

Chan et al. (1991) used seemingly unrelated regressions (SUR) to model CAPM excess returns as functions of traditional fundamental variables such as earnings, book values and cash flows relative to price, denoted as EP, BP and CP. Moreover, size was measured as the natural logarithm of market capitalization (LS).[1] Betas were estimated simultaneously, and cross-sectional correlations of residuals were addressed. When fractal portfolios were constructed by sorting on the EP ratio, the highest EP quintile portfolio outperformed the lowest EP quintile portfolio, and the EP effect was not statistically significant. The portfolios composed of and sorted by the highest BP and CP outperformed the portfolios composed of the lowest BP and CP stocks. In the authors' multiple regressions, the size and book-to-market variables were positive and statistically significant. The EP coefficient was negative and statistically significant at the 10% level. Applying an adaptation of the Fama and MacBeth (1973) time series of portfolio cross-sections to the Japanese market produced negative and statistically significant coefficients on EP and size, but positive and statistically significant coefficients for the BP and CP variables. Chan et al. (1991, p. 1760) summarized their findings as follows: "The performance of the book-to-market ratio is especially noteworthy; this variable is the most important of the four variables investigated".

Bloch et al. (1993) built fundamental-based stock selection models for Japanese and United States stocks. The investable stock universe was the first section, non-financial Tokyo Stock Exchange common stocks from January 1975 to December 1990 in Japan, and the 1000 largest market-capitalized common stocks from November 1975 to December 1990 in the United States. They found that a series of Markowitz (1952, 1959) mean–variance efficient portfolios using the higher EP values in Japan underperformed the universe benchmark, whereas the BP, CP, and SP (sales-to-price, or sales yield) variables outperformed the universe benchmark. For the United States, the optimized portfolios using the BP, CP, SP, and EP variables outperformed the U.S. S&P 500, providing support for the Graham and Dodd concept of using the relative rankings of value-focused fundamental ratios to select stocks.[2] Bloch et al. (1993) used relative ratios as well as current ratio values. Not only might an investor want to purchase a low P/E stock, one might also wish to purchase when the ratio is at a relatively low value compared to its historical value, in this case a low P/E relative to its average over the last five years. Bloch et al. (1993) estimated Eq. (1) in order to assess empirically the relative explanatory power of each of the eight value ratios in the equation:

$$\begin{aligned} TR = {} & w_0 + w_1 EP + w_2 BP + w_3 CP + w_4 SP \\ & + w_5 REP + w_6 RBP + w_7 RCP + w_8 RSP + e_t. \end{aligned} \tag{1}$$

Given concerns about both outlier distortion and multicollinearity, Bloch et al. (1993) tested the relative explanatory and predictive merits of alternative regression estimation procedures: OLS, robust regression using the Beaton and Tukey (1974) bi-square criterion to mitigate the impact of outliers, latent roots to address the issue of multicollinearity (see Gunst, Webster, & Mason, 1976), and

[1] Chan et al. (1991) define cash as the sum of earnings and depreciation, without explicit correction for other noncash revenue or expenses.

[2] One finds the Price/Earnings, Price/Book and Price/Sales ratios listed among the accounting anomalies by Levy (1999, p. 434). Levy also discusses the dividend yield as a (positive) stock anomaly. Malkiel (1996) cites evidence in support of buying low P/E, low P/B, and high D/P (dividend yield) stocks for a good performance, provided that the low P/E stocks have modest growth prospects (pp. 204–210). Malkiel speaks of a "double bonus"; that is, if growth occurs, earnings increase and the price-to-earnings multiple may increase, driving the price up even further. Of course, should growth fail to occur, both earnings and the P/E multiple may fall.

weighted latent roots, denoted WLRR, a combination of robust and latent roots. Bloch et al. (1993) used the estimated regression coefficients to construct a rolling horizon return forecast. The predicted returns and predictions of risk parameters were used as inputs for a mean–variance optimizer (see Markowitz, 1987) to create mean–variance efficient portfolios in financial markets in both Japan and the United States. Bloch et al. (1993) reported several results. First, they compared OLS and WLRR techniques, inputting the expected return forecasts produced by each method into a mean–variance optimizer. The WLRR-constructed composite model portfolio produced higher Sharpe ratios and geometric means than the OLS-constructed composite model portfolio in both Japan and the United States, indicating that controlling for both outliers and multicollinearity is important when using regression-estimated composite forecasts. Second, Bloch et al. (1993) quantified the survivor bias and found that it was not statistically significant in either Japan or the United States for the period tested. Third, they investigated period-to-period portfolio revision and found that tighter turnover and rebalancing triggers led to higher portfolio returns for value-based strategies. Finally, Markowitz and Xu (1994) developed a test for data mining. In addition to testing the hypothesis of data mining, the test can also be used to estimate and assess the expected differences between the best test model and the average of simulated policies.

In a thorough assessment of value versus growth in the United States, Lakonishok et al. (1994) examined the intersection of the Compustat and CRSP databases for annual portfolios for NYSE and AMEX common stocks, April 1963 to April 1990. Their value measures were three current value ratios: EP, BP and CP. Their growth measure was the five-year average annual growth of sales (GS). They performed three types of tests: a univariate ranking into annual decile portfolios for each of the four variables, bivariate rankings on CP (value) and GS (growth, glamour), and finally a multivariate regression adaptation of the Fama and MacBeth (1973) time series pooling of cross-sectional regressions. The univariate regression coefficient for GS was significantly negative. The EP, BP, and CP coefficients were all significantly positive. When Lakonishok et al. performed a multivariate regression using all four variables, they found significantly positive coefficients for BP and EP (but not CP), and significantly negative coefficients for GS. Lakonishok et al. (1994) concluded that buying out-of-favor value stocks outperformed growth (glamour) stocks during the period April 1968 to April 1990, that future growth was difficult to predict from past growth alone, that the actual future growth of the glamour stocks was much lower than past growth, relative to the growth of value stocks, and that the value strategies were not significantly riskier than growth (or 'glamour') strategies ex post.

Bloch et al. (1993) wrote their manuscript in 1991. At the time of the original estimation of Eq. (1), the international Institutional Estimation Brokerage Service (I/B/E/S) was only four years old, having started in 1987, and did not have sufficient data for model building and testing. The original international database consisted primarily of earnings forecasts (means, medians and standard deviations) of large (in terms of market capitalization) securities. The domestic I/B/E/S database was created in 1976, and included a well-established body of literature on earnings forecasting analysis, testing, and portfolio construction, published by Bruce and Epstein (1994). The Bruce and Epstein volume reprinted a study reporting the ineffectiveness of earnings forecasting in creating portfolios that could generate excess returns over the period 1972–1976 (Elton, Gruber, & Gultekin, 1981). However, in the same study, Elton et al. (1981) reported the effectiveness of earnings forecast revisions in creating portfolios that are capable of generating excess returns. The Bruce and Epstein volume also reprinted a study by Hawkins, Chamberlain, and Daniel (1984) which reported large excess returns for domestic stocks, which have the largest positive monthly earnings revisions for the period 1975–1980. Wheeler (1994) developed and tested a United States-only stock strategy in which analyst forecast revision breadth, defined as the number of upward forecast revisions less the number of downward forecast revisions, divided by the total number of estimates, was the criterion for stock selection. Wheeler found statistically significant excess returns from the breadth strategy. Thus, earnings forecasts per share, earnings forecast revisions, and earnings forecast breadth had all been documented by 1994. Guerard, Gultekin, and Stone (1997) created a composite forecasting variable consisting of consensus analysts' forecasts, forecast revisions and the breadth variables, which they referred to as a proprietary growth variable, PRGR, and reported that the composite earnings variable, when added to Eq. (1) as a ninth variable, averaged a relative weight of 33%. This result complements that of Lakonishok et al. (1994) in showing that rank-ordered portfolio returns have significant value and growth components. Guerard (1997) reported the dominance of the (same) consensus earnings efficiency variable, referred to as CTEF, relative to analysts' revisions, forecasted earnings yields, and breadth in generating excess returns. Guerard and Mark (2003) tested analysts' revisions, forecasted earnings yields, breadth, and CTEF using a multi-factor risk model, the Barra USE2 risk model, see Grinold and Kahn (1999) and Rudd and Clasing (1982). Guerard and Mark (2003) reported that forecasted earnings per share produced positive, but statistically insignificant, excess returns (total active returns), in the Barra system. Asset selection was negative for United States stocks in the 1990–2001 Frank Russell stock universe using forecasted earnings yields. Similarly, Guerard and Mark (2003) reported that forecast earnings revisions produced positive, but statistically insignificant, excess returns that were positively (but not statistically) associated with earnings yields. Breadth and CTEF were positively and statistically associated with earnings yields and smaller-sized stocks (another Barra risk model factor), but produced statistically significant excess returns and asset selection. Moreover, the CTEF produced larger excess returns and better asset selection than forecasted earnings yields, revisions, or breadth. Clearly, earnings forecasts were associated with United States stock returns and should be added to Eq. (1). For an excellent summary of the earnings forecasting literature, the reader is referred to Ramnath, Rock, and Shane (2008).

Momentum investing was being studied by academics at about the same time that earnings forecasting studies were being published. Arnott (1979) and Brush and Boles (1983) found statistically significant power in the relative strength. Brush and Boles' analysis was particularly valuable, because it reported that the short-term monthly price momentum model, taking the price at time $t-1$ divided by the price 12 months ago, $t-12$, was associated with total returns. Brush and Boles found that beta adjustments enhanced the predictive power slightly in the six- to twelve-month periods. Fama and French's (1992, 1995, 2008) price momentum variable uses the price two months ago divided by the price twelve months ago, thus avoiding the well-known return or residual reversal effect. We refer to it as FFPM. Fama and French's studies find significant stock price anomalies, and Brush (2007) and Korajczyk and Sadka (2004) confirm the findings after considering transaction costs. Lesmond, Schill, and Zhou (2004) found that price momentum returns did not exceed the transaction costs. The vast majority of studies have found that the use of three-, six-, and twelve-month price momentum variables, often defined as intermediate-term momentum variables, is associated statistically significantly with excess returns. Momentum is associated closely with excess returns in the academic literature, and should be added to Eq. (1). Further evidence on the anomalies is provided by Levy (1999). Guerard, Xu, and Gultekin (2012) added the Guerard et al. (1997) composite earnings forecasting variable CTEF and the Fama and French FFPM variable to the equation, to create a ten-factor stock selection model for the United States expected returns, which they referred to as the USER model.

$$TR_{t+1} = a_0 + a_1EP_t + a_2BP_t + a_3CP_t + a_4SP_t + a_5REP_t + a_6RBP_t + a_7RCP_t + a_8RSP_t + a_9CTEF_t + a_{10}PM_t + e_t, \quad (2)$$

where:

EP = [earnings per share]/[price per share] = earnings-price ratio;

BP = [book value per share]/[price per share] = book-price ratio;

CP = [cash flow per share]/[price per share] = cash flow-price ratio;

SP = [net sales per share]/[price per share] = sales-price ratio;

REP = [current EP ratio]/[average EP ratio over the past five years];

RBP = [current BP ratio]/[average BP ratio over the past five years];

RCP = [current CP ratio]/[average CP ratio over the past five years];

RSP = [current SP ratio]/[average SP ratio over the past five years];

CTEF = consensus earnings-per-share I/B/E/S forecast, revisions and breadth;

PM = price momentum; and

e = randomly distributed error term.

Table 1
Information coefficients of FSGLER variables.

(ICs)		
Variable	1997–2011 IC (t)	2003–2011 IC (t)
EP	0.037 (6.21)	0.029 (4.75)
FEP	0.040 (6.67)	0.032 (5.85)
CTEF	0.035 (10.42)	0.033 (8.68)
GLER	0.045 (6.98)	0.036 (5.41)

The USER model produced highly statistically significant active returns and stock selections. Moreover, the USER model also passed the Markowitz and Xu (1994) data mining corrections (DMC) test, indicating that the USER return was statistically different from the average of the approximately 21 models that were tested. We will employ the DMC test in Section 5.

Guerard et al. (2013) estimated Eq. (2) for all global stocks included in the FactSet database over the period January 1997–December 2011. They referred to the global expected returns model as the GLER model. The GLER model produced highly statistically significant active returns and better stock selections than the USER model over the corresponding period. That is, global stock selection models outperformed domestic stock selection models. Thus, United States investors should prefer global portfolios in order to maximize portfolio returns.

3. Building and testing stock selection models

How does one develop, estimate, and test a global stock selection model? We use the Guerard et al. (2013) database of global stocks included on the FactSet database during the period January 1997–December 2011. The number of stocks grows to approximately 16,000 during the period 1997–2011. Guerard et al.'s (2013) universe was restricted to global stocks that were covered by at least two analysts, which reduced the number to approximately 7000–8000 stocks. One can survey the academic and practitioner literature, as we have done, and calculate information coefficients for the equity universe within which one seeks to manage assets. Information coefficients, ICs, are estimated by ranking strategies and the subsequent monthly returns. We estimate one-month IC in this analysis. There is strong support for the earnings expectations variables and the fundamental variables (particularly earnings and cash flow). An objective examination of the reported ICs, as shown in Table 1, leads one to identify CTEF, EP, and CP as leading variables for inclusion in stock selection models.

The results support the low P/E (high earnings yield) approach to value investing advocated by Graham et al. (1934) and Graham, Dodd, and Cottle (1962), and validate the cross-sectional return anomaly found by Basu (1977). They marginally (only in 2003–2011) support Fama and French's (1992, 1995) finding that the book-to-market ratio is an important variable for explaining the cross-section of security returns. While the EP and BP variables are significant in explaining returns, the majority of the forecasting performance is attributable to the other model variables, namely the relative earnings-to-price, relative cash-to-price, relative sales-to-price, and earnings forecast

Table 2
Top/bottom decile spreads of FSGLER variables.

Variable	Top 3 decile spreads (t)	Annualized top 3 decile spreads	Top decile spreads (t)	Annualized top decile spreads
1997–2011				
EP	0.42% (1.66)	4.43%	0.20% (0.66)	1.40%
BP	0.50 (1.67)	5.21	0.96 (1.45)	9.54
FEP	0.50 (1.95)	5.38	0.54 (2.02)	5.11
CTEF	0.72 (5.85)	8.85	1.16 (7.27)	14.54
EWC	0.70 (3.67)	8.37	1.06 (3.55)	12.36
GLER	1.12 (4.54)	13.55	1.48 (3.67)	17.19
2003–2011				
EP	0.23% (0.80)	2.267	0.25% (1.08)	2.65
BP	0.80 (1.78)	8.74	0.47 (1.57)	5.21
FEP	0.38 (1.33)	4.12	0.23 (1.39)	2.66
CTEF	1.07 (6.48)	13.37	0.58 (4.88)	7.12
EWC	0.97 (5.79)	12.07	0.60 (1.83)	7.41
GLER	1.33 (3.98)	16.32	0.96 (4.59)	11.78

variables. A regression weighting of the GLER factors, using the weighted principal components regression discussed by Guerard et al. (2013), produces a higher IC than the equally-weighted ten-factor model, denoted EWC. The consensus earnings forecasting variable, CTEF, dominates the top/bottom (one and three) decile spreads.[3] See Table 2.

The regression weighting model produces higher decile spreads than the EWC model. We refer to the IC and decile spread tests as a Level I model of portfolio statistical significance. The GLER model can be an input into an optimization system for creating optimized portfolios.

4. Efficient APT portfolio construction

The mean–variance (MV59) portfolio construction and management can be summarized as:

$$\text{minimize } w^T C w - \lambda \mu^T w, \tag{3}$$

where μ is the expected return vector, C is the variance–covariance matrix, w is the portfolio weights, and λ is the risk-return tradeoff parameter. The estimation of C is usually done by a multifactor model, in which the individual stock return R_j of security j at time t, dropping the subscript t for time, may be written like this:

$$R_j = \sum_{k=1}^{K} \beta_{jk} \tilde{f}_k + \tilde{e}_j. \tag{4}$$

The nonfactor, or asset-specific, return on security j, $\tilde{e}_j$, is the residual risk of the security after removing the estimated impacts of the K factors. The term f_k is the rate of return on factor k. The factor model simplifies the C as the sum of the systematic risk covariance and diagonal specific variances,

$$C = \beta C_{f,f} \beta' + \Sigma. \tag{5}$$

Accordingly, the portfolio risk is decomposed into the systematic risk and specific risk

$$\begin{aligned} \sigma_p^2 &= w' \beta C_{f,f} \beta' w + w' \Sigma w \\ &= \sigma_{\beta P}^2 + \sigma_{SP}^2. \end{aligned} \tag{6}$$

If the investor is more concerned about tracking a particular benchmark, the mean–variance optimization in Eq. (3) can be reformulated as a mean–variance tracking error at risk (MVTaR) optimization:

$$\text{minimize } (w - w_b)^T C (w - w_b) - \lambda \mu^T (w - w_b), \tag{7}$$

where w_b is the weight vector of the benchmark. One can also add equal active weighing constraints (EAW):

$$|w_j - w_{(b)j}| \le x, \quad \text{for all } j. \tag{8}$$

The MVTaR with constraints in Eq. (8) will be referred to as EAWxTaR. The total tracking error can be decomposed into the systematic tracking error and the specific tracking error:

$$\begin{aligned} \sigma_{pTE}^2 &= (w - w_b)' \beta C_{f,f} \beta' (w - w_b) \\ &\quad + (w - w_b)' \Sigma (w - w_b) \\ &= \sigma_{\beta PTE}^2 + \sigma_{SPTE}^2. \end{aligned} \tag{9}$$

Multi-factor risk models evolved in the works of King (1966), Rosenberg (1974), Ross (1976), and Ross and Roll (1980). The different choices of factors lead to different risk model products. The domestic Barra risk model based on company fundamental data (like BP and size, as discussed in Section 2) was developed by Rosenberg (1974) and Rosenberg and Marathe (1979), and was discussed thoroughly by Grinold and Kahn (1999) and Rudd and Clasing (1982). The Barra attribution analysis is used in this analysis in order to determine the statistical significance of stock selection. The Sunguard APT model, developed by Blin and Bender, followed the Roll factor theory, and estimated more than 20 orthogonal factors based on 3.5 years of weekly stock returns data. Blin, Bender, and Guerard

[3] Asness, Moskowitz, and Pedersen (2013) and Berger, Israel, and Moskovitz (2009) find that an equally-weighted composite model of 50/50 value (as measured by the book value) and momentum is effective for modeling equity returns. Larry Fisher was a long-time resident of Chatham, NJ, and lived one street away from the primary author of this study. During his 1991 CRSP seminar presentation, Fisher told Guerard that the value-based strategy of Eq. (1) was merely a test of the CRSP momentum strategy. The estimation of Eq. (2) addresses the answer to Professor Fisher's observation more completely.

Table 3
Efficient frontier of the global stock selection model with various portfolio optimization techniques 1999–2011.

APT risk model							
Earnings model or component	Mean–variance methodology	Lambda	Annualized return	Standard deviation	Sharpe ratio	Information ratio	Tracking error
GLER	M59	1000	15.84	24.97	0.590	0.78	13.11
		500	16.34	24.85	0.590	0.82	12.08
		200	16.37	24.38	0.610	0.85	12.68
		100	15.90	24.61	0.580	0.81	12.66
		5	10.11	19.36	0.440	0.51	8.81
Benchmark			5.59		0.240		
GLER	TaR	1000	16.10	21.93	0.660	0.94	11.18
		500	15.91	21.99	0.651	0.90	11.44
		200	16.09	20.95	0.691	0.97	10.83
		100	14.18	21.24	0.591	0.77	11.23
		5	8.51	20.03	0.344	0.33	8.75
GLER	EAWTaR2	1000	14.80	21.96	0.600	0.94	11.07
		500	14.30	21.65	0.590	0.80	10.87
		200	14.15	20.92	0.600	0.85	10.04
		100	13.49	20.82	0.570	0.80	9.84
		5	10.77	20.79	0.440	0.43	12.18

(1997) and Guerard (2012) demonstrated the effectiveness of Sungard APT systems in portfolio construction and management.

Let us examine the use of the Sungard APT model for creating monthly portfolios using the GLER stock selection model with the assumption of a 150-basis point transaction cost each way and an 8% monthly turnover for the 1997–2011 timeframe. We use Guerard et al.'s (2013) global FactSet universe, consisting of stocks covered by at least two analysts. As lambda rises, the expected return of the portfolio rises and the number of securities in the portfolio declines.

An increase in lambda serves to produce portfolios with higher geometric means (GM), Sharpe ratios (ShR), and information ratios (IRs). If one seeks to maximize the geometric mean of a portfolio, consistent with Latane (1959) and Markowitz (1976), then one should employ a lambda of at least 200.[4] An examination of Table 3 shows that the Sharpe ratio is maximized by a lambda of 200, as was reported by Guerard et al. (2013). We show three sets of results in Table 3, generated by (1) MV59, (2) a practitioner's variation of MVTaR that weights the APT systematic risk at three times the importance of the specific risk, and (3) EAW2TaR, where x in the constraints equation (Eq. (8)) is set to two. The MV59, MVTaR, and EAW2TaR portfolio methodologies all show that one should never use a lambda of less than 100 if the asset manager seeks to maximize any portfolio measurement criterion. The efficient frontiers of the MV59, MVTaR, and EAW2TaR portfolios report substantial excess returns for any given level of risk. Moreover, for the GLER expected returns model, the MVTaR optimization technique produces higher geometric means, Sharpe ratios, and information ratios than the MV59 and EAW2TaR techniques. We run a large (seemingly infinite) set of portfolio efficient frontiers, varying the ratio of systematic risk to total risk,[5] and find that the tracking error at risk formulation is an optimal solution for the GLER data, at least for this specific time frame. However, we remind readers that there is an infinite set of portfolios that lie on or near the efficient frontier.

Guerard et al. (2013) reported that the portfolio active returns, or excess returns, of 1093 basis points were highly statistically significant (with a t-statistic of 3.85), and consisted of factor contributions (701 basis points, with a t-statistic of 3.31) and specific returns (391 basis points, with a t-statistic of 2.07) over the period 1999–2011. One refers to the decomposition of excess returns as an "attribution analysis", see Grinold and Kahn (1999). Most often, attribution analysis is created using a fundamental data-based risk model. Guerard et al. (2013) used the Axioma worldwide fundamental risk model, AX-WW2.1, or FUND, which consists of exchange rate sensitivity, growth, leverage, liquidity, medium-term momentum, short-term momentum, size, value, and volatility. The GLER model factor returns consisted of the medium-term momentum (478 basis points with a t-statistic of 6.95), value (157 basis points with a t-statistic of 5.44), and growth (77 basis points with a t-statistic of 5.21). The fundamental risk model most commonly referenced and used is the MSCI Barra GEM3 (global equity model); see Menchero, Morozov, and Shepard (2010) and Rudd and Clasing (1982) for descriptions of Barra risk model estimations. One can create an infinite number of portfolios that beat the market, once one has a statistically significant expected return input, and preferably one that is not correlated with risk factors. Wormald and van der Merwe (2012) and Shao, Rachev, and Mu (2015) are alternative formulations of optimization that

[4] The authors believe that the use of lambdas that are less than the levels that maximize the geometric mean or the Sharpe ratio is due to investors' preferences. The authors prefer to maximize the GM and ShR criteria, even if the tracking errors are larger than those of enhanced-index strategies. They refer to the use of larger lambdas as "gird your loins" and/ or "put on your big boy investment pants" strategies. One of the authors, John Guerard, refers to the use of lambdas less than 75 as being for "wimpy index huggers".

[5] Readers may request information regarding the set of additional trade-off curves and analyses from the corresponding author, John Guerard.

are very useful in creating efficient frontiers using earnings forecasting data. We refer to the creation of portfolios with a multi-factor model and the generation of the efficient frontier as a Level II test of portfolio construction.

5. A further test of data mining corrections

In the practical world of Wall Street, it is conventional wisdom to cut your historical backtested excess returns in half; that is, if your backtested excess return (the portfolio geometric mean return less the geometric mean of the benchmark) was 6%, or 600 basis points, an investment manager and/or a client might expect 3% excess returns in the future. How do we justify this cutoff?

Markowitz and Xu (1994) proposed three statistical models for estimating the cutoff, which are close to half.

In particular, model II assumes that the modeler tests N models for T periods. Let y_{it} be the logarithm of one plus the return for the ith portfolio selection model in period t, with the form

$$y_{it} = \mu_i + z_t + \varepsilon_{it}, \quad (10)$$

where μ_i is a model effect, z_t is a period effect, and ε_{it} is a random deviation. The random deviation of the return, ε_{it}, has a zero mean and is uncorrelated with the model effect, μ_i and other model random effects. Then, the best linear estimate of the unknown μ_i is

$$\hat{\mu}_i = E\mu + \beta\,(\bar{r}_i - E\mu) \quad (11)$$

$$\beta = \frac{\mathrm{cov}(\bar{r}_i, \mu)}{\mathrm{Var}(\bar{r}_i)}, \quad (12)$$

where β is the regression coefficient of μ_i as a function of $\bar{r}_i$, the sample mean of method i, and $E\mu$ is the expected average performance of all models. In practice, $E\mu$ is estimated by the sample grand average

$$\bar{r} = \sum_{i=1}^{N} \bar{r}_i / n. \quad (13)$$

The Markowitz–Xu DMC test does not use a "holdout period", as it can be data mined routinely as well; that is, one can vary the estimation and holdout periods to generate the desired conclusion. Markowitz and Xu (1994) tested the DPOS strategies of Bloch et al. (1993), and reported a β of 0.59, which is statistically significant; that is, approximately 59% of the excess returns could be expected to continue. Alternative portfolio models were created using the factors discussed in Eq. (2) as tilt factors. The GLER variable analysis passes the data mining corrections test criterion for the global market, indicating that the stock selection and portfolio construction methodologies produce superior returns that cannot be due to chance. The GLER variable has a data mining corrections coefficient of 0.74, and is highly statistically significant, having a F-value of 1.9. Thus, one could expect 74% of the excess returns on the GLER model relative to the average return to be continued. More importantly, the GLER model produced a higher geometric mean than an average model that could have been used to manage an equity portfolio in the global equity market over the period January 1997–December 2011. The Markowitz and Xu (1994) data mining corrections test is referred to as a Level III test. The GLER model passes all three levels of hypothesis testing: (1) the model and its components have statistically significant information coefficients; (2) the strategy produces excess returns after transaction costs; and (3) the strategy produces a significantly higher geometric mean than the average model that could have been used to manage assets in the universe considered.

6. The alpha alignment factor: an application to global earnings forecasting

Several practitioners have decided to perform a "post-mortem" analysis of mean–variance portfolios, attempted to understand the reasons for the deviation of ex-post performances from ex-ante targets, and used their analysis to suggest enhancements to mean–variance optimization inputs, in order to overcome the discrepancy. Lee and Stefek (2008) and Saxena and Stubbs (2012) define this as a factor alignment problem (FAP), which arises as a result of the complex interactions between the factors used for forecasting expected returns, risks and constraints. While predicting expected returns is exclusively a forward-looking activity, risk prediction focuses on explaining the cross-sectional variability of returns, mostly by using historical data. Expected-return modelers are interested in the first moment of the equity return process, while risk modelers focus on the second moments. These differences in ultimate goals inevitably introduce different factors for expected returns and risks. Even for the "same" factors, expected-return and risk modelers may choose different definitions for good reasons. Saxena and Stubbs (2012) reported that the earning-to-price (E/P) and book-to-price (B/P) ratios used in the USER Model and the Axiom Risk Model have average misalignment coefficients of 72% and 68%, respectively. While expected-return and risk models are indispensable components of any active strategy, there is also a third component, namely the set of constraints that is used to build a portfolio. Constraints play an important role in determining the composition of the optimal portfolio. Equal active weighting (EWA) constraints are one type of constraint. Most real-life quantitative strategies have other constraints that model desirable characteristics of the optimal portfolio. For example, a client may be reluctant to invest in stocks that benefit from alcohol, tobacco or gambling activities on ethical grounds, or may constrain their portfolio turnover so as to reduce their tax burden.

The naïve application of the optimizations in Eqs. (3) and (7) has the unintended effect of magnifying the sources of misalignment. The optimized portfolio underestimates the unknown systematic risk of the portion of the expected returns that is not aligned with the risk model. Consequently, it overloads the portion of the expected return that is uncorrelated with the risk factors. The empirical results in a test-bed of real-life active portfolios based on client data show clearly that the above-mentioned unknown systematic risk is a significant portion of the overall systematic risk, and should be addressed accordingly.

Sivaramakrishnan and Stubbs (2013) proposed the creation of a custom risk model by combing the factors used in both the expected-return and risk models, which does not address the factor alignment problem that is due to constraints. Saxena and Stubbs (2012) proposed that the risk variance–covariance matrix C be augmented with additional auxiliary factors in order to complete the risk model. The augmented risk model has the form of

$$C_{new} = C + \sigma_{\underline{\alpha}}^2 \underline{\alpha} \cdot \underline{\alpha}' + \sigma_{\underline{\gamma}}^2 \underline{\gamma} \cdot \underline{\gamma}', \tag{14}$$

where $\underline{\alpha}$ is the alpha alignment factor (AAF), σ_α is the estimated systematic risk of $\underline{\alpha}$, $\underline{\gamma}$ is the auxiliary factor for constrains, and σ_γ is the estimated systematic risk of $\underline{\gamma}$. The alpha alignment factor $\underline{\alpha}$ is the unitized portion of the uncorrelated expected-return model, i.e., the orthogonal component, with risk model factors.

Saxena and Stubbs (2012) applied their AAF methodology to the USER model, running a monthly backtest based on the above strategy over the time period 2001–2009 for various tracking error values of σ chosen from {4%, 5%...8%}. For each value of σ, the backtests were run on two setups, which were identical in all respects except one, namely that only the second setup used the AAF methodology ($\sigma_\alpha = 20\%$). Axioma's fundamental medium-horizon risk model (US2AxiomaMH) is used to model the active risk constraints. Saxena and Stubbs (2012) analyzed the time series of misalignment coefficients of alpha, implied alpha and the optimal portfolio, and found that almost 40%–60% of the alpha is not aligned with the risk factors. The alignment characteristics of the implied alpha are much better than those of the alpha. Among other things, this implies that the constraints of the above strategy, especially the long-only constraints, play a proactive role in containing the misalignment issue. In addition, not only do the orthogonal components of both the alpha and the implied alpha have systematic risk, but the magnitude of the systematic risk is comparable to that of the systematic risk associated with a median risk factor in US2AxiomMH. Saxena and Stubbs (2012) showed the predicted and realized active risks for various risk target levels, and noted the significant downward bias in risk prediction when the AAF methodology is not employed.[6] The realized risk-return frontier demonstrates that not only does using the AAF methodology improve the accuracy of risk prediction, it also moves the ex-post frontier upwards, thereby giving ex-post performance improvements. In other words, the AAF approach recognizes the possibility of missing systematic risk factors and makes amends to the greatest extent that is possible without a complete recalibration of the risk model that accounts for the latent systematic risk in alpha factors explicitly. In the process of doing so, the AAF approach not only improves the accuracy of risk prediction, but also makes up for the lack of efficiency in the optimal portfolios.

We re-examine the FactSet-based GLER database and test the usefulness of the alpha alignment factor in two applications. First, we create GLER portfolios using the Axioma world-wide statistically-based risk model and the Axioma world-wide fundamentally-based risk model, discussed in the attribution analysis.[7] Guerard (2013) created efficient frontiers using both of the Axioma risk models, and found that the statistically-based Axioma risk model, STAT, produced higher geometric means, Sharpe ratios, and information ratios than the Axioma fundamental risk model, FUND. We report a larger set of tracking error optimizations in Table 4, with the same result. An examination of Table 4 reveals that the geometric means and Sharpe ratios increase with the targeted tracking errors; however, the information ratios are higher in the lower tracking error range of 3%–6%, with at least 200 stocks, on average, in the optimal portfolios. We find that statistically-based risk models using principal components, such as Sungard APT and Axioma, produce more efficient trade-off curves than fundamentally-based risk models using our variables.

The application of the AAF, chosen initially to be 50%, is shown in Table 4. We find that risk is underestimated substantially at higher targeted tracking errors, with the AAF producing higher Sharpe ratios and information ratios in both fundamental and statistical risk model tests, particularly in the 7%–10% targeted tracking error range.[8]

In the second AAF application, we construct portfolios with CTEF as the expected-return model and the Axioma world-wide statistical risk (STAT) and fundamental risk (FUND) models under conditions identical to those of the GLER model. We report that portfolios constructed using the STAT model dominate those constructed using the FUND model, see Table 5 and footnote 9. The STAT model procedure increases the number of securities in the optimal portfolios substantially, see Table 5. The CTEF variables

[6] The bias statistic shown is a statistical metric that is used to measure the accuracy of risk prediction; if the ex-ante risk prediction is unbiased, then the bias statistic should be close to 1.0. Clearly, the bias statistics obtained without the aid of the AAF methodology are significantly above the 95% confidence interval, which shows that the downward bias in the risk prediction of optimized portfolios is statistically significant. The AAF methodology recognizes the possibility of inadequate systematic risk estimation, and guides the optimizer to avoid taking excessive unintended bets.

[7] The Axioma world-wide equity risk factor model (AX-WW2.1) seeks to forecast the medium-horizon risk, or risk 3–6 months ahead. The equity risk factor, or fundamental, model uses nine style factors: exchange rate sensitivity, growth (historical earnings and sales growth), leverage (debt-to-assets), liquidity (one-month trading volume divided by market capitalization), medium-term momentum (cumulative returns of the past year, excluding the previous month), short-term momentum (last-month return), size (natural logarithm of issuer market capitalization), value (book-to-price and earnings-to-price ratios), and volatility (three-month average of absolute returns divided by the cross-sectional standard deviation). The Axioma statistical risk model estimates 20 factors using principal components.

[8] Beheshti (2015) estimated alpha alignment factor models for 20% for CTEF, and found that AAF portfolios dominated non-AAF portfolios over 85% of the portfolio permutations. Moreover, in an examination of global portfolios using WRDS data, referred to by Xia, Min, and Deng (2015), Markowitz suggested graphing the Sharpe ratios and information ratios in order to identify possible "optimal" AAF levels. The resulting graph suggested that AAF levels of 20% and 40% were virtually identical in predictive power; all AAF levels (10, 20, 30,...,90) produced better results than on-AAF portfolios. The AAF level of 50% reported for these data produces information ratios that are virtually identical to those from the AAF level of 20% reported in a follow-up study using ITG cost curves for portfolio construction over the period 2001–2011.

Table 4
Axioma WRDS global data.

GLER model
Simulation period: Jan. 1999–Dec. 2011
Transactions costs: 150 basis points each way, respectively

Return model	Risk model	Tracking error	No AAF					AAF				
			Sharpe ratio	Information ratio	Ann. active return	Ann. active risk	N	Sharpe ratio	Information ratio	Ann. active return	Ann. active risk	N
GLER	STAT	4	0.448	1.247	8.72	6.99	216	0.290	1.159	4.79	4.14	516
		5	0.511	1.119	10.52	8.77	204	0.359	1.230	6.37	5.18	442
		6	0.516	1.089	11.02	10.12	188	0.397	1.145	7.43	6.49	383
		7	0.552	1.074	12.29	11.44	185	0.464	1.179	9.09	7.71	340
		8	0.605	1.111	14.14	12.73	177	0.532	1.236	10.94	8.86	304
	FUND	4	0.286	0.882	4.97	5.63	221	0.230	1.009	3.53	3.50	488
		5	0.320	0.841	5.84	6.94	199	0.269	0.971	4.45	4.59	414
		6	0.356	0.827	6.91	6.91	196	0.306	0.952	5.39	5.66	357
		7	0.414	0.885	8.45	8.45	188	0.344	0.946	6.36	6.72	318
		8	0.427	0.845	8.99	8.99	182	0.407	1.012	7.97	7.88	291

Table 5
Global earnings forecasting.

IBES global universe with at least two analysts
Axioma statistical risk model

Earnings model or component	Risk model	Targeted tracking error	Annualized return	Standard deviation	Active return	Active risk	Sharpe ratio	Information ratio	Number stocks
CTEF	Fundamental	3	6.02	18.63	4.74	3.21	0.323	1.478	1423
		4	7.64	19.03	6.36	4.16	0.402	1.578	1647
		5	7.85	19.77	6.57	4.98	0.397	1.321	1737
		6	9.78	20.15	8.50	5.78	0.485	1.470	1884
		7	10.56	20.74	9.28	6.51	0.509	1.426	1978
		8	11.71	20.64	10.43	6.90	0.567	1.511	2035
		9	12.45	21.02	11.17	7.21	0.593	1.550	2097
		10	12.82	20.90	11.55	7.67	0.614	1.504	2108
CTEF	Statistical	3	8.75	19.47	7.47	4.60	0.449	1.624	1694
		4	9.85	20.16	8.57	5.62	0.489	1.526	1740
		5	11.21	20.79	9.93	6.26	0.539	1.586	1909
		6	13.67	21.04	12.39	6.84	0.650	1.817	1956
		7	14.72	21.36	13.44	7.97	0.689	1.687	2072
		8	14.81	21.22	13.53	8.44	0.698	1.602	2112
		9	16.35	21.30	15.07	8.55	0.768	1.764	2129
		10	16.11	21.05	14.83	8.56	0.765	1.733	2133
CTEF	Statistical	3	5.69	18.28	4.41	3.39	0.312	1.302	129
		4	7.09	18.55	5.81	4.43	0.382	1.312	73
		5	7.48	18.22	6.20	4.61	0.411	1.343	70
		6	8.60	18.87	7.32	5.48	0.456	1.335	70
		7	9.13	19.21	7.85	5.73	0.474	1.370	70
		8	11.50	19.04	10.22	6.98	0.604	1.464	70
		9	10.79	19.15	9.51	6.54	0.563	1.454	70
		10	10.16	19.59	8.88	7.30	0.519	1.216	70

require more stocks than the GLER model in the Axioma simulations. We limit the number of securities to only 70 stocks each month and obtain a more investable solution that is still consistent with the risk-return tradeoff. As the tracking errors rise, the Sharpe ratios generally also rise. The information ratios tend to support the creation of portfolios with the lower tracking errors of the GLER model.

One notes an extremely import result in Table 5 with regard to the constraint on the number of stocks: the active risk of the holdings-constrained CTEF portfolios is less than the targeted tracking errors. Thus, the AAF procedure should not be used. The optimal CTEF portfolio construction technique uses the Axioma statistical risk model with constraints on the number of holdings. The Sharpe ratios and information ratios on the CTEF model in Table 5 exceed those on the GLER model. The consensus earnings efficiency, CTEF, has dominated stock returns in global markets over the past 12 years. Earnings forecasting has been rewarded in global markets.

7. Conclusions

Investing based on analysts' expectations, fundamental data, and momentum variables is a good investment strategy in the long-run. Stock selection models often use momentum, analysts' expectations, and fundamental data. We find support for composite modeling using these sources of data, as well as evidence supporting the use of APT multi-factor models for portfolio construction and risk control. We develop and estimate three levels of testing for stock selection and portfolio construction. The use of multi-factor risk-controlled portfolio returns allows us to reject the data mining corrections test null hypothesis. Some readers may ask why the authors ended their analysis in 2011. The authors have updated their research through December 2013 and found similar results. Interested readers may request updated information from the corresponding author. The anomalies literature can be applied in real-world global portfolio construction.

Acknowledgments

The authors appreciate the comments of Martin J. Gruber, the referee, Anureet Saxena, and Robert Stubbs. Research conversations with Bernell Stone and Mustafa Gultekin enhanced our analysis. Vishnu Anand and Chris Martin of Axioma were extremely helpful in helping the authors use Axioma, particularly Chris' work on limiting the numbers of securities (names) in the portfolios. Any errors remaining are the responsibility of the authors.

References

Arnott, R. (1979). Relative strength revisited. *Journal of Portfolio Management*, *5*, 19–23.

Asness, C., Moskowitz, T., & Pedersen, L. (2013). Value and momentum everywhere. *Journal of Finance*, *68*, 929–985.

Basu, S. (1977). Investment performance of common stocks in relation to their price earnings ratios: a test of market efficiency. *Journal of Finance*, *32*, 663–682.

Beaton, A. E., & Tukey, J. W. (1974). The fitting of power series, meaning polynomials, illustrated on bank-spectroscopic data. *Technometrics*, *16*, 147–185.

Beheshti, B. (2015). A note on the integration of the alpha alignment factor and earnings forecasting models in producing more efficient Markowitz frontiers. *International Journal of Forecasting*, *31*, 582–584.

Berger, A. L., Israel, R., & Moskovitz, T. J. (2009). *The case for momentum investing*. AQR White Paper.

Blin, J. M., Bender, S., & Guerard, J. B., Jr. (1997). Earnings forecasts, revisions and momentum in the estimation of efficient market-neutral Japanese and U.S. portfolios. In A. Chen (Ed.), *Research in finance, Vol. 15* (pp. 93–114). Greenwich, CT: JAI Press.

Bloch, M., Guerard, J. B., Jr., Markowitz, H. M., Todd, P., & Xu, G.-L. (1993). A comparison of some aspects of the U.S. and Japanese equity markets. *Japan and the World Economy*, *5*, 3–26.

Bruce, B., & Epstein, C. B. (1994). *The handbook of corporate earnings analysis*. Chicago: Probus Publishing Company.

Brush, J. S. (2007). A flexible theory of price momentum. *Journal of Investing*, *16*, 36–42.

Brush, J. S., & Boles, K. E. (1983). The predictive power in relative strength and CAPM. *Journal of Portfolio Management*, *9*, 20–23.

Chan, L. K. C., Hamao, Y., & Lakonishok, J. (1991). Fundamentals and stock returns in Japan. *Journal of Finance*, *46*, 1739–1764.

Elton, E. J., Gruber, M. J., & Gultekin, M. (1981). Expectations and share prices. *Management Science*, *27*, 975–987.

Fama, E. F., & French, K. R. (1992). Cross-sectional variation in expected stock returns. *Journal of Finance*, *47*, 427–465.

Fama, E. F., & French, K. R. (1995). Size and the book-to-market factors in earnings and returns. *Journal of Finance*, *50*, 131–155.

Fama, E. F., & French, K. R. (2008). Dissecting anomalies. *Journal of Finance*, *63*, 1653–1678.

Fama, E. F., & MacBeth, J. D. (1973). Risk, return, and equilibrium: empirical tests. *Journal of Political Economy*, *81*, 607–636.

Grinold, R., & Kahn, R. (1999). *Active portfolio management*. New York: McGraw-Hill/Irwin.

Graham, B., Dodd, D., & Cottle, S. (1934). *Security analysis: principles and technique* (1st ed.). New York: McGraw-Hill Book Company.

Graham, B., Dodd, D., & Cottle, S. (1962). *Security analysis: principles and technique* (4th ed.). New York: McGraw-Hill Book Company.

Guerard, J. B. (1997). Is there a cost to be socially responsible in investing? *Journal of Forecasting*, *16*, 475–490.

Guerard, J. B. (2012). Global earnings forecast efficiency. *Research in Finance*, *28*, 19–47.

Guerard, B., Jr. (2013). *Introduction to financial forecasting in investment analysis*. New York: Springer.

Guerard, J. B., Jr., Gultekin, M., & Stone, B. K. (1997). The role of fundamental data and analysts' earnings breadth, forecasts, and revisions in the creation of efficient portfolios. In A. Chen (Ed.), *Research in finance, Vol. 15*.

Guerard, J. B., Jr., & Mark, A. (2003). The optimization of efficient portfolios. In A. Chen (Ed.), *Research in finance, Vol. 20*.

Guerard, J. B., Jr., Rachev, R. T., & Shao, B. (2013). Efficient global portfolios: big data and investment universes. *IBM Journal of Research and Development*, *57*(5), Paper 11.

Guerard, J. B., Jr., Xu, G., & Gultekin, M. N. (2012). Investing with momentum: the past, present, and future. *Journal of Investing*, *21*, 68–80.

Gunst, R. F., Webster, J. T., & Mason, R. L. (1976). A comparison of least squares and latent root regression estimators. *Technometrics*, *18*, 75–83.

Haugen, R., & Baker, N. (2010). Case closed. In J. B. Guerard (Ed.), *The handbook of portfolio construction: contemporary applications of Markowitz techniques*. New York: Springer.

Hawkins, E. H., Chamberlain, S. C., & Daniel, W. E. (1984). Earnings expectations and security prices. *Financial Analysts Journal*, *40*(5), 24–38, 74.

King, B. F. (1966). Market and industry factors in stock price behavior. *Journal of Business*, *39*, 139–191.

Korajczyk, R. A., & Sadka, R. (2004). Are momentum profits robust to trading costs? *Journal of Finance*, *59*, 1039–1082.

Lakonishok, J., Shleifer, A., & Vishny, R. W. (1994). Contrarian investment, extrapolation and risk. *Journal of Finance*, *49*, 1541–1578.

Latane, H. A. (1959). Crietria for choice among risky ventures. *Journal of Politcal Economy*, 67, 144–155.

Lee, J. H., & Stefek, D. (2008). Do risk factors eat alphas? *Journal of Portfolio Management*, *34*(4)), 12–25.

Lesmond, D. A., Schill, M. J., & Zhou, C. (2004). The illusory nature of trading profits. *Journal of Financial Economics*, *71*, 349–380.

Levy, H. (1999). *Introduction to investments* (2nd ed.). Cincinnati: South-Western College Publishing.

Malkiel, B. (1996). *A random walk down Wall Street* (6th ed.). New York: W.W. Norton & Company.

Markowitz, H. M. (1952). Portfolio selection. *Journal of Finance*, *7*, 77–91.

Markowitz, H. M. (1959). *Portfolio selection: efficient diversification of investment, Cowles foundation monograph Vol.16*. New York: John Wiley & Sons.

Markowitz, H. M. (1976). Investment in the long run: new evidence for an old rule. *Journal of Finance*, *31*, 1273–1286.

Markowitz, H. (1987). *Mean-varance analysis in portfolio choice and capital markets*. London: Basil Blackwell.

Markowitz, H. M., & Xu, G. L. (1994). Data mining corrections. *Journal of Portfolio Management*, *21*, 60–69.

Menchero, J., Morozov, A., & Shepard, P. (2010). Global equity modeling. In J. B. Guerard (Ed.), *The handbook of portfolio construction: contemporary applications of Markowitz techniques*. New York: Springer.

Ramnath, S., Rock, S., & Shane, P. (2008). The financial analyst forecasting literature: a taxonomy with suggestions for further research. *International Journal of Forecasting*, *24*, 34–75.

Rosenberg, B. (1974). Extra-market components of covariance in security returns. *Journal of Financial and Quantitative Analysis*, *9*, 263–274.

Rosenberg, B., & Marathe, V. (1979). Tests of capital asset pricing hypotheses. In H. Levy (Ed.), *Research in finance, Vol. 1*.

Ross, S. A. (1976). The arbitrage theory of capital asset pricing. *Journal of Economic Theory*, *13*, 341–360.

Ross, S. A., & Roll, R. (1980). An empirical investigation of the arbitrage pricing theory. *Journal of Finance*, *35*(2), 1071–1103.

Rudd, A., & Clasing, H. K. (1982). *Modern portfolio theory: the principles of investment management*. Homewood, IL: Dow-Jones Irwin.

Saxena, A., & Stubbs, R. A. (2012). An empirical case study of factor alignment using the USER model. *Journal of Investing*, *21*, 25–44.

Shao, B. P., Rachev, S. T., & Mu, Y. (2015). Applied mean ETL optimization using earnings forecasting. *International Journal of Forecasting*, *31*, 561–567.

Sivaramakrishnan, K., & Stubbs, R. A. (2013). Improving the investment process with a custom risk model: a case study with the GLER model. *Journal of Investing*, *22*, 129–147.

Wheeler, L. B. (1994). Changes in consensus earnings estimates and their impact on stock returns. In B. Bruce & C. B. Epstein (Eds.), *The handbook of corporate earnings analysis*. Chicago: Probus Publishing Company.

Williams, J. B. (1938). *The theory of investment value*. Cambridge: Harvard University Press.

Wormald, L., & van der Merwe, M. (2012). Constrained optimization for portfolio construction. *Journal of Investing*, *21*, 44–59.

Xia, H., Min, H., & Deng, S. (2015). Effectiveness of earnings forecasts in efficient global portfolio construction. *International Journal of Forecasting*, *31*, 568–574.

John B. Guerard is Director of Quantitative Research at McKinley Capital Management, in Anchorage, Alaska. He earned his AB in Economics from Duke University, his MA in Economics from the University of Virginia, MSIM from the Georgia Institute of Technology, and Ph.D. in Finance from the University of Texas, Austin. Mr. Guerard has published several monographs, including *Quantitative corporate finance* (Springer, 2007, with Eli Schwartz) and *Introduction to financial forecasting in investment analysis* (Springer, 2013), and edited *The handbook of portfolio construction: contemporary applications of Markowitz techniques* (Springer, 2010). John serves an Associate Editor of the *Journal of Investing* and the *International Journal of Forecasting*.

Harry Markowitz is the Chief Architect at Guidedchoice.com in San Diego, CA, and a quantitative research scientific advisor at McKinley Capital Management LLC in Anchorage, AK. He is a Nobel Laureate and the father of modern portfolio theory, and was named "Man of the Century" by *Pensions and Investments* magazine. He has received the prestigious John von Neumann Theory Prize for his work in portfolio theory, sparse matrix techniques, and the SIMSCRIP programming language. Dr. Markowitz earned his Ph.D. from the University of Chicago.

GanLin Xu is the Chief Technology Officer of Guidedchoice.com, where he leads a team of finance, economics, and mathematics experts to develop Guidedchoice's financial methodology, software, and systems. Dr. Xu earned his Ph.D. from Carnegie Mellon University. His research on portfolio theory has been published in various journals. He is a quantitative research scientific advisor at McKinley Capital Management LLC in Anchorage, AK.

https://doi.org/10.1142/9789811222634_0006

Chapter 6

Truly Active Management Requires a Commitment to Excellence: Portfolio Construction and Management with FactSet

Bijan Beheshti

FactSet Research Systems Inc.
San Francisco, CA, USA

John B. Guerard, Jr.

McKinley Capital Management, LLC
Anchorage, AK 99503, USA
jguerard@mckinleycapital.com

Chris Mercs

FactSet Research Systems Inc.
San Francisco, CA, USA

Financial anomalies have been studied in the U.S. Recent evidence suggests that financial anomalies have diminished in the U.S. and possibly in non-U.S. portfolios. Have the anomalies changed and are they persistent? Have historical and earnings forecasting data been a consistent and highly statistically significant source of excess returns? We test many financial anomalies of the 1980–1990s and report that several models and strategies continue to produce statistically significant excess returns. We test a large set of U.S. and global variables over the past 16 years. We report that many of these fundamental, earnings forecasts, revisions, and breadth and momentum, and cash deployment strategies maintained their statistical significance during the 2003–2018 time period. Moreover, the earnings forecasting model and robust regression estimated that composite model excess returns are greater in non-U.S. and global markets than in the U.S. markets.

Keywords: Portfolio Optimization, Earnings Forecasting, Robust Regression, Efficient Portfolios.

1. Introduction

The purpose of this study is to document the existence and effectiveness of variables reported as financial anomalies in 2003 time period and test whether these reported anomalies are statistically significant during the 2003–2017 time periods. One must create optimal portfolios to assess the predictive power of financial anomalies. We report results working exclusively on the FactSet Research Systems, Inc. (FactSet) platform. We report a "one-button" approach to portfolio construction and management that is consistent with the teachings of Harry Markowitz and William F. Sharpe, the creators of Modern Portfolio Theory (MPT). On the FactSet platform, we pull down FactSet Fundamentals financial data, the I/B/E/S earnings history, create fundamental ratios and data, run robust regression to implement a statistically significant stock selection model, create portfolios, and assess the portfolios over time (i.e. backtest the strategies). We report the expected returns modeling work of Elton *et al.* (1981), Ziemba and Schwartz (1992), and Guerard *et al.* (2003, 2013, 2014, 2015, 2018) that continue to drive stock returns. What do we add to an extensive anomaly literature? We test portfolio anomalies in a post-publication setting. We report three results: (1) many of the reported financial anomalies published in 1993–2003 time period maintained their statistically significant active (or excess) returns; (2) the anomalies are greater in non-U.S. markets than in the U.S.; and (1) transactions costs do not destroy the excess returns. The authors report highly statistically significant excess returns above transactions costs, and data mining corrections adjustments in U.S. and non-U.S. stocks during the 2003–2018 time period, using models published by the authors in 1993 and 1997, modeled with the FactSet Research Systems, Inc.

This chapter is composed of four sections. Section 1 addresses what we knew in 1991–2003, with regard to the reported fundamental data, earnings forecasting, composite modeling of earnings forecasting, and fundamental variables, and what risk models were available for creating and monitoring the effectiveness of optimized portfolios. This section presents a brief literature review of the fundamental variables used in modeling stock returns in the 1991–2003 time period, including the earnings forecasting models and fundamentally based stock selection models. Section 2 examines Markowitz optimization and the use of Barra and Axioma Risk Models used in the analysis. Section 3 inquires if a bottom-up stock picker's world has changed post-2003 or post-Global Financial Crisis periods by estimating the models of stock selection. Section 4 presents summaries and conclusions and thoughts regarding future research and testing.

2. What we Knew in the 1991 Tests of Fundamental Data

In 1991, Harry Markowitz developed an equity research group, DPOS, at Daiwa Securities Trust Company, in Jersey City, NJ. Financial modeling used traditional fundamental variables, such as earnings-to-price, book value-to-price, cash flow-to-price, sales-to-price, cash flow-to-price, small size, institutional holdings, earnings forecasts, revisions, recommendations, and breadth; earnings surprises, and dividend yield variables identified in Dimson (1988) and Jacobs and Levy (1988); and ongoing conversations with William (Bill) Ziemba as anomalies.[1] Testing and reporting on financial anomalies in October 2018, we find that many of Jacobs and Levy (1988), Guerard *et al.* (1993), Chan, Hamao, and Lakonishok (1991), and Haugen and Baker (1996) variables have continued to produce statistically significant Active and Specific Returns in the post-publication period, i.e. the 2003–2018 (and later) time periods. The forecasted earnings acceleration variable has produced statistically significant Active and Specific Returns in the post-Global Financial

[1]Bloch *et al.* (1993), Guerard, Markowitz, Todd, and Xu (1993), Ziemba and Schwartz (1992), and Chan *et al.* (1991) specifically addressed many of the earlier reported non-U.S. anomalies and/or compared U.S. and non-U.S. anomalies.

Crisis Period. The composite model of earnings, price momentum, and fundamental data is a consistent source of alpha in the U.S. and international markets. Excess returns are greater in international stocks than in U.S. stocks.

Bloch *et al.* (1993) built fundamental-based stock selection models for Japanese and U.S. stocks. What did we know in 1991? The DPOS Group was well versed in the low PE or high earnings-to-price, EP, high book value-to-price, high cash flow-to-price, high sales-to-price, net current asset value, and the earnings forecasting models in Graham and Dodd (1934), Graham *et al.* (1962), Elton and Gruber (1972a, 1972b), Latane *et al.* (1975), Jacobs and Levy (1988), and Dimson (1988).[2] DPOS built stock selection models and created the Markowitz mean–variance (MV) Efficient Frontiers for U.S. and Japanese stock markets. The investable stock universe was the first section, non-financial Tokyo Stock Exchange common stocks from January 1975 to December 1990 in Japan and the 1,000 largest market-capitalized common stocks from November 1975 to December 1990 in the U.S.

Eight factors were used in the quarterly, cross-sectional regressions in Japan and the U.S. Bloch *et al.* (1993) estimated Eq. (9) to assess empirically the relative explanatory power of each of the eight variables in the equation to estimate the determinants of total stock returns, TR. We refer to this model as REG8.

$$\begin{aligned} \mathrm{TR} = {} & w_0 + w_1\mathrm{EP} + w_2\mathrm{BP} + w_3\mathrm{CP} + w_4\mathrm{SP} + w_5\mathrm{REP} \\ & + w_6\mathrm{RBP} + w_7\mathrm{RCP} + w_8\mathrm{RSP} + e_t \end{aligned} \quad (1)$$

[2]Nerlove (1968) reported the statistical significance of the growth sales and earnings in association with stock returns. The major papers on the combination of value ratios for the prediction of stock returns (including at least CP and/or SP) include those of Jacobs and Levy (1988), Chan *et al.* (1991), Fama and French (1992 and 2008), and Bloch *et al.* (1993). Lakonishok *et al.* (1994) and Haugen and Baker (1996) later produced highly cited variable testing which confirmed that fundamental variables enhanced portfolio returns over the long run. Our point is that this brief survey of anomalies is to acknowledge that Jacobs and Levy (1988), *Chan et al.* (1991), Bloch *et al.* (1993), and Ziemba and Schwartz (1992) were correct in their Berkeley Program in Finance and *Q*-Group presentations of the early 1990s on the inefficiencies of stock markets.

where

$$\begin{aligned}
\text{EP} &= [\text{earnings per share}]/[\text{price per share}] \\
&= \text{earnings} - \text{price ratio;} \\
\text{BP} &= [\text{book value per share}]/[\text{price per share}] \\
&= \text{book} - \text{price ratio;} \\
\text{CP} &= [\text{cash flow per share}]/[\text{price per share}] \\
&= \text{cash flow} - \text{price ratio;} \\
\text{SP} &= [\text{net sales per share}]/[\text{price per share}] = \text{sales} - \text{price ratio;} \\
\text{REP} &= [\text{current EP ratio}]/[\text{average EP ratio over the past 5 years}]; \\
\text{RBP} &= [\text{current BP ratio}]/[\text{average BP ratio over the past 5 years}]; \\
\text{RCP} &= [\text{current CP ratio}]/[\text{average CP ratio over the past 5 years}]; \\
&\quad \text{and} \\
\text{RSP} &= [\text{current SP ratio}]/[\text{average SP ratio over the past 5 years}].
\end{aligned}$$

Given the concerns about both outlier distortion and multicollinearity, Bloch *et al.* (1993) tested the relative explanatory and predictive merits of alternative regression estimation procedures: OLS; robust regression using the Beaton and Tukey (1974) bi-square criterion to mitigate the impact of outliers; the presence of highly correlated variables (latent root regression to address the issue of the highly correlated variables, known as multicollinearity) (see Gunst *et al.*, 1976); and weighted latent roots, denoted WLRR, a combination of robust and latent roots. Bloch *et al.* (1993) used the estimated regression coefficients to construct a rolling horizon return forecast. The predicted returns and predictions of risk parameters were used as inputs for an MV optimizer (see Markowitz, 1959, 1987) to create MV efficient portfolios in financial markets in both Japan and the U.S. The DPOS analysis found that a series of Markowitz (1952, 1959, 1976) MV efficient portfolios produced statistically significant excess returns. First, they compared OLS and robust regression techniques, inputting the expected return forecasts produced by each method into an MV optimizer. The robust regression-constructed composite model portfolio produced higher Sharpe ratios and geometric means than the OLS-constructed composite model portfolio in both Japan and the U.S., indicating that controlling for both outliers and multicollinearity is important. Second, Bloch *et al.* (1993) quantified the survivor bias (including dead companies in the database) and found that it was not statistically significant in either Japan or the U.S. for the period tested. Third, they investigated period-to-period portfolio revision and found that tighter turnover and rebalancing triggers led to higher portfolio returns for value-based strategies. Finally, Markowitz and Xu (1994) developed a test for data mining.[3] In addition to testing the hypothesis of data mining, the test can also be used to estimate and assess the expected differences between the best test model and the average of simulated policies. We will refer to the eight-factor model as REG8, or the Markowitz model, in this analysis.

Studies of the effectiveness of corporate earnings forecasting variables, reported in Cragg and Malkiel (1968), Elton and Gruber, and Gultekin (1981), DeBondt and Thaler (1989), Wheeler (1994), and Guerard and Stone (1992) were reprinted in Bruce and Epstein (1994).[4] Analysts' forecasts of earnings per share (eps), eps revision, and the direction of eps forecast revisions were incorporated into the Institutional Broker Estimation Services (I/B/E/S) in-print

[3]Bloch *et al.* (1993) wrote their article in 1991. At the time of the original estimation of eight-factor regression model, the international Institutional Estimation Brokerage Service (I/B/E/S) was only 4 years old, having started in 1987, and did not have sufficient data for model building and testing such that the models with earnings forecasts could pass the Markowitz and Xu (1994) Data Mining Corrections test.

[4]The studies by Bruce and Epstein (1994) and Brown (2000) contain much of the rich history of earnings forecasting and the resulting excess returns. Researchers such as Elton *et al.* (1981, 1984) developed the I/B/E/S database and published the initial research and Hawkins *et al.* (1984) also published his studies in 1984. The Elton *et al.* (1981) paper is one of the most influential analysis in earnings forecasting and security analysis. Guerard *et al.* (1993) employed Toyo Keizai earnings forecasts in Japan because of the limitations of the non-U.S. I/B/E/S database. The Toyo Keizai earnings forecasts enhanced portfolio returns by over 200 basis points annually. The GPRD team was well aware of the return enhancement of I/B/E/S forecasts in U.S. stocks, see Guerard and Stone (1992). The Guerard and Stone research was sponsored by the Institute for Quantitative Research in Finance, the "*Q*-Group", circa 1985. Womack (1996), Guerard *et al.* (1997, 2015), and Ball and Ghysels (2018), are among the thousands of studies of analysts' forecasting efficiency and how analysts' forecasts enhance portfolio returns.

database in July 1972. The I/B/E/S database has computer-readable data from January 1976, domestically, and January 1987.[5] In 1993, the best and longest source of Japanese earnings forecasts was the Toyo Keizai database. We present evidence in this section that the I/B/E/S database has been a source of highly statistically significant excess returns. We refer the reader to Brown (2000) which contains about 570 abstracts of I/B/E/S studies. Guerard *et al.* (1997) reported that analysts' forecast variables enhanced portfolio returns over the long run. By 1997, we knew that CTEF, a composite model of earnings forecasts, revisions, and breadth, the agreement among analysts' revisions, was highly statistically significantly correlated with stock returns. Guerard and Mark (2003) published that CTEF, and a nine-factor model, denoted REG9, composed of REG8 plus CTEF was also highly (statistically) significantly correlated with stock returns. By 2003, Guerard and Mark were pushing CTEF, REG8, and REG9 for stock selection modeling, using the Barra risk model. In 1975, Barr Rosenberg and his associates introduced the Barra U.S. Equity Model, often denoted USE1.[6] There were

[5]The newly created non-U.S. I/B/E/S database did not have enough data in 1991–1994 to pass the Markowitz–Xu data mining test for its use in Japan.

[6]The Barra USE1 Model predicted risk, which required the evaluation of the firm's response to economic events, which were measured by the company's fundamentals. There were six descriptors, or risk indexes, in the Barra model. These descriptors were composite variables primarily based on the statistically significant variables in Rosenberg and McKibben (1973). Rosenberg and Marathe (1979), Rudd and Rosenberg (1979), and Rudd and Clasing (1982) are excellent references for how the Barra equity model is constructed. Barra is a proprietary model; that is, the composite model weights are not disclosed. Thus, there were nine factors in the Index of Market Variability, including the historic beta estimate, historic sigma estimate, share turnover for 3 months, trading volume, the log of the common stock price, and a historical alpha estimate, and cumulative range over 1 year, but without coefficients, one cannot reproduce the model. One can correlate an investment manager's variables with the risk indexes, as we will discuss later in the chapter. The Index of Earnings Variability included the variance of earnings, variance of cash flow, and the covariability of earnings and price. The Index of Low Valuation and Unsuccess included the growth in earnings per share, recent earnings change, relative strength (a price momentum variable), the book-to-price ratio, dividend cuts, and the return of equity. The Index of Immaturity and Smallness included the log of total assets, the log of market capitalization, and net plant/common equity. The Index of Growth Orientation included the dividends-to-earnings ratio (the payout ratio), dividend yield, growth in total assets, the earnings-to-price (ep) multiple, and the typical ep ratio over the past 5 years. The Graham and Dodd low P/E investment manager would

39 industry variables in the Barra USE1 model. How are the data manipulated and/or normalized to be used in the Barra USE1 model? First, raw data are normalized by subtracting a mean and dividing through by the variable standard deviation; however, the mean subtracted is the market capitalization-weighted mean for each descriptor for all securities in the S&P 500.[7] The monthly residual risk factors are calculated by regressing residual returns (the stock excess return less the predicted beta times the market excess return) versus the six risk indexes and the industry dummy variables.[8] The domestic Barra E3 (USE3, or sometimes denoted US-E3) model, with some 15 years of research and evolution, uses 13 sources of factor, or systematic, exposures. The sources of extra-market factor exposures are volatility, momentum, size, size nonlinearity, trading activity, growth, earnings yield, value, earnings variation, leverage,currency sensitivity, dividend yield, and non-estimation universe.[9]

"load up" on the Index of Growth Orientation and would offer investors positive asset selection (good stock picking) only if the portfolio weights differed from weights on the "Growth" Index components. The "Index of Financial Risk" included leverage at market and book values, debt-to-assets ratio, and cash flow-to-current liabilities ratio.

[7]The relevant variable standard deviation is not the universe standard deviation of each variable, but the standard deviation of the variables for companies with market capitalizations exceeding $50 million. A final transformation occurs when the normalized descriptor is scaled such that its value is one standard deviation above the S&P 500 mean. Every month, the monthly stock return in the quarter is regressed as a function of the normalized descriptors. If the firm is typical of the S&P 500 firms, then most of the scaled descriptor values and coefficients should be approximately zero.

[8]See Rudd and Clasing (1982), p. 115, for the USE1 descriptors.

[9]There is an equally extensive body of literature on the impact of price momentum variables on the cross-section of stock returns. Price momentum, or the non-random character of stock market prices, has been studied since Bachelier in 1900, but the availability of much of the early, pre-1964 research was made far more accessible in Cootner (1964). Guerard and Mark (2003) did not use price momentum in their stock selection model. The Barra risk model contained a price momentum factor risk premium and thus one might not expect momentum to be significant with a risk model incorporating the variable. Influential recent researchers such as Conrad and Kaul (1993, 1998), Jagadeesh and Titman (1993), and Lo *et al.* (2000) extended the technical analysis and price momentum literature. Most importantly for our analysis, Conrad and Kaul (1998) reported the mean reversion of stock returns in the very short run, one week or one month, and the medium-term persistence of momentum to drive stock prices higher in the 3-, 6-, 9-, 12-, and 18-month time horizons over the 1926–1988 and 1926–1989 time

There was extensive body of literature on the impact of price momentum variables on the cross-section of stock returns. Price momentum, or the non-random character of stock market prices, has been studied since Bachelier in 1900, but the availability of much of the early, pre-1964 research was made far more accessible in Cootner (1964).[10] Later, and in both the U.S. and international stock market analyses, Guerard *et al.* (2014) and the Fama and French (1998) PM122 variable, defined as $P(t-2)/P(t-12)$, to the stock selection model, developed a 10-factor stock selection model for the U.S. expected returns, which they referred to as the USER model.[11] Guerard *et al.* (2013) and Guerard and Mark (2018) applied the 10-factor model to global stocks, referring to the model as GLER, or REG10. See Eq. (2).

$$\begin{aligned}\mathrm{TR}_{t+1} &= a_0 + a_1\mathrm{EP}_t + a_2\mathrm{BP}_t + a_3\mathrm{CP}_t + a_4\mathrm{SP}_t + a_5\mathrm{REP}_t + a_6\mathrm{RBP}_t \\ &\quad + a_7\mathrm{RCP}_t + a_8\mathrm{RSP}_t + a_9\mathrm{CTEF}_t + a_{10}\mathrm{PM}_t + e_t, \end{aligned} \tag{2}$$

where

$$\begin{aligned}\mathrm{EP} &= [\text{earnings per share}]/[\text{price per share}] \\ &= \text{earnings} - \text{price ratio};\end{aligned}$$

periods. Jagadeesh and Titman (1993) constructed portfolios based on 6 months of positive price momentum, held the portfolios for 6 months, and earned excess returns of 12.01% over the 1965–1989 time period. Medium-term momentum is an important, and persistent, risk premium. In the very long run, 24 and 36 months in Conrad and Kaul (1998), momentum returns become very negative. Lo *et al.* (2000) produced a definitive study of technical analysis over the 1962–1996 time period and found that technical patterns produced incremental returns, particularly for NASDAQ stocks. Price momentum and technical analysis variables enhanced portfolio returns over the long run, although the majority of the academic studies did not use the Barra model, which dominated the asset management industrial use.

[10]The classic Cootner edited volume reprinted the works of Bachelier (translated), Kendall, Osborne, Working, Cowles, Granger, Fama, Mandelbrot, and Samuelson, among others. It is interesting to note that these researchers published in economic, business, statistical, operations research, and industrial management journals. The Cootner volume papers reported evidence of efficient and inefficient markets. The reader is referred to Lo *et al.* (2000) for a definitive (but dated) test of price momentum in the U.S.

[11]Brush and Boles (1983) and Brush (2001) tested a PM121 price momentum variable, defined as P(t − 1)/P(t − 12). The Brush PM121 model was useful in the U.S. market but not useful in Japan.

$$
\begin{aligned}
\text{BP} &= [\text{book value per share}]/[\text{price per share}] \\
&= \text{book} - \text{price ratio;} \\
\text{CP} &= [\text{cash flow per share}]/[\text{price per share}] \\
&= \text{cash flow} - \text{price ratio;} \\
\text{SP} &= [\text{net sales per share}]/[\text{price per share}] = \text{sales} - \text{price ratio;} \\
\text{REP} &= [\text{current EP ratio}]/[\text{average EP ratio over the past 5 years}]; \\
\text{RBP} &= [\text{current BP ratio}]/[\text{average BP ratio over the past 5 years}]; \\
\text{RCP} &= [\text{current CP ratio}]/[\text{average CP ratio over the past 5 years}]; \\
\text{RSP} &= [\text{current SP ratio}]/[\text{average SP ratio over the past 5 years}]; \\
\text{CTEF} &= \text{consensus earnings-per-share I/B/E/S forecast, revisions,} \\
&\quad \text{and breadth;} \\
\text{PM122} &= \text{price momentum; and} \\
e &= \text{randomly distributed error term.}
\end{aligned}
$$

Guerard *et al.* (2013, 2015) estimated the 10-factor model for all global stocks included in the FactSet database over the period January 1997 to December 2011. Bloch *et al.* (1993) used the Beaton–Tukey bi-square robust regression weighting scheme, as part of their regression analysis, which they denoted WLRR. The Beaton–Tukey bi-square is one of the several schemes analyzed in Andrews *et al.* (1972). The Andrews *et al.* (1972) volume reported that most robust regression modeling techniques produce similar median forecasting errors, which are substantially lower than the OLS median forecasting errors. Guerard and Mark (2020, forthcoming) updated the GLER model simulation period to the 1996–2016 time period. The GLER model produced highly statistically significant active returns and better stock selections than the USER model over the corresponding period.[12] The earnings forecasting model, CTEF, continued to produce statistically significant Active Returns and Specific Returns (stock selection) during the 1996–2016 time period.

[12]That is, global stock selection models outperformed domestic stock selection models. Thus, U.S. investors should prefer global portfolios in order to maximize portfolio returns.

The I/B/E/S database continues to be a great source of statistically significant excess returns for stocks.

The identification of influential data is an important component of regression analysis. The modeler can identify outliers, or influential data, and re-run the ordinary least squares regressions on the re-weighted data, a process referred to as robust (ROB) regression. In ordinary least squares (OLS), all data are equally weighted. The weights are 1.0. In robust regression, the larger is the OLS residual, the smaller is the weight of the observation in the robust regression. In robust regression, several weights may be used. In fact, the authors have tested 7–8 weighting functions and Guerard *et al.* (2019) reported finding no statistically significant differences in simulated portfolios using the robust regression-weighted GLER model with the Beaton–Tukey bi-square, Huber, Hampel, Fair, and Tukey and Yohai Optimal Influence Function (OIF) weightings. The Huber and Tukey bi-square weightings are derived upon bounded loss functions and have smooth psi-functions which produce a unique solution, see Huber (1981), Maronna *et al.* (2006), and Maronna *et al.* (2019). The starting point, OLS estimates in Bloch *et al.* (1993), influences the number of iterations, but not the final result, see Maronna *et al.* (2006, 2019).[13]

The recent literature on financial anomalies is summarized in Fama and French (2008), Levy (2012), Guerard *et al.* (2013, 2014, 2015), Jacobs and Levy (2017), Chu *et al.* (2017), and Grinblatt (2019).

3. Markowitz Risk Modeling with Barra and Axioma Risk Models: Constructing MV Efficient Frontiers

The Markowitz (1952, 1959) portfolio construction approach seeks to identify the efficient frontier, the point at which returns are maximized for a given level of risk, or risk is minimized for a given level of return. The portfolio expected return, $E(R_p)$, is calculated by taking the sum of the security weights multiplied by their respective

[13] John Guerard thanks Doug Martin for a detailed conversation regarding this point.

expected returns. The portfolio standard deviation is the sum of the weighted covariances, i.e.

$$E(R_p) = \sum_{i=1}^{N} x_i E(R_i) = \sum_{i=1}^{N} x_i \mu_i \tag{3}$$

$$\sigma_p^2 = \sum_{i=1}^{N} \sum_{j=1}^{N} x_i x_j c_{ij}, \tag{4}$$

where μ is the expected return vector, C is the variance–covariance matrix, and x is the portfolio weights.

The efficient frontier can be traced out by

$$\text{minimize}_{\{x_i \geq 0,\, x_i \leq \bar{u}\}}\ x^T C x - \lambda \mu^T x, \tag{5}$$

where λ is the risk–return trade-off parameter and $\bar{u}$ is the fixed upper bound. Bloch *et al.* (1993) created efficient frontiers using a purely full historical covariance matrix.

Sharpe (1963) developed the Diagonal Model which reduced the computing time of the RAND QP (quadratic programming) code on the IBM 7090 computer from 33 minutes to 30 seconds for a 100-stock example. In the Diagonal Model, Sharpe modeled stock returns are related through common relationships of an underlying factor or index. Sharpe specifically suggested variables such as the level of the stock market, Gross National Product (GNP), or a price index.[14]

Rudd and Rosenberg (1979) published a paper, *Realistic Portfolio Optimization*, that enhanced the portfolio optimization by introducing transactions costs into the portfolio optimization analysis. Moreover, and more importantly, Rudd and Rosenberg (1979) introduced

[14]Harry Markowitz (1959) anticipated the Diagonal Model in footnote 1, page 100, of Chapter 4 in his book *Portfolio Selection: Efficient Diversification of Investment*, where the return of a security can be expressed as a function of the value of an index. Given that Sharpe's Diagonal Model paper had four references, three of which were Markowitz publications, one can clearly understand that modern portfolio theory was developed in large part due to the interactions of these great thinkers. It is little wonder they shared the Noble Prize. Elton and Gruber (1980) and Elton *et al.* (2007) brought the correlation coefficients and covariances and beta relationships to a far greater audience, MBA students. The Elton and Gruber texts are excellent books (the first and seventh editions) that greatly enhanced multi-factor risk explanations, particularly in integrating stock betas.

the idea of using of the Barra multi-factor risk model parameters *in lieu* of using only the historic covariances among stock returns. Muller (1993) reported the use of the Barra E2 model in portfolio optimization. The Barra optimization model was an industry standard.

The Barra risk model was a multi-factor risk model that built upon the inadequacies of the Capital Asset Pricing Model. The multiple-factor risk model builds upon the Capital Asset Pricing Model (CAPM) framework of Sharpe (1964), Lintner (1965), Mossin (1996, 1973), and Levy (1999, 2012). The Barra risk model has been tested with another commercially available risk model, which is the Axioma Risk Model. The Axioma Robust Risk Model[15] is a multi-factor risk model, in the tradition of the Barra model. Axioma offers both U.S. and world fundamental and statistical risk models. The Axioma Risk Models use several statistical techniques to efficiently estimate factors. The ordinary least squares residuals (OLS) of beta estimations are not of constant variance; that is, when one minimizes the sum of the squared residuals to estimate factors using OLS, one finds that large assets exhibit lower volatility than smaller assets. Axioma uses a weighted least squares (WLS) regression, which scales the asset residual by the square root of the asset market capitalization (to serve as a proxy for the inverse of the residual variance). Robust regression, using the Huber M Estimator, addresses the issue and problem of outliers. (Asymptotic) Principal components analysis (PCA) is used to estimate the statistical risk factors. A subset of assets is used to estimate the factors and the exposures and factor returns are applied to other assets. Guerard *et al.* (2015) tested CTEF and a 10-factor regression-based model of global expected returns, GLER, during the 1997–2011 time period. The authors reported that the geometric means and Sharpe ratios increase with the targeted tracking errors; however, the information ratios are higher in the lower tracking error range of 3–6%, with at least 200 stocks, on average, in the optimal portfolios. They reported that statistically based risk models using principal components, such

[15] *Axioma Robust Risk Model Handbook*, January 2010.

as Sungard APT and Axioma, produce more efficient trade-off curves than fundamentally based risk models using our variables.[16] Guerard and Mark (2020, forthcoming) validated the continued statistical significance of CTEF and REG9 using Axioma Medium-Term U.S. Model, version 3.[17]

---

[16]Blin *et al.* (1997) and Guerard (2012) demonstrated the effectiveness of the APT, Sungard APT, and FIS APT systems in portfolio construction and management. The estimation of security weights, w, in a portfolio is the primary calculation of Markowitz's portfolio management approach. The issue of security weights will now be considered from a different perspective. The security weight is the proportion of the portfolio's market value invested in the individual security. The active weight of the security is calculated by subtracting the security weight in the (index) benchmark, b, from the security weight in the portfolio, p. The marginal security systematic volatility is the partial derivative of the systematic volatility of the portfolio relative to the security weight. In the King's English, the marginal tracking error measures the sensitivity of the tracking error relative to the marginal change in the security active weight. If a position taken in a security leads to an increase in the portfolio's volatility, then the security is said to create a positive contribution to risk. A negative contribution to risk occurs when a security reduces the portfolio volatility such as a long position on a security with a negative beta or a short position on a security with a positive beta. Obviously, the contribution to risk depends upon the security weight and the security's beta to the overall portfolio. The security contribution to tracking error reflects the security's contribution to the tracking error of a portfolio considering the security return that is undiversified at the active portfolio level. The portfolio Value-at-Risk (VaR) is the expected maximum loss that a portfolio could produce over 1 year. The APT measure of portfolio risk estimating the magnitude that the portfolio return may deviate from the benchmark return over one year is referred to as TaR, or "Tracking-at-Risk". TaR is composed of systematic and specific components. What is the economic importance of tracking error at risk? First, TaR helps the assert manager assess the downside risk. Second, by optimizing portfolios where systematic risk is more important than specific risk, one produces high Information Ratios, IRs, than equally weighting systematic and specific risk or using only total risk (Markowitz, 1959). TaR specifically addresses fat tails in stock return distributions. Third, as portfolios becomes diversified, the R-squared statistics of portfolio returns increase, and the optimal TaR ratio to relative tracking errors increase, to 1.645 (unsystematic risk is weighted 0.345). Guerard *et al.* (2013, 2015) reported the highly statistically significant excess returns (and specific returns) effectiveness of an APT MVTaR optimization analysis of CTEF in global markets during the 1997–2011 time period and Guerard *et al.* (2014) reported CTEF effectiveness in U.S. markets over the corresponding time period.

Guerard *et al.* (2013, 2015) reported the highly statistically significant excess returns (and specific returns) effectiveness of an APT MVTaR optimization analysis of CTEF in global markets during the 1997–2011 time period and Guerard *et al.* (2014) reported CTEF effectiveness in the U.S. markets over the corresponding time period.

[17]Guerard and Mark (2018) reported monthly Axioma attribution statistics which, in the case of CTEF, indicates that the forecasted earnings acceleration variable loads on

4. The Existence and Continued Persistence of Financial Anomalies, 2003–2018

Guerard *et al.* (2015) reported three levels of testing investment strategies.[18] The first level is the information coefficient, IC, of a strategy in which the subsequent ranked returns are regressed as a function of the ranked financial strategy. The regression coefficient is the IC which is a randomly distributed variable to test the statistical significance of the individual variable or composite model strategies. The second level of investment testing is to estimate, with transactions costs, the Markowitz efficient frontier, by varying either the lambda or the targeted tracking error. The third level of testing is to apply the Markowitz and Xu (1994) Data Mining Corrections, DMC, to test whether the strategy is statistically different from any model that could have been used. Moreover, the regression coefficient of the DMC test indicates how much excess returns could be

---

Medium-Term Momentum (0.257), Growth (0.151), and Value (0.469) and that mean–variance CTEF and REG10 portfolios produced approximately 300–350 basis points of Specific Returns for the 20-year time periods. In the U.S. portfolios, equally weighted 125-stock portfolios outperform mean–variance (MV) 4% portfolios. In the non-U.S. and EAFE universes, Guerard and Mark (2018) reported that the CTEF ICs were higher than the REG10 or GLER ICs in their 10-, 5-, 3-, and 1-year time sub-periods. The CTEF and REG10 produced approximately 400–500 basis points of Active Returns and about 250 basis points of Specific Returns. The non-U.S. portfolios offer more stock selection than U.S. portfolios with the addition of the REG8 plus CTEF (denoted REG9) and REG10 factors. The t-statistic on the risk stock selection effect in non-U.S. portfolios is maximized with ranked CTEF. The t-statistics on the risk stock selection effect is statistically significant for REG10, although the t-statistic on the risk stock selection effect in the non-U.S. portfolios is only statically significant at the 10% level. Guerard and Mark (2018) reported that only ranked CTEF is statistically significant in the U.S., whereas globally, ranked CTEF and REG10 are statistically significant in Total Active Returns and Risk Stock Selection Returns.

[18]The first level is the information coefficient, IC, of a strategy in which the subsequent ranked returns are regressed as a function of the ranked financial strategy. The regression coefficient is the IC, which is a randomly distributed variable to test the statistical significance of the individual variable or composite model strategies. The second level of investment testing is to estimate, with transactions costs, the Markowitz efficient frontier, by varying either the lambda or the targeted tracking error. The third level of testing is to apply the Markowitz and Xu (1994) Data Mining Corrections, DMC, to test whether the strategy is statistically different from any model that could have been used. Moreover, the regression coefficient of the DMC test indicates how much excess returns could be continued into the future, holding everything else constant.

continued, holding everything else constant. We seek to maximize the Geometric Mean (GM), Information Ratios (IRs), and Sharpe Ratios (ShRs). We rank our variables from low to high, and 99 is preferred.

One must use transactions costs in one's portfolio construction and management in industry. Our portfolio optimization models employ a piecewise linear transaction cost model by ITG, specifically the Non-Discretionary ITG ACE Optimal 0.7 Trade Urgency model. In the unlikely event that a security is not covered by the model, we assume a conservative default buy and sell cost of 150 basis points. We refer the reader to the white paper *ITG ACE — Agency Cost Estimator: A Model Description* (2007) for a detailed review of the transaction cost model methodology. We will review some basic definitions here. "Non-discretionary" estimates are calibrated to observed transaction costs for a subset of the ITG Peer Group Database which do not exhibit opportunistic characteristics. Non-discretionary trades will typically have higher transaction costs than discretionary trades. "ITG ACE Optimal" strategies are determined by creating a trade-off between minimizing expected cost and standard deviation of cost with respect to trade urgency. The trade urgency range is between 0 and 1, with 0.7 reflecting an aggressive strategy that weighs minimizing risk (standard deviation of estimated trade cost) above minimizing transaction cost. The model described here is used to estimate the transaction costs during each rebalance period throughout the portfolio construction process for all our model portfolios.[19]

[19]The FactSet Portfolio Analytics System is used as the calculation engine behind our performance attribution results. Transaction costs generated from the ITG model described above are used to determine the "Risk Transaction Effect" calculated by FactSet. Factor returns and exposures from the Axioma Risk Models are used to calculate the "Risk Factors Effect", "Risk Factors Effect T-Stat", and "Compounded Factor Impact" columns produced by FactSet. The portfolio's Total Effect is calculated using FactSet's Daily Valuation method, a CFA Institute/PPS transactions-based performance calculation methodology shown as follows:

$$[(\mathrm{EMV}+\mathrm{ACCRe})(\mathrm{BMV}+\mathrm{ACCRb})(\mathrm{FEE}+\mathrm{PRCHSALEINCCPNPRIN})]/(\mathrm{BMV}+\mathrm{ACCRb}) \quad (6)$$

The initial data used in this analysis are the Morgan Stanley Capital International (MSCI) Index constituent data for the All Country World (ACW) Index, the MSCI Non-U.S. (XUS) Index, the MSCI Japanese (JP) Index, MSCI China A-Shares Index, and MSCI

This total effect can be further decomposed into four underlying effects as previously highlighted in Tables 2 and 3.

The statistical significance of two of these effects, factor and stock specific, are also presented as T-Stats.

Risk Factors Effect: The overall excess return explained by the active exposures to the factors in the risk model. It is calculated by compounding the calculation period results for the sum of each factor's Active Exposure multiplied by its Factor Return. This effect can be further decomposed down to individual risk model factors.

Risk Stock Specific Effect: The portion of the active return that is not explained by the risk model, often referred to as stock selection skill.

Risk Total Effect − Risk Factors Effect.

Risk Total Effect: The overall active performance of the portfolio gross of transaction costs. It is equal to

Risk Stock Specific Effect + Risk Factors Effect.

At the asset level, this can be expressed by the following formula:

$$r_i = r_f + \epsilon_i = \sum_{k=1}^{K} x_i k f k + \epsilon_i$$

r_i : Standalone asset total return

r_f : Standalone factors effect

ϵ_i : Asset specific returns

$x_{i,k}$: Asset raw factor exposure to factor k

f_k : Raw factor return of factor k (7)

Risk Transaction Effect: The performance impact of fees, trading costs, and execution price relative to close price.

Risk Stock Specific and Factors Effect T-Stat: Tests whether the average return is statistically different than zero.

The calculation is as follows:

(Average Return − 0)/(Model Standard Deviation/Square Root of the number of periods)

To calculate cumulative effects over time, FactSet applies compounding algorithms to standalone effects. Our portfolios use the Residual Free Portfolio Cumulative compounding algorithm with attribution effects, also known as the GRAP Method or the Frongello Method. The results will produce a total effect that equals the difference between the geometrically linked portfolio and benchmark total returns.

$$e_{i'} = (e_{i-1'})(1 + \text{BR}_i/100) + (e_i)(1 + \text{PR}_{i-1'}/100) \tag{8}$$

Emerging Markets (EM) Index, and Russell 3000 (R3) Index, for the 12/2002–11/2018 time period. In a second analysis, we require stocks to be covered by at least two analysts on the Institutional Brokerage Estimate Services (I/B/E/S) universe in the ACW and CH analyses. McKinley Capital Management (MCM) maintains a factor database of approximately 70 factors since 1999. We show that CTEF, the most statistically significant model used for stock selection, published in 1997, has been one of the 2–3 most dominant variables in the MCM in all MSCI universes up until September 2019 (please see the Appendix of Guerard and Markowitz (2018)).[20] We test five sets of expected returns, CTEF, REG8, REG9, and REG10, for the six index constituent universes. We use data only as they are known (or more exactly, our portfolios are tested out-of-sample).

We report an Alpha Tester set of non-U.S. stock results in Table 1. The CTEF variable, REG8, REG9, and REG10 models produced statistically significant Active Returns for 12/2002–11/2018. The FactSet alpha Tester analysis, as a default, equals weights stocks according to the variable fractiles (such as quintiles, in our reported results). The Bloch *et al.* (1993) universes, the R1000 and (MSCI) Japan-only universes report the REG8 model produced over 200 basis

---

where

$e_{i'}$ = cumulative attribution effect through period i;
$e_{i-1'}$ = cumulative attribution effect in period $i-1$;
BR_i = benchmark return in period i;
e_i = attribution effect in period i;
$\mathrm{PR}_{i-1'}$ = cumulative portfolio return through period $i-1$.

All portfolio attribution results are annualized by taking the arithmetic difference of the annualized portfolio and annualized benchmark returns. This method produces annualized attribution effects while maintaining their additive property so that

$$\begin{aligned}&\text{Annualized Stock Specific Effect} + \text{Annualized Factors Effect}\\&\quad + \text{Annualized Transaction Effect} = \text{Annualized Total Effect}\end{aligned} \tag{9}$$

[20]The models discussed in Guerard and Markowitz (2019), written for 84,000 Certified Financial Planners, stressed that the models identified by the authors well before the 2003–11/2018 were highly statistically significant post-publication. The models that passed the Markowitz-Xu (1994) Data Mining Corrections test in 1994 and 1997, continued to be statistically significant for another 25 years.

Table 1. Alpha testing model summary — Japan.

Model	Client:/Quant/Japan Ranked 8_9_10
Universe	ISAV(OFDB(CLIENT:/QUANT/JAPAN2_RANKED_SMOOTHED,MFR_SMOOTHED_8F,0))=1
Benchmark	ISON_MSCI_REGION(939200,0,CLOSE)=1
Date Range	31-Jan-2003 - 30-Nov-2018: 1 - Month Rebalance
Main Return	1 - Month Forward: Equal Weighted
Univ Return (%)	0.68
Bench Return (%)	0.68

Factor 1	8 Factor JP
Factor 2	9 Factor JP
Factor 3	10 Factor JP
Factor 4	EP JP
Factor 5	CTEF JP

First - Last Fractile Cumulative Return

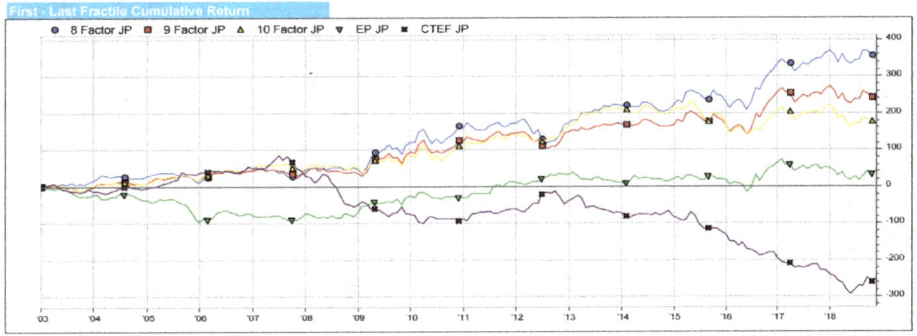

Average Information Coefficients

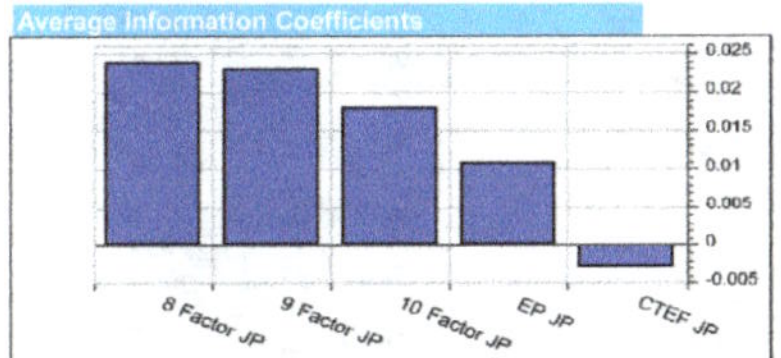

Factor Comparison

Factor	F1-FN Return	Avg IC	Avg IC T-Stat	Std Dev of ICs
8 Factor JP	0.446	0.024	0.472	0.163
9 Factor JP	0.283	0.023	0.447	0.155
10 Factor JP	0.240	0.018	0.349	0.154
EP JP	-0.003	0.011	0.215	0.149
CTEF JP	-0.389	-0.003	-0.065	0.149

Fractile 1 Regression Statistics

Factor	Alpha	T-Stat Alpha	Beta	T-Stat Beta	Residual Risk	Information Ratio	Sharpe Ratio	% Total Turnover	Ann. Excess vs. Bench	Std. Dev. Excess vs. Bench
8 Factor JP	0.203	1.476	1.078	35.209	1.889	0.449	0.175	19.209	2.987	1.921
9 Factor JP	0.139	1.126	1.059	38.349	1.702	0.346	0.166	21.649	2.065	1.723
10 Factor JP	0.038	0.328	1.062	41.656	1.572	0.160	0.147	24.453	0.883	1.597
EP JP	-0.043	-0.318	1.032	34.596	1.839	-0.065	0.128	10.929	-0.412	1.845
CTEF JP	-0.201	-1.592	1.096	38.949	1.735	-0.274	0.098	16.526	-1.695	1.788

Notes: In the Alpha Testing Model, 8 Factor = REG8; In the Alpha Testing Model, 9 Factor = REG9; In the Alpha Testing Model, 10 Factor = REG10.

points, annualized returns over the benchmark, without Markowitz MV optimization or transactions costs. The XUs and EM Alpha Testers report statistically significant stock selection in XUS and EM universes for CTEF and REG10 variables; in fact, in the EM universe, CTEF, REG8, REG9, and REG10 are statistically significant. The Alpha Tester analysis is a similar (alternative) test to the Information Coefficients, ICs, reported in Guerard *et al.* (2015) in Level I testing.

Our simulation conditions assume 8% monthly turnover, 35 basis point threshold positions, an upper bound in mean–variance optimization of 4% on security weights, and ITG transactions costs.[21] We use the MV optimization techniques. Our portfolio simulations reported in Table 2 use the Axioma Fundamental Risk Model. The optimizations use the ITG transaction cost curves discussed in Borkovec *et al.* (2010). ITG transaction costs have been taken out of the portfolio returns reported in Table 2. The financial anomalies of EP, BP, CP, SP, CTEF, and PM are reflected in Tables 3–5 which report the REG10 results. In the CTEF-optimized portfolios outperform in 70% and 77% of the years, respectively. Financial anomalies, as published in 1993 and 2003, continue to outperform, with slightly reduced winning percentages, from 83% in 1993 to 77% in 2018. Is that enough for investors? Should that be enough for investors? The excess returns reported in Table 2, particularly for targeted

tracking errors of 6% and 8% should satisfy investors who seek to maximize the Geometric Mean and the utility of terminal wealth.[22]

[21]ITG estimate our transaction costs to be about 60 basis points, each way, for 2011–2015.

[22]Fama (1991) hypothesized that anomalies could not be effectively tested because of changing asset pricing models and the number of factors in multi-factor models. Barillas and Shanken (2018) addressed the issue of changing risk models and factors. We have addressed these issues in two previous studies and are currently addressing a third issue. First in Guerard and Mark (2003), we established what Barra USE models were known at that time; there was no look-ahead bias in risk models. Second, in Guerard and Mark (2018) we used the Boolean signal portfolio construction process in which we buy attractively ranked stocks and sell them when they fell through pre-determined level (buy stocks with CTEF or REG10 scores of at least 85 and higher, where 0 is least preferred and 99 is most preferred and sell at 70, holding in equally weighted portfolios). The Boolean signal treats re-enforced the mean–variance

Table 2. Alpha testing model summary — R1000.

Model	Client:/Quant/R1000 Ranked 8_9_10	**Factor 1**	8 Factor R1
Universe	ISAV(OFDB(CLIENT:/QUANT/R1000_RANKED_SMOOTHED,MFR_SMOOTHED_8F,0))=1	**Factor 2**	9 Factor R1
Benchmark	FG_CONSTITUENTS(R.1000,0,CLOSE)=1	**Factor 3**	10 Factor R1
Date Range	31-Jan-2003 - 30-Nov-2018: 1 - Month Rebalance	**Factor 4**	EP R1
Main Return	1 - Month Forward: Equal Weighted	**Factor 5**	CTEF R1
Univ Return (%)	0.91		
Bench Return (%)	0.89		

First - Last Fractile Cumulative Return

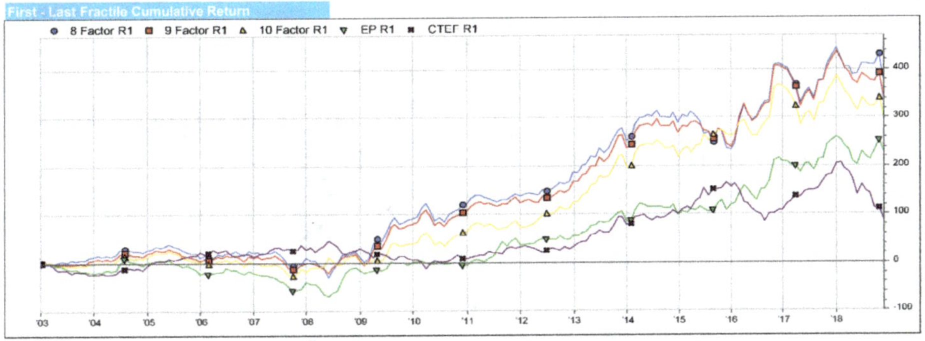

Average Information Coefficients

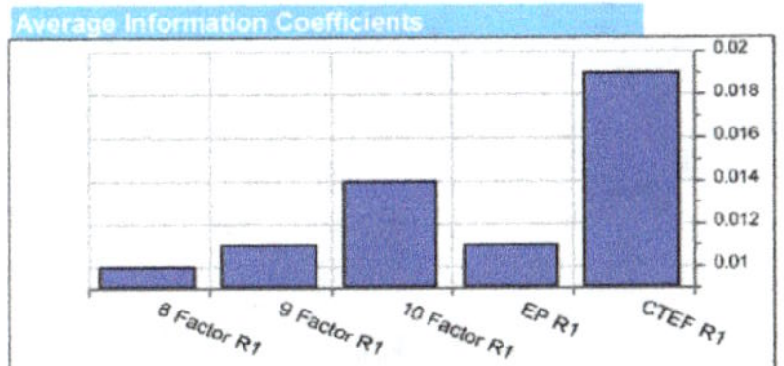

Factor Comparison

Factor	F1-FN Return	Avg IC	Avg IC T-Stat	Std Dev of ICs
8 Factor R1	0.346	0.010	0.298	0.125
9 Factor R1	0.297	0.011	0.338	0.119
10 Factor R1	0.227	0.014	0.412	0.116
EP R1	0.176	0.011	0.331	0.113
CTEF R1	0.011	0.019	0.564	0.101

Fractile 1 Regression Statistics

Factor	Alpha	T-Stat Alpha	Beta	T-Stat Beta	Residual Risk	Information Ratio	Sharpe Ratio	% Total Turnover	Ann. Excess vs. Bench	Std. Dev. Excess vs. Bench
8 Factor R1	0.041	0.286	1.157	38.683	2.018	0.298	0.175	16.403	2.206	2.138
9 Factor R1	0.059	0.439	1.138	41.210	1.862	0.327	0.180	17.921	2.216	1.958
10 Factor R1	0.117	1.055	1.039	45.276	1.548	0.333	0.196	20.846	1.769	1.534
EP R1	0.002	0.014	1.091	41.549	1.771	0.154	0.172	10.315	0.963	1.802
CTEF R1	0.035	0.373	0.982	50.741	1.305	0.023	0.184	15.924	0.100	1.281

Notes: In the Alpha Testing Model, 8 Factor = REG8; In the Alpha Testing Model, 9 Factor = REG9; In the Alpha Testing Model, 10 Factor = REG10.

Table 3. Alpha testing model summary — XUS.

Model	Client:/Quant/Ranked 8_9_10	**Factor 1**	8F MFR
Universe	ISAV(OFDB(CLIENT:/QUANT/RANKED_8_9_10_SMOOTHED.OFDB,MFR_SMOOTHED_8F,0))=1	**Factor 2**	9F MFR
Benchmark	ISON_MSCI_REGION(899901,0,CLOSE)=1	**Factor 3**	10F MFR
Date Range	31-Jan-2003 - 30-Nov-2018: 1 - Month Rebalance	**Factor 4**	EP Rank
Main Return	1 - Month Forward: Equal Weighted	**Factor 5**	CTEF Rank
Univ Return (%)	0.85		
Bench Return (%)	0.83		

First - Last Fractile Cumulative Return

Average Information Coefficients

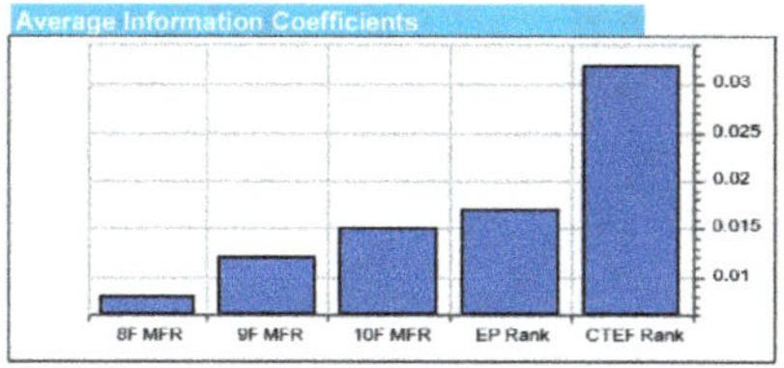

Factor Comparison

Factor	F1-FN Return	Avg IC	Avg IC T-Stat	Std Dev of ICs
8F MFR	0.231	0.008	0.320	0.102
9F MFR	0.334	0.012	0.510	0.097
10F MFR	0.359	0.015	0.630	0.092
EP Rank	0.355	0.017	0.720	0.092
CTEF Rank	0.710	0.032	1.320	0.071

Fractile 1 Regression Statistics

Factor	Alpha	T-Stat Alpha	Beta	T-Stat Beta	Residual Risk	Information Ratio	Sharpe Ratio	% Total Turnover	Ann. Excess vs. Bench	Std. Dev. Excess vs. Bench
8F MFR	0.094	0.875	1.042	51.446	1.479	0.290	0.165	18.380	1.500	1.496
9F MFR	0.145	1.452	1.046	55.538	1.375	0.452	0.175	19.612	2.183	1.396
10F MFR	0.190	2.186	1.017	62.279	1.192	0.583	0.186	22.538	2.414	1.195
EP Rank	0.019	0.175	1.205	57.760	1.522	0.379	0.149	21.655	2.453	1.870
CTEF Rank	0.274	3.798	1.089	80.095	0.992	1.141	0.198	93.141	4.343	1.099

Notes: In the Alpha Testing Model, 8 Factor = REG8; In the Alpha Testing Model, 9 Factor = REG9; In the Alpha Testing Model, 10 Factor = REG10.

Table 4. Alpha testing model summary — R3000.

Model	Client:/Quant/US Ranked 8_9_10	**Factor 1**	REG8 US
Universe	ISAV(OFDB(CLIENT:/QUANT/US_RANKED_SMOOTHED,MFR_SMOOTHED_REG8,0))=1	**Factor 2**	REG9 US
Benchmark	FG_CONSTITUENTS(R.3000,0,CLOSE)=1	**Factor 3**	REG10 US
Date Range	31-Jan-2003 - 30-Nov-2018: 1 - Month Rebalance	**Factor 4**	EP US
Main Return	1 - Month Forward: Equal Weigh	**Factor 5**	CTEF US
Univ Return (%)	0.83		
Bench Return (%)			

First - Last Fractile Cumulative Return

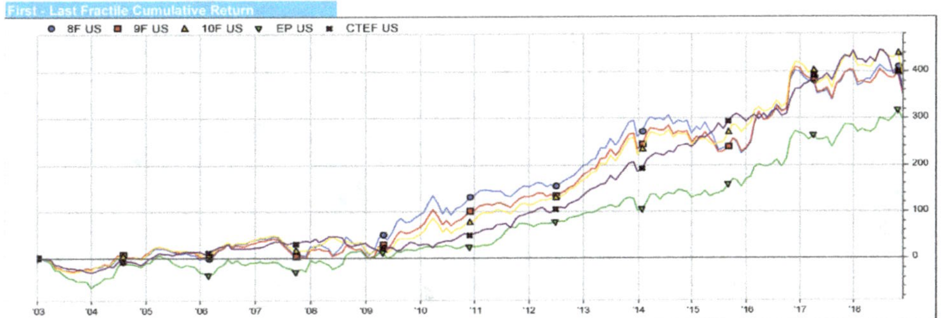

Average Information Coefficients

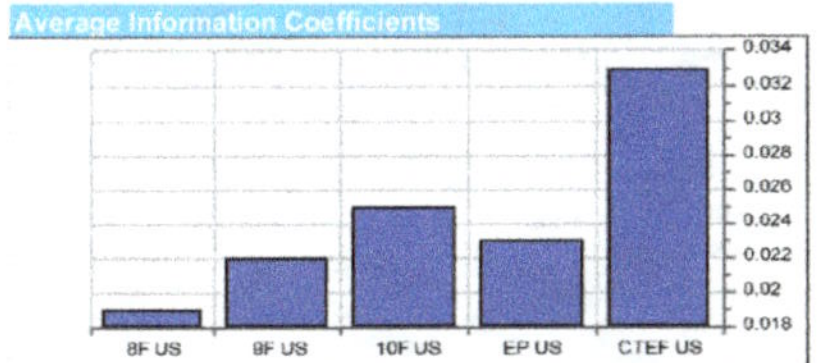

Factor Comparison

Factor	F1-FN Return	Avg IC	Avg IC T-Stat	Std Dev of ICs
REG8 US	0.380	0.019	0.954	0.102
REG9 US	0.354	0.022	1.112	0.096
REG10 US	0.372	0.025	1.292	0.095
EP US	0.262	0.023	1.208	0.103
CTEF US	0.342	0.033	1.687	0.076

Fractile 1 Regression Statistics

Factor	Alpha	T-Stat Alpha	Beta	T-Stat Beta	Residual Risk	Information Ratio	Sharpe Ratio	% Total Turnover	Ann. Excess vs. Bench	Std. Dev. Excess vs. Bench
REG8 US	0.074	0.510	1.125	42.995	2.003	0.288	0.146	15.729	2.116	2.120
REG9 US	0.098	0.735	1.096	45.991	1.824	0.320	0.152	16.762	2.104	1.901
REG10 US	0.169	1.488	1.013	49.694	1.561	0.380	0.169	18.906	2.055	1.563
EP US	0.064	0.507	1.019	44.820	1.742	0.136	0.149	10.451	0.822	1.745
CTEF US	0.190	2.218	0.928	60.431	1.176	0.313	0.180	16.815	1.347	1.242

Notes: In the Alpha Testing Model, 8 Factor = REG8; In the Alpha Testing Model, 9 Factor = REG9; In the Alpha Testing Model, 10 Factor = REG10.

Table 5. Alpha testing model summary — EM.

Model	Client:/Quant/EM Ranked 8_9_10	**Factor 1**	8 Factor EM
Universe	ISAV(OFDB(CLIENT:/QUANT/EM_RANKED_SMOOTHED,MFR_SMOOTHED_8F,0))=1	**Factor 2**	9 Factor EM
Benchmark	ISON_MSCI_REGION(891800,0,CLOSE)=1	**Factor 3**	10 Factor EM
Date Range	31-Jan-2003 - 30-Nov-2018: 1 - Month Rebalance	**Factor 4**	EP EM
Main Return	1 - Month Forward: Equal Weighted	**Factor 5**	CTEF EM
Univ Return (%)	0.97		
Bench Return (%)	0.94		

First - Last Fractile Cumulative Return

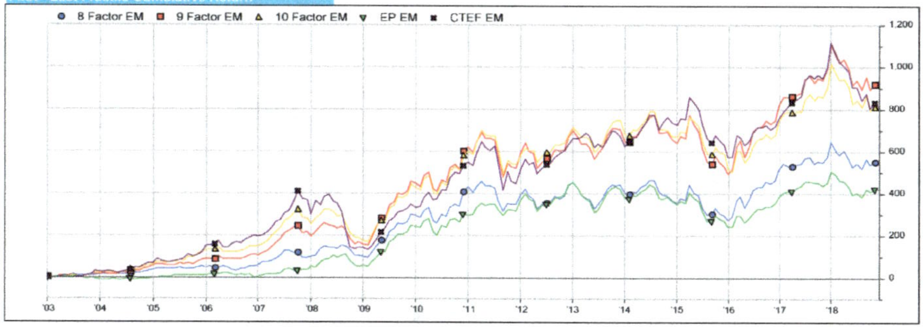

Average Information Coefficients

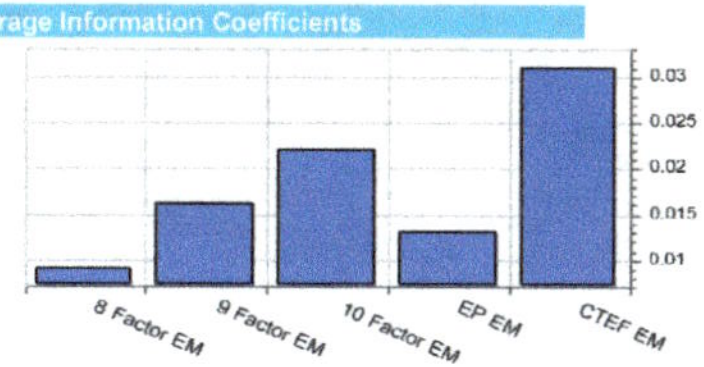

Factor Comparison

Factor	F1-FN Return	Avg IC	Avg IC T-Stat	Std Dev of ICs
8 Factor EM	0.420	0.009	0.246	0.108
9 Factor EM	0.642	0.016	0.451	0.101
10 Factor EM	0.612	0.022	0.598	0.095
EP EM	0.319	0.013	0.370	0.080
CTEF EM	0.673	0.031	0.821	0.081

Fractile 1 Regression Statistics

Factor	Alpha	T-Stat Alpha	Beta	T-Stat Beta	Residual Risk	Information Ratio	Sharpe Ratio	% Total Turnover	Ann. Excess vs. Bench	Std. Dev. Excess vs. Bench
8 Factor EM	0.217	1.959	1.049	59.300	1.520	0.589	0.176	18.027	3.164	1.550
9 Factor EM	0.368	3.575	1.063	64.625	1.415	1.036	0.198	19.103	5.274	1.469
10 Factor EM	0.320	3.237	1.044	66.084	1.359	0.919	0.192	21.179	4.417	1.387
EP EM	0.169	1.654	1.071	65.742	1.401	0.570	0.168	10.453	2.904	1.470
CTEF EM	0.279	2.988	1.115	74.763	1.282	0.960	0.182	16.780	4.887	1.470

Notes: In the Alpha Testing Model, 8 Factor = REG8; In the Alpha Testing Model, 9 Factor = REG9; In the Alpha Testing Model, 10 Factor = REG10.

Several more results should be pointed to our readers in Table 6, where models within stock universes are ranked by specific returns: (1) CTEF is highly statistically significant in non-U.S., EM, and China A-Shares universes; (2) REG8 is statistically significant in all stock universes; (1) REG10 Active Returns dominate in non-U.S., EM, and China A-Shares portfolios.

In the MSCI All Country World ex-U.S. universe, during the 12/2002–11/2018 time period, the ranked EP and CTEF variables produced highly statistically significant Active Returns (Risk Total Effect) and Specific Returns (see Table 6). Modern robust statistics minimize a scale measure of residuals insensitive to large residuals, such as the median of the absolute residuals, see Maronna *et al.* (2019). The least median squares (LMS) estimator was introduced by Hampel (1975) and Rousseeuw (1984). When we use a very large efficiency measure, such as 99%, large outliers have virtually no influence on the regression estimates. FactSet uses the *R* system for robust regression modeling. The larger the efficiency, the larger the bias under contamination, and there can be a trade-off between normal efficiency and contamination by outlier bias.[23]

The role of historical and forecasted earnings in the non-U.S. universe is well documented, as in Guerard *et al.* (2015). The CTEF portfolio Geometric Means, Sharpe Ratios, and IRs are followed by REG8, REG9, and REG10 (see Table 6). The CTEF, REG8, and REG9 variables produced statistically significant portfolio Active

---

portfolio results. The mean–variance portfolios, with a specified upper bound on stock weights and positive holdings for long-only portfolios produced very reasonable (possible) weights. We do not believe the Brennan-Lo (2011) footnote that repeats the impossible mean–variance optimized portfolios tales told by Wall Street portfolio managers. The Axioma attribution of the Boolean signal portfolios attributed all Active Returns to stock selection in the CTEF model and the majority of the REG10 model Active Returns were due to Specific Returns, or asset selection. Finally, we are testing whether it makes a difference as to whether we use a (1) mean–variance tracking error at-risk model, stressing systematic risk minimization; (2) a mean–variance model without factors (MVM59), using only total risk; or (1) a mean–variance model using only systematic risk.

[23]The SAS robustreg procedure uses an 85% efficiency default level as a result of Maronna *et al.* (2006). We use 99% because of research conversations with Doug Martin, the publication of Maronna *et al.* (2019), and the resulting higher portfolio simulation Sharpe Ratios.

Table 6. Portfolio dashboard mean-variance optimization AXIOMA fundamental risk mode 11/2002–11/2018.

Portfolios	Sharpe Ratio	Info Ratio	Risk Stock Specific Effect	Risk Stock Specific Effect T-Stat	Risk Factors Effect	Risk Factors Effect T-Stat	Risk Total Effect	Risk Transaction Effect	Total Effect	Earnings Yield	Growth	Medium-Term Momentum
R3000_REG9_8TE	0.68	0.38	3.01	**2.04**	0.06	0.55	3.07	−1.20	1.88	**0.29**	−0.15	−0.21
R3000_REG8_6TE	0.60	0.18	1.86	**1.66**	−0.88	−0.24	0.98	−0.94	0.04	**−0.31**	−0.15	−0.28
R3000_CTEF_8TE	0.75	**0.52**	1.61	1.36	3.30	2.24	4.92	−2.26	2.65	**1.81**	0.07	1.41
R3000_REG8_8TE	0.51	0.06	1.77	1.36	−1.53	−0.50	0.24	−1.28	−1.03	**−0.74**	−0.18	−0.41
R3000_REG9_6TE	0.64	0.25	1.35	1.14	0.15	0.55	1.50	−1.12	0.38	**0.43**	−0.13	−0.15
R3000_CTEF_6TE	0.71	0.42	0.35	0.57	2.59	2.26	2.95	−1.55	1.39	**1.66**	0.06	1.07
R3000_CTEF_4TE	0.72	0.42	−0.02	0.20	2.03	2.73	2.02	−0.92	1.10	**1.29**	0.03	0.72
R3000_REG9_4TE	0.62	0.12	0.02	0.05	0.31	0.67	0.33	−0.55	−0.22	**0.53**	−0.11	−0.02
R3000_REG8_4TE	0.58	0.02	−0.06	−0.05	−0.11	0.17	−0.17	−0.45	−0.62	**0.10**	−0.11	−0.19
R3000_REG10_8TE	0.53	0.08	−0.42	−0.14	0.85	0.86	0.43	−1.96	−1.54	**0.61**	−0.17	0.28
R3000_REG10_4TE	0.62	0.12	−0.17	−0.17	0.52	0.89	0.35	−0.81	−0.46	**0.71**	−0.16	0.18
R3000_REG10_6TE	0.53	−0.01	−0.88	−0.62	0.53	0.68	−0.35	−1.33	−1.68	**0.67**	−0.17	0.18
R1000_REG8_6TE	0.69	0.30	2.52	**2.07**	−0.55	0.16	1.97	−0.88	1.10	**0.08**	−0.09	−0.28
R1000_REG8_8TE	0.58	0.13	2.36	1.57	−1.40	−0.18	0.96	−1.10	−0.15	**−0.03**	−0.11	−0.39
R1000_REG8_4TE	0.71	0.27	0.81	1.00	0.44	0.84	1.25	−0.43	0.82	**0.31**	−0.07	−0.21
R1000_REG9_8TE	0.58	0.15	1.25	0.99	0.07	0.59	1.32	−1.15	0.17	**0.55**	−0.15	−0.25
R1000_CTEF_4TE	0.75	0.44	0.63	0.89	1.53	2.34	2.16	−0.69	1.47	**1.18**	0.01	0.62
R1000_REG10_6TE	0.66	0.19	0.75	0.68	0.41	0.70	1.16	−0.95	0.20	**0.75**	−0.09	0.19
R1000_CTEF_6TE	0.73	0.39	0.47	0.66	2.23	2.04	2.70	−1.00	1.70	**1.62**	0.03	0.91
R1000_CTEF_8TE	0.72	0.40	0.29	0.57	2.89	2.09	3.18	−2.08	1.10	**1.72**	0.05	1.21
R1000_REG9_6TE	0.61	0.13	0.54	0.46	0.31	0.71	0.85	−1.04	−0.19	**0.57**	−0.16	−0.15
R1000_REG9F_4TE	0.67	0.19	0.10	0.21	0.73	1.16	0.83	−0.74	0.10	**0.57**	−0.07	−0.03
R1000_REG10_8TE	0.58	0.09	−0.15	0.02	0.62	0.75	0.47	−0.86	−0.39	**0.84**	−0.08	0.46
R1000_REG10_4TE	0.66	0.14	−0.34	−0.29	1.01	1.41	0.66	−0.76	−0.10	**0.71**	−0.08	0.23

Portfolios	Sharpe Ratio	Info Ratio	Risk Specific Effect	Risk Stock Effect T-Stat	Factors Effect	Risk Effect T-Stat	Total Effect	Risk Transaction Effect	Total Effect	Earnings Yield	Growth	Medium-Term Momentum
ALLXUS_CTEF_6TE	0.85	**1.45**	9.35	**6.89**	5.58	6.80	14.93	–4.16	10.77	**0.69**	–0.18	**3.25**
ALLXUS_CTEF_8TE	0.91	**1.44**	11.51	**6.60**	5.24	5.27	16.74	–4.98	11.76	**0.70**	–0.26	**4.08**
ALLXUS_CTEF_4TE	0.70	**1.26**	6.40	**5.77**	4.66	7.71	11.05	–3.07	7.98	**0.67**	–0.10	**2.05**
ALLXUS_REG10_6TE	0.65	**1.21**	4.16	**3.53**	7.23	6.53	11.39	–4.27	7.12	**0.36**	0.08	**2.22**
ALLXUS_REG10_4TE	0.49	**1.07**	2.66	**3.09**	4.67	5.85	7.33	–3.06	4.26	**0.36**	0.09	**1.27**
ALLXUS_REG10_8TE	0.70	**1.14**	4.41	**2.98**	8.72	6.12	13.13	–4.88	8.26	**0.44**	0.08	**2.87**
ALLXUS_REG8_8TE	0.39	0.45	5.53	**2.93**	5.29	4.65	10.82	–5.44	5.38	**–0.18**	0.42	**0.85**
ALLXUS_REG8_6TE	0.44	**0.61**	2.61	0.59	5.33	4.68	7.94	–4.34	3.60	**0.34**	0.11	**0.15**
ALLXUS_REG9_8TE	0.60	**0.93**	1.03	–0.78	10.85	7.01	11.89	–4.75	7.14	**0.66**	0.08	**0.95**
ALLXUS_REG9_6TE	0.56	**0.95**	1.34	–0.84	8.59	7.25	9.93	–3.92	6.01	**0.63**	0.06	**0.65**
ALLXUS_REG8_4TE	0.44	**0.82**	2.89	–0.89	3.09	3.95	5.98	–3.42	2.56	**0.30**	0.11	**–0.21**
ALLXUS_REG9_4TE	0.48	**1.02**	1.39	–2.08	5.06	6.62	6.45	–2.88	3.56	**0.50**	0.06	**0.43**

Portfolios	Sharpe Ratio	Info Ratio	Risk Stock Specific Effect	Stock Specific Effect T-Stat	Risk Factors Effect	Risk Factors Effect T-Stat	Risk Total Effect	Risk Transaction Effect	Total Effect	Earnings Yield	Growth	Medium-Term Momentum
EM_REG8_4TE	0.51	0.31	3.99	**2.38**	1.79	2.11	5.78	–2.05	3.73	**0.25**	0.26	**–0.85**
EM_REG9_4TE	0.55	0.49	3.45	**2.20**	3.28	3.60	6.73	–2.11	4.63	**0.43**	0.16	**–0.19**
EM_CTEF_8TE	0.59	**0.61**	3.54	**2.18**	5.76	3.64	9.30	–3.58	5.72	**0.87**	–0.02	**2.69**
EM_CTEF_4TE	0.58	**0.72**	3.20	**2.16**	3.84	4.42	7.04	–2.10	4.94	**0.63**	–0.09	**1.51**
EM_CTEF_6TE	0.60	**0.65**	3.67	**2.13**	4.67	4.02	8.34	–2.75	5.59	**0.80**	–0.06	**2.13**
EM_REG9_8TE	0.51	0.30	3.40	**1.73**	5.09	3.31	8.50	–3.62	4.88	**0.38**	0.21	**0.25**

(Continued)

Table 6. (*Continued*)

Portfolios	Sharpe Ratio	Info Ratio	Risk Stock Specific Effect	Stock Specific Effect T-Stat	Risk Factors Effect	Risk Factors Effect T-Stat	Risk Total Effect	Risk Transaction Effect	Total Effect	Earnings Yield	Growth	Medium-Term Momentum
EM_REG8_6TE	0.44	0.06	3.30	1.64	2.32	2.17	5.63	–2.79	2.83	**0.13**	0.32	**–0.99**
EM_REG10_4TE	0.54	0.45	2.25	1.58	4.06	4.24	6.31	–1.92	4.39	**0.44**	0.17	**0.53**
EM_REG9_6TE	0.48	0.22	2.62	1.54	4.37	3.49	6.99	–2.80	4.19	**0.41**	0.18	**–0.09**
EM_REG8_8TE	0.43	0.10	3.37	1.36	2.59	2.27	5.96	–3.52	2.44	**0.00**	0.41	**–0.78**
EM_REG10_6TE	0.52	0.33	1.33	1.07	5.63	4.17	6.96	–2.96	4.00	**0.41**	0.23	**0.93**
EM_REG10_8TE	0.49	0.24	0.30	0.59	6.34	3.68	6.64	–3.54	3.10	**0.39**	0.24	**1.32**
JAPAN_REG8_8TE	0.56	**0.54**	5.64	**4.00**	–0.18	0.44	5.46	–2.24	3.26	–0.39	0.28	–0.75
JAPAN_REG8_6TE	0.54	**0.51**	4.73	**3.74**	–0.23	0.20	4.50	–1.49	3.04	–0.34	0.25	–0.72
JAPAN_REG8_4TE	0.50	**0.46**	2.75	**2.88**	0.17	0.63	2.92	–0.79	2.17	–0.16	0.18	–0.58
JAPAN_REG9_8TE	0.42	0.28	2.14	**1.65**	0.74	1.34	2.87	–2.00	0.95	–0.05	0.22	–0.44
JAPAN_REG9_4TE	0.44	0.31	1.54	1.59	0.55	1.45	2.09	–0.82	1.32	0.05	0.13	–0.33
JAPAN_REG9_6TE	0.41	0.25	1.83	1.50	0.44	1.04	2.27	–1.35	0.98	–0.03	0.19	–0.44
JAPAN_REG10_8TE	0.38	0.19	0.23	0.44	1.48	1.98	1.71	–1.80	–0.01	–0.02	0.19	0.11
JAPAN_REG10_6TE	0.37	0.16	–0.13	0.14	1.40	2.01	1.26	–1.48	–0.16	0.03	0.19	0.07
JAPAN_CTEF_8TE	0.35	0.15	–0.93	–0.01	2.20	2.50	1.28	–6.73	–5.40	0.56	–0.25	1.29
JAPAN_CTEF_6TE	0.12	0.09	–0.90	–0.18	2.32	3.13	1.42	–3.87	–2.38	0.56	–0.18	1.19
JAPAN_CTEF_4TE	0.30	0.19	–0.82	–0.38	1.96	3.97	1.13	–1.35	–0.17	0.53	–0.13	0.96
JAPAN_REG10_4TE	0.35	0.07	–0.97	–0.76	1.39	2.70	0.42	–1.06	–0.58	0.08	0.11	0.08

Portfolios	Sharpe Ratio	Info Ratio	Risk Stock Specific Effect	Risk Stock Specific Effect T-Stat	Risk Factors Effect	Risk Factors Effect T-Stat	Risk Total Effect	Risk Transaction Effect	Total Effect	Earnings Yield	Growth	Medium-Term Momentum
CHINAA_CTEF_4TE	0.60	**1.23**	7.12	**6.75**	2.22	6.32	9.35	−1.74	7.68	**0.34**	−0.08	0.55
CHINAA_CTEF_6TE	0.59	**1.05**	7.30	**5.16**	2.54	5.31	9.84	−2.39	7.52	**0.34**	−0.12	0.78
CHINAA_CTEF_8TE	0.57	**0.95**	7.19	**4.87**	2.75	4.98	9.94	−2.61	7.40	**0.35**	−0.13	0.89
CHINAA_REG10_4TE	0.51	**0.87**	4.62	**4.43**	2.31	5.60	6.93	−1.78	5.19	**0.22**	0.19	−0.06
CHINAA_REG9_4TE	0.44	**0.54**	3.45	**3.41**	1.42	3.77	4.88	−1.66	3.24	**0.17**	0.19	−0.51
CHINAA_REG10_6TE	0.52	**0.72**	4.77	**3.31**	3.06	5.51	7.84	−2.51	5.39	**0.28**	0.24	−0.05
CHINAA_REG8_4TE	0.42	0.47	3.17	**3.29**	1.29	3.29	4.47	−1.65	2.83	**0.12**	0.20	−0.74
CHINAA_REG10_8TE	0.50	**0.63**	4.38	**2.89**	3.18	5.05	7.56	−2.79	4.83	**0.30**	0.26	−0.01
CHINAA_REG8_6TE	0.41	0.39	3.45	**2.67**	1.49	2.84	4.94	−2.41	2.58	**0.11**	0.28	−0.91
CHINAA_REG8_8TE	0.41	0.37	3.65	**2.56**	1.64	2.75	5.30	−2.67	2.67	**0.10**	0.33	−0.91
CHINAA_REG9_8TE	0.41	0.38	3.40	**2.40**	1.76	3.06	5.16	−2.63	2.57	**0.18**	0.27	−0.55
CHINAA_REG9_6TE	0.42	0.42	3.18	**2.37**	1.82	3.52	5.01	−2.37	2.69	**0.18**	0.24	−0.58

REG8 = OIF99 Regression(EP,BP,CP,SP,REP,RBP,RCP,RSP)
REG9 = OIF99 Regression(EP,BP,CP,SP,REP,RBP,RCP,RSP,CTEF)
REG10 = OIF99 Regression(EP,BP,CP,SP,REP,RBP,RCP,RSP,CTEF,PM71)
BOLD IRs exceed 0.50
BOLD Risk Stock Specific T-Stat is statistically significant

Total returns and Stock Specific returns in the non-U.S. universe. The CTEF, REG8, REG9, and REG10 MV portfolios produce statistically significant portfolio Active and Specific returns. If one uses the largest 5000 market-capitalized non-U.S. stocks for the corresponding period, the CTEF, REG8, REG9, and REG10 MV portfolios produce statistically significant portfolio Active and Specific Returns. However, only CTEF produces higher Specific Returns than in the index constituent universe. The risk index returns for the size and value factors create higher Active Returns in the larger non-U.S. universe for the 2002–11/2018 time period. In the Russell 3000 (R3) universe, only the ranked CTEF portfolios produced statistically significant portfolio Active and Specific Returns. The R3 EP, REG8, REG9, and REG10 MV portfolios did not produce consistently statistically significant portfolio Active returns and significant Stock Specific Returns for the 1/2003–11/2018 time period. Only the REG8 and REG9 produced statistically significant stock selection at 6% and 8%targeted tracking errors, respectively. In the Russell 1000 (R1) universe, only the ranked CTEF portfolios produced statistically significant portfolio Active Returns. The important result of the empirical update is that CTEF, REG8, REG9, and REG10 MV portfolios produce statistically significant portfolio Active Returns and significant Stock Specific Returns for the 12/2002–11/2018 time period in foreign markets.[24] No U.S. portfolio should be run

[24]Before closing the discussion of MV analysis, it is important to respond to Brennan and Lo (2012) whose article on portfolio optimization will be regarded as a modern classic. In a footnote, Brennan and Lo repeat comments of practitioners who claim the MV analysis produces absurd solutions. It is our experience, with our variables, that this is not a valid claim. A simple test was performed for the January 2003 to December 2016 time period. We produce monthly ranked CTEF variables for the Russell 3000 (R3) and World Investable ex-U.S. (XUS) index constituents. We prefer to buy higher ranked stocks (85–99) and sell those with lower scores, such as 70. The R3 and XUS models correctly rank-order stocks; that is, to buy R3 stocks exceeding 85, hold them in equally weighted portfolios until their monthly CTEF score falls below 70, produced an annualized Active Return of 6.88%, composed of a highly statistically significant stock selection (Specific Returns). A similar test to buy XUS stocks exceeding 85, which holds them in equally weighted portfolios until their monthly CTEF score falls below 70, produced annualized Active Returns of 8.15% (see Table 30.11 from the book by Brennan and Lo (2012). We refer to the "buy, hold, sell" test as the Boolean Signal test. The Boolean Signal "buy at 85 and sell at 70" XUS and R3 portfolios are analyzed in the Axioma attribution system

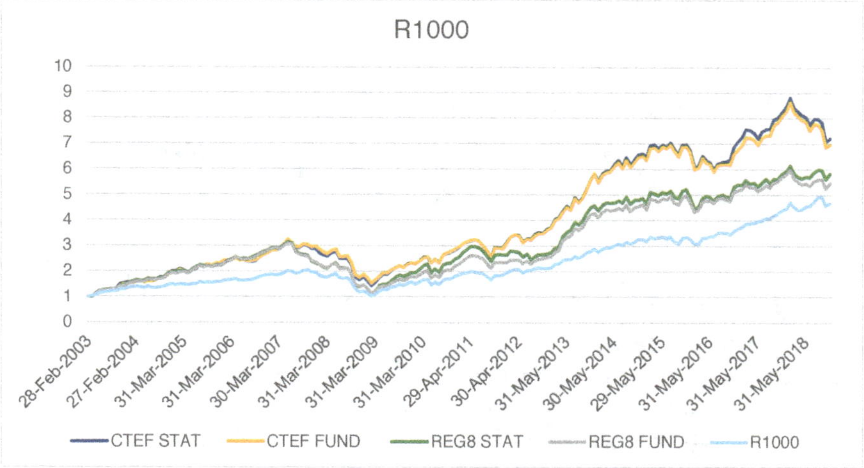

Fig. 1(a). Large cap U.S. stock portfolios.

with a tracking error of less than 6% if one wants to outperform the market.[25] Moreover, as reported by Guerard *et al.* (2015) and Beheshti (2015), the CTEF and REG9 Efficient Frontier portfolios produced with the Axioma Statistical Risk Model outperform the Axioma Fundamental Risk Model Efficient Frontier portfolios (see Figs. 1(a)–1(e)).

---

and produce highly statistically significant Active Returns and Specific Returns for the 2003–2016 period as well as the 2012–2016 post-Global Financial Crisis period. In fact, in the post-GFC time period, all ranked CTEF Active returns are Specific returns. In the 2003–2016 time period, all R3-ranked CTEF Active Returns (6.88%) are Specific Returns (7.24%); whereas the majority of non-U.S.-ranked CTEF Active Returns (8.15%) are Specific Returns (5.02%). We believe that the Boolean Signal test confirms the validity of MV application. The world is changing; but as bottom-up quantitative stock pickers, we report that MV models which were statistically significant for 1990–2001 in Guerard and Mark (2003) continue to be statistically significant in 1996–2016, 2003–2017, and the post-Global Financial Crisis period. Models cannot be perfect, but they can, and for practitioners, should be statistically significant.

[25]Another means to analyze the updated non-U.S. and R3 portfolios is to directly compare Information Ratios, Sharpe Ratios, and Draw Downs, DD. Draw-downs do not vary as much as one might expect from varying targeted tracking errors. In non-U.S. portfolios, the Sharpe Ratios and IRs are maximized at a targeted 6% level with CTEF and 8% with REG9. In the U.S., the maximum TE of 8% maximizes the Sharpe Ratios and Information Ratios.

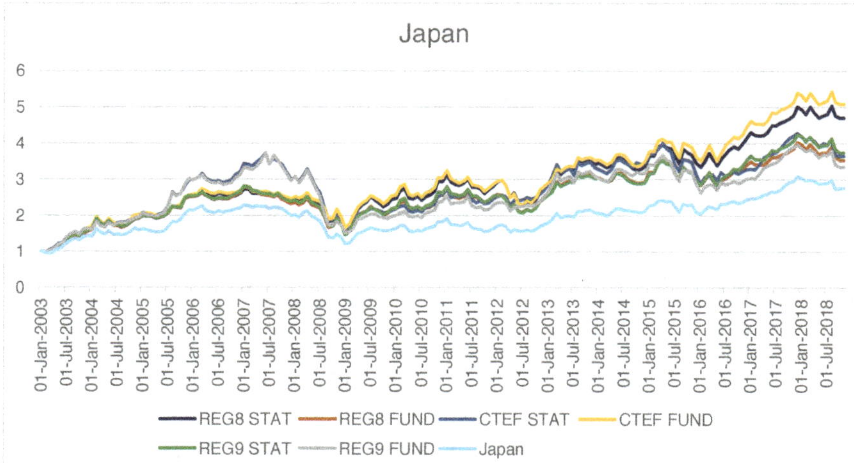

Fig. 1(b). MSCI Japan stock portfolios.

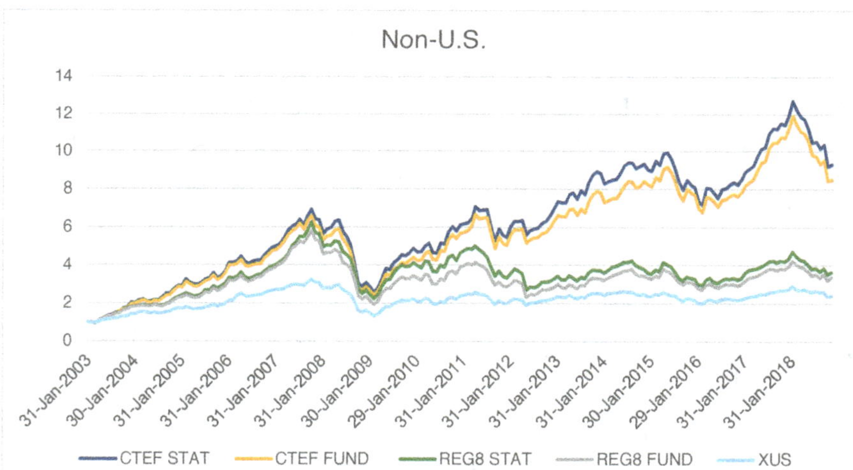

Fig. 1(c). MSCI non-U.S. stock portfolios.

We have shown how forecasted earnings acceleration produces a highly statistically significant stock selection in non-U.S. and U.S. stock universes. CTEF, REG8, REG9, and REG10 models optimized

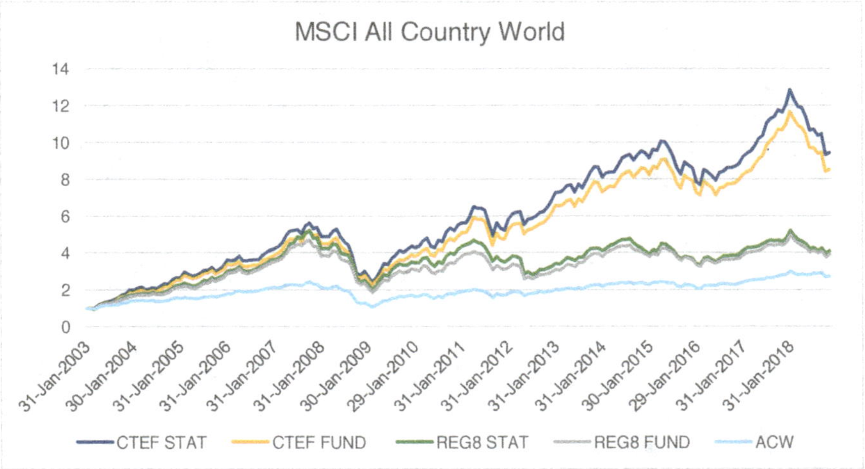

Fig. 1(d). MSCI all-world (Global) stock portfolios.

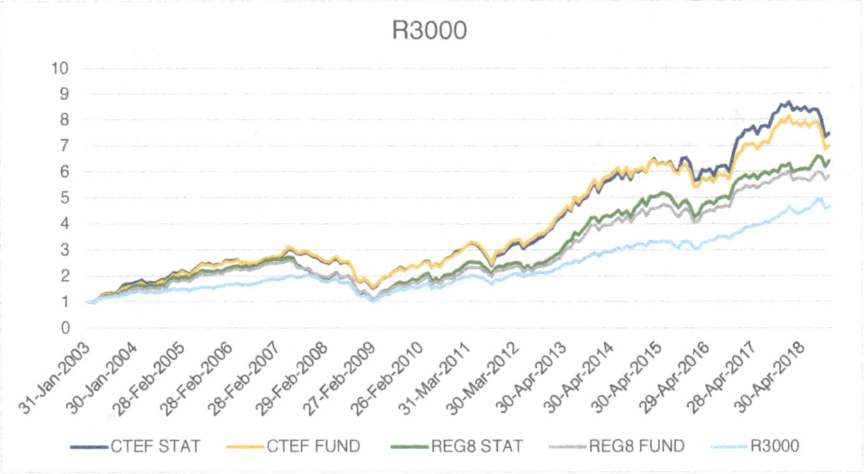

Fig. 1(e). Russell 3000 U.S. stock portfolios.

portfolios produce higher Active and Specific Returns in non-U.S. stocks, whereas only CTEF consistently produces statistically significant Specific Returns in U.S. The non-U.S. CTEF and REG9 models outperform in 80% of the years, post-publication of 2003. The U.S. CTEF and REG9 models outperform in 60% of the years.

Table 7. Donut portfolio analysis time period: 12/2002–11/2018.

Portfolios	Risk Stock Specific Effect	Risk Stock Specific Effect T-Stat	Risk Factors Effect	Risk Factors Effect T-Stat	Risk Total Effect	Risk Transaction Effect	Total Effect	Earnings Yield	Growth	Medium-Term Momentum
ACW_DONUT_CTEF_STAT_6TE	4.43	**3.65**	3.00	**3.11**	7.42	–3.96	3.46	0.69	–0.11	2.67
EM_DONUT_CTEF_STAT_6TE	1.82	1.94	4.37	**3.94**	6.19	–2.95	3.25	0.59	–0.03	2.09
XUS_DONUT_CTEF_STAT_6TE	3.14	**3.27**	4.18	**3.73**	7.32	–4.56	2.76	0.72	–0.13	2.63
EM_DONUT_CTEF_FUND_6TE	1.49	1.76	4.00	**4.01**	5.49	–2.83	2.66	0.60	–0.03	2.00
ACW_DONUT_CTEF_FUND_6TE	3.93	**3.17**	2.19	**2.66**	6.12	–3.76	2.36	0.66	–0.16	2.53
XUS_DONUT_CTEF_FUND_6TE	2.46	**2.72**	3.82	**3.48**	6.28	–4.34	1.94	0.72	–0.18	2.48
EM_DONUT_REG9_STAT_6TE	0.27	0.79	4.57	**3.76**	4.83	–3.15	1.68	0.27	0.25	0.06
EM_DONUT_REG9_FUND_6TE	0.31	0.71	3.82	**3.60**	4.14	–2.92	1.22	0.27	0.20	–0.03
XUS_DONUT_REG9_STAT_6TE	0.51	0.58	2.85	**2.87**	3.35	–4.03	–0.68	0.21	0.06	0.30
ACW_DONUT_REG9_STAT_6TE	–0.50	–0.21	2.78	**2.47**	2.29	–3.51	–1.22	0.15	0.01	0.42
XUS_DONUT_REG9_FUND_6TE	0.18	0.51	2.30	**2.39**	2.48	–3.86	–1.38	0.19	0.06	0.23
ACW_DONUT_REG9_FUND_6TE	–0.57	–0.27	2.34	**2.29**	1.77	–3.21	–1.43	0.17	–0.03	0.29

Portfolios	Risk Stock Specific Effect	Risk Stock Specific Effect T-Stat	Risk Factors Effect	Risk Factors Effect T-Stat	Risk Total Effect	Risk Transaction Effect	Total Effect	Earnings Yield	Growth	Medium-Term Momentum
R3000_DONUT_CTEF_STAT_6TE	0.38	0.54	3.39	**2.33**	3.78	–1.84	1.94	1.53	0.00	1.27
R3000_DONUT_CTEF_FUND_6TE	0.56	0.74	2.71	**2.22**	3.27	–1.52	1.74	1.49	0.04	1.06
R3000_DONUT_REG9_STAT_6TE	2.43	1.79	0.19	0.59	2.62	–1.85	0.77	0.23	–0.17	–0.25
R3000_DONUT_REG9_FUND_6TE	1.23	1.06	0.40	0.68	1.63	–1.43	0.20	0.36	–0.14	–0.14

BOLD Denotes Statistically significant at 5% Level.

We modify the Domowitz and Moghe (2018) "Donut" strategy to accommodate the five largest market-capitalized stocks within the MSCI non-U.S., Global, and Russell 3000 index constituents to become the "holes" in the donut. We optimize the portfolios such that the sum of the market-capitalized weights of the top five stocks is within 2% of the sum of the respective stock benchmark weights. The remaining stocks that are optimized within a traditional Markowitz MV are within 3% of the index weights. Donuts are not an optimal solution compared to traditional optimization; however, there is no lesser possibility of portfolio implementation shortfall. The reader is referred to Table 7.

The CTEF and REG9 Efficient Frontier Donut portfolios produced with the Axioma Statistical Risk Model outperform the Axioma Fundamental Risk Model Efficient Frontier Donut portfolios (see Fig. 2). In the real world of asset management, it may well be better to be near-optimal in portfolio construction and its implementation than optimal in portfolio construction and avoid needless debate regarding the relative risk of large benchmark weight stocks.

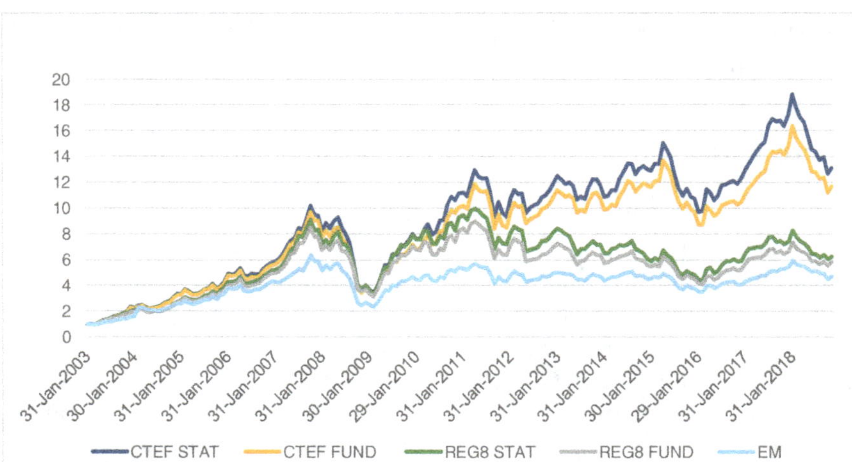

Fig. 2. MSCI emerging markets stock portfolios.

5. Summary and Conclusions

We report that an earnings forecasting model continues to produce statistically significant asset selection in global stocks, 2003–11/2018. Regression models of fundamental factors and earnings forecasting factors continue to enhance portfolio returns. Momentum enhances portfolio returns primarily in non-U.S. equity markets. We report that the Markowitz MV optimization is particularly efficient for producing efficient frontiers using a forecasted earnings acceleration model, CTEF, and a composite, robust regression-based 10-factor model, REG10. Have markets and stock selection models changed since Bloch *et al.* (1993) and Guerard and Mark (2003) published their studies? No, CTEF, REG9, and REG10 still dominate most other models. The authors believe that financial anomalies exist, persist, and most likely will exist. We report all results produced by the FactSet Research Systems, Inc., platform. Are markets efficient? No, not completely, but significant databases and computers are required to outperform.

Acknowledgment

The authors thank Ross Sharp, formerly of FactSet, who created the R-robust regression script.

References

Barillas, F. and Shanken, J. (2018). Comparing asset pricing models. *Journal of Finance* **73**, 715–755.

Beheshti, B. (2015). A note on the integration of the alpha alignment factor and earnings forecasting models in producing more efficient Markowitz frontiers. *International Journal of Forecasting* **31**, 582–585.

Blin, J. M., Bender, S., and Guerard, J. B., Jr. (1997). Earnings forecasts, revisions and momentum in the estimation of efficient market-neutral Japanese and U.S. portfolios. In A. Chen (Ed.), *Research in Finance* **15**.

Bloch, M., Guerard Jr., J. B., Markowitz, H. M., Todd, P., and Xu, G. -L. (1993). A comparison of some aspects of the U.S. and Japanese equity markets. *Japan and the World Economy* **5**, 3–26.

Borkovec, M., Domowitz, I., Kiernan, B., and Serbin, V. (2010). Portfolio optimization and the cost of trading. *Journal of Investing* **19**, 63–76.

Brennan, T. J. and Lo, A. (2010). Impossible frontiers. *Management Science* **56**, 905–923.

Brush, J. (2001). *Price momentum: A twenty-year research effort.* Columbine Newsletter.

Bruce, B. and Epstein, C. B. (1994). *The Handbook of Corporate Earnings Analysis.* Chicago: Probus Publishing Company.

Chan, L. K. C., Hamao, Y., and Lakonishok, J. (1991). Fundamentals and stock returns in Japan. *Journal of Finance* **46**, 1739–1764.

Chu, Y., Hirschleifer, D., and Ma, L. (2017). The casual effect of limits on arbitrage on asset pricing models. *NBER Working Paper No.* 24144. http://www.nber.org/papers/w24144.

Conrad, J. and Kaul, G. (1989). Mean reversion in short-horizon expected returns. *Review of Financial Studies* **2**, 225–240.

Conrad, J. and Kaul, G. (1993). Long-term market overreaction or biases in compound returns. *Journal of Finance* **59**, 39–63.

Conrad, J. and Kaul, G. (1998). An anatomy of trading strategies. *Review of Financial Studies* **11**, 489–519.

Cootner, P. (1964). *The Random Character of Stock Market Prices.* Cambridge: MIT Press.

Dimson, E. (1988). *Stock Market Anomalies.* Cambridge: Cambridge University Press.

Domowitz, I. and Moghe, A. (2018). Donuts: A picture of optimization applied to fundamental portfolios. *Journal of Portfolio Management* **44**, 103–113.

Elton, E. J. and Gruber, M. J. (1972). *Security Analysis and Portfolio Analysis.* Englewood Cliffs: Prentice-Hall, Inc.

Elton, E. J., Gruber, M. J., and Gultekin, M. (1981). Expectations and share prices. *Management Science* **27**, 975–987.

Elton, E. J. and Gruber, M. J. (1980). *Modern Portfolio Theory and Investment Analysis.* John Wiley & Sons, Inc.

Elton, E. J., Gruber, M. J., Brown, S. J., and Goetzman, W. N. (2007). *Modern Portfolio Theory and Investment Analysis.* John Wiley & Sons, Inc., Seventh Edition.

Fama, E. F. (1991). Efficient capital markets II. *Journal of Finance* **46**, 1575–1617.

Fama, E. F. and French, K. R. (1992). Cross-sectional variation in expected stock returns. *Journal of Finance* **47**, 427–465.

Fama, E. F. and French, K. R. (2008). Dissecting anomalies. *Journal of Finance* **63**, 1653–1678.

Grinold, R. and Kahn, R. (1999). *Active Portfolio Management.* New York: McGraw-Hill/Irwin.

Graham, B. and Dodd, D. (1934). *Security Analysis: Principles and Technique* (1st Ed.). New York: McGraw-Hill Book Company.

Graham, B., Dodd, D., and Cottle, S. (1962). *Security Analysis: Principles and Technique*. New York: McGraw-Hill Book Company, 4th edition.

Graham, B. (1973). *The Intelligent Investor*. New York: Harper & Row.

Guerard, J. B., Jr. and Stone, B. K. (1992). Composite forecasting of annual corporate earnings. In A. Chen (Ed.), *Research in Finance* **10**.

Guerard, J. B., Jr., Gultekin, M., and Stone, B. K. (1997). The role of fundamental data and analysts' earnings breadth, forecasts, and revisions in the creation of efficient portfolios. In A. Chen (Ed.) *Research in Finance* **15**, 69–91.

Guerard, J. B., Jr. and Mark, A. (2003). The optimization of efficient portfolios: The case for an R&D quadratic term. In *Research in Finance* **20**, A. Chen, editor, 213–247.

Guerard, J. B., Jr., Markowitz, H. M., and Xu, G. (2014). The role of effective corporate decisions in the creation of efficient portfolios. *IBM Journal of Research and Development* **58**, 6.1–6.11.

Guerard, J. B., Jr., Rachev, R. T., and Shao, B. (2013). Efficient global portfolios: big data and investment universes. *IBM Journal of Research and Development* **57**(3), Paper 11.1–11.11.

Guerard, J. B., Jr., Markowitz, H. M., and Xu, G. (2015). Earnings forecasting in a global stock selection model and efficient portfolio construction and management. *International Journal of Forecasting* **31**, 550–560.

Guerard, J. B., Jr. and Markowitz, H. M. (2018). The existence and persistence of financial anomalies: What have you done for me lately? *Financial Planning Review* **1**(3–4), https://doi.org/10.1002/cfp2.1022.

Guerard, J. B., Markowitz, H. M. and Wang, E. (2018). Global portfolio construction with emphasis on conflicting strategies to maximize stockholder wealth, *Annals of Operations Research* 267, 203–219.

Guerard, J. B., Jr. and Mark, A. (2020). Earnings forecasts and revisions, price momentum, and fundamental data: Further explorations of financial anomalies, in C. F. Lee, Editor, *Handbook of Financial Econometrics*. Singapore, World Scientific Handbook in Financial Economics, forthcoming.

Gunst, R. F., Webster, J. T., and Mason, R. L. (1976). A comparison of least squares and latent root regression estimators. *Technometrics* **18**, 75–83.

Harvey, C. R., Lin, Y., and Zhu, H. (2016). The cross-section of expected returns. *Review of Financial Studies* **29**(1), 5–69.

Haugen, R. A. and Baker, N. (1996). Communality in the determinants of expected results. *Journal of Financial Economics* **41**, 401–440.

Hawkins, E. H., Chamberlain, S. C., and Daniel, W. E. (1984). Earnings expectations and security prices. *Financial Analysts Journal* **40**(3), 24–38.

Hochbaum, D. S. (2018). Machine learning and data mining with combinatorial optimization algorithms. *INFORMS Tutorials in Operations Research.* Published online: 19 Oct. 2018: 109–129.

Hong, H., Kubik, J. D., and Solomon, A. (2000). Security analysts' career concerns and the herding of earnings forecasts. *Rand Journal of Economics* **31**, 121–144.

Hong, H. and Kubik, J. D. (2003). Analyzing the analysts: Career concerns and biased earnings forecasts. *Journal of Finance* **58**, 313–351.

ITG (2007). *ITG ACE — Agency Cost Estimator: A Model Description*, Unpublished ITG Working Paper.

Jacobs, B. I. and Levy, K. (1988). Disentangling equity return regularities: New insights and investment opportunities. *Financial Analysts Journal* **44**, 18–43.

Jacobs, B. I. and Levy, K. (2017). *Equity Management: The Art and Science of Modern Quantitative Investing.* New York: McGraw-Hill. Second Edition.

Jagadeesh, N. and Titman, S. (1993). Returns to buying winners and selling losers: Implications for stock market efficiency. *Journal of Finance* **48**, 65–91.

Konno, H. and Yamazaki, H. (1991). Mean-absolute deviation portfolio optimization and its application to the Tokyo stock market. *Management Science* **37**, 519–537.

Korajczyk, R. A. and Sadka, R. (2004). Are momentum profits robust to trading costs? *Journal of Finance* **59**, 1039–1082.

Lakonishok, J., Shleifer, A., and Vishny, R. W. (1994). Contrarian investment, extrapolation and risk. *Journal of Finance* **49**, 1541–1578.

Latane, H. A., Tuttle, D. and Jones, C. P. (1975). *Security Analysis and Portfolio Management*, New York: Roland Press, revised edition

Levy, H. (1999). *Introduction to Investments* Cincinnati: South-Western College Publishing. Second Edition.

Levy, H. (2012). *The Capital Asset Pricing Model in the 21st Century.* Cambridge: Cambridge University Press.

Lintner, J. (1965). The valuation of risk assets and the selection of risky investments in stock portfolios and capital budgets, *Review of Economics and Statistics* 47, 51–68.

Lo, A. W., Mamaysky, H., and Wang, J. (2000). Foundations of technical analysis: Computational algorithms, statistical inference, and empirical implementation. *Journal of Finance* **60**, 1705–1764.

Lo, A. (2017). *Adaptive Markets.* Princeton: Princeton University Press.

Malkiel, B. (1996). *A Random Walk Down Wall Street* (6th Edn.). New York: W.W. Norton & Company.

Markowitz, H. M. (1952). Portfolio selection. *Journal of Finance* **7**, 77–91.

Markowitz, H. M. (1959). *Portfolio Selection: Efficient Diversification of Investment.* Cowles Foundation Monograph No. 16. New York, John Wiley & Sons.

Markowitz, H. (1987). *Mean-Variance Analysis in Portfolio Choice and Capital Markets.* London: Basil Blackwell.

Markowitz, H. M. (1976). Investment in the long run: New evidence for an old rule. *Journal of Finance* **31**, 1273–1286.

Maronna, R. A., Martin, R. D., and Yohai, V. J. (2006). *Robust Statistics; Theory and Methods.* New York: Wiley.

Maronna, R. A., Martin, R. D., Yohai, V. J., and Salibian-Barrera, M. (2019). *Robust Statistics; Theory and Methods (with R).* New York: Wiley.

Mossin, J. (1966). "Equilibrium in a Capital Asset Market." *Econometrica* 34, 768–783.

Mossin, J. (1973). *Theory of Financial Markets.* Englewood Cliffs, NJ: Prentice-Hall, Inc.

Muller, P. (1993). Empirical tests of biases in equity portfolio optimization. In S. A. Zenios (Ed.), *Financial Optimization.* Cambridge: Cambridge University Press.

Ramnath, S., Rock, S., and Shane, P. (2008). The financial analyst forecasting literature: A taxonomy with suggestions for further research. *International Journal of Forecasting* **24**, 34–75.

Rosenberg, B. and McKibben, W. (1973). The reduction of systematic and specific risk in common stocks. *Journal of Financial and Quantitative Analysis* **8**, 317–333.

Rosenberg, B. and Marathe, V. (1979). Tests of capital asset pricing hypotheses. In H. Levy (Ed.), *Research in Finance,* **1**.

Rudd, A. and Rosenberg, B. (1979). Realistic portfolio optimization. In E. Elton and M. J. Gruber (Eds.), *Portfolio Theory, 25 Years After.* Amsterdam: North-Holland.

Rudd, A. and Clasing, H. K. (1982). *Modern Portfolio Theory: The Principles of Investment Management.* Homewood, IL: Dow-Jones Irwin.

Sharpe, W. F. (1963). A simplified model for portfolio analysis. *Management Science* **9**, 277–293.

Sharpe, W. F. (1964). Capital asset prices: A theory of market equilibrium under conditions of risk. *Journal of Finance* **19**, 425–442.

Wheeler, L. B. (1994). Changes in consensus earnings estimates and their impact on stock returns. In B. Bruce and C. B. Epstein (Eds.), *The Handbook of Corporate Earnings Analysis* (Chicago: Probus).

Ziemba, W.T. and S. Schwartz. 1992. *Invest Japan.* Chicago: Probus.

https://doi.org/10.1142/9789811222634_0007

Chapter 7

The Hillcrest Management Sentiment Indicator

Brian Bruce

CEO & CIO, Hillcrest Asset Management, USA

Douglas Stark

Managing Director, Hillcrest Asset Management, USA

The advent of big data has created new opportunities for money managers. In the field of earnings expectations big data will fuel the next leap forward in modeling. The first breakthrough in the field was the creation of quantitative models using expectations of future earnings collected from analysts. The earnings surprise model was the first model to take advantage by comparing expectations to actual earnings. Next came the earnings revision models which looked at how estimates changed over time. Both proved highly predictive of future firm performance. Models since then have been limited to manipulating the data collected by vendors and put into databases. Big data allows money managers to bypass the data vendors and collect information directly from the source. In the case of earnings expectations, managers can get information directly from company management in the form of earnings call transcripts. This information can be processed by the manager to create signals that are as powerful as the original earnings surprise and earnings revision signals.

Keywords: text reading, big data, earnings surprise, guidance, behavior, quant

Brian and Doug were first introduced to investing using behavioral concepts in 1990 at the State Street. They joined at a time when new research was being done to revamp the global forecasting model.

Besides the usual valuation data, the team was starting to look at I/B/E/S estimates. Estimate data had been successfully integrated into the U.S. active management process the previous year. We built what is likely the first global earnings revision model. Earnings revision models were the first use of behavioral concepts in money management, but it took us another 8 years to realize it and understand what behavioral finance was.

By 1994, Brian collected the abundance of articles and created *The Handbook of Corporate Earnings Analysis*. The handbook was the first book to address the topic of earnings estimates and included articles from the leading thinkers in quantitative management. One of the speakers at the final Corporate Earnings Analysis Seminar was Mark Bradshaw, an accounting professor from Harvard Business School. After the seminar, Mark and Brian met and decided that the time was right for a behavioral book that addressed the use of earnings and earnings estimate data in picking stocks. We chronicled the field of using behavioral data in our 2004 publication, *Analysts, Lies and Statistics*, which went on to become required reading for all new analysts at *Morningstar*. The book covered popular issues regarding the use of earnings and earnings estimate data in picking stocks. Since then, the number of people using estimate data has grown from a small group of fanatics to the mainstream investment community.

Initially, investors looked at earnings revision data over time. Estimates going back 6 months had power. Then as more investors started to follow revisions, the timeframe became shorter. By the mid-2000s, most investors were looking at only the most recent informational cluster, i.e. the revisions since the last public earnings announcement by the company. As the timeframe shortened and all the quants started to look at the same data, the crowding in these factors caused them to be underproductive. The quant meltdown that happened in the late 2000s was caused due to the following reasons:

1. No style ever works all the time including quants. Quants worked well in the mid-2000s and attracted lots of assets. By 2007, a lot of aspects were being managed by quants that when the period of underperformance hit, it hit a lot of managers and assets at the same time.
2. The main reason for many quants to fail is that they believe they can model themselves out of any problem. Different factors drove performance in the last half of 2008 and first quarter of 2009 versus the last three quarters of 2009. What is the traditional quant solution? Rotate quant model factors faster. This totally ignores whether or not you can predict which factors will work going forward.
3. Quants rely on historical data to make their decisions. This causes them to fall victim to the behavioral bias of framing. Framing refers to perception of a situation being based on how information is presented. How did framing affect the quants? One way is the use of quantitative metrics to control risk in quant portfolios. A well-known, enhanced index manager used history-based metrics to predict that their portfolio returns would be unlikely to fall by more than 1.5% relative to their benchmark. Instead, they underperformed by over 4%. How did these tools to control risk fail? When you frame results based on how information is presented, risk measures like expected tracking error appear to give probabilities for the future. The failure occurs when the future is different from the past.

The response for many quants was to look for data that not everyone had access to. Conveniently at this time, the available data were expanding (see Fig. 1).

This data growth allowed quants to find data that was not in traditional investment databases. Firms started to adopt these data (known as big data) at a very quick pace. From 2015 to 2017, usage of big data went from under 20% to over 50% (see Fig. 2).

Using data not in databases or using data in a unique way is how we have been able to thrive in this fast-changing industry.

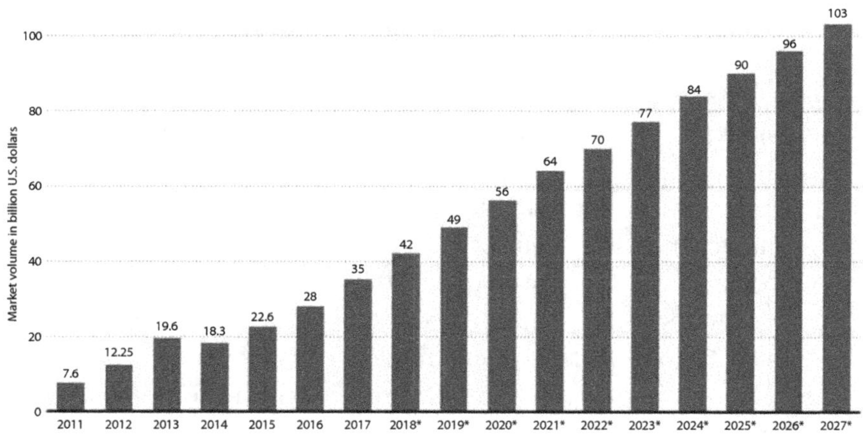

Fig. 1. Big data market size revenue forecast worldwide from 2011 to 2027 (in billion U.S. dollars).

1. Earnings Surprise

When we started Hillcrest, we made a decision to not include earnings surprise as a factor in our investment process. Earnings surprise had been a staple of many investment strategies for years. The logic of this factor is excellent. When companies did better than expectations, it was a sign that the company's prospects were improving and would lead to increased revisions and subsequent positive earnings surprises in the future. It was also considered a sign the company was doing well and that management was positive about the future of the firm.

Not surprisingly, the behavioral result was that company management noticed the stock price benefit of a positive earnings surprise and started managing the earnings to create them. The result was that earnings surprise quit having a significant informational benefit to portfolio managers, and any surprise could either be the result of true improvement in the company or just accounting tricks to

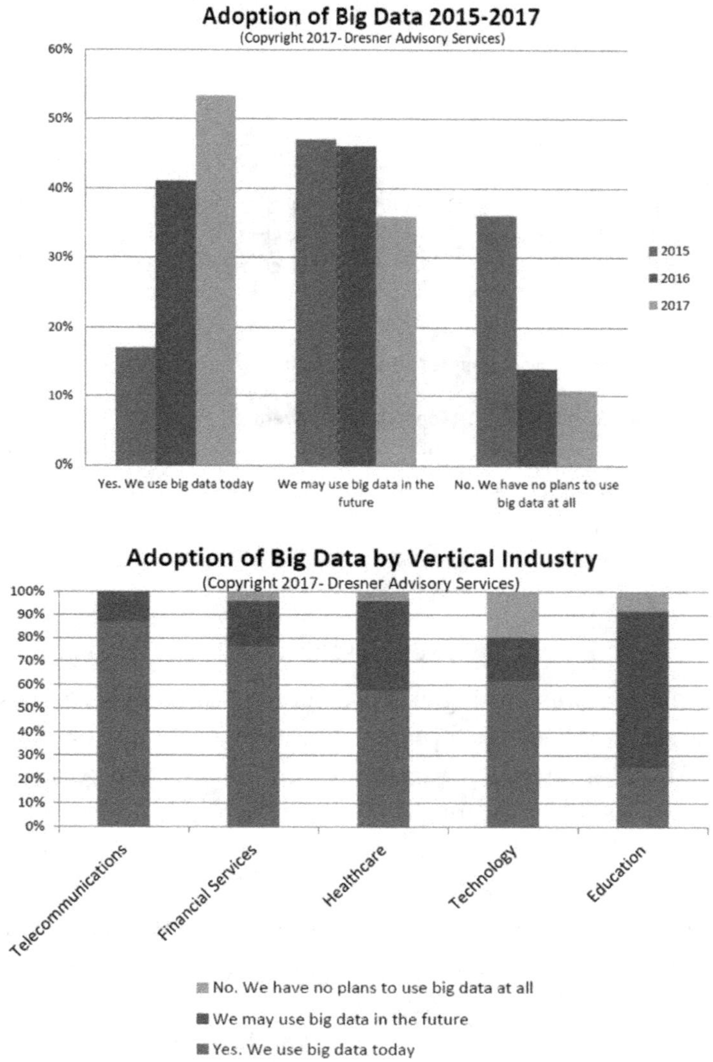

Fig. 2. Adoption of big data.

increase earnings. Thus, Hillcrest avoided the use of earnings surprise in our investment process. Figure 3 shows that earnings surprise measured as SUE added no value over the 8 years ending Q4 2015.

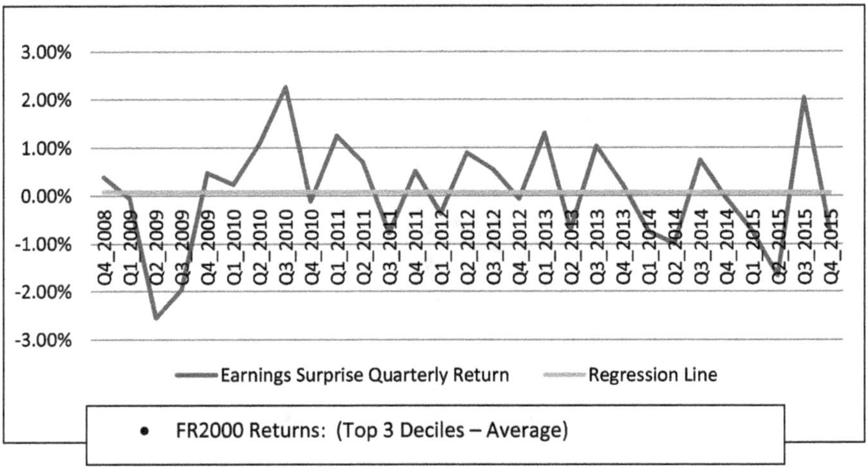

Fig. 3. Quarterly returns for earnings surprise (volatility with little return). *Source*: Hillcrest Asset Management.

During this period, we began noticing the following:

1. The market was paying more attention to sales surprises than earnings surprises. It became apparent that the market reaction to sales surprises was more important than earnings surprises. This was possibly due to the fact that sales are harder to manipulate and thus are a better evidence of the company's situation.
2. Our fundamental analysis often linked companies that had a series of positive earnings and sales surprises. These were the companies that were the best long-term investments for our strategy. This was in contrast to most managers who focused exclusively on the most recent data. For our analysts, a series of consecutive beats was evidence of the quality of management and the popularity of their products.
3. If companies changed guidance concurrently with earnings announcements, the reaction to the guidance superseded any surprise. This was particularly noticeable when guidance and the surprise were in opposite directions.

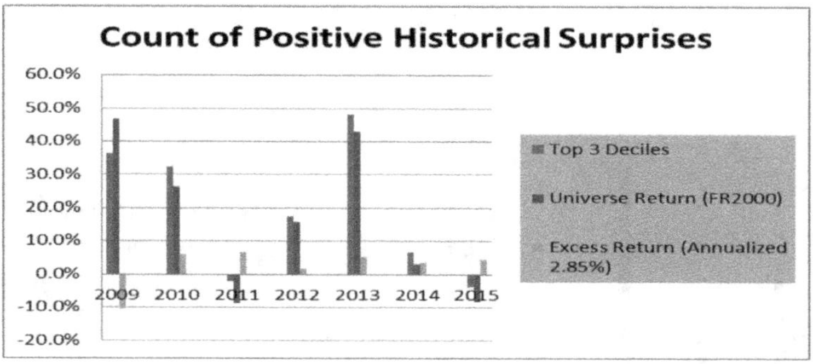

Fig. 4. Count of positive historical surprises.
Source: Hillcrest Asset Management.

4. Companies with major problems were beginning to release negative guidance changes during the quarter when nobody was watching, with the result that the lower guidance gave them a chance to get an earnings surprise at quarter end. The market was usually not fooled.

More small companies were issuing guidance each year. To examine these new facts, we first analyzed the benefits of finding companies that consistently had positive surprises in both earnings and sales over the last five quarters. Instead of just using the latest surprise numbers, there was a definite improvement in performance by including more historical information. Behaviorally, this fits with the "Recency Bias" that pervades our industry. Looking at only the most recent data does not give a clear picture of the likelihood of future results. Generally, any company may have one positive surprise, but quality companies create a series of them. Figure 4 shows the results. This factor outperformed in 6 of 7 years and added 2.85% annualized.

Second, we analyzed the performance of company earnings and guidance changes. We were very interested in whether these changes had a greater or lesser impact on stock performance versus traditional surprise metrics (see Fig. 5). The results were dramatic with earnings guidance changes adding value during all 7 years, and sales guidance

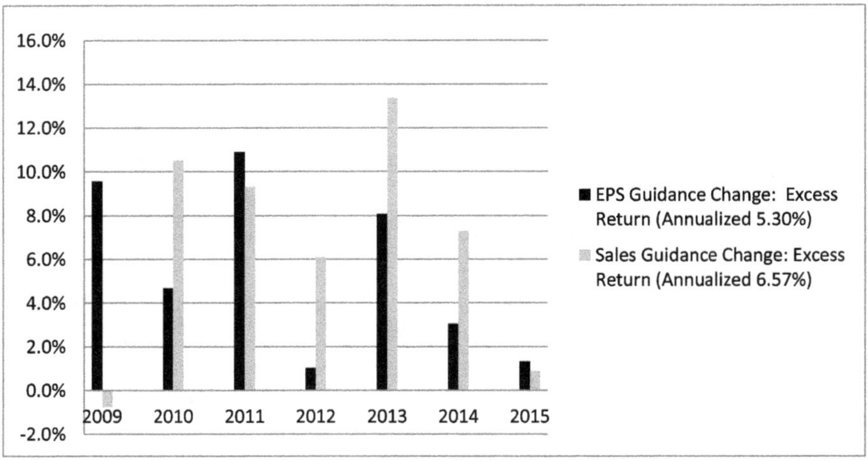

Fig. 5. Guidance change (excess return (top 3 deciles – average)).
Source: Hillcrest Asset Management.

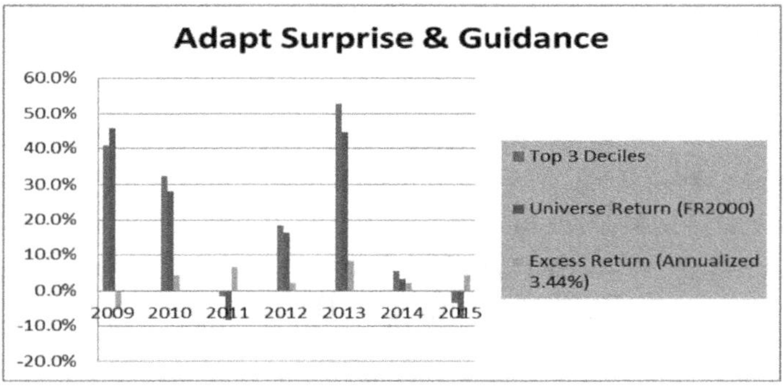

Fig. 6. Adapt, surprise and guidance.
Source: Hillcrest Asset Management.

adding value in 6 of 7 years. Both sales and earnings guidance changes added over 5% to returns.

We combined the different surprise factors to create an overall surprise factor, which we called Behaviorally Adapted Surprise and Guidance. The returns for the adapted factor over the test period were 3.44% excess return annualized, which can be seen in Fig. 6.

Earnings surprise has been a poor factor to use over the last decade. However, when combined with guidance changes, sales surprises, and using a longer term focus to find companies that are continually outperforming expectations, a behaviorally adapted factor can be created which can add a significant value to a portfolio.

2. Utilizing New Data

We then asked ourselves if there was more that we could do. We liked the concept behind surprise showing that the firm was doing better than current analyst expectations. We wanted to see if we could utilize new data and new techniques to create an indicator showing firms that could do better than expectations. We realized that behavioral insights are not just a series of models but an approach to investing that starts with philosophy, permeates stock selection, and continues all the way to portfolio construction. The only specific behavioral sentiment models that have been developed have been with us for a long time: earnings revision and earnings surprise (for a history, see by Bruce and Bradshaw, 2004). We decide to look at using non-database information to create an indicator of sentiment. A paper about text reading had been submitted to *The Journal of Behavioral Finance* (where Brian Bruce is the editor) and a leading data vendor had started text reading news feeds. Hillcrest is now text reading by a proprietary analysis of the sentiment of the management team of each company.

The quest for an accurate understanding of all types of company sentiment has long been an alluring goal of investors. Irrespective of whether a company is cheap or expensive, growing or declining, sentiment is a prominent determinant of the direction of stock prices. An accurate analysis of sentiment can make or break an investment strategy. At Hillcrest, we aspire to determine the sentiment of investors outside the company as well as the more elusive sentiment within the company. These can provide information that is not contained in the price.

Since Brian Bruce and Doug Stark built the first global earnings revision models at State Street in the early 1990s, it has become a factor in virtually all model-driven strategies. This model is the most popular method of determining investor sentiment. No new behavioral sentiment indicators were created until recently. A study done by UBS, "Online Search Frequency, Information Asymmetry, and Market Liquidity", uses a sentiment tool from a leading data vendor. According to the data vendor, their new tool analyzes news providing improved buy/hold/sell signals within milliseconds. They anticipate that users will be traders, market makers, and quant hedge funds. The big problem with news sentiment indicators is the ephemeral nature of news which can turn from positive to negative multiple times daily. This is exemplified in the new tool mentioned earlier which provides signals within milliseconds. Hillcrest believes it is impractical and costly to find a way to incorporate such short-term information into a long-term strategy, such as ours, that has a holding period measured in years.

3. Hillcrest Research into Internal Company Sentiment

Our goal when starting this research was to find a method of measuring the highly elusive sentiment within the company or, in other words, to determine whether the people working there have a strong belief in their products, personnel, and leadership. Without working at a company, it is difficult to ascertain the morale of the people developing, producing, and marketing the products sold. But as any reader of the Dilbert comics knows, the morale of the people working at a firm is one indicator of the long-term success or failure, and it was the long-term results that we were interested in.

Finding a plentiful source of insight into companies led us to considering earnings call transcripts. The transcripts had all of the necessary ingredients. They were produced on a consistent basis, followed a standard format (review of financials, new products, problems, and Q&A) which allowed for comparison between companies, and were not over-analyzed by the investment community.

For our initial investigation, we created a proprietary scoring system to compare the number of positive phrases or statements in each earning call transcript, versus negative phrases or statements, the idea being that companies where the executives were nervous, apprehensive, or concerned would have a higher percentage of negative statements. This methodology was showing positive results, when we noticed, because of exposure to academic papers and reading the transcripts, an area of opportunity that deserved our attention.

4. The Art of Deflection

One of our favorite political axioms is "Never answer the question you are asked, answer the question you wish you were asked". Luckily, our business leaders are not as adept at obfuscation and de-clarification as our politicians, but they didn't get to the top of the business world without being able to deftly focus on those aspects that make them look good.

The second phase of our research focused on determining when the managers are consciously or subconsciously hiding lingering doubts about potential problems. Whether these are problems such as an inventive new competitor, or an internal problem that they hope will find a solution by the next quarterly report, they don't want to talk about it so they hide it by talking about something positive. To determine if we could find these situations, we developed "Deflection Phrases", where the manager is deflecting attention away from something they don't want to talk about or deflecting blame so that they will not be implicated. Table 1 shows some samples of deflection phrases, as well as positive and negative phrases.

Deflection phrases fall into two major categories: the first is the use of qualifying statements, e.g. things aren't "good" they are "mostly good". These qualifiers allow management to focus on the "good" while ignoring the parts that don't qualify as "mostly". Of course, as investors we are interested in the information that the management is ignoring. The second category of deflection phrases is blame avoidance, where management has lingering doubts about the future and is trying to limit the amount of blame that is attributed

Table 1. Sample words and phrases used in earnings call analysis.

Positive Phrases	Negative Phrases	Deflection Phrases
Great	Collapse	Unexpected
Innovation	Breakdown	Mostly Positive
Leading Edge	Decreasing Market Share	Do Not Wish to Comment
Profit Growth	Below Expectations	Previous Management Policies

Source: Hillcrest Asset Management.

to them personally. In blame avoidance, you see such words as "unexpected", which we translate into "it is not my fault, it was unexpected".

5. Deflection Performance

Deflection phrases, by their very nature, are expected to have significantly more power on the downside than the upside. At Hillcrest, we also expected that because deflection phrases looked for unseen problems that had not surfaced, the returns would be delayed into future quarters as the problems started to become noticed. This delay was perfect for our long-term investment strategy. The results of our research confirms what we expected as is shown in the following graph which look at the bottom two deciles (the worst scoring companies in our deflection score). The data continue to show power even 12 months after the Earnings Call Transcript was analyzed (see Fig. 7).

Our analysis of the informational value of analyzing Management Sentiment is shown in Fig. 8. Our Management Sentiment Indicator shows power in both finding companies that will outperform as well as companies that have potential problems and should be avoided.

The above chart shows strong returns to the top two deciles of management sentiment over our backtest period.

Our Hillcrest Management Sentiment behavioral factor confirms our belief that analyzing earnings call transcripts is a profitable

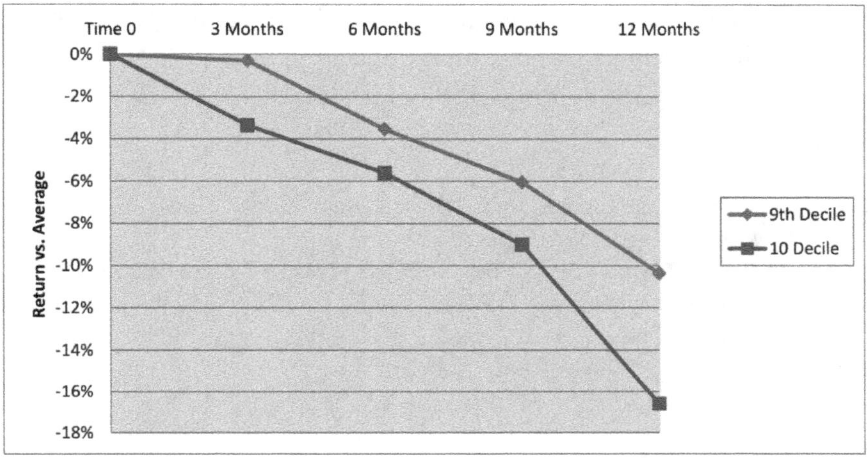

Fig. 7. Performance of bottom 2 deciles hillcrest deflection score.
Source: Hillcrest Asset Management.

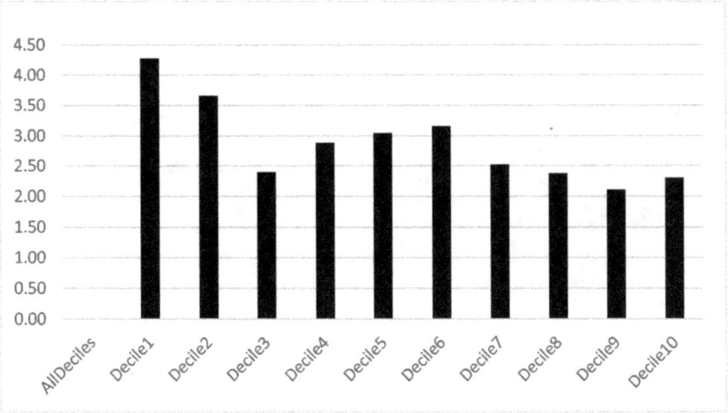

Fig. 8. Backtest results.
Source: Hillcrest Asset Management.

way to determine the internal sentiment within a company and that sentiment provides evidence of future returns. At Hillcrest, we continue to look for ways to exploit our unique knowledge of behavioral finance and the cognitive decision biases that affect executives, analysts, and money managers. We use this information to make constant improvements to our investment process.

References

Brian, R. B. and Charles, B. E. (1994). *The Handbook of Corporate Earnings Analysis*. Chicago: Probus Publishing Company.

Brian, R. B. and Mark, T. B. (2004). *Analysts, Lies and Statistics*. New York, NY: Institutional Investor Books.

Part II

Financial Anomalies and Calendar Effects

https://doi.org/10.1142/9789811222634_0008

Chapter 8

SEASONALITY EFFECTS IN JAPANESE FUTURES MARKETS*,†

William T. Ziemba

Yamaichi Research Institute, Tokyo
University of Tsukuba and
University of British Columbia

This paper investigates seasonal regularities in the security price returns on the first section of the Tokyo Stock Exchange. The research uses data from the futures markets in Singapore for the Nikkei Dow 225 index and in Osaka for the Kabusaki 50 index. The questions of main concern are whether or not the seasonal anomalies observed in the spot markets are maintained, are they anticipated in the futures markets, and do the futures market anticipations alter the character of the seasonal regularity. Results are presented concerning day of the week, monthly, holiday, turn of the month and year and first half of the month effects. The conclusions are tentative because the futures markets have only a short history to date.

1. INTRODUCTION

The Japanese country and economy were devastated in WWII. After the war the country was occupied and plans were set for a rebuilding. The stock markets reopened in 1949. The early years were difficult but the hard work and internal savings for investment paid off as the country's products gained more and more acceptance abroad. The full fruits of the economic miracle of Japan are now well known and feared in the west. Since 1980 the transfer of wealth to Japan from the U.S and others has been very large indeed. Figure 1 shows this through the world stock market capitalizations in October 1980 and September 1988. Europe's share of the world's stock markets has stayed about constant (21% in 1988 versus 20% in 1980), the U.S. share has dropped from

*Without implicating them I would like to thank my colleagues at the Yamaichi Research Institute particularly A. Komatsu and H. Shintani for their help and useful discussions on anomalous behavior in Japanese security markets. Thanks are also due to Warren Bailey and Sandra Schwartz for helpful comments on an earlier draft of this paper. This research was conducted at the Yamaichi Research Institute with the advice of William T. Ziemba. All the rights to the research belong to the Yamaichi Research Institute. I thank the Yamaichi Research Institute for permission to publish the results. This research was also partially supported by the Social Sciences and Humanities Research Council of Canada, and the Centre for International Business Studies, University of British Columbia.

†This chapter originally appeared in *Pacific-Basin Capital Investment Research,* Chapter 12, by S. G. Rhee and R. P. Chang (Eds.), 1990, pp. 379–407, © 1990 Elsevier Science Publishers.

53% to 31% and the rest of the world's is now 6% compared to 12% in 1980. Meanwhile, Japan's share has increased from 15% to 42% Net assets of Japan were $11.5 billion at the end of 1980 and those of the U.S. were $106.3 billion. By 1987 Japan's net assets grew over 20 fold to $240.7 billion. Meanwhile U.S. private and public assets fell by a negative $368.2 billion. There is much talk in the press about the U.S. trade and budget deficits. Indeed the public's deficit was $148.9 billion at the end of 1987. But the private sector of the U.S. is also $219.3 billion in the red.

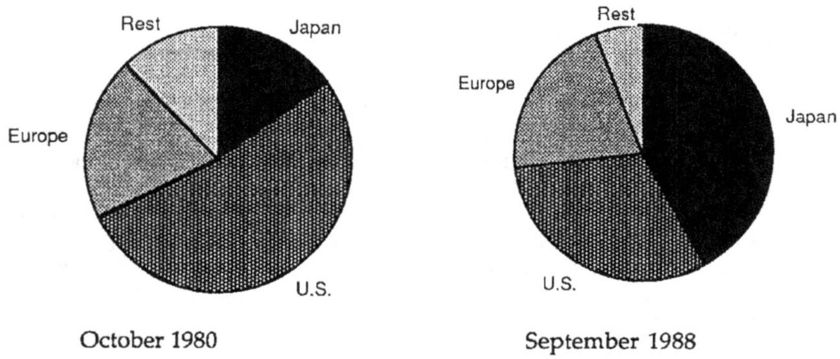

Figure 1: Stock Market Capitalizations

There has been a huge increase in Japanese stock prices. A standard measure of the market is the Nikkei Dow index. This index is analogous to the Dow Jones Industrial Average in the U.S. Its value at any time is the sum of the prices of the 225 stocks in the index divided by the current divisor which is adjusted over time to account for stock splits, rights offerings, etc. The index stood at ¥176.21 on the date of its original investment, May 16, 1949. By the end of the year the index had fallen to ¥109.9. But by the end of December 1988 the index had increased to ¥30,159. The divisor which began at 225 was then 10.289. The increase over the 38+ years was 171.15 times not counting dividends and taxes. In U.S. dollars the increase was a remarkable 489.59 times. The increase has not been straight up. Over this period there have been twenty corrections of 10% or more and nine of over 20%. For details see Ziemba and Schwartz (1990). Table 1 shows the closing prices of the ND index plus the value of the yen/dollar exchange rate year by year plus the gains in yen and dollars for the ND index.

The major stock market in Japan is the Tokyo Stock Exchange. The TSE has over 85% of the value and trading volume of the whole market which is also traded in Osaka, Nagoya and five other smaller exchanges. The stocks in the Nikkei Dow comprise about 50% of the market value and about 75% of the

Table 1: Yearly Yen Closing Prices of the Nikkei Dow and Yen/Dollar Exchange Rates, 1949-88

End of Year	ND	Yen/$	Current Value of 1¥ invested in 1949 in ¥	Current Value of 1$ invested in 1949 in$
1949	109.9	360.00	0.62	0.62
1950	101.9	360.00	0.58	0.58
1951	166.1	360.00	0.94	0.94
1952	362.6	360.00	2.06	2.06
1953	377.9	360.00	2.14	2.14
1954	356.1	360.00	2.02	2.02
1955	425.7	360.00	2.42	2.42
1956	549.1	360.00	3.12	3.12
1957	474.5	360.00	2.69	2.69
1958	666.5	360.00	3.78	3.78
1959	874.9	360.00	4.97	4.97
1960	1356.7	360.00	7.70	7.70
1961	1432.6	360.00	8.13	8.13
1962	1420.4	360.00	8.06	8.06
1963	1225.1	360.00	6.95	6.95
1964	1216.5	360.00	6.90	6.90
1965	1417.8	360.00	8.05	8.05
1966	1452.1	360.00	8.24	8.24
1967	1283.5	360.00	7.28	7.28
1968	1714.9	360.00	9.73	9.73
1969	2359.0	360.00	13.39	13.39
1970	1987.1	360.00	11.28	11.28
1971	2713.7	314.80	15.40	17.61
1972	5207.9	302.00	29.56	35.23
1973	4306.8	280.00	24.44	31.42
1974	3817.2	300.95	21.66	25.91
1975	4358.6	305.15	24.74	29.18
1976	4990.8	292.80	28.32	34.82
1977	4865.6	240.00	27.61	41.42
1978	6001.8	194.60	34.06	63.01
1979	6569.5	239.70	37.28	55.99
1980	7116.4	203.00	40.39	71.62
1981	7681.8	219.90	43.59	71.37
1982	8016.7	235.00	45.50	69.69
1983	9893.8	232.20	56.15	87.05
1984	11542.6	251.10	65.50	93.91
1985	13113.3	200.50	74.42	133.62
1986	18701.3	160.05	106.13	238.72
1987	21564.0	123.00	122.38	358.18
1988	30159.0	125.85	171.15	489.59
April 19. 1989	33185.15	132.36	188.32	512.22

trading volume on the first section of the TSE. The second section has only a few percent of the value and volume so the first section and the Nikkei Dow give onea good indication of the whole market. The first section's capitalization is currently about Y490 trillion which is more than all the stock exchanges in the U.S. The ND index suffers from the same problems as the DJIA. A more representative index of the whole market is the TOPIX which is a value weighted index of all, some 1135, stocks on the first section. It is analogus to the NYFE index in the U.S. Relative to the TOPIX, the ND has a beta (using data from Octover 1983 to October 1988) of about 0.84 so it is less variable than the overall market. The TSE is highly regulated with detailed and cumbersome listing procedures, price and margin limits and the like. Trading is dominated by the institutions including the life insurance companies and made largely through the big four: Nomura, Nikko, Daiwa and Yamaichi. Although there are some 45 foreign brokerage firms in Japan they handle only about 2% of the trading volume. In contrast, Nomura alone has about 30% of the trading volume. Although the foreign firms are very active in program trading and the like the lack of commission business has led to massive losses. Only ten of the 45 had profits in 1988 and the profits of these were small compared to those of the big four.[1]

The Japanese stock market is not well understood and is therefore avoided in the U.S. Despite sharply rising prices and a firming yen, there was net selling by foreigners from 1984 to mid 1988. Fears of extraordinary high PE ratios, land prices beyond belief and the like abound as has been described in Ziemba and Schwartz (1990). A few key points are:

- there are extraordinary high correlations between land prices particularly of commercial land and stock prices, see also Ziemba (1989b)
- much of the stock holdings are to cement business relationships and are never traded
- there is a great preference by the Japanese corporations and individuals to accumulate land and a strong feeling not to sell it ever
- the value of the stocks is much less, even with their high PE ratios based on trailing earnings of some 50-70 times, than the value of the land and stock holdings they own not to mention the value of the assets in businesses they are in. Tobin's Q, the percent of the assets that the stocks are worth is about 70% for the ND.
- the PE ratios are not generally as useful a measure of stock value as in the U.S. because of the nontrading, undervaluation of land and other buildings, stock holding and other assets. Still there is a small but significant low PE effect separate from other valuation descriptors

The impending crash that many U.S. and other foreign observers see as inevitable may take a while to materialize if at all. The confidence level of the Japanese in their markets is high and for good reason. Sharply rising earnings growth, GNP growth of about 6% in 1988, 4.5% in 1989 (estimated), low

[1]Japanese firms are not doing well in the U.S either.

interest and inflation rates, a strong yen, huge balance of trade and the like are cited as reasons (and used as explanatory variables in econometric prediction equations) for this strength. Japanese investors prefer to buy on weakness rather than on strength. That is the reverse of the majority of U.S. investors.

The stock market is opening up quickly with a whole host of derivative instruments[2] recently added and planned. There are now four index futures contracts trading and options on futures indices are scheduled to be traded later in 1989. Details on these contracts and their early histories appear in Ziemba and Schwartz (1990).

There is not much literature yet on Japanese anomalies.[3] Part of the reason for this is a lack of interest in such studies by the big Japanese brokerage firms who are unaware and suspicious of their potential use. Also these firms do not generally publish much of their research findings even in Japanese. Recently, however, U.S. and Japanese researchers have been studying these markets. The thrust has been mainly to ascertain the similarities and differences with the analogous results in U.S. markets. Some of the main references are Hawawani (1988a,b), Jaffe and Westerfield (1985a,b), Kato (1988a,b), Kato and Schallheim (1985), Kunimura (1984), Ikeda (1985, 1988) and Nakumura and Terada (1984). Kato, Schwartz, and Ziemba (1989) have surveyed the research and presented new results on day of the week effects in Japanese security markets. Other research works on the Japanese stockmarket are Bailey (1989), Brenner, Subrahmanyam and Uno (1987, 1988), Elton and Gruber (1988, 1989), Hamao (1988, 1989), Kunimura (1984), Hiraki, Aggarwal and Rao (1988), Komatsu and Ziemba (1989), Lau, Quay and Ramsey (1974), Roehl (1985), Pettway and Tapley (1984), Suzuki (1988) and Schoenfeld (1988).

Ziemba (1989a) had access to data on the entire 38+ years of the ND and TOPIX indices and used it to study holiday, monthly, turn of the month and year, first half of the month and Golden Week effects on the first section of the TSE. There are strong and pervasive security market regularities that with some changes because of the institutions involved are analogous to many U.S. findings. The purpose of this paper is to investigate how the new index futures markets are affecting these anomalies. The specific data used are from two of these futures contracts: the SIMEX, ND225 futures traded on the Singapore International Monetary Exchange and the Kabusaki 50 index traded on the Osaka Stock Exchange. These contracts began trading on September 3, 1986 and June 6, 1987, respectively. The newest futures contracts, based on the TOPIX traded on the TSE, and the ND traded on the OSE began trading on September

[2]For a survey of the U.S. derivative instruments and some of the theory behind them see Rubinstein (1987).

[3]The U.S. literature on seasonal regularities is now extremely voluminous. Surveys and list of references appear in Schwert (1983), Keim (1986), Jacobs and Levy (1988) and the books by Dimson (1988) and Ziemba (1990).

3, 1988. In this paper we investigate the SIMEX, and Kabusaki data up to September 19 and 20, respectively, which is 557 trading days for the SIMEX and 352 for the Kabusaki.

Figure 2 shows the volume on the SIMEX and Kabusaki 50 during and after the period of this study. Similarly, Figure 3 shows the volume of the two new contracts. The main point is that the new contracts essentially replaced the Kabusaki 50 and its trading volume shrank to almost nothing and it has remained at this low level of activity. Meanwhile the SIMEX had an increase in volume part of which is increased programmed trading. The papers by Brenner, Subrahmanyam and Uno (1987, 1988) study arbitrage programmed trading strategies between the SIMEX and Kabusaki for the early part of the history before September 1988. See also Chapter 13 in Ziemba and Schwartz (1990). The Kabusaki is a price weighted package of 50 stocks traded on the TSE and OSE designed to track the ND. It has a daily limit price move of 3% in either direction. Hence in a market crash, it does not trade. The SIMEX has no such price limits and had a huge fall on crash day October 20, 1987. It now has a daily price limit change of 15%

Singapore time is one hour behind Tokyo time, hence to correspond to Tokyo's 9:00 a.m. opening, the SIMEX begins trading at 8 a.m. During the time of this study, the TSE was open for trading from 9:00-11:00 a.m. and 1:00-3:00 p.m., and 9:00-11:00 a.m. on the first, fourth and fifth (if there is one) Saturdays of the month. As of the beginning of February 1989 there was no Saturday trading on the TSE with trading in the afternoon from 12:30-3:00 pm with extra trading on the previously closed days December 28 and 29. SIMEX does not close for lunch and trades continuously from 8 a.m. to 2:15, an extra fifteen minutes after Tokyo's close. This is much the same as the extra time futures on the S&P 500 and other indices trade following the close of the New York Stock Exchange. Most of the trading days on the TSE and SIMEX are comparable but occasionally one of them has a different holiday. In the initial period until May 23, 1987 SIMEX did not trade on Saturdays.

The SIMEX has a spot contract for the ND that is rarely traded, plus four futures contracts that mature on the quarter months, as do the Kabusaki and U.S. futures contracts, of March, June, September and December. The contracts mature on the third Wednesday of the month and they are settled in cash based on the closing value of the ND. The Kabusaki is settled on the fifteenth day of each contract month with the delivery of the basket of stocks. Throughout most of its trading history the SIMEX traded at a discount from fair value and often the Kabusaki was at a premium. There simply was not enough arbitrage trading to keep the prices in line. I refer the reader to the cited references and also Schoenfeld (1988) who among other accomplishments was the first westerner to trade on the SIMEX.

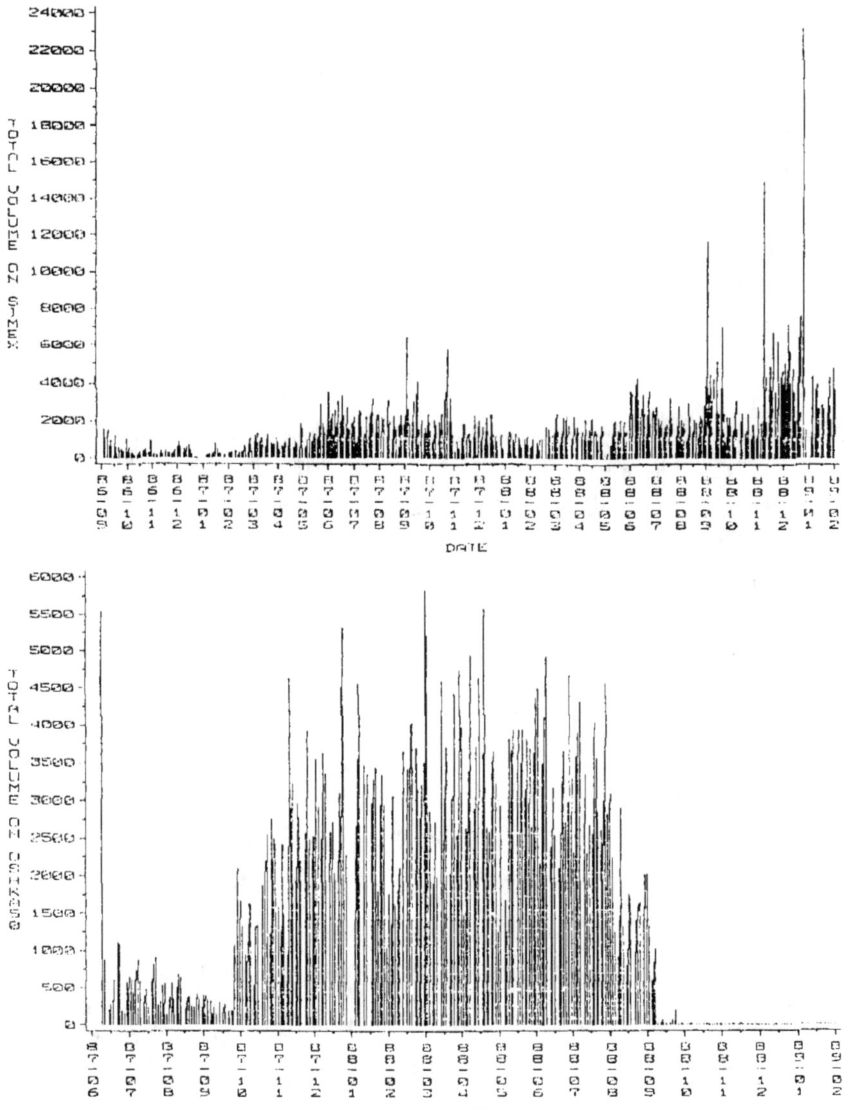

Figure 2: Trading Volume of the SIMEX and Kabusaki Futures Contracts for their Inception through the End of January 1989.

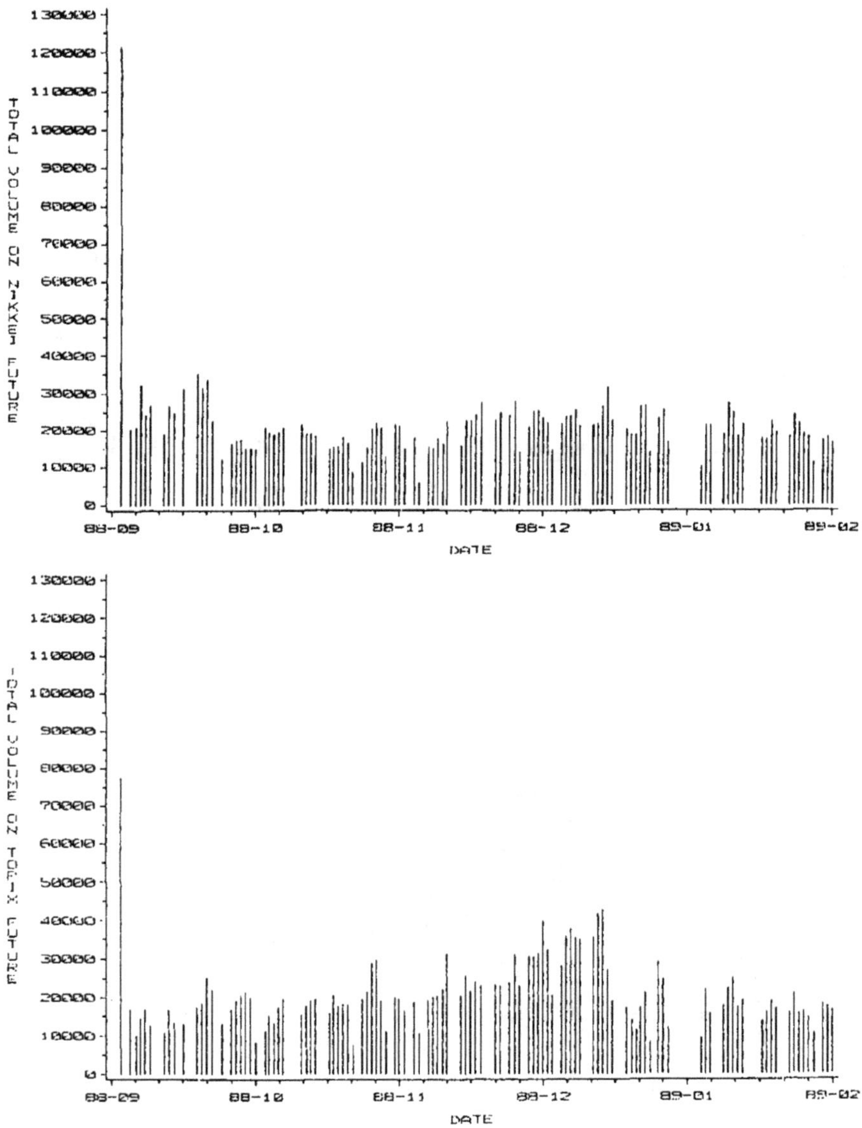

Figure 3: Trading Volume of the ND and TOPIX Futures Contracts Traded on the OSE and TSE, September 3, 1988 to January 31, 1989.

The plan of the paper is to describe in turn each of the spot anomalies and then investigate their current effects in the futures and spot markets. The conclusions reached are tentative because these data sets are still small but they are suggestive. In general, the anomalies still seem to be there, although they are anticipated in the markets to some extent and this has shifted their effects somewhat.

2. Days of the Week Effect

A survey of the days of the week effect in the spot Japanese stock markets along with some new results investigating the ND and TOPIX indices for the entire 1949-88 period appears in Kato, Schwartz and Ziemba (1989). The major research papers investigating the day of the week effects using data from the 1970s and 1980s are Ikeda (1985, 1988) in Japanese, Kato (1988a,b), Kato and Schallheim (1988), and Jaffe and Westerfield (1985a,b). Some of the main conclusions of this research are:

- There is a strong day of the week effect. Wednesdays and Saturdays are strongly positive, Thursdays and Fridays are mildly positive, Mondays are about neutral, and Tuesdays are especially negative. Until the end of January 1989, Saturday trading occurs for a half day on the first, fourth, and (if applicable) the fifth week of the month.

- For the period 1978-87, Wednesdays gain 0.145% and Saturdays 0.14% each about triple the average gain of 0.058%. This is counterbalanced by the nearly even Mondays which return 0.004% on average and a loss of 0.09% on Tuesdays. Thursdays and Fridays return 0.065% and 0.105%, respectively.

- Except for Saturdays which open up and rise all day, on average, most of the gains occur at night. Except for a brief rise early in the day and a little kick at the end all the other days have negative returns during trading hours.

- Saturday trading affects the market in significant ways. Indeed the market seems affected by whether or not Saturday trading occurs. For example, with Saturday trading on the first, fourth and fifth weeks of the month during the sample period, the following Mondays are positive. But without Saturday trading Mondays are negative. Tuesdays are always negative except in the third week of the month when there is no Saturday trading both in this week and the proceeding week. In this case Mondays are especially negative losing 0.35% on average while Tuesdays gain back 0.19% of this.

- In total, Monday-Tuesday trading losses in Japan are about 0.09% which is similar to the Monday losses coupled with Tuesday's mildly positive gain in New York for a Monday-Tuesday return of about -.11%. Correlations between the New York and Tokyo's Dow's vary by time period but these relationships are more or less becoming stronger over time. What is consistent is that New York's effect on Tokyo is stronger than the reverse. For the period 1980-87 the correlation between the previous day's return in New York and the close-to-open returns in Tokyo was 53.6%. The reverse effect, the correlation between Tokyo's close-to-close and New York's close-to-open is only about 11%.

Table 2 sumarizes the recent effects using 1978-87 data and the effects of Saturday trading.

Table 2: Effects of Saturday Trading on the TOPIX, April 4, 1978-June 18, 1987

Week	Trading Ends This Week	Trading Ends Last Week	Mon	Tues	Wed	Thur	Fri	Sat	Sample Size
1st,5th A1	Sat	Sat	0.0198	-0.1072	0.1790	0.0581	0.0605	0.1678	1406
4th A2	Sat	Fri	-0.1008	-0.1102	0.1074	0.0306	0.1582	0.0793	649
2nd B1	Fri	Sat	0.1135	-0.0649	0.0980	0.0933	0.1341		539
3rd B2	Fri	Fri	-0.3489	0.1931	0.2479	0.2609	0.2193		58
	All Weeks		0.0039	-0.0902	0.1449	0.0648	0.1049	0.1397	2652
Sample Size			449	464	464	465	467	343	2652

(Source: Kato 1988a)

Pieptea and Prisman (1988) and others such as Cornell (1985) have found that in the U.S. markets Mondays fall is fully anticipated in the futures markets using the S&P500 index. The futures market tends to fall in the last hour or so of trading so that even as the spot market is rising the futures are moving lower to anticipate Monday's decline. For the period March 18, 1983 to June 27, 1986 Pieptea and Prisman found the following results:

	Mon	Tues	Wed	Thur	Fri
Mean Annualized Return in Spot Market	-4.93	42.33	3.16	23.50	32.59
its Standard Deviation	2.11	2.45	2.41	1.97	2.23
Mean Annualized Return in Futures Market of the Nearest Contract	19.35	9.10	4.83	23.57	6.75
its Standard Deviation	2.09	2.46	2.48	2.07	2.12

Figure 4 and Table 3 compare the day of the week effects on the spot ND in Tokyo with the futures market on the Nikkei Dow at the SIMEX in Singapore. Similarly Figure 5 and Table 4 compare the effects on the Osaka 50 futures, the Osaka 50 spot and the Nikkei Dow spot.

Table 3: Days of the Week Effects in the ND Spot Market in Tokyo and the SIMEX Futures Markets in Singapore, Sept 3, 1986 to Sept 19, 1988

	SIMEX futures				*ND spot*			
	Sample	Mean		%	Sample	Mean		%
Day	Size	Return	t-Statistic	Positive	Size	Return	t-Statistic	Positive
All	532	0.094	1.00	56.8	557	0.082	1.50	56.6
Mon	102	-0.223	-1.52	46.1	100	-0.301*	-2.93	44.0
Tues	104	-0.137	-0.47	57.7	99	-0.120	-0.68	50.5
Wed	101	0.029	0.20	58.4	100	0.251	1.74	60.0
Thur	101	0.534	1.90	59.4	101	0.305*	3.08	64.4
Fri	99	0.207	1.39	62.6	102	0.174	1.54	59.8
Sat	25	0.383	1.09	56.0	55	0.258*	1.96	63.6

In this and succeeding tables, * indicates that a coefficient is significantly different from zero at the 5% level, ** at 1% and *** at 0.1%.

Figure 4: Days of the Week Effects in the ND Spot Market in Tokyo and the SIMEX Futures Markets in Singapore, Sept 3, 1986 to Sept 19, 1988

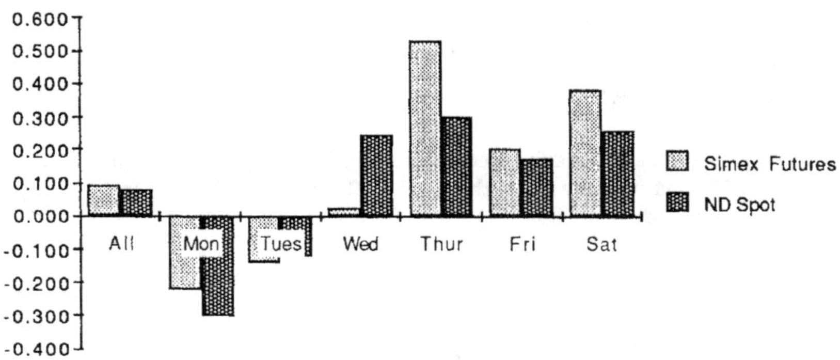

Table 4: Days of the Week Effects in the ND Spot Market and the Osaka 50 Spot Market in Tokyo and the Osaka 50 Kabusaki Futures in Osaka, June 6, 1987 to Sept 20, 1988

	Osaka 50 Futures				*Osaka 50 Spot*			
Day	Sample Size	Mean Return	t-Statistic	% Positive	Sample Size	Mean Return	t-Statistic	% Positive
All	352	-0.020	-0.30	49.4	353	0.000	0.00	52.1
Mon	65	-0.329*	-2.35	38.5	65	-0.347*	-2.50	38.5
Tues	62	0.205	1.20	54.8	63	-0.173	-0.62	60.3
Wed	64	0.018	0.10	51.6	64	0.275	1.15	53.1
Thur	63	-0.012	-0.09	50.8	63	0.173	1.31	55.6
Fri	64	0.007	0.04	46.9	64	-0.025	-0.15	46.9
Sat	34	0.018	0.08	58.8	34	0.190	0.90	64.7

	ND Spot			
Day	Sample Size	Mean Return %	t-Statistic	% Positive
All	353	0.033	0.45	56.4
Mon	65	-0.254	-1.93	46.1
Tues	63	-0.196	-0.75	52.4
Wed	64	0.318	1.57	59.4
Thur	63	0.204	1.79	63.5
Fri	64	0.059	0.39	56.3
Sat	34	0.107	0.62	64.7

Figure 5: Days of the Week Effects in the ND Spot Market and the Osaka 50 Spot Market in Tokyo and the Osaka 50 Kabusaki Futures in Osaka, June 6, 1987 to Sept 20, 1988

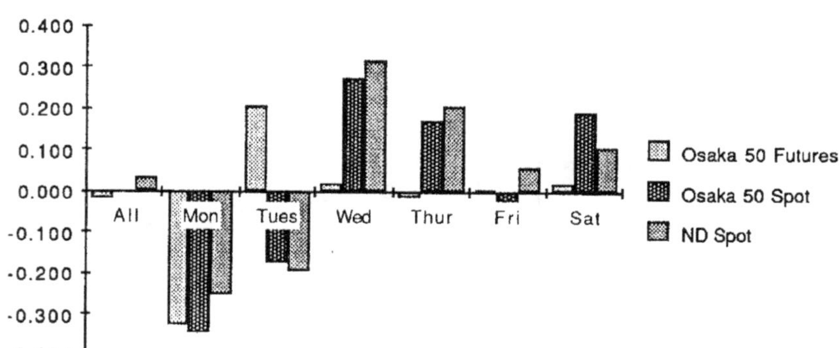

The spot effect of weak Mondays and Tuesdays and strong Wednesday to Saturday is continuing. Wednesdays are the strongest days followed by Thursdays and Saturdays in the spot market. The Simex futures in Singapore look just like the spot market in Tokyo except in the Wednesday -Thursday period. Possibly this market is following rather than leading, although other evidence suggests the leading hypothesis. The futures seem to rise and fall with the spot. The Osaka 50 seems to anticipate the days of the week effect. Saturdays hardly rise at all in the futures markets despite the spot gains thus anticipating Monday's fall. Then these futures fall on Monday to anticipate a further fall on Tuesday. They then rise on Tuesday to anticipate the gains on Wednesday, Thursday, Friday and Saturday. They are then flat until the fall the next Monday.

3. HOLIDAY EFFECTS

The main references on the holiday effect in U.S. spot markets are Ariel (1988), Lakonishok and Smidt (1989), Zweig (1986) and the survey in Ziemba (1990). These authors found a very strong effect: days before holidays have significantly higher returns than other days. The effect is relatively strongest for large capitalized stocks although the total preholiday returns is higher for the small stocks because of the small firm effect. Indeed for the 90 year Lakonishok and Smidt DJIA sample from 1897-1986 these eight or so days return more than half the non-dividend return over the whole year. Trading days before the preholiday and after the holiday do not have significantly higher returns. Indeed these days particularly the post holidays have lower returns on average. Ziemba (1989a) has investigated similar effects on the TSE. In Japan there are about twelve holidays each year compared with about eight in the U.S. For the Nikkei Dow from 1949-88, I found that the mean daily returns could be estimated by

$$R = \underset{(3.745)}{0.0352} + \underset{(1.491)}{0.0799}\,Day_{-3} + \underset{(0.424)}{0.0222}\,Day_{-2} + \underset{(3.709)}{0.1894}\,Day_{-1} - \underset{(-1.334)}{0.0663}\,Day_{+1} + \underset{(0.023)}{0.00114}\,Day_{+2},$$

where Day_{-3} is the dummy for the separate effect of trading day -3, etc. The pre-holiday with an extra mean return of 0.1894% per day is statistically significant with a t-static of 3.709 and none of the other days have returns that are significantly different from b_0. The effect of the +1 day is negative, although the coefficient is not significant. Their total returns are slightly positive, 0.0068% which is less than a typical day. In total, the preholidays return 0.2246 per day versus 0.049% on a typical non-preholiday with lower risk measured by the standard deviation, 0.794% versus 0.979%. The preholidays also improve every day of the week, for the Japanese stocks see Ziemba (1989a), just as Lakonishok and Smidt (1989) found for the DJIA.

Figure 6 and Table 5 show the spot holiday effect on the ND and on the SIMEX futures market for the period of the SIMEX data, September 3, 1986 to September 19, 1988 some 557 trading days. The preholidays have gains on 78% of the days which is much higher than for the other days. The mean returns are high, averaging 0.276% per day which is nearly four times the return on other days. However, the t statistic of 1.57 is not significant except at the 13% level. Moreover, the third day before the holiday has even higher returns. The other days around the preholiday have low returns as expected.

In the futures markets the SIMEX anticipates the holiday effect on the 3rd day before the holiday. This anticipation seems to affect the spot market so the spot prices rise on -3 taking out some of the gains that would normally occur on the preholiday. The return in the SIMEX futures market on the preholiday is in fact slightly negative again reinforcing the fact that the preholiday effect is anticipated.

Table 5: Holiday Effect on SIMEX Sept 1986-Sept 1988

	ND Spot on TSE				*ND Futures on SIMEX*			
Day	Sample Size	Mean Return %	t-statistic	% Positive	Sample Size	Mean Return %	t-statistic	% Positive
All	557	0.082	1.50	56.6	508	0.098	1.00	56.9
3rd PH	21	0.370	1.38	57.1	17	0.684	1.62	64.7
2nd PH	22	-0.083	-0.30	50.0	20	0.014	0.04	45.0
PH	23	0.276	1.57	78.3	18	0.225	0.48	66.7
AH	23	-0.001	0.00	56.5	21	0.445	1.25	61.9
2nd AH	21	0.092	0.48	52.4	21	0.320	1.07	66.7
Others	447	0.071	1.12	55.9	411	0.063	0.55	56.0

Figure 6: Holiday Effect on SIMEX Sept 1986-Sept 1988

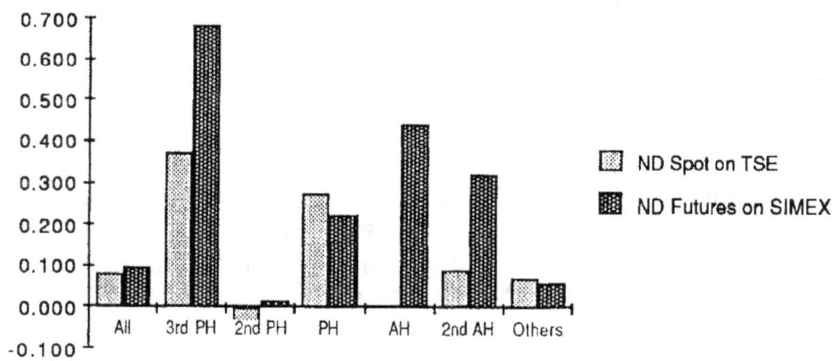

Figure 7 and Table 6 investigate the holiday effect from the Kabusaki Osaka 50 index for the period June 6, 1987 to September 20, 1988. In the spot market on the TSE the effect is similar to the historical record. The preholiday returns average 0.50% per day and the index increases 75% of the time. The gain is significant at the 5% level. The third trading day before the holiday has high returns but they are not significant. In the futures markets the return is only significant at the 5% level on the preholiday. The returns were high around the holiday periods in this sample with the days outside the pre and post holidays having negative returns. There is no evidence of the future market anticipating the holiday effect.

Table 6: Holiday Effect on the Kabusaki 50 Sept 1986-Sept 1988

	Kabusaki 50 Spot on TSE				Kabusaki 50 Future on TSE			
Day	Sample Size	Mean Return	t-Statistic	% Positive	Sample Size	Mean Return	t-Statistic	% Positive
All	353	-0.001	0.00	52.1	352	-0.020	-0.30	49.4
3rd PH	12	0.340	0.68	58.3	12	0.324	0.61	41.7
2nd PH	11	0.021	0.04	45.5	11	-0.206	-0.42	45.5
PH	12	0.499**	3.68	75.0	12	0.391*	2.27	66.7
AH	12	-0.022	-0.07	50.0	12	0.284	1.03	50.0
2nd AH	11	0.243	0.74	63.6	11	0.324	0.68	63.6
Others	295	-0.043	-0.46	50.8	294	-0.070	-0.94	48.6

In the spot market, the holiday effect for this sample of data of a year plus is not working in the usual fashion. The preholiday is strong but not dominant compared to the other days around the holiday. In fact for the SIMEX trading period the ND spot has risen most on the 3rd day before the holiday not on the preholiday. For the period that the Osaka 50 has been trading, the preholiday has the highest returns on the ND and these results are highly significant. The Osaka 50 also seems to have a strongly positive effect on the -3 preholiday trading day although these coefficients are not significant. So there may be some anticipation of the effect but with the small sample one cannot conclude much.

Figure 7: Holiday Effect on the Kabusaki 50 Sept 1986-Sept 1988

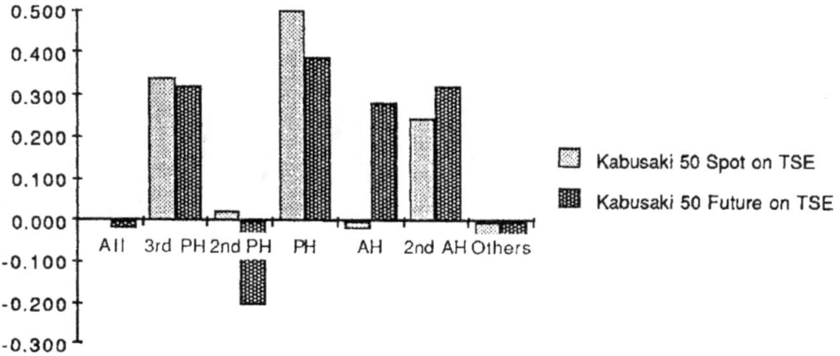

4. Turn of the Month and First Half of the Month Effects

The U.S. turn of the month effect occurs on trading days -1 to +4, see Ariel (1987) for an analysis of the spot data from 1963-82 and Sick and Ziemba (1989) for an analysis of futures data from 1982-88. The gains in this period are very high and contribute a very large percentage of the total monthly returns. The return in this *week*, coupled with that in the second week of the month, roughly trading days +5 to +8 or +10, essentially amounts to *all* the gains in the spot stock market during 1960-88. The rest of the month is essentially noise and at best provides zero returns. The reason(s) for this effect are not fully known but part of the story is that people receive their salaries on or around the -1 day as well as their stock account statements so they have funds to invest in stocks. There are also the portfolio balancing and renewal effects. When would one expect the turn-of-the-month to be in Japan? Many companies pay their salaries around the 25th of the month. Indeed, Ziemba (1989a) found similar turn of the month and first half of the month effects on the TSE. These effects are in the trading periods -5 to +2 and +3 to +7. For the ND from 1949-88 the period with trading days -5 to +2 receives the bulk of the month's return and each of these day's return is significant at the 5% level or better. Days +3 to +7 have positive returns and the rest of the month is noise; see Table 7 and Figure 8. Because of the pecularities of the Japanese market including Saturday trading day, +22 corresponds to a -5 day once a year or for 39 times in that many years. Since Japan had more trading days because of the two or three Saturdays that were trading each month these periods are correspondingly lengthened. In the first half of the month the mean return is 0.01142% per day while in the second half it is an insignifiant 0.00048% per day.

Table 7: Turn-of-the-Month Data, 1949-1988

Trading Day	Sample Size	Mean Return, %	t-Statistic	Trading Day	Sample Size	Mean Return, %	t-Statistic
-5	471	.0899*	2.75	9	471	.1065*	2.46
-4	471	.1041*	2.65	10	471	.0620	1.58
-3	471	.1733**	3.82	11	471	.0395	1.05
-2	471	.1334**	3.18	12	471	-.0196	-0.50
-1	471	.2255***	5.36	13	471	.0115	0.24
1	471	.0980*	2.43	14	471	-.0042	-0.10
2	471	.1006*	2.47	15	471	-.0306	-0.54
3	471	.0307	0.72	16	471	.0716	1.35
4	471	.0592	1.15	17	471	-.0498	-1.20
5	471	.0358	0.81	18	429	-.0207	-0.49
6	471	-.0005	-0.01	19	350	.0162	0.36
7	471	.0357	0.09	20	229	-.0286	-0.48
8	471	-.0585	-1.34	21	118	-.0476	-0.46
				22	39	.0562	0.45

	trading days	
1st Half	22-7	.01142
2nd Half	8-21	.00048

Source: Yamaichi Research Institute reported in Ziemba (1989a).

Figure 8: Turn-of-the-Month Data, 1949-1988

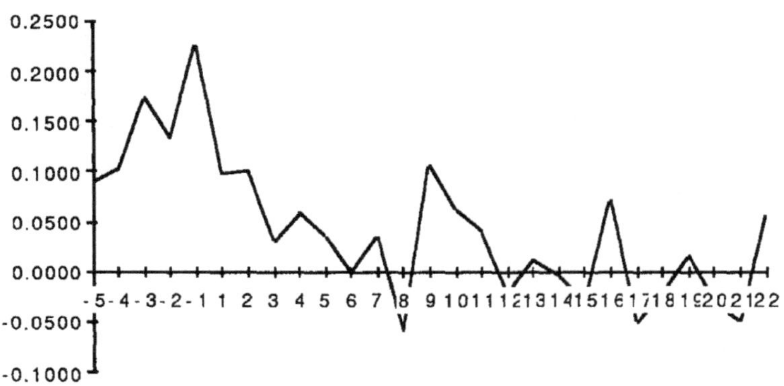

The turn of the month effect with high returns on days -5 to +2 seems to still be there but the SIMEX and Osaka 50 futures markets totally anticipate the effect. On the SIMEX, days -8 to -5 have all the gains of about 2.8% per month on average. This is a huge average gain in only four days. This is the whole turn of the month effect with the rest of the period about even. Although lower than in the futures markets, the spot market also has large gains on days -8 to -5. But the spot gains in the -5 to +2 period are still abnormally high. On the Osaka 50 futures market the anticipation seems to be on days -7, -6 and -5 with a total gain of about 1%. Both markets lose back much of the gain on -4 and -3. The effect in the spot market is similar to that mentioned above for the ND. The SIMEX seems to lead the Osaka 50 futures and the spot ND in this effect. Table 8 and Figure 9 describe the results. Since there is only one or two turn of the years this data is lumped in with that for the other months. These were calculated separately, but this does not seem to change the results much.

Table 8: The Turn of the Month Effect on the ND

	ND Spot on TSE				ND Futures on SIMEX			
Day	Sample Size	Mean Return	t-Statistic	% Positive	Sample Size	Mean Return	t-Statistic	% Positive
-7	24	0.432*	2.17	66.7	22	0.668*	2.18	68.2
-6	24	-0.095	-0.40	62.5	21	-0.061	-0.19	57.1
-5	24	0.333*	1.99	62.5	22	0.625*	1.96	54.5
-4	24	0.347*	2.00	62.5	23	-0.356	-1.02	47.8
-3	24	-0.100	-0.40	54.2	18	0.445	0.15	61.1
-2	24	0.315	1.10	70.8	20	0.349	0.84	65.0
-1	24	0.161	0.79	50.0	18	-0.448	-0.90	33.3
1	24	0.142	0.69	66.7	19	0.256	0.76	57.9
2	24	0.689	0.31	54.2	21	0.314	1.32	61.9
3	24	0.160	0.55	41.7	24	0.355	0.99	54.2
4	25	0.261	1.61	68.0	21	0.103	0.45	57.1
5	25	0.112	0.69	60.0	24	0.244	1.15	54.2
6	25	-0.869	-0.64	40.0	20	-0.106	-0.51	55.0
7	25	0.963	0.46	56.0	23	-0.438	-0.14	56.5
8	25	-0.046	-0.02	56.0	25	0.252	0.97	60.0
9	25	0.534*	2.50	76.0	25	0.297	1.40	76.0
10	25	0.227	1.09	64.0	24	0.358	1.75	66.7
11	25	-0.097	-0.47	56.0	25	0.158	0.07	68.0
12	25	-0.341	-1.93	40.0	25	-0.383*	-2.12	40.0
13	25	-0.019	-0.10	48.0	24	0.043	0.17	41.7
14	24	0.154	0.79	58.3	22	0.933	0.35	68.2
15	24	-0.601	-0.92	54.1	23	-0.923	-0.72	60.9
16	24	0.446	1.04	62.5	21	0.012	0.07	61.9
17	24	0.022	0.92	62.5	24	1.472	1.32	66.7

Figure 9: The Turn of the Month Effect on the ND

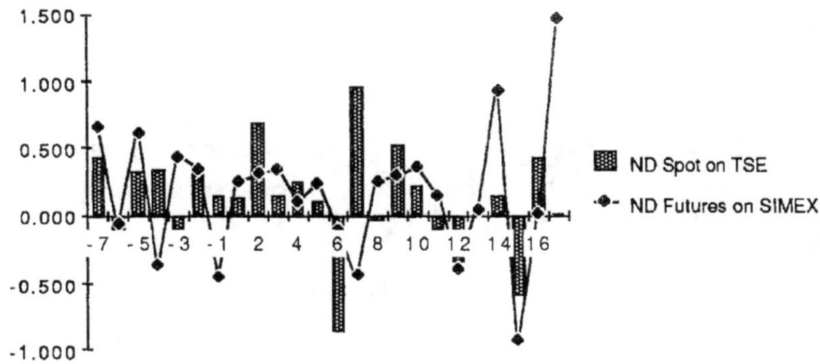

Table 9: The Turn of the Month Effect on the Osaka 50

	Osaka 50 Spot on TSE				Osaka 50 Futures on OSE			
Day	Sample Size	Mean Return	t-Statistic	% Positive	Sample Size	Mean Return	t-Statistic	% Positive
-7	15	0.391	1.41	66.7	15	0.270	1.26	60.0
-6	15	-0.185	-0.53	66.7	15	-0.082	-0.21	60.0
-5	15	0.380	1.44	66.7	15	0.702	1.41	53.3
-4	15	0.263	1.19	66.7	15	-0.548	-1.45	46.7
-3	15	-0.217	-0.78	46.7	15	-0.253	-0.82	40.0
-2	15	0.330	0.95	80.0	15	0.131	0.27	66.7
-1	15	0.110	0.45	53.3	15	0.054	0.19	53.3
1	15	-0.029	-0.12	66.7	15	-0.062	-0.16	53.3
2	15	0.197	0.85	60.0	15	0.121	0.40	46.7
3	15	0.083	0.19	26.7	15	0.120	0.24	33.3
4	15	-0.030	-0.19	60.0	15	0.086	0.29	46.7
5	15	0.100	0.51	66.7	15	0.049	0.19	60.0
6	15	-0.225	-1.21	26.7	15	-0.305	-1.27	33.3
7	15	0.058	0.18	53.3	15	0.117	0.28	53.3
8	15	-0.115	-0.41	53.3	15	-0.037	-0.20	40.0
9	16	0.517	1.86	75.0	16	0.361	1.62	68.8
10	16	0.493	1.75	81.3	16	0.446	1.86	75.0
11	16	0.118	0.94	62.5	16	0.028	0.18	50.0
12	16	-0.306*	-2.16	43.8	16	-0.259	-1.33	43.8
13	16	0.011	0.07	43.8	16	-0.015	-0.07	31.3
14	16	-0.108	-0.43	43.8	16	-0.274	-1.11	50.0
15	15	-0.940	-0.91	60.0	14	0.007	0.02	57.1
16	15	0.606	0.93	60.0	15	-0.068	-0.24	60.0
17	15	-0.083	-0.27	53.3	15	-0.255	-0.69	46.7

Figure 10: The Turn of the Month Effect on the Osaka 50

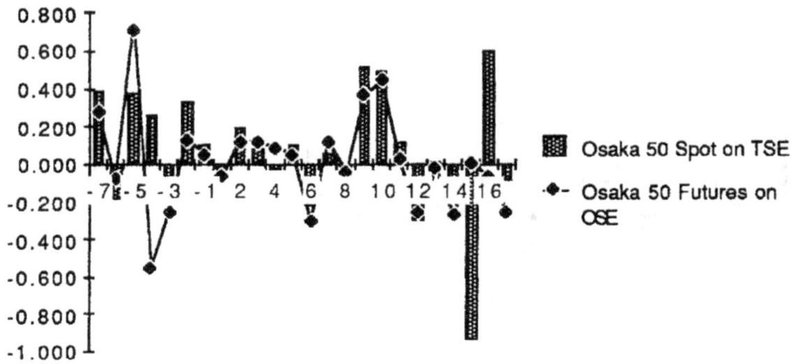

5. First Half of the Month

The effect that most or all of the gains on the TSE occur on trading days -5 to +7 seems to be working according to the script in the spot market. It is as well in the Osaka 50 futures market. The SIMEX futures though seems to at least partially smooth out the returns. This first half has higher returns by a 50% margin but it does not have *all* the gains. The following strategy would have been profitable during the sample period: buy the SIMEX on the close of -9, sell on the open of -5; on the Osaka 50, buy on the close of -8 and sell on the open of -5.

Table 10: Test of the hypothesis that first half of month has all the returns.

half	N	Mean %	Std Dev	Std Error
1	292	.15	1.023	0.0598
2	265	.008	1.355	0.0942

The F test with 264 and 291 degrees of freedom indicates that with F=2.25 the variances are equal at the 0.1% level. The t test with equal variances then indicates that the first half of the month has all the gains with 19.24% confidence using a pooled variance with 555 degrees of freedom.

Table 11: The First Half of the Month Effect on the ND

	ND Spot on TSE				ND Futures on SIMEX			
Day	Sample Size	Mean Return %	t-Statistic	% Positive	Sample Size	Mean Return	t-Statistic	% Positive
All	557	0.082	1.50	56.5	508	0.098	1.00	56.9
1st Half	292	0.150*	2.51	57.1	253	0.119	1.29	54.9
2nd Half	265	0.008	0.08	55.8	255	0.077	0.45	58.8

Figure 11: The First Half of the Month Effect on the ND

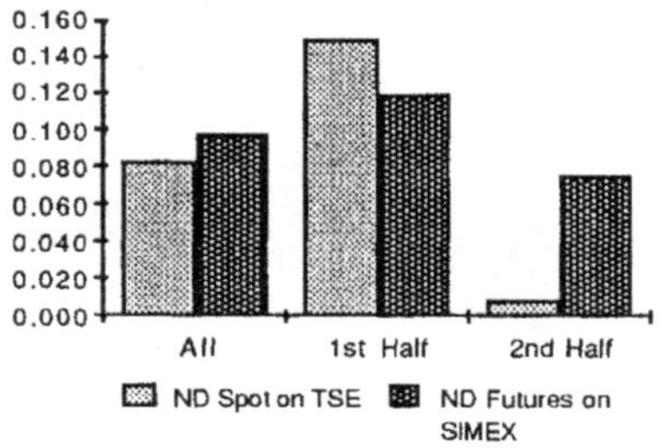

Figure 12: The First Half of the Month Effect on the Osaka 50

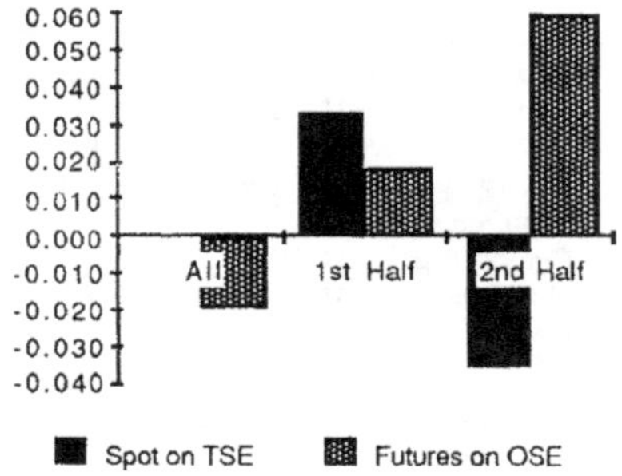

Table 12: The First Half of the Month Effect on the Osaka 50

	Spot on TSE				Futures on OSE			
Day	Sample Size	Mean Return	t-Statistic	% Positive	Sample Size	Mean Return	t-Statistic	% Positive
All	553	-0.000	-0.00	52.1	352	-0.020	-0.30	49.4
1st Half	180	0.034	0.37	52.8	180	0.018	0.17	48.9
2nd Half	173	-0.036	-0.25	51.4	172	0.060	-0.71	50.0

6. THE MONTHLY EFFECT

Because of its length of about 30 days one would expect the futures markets to closely mirror the spot markets over a monthly period. Research on the spot market in Japan appears in Hawawani (1988b), the data of Horimoto (1988) reported in Ziemba (1989a) along with additional data reported there. These results are summarized in Table 13.

Table 13: Monthly Effects on the Tokyo Stock Exchange

	Hawawani (1988) 373-566 stocks Jan 1955-Dec 1985 Equally Weighted			Horimoto (1988) All TSE 1st Section, 1965-87 Equally Weighted	Ziemba (1989a) ND 225 1949-88 Price Weighted		
Average Monthly Return Over	Sample Size	Mean Monthly Return	t statistic	Mean Monthly Return	Sample Size	Mean Daily Return	t statistic
All months	372	1.60%*	6.40	1.76	11529	0.0482***	5.56
all but January	341	1.24%***	4.75	1.42	na	na	na
January	31	5.58%***	13.17	5.44	885	0.1816***	5.80
February	31	1.00	1.85	1.71	905	0.0549	1.87
March	31	2.90%**	3.77	2.88	986	0.0457	1.50
April	31	0.51	0.57	0.82	947	0.0623*	2.10
May	31	0.18	0.20	1.29	956	0.0074	0.27
June	31	2.51%***	4.59	2.83	1011	0.0641*	2.39
July	31	0.65	0.75	1.12	1043	0.0083	0.27
August	31	0.92	0.85	1.16	1038	0.0790**	2.96
September	31	0.13	0.17	0.28	931	0.0059	-0.22
October	31	0.52	0.48	0.17	998	0.0088	0.24
November	31	1.81	1.76	1.11	910	0.0371	1.27
December	31	2.48%**	3.02	2.27	919	0.0470	1.37

January, March, June and December have had the highest mean returns in that order in both Hawawani's and Horimoto's samples. Also September and October had the lowest returns. Ziemba's longer data set shows similar very high returns in January, and the low September and October returns. But there are differences in the other months from the Hawawani and Horimoto samples. The sample sizes for Horimoto's data are unavailable.

There is only one January in the Osaka 50 data and two in the SIMEX data but the daily data used do give us some results that are significant at the 5% level. Tables 14 and 15 and Figures 13 and 14 describe the results.

Table 14: The Monthly Effect on the ND Spot and the SIMEX

	ND Spot on TSE				ND Futures on SIMEX			
Month	Sample Size	Mean Return	t-Statistic	% Positive	Sample Size	Mean Return	t-Statistic	% Positive
all days	532	0.094	1.00	56.8	557	0.082	1.50	56.6
Jan	39	0.380*	1.97	61.5	42	0.396*	2.24	69.0
Feb	40	0.226*	2.06	62.5	43	0.232*	2.26	65.1
Mar	44	0.205	1.79	68.2	48	0.164	1.53	64.6
Apr	41	0.254	1.34	63.4	46	0.272	1.87	60.9
May	37	0.204	0.90	59.5	43	0.154	1.02	55.8
Jun	46	-0.003	-0.02	60.9	48	-0.032	-0.29	54.2
Jul	48	-0.002	-0.01	50.0	49	0.064	0.40	57.1
Aug	45	0.128	0.87	46.7	49	0.066	0.65	53.1
Sep	57	-0.079	-0.47	54.4	54	-0.027	-0.20	57.4
Oct	47	-0.242	-0.26	51.0	49	-0.283	-0.64	44.9
Nov	43	0.204	0.85	58.1	42	0.134	0.65	57.1
Dec	45	0.014	0.08	48.9	44	-0.066	-0.52	40.9

Figure 13: The Monthly Effect on the ND Spot and the SIMEX

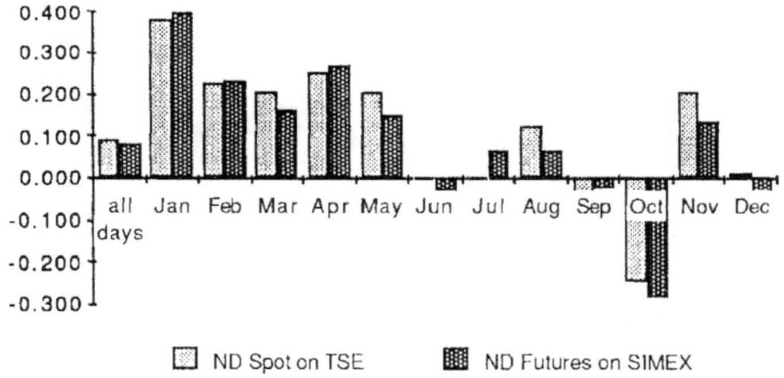

Table 15: The Monthly Effect on the Osaka 50

	ND Spot on TSE				*Osaka 50 Spot on TSE*			
Month	Sample Size	Mean Return	t-Statistic	% Positive	Sample Size	Mean Return	t-Statistic	% Positive
all days	353	0.033	0.45	56.4	353	-0.000	-0.00	52.1
Jan	21	0.465	1.42	66.7	21	0.410	1.07	57.1
Feb	20	0.284**	3.21	72.7	20	0.254*	2.40	63.6
Mar	24	0.167	1.20	58.3	24	0.124	0.77	45.8
Apr	23	0.204	1.87	65.2	23	0.159	1.09	69.6
May	21	-0.014	-0.09	52.4	21	-0.219	-1.22	38.1
Jun	40	-0.086	-0.69	52.5	40	-0.084	-0.59	52.5
Jul	49	0.064	0.40	57.1	49	0.026	0.14	61.2
Aug	49	0.066	0.65	53.1	49	0.055	0.46	53.1
Sep	36	0.020	0.15	61.1	36	0.044	0.26	50.0
Oct	25	-0.351	-0.43	56.0	25	-0.399	-0.45	48.0
Nov	21	-0.118	-0.31	47.6	21	-0.137	-0.33	38.1
Dec	22	-0.226	-1.08	36.4	22	-0.256	-1.00	36.4

Osaka 50 Futures on OSE

Month	Sample Size	Mean Return	t-Statistic	% Positive
all days	353	-0.020	-0.28	49.4
Jan	21	0.358	0.95	52.4
Feb	20	0.244*	2.68	68.2
Mar	24	0.162	1.04	50.0
Apr	23	0.170	1.14	65.2
May	21	-0.280	-1.50	42.9
Jun	40	0.076	-0.65	47.5
Jul	49	-0.081	-0.47	51.0
Aug	49	0.097	0.86	46.9
Sep	36	0.008	0.05	55.6
Oct	25	-0.494	-0.84	33.3
Nov	21	-0.121	-0.27	42.9
Dec	22	-0.256	-0.92	36.4

Figure 14: The Monthly Effect on the Osaka 50

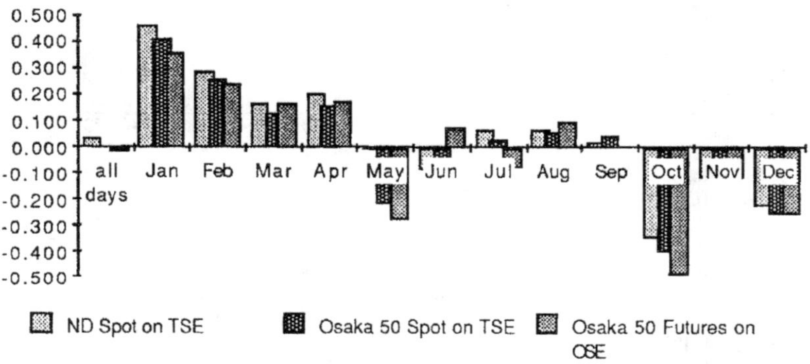

7. TURN OF THE YEAR - JANUARY EFFECT

The turn of the year effect based on the ND for 1949-88 is very strong. Days -7 to +14 all have positive returns that average 0.142% per day for a cumulative return of about 3% in this twenty-one day period. There is only one turn of the year in the Osaka 50 data and only two in the SIMEX data. In the spot data for the thirty-nine years from 1949 to 1988 trading days -8 to +14 all have positive returns. Four of these days have gains in excess of 0.4% and seven others have gains of more than 0.2%. See Table 16 and Figure 15.

For the 1987 and 1988 turn of the years there are modest gains but nothing like the long historical record. In addition many of the days have negative returns. The +2 and +3 days had a total return of about 9% on the Osaka 50. Volatility was very high. The Osaka 50 futures and spot prices are very consistent. All in all the Turn of the Year effect did not seem as strong as usual in 1987 and 1988. Perhaps the October 1987 crash's effect on 1987 was a contributing factor to this.

Table 16: Rates of Return for the Thirty-Nine Turn of the Years, ND, 1949-1988 and for the one turn of the year in the Osaka 50 Futures data set and the two turns of the year in the SIMEX data set

Trading Day	ND Spot Mean Return, %	t-Statistic	Osaka 50 Futures	SIMEX Futures	ND Spot SIMEX data	ND Spot Osaka data	Osaka 50 Spot
-15	0.0292	0.24	-0.411	0.110	-0.424	-0.273	-0.411
-14	-0.0603	-0.38	1.305	0.705	1.330	1.727	1.516
-13	-0.2631	-1.29	-1.265	-0.236	-0.646	-1.053	-1.535
-12	0.2210	0.72	0.083	0.279	0.028	-0.476	-0.680
-11	-0.1036	-0.90	0.413	0.117	-0.284	-0.347	-0.259
-10	0.0202	0.09	-0.165	-0.059	0.324	-0.120	-0.176
-9	-0.1197	-0.54	0.577	1.176	-0.049	0.352	0.855
-8	0.0347	0.17	0.000	-0.575	-0.488	-0.318	-0.449
-7	0.1413	0.76	0.328	0.553	0.835	0.569	0.868
-6	0.1738	1.31	-0.449	-0.510	-0.746	-0.940	-1.018
-5	0.1303	1.08	-0.164	-0.266	-0.149	-0.207	-0.184
-4	0.4683***	4.48	-0.534	0.063	-0.081	-0.663	-0.327
-3	0.4413*	2.49	-2.188	0.000	-1.277	-1.874	-2.412
-2	0.0613	0.39	-3.757	-5.795	-1.204	-2.656	-3.239
-1	0.2457*	2.01	-0.263	-0.550	-0.246	0.142	0.917
1	0.0369	0.22	-1.671	1.653	-0.486	-1.609	-2.329
2	0.1539	0.91	2.683	2.463	1.153	1.689	1.553
3	0.3812	1.92	6.272	-0.138	2.567	5.633	6.657
4	0.246	1.46	-0.656	0.202	-0.165	0.007	-0.312
5	0.4067*	2.74	0.248	-1.223	0.261	0.353	-0.184
6	0.0856	0.68	-1.482	-0.473	-1.019	-1.286	-1.389
7	0.2546	1.51	-0.084	-0.420	-0.232	0.207	0.335
8	0.0985	0.74	-1.212	2.119	-0.015	-1.326	-1.494
9	0.4007*	2.91	1.185	0.766	1.597	1.248	1.302
10	0.2736*	2.50	1.589	0.186	0.780	1.356	1.443
11	0.2243*	1.95	-0.865	-0.235	0.047	-0.053	-0.144
12	0.0375	0.32	-0.332	-0.456	0.432	-0.240	-0.119
13	0.1101	0.98	-0.917	na	-0.416	-0.582	-0.357
14	0.2180*	2.04	0.883	1.007	0.563	0.732	0.285
15	-0.0334	-0.14	0.542	0.658	0.757	1.087	1.157

Figure 15: Rates of Return for the Thirty-Nine Turn-of-the Years, ND, 1949-88

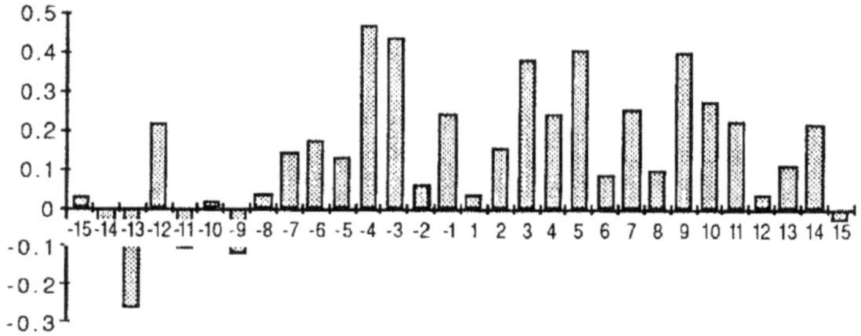

REFERENCES

Ariel, Robert A. (1987) A Monthly Effect in Stock Returns, *Journal of Financial Economics, 18:* 1-14.

Ariel, Robert A. (1988) High Stock Returns before Holidays, working paper, Baruch College.

Bailey, Warren (1989) The Market for Japanese Stock Index Futures: Some Preliminary Evidence, *Journal of Futures Markets,* forthcoming.

Brenner, Menachem, Marti G. Subrahmanyam, and Jun Uno (1987) Arbitrage Opportunities in the Nikkei Spot and Futures Markets, working paper, Graduate School of Business, New York University, November.

Brenner, Menachem, Marti G. Subrahmanyam, and Jun Uno (1988) Arbitrage in the Japanese Stock Index Futures Markets, working paper, Graduate School of Business, New York University.

Cornell, Bradford (1985) The Weekly Pattern in Stock Returns: Cash versus Futures: A Note, *The Journal of Finance, XL:* 583-588.

Dimson, E., ed. (1988) *Stock Market Regularities,* Cambridge University Press.

Elton, Edwin J. and Martin J. Gruber (1988) Multi-Index Risk Model, *Japan and the World Economy 1,* 44.

Elton, Edwin J. and Martin J. Gruber, eds. (1989) *Japanese Capital Markets,* Ballinger, forthcoming.

Hamao, Yasushi (1988) An Empirical Examination of the Arbitrage Pricing Theory Using Japanese Data, *Japan and the World Economy 1,*:45-61.

Hamao, Yasushi (1989) Fifteen-year Performance of Japanese Capital Markets, *Journal of Portfolio Management,* Winter: 21-26.

Hawawini, Gabriel (1988a) Market Efficiency and Equity Pricing: International Evidence and Implications for Global Industry, working paper, INSEAD, Fontainbleau, March.

Hawawini, Gabriel (1988b) Stock Market Anomalies and the Pricing of Equity on the Tokyo Stock Exchange, working paper, INSEAD, Fontainbleau, France, May.

Hiraki, Takato, Raj Aggarwal and Ramesh P. Rao (1988) Stock Market Anomalies and Investors Behavior in Japan, Working Paper, International University of Japan.

Horimoto, Saburo (1988) Private correspondence using raw results from forthcoming paper.

Ikeda, M. (1985) The Day of the Week Effects and Monthly Effects in the Tokyo Stock Exchange, Working Paper, University of Tokyo

Ikeda, M. (1988) Day of the Week Effects and the Mixture of Normal Distributions Hypothesis, *Japan Financial Review, Vol 8:* 27-53.

Jacobs, Bruce I. and Kenneth N. Levy (1988) Disentangling Equity Return Regularities: New Insights and Investment Opportunities, *Financial Analysts Journal*, May-June, pp 18-43.

Jaffe, J. and R. Westerfield (1985a) The Weekend Effect in Common Stock Returns: The International Evidence, *Journal of Finance* 40, 433-454.

Jaffe, J. and R. Westerfield (1985b) Patterns in Japanese Common Stock Returns: Day of the Week and Turn of the Year Effects, *Journal of Financial and Quantitative Analysis* 20, 243-260.

Kato, Kiyoshi (1988a) Weekly Patterns in Japanese Stock Returns, Working Paper, Nanzan University, Nagoya, Japan, April.

Kato, Kiyoshi (1988b) A Further Investigation of Anomalies on the Tokyo Stock Exchange, Working Paper, Nanzan University, Nagoya, Japan, August.

Kato, Kiyoshi and Yoshii Iihara (1988) Valuation of Japanese Warrants and Convertibles, Working Paper, Nanzan University

Kato, Kiyoshi and James S. Schallheim (1985) Seasonal and Size Anomalies in the Japanese Stock Market, *Journal of Financial and Quantitative Analysis*, 20, 2, 243-272.

Kato, Kiyoshi, S. L. Schwartz and William T. Ziemba (1989) Day of the Week Effects in Japanese Stocks, in Edwin J. Elton and Martin J. Gruber, eds, *Japanese Capital Markets*, Ballinger, forthcoming..

Komatsu, Asaji and William T. Ziemba (1989) Some Tests of Plausible Causes for Anomalous Behavior in Japanese Security Markets, working paper, Yamaichi Research Institute.

Kunimura, Michio (1984) The Information Content of Forecasts by Corporate Officials and by Financial Analysts in the Japanese Capital Market, Working Paper No. 84-3 U.S.-Japan Management Studies Center, University of Pennsylvania.

Lakonishok, Josef and Seymour Smidt (1989) Are Seasonal Anomalies Real? A Ninety-Year Perspective, *Review of Financial Studies,* forthcoming.

Lau, S., S. Quay and C. Ramsey (1974) The Tokyo Stock Exchange and the Capital Asset Pricing Model, *Journal of Finance* 28 (May), 507-514.

Nakamura, Takeo and Nobaru Terada (1984) The Size Effect and Seasonality in Japanese Stock Returns, unpublished manuscript, Institute for Quantitative Research in Finance.

Pettway, R. and T. Tapley (1984) The Tokyo Stock Exchange: An Analysis of Stock Market Prices, *Keio Business Review,* 75-93.

Pieptea, Dan R. and Eliezer Prisman (1988) The Monday Effect and Speculative Opportunities in the Stock-Index Futures Market, mimeo, University of Texas, Dallas.

Ritter, Jay and Navin Chopra (1989) Portfolio Rebalancing and the Turn of the Year Effect, *Journal of Finance, 44:* 149-166..

Roehl, Tom (1985) Data Sources for Research in Japanese Finance, *Journal of Financial and Quantitative Analysis* 20, 2.

Rubinstein, Mark (1982) Derivative Assets Analysis, *Journal of Economic Perspectives Vol 1:* 73-93.

Schoenfeld, Steven A. (1988) The Coming Explosion of the Japanese Futures Markets, *Intermarket,* September 22-26.

Sick, Gordon and William T. Ziemba (1989) The Turn of the Year Effect in U.S. Futures Markets,1982-1989, Working Paper, University of British Columbia.

Suzuki, Yoshio (1988) *The Japanese Financial System,* Oxford, England, Oxford University Press.

Ziemba, William T. (1990) *Strategies for Making and Keeping Excess Profits in the Stock Market,* New York, William Morrow.

Ziemba, William T. with S. L. Schwartz (1990) *Investing in Japan,* forthcoming.

Ziemba, William T. (1989a) Japanese Security Market Regularities: Monthly, Turn of the Month and Year, Holiday and Golden Week Effects, Yamaichi Research Institute, Tokyo.

Ziemba, William T. (1989b) The Chicken or the Egg: Land and Stock Prices in Japan, Yamaichi Research Institute, Tokyo.

Zweig, Martin (1986) *Winning on Wall Street,* New York, Warner Books.

https://doi.org/10.1142/9789811222634_0009

Chapter 9

Sell-in-May-and-Go-Away in the U.S. Equity Index Futures Markets, 1993–2019

Constantine Dzhabarov

Consultant, Surrey, BC, Canada
Canada info@alphalake.com

William T. Ziemba

Alumni Professor of Financial Modeling and Stochastic Optimization (Emeritus), University of British Columbia, Vancouver, BC and Distinguished Visiting Research Associate, Systemic Risk Center, London School of Economics, United Kingdom
wtzimi@mac.com

The period May 1 to the turn of the month of November (−6 trading day of October) has historically produced negligible returns. The rest of the year (late October to the end of April) has essentially all the year's gains. We show that there is a statistically significant difference and conclude that the strategy *go to cash in the weak period and go long in the strong period* has about $1\frac{1}{2}$ times the returns of buy and hold for large cap S&P 500 index and 2 times for the small cap Russell 2000 index during the period 1993–2019 in the index futures markets. Graphs and tables of returns for the entire 1993–2019 period are shown. The 2016–2019 time period had very high returns. For the S&P 500, buy and hold and sell in May had essentially identical returns. The Russell 2000 sell in May is higher than buy and hold but with only 3 years data it is not statistically significantly higher than buy and hold.

Keywords: Calendar anomalies, sell-in-May effect, monthly small cap and large cap returns, equity futures markets.

1. Sell-in-May-and-Go-Away

August, September, and October have historically had low stock market returns with many serious declines or crashes occurring in these months. The months of November to February have historically had higher than average returns; see, for example, Gultekin and Gultekin (1983) and various papers in Keim and Ziemba (2000), Ziemba (2012), and the tables in this chapter. This suggests the strategy to avoid the bad months and be in cash then and only be long the stock market in the good months. Sell-in-May-and-go-away, which is sometimes called the *Halloween Effect*, is one such strategy that is often discussed in the financial press. This paper studies U.S. equity futures markets. Dzhabarov *et al.* (2018) studies international markets. See also the international update in this handbook (Dzhabarov *et al.*, 2020)

For the S&P 500, a buy and hold strategy turns $1 on February 4, 1993 into $6.71 on October 25, 2019; whereas, sell-in-May-and-move-into-cash had a final wealth of $9.28, some 38.2% higher. For sell in May (SIM), this counts interest (Fed funds effective monthly rate) and for the buy and hold this counts dividends (which for futures are capital gains). For the small cap Russell 2000, the final wealths were $6.67 and $12.61, respectively, some 89.0% higher.

Figures 1 and 2 show this strategy using the rule "sell on the first trading day in May and buy on the 6th trading day before the end of October", for the S&P 500 and Russell 2000 index futures for the years 1993–2019, respectively. This rule did indeed beat a buy and hold strategy by about $1\frac{1}{2}$ times and 2 times in final wealth with lower standard deviation risk, respectively. Tables 1 and 2 show the monthly returns, respectively, for those 26 years to the end of October 2019. The strategy worked in most but not all years and in strategy design can be combined with other effects depending upon market conditions.

This advantage is greater in absolute total returns, but the percentage advantage was not as high as it was going to in 2016. For example, the current advantage for the S&P 500 was 38.2% versus 84.2% from 1993–2016 and for the Russell 2000 the advantage was 89.0% versus 147.1%. This was caused by the huge rise of equity

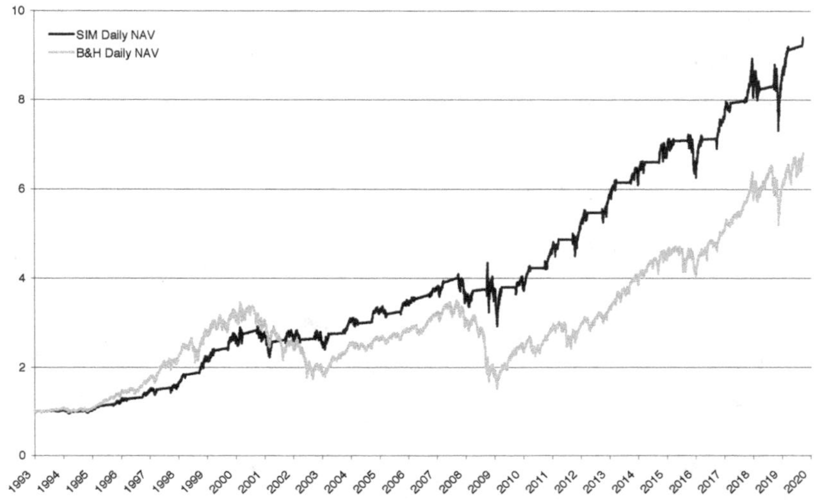

Fig. 1. S&P 500 Futures Sell in May (SIM) and B&H Cumulative Returns Comparison: 1993–2019. (Entry at close on 6th day before end of October. Exit 1st day of May.)

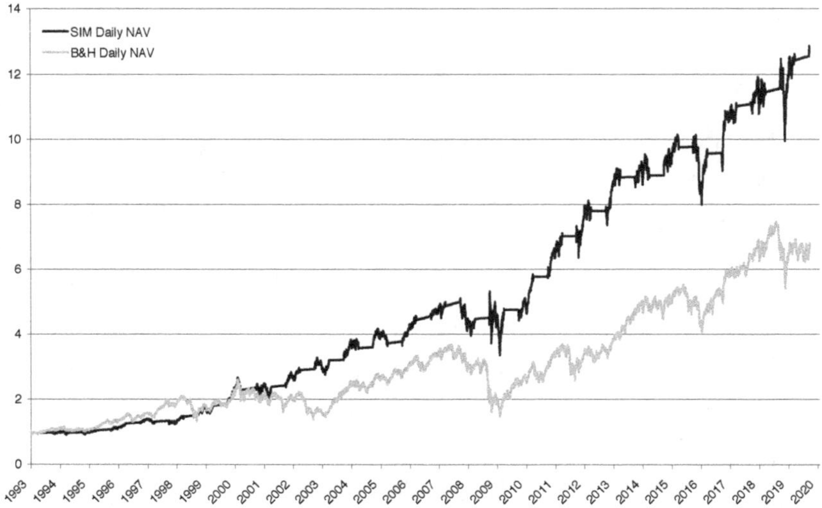

Fig. 2. Russell 2000 Futures (SIM) and B&H Cumulative Returns Comparison: 1993–2019. (Entry at close on 6th day before end of October. Exit 1st day of May.)

Table 1. Data by month for sell-in-May-and-go-away versus buy and hold for the S&P 500 equity index futures, 1993–2019.

SIM Trading in SP500 futures contract. Geometrically Linked Returns. Entry at Close on 6th Business Day before End of October, Exit Close of 1st Business Day of May.																
	Jan	Feb	Mar	Apr	May	Jun	Jul	Aug	Sep	Oct	Nov	Dec	Mthly Avg	StDev	t	Geom r
1993		−1.28%	1.89%	−3.08%	1.05%	0.28%	0.26%	0.27%	0.26%	1.18%	−1.32%	1.10%	0.05%	0.014	0.127	0.50%
1994	3.16%	−3.23%	−4.16%	0.81%	0.88%	0.35%	0.34%	0.41%	0.39%	3.41%	−4.71%	1.63%	−0.06%	0.026	−0.079	−1.10%
1995	2.35%	2.75%	3.96%	2.45%	0.22%	0.50%	0.51%	0.50%	0.47%	−0.52%	4.01%	1.84%	1.59%	0.015	3.621	20.64%
1996	3.15%	0.05%	2.04%	0.55%	0.68%	0.41%	0.50%	0.44%	0.46%	1.19%	6.85%	−1.81%	1.21%	0.021	1.967	15.23%
1997	5.78%	0.37%	−4.10%	5.91%	0.35%	0.48%	0.48%	0.45%	0.49%	−1.76%	3.34%	2.53%	1.19%	0.029	1.446	14.80%
1998	0.89%	6.35%	5.71%	0.78%	1.36%	0.49%	0.48%	0.48%	0.46%	3.23%	5.18%	7.14%	2.71%	0.026	3.552	37.39%
1999	2.89%	−3.59%	4.68%	3.34%	2.03%	0.44%	0.42%	0.45%	0.44%	5.61%	1.11%	6.66%	2.04%	0.028	2.522	26.89%
2000	−5.61%	−2.07%	10.44%	−1.93%	−0.09%	0.54%	0.56%	0.56%	0.53%	3.03%	−8.29%	0.64%	−0.14%	0.046	−0.107	−2.77%
2001	3.20%	−9.80%	−5.56%	7.25%	1.79%	0.32%	0.34%	0.32%	0.25%	−2.06%	7.48%	0.81%	0.36%	0.048	0.261	3.09%
2002	−1.64%	−2.08%	3.82%	−6.27%	1.19%	0.14%	0.16%	0.15%	0.15%	0.67%	5.71%	−6.10%	−0.34%	0.035	−0.342	−4.65%
2003	−2.75%	−1.61%	0.73%	8.16%	−0.02%	0.11%	0.09%	0.08%	0.09%	1.97%	0.79%	4.86%	1.04%	0.029	1.243	12.72%
2004	1.87%	1.30%	−1.72%	−1.67%	0.97%	0.09%	0.10%	0.13%	0.13%	3.25%	3.88%	3.37%	0.97%	0.018	1.829	12.14%
2005	−2.64%	1.90%	−1.68%	−2.15%	0.68%	0.25%	0.26%	0.32%	0.30%	0.87%	3.41%	0.30%	0.15%	0.017	0.315	1.69%
2006	2.30%	−0.09%	1.63%	0.97%	−0.18%	0.42%	0.45%	0.45%	0.42%	0.25%	1.42%	1.82%	0.82%	0.008	3.579	10.28%
2007	1.02%	−2.36%	1.58%	4.00%	0.73%	0.42%	0.47%	0.43%	0.39%	2.52%	−4.58%	−0.44%	0.35%	0.022	0.553	3.99%
2008	−6.61%	−3.50%	−0.55%	4.68%	2.01%	0.17%	0.17%	0.16%	0.16%	11.77%	−7.44%	0.54%	0.13%	0.050	0.090	0.22%
2009	−8.62%	−10.74%	8.25%	9.46%	0.72%	0.02%	0.01%	0.01%	0.01%	−4.07%	5.98%	1.45%	0.21%	0.060	0.119	0.47%
2010	−3.63%	3.08%	5.60%	1.56%	1.30%	0.02%	0.02%	0.02%	0.02%	−0.07%	−0.01%	6.22%	1.18%	0.027	1.509	14.62%
2011	2.35%	3.41%	−0.38%	2.93%	−0.14%	0.01%	0.01%	0.01%	0.01%	0.18%	−0.26%	0.53%	0.72%	0.013	1.847	8.88%
2012	4.44%	4.30%	2.84%	−0.68%	0.50%	0.01%	0.01%	0.01%	0.01%	0.12%	0.54%	0.40%	1.04%	0.018	2.042	13.06%
2013	5.15%	1.34%	3.26%	1.89%	−0.93%	0.01%	0.01%	0.01%	0.01%	0.15%	3.03%	2.05%	1.33%	0.018	2.565	17.00%
2014	−3.50%	4.56%	0.38%	0.71%	0.00%	0.01%	0.01%	0.01%	0.01%	2.64%	2.73%	−0.67%	0.57%	0.020	0.985	6.86%
2015	−3.12%	5.75%	−2.00%	0.88%	1.10%	0.01%	0.01%	0.01%	0.01%	0.38%	0.29%	−2.13%	0.10%	0.022	0.158	0.94%
2016	−5.17%	−0.03%	6.32%	0.37%	0.77%	0.03%	0.03%	0.04%	0.03%	−1.10%	3.71%	1.70%	0.56%	0.027	0.710	6.48%
2017	1.71%	3.88%	−0.15%	0.90%	0.34%	0.09%	0.10%	0.10%	0.09%	0.29%	2.92%	1.06%	0.95%	0.013	2.557	11.85%
2018	5.60%	−3.94%	−2.63%	0.15%	0.34%	0.15%	0.17%	0.16%	0.15%	1.92%	1.74%	−9.18%	−0.45%	0.036	−0.431	−5.94%
2019	7.96%	2.97%	1.91%	3.90%	−0.66%	0.19%	0.22%	0.18%	0.18%	1.18%			1.80%	0.026	2.196	19.19%
Average	0.40%	−0.09%	1.56%	1.70%	0.63%	0.22%	0.23%	0.23%	0.22%	1.34%	1.44%	1.01%	0.74%			
StDev	0.043	0.042	0.039	0.035	0.007	0.002	0.002	0.002	0.002	0.029	0.041	0.035				
t	0.480	−0.107	2.104	2.534	4.420	6.060	6.094	6.143	6.129	2.423	1.810	1.487				

B&H Trading in S&P500 futures contract. Geometrically Linked Returns.

	Jan	Feb	Mar	Apr	May	Jun	Jul	Aug	Sep	Oct	Nov	Dec	Mthly Avg	StDev	t	Geom r
1993		−1.28%	1.89%	−3.08%	2.61%	0.20%	−0.67%	3.40%	−0.84%	1.89%	−1.32%	1.10%	**0.36%**	0.020	0.594	3.78%
1994	3.16%	−3.23%	−4.16%	0.81%	1.30%	−2.44%	3.11%	3.31%	−2.13%	2.67%	−4.71%	1.63%	−0.06%	0.031	−0.065	−1.20%
1995	2.35%	2.75%	3.96%	2.45%	3.21%	2.59%	2.92%	−0.05%	4.50%	−0.74%	4.01%	1.84%	**2.48%**	0.016	5.528	34.05%
1996	3.15%	0.05%	2.04%	0.55%	1.85%	1.48%	−5.08%	1.39%	6.15%	2.64%	6.85%	−1.81%	**1.60%**	0.032	1.742	20.38%
1997	5.78%	0.37%	−4.10%	5.91%	5.95%	4.66%	7.60%	−5.73%	5.69%	−3.20%	3.34%	2.53%	**2.40%**	0.045	1.844	31.51%
1998	0.89%	6.35%	5.71%	0.78%	−2.54%	4.79%	−1.75%	−15.05%	7.55%	7.72%	5.18%	7.14%	**2.23%**	0.065	1.185	27.21%
1999	2.89%	−3.59%	4.68%	3.34%	−2.94%	6.51%	−2.91%	−1.60%	−1.64%	5.98%	1.11%	6.66%	**1.54%**	0.040	1.352	19.16%
2000	−5.61%	−2.07%	10.44%	−1.93%	−4.29%	3.23%	−1.99%	5.78%	−4.50%	−0.86%	−8.29%	0.64%	−0.79%	0.052	−0.525	−10.39%
2001	3.20%	−9.80%	−5.56%	7.25%	0.08%	−1.35%	−1.83%	−6.60%	−8.05%	1.63%	7.48%	0.81%	−1.06%	0.056	−0.654	−13.59%
2002	−1.64%	−2.08%	3.82%	−6.27%	−0.90%	−7.25%	−7.94%	0.50%	−11.04%	8.64%	5.71%	−6.10%	−2.04%	0.060	−1.184	−23.52%
2003	−2.75%	−1.61%	0.73%	8.16%	5.15%	1.04%	1.64%	1.86%	−1.35%	5.57%	0.79%	4.86%	**2.01%**	0.033	2.106	26.20%
2004	1.87%	1.30%	−1.72%	−1.67%	1.39%	1.69%	−3.45%	0.27%	0.98%	1.38%	3.88%	3.37%	**0.77%**	0.021	1.261	9.42%
2005	−2.64%	1.90%	−1.68%	−2.15%	2.92%	0.27%	3.45%	−1.25%	1.06%	−1.98%	3.41%	0.30%	**0.30%**	0.023	0.463	3.39%
2006	2.30%	−0.09%	1.63%	0.97%	−3.33%	0.57%	0.19%	1.86%	3.05%	2.81%	1.42%	1.82%	**1.10%**	0.017	2.240	13.83%
2007	1.02%	−2.36%	1.58%	4.00%	2.99%	−1.14%	−3.53%	1.01%	4.16%	1.09%	−4.58%	−0.44%	**0.32%**	0.028	0.390	3.42%
2008	−6.61%	−3.50%	−0.55%	4.68%	1.05%	−8.53%	−1.09%	1.22%	−8.86%	−17.25%	−7.44%	0.54%	−3.86%	0.061	−2.198	-39.07%
2009	−8.62%	−10.74%	8.25%	9.46%	5.53%	−0.28%	7.53%	3.59%	3.26%	−1.89%	5.98%	1.45%	**1.96%**	0.064	1.057	23.40%
2010	−3.63%	3.08%	5.60%	1.56%	−8.02%	−5.69%	6.98%	−4.55%	8.43%	3.78%	−0.01%	6.22%	**1.15%**	0.055	0.725	12.81%
2011	2.35%	3.41%	−0.38%	2.93%	−1.16%	−2.11%	−2.06%	−5.49%	−7.53%	10.95%	−0.26%	0.53%	**0.10%**	0.047	0.071	−0.03%
2012	4.44%	4.30%	2.84%	−0.68%	−6.06%	3.61%	1.34%	2.22%	2.07%	−1.91%	0.54%	0.40%	**1.09%**	0.030	1.273	13.37%
2013	5.15%	1.34%	3.26%	1.89%	2.31%	−1.82%	5.08%	−2.93%	2.64%	4.58%	3.03%	2.05%	**2.22%**	0.025	3.086	29.65%
2014	−3.50%	4.56%	0.38%	0.71%	2.32%	1.61%	−1.41%	3.98%	−1.79%	2.34%	2.73%	−0.67%	**0.94%**	0.024	1.329	11.48%
2015	−3.12%	5.75%	−2.00%	0.88%	1.30%	−2.45%	2.14%	−6.16%	−3.07%	8.64%	0.29%	−2.13%	**0.01%**	0.041	0.006	−0.83%
2016	−5.17%	−0.03%	6.32%	0.37%	1.74%	−0.22%	3.73%	0.06%	−0.42%	−1.87%	3.71%	1.70%	**0.83%**	0.030	0.970	9.87%
2017	1.71%	3.88%	−0.15%	0.90%	1.29%	0.41%	1.95%	0.09%	1.86%	2.25%	2.92%	1.06%	**1.51%**	0.012	4.467	19.67%
2018	5.60%	−3.94%	−2.63%	0.15%	2.21%	0.60%	3.51%	3.02%	0.58%	−7.12%	1.74%	−9.18%	−0.46%	0.044	−0.356	−6.38%
2019	7.96%	2.97%	1.91%	3.90%	−6.64%	6.96%	1.29%	−1.93%	1.84%	1.92%			**2.02%**	0.042	1.536	21.18%
Average	**0.40%**	−0.09%	**1.56%**	**1.70%**	**0.35%**	**0.26%**	**0.70%**	−0.66%	**0.10%**	**1.47%**	**1.44%**	**1.01%**	0.68%			
StDev	0.043	0.042	0.039	0.035	0.036	0.037	0.039	0.044	0.050	0.055	0.041	0.035				
t	0.480	−0.107	2.104	2.534	0.492	0.359	0.936	−0.774	0.100	1.383	1.810	1.487				

Table 2. Data by month for sell-in-May-and-go-away versus buy and hold for the Russell 2000 equity futures, 1993–2019.

SIM Trading in Russell 2000 futures contract. Geometrically Linked Returns. Entry at Close on 6th Business Day before End of October, Exit 1st Business Day of May.

	Jan	Feb	Mar	Apr	May	Jun	Jul	Aug	Sep	Oct	Nov	Dec	Mthly Avg	StDev	t	Geom r
1993		−4.11%	2.63%	−3.00%	1.02%	0.28%	0.26%	0.27%	0.26%	1.45%	−4.21%	4.15%	−0.09%	0.027	−0.113	−1.35%
1994	2.97%	−1.33%	−4.34%	−0.40%	1.66%	0.35%	0.34%	0.41%	0.39%	2.11%	−4.69%	2.91%	**0.03%**	0.025	0.046	0.05%
1995	−1.57%	4.21%	1.42%	2.41%	0.13%	0.50%	0.51%	0.50%	0.47%	−1.37%	4.48%	3.20%	**1.24%**	0.020	2.179	15.69%
1996	−0.23%	1.60%	3.55%	4.63%	1.08%	0.41%	0.50%	0.44%	0.46%	−0.10%	3.92%	2.08%	**1.53%**	0.017	3.185	19.77%
1997	2.07%	−2.82%	−4.14%	−0.01%	1.73%	0.48%	0.48%	0.45%	0.49%	−2.38%	−1.01%	2.20%	−0.21%	0.020	−0.357	−2.67%
1998	−2.33%	7.35%	5.24%	0.01%	0.93%	0.49%	0.48%	0.48%	0.46%	4.01%	4.37%	6.94%	**2.37%**	0.031	2.660	31.80%
1999	0.41%	−7.88%	1.31%	8.67%	1.59%	0.44%	0.42%	0.45%	0.44%	2.58%	4.77%	12.72%	**2.16%**	0.050	1.488	27.52%
2000	−2.78%	16.94%	−5.93%	−6.67%	3.34%	0.54%	0.56%	0.56%	0.53%	2.82%	−10.19%	8.57%	**0.69%**	0.072	0.333	5.69%
2001	4.30%	−7.17%	−3.60%	6.81%	1.69%	0.32%	0.34%	0.32%	0.25%	0.22%	7.55%	6.14%	**1.43%**	0.043	1.154	17.40%
2002	−1.21%	−2.89%	8.11%	0.73%	0.60%	0.14%	0.16%	0.15%	0.15%	2.29%	8.78%	−5.71%	**0.94%**	0.041	0.804	10.92%
2003	−2.90%	−3.12%	1.10%	9.38%	0.21%	0.11%	0.09%	0.08%	0.09%	4.38%	3.44%	1.96%	**1.24%**	0.034	1.275	15.19%
2004	4.25%	0.81%	0.85%	−5.21%	0.66%	0.09%	0.10%	0.13%	0.13%	3.20%	8.49%	3.12%	**1.39%**	0.032	1.478	17.30%
2005	−4.37%	1.49%	−2.64%	−5.99%	1.08%	0.25%	0.26%	0.32%	0.30%	0.34%	4.45%	0.03%	−0.37%	0.028	−0.467	−4.79%
2006	8.61%	−0.64%	5.44%	−0.39%	−0.63%	0.42%	0.45%	0.45%	0.42%	0.84%	2.14%	0.94%	**1.50%**	0.028	1.880	19.14%
2007	1.20%	−1.21%	1.67%	1.35%	0.60%	0.42%	0.47%	0.43%	0.39%	2.45%	−7.56%	0.36%	**0.05%**	0.026	0.065	0.21%
2008	−7.41%	−3.94%	0.47%	3.99%	1.82%	0.17%	0.17%	0.16%	0.16%	16.38%	−11.89%	5.33%	**0.45%**	0.069	0.226	2.87%
2009	−11.11%	−12.22%	8.44%	15.52%	−0.15%	0.02%	0.01%	0.01%	0.01%	−6.56%	3.10%	7.72%	**0.40%**	0.080	0.174	1.34%
2010	−3.67%	4.48%	7.84%	5.67%	2.04%	0.02%	0.02%	0.02%	0.02%	0.03%	3.46%	7.68%	**2.30%**	0.036	2.242	30.49%
2011	−0.27%	5.47%	2.28%	2.64%	−1.30%	0.01%	0.01%	0.01%	0.01%	1.11%	−0.35%	0.29%	**0.83%**	0.018	1.555	10.16%
2012	7.09%	2.38%	2.19%	−1.55%	−0.33%	0.01%	0.01%	0.01%	0.01%	0.44%	0.54%	3.16%	**1.16%**	0.023	1.764	14.58%
2013	6.32%	1.12%	4.25%	−0.40%	−2.54%	0.01%	0.01%	0.01%	0.01%	−1.72%	4.00%	1.73%	**1.07%**	0.026	1.421	13.15%
2014	−2.85%	4.75%	−0.96%	−4.01%	0.03%	0.01%	0.01%	0.01%	0.01%	4.99%	0.05%	2.48%	**0.38%**	0.026	0.492	4.21%
2015	−3.29%	6.06%	1.40%	−2.60%	0.65%	0.01%	0.01%	0.01%	0.01%	−0.26%	3.25%	−5.39%	−0.01%	0.030	−0.012	−0.60%
2016	−8.85%	0.03%	7.55%	1.62%	0.91%	0.03%	0.03%	0.04%	0.03%	−2.79%	11.18%	2.62%	**1.03%**	0.049	0.729	11.68%
2017	0.19%	1.88%	−0.04%	1.01%	0.79%	0.09%	0.10%	0.10%	0.09%	0.17%	2.85%	−0.58%	**0.55%**	0.010	2.008	6.80%
2018	2.56%	−4.11%	1.37%	0.76%	0.71%	0.15%	0.17%	0.16%	0.15%	3.03%	1.50%	−12.09%	−0.47%	0.041	−0.400	−6.40%
2019	11.21%	5.02%	−2.01%	3.26%	−0.84%	0.19%	0.22%	0.18%	0.18%	0.83%			**1.82%**	0.039	1.495	19.06%
Average	−0.06%	**0.45%**	**1.61%**	**1.42%**	**0.65%**	**0.22%**	**0.23%**	**0.23%**	**0.22%**	**1.43%**	**1.63%**	**2.41%**	0.86%			
StDev	0.052	0.057	0.039	0.050	0.012	0.002	0.002	0.002	0.002	0.039	0.056	0.049				
t	−0.062	0.410	2.135	1.486	2.869	6.060	6.094	6.143	6.129	1.912	1.491	2.481				

B&H Trading in Russell 2000 futures contract. Geometrically Linked Returns.

	Jan	Feb	Mar	Apr	May	Jun	Jul	Aug	Sep	Oct	Nov	Dec	Mthly Avg	StDev	t	Geom r
1993		−4.11%	2.63%	−3.00%	4.04%	1.55%	0.57%	3.97%	2.54%	2.99%	−4.21%	4.15%	**1.01%**	0.033	1.027	11.11%
1994	2.97%	−1.33%	−4.34%	−0.40%	−1.09%	−3.42%	2.02%	5.45%	−0.54%	−0.35%	−4.69%	2.91%	−0.23%	0.031	−0.261	−3.29%
1995	−1.57%	4.21%	1.42%	2.41%	2.26%	4.68%	5.33%	1.46%	1.86%	−5.01%	4.48%	3.20%	**2.06%**	0.029	2.450	27.15%
1996	−0.23%	1.60%	3.55%	4.63%	3.21%	−3.59%	−9.10%	5.05%	4.20%	−1.46%	3.92%	2.08%	**1.15%**	0.042	0.958	13.66%
1997	2.07%	−2.82%	−4.14%	−0.01%	10.37%	4.81%	4.17%	2.06%	7.77%	−4.55%	−1.01%	2.20%	**1.74%**	0.046	1.314	21.67%
1998	−2.33%	7.35%	5.24%	0.01%	−6.28%	1.29%	−9.21%	−19.83%	8.54%	4.31%	4.37%	6.94%	**0.03%**	0.083	0.014	−3.65%
1999	0.41%	−7.88%	1.31%	8.67%	1.80%	4.80%	−3.79%	−3.87%	0.51%	0.54%	4.77%	12.72%	**1.67%**	0.056	1.028	19.92%
2000	−2.78%	16.94%	−5.93%	−6.67%	−6.58%	9.91%	−3.18%	6.11%	−1.77%	−5.10%	−10.19%	8.57%	−0.06%	0.084	−0.023	−4.30%
2001	4.30%	−7.17%	−3.60%	6.81%	1.95%	3.12%	−4.88%	−3.58%	−13.45%	5.57%	7.55%	6.14%	**0.23%**	0.066	0.120	0.27%
2002	−1.21%	−2.89%	8.11%	0.73%	−4.62%	−4.97%	−15.26%	−0.41%	−7.28%	3.03%	8.78%	−5.71%	−1.81%	0.067	−0.940	−21.68%
2003	−2.90%	−3.12%	1.10%	9.38%	10.64%	1.67%	6.18%	4.48%	−1.93%	8.30%	3.44%	1.96%	**3.27%**	0.047	2.413	45.41%
2004	4.25%	0.81%	0.85%	−5.21%	1.50%	4.24%	−6.86%	−0.65%	4.73%	1.83%	8.49%	3.12%	**1.43%**	0.042	1.165	17.36%
2005	−4.37%	1.49%	−2.64%	−5.99%	6.26%	4.19%	6.07%	−2.19%	0.73%	−3.41%	4.45%	0.03%	**0.39%**	0.042	0.319	3.72%
2006	8.61%	−0.64%	5.44%	−0.39%	−6.06%	1.29%	−3.68%	2.43%	1.44%	5.31%	2.14%	0.94%	**1.40%**	0.040	1.221	17.19%
2007	1.20%	−1.21%	1.67%	1.35%	3.61%	−0.75%	−7.26%	1.77%	2.32%	2.35%	−7.56%	0.36%	−0.18%	0.036	−0.171	−2.86%
2008	−7.41%	−3.94%	0.47%	3.99%	4.35%	−7.61%	3.44%	3.41%	−8.31%	−20.92%	−11.89%	5.33%	−3.26%	0.082	−1.380	−35.52%
2009	−11.11%	−12.22%	8.44%	15.52%	3.00%	1.18%	9.60%	2.84%	5.47%	−6.83%	3.10%	7.72%	**2.23%**	0.084	0.915	25.31%
2010	−3.67%	4.48%	7.84%	5.67%	−7.60%	−8.06%	6.88%	−7.39%	12.12%	4.11%	3.46%	7.68%	**2.13%**	0.070	1.058	25.39%
2011	−0.27%	5.47%	2.28%	2.64%	−1.86%	−2.64%	−3.62%	−8.71%	−11.66%	15.25%	−0.35%	0.29%	−0.27%	0.068	−0.136	−5.56%
2012	7.09%	2.38%	2.19%	−1.55%	−6.60%	4.51%	−1.36%	3.38%	2.87%	−2.17%	0.54%	3.16%	**1.20%**	0.036	1.143	14.59%
2013	6.32%	1.12%	4.25%	−0.40%	4.02%	−0.85%	7.00%	−3.15%	6.07%	2.46%	4.00%	1.73%	**2.71%**	0.031	2.991	37.18%
2014	−2.85%	4.75%	−0.96%	−4.01%	0.85%	5.04%	−6.18%	5.08%	−6.55%	6.78%	0.05%	2.48%	**0.37%**	0.046	0.283	3.38%
2015	−3.29%	6.06%	1.40%	−2.60%	2.29%	0.49%	−1.22%	−6.29%	−5.32%	5.69%	3.25%	−5.39%	−0.41%	0.043	−0.332	−5.76%
2016	−8.85%	0.03%	7.55%	1.62%	2.29%	−0.52%	6.07%	1.79%	0.77%	−4.73%	11.18%	2.62%	**1.65%**	0.053	1.086	19.92%
2017	0.19%	1.88%	−0.04%	1.01%	−2.10%	3.30%	0.71%	−1.40%	6.31%	0.66%	2.85%	−0.58%	**1.07%**	0.023	1.616	13.25%
2018	2.56%	−4.11%	1.37%	0.76%	5.88%	0.80%	1.51%	4.08%	−2.29%	−11.11%	1.50%	−12.09%	−0.93%	0.056	−0.572	−12.21%
2019	11.21%	5.02%	−2.01%	3.26%	−8.01%	6.86%	0.61%	−5.23%	2.06%	2.52%			**1.63%**	0.057	0.910	15.89%
Average	−0.06%	**0.45%**	**1.61%**	**1.42%**	**0.65%**	**1.16%**	−0.57%	−0.35%	**0.42%**	**0.23%**	**1.63%**	**2.41%**	0.74%			
StDev	0.052	0.057	0.039	0.050	0.052	0.043	0.061	0.057	0.061	0.069	0.056	0.049				
t	−0.062	0.410	2.135	1.486	0.646	1.415	−0.485	−0.314	0.353	0.170	1.491	2.481				

prices in the period 2016–2019. In this 3-year period, the sell-in-May-and-buy-and-hold strategies have essentially equivalent gains. For the Russell 2000, the SIM strategy had higher gains than buy and hold but with just 3 years' data, it is not significantly higher statistically.

2. Statistical Tests

To show statistical significance, we tested the following three hypotheses:

1. Is the mean return for SIM higher than buy and hold for the S&P 500?
2. Is the mean return for SIM higher than buy and hold for the Russell 2000?
3. Is the SIM Russell 2000 mean return greater than the SIM S&P 500 mean return?

The essence is to show that the returns during October to May are more than those from May to October and that it is true for both the S&P 500 and the Russell 2000 with the small caps higher with the SIM strategy.

The CME began trading Russell 2000 futures in February 1993. Since we used both S&P 500 and Russell 2000 for our analysis, February 1993 was chosen as a starting point to have fair comparisons.

In testing the null hypothesis regarding the equality of mean rates of return in two populations, the null and alternative hypotheses are

$$H_0 : r_{\text{B\&H}} - r_{\text{SIM}} \geqslant 0,$$

$$H_a : r_{\text{B\&H}} - r_{\text{SIM}} < 0.$$

The first population (B&H) average is the daily rate of return (r_1) in the period with entry at the close of the first trading day in May and exit at the close of the sixth trading day before the end of October. The second population (SIM) average is the daily rate of return (r_2) in the period with entry at the close of the sixth trading day before the end of October and exit at the close of the first trading day in May next year. The dataset for the analysis is from February

5, 1993 to October 25, 2019, some 6,767 days. The test considers two independent groups of returns that are assumed to follow normal distributions. The sample sizes are $n_1 = 3{,}315$ and $n_2 = 3{,}451$ days and their variances are ${s_1}^2$ and ${s_2}^2$, respectively.

The data show that cumulative returns for SIM are higher than the cumulative returns for B&H, hence a one-tail test is appropriate. To prove the hypothesis that the SIM mean returns are significantly higher than those for the B&H strategy, the null hypothesis that the SIM mean returns are significantly lower or equal to those for B&H strategy was tested and a two-sample, independent, one-tail Z test at the 0.05 level of significance was conducted.

$$Z = \frac{\bar{r}_{\text{B\&H}} - \bar{r}_{\text{SIM}}}{\sqrt{\frac{s^2_{\text{B\&H}}}{n^2_{\text{B\&H}}} + \frac{s^2_{\text{SIM}}}{n^2_{\text{SIM}}}}}.$$

The Z-score for the SP futures was −1.95, which is in the rejection area whose cutoff is −1.645. The P-value was 0.0256, which is lower than 5%. The null hypothesis is thus rejected and the conclusion is that the average daily return for SIM strategy is significantly higher than average daily return for B&H strategy. The Z-score for the Russell 2000 futures was −2.15, which is in the rejection area whose cutoff is −1.645. The P-value was 0.0158, which is lower than 5%. The null hypothesis is rejected and the conclusion is that the average daily return for the SIM strategy is significantly higher than the average daily return for the B&H strategy.

To test whether we can fail to reject the hypothesis that the SIM Russell 2000 mean returns are not equal to the SIM S&P 500 mean returns, the null hypothesis that the SIM Russell 2000 mean returns are equal to the SIM S&P 500 mean returns is tested using a two-sample, independent two-tail Z test at the 0.05 level of significance. The Z-score for the test is −0.30, whose cutoff is −1.96 and the p-value was 0.7642. Based on the results, the null-hypothesis cannot be rejected.

We use a one-tail test to determine if there is a relationship between the returns, either higher or lower. Figures 1 and 2 show that the SIM futures cumulative return steadily outperforms the B&H

returns. The S&P 500 buy and hold strategy turns \$1 on February 4, 1993 into \$6.71; whereas, sell-in-May-and-move-into-cash, counting interest (Fed funds effective monthly rate for sell in May) and dividends for the buy and hold, had a final wealth of \$9.28, some 38.2% higher. For the Russell 2000, the final wealth were \$6.67 and \$12.61, respectively, some 84.0% higher.

When the SIM is in the market, the daily returns are the same as B&H strategy, but during the other period we are not in the market, the daily returns are different for the two strategies. The reason for the difference in cumulative returns is caused by the lower stock market returns during the SIM cash period. As this is directional, a one-tail test is appropriate. Even a more conservative two-tail test with $z = -1.95$ gives a P-value for the S&P 500 futures of 0.0512, which is slightly above the 0.05 cutoff. For the Russell 2000 futures, with $z = -2.15$ the p-value was 0.0316 which passes the test so we reject the null-hypothesis even with a two-tail test.

In the last 3 years 2017–2019 with President Trump, there was a large increase in stock prices. We tested the equality of the mean rates of return of B&H and SIM for the S&P 500 and Russell 2000 for this period. The assumptions and hypotheses were the same as for the longer period, 1993–2019, but the test used was two tailed. The total period for the analysis from January 2, 2017–October 25, 2019 was 716 days. The Z-score for S&P 500 futures was −0.50 with a cutoff of −1.96 and p value of 0.7642. The Z-score for Russell 2000 futures was −0.64, with a cutoff of −1.96 and p value of 0.5222. Hence, the null hypothesis cannot be rejected for both cases and B&H and SIM were statistically equal even though the Russell 2000 SIM was higher than its B&H.

Future rollover costs were not taken into account. While they were a significant cost in the 1990s, current commissions for a round trip are under \$5. The data uses the front month contract. In real trading, one could use only two rollovers a year, getting a position in the December contract in October, rolling over into the June contract at expiration into December and exiting position in May. This would possibly have larger bid–ask spreads and be less liquid. The point is that this cost is minor.

3. Discussion

Various hypotheses for the SIM effect have been proposed. Doeswijk (2005) reviews two prominent ones. Bouman and Jacobsen (2002) confirm the empirical and historical basis of the maxim, finding that the SIM effect holds in 36 of the 37 countries included in their analysis. They consider vacation timing as a potential cause of the SIM effect, suggesting the timing of summer vacations may cause temporal variation in appetites for risk aversion. However, they find evidence of the SIM effect in their subset of Southern hemisphere countries, which under their hypothesis would be expected to have a different seasonal pattern.

Another hypothesized link between seasonality and stock returns is the Seasonal Affective Disorder (SAD), which was studied by Kamstra *et al.* (2003) and Garrett *et al.* (2004). SAD is a disorder in which the shorter, relatively sunless days of fall and winter cause depression, which some recent research links to an unwillingness to take risk. Kamstra *et al.* (2003) conclude that the SAD explanation does not lead to a profitable trading strategy because the risk premium varies with the seasonal effects. Like the vacation timing hypothesis, Doeswijk (2005) found the SAD hypothesis insufficient because SAD is known to start as early as September so the historically high November returns cannot be explained.

After discussing these two hypotheses, Doeswijk (2005) offers a new hypothesis to explain the SIM effect. He posits that, in the fourth quarter of each year, investors are overly optimistic about the upcoming year. This excessive optimism leads to attractive initial returns followed by a renewed realism that readjusts expectations. Unlike the SAD hypothesis, which suggests a varying risk premium, the Optimism Cycle hypothesis reflects a constant risk premium but a varying perception of the economic outlook. To test this hypothesis, Doeswijk ran three analyses: (1) the global zero-investment seasonal sector-rotation strategy, (2) the seasonality of earnings growth revisions, and (3) the initial returns of IPOs as a proxy for investor optimism.

According to the Optimism Cycle, investors are over-optimistic at the end and beginning of the year. If this hypothesis is correct, a winning investment strategy is going long in cyclical stocks and short in defensive stocks during the winter period from November through April (winter) and following the opposite strategy from May through October (summer). (These stock groups are chosen for their relative exposure to the general economy, with cyclical stocks having a high exposure and defensive stocks a low exposure.) To test this strategy, Doeswijk uses the MSCI World index of global stock returns from 1970 to 2003 and tests the data as a whole, in two 17-year sub-periods, using several variations on timing of the winter period, and various sector definitions. The study runs regressions using monthly market capitalization-weighted price return indices and their monthly log returns.

Doeswijk (2005) found that, on average during the study period, winter returns are a significant 7.6% higher than summer returns and the strategy is successful in 65% of the years. On a monthly basis, the average performance of the global zero-investment strategy is 0.56%, which is significant at the 1% confidence level. Using further regression analysis techniques, Doeswijk (2005) also isolates the market timing effects from the seasonality and found that seasonality alone accounts for approximately half of the excess returns.

Like the Optimism Cycle strategy, both other analyses in the Doeswijk study support the Optimism Cycle hypothesis. Doeswijk (2005) found that expected earnings growth rates follow a seasonal cycle and that these changes have an effect on stock performance. The third analysis uses initial IPO returns, which show a remarkable seasonality, as a proxy for investor confidence. Using this investor confidence proxy as an independent variable, the regression result for remaining excess return is not statistically significant, which supports the Optimism Cycle hypothesis.

Along with the three supporting analyses, Doeswijk (2005) explains a qualitative argument in favor of his Optimism Cycle hypothesis. He argues that, since this phenomenon is one based on an aspect of human psychology, it tricks investors into repeating the same biases every year. Importantly, this cycle of optimism and pessimism is not generally accepted, which Doeswijk argues allows for investors who understand it to profit from it as a free lunch until it is more widely accepted and the arbitrage opportunity is absorbed into the market.

Ziegler and Ziemba (2015) also studied the effect of weather on the SIM research in many countries and found that when the weather is good, the returns are higher on average. Additional references related to this SIM phenomenon are Agrrawal and Skaves (2015), Bee *et al.* (2016), Dzhabarov and Ziemba (2010), Fiore and Saha (2015), Jacobsen and Visaltanachoti (2009), Keloharju and Linnainmaa (2015), Patel and Sewell (2015), Swinkels and van Vliet (2012), Witte (2012), and Zhang and Jacobsen (2012).

4. Conclusions

Whatever the reasons, it is clear that there is some SIM anomaly effect in U.S. and other equity markets. See Dzhabarov *et al.* (2019). Receiving double or more final wealth with less standard deviation risk and a higher Sharpe ratio indicates that the strategy adds value on average. Given tax considerations, implementation of this could be done by shorting index futures, which is simpler than exiting equity positions for onshore accounts. For offshore accounts, investing in futures and exiting during the May–October period is likely best.

Acknowledgment

Thanks go to Alexandre Ziegler for helpful comments on an earlier version of this chapter.

References

Agrrawal, P. and Skaves, M. (2015). Seasonality in stock and bond ETFs (2001–2014): The months are getting mixed up but Santa delivers on time. *Journal of Investing* **24**(3).

Bee, M., Dupuis, D. J., and Trapin, L. (2016). US stock returns: Are there seasons of excesses? *Quantitative Finance*, **16**, 1–12.

Bouman, S. and Jacobsen, B. (2002). The Halloween indicator, sell in May and go away: Another puzzle. *American Economic Review* **92**(5), 618–1635.

Doeswijk, R. (2005). The optimism cycle: Sell in May. *De Economist* **156**(2), 175–200.

Dzhabarov, C. and Ziemba, W. T. (2010). Do seasonal anomalies still work? *Journal of Portfolio Management* **36**(3), 93–104.

Dzhabarov, C., Ziegler, A., and Ziemba, W. T. (2018). Sell in May and Go away, the evidence in the international equity index futures markets. *Quantitative Finance* **18**(2), 171–181.

Dzhabarov, C., Ziegler, A., and Ziemba, W. T. (2019). Sell in May and Go Away, the international evidence to 2019. Working Paper.

Dzhabarov, C., Ziegler, A., and Ziemba, W. T. (2020). Sell in May and Go Away, the international evidence this volume, Chapter 12.

Fiore C. and Saha, A. (2015). A tale of two anomalies: Higher returns of low-risk stocks and return seasonality. *Financial Review* **50**(2), 257–273.

Garrett, I., Kamstra, M., and Kramer, L. A. (2004). Winter blues and time variation in the price of risk. *Journal of Empirical Finance* **12**(2), 291–316.

Gultekin, M. and Gultekin, N. B. (1983). Stock market seasonality: International evidence. *Journal of Financial Economics* **12**, 469–481.

Jacobsen, B. and Visaltanachoti, N. (2009). The Halloween effect in US sectors. *Financial Review* **44**(3), 437–459.

Kamstra, M. J., Kramer, L. A., and Levi, M. D. (2000). Losing sleep at the market: The daylight-savings anomaly. *American Economic Review* **90**, 1005–1011.

Kamstra, M. J., Kramer, L. A., and Levi, M. D. (2003). Winter blues: A SAD stock market cycle. Federal Reserve Bank of Atlanta Working Paper No. 2002–2013a Sauder School of Business Working Paper.

Keim, D. B. and Ziemba, W. T. (Eds.) (2000). *Security Market Imperfections in World Wide Equity Markets.* Cambridge University Press.

Keloharju, M. and Linnainmaa, J. T. (2015). Return seasonalities. *The Journal of Finance.*

Patel, N. and Sewell, M. (2015). Calendar anomalies: A survey of the literature. *International Journal of Behavioural Accounting and Finance* **5**(2), 99–121.

Swinkels, L. A. P. and van Vliet, P. (2012). An anatomy of calendar effects. *Journal of Asset Management* **13**(4), 271–286.

Witte, H. D. (2012). Outliers and the Halloween effect: Comment on Maberly and Pierce. *Econ Journal Watch* **7**(1), 91–98.

Zhang, C. Y. and Jacobsen, B. (2012). Are monthly seasonals real? A three century perspective. *The Review of Finance.*

Ziegler, A. and Ziemba, W. T. (2015). Sell in may and go away and the weather. Working Notes, University of Zurich.

Ziemba, W. T. (2012). *Calendar Anomalies and Arbitrage* World Scientific Publishing, Singapore.

https://doi.org/10.1142/9789811222634_0010

Chapter 10

Japanese security market regularities

Monthly, turn-of-the-month and year, holiday and golden week effects*

William T. Ziemba

University of British Columbia, Vancouver, BC, V6T 1Y8, Canada

Abstract: This paper investigates evidence on several seasonal regularities in the security price returns on the Tokyo Stock Exchange. The study uses data on the NSA and TOPIX market indices from 1949–88. Results are presented concerning monthly, turn-of-the-month and first-half-of-the-month, turn-of-the-year, holiday and golden week effects on the TSE.

Keywords: Seasonal regularities, monthly effects, turn-of-the-month effects, turn-of-the-year effects, holiday effects, golden week effects, NSA market indices, TOPIX market indices.

1. Introduction

Research in English on Japanese anomalies is quite recent. Part of the reason for this is a lack of interest in such studies by the big Japanese brokerage firms who are unaware and suspicious of their potential use. These firms do not like to publish their research findings even in Japanese. Recently, however, U.S. and Japanese researchers have been studying these markets. The thrust has been mainly to ascertain the similarities and differences with the analogous results in U.S. markets. Kato, Schwartz and Ziemba (1989) have surveyed the research and presented new results on day-of-the-week effects in Japanese security markets. Other aspects of Japanese security markets are discussed in Elton and Gruber (1989), Ziemba and Schwartz (1991) and

* Without implicating them I would like to thank A. Komatsu and H. Shintani of the Yamaichi Research Institute for their help and useful discussions on anomalous behavior in Japanese security markets. This paper is based on research originally conducted at the Yamaichi Research Institute, Tokyo. Their support is gratefuly acknowledged as is their permission to publish these findings. This research was also partially supported by the Social Sciences and Humanities Research Council of Canada, and the Centre for International Business Studies, University of British Columbia. Thanks are also due to M. Brennan, S.L. Schwartz and two anonymous referees for helpful comments on an earlier draft.

[†]This article originally appeared in *Japan and the World Economy* **3**, 119–146, 1991, © 1991 by Elsevier Science Publishers.

Ziemba, Bailey and Hamao (1991). The U.S. literature on seasonal regularities is surveyed in Schwert (1983), Keim (1986), Jacobs and Levy (1988) and the books by Dimson (1988) and Ziemba (1992).

To begin our study of seasonal regularities and to provide background for the reader, the paper begins with a survey of recent work on the January, monthly and size effect literature which is based on data for subsets of the 1949–88 periods for the first section of the (TSE). Since the first section of the TSE has about 86% of the trading values and volume, its study provides a good measure of the whole market. As of December 1988 the first section of the TSE had a capitalization of about ¥450 trillion which was more than the value of all the stock exchanges in the U.S. This survey is then complemented by evaluating the monthly effects over the whole sample period. New results on the other effects are discussed in succeeding sections of the paper. The basic efficient markets working hypothesis is that *all days are equivalent* and have the same mean returns. The seasonality results show that there are significant departures from this. An attempt is made to discuss why such departures occur for the various effects. The answers seem to be a combination of cash flows, institutional and cultural factors and differences in risk.

2. The January and monthly effects

There seems to be a January effect in Japan similar to that in the U.S., Canada and many other countries. In Japan, the effect is not based on tax loss selling. For individuals, there were no taxes on capital gains or credits on losses during the period of this study. Corporations must pay taxes on capital gains but each firm can choose its own tax year and the majority are in March not at the turn of the year.

In addition to excess gains in January particularly for small stocks, there are excess gains in June for small stocks. A major reason for these gains seems to be the large semi-annual bonuses paid by most Japanese companies in December and June. The precise dates vary but it is typical to pay these bonuses early in the month. For example, the big brokerage firms pay these bonuses near the beginning of the month. These bonuses can amount to as much as three months salary and they are steeped in tradition. They provide a great measure of flexibility to Japanese corporations facing economic swings. Employees purchase gifts – called *Ochugen* in the summer and *Oseibo* in the winter. They also invest some of their considerable savings in the stock market and this boosts the prices. Earnings forecasts may also be a factor. Corporate officers often make their earnings forecasts in May and financial analysts make theirs in March, June, September and December; see Kunimura (1984). Darrough and Harris (1991) and Ziemba (1990) show the strong effects of earnings on stock prices. Whether or not the timing of earnings forecasts injects a seasonality effect in the market is not well understood. There is, however, a tendency to delay bad news and accelerate good news which may be a factor in the turn-of-the-month effect.

Kato and Schallheim (1985) studied the monthly returns in Japan during the twenty-nine year period 1952 to 1980. The number of firms with clear data ranged from 529 in 1964 to 844 in 1980. Those firms that were delisted or had other data irregularities had similar monthly effects to those firms in the sample. Equally and value weighted indices were constructed from the Nissho Monthly Stock Price file (1952–80) and the Nikkei Needs Financial Data file (1964–81). They found that there was a small firm effect: the average monthly return for the equally weighted index (EWI) was 0.42% higher than the value weighted index (VWI). This yearly edge of $(1.0042)^{12} - 1 = 5.16\%$ is similar to that found in the U.S. in this period. The 5.16% is an overstatement of the actual buy and hold mean return difference due to the bias discussed in Roll (1983b). However, only the post 1964 period has the small firm effect in Japan. This is similar to the U.S. [see, e.g. Ziemba (1992) for precise results and references]. In Japan this also corresponds to the opening up of the Japanese economy to foreign investors. There is also a strong January seasonal effect in both the equally and value weighted indices of 7.08% and 4.48%, respectively, relative to the other months. The mean return difference was larger in the 1952–63 period, 8.27% and 5.99%, respectively, than in the 1964–80 period, which gained 6.24% and 3.41%, for the EWI and VWI, respectively. From 1964 to 1980 Kato and Schallheim found the mean return differences in January returns to be size dependent. For the equally weighted index, the excess gain in January relative to the other months ranged from 8.68% for the smallest decile firms and 3.18% for the largest decile firms with the other firms being

Largest	2	3	4	5	6	7	8	9	Smallest
3.18	3.82	4.42	6.25	6.12	7.16	8.15	8.20	8.55	8.68

For the value weighted index the January versus the rest of the year mean return differences were

Largest	2	3	4	5	6	7	8	9	Smallest
−0.98	−0.19	0.61	1.19	2.18	3.34	4.05	4.38	4.87	5.16

Analogous to the U.S. Value Line-S&P500 spread gains in January, see Clark and Ziemba (1987) and Vander Cruyssen and Ziemba (1991), Kato and Schallheim computed the mean return difference between the equally and value weighted indices by portfolio size. This is not the best measure for the small versus large firm spread but one that gleans the effect. The spread in January excess returns relative to the CAPM model using equally and value weighted indices were

	Largest	2	3	4	5	6	7	8	9	Smallest
EW	−2.48	−2.01	−1.44	−0.84	−0.52	0.53	1.08	1.40	1.82	2.02
VW	−0.98	−0.19	0.61	1.49	2.18	3.34	4.05	4.38	4.87	5.16

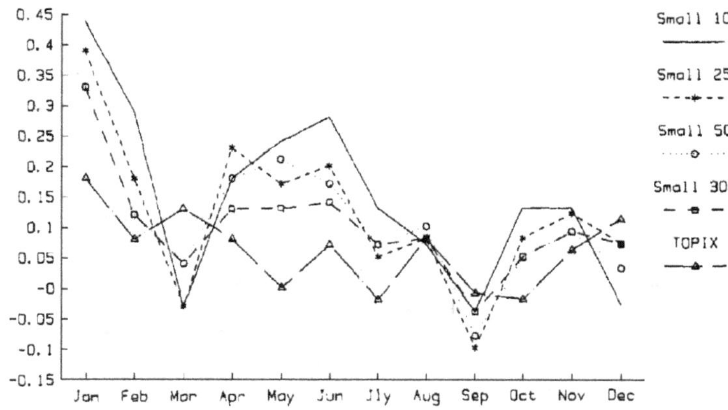

Fig. 1. Mean daily returns by month in Percent for various small stock portfolios versus the TOPIX, 1975–88.

Source: Yamaichi Research Institute.

The monthly size effect is shown in fig. 1 using our updated data from 1975 to 1988 using daily returns for the smallest 10, 25, 50 and 300 stocks and the TOPIX. Kato and Schallheim also found elements of June effect. So does the more recent data. Both January and June have significantly higher returns than the other months for small firms. Actual calculations appear in Kato (1990b) and Jaffe and Westerfield (1985a, b).

Another study (unpublished and in Japanese) by Horimoto (1988) based on monthly return data on the equally weighted index is described in tables 1 and 2 for all the stocks on the first section of the TSE from January 1965 to December 1987. Table 1 indicates that the smallest decile stocks gained 9.53% in January on average which is 7.21% more than the largest decile stocks. The smallest stocks also gained 4.34% more, on average, than the largest stocks in June. March and December are strong months relatively for the big stocks probably because of window dressing and corporate dividend and reporting effects. By month the highest average returns on the TSE were in January, followed in order by March, December and June. There seem to be two windows of opportunity for small stock buyers. The period January and February has a higher mean return of about 8.6% and the April to July period has one of about 8.2%. Small stocks are not in favor by the big four securities companies hence they have not encouraged their clients to bid up these prices to close these rather large differences in small versus large firm average returns. The data also show clearly the observation that September and October are typically weak months for all stocks. Risks in small stocks are higher than in big stocks as measured by the standard deviations shown in

Table 1

Mean returns in percent of ten size deciles on the first section of the TSE, by month 1965–87.

Firm decile size		Jan.	Feb.	Mar.	Apr.	May	June	July	Aug.	Sep.	Oct.	Nov.	Dec.	Mean	St dev stocks	St dev index
Smallest	1	9.538	2.108	1.289	1.305	2.536	5.308	2.759	1.543	−0.426	1.135	1.081	2.625	2.567	6.107	2.591
	2	7.704	2.379	2.064	0.622	1.818	4.436	2.155	0.859	−0.261	0.568	1.083	2.350	2.148	5.186	2.126
	3	6.993	1.796	1.908	0.697	1.876	3.963	2.374	0.881	0.229	0.327	1.036	2.140	2.018	5.005	1.879
	4	6.303	1.568	2.882	0.790	1.042	3.403	0.670	0.877	−0.270	0.545	0.831	2.102	1.729	4.843	1.774
	5	5.931	2.002	3.162	0.681	1.250	2.603	1.126	1.315	0.258	0.224	0.860	2.052	1.789	4.811	1.586
	6	4.866	1.938	3.194	0.795	1.350	2.390	0.816	1.289	−0.001	−0.365	1.255	2.098	1.635	4.513	1.419
	7	4.596	1.706	3.315	0.875	0.800	2.506	0.327	1.388	0.580	0.000	0.898	1.759	1.563	4.422	1.338
	8	3.232	1.373	3.527	0.934	0.619	1.454	0.232	1.457	0.830	−0.104	1.215	1.906	1.390	4.100	1.085
	9	2.850	1.446	3.663	0.551	0.714	1.281	0.290	0.739	0.742	−0.156	1.579	2.567	1.356	4.351	1.141
Largest	10	2.332	0.774	3.763	0.934	0.899	0.966	0.461	1.213	1.129	−0.430	1.295	3.142	1.373	4.808	1.163
Mean		5.435	1.709	2.877	0.818	1.290	2.831	1.121	1.156	0.281	0.174	1.113	2.274	2.757	4.815	1.610

Source: Adapted from Horimoto (1988).

Table 2
Standard deviations of ten size deciles on the first section of the TSE, by month 1965–87.

Firm decile size		Jan.	Feb.	Mar.	Apr.	May	June	July	Aug.	Sep.	Oct.	Nov.	Dec.	Mean	
														St dev of stock	St dev decile
Smallest	1	4.752	3.897	4.298	6.024	7.443	5.197	5.334	8.000	4.849	6.648	5.381	4.941	5.564	1.244
	2	3.747	3.604	4.268	5.063	5.812	4.399	4.392	6.829	4.400	5.350	5.546	3.945	4.780	0.958
	3	3.518	3.078	4.053	4.647	5.381	4.840	3.844	7.276	4.322	5.642	4.991	4.152	4.645	1.115
	4	2.835	2.516	4.431	5.279	5.101	4.002	3.658	7.470	3.940	5.169	5.332	3.630	4.447	1.336
	5	3.107	3.130	4.023	5.047	5.198	3.255	2.823	7.704	4.008	5.080	5.553	3.876	4.484	1.320
	6	2.530	3.405	3.530	4.720	4.501	3.272	3.475	6.838	4.149	5.334	5.276	3.830	4.238	1.173
	7	2.349	3.232	3.804	5.546	4.592	3.270	3.685	6.808	3.750	4.835	4.771	3.269	4.159	1.213
	8	2.478	3.275	3.765	4.463	4.266	2.753	3.559	6.073	3.832	4.819	3.677	3.239	3.933	0.996
	9	2.107	3.638	5.191	4.609	4.501	2.511	3.861	6.204	3.305	4.751	5.275	3.809	4.147	1.179
Largest	10	3.777	3.896	5.465	5.568	3.964	2.779	4.757	5.862	4.265	5.249	5.860	4.748	4.683	0.966
Mean		3.120	3.367	4.283	5.097	5.076	3.628	4.039	6.906	4.082	5.288	5.266	3.944	4.508	1.150

Source: Adapted from Horimoto (1988).

table 2. However, the risks in January and June are lower than in most other months and are below the mean monthly standard deviation. They are also not much higher than the average standard deviations by month for all ten of the deciles. Small firms in Japan in recent years have had low beta values. One can conjecture that the low betas are probably due to thin trading and the bias that this gives to beta estimates that are not computed using the Dimson or Scholes–Williams estimation methods. However, upon calculation these differences are minor. The small stocks simply do not move with the market indices in a regular pattern. For details, see Ziemba and Schwartz (1991). The advent of programmed trading once futures contracts were available on the SIMEX in 1986 and later in Japan has accentuated this disassociation of the small stocks from the NSA index.

For the five-year period July 1983 to June 1988 the average beta for the NSA (relative to the TOPIX's 1.00) estimated by the TSE was 0.84. For the largest capitalized stocks it was 1.16, for the medium caps 0.48 and for the smallest stocks only 0.37. For this study small firms were defined to be those with less than 60 million shares outstanding, medium sized firms with 60 to 200 million shares and large firms more than 200 million shares. The TOPIX index is a value weighted average of all, some 1135, stocks on the first section of the TSE. The NSA is a price weighted average of 225 well known stocks. Its value is computed like the Dow Jones Industrial Average (DJIA) by adding up the values and dividing by the current divisor. More details on these indices appear in Ziemba and Schwartz (1991). These results are shown in fig. 2 using

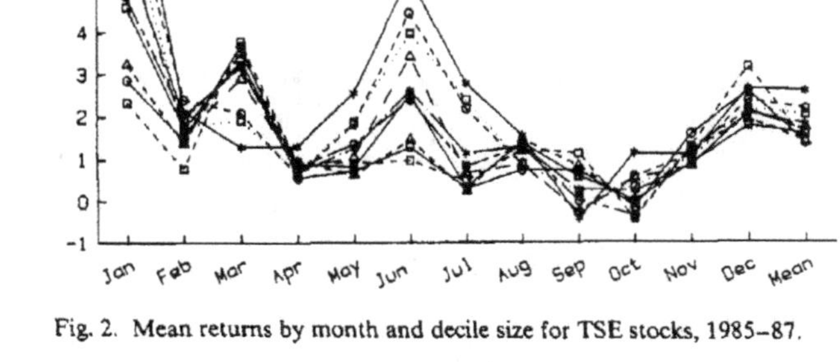

Fig. 2. Mean returns by month and decile size for TSE stocks, 1985–87.

Source: Constructed from data compiled by Horimoto (1988).

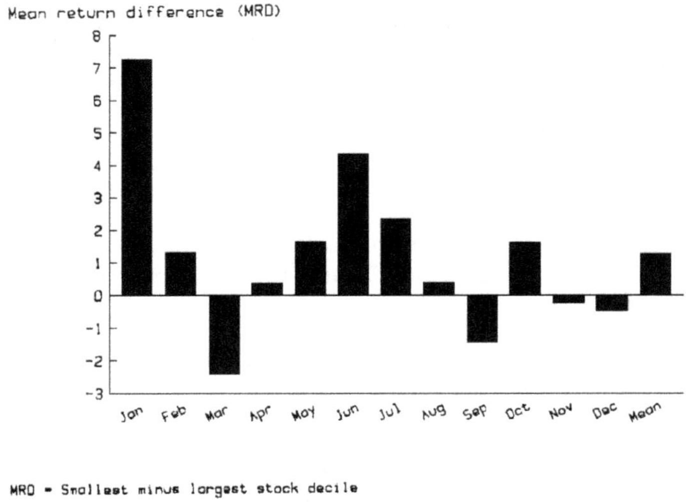

Fig. 3. Mean return differences by month and decile size for TSE stocks, 1985–87.

Source: Constructed from data compiled by Horimoto (1988).

capitalization deciles. Fig. 3 shows the monthly small firm minus large firm return differences.

Kato (1990a) investigated the small-firm effect using daily returns on all TSE stocks, namely the value-weighted TOPIX index, from 1974, when there were 806 securities, to 1987 when there were 1069 securities. He used yearly rebalancing on portfolio size and ranked the securities into five size categories with 1 denoting the smallest capitalized stocks and 5 the largest. The average firm sizes for these groups were 773 million yen to 32,689 million yen, respectively. Table 3 describes the results.

The small stocks outgain the big stocks by a two to one margin and the gain

Table 3
Mean returns for size related portfolios, TOPIX, 1974–1987.

Firm size	Average market value (¥ million)	Mean return		
		Close to close	Close to open	Open to close
Smallest	773	0.1492	0.1784	−0.0295
2	1,716	0.1058	0.1545	−0.0489
3	3,275	0.0859	0.1354	−0.0495
4	6,554	0.0764	0.0976	−0.0213
Largest	32,689	0.0653	0.0483	0.0168

Source: Kato (1990a).

Table 4
Average monthly returns on a portfolio containing all the stocks in the sample (from 373 to 566 stocks) over the period January 1955–December 1985.

Average monthly return over	Sample size	Equally-weighted portfolio value-weighted portfolio			
		Average return	t-Statistic	Average return	t-Statistic
All months	372	1.60% ***	6.40	1.84% ***	7.55
All months but January	341	1.24% ***	4.75	1.61% ***	6.22
January	31	5.58% ***	13.17	4.36% ***	9.85
February	31	1.00%	1.85	0.99%	1.73
March	31	2.90% ***	3.77	3.85% ***	4.48
April	31	0.51%	0.57	1.01%	1.23
May	31	0.18%	0.20	0.86%	0.91
June	31	2.51% **	4.59	2.43% ***	4.09
July	31	0.65%	0.75	0.44%	0.51
August	31	0.92%	0.85	1.05%	1.09
September	31	0.13%	0.17	1.28%	1.85
October	31	0.52%	0.48	0.49%	0.56
November	31	1.81%	1.76	2.42% *	2.27
December	31	2.48% **	3.02	2.87% **	3.25

[a] In this and succeeding tables * indicates that the average return is significantly different from zero at the 5 percent level, with a two-tail test, ** at the 1% level and *** at the 0.1% level.
Source: Hawawini (1991).

is monotonic in size. So the usual size effect was present in Japan during 1974–87. Like in the U.S. the yearly size effect is not present during 1983–87. However, even in this period small firms do have much higher absolute and risk adjusted returns in January and June. Interestingly all the gains occur in the non-trading period at night as the close-to-open returns are statistically at least as high as the total, i.e., close-to-close returns. The returns during the day provide no gains at all and in fact are slightly negative except for the highest capitalized stocks. This finding is somewhat akin to Keim and Smirlock's (1987) results for U.S. stocks who found that the major gain in the Value Line small stock index was mostly at night and there were larger gains during the day for the large cap S&P500 index. See Kato (1990a) for an analysis of these effects by day of the week in January and other months and Kato, Schwartz and Ziemba (1989) for some plausible reasons for this behavior.

Additional insight has been provided by Hawawini (1988, 1991). His study used monthly data for the 31 years January 1955 to December 1985. The firms he considered trade on the first section of the TSE. There were 373 firms which traded continuously during this entire period and 566 which traded in the second half, January 1970–December 1985. The effect across months appears in table 4. January has the highest returns for small stocks (the equally-weighted index) averaging 5.58% per month. The big stocks (the value weighted index) do nearly as well, returning 4.36% per month. June and

Table 5
Risk and return characteristics of the largest and smallest size portfolios partitioned into four sub-portfolios ranked by decreasing magnitude of their beta coefficient risk TSE, January 1955–December 1985. [a]

Average portfolio size (in millions)	Sub-portfolios ranked by risk		Average monthly return	
	Risk (beta)	Size (¥ millions)	All year	January
¥ 164,716	1.44	¥ 158,275	1.29%	6.20%
largest	0.89	¥ 179,708	0.77%	3.33%
quintile	0.57	¥ 160,110	0.61%	2.74%
	0.21	¥ 160,772	0.69%	1.14%
¥ 4942	1.97	¥ 5,406	2.02%	12.40%
smallest	1.37	¥ 4,776	1.34%	8.16%
quintile	0.97	¥ 4,710	1.35%	5.75%
	0.43	¥ 4,876	1.42%	2.51%

[a] All beta coefficients and mean returns are significantly different from zero at the 5% level.
Source: Hawawini (1991).

December, the bonus months also have high returns in the $2\frac{1}{2}\%$ range, and March has high returns as well, namely 2.90% and 3.85% for the small and big stocks, respectively.

The January effect and the excess gains of small stocks over big stocks are beta dependent. The small stocks have higher returns than the big stocks and the more so the higher the β is. The smallest stocks with the highest βs return 12.40% in January versus only 1.14% for the largest stocks with the lowest βs. Table 5 shows this effect which is analogous to that observed on U.S. stocks. See, Ritter and Chopra (1989). A strategy to exploit this is to invest in small stocks in January especially those with high betas and then if your transactions costs are small moving into big stocks for the rest of the year. For the period 1975 to 1984 without transactions costs one has returns in U.S. dollars as listed in table 6.

The strategy of being in small stocks in January and big stocks otherwise has lower risk than even big stocks throughout the year and nearly as high mean returns as being in small stocks all the time. Adding transactions costs

Table 6
Returns from various investment strategies on the TSE, January 1955 to December 1985.

Strategy	Arithmetic mean	Geometric mean	Standard deviation using arith. mean
TOPIX	18%	17%	18%
Bottom quintile on TSE 1st Section	28%	22%	38%
Bottom quintile in Jan. and TOPIX rest of year	22%	21%	14%

Source: Hawawini (1991).

Table 7
Mean daily return, standard deviation, and percent positive returns by month of the NSA, 1949–1988.

Month	Sample size	Mean return, %	Standard deviation of return, %	t-Statistic	p-Statistic	% Positive returns
All days	11529	0.0482 ***	0.0933	5.56	0.0001	54.3
January	885	0.1816 ***	0.0926	5.80	0.0001	60.7
February	905	0.0549	0.0886	1.87	0.0622	56.7
March	986	0.0457	0.0955	1.50	0.1335	55.0
April	947	0.0623 *	0.0913	2.10	0.0359	54.2
May	956	0.0074	0.0835	0.27	0.7843	53.1
June	1011	0.0641 *	0.0852	2.39	0.0169	56.8
July	1043	0.0083	0.1012	0.27	0.7904	52.3
August	1038	0.0790 **	0.0859	2.96	0.0032	55.2
September	931	0.0059	0.0820	−0.22	0.8252	51.6
October	998	0.0088	0.1150	0.24	0.8089	50.9
November	910	0.0371	0.0879	1.27	0.2031	52.4
December	919	0.0470	0.1038	1.37	0.1706	53.8

Source: Yamaichi Research Institute.

for the extra round trip transaction would reduce the difference in specific returns by 1–2% per year, but would not change the conclusion that the *January small stock, TOPIX rest of year strategy* dominates the *TOPIX alone strategy*. Additional research on these types of strategies appears in Ziemba and Schwartz (1991).

3. The monthly effect on the NSA and TOPIX market indices, 1949–88

Table 7 gives the monthly returns on the NSA[1] from 1949–1988 (September). The data in this section are over longer periods than that discussed above, namely, the entire 1949–1988 sample period. January has by far the highest returns and all months are positive except for September which is just slightly negative. With January excluded one cannot reject the hypothesis of equal mean returns in all months. January has significantly higher returns than the other months. The market increased 60.7% of the days compared to 54.3% in all months (including January). The other months have similar behavior with September and October having the lowest returns. Even then more days rise than fall.

[1] The NSA is a price weighted average of 225 stocks on the first section of the TSE. It is computed like the DJIA by simply adding up the values of the 225 stocks and dividing by the current divisor, which was 10.289 as of the end of December 1988. The NSA then had a beta of 0.84 relative to the TOPIX index.

Table 8
Mean daily return standard deviation, and percent positive returns by month of the NSA, 1949–1959.

Month	Sample size	Mean return, %	Standard deviation of return, %	t-Statistic	p-Statistic	% Positive returns
All days	3193	0.0565 **	1.119	2.85	0.0044	53.6
January	232	0.1990 *	1.302	2.33	0.0207	59.9
February	239	0.0495	1.284	0.60	0.5519	57.2
March	256	−0.1284	1.290	−1.59	1128	47.7
April	247	0.1446 *	1.068	2.13	0.0343	52.2
May	262	0.0142	0.863	0.27	0.7904	50.7
June	283	0.0192	0.952	0.34	0.7350	54.4
July	291	0.0897	1.441	1.06	0.2895	54.4
August	292	0.2482 ***	0.798	5.31	0.0001	59.6
September	273	0.0330	0.813	0.67	0.5044	55.3
October	292	0.0481	0.968	0.85	0.3965	52.1
November	262	0.0031	0.939	0.05	0.9574	48.1
December	264	−0.0460	1.453	−0.51	0.6077	52.3

Source: Yamaichi Research Institute.

To investigate the changing patterns, tables 8–11 consider the past four decades. The main differences are:
(a) During the 1950s August had very high returns, surpassing even January, while December was slightly negative and March was significantly negative. Both January and August had gains on about 60% of the days, while March had losses on more days than gains.

Table 9
Mean daily return, standard deviation, and percent positive returns by month of the NSA, 1960–1969.

Month	Sample size	Mean return, %	Standard deviation of return, %	t-Statistic	p-Statistic	% Positive returns
All days	3000	0.0368 *	0.868	2.33	0.0201	52.8
January	232	0.2170 ***	0.725	4.56	0.0001	62.9
February	241	0.0271	0.673	0.62	0.5327	52.7
March	258	0.0483	0.958	0.81	0.4187	51.6
April	248	0.0465	0.770	0.95	0.3424	51.6
May	246	−0.0128	0.864	−0.23	0.8170	53.3
June	257	0.0906	0.933	1.56	0.1211	56.8
July	265	−0.0592	0.920	−1.05	0.2957	51.3
August	267	0.0139	0.783	0.29	0.7728	48.7
September	246	−0.0362	0.856	−0.66	0.5079	47.6
October	260	−0.0135	0.101	−0.22	0.8298	49.2
November	240	0.0448	0.944	0.74	0.4631	52.9
December	240	0.0965	0.868	1.72	0.0866	56.7

Source: Yamaichi Research Institute.

Table 10
Mean daily return, standard deviation, and percent positive returns by month of the NSA, 1970–1979.

Month	Sample size	Mean return, %	Standard deviation of return, %	t-Statistic	p-Statistic	% Positive returns
All days	2892	0.0391 *	0.853	2.46	0.014	55.3
January	224	0.1370 *	0.830	2.47	0.014	59.4
February	225	0.1075	0.830	1.94	0.053	59.1
March	252	0.1158 **	0.064	2.87	0.004	60.3
April	239	−0.0555	1.016	−0.84	0.399	51.9
May	240	0.0219	0.810	0.42	0.676	56.7
June	251	0.0794	0.834	1.51	0.133	57.8
July	258	0.0193	0.628	0.49	0.622	52.3
August	259	−0.0686	1.089	−1.01	0.324	55.2
September	232	0.0749	0.758	0.15	0.880	51.3
October	249	−0.0915	0.989	−0.15	0.884	49.8
November	230	0.0335	0.812	0.63	0.532	54.3
December	233	0.0977	0.898	1.66	0.098	55.4

Source: Yamaichi Research Institute.

(b) In the 1960's January was very strong, having average returns of about 0.21% per day and the market advanced about 63% of the time. After January, the market had a reasonable showing in the first half and then fell in the second half of the year but managed to close positively in December. The

Table 11
Mean daily return, standard deviation, and percent positive returns by month of the NSA, 1980–1988.

Month	Sample size	Mean return, %	Standard deviation of return, %	t-Statistic	p-Statistic	% Positive returns
All days	2444	0.0625 ***	0.8242	3.75	0.000	56.1
January	197	0.1658 ***	0.6825	3.41	0.001	60.4
February	200	0.0361	0.5209	0.98	0.328	58.5
March	220	0.1648 **	0.7471	3.27	0.001	61.8
April	213	0.1175 *	0.7212	2.38	0.018	62.4
May	208	0.0060	0.8006	0.11	0.914	51.9
June	220	0.0738	0.6054	1.81	0.072	58.6
July	229	−0.0292	0.7747	−0.57	0.569	50.2
August	220	0.1074 *	0.6612	2.41	0.017	57.3
September	180	−0.0406	0.8047	−0.68	0.499	51.7
October	197	0.0027	1.6574	0.02	0.982	52.8
November	178	0.0814	0.7784	1.40	0.165	55.6
December	182	0.0516	0.5936	1.17	0.242	50.0

Source: Yamaichi Research Institute.

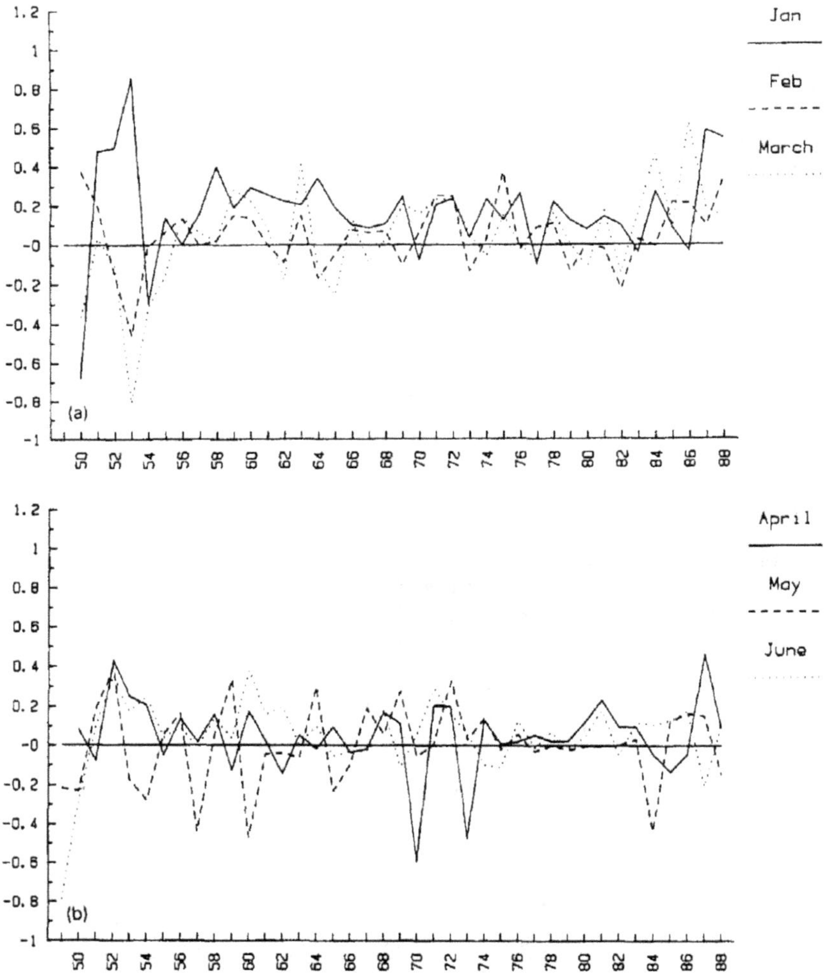

Fig. 4a. Mean return in percent by month of the year, 1949–1988. (a) During January to March on the TOPIX Index. (b) During April to June on the TOPIX Index. (c) During January to March on the NSA Index. (d) During April to June on the NSA Index.

Source: Yamaichi Research Institute.

bonus month of June was positive and the market rose about 57% of the time then. The July–November period was very weak.

(c) In the 1970s January again had the highest returns and again June and

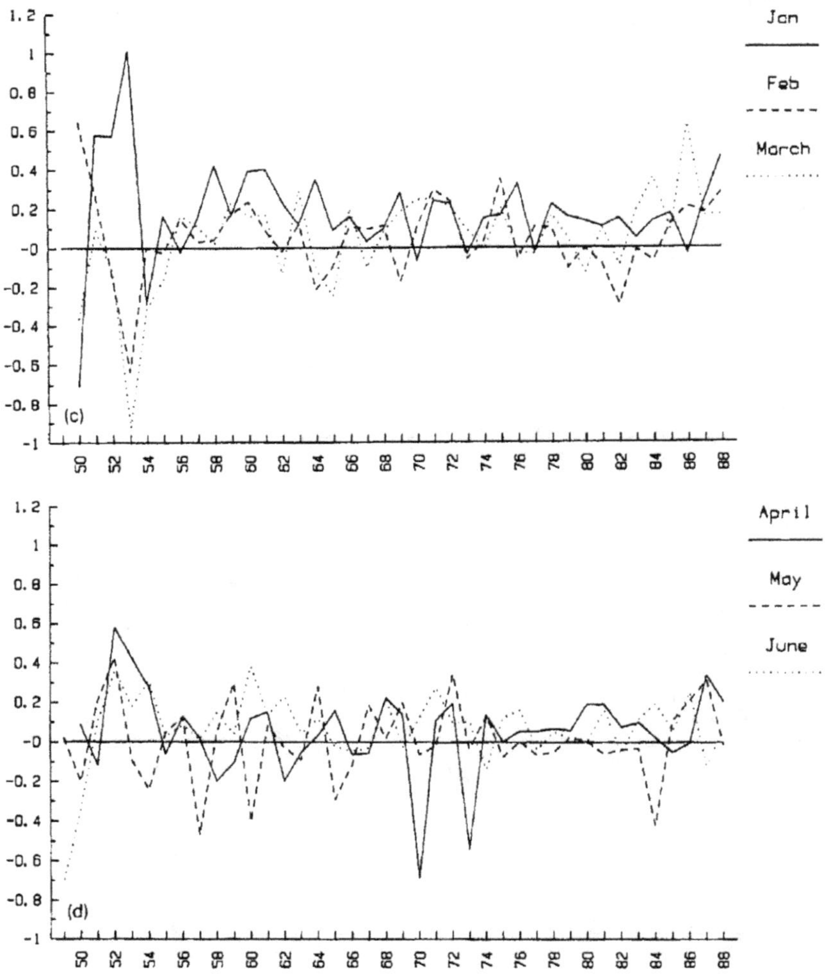

Fig. 4 (continued).

December had strong returns. The second half of the year, July–November was again weak with net losses in this period although the market did manage to close higher on more than half of the days. February and March were strong and had returns above December and nearly as high as January. The market was up about 60% in these months similar to January's performance. (d) In the 1980s January again had the highest return but only marginally

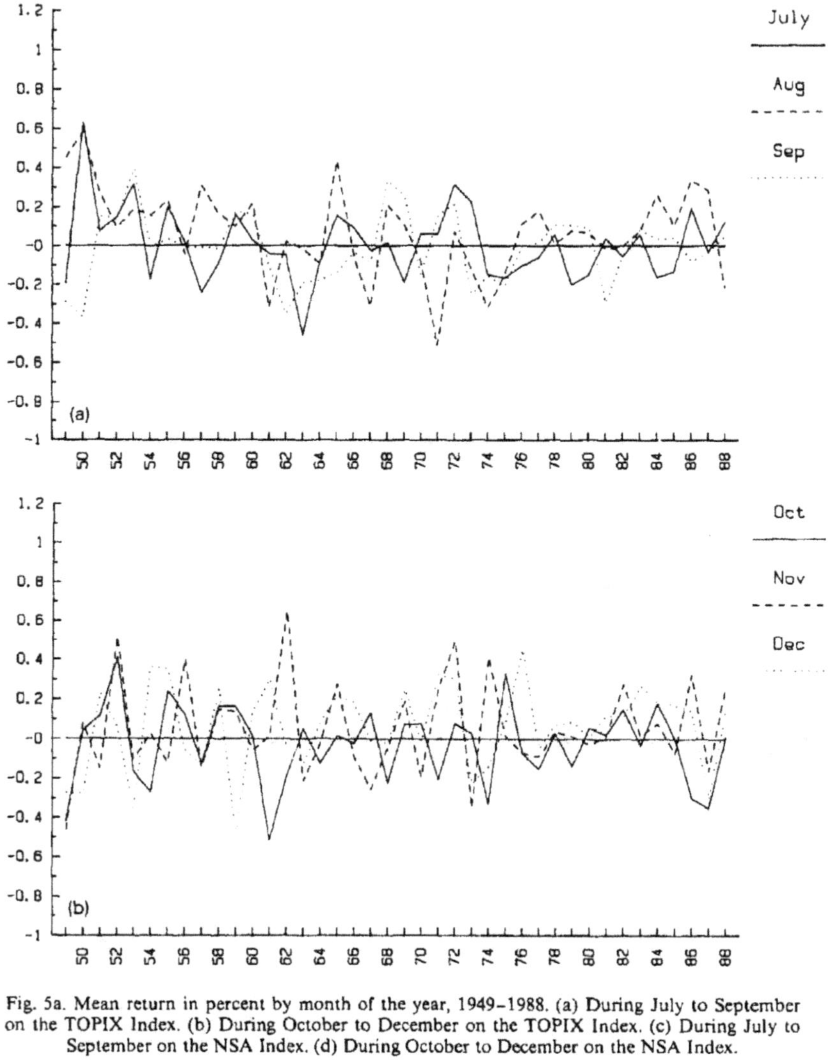

Fig. 5a. Mean return in percent by month of the year, 1949–1988. (a) During July to September on the TOPIX Index. (b) During October to December on the TOPIX Index. (c) During July to September on the NSA Index. (d) During October to December on the NSA Index.

Source: Yamaichi Research Institute.

above March. July was weak again as was the September–October period. Other months, such as April, August, November and December, had strong returns.

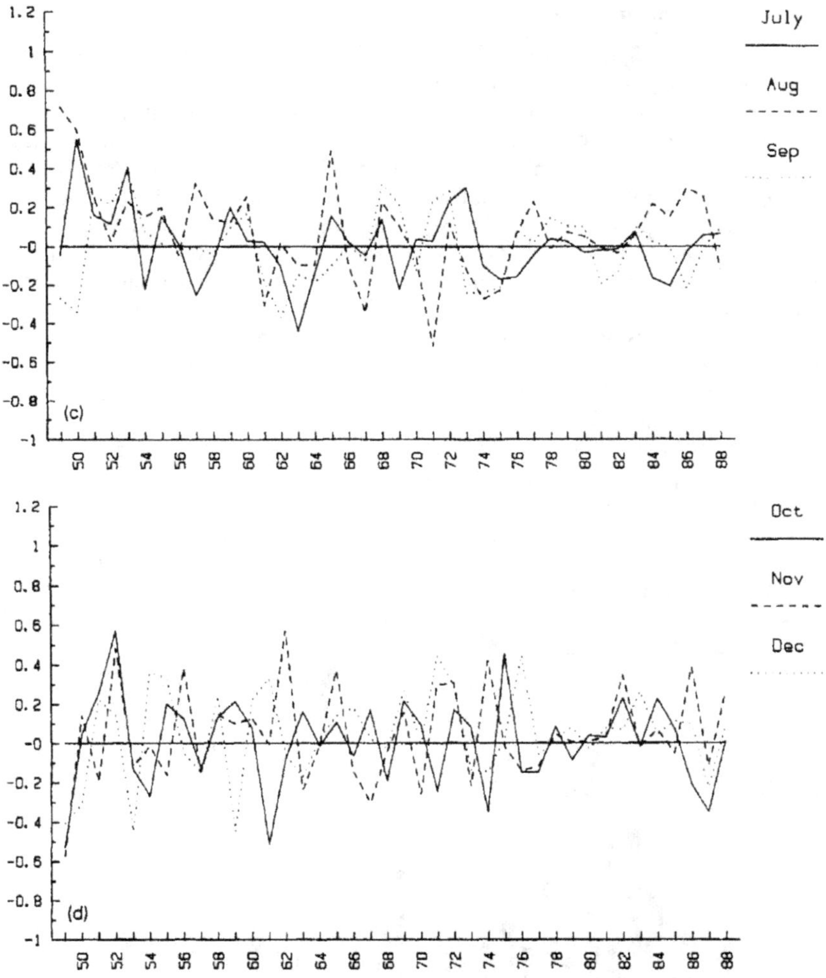

Fig. 5 (continued).

(e) The decades returned 0.056%, 0.037%, 0.039%, and 0.062%, respectively for an average gain over the 39 years of 0.048% per day.

Figs. 4a–d and 5a–d provide the monthly returns year by year for the TOPIX and the NSA from 1949 to 1988. These results are more variable than the aggregated results but yield similar conclusions.

4. Turn-of-the-month effect

In the United States the returns on trading days −1 to +4 of each month dominate the other days. This is referred to as the turn-of-the-month effect. The return in this period, coupled with that in the second week of the month, roughly trading days +5 to +8 or +10, essentially amounts to *all* the gains in the spot stock market in the period of the 1960s, 70s and 80s. See Ariel (1987) for spot data for the period 1963–82 and Sick and Ziemba (1991) for futures data for 1982–91. The rest of the months' returns is essentially noise and at best provides zero returns. The reason(s) for this effect are not fully known but part of the story is likely that people receive their salaries on or around the −1 day and they receive their stock account statements so they have funds to invest in stocks. There are also portfolio balancing effects. When would one expect the turn-of-the-month to be in Japan? Most companies pay their salaries on the 25th of the month. Does the turn-of-the-month start then and is it similar to that in the U.S.?

Figure 6 displays the daily returns over the 27 possible trading days each month in Japan for the NSA, 1949–1988. There are higher returns in Japan's turn-of-the-month: −5 to +2,. a seven-day trading period. Each of these days has returns of 0.10% or more on average and these returns are all statistically significant at the 5% level. The −1 day has very high returns, as in the U.S. The mean returns are over 0.22%, making its effect about as strong as a pre-holiday, namely providing returns about five times as large as on a typical trading day. The first-half-of-the-month effect, namely days −5 to +7, a twelve-day trading period, is also present. The fifteen-day period +8 to +17

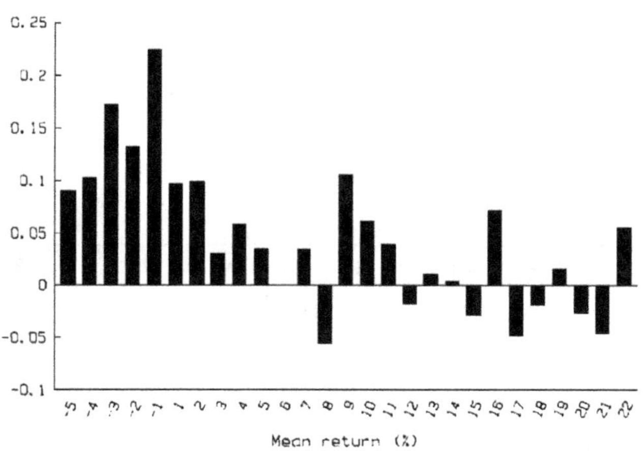

Fig. 6. Mean rates of return in percent by trading day-of-the-month, NSA, 1949–1988.

Source: Yamaichi Research Institute.

Table 12
Turn-of-the-month data, 1949–1988.

Trading day	Sample size	Mean return, %	Standard deviation return, %	Maximum return, %	Minimum return, %	Median return, %	*t*-Statistic
−5	471	0.0899 **	0.710	3.650	−2.578	0.0831	2.75
−4	471	0.1041 **	0.853	5.321	−2.853	0.1197	2.65
−3	471	0.1733 ***	0.984	4.118	−4.216	0.2365	3.82
−2	471	0.1334 ***	0.911	4.555	−6.734	0.1392	3.18
−1	471	0.2255 **	0.914	2.750	−8.686	0.3005	5.36
1	471	0.0980 *	0.875	4.501	−3.987	0.1563	2.43
2	471	0.1006 *	0.884	3.673	−4.849	0.1313	2.47
3	471	0.307	0.924	5.633	−4.368	0.0202	0.72
4	471	0.0592	1.113	11.149	−9.997	0.0437	1.15
5	471	0.0358	0.957	6.307	−10.649	0.0305	0.81
6	471	−0.0005	0.811	4.41	−3.899	−0.0092	−0.01
7	471	0.0357	0.838	3.471	−4.600	0.0573	0.09
8	471	−0.0585	0.945	4.554	−8.218	0.0112	−1.34
9	471	0.1065 *	0.940	6.877	−4.716	0.1085	2.46
10	471	0.0620	0.852	4.795	−4.399	0.0570	1.58
11	471	0.0395	0.813	5.394	−4.025	0.0566	1.05
12	471	−0.0196	0.850	4.681	−6.970	0.0531	−0.50
13	471	0.0115	1.055	11.289	−7.680	0.0201	0.24
14	471	−0.0042	0.912	6.408	−3.542	0.0218	−0.10
15	471	−0.0306	1.237	6.138	−14.901	0.0616	−0.54
16	471	0.0716	1.148	9.888	−7.493	0.871	1.35
17	471	−0.498	0.888	4.716	−4.253	−0.0380	−1.20
18	429	−0.0207	0.870	3.582	−4.930	0.0206	−0.49
19	350	0.0162	0.841	3.924	−5.032	−0.0344	0.36
20	229	−0.0286	0.899	4.604	−4.705	−0.0104	−0.48
21	118	−0.0476	0.354	3.600	−6.610	0.0680	−0.46
22	39	0.0562	0.778	2.008	−1.732	0.0079	0.45
Trading days							
1st half	22 − 7	0.01142					
2nd half	8 − 21	0.00048					

Source: Yamaichi Research Institute.

and −10 to −6 amounts to a second half of the month which has returns that are at best noise. In fact, these returns are negative, on average. The hypothesis that these returns are less than or equal to zero cannot be rejected at the 5% level.

It is a difficult to compare the days consistently, as each month in Japan is lightly different. For example, Saturdays trade on the first, fourth and fifth (if there is one) week of the month. Table 12 shows the −5 to +2 and −5 to +7 periods more clearly. These periods have the highest returns. The remainder of the month, starting either on day +8 or possibly on +12 has zero or negative returns. This is striking, since the average day during these 39 years had returns of nearly 0.05% per day.

The numerical data of table 12 appears in fig. 6. If we let day +22 be in our turn-of-the-month, then the 22, −5 to +7 period returns more than 1% a month, namely 1.142%, on average while in the +8 to +21 period (+8 to +17 and −10 to −6 in the other counting) the returns are slightly positive but they are insignificant from zero return of only 0.0482%, on average, which is only one in 23.7 times as much as in the turn of the month. The days of the week have a considerable effect on mean stock returns; see Kato, Schwartz and Ziemba (1989) and Kato (1990a). Hence the turn-of-the-month effect is commingled with the days-of-the-week effect. Ziemba and Schwartz (1991) present the results of a 52-variable model to separate out these effects to develop *seasonality calendars* to evaluate and rank all the days on a common basis.

Discussions with experienced brokerage executives provided the following list of plausible reasons for the turn-of-the-month effect. They involve financial flows or institutional arrangements that collectively seem to cause the effect. To test these hypotheses rigorously would require considerable statistical ingenuity and data collection effort.

- Most salaries are paid on days 20–25 of the month with the 25th being especially popular. This leads to buying pressure on the 25th.
- There is portfolio window dressing on day −1.
- Security firms can invest for their own accounts in amounts based on their capitalization. Since their capitalization usually rises each month and is computed at the end of the month, there is buying as early as on day −3 to account for this (because of the three day settlement process on the TSE).
- Large brokerage firms have a sales push that lasts 7 to 10 days and this starts on day −3.
- Employment stock holding plans and mutual funds receive money in this period to invest, starting around day −3.
- People buy mutual funds with their pay which they receive on calendar days 15 to 25 of the month; then these funds are invested in stocks with a lag, so most of the buying occurs on days −5 to +2.

5. Holiday effects

There is a holiday effect in Japanese securities similar to that in U.S. securities as documented by Ariel (1988). See also French and Roll (1986), Lakonishok and Smidt (1989), Zweig (1986) and Ziemba (1991). The mean return on all days on the NSA from 1949–1988 is 0.048% per day. On the pre-holidays the return is about five times as high: 0.246% per day. Moreover the risk as measured by the standard deviation is also lower: 0.794% versus 0.979% per day, respectively. As in the U.S. there are no abnormal gains on the days around holidays except for the pre-holiday trading day. For example,

Table 13
Holiday effects on the NSA, 1949–1988.

Day	Sample size	Minimum return, %	Maximum return, %	Mean return, %	Standard deviation, %	t-Statistic
Pre-holiday	408	−5.4069	3.0631	0.2461 ***	0.7943	6.26
Non pre-holiday	7143	−14.9009	11.2893	0.0489 ***	0.9786	4.22
Days after holidays	408	−8.6856	4.7122	0.0068	0.9893	0.14
Pre-holidays, Fridays and Saturdays preceding market closing	2268	−6.6101	6.8765	0.1561 ***	0.7242	10.27
Days after holidays and weekends	2268	−8.6856	5.3938	−0.0480 *	0.9473	−2.41

Source: Yamaichi Research Institute.

the days following holidays had returns of 0.0067% per day on the NSA during 1949–1988 which is less than a typical day. A regression shows this:

$$\underset{(3.745)}{R = 0.0352} \underset{(1.491)}{+0.0799\,Day-3} \underset{(0.424)}{+0.0222\,Day-2} \underset{(3.709)}{+0.1894\,Day-1} \underset{(-1.334)}{-0.0663\,Day+1} \underset{(0.023)}{+0.00114\,Day+2}$$

where R is the daily return and the effects of trading days -3 to $+2$ are separated out using 0, 1 variables for these coefficients. Only the pre-holiday with a mean return of 0.1894% per day is statistically significant with a t-static of 3.709.

If we lump Fridays without Saturday trading and Saturdays in as *special pre-holidays* then the average return over the thirty-nine years is still 0.156% per day and the trading day after special and regular holidays has negative returns namely −0.048%. This is mostly the effect of the negative Mondays. See Kato, Schwartz and Ziemba (1989) or Kato (1990a). In Japan, Tuesdays are negative, on average, but not when there is Saturday trading the previous week. Then Monday is strongly negative, on average. These results are summarized in table 13.

Table 14 shows that pre-holidays improve every day of the week. Lakonishok and Smidt (1989) found similar results in their 90-year Dow Jones Industrial Average study. Even Mondays and Tuesdays are positive if they are pre-holidays. Wednesdays, Thursdays, Friday and Saturdays have extremely high returns if they are pre-holidays. These days have positive returns about 70% of the time. Saturday trading has varied considerably over the years with the trend towards fewer and fewer open Saturdays. During the sample period, Saturdays were open about 90% of the weeks. Saturdays were closed for trading as of February 1989. For more on the day-of-the-week effects in Japan, see Kato (1990a), Kato, Schwartz and Ziemba (1989) and Amihud and Mendelson (1989).

Table 14
Mean daily return, standard deviation and percent positive returns on pre-holidays by days of the week of the NSA, 1949–1988. [a]

	Sample size	Mean return, %	Standard deviation, %	t-Statistic	p-Statistic	Median return	% Positive returns
All Mondays	1937	−0.589 **	0.9500	−2.73	0.0064	0.0189	50.9
All Tuesdays	1959	−0.0419	0.9586	−1.93	0.0532	−0.0373	47.4
All Wednesdays	1960	0.1164 ***	0.9722	5.30	0.0001	0.1212	56.9
All Thursdays	1959	0.0871 ***	1.0234	3.77	0.0002	0.0676	55.1
All Fridays	1959	0.0544 **	0.9174	2.62	0.0087	0.0700	54.6
All Saturdays	1755	0.1409 ***	0.7043	8.38	0.0001	0.1483	61.9
Mon. before holidays	59	0.3106 **	0.7698	3.10	0.0030	0.3788	76.3
Tues. before holidays	59	0.0103	0.7866	0.10	0.9198	0.1192	57.6
Weds. before holidays	58	0.1600	1.0388	1.17	0.2456	0.1955	69.0
Thurs. before holidays	60	0.1868 **	0.7860	2.82	0.0064	0.2986	73.3
Fri. before holidays	71	0.3821 ***	0.7944	4.05	0.0001	0.3411	74.6
Sat. before holidays	101	0.2758 ***	0.6242	4.44	0.0001	0.2468	64.4
1	256	0.2097 ***	0.7324	4.58	0.0001	0.1574	62.5
2	1703	0.0310	0.9401	1.36	0.1731	0.0522	53.4
3	18	0.2648	0.8151	1.38	0.1859	0.4115	77.8
4	56	0.1895 *	0.5595	2.53	0.0141	0.2139	66.1

1 = Fridays before a no-trading Saturday; 2 = Fridays before a trading Saturday; 3 = Fridays before no-trading Saturday and no-trading Monday; 4 = Saturdays before no-trading Monday (Saturdays before a Monday holiday).

Source: Yamaichi Research Institute.

Table 15 shows the effect of the pre-holidays as separate from the day-of-the-week effects. The regression estimates show that the pre-holiday effect is the largest, about 0.246% per day. Mondays and Tuesdays are negative as expected. Since these estimates use the entire 39 years of the NSA, Wednesdays' returns are slightly less than Saturdays' and these two days return the bulk of the week's return. All the coefficients are significant at the 5% level.

Table 15
Day of the week and pre-holiday effects on the NSA, 1949–1988.

Effect	Mean return, %	Standard deviation, %	t-Statistic	p-Statistic
Monday	−0.0705 **	0.0214	−3.29	0.0010
Tuesday	−0.0435 *	0.0213	−2.04	0.0412
Wednesday	0.1151 ***	0.0213	5.40	0.0001
Thursday	0.0807 ***	0.0213	3.79	0.0002
Friday	0.0420 *	0.0214	1.97	0.0492
Saturday	0.1327 ***	0.0229	5.81	0.0001
Pre-holiday	0.2461 ***	0.0460	5.35	0.0001

Source: Yamaichi Research Institute.

Table 16
Mean daily return, standard deviation on pre-holidays, NSA, 1949–1988.

Holiday	Advances	Mean return, %	Standard deviation, %	Minimum return, %	Maximum return, %	t-Statistic
January 1	32/39	0.2457	0.7625	−3.38	1.269	2.01
January 15	32/39	0.4711 **	0.7157	−2.04	1.947	4.11
February 11	15/22	0.3011 *	0.5326	−0.42	1.810	2.65
February 20	21/39	0.0687	0.6213	−1.50	1.912	0.69
April 29	25/39	0.2272	0.8313	−2.96	2.731	1.71
May 3	31/39	0.4989 ***	0.6700	−0.74	3.063	4.65
May 5	30/39	0.3884 ***	0.6184	−0.66	2.188	3.92
September 15	14/22	0.0154	0.7309	−2.48	0.670	0.10
September 23	27/39	0.2341 **	0.4866	−0.92	1.310	3.00
October 10	12/22	−0.2487	1.4389	−5.41	1.256	−0.81
November 3	24/39	0.2987 *	0.8684	−1.27	2.770	2.15
November 23	25/39	0.2414	0.9711	−2.18	2.585	1.55

Source: Yamaichi Research Institute.

Table 17
Mean return per day around the time of the golden week NSA, 1949–1988.

Date	Sample size	Mean return, %	t-Statistic	p-Statistic
April 20	32	−0.1285	−0.73	0.4691
April 21	32	−0.0234	−0.18	0.8617
April 22	33	0.0576	0.34	0.6963
April 23	34	−0.0024	−0.01	0.9888
April 24	33	0.1133	1.23	0.2291
April 25	34	0.1339	0.92	0.3664
April 26	33	0.2922 *	2.10	0.0433
April 27	33	0.1277	0.74	0.4639
April 28	34	0.2148	1.41	0.1685
April 30	31	−0.1418	−0.47	0.6448
May 01	33	0.4312 *	2.69	0.0113
May 02	34	0.5359 ***	4.47	0.0001
May 04	30	0.3255 **	2.96	0.0060
May 06	31	−0.0976	−0.60	0.5516
May 07	34	0.0903	0.87	0.3892
May 08	33	−0.1326	−0.79	0.4260
May 09	33	−0.1174	−0.91	0.3671
May 10	32	−0.0350	−0.23	0.8170
May 11	32	0.0282	0.28	0.7924
May 12	33	−0.0701	−0.70	0.4905
May 13	33	−0.1336	−1.02	0.3134
May 14	33	−0.2421	−1.75	0.0889
May 15	31	−0.2111	−1.70	0.0989
May 16	32	−0.0635	−0.50	0.6235
May 17	32	−0.2209	−1.39	0.1755
May 18	33	−0.3210 *	−2.20	0.0355
May 19	34	−0.2898	−1.47	0.1509
May 20	32	0.0081	0.06	0.9551
May 21	32	0.3553	1.57	0.1274

Table 18
Rates of return for the 39 turn-of-the years, NSA, 1949–1988.

Trading day	Mean return, %	Standard deviation, %	t-Statistic	p-Statistic
−15	0.0292	0.7566	0.24	0.8108
−14	−0.603	0.9834	−0.38	0.7037
−13	−0.2631	1.2660	−1.29	0.2022
−12	0.2210	1.9265	0.72	0.4782
−11	−0.1036	0.7214	−0.90	0.3754
−10	0.0202	1.2598	0.09	0.9209
−9	−0.1197	1.3817	−0.54	0.5918
−8	0.0347	1.2604	0.17	0.8643
−7	0.1413	1.1679	0.76	0.4538
−6	0.1738	0.8303	1.31	0.1990
−5	0.1303	0.7532	1.08	0.2868
−4	0.4683 ***	0.6526	4.48	0.0001
−3	0.4413 *	1.1038	2.49	0.0170
−2	0.0613	0.9883	0.39	0.7005
−1	0.2457	0.7625	2.01	0.0513
1	0.0369	1.0594	0.22	0.8289
2	0.1539	1.0529	0.91	0.3670
3	0.3812	1.2409	1.92	0.0626
4	0.2460	1.0516	1.46	0.1523
5	0.4067 *	0.9277	2.74	0.0093
6	0.0856	0.7856	0.68	0.5005
7	0.2546	1.0541	1.51	0.1397
8	0.0985	0.8342	0.74	0.4655
9	0.4007 **	0.8602	2.91	0.0060
10	0.2736 *	0.6824	2.50	0.0167
11	0.2243	0.7166	1.95	0.0580
12	0.0375	0.7256	0.32	0.7489
13	0.1101	0.7036	0.98	0.3309
14	0.2180 *	0.6674	2.04	0.0484
15	−0.0334	1.4171	−0.14	0.8837

The standard deviations are coincidently extremely close for all days of the week except for the pre-holidays.

Are some pre-holidays better than others? Table 16 investigates this for the twelve holidays. Most of the pre-holidays have high returns. The exceptions are September 15 which is just barely positive and October 10 which is negative. This is not surprising as the earlier research showed very poor returns in these months over the years.

6. The golden week effect

In late April and early May there are three holidays in a one-week period referred to as *The Golden Week*. The holidays are on April 29, May 3 and May 5. Hence, one would expect that April 28, May 2 and May 4 would have strong returns. Also, in relation to the Christmas holiday period, as Lakonishok and Smidt (1989) found for the DJIA in the U.S., other days in this period likely will have large returns as well. The results for the NSA 1949–1988 data displayed in table 17 shows that the three pre-holidays have high returns. April 28 returns, on average, 0.215%, May 2 a whopping 0.536% and May 4 0.326%. The in-between day, May 1, a +1 day, and a −2 pre-holiday, returns an extremely high 0.431%. The post-holiday day is poor; not surprisingly it returns a negative 0.142%. It is an exception to the observed fact that the −1 day of the month is extremely positive. A change in 1989 may affect this. This is the closing of the market on May 4 to make a three-day break. With only two instead of three pre-holidays the total return in this period may be sufficient for −1 to be strong as usual. This was the case in 1989 and 1990.

7. Turn-of-the-year effect

Based on our discussion of the turn-of-the-month effect, one would expect the turn-of-the-year effect to begin around day −5 and run to the middle of January. The data shown in table 18 indicate that the effect seems to start on day −7 when the mean return is 0.142% per day. The effect then has positive returns on every trading day until +14. Many of the days have phenomenal average returns: −4 is 0.468%, −3 is 0.441%, −1 is 0.246%, +3 is 0.381%, +5 is 0.407%, +7 is 0.255%, +9 is 0.401%, +10 is 0.274%, +11 is 0.224%, and +14 is 0.218%. This is with the 39 years of NSA data from 1949–1988. There are no small-firm indices readily available in Japan. Given the results discussed earlier that the small firms would probably have even higher returns. The cumulative average return on these 21 trading days is about 3% for the NSA.

The −1 day, the final trading day of the year, is the start of the U.S. turn-of-the-month effect, how important is it in Japan? Its return, by itself, is about 0.198% per day, or more than four times the average day's return of about 0.0476% as shown by the regression model:

		Mean return %	t-Statistic	p-Statistic
b_0	Typical day	0.0476 ***	5.47	0.0001
b_1	−1's	0.1981	1.32	0.1856

where

$$b_1 = \begin{cases} 1 & \text{for } -1 \text{ day of the month} \\ 0 & \text{otherwise} \end{cases}$$

The following regression model separates out the −1 of the year effect, from the −1 of each other month and the pre-holiday effect. The results show that each of these three effects is quite similar in size, returning about 0.2% per day. At least one third of the total mean returns amounts to −1's and pre-holidays which is similar to what Lakonishok and Smidt (1989) found for the Dow Jones Industrial Average over the 90 years from 1897 to 1986.

		Mean return	t-Statistic	p-Statistic
b_0	Typical day	0.0341 ***	3.78	0.0002
b_1	−1 of the year	0.2116	1.42	0.1568
b_2	−1 of the month	0.1822 ***	3.95	0.001
b_3	Pre-holidays	0.2121 ***	4.30	0.0001

$$b_1 = \begin{cases} 1 & \text{for last trading day of December} \\ 0 & \text{otherwise} \end{cases},$$

$$b_2 = \begin{cases} 1 & \text{for-1 day of the month except for January} \\ & \quad \text{and pre-holidays} \\ 0 & \text{otherwise} \end{cases},$$

$$b_3 = \begin{cases} 1 & \text{pre-holidays except-1 day of year} \\ 0 & \text{otherwise} \end{cases}$$

8. Conclusion

The results show that the seasonality regularities in Japan during the 1949–88 period were quite similar to the corresponding effects in U.S. security markets. Differences occur because of alternative institutional and cultural patterns in Japan. For example, the turn-of-the-month effect which indicates higher returns on trading days −1 to +4 in the U.S. is paralleled in Japan with days −5 to +2. The returns on these days were about two thirds of the total monthly return. The rest of the return in each country was earned on days +5 to +9 in the U.S. and +3 to +7 in Japan. For the balance of the month in each country, the returns are statistically less than or equal to zero. The turn-of-the-year effect was also similar to that in the U.S. except it was longer in December and in January.

The holiday effect is also similar with strong gains on pre-holiday trading days and negative returns on the post-holiday trading days. The Golden Week effect in early May is unique to Japan. It is interconnected with the holiday effect since during the sample study period 1949–88 there were three holidays during Golden Week. The strongest days of the year in Japan as in the U.S. are the pre-holidays and the −1 days for all twelve months. These days have a mean return of about 0.20% per day.

The small stock January effect in Japan was similar to that in the U.S. despite the fact that there were no capital gains for individuals during the period. Japan also has a strong June effect for small stocks. Large bonuses paid to workers just prior to these stock rises seem to be at least a part of the cause of the high returns in these months.

Students and practitioners of the Japanese stock market can utilize the seasonal regularities for several purposes. One is in the construction of seasonality calendars that rank the days of the years on a +4 (the best) to −4 (the worst). This is discussed in Ziemba and Schwartz (1991). The evidence is that such seasonality calendars do show violations of market efficiency with the high rated day having significantly higher returns than the low rated days at high levels of significance. The seasonal regularities along with the small stock effect can also be used to construct anomaly portfolios which is also discussed in Ziemba and Schwartz (1991).

References

Amihud, Y. and H. Mendelson, 1989, Market microstructure and price discovery on the Tokyo stock exchange, Japan and the World Economy 1, no. 4, 341–370.

Ariel, R.A., 1987, A monthly effect in stock returns, Journal of Financial Economics 17, 161–174.

Ariel, R.A., 1988, High stock returns before holidays, Working paper (Baruch College, City University of New York, New York).

Clark, R. and W.T. Ziemba, 1987, Playing the turn of the year effect in the futures markets, Operations Research 35, 798–813.

Darrough, M. and T. Harris, 1991, Do management forecasts of earnings affect stock prices in Japan?, in: W.T. Ziemba, W. Bailey and Y. Hamao, eds., Japanese financial market research (North-Holland, Amsterdam).

Dimson, E., ed., 1988, Stock market regularities (Cambridge University Press, Cambridge, MA).

Elton, E.J. and M.J. Gruber, eds., 1989, Japanese capital markets (Harper and Row, New York).

French, K. and R. Roll, 1986, Stock return variances: The arrival of information and the reaction of traders, Journal of Financial Economics 17, 5–26.

Hawawini, G., 1988, Market efficiency and equity pricing: International evidence and implications for global industry, in: P.H. Aron, ed., Global investing: A guide to international security analysis and portfolio management (Wiley, New York).

Hawawini, G., 1991, Stock market anomalies and the pricing of equity on the Tokyo stock exchange, in: W.T. Ziemba, W. Bailey and Y. Hamao, eds., Japanese financial market research (North-Holland, Amsterdam).

Horimoto, S., 1988, Private correspondence using raw results from forthcoming paper.

Jacobs, B.I. and K.N. Levy, 1988, Disentangling equity return regularities: New insights and investment opportunities, Financial Analysts Journal, May–June, 18–43.

Jaffe, J. and R. Westerfield, 1985a, The weekend effect in common stock returns: The international evidence, Journal of Finance 40, 433–454.

Jaffe, J. and R. Westerfield, 1985b, Patterns in Japanese common stock returns: Day of the week and turn of the year effects, Journal of Financial and Quantitative Analysis 20, 243–260.

Kato, K., 1990a, Weekly patterns in Japanese stock returns, Management Science 36, 1031–1043.

Kato, K., 1990b, Being a winner in the Tokyo stock market: The case for an anomaly fund, Journal of Portfolio Management, forthcoming.

Kato, K. and J.S. Schallheim, 1985, Seasonal and size anomalies in the Japanese stock market, Journal of Financial and Quantitative Analysis 20, no. 2, 243–272.

Kato, K., S.L. Schwartz and W.T. Ziemba, 1989, Day of the week effects in Japanese stocks, in: E.J. Elton and M.J. Gruber, eds., Japanese capital markets (Harper and Row, New York) 249–281.

Keim, D.B., 1986, The CAPM and equity return regularities, Financial Analysis Journal 42, 19–34.

Keim, D.A. and M. Smirlock, 1987, The behavior of intraday stock index futures prices, Advances in Futures and Options Research 2, 143–166.

Kunimura, M., 1984, The information content of forecasts by corporate officials and by financial analysts in the Japanese capital market, Working paper no. 84-3 (U.S.–Japan Management Studies Center, University of Pennsylvania, Philadelphia, PA).

Lakonishok, J. and S. Smidt, 1989, Are seasonal anomalies real? A ninety-year perspective, Review of Financial Studies 1, 403–425.

Nakamura, T. and N. Terada, 1984, The size effect and seasonality in Japanese stock returns, Unpublished manuscript (Institute for Quantitative Research in Finance).

Ritter, J. and N. Chopra, 1989, Portfolio rebalancing and the turn of the year effect, Journal of Finance 44, 149–166.

Roll, R., 1983a, Vas ist dat, Journal of Portfolio Management, Winter, 18–28.

Roll, R., 1983b, On computing mean returns and the small firm premium, Journal of Financial Economics 12, 371–386.

Sick, G. and W. T. Ziemba, 1991, The turn of the year effect in U.S. futures markets, 1982–1990, Working paper (University of British Columbia, Vancouver).

Vander Cruyssen, B. and W.T. Ziemba, 1991, The turn of the year effect in the futures markets, Interfaces, forthcoming.

Williams, J., 1987, Financial anomalies under rational expectations: A theory of the annual size and related effects, Working paper (New York University, New York).

Ziemba, W.T., 1990, Fundamental factors in Japanese stock market returns: 1979 to 1989, Presentation to Berkeley Program in Finance, Santa Barbara, CA, Sept.

Ziemba, W.T., 1992, Strategies for making and keeping excess profits in the stock market (William Morrow, New York) forthcoming.

Ziemba, W.T. and S.L. Schwartz, 1991, Investing in Japan (Probus Publishing, Chicago, IL) forthcoming.

Ziemba, W.T., W. Bailey and Y. Hamao, eds., 1991, Japanese financial market research (North-Holland, Amsterdam) forthcoming.

Zweig, M., 1986, Winning on Wall Street (Warner Books, New York).

https://doi.org/10.1142/9789811222634_0011

Chapter 11

World wide security market regularities*,†

William T. Ziemba
Faculty of Commerce, University of British Columbia, Vancouver, BC, Canada V6T 1Y8

Abstract: This paper is a brief survey of systematic violations of security market efficiencies in the US, Japan and other world wide equity markets. These security market regularities or anomalies seem to occur because of cash flow, institutional constraints and policies, investor behavior and sentiment, the slowness of markets to react to new information, the timing of favorable or unfavorable information flows and market maker supply–demand balances and optimal bid–ask spreads. While such anomalies are controversial and difficult to measure precisely as well as being variable over time, the persistence of many of these market regularities is of considerable interest to researchers and financial traders.

Keywords: Finance; Investment; Forecasting; Behavior; Empirical statistics

Introduction

One of the hallmarks of modern financial economics is the efficient market hypothesis. Is the current price the correct price? Is the current price useful in predicting future prices? Such questions abound. Research began in earnest in the early 1960s and a voluminous literature has evolved. Fama (1970, 1991) has surveyed the literature and also pointed out the difficulty of defining and testing for market efficiency. Such a test, as stressed by Roll (1977) if properly undertaken, is a joint hypothesis concerning efficiency and the validity of an equilibrium pricing model such as the capital asset or arbitrage pricing models.

Over the years market efficiency has evolved from studying weak, semi-strong and strong form efficiency in which prices fully reflect price information, all publicly available information and all information, respectively, to studies of the predictability of returns based on fundamental variables, event studies of the adjustment of prices to specific public announcements and tests for private information. The evidence is that future returns are predictable from past returns, dividend yields and term structure variables. This apparent violation of weak form efficiency of the constant expected returns model is confounded by the joint hypothesis problem of whether there is rational variation over time in expected returns or systematic deviations from fundamental value. Various security market regularities or anomalies can then be seriously analyzed as surveyed in the books by Dimson (1988), Haugen (1994), Thaler (1992) and Ziemba (1988, 1994, 1994a).

Anomalies that yield higher short term returns seem to occur for six basic reasons: a) increased cash flows just prior to and during the anomalous period a portion of which is invested in equities; b) institutional constraints and policies such as pension funds investments made on the last day of the month; c) behavioral considerations such as investor sentiment leading to excess purchase

Correspondence to: Prof. W.T. Ziemba, Faculty of Commerce, University of British Columbia, Vancouver, BC, Canada V6T 1Y8.

* Presented as a tutorial at the Euro XII/TIMS XXXI Helsinki, Finland, July 1992.

†This article originally appeared in *European Journal of Operational Research* **74**, 198–229, 1994, © 1994 by Elsevier Science Publishers.

or sale of equities in related but different securities; d) the timing of favorable and unfavorable information flows such as the delays in reporting bad news; 5) the slowness of the market to react to new information such as earnings changes, and favorable or unfavorable publicly available ranking changes; and 6) market maker supply–demand balances and optimal bid–ask spreads. While arguments may be made that increased returns may be occurring because of increased risk, which is difficult or impossible to measure accurately, there is very strong evidence that most or all the gains in equity markets actually occur during a small subset of the year's trading days, namely, the seasonally anomalous periods. Ritter and Chopra (1989) and Cadsby (1992) show, for example, that the only periods where higher risk as measured by the capital asset pricing model's beta is rewarded with higher equity returns is precisely at the anomalous periods such as the trading day before holidays, at the end of the week, at the turn of the month, in the first two weeks of January for small stocks, etc. Event studies are more straight forward and less controversial since they are able to provide more clear cut evidence of the effect of the new information. Regarding strong form tests there is considerable evidence that corporate insiders have private information that is not fully reflected in current prices.

This is a brief survey of some of the evidence concerning departures from security market efficiency in the US, Japanese and other world wide equity markets. Capitalization varies year by year but one may conveniently think of the world's equity markets as approximately: US two fifths, Japan a quarter, Europe a quarter and the rest of the world about one tenth. The United Kingdom is the world's third largest market with about a third of Europe's share. A survey of many of these topics appears in Hawawini and Keim (1994). Blume and Siegel (1992) survey various theories of security pricing and their relationship with the structure of markets. I do not specifically discuss why particular countries have had higher returns over time than others. Roll (1992) shows that these differences are largely explained by the diversification aspects of index construction, industrial structure and exchange rate behavior. Ferson and Harvey (1992) show that lagged beta factors are useful in predicting returns in major security markets. Froot and Thaler (1990) and Eaker and Grant (1990) discuss currency hedging of international portfolios. They show the advantage of selectively hedging only those currencies trading at a forward premium while not hedging currencies trading at a forward discount. Jorion (1989) shows the advantage of foreign investing. In particular, the optimal amount of foreign investment is much greater than current allocations. Departures from market efficiency are classified here as seasonal regularities and cross sectional fundamental factors that explain equity returns. Of great interest is the robustness of the specific effect over time across various countries and a proper explanation of the reasons for the departures (if there is one) from efficiency however, it may be defined. Merton (1985), Lo and MacKinlay (1990), Black (1986, 1992) and Markowitz (1992) discuss data mining and the dangers of searching for supposedly predictable trends from a large amount of data with many potential hypotheses without ex ante explanations. These dangers are real and are to be taken seriously in the application of results such as those that follow.

Efficient market theory and the capital asset pricing model

Theoretically, the value of a financial asset must equal the present value of its cash flows. Over a finite horizon, the present value of the terminal value should be added. Gordon and Shapiro (1956) and Gordon (1962) formalized this into the dividend discount model for the price p of the security:

$$p = \frac{d}{i-g}$$

assuming that the dividend rate d, the discount rate i and the growth rate of dividends g are constants.

Such models and their generalizations to allow nonstationarity are useful but one must have good estimates of the parameters into the future and errors in $i-g$ are magnified in the estimate of p. French and Poterba (1991) and Ziemba and Schwartz (1991, chapter 5) utilize such hair trigger models to value the Japanese stock market.

The British statistician Maurice Kendall postulated the efficient market hypothesis in 1953. Price changes were assumed to follow a random walk. Kendall found considerable support for the hypothesis by examining British stock prices as well as US commodity prices. Kendall's work ushered in the efficient market era which is well represented by the important early studies by Roberts (1959, 1967), Black, Jensen and Scholes (1972), Cootner (1964), Fama (1965) and Mandelbrot (1963). This literature is surveyed by Fama (1970).

An excellent recent survey of the past twenty years of voluminous activity studying efficient market theory and empirical tests is Fama (1991); see also the discussion in Blume and Siegel (1992). The hypothesis' theoretical underpinnings date at least to Bachelier in 1900 and the term random walk to Pearson in 1905. The capital asset pricing model developed by Sharpe (1964), Lintner (1965) and Mossin (1966) provided a method to price individual stocks in an efficient market. The expected return on a stock was then simply the risk free return plus the stocks beta (covariance with the market relative to market variance) times the excess mean return of the market over the risk free rate. T-bills substitute well for the risk free asset. The CAPM was also the basis and motivation for index funds since the market was essentially the index. It was John McQuown and Bill Sharpe's early work at Wells Fargo in San Francisco, plus the CAPM theory, that pioneered the current large scale worldwide activity in this area.

Roll (1977) showed how difficult it was to properly test for market efficiency. A test of market efficiency and an equilibrium model of asset return must be made jointly. This also raised the question of the definition of the market and how to measure it. Betas, which give the sensitivity of a stock to market movements, are only relative to the given market index used.

The CAPM is a single variable model. Its introduction into modern portfolio theory had as much impact as Markowitz's theory of portfolio

Table 1
Fundamental variable effects on US equity prices, univariate and multivariate

Return factor	Univariate effect		Multivariate effect		Multivariate effect		Multivariate effect	
	Monthly mean	*t*-stat	Monthly mean	*t*-stat	January mean	*t*-stat	Non-January mean	*t*-stat
Low P/E	0.59	3.4	0.46	4.7	0.09	0.5	0.49	4.7
Small Size	0.15	2.3	0.12	2.7	0.14	1.3	0.12	2.5
Yield	−0.01	−0.1	0.03	0.5	0.67	3.4	−0.03	−0.4
Zero Yield	0.00	0.0	0.15	1.3	1.00	1.9	0.08	0.6
Neglect	0.14	1.9	0.10	1.7	0.36	1.8	0.08	1.3
Low Price	−0.01	−0.1	0.01	0.2	0.38	2.0	−0.02	−0.4
Book/Price	0.17	1.4	0.09	1.2	0.51	2.4	0.05	0.7
Sales/Price	0.17	3.1	0.17	3.7	0.05	0.2	0.18	4.1
Cash/Price	0.36	2.7	0.04	0.6	−0.15	−2.0	0.05	0.8
Volatility (S.D.)	0.16	0.6	0.07	0.6	0.62	2.1	0.02	0.2
Beta	−0.01	0.0	0.04	0.3	−0.05	−0.1	0.05	0.4
Coskewness	0.09	0.6	0.04	0.7	0.10	0.5	0.04	0.6
Controversy	−0.33	−2.1	−0.05	−0.8	−0.01	−0.1	−0.06	−0.8
Trend in Ear. Ests (−1)	0.48	4.8	0.51	8.1	0.60	3.8	0.50	7.5
Trend in Ear. Ests (−2)	0.40	4.4	0.28	4.9	0.25	1.6	0.29	4.7
Trend in Ear. Ests (−3)	0.29	3.0	0.19	3.8	0.13	0.6	0.19	3.8
Earn. Surprise (−1)	0.44	2.1	0.48	3.7	1.36	1.6	0.42	3.4
Earn. Surprise (−2)	0.47	1.8	0.18	0.8	0.14	2.0	0.18	0.7
Earn. Surprise (−3)	−0.03	−0.1	−0.21	−1.1	−0.01	0.0	−0.22	−1.1
Earn. Torpedo	0.00	0.0	−0.10	−1.7	0.08	0.3	−0.12	−1.9
Relative Strength	0.30	1.4	0.34	3.5	−0.13	−0.2	0.39	1.0
Res. Reversal (−1)	−0.54	−4.9	−1.08	−17.8	−1.38	−6.0	1.06	−16.8
Res. Reversal (−2)	−0.13	−1.4	−0.37	−8.1	−0.56	−2.5	−0.35	−7.7
Short Term Tax	−0.08	−0.4	−0.04	−0.4	0.38	1.8	−0.08	−0.7
Long Term Tax	−0.29	−1.6	0.00	−0.1	0.78	3.2	−0.07	−1.2

Source: Jacobs and Levy (1988a). −1 means one month lagged, etc. The effect is the mean change in expected return from a one standard deviation tilt in the direction of the given factor.

selection (1952, 1959). Markowitz's contribution was to provide an operational way to measure risk and to compute efficient portfolios that maximized return for fixed levels of risk. Both Sharpe and Markowitz were awarded the Nobel prize for their contributions to the field of financial economics in 1990. Various multifactor equilibrium models exist with the theoretical support greatest for Ross's (1976) arbitrage pricing theory (APT). A survey of research work on the APT appears in Connor and Korajzyk (1994). We now turn to empirical work on multifactor models.

Multiple factor models

The various fundamental and seasonal effects are interrelated and it is useful to attempt to isolate the pure effects of particular variables on equity returns. Table 1 from Jacobs and Levy (1988a) shows this for various monthly adjusted fundamental factors for the US market using 1970s and 1980s data. The univariate and multivariate effects for twenty-five normalized variables throughout the year and in and outside of January are isolated along with coefficient t-values. For a variety of reasons, January is the highest return month for small capitalized stocks and provides a strong signal for all stocks as discussed below. Very significant factors are low price to earnings, small capitalization, high sales to price, high cash flow to price, trends in earnings (current and lagged one or two months) and residual reversal (a mean reversal concept). In January, the two strongest effects were return

Table 2
Univariate and multivariate fundamental variable effects on Japanese Tokyo stock exchange section I stocks, June 1979–August 1989

Factor	Univariate effect			Multivariate effect		
	Rank	Monthly mean	t-statistic	Rank	Monthly mean	t-statistic
Earnings growth relative to price	13	0.00820	8.74	1	0.00788	7.85
Last month's excess return	11	−0.00350	−3.04	2	−0.00693	−3.65
Relative return strength	26	−0.00649	−3.85	3	−0.00645	−3.42
Current minimum past book value/price	19	−0.00165	−1.39	4	−0.00397	−2.87
Current price relative to past highs	25	−0.00279	−1.47	5	0.00363	2.86
Low P/E	22	−0.00038	−0.30	6	0.00385	2.69
Small cap	29	−0.00396	−2.24	7	−0.00429	−2.21
Shares	27	−0.00017	−0.07	8	0.00382	1.87
Volatility (S.D.)	28	−0.00434	−3.02	9	−0.00234	−1.72
Book/price	18	0.00398	3.31	10	0.00124	1.68
Acceleration of dividends/price	3	0.00065	1.31	11	0.00105	1.49
Two year acceleration of dividends/price	10	−0.00122	−0.18	12	−0.00136	−1.45
Acceleration of dividend payment ratio	8	0.00110	0.94	13	0.00281	1.35
Acceleration of relative strength	6	−0.00233	−1.92	14	0.00250	1.22
Sales acceleration/price	21	−0.00117	−1.29	15	−0.01645	−1.20
Beta	4	−0.00104	−0.45	16	0.00223	1.11
Two year acceleration of dividend payout ratios	1	0.00013	0.12	17	−0.00147	−1.00
Sales growth/price	21	−0.00117	−1.29	18	0.00109	0.93
Percent of shares held by individuals	14	0.00240	2.50	19	0.00046	0.84
Zero dividend factor	7	0.60613	1.88	20	0.00184	0.83
Sales/price	24	0.00416	2.98	21	0.00072	0.67
Next to last month's excess return	12	−0.00195	−1.46	22	−0.00846	−0.63
Acceleration of book value/price	15	0.00017	0.19	23	0.00097	0.60
Earnings change/price	20	0.00094	0.96	24	0.00092	0.53
Dividend/price	30	0.00233	2.50	25	0.00033	0.38
Low price	23	−0.00719	−3.04	26	−0.00068	−0.34
Excess return variable	2	−0.00384	−3.99	27	0.00025	0.19
Acceleration of earnings/price	16	0.00263	3.25	28	0.00020	0.18
Par variable	5	−0.00370	−0.02	29	−0.00042	−0.09
Dividend/earnings	9	0.00033	0.22	30	−0.00012	−0.07

Source: Ziemba (1990), Ziemba and Schwartz (1991).

Table 3
Returns from use of model in Table 2 with yearly re-estimations

Portfolio	Value of ¥1 invested in Jan 85 at end of Sept 89	Annualized return in %	Monthly mean return, %	St. dev. of monthly returns
Best 50	7.57	53.1	3.76	5.57
Best 100	7.12	51.2	3.64	5.36
Best 200	6.54	48.5	3.48	5.17
Best 300	6.16	46.6	3.37	5.13
Best 400	5.84	45.0	3.26	5.02
Best 500	5.54	43.4	3.16	4.88
Equally weighted TSE-1	4.44	36.8	2.80	4.17
Nikkei	3.09	26.8	2.09	4.42
TOPIX	2.96	25.7	2.04	4.96

Source: Ziemba (1990), Ziemba and Schwartz (1991).

reversals for stocks with long term tax losses and high returns to stocks with either high yields or no dividends at all. The coefficients estimate the mean returns for a one standard deviation tilt in the direction of the given factor.

Table 2 from Ziemba and Schwartz (1991) based on Ziemba (1990) shows similar results for Japan for the period June 1979 to August 1989 using monthly data for the first section of the Tokyo stock exchange. The multivariate and univariate effects of the variables with t-values are shown here.

The most important factors explaining Japanese stock returns in the 1980s were similar to those in US markets, namely earnings growth projections, mean reversion variables, low price to book and to earnings and low capitalization.

The fact that anomalies exist is born out by the fact that results similar to those in Tables 1 and 2 form the basis of proprietary investment management models used to trade securities and create profitable hedges. For example, models using elements similar to the results in Tables 1 and 2 are used in proprietary trading by Jacobs and Levy Investment Management and Buchanan Partners, Ltd, London, England, respectively. Several firms, most notably BARRA, in Berkeley, California, estimate and lease factor models for various countries. The hope is that by using such models, superior returns will be obtained. Table 3 and Figure 1 provide the results of using the model defined in Table 2 readjusted year by year from 1985 to September 1989 to rank the best stocks in Japan. For example, for stocks in 1987 the model was estimated using data up to December 1986. The results indicate that the portfolios of the highest ranking stocks have returns significantly higher than the portfolios of the Topix and Nikkei Stock Average market indices. Topix includes all Tokyo stock exchange section one stocks value weighted and the NSA is the price weighted average of 225 large companies. Because of its value weighting, the Topix is a larger capitalized index. Recent experience shows that models of this type have been quite effective even in the steep 1990–94 declines in the Japanese stock market. [1] Essentially all the variable factors used in Tables 1 and 2 have been extensively studied by previous researchers in isolation or in small groups.

An important and controversial research area is that of mean reversion and the time period of the reversion. Key references are Poterba and Summers (1988), Kim, Nelson and Startz (1991), DeBondt and Thaler (1985, 1987, 1989) and Thaler (1992). Some of this research is discussed below. The essence of the research is that securities that have had very high or very low short or long term returns tend to have lower or higher returns than average, respectively, in succeeding time intervals.

The small firm and January effects

The size effect measured by market capitalization has been of particular interest. Key refer-

[1] The 1990–92 decline in Japanese stock and speculative land prices and their relationships is studied along with the past behavior of these markets in Stone and Ziemba (1993).

Table 4
Excess returns of smallest market capitalization decile stocks over decile 2 to 10 stocks on NYSE by month, 1926 to 1987

DecNe	Jan	Feb	Mar	Apr	May	Jun	Jul	Aug	Sep	Oct	Nov	Dec	Total (Jan–Dec)
2	1.16	0.16	−0.05	−0.40	0.05	0.00	0.00	0.09	0.04	0.06	0.32	0.20	1.52
	51	34	21	24	35	32	30	30	29	33	41	38	
3	1.46	0.09	0.02	−0.34	−0.21	−0.13	0.12	−0.18	0.16	−0.29	0.33	0.03	1.15
	46	38	29	24	25	28	30	32	32	30	41	31	
4	1.85	0.36	−0.11	−0.09	−0.05	−0.13	0.21	0.22	0.38	0.47	0.56	0.06	2.80
	49	31	32	27	30	29	31	37	34	21	39	29	
5	2.89	0.33	−0.22	−0.42	−0.16	−0.16	0.25	0.30	0.13	−0.60	0.39	0.16	2.89
	49	36	28	26	26	28	29	34	28	28	33	31	
6	3.43	0.29	−0.30	−0.36	0.09	−0.47	0.16	0.36	0.22	−0.90	0.58	−0.04	2.94
	53	36	31	25	25	24	32	31	31	28	35	30	
7	4.11	0.60	−0.23	−0.23	0.28	−0.46	0.27	0.04	0.15	−0.65	0.30	0.44	3.68
	52	40	34	20	28	23	31	32	33	27	31	25	
8	5.42	0.69	−0.47	−0.46	0.21	−0.69	0.35	−0.05	−0.23	−0.83	0.39	−0.65	3.69
	51	40	29	24	25	24	32	26	32	29	32	28	
9	7.06	0.87	−0.06	−0.40	0.20	−0.71	0.45	0.13	−0.00	−0.91	0.22	−1.07	5.67
	56	36	34	25	27	24	33	29	29	27	30	24	
10	10.27	0.94	−0.94	−0.30	0.37	−0.64	0.69	−0.07	0.03	−1.23	−0.27	−1.26	8.40
	57	32	26	23	29	24	32	26	30	24	23	24	

Source: Ibbotson and Associates (1988).

ences for US studies are Banz (1981), Reinganum (1981), Roll (1983), Blume and Stambaugh (1983), Keim (1983), Jaffe, Keim and Westerfield (1989), Reinganum (1990), Jegadeesh (1992) and Dyl and Maberly (1992). Table 4 from Ibbotson and Associates shows the relative returns by month of various decile NYSE stocks from 1926 to 1987. While there is a substantial size effect (smallest minus largest decile returns) of 8.40% per year over these 62 years, the whole gain is in January which returned 10.27%. Indeed, the small firm effect is strong in many years (for example 1962–1983, 1990–92) and very weak in others (for example 1983–85, 1988–90). However, the January excess returns of small over large capitalized stocks are positive in almost every year (also as discussed below small stocks have greatly outpreformed during democratic administrations as shown by Hensel and Ziemba (1993b)). Table 4 indicates that the smallest decile stocks had higher returns than the largest decile stocks in 57 of the 62 years (and the last seven from 1988–94)

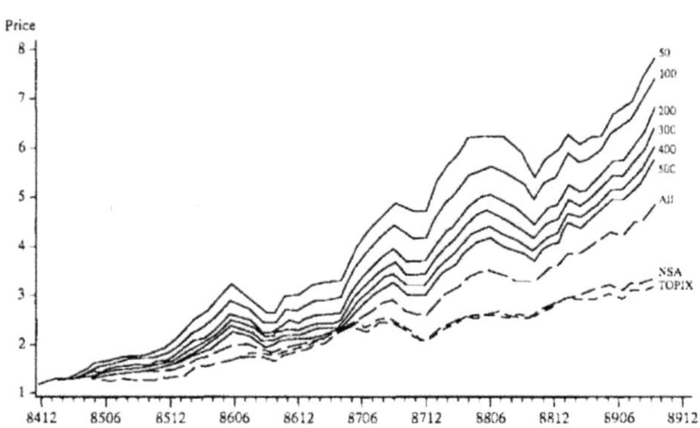

Figure 1. Cumulative performance of ¥1 invested in the best 50, 100, 200, 300, 400, 500 and all equally weighted TSE-I stocks versus the Topix and NSA225, monthly revisions of data and model, January 1985 to September 1989. Source: Ziemba (1990), Ziemba and Schwartz (1991)

Table 5
Mean return difference between equally and value weighted indices

	Last day of December	January trading day during 1963–1978			
		First	Second	Third	Fourth
Mean return	0.5647	1.186	0.6067	0.6107	0.4527
t-statistic	(4.72) [a]	(8.39)	(3.86)	(3.96)	(3.05)

[a] *t*-statistics in ( ).
Source: Roll (1983).

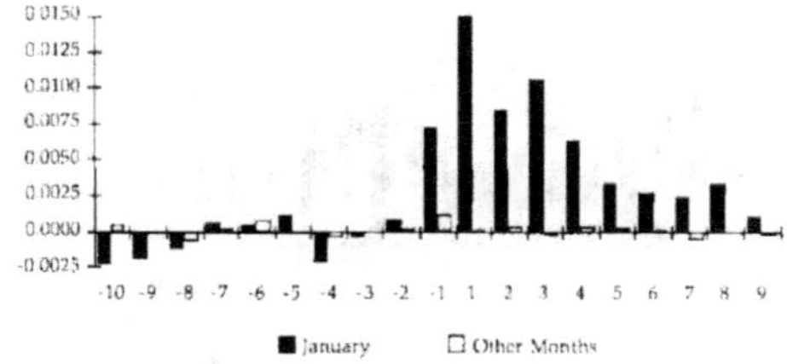

Figure 2. Excess returns on small stocks, mean daily percent returns, smallest minus largest decile, 1971–85. Source: Ritter (1988)

whereas the outperformance in other months is not statistically significant and indeed there is no outperformance at all. A figure showing the more recent years appears in Ziemba (1994). Table 5 shows the small stock premium measured as the difference between equally and value weighted indices of all NYSE stocks for 1963–78 for trading days −1 to +4. The mean difference in these five days was over 3% during this 16 year period.

Figures 2 and 3 supplement this and show that for the period 1971–85 small stock returns greatly exceeded large stock returns on trading days −1 to +9 in January and much of the explanation for this difference ($R^2 = 0.48$) is the difference in the buy–sell ratios of individual investors. [2] There is no such effect in any other month. A survey of the small firm/January effect literature along with methods to invest in this regularity in the futures markets since 1982 appears in Clark and Ziemba (1987) which was updated to 1993–94 in Ziemba (1994b). They document the success of a strategy of going long the small capitalized stocks

[2] Asaji Komatsu, of the Yamaichi Research Institute in Tokyo, and the author investigated the explanatory power of the buy–sell ratios of individual investors on Japanese security returns. This variable explained about 11% of the variation in the excess returns of small versus large capitalized stocks using data from the 1970s and 1980s.

Table 6
International evidence of seasonality in the size premium

	Country					
	Belgium	Finland	France	Japan	Taiwan	UK
Test period	1969–1983	1970–1983	1968–1980	1965–1987	1979–1986	1958–1982
Number of securities	170	40	201	First section TSE	53 to 72	All LSE
Number of size portfolios	5	5	5	10	5	10
Market value largest portfolio / Market value smallest portfolio	188	113	83	NA	17	182
January return (%) on:						
Smallest portfolio	5.4	5.9	3.7	9.5	NA	2.3
Largest portfolio	3.0	2.5	4.4	2.3	NA	3.6
January size-premium	2.4	3.4	−0.7	7.2	3.4	−1.3
Rest-of-the-year monthly return (%) on:						
Smallest portfolio	0.8	1.8	1.4	1.9	NA	1.2
Largest portfolio	0.4	1.0	0.7	1.3	NA	0.7
Rest-of-the-year size-premium (%)	0.4	0.8	0.7	0.6	0.3	0.5

TSE = Tokyo Stock Exchange; LSE = London Stock Exchange; NA = Not Available.
All monthly mean returns are significantly different from zero at the 5% level.
The January size-premium is significantly different from zero only in Belgium, Finland, Taiwan and Japan.
Monthly mean returns are not significantly different from zero for the largest portfolio.
Source: Hawawini and Keim (1994) from original data.

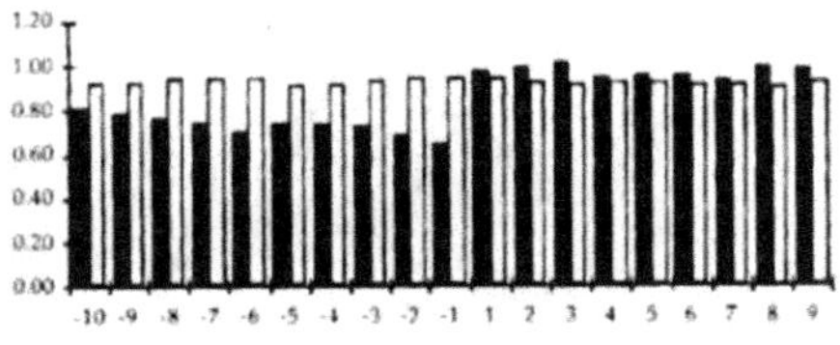

Figure 3. Mean buy–sell ratio of individual investors at Merrill Lynch, 1971–85. Source: Ritter (1988)

and short the large caps using the Value Line and S&P500 futures contracts. While the futures market seems to anticipate the effect in mid to late December, the cash effect has remained very similar to that in previous years and has not been anticipated by those knowledgeable in trading this effect in the futures markets. Indeed the years 1990/91 to 1993/94 have produced very strong effects with 1992/93 the largest in the past two decades and 1993/94 nearly as strong. This is consistent with the evidence in Hensel and Ziemba (1993b) that the small capitalized stocks have outpreformed large capitalized stocks when democrats are in the White House. The advantage, which seems to hinge on the different approach of Democrats and Republicans to small and large businesses, has been greatest in the first year of administrations. This small minus large stock advantage during democratic administrations averaged 15.12% in the first year, 8.25% in the first two years and 7.87% over the four years from 1937–1992 and even more during the period 1929–1992.

The small firm effect and its relationship to the January effect has been studied in numerous countries. Table 6 from Hawawini and Keim (1994) shows results from Belgium, Finland, France, Japan, Taiwan and the United Kingdom. The January size premium was significantly different from zero in Belgium, Finland, Taiwan and Japan. However, there was no size premium in France and the United Kingdom. The data used for these studies while fairly extensive ends at the beginning of the 1980s. In this table all monthly returns are significantly different from zero except the largest portfolio outside of January. Figure 4 shows the January size premium in twenty one countries during 1991 and 1992. There was a January size premium in the US in these years but this was not world wide.

Using data up to 1989 indicates that the size effect in Japan seems to occur twice each year with each excess of small over large stock returns occurring at the time of the semi-annual December and June bonuses. Each of these bonuses amount to about one sixth of a typical worker's annual salary and some of these funds may well price pressure small capitalized stock because the increased buying of stocks with low volume increases their prices. The evidence in Ziemba and Schwartz (1991) and Kato (1991) is that the size effect on the first section of the Tokyo stock exchange from 1969 to 1987 was 8.6% in January and February and 8.2% in April to July. For anomalies to persist, the reason for them such as increased cash flows into stocks during various periods must continue. During the steep decline

Figure 4. Difference between small and large cap stocks in local currency in January, 1991 and 1992. Source: Morgan Stanley data

and high volatility in the Japanese stock market from 1990 to 1993 individual investors have been simply afraid to buy stocks. Their cash flows have gone into bounds and cash instruments not into stocks. Indeed Bell and Ziemba (1993) found that the only anomaly that was still present in Japan in the this period was the fact that all gains in the stock market are at night in the close to open returns. The absence of anomalies has modified the behavior of Japanese security markets.

Low price to earnings, sales, book value and cash flow effects

Low price to earnings stocks are natural choices for investors since the major reason to be in business is to generate earnings. Early proponents of such strategies were the famous value investors Graham and Dodd (1934). Studies by Nicholson (1960), Basu (1977, 1983), Reinganum (1981), Peavy and Goodman (1983), Jaffe, Keim and Westerfield (1990), Fama and French (1991) in the US, Levis (1990) in the UK, Aggarwal, Rao and Hiraki (1988) and Ziemba and Schwartz (1991) for Japan, Chou and Johnson (1990) and Ma and Shaw (1990) for Taiwan, and Gillan (1990) for New Zealand find significant price earnings effects. The highest return strategies are usually these that invest in stocks with low price earnings ratios relative to their own historical values and those of stocks similar industries. Strategies that attempt to eliminate general market risk by going long such stocks and short the high PER stocks generally have high returns and low risk. Peavy and Goodman (1983) found this to be 20.8% per year during 1970–80. Hawawini and Keim (1994) using data from 1962 to 1989 show that although the lowest price earning ratio stocks have the highest average returns in total or risk adjusted using the capital asset pricing model securities with negative earnings have even higher average returns; see Table 7. But these returns have considerable risk. For example, negative earnings stocks have average betas of 1.46 versus 1.01 for the lowest price earnings ratio stocks. These stocks also have low prices and low capitalization. After risk adjustment they still have very high returns but they are significantly below the lowest decile price earnings ratio stocks. Negative earnings stocks are also highly correlated with small capitalized effects which again brings back the advantage of analyses like Tables 1 and 2. See also Jaffe, Keim and Westerfield (1989).

Ettredge and Fuller (1991) investigated this further concentrating on the risk aspects. Using data from 1973–82 on the NYSE and ASE they find that stocks with negative earnings on April 1 and held for one year have mean returns that average 11.8% above the market index. Large earnings gains, which average 34.8%, seem to be the reason behind the increase in stock prices. The 11.8% excess gain can be decomposed into a 7.7% negative earnings effect and a 4.1% size effect. Repeat losers have even higher mean returns than first time losers. They had mean excess returns of 19.5% above the market index. The effects of firms and second time losers seems to

Table 7
Mean monthly returns and other attributes for the NYSE and AMEX from April 1962 to December 1989 using portfolios formed on the basis of the ratio of price/earnings created on March 31 and revised after each twelve months

P/B portfolio	Mean return	Std. dev. return	Beta	Mkt. cap. ($mil)	P/B	Price ($)
Negative	1.55	8.68	1.46	141.8	−37.7	10.57
Lowest	0.79	5.61	1.09	888.4	2.7	37.55
2	0.90	5.06	1.05	938.4	5.0	38.02
3	0.91	4.94	1.03	849.1	6.4	35.38
4	0.87	4.60	0.95	913.9	7.5	31.91
5	0.79	4.81	0.98	913.5	8.5	31.22
6	0.97	4.65	0.94	808.0	9.4	29.68
7	1.05	4.69	0.96	682.3	10.5	28.11
8	1.13	4.64	0.87	777.8	11.7	27.47
9	1.34	4.65	0.89	656.5	13.3	25.07
Highest	1.25	5.48	1.01	569.8	18.9	21.82

Source: Hawawini and Keim (1994).

Table 8
Mean monthly returns and other attributes for the NYSE and AMEX from April 1962 to December 1989 using portfolios formed on the basis of the ratio of price/book created on March 31 and revised after each twelve months

P/B portfolio	Mean return	Std. dev. return	Beta	Mkt. cap. ($mil)	P/B	Price ($)
Negative	1.66	8.37	1.29	119	−7.07	13.62
Lowest	1.49	5.63	1.04	261	0.57	15.98
2	1.46	4.98	0.95	401	0.83	19.99
3	1.08	4.66	0.90	620	1.00	23.56
4	1.12	4.32	0.83	668	1.15	25.72
5	0.96	4.56	0.90	641	1.31	26.94
6	0.82	4.45	0.91	835	1.52	29.97
7	0.86	4.79	0.98	752	1.80	31.45
8	0.93	4.87	1.02	813	2.20	33.93
9	0.85	5.25	1.11	1001	2.95	37.48
Highest	0.91	5.19	1.05	1430	8.17	46.66

Source: Hawawini and Keim (1994).

be caused by bad market sentiment and their subsequent bounce and lower estimates of earnings then reality.

Evidence of a low price to sales effect has been found for the US market by Senchack and Martin (1987) and for Japan by Aggarwal, Rao and Hiraki (1989). Hawawini and Keim (1994) present evidence on price to cash flow (earnings plus depreciation). Finally several authors including Stattman (1980), Rosenberg, Reid and Lanstein (1985), Keim (1988), Fama and French (1991) and Hawawini and Keim (1994) have found statistically significant evidence of a low price to book value per share effect. Hawawini and Keim, using data from April 1962 to December 1989, found the results in Table 8. There was a strong price to book effect in this period with the lowest P/B stocks returning 1.66% per month with lower beta versus 0.85% for the highest P/B stocks. As with the low price earnings and low price to cash flow, see tables in Hawawini and Keim (1994), negative price to book equities have the highest returns. This latter is an example of the winner–loser effect studied by DeBondt and Thaler (1985, 1987); see also Ball and Kothari (1989), Fama and French (1988a), Chan (1988), Zarowin (1989, 1990), Thaler (1992), and Chopra, Lakonishok and Ritter (1992). There is considerable evidence that US stocks that have had very poor performance over a long period, such as five years, have much higher returns in subsequent years, especially in January. However, there seems to be a difference between extreme winners and losers over one versus five year periods. While the evidence points strongly to reversals for the latter, the former seem to continue their losing or winning trends, see Jegadeesh and Titman (1991).

Similar results do not seem to occur in Canada. Kryzanowski and Zhang (1992) found that the continuation hypothesis holds for the following one and two years so that losers continue to lose and winners win. But there is no reversal over subsequent five to ten year periods.

Figure 5 shows the effect using monthly return data for all NYSE stocks from 1926 to 1982. Porfolios of the 35 most extreme losers and winners were formed over five year periods. These portfolios returns were evaluated for the following five years. This was done year by year as well as through an averaging process. The returns for both winners and losers are mean reverting. The subsequent outperformance of the losers is much greater than the subsequent underperformance

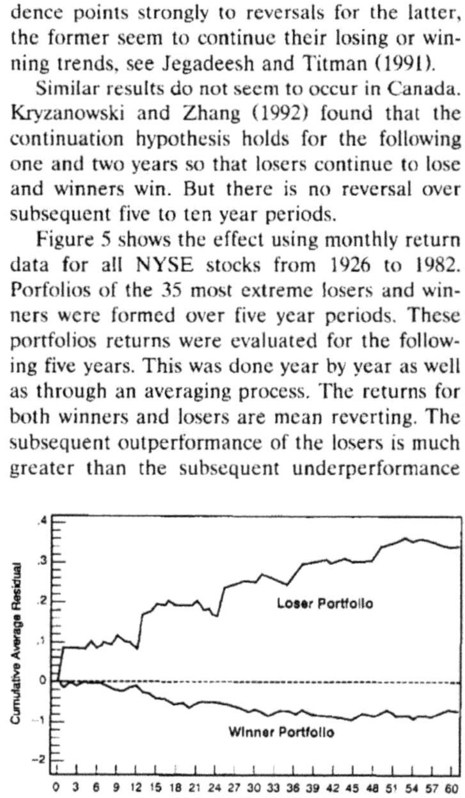

Figure 5. Cumulative excess returns for winner and loser portfolios. Source: De Bondt and Thaler (1985)

for the winners. One can see the sharp upward return movements in the five Januarys on the graph. Differences in beta risks do not explain the phenomenon. The losers are, on average, smaller firms and also have low price and low price to earnings, etc. Space limitations prohibit a full discussion of the interaction of the various effects and also their relationship with seasonality effects which I now turn to. On this see Jaffe, Keim and Westerfield (1989), Fama and French (1991), Hawawini and Keim (1994) and the results in Table 1 and 2. See also Reinganum (1988) who has studied factors that lead to extremely higher medium term returns for specific stocks.

Seasonality effects

There is considerable research on seasonality patterns in US, Japan and other world wide security markets. The focus has been on day of the week, holiday, turn of the month and year and related effects. As with the fundamental variables, the effects are interrelated. Hence, to understand them better, isolated analysis plus joint effects research is suggested. In the case of fundamental variables, one can estimate, as in Tables 1 and 2, multivariate equations to attempt to use the various effects to improve on investment predictions concerning individual securities. For the seasonal effects, one may construct seasonality calendars that attempt to improve on investment prediction for market indices such as small and large capitalized. There is some evidence that taken together such calendars can provide forecasts that separate out the days of the year into the most and least favorable for stocks with intermediate gradations. Ziemba and Schwartz (1991) have attempted to do this for Japan following on the work in Ziemba (1988, 1994a). A fifty-two variable model was developed to attempt to capture day of the week, holiday, January, turn of the year, turn of the month, monthly, Golden Week, and the small firm effect. The t-statistics are very high leading to a rejection of the hypothesis that the days ranked +1 to +4 (i.e., one standard deviation above average or more) have lower mean returns, than the days ranked −1 to −4. The model was estimated in several ways for the years 1984, 1985, ..., 1989 using data for 5, 10, 20 or all the data back to 1949, using all coefficients or all coefficients that

Table 9
Summary of the seasonality calendar results, January 1988 to end of January 1989

Rank	Sample size	Mean daily returnNSA225	Mean daily return Topix	St. dev. on NSA	St. dev. on Topix
−4	14	0.213	0.166	0.455	0.409
−3	19	−0.129	−0.080	0.517	0.538
−2	6	0.281	0.240	0.668	0.732
−1	7	0.104	0.002	0.781	0.834
0	27	−0.111	−0.117	0.675	0.687
1	79	0.132	0.081	0.627	0.659
2	71	0.067	0.085	0.650	0.676
3	30	0.154	0.149	0.610	0.595
4	40	0.478	0.512	1.060	1.224
Categories to be compared:					
4 3	70	0.339	0.356	0.904	1.014
−4 −3	33	0.016	0.025	0.514	0.496
2 1	150	0.102	0.083	0.637	0.665
−2 −1	13	0.186	0.112	0.706	0.765
4 3	70	0.339	0.356	0.904	1.014
2 1	150	0.102	0.083	0.637	0.665
−2 −1	13	0.186	0.112	0.706	0.765
−4 −3	33	0.016	0.025	0.514	0.496
4 3 2 1	220	0.177	0.170	0.738	0.801
−4 −3 −2 −1	46	0.064	0.049	0.572	0.577

Source: Ziemba and Schwartz (1991).

Table 10
International evidence of daily seasonality in stock market returns in percent

Country	Period	Index [b]	Mon	Tues	Wed	Thurs	Fri	Sat
Australia	1975–84	EW1	0.044	−0.116 *[a]	0.450	0.198 *	0.157 *	
Belgium	1977–85	VW1	0.098 *	−0.032	0.041 *	0.111 *	0.130 *	
Belgium	1977–85	EW1	0.080 *	0.026 *	0.046 *	0.044 *	0.062 *	
Canada	1969–84	TC	−0.157 *	−0.003	0.073 *	0.075 *	0.094 *	
Finland	1977–82	VW1	0.086 *	0.066 *	0.030	0.070 *	0.074 *	
France	1977–89	VW1	−0.050	0.139 *	0.126 *	0.133 *	0.100 *	
France	1977–89	EW1	0.083 *	0.117 *	0.122 *	0.117 *	0.013	
Germany	1970–85	VW1	−0.085 *	0.008	0.044	0.060 *	0.099 *	
Germany	1970–85	EW1	0.005	−0.026	0.031	0.066	0.107 *	
Greece	1978–86	VW1	0.070 *	−0.058	−0.073 *	0.041	0.160 *	
Japan	1949–88	VW1	−0.071 *	−0.044 *	0.115 *	0.081 *	0.042 *	0.133 *
Korea	1980–84	VW1	−0.072 *	−0.087 *	0.087 *	0.014 *	0.120 *	0.230 *
Singapore	1969–84	ST	−0.036	−0.107 *	0.079 *	0.121 *	0.100 *	
Spain	1979–83	VW1		−0.072 *	0.003	0.037	0.071 *	
UK	1969–84	FT-A	−0.095 *	0.106 *	0.090 *	0.011	0.044	
US	1928–52	S&P	−0.223 *	0.076 *	0.084 *	0.066	0.029	0.147 *
US	1952–82	S&P	−0.154 *	0.026	0.103 *	0.036 *	0.092 *	

[a] * Indicates returns that are significantly different from zero at the 5% level, VMI and IWI indicate value and equally weighted indices, respectively.

[b] TC = Toronto composite index. The Tokyo stock exchange is closed on Saturdays since February 1989. ST = Straits Times index. FT-A = Financial Times all share index.

Source: Hawawani and Keim (1994).

were statistically significant at the 20% or 5% level. In all cases the higher ranked days such as those before holidays, in January, at the turn of the month, etc. had higher returns than those in the second half of the month, on Mondays or in October. The results for January 1988 to the end of January 1989 appear in Table 9 using all the data and all the coefficients. The hypothesis that the +3 and +4 days have returns higher than the −3 and −4 days is significant for the NSA at the 94% level and for the Topix at the 92% level. Generally speaking the results are as expected but standard deviations are high and many hypotheses are not significant at conventional levels for this short period.

There is strong evidence that stock prices fall on Mondays and rise on other days. Table 10 from Hawawini and Keim (1994) shows the evidence from 13 countries. An interesting observation is that all the 1929–32 stock market decline some 87% from peak to valley occurred on weekends and on the following Monday. There were

Table 11
International evidence of seasonality in stock market returns, monthly mean returns, 1959–1979

Country	Jan	Feb	Mar	Apr	May	Jun	July	Aug	Sept	Oct	Nov	Dec	All
Australia	2.65	−0.58	0.51	0.84	0.97	0.43	0.66	−0.37	−2.39	2.13	−0.85	3.99	0.67
Belgium	3.20	1.09	0.40	1.48	−1.36	−0.84	1.44	−1.17	−1.87	−0.69	0.42	−0.09	0.17
Canada	2.90	0.07	0.79	0.41	−0.96	−0.30	0.69	0.60	−0.06	−0.82	1.44	2.61	0.61
Finland	3.62	2.09	2.63	0.95	−0.02	1.55	2.53	0.97	−0.76	0.77	0.61	2.51	0.45
France	3.72	−0.18	1.98	0.94	−0.66	−1.90	1.53	1.03	−1.21	−0.72	0.43	0.15	1.43
Japan	3.53	1.13	1.88	0.30	0.90	2.06	−0.32	−0.83	−0.13	−0.98	1.65	1.80	0.92
Spain	2.24	1.29	0.32	1.59	−1.87	0.06	0.79	1.29	−1.64	0.19	−0.44	−0.01	0.32
UK	3.40	0.69	1.25	3.13	−1.21	−0.17	−1.11	1.88	0.24	0.80	−0.61	2.06	0.85
UK FT-A	3.06	0.79	1.15	3.57	−1.00	−0.85	−0.22	2.62	0.03	1.26	0.16	2.34	1.08
US	1.04	−0.41	1.27	0.96	−1.38	−0.56	0.14	0.34	−0.79	0.78	1.03	1.42	0.32
NYSE, equally weighted	5.08	0.55	1.55	0.44	−1.42	−1.00	0.73	0.72	−0.42	−0.79	1.79	1.37	0.72

Source: Gultekin and Gultekin (1983).

gains on average from Monday's close to Friday's close. Monday's decline seems to have an influence from the existence of a two day trading break. Table 12 indicates that along with holidays, returns are high before the break in trading and low after it. Ziemba (1993) investigated the difference between one and two day weekends in Japan that is with or without Saturday trading. Returns are negative on Mondays after two day breaks and negative on Tuesdays after one day breaks. Accumulation of sell orders by individual investors when they have time to formulate them on weekends is offered as the cause for this effect. Osborne (1962) and Miller (1988) argued this for US markets as well. Lakonishok and Maberly (1990) have provided a test with NYSE odd-lot sales and purchases, sales and purchases of cash-account customers of Merrill–Lynch and NYSE block transactions. They found that Monday had the lowest trading volume. Institutional trading is the lowest on Monday of all trading days but individual trading on Monday is the highest relative to other days of the week. Individuals tend to sell more on Mondays. For example, odd-lot sales minus odd lot purchases relative to NYSE volume was 29% higher during 1962–86 on Monday than the average of Tuesday to Friday. Theoretical arrangements that lead to imbalances on different days in trading volume, mean returns and volatility based on the interaction of various traders have been made by Admati and Pfleider (1988, 1989).

Interestingly as soon as Saturday trading ended in Japan the end of January 1989, the day of the week effect became like the US with larger declines on Mondays and rises on Tuesdays. See Table 9 and Ziemba and Schwartz (1991).

Stock prices tend to rise in January and the early part of the year and then at the end of the year with May and June and especially September and October being weak months. Table 11 from Gultekin and Gultekin (1983) shows the effect in ten major stock markets for the twenty one years from 1959 to 1979.

Holiday effects

There has been a very strong holiday effect in US markets throughout the twentieth century. Ariel (1984, 1990), Zweig (1986), Lakonishok and Smidt (1988) have documented this. For example, for the ninety years from 1897 to 1986, Lakonishok and Smidt found that fully 51.5% of the non-dividend returns on the Dow Jones industrials were made on the approximately eight preholidays. Figure 6a shows the mean returns on the eight preholidays for the S&P500 from 1980–92. Ariel using data from 1963–82 found a very strong effect with the average preholiday having returns that were about 23 times an average day for large capitalized stocks measured by a value weighted index of all NYSE stocks. Small capitalized stocks (equally weighted NYSE stocks) had returns 14 times larger but since this period was one of extremely high small stock returns, the actual returns exceeded the large capitalized securities. Lakonishok and Smidt also found that preholidays are associated with higher mean returns on all days of the week compared to average returns those days. Investigation of the holiday effect in Japan by Ziemba (1991) yields very similar results. Using daily data on the Nikkei stock average from May 1949 when the market opened up after World War II to 1988, he found that the typical preholiday had returns of about five times the average non-preholiday trading day, namely 0.246% versus 0.0489%.

A regression to separate out the effects on trading days −3 to +2 around a holiday using 0–1 variables led to the daily return

$$\begin{aligned} R = {} & \underset{(3.745)}{0.0352} + \underset{(1.491)}{0.0799}\,\text{day}_{-3} + \underset{(0.424)}{0.0222}\,\text{day}_{-2} \\ & + \underset{(3.709)}{0.1894}\,\text{Day}_{-1} - \underset{(-1.334)}{0.0663}\,\text{Day}_{+1} \\ & + \underset{(0.023)}{0.00114}\,\text{Day}_{+2}. \end{aligned}$$

The only day whose return effect is statistically different from zero was the preholiday. The day after holidays has negative returns which are significant at low confidence levels. Investigation of the relationship between the holiday and day of the week effects led to the results in the tables. Preholidays when lumped with pseudo-preholidays namely Fridays and Saturdays preceding market closings have high returns and a 10.27 t-statistic. With this additional data, the post holidays and Mondays have statistically significant negative returns, see Table 12. The preholidays

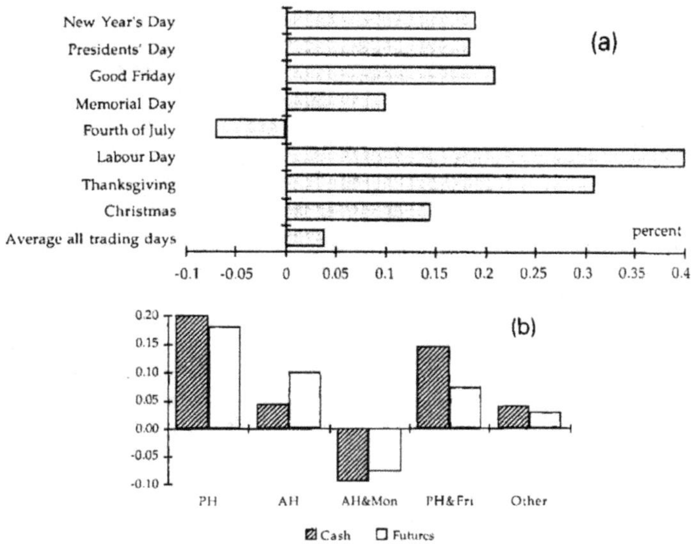

Figure 6(a). Mean percentage returns on the preholidays for the S & P500, 1980–92. Source: *The Economist* (1992) (b) Holiday effects in the UK, mean daily percent returns.

had higher returns on every day of the week as shown in Table 13. Moreover, the returns are consistently positive in months with high mean returns in Japan such as January but not so for the lower mean months of September and October; see Table 14. Finally an investigation of the futures markets effects by Ziemba (1989) led to the conclusion that the futures markets during 1986–88 anticipated the holiday effect on the third trading day before the holiday and this anticipation led to price rises on the −3 day to take some of the expected preholiday gains.

The period in late April to early May is referred to as Golden Week in Japan. There were holidays on April 29 and May 3 and 5 during the sample period data in Ziemba (1991). The preholidays all had very high mean returns: 0.215% on April 28, 0.536% on May 2 and 0.326% on May 4.

The holiday effect seems to be similar in the UK as well. Table 15 and Figure 6b show results

Table 12
Holiday effects on the NSA, 1949–1988

Day	Sample size	Minimum return, %	Maximum return, %	Mean return, %	Standard deviation, %	t-statistic
Pre-holiday	408	−5.41	3.06	0.2461	0.79	6.26
Non pre-holiday	7143	−14.90	11.29	0.0480	0.98	4.22
Days after holidays	408	−8.69	4.71	0.0068	0.99	0.14
Pre-holidays, Fridays and Saturdays preceding market closing	2268	−6.61	6.88	0.1561	0.72	10.27
Days after holidays and weekends	2268	−8.69	5.39	−0.0480 *	0.95	−2.41

Source: Ziemba (1991).

Table 13
Mean daily return, standard deviation and percent positive returns on pre-holidays by days of the week of the NSA, 1949–1988

	Sample size	Mean return, %	t-statistic	Positive returns, %
All Mondays	1937	−0.0589	−2.73	50.9
All Tuesdays	1959	−0.0419	−1.93	47.4
All Wednesdays	1960	0.1164	5.30	56.9
All Thursdays	1959	0.0871	3.77	55.1
All Fridays	1959	0.0544	2.62	54.6
All Saturdays	1755	0.1409	8.38	61.9
Mon. before holidays	59	0.3106	3.10	76.3
Tues. before holidays	59	0.0103	0.10	57.6
Weds. before holidays	58	0.1600	1.17	69.0
Thurs. before holidays	60	0.1868	2.82	73.3
Fri. before holidays	71	0.3821	4.05	74.6
Sat. before holidays	101	0.2758	4.44	64.4
1 [a]	256	0.2097	4.58	62.5
2	1703	0.0310	1.36	53.4
3	18	0.2648	1.38	77.8
4	56	0.1895 *	2.53	66.1

[a] 1 = Fridays before a no-trading Saturday; 2 = Fridays before a trading Saturday; 3 = Fridays before a no-trading Saturday and no-trading Monday; 4 = Saturdays before a no-trading Monday and Saturdays before a Monday holiday.
Source: Ziemba (1991).

from the cash and futures markets from 1984 to 1992. The preholidays have returns that average about five times a typical day. As in the US and Japan, there is some anticipation in the futures markets that tends to shift the return distributions. Arbitrage trading is less active in the UK than in the US and this may be the reason that the effect is less pronounced in the UK. As in the other countries, the after holidays combined with Mondays are negative.

The turn of the month effect

There is strong evidence for a turn of the month effect in US, Japanese and other security markets. Market advisors such as Merrill (1966), Fosback (1976) and Hirsch (1986) have argued that stocks advance at the turn of the month. The five days consisting of the last trading day of the previous month (−1) and the first four trading days of the new month (+1 to +4) are referred

Table 14
Mean daily return, standard deviation on pre-holidays, NSA, 1949–1988

Holiday	Advances	Mean return, %	Minimum return, %	Maximum return, %	t-statistic
January 1	32/39	0.2457	−3.38	1.27	2.01
January 15	32/39	0.4711	−2.04	1.95	4.11
February 11	15/22	0.3011	−0.42	1.81	2.65
March 21	21/39	0.0687	−1.50	1.91	0.69
April 29	25/39	0.2272	−2.96	2.73	1.71
May 3	31/39	0.4989	−0.74	3.06	4.65
May 5	30/39	0.3884	−0.66	2.19	3.92
September 15	14/22	0.0154	−2.48	0.67	0.10
September 23	27/39	0.2341	−0.92	1.31	3.00
October 10	12/22	−0.2487	−5.41	1.26	−0.81
November 3	24/39	0.2987	−1.27	2.77	2.15
November 23	25/39	0.2414	−2.18	2.59	1.55
December 23					

Source: Ziemba (1991).

Table 15
Holiday effects in the UK

Day [a]	Cash market Data period: May 4, 1984 to May 10, 1992			Futures market Data period: May 4, 1984 to July 17, 1992		
	Sample size	Average return %	t-stat	Sample size	Average return %	t-stat
PH	49	0.198	1.912	50	0.182	1.097
AH	49	0.044	0.365	50	0.103	0.573
AH&M	427	−0.095	−1.861	437	−0.078	−1.130
PH&FRI	428	0.144	3.544	438	0.079	1.477
Other	1928	0.410	1.911	1975	0.031	1.190

[a] PH = preholiday (−1);
AH = after holiday (+1);
AH&M = Monday;
PH&FRI = Friday;
Other = rest of days.

to as the turn of the month. Ariel (1987) documented this for small land large capitalized stocks measured by equally and value weightings, respectively, of all NYSE stocks from 1963 to 1981, see Figure 7. See Table 5 for the January returns on these days from 1963 to 1979.

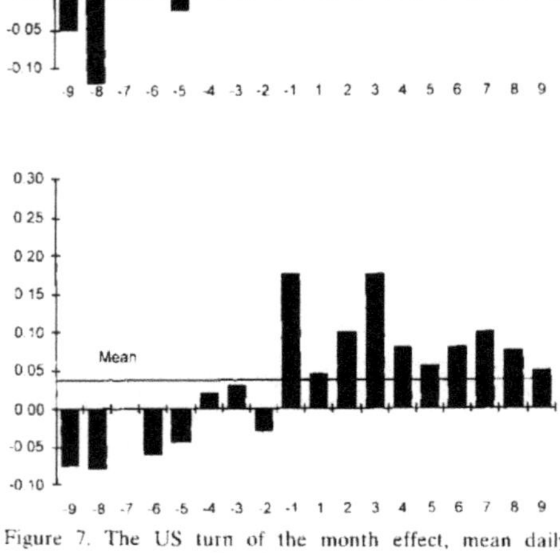

Figure 7. The US turn of the month effect, mean daily percent returns on trading days −9 to +9, 1963–81. Source: Ariel (1987)

The rest of the market gains during 1963–81 occurred in the second week of the month. The first half of the month, namely trading day −1 to +9 had all the gains and the second half of the month had no returns at all. For these 19 years, Ariel (1987) found the following portfolio gains: [3]

	Equally weighted	Value weighted
First half of trading month	2552.40%	565.40%
Last half of trading month	−0.25%	−33.80%
Nineteen years	2545.90%	339.90%

Lakonishok and Smidt (1988) reported that over the ninety year period 1897–1986, the large capitalized Dow Jones industrials rose 0.475% during the four day period −1 to +3 each month whereas the average gain for a four day period is 0.061%. There was an increase in prices over 56% of the time. The average gain per month over these 90 years was 0.349%. Hence aside from these four days at the turn of the month, the DJIA actually fell.

The effect has continued in recent years even in the presence of index futures contracts which have been trading since 1982. Hensel, Sick and Ziemba (1994) found the results presented in Table 16 and Figure 8. Consistent with the previous evidence about two thirds of the month's gains occur on trading days −1 to +4, the turn of the month, and the rest of the month's gains occur on trading days +5 to +9 so that all or

[3] One also sees the strong small firm effect during these years as the equally weighted index rose over seven times as much as the value weighted large capitalized index.

Table 16
The US turn of the month effect: average daily returns and t-values for the hypothesis that returns are greater than zero and the mean return, respectively, in the cash and futures markets for small and large capital stocks during the turn of the month, first half of the month, and rest of the month. May 1982–April 1992

	Average daily returns (%)				t-values (Ho: return = 0)				t-values (Ho: ret diff = 0)			
	TOM	FH	ROM	All days	TOM	FH	ROM	All days	TOM	FH	ROM	All days
	−1 to 4	−1 to 9	10 to −2	−1 to −1	−1 to 4	−1 to 9	10 to −2	−1 to −1	−1 to 4	−1 to 9	10 to −2	−1 to −1
(a) Cash market data												
Value Line index:									*Avg daily VL index ret = 0.0388*			
January	0.5483	0.2547	0.1087	0.1769	4.40	2.61	1.42	2.89	4.08	2.21	0.91	2.26
February	0.3839	0.2479	0.1030	0.1784	4.00	3.61	1.56	3.72	3.59	3.04	0.97	2.91
March	0.3229	0.1712	0.0099	0.0842	3.99	2.94	0.18	2.11	3.51	2.28	−0.53	1.14
April	0.0054	0.0161	0.0051	0.0104	0.06	0.22	0.09	0.22	−0.36	−0.31	−0.57	−0.81
May	0.1464	0.1147	−0.0084	0.0494	1.96	2.16	−0.14	1.20	1.44	1.43	−0.77	0.26
June	0.2203	0.0709	0.0006	0.0336	2.63	1.18	0.01	0.75	2.16	0.53	−0.58	−0.12
July	0.0278	0.0416	−0.0927	−0.0291	0.31	0.68	−1.59	−0.69	−0.12	0.05	−2.26	−1.60
August	−0.0212	0.0036	0.0864	0.0493	−0.15	0.04	1.07	0.81	−0.42	−0.38	0.59	0.17
September	0.0495	−0.0804	−0.0801	−0.0802	0.53	−1.04	−1.40	−1.68	0.11	−1.54	−2.07	−2.49
October	0.1272	0.0422	−0.3121	−0.1518	1.34	0.55	−1.61	−1.35	0.93	0.04	1.81	−1.70
November	0.3421	0.2321	−0.0711	0.0768	2.33	2.46	−1.07	1.32	2.06	2.05	−1.65	0.65
December	0.0521	0.0170	0.1410	0.0819	0.39	0.22	1.70	1.44	0.10	−0.28	1.23	0.76
All months	0.1837	0.0943	−0.0112	0.0388	5.84	4.30	−0.44	2.27	4.61	2.10	−1.95	0.00
All except Jan	0.1506	0.0797	−0.0225	0.0261	4.70	3.59	0.83	1.47	3.49	1.84	−2.26	−0.72
S&P 500 index:									*Avg daily S&P index ret = 0.0501*			
January	0.2730	0.0716	0.1371	0.1065	1.75	0.58	1.46	1.40	1.43	0.17	0.93	0.74
February	0.2116	0.1471	0.0909	0.1202	1.79	1.68	1.01	1.93	1.36	1.11	0.46	1.12
March	0.2220	0.0987	0.0297	0.0615	2.01	1.28	0.41	1.16	1.56	0.63	−0.28	0.22
April	0.0308	0.0432	0.0680	0.0560	0.24	0.42	0.82	0.86	−0.15	−0.07	0.22	0.09
May	0.1393	0.0872	0.0377	0.0609	1.35	1.15	0.48	1.11	0.86	0.49	−0.16	0.20
June	0.2074	0.0579	0.0521	0.0548	1.70	0.67	0.65	0.94	1.29	0.09	0.03	0.08
July	−0.0456	0.0348	−0.0332	−0.0009	−0.37	0.44	−0.44	−0.02	−0.78	−0.19	−1.11	−0.94
August	0.0234	0.0540	0.1129	0.0865	0.15	0.54	1.11	1.21	−0.17	0.04	0.62	0.51
September	0.0138	−0.0961	−0.0443	−0.0698	0.10	−0.97	−0.56	−1.11	−0.26	−1.48	−1.19	−1.90
October	0.2029	0.1256	−0.1763	−0.0397	1.43	1.24	−0.69	−0.27	1.08	0.74	−0.89	−0.61
November	0.2776	0.1500	−0.0718	0.0364	1.89	1.38	−0.78	0.51	1.55	0.92	−1.33	−0.19
December	0.1323	0.1073	0.1531	0.1313	0.78	1.05	1.66	1.91	0.48	0.56	0.11	1.18
All months	0.1407	0.0734	0.0290	0.0501	3.59	2.65	0.88	2.30	2.31	0.84	−0.64	0.00

(b) Futures market data

Value Line futures:									*Avg daily VL futures ret = 0.0321*			
January	0.5367	0.1926	0.1327	0.1606	3.43	1.32	27	1.82	3.22	1.10	0.96	1.46
February	0.3537	0.2115	0.0859	0.1510	2.38	2.02	93	2.15	2.17	1.72	0.58	1.70
March	0.2795	0.1467	−0.0165	0.0584	2.25	1.84	0.21	1.05	1.99	1.44	−0.63	0.47
April	0.0419	0.0186	−0.0247	−0.0039	0.26	0.15	−0.25	−0.05	0.06	−0.11	−0.58	−0.45
May	0.1362	0.1228	−0.0043	0.0551	1.36	1.62	−0.05	0.99	1.04	1.20	−0.45	0.41
June	0.1601	0.0709	−0.0067	0.0298	1.29	0.80	−0.07	0.47	1.03	0.44	−0.42	−0.04
July	0.0204	0.0715	−0.1144	−0.0267	0.13	0.68	−1.36	−0.40	−0.07	0.38	−1.74	−0.88
August	−0.1085	−0.0306	0.0844	0.0329	−0.52	−0.24	0.75	0.39	−0.67	−0.50	0.47	0.01
September	−0.0024	−0.0974	−0.0996	−0.0985	0.02	−0.90	−1.06	−1.38	−0.24	−1.19	−1.41	−1.83
October	0.1516	0.0853	−0.3130	−0.1336	0.94	0.74	−1.12	−0.82	0.74	0.46	−1.24	−1.62
November	0.2528	0.2404	−0.1097	0.0602	1.36	1.99	−1.08	0.76	1.19	1.72	−1.40	0.35
December	0.1488	0.0318	0.1833	0.1115	1.02	0.35	1.80	1.63	0.80	0.00	1.48	1.16
All months	0.1642	0.0887	−0.0186	0.0321	3.69	2.82	−0.51	1.32	2.97	1.80	−1.39	0.00
All except Jan	0.1304	0.0792	−0.0328	0.0202	2.82	2.50	−0.85	0.80	2.13	1.49	−1.68	−0.47
S & P 500 futures:									*Avg daily S & P futures ret = 0.0360*			
January	0.2437	0.0485	0.1186	0.0859	1.38	0.33	1.13	0.98	1.18	0.09	0.79	0.57
February	0.2042	0.1396	0.0738	0.1079	1.47	1.38	0.77	1.55	1.21	1.03	0.39	1.03
March	0.1839	0.0743	−0.0060	0.0308	1.62	0.90	−0.07	0.53	1.30	0.47	−0.52	−0.09
April	0.0111	0.0170	0.0480	0.0331	0.07	0.14	0.52	0.44	−0.16	−0.15	0.13	−0.04
May	0.1235	0.0871	0.0254	0.0542	1.15	1.07	0.30	0.91	0.81	0.63	−0.12	0.31
June	0.1585	0.0484	0.0493	0.0489	1.11	0.49	0.52	0.72	0.86	0.12	0.14	0.19
July	−0.0053	0.0566	−0.0649	−0.0073	−0.03	0.59	−0.79	−0.12	−0.26	0.21	−1.23	−0.69
August	−0.0243	0.0383	0.0987	0.0716	−0.13	0.33	0.89	0.89	−0.32	0.02	0.57	0.44
September	−0.0163	−0.1185	−0.0529	−0.0852	−0.10	−1.03	−0.56	−1.15	−0.33	−1.34	−0.95	−1.64
October	0.1708	0.1284	−0.1972	−0.0505	1.02	1.07	−0.55	−0.25	0.80	0.77	−0.65	−0.42
November	0.2680	0.1499	−0.1122	0.0150	1.49	1.18	−1.07	0.18	1.29	0.90	−1.41	−0.25
December	0.2097	0.1094	0.1494	0.1303	1.22	1.05	1.45	1.78	1.01	0.70	1.10	1.29
All months	0.1273	0.0649	0.0100	0.0360	2.83	2.03	0.24	1.34	2.03	0.91	−0.62	0.00
All except Jan	0.1167	0.0664	−0.0002	0.0314	2.51	2.06	0.00	1.11	1.74	0.94	−0.80	−0.16

Source: Hensel, Sick and Ziemba (1994).

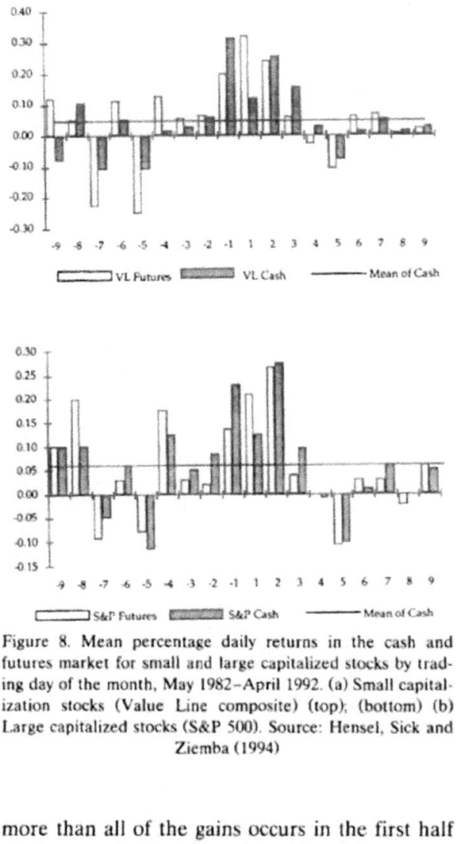

Figure 8. Mean percentage daily returns in the cash and futures market for small and large capitalized stocks by trading day of the month, May 1982–April 1992. (a) Small capitalization stocks (Value Line composite) (top); (bottom) (b) Large capitalized stocks (S&P 500). Source: Hensel, Sick and Ziemba (1994)

more than all of the gains occurs in the first half of the month. The second half is at best noise. The effect is monthly dependent with the largest gains in January and size dependent with the small capitalized value line index of about 1650 stocks having higher means and lower standard deviations than the large capitalized S&P500 index. There is partial anticipation in the futures market as shown in Figure 8. For the small capitalized value line index, the cash effect on day −1 is partially anticipated on days −4 to −2. Then the effect in the cash market on days +2 and +3 is partially anticipated on day +1. Hence the cash market effect on days −1 to +4 is as Ariel found for the 1963 to 1981 data with small gains on days −4 to −2. For the large capitalized S&P500 index, the results are similar except that there are higher returns in the cash market in the anticipation period (−4 to −2) and lower returns in the −1 to +4 period. As Lakonishok and Smidt found, there are insignificant gains on day +4 except in January. Heavy arbitrage trading in the S&P500 is offered as the cause for this shift. Once the futures moves on day −4, the cash moves as well through the arbitrage of selling expensive futures and buying cheaper stocks. There is less anticipation in the Value Line, especially in the anticipation cash market because the Value Line is too difficult to arbitrage with its 1650 stocks many of which are very small with low volumes.

Hensel, Sick and Ziemba (1994) computed the growth on one dollar over the 10 years of their sample in the cash and futures markets for small and large capitalized stocks during the turn, first half, and the rest of the month as well as during all days by month. These values show the compounded effects of monthly as well as intramonth seasonality during the TOM, FH and ROM subperiods and the futures anticipation. The results show very high returns during TOM for most months especially for the Value Line. The second half of many months are very negative with the worst month being October when $1 in 1982 became 68¢ for the small stocks and about 80¢ for the large stocks in 1992. Meanwhile in January's TOM the $1 grew to $1.32 for small stocks and $1.15 for large stocks using only five days per year. Table 16 shows the details for the cash market. The futures results are similar and appear in Hensel, Sick and Ziemba (1994). Additional results on the S&P cash market from 1928 to 1993 appear in Hensel, Sick and Ziemba (1993).

The reasons for the turn of the month effect are several but they are largely cash flow and institutionally based. The US economy works on a system where much money is paid on the −1 day such as salaries and bills and debt payments. In additions to some of this money being invested in the stock market, there are institutional corporate and pension fund purchases at that time. These cash flows vary by month and lead to higher average returns in January which has the highest cash inflow. Ogden (1990) presents some empirical support of this hypothesis and related monetary actions for US markets. Another factor in this effect seems to be behavioral. One manifestation is that bad news such as that relating to earnings announcements is delayed and announced late in the month while good news is released promptly at the beginning of the month; see Penman (1987).

Hensel, Sick and Ziemba (1994) also found that the return distributions were very different during TOM, FH and ROM. In the cash market, the normality of the first half price changes cannot be rejected, but the returns were non-normal during the turn-of-the-month and the rest of the month. The high returns during TOM and low returns during ROM in the cash market apparently lead to the rejection of normality because of their skewness. The smoothing effect of the futures anticipation yields distributions that are not skewed enough to reject the normality hypothesis. As Ariel (1987) found for the 1963 to 1981 data, the higher returns during TOM and ROM are caused by a slight shifting of the return distribution and not by a few outliers.

The turn of the month is similar in Japan except that the dates change with the turn being days −5 to +2, with +3 to +7 being the rest of the first half of the month. Ziemba (1989, 1991) investigated this; see also the more detailed summary in Ziemba and Schwartz (1991). The reasons for the effect in Japan seem to be:

- Most salaries are paid during the period of the 20–25th day of the month, with the 25th being especially popular.
- There is portfolio window dressing on day −1.
- Security firms can invest for their own accounts on amounts based on their capitalization. Since their capitalization usually rises each month and is computed at the end of the month, there is buying on day −3 to account for this. Buying is done as soon as possible.
- Large brokerage firms have a sales push that lasts 7 to 10 days and this starts on day −3.
- Employment stock holding plans and mutual funds receive money in this period to invest, starting around day −3.
- Individual investors buy mutual funds with their pay, which they receive on calendar days 15 to 25 of the month; the funds then invest in stocks with a lag, so most of the buying occurs on days −5 to +2.
- For low liquidity stocks, buying occurs over several days by dealing in accounts to minimize price pressure effects.

Using data on the NSA from 1949 to 1988 Ziemba (1991) found that all of the days −5 to +2 had significantly positive returns as shown in Table 17 and Figure 9. As in the US all the gains occurred in the first half of the month and the second half had zero or negative returns.

Ziemba (1989) investigated the futures market trading outside Japan on the Simex in Singapore on the turn of the month and other anomalous effects in Japanese security markets during the period September 1986 to September 1988 before there was futures trading on the NSA or Topix in Japan. He found that the spot effect was consistent with past data so the futures market did not alter the effect. However, the futures market in Singapore totally anticipated the effect on days −8 to −5 with a total average rise on 2.8%. Then when the effect occurred on days −5 to +2

Table 17
Growth of $1 investment in the cash market for small and large capitalized stocks in various periods, May 1982 to April 1992

	Growth of $1 investment			
	TOM −1 to 4	FH −1 to 9	ROM 10 to −2	All days −1 to −1
Value Line cash market:				
January	1.31539	1.29004	1.13193	1.46024
February	1.21160	1.28128	1.09938	1.40861
March	1.17520	1.18676	1.01164	1.20057
April	1.00272	1.01623	1.00556	1.02187
May	1.07595	1.12155	0.99050	1.11089
June	1.11645	1.07345	1.00064	1.07413
July	1.01399	1.04248	0.90220	0.94053
August	0.98944	1.00359	1.11211	1.11610
September	1.02506	0.92279	0.92078	0.84969
October	1.06565	1.04312	0.68550	0.71505
November	1.18652	1.26119	0.92802	1.17041
December	1.02641	1.01711	1.16779	1.18778
All months	3.01108	3.10035	0.86112	2.66979
All except Jan	2.28912	2.40330	0.76076	1.82832
S & P 500 cash market:				
January	1.14627	1.07421	1.16913	1.25589
February	1.11162	1.15848	1.08725	1.25956
March	1.11741	1.10378	1.03535	1.14280
April	1.01551	1.04413	1.07551	1.12298
May	1.07212	1.09108	1.04347	1.13851
June	1.10926	1.05961	1.06061	1.12383
July	0.97746	1.03546	0.96383	0.99801
August	1.01177	1.05548	1.14891	1.21266
September	1.00693	0.90834	0.95544	0.86786
October	1.10680	1.13381	0.80792	0.91603
November	1.14888	1.16187	0.92741	1.07753
December	1.06837	1.11331	1.18344	1.31753
All months	2.32626	2.41413	1.46965	3.54792
All except Jan	2.02942	2.24736	1.25705	2.82503

Source: Hensel, Sick and Ziemba (1994).

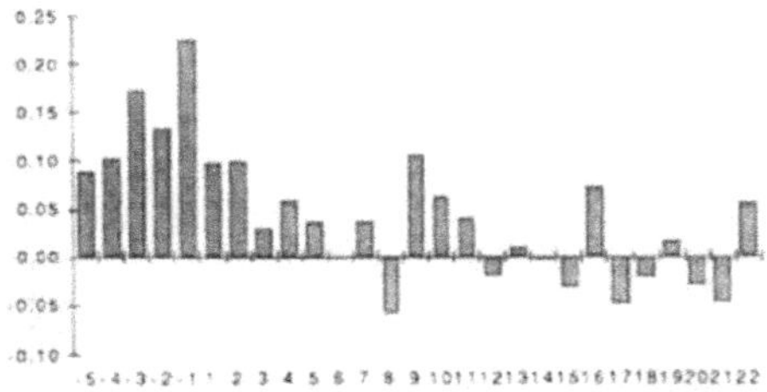

Figure 9. Rate of return by trading day-of-the-month, NSA, 1949–1988. Source: Ziemba (1991)

Table 18
Mean returns in percent on the NSA by trading day of the month, 1949–1988

Trading day	Sample size	Mean return, %	*t*-statistic
−5	471	0.0899	2.75
−4	471	0.1041	2.65
−3	471	0.1733	3.82
−2	471	0.1334	3.18
−1	471	0.2255	5.36
1	471	0.0980	2.43
2	471	0.1006	2.47
3	471	0.0307	0.72
4	471	0.0592	1.15
5	471	0.0358	0.81
6	471	−0.0005	−0.01
7	471	0.0357	0.09
8	471	−0.0585	−1.34
9	471	0.1065	2.46
10	471	0.0620	1.58
11	471	0.0395	1.05
12	471	−0.0196	−0.50
13	471	0.0115	0.24
14	471	−0.0042	−0.10
15	471	−0.0306	−0.54
16	471	0.0716	1.35
17	471	−0.0498	−1.20
18	429	−0.0207	−0.49
19	350	0.0162	0.36
20	229	−0.0286	−0.48
21	118	−0.0476	−0.46
22	39	0.0562	0.45

Source: Ziemba (1991).

and the spot market gained 1.7%, the futures market was flat; see Figure 10.

Cadsby and Ratner (1991) investigated turn of the month and holiday effects in the US, Canada, the UK, Australia, Switzerland, West Germany, Japan, Hong Kong, Italy and France. Their use of −1 to +4 as the turn of the month in all these countries makes their results hard to interpret since there may be cash flow and institutional constraint date alterations as in Japan. Still they find a significant turn of the month in most countries as shown in Figure 11.

A good example of a significant turn-of-the-month effect with different dates is that in Italy. The month there essentially starts on the 15th (approximately) and all trades from then up to the following 14th are settled on the last trading date of that calendar month. This system leads to high returns from the 15th to the end of that calendar month and low or negative returns from the +1 day to the 14th; see Barone (1990). Not surprisingly, Italy has not had high returns on days −1 to +4 and does not appear in Figure 11.

I investigated more recent data from the UK in addition to futures market data. Their results from 1984–92 show a significant turn-of-the-month effect. Anticipation in the futures markets on trading day −3 provides a TOM from −3 to +3 as shown in Table 19 and Figure 12. As with other countries, the effect is monthly dependent and the strongest months are similar to those in

Spot Data 1949-88

	trading days	
1st Half	22-7	.01142
2nd Half	8-21	.00048

Futures Market Effects: 1986-88

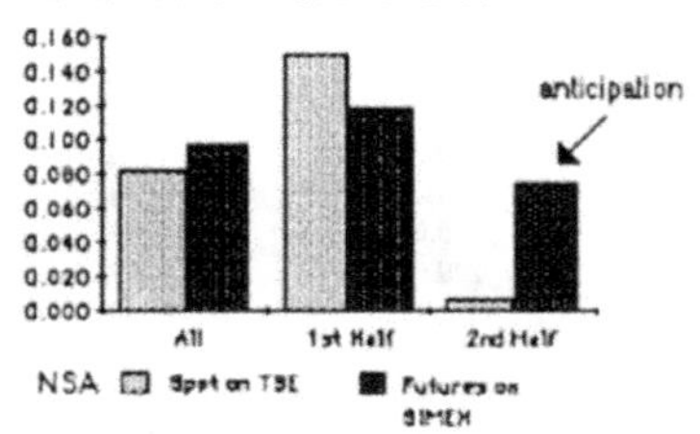

Figure 10. Daily rates of return in the first and second halves of the month in Japan, cash data, 1949–1988, futures market effects 1986–88. Source: Ziemba (1989)

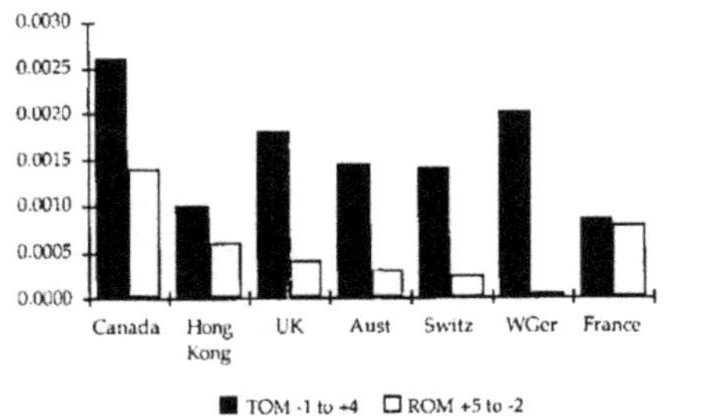

Figure 11. International turn-of-the-month-effects. Daily rates of return in % for Canada (1/75–12/87), Hong Kong (1/80–89), UK (8/83–6/88), Australia (1/80–8/89), Switzerland (1/80–8/89), West Germany (1/80–8/89), and France (1/80–8/89). Source: Cadsby and Ratner (1991)

the US with the early months especially January and the late months the strongest.

The turn-of-the-month effect seems to be a worldwide phenomenon. The paper by Martikainen, Perttunen and Ziemba (1994), although it only considers the brief period from January 1988 to January 1990, shows this with various indices for a variety of regions of the world. They also found that returns on individual days during

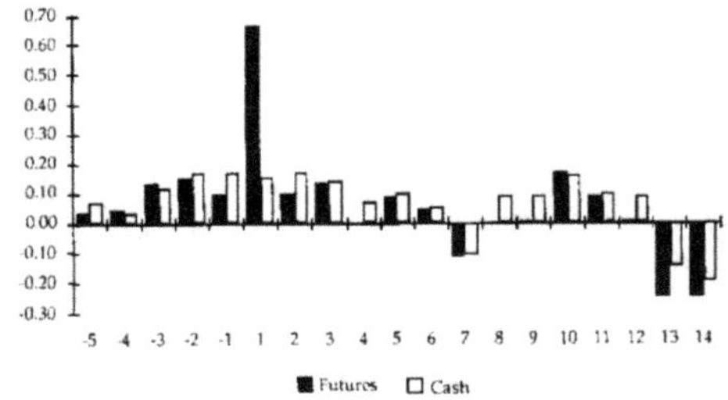

Figure 12. The turn-of-the-month effect in the UK, mean percent returns on trading days −5 to +14, 1984–1992.

TOM, especially −1, were high. The latter averaged 0.41% per day over 24 countries with a t value of 3.89 and was the only trading day with a mean return different from zero.

The January barometer

Around the world, January returns are generally very high. In many countries and particularly in the US markets, small stocks greatly outperform large stocks in January. For large capital-

Table 19
The turn-of-the-month effect in the UK, 1984–1992

Trading day	Futures market Data period: May 4th, 1984 –July 17th, 1992			Cash market Data period: May 4th, 1984 –May 10th, 1992		
	Sample size	Average return %	t-statistic	Sample size	Average return %	t-statistic
−5	98	−0.025	−0.252	96	−0.063	−0.603
−4	98	−0.035	−0.363	96	−0.017	−0.194
−3	98	0.127	1.201	96	0.104	1.228
−2	98	0.161	1.505	96	0.176	2.076
−1	98	0.105	0.795	96	0.158	1.767
1	98	0.633	4.830	96	0.163	1.966
2	98	0.094	0.930	96	0.171	2.062
3	98	0.118	1.266	96	0.125	1.625
4	98	−0.007	−0.066	96	0.050	0.598
5	98	0.065	0.669	96	0.092	1.101
6	98	0.037	0.359	96	0.042	0.469
7	98	−0.105	−1.038	96	−0.093	−1.112
8	98	0.004	0.033	96	0.058	0.547
9	98	0.004	0.043	96	0.080	0.932
10	98	0.152	1.662	96	0.144	1.929
11	98	0.069	0.640	96	0.089	1.114
12	98	0.004	0.044	96	0.084	1.080
13	98	−0.239	−1.185	96	−0.146	−1.126
14	98	−0.253	−1.806	96	−0.198	−1.354

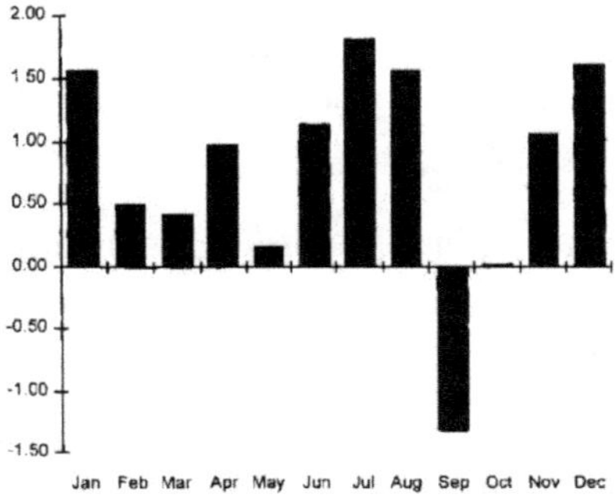

Figure 13. S&P500 percentage returns by month, from February 1928 to June 1993. Source: Ibbotson and Associates; data in Hensel and Ziemba (1993a)

ized stocks, January returns have been higher than average but not higher than many other months. For example, for the sixty-five years from January 1928 to June 1993, fully six other months have similar returns as shown in Figure 13.

However, January seems to be a valuable signal for the whole year.

If large stocks have positive returns in January, then it is likely that the market as a whole will rise in the rest of that year (ROY). Yale Hirsch (1986) has called this the January barometer. The supposition is that:
if the market rises in January, then it will rise in the rest of the year; but if it falls in January, then there will be a decline or a flat market in the rest of that year.

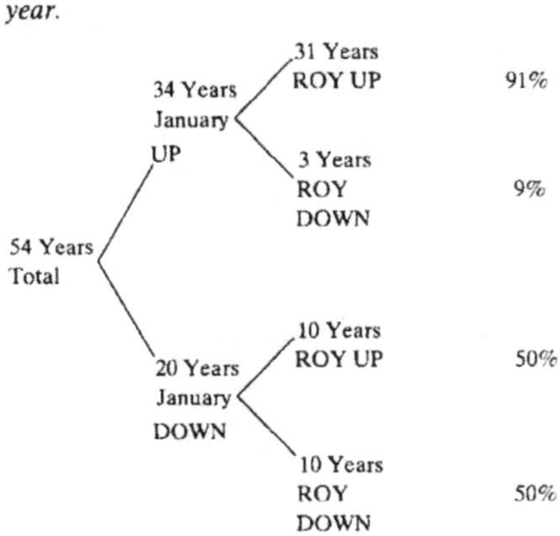

Table 20 from Hensel and Ziemba (1993a) has the results for the 54 years 1940–93.

When the return in January was positive, the rest of the year was up 91% of the time. This compares with only 76% of all years that the rest of the year was up.

When the return in January was negative, the rest of the year was down 50% of the time. Thus even in years when January is down, the rest of the year is equally likely to be up or down.

January 1994 had a gain of 3.2% hence a gain in the rest of 1994 is predicted.

Time of day effects

Harris (1986a) has documented a time of day effect for NYSE securities. Figure 14 shows the typical behavior using all NYSE stocks from 1981 to 1983. Consistent with the day of the week finding there are share price rises on Tuesday to Friday and declines on Mondays. Price action occurs mostly in the first 45 minutes and then there is little movement until a sharp rise near the close of trading. Harris (1986b) discusses this latter move and details the very high percentage of final trades that are at price increases. The percentage of stocks advancing on their last trade of the day is usually above 80%. As pointed out by Kevin Rowe, this may be largely attributed to specialists book balancing to end the day. Admati and Pffeidler (1988, 1989) present a formal theory that attempts to explain the intra and inter day changes based on the trading of participants with differential information.

Japanese stocks seem to have all their gains during the non trading period at night. Table 21 using data on the Topix from 1974–87 with yearly rebalancing shows this in a rising market and Table 22 for a declining market. The effect seems to be broker related with solicitations of buy orders obtained after market closing on the previous day that are executed on the open in the cash and futures market. Table 21 also illustrates the size effect in which the smallest capitalized quintile had returns more than twice as high as the largest capitalized quintile. Table 22 shows that even though the NSA fell over 50% from January 1990 to March 1992 there were net gains at night. Bell and Ziemba (1993) show that this has continued in the remainder of 1992. Keim and Smir-

Table 20
The January barometer 1940–1993

Year	S&P500 (%) Jan	S&P500 (%) Rest of year	Direction of signal		Did it work?
			Jan	Rest of year	
1993	0.7	6.3	up	up	yes
1992	−1.9	4.3	down	up	no
1991	4.3	22.3	up	up	yes
1990	−6.9	3.7	down	up	no
1989	7.0	20.4	up	up	yes
1988	4.2	11.4	up	up	yes
1987	12.6	−7.5	up	down	no
1986	0.4	16.5	up	up	yes
1985	7.4	20.5	up	up	yes
1984	−0.7	6.7	down	up	no
1983	3.4	16.9	up	up	yes
1982	−1.6	21.0	down	up	no
1981	−4.5	−0.6	down	down	yes
1980	5.9	22.2	up	up	yes
1979	4.1	12.8	up	up	yes
1978	−6.1	12.5	down	up	no
1977	−5.0	−2.4	down	down	yes
1976	11.3	10.1	up	up	yes
1975	11.8	19.8	up	up	yes
1974	−0.9	−29.9	down	down	yes
1973	−1.6	−14.2	down	down	yes
1972	1.9	15.5	up	up	yes
1971	4.1	9.3	up	up	yes
1970	−7.7	11.7	down	up	no
1969	−0.7	11.7	down	up	no
1969	−0.7	−8.2	down	down	yes
1968	−4.3	14.8	down	up	no
1967	7.7	13.8	up	up	yes
1966	0.6	−11.2	up	down	no
1965	3.4	8.3	up	up	yes
1964	2.8	12.5	up	up	yes
1963	4.9	15.6	up	up	yes
1962	−3.7	−5.4	down	down	yes
1961	6.3	17.6	up	up	yes
1960	−7.3	7.7	down	up	no
1959	0.5	10.8	up	up	yes
1958	4.4	31.7	up	up	yes
1957	−4.1	−7.3	down	down	yes
1956	−3.5	9.9	down	up	no
1955	2.0	25.5	up	up	yes
1954	5.2	37.1	up	up	yes
1953	−0.5	−0.5	down	down	yes
1952	1.8	15.1	up	up	yes
1951	6.2	15.3	up	up	yes
1950	1.9	25.6	up	up	yes
1949	0.4	16.8	up	up	yes
1948	−3.9	9.2	down	up	no
1947	2.5	3.0	up	up	yes
1946	6.9	−15.3	up	down	no
1945	1.6	29.5	up	up	yes
1944	1.7	16.3	up	up	yes
1943	7.1	15.9	up	up	yes
1942	1.6	16.9	up	up	yes
1941	−4.7	−7.6	down	down	yes
1940	−3.4	−6.9	down	down	yes

Source: Hensel and Ziemba (1993a).

lock (1987) found consistent but not as sharp results in the US for small stocks with the Value Line small capitalized index having its major gains at night.

Can professional fund managers beat the market averages?

The evidence presented in this review is potentially useful in the design and implementation of superior portfolio management strategies. In particular, the aim is to have higher average returns with no higher risk than the market averages. Shukla and Trzcinka (1992) survey methods to evaluate managed portfolio performance. Various authors such as Cowles (1933), Sharpe (1966), Jensen (1968), Brown, Friend, Herman and Vickers (1962), Friend, Blume and Crockett (1970), Henriksson (1984), Brinson, Hood and Beebower (1986), Grinblatt and Titman (1989), Elton et al. (1991), and Lakonishok, Shleifer and Vishny (1992) have found that professional and pension fund managers do not usually outperform their benchmark portfolios once transactions costs and fees are considered. Table 23 shows the usual behavior.

This and as suggested by the capital asset pricing model's conclusion to hold stocks in weights proportional to their capitalization provides a strong case for index funds. Indeed, there is much support for this view in the pension fund management industry and hundreds of billions of dollars are so managed. Wells Fargo in San Francisco alone so manages a sum in the $100 billion range.

The reasons why index funds typically outperform active management are:

- The market averages stay fully invested at all times, never missing market moves nor paying commissions for stock changes and market timing.

Table 21
Topix mean returns for size related portfolios, 1974–1987

Firm size	Average market Value (¥ million)	Mean return		
		Close to Close	Close to Open	Open to Close
Smallest	773	0.1492	0.1784	−0.0295
2	1,716	0.1058	0.1545	−0.0489
3	3,275	0.0859	0.1354	−0.0495
4	6,554	0.0764	0.0976	−0.0213
Largest	32,689	0.0653	0.0483	0.0168

Source: Kato (1990).

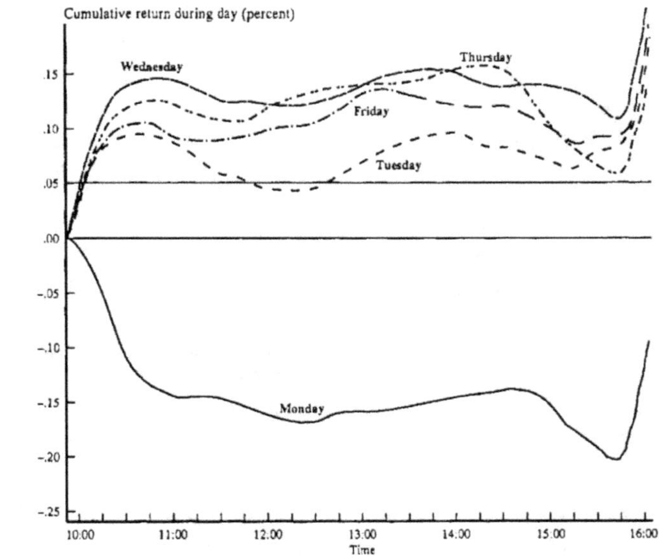

Figure 14. The time of day effect on the MYSE. Source: Harris (1986a)

• When funds get behind the index, they often make hasty moves to try to catch up and, more often than not, this puts them further behind.

• Portfolio managers have a tendency to window dress at reporting times, adding to turnover and commissions.

• Since the managers collectively more or less *are* the market (with individual investors forming

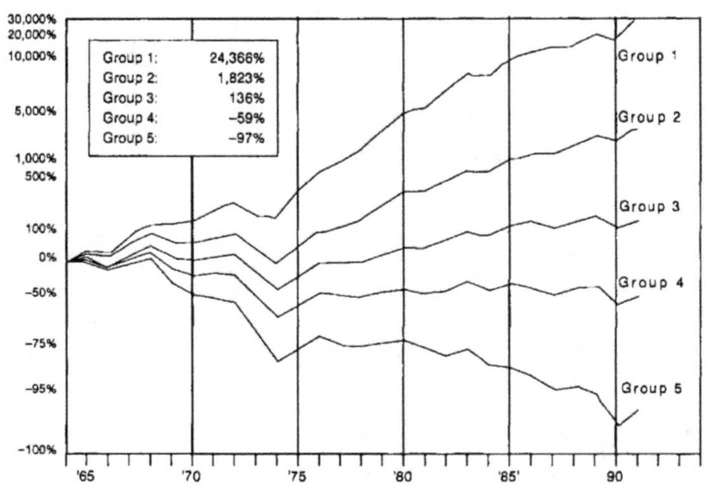

Figure 15. Value Line timeliness rankings, revised weekly, April 16, 1965 to December 27, 1991. Source: Value Line Investment Survey

Table 22
Mean returns in percent during the day and night by month in Japan, NSA, January 1990–March 1992

Month	Mean return	
	Close to Open	Open to Close
All days	0.001150	−0.002390
Jan	0.003870	−0.005780
Feb	−0.003850	0.003768
Mar	0.001790	−0.005670
Apr	−0.000130	−0.000540
May	0.003120	−0.001650
Jun	0.007450	−0.010220
Jul	−0.000960	0.000638
Aug	0.006120	−0.011000
Sep	−0.008440	0.005170
Oct	−0.002300	0.006320
Nov	0.010820	−0.015820
Dec	−0.003640	0.005923

Source: Bell and Ziemba (1993).

less and less of the market each year) the indices, on average, beat half of the fund managers. Then with commissions, fees, and these other reasons, only the 25% to 40% typically beat the market averages (which does quite well with a lot less work).

• The fund managers take fees; the averages work for free.

• The fund managers' goals may get in the way of the fund's best interests. This is the so-called agency problem.

• Portfolio managers tend to follow each other's moves. They tend to move the market which gains the full amount, and they can easily be a little behind.

Hence although the evidence in this review suggests methods and strategies for beating market averages [4] it is clear that only a small number of managers are able to successfully implement such strategies over a long period of time. [5]

[4] My own experience with a small private mutual fund based on anomalies has been encouraging. In 76 months from October 1987 to January 1994, the fund averaged 27.3% annualized (net of fees) with a standard deviation of 13.2%. Experience, size and diversification are important in such funds and the 1991–94 results were superior providing a similar mean return but with the much lower standard deviation of 8.1%.

[5] Lakonishok, Shleifer and Vishny (1992) used a data base on all 769 all-equity pension funds followed by SEI, a financial services company that specialized in evaluating the performance of pension plans and in recommending money managers. The results for 1983–89 for these managers, who collectively managed $124 billion as of the end of 1989 was underperformance of the S & P500 by 1.3% per year before management fees which averaged 0.5%. Hence, the average active manager subtracted rather than added value. However, Hendricks, Patel and Zeckhauser (1991) show that managers that have had outperforming track records tend to continue to outperform. Ippolito (1989, 1992) and Goetzmann and Ibbotson (1991) also confirm the existence of superior managers. Brown et al. (1992) show the effect of survivorship bias in such studies and how it over estimates the true return.

Table 23
Sector Median Returns of Hong Kong Based Funds Compared with Market Average, January 1 to November 30, 1988

Class of fund	Outperforming median return, %	Reference market average	Number of funds	
			% Change	Market average
Japanese equity funds	19.1	TSE Index	34.9	4 of 30
Hong Kong equity funds	24.4	Hang Seng index	20.8	9 of 15
Australian equity funds	23.1	All-ordinaries index	43.3	1 of 11
Singapore/Malaysian equity funds	25.8	FT Actuaries Singapore	25.9	3 of 7
Asean equity funds	41.4	FT Actuaries HK and Singapore	27.7	11 of 13
Far East equity funds	22.1	FT Actuaries Pacific	35.1	3 of 20
US equity funds	7.6	S&P Composite	14.0	5 of 25
British equity funds	6.8	FT All Shares Index	10.9	4 of 19
European equity funds	13.0	FT Actuaries Europe	13.9	7 of 15
International managed funds	9.4	FT Actuaries World	23.1	0 of 6
British gilt funds	1.0	FT All Stock Bond index	5.0	1 of 6
			(28.7%)	48 of 167

Source: Ziemba and Schwartz (1991).

Table 24
Value line timeliness rankings (%), revised weekly, April 16, 1965 to December 27, 1991

	Group					
	1	2	3	4	5	1-5
'65	26.6	16.5	6.7	−0.4	−3.2	32.0
'66	−5.5	−6.2	−13.9	−15.7	−18.2	12.7
'67	53.4	36.1	27.1	23.8	21.5	31.9
'68	37.1	26.9	24.0	20.9	11.8	25.3
'69	−10.4	−17.5	−23.8	−33.3	−44.9	34.5
'70	7.3	−3.2	−8.0	−16.3	−23.3	30.6
'71	30.8	13.7	9.3	8.4	−5.5	36.1
'72	12.6	7	3.5	−7.1	−13.4	26.9
'73	−13.1	−23.9	−33.8	−31.8	−43.8	24.1
'74	−11.1	−29.5	−34.1	−40.6	−55.7	44.6
'75	75.6	47.4	40.7	39.3	40.9	34.7
'76	54.0	31.2	29.0	28.8	26.7	27.3
'77	26.6	13.4	1.3	−6.9	−17.6	41.2
'78	32.6	18.3	3.0	−3.8	−3.2	35.8
'79	54.7	38.0	20.7	12.8	10.4	41.8
'80	52.6	35.7	15.4	7.4	2.9	49.7
'81	13.6	1.8	−3.3	−8.7	−21.4	35.0
'82	50.6	31.0	17.9	5.1	−10.9	61.5
'83	40.9	19.1	20.2	25.0	19.0	21.9
'84	−2.1	−0.8	−5.6	−17.4	−81.0	28.9
'85	47.0	30.7	22.8	11.4	5.6	41.4
'86	22.9	14.4	7.7	−6.6	−19.6	42.5
'87	5.4	−2.4	−12.6	−15.8	−28.0	11.4
'88	9.5	20.4	16.1	17.6	11.4	(1.9)
'89	27.9	28.5	13.7	2.6	−19.2	47.1
'90	−10.4	−10.2	−24.4	−33.7	−45.5	35.1
'91	55.4	34.1	18.9	16.7	25.5	29.9
'65–'91	24.366	1823	136	−59	−97	

Source: Value Line Investment Survey.

The Value Line enigma

There is considerable evidence that the rankings made by the Value Line Investment Survey actually do have value to investors. Each week stocks in their universe (about 1650) are ranked into five groups based on their projected timeliness for the subsequent year. Table 24 and Figure 15 show the theoretical results not counting transactions costs, dividends or taxes, of the strategies of holding all #1, #2, #3, #4 and #5 ranked stocks and rebalancing whenever there is a rank change for the period April 16, 1965 to December 27, 1991. On the surface, the results are impressive. Long positions in #1s averaged 24.2% over these 27 years. Moreover, a close to beta equal zero market neutral strategy that went long #1s and short #5s averaged 33.7% returns with an annualized standard deviation of 12.2% and had only one losing year. A strategy of going long #1s and holding for one year and then rebalancing had average returns of 16.6% over the 27 years. Several academics such as Black (1973), Copeland and Mayers (1982), Stickel (1985), Huberman and Kandel (1987, 1990) and Affleck-Graves and Mendenhall (1992) have studied the reported results and in general confirm the superior behavior of the Value Line ranking model.

Several questions arise. Why is Value Line able to beat the market with publicly available information and rankings? How reliable are the rankings? How should one implement such a strategy with actual funds?

On the first question, it is known that Value Line's model uses several elements that include price momentum, size and earnings variables. Analysis of rankings by Stickel (1985) concluded that the rankings were better than chance so that Value Line's model has information that is not fully reflected in current stock prices. Copeland and Mayers (1982) show that excess returns peak at about thirteen weeks from the time a rank change is made. Hence, there is a lag effect. Ball and Brown (1968), Bernard and Thomas (1989, 1990) and Abarbanell and Bernard (1992) have studied such stale information effects regarding earnings. There is considerable evidence that the market does not immediately factor new earnings information instantaneously. In particular even after three days after quarterly earnings announcements stock prices have not adjusted to the new information. Jennings and Starks (1986) show that the speed of adjustment to quarterly earnings information is faster if options are traded in the stock. Affleck-Graves and Mendehall (1992) show that a substantial portion of Value Line's superior performance is from rank changes involving earning surprises of small capitalized firms. A good strategy for fund managers is thus to invest in Value Line #2 stocks that have just reported earnings surprises, many of these stock will be elevated to #1 stocks shortly.

There is superior long run performance of the Value Line #1s in comparisons with the #5s. However, occasionally the rankings do not produce higher returns. This is usually in January and the first quarter and is likely associated with the DeBondt-Thaler winner-loser effect and the January small firm effect. Value Line #5s are likely to be losers such as negative earnings stocks and they may have high returns in the next January.

Despite the superior performance, there have been very few mutual funds that have had successful implementations of the long #1 or long #1–short #5 strategy with real money. Obtaining precise transactions costs is difficult as is the ability to put on the positions before the market moves as there are over 100,000 copies of the Value Line Investment Survey as well as computer disks and on line service available to investors each week. I have been implementing a version of the Value Line neutral investment strategy since April 1991, using put and call option sales for Global Securities, a Vancouver investment firm. The preliminary results are encouraging and the investors have had returns that have beaten the market averages with lower risk. In the 33 months until the end of December 1993, the annualized net rate of return was 18.9% which greatly exceeds the S&P500 with dividends. During the first half of 1992 the Value Line system was in a period where the rankings failed because the market favored value stocks rather than the growth stocks that the model favors. The option sale strategy was successful in this period. However, implementations that were long and short probably produced losses.

Final remarks

Behavioral factors along with cash flows and institutional constraints and policies are important reasons for anomalous behavior. Investor sentiment, however it may be defined (such as by the level of new IPOs, see Ritter, 1991), greatly affects stock prices. For example, Bailey and Lim (1992) found that the discounts and premiums of closed end country funds traded on the NYSE and ASE depend upon the current returns in the US rather than the returns in the foreign country. Hence the returns of say the Australian, Brazil, France or Italy funds tend to have higher short term correlations with the S&P500 than the home market indices.

Lee, Shliefer and Thaler (1991) using data from 1965–85 showed that the discounts on premiums of general closed end mutual funds seem to be dependent upon general market sentiment which includes seasonality effects rather than the specific holdings of the fund. For example, discounts shrink in January when there are high small stock returns. Yet Brauer and Chang (1989) found that the funds' underlying assets had no January small firm effect. The results seem to be based on the existence of two types of investors: rational traders, who invest based on fundamentals, and noise traders who base their investments at least in part on the basis of irrational factors that can be overly optimistic or pessimistic about the future; see DeLong, Shleifer, Summer and Waldmann (1990) and DeLong and Shleifer (1992).

Bell and Ziemba (1993) and Ziemba (1994a) found that the anomalies fail to behave as expected during periods of extreme market volatility. Ziemba studied the US markets during the buildup and subsequent 1987 stock market crash and Bell and Ziemba study the Japanese market during the 1990–92 decline of over 60%. In both cases market sentiment factors were dominant and cash flow considerations secondary. In the case of Japan the cash flows were substantial but they did not become invested in the stock market because investors expectation of future returns was negative.

This survey covers several anomaly topics for US and several other equity markets. Effects in other markets such as interest rates (see Froot, 1993), bond and commodity prices are fruitful areas of study. So are the effects of various events such as stock splits, [6] and S&P500 additions and deletions. Some of these topics are discussed in Ziemba (1994a).

Acknowledgements

This research was partially supported by the Social Sciences and Humanities Research Council of Canada, Buchanan Partners, London and the Frank Russell Company. Without implicating them I would like to thank Chris Hensel, Victor Lo, Alan Mercer, Peregrine Moncreiffe, John Mulvey, Peter Newman, Douglas Ohlman, Kevin Rowe, Sandra L. Schwartz, Gordon Sick, Andrew

[6] See Brennan and Copeland (1988a, b), Dravid (1987), Ohlson and Penman (1985) and Wiggins (1992).

L. Turner, and Edward O. Thorp for helpful comments on an earlier version of this review and for useful discussions on this topic.

References

Abarbenell, J.S., and Bernard, V.L. (1992), "Test of analysts' overreaction/underaction to earnings information as an explanation for anomalous stock price behavior", *Journal of Finance* 37, 1181–1227.

Admati, A.R., and Pfleiderer, P. (1988), "A theory of intraday patterns: Volume and price variability", *Review of Financial Studies* 1, 3–10.

Admati, A.R., and Pfleiderer, P. (1989), "Divide and conquer: A theory of intra-day and day of the week mean effects," *Review of Financial Studies* 2, 189–223.

Affleck-Graves, J., and Mendenhall, R. (1992), "The relation between the value line enigma and post earnings announcement drift", *Journal of Financial Economics*, forthcoming.

Aggarwal, R., Rao, R.P., and Hiraki, T. (1988), "Japanese equity returns: Empirical evidence of skewness and kurtosis", Working Paper, John Carroll University, University Heights, OH.

Aggarwal, R., Hiraki, T., and Rao, R.P. (1988), "Price/earnings ratios and equity returns on the Tokyo Stock Exchange: A note", Working Paper, John Carroll University, University Heights, OH.

Aggarwal, R., Rao, R.P., and Hiraki, T. (1989), "Price/sales ratios and equity returns on the Tokyo Stock Exchange: An empirical study", Working Paper, John Carroll University, University Heights, OH.

Ariel, R.A. (1984), "High stock returns before holidays", Mimeo, Sloan School of Management, MIT.

Ariel, R.A. (1987), "Monthly effect in stock returns", *Journal of Financial Economics* 18, 1–14.

Ariel, R.A. (1990), "High stock returns before holidays: Existence and evidence on possible causes", *Journal of Finance* 45, 1611–1626.

Bachelier, L. (1900), *Théorie de la Speculation*, Gauthier-Villars, Paris.

Bailey, W., and Lim, J. (1992), "Evaluating the diversification benefits of the new country funds", *Journal of Portfolio Management*, Spring, 74–80.

Ball, R. (1978), "Anomalies in relationships between securities' yields and yield-surrogates", *Journal of Financial Economics* 6, 103–126.

Ball, R., land Brown, P. (1968), "An empirical evaluation of accounting income numbers", *Journal of Accounting Research* 6/2, 159–178.

Ball, R., and Kothari, S. (1989), "Nonstationary expected returns: Implications for tests of market efficiency and serial corelation in returns", *Journal of Financial Economics* 25, 51–74.

Banz, R.W. (1981), "The relationship between return and market value of common stocks", *Journal of Financial Economics* 9, 3–18.

Barone, E. (1990), "The Italian stock market: Efficiency and calendar anomalies", Working Paper, Centre for Research in Finance – IMI Group, No 1, February.

Basu, S. (1977), "Investment performance of common stocks in relation to their price–earnings ratios: A test of the efficient market hypothesis", *Journal of Finance* 32, 663–682.

Basu, S. (1983), "The relationship between earnings' yield, market value and return for NYSE common stocks: Further evidence", *Journal of Financial Economics* 12, 129–156.

Bell, D., and Ziemba, W.T. (1993), "Investigation of seasonal anomalies on the Tokyo stock exchange, 1990–93", Mimeo, University of British Columbia.

Bernard, V.L., and Thomas, J.K. (1989), "Post-earnings-announcement drift: Delayed price response or risk premium?", *Journal of Accounting Research* 27 (Supplement), 1–36.

Bernard, V.L., and Thomas, J.K. (1990), "Evidence that stock prices do not fully reflect the implications of current earnings for future earnings", *Journal of Accounting and Economics* 13, 305–340.

Black, F. (1973), "Yes, Virginia, there is hope: Tests of the Value LIne ranking system", *Financial Analysts Journal* 29/5, 10–14.

Black, F. (1986), "Noise", *Journal of Finance* 41, 10–14.

Black, F. (1992), "Estimating expected returns", Mimeo, Goldman Sachs, New York.

Black, F., Jensen, M., and Scholes, M. (1972), "The capital asset pricing model: Some empirical tests", in: M. Jensen (ed.), *Studies in the Theory of Capital Markets*, Praeger, New York.

Blume, M.E. (1980), "Stock returns and dividend yields: Some more evidence", *Review of Economics and Statistics* 62, 567–577.

Blume, M.E., and Siegel, J.J. (1992), "The theory of security pricing and market structure", *Journal of Financial Markets, Institutions and Instruments* 1, 1–58.

Blume, M.E., and Stambaugh, R.F. (1983), "Biases in computed returns an application to the size effect", *Journal of Financial Economics* 12, 387–404.

Brauer, G.A., and Chang, E. (1989), "Return seasonality in stocks and their underlying assets: Tax loss selling versus information expectations", Mimeo, University of Washington.

Brennan, M.J., and Copeland, T.E. (1988a), "Stock splits, stock prices and transactions costs", *Journal of Financial Economics* 22, 83–101.

Brennan, M.J., and Copeland, T.E. (1988b), "Beta changes around stock splits: A note", *Journal of Finance* 43, 1009–1013.

Brinson, G.L., Hood R., and Beebower, G. (1986), "Determinants of portfolio performance", *Financial Analysts Journal* 43, 39–44.

Brown, F.E., Friend, I., Herman, E.S., and Vickers, D. (1962), "A study of mutual funds", in: *Report of the Committee on Interstae and Foreign Commerce*, US Government Printing Office, Washington, DC.

Brown, S.J., Goetzmann, W., Ibbotson, R.G., and Ross, S.A. (1992), "Survivorship bias in performance studies", *Review of Financial Studies* 5, 553–580.

Cadsby, C.B. (1992), "The CAPM and the calendar: Empirical anomalies and the risk-return relationship", *Management Science* 38, 1543–1561.

Chan, K.C. (1988), "On the contrarian investment strategy", *Journal of Business* 61, 147–163.

Chopra, N., Lakonishok, J., and Ritter, J. (1992). "Performance measurement methodology and the question of whether stocks overract", *Journal of Financial Economics* 31, 235–268.

Clark, R., and Ziemba, W.T. (1987), "Playing the turn-of-the-year effect with index futures", *Operations Research* 35, 799–813.

Connor, G., and Korajzyk, R. (1994), "Arbitrage pricing theory", in: R. Jarrow, V. Maksimovic and W.T. Ziemba (eds.), *Finance*, North-Holland, Amsterdam, forthcoming.

Coother, P. (ed.) (1964), *The Random Character of Stock Market Prices*, MIT Press, Cambridge, MA.

Copeland, T., and Mayers, D. (1982). "The Value Line enigma (1965–1978): A case study of performance evaluation issues", *Journal of Financial Economics* 1, 289–321.

Cowles, A. (1933), "Can stock market forecasters forecast?", *Econometrica* 1/3, 309–324.

DeBondt, W.R.M., and Thaler, R.H. (1985), "Does the stock market overreact?", *Journal of Finance* 40, 793–805.

DeBondt, W.R.M., and Thaler, R.H. (1987), "Further evidence on investor overreaction and stock market seasonality", *Journal of Finance* 42, 557–581.

DeBondt, W.R.M., and Thaler, R.H. (1989), "A mean reverting walk down Wall Street", *Journal of Economics Perspectives* 3, 189–202.

DeLong, J.B. (1992), "Closed-end fund discounts", *Journal of Portfolio Management*, Winter, 46–53.

De Long, J.B., Shleifer, A., Summers, L.H., and Waldmann, R.J. (1990), "Positive feedback investment strategies and destabilizing rational speculation", *Journal of Finance* 45, 379–395.

Dimson, E. (ed.) (1988), *Stock Market Regularities*, Cambridge University Press, Cambridge, UK.

Dravid, A.R. (1987), "A note on the behavior of stock returns around ex-dates of stock distribution", *Journal of Finance* 42, 163–168.

Dyl, E.A., and Maberly, E.D. (1992) "Odd-lot transactions around the turn of the year and the January effect", *Journal of Financial and Quantitative Analysis* 27, 591–604.

Eaker, M.R., and Grant, D.M. (1990), "Currency hedging strategies for internationaly diversified portfolios", *Journal of Portfolio Management*, Fall, 30–32.

Elton, E.J., et al. (1992), "Efficiency with costly information: A reinterpretation of evidence from managed portfolios", *Review of Financial Studies* I, P.

Ettredge, M., and Fuller, R.J. (1991), "The negative earnings effect", *Journal of Portfolio Management*, Spring, 27–33.

Fama, E.F. (1965), "The behavior of stock market prices", *Journal of Business* 38, 34–105.

Fama, E.F. (1970), "Efficient capital markets: A review of theory and empirical work", *Journal of Finance* 25, 383–417.

Fama, E.F. (1991), "Efficient capital markets: II", *Journal of Finance* 46, 1575–1617.

Fama, E.F., and French, K.R. (1988a), "Permanent and temporary components of stock prices", *Journal of Political Economy* 96, 246–273.

Fama, E.F., and French, K.R. (1988b), "Dividend yields and expected stock returns", *Journal of Financial Economics* 22, 3–25.

Fama, E.F., and French, K.R. (1992), "Cross-sectional variation in expected stock returns", *Journal of Finance* I, P.

Ferson, W.E., and Harvey, C.R. (1992), "The risk and predictability of international equity returns", Mimeo, Duke University.

French, K.R., and Poterba, J.M. (1991), "Were Japanese stock prices too high?", *Journal of Financial Economics* 25, 337–363.

Friend, I., Blume, M., and Crockett, J. (1970), *Mutual Funds and Other Institutional Investors*, McGraw-Hill, New York.

Froot, K. (1993), "Short rates and expected asset returns", *Journal of Finance*, forthcoming.

Froot, K., and Thaler, R. (1990), "Foreign exchange", *Journal of Economic Perspectives* 4, 179–92.

Goetzmann, W., and Ibbotson, R. (1991), "Do winners repeat? Patterns in mutual fund behavior", Mimeo, Yale University.

Gordon, M.J. (1962), *The Investment, Financing and the Valuation of the Corporation*, Irwin, Homewood, Il.

Gordon, M.J., and Shapiro, E. (1956), "Capital equipment analysis: The required rate of profit", *Management Science* 3, 102–10.

Graham, B., and Dodd, D.L. (1934), *Security Analysis: Principles and Technique*, McGraw-Hill, New York.

Grinblatt, M., Titman, S. (1989), "Mutual fund performance: An analysis of quarterly portfolio holdings", *Journal of Business* 62, 393–416.

Haugen, R.A. (1994), *New Finance: The Case against Efficient Markets*, Prentice Hall, New York.

Harris, L. (1986a), "A transaction data study of weekly and intradaily patterns in stock returns", *Journal of Financial Economics* 16, 99–117.

Harris, L. (1986b), "How to profit from intradaily stock returns", *Journal of Portfolio Management*, Winter, 61–64.

Hawawini, G., and Keim, D. (1994), "On the predictability of common stock returns: World-wide evidence", in: R. Jarrow, V. Maksimovic and W.T. Ziemba (eds.), *Finance*, North Holland, Amsterdam.

Hendricks, D., Patel, J., and Zeckhauser, R. (1991) "Hot hands in mutual funds: The persistence of performance, 1974–88", Kennedy School of Government, Harvard University.

Hensel, C.R., Sick, G.A., and Ziemba, W.T. (1993), "The turn of the month effect in the S&P500, 1926–93", Mimeo, University of British Columbia.

Hensel, C.R., Sick, G.A., and Ziemba, W.T. (1994), "The turn of the month effect in the US index futures markets, 1982–92", *Review of Futures Markets* (in press).

Hensel, C.R., and Ziemba, W.T. (1993a), "The January barometer", Mimeo, Frank Russell Company.

Hensel, C.R., and Ziemba, W.T. (1993b), "Returns after presidential elections 1928–1993", Mimeo, Frank Russell Company.

Hirsch, Y. (1986), *Don't Sell Stocks on Monday*, Facts on File Publications, New York.

Huberman, G., and Kandel, S. (1987), "Value Line rank and firm size", *Journal of Business* 60/4, 577–589.

Huberman, G., and Kandel, S. (1990), "Market efficiency and Value Line's record", *Journal of Business* 63/2, 187–216.

Ibbotson and Associates (1989), "Stocks, bonds, bills and inflation: 1926–88", Chicago, Il.

Ippolito, R.A. (1989)", Efficiency with costly information: A study of mutual fund performance, 1965–1984", *Quarterly Journal of Economics* 104–1; 1–23.

Ippolito, R.A. (1992), "Consumer reaction to measures of poor quality: Evidence from the mutual fund industry", *Journal of Law and Economics* 35, 45–70.

Jacobs, B.I., and Levy, K.N. (1988a), "Disentangling equity return regularities: New insights and investment opportunities", *Financial Analysts Journal* 44, 18–43.

Jacobs, B.I., and Levy, K.N. (1988b), "On the value of value", *Financial Analysts Journal* 44, 47–62.

Jacobs, B.I., and Levy, K.N. (1988c), "Calendar anomalies: Abnormal returns at calendar turning points", *Financial Analysts Journal* 44, 28–39.

Jaffe, J.D., Keim, B., and Westerfield, R. (1989), "Earnings yields, market values and stock returns", *Journal of Finance* 44, 135–148.

Jegadeesh, N. (1990), "Evidence of predictable behavior of security returns", *Journal of Finance* 45, 881–898.

Jegadeesh, N. (1992), "Does market risk really explain the size effect?", *Journal of Financial and Quantitative Analysis* 27, 337–351.

Jegadeesh, N., and Titman, S. (1991), "Returns to buying winners and selling losers: Implications for stock market efficiency", Mimeo, UCLA.

Jennings, R., and Starks, L. (1986), "Earnings announcements, stock price adjustment and the existence of option markets", *Journal of Finance* 61, 107–125.

Jensen, M. (1968), "The performance of mutual funds in the period 1945–64", *Journal of Finance* 23/2, 389–416.

Jorion, P. (1989), "Asset allocation with hedged and unhedged foreign stocks and bonds", *Journal of Portfolio Management*, Summer, 49–54.

Kato, K. (1990a), "Weekly patterns in Japanese stock returns", *Management Science* 36, 1031–1043.

Kato, K. (1990b), "Being a winner in the Tokyo stock market: The case for an anomaly fund", *Journal of Portfolio Management*, Summer, 52–56.

Keim, D.B. (1983), "Size related anomalies and stock return seasonality", *Journal of Financial Economics* 12, 13–32.

Keim, D.B. (1985), "Dividend yields and stock returns", *Journal of Financial Economics* 14, 433–489.

Keim, D.B. (1988), "Stock market regularities: A synthesis of the evidence and explanations", in: E. Dimson (ed.), *Stock Market Anomalies*, Cambridge University Press, Cambridge, UK.

Keim, D.B., and Smirlock, M. (1987), "The behavior of intraday stock index futures prices", *Advances in Futures and Options Research* 2, 143–166.

Kim, M.J., Nelson, C.R., and Startz, R. (1991) "Mean reversion in stock prices? A reappraisal of the empirical evidence", *Revies of Economic Studies* 58, 515–528.

Lakonishok, J., and Maberly, E. (1990), "The weekend effect: Trading patterns of individual and institutional investors", *Journal of Finance* 45, 231–243.

Lakonishok, J., and Smidt, S. (1988), "Are seasonal anomalies real? A ninety-year perspective", *Review of Financial Studies* 1, 403–425.

Lakonishok, J., Shleifer, A., and Vishny, R.W. (1992), "The structure and performance of the money management industry", in: *Brookings Papers: Microeconomics* 1992, 339–391.

Lee, C., Shleifer, A., and Thaler, R. (1991), "Investor sentiment and the closed-end fund puzzle", *Journal of Finance* 46, 75–110.

Lehmann, B. (1990), "Fads, Martingales and market efficiency", *Quarterly Journal of Economics* I, P.

Lintnes, J. (1965), "The valuation of risky assets and the selection of risky investments in stock portfolios and capital budgets", *The Review of Economics and Statistics* 47, 13–37.

Lo, A.W., and MacKinlay, A.C. (1990), "Data-snooping biases in tests of financial asset pricing models", *Review of Financial Studies* 3, 431–467.

Mandelbrot, B.B. (1963), "The variation of certain speculative prices", *Journal of Business* 36, 394–419.

Markowitz, H.M. (1952), "Portfolio selection", *Journal of Finance* 6, 77–91.

Markowitz, H.M. (1959), *Portfolio Selection: Efficient Diversification of Investments*, Wiley, New York.

Markowitz, H.M. (1992), "Data mining", Mimeo, Daiwa Securities, Jersey City, NJ.

Martikainen, T., Perttunen, J., and Ziemba, W.T. (1994), *Finanzmarkt und Portfolio Management* (in press).

Merrill, A.A. (1966), "Behavior of prices on Wall Street", *Journal of Finance* 21, 13–21.

Merton, R.C. (1985), "On the current state of stock market rationality hypothesis", in: R. Dornbusch and S. Fischer (eds.), *Macroeconomics and Finance*, MIT Press, Cambridge, MA.

Miller, E., M. (1988), "Why a weekend effect?", *Journal of Portfolio Management* 15, 42–48.

Mossin, J. (1966), *Equilibrium in a Capital Market*, Econometrica.

Nicholson, S.F. (1960), "Price–earnings ratios", *Financial Analysis Journal*, July/August, 43–50.

Ogden, J.P. (1990), "Turn of the month evaluations of liquid profits and stock returns: A common explanation for the monthly and January effects", *Journal of Finance* 45, 1259–1272.

Ohlson, J.A., and Penman, S.H. (1985), "Volatility increases subsequent to stock splits: An empirical aberration", *Journal of Financial Economics* 14, 251–266.

Peavy, III, J.W., and Goodman, D.A. (1983), "Industry-relative price–earnings ratios as indicators of investment returns", *Financial Analysts Journal* 39, 60–66.

Reinganum, M.R. (1981), "Misspecification of capital asset pricing: empirical anomalies based on earnings yields and market values", *Journal of Financial Economics* 9, 19–46.

Reinganum, M.R. (1988), "The anatomy of a stock market winner", *Financial Analysts Journal*, March/April, 16–28.

Reinganum, M.R. (1990), Market microstructure and asset pricing: An empirical investigation of NYSE and NASDAQ securities", *Journal of Financial Economics* 28, 127–148.

Ritter, J. (1988), "The buying and selling behavior of individual investors at the turn of the year", *Journal of Finance* 43, 701–717.

Ritter, J. (1991), "The long-run performance of initial public offerings", *Journal of Finance* 46/1, 3–27.

Ritter, J., and Chopra, N. (1989), "Portfolio rebalancing and the turn of the year effect", *Journal of Finance* 44, 149–166.

Roberts, H.V. (1959), "Stock market patterns and financial analysis: Methodological suggestions", *Journal of Finance* 14/1, 1–10.

Roberts, H.V. (1967), "Statistical versus clinical prediction of the stock market", Mimeo, University of Chicago.

Roll, R. (1977), "A critique of the asset pricing theory's test; Part I: On past and potential testability of the theory", *Journal of Financial Economics* 4, 129–176.

Roll, R. (1983), "Vas ist dat: The turn of the year effect and the return premia of small firms", *Journal of Portfolio Management* 9, Winter, 18–28.

Roll, R. (1992), "Industrial structure and the comparative behavior of international stockmarket indices", *Journal of Finance* 47, 3–41.

Rosenberg, B., Reid, K., and Lanstein, R. (1985), "Persuasive evidence of market inefficiency", *Journal of Portfolio Management* 11, 9–16.

Senchak, A.J., and Martin, J.D. (1987), "The relative performance of the PSR and the PER investment strategies", *Financial Analysts Journal* 43, 46–56.

Sharpe, W.F. (1964), "Capital asset prices: A theory of market equilibrium under conditions of risk", *Journal of Finance* 19/3, 425–442.

Sharpe, W.F. (1966), "Mutual fund performance", *Journal of Business* 39/1 Part II, 119–138.

Shukla, R., and Trzcinka, C. (1992), "Performance measurement of managed portfolio financial markets", *Financial Market, Institutions and Instruments* 1/4, 1–58.

Stattman, D. (1980), "Book values and expected stock returns", Unpublished MBA Honors Paper, University of Chicago.

Stickel, S. (1985), "The effect of Value Line investment survey rank changes on common stockprices", *Journal of Financial Economics*, 121–144.

Stone, D., and Ziemba, W.T. (1993), "Land and stock prices in Japan", *Journal of Economic Perspectives*, Summer, 149–165.

Thaler, R.H. (1992), *The Winner's Curse*, The Free Press, New York.

Wiggins, J.B. (1992), "Beta changes around stock splits revisited", *Journal of Financial and Quantitative Analysis* 27, 631–640.

Zarowin, P. (1990), "Size, seasonality, and stock market overreaction", *Journal of Financial and Quantitative Analysis* 25, 113–125.

Ziemba, W.T. (1988), "Strategies for making and keeping excess profits in the stock market", Mimeo, forthcoming for William Morrow, New York, 1994a.

Ziemba, W.T. (1989), "Seasonality effects in Japanese futures markets", in: Rhee and Chang (eds.), *Research on Pacific Basin Security Markets*, North-Holland, Amsterdam.

Ziemba, W.T. (1990), "Cumulative effects of fundamental variables on the Tokyo Stock Exchange: 1979–89", Working Paper, University of British Columbia, Vancouver, Canada. Shortened version in *Investing*, February, 1991.

Ziemba, W.T. (1991), "Japanese security market regularities: Monthly, turn of the month and year, holiday and Golden Week effects", *Japan and the World Economy* 3, 119–146.

Ziemba, W.T. (1993), "Comment on 'Why a weekend effect?'", *Journal of Portfolio Management*, Winter, 93–99.

Ziemba, W.T. (1994b), "Investing in the turn of the year effect in the futures markets", *Interfaces* May–June, in press.

Ziemba, W.T., and Schwartz, S.L. (1991), *Invest Japan: The Structure, Performance and Opportunities of the Stock, Bond and Fund Markets*, Probus Publishing, Chicago, Il.

Ziemba, W.T., Bailey, W., and Hamao, Y. (eds.) (1991), *Japanese Financial Market Research*, North-Holland, Amsterdam.

Zweig, M. (1986), *Winning on Wall Street*, Warner Books, New York.

https://doi.org/10.1142/9789811222634_0012

Chapter 12

Sell-in-May-and-Go-Away: The International Evidence

Constantine Dzhabarov
Consultant, Surrey, BC, Canada
info@alphalake.com

Alexandre Ziegler
Department of Banking and Finance, University of Zurich, Switzerland
alexandre.ziegler@bf.uzh.ch

William T. Ziemba
Alumni Professor of Financial Modeling and Stochastic Optimization (Emeritus), University of British Columbia, Vancouver, BC and Distinguished Visiting Research Associate, Systemic Risk Center, London School of Economics, United Kingdom
wtzimi@mac.com

We investigate the *Sell-in-May-and-Go-Away* effect using equity index futures data for the U.S. and 24 international markets. The *Sell-in-May* seasonality is pervasive: in no country do returns from investing in the summer months exceed those from investing in the winter months, and investing using the "Sell-in-May" strategy earns higher returns than the "Buy-and-Hold" strategy in 21 of the 25 markets. Investigating returns by calendar month reveals that the worst month of the year occurs during the summer period in all markets, and the best month occurs during the winter period in all markets except two. In addition to higher returns, the winter period also has lower risk than the summer period, making Sharpe ratios in winter quite attractive. Contrary to conventional wisdom, in two-thirds of countries, the largest Sharpe ratios do not accrue at year-end but rather in April, reflecting the combination of high returns and low volatility during that month.

Keywords: Stock market, calendar anomalies, equity futures markets.

1. Sell-in-May-and-Go-Away

Sell-in-May-and-Go-Away, which is sometimes called the *Halloween Effect*, is an old market adage that recommends investing in the stock market from late October to early May and in cash from early May to late October. As odd as it may seem, the adage is far from unfounded. Indeed, August, September, and October have historically been challenging months for stock market investors, with September having the lowest average returns of all months and many serious declines or crashes occurring in October. By contrast, the months of November–April have historically had higher than average returns; see, for example, Gultekin and Gultekin (1983) and various papers in Keim and Ziemba (2000) and Ziemba (2012). *Sell-in-May-and-Go-Away*, which is often discussed in the financial press, is a simple strategy seeking to take advantage of this seasonality.[1]

In a recent paper, Dzhabarov *et al.* (2018) investigate the profitability of the "Sell-in-May" strategy using equity index futures contracts for 16 countries and the Eurozone. Using data from the different contracts' inception through the end of October 2017, they document that "Sell-in-May" strategies exhibit a strong outperformance in most countries, with Hong Kong being a notable exception. They also report that in addition to having higher average returns, the winter months also have lower risk than the summer months, making stock market investments during this period quite attractive. Finally, they find that while the profitability of "Sell-in-May" strategies has weakened slightly following the increased publicity

[1]Return seasonalities have been discussed in several academic papers including Agrrawal and Skaves (2015), Bee *et al.* (2016), Garrett *et al.* (2004), Kamstra *et al.* (2000, 2003), Fiore and Saha (2015), Patel and Sewell (2015), Swinkels and van Vliet (2012), and Zhang and Jacobsen (2013). Studies focusing on the "Sell-in-May" phenomenon include Bouman and Jacobsen (2002), Doeswijk (2005), Dzhabarov and Ziemba (2010, 2017, 2019), Jacobsen and Visaltanachoti (2009), and Witte (2012).

around them, seasonal differences in average returns are still present in most countries over the more recent 2003–2017 period.

In this chapter, we broaden the analysis in Dzhabarov *et al.* (2018) in three respects. First, we investigate an additional eight countries, mostly developing markets, for which liquid equity index futures contracts are available over a relatively long period. Second, we analyze average returns and Sharpe ratios by calendar month and find that while there is heterogeneity across countries, the months of August, September, and October tend to be particularly unattractive for stock market investments, with August and September having low average returns and October having high volatility. Third, we extend the sample period through the end of October 2019.

The chapter is organized as follows. Section 2 describes the data underlying our analysis and a simple method to assess the outperformance of the "Sell-in-May" strategy using equity index futures data. Section 3 documents the strategy's outperformance around the world, and Section 4 assesses its statistical significance. Section 5 investigates average returns by calendar month. Section 6 shows that return volatility also exhibits seasonal variation, resulting in Sharpe ratios that vary widely between the winter and summer periods. Section 7 discusses a number of possible explanations for the "Sell-in-May" effect, and Section 8 shows that in spite of the increased publicity around them in recent years, seasonal differences in average returns are still present in most countries. Section 9 concludes.

2. Data and Performance Measurement Methodology

We use daily equity index futures prices for 24 countries plus the Eurozone from Bloomberg. We include countries for which liquid stock index futures are available. The markets covered are the main markets followed by investors, namely those included in the "World Equity Index Futures" (WEIF) page on Bloomberg as of early November 2019 (16 countries plus the Eurozone), as well as eight others for which liquid futures are available over a relatively long period, namely India, Norway, Russia, South Africa, South Korea, Taiwan, Thailand, and Turkey.

The data are adjusted for rollovers, which are assumed to take place on the penultimate day of trading for each contract (usually the Thursday preceding the third Friday of March, June, September, and December unless the third Friday is a holiday, in which case the rollover is performed on Wednesday). For each country, we use data from the first day that data are available in Bloomberg through October 31, 2019. The list of countries considered in our analysis, the names of the underlying indices, the tickers of the corresponding futures contracts as of early November 2019, the start date of the sample, and the number of available trading days for each country are reported in Table 1. All indices in our sample are large cap indices.

Using futures data has the advantage of making the analysis of return seasonalities and the profitability of strategies exploiting them particularly simple and intuitive. Indeed, since futures are unfunded positions, their returns are by definition excess returns. Moreover, by no-arbitrage, returns on equity index futures are equal to the total return on the underlying index (including dividends) minus the return on the riskless asset. Accordingly, futures returns capture the entire equity premium. Thus, positive average returns (geometric average ordinary returns or arithmetic average log returns) during a given period mean that being invested in futures earned higher returns than being invested in cash during that period. Conversely, negative average returns imply that being invested in cash would have been the better option.

In addition to its analytical convenience, the use of futures is also attractive from an implementation standpoint. Indeed, futures have low transaction costs, can be rolled over conveniently using spread trades for which bid–ask spreads are especially narrow, and are tax-efficient for offshore investors because they avoid withholding taxes on dividends that investments in index ETFs would incur. Futures are therefore generally the preferred instrument when implementing the strategies described in this chapter.

Table 1. Countries and underlying stock indices considered in the analysis.

Country	Underlying index	Futures ticker	Start date	Number of observations
Australia	S&P/ASX 200	XP	5/2/2000	5,009
Brazil	Bovespa	BZ	7/12/1995	6,007
Canada	TSX 60	PT	9/7/1999	5,063
China	CSI 300	IFB	4/16/2010	2,319
Eurozone	EuroStoxx 50	VG	6/22/1998	5,441
France	CAC 40	CF	12/7/1988	7,859
Germany	DAX	GX	11/23/1990	7,326
Hong Kong	Hang Seng	HI	4/1/1992	6,819
India	Nifty 50	NZ	6/13/2000	4,806
Italy	MIB	ST	3/22/2004	3,967
Japan	Nikkei	NK[a]	9/5/1988	7,653
Mexico	IPC	IS	5/3/1999	5,164
Netherlands	AEX	EO	1/2/1989	7,860
Norway	OBX	OI	7/8/1993	5,951
Russia	RTS	VE	8/4/2005	3,554
South Africa	FTSE/JSE Top 40	AI	5/16/1994	6,352
South Korea	KOSPI 200	KM	5/4/1996	5,922
Spain	IBEX 35	IB	7/21/1992	6,888
Sweden	OMX Stockholm 30	QC	2/14/2005	3,701
Switzerland	SMI	SM	12/22/1997[b]	5,495
Taiwan	TAIEX	FT	7/22/1998	5,313
Thailand	SET 50	BC	5/2/2006	3,300
Turkey	Borsa Istanbul 30	A5	5/3/2005	3,641
UK	FTSE 100	Z	2/26/1988	8,068
U.S.	S&P 500	SP/ES[c]	4/21/1982	9,527

Notes: [a]Several futures contracts are available on the Nikkei. Two contracts (one in Yen and one in USD) are traded on the Chicago Mercantile Exchange, and one contract (in Yen) is traded on the Osaka Stock Exchange (OSE). Our analysis uses the OSE contract because of the longer sample period.

[b]Data for Switzerland is actually available from 10/28/1991. However, data are missing between 12/15/1994 and 12/22/1997. In order to avoid this gap, our analysis for Switzerland begins on 12/22/1997.

[c]Two futures contracts are available on the S&P 500: the legacy contract, which was introduced in April 1982, and the E-mini contract, which was introduced in September 1997. The E-mini contract became popular very quickly and its trading volume soon exceeded that of the legacy contract. In our analysis, we use the legacy contract through the end of 1998 and the E-mini contract thereafter.

3. Performance of "Sell-in-May" Strategies around the World

Figure 1 reports the cumulative log returns (expressed in percentage points) from investing in S&P 500 index futures from their launch on April 21, 1982 through October 31, 2019. Three strategies are considered. In the "Buy-and-Hold" strategy, the investor is fully invested all the time. The "Sell-in-May" strategy is long index futures from the close of the sixth trading day before the end of October through the close of the first business day in May and in cash the rest of the

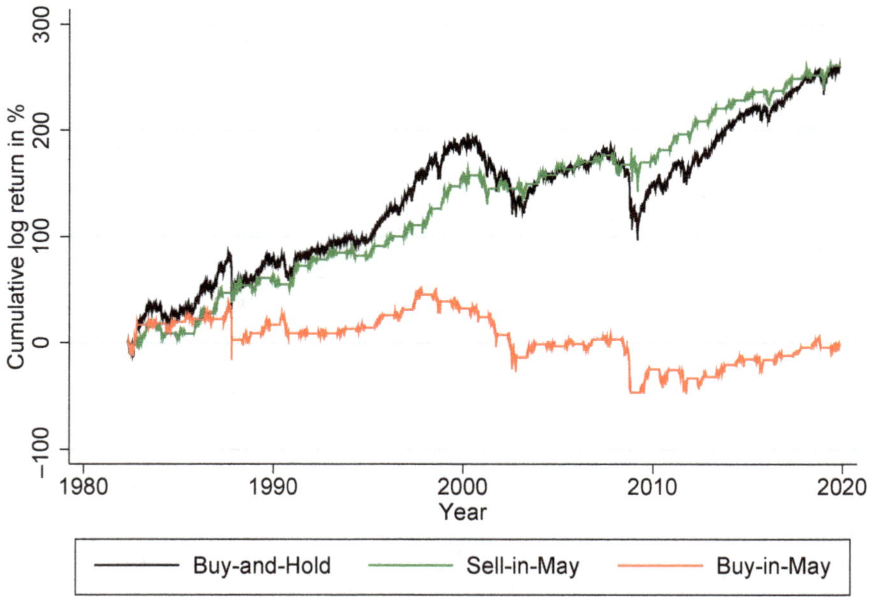

Fig. 1. Cumulative returns from investing in S&P 500 index futures.

Note: This figure reports the cumulative log excess returns in percentage points from investing in S&P 500 index futures using three strategies. In the "Buy-and-Hold" strategy, the investor is fully invested all the time. The "Sell-in-May" strategy is long index futures from the close of the sixth trading day before the end of October through the close of the first business day in May and in cash the rest of the time. The "Buy-in-May" strategy does the reverse — invest in index futures from the close of the first trading day in May through the close of the sixth business day in October and in cash the rest of the time. The sample period ranges from the launch of S&P 500 index futures on April 21, 1982 through October 31, 2019.

time. The "Buy-in-May" strategy does the reverse — invest in index futures from the close of the first trading day in May through the close of the sixth business day before the end of October and in cash the rest of the time. The results in Fig. 1 show that during our 37-year sample, the entire equity premium was earned during the winter months.[2]

Figure 2 reports the results of similar computations for the 24 other indices in our dataset. The return seasonality is pervasive, since in no country does the cumulative return from investing in the summer months exceed that from investing in the winter months. Moreover, the "Sell-in-May" strategy earns higher returns than the "Buy-and-Hold" strategy in all markets except Australia, Hong Kong, India, and Turkey, with the summer months in Australia and Turkey making a negligible positive contribution to overall returns.

Arguably, the presence of the "Sell-in-May" effect in most countries could merely reflect the high correlations in daily stock market returns across countries. What speaks against this interpretation is the fact that year after year, large discrepancies in stock index returns can be observed across countries over longer periods such as a few months or a year. Yet, no single country in our sample, even in the Southern hemisphere, exhibits higher returns in the May–October period than in the November–April period.

In some markets such as Brazil, France, Germany, Japan, the Netherlands, South Korea, and Switzerland, the "Buy-in-May" strategy generates sizable negative cumulative returns during the sample period. For example, in both France and Germany, investing in stocks from May to October only would have generated a cumulative log return close to −100%, corresponding to a wealth loss of over 60%. For Brazil, Japan, and South Korea, the cumulative log return from stock index futures investments in the summer months is even worse, at around −140%, implying a wealth loss of over 75%.

[2]For brevity, throughout the chapter we often refer to the period from the close of the sixth trading day before the end of October through the close of the first business day in May as the "winter" or the "November–April" period. Similarly, we refer to the period from the close of the first trading day in May to the close of the sixth business day before the end of October as the "summer" or the "May–October" period.

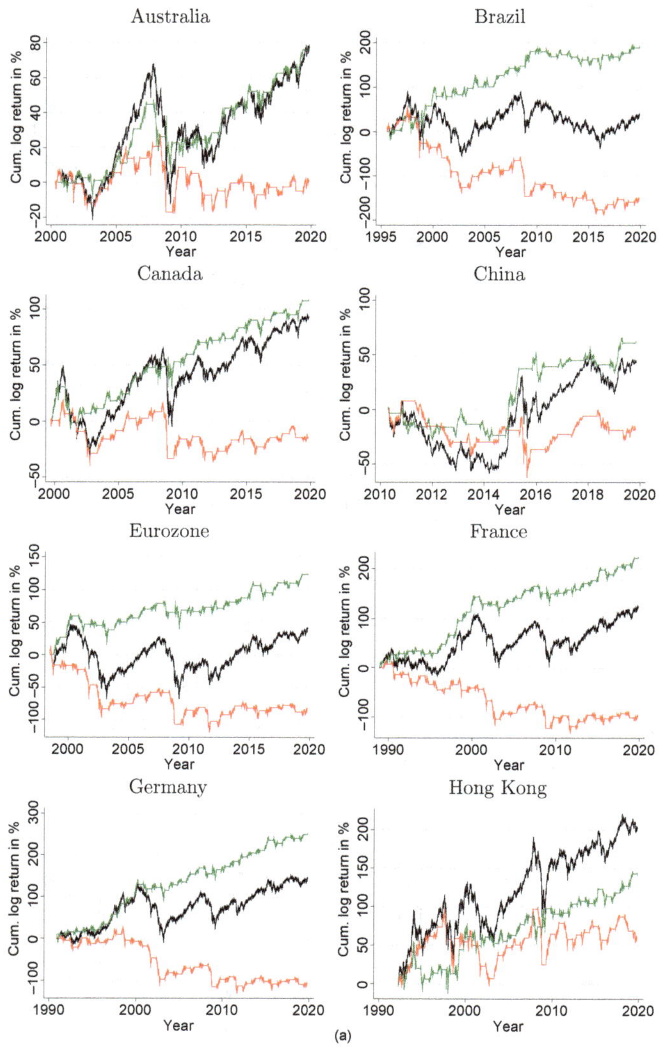

(a)

Fig. 2. Cumulative returns from investing in index futures in the different markets. (*Continued*)

Note: This figure reports the cumulative log excess returns in percentage points from investing in index futures. The same three strategies as in Fig. 1 are considered: a “Buy-and-Hold” strategy, in which one is fully invested all the time, a “Sell-in-May” strategy, in which one is invested from the close of the sixth trading day before the end of October through the close of the first business day in May and in cash the rest of the time, and a “Buy-in-May” strategy, doing the reverse. The sample period for each market ranges from the start date reported in Table 1 through October 31, 2019.

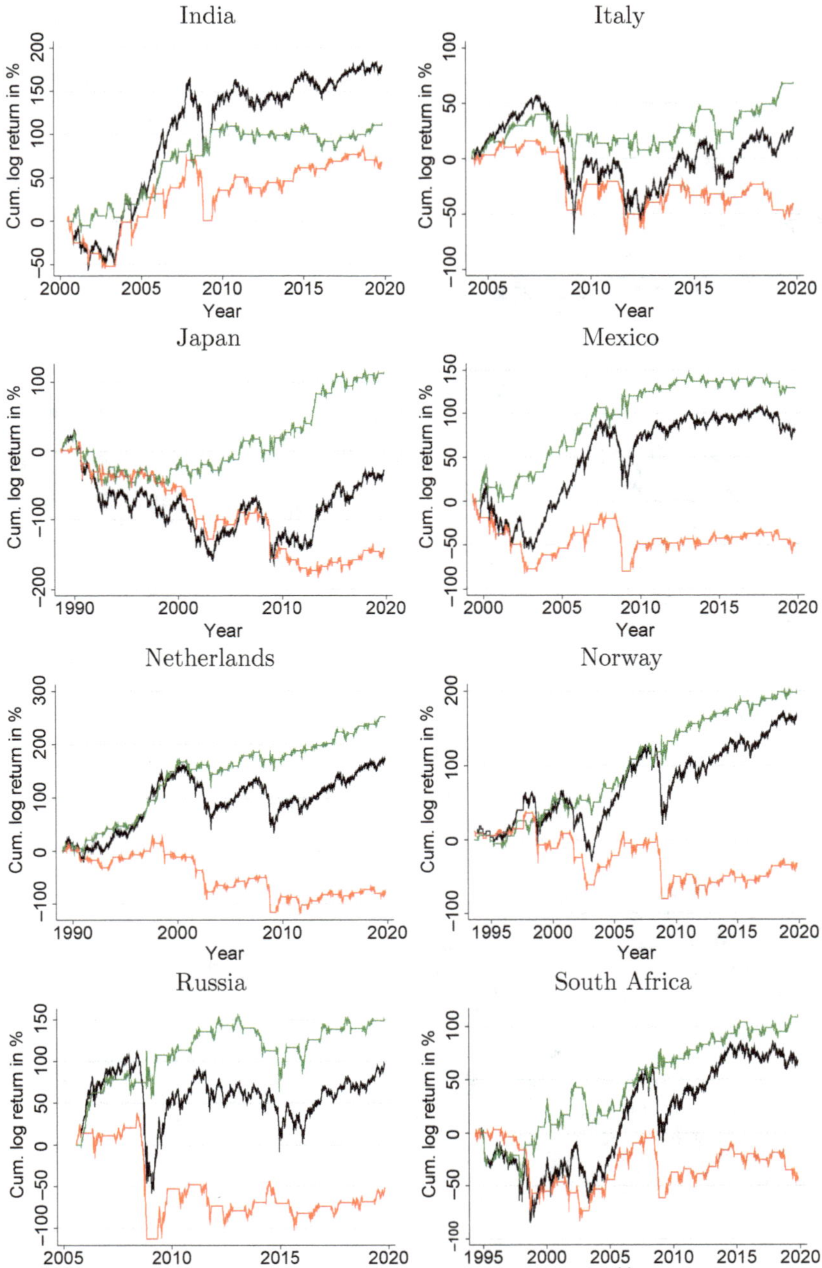

(b)

Fig. 2. (*Continued*)

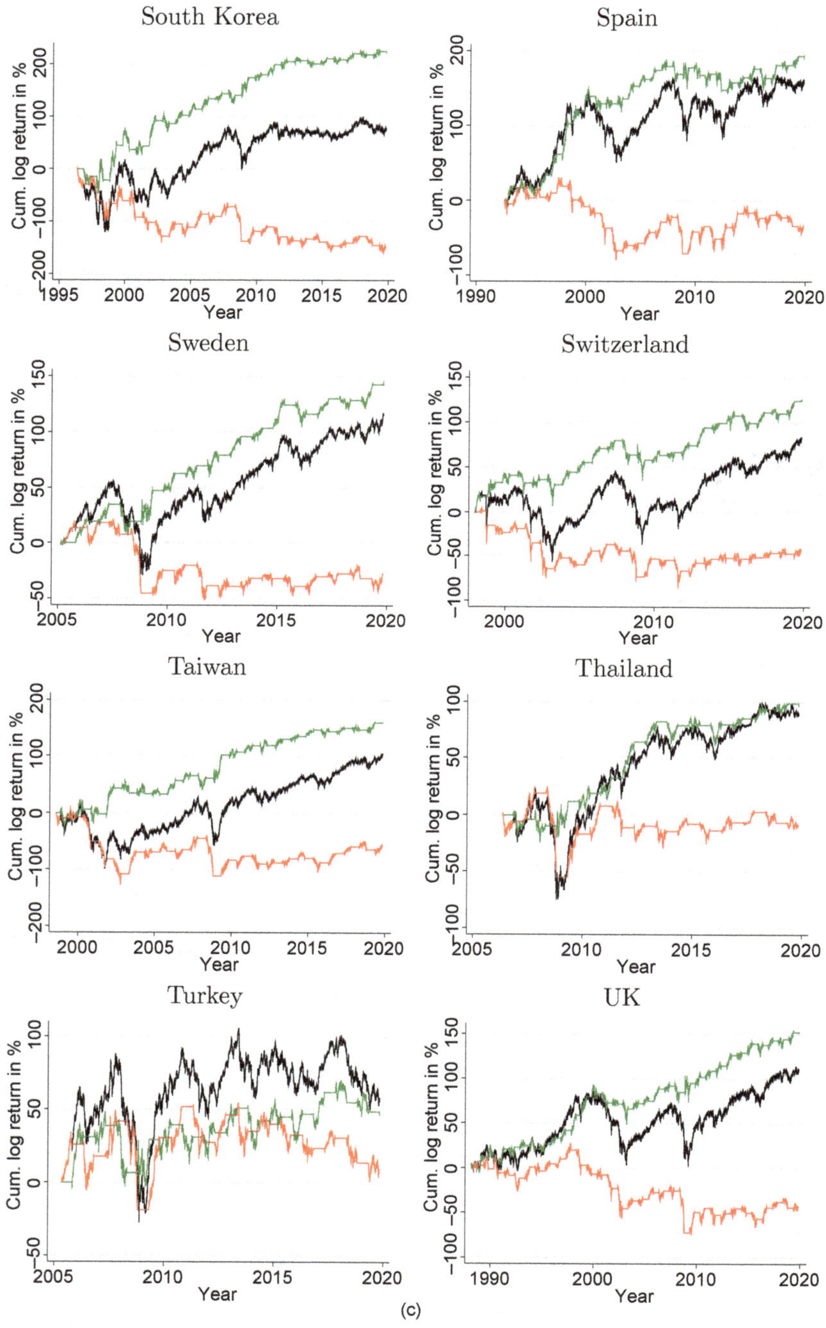

Fig. 2. (*Continued*)

4. Statistical Tests

In order to assess the statistical significance of these results, for each country we perform two-sample t-tests that average log returns in the November–April period are equal to those in the May–October period. Since prior evidence and Figs. 1 and 2 show that cumulative returns for "Sell-in-May" are higher than the cumulative returns for "Buy-in-May", a one-tail test is appropriate. The null and alternative hypotheses are

$$\begin{aligned} H_0 &: \ \bar{r}_W - \bar{r}_S \leq 0, \\ H_a &: \ \bar{r}_W - \bar{r}_S > 0, \end{aligned}$$

where $\bar{r}_W$ (for winter) denotes average daily log returns in the period with entry at the close of the sixth trading day before the end of October and exit at the close of the first trading day in May of the following year and $\bar{r}_S$ (for summer) denotes average daily log returns in the period with entry at the close of the first trading day in May and exit at the close of the sixth trading day before the end of October. The test statistic is

$$Z = \frac{\bar{r}_W - \bar{r}_S}{\sqrt{\frac{\sigma_W^2}{n_W} + \frac{\sigma_S^2}{n_S}}},$$

where σ_W and σ_S denote the sample standard deviations of daily log returns in the winter and summer periods and n_W and n_S the number of trading days in both subsamples, respectively.

While the above Welch test is intuitively appealing since it is based on the difference in average returns between periods — a measure of how much better expected returns in winter are compared to those in summer — it rests on the normality assumption. For robustness, we therefore also perform the corresponding nonparametric Mann–Whitney test for equality in central tendency.

Table 2 reports the average daily log returns for the May–October and November–April periods in the different markets, the difference in average returns between periods, and the p-values of the above

Table 2. Return seasonality in the different markets.

Country	November–April	May–October	Difference	t-test p-value	MW p-value
Australia	3.01	0.05	2.96	0.1420	0.2592
Brazil	6.28	−5.04	11.33	0.0154**	0.0274**
Canada	4.12	−0.62	4.74	0.0716*	0.0655*
China	5.32	−1.50	6.82	0.1401	0.1673
Eurozone	4.54	−3.03	7.57	0.0310**	0.0352**
France	5.53	−2.52	8.05	0.0044***	0.0085***
Germany	6.71	−2.91	9.62	0.0016***	0.0036***
Hong Kong	4.18	1.79	2.39	0.2832	0.2933
India	4.69	2.81	1.88	0.3283	0.4455
Italy	3.44	−2.48	5.50	0.1172	0.1016
Japan	2.90	−3.79	6.69	0.0259**	0.0328**
Mexico	5.07	−1.84	6.91	0.0285**	0.0700*
Netherlands	6.27	−2.01	8.28	0.0024***	0.0055***
Norway	6.51	−1.09	7.60	0.0271**	0.0575*
Russia	8.43	−2.96	11.39	0.0845*	0.1609
South Africa	3.48	−1.35	4.83	0.0804*	0.0806*
South Korea	7.47	−5.05	12.52	0.0055***	0.0040***
Spain	5.58	−0.99	6.57	0.0306**	0.0379**
Sweden	7.68	−1.47	9.15	0.0217**	0.0771*
Switzerland	4.47	−1.58	6.05	0.0314**	0.0270**
Taiwan	6.04	−2.13	8.17	0.0254**	0.0165**
Thailand	5.97	−0.52	6.48	0.1102	0.0693*
Turkey	2.54	0.52	2.02	0.3637	0.4827
UK	3.70	−1.08	4.78	0.0264**	0.0829*
U.S.	5.41	−0.04	5.45	0.0130**	0.0085***

Note: This table reports the average daily log returns for the May–October and November–April periods in the different markets, the difference in average returns between periods, as well as the p-values of two sample t-tests with unequal variances that average returns in the winter months do not exceed those in the summer months and of the corresponding nonparametric Mann–Whitney (MW) test. All returns are measured in basis points, and p-values are for one-sided test. *, **, and *** denote statistically significant differences in average returns or central tendency at the 10%, 5%, and 1% levels, respectively.

t-test that average returns in the winter months do not exceed those during the summer months and of the corresponding nonparametric Mann–Whitney test. The t-test results provide strong evidence that average returns in the winter months exceed those in the summer months. Indeed, the difference in returns between the winter and summer months is significant at the 5% level or higher in 15 of the 25 markets considered. Three additional countries — Canada, Russia, and South Africa — have return differences that are statistically different at the 10% level. Although the significance is somewhat weaker, a similar picture emerges when considering the results of the Mann–Whitney test: the winter months exhibit higher returns than the summer months at the 5% level or higher in 11 of the 25 markets, and at the 10% level in an additional seven countries.

Even in markets where the difference in returns is not statistically significant, the point estimates of average returns in winter lie above those for summer. Strikingly, and in line with the results in Fig. 2, in no single country do returns in the summer months exceed those in the winter months, and average returns in the May–October period are negative in 21 of the 25 markets.

5. Returns by Calendar Month

In this section, we take a closer look at the return seasonality by considering average daily returns from a long index futures position by calendar month. To be consistent with the "Sell-in-May" strategy, we include the return on the first trading day of May in the April average, and the returns of the last five trading days in October in the November average.

Figure 3 presents the results for the S&P 500 index. Bars corresponding to the winter period appear in light gray, and those corresponding to the summer period, in dark gray. Only 3 months exhibit negative average returns: August, September, and October, with September being by far the worst month of the year.[3]

Figure 4 presents the results of similar computations for the other 24 markets. The worst month of the year occurs during the summer period in all markets, and the best month occurs during the winter period in 22 of the 24 markets, the two exceptions being China (October) and Turkey (July). September is the worst month in 7 of

[3]The turn-of-the-month effect is particularly strong on U.S. markets in October. If the last five trading days in October are included in the October average rather than in the November average, mean returns for October are positive.

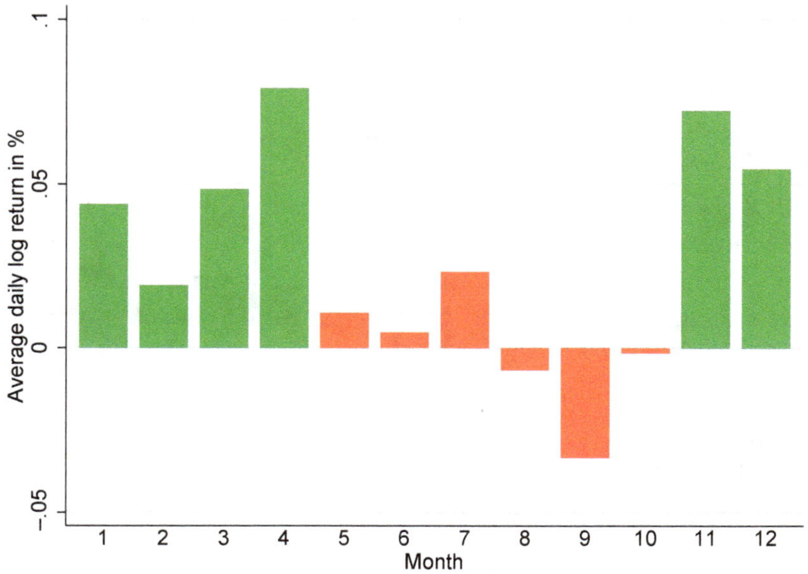

Fig. 3. Average daily returns from investing in S&P 500 index futures by calendar month.

Note: This figure reports average daily log excess returns in percentage points from investing in S&P 500 index futures by calendar month. The first trading day in May is included in the April average and the last five trading days in October are included in the November average. The sample period ranges from the launch of S&P 500 index futures on April 21, 1982 through October 31, 2019.

the 24 markets, while August has the lowest returns in 5 of the 24 markets, and October, in 4 of the 24 markets. Thus, including the US, the worst month of the year lies in the August–October period in 17 of the 25 markets, confirming that late summer and early autumn are the worst periods to be invested in stocks.

6. Beyond Average Returns: Seasonality in Risk and Sharpe Ratios

As does most of the literature, the above analysis focuses on average returns. Yet, an investor's optimal exposure to risky assets is driven not just by expected returns *per se*, but by the attractiveness of the risk–return tradeoff. To the extent that the higher returns in the

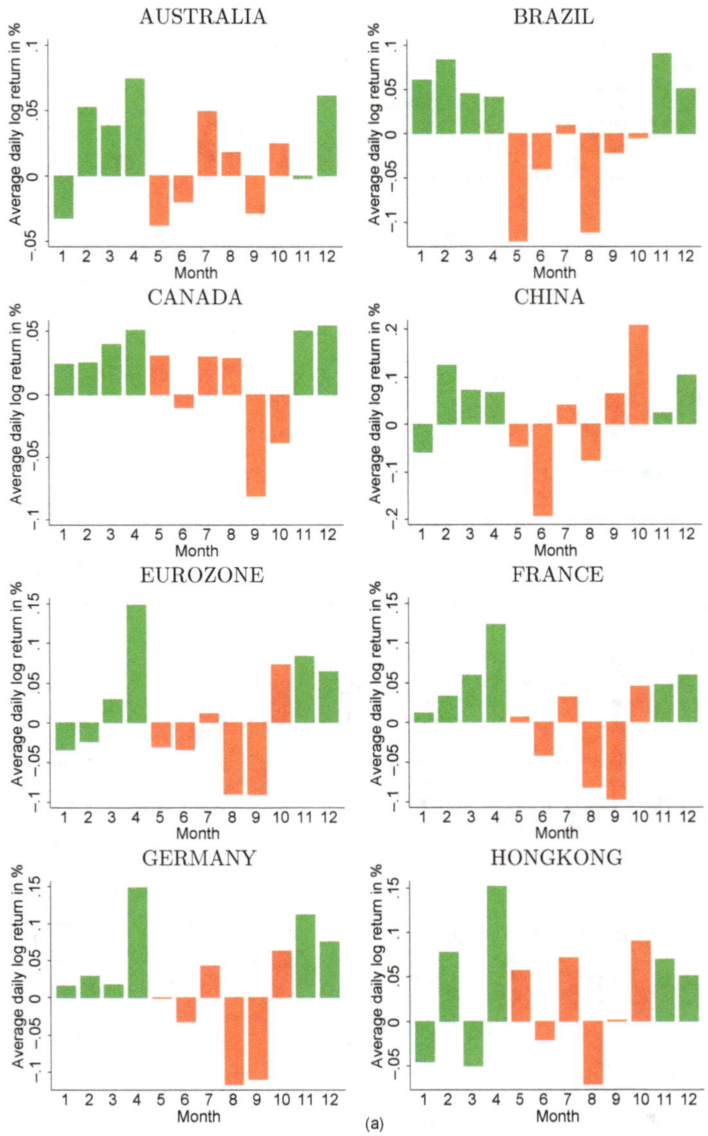

Fig. 4. Average daily returns by calendar month from investing in index futures in the different markets. (*Continued*)

Note: This figure reports average daily log excess returns in percentage points from investing in index futures each month. The first trading day in May is included in the April average and the last five trading days in October are included in the November average. The sample period for each market ranges from the start date reported in Table 1 through October 31, 2019.

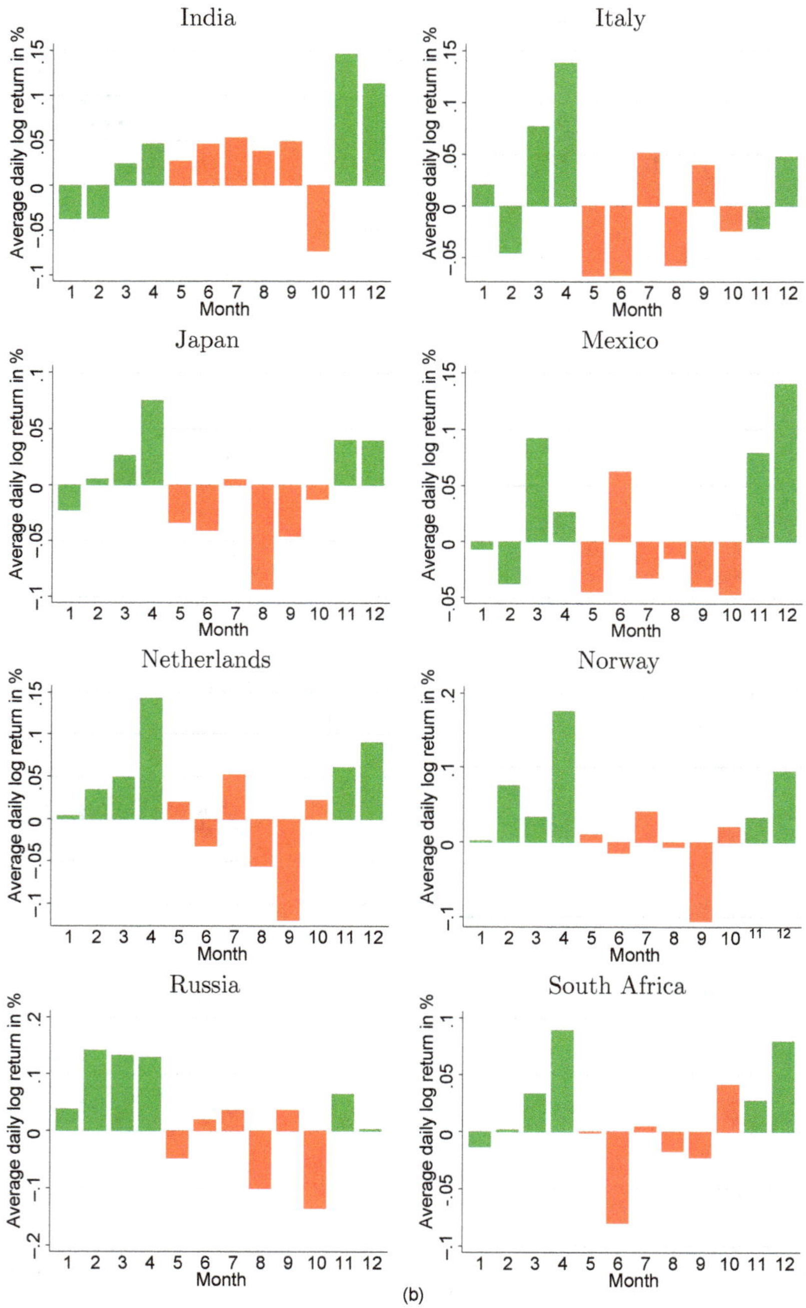

Fig. 4. (*Continued*)

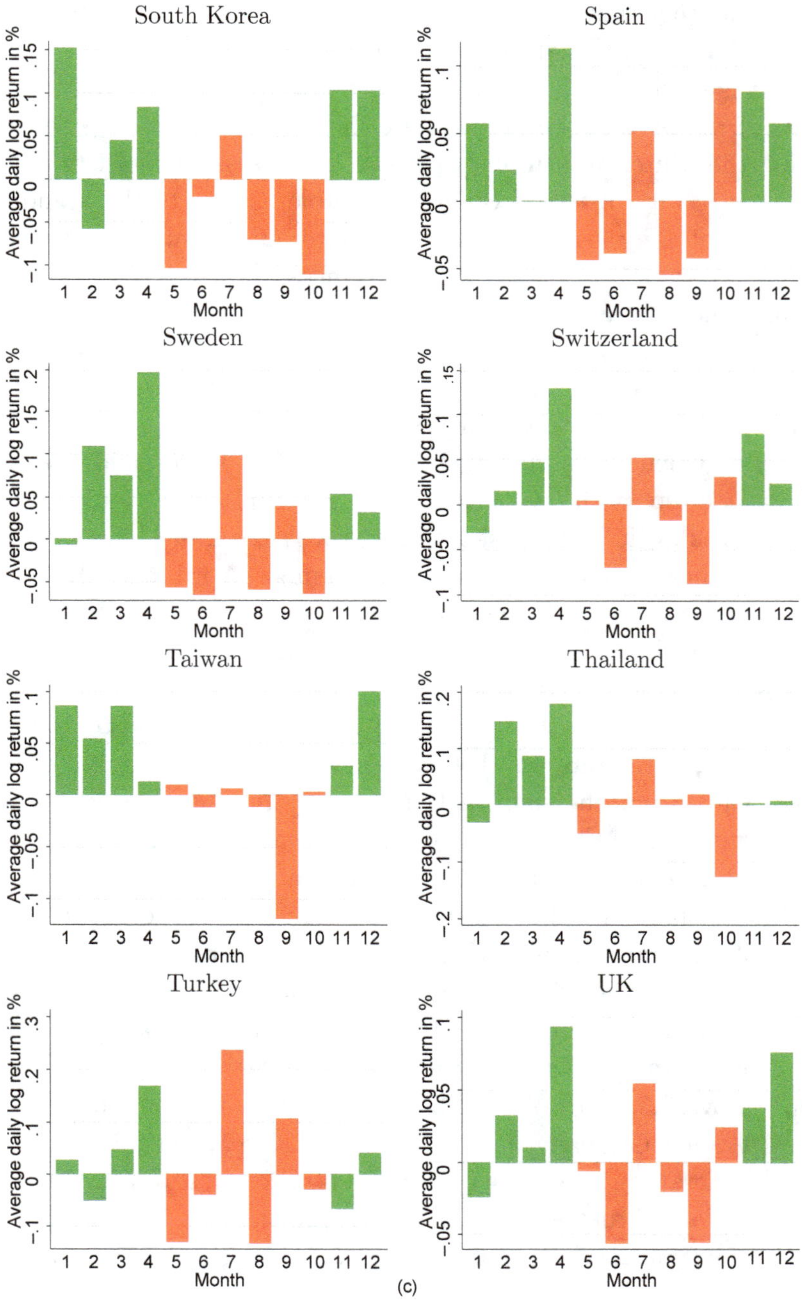

Fig. 4. (*Continued*)

winter months reflect higher risk, increasing one's exposure to stocks during that period would not be attractive.

In this section, we investigate whether a "Sell-in-May" effect also exists for risk. To do so, we compute the volatility of futures returns during the winter and summer periods and assess the statistical significance of any observed difference. Table 3 reports the standard deviation of daily log returns during winter and summer in percentage points, the ratio of the return variances in the winter versus the summer months, and the results of two different tests of whether the variances in both periods are identical. The first is the standard variance ratio test, which assumes normally distributed returns. The second is the Levene test, which is robust to outliers. Since we have no prior evidence on the relative riskiness of winter and summer returns, we report the p-values for two-sided tests.

The results in Table 3 show that risk is generally higher in the May–October period than in the November–April period. When using the variance ratio test, 15 out of 25 markets exhibit statistically significant higher risk in the summer months than in the winter months at the 1% level. When using the Levene test, risk is significantly higher at the 5% level or higher for 9 of the 25 markets. Hong Kong is the only market for which risk is significantly higher in the winter months than in the summer months. The lower risk in the winter months in most countries makes the higher average returns documented in Table 2 even more attractive.

Combining the results in Tables 2 and 3, Table 4 reports the annualized Sharpe ratios from index futures investments in the different markets during the winter and summer months. The combination of higher average returns and lower risk makes investing in stock index futures during the winter months quite attractive, with Sharpe ratios above 0.5 in 18 of the 25 markets. In some markets such as Brazil, France, Germany, Japan, and South Korea, the May–October period generates sizable negative Sharpe ratios that are in absolute value similar to those of buy-and-hold investments in some of the best performing markets in our sample, and larger than the Sharpe

Table 3. Risk seasonality in the different markets.

Country	Standard deviation Nov.–Apr.	May–Oct.	Variance ratio	p-value	Levene F-statistic	p-value
Australia	0.93	1.02	0.8404	0.0000***	7.6619	0.0057***
Brazil	2.03	2.03	0.9976	0.9473	0.4022	0.5260
Canada	1.17	1.13	1.0576	0.1596	0.0636	0.8008
China	1.42	1.62	0.7639	0.0000***	0.5757	0.4481
Eurozone	1.43	1.55	0.8510	0.0000***	5.3014	0.0213**
France	1.30	1.42	0.8325	0.0000***	9.6543	0.0019***
Germany	1.36	1.43	0.9142	0.0066***	2.2938	0.1299*
Hong Kong	1.83	1.62	1.2798	0.0000***	13.8367	0.0002***
India	1.39	1.53	0.8257	0.0000***	1.5783	0.2091
Italy	1.41	1.50	0.8868	0.0075***	2.1842	0.1395
Japan	1.52	1.49	1.0367	0.2649	4.5129	0.0337**
Mexico	1.31	1.30	1.0231	0.5612	0.0084	0.9271
Netherlands	1.25	1.35	0.8527	0.0000***	7.3872	0.0066***
Norway	1.45	1.59	0.8353	0.0000***	3.6687	0.0555*
Russia	2.39	2.54	0.8808	0.0075***	0.0003	0.9868
South Africa	1.40	1.34	1.0861	0.0200*	0.1899	0.6630
South Korea	1.92	1.87	1.0540	0.1528	0.7607	0.3831
Spain	1.39	1.52	0.8410	0.0000***	4.9646	0.0259**
Sweden	1.36	1.40	0.9439	0.2148*	2.3347	0.1266
Switzerland	1.12	1.28	0.7705	0.0000***	4.8023	0.0285**
Taiwan	1.52	1.53	0.9825	0.6495	0.6026	0.4376
Thailand	1.47	1.57	0.8770	0.0078***	4.9754	0.0258**
Turkey	1.71	1.77	0.9335	0.1423	0.0365	0.8485
UK	1.06	1.15	0.8420	0.0000***	6.5998	0.0102**
U.S.	1.13	1.26	0.8043	0.0000***	0.1338	0.7145

Note: This table reports the standard deviation of daily log returns for the May–October and November–April periods in the different markets, and the results of two different tests of whether the variances in both periods are identical. The first is the standard variance ratio test, which assumes normally distributed returns. The second is the Levene test, which is robust to outliers. Standard deviations are reported in percentage points, and p-values are for a two-sided test. *, **, and *** denote statistically significant differences in risk between winter and summer at the 10%, 5%, and 1% levels, respectively.

Table 4. Sharpe ratio seasonality in the different markets.

	Average return		Standard deviation		Annualized Sharpe ratio	
Country	Nov.–Apr.	May–Oct.	Nov.–Apr.	May–Oct.	Nov.–Apr.	May–Oct.
Australia	3.01	0.05	0.93	1.02	0.51	0.01
Brazil	6.28	−5.04	2.03	2.03	0.49	−0.39
Canada	4.12	−0.62	1.17	1.13	0.56	−0.09
China	5.32	−1.50	1.42	1.62	0.60	−0.15
Eurozone	4.54	−3.03	1.43	1.55	0.50	−0.31
France	5.53	−2.52	1.30	1.42	0.68	−0.28
Germany	6.71	−2.91	1.36	1.43	0.78	−0.32
Hong Kong	4.18	1.79	1.83	1.62	0.36	0.18
India	4.69	2.81	1.39	1.53	0.54	0.29
Italy	3.44	−2.48	1.41	1.50	0.39	−0.26
Japan	2.90	−3.79	1.52	1.49	0.30	−0.40
Mexico	5.07	−1.84	1.31	1.30	0.61	−0.22
Netherlands	6.27	−2.01	1.25	1.35	0.80	−0.24
Norway	6.51	−1.09	1.45	1.59	0.71	−0.11
Russia	8.43	−2.96	2.39	2.54	0.56	−0.18
South Africa	3.48	−1.35	1.40	1.34	0.39	−0.16
South Korea	7.47	−5.05	1.92	1.87	0.62	−0.43
Spain	5.58	−0.99	1.39	1.52	0.64	−0.10
Sweden	7.68	−1.47	1.36	1.40	0.90	−0.17
Switzerland	4.47	−1.58	1.12	1.28	0.63	−0.20
Taiwan	6.04	−2.13	1.52	1.53	0.63	−0.22
Thailand	5.97	−0.52	1.47	1.57	0.65	−0.05
Turkey	2.54	0.52	1.71	1.77	0.24	0.05
UK	3.70	−1.08	1.06	1.15	0.55	−0.15
U.S.	5.41	−0.04	1.13	1.26	0.76	−0.01

Note: This table reports average daily log returns, the standard deviation of daily log returns, and the annualized Sharpe ratio for the May–October and November–April periods in the different markets. Average returns are reported in basis points and standard deviations in percentage points.

ratios of buy-and-hold investments in these five markets.[4] Thus, as was already apparent in Fig. 2, investing in these five markets between May and October led to sizable losses during our sample period.

[4]For example, the unconditional annualized Sharpe ratio from an investment in the U.S. market is 0.36. The unconditional Sharpe ratios for Brazil, France, Germany, Japan, and South Korea are 0.05, 0.19, 0.23, −0.04, and 0.11, respectively.

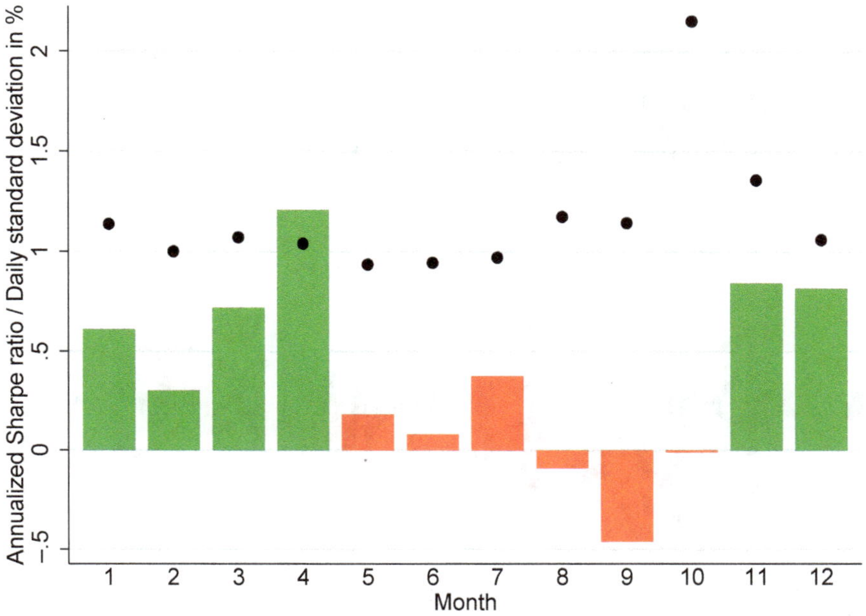

Fig. 5. Annualized Sharpe ratios (bars) and daily return standard deviations in percent (dots) from investing in S&P 500 index futures by calendar months.

Note: This figure reports annualized Sharpe ratios (bars) and daily return standard deviations in percent (dots) from investing in S&P 500 index futures by calendar months. The first trading day in May is included in the April values and the last five trading days in October are included in the November values. The sample period ranges from the launch of S&P 500 index futures on April 21, 1982 through October 31, 2019.

Figures 5 and 6 report the annualized Sharpe ratios (bars) and daily percentage return standard deviations (dots) by calendar months from investing in equity index futures for the S&P 500 index and the 24 other markets, respectively. As was the case in Figs. 3 and 4, bars corresponding to the winter period appear in light gray, and those corresponding to the summer period, in dark gray. For most countries, the seasonal patterns for Sharpe ratios are quite similar to those for average returns reported in Figs. 3 and 4, reflecting the fact that differences in risk across months are not very strong. Nevertheless, the figures reveal that in most countries, return volatility tends to be lower in the spring and at year-end and higher in the fall.

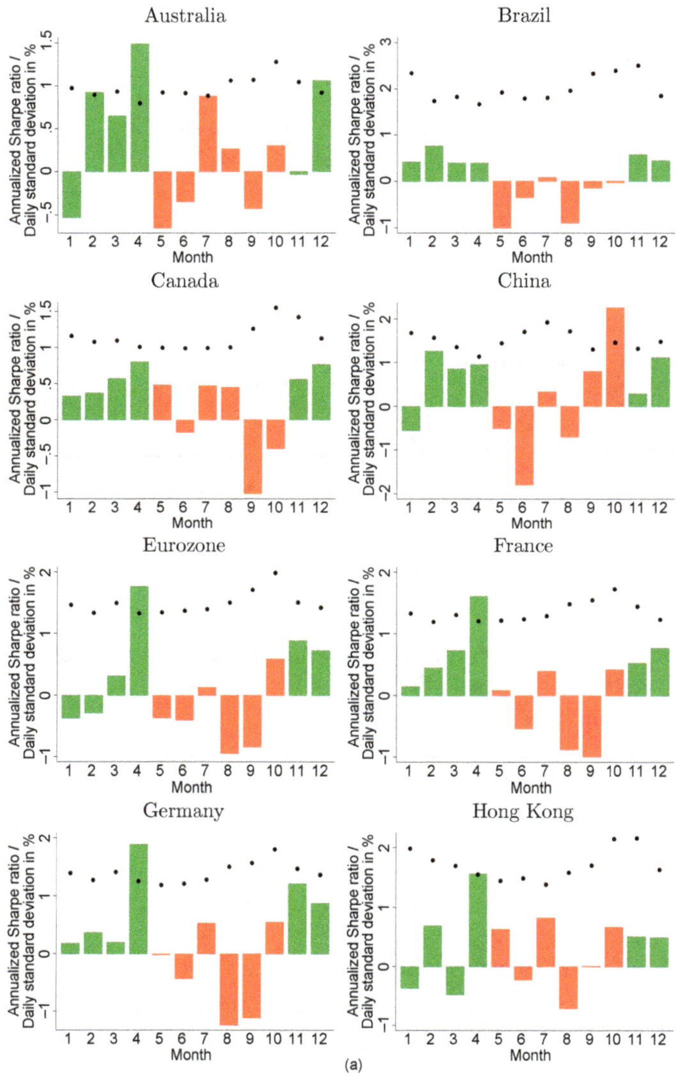

Fig. 6. Annualized Sharpe ratios (bars) and daily return standard deviations in percent (dots) from investing in index futures in the different markets by calendar months. (*Continued*)

Note: This figure reports annualized Sharpe ratios (bars) and daily return standard deviations in percent (dots) from investing in index futures each month. The first trading day in May is included in the April values and the last five trading days in October are included in the November values. The sample period for each market ranges from the start date reported in Table 1 through October 31, 2019.

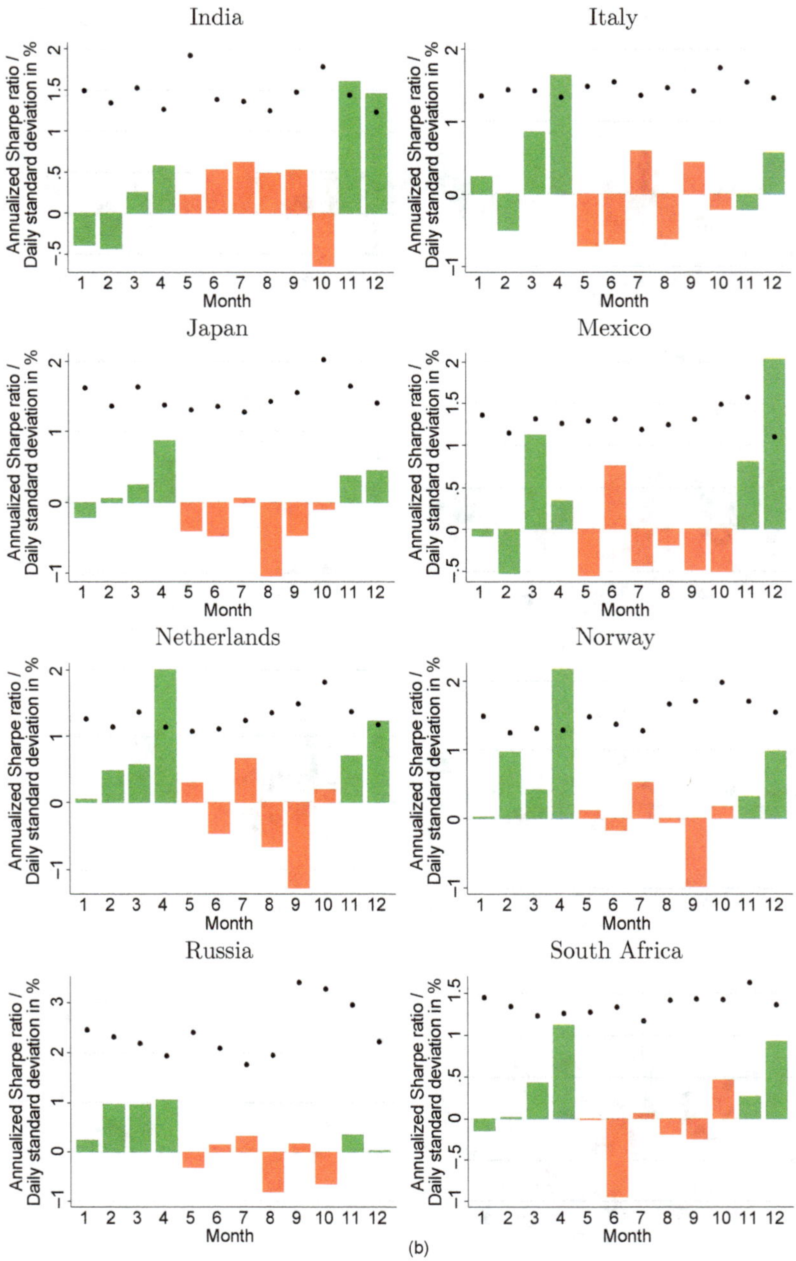

Fig. 6. (*Continued*)

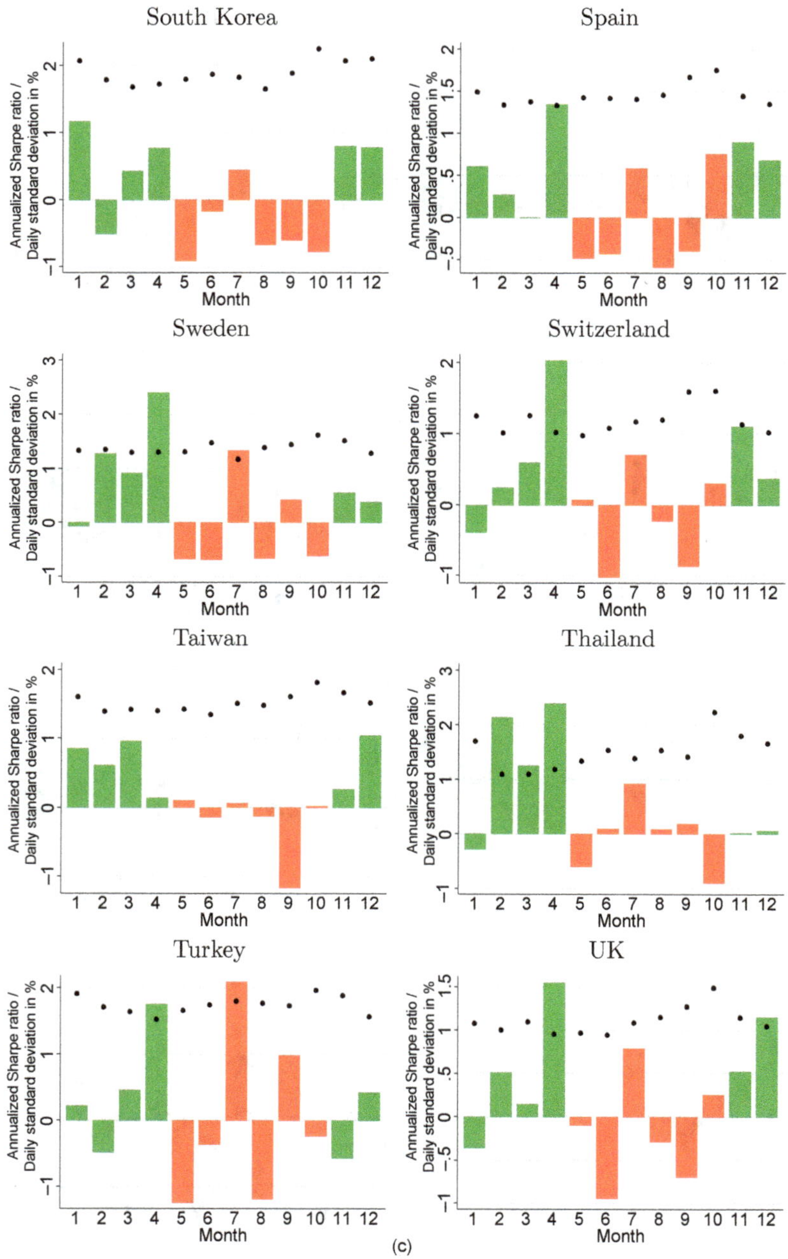

Fig. 6. (*Continued*)

The strikingly large volatility during the month of October for S&P 500 index futures reflects the impact of the 1987 stock market crash and the 2008 financial crisis. Contrary to conventional wisdom, in many countries (namely 17 of the 25 markets), the largest Sharpe ratios do not accrue at year-end but rather in April, reflecting the combination of high returns and low volatility during that month. As was the case for average returns, China and Turkey are notable exceptions to these patterns, with the highest Sharpe ratios observed in October and July, respectively.

7. Theoretical Explanations for the "Sell-in-May" Effect

A number of explanations for the "Sell-in-May" effect have been suggested in the literature. Bouman and Jacobsen (2002) confirm the empirical and historical basis of the maxim, finding that the "Sell-in-May" effect is present in 36 of the 37 countries included in their analysis. They consider the summer holiday period as a potential cause of the effect, as investors' willingness to take risk may be reduced during vacation periods. Two facts cast doubt as to the validity of this explanation. First, Bouman and Jacobsen (2002) find evidence of the "Sell-in-May" effect in their subset of Southern hemisphere countries, which under their hypothesis would be expected to have a different seasonal pattern. The same holds in our sample, where all three Southern hemisphere countries have higher returns in winter than in summer (see Table 2 and Fig. 2). Second, the vacation timing explanation cannot account for the fact that, as shown in Figs. 3 and 4, the worst month for the stock market is not July or August, but September.

Another explanation for return seasonalities that has been proposed is the Seasonal Affective Disorder (SAD), which is studied in Kamstra *et al.* (2003) and Garrett *et al.* (2004). SAD is a disorder in which the shorter, relatively sunless days of fall and winter cause depression, which some recent research links to an unwillingness to take risk. Kamstra *et al.* (2003) conclude that the SAD explanation does not lead to a profitable trading strategy because the risk premium varies with the seasonal effects. While the fact that SAD starts as early as September could explain why September returns are that low, SAD persists well into the fall, so it cannot explain the historically high November returns. Nor is this explanation consistent with the fact that the "Sell-in-May" effect is also observed in Southern hemisphere countries.

After reviewing these two candidate explanations, Doeswijk (2005) offers a new hypothesis for the "Sell-in-May" phenomenon. He posits that, in the fourth quarter of each year, investors are overly optimistic about the upcoming year. This excessive optimism leads to attractive initial returns followed by a renewed realism that readjusts expectations. Unlike the SAD hypothesis, which suggests a time-varying risk premium, the Optimism Cycle hypothesis reflects a constant risk premium but a varying perception of the economic outlook. To test this hypothesis, Doeswijk (2005) investigates whether three of its implications hold empirically: (1) the profitability of a global zero-investment seasonal sector-rotation strategy; (2) the seasonality of earnings growth revisions; and (3) the initial returns of IPOs as a proxy for investor optimism.

If the excessive optimism hypothesis is correct, an investment strategy going long in cyclical stocks and short in defensive stocks during the period from November through April (winter) and following the opposite strategy from May through October (summer) should be profitable. (These stock groups are chosen for their relative exposure to the general economy, with cyclical stocks having a high exposure and defensive stocks a low exposure.) Doeswijk tests this strategy using the MSCI World index of global stock returns both for his entire sample period from 1970 to 2003 and for two 17-year sub-periods. He considers several variations in timing of the winter period and various sector definitions.

Doeswijk finds that during the study period, average winter returns are a significant 7.6% higher than summer returns and the strategy is successful in 65% of the years. On a monthly basis, the average performance of the global zero-cost investment strategy is 0.56% and statistically significant at the 1% level. Using regression techniques, Doeswijk isolates the market timing effects from the seasonality and finds that seasonality alone accounts for approximately half of the excess returns.

The two other analyses in the Doeswijk study also support the Optimism Cycle hypothesis. Specifically, Doeswijk finds that expected earnings growth rates follow a seasonal cycle and that these changes have an effect on stock performance. His third analysis reveals that initial IPO returns exhibit the hypothesized seasonality. Using these initial returns as a proxy for investor confidence, he shows that the remaining excess returns are not statistically significant, again supporting the Optimism Cycle hypothesis.

Along with the three supporting analyses, Doeswijk provides a qualitative argument in favor of his Optimism Cycle hypothesis. He argues that, since this phenomenon is based on an aspect of human psychology, it tricks investors into repeating the same biases every year. Importantly, this cycle of optimism and pessimism is not generally accepted, which Doeswijk argues allows investors who understand it to profit from it as a "free lunch" until it is more widely accepted and the arbitrage opportunity is absorbed into the market.

8. Post-Publication Performance

As the preceding discussion suggests, one would expect anomalies that have been publicized and become widely accepted to be arbitraged away over time. For example, in a study of 97 variables shown to predict cross-sectional stock returns in the literature, McLean and Pontiff (2016) find that the returns of portfolios formed based on these variables are 26% lower out-of-sample and 58% lower post-publication.

In this section, we investigate whether the "Sell-in-May" effect has vanished post-publication. To do so, we repeat the analysis in Section 3 for the 2003–2019 period. While "Sell-in-May" is an old market adage, the Bouman and Jacobsen (2002) study documenting the "Sell-in-May" effect empirically was published in the highly regarded *American Economic Review* in 2002. Hence, it should have become reasonably widely accepted by early 2003, and we therefore use 2003 as the beginning of our sample period.

The results for the U.S. market are reported in Fig. 7 and those for the other markets, in Fig. 8. Consider first the results for the

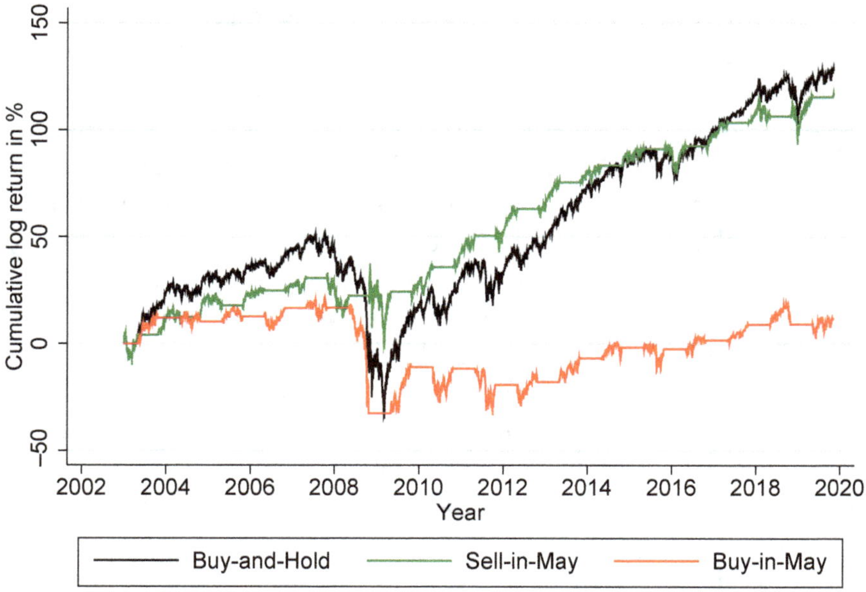

Fig. 7. Cumulative returns from investing in S&P 500 index futures for the period 2003–2019.

Note: This figure reports the cumulative log excess returns in percentage points from investing in S&P 500 index futures using the same three strategies as in Fig. 1. In the "Buy-and-Hold" strategy, the investor is fully invested all the time. The "Sell-in-May" strategy is long index futures from the close of the sixth trading day before the end of October through the close of the first business day in May and in cash the rest of the time. The "Buy-in-May" strategy does the reverse. The sample period ranges from January 2, 2003 through October 31, 2019.

U.S. market. Although the May–October period generated positive returns in a number of years, the cumulative excess return earned by the "Buy-in-May" strategy during the 17 years considered is very low. Accordingly, over the 2003–2019 period, the "Buy-and-Hold" strategy generated marginally higher returns than the "Sell-in-May" strategy. Nevertheless, having avoided most of the large drawdowns that occurred during the period, the "Sell-in-May" strategy has substantially better risk-adjusted returns.

As can be seen in Fig. 8, during the 2003–2019 period, the summer months generated positive excess returns in several markets, notably

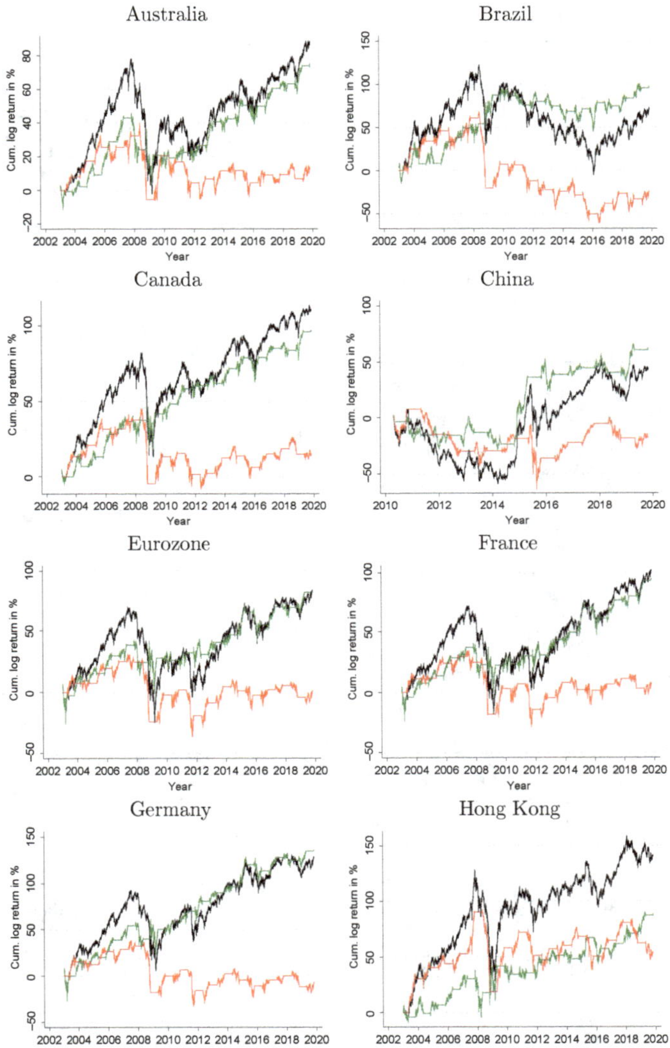

(a)

Fig. 8. Cumulative returns from investing in index futures in the different markets for the period 2003–2019. (*Continued*)

Note: This figure reports the cumulative log excess returns in percentage points from investing in index futures. The same three strategies as in Fig. 1 are considered: a "Buy-and-Hold" strategy, in which one is fully invested all the time, a "Sell-in-May" strategy, in which one is invested from the close of the sixth trading day before the end of October through the close of the first business day in May and in cash the rest of the time, and a "Buy-in-May" strategy, doing the reverse. The sample period for each market ranges from the later of (i) January 2, 2003 and (ii) the start date reported in Table 1 through October 31, 2019.

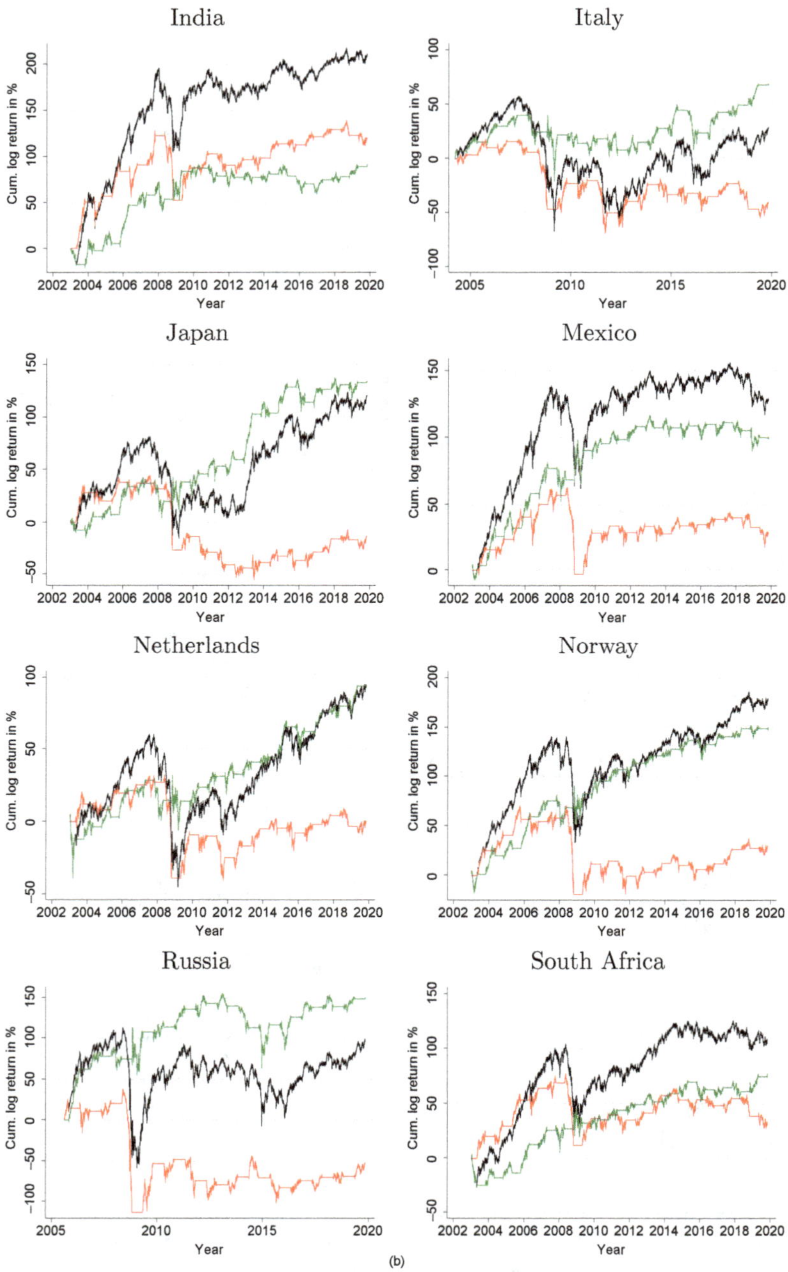

Fig. 8. (*Continued*)

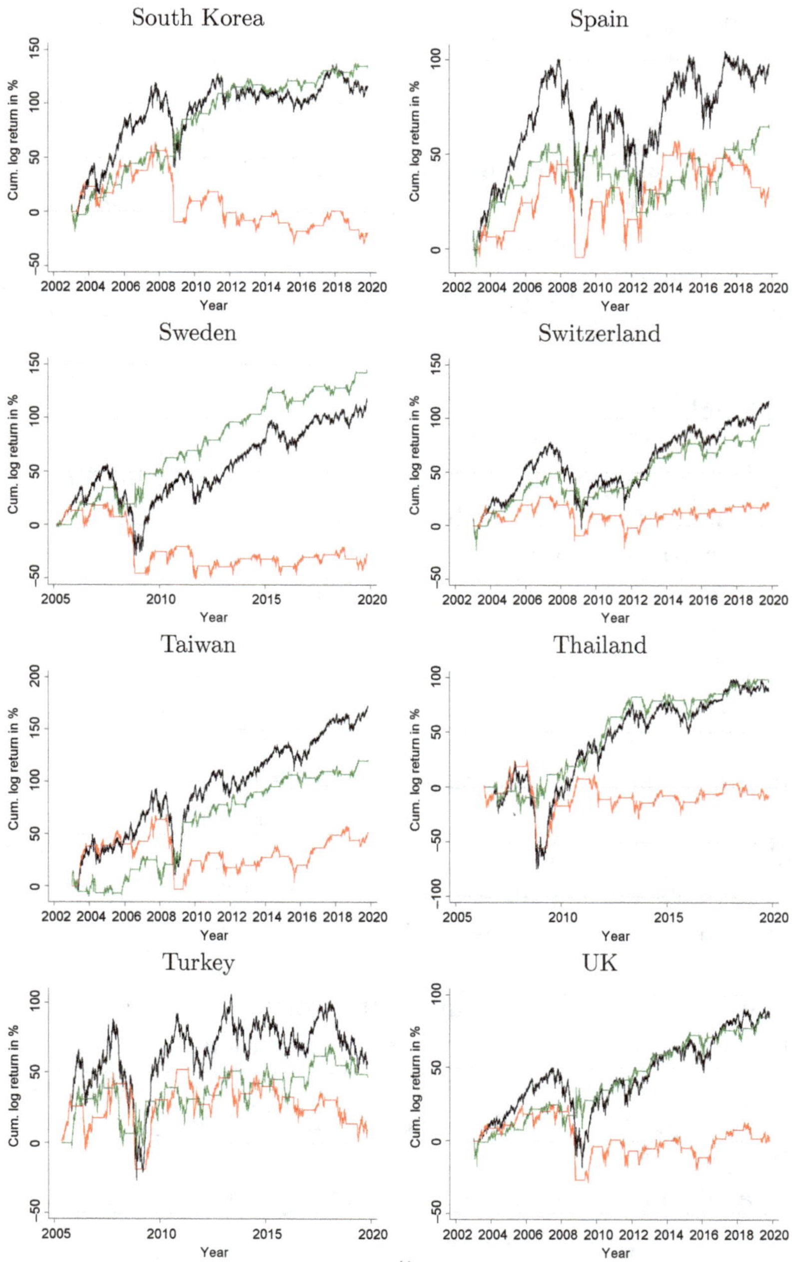

(c)

Fig. 8. (*Continued*)

Australia, Canada, Hong Kong, India, Mexico, South Africa, Spain, and Taiwan. Moreover, the large negative cumulative returns of the summer months documented in Fig. 2 are no longer apparent. Nevertheless, the cumulative returns during the summer months in most countries are close to zero or negative, and the "Buy-in-May" strategy does much worse than the "Sell-in-May" strategy in all markets except India. Thus, although it may have weakened slightly in recent years, the "Sell-in-May" effect appears to have, so far, survived the publicity around it.

9. Conclusions

Whatever its causes, it is clear that the "Sell-in-May" effect is present in equity and equity futures markets around the globe. The November–April period exhibits not just higher average returns, but also lower risk than the May–October period. Accordingly, the Sharpe ratios from investing in stock index futures between the turn of the month of November (six trading days before the end of October) and the first trading day in May are quite attractive.

Strong seasonality is also apparent in average returns and Sharpe ratios computed by calendar months. Specifically, the worst month of the year in terms of average returns occurs during the summer period in all markets, and the best month occurs during the winter period in all markets except China and Turkey. Even more strikingly, the worst month of the year lies during the August–October period in two-thirds of the countries considered in this study, confirming that late summer and early autumn are the worst periods to be invested in stocks. By contrast, and contrary to conventional wisdom, in two-thirds of countries, the largest Sharpe ratios do not accrue at year-end but rather in April, reflecting the combination of high returns and low volatility during that month.

In a number of countries, being invested in the stock market during the summer months has historically generated not just sub-par returns, but substantial losses. These large negative returns are no longer apparent in the period following the increased publicity around the "Sell-in-May" effect at the beginning of this century.

Nevertheless, the cumulative returns during the summer months remain close to zero or negative in the more recent period in most countries, and the "Buy-in-May" strategy does much worse than the "Sell-in-May" strategy in almost all markets in our sample. Thus, although it may have weakened slightly in recent years, the "Sell-in-May" effect appears to have, so far, survived the publicity around it.

References

Agrrawal, P. and Skaves, M. (2015). Seasonality in stock and bond ETFs (2001–2014): The months are getting mixed up but santa delivers on time. *Journal of Investing* **24**(3), 129–143.

Bee, M., Dupuis, D. J., and Trapin, L. (2016). US stock returns: Are there seasons of excesses? *Quantitative Finance* **16**(9), 1453–1464.

Bouman, S. and Jacobsen, B. (2002). The Halloween indicator, sell in May and go away: Another puzzle. *American Economic Review* **92**(5), 1618–1635.

Doeswijk, R. (2005). The optimism cycle: Sell in May. *De Economist* **156**(2), 175–200.

Dzhabarov, C. and Ziemba, W. T. (2010). Do seasonal anomalies still work? *Journal of Portfolio Management* **36**(3), 93–104.

Dzhabarov, C. and Ziemba, W. T. (2017). Sell-in-May-and-go-away in the equity index futures markets. *Wilmott Magazine* **92**, 12–16.

Dzhabarov, C. and Ziemba, W. T. (2019). *Sell-in-May-and-go-away in US Equity Index Futures Markets.* Mimeo.

Dzhabarov, C., Ziegler A., and Ziemba, W. T. (2018). Sell in May and go away: The evidence in the international equity index futures markets. *Quantitative Finance* **18**(2), 171–181.

Fiore C. and Saha, A. (2015). A tale of two anomalies: Higher returns of low-risk stocks and return seasonality. *Financial Review* **50**(2), 257–273.

Garrett, I., Kamstra, M., and Kramer, L. A. (2004). Winter blues and time variation in the price of risk. *Journal of Empirical Finance* **12**(2), 291–316.

Gultekin, M., and Gultekin, N. B. (1983). Stock market seasonality: International evidence. *Journal of Financial Economics* **12**, 469–481.

Jacobsen, B. and Visaltanachoti, N. (2009). The Halloween effect in US sectors. *Financial Review* **44**(3), 437–459.

Kamstra, M. J., Kramer, L. A., and Levi, M. D. (2000). Losing sleep at the market: The daylight-savings anomaly. *American Economic Review* **90**(4), 1005–1011.

Kamstra, M. J., Kramer, L. A., and Levi, M. D. (2003). Winter blues: A SAD stock market cycle. *American Economic Review* **93**(1), 324–343.

Keim, D. B. and Ziemba, W. T. (Eds.) (2000). *Security Market Imperfections in World Wide Equity Markets.* Cambridge University Press, Cambridge, UK.

McLean, R. D. and Pontiff, J. (2016). Does academic research destroy stock return predictability? *Journal of Finance* **71**(1), 5–32.

Patel, N. and Sewell, M. (2015). Calendar anomalies: a survey of the literature. *International Journal of Behavioural Accounting and Finance* **5**(2), 99–121.

Swinkels L. A. P. and van Vliet, P. (2012). An anatomy of calendar effects. *Journal of Asset Management* **13**(4), 271–286.

Witte, H. D. (2012). Outliers and the Halloween effect: Comment on Maberly and Pierce. *Econ Journal Watch* **7**(1), 91–98.

Zhang, C. Y., and Jacobsen, B. (2013). Are monthly seasonals real? A three century perspective. *The Review of Finance* **17**(5), 1743–1785.

Ziemba, W. T. (2012). *Calendar Anomalies and Arbitrage.* World Scientific.

https://doi.org/10.1142/9789811222634_0013

Chapter 13

Seasonal Effects, Trends and Pre-Announcement Drifts: Turning Anomalies into Investment Strategies

Blair Hull, Petra Bakosova and Alexander Kment*

Hull Tactical, Chicago, IL 60604, USA

We revisit a series of popular anomalies: seasonal, announcements, and momentum. We confirm statistical significance and persistence of these effects and propose useful investment strategies to incorporate this information. We investigate the creation of a seasonal anomaly and trend model composed of the Sell-in-May (SIM or the Halloween effect), Turn of the Month (TOM), Federal Open Market Committee pre-announcement drift (FOMC), and State Dependent Momentum (SDM). Using the total return S&P 500 dataset starting in 1975, we estimate the parameters of each model on a yearly basis based on an expanding window, and then proceed to form, in a walk forward manner, an optimized combination of the four models using a return to risk optimization procedure. We find that a real-time optimized strategy of the aforementioned four market anomalies produced 9.13% annualized returns with 5.19% volatility and a Sharpe ratio of 0.85. This strategy exceeds the Sharpe ratio of Buy-and-Hold in the same period by more than 100%. Furthermore, the strategy also shows low correlation to a number of popular investment approaches including previously published market-timing models.

---

*Blair Hull founded Hull Trading Company in 1985 and sold it to Goldman Sachs in 1999. In 2013, Hull founded HTAA, LLC ("Hull Tactical", www.hulltactical.com), a registered investment adviser, to establish an actively managed ETF listed on the NYSE. The ETF utilizes advanced algorithms, macroeconomic variables, and technical indicators to anticipate future market returns. Petra Bakosova serves as the Chief Operating Officer at Hull Tactical. Alexander Kment is a financial engineer at Hull Tactical.

1. Introduction

Academic literature on stock market anomalies is voluminous, yet few papers look at practical ways to combine this information. In this chapter, we combine seasonal anomalies, Fed announcements, and trends in a walk-forward way. Numerous papers present compelling evidence on seasonal effects of the market, with TOM and the Halloween effect being the most convincing. At the same time, there appears to be an excess return prior to Fed meetings. We combine these effects with the new trend indicator to create an effective model that beats Buy-and-Hold. This Seasonal Anomaly and Trend Model is then combined in an ensemble with other market-timing models to produce an even more powerful strategy.

Following the work of Hull and Qiao (2017) and Hull *et al.* (2017), we present a novel market-timing strategy. However, instead of forecasting market excess returns, we focus on predictability stemming from seasonal, trend, and drift anomalies. Unlike those studies, this chapter aims to discuss the use of discrete variables and deterministic models. None of these are new topics in the academic literature. To name a few existing studies, Swinkels and Van Vliet (2012) and Ziemba (2012) discuss the use of calendar anomalies, and Jensen *et al.* (1996) introduce a monetary policy indicator as a predictor for market returns. However, in addition to showing statistical significance of individual effects, we aim to build a robust model using multiple anomalies that will outperform the Buy-and-Hold strategy.

The contribution of our chapter to the literature is threefold. First, we propose a calibration method for individual anomalies. Most existing studies pick fixed start and end dates for calendar anomalies, but our technique offers annual calibration using Sharpe Ratio as the objective function. Second, our chapter serves as a cookbook for investors. While many papers on anomalies end with discussing their statistical significance or the lack thereof, we discuss implementation with consideration of realistic leverage available to retail clients, realistic trading costs, and problems arising from trying to allocate capital to multiple anomalies. Third, many investors might already have an allocation in more traditional macro strategies and are curious to see whether these could be enhanced by addition of seasonal trends, pre-announcement drift, and momentum strategies. This chapter combines these anomalies with existing market-timing strategies and some popular investment approaches to illustrate the potential of such ensembles.

We start with four robust seasonal anomalies and some of their variations, and propose a simple deterministic trading strategy for each. Then we introduce three different options of combining these four strategies. First, we look at the mean–variance optimization algorithm (Markowitz, 1952), and second, we perform a grid search on model weights to look for optimal combinations of signals rather than using portfolio optimization based on the covariance structure. Last, we consider a simple equal weight portfolio for comparison. Simultaneously, we combine all strategies on a real-time basis. Welch and Goyal (2008) demonstrate that many predictors perform poorly out-of-sample and even in the late in-sample period. By only including strategies on anomalies after they have been described, we are only looking at true out-of-sample periods and are able to demonstrate that their value for an investor's portfolio is meaningful and valuable. The results are as follows. From 1976 to 2017, the equally weighted model produces the highest Sharpe ratio (0.89 compared to 0.76 of the grid search algorithm and 0.81 for the mean–variance algorithm). However, the grid search model produces the highest Sharpe ratio of 0.86 in a more recent period (1996–2017), compared to 0.81 and 0.79 for equal weight and mean–variance algorithm, respectively. In the real-time setting from 1976 to 2017, the equally weighted model and the mean–variance algorithm produce Sharpe ratios of 0.65 and 0.55, respectively, which is considerably lower than the 0.85 attained by the grid search algorithm. The grid search model also dominates the more recent period in the real-time setting, with a Sharpe ratio of 0.82, compared to 0.62 and 0.57 for equal weight and mean–variance algorithm, respectively. There is a noticeable difference between the non-real-time and real-time backtests, especially for the equal weight and mean–variance optimized models. But it is important to note that the real-time models still differ from the Buy-and-Hold benchmark in a statistically significant way; the equal weight real-time model at 1% significance level, and the mean–variance optimized real-time model at 5% significance level. The univariate strategies are restricted to be between 0% and 150% invested in S&P 500. We maximize the backtested Sharpe ratio in our analysis, since this metric is rather invariant to scaling. Investors wishing to deploy these models in their portfolios can subsequently choose a level of leverage based on their risk preferences.

The seasonal trend model also enhances the market-timing models of Hull and Qiao (2017) and Hull *et al.* (2017). A simple strategy which combines all three models almost triples the Sharpe ratio of Buy-and-Hold between 2003 and 2017 (this period was selected to match the out-sample period of Hull *et al.* (2017)). The combined strategy produces a Sharpe ratio of 1.26, with annualized returns of 18.07% and 13.26% volatility.

This chapter fits into the literature on return predictability and seasonal anomalies. Calendar anomalies in equity returns have been documented in published papers by a number of authors, most of whom found them significant. The SIM phenomenon, or Halloween effect, was documented among others by Bouman and Jacobsen (2002), Jacobsen and Visaltanachoti (2009), Jacobsen and Zhang (2014), and Maberly and Pierce (2004). Bouman and Jacobsen (2002) trace this phenomenon all the way back to 1964, with a quote from the Financial Times: "The Stock Exchange world is in a sort of twilight state at the moment. The potential buyers seem to have 'sold in May and gone away'. ..." The TOM effect was documented by Jacobs and Levy (1988), Lakonishok and Smidt (1988), and more recently by McConnell and Xu (2008). Empirical evidence was provided by Haug and Hirschey (2006) and Zhang and Jacobsen (2017) on the January effect, and by Cross (1973) on the weekend effect, and by Ariel (1990) on the holiday effect. A short early review of such anomalies was published by Thaler (1987) and Dimson (1988) and updated to discuss more recent data and relative importance of various effects by Swinkels and Van Vliet (2012). It is difficult to identify the continuing causes of such anomalies, assuming they have persisted to the present, and we do not try to do so at this time.

Similar to seasonal effects, statistically significant anomalies in expected returns have been mentioned in the academic literature in relation to pre-announcement drifts. Lucca and Moench (2015) popularized the abnormal pre-FOMC announcement returns, and Azar and Lo (2016) discuss refining this phenomenon using Twitter sentiment data. The discovery of a relationship between FOMC announcements and equity returns predates both of the studies and can be traced to Bernanke and Kuttner (2003).

We also include a momentum indicator in this chapter. While momentum is not related to any specific time period, or to any specific market event (such as earnings announcements), it falls into the category of well-documented phenomena unexplained by current risk models. The literature on momentum is vast, with some of the seminal work attributed to Moskowitz *et al.* (2012). We find the expansion of the momentum indicator into different market states described in Huang *et al.* (2017) particularly useful. Cootner (1962) documents the use of a 200-Day MA indicator for trade momentum, and helps us place the discovery of this trading rule on the historical timeline.

Hull and Qiao (2017) and Hull *et al.* (2017) propose market-timing strategies to illustrate economic importance of return predictability. Hull and Qiao (2017) focus on 6-month future market excess returns. They combine 20 well-known return predictors using correlation screening and use an ordinary least squares model to forecast future market excess return. Hull *et al.* (2017) consider 15 return predictors, and use weighted least squares (WLS) regression with stepwise variable selection to build a forecasting model for next month's market excess returns. They also find that the combination of the one-month strategy with the six-month model of Hull and Qiao (2017) does better than the individual models separately. A portfolio of equal investments in these two strategies results in 15.25% annualized returns with a Sharpe ratio of 1.19, and a maximum drawdown of 14.33%. The improvement relative to individual models in risk-adjusted return for the combined model results from diversification across models. The one-month and six-month models complement each other. Drawdowns for each strategy occur at different times, and the two strategies underperform Buy-and-Hold in different years. Combining the two market-timing strategies forms a more stable and robust portfolio than either stand-alone strategy.

The remainder of this chapter is organized as follows. We describe our data sources in Section 2 and analyze the robustness of our anomalies in Section 3. In Section 4, we explain how to utilize the statistical results presented in Section 3 into univariate trading strategies and how to combine these univariate strategies into an optimized trading system. We proceed with an evaluation of potential benefits of combining seasonal trends with other market-timing models in Section 5. Section 6 concludes and suggests potential future research.

2. Data

We fit our models on the equity risk premium (ERP) which is defined as the difference between the S&P 500 return and the risk-free rate. We use the total return S&P 500 dataset starting in 1960 and the three-month Treasury bill rate as a proxy for the risk-free rate. Besides the FOMC meeting dates, no other data are needed to construct and optimize the four strategies. In Section 5, we use signal data as described in referenced papers. To simplify all comparisons, we use all data from 1960 onward to describe the anomalies, we start all univariate strategies in 1975, and all combinations of univariate strategies in 1976.

3. Market Anomalies

This section revisits various types of commonly known market anomalies, updates their results, and comments on their persistence throughout time.

3.1. *Seasonal anomalies*

3.1.1. *Turn of the month*

Hensel and Ziemba (1996) define TOM as the period from the last day of the month and first four trading days of the new month. Their paper also explores various hypotheses behind the existence of this phenomenon. For example, U.S. companies make substantial payments to private investors in form of salaries and debt interests (Ogden, 1990). More recent work by Etula *et al.* (2017) also leans toward the liquidity explanation behind this effect, arguing that many of the largest transfers such as pensions and dividends are clustered around the TOM, thus creating a significant systemic liquidity demand (followed by a liquidity surplus). Such demand for liquidity results in temporarily increased cost of long-term debt capital and is demonstrated by depressed stock and bond prices. Ensuing liquidity surplus elevates stock and bond prices again. Another proposed explanation looks at the way companies put off announcing bad news toward the end of the month (Penman, 1987). We see that while all of these theories seem intuitive and based on empirical evidence, none of them restrict the effect to the exact five days, usually discussed in academic literature, which leads us to loosen the time constraint and examine a broader set of start and end dates. We examine the duration of this effect by observing excess returns up to four trading days before the end of the month and up to four trading days after the end of the month, all in all 9 days. Table 1 shows excess return distribution characteristics on TOM days vs. other days for various parameters of TOM.

Figure 1 shows a heat map of differences between the average daily excess return on TOM days and non-TOM days. We observe a concentrated occurrence of positive excess returns on all combinations of start days between 0 and 4 days before the end of the month, and end days of 0 to 4 days after the end of the month. This is consistent with academic literature and serves as a robustness test for the model parameters.

Table 1. TOM effect (1960–2017). TOM portfolio is fully invested on days that fall into the following range: $(T - n_{\text{start}}, T + n_{\text{end}})$, where T is the last trading day of each month. The non-TOM portfolio is invested in cash on these days, and fully invested otherwise.

n_{start}	n_{end}	$\bar{r}_{\text{TOM}}$ [%]	$\text{sd}(r_{\text{TOM}})$ [%]	$\bar{r}_{\text{other}}$ [%]	$\text{sd}(r_{\text{other}})$ [%]	$\bar{r}_{\text{TOM}} - \bar{r}_{\text{other}}$ [%]
0	1	0.0995	1.0182	0.0173	1.0033	0.0822***
1	1	0.0798	1.0178	0.0161	1.0025	0.0637***
2	1	0.0743	1.0091	0.0136	1.0037	0.0607***
3	1	0.0732	1.0109	0.0101	1.0027	0.0630***
4	1	0.0505	1.0122	0.0150	1.0019	0.0355*
0	2	0.0964	0.9972	0.0133	1.0058	0.0831***
1	2	0.0824	1.0022	0.0117	1.0052	0.0707***
2	2	0.0775	0.9983	0.0088	1.0065	0.0687***
3	2	0.0760	1.0016	0.0048	1.0056	0.0712***
4	2	0.0562	1.0041	0.0096	1.0051	0.0466***
0	3	0.0934	0.9803	0.0091	1.0100	0.0843***
1	3	0.0828	0.9877	0.0071	1.0097	0.0757***
2	3	0.0787	0.9869	0.0038	1.0114	0.0749***
3	3	0.0772	0.9914	−0.0009	1.0107	0.0781***
4	3	0.0597	0.9949	0.0039	1.0105	0.0558***
0	4	0.0771	0.9866	0.0089	1.0101	0.0682***
1	4	0.0710	0.9916	0.0068	1.0097	0.0642***
2	4	0.0691	0.9903	0.0032	1.0115	0.0660***
3	4	0.0691	0.9938	−0.0019	1.0109	0.0709***
4	4	0.0544	0.9966	0.0032	1.0107	0.0512***

Note: *, **, and *** denote significance at the levels of 10%, 5%, and 1%, respectively.

3.1.2. *Sell-in-May*

Explanations behind the existence of the SIM effect often revolve around vacation behavior of investors (Bouman and Jacobsen, 2002). Doeswijk (2008) proposes that investors' irrational optimism for the upcoming year explains abnormal returns in the fourth quarter, but this optimism turns into pessimism when confronted with reality several months into the next year and the stock markets experience a summer lull. Chan and Marsh's (2017) is to our knowledge the most recent work contributing to the SIM effect discussion, arguing that the effect captures risk premium surrounding political uncertainty around elections, in particular midterm election (3rd year or

Fig. 1. Heat map of the difference between the mean excess return on TOM days and the mean excess return on other days for various start and end date combinations. TOM days are defined as days that fall into the following range: $(T - n_{\text{start}}, T + n_{\text{end}})$, where T is the last trading day of the month.

a political cycle). Because of the convincing statistical evidence presented by Chan and Marsh (2017), we follow their methodology in our approach. In spite of the fact that our strategy will only follow the pattern or investing in the market in the winter months once every four years, we will still refer to the strategy as "Sell-in-May". We go beyond the dates proposed in the popular saying suggesting that investors sell-in-May-and-go-away, and consider a wider range of starting and ending dates; April 1 to June 15 for start dates and September 1 to November 15 for end dates resulting in 5776 possible combinations. We split our return dataset into two sets, a SIM set, containing all returns that fall between the start date and end date of the SIM period and a non-SIM set, which comprises days not included in the SIM set. Each parameter combination yields a different pair of the two sets for which we calculate Sharpe ratios. Figure 2 shows the empirical distribution of the Sharpe ratios for both sets and a clear separation of the annualized "3rd year winter" and "other" Sharpe ratios is visible. However, this figure is purely an

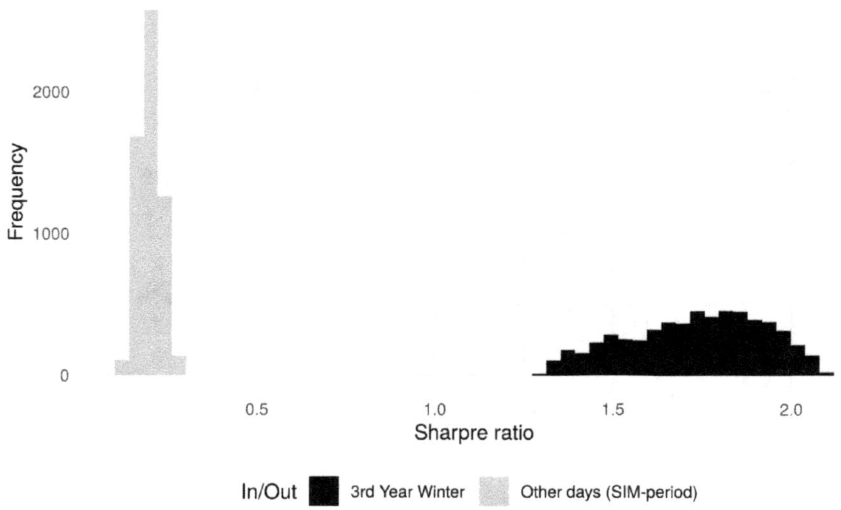

Fig. 2. Histograms of SIM annualized Sharpe ratios for the 5,776 possible start–end date combinations. The dark bars are Sharpe ratios of portfolios invested during the winter months following a midterm election and light bars are Sharpe ratios on portfolios which are fully invested rest of the time. "3rd Year Winter" and "Other days" are defined by all the combinations of start and end days we tested.

illustration of the effect and its robustness toward the choice of start and end dates and does not actually tell us how to determine the optimal trading strategy. For the purposes of the real-time trading strategy, however, we cannot use these findings and fall back to the strategy that does not have a condition on election cycle.

3.1.3. *January effect*

The January effect was first documented and named by Wachtel (1942). The common explanations of its existence revolve around tax-motivated selling in December or unusual demand for cash before Christmas (Wachtel, 1942). Both hypotheses would cause price depression in December followed by a return to "normal" in January. The January effect is one of the older documented seasonal anomalies but more recent studies posit that the effect has been subsumed by the TOM effect (Swinkels and Van Vliet, 2012). We test this theory by examining the value of staying long after the TOM period.

We looked at the average excess return earned in January relative to the rest of the year. We allow the January effect to begin up to 4 days before the beginning of the month and end any time in the first 30 days of the year. Studying the difference between the mean return on January effect days and mean return on non-January effect days for various start and end dates showed that the only significant returns were gained during the last four trading days in December and first four trading days in January, which coincide with the TOM period. All in all our observations match those of Swinkels and Van Vliet (2012) who concluded that January effect is subsumed by other seasonal anomalies. Therefore, we conclude that we can capture all relevant information in our TOM effect and do not proceed with the January effect any further.

3.1.4. *Weekend effect*

The weekend effect has been observed in many studies, but few offer an actual hypothesis about its origin. Chen and Singal (2003) argue that short-sellers close their positions on Fridays, which causes prices to be pushed upwards and deflate again on Mondays when they reopen their positions. We test being flat on Mondays, and also staying out of the market the days before or after Monday to see how concentrated around Monday the effect actually is. Table 2 shows empirical results demonstrating the statistical significance of the difference between mean daily excess return on Turn of the Week (TOW) days and mean excess return on other days. We replicate the results of the original study by Cross (1973) by showing that the average daily excess return on or around Mondays is substantially lower than on other days. However, we see that these excess returns are only barely negative. This observation, coupled with expectations about trading cost on a strategy with around 5200% annual turnover (100% turnover every week) suggests that implementing the weekend effect in a trading strategy would not be fruitful and we abandon this idea.

Table 2. Weekend effect, 1970–2017. N_{start} shows the first day when we are flat, and n_{end} shows the last. "Other" subsets include days when we are invested in the market. "TOW" subset includes flat days.

n_{start}	n_{end}	$\bar{r}_{\text{TOW}}$ [%]	sd(r_{TOW}) [%]	$\bar{r}_{\text{other}}$ [%]	sd(r_{other}) [%]	$\bar{r}_{\text{TOW}} - \bar{r}_{other}$ [%]
1	1	−0.0468	1.1652	0.044	0.9578	−0.0908***
2	1	0.0009	1.052	0.0423	0.97	−0.0414**
3	1	0.0073	1.0218	0.0545	0.976	−0.0471***
1	2	0.0028	1.0773	0.041	0.9502	−0.0382**
2	2	0.0181	1.0285	0.0368	0.965	−0.0187
3	2	0.0185	1.0117	0.0575	0.9713	−0.0390*
1	3	0.0224	1.0368	0.0296	0.9505	−0.0072
2	3	0.0288	1.0096	0.0078	0.9825	0.021

Note: *, **, and *** denote significance at the levels of 10%, 5%, and 1%, respectively.

3.2. *Announcement drifts*

3.2.1. *Federal Open Market Committee*

Lucca and Moench (2015) offer historic background for the FOMC meeting. According to the study, members of this monetary policy-making body have met eight times per year at regularly scheduled meetings to discuss and make monetary policy decisions since the 1980s. Prior to the 1980s, these meetings occurred even more frequently. In 1994, the committee started announcing their decisions to the public around 2:15 pm Eastern Time. Prior to 1994, investors had to infer these decisions through the open market operations as no decisions were announced. The same study by Lucca and Moench (2015) also finds that since 1994, the S&P 500 index has increased on average 49 bps in the 24 hours prior to the FOMC announcement, thus making up 80% of the annual realized excess stock returns between 1994 and 2015. According to their research, these pre-announcement returns are robust to small sample bias or outliers and appear across industry and size portfolios. The same study also finds that the results do not significantly differ across monetary cycles of easing and tightening but they do vary depending on the prevailing level of uncertainty in the market during the pre-announcement period, as proxied by the VIX index. This appears to partially confirm the hypothesis that this return anomaly may reflect the premium required by equity investors for bearing non-diversifiable risk. Additionally, Lucca and Moench (2015) find that a flatter yield curve coincides with larger gains, which may suggest a premium for the uncertainty of a rates lift-off and the beginning of a monetary tightening cycle. This section describes our replication methodology and presents the results updated through 2017. The original research proposes a strategy that goes long at 2 pm ET the day before the FOMC announcement and stays long until 2 pm ET the day of the announcement. Our contribution is expanding this work to discuss potential value of this anomaly in trading systems that only rebalance at the end of the day, and showing recent performance of strategies utilizing this signal. We only consider scheduled meetings and exclude unscheduled meetings from our analysis since the market participants do not know about them. We show that the effect is robust with respect to the exact timing and a close-to-close (4 pm ET) strategy is sufficient to capture the drift and provides significant excess returns even in recent times.

Table 3 shows Sharpe ratio comparisons for different versions of the FOMC strategy. In addition to testing end of the day execution, we also check whether traders have become aware of the effect and bid the market up the day prior. However, our results indicate that entering the market two days before the announcement does not improve performance. We also look at subsets of the dataset to see how robust these results are in more recent periods. We break down the experiment into two periods: 1994–2009 and 2010–2017. We find that the average daily return difference in the most recent period is only 0.1514% compared to 0.3328% during the 1994–2009 era, and is no longer statistically significant. However, these sub-periods only include a small number of data points so we do not claim that the FOMC pre-announcement drift has disappeared.

3.2.2. *U.S. macroeconomic announcements*

Kurov *et al.* (2015) explore intraday pre-announcement drifts for major U.S. macroeconomic announcements, and find that seven out of 21 market-moving announcements show evidence of informed

Table 3. FOMC pre-announcement drift effect 1994–2017.

	SR_{FOMC}	$SR_{non-FOMC}$	$\bar{r}_{FOMC} - \bar{r}_{other}$ [%]
2pm S&P 500 Index	5.60	0.34	0.3604***
3pm S&P 500 Index	6.54	0.34	0.3748***
4pm S&P 500 Index	4.13	0.38	0.2664***
SPY	4.11	0.34	0.2723***
1-day ahead SPY	1.68	0.41	0.1186
2-day SPY	2.76	0.29	0.2021***

Note: *, **, and *** denote significance at the levels of 10%, 5%, and 1%, respectively. The first two columns compare Sharpe ratios of days with FOMC announcements (or the day before in case of "1-day ahead SPY"), with other days. The third column shows the average daily return difference of these two sets. The first three rows assume entering a long position at a specific time (all times are displayed in Eastern Time Zone), and selling 24 hours later. The fourth row shows simulated results obtained by using the closing auction prices of the SPY ETF, and therefore we expect the results to be very similar to 4pm ET trading. Row five is based on the close-to-close SPY return realized on the day before the announcement. The 1-day ahead strategy (fifth row) tests entering a long position two days before the announcement and selling day before the announcement. 2-day SPY strategy (sixth row) combines the strategies from rows four and five.

trading, meaning that the price drifts in the direction of the post-announcement level up to 30-minute before the announcement. While this information is certainly useful for intraday traders, we explore the possibility that a risk-based inter-day drift similar to that of the FOMC announcements is present. We focus on two widely watched macroeconomic announcements: the Civilian Unemployment Rate and the Producer Price Index. The Bureau of Labor Statistics announces the seasonally adjusted civilian unemployment rate on the first Friday of every month at 8:30 am ET, and the Producer Price Index is also released monthly, typically mid-month though not on a specific day. However, the bureau makes announcement dates known in advance and they are widely available on various financial websites. We explore intraday drifts, as well as drifts starting up to two days before the announcement. Similarly to the FOMC pre-announcement drift, we observe that the magnitude of the effect is comparable using either intraday execution with a 24-hour holding period or end of day trading. However, the magnitude of these effects is smaller. The average daily excess return difference for end of day trades is only 3 bps on PPI announcement days and 11 bps on unemployment announcement days, compared to 27 bps for the FOMC announcement. Duyvesteyn *et al.* (2011) study these and other macroeconomic announcements and conclude that the announcement surprise rather than the announcement itself is predictive of returns. This is certainly a plausible idea worthy of further research because it offers an explanation why we were not able to confirm pre-announcement drift in many macroeconomic announcements.

3.2.3. *Trend models*

Many trend models and many enhancements to trend models have been published in academic literature as well as in professional forums. (Faber, 2007, is to this day the most downloaded paper on SSRN.) Investors like trend models because they seek tail risk protection and trend models have historically accomplished this task without the need to invest in derivatives (only options protect against tail risk by design). Investors also dislike trend models because this tail risk protection comes at a cost, the cost being the tendency to miss beginnings of market rallies resulting in a lower return compared to Buy-and-Hold. One of the most popular, if not the most popular momentum indicator is the 200-day moving average as discussed by Faber (2007). We examined the robustness of this approach with respect to the choice of the length of the SMA on average excess returns for this binary approach (long when price is above the moving average and flat when price is below the moving average). We allowed the N in the N-day moving average to range between 20 and 400 days. We find the sign of the effect to be consistent in every studied scenario, with the largest effects occurring when N was between 220 and 260 days. The effect was statistically significant on the 10% significance level in these cases. Other seminal work in this area includes the proposed use of principal component analysis to reduce the dimensionality and extract value from a variety of technical indicators (Neely *et al.*, 2014).

4. Trading Strategies

The rest of this chapter deals with practical issues of an investor trying to improve the performance of a portfolio by incorporating these anomalies into a trading system. While academic literature has documented the statistical and economic theories surrounding these effects, the question of how to use these anomalies optimally in a trading system is uncharted territory. At no point do we claim that the signals and strategies are optimal or extract the most edge out of these anomalies. To paraphrase George Box: "All strategies are wrong, but some are useful." For the purpose of this chapter, we refer back to our original question: "Can we beat Buy-and-Hold (on a risk-adjusted or absolute basis) by incorporating additional information into our trading system into a market-timing strategy?" We further expand the question to asking whether we could have beaten the market since 1976 using only strategies known to the public at any given time.

In a market-timing strategy, we are faced with the decision to allocate between the risk-free asset and the market portfolio. Having the risk-free asset available is important in this case as all the strategies have significant periods during which they are not invested in the market portfolio. We aim to eliminate forward looking bias from our backtests by estimating all model parameters in a walk forward manner. Our dataset starts in 1960, and we start making forecasts from 1975. We re-estimate our parameters annually and use an expanding window. This means we optimize the model parameters using data from 1960 to 1974 and trade with these parameters for all of 1975. At the end of 1975, we re-estimate the parameters and use them for trading in 1976. We continue these annual refits all the way to 2016. This way we are able to generate out-of-sample predictions from 1971 to 2017, the last full year included in our data.

We assume that we enter the market at the close. This makes our backtest more relevant for practical purposes since closing prices are actual tradeable prices which can be realized by entering the closing auction. For our backtest, we assume trading costs of 2.5 basis points for each dollar market portfolio bought or sold. For example, with the SPY ETF priced at $250 per share, this would imply trading cost of 0.625 cents per share. Considering that many retail brokers now offer commissions of 0.5 cents or less per contract traded, our transaction costs are in line with prices offered to clients even after accounting for the SEC fee ($13.00 per $1 million dollar notional traded). We also did not have to account for slippage, because many brokers now offer guaranteed market on close (MOC) price to their clients for liquid products. We cap all signals between 0% and 150%. The lower bound of this constraint is motivated by Campbell and Thompson (2005), who demonstrate value of capping ones' predictions at zero instead of trying to forecast negative ERP. As for the upper bound, we wanted to balance two goals. We wanted to allow for leverage, knowing that our strategies trade infrequently and thus carry less risk than Buy-and-Hold, but we also wanted to keep the leverage within reach of most investors. We keep the same restrictions on our combined signals in Section 4.1 to be consistent.

Section 4.1 shows the resulting portfolios for each strategy. Whenever we say we "buy the market", or "enter a position" or "go long", we mean that we buy shares of an S&P 500 tracking instrument such as the SPY ETF or E-mini S&P 500 futures. Our exposure to S&P 500 at the end of each trading day is determined by our strategy signal. Whenever we say we "exit the market" or "go flat", it means we sell our S&P 500 instrument and acquire short-term government bonds with the proceeds.

4.1. *Univariate trading strategies*

4.1.1. *TOM strategy*

We propose the following simple trading strategy. We define a TOM period during which we are long the market portfolio. All other days we hold the risk-free asset. This strategy has two parameters that we optimize for, the start date and the end date of the TOM period. We are always long on the last trading day of the month. The start date parameter determines how many days before the last trading day of the month we are long and the end date parameter determines how many days after the last trading days of the month we are long. We constrain both the parameters to lie between 0 and 8 days. Thus, the shortest possible TOM period is one day (last trading day of the month) and the longest is 17 days (8 days before and 8 days after the last trading day.) The optimization rule we use chooses a combination of start and end dates that maximizes the Sharpe ratio of the strategy. The optimal parameters change little from refit to refit and for the most part, it is optimal to begin between 0 and 3 days before the end of the month, and sell out of the position between 3 and 7 trading days after the beginning of the following month. Since the strategy holds the risk-free asset for most of the time, it lags the Buy-and-Hold strategy in terms of return. However, on a risk-adjusted basis, it actually outperforms as indicated by the higher Sharpe ratio. Figure 3 shows the evolution of the optimal strategy parameters and Fig. 4 shows a wealth accumulation for the strategy and the Buy-and-Hold benchmark.

4.1.2. *SIM strategy*

For the SIM strategy, we want to be invested in the market in days outside of the SIM period and hold the risk-free asset during the

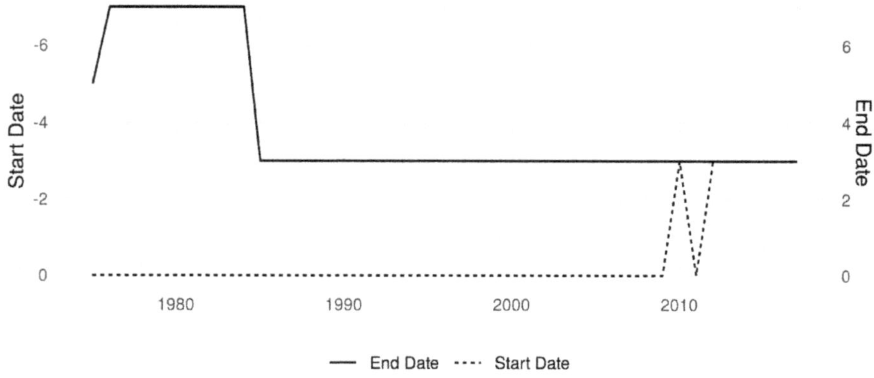

Fig. 3. Evolution of the optimal start and end dates for the TOM Strategy. Start date shows how many days before the last trading day of the month we enter the market, and end date shows how many days after the beginning of the month we stay long.

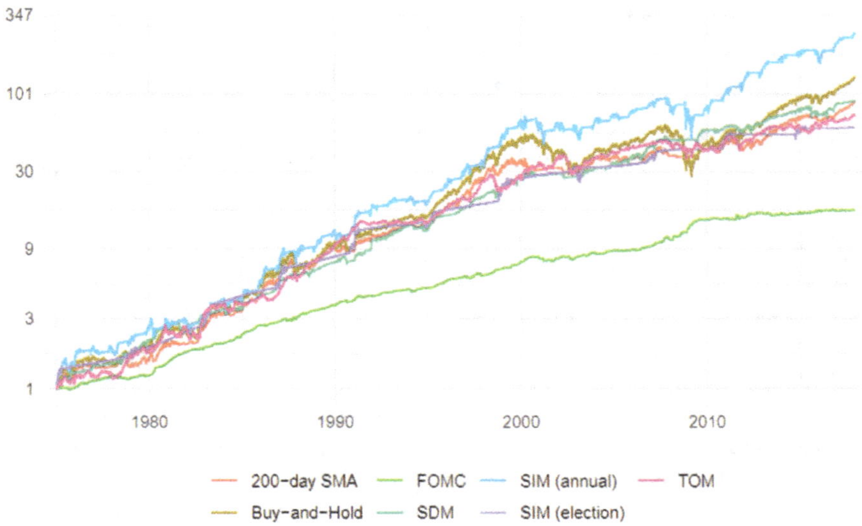

Fig. 4. Wealth accumulation of the TOM, SIM (election), SIM (annual), FOMC, SDM and simple 200-day moving average strategies. Note that y-axis has a logarithmic scale.

SIM period. We perform a similar search for the SIM strategy as we did for the TOM strategy. That is, we optimize the start and end date parameters of the SIM period to maximize the Sharpe ratio. We allow the SIM period to start on April 1 the earliest and last till November 15 at most. Again, we report optimal parameters and show a wealth accumulation plot of this approach. The optimal start dates selected in our backtest range between April 29 and May 10, with May 6 being the most frequently chosen start date. The optimal end date is also stable, ranging between October 4 and October 28. Figure 4 shows the wealth accumulation plot relative to Buy-and-Hold for this strategy and Fig. 5 shows the evolution of the optimal trading parameters from refit to refit. For the real-time model, we follow the original conventional wisdom as closely as possible in order to not introduce information from later periods. Therefore, instead of optimizing entry and exit dates, we simply reduce our market exposure to zero on May 1st and return to being 150% invested on October 31st each year.

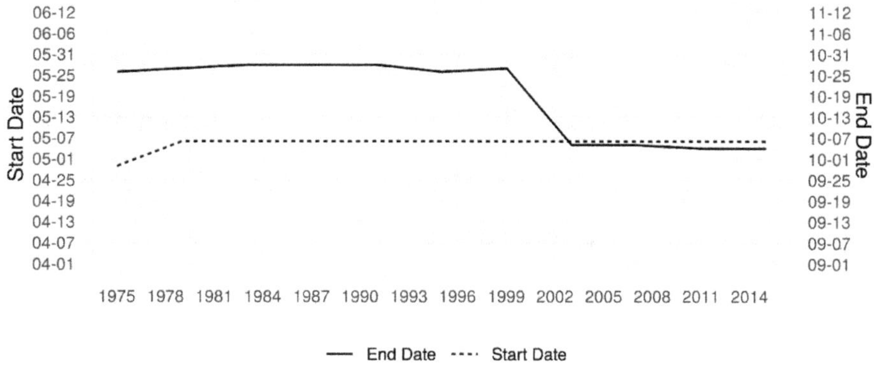

Fig. 5. Evolution of the optimal start and end dates for the SIM Strategy. Start date shows the date when we sell our positions and exit the market, and end date shows the date we return.

4.1.3. *FOMC strategy*

For the FOMC strategy, we do not perform an optimization *per se*. Our prior analysis revealed that a significant pre-announcement premium exists on announcement days. We harvest this anomaly by going long on the market portfolio at the close of the day before the announcement and exiting the position at the close of the day of the announcement.

Figure 4 shows cumulative wealth for the FOMC strategy vs. Buy-and-Hold. Once again, we see a wealth plot that smooths out the big drawdowns of Buy-and-Hold but struggles to keep up with the return, because it only invests in the market about 8 days every year.

4.1.4. *State dependent momentum strategy*

We follow the steps in Huang *et al.* (2017) and compare the resulting strategy to the simple 200 day moving average indicator (Faber, 2007). We forecast the 1-month ERP in two different regimes depending on whether the S&P 500 index level is above or below its 200-day moving average. Figure 4 shows wealth accumulation for two simple momentum strategies vs. Buy-and-Hold. Even without seeing the complete performance statistics, we can observe that the two momentum strategies have fairly similar cumulative returns, perhaps with the SDM having a slightly lower volatility and thus a slightly higher Sharpe Ratio. The choice between these two models does not impact our conclusions in a significant way but we proceed with the SDM model because of its added ability to distinguish between market regimes. However, for the purposes of evaluating the real-time strategy, we can only use the traditional 200-day moving average indicator.

4.2. *Performance*

Table 4 summarizes the backtested results of the univariate strategies. We observe certain similarities among all our univariate trading strategies. They all improve the Sharpe ratio over Buy-and-Hold. The SDM strategy has the highest Sharpe ratio of 0.7 compared to 0.42 for Buy-and-Hold on the 1975–2017 period. On the one hand, our strategies all significantly reduce volatility compared to Buy-and-Hold, with FOMC having the lowest volatility of 4.67% compared to 17.13% for Buy-and-Hold. This is an expected effect, since all our strategies are invested in the risk-free asset for significant portions of time. On the other hand, the same strategies tend to trail Buy-and-Hold the most in terms of annualized average returns. The only strategy that is able to beat the return of Buy-and-Hold is the annual SIM Model, with an annualized average return of 13.80% compared to 11.99% for Buy-and-Hold. The SDM strategy and the simple 200-day moving average strategy are more or less able to keep up with the market as well, with annualized average returns of 11.05% and 11.01%, respectively. Another observation is that all proposed strategies have a low CAPM beta, ranging from 0.05 to 0.68, and all of them achieve a positive annualized alpha (between 1.74% and 4.28%). It is also important to keep in mind that these results were calculated using data between 1975 and 2017, and the FOMC did not start holding meetings in the form we know today until 1980 and their decisions were not publicly announced until 1994.

Table 4. Performance statistics of all univariate strategies, 1975–2017. The statistical significance of performance difference relative to Buy-and-Hold in terms of the Sharpe ratio is tested using the Ledoit and Wolf (2008) test.

	TOM	SIM (election)	SIM (annual)	SDM	200-day SMA	FOMC	Buy-and-Hold
CAGR [%]	10.46	9.98	13.8	11.05	11.01	6.71	11.99
Total Return [%]	7127.75	5901.45	25940.69	8984.29	8863.1	1539.13	12996.79
Volatility [% Ann.]	12.02	8.41	17.34	8.83	11.86	4.67	17.13
Sharpe	0.47	0.62**	0.51	0.7***	0.52***	0.44	0.42
Return/Risk	0.87	1.19	0.8	1.25	0.93	1.44	0.7
maxDrawdown [%]	26.41	21.01	48.15	15.45	22.97	7.63	55.2
Time Under Water [days]	862	883	1500	689	1416	561	1805
CAPM [alpha] [% Ann.]	3.48	4.07	4.28	3.76	2.7	1.74	
CAPM [beta]	0.33	0.16	0.68	0.32	0.48	0.05	

Note: *, **, and *** denote significance at the levels of 10%, 5%, and 1%, respectively.

4.3. *Combining anomalies*

Section 4.1 presented the potential of individual strategies for exploiting market anomalies. While the performance of the individual trading strategies does not justify the allocation of an investor's total wealth to any one strategy, a combination of these trading signals might be able to outperform Buy-and-Hold not only in terms of risk-adjusted performance but also other metrics and therefore present itself as a viable alternative. There are a few reasons to combine multiple strategies rather than picking the one that performed best in a backtest. First of all, any backtest is sample specific and there is always uncertainty about true performance of any given strategy. Secondly, Harry Markowitz famously pointed out that diversification is the only free lunch in investing (Markowitz, 1952). If we can present multiple strategies with positive alpha and correlation of less than 100%, there is always added value in extracting information from more than one of them.

There is a wrong and a not so wrong way of optimizing the portfolios. Just like any other model parameters, model weights in an ensemble are subject to forward looking bias. The wrong way would be to use the in-sample signals of our strategies at any given point or to just optimize the weights once, at the end of our dataset, and expect the ensemble strategy to perform equally well in the future. A less wrong way would be to use the returns of the "actual" portfolios (i.e., the portfolios formed after the optimization of their parameters). This would more closely represent the out-of-sample performance of the four strategies. This mean–variance portfolio optimization approach provides a basic solution, but there are a few issues preventing us from being able to accurately optimize our trading system. The high parameter uncertainty associated with the low trading frequency of the proposed trading strategies limits our confidence in the stability of the mean–variance portfolio optimization. Additionally, mean–variance optimization assumes that we have a good estimate of the correlation matrix of our portfolios. Lastly, these algorithms only optimize the resulting portfolio's return on risk characteristic without regard to potential capital underutilization. While we cannot mitigate the problem caused by the sparsity of data, we propose a method that is less sensitive to correlation matrix estimation accuracy and allows a better capital usage. We can perform a grid search across individual model weights, and the sum of all weights to find a combination that meets our needs. Regardless of the choice of ensemble method, we see that all proposed strategies seem to add value to an investor's portfolio, especially when considering risk-adjusted returns. Table 4 summarizes our univariate results net of transaction fees.

When ensembling different trading strategies, three ways of introducing look-ahead bias come into mind. The first way is by means of including trading strategies which have been proven to work on data prior to their discovery when selecting the ensembling universe. This is also known as discovery bias. To mitigate this kind of look-ahead bias, we only include strategies once their underlying anomalies have been published. The second way to introduce look-ahead bias is by using the same data that were used to estimate the parameters of the ensembling technique to generate the ensemble signal on which we measure our performance. We eliminate this bias by performing our analysis in a walk-forward manner. The third way is by only including strategies that still work at the end of the data sample. This is known as survivorship bias and is particularly difficult to address. In a perfect world, at any point we would be able to include strategies that were perceived as profitable by investors and only remove them once there was a sufficient statistical evidence to the contrary. Novy-Marx (2016) discusses the risks and potential problems associated with combining variables that may suffer from such look-ahead bias in greater depth. We acknowledge this shortcoming of our paper. The one potentially redeeming quality of our approach is the annual optimization which, at least in theory, allows the model to reduce weights of anomalies that have consistently underperformed and allocate capital to more robust ones instead.

A reasonable realistic timeline for a real-time strategy exploiting the anomalies considered in this chapter would be as follows. In 1975, investors were aware of two of our anomalies: SIM and Momentum (captured by the 200 MA crossover as described by Cootner

(1962)). By 1988, the TOM effect had been confirmed by a number of studies. The basic momentum approach could have been augmented to include the state-dependent estimation starting in 2013. The FOMC pre-announcement drift was first described in October 2003 by Bernanke and Kuttner (2003), so an attentive investor could have implemented it in 2004. The political uncertainty explanation of the SIM phenomena was not widely available until 2017, so we will not include the political uncertainty version in the real-time trading strategy.

4.3.1. *Equal weight*

Empirical results of portfolio optimization problems show that it is surprisingly difficult to outperform equally weighted strategies (Fugazza *et al.*, 2015). Therefore, we test an equal weighted portfolio of our four univariate strategies. Figure 6 shows the performance of this portfolio. While the risk properties of the strategy resulting from

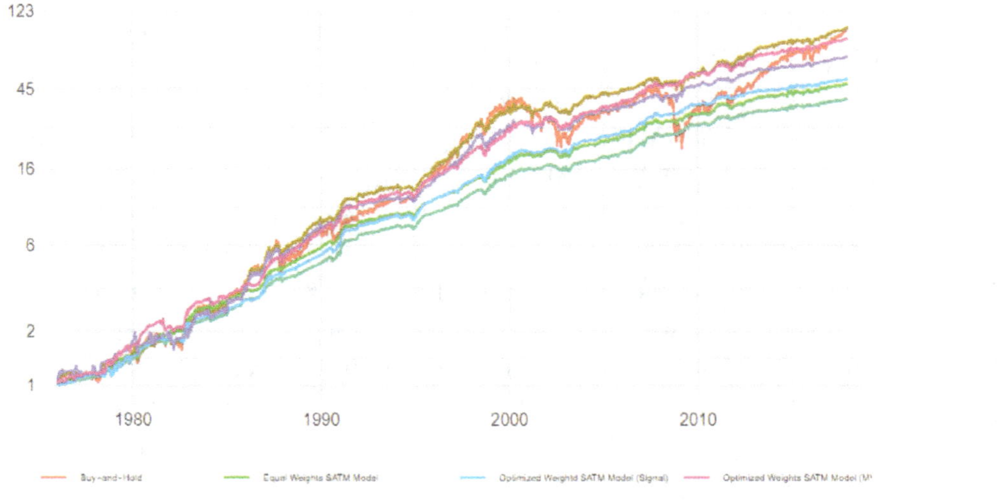

Fig. 6. Simulated performance of the four different anomaly combination strategies vs. Buy-and-Hold (1976–2017). Optimized weights SATM Model (MV) stands for mean–variance optimized, and optimized weights SATM Model (signal) denotes portfolio of the grid search optimized signals. Note that y-axis has a logarithmic scale.

this approach are attractive compared to Buy-and-Hold, we are faced with lower expected returns as a result of the capital underutilization described in Section 4.3. We also show the results of a real-time equal weight approach which adds strategies in an equal weight manner according to the timeline described above. In the real-time setting, the weight is equally split between strategies available at any given point. Initially, SIM and MOM received 50% each. In 1988, TOM was added and each of the three strategies received a 33% weight. FOMC was last to enter, in 2004, and each strategy is allocated 25% weight from that point.

4.3.2. *Mean–variance optimization*

We can treat our strategies as assets and combine them using mean–variance portfolio optimization (Markowitz, 1952). There are issues with this approach, such as estimation errors, especially on small time samples, or relative low trading frequencies of our strategies, that lead to more parameter uncertainty. For example, the FOMC trades only eight times a year. For this reason, we imposed bounds of 0% and 100% on weights of all our strategies. These weights are not very restrictive, but they ensure we will not use a negative weight on some of our signals, and compensate by over-inflating the weight of other signals. We estimate these weights in a walk-forward manner, similar to that described in Section 4. As a result, similar to the individual strategies, the combined signal ranges between 0% and 150%. Figure 7 shows how the optimal weights change year after year as we expand our sample. Figure 8 shows how the optimal weights change year after year if we only include strategies once they have been documented in the academic literature. Optimal weights are calculated at the end of each year and used for trading for the following year.

4.3.3. *Optimizing the signal combination*

The alternative portfolio optimization algorithm works on the trading signals rather than the returns. There are two ways in which one can look at combining the strategies described in this chapter.

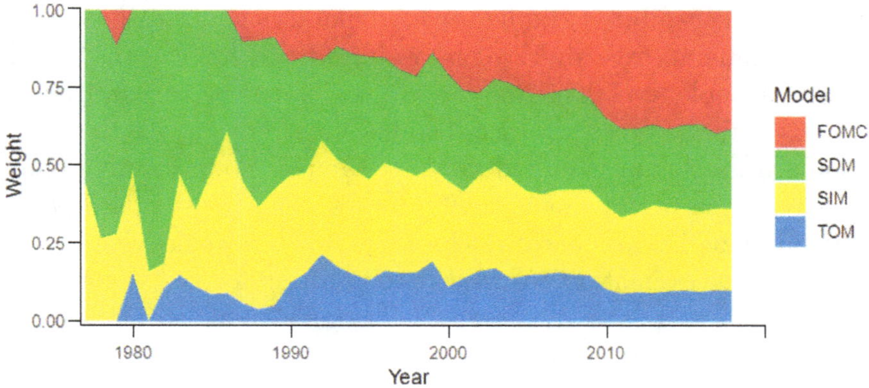

Fig. 7. Evolution of the optimal weights when all four strategies are included with weights between 0% and 100%, with the sum of all weights set equal to 100%.

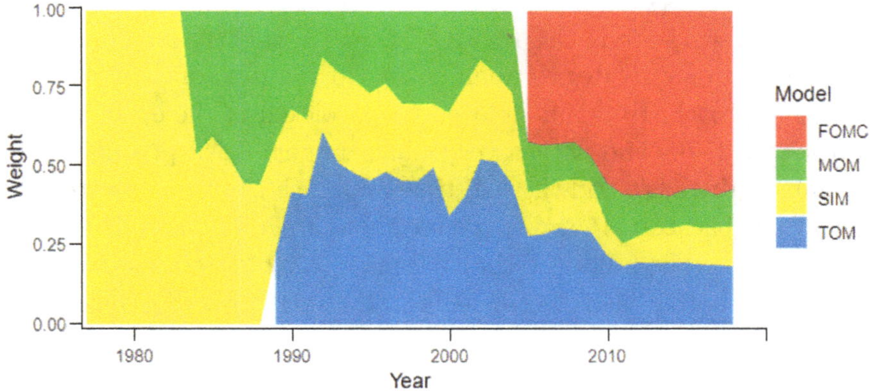

Fig. 8. Evolution of the optimal weights when all four strategies are included on real-time basis, showing only post-discovery performance, with weights between 0% and 100%, with the sum of all weights set equal to 100%.

The first one is to treat each trading strategy as an asset with its own return characteristics and perform a standard portfolio optimization technique, such as mean–variance optimization, on the return series. The second approach is to realize that the strategies trade the same asset and that not 100% of the capital allotted to a strategy is being used by each strategy at any point in time. Capital usage of the strategies is dynamic, meaning that when one strategy does not need the capital, it can be used by another one. In case the signals overlap and excessive leverage is introduced, we cap the signal at a reasonable level. This way we are not bound by the covariance matrix of the strategy returns. The question remains whether this approach is also able to perform out-of-sample. However, we do not see any reason why it should perform worse than the standard portfolio optimization approach which suffers from the same uncertainty in parameter estimation. We end up optimizing for the set of optimal weights using the grid search algorithm. We allow the weights of the individual strategies to range between 0% and 100% and cap the combined signals at 150%. 150% is chosen because it is a reasonable number for the amount of leverage an average investor is able to take on.

Figure 9 shows results of this optimization and Fig. 10 shows the real-time version of this approach. Compared to Fig. 7, we see that in recent periods the FOMC receives a slightly larger weight relative to other strategies, mainly due to the dynamic capital use of this approach. Buy-and-Hold only gets picked in the optimal mix in the late 1970s and with a very small weight. Unsurprisingly, the weights of the basic and the real-time approach converge toward the end of our backtest. However, we see that the FOMC and TOM are only added to the mix once they become available to investors. It is also worth noting that the real-time SIM strategy had a relatively

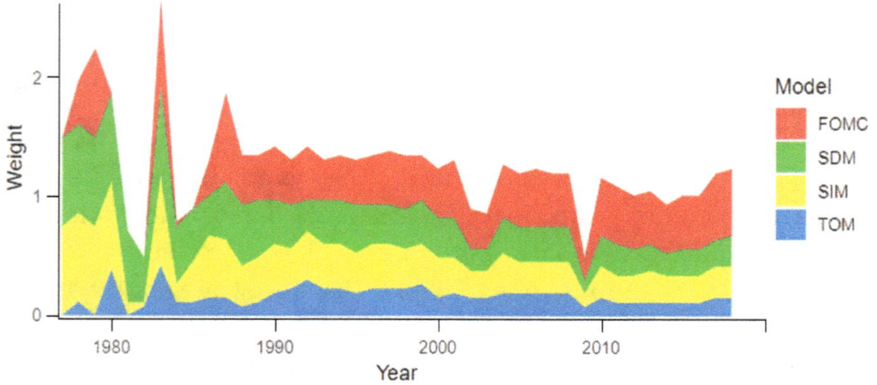

Fig. 9. Evolution of the optimal weights of a grid search optimization procedure.

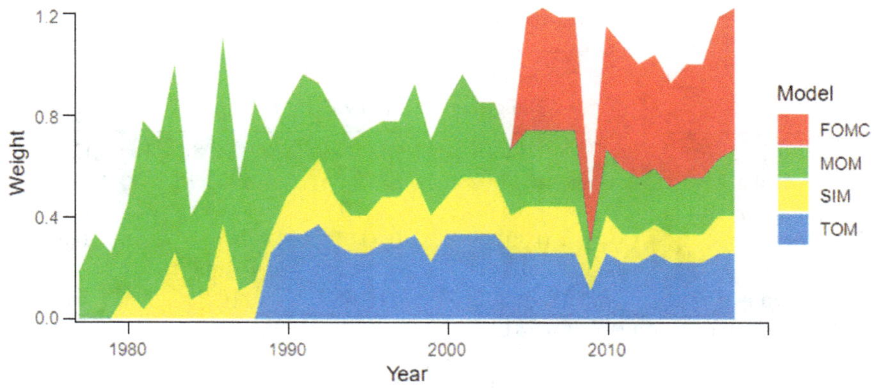

Fig. 10. Evolution of the optimal weights of a grid search optimization procedure. This version of the procedure only includes strategies once they have been described in academic literature and mimics behavior of a real investor who can only include new strategies after they have been discovered.

low weight compared to its basic counterpart. Part of the reason is that the basic approach uses the improved version based on political uncertainty around election cycles.

4.3.4. *Performance*

Table 5 shows performance metrics for various portfolios formed from the univariate strategies between 1976 and 2017, and compares them to Buy-and-Hold, and Fig. 6 shows wealth accumulation of the four strategies for the same time period. It shows three options: an equally weighted portfolio of all strategies, a mean–variance (MV) optimized portfolio of all strategies, and a portfolio of grid search optimized signal combination. We note that all four strategies outperform Buy-and-Hold in terms of Sharpe ratio, with the equally weighted strategy and the mean–variance optimized strategy scoring the highest in this metric, 0.89 and 0.81, respectively. The volatility and drawdowns of all proposed strategies are substantially lower than those of Buy-and-Hold. Between 1976 and 2017, Buy-and-Hold incurred a maximum drawdown of 55.20% with an annual volatility of 17.17%. In comparison, the maximum drawdowns of our strategies range between 9.37% and 15.63%.

Table 5. Performance statistics of all combined strategies, 1976–2017.

	Equal Weight	Optimized (MV)	Optimized (Signal)	Buy-and-Hold
CAGR [%]	9.62	11.14	9.78	11.51
Total Return [%]	4644.62	8372.65	4953.18	9627.54
Volatility [% Ann.]	5.48	7.79	6.59	17.17
Sharpe	0.89***	0.81***	0.76***	0.39
Return/Risk	1.76	1.43	1.49	0.67
maxDrawdown [%]	9.37	15.63	10.29	55.2
Time Under Water [days]	312	360	313	1805
CAPM [alpha] [% Ann.]	3.23	4.05	3.28	
CAPM [beta]	0.21	0.3	0.23	

Note: *, **, and *** denote significance at the levels of 10%, 5%, and 1%, respectively. Optimized (MV) stands for mean–variance optimized, and Optimized (Signal) denotes portfolio of grid search optimized signals. The statistical significance of performance difference relative to Buy-and-Hold in terms of the Sharpe ratio is tested using the Ledoit and Wolf (2008) test.

We are also interested in how the strategies held up in the more recent period, in particular, the period between 1996 and 2017. The good news is that the returns or volatility do not differ significantly on the more recent subset pointing to stable performance of all described strategies. Furthermore, we see that all four strategies outperform Buy-and-Hold in terms of Sharpe ratio, with the grid search optimized strategy and the equally weighted strategy scoring the highest in this metric, 0.86 and 0.81, respectively. We also observe that the volatility and drawdowns of all proposed strategies are substantially lower than those of Buy-and-Hold. Between 1996 and 2017, Buy-and-Hold incurred a maximum drawdown of 55.20% with an annual volatility of 19.24%. In contrast, the maximum drawdowns of our strategies range between 8.64% and 14.23%, which is less than one third of that of Buy-and-Hold. As we previously mentioned, we worried that ensemble optimization algorithms may suffer from the capital underutilization problem, and resulting underperformance in terms of returns. We do not actually observe this phenomenon when we look at the equal weight and mean–variance optimized strategy. All three strategies offer similar returns, ranging between 6.98% and

8.38% annually, and trail the annualized return of Buy-and-Hold, which was 8.82%. Aside from returns and volatilities, there are a few important metrics all money managers should consider when making decisions for their clients. Time under water, for example, measures how quickly a strategy recovers from its largest drawdown. It took Buy-and-Hold more than 7 years to recover from its largest drawdown compared to less than 2 years for all our proposed strategies. Furthermore, allocators typically look for unique sources of returns, uncorrelated to general market moves, known as "alpha". A quick look at the performance of all our strategies shows that a significant portion of their returns is unrelated to the broad market. Annualized alphas of our strategies range between 3.17% and 4.03%, with the highest alpha occurring in our mean–variance optimized portfolio.

As impressive as these signal combinations may seem, they offer little value to practitioner's without addressing the issue of discovery bias. Welch and Goyal (2008) among others suggest that many market-timing predictor strategies fail to produce statistically significant outperformance after they have been discovered and documented. The explanations behind these phenomena usually fall into two categories: either the market priced in the new anomaly as soon as it became aware of its existence, or, the anomaly was sample specific and not present in subsequent time periods. To realistically estimate potential value of a seasonal and trend model, we have to account for this effect and evaluate strategies created on a real-time basis. By real time, we mean strategies only implement new anomalies after they have been discovered. Table 6 shows the performance metrics between 1976 and 2017. During the 1976–2017 time period, the maximum drawdowns of our real-time strategies range between 8.75% and 24.50%. All three real-time strategies offer similar returns, ranging between 9.13% and 11.52% annually, and trail the annualized return of Buy-and-Hold which was 11.51%. While returns of the real-time strategies are comparable to those constructed on entire signal history, we observe that these strategies tend to have higher volatility, which leads to lower Sharpe Ratios. Annualized alphas of our real-time strategies range between 2.82% and 3.32%, with the highest alpha occurring in our signal optimized portfolio.

Table 6. Performance statistics of all real-time combined strategies, 1976–2017.

	Equal Weight Real-time (RT)	Optimized RT (MV)	Optimized RT (Signal)	Buy-and-Hold
CAGR [%]	11.52	10.54	9.13	11.51
Total Return [%]	9692.55	6660.51	3826.87	9627.54
Volatility [% Ann.]	10.32	10.43	5.19	17.17
Sharpe	0.65***	0.55**	0.85***	0.39
Return/Risk	1.12	1.01	1.76	0.67
maxDrawdown [%]	18.85	24.5	8.75	55.2
Time Under Water [days]	495	734	312	1805
CAPM [alpha] [% Ann.]	3.32	2.82	2.91	
CAPM [beta]	0.46	0.42	0.19	
Alpha/Drawdown	0.18	0.11	0.33	
Drawdown/Volatility	1.83	2.35	1.69	3.21

Note: *, **, and *** denote significance at the levels of 10%, 5%, and 1%, respectively. Optimized (MV) stands for mean–variance optimized, and Optimized (Signal) denotes portfolio of grid search optimized signals. The statistical significance of performance difference relative to Buy-and-Hold in terms of the Sharpe ratio is tested using the Ledoit and Wolf (2008) test.

However, both the alpha and drawdowns are sensitive to scaling. If we want to comment on which strategy offers the most potent source of information, we need to introduce some new, scaled, metrics or scale all combined strategies to the same level of volatility. We introduce two such metrics: alpha-to-drawdown ratio and volatility-adjusted drawdown. Alpha-to-drawdown ratio helps investors understand the relative cost of any excess alpha. For example, if a strategy offers 3% alpha with a 10% max drawdown, it would be hard to argue that an investor should pick a strategy with 3.3% alpha and 20% maximum drawdown. Similarly, not all volatility is bad, but investors may want to know how a strategy's volatility relates to its maximum drawdown. Dividing maximum drawdown by volatility makes the relationship obvious and comparison of strategies simple. Even though three combined strategies outperform Buy-and-Hold, the grid search optimized real-time strategy (Optimized RT (Signal)) offers the best trade-off between alpha, drawdown, and volatility. We will continue the rest of this chapter by referring to it as the Seasonal Anomaly and Trend Model.

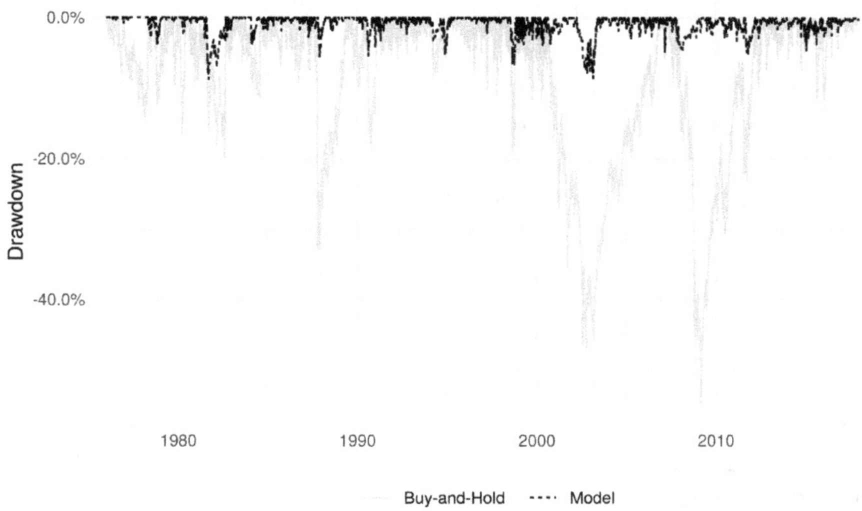

Fig. 11. Drawdowns from peak equity attained of the optimized portfolio of the four strategies vs. Buy-and-Hold, 1976–2017.

4.3.5. *Drawdown analysis*

One of the main incentives to adopt market timing is its perceived ability to be able to reduce the large drawdowns that occur around market crashes. In Fig. 11, we compare the drawdowns of our combined strategy to those of the Buy-and-Hold strategy. It is useful to keep in mind that a portion of our model contains a trend following strategy. Therefore, we expect to see the beginnings of strategy drawdowns coincide with some of the market drawdowns, but overall suffer less drastic losses and recover much faster. We observe precisely this pattern in 2002, 2007, and 2011. We see that all drawdowns are limited to less than 10% even during times when the market lost about 49% and 55%, in 2002 and 2007. The largest drawdown actually occurs during 1981-08-12–1982-09-03 period and is equal to −8.75%.

5. Combining SATM with Other Strategies

In this section, we revisit the results of Hull *et al.* (2017) and Hull and Qiao (2017) and compare a combination of their 6-month ERP model and 1-month ERP model to the SATM strategy. In addition, we also discuss overlaying the SATM strategy on top of two popular investment approaches: factor investing, represented by a Fama–French portfolio formed on small stocks with high book-to-market ratio (Small-Value (SV)), and risk parity (RP), represented by the Salient Risk Parity index. We discuss potential diversification benefits and increases in model confidence resulting from combining different models into a trading system. Table 7 offers insights into the potential value of combining the SATM with all aforementioned approaches.

SATM's Sharpe ratio for the 2003–2017 period is 1.07, which is comparable to that of the combination of 6-month model and 1-month model (1.19). However, SATM has a much longer backtest, giving us more confidence in its performance, and its signals only moderately correlated with the other two market-timing models. These two facts make a strong argument why all three models should be combined into one market-timing strategy. The longer backtest is important, because the previous two models suffered from having relatively short out-of-sample periods which coincided with the most opportune time to be a market timer. However, the SATM model survives a number of major market rallies further supporting the hypothesis that the Buy-and-Hold strategy can be enhanced by including additional market information. Unlike most macro and fundamental market-timing strategies which tend to be contrarian in nature, the seasonal effects in SATM are market cycle-independent, and the momentum component of SATM trends with the market. As a result, the SATM model performs relatively well in market rallies and has moderate correlations with other market-timing models. As we can see, SATM could also be a useful tool for investors who are not pursuing other market-timing strategies. By combining SATM with the SV strategy resulted in additional % of annual alpha during 2003–2017. Similarly, combining SATM with the Risk Parity strategy resulted in additional % of annual alpha during 2003–2017. These estimates are not as precise as our discussion of combination of the market-timing strategies since we do not have detailed information about costs and exposures of the SV and RP strategies. Nevertheless,

Table 7. Performance statistics (2003–2017) for combination of market-timing strategies.

	SATM	(1M+6M)/2	(1M+6M)/2 + 0.5*SATM	SV	SV + 0.5*SATM	RP	RP + 0.5*SATM	Buy-and-Hold
CAGR [%]	6.45	15.25	18.07	13.04	16.3	7.91	11.3	10.3
Total Return [%]	151.36	710.4	1055.99	508.77	825.63	207.16	384.26	324.27
Volatility [% Ann.]	4.88	11.69	13.26	23.68	25.08	8.71	9.76	18.16
Sharpe	1.07***	1.19***	1.26***	0.5	0.6	0.77	1.03*	0.5
Return/Risk	1.32	1.3	1.36	0.55	0.65	0.91	1.16	0.57
maxDrawdown [%]	5.17	14.33	14.84	65.8	64.8	30.64	29.63	55.2
Time Under Water [days]	312	329	327	968	727	842	602	1411
CAPM [alpha] [%Ann.]	3.58	9.73	11.52	2.08	4.44	4.61	6.97	
CAPM [beta]	0.16	0.39	0.47	1.15	1.23	0.22	0.3	

Note: *, **, and *** denote significance at the levels of 10%, 5%, and 1%, respectively. First column shows performance of SATM model. The second column shows an equally weighted combination of the 6-month and 1-month model. The third columns adds a SATM overlay ($0.5\times$SATM signal) to this combination. Columns four and five compare a Small/Value strategy with a Small/Value strategy overlaid with the SATM signal. Columns six and seven compare a Risk Parity strategy with a Risk Parity strategy overlaid with the SATM signal. Last column shows the performance of Buy-and-Hold. The significance of outperformance relative to Buy-and-Hold in terms of the Sharpe ratio is tested using the Ledoit and Wolf (2008) test.

Table 8. Correlations of the three market-timing strategies for 2003–2017.

	SATM	6M	1M	SV	RP
SATM	1.00	0.31	0.62	0.54	0.31
6M	0.31	1.00	0.44	0.34	0.17
1M	0.62	0.44	1.00	0.63	0.32
SV	0.54	0.34	0.63	1.00	0.41
RP	0.31	0.17	0.32	0.41	1.00

we mention them to illustrate value of diversification on a broader set of investment strategies.

Table 8 shows correlations of all strategy signals. The correlation between SATM and the 6-month model is 31% and the correlation between SATM and the monthly model is 62%. SATM also shows a low correlation to the Small Value and to the Risk Parity strategy (54% and 31%, respectively). The optimal allocation of an investor's wealth into all these strategies is beyond the scope of this chapter and we may revisit the issue in a future publication.

5.1. *Performance of the combined signal*

Since we do have detailed information about the two market-timing strategies, for the purpose of further analysis, we simply add an SATM overlay to an equally weighted combination of the two trading signals, which we refer to as the combined strategy for the remainder of the chapter. The combination is evaluated in Table 7.

Figure 12 shows the wealth accumulation of the combined strategy relative to Buy-and-Hold. The outperformance is not economically significant in the bull market of the early 2000s but becomes more pronounced in the volatile period during the Global Financial Crisis (GFC) and in the jittery markets of 2011–2012. A closer look at the strategy's performance throughout the time can be seen in Fig. 13. We look at the 1-year rolling outperformance of our SATM strategy and our combined strategy between 2003 and 2017. In addition to wanting to limit their drawdowns, investors prefer strategies that offer relatively stable outperformance as opposed to only performing

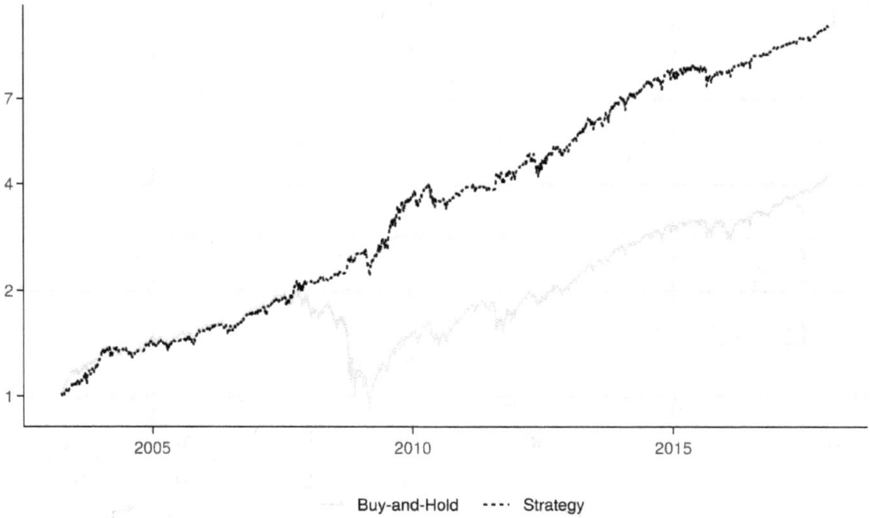

Fig. 12. Wealth accumulation of the combined strategy. Note that y-axis has a logarithmic scale.

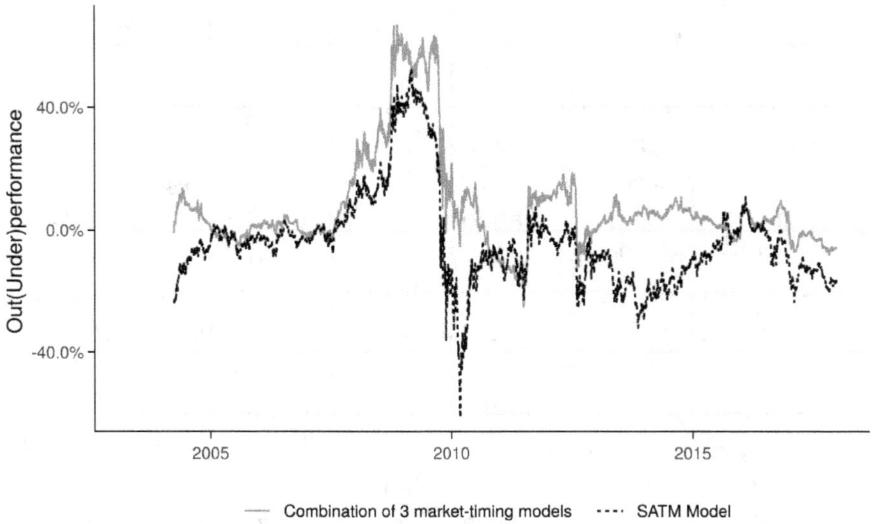

Fig. 13. One-year rolling out (under) performance.

well in certain regimes or scenarios. We observe that the combined strategy offers much more consistent performance and balances out the underperformance of the SATM model in 2010–2011.

6. Conclusions

This chapter differs from previous market-timing models of Hull and Qiao (2017) and Hull *et al.* (2017) in the sense that it does not forecast future equity risk premia but uses a deterministic trading system to utilize various market anomalies to enhance investor returns. However, similar to previous work on market timing, this chapter addresses issues with signal robustness and walk-forward analysis. We do not claim to have found and exploited all useful market anomalies, but we do offer readers a quick guide to test and implement their own research ideas. More importantly, we demonstrate their post-discovery robustness by building a real-time seasonal and trend strategy.

One elegant feature of a strategy that only invests in S&P 500 index instruments is that it does not require investment into illiquid instruments, or instruments with high short costs or management fees which reduces implementation cost and liquidity risks. We believe the continued stigma associated with market timing reduces the risk of the strategy becoming a crowded trade. A simple strategy which combines all three models almost triples the Sharpe ratio of Buy-and-Hold between 2003 and 2017. The combined strategy produces a Sharpe ratio of 1.26, with annualized returns of 18.07%, 13.26% volatility, and maximum drawdown of 14.71%. Even the SATM strategy by itself offers attractive performance. It produces 9.13% annualized returns with 5.19% volatility and resulting Sharpe ratio of 0.85 between 1976 and 2017, thus exceeding the Sharpe ratio of Buy-and-Hold for the same period by more than 100%.

As we continue to expand the debate on economic benefits of combining various market-timing strategies, we open a Pandora's Box of issues ranging from different signal histories, through frequencies, and model types. So far, with the exception of discussing the differences in weights recommended by a mean–variance portfolio optimization algorithm and by a grid search algorithm, we largely avoided talking about optimal ways of scaling and combining our strategies. We do not think this topic is inconsequential or unimaginative. Quite the contrary, we think this topic deserves a separate, well-thought-out discussion and we may address it in future research.

Also, this deviation away from ERP forecasting does not mean we have exhausted potential research into this area. This model demonstrates that excess returns can be captured by models with very short holding periods and we will continue to research and discuss additional short-term models. By discussing a multitude of approaches to market timing, we intend to help alleviate some of its stigma and encourage a discussion on this topic by a wider audience.

Acknowledgments

We would like to thank Alexios Galanos for contributing to the original research on this model and John Blin, Rick Anderson, Jim Lodas, Bill Swan, Dirk Eddelbuettel, and Xiao Qiao for helpful comments. The views expressed are those of the individual authors and do not necessarily reflect official positions of Hull Tactical. All errors are our own.

References

Ariel, R. A. (1990). "High stock returns before holidays: Existence and evidence on possible causes. *The Journal of Finance* **45**(5), 1611–1626.

Asness, C., Frazzini, A., Israel, R., and Moskowitz, T. (2014). Fact, fiction, and momentum investing. *Journal of Portfolio Management* **40**(5), 75.

Azar, P. D. and Lo, A. W. (2016). The wisdom of Twitter crowds: Predicting stock market reactions to FOMC meetings via Twitter feeds. *Journal of Portfolio Management* **42**(5), 123.

Bernanke, B. S. and Kuttner, K. N. (2003). What Explains the Stock Market's Reaction to Federal Reserve Policy? SSRN Scholarly Paper ID 890610.

Bouman, S. and Jacobsen, B. (2002). The Halloween indicator, "Sell in May and Go Away": Another puzzle. *The American Economic Review* **92**(5), 1618–1635.

Chan, K. F. and Marsh, T. (2017). Sell-in-May in Pre-Election Years, Market Premiums and Political Uncertainty: Two Centuries of Evidence. SSRN Scholarly Paper, No. ID 2903067 (October).

Chen, H. and Singal, V. (2003). Role of speculative short sales in price formation: The case of the weekend effect. *The Journal of Finance* **58**(2), 685–705.

Cochrane, J. H. (2008). The dog that did not bark: A defense of return predictability. *The Review of Financial Studies* **21**(4), 1533–1575.

Cootner, P. H. (1962). *Stock Prices: Random Vs. Systematic Changes.* Industrial Management Review **3**(2), 24–45.

Cross, F. (1973). The behavior of stock prices on fridays and mondays. *Financial Analysts Journal* **29**(6), 67–69.

Dimson, E. (1988). *Stock Market Anomalies.* Cambridge: Cambridge University Press.

Doeswijk, R. Q. (2008). The optimism cycle: sell in May. *De Economist* **156**(2), 175.

Etula, E., Rinne, K., Suominen, M., and Vaittinen, L. (2017). Dash for Cash: Monthly Market Impact of Institutional Liquidity Needs." SSRN Scholarly Paper ID No. 2528692.

Faber, M. T. (2007). A quantitative approach to tactical asset allocation. *The Journal of Wealth Management* **9**.

Fugazza, C., Guidolin, M., and Nicodano, G. (2015). Equally weighted vs. long-run optimal portfolios. *European Financial Management* **21**(4), 742–789.

Haug, M. and Hirschey, M. (2006). The January effect. *Financial Analysts Journal* **62**(5), 78–88.

Hensel, C. and Ziemba, W. (1996). Investment results from exploiting turn-of-the-month effects. *Journal of Portfolio Management* **22**, 17–23.

Huang, D., Jiang, F., Tu, J., and Zhou, G. (2017). Forecasting Stock Returns in Good and Bad Times: The Role of Market States. SSRN Scholarly Paper ID 2188989.

Hull, B. and Qiao, X. (2017). A practitioner's defense of return predictability. *The Journal of Portfolio Management* **43**(3), 60–76.

Hull, B., Qiao, X., and Bakosova, P. (2017). Return Predictability and Market-Timing: A One-Month Model. SSRN Scholarly Paper ID 3050254.

Jacobs, B. I. and Levy, K. N. (1988). Calendar anomalies: Abnormal returns at calendar turning points. *Financial Analysts Journal* **44**(6), 28–39.

Jacobsen, B. and Visaltanachoti, N. (2009). The Halloween effect in U.S. sectors. *Financial Review* **44**(3), 437–459.

Jacobsen, B. and Zhang, C. Y. (2014). The Halloween Indicator, "Sell in May and Go Away": An Even Bigger Puzzle. ID 2154873.

Jegadeesh, N. and Titman, S. (1993). Returns to buying winners and selling losers: Implications for stock market efficiency. *The Journal of Finance* **48**(1), 65–91.

Kurov, A., Sancetta, A., Strasser, G. H., and Halova Wolfe, M. (2015). Price Drift Before U.S. Macroeconomic News: Private Information About Public Announcements? **881**.

Lakonishok, J. and Smidt, S. (1988). Are seasonal anomalies real? A ninety-year perspective. *The Review of Financial Studies* **1**(4), 403–425.

Ledoit, O. and M. Wolf 2008. Robust performance hypothesis testing with the Sharpe ratio. *Journal of Empirical Finance* **15**(5), 850–859.

Lucca, D. O. and Moench, E. (2015). The pre-FOMC announcement drift. *The Journal of Finance* **70**(1), 329–371.

Maberly, E. D. and Pierce, R. M. (2004). Stock market efficiency withstands another challenge: Solving the "Sell in May/Buy After Halloween" puzzle. *Econ Journal Watch* **1**(1), 29–46.

Markowitz, H. (1952). Portfolio selection. *The Journal of Finance* **7**(1), 77–91.

McConnell, J. J. and Xu, W. (2008). Equity returns at the turn of the month. *Financial Analysts Journal* **64**(2), 49–64.

Moskowitz, T. J., Ooi, Y. H., and Pedersen, L. H. (2012). Time series momentum. *Journal of Financial Economics* **104**(2), 228–250.

Neely, C. J., Rapach, D. E., Tu, J., and Zhou, G. (2014). Forecasting the equity risk premium: The role of technical indicators. *Management Science* **60**(7), 1772–1791.

Novy-Marx, R. (2016). "Testing Strategies Based on Multiple Signals." Simon Graduate School of Business, University of Rochester; available at http://rnm.simon.rochester.edu/research/MSES.pdf.

Ogden, J. P. (1990). Turn-of-month evaluations of liquid profits and stock returns: A common explanation for the monthly and January effects. *The Journal of Finance* **45**(4), 1259–1272.

Penman, S. H. (1987). The distribution of earnings news over time and seasonalities in aggregate stock returns. *Journal of Financial Economics* **18**(2), 199–228.

Swinkels, L. and Vliet, P. V. (2012). An anatomy of calendar effects. *Journal of Asset Management* **13**(4), 271–286.

Thaler, R. H. (1987). Anomalies: Weekend, holiday, turn of the month, and intraday effects. *Journal of Economic Perspectives* **1**(2), 169–177.

Wachtel, S. B. (1942). Certain observations on seasonal movements in stock prices. *The Journal of Business* **15**, 184–193.

Welch, I. and Goyal, A. (2008). A comprehensive look at the empirical performance of equity premium prediction. *The Review of Financial Studies* **21**(4), 1455–1508.

Ziemba, W. T. (2012). *Calendar Anomalies and Arbitrage.* World Scientific Books. World Scientific Publishing Co. Pte. Ltd.

Zhang, C. Y. and Jacobsen, B. (2017). Are monthly seasonals real? A three century perspective. Review of Finance **17**(5), 1743–1785

https://doi.org/10.1142/9789811222634_0014

Chapter 14

Sebastien Lleo and William T Ziemba

Stock Market Crashes in 2006–2009: Were We Able to Predict Them?[1,*]

We investigate the stock market crashes in China, Iceland, and the US in the 2006-2009 period based on the results in Lleo and Ziemba (2012). The bond stock earnings yield difference model is used as a prediction tool. Historically, when the measure is too high, meaning that long bond interest rates are too high relative to the trailing earnings over price ratio, then there usually is a crash of 10% or more within four to twelve months. The model did in fact predict all three crashes. Iceland had a drop of fully 95%, China fell by two thirds and the US by 57%.

Background

The second author started using the bond stock earnings yield model while in Tokyo consulting at the Yamaichi Research Institute in 1988 and early results are in Ziemba and Schwartz (1991). Later studies are Ziemba (2003) which discusses, in particular, the internet bubble crash of 2000-2002, Koivu, Pennanen and Ziemba (2005) which discusses co-integration of the crash measure and the stock markets in Germany, UK and the US and Lleo and Ziemba (2012) which discusses the 2006-2009 crashes in China, Iceland and the US. The model relates the yield on stocks (measured by the ratio of earnings to stock prices) to the yield on nominal Treasury

[1]Edited from *Wilmott*, November 2009.

*This article originally appeared in *Investment in the Modern Age,* Chapter 21, by R. E. Ziemba and W. T. Ziemba (2013), World Scientific Series in Finance: Volume 6, pp. 257–287, World Scientific: Singapore.

bonds. The theory behind the model is that an optimal asset allocation between stocks and bonds is related to their relative yields and when the bond yield is too high, a market adjustment is needed and there is a shift out of stocks into bonds. If the adjustment is large, it causes an equity market correction (a decline of 10% within one year). Hence, there is a short term negative equity risk premium (ERP). A study of the October 1987 stock market crash illustrated the model and it was from this episode that the model was discovered in Ziemba's crash study group. Table 21.1 and Figure 21.1 show that the model went into the danger zone, that is the measure was above an upper confidence limit, in April 1987 with a spread of 3.39. The S&P500 was then at 289.32. By the end of September the S&P500 was at 318.66 with the measure higher at 4.14. After the crash at the end of October, the S&P500 had fallen to 245.01 with the spread falling out of the danger zone to 1.64. Table 21.1 has beginning of months values. Continuous daily values are in Figure 21.1 and one sees a sharp move up in the measure to 4.42, in September 1987 way above the upper limit .

Fig. 21.1 Bond and stock price earnings yield differential model for the S&P500, 1980-1990, Source: Ziemba and Schwartz, 1991

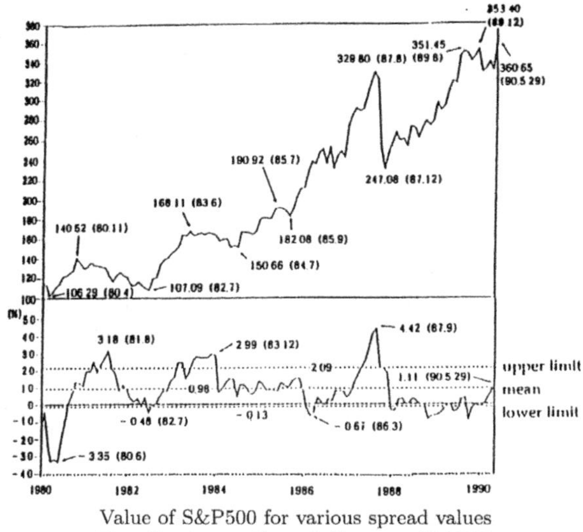

Value of S&P500 for various spread values		
Date/level	Spread, %	S&P500
May 29, 1990	1.11	360.65
Mean	0.98	355.00
Upper limit	2.09	415.00
Lower limit	-0.13	309.00

There are various ways that one can compute the upper and lower limits but my experience is that with the various approaches, all of which use out of sample prior data, one usually has the same conclusion. In Figure 21.1, the limits are simply the

Table 21.1: S&P500 index, PE ratios, government bond yields and the yield premium over stocks, January 1984 to August 1988. Source: Ziemba and Schwartz (1991)

		S&P Index	PER	(a) 30 Yr G bd	(b) 1/pe,%	(a)-(b)
1986	Jan	208.19	14.63	9.32	6.84	2.48
	Feb	219.37	15.67	8.28	6.38	1.90
	Mar	232.33	16.50	7.59	6.06	1.53
	Apr	237.98	16.27	7.58	6.15	1.43
	May	238.46	17.03	7.76	5.87	1.89
	Jun	245.30	17.32	7.27	5.77	1.50
	Jul	240.18	16.31	7.42	6.13	1.29
	Aug	245.00	17.47	7.26	5.72	1.54
	Sep	238.27	15.98	7.64	6.26	1.38
	Oct	237.36	16.85	7.61	5.93	1.68
	Nov	245.09	16.99	7.40	5.89	1.51
	Dec	248.60	16.72	7.33	5.98	1.35
1987	Jan	264.51	15.42	7.47	6.49	0.98
	Feb	280.93	15.98	7.46	6.26	1.20
	Mar	292.47	16.41	7.65	6.09	1.56
	Apr	289.32	16.22	9.56	6.17	3.39
	May	289.12	16.32	8.63	6.13	2.50
	Jun	301.38	17.10	8.40	5.85	2.55
	Jul	310.09	17.92	8.89	5.58	3.31
	Aug	329.36	18.55	9.17	5.39	3.78
	Sep	318.66	18.10	9.66	5.52	4.14
	Oct	280.16	14.16	9.03	7.06	1.97
	Nov	245.01	13.78	8.90	7.26	1.64
	Dec	240.96	13.55	9.10	7.38	1.72
1988	Jan	250.48	12.81	8.40	7.81	0.59
	Feb	258.10	13.02	8.33	7.68	0.65
	Mar	265.74	13.42	8.74	7.45	1.29
	Apr	262.61	13.24	9.10	7.55	1.55
	May	256.20	12.92	9.24	7.74	1.50
	Jun	270.68	13.65	8.85	7.33	1.52
	Jul	269.44	13.59	9.18	7.36	1.82
	Aug	263.73	13.30	9.30	7.52	1.78

trailing mean plus or minus a standard deviation measure so the one sided limits hold 95% of the probability.[2]

[2]Using a different index rather than the S&P500 has the same conclusion but slightly different results. Berge, Consigli and Ziemba (2008) used the MSCI index. The danger zone was entered in May 1987 and the correction occurred in October, four months later. During June, July and August investors kept rebalancing their portfolios from the bond to the equity market (MSCI TRI + 13.87% over the quarter) then the equity market fell 31.80% in the following quarter (September to November 1987) with the major decline in October.

Moving Average and Signal Chart

In the following sections[3] we use a moving average and a rolling horizon standard deviation to establish the confidence levels. The h-day moving average at time t, denoted by μ_t^h, and the corresponding rolling horizon standard deviation σ_t^h are

$$\mu_t^h = \frac{1}{h}\sum_{i=1}^{h} x_{t-i}$$

$$\sigma_t^h = \sqrt{\frac{1}{h}\sum_{i=1}^{h}(x_{t-i} - \mu_t^h)^2}$$

Using rolling horizon means and standard deviations provide data consistency. This is used to compute confidence levels for the BSEYD measure. In particular, rolling horizon mean and standard deviation are not overly sensitive to the starting date of the bond yield or stock market data, or to the overall number of data points. However, the choice of the horizon parameter h is subjective.

For the analysis of the US market, we use a five year horizon, so $h = 1260$ as longer time horizons tend to generate a robust signal and eliminate false positives. Five years of historical bond and stocks data may be a difficult requirement outside of major markets. For Iceland and China, a one year rolling horizon was used with the confidence level tightened in order to eliminate false positives.

The figures show the signal calculated, respectively, on a standard one-tail 95% normal distribution based confidence level and on an application of Cantelli's inequality for arbitrary non-normally distributed returns. The conclusions are similar: over the period January 1, 1995 to October 19, 2011, two crash signals occurred: one in June 1999 and the other in June 2007 (as discussed below).
An examination of the BSEYD spread distributions reveals their non-Normal nature (see Figures 21, 21, 21.11 and 21.18). As a result, standard confidence intervals which are based on a Gaussian assumption may prove inaccurate. In this case, we use Cantelli's inequality, a one-tailed version of Chebyshev's inequality, to derive a 'worst case' confidence level (see, for example, Problem 7.11.9 in Grimmett and Stirzaker, 2001).

Cantelli's inequality relates the probability that the distance between a random variable X and its mean μ exceeds a number $k > 0$ of standard deviations σ to this distance

$$P\left[X - \mu \geq k\sigma\right] \leq \frac{1}{1 + k^2}$$

[3]The rest of this chapter is a summary of the results in Lleo and Ziemba (2012).

or alternatively

$$P\left[X - \mu \geq \sigma\sqrt{\frac{1}{\alpha} - 1}\right] \leq \alpha$$

where $\alpha = \frac{1}{1+k^2}$. The parameter α provides an upper bound for a one-tailed confidence level on any distribution, regardless of how different it is from a Normal distribution.

We use Cantelli's inequality with a one-tail confidence level to assess the relative strength of a signal. Using the one-tail confidence level, we obtain the crash signal. We then find the Cantelli probability α giving us a similar signal date. To generate the same signal as a standard 95% confidence level, we need to select $\alpha = 27\%$ in Cantelli's inequality. Similarly, to generate the same signal as a standard 99% confidence level, we need to select $\alpha = 15.60\%$

In the case of China, as discussed below, we used a standard 99% confidence level to determine the signal. Based on Cantelli's inequality, we expect in the worst case to have a crash signal 15.60% of the time. Retrospectively, Cantelli's inequality is rather severe since it places the threshold for a signal at a BSEYD spread of 3% or above, on 520 consecutive trading days from September 9, 2007 to February 2, 2009 out of the 2099 days (i.e. 24.77% of days) where this measure was computed. By contrast, if we consider the distribution over the entire period, we observe that the spread only exceeded 2.52% on 0.03% of all instances. To conclude, a standard 99% confidence level would have been sufficient to determine a clear crash signal.

In the case of Iceland, we use a 95% confidence level to determine the signal, Cantelli's inequality suggests a worst case probability that 27% of observations could result in a signal. However, lowering the Cantelli probability α from 27% to 20% (corresponding roughly to a standard 97.7% confidence level) does not result in significant loss of responsiveness of the signal, at least for Glitnir and Kaupthing (see Figures 21.13b,d).

The idea behind the BSEYD model is that a crash signal should occur whenever

$$BSEYD(t) > CL(t)$$

where $CL(t)$ represents a one-tail confidence level. The level CL acts as a time-varying threshold for the crash signal.

There is a crash signal whenever

$$SIGNAL(t) = BSEYD(t) - CL(t) > 0.$$

Graphically, the threshold for the crash signal is a horizontal line with value 0, as shown below in Figures 21.5(b), 21.6(b), 21 and 21.13. These graphs show a calculation of $SIGNAL(t)$ based respectively on a standard one-tail 95% confidence level and on an application of Cantelli's inequality.

Lleo and Ziemba (2013) give an historical account of his use of this model from 1988 to 2012 in the US, Japan and other countries. In Japan, the signal was in the danger zone twelve times from 1948 to 1988 and each time the Nikkei Stock Average index fell at least 10% from the level when the signal was reached. During this forty year period, the index had twenty such falls of which eight occurred for reasons other than high interest rates relative to earnings. The BSEYD model also predicted the -56% crash that started in January 1990 with a signal further in the danger zone than at any time since 1948.

The Fed model, which is the ratio not the difference like the original BSEYD model, is mathematically equivalent to the BSEYD model, as now shown.

The Fed model in its original 1996 form states the dependence of a fair stock price level $\tilde{p}(t)$ at time t to the expected earnings, $E(t)$, and the most liquid (10- or 30-year) Treasury bond rate $r(t)$. Earnings expectations are incorporated in prices and discounted via

$$\tilde{p}(t) = \frac{E(t)}{r(t)}, t = 1, 2, \ldots. \tag{21.1}$$

Equity earnings per share $\gamma(t)$ is the expected earnings for a unit investment in the stock market with equity shares, $S(t)$, namely

$$\gamma(t) = \frac{E(t)}{S(t)}. \tag{21.2}$$

Then

$$S(t) = \frac{E(t)}{\gamma(t)}.$$

There is a direct relationship between the equity yield in Equation (21.2) and the long bond rate in Equation (21.1) . The ratio of the current market value to the theoretical value is the Fed model bond stock yield ratio BSYR(t)

$$\frac{S(t)}{\tilde{p}(t)} = \frac{E(t)/\gamma(t)}{E(t)/r(t)} = \frac{r(t)}{\gamma(t)} = BSYR(t). \tag{21.3}$$

The bond stock earnings yield differential that we focus on in this paper is related to the valuation measure and the equity yield via

$$\frac{S(t)}{\tilde{p}(t)} - 1 = \frac{BSEYD(t)}{\gamma(t)}$$

$$BSEYD(t) = [BSYR(t) - 1]\gamma(t).$$

The differential reflects the difference between the current market value and its theoretical value. A more theoretically sound motivation for the predictive ability of the BSEYD is using the basic Gordon formula, where EP is the forward earnings yield (which Schwartz and Ziemba (2000) show is the best predictor of at least individual Japanese stock prices),

E/P - nominal yield = equity risk premium - real growth - inflation.

So the BSEYD can be used as a proxy for the unobservable right hand side economic variables.

For given equity yield the BSEYD and the BSYR can be used to identify zones of under and over valuation and forecast possible forthcoming market adjustments.

Koivu, Pennanen and Ziemba (2005) study the Fed model using a dynamic vector equilibrium correction model with data from 1980 to 2003 in the US, UK and Germany and show that the Fed model had predictive power in forecasting equity prices, earnings and bond yields. The model has been successful in predicting market turns, but in spite of its empirical success and simplicity, the model has been justifiabily criticized. First it does not consider the role played by time varying risk premiums in the portfolio selection process while it does consider a risk free government interest rate as the discount factor of future earnings. More seriously, the inflation illusion (the possible impact of inflation expectations on the stock market) as suggested by Modigliani and Cohn (1979) is not taken into consideration. Secondly, the model assumes the comparability of earning price ratios, a real quantity, with a nominal, bond induced, interest rate [Campbell and Vuolteenaho (2004), Asness (2000, 2003), and Ritter and Warr (2002) discuss these issues.] Consigli, MacLean, Zhao and Ziemba (2009) propose a stochastic model of equity returns based on an extension of the model inclusive of a risk premium in which market corrections are endogenously generated by the bond-stock yield difference. The model accommodates both cases of prolonged yield deviations leading to a long series of small declines in the equity market and the case, peculiar of recent speculative bubbles, of a series of corrections over limited time periods. The inclusion of the yield differential as a key driver of the market correction process is tested and the model is validated with market data.

Many of the critics focus on: 1) short term predicability that we know is weak as does Giot and Petitjean (2008), 2) simply do not focus on the long run value of the measure, or 3) dismiss it outright because of the nominal versus real minor flaw as does Montier (2011). Consigli, MacLean, Zhao and Ziemba (2009) use the model to estimate the current fair value of the S&P500. Of course, market and fair value can diverge for long periods. However, our concern is whether or not the model actually predicts stock market crashes, stock market rallies and good times to be in and out of stock markets. Berge, Consigli and Ziemba (2008) discuss the latter issue and found for five countries (US, Germany, Canada, UK and Japan) that the strategy stay in the market when it is not in the danger zone and move to cash otherwise provides about double the final wealth with less variance and a higher Sharpe ratio than a buy and hold strategy during 1975–2005 and 1980–2005. There is some limited predictability of stock market increases but the evidence supports the good use of the model to predict crashes. In this paper we study the period 2007–2009 for the US, China and Iceland, all of which had large crashes. Shiller (2006) observes, as we have in the past, that low PE periods seem to lead to higher future stock prices and high PE periods to lower future prices. But the evidence is that PE levels by themselves are not enough to call the crashes. The argument here is that it is usually the interplay of interest rates measured by the long bond with the PE ratios that gives the crash signal.

The Chinese Shanghai Stock Market Crash

Figure 21.2 shows the rise of the Shanghai stock index from January 2000 to June 2012. The market bottomed at 1011.50 on July 11, 2005. It then rose six-fold to peak at 6092.06 on October 16, 2007. Then there was a crash of 11.98% from 5180.51 to 4559.75 over the two day period January 21 and 22 followed by another 7.19% fall from 4761.69 to 4419.29 on January 28, 2008. Ultimately the index fell to 1706.70 on November 4, 2008 , a decline of over two thirds from the peak and 23.09% and 29.93% from the December 12 and 25, 2006 BSEYD danger signals at 2218.95 and 2435.76. Table 21.2 discusses highlights for the Shanghai index from 2005–12.

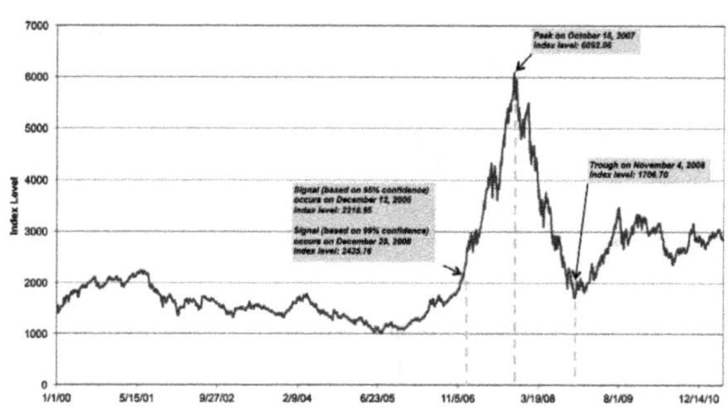

Fig. 21.2 The Shanghai stock exchange composite index, January 2000 to June 2012. Source: Lleo and Ziemba (2012)

Did the BSEYD model predict this crash? First, Figure 21 shows that the BSEYD measure is not normally distributed with fat right and even fatter left tails. The biggest declines are much larger than the biggest increases.

Figures 21.4(a) and 21.4(b) show that the model did in fact predict the crash. See also the signals hitting the danger level in Figures 21.5 and 21.6. It is a typical application of the model. The signal goes into the danger zone, then the market

Table 21.2: Highlights on the Shanghai Stock Index, 2005-2012. Source: Lleo and Ziemba (2012)

Date	Index Value	Comment
Dec 31, 2004	1266.50	
May 23, 2005	1070.84	The index was down 15.4% year-to-date
July 11, 2005	1011.50	Market bottom
Dec 31, 2005	1161.06	The index was down 8.3% in 2005
Dec 12, 2006	2218.95	95% confidence BSEYD crash signal occurs
Dec 25, 2006	2435.76	99% confidence BSEYD crash signal occurs
Dec 31, 2006	2675.47	The index was up 130.4% in 2006
May 29, 2007	4334.92	Local high of the market. The market was up 62% year-to-date
July 5, 2007	3615.87	Local low of the market. The market was still up 35.1% year-to-date
Oct 16, 2007	6092.06	Highest historical market close. The market was up 127.7% year-to-date
Nov 28, 2007	4803.39	Local low of the market. The market was still up 79.5%year-to-date
Dec 31, 2007	5261.56	Index was up 96.7% in 2007, but down 13.6% from its peak in October
Jan 14, 2008	5497.90	Local high of the market
Jan 18, 2008	5180.51	The index closes the week at 5180.51, which is 5.8% lower than than its local high on Jan 14
Jan 21, 2008	4914.43	The index experiences a one-day drop of 5.1% from 5180.51 to 4914.43
Jan 22, 2008	4559.75	The index experiences declines by 7.2% on this day, opening at 4914.43 to close at 4559.75
Jan 25, 2008	4761.69	The index recovers slightly to close the week at 4761.69
Jan 28, 2008	4419.29	The index drops by 7.2% from 4761.69 to 4419.29
Apr 18, 2008	3094.67	Local low of the market
May 5, 2008	3761.01	Local high of the market
Nov 4, 2008	1706.70	Global market minimum. The market was down by 72% peak to trough and 23.09% and 29.93% from the December 12 and 25 danger signal levels
Dec 31, 2008	1820.81	The market was down 65.4% in 2008
Aug 3, 2009	3471.44	Local high of the market. The market was up 103.4% from the trough
Aug 31, 2009	2667.75	Local low of the market
Nov 23, 2009	3338.66	Local high of the market
Dec 31, 2009	3277.14	The market was up 80% in 2009
Jul 5, 2010	2363.95	Local low of the market
Dec 31, 2010	2808.08	The market was down 14.3% in 2009
Jun 30, 2011	2762.08	The market was down about 1% year-to-date
August 31, 2011	2567.34	The market was down about 8.6% year-to-date
Sept 30, 2011	2359.22	The market was down about 16% year-to-date
Dec 31, 2011	2199.42	The market was down about 22% in 2011
June 30, 2012	2225.43	The market was up about 1% year-to-date

continues higher but within four to twelve months there is a crash of 10%+ from the value at the initial signal. In this case, the decline is much higher than 10%. Figure 21.4(a) uses a 95% confidence one sided moving average interval using prior data out of sample. The danger signal occurred on December 12, 2006, some ten months before the stock market peak on October 16, 2007 with the index at 6092.06. Figure 21.4(b) uses a 95% one sided confidence interval and gives the first danger signal on December 12, 2006 with the index at 2218.95. With a 99% one sided confidence interval, the danger signal was reached on December 25, 2006 with the index at 2435.76. The ultimate fall was to 1706.70 on November 4, 2008 about 30% below the index value of 2218.76 or 2435.76 of the crash signal. This signal and decline were a bit different than the usual case as it took almost two years to get the 10% plus crash and in the meantime the market almost tripled in value before the ultimate crash.

Figure 21.4 also illustrates the importance of the confidence level in relation to the rolling horizon of the moving average and the shape of the spread distribution. As pointed out in Section 2, a short time horizon of one year, combined with a lower

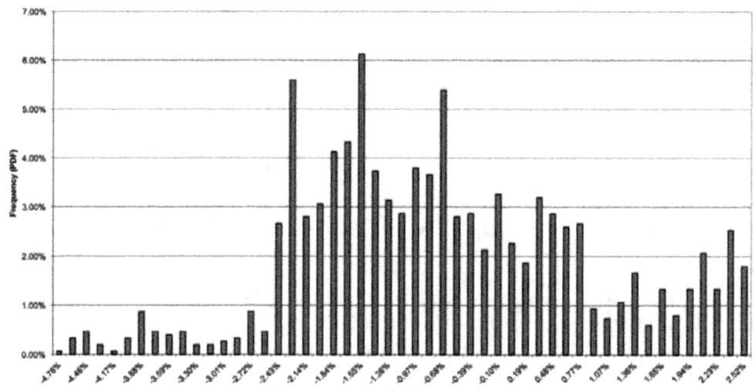

Fig. 21.3 Spread distribution of the BSEYD measure on the Shanghai Stock Exchange Composite. Source: Lleo and Ziemba (2012)

confidence level of 95% and the non-Gaussian nature of the spread distribution may result in false positives. An ex-post analysis reveals that the Gaussian-based 95% confidence spread for the Shanghai Stock Exchange Composite index over the entire period equals 1.78%. However, the actual 95% confidence level of the empirical distribution is 2.18%. In fact, a full 9.32% of all actual observations occur at or above 1.78%, a marked contrast from the 5% predicted by the Gaussian distribution. Raising the confidence level to 99% or increasing the rolling horizon does help reduce the impact of the shape of the distribution on the signal.

The Iceland stock market crash

Iceland is a small country with only about 300,000 people. From 2002 to 2007, the economy and asset prices rose dramatically with much leveraging of investments, especially by the banks. This led to high interest rates of about 10% long term and 16% short term. Eventually, it all collapsed in the wake of the 2007-2009 worldwide financial crisis. And the decline was a massive crash of -95% in the equity index and a currency collapse. The equity index, see Table 21.4, had 15 stocks in it with three of the banks having very high weighting: Kaupthing (26.5%), Landsbanki (13.0%) and Glitnir (12.3%) were more than half the market capitalization and Actavis Banki had 9.9%, and FL Banki another 6.7%. So the banks were close to two thirds of the index value. And index funds that tracked the market actually slightly over weight these banks to yield higher returns.

A brief discussion of Iceland

Both Iceland and China had gigantic stock price rises and falls which have a number of parallels with Japan in 1990. The difference though was that Iceland, like Ireland, had its economy essentially destroyed, while in China the impact was and will be

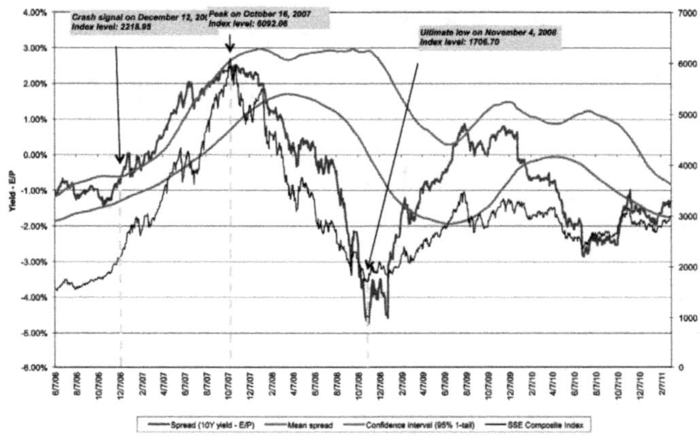

(a) First signal occurs on December 12, 2006. The market reaches its peak on October 16, 2007 and ultimate low on November 4, 2008 based on 95% confidence.

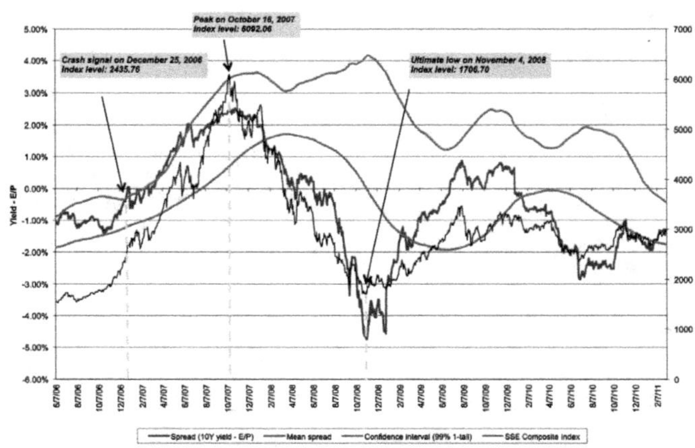

(b) First signal occurs December 25, 2006. The market reaches its peak on October 16, 2007 and ultimate low on November 4, 2008 based on 99% confidence.

Fig. 21.4 BSEYD danger signals for the Shanghai Stock Exchange Composite, 95% and 99% confidence. Source: Lleo and Ziemba (2012)

much less. The long term effects remain to be seen. We know Japan has yet to recover!

In the case of Iceland and Ireland (which, along with China, is discussed in Part III), the entire economy was levered way beyond its capacity to sustain ever higher real estate and stock prices with loans in foreign currency. Aliber (2008) describes it well and his prediction of trouble came to fruition. The Krona was rising until the crash because of its high interest rates and the apparent excess return from its

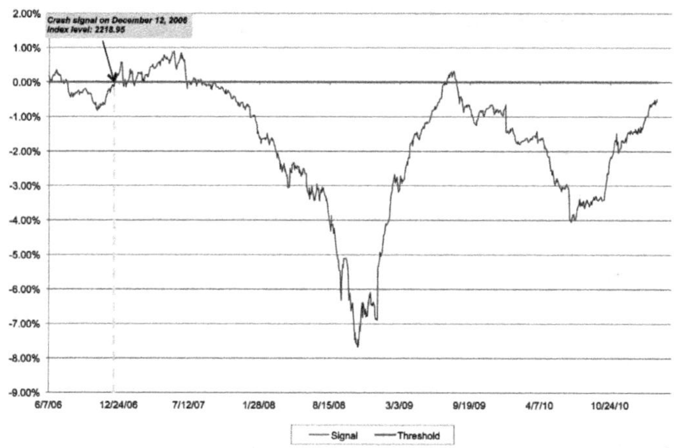

(a) Signal occurs on December 12, 2006 based on 95% confidence

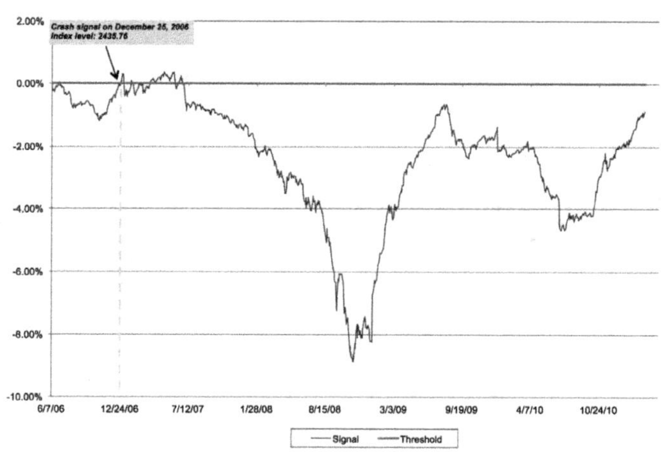

(b) Signal occurs on December 25, 2006 based on 99% confidence

Fig. 21.5 BSEYD danger signals for the Shanghai Stock Exchange Composite, Signals at 95% and 99% confidence. Source: Lleo and Ziemba (2012)

investment by locals and especially foreigners. In euro terms, it started 2008 at 90, was 130 on October 7, 2008 when the stock market was closed, then fell to 340 when trade was suspended, and then 290 in December 2008. The stock market fell 77% on October 14, 2008 after being closed since October 6th. Before the crisis, the market cap was 120% of GDP and only 20% after.

The Iceland crash occurred in October 2008. In Ziemba and Ziemba (2007) as of July 12, 2006 we had the results shown in Table 21.3 for the bond-stock model with the 16 non-financials in the danger zone but the 15 main stocks which focused on

(a) First signal occurs on December 25, 2006. The market reaches its peak on October 16, 2007.

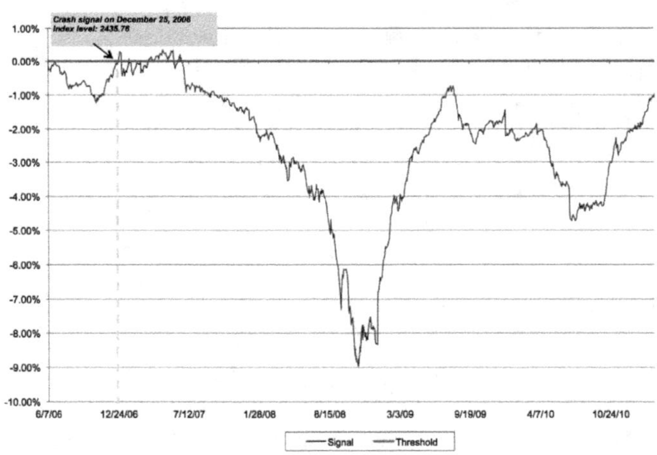

(b) Signal occurs on December 25, 2006 (based on Cantelli's inequality, α = 15%)

Fig. 21.6 BSEYD Cantelli danger signals for the Shanghai Stock Exchange Composite, Chart, Source: Lleo and Ziemba (2012)

the banks were not in the danger zone until 2008. The rate of increase of property prices was already dropping in mid 2006 but there were no losses yet with the property index up 4.8% in 2006. Short term interest rates, which were 13% in July 2006 were 14.25% in the fall of 2006 and went to 14.5% in December 2006, with projection to 16%.

Iceland was in a dangerous highly levered position. It was all predicated on a continual rise in the currency and asset prices with very high interest rates. They

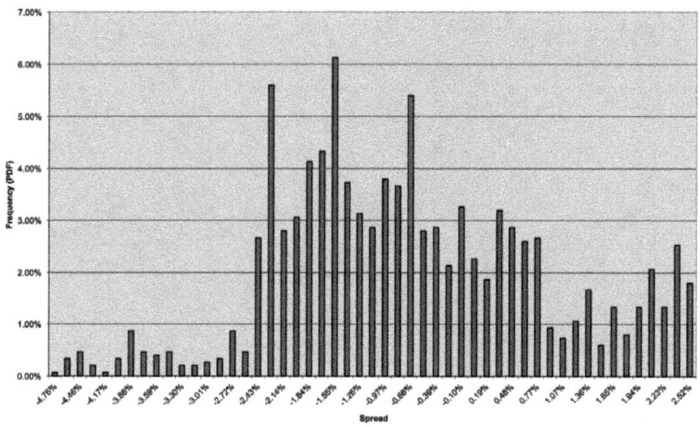

Fig. 21.7 Spread distribution of the BSEYD measure on the Shanghai Stock Exchange Composite using Cantelli inequality. Source: Lleo and Ziemba (2012)

Table 21.3: Bond-stock measure calculations in Iceland

index	16 nonfin	15 in index
A) PE ratio		11.1
B) Stock Return (1/A)	6.13%	9.01%
C) Bond Return (5 yr)	11.00%	9.4%
Crash Signal (C-B)	4.87%	0.39%

would have eventually had a decline, which might have been gradual, but the onslaught from the US and especially the UK economic troubles accelerated at the time of Lehman Brothers' bankruptcy putting the problem to a head. Then everyone rushed for the exits when the market was closed and there was the monumental 77% fall on October 15, 2008. Prices of the stocks and real estate had simply gotten way to high and all out of proportion to the real business of Iceland's companies. The economy was mostly financial services controlled by the big banks which made enormous profits to keep their PE ratios below the danger level but as profits declined and interest rates rose, the bond-stock model signaled the crash as did many other ways of looking at the economic health of the country. It was a highly over-levered hedge fund with Kelly bets way too high. Aliber (2008) argued that because of the skewed nature of Iceland's exports of goods and services - 50% fish related, and the small size of the domestic manufacturing sector, each increase of 1% of Iceland's exports led to a 1.2%+ increase in the krona exchange rate. The monies flowing in were borrowed in the wrong currencies - pound, euro, etc, not in krona, whose assumed continual rise would make it easier to pay off. So rather than matching currency loan to repayment, there was the added speculation in currencies. The same mistake was made by Thailand and other Asian countries in the 1997 currency crisis, borrowing in dollars rather than yen (again the low interest rate currency). There the dollar rose while in Iceland, the krona fell.

Household savings declined as a share of GDP and household consumption rose based on apparently higher household wealth in stock and real estate starting from the bottom of the US stock market in March 2003. The rapid real estate price boom led to a large increase in bank credit.

From 2002–2006 bank assets rose six-fold. In the same period, bank capital rose eight-fold mainly from gains on their stock holdings and the ratio of bank assets to the sum of demand and savings deposits rose from two to five (Aliber, 2008). New foreign currency debt was required to pay interest on the foreign loans. What was needed but never achieved was a trade surplus. Eventually the currency and stock and land markets had to collapse. There were many investors who had purchased Icelandic stocks with borrowed money that had a negative carry meaning that their interest payments were larger than their investment income. Some of these investors had to sell stock in the panic decline. Before the collapse Iceland had achieved the title of the happiest people on earth - they appeared to have good achieved the good life with lots of savings and assets but they ignored the toxic debt on which it was based. It was a classic overlevered, non diversified situation like the US and UK with high risk taking behavior; see Chapter 26 showing that this situation invariably leads to a crash. After this crash, it will be very painful to recover and be a low risk, low income country.

The Iceland financial crisis continues

The mouse that roared country of 316,000 people in a hikers and spa paradise seems to owe about $5.3 billion (3.9 billion euro) to some 400,000 Dutch and British investors for losses incurred by Icesave, the online branch of the Reykjavik bank Landsbanki. There is blame on both sides. The investors were greedy for the higher than market rates offered in Iceland which were encouraged by the Icelandic bank. Indeed, short term interest rates reached 16% in 2007/08. Landsbanki collapsed in October 2008. Of course, the depositors forgot that extra return usually has extra risk so the default is understandable.

While the Icelandic people consider themselves "proud people who wish to shoulder their obligations ...the commitments must be fair, reasonable and normal" according to Johanna Sigurdottir, the Icelandic prime minister. The British and Dutch governments have bailed out their greedy investors through each country's deposit guarantees and now want their money back. An issue is to lower the 5.5% interest rate. A referendum to pay some 48,000€ per Icelandic household (or over 10,000£ per person) was soundly rejected by over 90% of the people who voted. Since the deal would require each Icelander to pay about $135 per month for eight years (about 25% of an average four member family salary) it is clear the burden is too high and had to be rejected.

Iceland is part of Europe but not in the EU which they would like to join and they need the Dutch approval along with the other 26 member states. Since Iceland vows to pay up the result here likely is a bit lower settlement price. This is another example of the government bailing out Wall Street except the money will go to pay the losses not line the pockets of the Landsbanki executives as was done in the US. Fortunately, up to 90% of the money owed in collateralized through assets salvaged from Landsbanki. But Britain and the Netherlands want Iceland to provide a sovereign guarantee to pay any shortfall. Meanwhile, the world's future banker, China, is interested in emerging sea routes through the Arctic to shorten trade routes so this might help the Iceland economy, see Ward (2010). But Russia is keen to keep Iceland out of the EU as it regards Iceland as a fellow Arctic country.

The economic and political saga will continue. For more on Iceland as the crisis unfolded, see two chapters in Ziemba and Ziemba (2007). Ziemba and Ziemba looked into predicting this crash with the bond-stock model and when the book went to press in late 2007 the model was close but quite to the danger zone, but it got there in 2008 well before the actual collapse. Before the financial crisis of fall 2008 hit Iceland the stock market capitalization was about 120% of the country's GDP now it is 20%.

Table 21.4: Stock market index. Source: Glitnir (2006)

Weights				**Real rates of return**		
Company		**Fund**	**Index**		**Fund**	**Index**
1	Kaupthing Banki hf.	27.2%	26.5%	2005	56.5%	54.5%
2	Landsbanki Islands hf.	13.1%	13.0%	2004	49.1%	47.2%
3	Glitnir Banki hf.	12.5%	12.3%	2003	42.7%	40.7%
4	Straumur Burôarás Fjárfes	8.9%	8.9%	2002	20.7%	19.2%
5	Actavis Banki hf.	10.1%	9.9%	2001	-16.4%	-16.6%
6	FL Banki hf.	6.3%	6.2%	2000	-16.7%	-17.2%
7	Bakkavör Group hf.	4.0%	4.1%	1999	36.7%	36.4%
8	Avion Group hf.	3.7%	3.7%	1998	6.3%	3.4%
9	Mosaic Fashions hf.	2.7%	2.6%	1997	9.0%	10.2%
10	Ossur hf.	2.2%	2.2%	1996	44.1%	57.3%
11	Tryggingamiðtöðin hf.	2.1%	2.0%	1995	33.4%	31.1%
12	Dagsbrûn hf.	1.5%	1.5%			
13	Alfresca hf.	1.2%	1.2%			
14	Fjárfestingafélagið Atorka	1.0%	1.0%			
15	Grandi hf.	1.0%	1.0%			

Figure 21.8 shows the dramatic rise of the stock market particularly since 2003 and, similarly, Figure 21.9 shows how quickly the crash occurred. However, the notable sharp sell-offs, were, to a large extent, blips before the big crash and there was a question whether these investments could continue to produce similar returns, and if not, whether that would prompt investors to seek other markets.

Fig. 21.8 The 15 stocks in the Iceland equity index and their growth in real terms from 1997-2006. Source: Glitnir (2006)

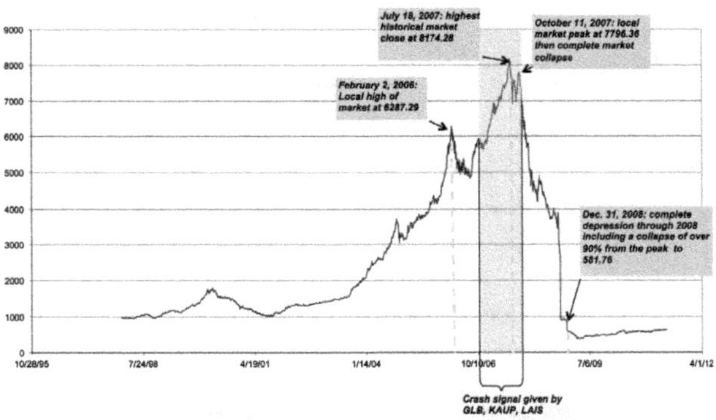

Fig. 21.9 OMX Iceland all share - price index, 1993 to November 2010. Source: Lleo and Ziemba (2012)

Figure 21.10 shows that in the fall of 2007, the long bond interest rates did get above 10% and that with an increase in the PE ratio respectively to 10.91 for Glitnir as of October 10, 11.09 for Kaupthing as of October 11 and 9.94 for Landsbanki as of October 17 the BSEYD spread signal did predict the massive crash. The market peaked at 8174.28 on July 18, 2007 starting in 2002 at 1180.75. Then it fell to 5803.55 by the end of December 2007. The complete collapse came in 2008 with the market falling about 90% to end 2008 at 581.76 and about -95% at the ultimate bottom on February 2, 1010 at 491.58. As of August 31, 2011 the market had fallen to 596.58. Table 21.5 summarizes the year by year story and Figure 21.9 shows the index values from 1998 to September 30, 2011.

Figure 21.11 shows the BSEYD spreads for the three top banks and Figures 21 and 21.13 show the bond-stock earnings yield crash measure from June 2004 to December 2008 for the three largest banks. Like China, the BSEYD distributions of these three largest banks are not normally distributed and have very fat left

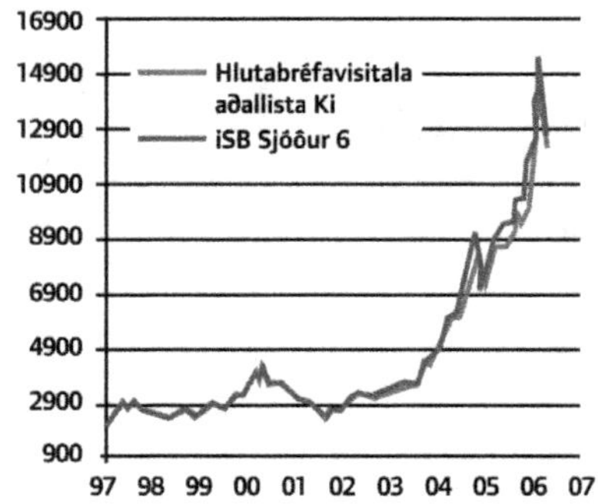

Fig. 21.8 The 15 stocks in the Iceland equity index and their growth in real terms from 1997-2006. Source: Glitnir (2006)

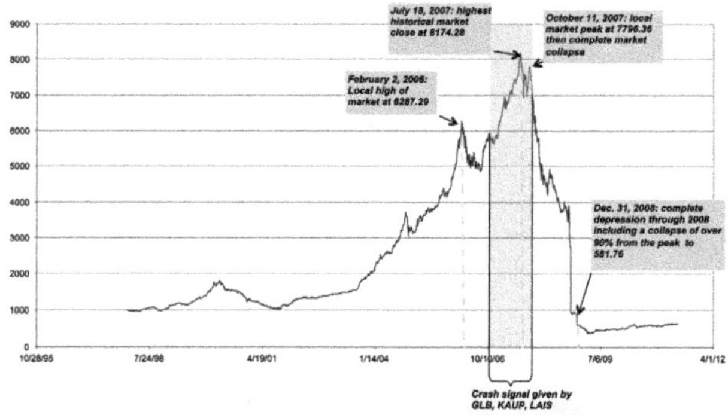

Fig. 21.9 OMX Iceland all share - price index, 1993 to November 2010. Source: Lleo and Ziemba (2012)

Figure 21.10 shows that in the fall of 2007, the long bond interest rates did get above 10% and that with an increase in the PE ratio respectively to 10.91 for Glitnir as of October 10, 11.09 for Kaupthing as of October 11 and 9.94 for Landsbanki as of October 17 the BSEYD spread signal did predict the massive crash. The market peaked at 8174.28 on July 18, 2007 starting in 2002 at 1180.75. Then it fell to 5803.55 by the end of December 2007. The complete collapse came in 2008 with the market falling about 90% to end 2008 at 581.76 and about -95% at the ultimate bottom on February 2, 1010 at 491.58. As of August 31, 2011 the market had fallen to 596.58. Table 21.5 summarizes the year by year story and Figure 21.9 shows the index values from 1998 to September 30, 2011.

Figure 21.11 shows the BSEYD spreads for the three top banks and Figures 21 and 21.13 show the bond-stock earnings yield crash measure from June 2004 to December 2008 for the three largest banks. Like China, the BSEYD distributions of these three largest banks are not normally distributed and have very fat left

Table 21.5: Highlights for the Iceland stock index ICEXI-OMZ 1998-2012 with start value = 1000 on December 31, 1997. Source: Lleo and Ziemba (2012)

Date	Index Value	Comment
Feb 11, 1998	977.58	
Dec 30, 1998	1046.58	
Dec 30, 1999	1511.86	Gain of 44.5% in 1999
Dec 28, 2000	1303.31	}
Dec 28, 2001	1180.75	} Weak market during US stock market weak period
Dec 30, 2002	1436.22	}
Dec 29, 2003	2064.05	Gain of 43.7% in 2003
Dec 30, 2004	3173.91	Gain of 53.8% in 2004
Dec 30, 2005	5107.49	Gain of 60.9% in 2005
Feb 2,2006	6287.29	Local high of market
Aug 2, 2006	4854.95	Local low of market
Dec 30, 2006	5857.50	Gain of 14.7% in 2006
July 18, 2007	8174.28	Global highest historical market close
Aug 16, 2007	6931.69	Market falls to local lows on day of US stock market turmoil when long-short funds had heavy losses
Oct 11, 2007	7796.36	Local market peak then complete market collapse
Dec 28, 2007	5803.35	Market down just slightly (-0.9%) in 2007 but 29% below the July 18, 2007 peak
Dec 30, 2008	581.76	Complete depression including a collapse of over 90% from the peak
Dec 30, 2009	496.48	Further fall in 2009
Feb 2, 2010	491.58	Global historical bottom of market
Nov 30, 2010	579.17	The market rallied back to make the yearly return nearly positive
Dec 30, 2010	569.19	Gain of 15.8% since global historical bottom but the index was still 93.0% below its historical high
Jan 31, 2011	624.97	Gain of 9.8% in January 2011
Jun 30, 2011	604.95	Gain of 23.0% since the global historical bottom but the index was still 92.5% below its historical high
Sept 30, 2011	596.58	Gain of 17.3% since the global historical bottom but the index was still 92.9% below its historical high
Dec 31, 2011	567.77	Gain of 15% since the global historical bottom but the index was still 93% below its historical high
June 30, 2012	677.75	Gain of 38% since the global historical bottom but the index was still 92% below its historical high

before the crash. Finally, for Landsbanki, the danger signal was on February 13, 2007. Figures 21b,d,f show the BSEYD using Cantelli's inequality to account for the non-normality of the BSEYD measure. Figure 21.13 shows the signal dates. We focus on the largest banks because they led the market into the collapse and they are a majority of the index weighting. The smallest cap stocks in the index were in the danger zone in 2006 but not the large banks and the overall index was not in the danger zone then as discussed in Ziemba and Ziemba (2007).

Comments on the crash signals for the three banks from Lleo and Ziemba (2012)

Glitnir:

- Signal from September 15, 2003 until December 23, 2003: on October 12, 2004, the share price reached 11.90. By November 2, 2004, the share had gone down to 10, a 15.97% drop.
- Faint signal from November 17, 2004 until November 19, 2004 and December 6, 2004: on February 18, 2005, the share price fell to 11.60. By March 3, 2005, the share had gone down to 11.60, a 7.20% drop.

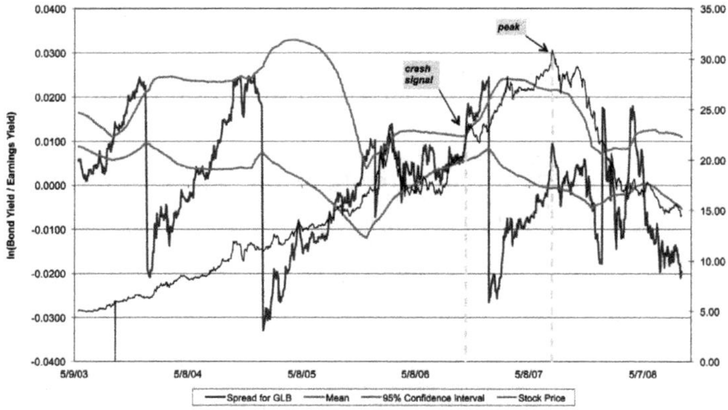

(a) BSEYD Chart (Indicator at 95% confidence): Glitnir. First crash signal occurs around October 17, 2006. The market reaches its peak on July, 20, 2007

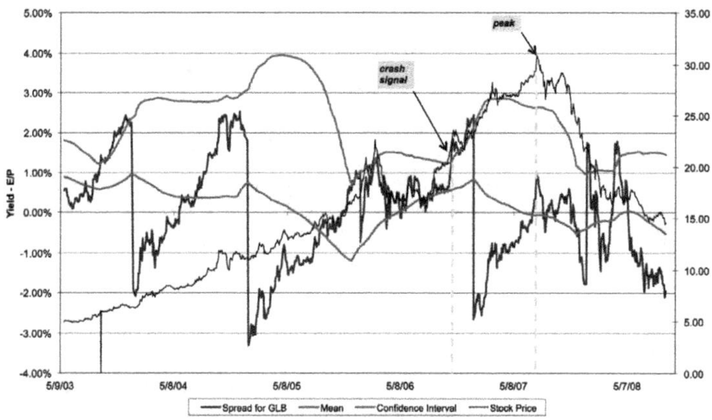

(b) BSEYD Chart (Indicator using Cantelli's Inequality, 20%): Glitnir. First crash signal occurs on October 17, 2006. The market reaches its peak on July, 20, 2007

Fig. 21.12 BSEYD Crash Indicators, Iceland. Source: Lleo and Ziemba (2012)

- Signal from November 22, 2005 until February 24, 2006 (with some interruptions): on October 12, 2004, the share price reached 22.60. By April 19, 2006, the share had gone down to 16.50, a 26.99% drop.
- Signal from October 17, 2006 (with PE ratio of 22.30) until December 27, 2006: announces the market crash.
- Signal from December 28, 2007 until January 8, 2008.
- Signal from March 26, 2008 until April 10, 2008.

(a) BSEYD Chart (Indicator at 95% confidence): Kaupthing. First signal occurs around October 2, 2007. The market reaches its peak on July 18, 2007 and a crash occurred on November 11, 2007.

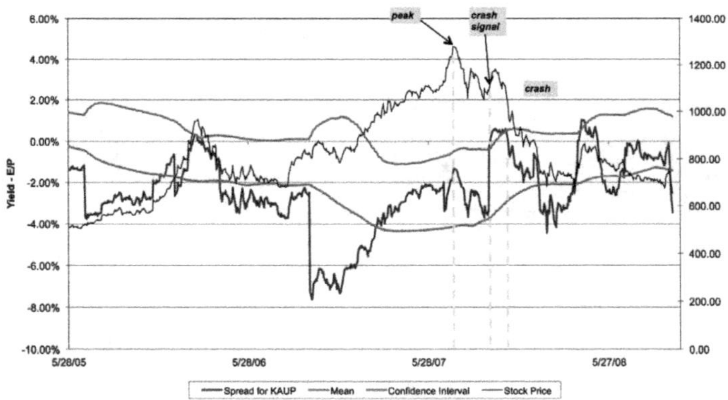

(b) BSEYD Chart (Indicator using Cantelli's Inequality, 20%): Kaupthing. First crash signal occurs on October 2, 2007. The market reaches its peak on July 18, 2007 and a crash occurred on November 11, 2007

Fig. 21.12 (Continued)

The crash signal analysis is basically according to the script except for the faint signal between November 17, 2004 until November 19, 2004 and December 6, 2004 for which we do not have a better explanation.

Kaupthing:

- Signal from February 7, 2006 until February 24, 2006: on October 26, 2006, the share price reached 868. By November 28, 2006, the share had fallen to 785, a 9.56% drop.
- The market reaches its peak on July 18, 2007 and a crash occurred on November 11, 2007.
- Signal from September 28, 2007 until November 5, 2007.
- Signal from March 26, 2008 until April 4, 2008.

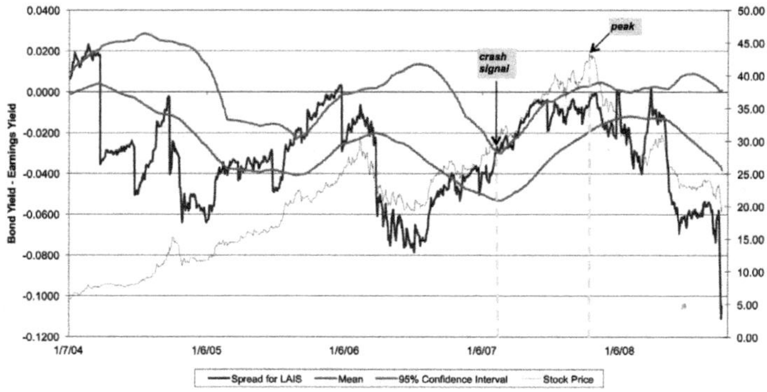

(c) BSEYD Chart (Indicator at 95% confidence): Landsbanki. First crash signal occurs around February 13, 2007. The market reaches its peak on October 17, 2007.

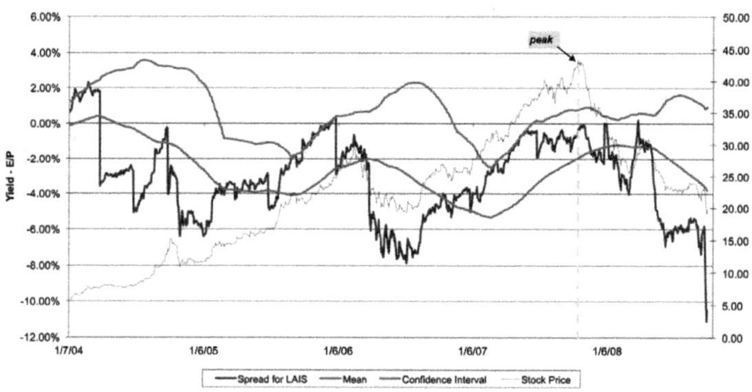

(d) BSEYD Chart (Indicator using Cantelli's Inequality, 20%): Landsbanki. Faint crash signal throughout the first half of 2007. The market reaches its peak on October 17, 2007.

Fig. 21.12 (Continued)

Landsbanki:

- Signal from January 15, 2004 until March 4, 2004: on October 11, 2004, the share price reached 15.28. By November 2, 2004, the share has fallen to 10.85, a 28.98% drop.
- Signal from August 30, 2005 until December 29, 2005 (with minor interruptions): on February 16, 2006, the share price reached 30.56. By May 3, 2006, the share has fallen to 20.05, a 34.39% drop.
- Signal from February 13, 2007 until March 13, 2007 and from March 30, 2007 until the June 28, 2007: market crash signal.
- The market reaches its peak on October 17, 2007.

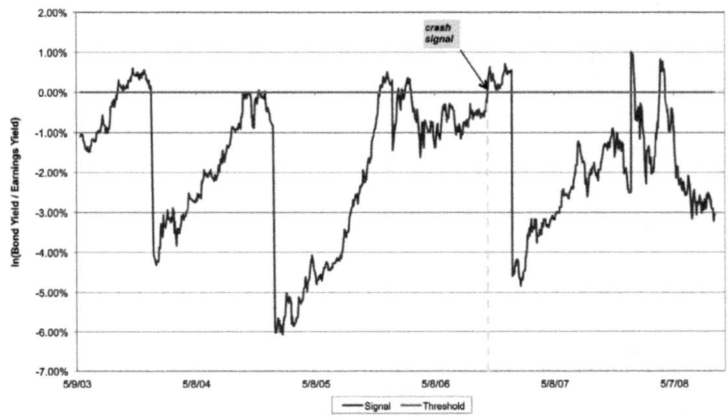

(e) Crash Signal Indicator (based on 95% confidence): Glitnir. First crash signal occurs around October 17, 2006. The market reaches its peak on July, 20 2007

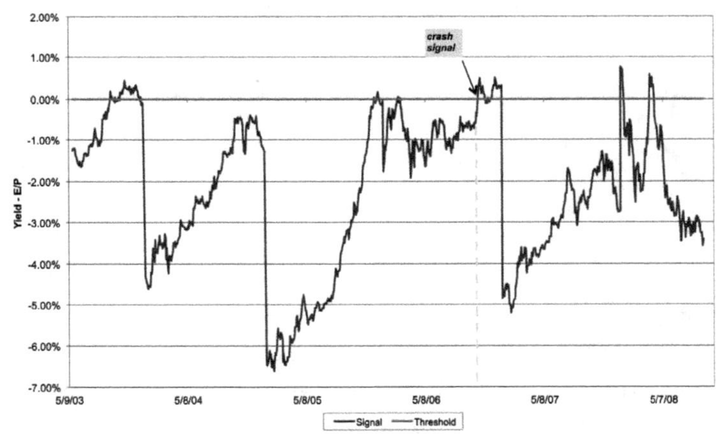

(f) Signal Chart (Indicator using Cantelli's Inequality, 20%): Glitnir. First crash signal occurs on October 17, 2006. The market reaches its peak on July, 20 2007

Fig. 21.13 Crash Indicators, Iceland. Source: Lleo and Ziemba (2012)

The crash model works out well for Landsbanki: the signal identifies the market crashes and two large declines. Although the signal could be clearer for Glitnir and Kaupthing, we do not observe any false positives.

The US 2007–2009 crash

In this section we investigate whether or not the bond-stock measure did predict the US 2007-2009 crash, including the devastating September 2008 to March 2009

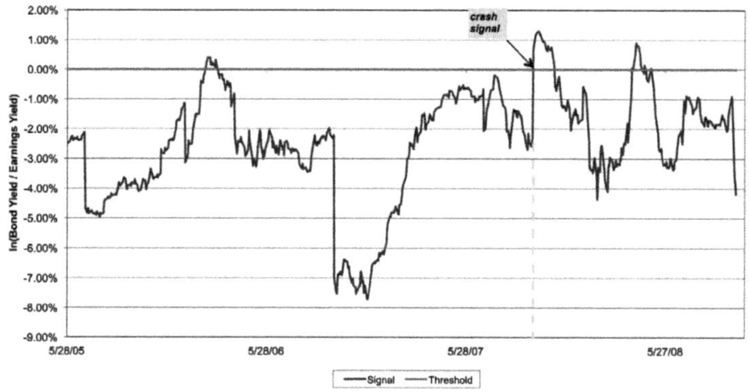

(a) Signal Chart (95% confidence): Kaupthing. First crash signal occurs around October 2, 2007. The market reaches its peak on July 18, 2007 and a crash occurred on November 11, 2007

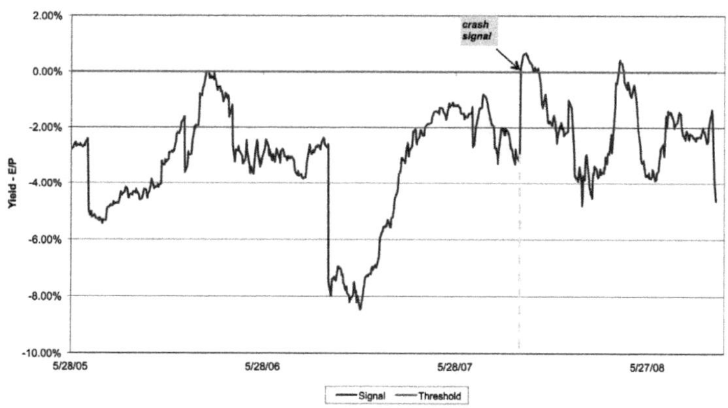

(b) Signal Chart (Indicator using Cantelli's Inequality, 20%): Kaupthing. First crash signal occurs on October 2, 2007. The market reaches its peak on July 18, 2007 and a crash occurred on November 11, 2007

Fig. 21.13 (Continued)

period. Table 21.7 shows the BSEYD at various periods from 2006 to 2011. In 2006 the weak economy led the Fed to dramatically reduce short term interest rates which tended to drop the long term rates that we use in the BSEYD calculations.

Table 21.6 considers the measure in five major countries on July 12, 2006. None of these major markets were in the danger zone then. Table 21.7 for the S&P500 has the calculations for the years from 2006 to 2011 on trailing price-earnings ratios that are usually used for these calculations and 2011 which uses Shiller's average inflation-adjusted earnings from the previous ten years. Figures 21.15ab show the S&P500 PE ratios (Shiller's calculation method) and the ten-year Treasury bond yield.

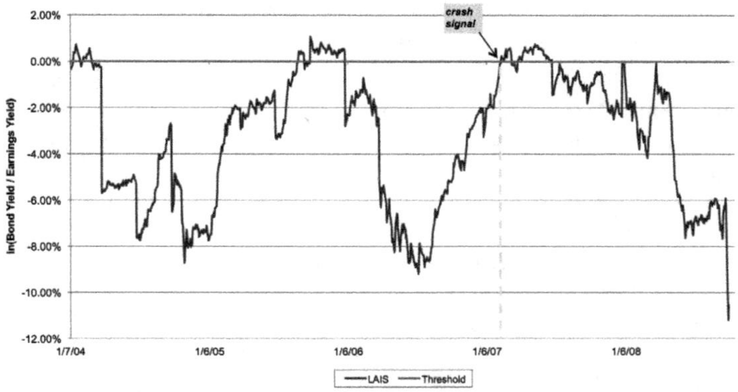

(c) Signal Chart (95% confidence): Landsbanki. First crash signal occurs around February 13, 2007. The market reaches its peak on October 17, 2007

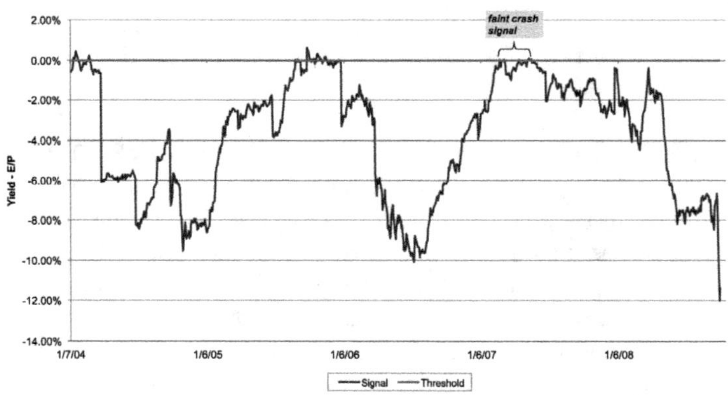

(d) Signal Chart (Indicator using Cantelli's Inequality, 20%): Landsbanki. Faint crash signal throughout the first half of 2007. The market reaches its peak on October 17, 2007

Fig. 21.13 (Continued)

Table 21.6: Long-bond (10 yr) versus earning yield differentials for major countries, July 12, 2006. Source: Ziemba and Ziemba (2007)

	S&P500	FTSE200	Nikkei225	CAC40	DAX30
Index	1259	5861	15249	4942	5638
A) PE ratio	16.86	16.61	36.26	13.82	13.33
B) Stock Return (1/A)	5.93%	6.02%	2.76%	7.24%	7.50%
C) Bond Return (10 yr)	5.10%	4.67%	1.94%	4.10%	4.09%
D) Crash Signal (C-B)	-0.83	-1.35	-0.82	-3.14	-3.41

Ex post it is clear that this stock market crash had a lot of components such as the first decline in aggregate US housing prices in more than thirty years, a subprime market collapsing because home buyers could not cover their mortgages, lots of suspect AAA rated packages of these mortgages and then a credit squeeze with much counter party risk with firms unwilling to lend money to others including supposedly sound financial institutions and the collapse of many large and previously sound financial institutions such as Bear Stearns, Freddie Mac, Fannie May and, the killer for the market, Lehman Brothers.

Table 21.7: BSEYD model calculations leading up to the 2007-2009 crisis in the S&P500. Source: Lleo and Ziemba (2012)

Date	Long Bond (10 years)	Trailing PE	1/PE, %	B-Y(pe)
Feb-06	4.49	20.00	5.00	(0.56)
Jun-07	5.15	17.00	5.98	(0.74)
Jun-08	4.14	18.00	5.55	(1.41)
May-09	3.70	33.30	3.00	0.70
May-10	3.41	20.47	4.89	(1.48)
Feb-11	3.59	23.83	4.20	(0.61)

Table 21.8 lists some of the main events regarding the S&P500 from 2006 to 2011. There are numerous books concerning this period plus many articles and columns. Ziemba has several in *Wilmott* that are discussed in this book. Starting in June 2007, he designed strategies and traded for an offshore BVI based hedge fund for a group headed by a top trader whose his hedge funds had investments in Bear Stearns and in June 2007 asked for his money back. That took three months and gave him a strong signal of danger. As an astute trader, he hedged and studied carefully the market situation through technical indicators that he has developed. Ziemba remembers his words to him starting in the summer of 2007 "this is the big one" ..."eventually the market will go to 660 on the S&P500". In the fall of 2007 the S&P500 was about 1500, see Figure 25.3. So this was a rather bold call but a private one and it turned out to be very accurate. Nouriel Roubini was predicting very boldly a serious financial meltdown starting in 2006 when the housing market was beginning its decline. He and other bears such as Yale Professor Robert Shiller are still (September 2012) pessimistic about the economy, real estate and financial markets. Dropping real estate has several depressive effects such as homeowners can no longer use house price gains to fund consumption, foreclosures, etc. The March 2009 low closing was 676.53 with an intraday low of 666.79 on March 6. The subsequent rally doubled the S&P500 to 1320.64 as of the end of June 2011 and 1362.16 to the end of June 2012 and to 1440.67 on September 30, 2012. There is considerable discussion regarding whether or not this rally is low interest rate related to the Fed quantitative easing, or only game in town since real estate, bonds and cash look unattractive. This is a case when the BSEYD signaled the rise in stock prices. A volatile period followed the rally, with a drop in the level of the S&P500 in August and September followed by a a stabilization in October.

Table 21.8: Highlights of the S&P500, January 1, 2006 to June 30, 2012. Source: Lleo and Ziemba (2012)

Date	Index Value	Comment
December 31, 2005	1248.29	
August 31, 2006	1303.82	Gain of 4.4% year-to-date
December 31, 2006	1418.30	Gain of 13.6% in 2006
February 26, 2007	1437.50	Local high of market
March 1, 2007	1374.12	Local low of market
June 7, 2007	1480.72	Bear Stearns suspends redemptions from one of its hedge funds
June 14, 2007	1522.97	BSEYD crash signal occurs
July 13, 2007	1552.50	Local high of market
July 31, 2007	1455.27	Bear Stearns liquidates two hedge funds
August 16, 2007	1411.27	Local low of market
October 9, 2007	1565.15	Market peak. Gain of 10.4% year-to-date
December 31, 2007	1468.35	Gain of 3.5% in 2007
March 17, 2008	1276.60	Local low of market
September 15, 2008	1192.70	Lehman Brothers files for bankruptcy protection
September 30, 2008	1166.36	Market down by 20.6% year-to-date
October 10, 2008	899.22	Local low of market
October 31, 2008	968.75	Market down by 16.9% in October
December 31, 2008	903.25	Market down by 38.5% in 2008
March 9, 2009	683.38	Lowest intraday: 666.79 on March 6, 2009
March 9, 2009	676.53	Market trough. The market was down by 56.8% peak to trough
July 28, 2009	979.62	Date Shepherd claimed that the S&P500 had a 723 PE ratio based on reported (real earnings) to the SEC on 10Q forms
December 31, 2009	1115.10	Market was down by 23.5% in 2009, but up by 64.8% since trough
April 23, 2010	1217.28	Local high
July 2, 2010	1022.58	Local low
December 31, 2010	1257.64	Gain of 12.8% in 2010, and of 23% since the local low of July 2, 2010
May 10, 2011	1357.16	Local high. Gain of 7.91% year-to-date and of 32.72% since the local low of July 2, 2010
August 31, 2011	1218.89	Loss of 3.1% year-to-date and of 10.2% since the local high of May 10, 2010
Sept 30, 2011	1131.42	Loss of 10.0% year-to-date and of 16.6% since the local high of May 10, 2010
Dec 31, 2011	1257.60	The index ends the year flat, but is still down 7.3% from the local high of May 10, 2010
June 30, 2012	1362.16	Gain of 8.3% year-to-date.

Did the BSEYD model predict the US crash? Figures 21.16 and 21.17 show that it did on June 14, 2007. As with China and Iceland, the BSEYD measure is not normally distributed but rather has fat tails especially on the downside as shown in Figure 21.18. The 95% confidence graphs with the crash danger signal is shown in Figure 21.16(a). The Cantelli's inequality version of the model, Figure 21.16(b), gives the danger signal on the same day, namely, June 14, 2007, see also Figures 21.17ab.

Let's go back to the BSEYD and whether or not it called the September 2008 to March 2009 crash. Figure 21.19 shows the S&P500 during the 2007-2009 period. Consider Table 21.9 which was published in the Maudlin weekly newsletter which has 1.5 million subscribers in May 2009. It shows how estimated earnings are dramatically falling. In March 2007, earnings for 2008 were forecast to be 92, during the course of 2008 the forecast was constantly revised downward. On July 25, 2008, the S&P500 earnings for 2008 were forecast to be 72.00 with the S&P500 at 1257.76 which gives a PE ratio of 17.47 which is not high enough to signal the September 2008 to March 2009 crash. But by February 20, 2009, the 2008 earnings

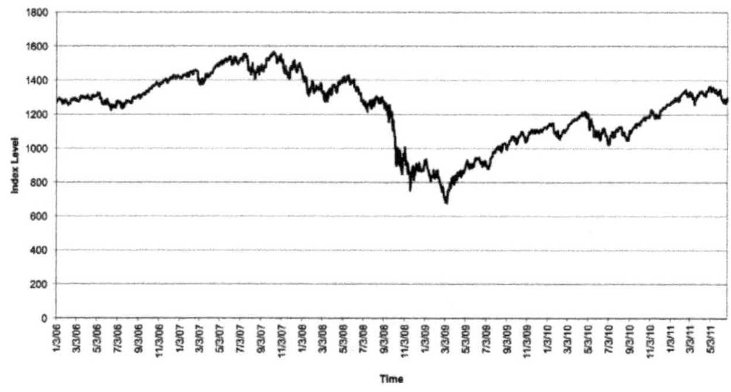

Fig. 21.14 The S&P500, January 1, 2006 to April 30, 2011

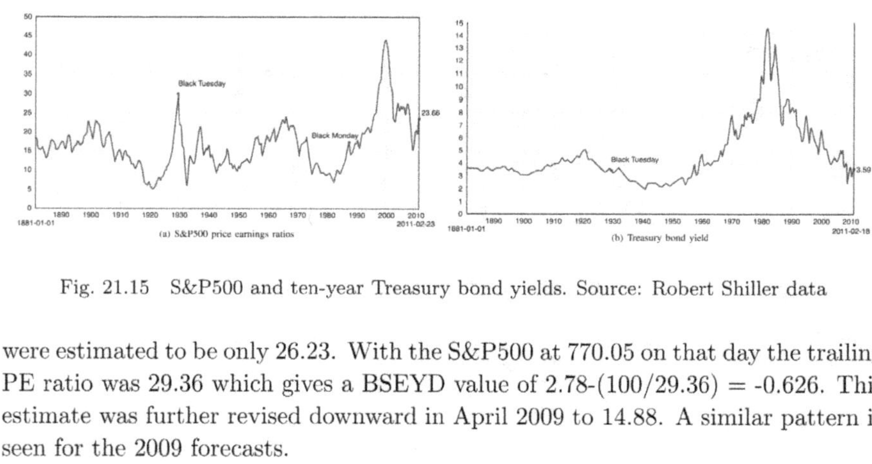

(a) S&P500 price earnings ratios

(b) Treasury bond yield

Fig. 21.15 S&P500 and ten-year Treasury bond yields. Source: Robert Shiller data

were estimated to be only 26.23. With the S&P500 at 770.05 on that day the trailing PE ratio was 29.36 which gives a BSEYD value of 2.78-(100/29.36) = -0.626. This estimate was further revised downward in April 2009 to 14.88. A similar pattern is seen for the 2009 forecasts.

Table 21.9: Earnings revisions for 2008 and 2009, analysts estimates of earnings in dollars. Source: Maudlin (2009)

Forecasts and estimates for 2008		. . . and forecasts for 2009	
Date	Earnings	Date	Earnings
March 2007	92.00	March 20, 2008	81.52
December 2007	84.00	April 9, 2008	72.60
February 2008	71.20	June 25, 2008	70.13
June 1, 2008	68.93	September 10, 2008	48.52
July 25, 2008	72.00	August 29, 2008	64.44
September 30, 2008	60.00	February 1, 2009	42.00
October 15, 2008	54.82	February 20, 2009	32.41
February 20, 2009	26.23	April 10, 2009	28.51
April 10, 2009	14.88		

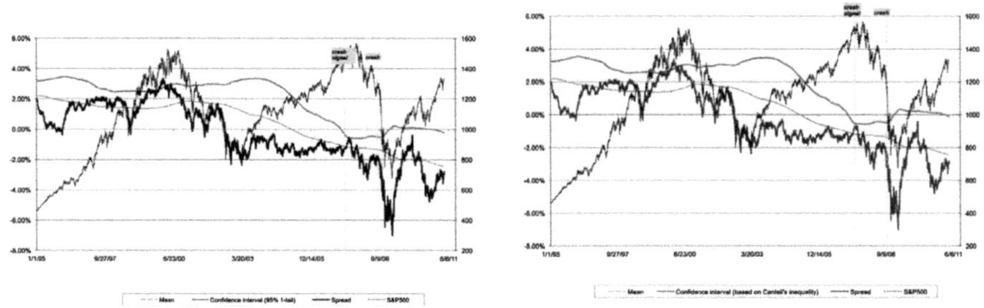

(a) Crash Indicator (95% confidence: S&P500 MA. Signal occurs on June 14, 2007. The market reaches its peak on October 9, 2007 and crashes in September 2008)

(b) Crash Indicator (Cantelli's Inequality): S&P500, MACI. Signal occurs on June 14, 2007. The market reaches its peak on October 9, 2007 and crashes in September 2008

Fig. 21.16 Crash Indicators, US. Source: Lleo and Ziemba (2012)

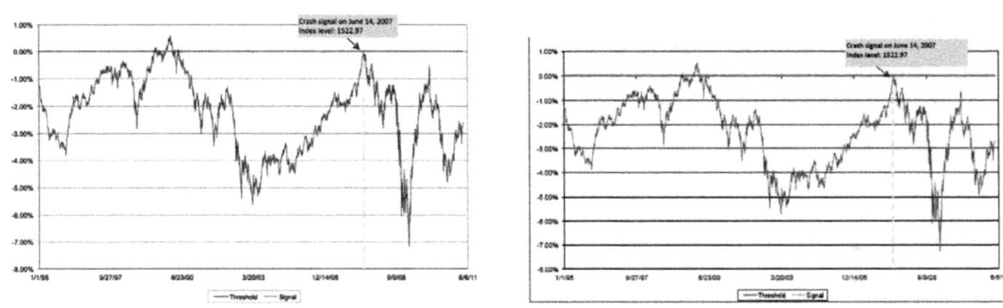

(a) Based on a standard 1-tail 95% confidence level, moving average normal distribution assumption

(b) Based on a standard 1-tail 95% confidence level, moving average fat tail distribution Cantelli's inequality assumption

Fig. 21.17 US crash signal occurs on June 14, 2007. Source: Lleo and Ziemba (2012)

Shepherd (2009) has the S&P500 PE ratio at 723 on July 28, 2009 four months into the rally that began in March 2009! The S&P500 was then 979.62, up nearly 50% from the March lows. This high PE ratio was based on reported real earnings from SEC 10Q filings. So what do we conclude here? Our conclusion is in Figure 21.20. The BSEYD model did not give any additional sell signals during 2008. The signal was on June 14, 2007 with the index at 1522.97 and the crash occurred in various phases with closing peak of 1565.15 on October 9, 2007 and a closing low of 676.53 on March 9, 2009, down some 56.8% from the peak. The conclusions are similar: over the period January 1, 1995 to April 6, 2011, two BSEYD crash signals occurred: one in June 1999 and the other in June 2007.

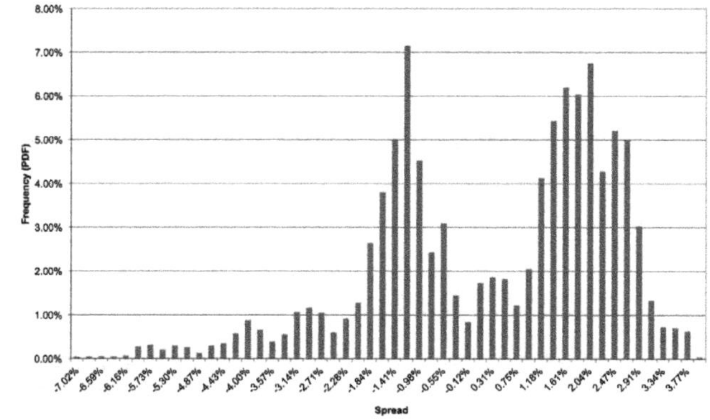

Fig. 21.18 Spread distribution of the BSEYD measure on the S&P500. Source: Lleo and Ziemba (2012)

Fig. 21.19 The S&P500, January 1, 2007 to December 31, 2009. Source: Lleo and Ziemba (2012)

Logarithmic Model

Koivu, Pennanen and Ziemba (2005) use a logarithmic version of the BSEYD model. The question is does that model suggest anything new for our analysis? The logarithmic model is based on the Fed model bond stock yield ratio

$$\ln BSEYR(t) = \ln\left(\frac{r(t)}{\gamma(t)}\right) = \ln r(t) - \ln \gamma(t). \tag{21.4}$$

For China and Iceland, both measures produce similar results which are available from the authors. The pattern and timing of the crash signals nearly coincide for all three Icelandic banks. In China, the lnBSEYR generates a slightly earlier signal than the BSEYD.

In the US, the result of the lnBSEYR and of the BSEYD measures are also broadly similar. A signal precedes both the internet-related crash of 2000 and

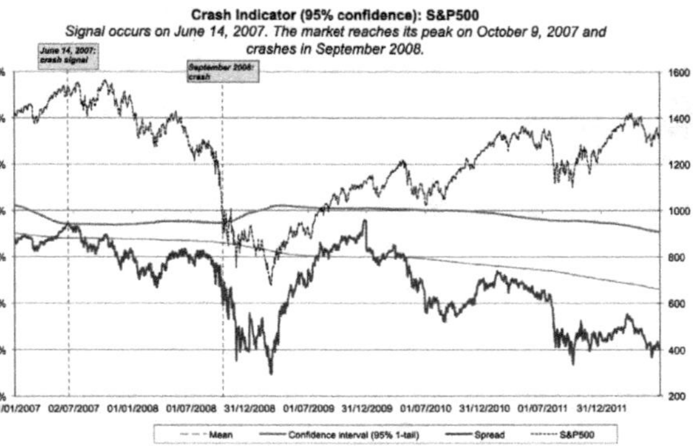

Fig. 21.20 Crash Indicator (95% confidence): S&P500. Source: Lleo and Ziemba (2012)

the credit crunch crash of 2008. In addition, the logarithmic lnBSYR(t) measure generates a signal in April 1998, ahead of a 19% decline from July 17th to August 31st. However, neither measure predicted the market decline of 2002. This is a combined result of the relatively low level reached by the two measures in 2001 compared to 1999, and of the increase in the confidence level starting in 2000.

Final remarks

The bond stock earnings yield model has been shown to be useful in a number of contexts. First, using it for being in or out of the market over long investment periods has been shown to produce about double the returns of buy and hold with lower risk in five major countries as shown in the next chapter. Secondly, over the years, the model has predicted many significant stock market crashes such as those in China, Iceland and the US during 2007-2009. Finally it has possible, but less clear, use concerning when to re-enter markets after a crash.

Part III

Efficient Portfolio Construction

https://doi.org/10.1142/9789811222634_0015

Chapter 15

Efficient global portfolios: Big data and investment universes*

J. B. Guerard, Jr.
S. T. Rachev
B. P. Shao

In this analysis of the risk and return of stocks in the United States and global markets, we apply several portfolio construction and optimization techniques to U.S. and global stock universes. We find that (1) mean-variance techniques continue to produce portfolios capable of generating excess returns above transaction costs and statistically significant asset selection, (2) optimization techniques minimizing expected tail loss are statistically significant in portfolio construction, and (3) global markets offer the potential for greater returns relative to risk than domestic markets. In this experiment, mean-variance, enhanced-index-tracking techniques, and mean-expected tail-loss methodologies are examined. Global equity data and the vast quantity (and quality) of the data relative to U.S. equity modeling have been discussed in the literature. We estimate expected return models in the U.S. and global equity markets using a given stock-selection model and generate statistically significant active returns from various portfolio construction techniques.

Introduction

In this study, we apply several portfolio construction and optimization techniques to U.S. and global stock universes. Global equity data and the vast quantity (and quality) of the data relative to U.S. equity modeling have been discussed in the literature. We estimate expected return models in the U.S. and global equity markets using a given stock-selection model and generate statistically significant active returns from various portfolio construction techniques.

This paper is organized as follows. In the section "Constructing mean-variance efficient portfolios," we introduce the reader to the risk and return tradeoff analysis. In the section "Extensions to the mean-variance optimization model," we discuss the Markowitz enhanced-index-tracking (EIT) portfolio construction model in which security weights are an absolute deviation from the security weight in the index. We refer to the absolute deviation from the benchmark weight enhanced-index portfolio construction weight as the equal active weighting (EAW) portfolio construction model. In the section "Arbitrage pricing theory multi-factor models in business," we discuss the theory of multi-factor risk models. In the section "A general stock-selection model for U.S. and global equity markets," we discuss our data sources and the construction and estimation of a general stock-selection model for U.S. and global securities. In the section "Extension to mean-ETL optimization model," we discuss mean-expected tail-loss (ETL) optimization. In the section "Portfolio simulation results with the U.S. Expected Returns (USER) and Global Expected Returns (GLER) models," we discuss portfolio construction and simulation, and present the empirical results. In the conclusion, we offer conclusions and a summary.

We report that (1) mean-variance (MV) techniques continue to produce portfolios capable of generating excess returns above transactions costs and statistically significant asset selection, (2) optimization techniques minimizing expected tail loss are statistically significant in portfolio construction, and (3) global markets offer the potential for greater returns relative to risk than domestic markets. In this experiment, MV, EIT techniques, and mean-ETL methodologies are examined.

H. M. Markowitz developed a portfolio construction model to achieve the maximum return for a given level of risk or the minimum risk for a given level of return [1–4]. It has long been noted by B. Solnik [5, 6] that investors should diversify internationally rather than domestically, and

---

* This article originally appeared in *IBM Journal of Research and Development* **57**(5), 11:1–11:11, 2013, ©2013 by International Business Machines Corporation.

the number of international securities is much larger than the securities of the U.S. market, aiding diversification. To better extend the portfolio construction methodology and techniques used for the U.S. market to the international market, we briefly review the applied U.S. equity investment research presented in Guerard et al. [7] and Tsuchida et al. [8]. Creating portfolios using statistics-based risk models for the U.S. and global markets, we test whether global markets offer the potential for greater returns relative to risk than domestic markets. We test MV, EIT techniques, and mean-ETL methodologies on the global assets.

In constructing efficient portfolios, the security weights are the primary decision variables to be solved. Second, we test whether the MV optimization technique using the portfolio variance as the relevant risk measure dominates the risk/return tradeoff curve using a variation of the MV optimization model that emphasizes systematic (or market) risk, the MV Tracking Error at Risk (MVTaR) optimization, and mean-ETL portfolio optimization. A statistics-based Principal Components Analysis model is used to estimate and monitor portfolio risk.

A measure of the tradeoff between the portfolio expected return and risk (as measured by the portfolio standard deviation) is typically denoted by the Greek letter lambda (λ). Generally, the higher the lambda, the higher is the ratio of portfolio expected return to portfolio standard deviation. We assume that the portfolio manager seeks to maximize the portfolio geometric mean (GM) and Sharpe ratio as put forth in Latane [9] and Markowitz [3, 10].

Summary and findings

We report that the Markowitz MV optimization technique, the EIT optimization technique, and the MVTaR optimization technique are appropriate tools for portfolio construction for the U.S. Expected Returns (USER) and Global Expected Returns (GLER) data. Global portfolios dominate domestic portfolios with regard to the return-to-risk statistics for the 1999 to 2011 period. The Markowitz approach to portfolio construction and management is 60 years old and remains an integral tool of investment research.

Constructing mean-variance efficient portfolios

Portfolio construction and management, as formulated in Markowitz, seeks to identify the efficient frontier, the point at which the portfolio return is maximized for a given level of risk, or equivalently, portfolio risk is minimized for a given level of portfolio return. The portfolio expected return, denoted by $E(R_P)$, is calculated from the sum of the security weights multiplied by their respective expected returns:

$$E(R_P) = \sum_{i=1}^{N} w_i E(R_i), \tag{1}$$

where N is the number of candidate securities, w_i is the weight for security i, and $\sum_{i=1}^{N} w_i = 1$ indicating that the portfolio is fully invested. $E(R_i)$ is the expected return for security i. The portfolio standard deviation σ_P is the square root of portfolio variance σ_P^2, which is the sum of the weighted securities covariance:

$$\sigma_P^2 = \sum_{i=1}^{N}\sum_{j=1}^{N} w_i w_j \sigma_{ij}, \tag{2}$$

where σ_{ij} is the covariance of returns for security i and security j.

The Markowitz framework measures risk as the portfolio standard deviation, a measure of dispersion or total risk. One seeks to minimize risk, as measured by the covariance matrix in the Markowitz framework, holding constant expected returns. The decision variables estimated in the Markowitz model are the security weights. The Markowitz model minimized the total risk, or variance, of the portfolio. Investors are compensated for bearing total risk.

Extensions to the mean-variance optimization model

We introduce two extensions to the MV approach: an EIT optimization technique and a tracking error at risk optimization technique. Markowitz [4] rewrites the general portfolio construction model variance, V, to be minimized as

$$V = (\mathbf{X} - \mathbf{W})^{\mathrm{T}}\mathbf{C}(\mathbf{X} - \mathbf{W}), \tag{3}$$

where $\mathbf{W}^{\mathrm{T}} = (W_1, \ldots, W_n)^{\mathrm{T}}$ is the vector of weights of an index of returns, $\mathbf{X}$ are the portfolio weights, and $\mathbf{C}$ are the covariance of returns. $(\cdot)^{\mathrm{T}}$ is the transpose. Guerard et al. [11] reported the efficiency of the EIT procedure is minimizing realized tracking errors.

One creates portfolios by allowing portfolio weights to differ from index weights by plus or minus 1% up to 5%, each portfolio denoted by EAW followed by a number indicating the percent. Obviously, one can use an infinite set of EAW variations. Guerard et al. [12] employed MV and EIT optimization techniques to test whether EAW strategies of 1%, 2%, 3%, 4%, and 5% (weight deviations from the index, or benchmark, weights) outperform MV strategies using 4% and 7% maximum security weights. Guerard et al. [12] also reported that MV portfolios produced higher information ratios and Sharpe ratios than EAW portfolios with weights less than EAW4 (portfolio weights are allowed to differ from index weights by ±4%). Thus, the traditional Markowitz MV is (still) quite relevant in the world of business.

Arbitrage pricing theory multi-factor models in business

Earlier, we introduced the reader to the Markowitz model in which investors are compensated for bearing the total risk of the portfolio. Implicit in the development of the Capital Asset Pricing Model by Sharpe [13], Lintner [14], and Mossin [15] is that investors are compensated for bearing systematic or market risk, not total risk. Systematic risk is measured by the beta of a stock. Beta is the slope of the market model in which the stock return is regressed as a function of the market return. Sharpe [16] proposed what he refers to as the diagonal model to simplify the computations in constructing portfolios. An investor is not compensated for bearing risk that may be diversified away from the portfolio, but rather portfolio risk as measured by factor exposures.

Multi-factor risk models evolved in the works of Rosenberg [17], Ross [18], and Ross and Roll [19]. The fundamentally based domestic Barra risk model was developed in Rosenberg, Rosenberg, and Marathe [20] and thoroughly discussed in Rudd and Clasing [21] and Grinold and Kahn [22]. Barra attribution is used in this analysis to access stock-selection statistical significance. The Barra model remains the industry standard for risk model. The total excess return for a multiple-factor model in the Rosenberg methodology for security j may be written as follows:

$$R_j = \sum_{k=1}^{K} \beta_{jk}\widetilde{f}_k + \widetilde{e}_j. \quad (4)$$

The nonfactor, or asset-specific return $\widetilde{e}_j$ on security j, is the residual risk of the security after removing the estimated impacts of the K factors. The term $\widetilde{f}_k$ is the rate of return on factor k, and β_{jk} is factor beta of security j on factor k. An extensive review of factor risk models can be found in Connor and Korajczyk [23].

Guerard [24] demonstrated the effectiveness of the Blin and Bender arbitrage pricing theory (APT) and Sungard APT systems in portfolio construction and management. The determination of security weights, the ws, in a portfolio are the primary calculation of the Markowitz portfolio management approach. The security weight is the proportion of the portfolio value invested in the individual j security.

The portfolio weight of security j is calculated as:

$$w_{(\mathrm{P})j} = \frac{MV_j}{MV_\mathrm{P}}, \quad (5)$$

where MV_j is the market value of security j, and MV_P is the market value total portfolio.

The active weight of the security j, $w_{(\mathrm{a})j}$ is calculated by subtracting the security weight in the (index) benchmark b, $w_{(\mathrm{b})j}$, from the security weight in the portfolio:

$$w_{(\mathrm{a})j} = w_{(\mathrm{P})j} - w_{(\mathrm{b})j}. \quad (6)$$

Blin and Bender created their Advanced Portfolio Technologies company, and its *Analytics Guide* [25, 26], which built upon the mathematical foundations of their APT system, published in Blin et al. [27]. Our review draws upon the *Advanced Portfolio Technologies Analytics Guide*. Volatility can be decomposed into independent variance components, systematic risk, and specific risk:

$$\sigma_\mathrm{P}^2 = \sigma_{\beta\mathrm{P}}^2 + \sigma_{\mathrm{SP}}^2, \quad (7)$$

where σ_P^2 is the total portfolio variance, $\sigma_{\beta\mathrm{P}}^2$ is the systematic portfolio volatility, and σ_{SP}^2 is the specific portfolio volatility.

Tracking error is a measure of volatility applied to the active return of funds (portfolio) benchmark with respect to an index. Portfolio tracking error is defined as:

$$\begin{aligned}\sigma_{\mathrm{te}} &= \sqrt{\mathrm{Var}(\mathbf{r}_\mathrm{P} - \mathbf{r}_\mathrm{b})} \\ &= \sqrt{E[(\mathbf{r}_\mathrm{P} - \mathbf{r}_\mathrm{b}) - E(\mathbf{r}_\mathrm{P} - \mathbf{r}_\mathrm{b})]^2},\end{aligned} \quad (8)$$

where σ_{te} is the square root of the variance of annualized tracking error, and $\mathbf{r}_\mathrm{P}$ and $\mathbf{r}_\mathrm{b}$ are the actual (annual) portfolio return and benchmark return, respectively. Systematic tracking error of a portfolio is a forecast of the portfolio active annual returns as a function of the securities returns associated with APT risk (factor) model components. The difference in APT portfolio returns versus a benchmark return at time t can be written as:

$$d_{\mathrm{P,b}}^{(t)} = \left. \sum_{i=1}^{n_\mathrm{P}} \mathbf{w}_{(\mathrm{P})i}\mathbf{r}_{ti} - \sum_{j=1}^{n_\mathrm{b}} \mathbf{w}_{(\mathrm{b})j}\mathbf{r}_{tj} \right), \quad (9)$$

where n_P is the number of securities in the portfolio, and n_b is the number of securities in the portfolio benchmark. $\mathbf{r}_{ti}$ and $\mathbf{r}_{tj}$ are the returns of security i and j at time t, respectively.

Although portfolios often contain stocks not in the benchmark, we can make $n_\mathrm{P} = n_\mathrm{b} = m$ by inserting zeros in the weights when appropriate. Let us define column vectors $\mathbf{w}_\mathrm{P}$ and $\mathbf{w}_\mathrm{b}$ for given portfolio and benchmark portfolios, respectively. Row vector $\mathbf{r}_t$ denotes the security returns at time t. Then, difference in APT portfolio returns can be rewritten as:

$$d_{\mathrm{P,b}}^{(t)} = \mathbf{r}_t \cdot (\mathbf{w}_\mathrm{P} - \mathbf{w}_\mathrm{b}). \quad (10)$$

Blin and Bender mimic the APT model in the *Analytics Guide*:

$$\begin{aligned}\sigma_{\mathrm{P,b}}^2 &= \mathrm{Var}(\mathbf{d}_{\mathrm{P,b}}) \\ &= (\mathbf{w}_\mathrm{P} - \mathbf{w}_\mathrm{b})^\mathrm{T}(\mathbf{B}^\mathrm{T}\mathbf{B} + \Sigma)(\mathbf{w}_\mathrm{P} - \mathbf{w}_\mathrm{b}),\end{aligned} \quad (11)$$

where $\mathbf{B}$ is the $k \times m$ matrix of factor loading, and $\Sigma = \mathbf{e}'\mathbf{e}$ is the $m \times m$ diagonal matrix of the specific risk loading. $\mathbf{d}_{\mathrm{P,b}} = [d_{\mathrm{P,b}}^{(1)}, \ldots, d_{\mathrm{P,b}}^{(T)}]$, where T in the superscript represents the number of data points, and $(\cdot)^\mathrm{T}$ in Eq. (11)

is the transpose. Thus, the annualized APT calculated portfolio error versus a benchmark is

$$\sigma_{P,b} = \sqrt{52(\mathbf{w}_P - \mathbf{w}_b)^T(\mathbf{B}^T\mathbf{B} + \Sigma)(\mathbf{w}_P - \mathbf{w}_b)} \quad (12)$$

$$\sigma_{ste} = \sqrt{52(\mathbf{w}_P - \mathbf{w}_b)^T\Sigma(\mathbf{w}_P - \mathbf{w}_b)} \quad (13)$$

and $\sigma^2_{P,b} - \sigma^2_{ste}$ is the systematic tracking variance of the portfolio, and its square root is the systematic tracking error. The number 52 here represents the average number of weeks in one year.

We can define the portfolio Value-at-Risk (VaR) as the probability that the value of the portfolio will decline, from its current value, V_0, by at least the amount $V(\alpha, T)$, where T is the time horizon, and α is a specified parameter, i.e., $\alpha = 0.05$ Then,

$$\begin{aligned} &\text{Prob}(V_T < V_0 - V(\alpha, T)) \leq 0.95 && \text{or} \\ &\text{Prob}(V_T < V_0 - V(\alpha, T)) \leq 0.05, && \text{if } \alpha = 0.95. \end{aligned} \quad (14)$$

The second case indicates that the probability that the value of the portfolio will decline by an amount $V(\alpha, T)$ within 30 days is at most 0.05.

Blin et al. [27] used a 20-factor beta model of covariances based on 3.5 years of weekly stock returns data. The Blin and Bender APT model followed the Ross factor theory, but Blin and Bender estimated at least 20 orthogonal factors. The tradeoff curves in Guerard [24] were created by varying lambda, a measure of risk-aversion, as a portfolio decision variable. Lambda measures the tradeoff between the portfolio expected return and risk. The Markowitz Efficient Frontier can be estimated by estimating a number of risk-aversion levels to estimate the risk-return tradeoff. A higher lambda leads to a higher ratio of portfolio expected return to portfolio risk. As lambda rises, the expected return of the portfolio rises and the number securities in the portfolio declines.

A general stock-selection model for U.S. and global equity markets

In 1991, Markowitz headed the Daiwa Securities Trust Global Portfolio Research Department (GPRD). The Markowitz team estimated stock-selection models using Graham and Dodd [28] fundamental valuation variables, earnings, book value, cash flow and sales, and relative variables, defined as the ratio of the absolute fundamental variable ratios divided by the 60-month averages of the fundamental variables. Bloch et al. [29] reported a set of approximately 200 simulations of U.S. and Japanese equity models. Guerard et al. [7] extended a stock-selection model, originally developed and estimated in Bloch et al. [29] by adding a price momentum (PM) and an analysts' expectations variable. The PM variable is the price in last month divided by the price 12 months prior, and the analysts' expectations variable involves the consensus I/B/E/S (Institutional Brokers' Estimate System) analysts' earnings forecasts and analysts' revisions composite analysts' efficiency variable, Consensus Temporary Earnings Forecasting (CTEF). Guerard [24] used the CTEF variable that is composed of forecasted earnings yield (FEP), earnings revisions (EREV), and EB (earnings breadth), which represents the direction of revisions and can also be identified as breadth, as created in Guerard et al. [30]. Guerard also reported domestic (U.S.) evidence that the predicted earnings yield is incorporated into the stock price through the earnings yield risk index. Moreover, CTEF dominates the historic low price-to-earnings effect, or high earnings-to-price (EP). The reader is referred to Guerard [30] for a more detailed analysis of the USER model. Fama and French [32–35] presented evidence to support the book-value-to-price (BP) and PM variables as anomalies. Guerard et al. [30] referred to the stock-selection model as a USER model. We can estimate an expanded stock-selection model to use as an input of expected returns in an optimization analysis at time t.

At time $t+1$, the stock-selection model estimated in this study, denoted as USER, is

$$\begin{aligned} TR_{t+1} = {} & a_0 + a_1 EP_t + a_2 BP_t + a_3 CP_t + a_4 SP_t + a_5 REP_t \\ & + a_6 \text{RBP}_t + a_7 RCP_t + a_8 RSP_t + a_9 CTEF_t + a_{10} PM_t + e_t \end{aligned} \quad (15)$$

where

EP	[earnings per share]/[price per share] = earnings – price ratio;
BP	[book value per share]/[price per share] = book value – price ratio;
CP	[cash flow per share]/[price per share] = cash flow – price ratio;
SP	[net sales per share]/[price per share] = sales – price ratio;
REP	[current EP ratio]/[average EP ratio over the past five years];
RBP	[current BP ratio]/[average BP ratio over the past five years];
RCP	[current CP ratio]/[average CP ratio over the past five years];
RSP	[current SP ratio]/[average SP ratio over the past five years];
CTEF	consensus earnings per share I/B/E/S forecast, revisions, and breadth;
PM	price momentum; and
e	randomly distributed error term.

The USER model is estimated using a weighted latent root regression (WLRR) analysis on Eq. (15) to identify variables statistically significant at the 10% level, and the model uses the normalized coefficients as weights and averages the variable weights over the past 12 months. The outlier-adjustment procedure is the Beaton-Tukey biweight procedure implemented and described in Bloch et al. [29].

The 12-month smoothing is consistent with the four-quarter smoothing in Bloch et al. [29]. Although EP and BP variables are significant in explaining returns, the majority of the forecast performance is attributable to other model variables, namely the relative earnings-to-price, relative cash-to-price, relative sales-to-price, PM, and earnings forecast variables. The CTEF and PM variables accounted for 44% of the weights in the USER model.

Extension to mean-ETL optimization model

Economists have been concerned with portfolio shortfall since 1959 when Markowitz addressed the topic in Chapter 9, "The Semi-Variance," in his *Portfolio Selection* [3]. Modern shortfall portfolio construction models, often referred to as "lower partial moments," are found in Bawa and Lindenberg [36], Jensen and King [37], King and Jensen [38], King [39], and Bertsimas et al. [40]. How to choose risk measure in a portfolio construction problem is an important part. The reason to choose ETL as a risk measure to construct a portfolio and compare with the GLER and the USER models is described in the following section.

Value-at-risk (VaR) has been a commonly used risk measure for a long time, which has an intuitive interpretation in practice. Artzner and Delbaen [41] proposed ETL as an alternative risk measure, which satisfies all the axioms of coherent risk measures, monotonicity, positive homogeneity, subadditivity, and the invariance property. In addition, ETL can be called Conditional Value at Risk (CVaR) or Expected Shortfall (ES). Compared with VaR, ETL is convex for all possible portfolios, which means that it always accounts for the diversification effect. ETL is defined as

$$ETL_\alpha(X) = \frac{1}{\alpha}\int_0^\alpha Var_p(X)dp, \tag{16}$$

where X is the returns, α is the tail probability, and $VaR_\alpha(X)$ is the value-at-risk of X:

$$Var_\alpha(X) = -\inf(x : P(X \le x) \ge \alpha). \tag{17}$$

ETL can be regarded as the average loss, or left tail, beyond the *VaR* threshold, and ETL can also be represented through a minimization formula [42]:

$$ETL_\alpha(X) = \min_{\theta \in R}\left(\theta + \frac{1}{\alpha}E(-X-\theta)_+\right), \tag{18}$$

where $(x)_+ = \max(x, 0)$.

In addition, ETL at tail probability α is one of the spectral risk measures, defined as

$$\rho_\phi(X) = \int_0^1 VaR_p(X)\phi(p)dp, \tag{19}$$

where $\phi(p)$, $p \in [0, 1]$ is the weighting function, or risk spectrum function. To ensure $\rho_\phi(X)$ to be a coherent risk measure, the risk spectrum function, $\phi(p)$, should satisfy the following criteria: $\phi(p) \ge 0$, $\phi(p)$ is nonincreasing, and $\int_0^1 \phi(p)dp = 1$. Rockafellar and Uryasev [42] have a more complete description of ETL properties.

In our mean-ETL portfolio optimization, we need to calculate the estimated ETL of scenarios, which are discrete return points, rather than a continuous function. For example, in this case, let $r_1, r_2, \ldots, r_S$ be the S scenario returns of the next time point, and we sort the scenario returns by $r_{(1)} \le r_{(2)} \le, \ldots, \le r_{(n)}$. Then, the ETL_α can be estimated by the following formula:

$$ETL_\alpha = -\frac{1}{\alpha}\left(\frac{1}{S}\sum_{k=1}^{\lceil S\alpha\rceil - 1} r_{(k)} + \left(\alpha - \frac{\lceil S\alpha\rceil - 1}{S}\right) r_{(\lceil S\alpha\rceil)}\right), \tag{20}$$

where $\lceil x\rceil$ means the smallest integer larger than x. Mean-ETL portfolio optimization will use this formula to calculate the estimated portfolio ETL from generated scenarios.

Multivariate normal tempered stable distribution (MNTS) is proposed here to capture the correlation between different securities. We can use independent normal tempered stable (NTS) innovation to model each stock individually. However, one of our targets is to construct a portfolio that can lower the downside risk and have a higher GLER value, and the correlation of GLER between different stocks has to be considered. Compared with NTS, MNTS has one more parameter—the covariance matrix $\boldsymbol{\rho}$ capturing the central dependence structure of the return MNTS distribution. The definition of MNTS of d dimensions can be defined as follows:

$$X = (X_1, X_2, \ldots, X_d) = \boldsymbol{\mu} + \boldsymbol{\beta}(CT - 1) + \boldsymbol{\gamma}\sqrt{CT}\boldsymbol{\varepsilon}, \tag{21}$$

where $\boldsymbol{\mu} = (\mu_1, \mu_2, \ldots, \mu_d)^T$, $\boldsymbol{\beta} = (\beta_1, \beta_2, \ldots, \beta_d)^T$, $\boldsymbol{\gamma} = (\gamma_1, \gamma_2, \ldots, \gamma_d)^T$, and $\boldsymbol{\gamma} > 0$.

CT is a classical tempered stable (CTS) subordinator with parameter (α, θ), where $\alpha \in (0, 1)$ and $\theta > 0$. $\boldsymbol{\varepsilon} = (\varepsilon_1, \varepsilon_2, \ldots, \varepsilon_d)^T$ is a d-dim standard normal distribution with covariance matrix $\boldsymbol{\rho}$, independent of the subordinator $CT > 0$. $(\cdot)^T$ is the transpose.

The autoregressive-moving-average (ARMA) generalized autoregressive conditional heteroskedastic (GARCH) and the multivariate normal tempered stable distribution (MNTS), denoted as ARMA-GARCH-MNTS, represent a flexible model for asset returns as it captures volatility clustering, heavy tails (the distributions are Pareto-stable-type except the very extreme tails, where it becomes exponential), skewness in any dimension, and a well-defined equivalent martingale measure. Model parameters can be estimated (via fast Fourier transformation) or calibrated; see Panorska and Mittnik [43]. To generate the scenarios at next time t, we propose the use of ARMA-GARCH-MNTS to model the changes of GLER. Fitting ARMA-GARCH-MNTS involves many parameters to estimate, and it is better to have longer in-sample data to fit the model. We propose the use of 120 months, or 10 years, of data as in-sample data to estimate the parameters in ARMA-GARCH-MNTS. First, we eliminate the securities that have too many missing points in out-of-sample data by requiring the maximum number of missing months in out-of-sample to be 10. In addition, all of the parameters are estimated for every out-of-sample month. To reduce the number of candidate securities and make use of the robust property of rankings, we select the stocks that have better performance over the last 5 months. Thus, at time t, we will choose the stocks with higher rankings from $t-5$ to $t-1$. We have a rolling window with a fixed length of 120 months to estimate the parameters of the ARMA-GARCH-MNTS model.

For convenience, we use $G_t^{(k)}$ to denote the GLER value of the k_t stock at time t, where $1 \le t \le T$ and $1 \le k \le N$. T and N are the number of data points and securities, respectively. $G_t^{(k)}$ are positive values because they are the monthly ranking of each stock. To apply ARMA-GARCH-MNTS to fit the data and generate scenarios, we perform the following transformations for security k at time t:

$$r_t^{(k)} = f(x) = \begin{cases} \log\left(G_t^{(k)}\right) - \log\left(G_{t-1}^{(k)}\right), & t \ge 2 \text{ and } k = 1, \ldots, N \\ 0, & t = 1 \text{ and } k = 1, \ldots, N, \end{cases} \quad (22)$$

where N denotes the number of securities in the portfolio.

We fit the ARMA-GARCH-MNTS model monthly transformed GLER data and then generate $S = 10,000$ scenarios of $r_t^{(k)}$. For convenience, we use $\hat{r}_t^{(k,s)}$ to denote the s-th scenario forecasting of k-th stock at time t. We want to maximize the GM of GLER and lower the downside risk. However, our forecasting model is applied to $r_t^{(k)}$, which is indicated in Eq. (22), instead of modeling on GLER directly. We generate the scenarios of $r_t^{(k)}$, and the following transformation is performed to obtain the scenarios of GLER $\widehat{G}_t^{(k,s)}$ from $\hat{r}_t^{(k,s)}$:

$$\widehat{G}_t^{(k,s)} = \exp\left(\hat{r}_t^{(k,s)} + \log\left(G_{t-1}^{(k)}\right)\right). \quad (23)$$

Here, $2 \le t \le T$, $1 \le k \le N$, and $1 \le s \le S$. T is the number of data points, N is the number of securities, and S is the number of scenarios.

After generating the scenarios of GLER values, $\widehat{G}_t^{(k,s)}$, we need to perform some transformations to ensure $0 \le \widehat{G}_t^{(k,s)} \le 99$. The stocks with the best performance will be 99, whereas the stocks with the worst performance will be 0. The approach we use here is to rank $\widehat{G}_t^{(k,s)}$ for each scenario s and then replace $\widehat{G}_t^{(k,s)}$ by the ranking. By using this approach, we can ensure $0 \le \widehat{G}_t^{(k,s)} \le 99$ while the relative advantages of better securities are staying the same. Then, at time t, we obtain the optimal weights by mean-ETL optimization from the scenarios generated by ARMA-GARCH-MNTS.

Here, mean-ETL optimization tries to maximize a utility function that includes the expected GLER and ETL_α of the scenarios. Thus, at time t the optimization problem can be described as follows:

$$\max_{\mathbf{w}_t} \frac{1}{S}\sum_{s=1}^{S} \mathbf{w}_t^{\mathrm{T}} \widehat{\mathbf{G}}_t^{(s)} - \lambda ETL_\alpha\left(\mathbf{w}_t^{\mathrm{T}} \widehat{\mathbf{G}}_t\right),$$

$$\text{subject to } 0.04 \ge \mathbf{w}_t \ge 0$$

$$\mathbf{e}_1^{\mathrm{T}} \mathbf{w}_t = 1 \quad (24)$$

where $\mathbf{w}_t$ is a column vector of optimal securities weights in the portfolio and $\widehat{\mathbf{G}}_t^{(s)}$ is a column vector that contains the s-th GLER scenario of all N securities:

$$\widehat{\mathbf{G}}_t^{(s)} = \left[\widehat{G}_t^{(1,s)}, \widehat{G}_t^{(2,s)}, \ldots, \widehat{G}_t^{(N,s)}\right]^{\mathrm{T}}$$

and $\widehat{\mathbf{G}}_t$ should be a matrix that consists of all S scenarios at time t:

$$\widehat{\mathbf{G}}_t = \left[\widehat{\mathbf{G}}_t^{(1)}, \widehat{\mathbf{G}}_t^{(2)}, \ldots, \widehat{\mathbf{G}}_t^{(S)}\right]_{N \times S}.$$

$(\cdot)^{\mathrm{T}}$ is the transpose. In our portfolio construction, α for ETL is chosen to be 1%, and the risk-averse parameter λ is chosen to be 1.

Portfolio simulation results with the USER and GLER models

Let us briefly review the Guerard et al. [30] Wharton Research Data Services (WRDS) USER model simulation to provide a baseline for comparison with the model in global markets during the 1999 to 2009 period. The portfolio returns of the USER model with APT MVTaR and a lambda of 200 are shown in **Table 1**. We report the Axioma attribution that the USER model produced a 10.7% annual active return, a result consistent with the Barra attribution results reported in Guerard et al. [7]. The active return is derived from a specific return of 16.3% annually. The active return has an Information Ratio of 1.12 and a t statistic of 3.68. Thus, the USER model is effective because of "bottom-up" stock selection. The APT-derived portfolios have active exposures to momentum, value, and size (0.49, 0.43, and -1.05, respectively) that are "priced" by the market to produce statistical significant portfolio factor returns with t statistics of 4.07, 4.24, and 2.9, respectively. The USER model portfolios have positive exposure to value and momentum, and smaller stocks are purchased. Similar factor exposures and statistically significant asset selection were found in the Tsuchida et al. [8] Mean-ETL portfolios using the USER series (Table 1). One can use WRDS Global Compustat data to estimate Eq. (15) weights. The WRDS GLER model, over the 1999 to 2009 period, produces an information ratio of 1.25 ($t = 3.92$) and excess returns of 13.18%, compared with WRDS USER excess returns of 10.7%. Global portfolios outperform the U.S.-only portfolios.

Table 1 Attribution of the USER model using the Axioma U.S. Fundamental Risk Model (USER). (IR: information ratio; HR: hit rate; T-stat: t statistics; n/a: not applicable. Adapted from [31].)

Local returns	*Return (geometric mean)*	*Risk (standard deviation)*	*IR*	*T-stat*	*Beginning no. of assets*	*End no. of assets*
Portfolio	0.095	0.221	n/a	n/a	94	92
Benchmark	-0.012	0.221	n/a	n/a	1854	1878
Active	0.107	0.096	1.115	3.683	1898	1922

Contributors to Active Return by Style

Style	*Contribution*	*Average weighted exposure*	*HR (% success)*	*Risk*	*IR*	*T-stat*
Size	0.042	−1.053	0.557	0.047	0.881	2.911
Medium-term momentum	0.026	0.486	0.748	0.021	1.232	4.071
Value	0.010	0.433	0.710	0.008	1.286	4.248
Market sensitivity	0.000	0.063	0.550	0.012	0.019	0.063
Exchange rate sensitivity	0.000	−0.357	0.580	0.007	0.027	0.090
Growth	−0.001	−0.044	0.443	0.002	−0.682	−2.252
Short-term momentum	−0.007	0.055	0.405	0.010	−0.735	−2.428
Leverage	−0.011	0.351	0.458	0.008	−1.298	−4.288
Liquidity	−0.046	−1.148	0.351	0.036	−1.269	−4.194
Volatility	−0.057	0.399	0.244	0.022	−2.591	−8.560

Contributors to Active Return by Sectors

Sectors	*Contribution*	*Average weighted exposure*	*HR (% success)*	*Risk*	*IR*	*T-stat*
Consumer Staples	0.007	−0.065	0.466	0.015	0.481	1.589
Energy	0.005	0.001	0.542	0.007	0.689	2.277
Industrials	0.005	-0.034	0.466	0.016	0.317	1.046
Health care	0.003	-0.032	0.550	0.014	0.240	0.793
Materials	0.002	0.031	0.595	0.011	0.186	0.615
Utilities	0.000	0.015	0.565	0.006	0.041	0.135
Consumer discretionary	−0.007	0.061	0.527	0.023	−0.294	−0.973
Information technology	−0.008	−0.108	0.405	0.035	−0.225	−0.743
Financials	−0.009	0.058	0.466	0.024	−0.360	−1.190
Telecommunication services	−0.010	0.071	0.496	0.016	−0.654	−2.160

In the world of business, one does not access academic databases annually, or even quarterly. Most industry analysis uses the FactSet database and the Thomson Financial I/B/E/S earnings forecasting database. We estimated the result of Eq. (15) for all securities on the Thomson Financial and FactSet databases, some 46,550 firms in December 2011. We estimated the GLER model from the FactSet universe for the 1990–2011 period and used FSGLER (FactSet Global Expected Return) to denote the expected return score. The average estimated GLER weights were as follows: $a_1(0.048)$, $a_2(0.069)$, $a_3(0.044)$, $a_4(0.047)$, $a_5(0.050)$, $a_6(0.032)$, $a_7(0.039)$, $a_8(0.086)$, $a_9(0.216)$, and $a_{10}(0.257)$.

In terms of information coefficients (ICs), the use of the WLRR procedure produces a higher IC for the models during the 1990-2009 time period, .044, versus the equally weighted IC of 0.035. The GLER model, compared with the USER model in Guerard et al. [7], has approximately the same ICs, but a t statistic of 6.91, statistically significant at the 5% level compared with the USER model t statistic of 5.77, also statistically significant at the 5% level, over the corresponding period. The IC test of statistical significance can be referred to as a Level I test. Further evidence on the anomalies is found in Levy [44]. The USER and GLER simulation conditions are identical to those described in Guerard et al. [7], which used monthly optimization with 8% turnover. Guerard et al.

Table 2 Barra attribution of APT-created FSGLER (global) portfolios, 2003 to 2011. (NoRC: no risk control model; MRC: moderate risk control model; SRC: strong risk control model; ACWG: All Country World Growth index; STD: portfolio standard deviation.)

	Portfolio Performance Criteria			
	NoRC	*MRC*	*SRC*	*ACWG benchmark*
Geometric mean	14.16%	13.75%	11.08%	4.56%
Information ratio	0.65	0.59	0.54	
Sharpe ratio	0.53	0.49	0.41	0.16
Excess returns	9.60%	9.19%	6.52%	
STD	23.20%	24.18%	22.71%	17.15%

Table 3 Attribution of FSGLER APT-created portfolios using the Axioma World Fundamental Risk Model. The term *local* refers to the domestic market.

Source of return	*Contribution*	*Average exposure*	*Hit rate*	*Risk*	*IR*	*T-stat*
Portfolio	12.62%			21.18%		
Benchmark	1.69%			19.59%		
Active	10.93%			8.53%	1.22	3.85
Factor contribution	7.01%			6.67%	1.05	3.31
Style	4.47%			6.24%	0.72	2.26
Exchange rate sensitivity	0.02%	0.014	43.70%	0.26%	0.08	0.27
Growth	0.77%	0.392	68.91%	0.46%	1.65	5.21
Leverage	−0.27%	0.064	47.06%	0.19%	−1.46	−4.59
Liquidity	0.34%	0.177	57.98%	0.64%	0.54	1.69
Medium-term momentum	4.78%	0.486	74.79%	2.17%	2.21	6.95
Short-term momentum	1.69%	0.025	47.90%	1.30%	1.30	4.11
Size	0.86%	−0.746	53.78%	4.57%	0.19	0.60
Value	1.57%	0.153	58.82%	0.91%	1.73	5.44
Volatility	−5.30%	0.501	36.13%	4.16%	−1.27	−4.01
Country	2.25%			2.11%	1.07	3.36
Industry	−0.46%			1.65%	−0.28	−0.88
Currency	0.35%			1.21%	0.29	0.90
Local	0.10%			0.28%	0.36	1.13
Market	0.31%			1.78%	0.17	0.54
Specific return	3.91%			5.95%	0.66	2.07

[7] also used 125 basis points, each way (i.e., for buying and selling stocks), of transactions cost in the United States, and we use 150 basis points, each way, in the global simulation. We restricted the simulations to securities covered by at least two I/B/E/S analysts, a real-world business simulation condition of McKinley Capital Management (MCM). We use the APT risk model and optimizer described in Blin et al. [27] to create portfolios during the 1999-2011 period by varying the portfolio lambda. One seeks to maximize the GM, Sharpe ratios, and information ratios of portfolios. We experimented with the Wormald and van der Merwe [45] risk control conditions. We find that the No Risk Control (NoRC) condition produced higher information ratios and GMs than the strong risk control (SRC), which is defined as systematic tracking error less than 2.3%, or mild risk control (MRC), which is defined as systematic tracking error less than 1.7%. These results are shown in **Table 2** for the 2003–2011 period. The benchmark is the Morgan Stanley

Table 4 Attribution of FSGLER mean-ETL model using the Axioma World Fundamental Risk Model. The term *style* refers to factor index variables.

Local returns	*Return*	*Risk*	*IR*	*T-stat*
Portfolio	0.139	0.224		
Benchmark	0.022	0.197		
Active	0.116	0.087	1.33	4.60
Contributor to active returns				
Specific return	0.093	0.042	2.15	7.41
Factor returns	0.026	0.077	0.34	1.18
Contributor to factor returns				
Style	0.029	0.055	0.52	1.80
Country	−0.012	0.040	−0.31	−1.06
Industry	0.018	0.021	0.52	1.81
Currency	−0.32	0.019	−0.17	−0.58
Local	0.030	0.035	0.35	2.95
Market	−0.06	0.038	−0.001	−0.59

Capital International All Country World Growth (MSCI ACWG) index.

We have established that the NoRC model was effective in the FSGLER universe. The portfolio returns of the FSGLER NoRC model with a lambda of 200 are shown in **Table 3**. We report that the GLER model produced a 12.62% annual return, a result consistent with the USER attribution results. The active return of 10.93% is derived from a factor return of 7.01% annually. The active return has an information ratio of 1.22 and a t statistic of 3.85. The active return is highly statistically significant.

The GLER model is effective because of stock selection. The APT-derived portfolios have active exposures to momentum, value, and size (0.49, 0.15, and −0.75, respectively), and the momentum and value factors are "priced" by the market to produce statistical significant portfolio factor returns with t statistics of 6.95, 5.44, and 0.60, respectively. The benchmark is the Russel Global Growth Index. The GLER model portfolios have positive exposure to value and momentum, and smaller stocks are purchased.

The active return of the mean-ETL model with lambda equal to 1 has an 8.73% annual active return, shown in **Table 4**, which has an information ratio of 1.33 and a t statistic of 4.60. The stock-selection model produces a statistically significant active return. The annual active return of the mean-ETL portfolio is larger than the return of the Russell Global Growth benchmark.

The USER and GLER portfolios and the respective attribution analyses report statistically significant active returns based on specific asset selection. APT and mean-ETL optimization techniques, and USER and GLER estimated stock-selection models, produce portfolios consistent with the maximization of the GM, Sharpe ratio, and information ratio.

Conclusions

We addressed several issues in portfolio construction and management using the Guerard et al. [7] USER data and its extension to a global database and estimation universe. We reported that the Markowitz MV optimization technique, the EIT optimization technique, and tracking error at risk models are appropriate for USER and GLER data. Global portfolios dominate domestic portfolios with regard to the return-to-risk statistics for the 1999-2011 period. The Markowitz approach to portfolio construction and management is 60 years old and remains an integral tool of investment research.

Acknowledgments

We thank Vishnu Anand, of Axioma, who ran the attribution analysis based on the Axioma Fundamental Risk Model. Earlier versions of this paper were presented at the Oxford-Man Institute of Quantitative Finance, University of Oxford, November 2012, and the 32nd International Symposium on Forecasting, Boston, June 2012.

References

1. H. M. Markowitz, "Portfolio selection," *J. Financ.*, vol. 7, no. 1, pp. 77–91, Mar. 1952.
2. H. M. Markowitz, "The optimization of a quadratic function subject to linear constraints," *Naval Res. Logist. Quart.*, vol. 3, no. 1/2, pp. 111–133, Mar.–Jun. 1956.
3. H. M. Markowitz, *Portfolio Selection: Efficient Diversification of Investment, Cowles Foundation Monograph no. 16.* New York, NY, USA: Wiley, 1959.

4. H. M. Markowitz, *Mean-Variance Analysis in Portfolio Choice and Capital Markets*. Oxford, U.K.: Blackwell, 1987.
5. B. Solnik, "Why not diversify internationally rather than domestically," *Financ. Anal. J.*, vol. 30, no. 4, pp. 48–54, Jul./Aug. 1974.
6. B. Solnik, *International Investments,* 4th ed. Reading, MA, USA: Addison-Wesley, 2000.
7. J. B. Guerard, Jr., M. N. Gultekin, and G. Xu, "Investing with momentum: The past, present, and future," *J. Invest.*, vol. 21, no. 1, pp. 68–80, Spring 2012.
8. N. Tsuchida, X. Zhou, and S. Rachev, "Mean-ETL portfolio selection under maximum weight and turnover constraints based on fundamental security factors," *J. Invest.*, vol. 21, no. 1, pp. 14–24, Spring 2012.
9. H. A. Latane, "Criteria for choice among risky ventures," *J. Polit. Econ.*, vol. 67, no. 2, pp. 144–155, Apr. 1959.
10. H. M. Markowitz, "Investment in the long run: New evidence for an old rule," *J. Financ.*, vol. 31, no. 5, pp. 1273–1286, Dec. 1976.
11. J. B. Guerard, Jr., M. Takano, and Y. Yamane, "The development of efficient portfolios in Japan with particular emphasis on sales and earnings forecasting," *Ann. Oper. Res.*, vol. 45, no. 1–4, pp. 91–108, Dec. 1993.
12. J. Guerard, Jr., E. Krauklis, and M. Kumar, "Further analysis of efficient portfolios with the USER data," *J. Invest.*, vol. 21, no. 1, pp. 81–88, Spring 2012.
13. W. F. Sharpe, "Capital asset prices: A theory of market equilibrium under conditions of risk," *J. Financ.*, vol. 19, no. 3, pp. 425–442, Sep. 1964.
14. J. Lintner, "The valuation of risk assets on the selection of risky investments in stock portfolios and capital investments," *Rev. Econ. Stat.*, vol. 47, no. 1, pp. 13–37, Feb. 1965.
15. J. Mossin, "Equilibrium in a capital asset market," *Econometrica*, vol. 34, no. 4, pp. 768–783, Oct. 1966.
16. W. F. Sharpe, "A simplified model for portfolio analysis," *Manage. Sci.*, vol. 9, no. 2, pp. 277–293, Jan. 1963.
17. B. Rosenberg, "Extra-market components of covariance in security returns," *J. Financ. Quant. Anal.*, vol. 9, no. 2, pp. 263–274, Mar. 1974.
18. S. A. Ross, "The arbitrage theory of capital asset pricing," *J. Econ. Theory*, vol. 13, no. 3, pp. 341–360, Feb. 1976.
19. S. A. Ross and R. Roll, "An empirical investigation of the arbitrage pricing theory," *J. Financ.*, vol. 35, no. 5, pp. 1071–1103, Dec. 1980.
20. B. Rosenberg and V. Marathe, "Tests of capital asset pricing hypotheses," in *Research in Finance*, H. Levy, Ed. Greenwich, CT, USA: JAI Press, 1979.
21. A. Rudd and H. K. Clasing, *Modern Portfolio Theory: The Principles of Investment Management.* Homewood, IL, USA: Dow-Jones Irwin, 1982.
22. R. Grinold and R. Kahn, *Active Portfolio Management.* New York, NY, USA: McGraw-Hill, 1999.
23. G. Conner and R. A. Korajczyk, "Factor models in portfolio and asset pricing theory," in *The Handbook of Portfolio Construction: Contemporary Applications of Markowitz Techniques*, J. Guerard, Ed. New York, NY, USA: Springer-Verlag, 2010.
24. J. Guerard, "Global earnings forecast efficiency," in *Research in Finance*. Bingley, U.K.: Emerald Group Publishing, 2012, pp. 19–47.
25. *APT Analytics Guide,* Sungard APT, London, U.K., 2005.
26. *APT Analytics Guide,* Sungard APT, London, U.K., 2011.
27. J. M. Blin, S. Bender, and J. B. Guerard, Jr., "Earnings forecasts, revisions and momentum in the estimation of efficient market-neutral japanese and U.S. portfolios," in *Research in Finance*, A. Chen, Ed. Greenwich, CT: JAI Press, Inc., 1997, pp. 93–114.
28. B. Graham and D. Dodd, *Security Analysis: Principles and Technique.* New York, NY, USA: McGraw-Hill, 1934.
29. M. Bloch, J. B. Guerard, Jr., H. M. Markowitz, P. Todd, and G. L. Xu, "A comparison of some aspects of the U.S. and Japanese equity markets," *Jpn. World Econ.*, vol. 5, no. 1, pp. 3–26, May 1993.
30. J. B. Guerard, Jr., M. Gultekin, and B. K. Stone, "The role of fundamental data and analysts' earnings breadth, forecasts, and revisions in the creation of efficient portfolios," in *Research in Finance*, A. Chen, Ed. Greenwich, CT: JAI Press, Inc., 1997, pp. 69–92.
31. J. B. Guerard, Jr., *Introduction to Financial Forecasting in Investment Analysis*. New York, NY, USA: Springer-Verlag, 2013.
32. E. F. Fama and K. R. French, "Cross-sectional variation in expected stock returns," *J. Financ.*, vol. 47, no. 2, pp. 427–465, Jun. 1992.
33. E. F. Fama and K. R. French, "Size and the book-to-market factors in earnings and returns," *J. Financ.*, vol. 50, no. 1, pp. 131–155, Mar. 1995.
34. E. F. Fama and K. R. French, "Multifactor explanations of asset pricing anomalies," *J. Financ.*, vol. 51, no. 1, pp. 55–84, Feb. 1996.
35. E. F. Fama and K. R. French, "Dissecting anomalies," *J. Financ.*, vol. 63, no. 4, pp. 1653–1678, Aug. 2008.
36. V. S. Bawa and E. B. Lindenberg, "Capital market equilibrium in a mean-lower partial moment framework," *J. Financ. Econ.*, vol. 5, no. 2, pp. 255–271, Nov. 1977.
37. D. L. Jensen and A. J. King, "Frontier: A graphical interface for portfolio optimization in a piecewise linear-quadratic risk framework," *IBM Syst. J.*, vol. 31, no. 1, pp. 62–70, Jan. 1992.
38. A. J. King and D. L. Jensen, "Linear-quadratic efficient frontiers for portfolio optimization," *Appl. Stoch. Models Data Anal.*, vol. 8, no. 3, pp. 195–207, Sep. 1992.
39. A. J. King, "Asymmetric risk measures and tracking models for portfolio optimization under uncertainty," *Ann. Oper. Res.*, vol. 45, no. 1–4, pp. 165–177, Dec. 1993.
40. D. Bertsimas, G. J. Lauprete, and A. Samarov, "Shortfall as a risk measure: Properties, optimzation and applications," *J. Econ. Dynam. Control*, vol. 28, no. 7, pp. 1353–1381, Apr. 2004.
41. P. Artzner and F. Delbaen, "Coherent measures of risk," *Math. Financ.*, vol. 9, no. 3, pp. 203–228, Jul. 1999.
42. R. T. Rockafellar and S. Uryasev, "Conditional value-at-risk for general loss distributions," *J. Bank. Financ.*, vol. 26, no. 7, pp. 1443–1471, Jul. 2002.
43. A. Panorska and S. Mittnik, "Stable GARCH models for financial time series," *Appl. Math. Lett.*, vol. 8, no. 5, pp. 33–37, Sep. 1995.
44. H. Levy, *Introduction to Investments,* 2nd ed. Cincinnati, OH, USA: South-Western College Publishing, 1999.
45. L. Wormald and E. van der Merwe, "Constrained optimization for portfolio construction," *J. Invest.*, vol. 21, no. 1, pp. 44–59, Spring 2012.

Received February 28, 2013; accepted for publication March 26, 2013

John B. Guerard, Jr. *McKinley Capital Management, LLC, Anchorage, AK 99503 USA (jguerard@mckinleycapital.com).* Dr. Guerard is Director of Quantitative Research at McKinley Capital Management, in Anchorage, Alaska. He earned his A.B. degree in economics from Duke University, M.A. degree in economics from the University of Virginia, M.S.I.M. degree from the Georgia Institute of Technology, and Ph.D. degree in finance from the University of Texas, Austin. He co-managed a Japanese equity portfolio with Harry Markowitz at Daiwa Securities Trust Company. Dr. Guerard has published several monographs, including *The Handbook of Financial Modeling* (Probus, 1989, with H.T. Vaught), *Corporate Financial Policy and R&D Management* (Wiley, 2006, second edition), *Quantitative Corporate Finance* (Springer, 2007, with Eli Schwartz), and *The Handbook of Portfolio Construction: Contemporary Applications of Markowitz Techniques* (Springer, 2010). He serves an Associate Editor of the *Journal of Investing* and *The International Journal of Forecasting*.

Svetlozar (Zari) Todorav Rachev *College of Business, Stony Brook University, Stony Brook, NY 11794 USA (svetlozar.rachev@stonybrook.edu).* Dr. Rachev is Professor of Finance at the College of

Business, Stony Brook University. He is also the Program Director, at the M.S. (Master of Science) Investment Risk Finance Program, Stony Brook University, and Frey Family Foundation Chair of Quantitative Finance, in the Department of Applied Mathematics and Statistics, SUNY-Stony Brook. Dr. Rachev earned his Ph.D. degree in mathematics at Lomonosov University (Moscow), and a Doctor of Science (Habilitation) in physics and mathematics at the Steklov Mathematical Institute. Dr. Rachev has published many models in quantitative finance, including *The Methods of Distances in the Theory of Probability and Statistics* (John Wiley, Finance, 2013, with L. B. Klebanov, S. Stoyanov, and F. Fabozzi), *Financial Models with Levy Processes and Volatility Clustering* (Springer, New York, 2011, with S.T. Kim, M. Bianchi, and F. Fabozzi), *Probability and Statistics for Finance* (John Wiley, Finance, 2010), *Advanced Stochastic Models, Risk Assessment and Portfolio Optimization: The Ideal Risk, Uncertainty, and Performance Measures* (Wiley, 2007, with S. Stoyanov and F. Fabozzi), and *Stable Paretian Models in Finance* (Wiley, New York, 2000, with S. Mittnik). Dr. Rachev's research areas cover non_Gaussian models in mathematical finance, financial econometrics, factor models for asset returns, market and credit risk management, operational risk assessment and forecast, and portfolio optimization and asset liability modeling.

Barret Pengyuan Shao *Applied Mathematics and Statistics, Stony Brook University, Stony Brook, NY 11794 USA (barretshao@gmail.com)*. Mr. Shao is a Ph.D. candidate in quantitative finance at SUNY Stony Brook University. He earned his B.S. degree in automatic control from Xiamen University and a B.S. degree in mathematical economics from Wangyanan Institute for Studies in Economics (WISE) in China.

https://doi.org/10.1142/9789811222634_0016

Chapter 16

Avoiding the Downside: A Practical Review of the Critical Line Algorithm for Mean–Semivariance Portfolio Optimization

Harry M. Markowitz

President at Harry Markowitz Company, 1010 Turquoise Street, San Diego, CA 92109, USA

David Starer

Director of Research at Constantia Capital, 17 Hendrickson Rd., Suite 100, Lawrenceville, NJ 08648, USA

Harvey Fram

Founder and Portfolio Manager at Constantia Capital, 17 Hendrickson Rd., Suite 100, Lawrenceville, NJ 08648, USA

Sander Gerber

Managing Partner, Chief Executive Officer, and Chief Investment Officer at Hudson Bay Capital Management, 777 Third Avenue, 30th Floor, New York, NY 10017, USA

Optimizing a portfolio to reduce exposure to downside risk can be difficult, and usually involves third or higher order statistical moments of the portfolio's return distribution. Mean–semivariance optimization simplifies this problem by using only the first two moments of the distribution and by penalizing returns below a predetermined reference. Although this penalty introduces a nonlinearity, mean–semivariance optimization can be performed easily and efficiently using the critical line algorithm

(CLA) provided that the covariance matrix is estimated from a historical record of asset returns. In practice, this proviso is not restrictive. This chapter reviews the theory of the CLA and presents sample computer code for applying the algorithm to mean–variance and mean–semivariance portfolio optimization. It also reviews a method for finding the efficient mean–semivariance portfolio for any given feasible desired expected portfolio return.

Keywords: Portfolio optimization, downside portfolio optimization, critical line algorithm, CLA, mean-semivariance.

1. Introduction

Mean–variance portfolio optimization continues to dominate asset management. In the majority of cases, it is the best method because, under widely applicable conditions, it maximizes the investor's utility (Levy and Markowitz, 1979), it is very easy to implement, and it is intuitively appealing.

Variance, however, is a symmetric measure; meaning that mean–variance optimization disfavors large positive returns as much as it disfavors large negative returns. Generally though, investors favor large positive returns, or positively skewed portfolio return distributions. Therefore, some would argue that mean–variance optimization should be augmented with methods that penalize only negative returns; i.e., with downside portfolio optimization. For this purpose, semivariance is a particularly useful measure of downside risk because it considers returns as risky only if they are below some reference return.

Despite its intuitive appeal, mean–semivariance optimization remains shrouded in mystery. This is primarily because of the difficulties raised by the apparent nonlinearity involved in the computation of semivariance. For example, Estrada (2008) states, "semivariance optimal portfolios cannot be determined without resorting to obscure numerical algorithms." In a similar vein, Cumova and Nawrocki (2011) state that mean–semivariance optimization "requires a laborious iterative process because the [semicovariance] matrix is endogenous and a closed form solution does not exist," and Cumova and Nawrocki (2014) say in part that mean–semivariance optimization "has traditionally been challenged by academic researchers because of the computational complexity of the asymmetric [semicovariance] matrix."

In reality, the mean–semivariance optimization problem was solved more than 60 years ago in Markowitz (1959), which showed that if an estimate of the covariance matrix is computed using time series of security returns, the great computational benefit of the Critical Line Algorithm (CLA) could be exploited to construct mean–semivariance efficient frontiers. Niedermayer and Niedermayer (2009) have shown that the CLA can be orders of magnitude faster than other algorithms for mean–variance optimization.

With the appropriate definition of new non-negative variables, Markowitz *et al.* (1992, 1993) showed how the mean–semivariance problem could be formulated such that a standard quadratic (i.e., mean–variance optimizer) could be used for the mean–semivariance problem as well.

In this chapter, we provide a review of the CLA for mean–variance and mean–semivariance optimization, as well as the method of Markowitz, Todd, Xu, and Yamane (1992, 1993) (the MTXY method) for mean–semivariance optimization. The primary reference for practical computation of the CLA itself is Chapter 13 of Markowitz and Todd (2000), which provides a Visual Basic implementation of the algorithm. Similar descriptions, such as those in Niedermayer and Niedermayer (2009) and Bailey and López de Prado (2013) have provided didactic and open-source versions in FORTRAN and Python. The contributions of this chapter are that we provide simple example code for the CLA applied to the mean–*semivariance* problem. Previously, only a brief description of the method has been available in Markowitz *et al.* (1992, 1993) with speed improvements and slightly more complicated extensions in Markowitz *et al.* (1992, 1993).

Our objective is to provide a step-by-step tutorial of the basic CLA, with the theory of each step clearly explained and tied to a specific block of computer code. To emphasize the flexibility of the CLA, we first review the CLA for mean–variance optimization with reference to a simple Python realization. We then build on the basic CLA and provide R code for mean–semivariance optimization.

Finally, we show how to solve the mean–semivariance optimization problem with modern convex optimization using the CVXR library (Boyd and Vandenberghe, 2004). We emphasize, however, that the computer code presented here is not intended for production purposes. It is merely illustrative.

One of the many benefits of the CLA is that it is amenable to very rapid computation using an efficient update of a certain matrix inverse when the components of that matrix change. The details of this update, based on the Sherman–Morrison–Woodbury formula (see, for example, Hager (1989) and references therein) are provided in Chapter 13 of Markowitz (1959). While very important for the purpose of obtaining fast code, the details of this matrix inverse update tend to hide the simplicity of the CLA. Therefore, in this chapter, we simply re-invert that matrix whenever needed. In practice, with modern computer hardware and software, and for typical institutional portfolios, the degradation in performance is not prohibitive. We also omit details of the initialization of the algorithm for general linear equality and inequality constraints. This merely requires standard linear programming, and again the details are available in Markowitz and Todd (2000).

In general, when considering whether to use mean–semivariance optimization instead of mean–variance optimization, analysts should be aware of the following compromise: semivariance is likely to exclude many periods. So the semicovariance estimate uses significantly fewer observations than the covariance estimate, and may therefore be less reliable. If the return distributions of assets are not significantly asymmetrical, positive return periods could also provide useful information on potential downside risk, and it may not be beneficial to exclude them.

2. The Critical Line Algorithm

The objective in portfolio optimization is to find the fraction x_i of investor wealth to be assigned to each asset i of n assets so as to maximize investor's utility subject to all constraints that the investor faces. In this section, we use the mean–variance approximation to utility (Levy and Markowitz, 1979). Let μ_{P} be the expected value of the portfolio's return, let σ_{P}^2 be the variance of the portfolio's return, and let $\lambda_{\mathrm{E}} \geq 0$ be a parameter under the investor's control that adjusts the trade-off between risk (variance) and return.[1] The mean–variance approximation to utility is

$$\mathcal{U} = \lambda_{\mathrm{E}}\mu_{\mathrm{P}} - \tfrac{1}{2}\sigma_{\mathrm{P}}^2. \tag{1}$$

The efficient frontier is the locus of all points in $(\sigma_{\mathrm{P}}, \mu_{\mathrm{P}})$-space corresponding to feasible portfolios that minimize σ_{P} for given μ_{P}, or maximize μ_{P} for given σ_{P}. Each point on the efficient frontier is the optimal pair $(\sigma_{\mathrm{P}}, \mu_{\mathrm{P}})$ for a given choice of λ_{E}. The CLA (Markowitz, 1987) is a computationally efficient method for finding the entire efficient frontier.

To understand the CLA, let μ_i be the expected return of security i, and let σ_{ij} or $\sigma_{i,j}$ be the covariance between the returns of securities i and j. Then the expected return and the variance of the portfolio's return are

$$\mu_{\mathrm{P}} = \sum_{i=1}^{n} \mu_i x_i, \quad \sigma_{\mathrm{P}}^2 = \sum_{i=1}^{n}\sum_{j=1}^{n} x_i \sigma_{ij} x_j.$$

Defining the mean vector $\boldsymbol{\mu}$, the portfolio weight vector $\boldsymbol{x}$, and the covariance matrix $\boldsymbol{C}$ as

$$\boldsymbol{\mu} = \begin{bmatrix} \mu_1 \\ \mu_2 \\ \vdots \\ \mu_n \end{bmatrix}, \quad \boldsymbol{x} = \begin{bmatrix} x_1 \\ x_2 \\ \vdots \\ x_n \end{bmatrix}, \quad \boldsymbol{C} = \begin{bmatrix} \sigma_{1,1} & \sigma_{1,2} & \cdots & \sigma_{1,n} \\ \sigma_{2,1} & \sigma_{2,2} & \cdots & \sigma_{2,n} \\ \vdots & & & \vdots \\ \sigma_{n,1} & \sigma_{n,2} & \cdots & \sigma_{n,n} \end{bmatrix},$$

we can also write the portfolio mean and variance as

$$\mu_{\mathrm{P}} = \boldsymbol{\mu}^{\top}\boldsymbol{x}, \quad \sigma_{\mathrm{P}}^2 = \boldsymbol{x}^{\top}\boldsymbol{C}\boldsymbol{x}.$$

[1] We can also interpret λ_{E} as a measure of risk tolerance.

The mean–variance approximation to utility in Equation (1) is then

$$\mathcal{U} = \lambda_{\mathrm{E}}\boldsymbol{\mu}^\top \boldsymbol{x} - \tfrac{1}{2}\boldsymbol{x}^\top \boldsymbol{C}\boldsymbol{x}. \tag{2}$$

Our objective, therefore, is to find the value of the weight vector $\boldsymbol{x}$ that maximizes (or equivalently that minimizes the negative of) the utility expressed in Equation (2).

The weights x_i are subject to constraints. By definition, since x_i is the fraction of the investor's wealth invested in security i, these weights must sum to 100%. This is the budget constraint, and it is written as

$$\sum_{i=1}^{n} x_i = 1.$$

Using more compact vector notation, with $\boldsymbol{\iota}$ being defined as a vector of ones whose dimension is determined from context, the budget constraint can be written as $\boldsymbol{\iota}^\top \boldsymbol{x} = 1$. The budget constraint is an example of one equation that can be included in a more general set of m linear equality constraints

$$\boldsymbol{A}\boldsymbol{x} = \boldsymbol{b} \tag{3}$$

for a given $m \times n$ constraint matrix $\boldsymbol{A}$ and $m \times 1$ constraint vector $\boldsymbol{b}$.

For the moment, consider the Lagrangian for minimizing the negative of the utility in Equation (2) subject only to the linear equality constraints. That is,

$$\mathcal{L}(\boldsymbol{x}, \boldsymbol{\lambda}|\lambda_{\mathrm{E}}) = \underbrace{\tfrac{1}{2}\boldsymbol{x}^\top \boldsymbol{C}\boldsymbol{x} - \lambda_{\mathrm{E}}\boldsymbol{\mu}^\top \boldsymbol{x}}_{\text{Objective}} - \boldsymbol{\lambda}^\top \underbrace{(\boldsymbol{A}\boldsymbol{x} - \boldsymbol{b})}_{\text{Constraint}}. \tag{4}$$

Here, $\boldsymbol{\lambda}$ is the $m \times 1$ Lagrange multiplier vector on the linear equality constraints.

In this case, the vector derivatives of the Lagrangian with respect to both $\boldsymbol{x}$ and $\boldsymbol{\lambda}$ must be equal to zero vectors. Differentiating the Lagrangian, we obtain

$$\frac{\partial \mathcal{L}}{\partial \boldsymbol{x}} = \boldsymbol{C}\boldsymbol{x} - \boldsymbol{\mu}\lambda_{\text{E}} + \boldsymbol{A}^{\top}\boldsymbol{\lambda}, \tag{5}$$

$$\frac{\partial \mathcal{L}}{\partial \boldsymbol{\lambda}} = \boldsymbol{A}\boldsymbol{x} - \boldsymbol{b}. \tag{6}$$

Setting these equations to zero to find the turning points of the Lagrangian, we get

$$\begin{bmatrix} \boldsymbol{C} & \boldsymbol{A}^{\top} \\ \boldsymbol{A} & \mathbf{O} \end{bmatrix} \begin{bmatrix} \boldsymbol{x} \\ \boldsymbol{\lambda} \end{bmatrix} = \begin{bmatrix} \boldsymbol{\mu} \\ \mathbf{0} \end{bmatrix} \lambda_{\text{E}} + \begin{bmatrix} \mathbf{0} \\ \boldsymbol{b} \end{bmatrix}, \tag{7}$$

where $\mathbf{O}$ is an appropriately dimensioned matrix of zeros, and $\mathbf{0}$ is an appropriately dimensioned vector of zeros.

Besides the linear equality constraints, the weights may also be subject to sets of linear inequality constraints in the form $\boldsymbol{F}\boldsymbol{x} \leq \boldsymbol{g}$. Inequality constraints can be converted into equality constraints with the addition of slack or surplus variables together with non-negativity constraints. Here, we will assume that such conversions have already been made, and consider only bounds on the minimum and maximum values of x_i. Specifically, define the $n \times 1$ minimum (down) vector $\boldsymbol{d}$ with elements d_i such that $x_i \geq d_i$. For example, the lower bound on a simple long-only portfolio is $d_i = 0$ for all i. Also define the $n \times 1$ maximum (up) vector $\boldsymbol{u}$ with elements u_i such that $x_i \leq u_i$. In vector form, $\boldsymbol{d} \leq \boldsymbol{x} \leq \boldsymbol{u}$.

We now consider the modifications of Equation (7) that are necessary to take account of the bounds. For a particular value of λ_{E} (i.e., for a point on a particular segment of the efficient frontier, as we shall discuss later), element i in the first block in Equation (7), or equivalently element i obtained when the derivative in Equation (5) is set to zero, is

$$\sum_{j=1}^{n} \sigma_{i,j} x_j + \sum_{j=1}^{m} a_{j,i} \lambda_j = \mu_i \lambda_{\text{E}} \text{ for } i \in \texttt{IN} \subseteq \{1, \ldots, n\}, \tag{8}$$

where $a_{j,i}$ is the element in row j and column i of $\boldsymbol{A}$. Importantly, this equation only holds for security i if the derivative $\partial \mathcal{L} / \partial x_i$ is zero for a value of x_i that lies between the upper bound u_i and lower bound d_i. We refer to the set of i for which these conditions hold as the IN set. For securities whose derivatives are zero for values outside of these bounds (i.e., for $i \notin \texttt{IN}$), the corresponding elements of Equation (8) do not hold, and must be modified.

First consider all securities i for which $\partial\mathcal{L}/\partial x_i$ would be zero at a value of x_i that is above the upper bound u_i. Such securities must be constrained to their upper bounds. We define UP to be the set of i for securities constrained like this. For these securities, since we can no longer set the derivatives equal to zero, we can ignore the previous contents of each equation $i \in \texttt{UP}$ in the top block of equation set (7). Instead, we use each equation i to impose the constraint $x_i = u_i$. Similarly, if $\partial\mathcal{L}/\partial x_i$ would be zero for a value of x_i that is below the lower bound d_i, we must constrain x_i to its lower bound. We define DN to be the set of i for securities constrained like this.

To impose these bounds for all $i \in \texttt{UP}$ or $i \in \texttt{DN}$ in the top block row of Equation (7):

S1. Replace row i of $\boldsymbol{C}$ with zeros, except in column i. Place a 1 at the intersection of row i and column i. Let $\bar{\boldsymbol{C}}$ be the resulting matrix after this replacement.

S2. Replace column i of $\boldsymbol{A}$ (i.e., row i of $\boldsymbol{A}^\top$) with zeros. Let $\bar{\boldsymbol{A}}$ be the resulting matrix after this replacement.

S3. Replace element i of $\boldsymbol{\mu}$ with zero. Let $\bar{\boldsymbol{\mu}}$ be the resulting vector after this replacement.

S4. Add a vector $\boldsymbol{k}$ to the right-hand side with entries $k_i = u_i$ if $i \in \texttt{UP}$, or $k_i = d_i$ if $i \in \texttt{DN}$, or $k_i = 0$ if $i \in \texttt{IN}$.

We therefore now have

$$\bar{\boldsymbol{C}}\boldsymbol{x} + \bar{\boldsymbol{A}}^\top\boldsymbol{\lambda} = \bar{\boldsymbol{\mu}}\lambda_E + \boldsymbol{k}. \tag{9}$$

This equation takes care of the first block equation in equation set (7) by ensuring that the derivatives $\partial\mathcal{L}/\partial x_i$ are equal to zero for $i \in \texttt{IN}$, and that the weights x_i are equal to their upper bounds for $i \in \texttt{UP}$ or lower bounds for $i \in \texttt{DN}$.

To maintain symmetry in the matrix in equation set (7), we should replace the $\boldsymbol{A}$ in the second block row with $\bar{\boldsymbol{A}}$. Equation ℓ in the second block row is

$$\sum_{j=1}^{n} a_{\ell,j} x_j = b_\ell \text{ for } \ell \in \{1, \ldots, m\}. \tag{10}$$

Analogous to $a_{i,j}$, let $\bar{a}_{i,j}$ be the element in row i and column j of$\bar{\boldsymbol{A}}$. From step S2 above, we know that if security i is bound with $i \in \texttt{UP}$ or $i \in \texttt{DN}$, we must have $\bar{a}_{i,k} = 0$ for all k. Therefore, to maintain equality in Equation (3), we need to add back these zeroed-out quantities with the appropriate bounds contained in $\boldsymbol{k}$ from step S4. Equation (10) therefore becomes

$$\sum_{j=1}^{n} \bar{a}_{\ell,j} x_j + \sum_{j=1}^{n} a_{\ell,j} k_j = b_\ell \text{ for } \ell \in \{1, \ldots, m\},$$

which is written in matrix form as

$$\bar{\boldsymbol{A}}\boldsymbol{x} = \boldsymbol{b} - \boldsymbol{A}\boldsymbol{k}.$$

Combining these two modifications of Equation (7), we find that we can account for securities in all sets (IN, UP, or DN) with the equation

$$\begin{bmatrix} \bar{\boldsymbol{C}} & \bar{\boldsymbol{A}}^\top \\ \bar{\boldsymbol{A}} & \mathbf{O} \end{bmatrix} \begin{bmatrix} \boldsymbol{x} \\ \boldsymbol{\lambda} \end{bmatrix} = \begin{bmatrix} \bar{\boldsymbol{\mu}} \\ \mathbf{0} \end{bmatrix} \lambda_{\mathrm{E}} + \begin{bmatrix} \mathbf{0} \\ \boldsymbol{b} \end{bmatrix} - \begin{bmatrix} \mathbf{0} \\ \boldsymbol{A}\boldsymbol{k} \end{bmatrix} \tag{11}$$

where $\bar{\boldsymbol{C}}$, $\bar{\boldsymbol{A}}$, $\bar{\boldsymbol{\mu}}$, and $\boldsymbol{k}$ are defined to have entries as follows:

$$\bar{\sigma}_{i,j} = \begin{cases} \sigma_{i,j} & \text{for } (i \in \texttt{IN}) \text{ and } (j \in \texttt{IN}), \\ 1 & \text{for } (i \notin \texttt{IN}) \text{ and } (i = j), \\ 0 & \text{otherwise.} \end{cases} \qquad k_i = \begin{cases} u_i \text{ for } i \in \texttt{UP}, \\ d_i \text{ for } i \in \texttt{DN}, \\ 0 \text{ otherwise,} \end{cases} \tag{12}$$

$$\bar{a}_{i,j} = \begin{cases} a_{i,j} & \text{for } j \in \texttt{IN}, \\ 0 & \text{otherwise.} \end{cases} \qquad \bar{\mu}_i = \begin{cases} \mu_i & \text{for } i \in \texttt{IN}, \\ 0 & \text{otherwise.} \end{cases} \tag{13}$$

For brevity, we define

$$\boldsymbol{M} = \begin{bmatrix} \boldsymbol{C} & \boldsymbol{A}^\top \\ \boldsymbol{A} & \mathbf{O} \end{bmatrix} \text{ and } \bar{\boldsymbol{M}} = \begin{bmatrix} \bar{\boldsymbol{C}} & \bar{\boldsymbol{A}}^\top \\ \bar{\boldsymbol{A}} & \mathbf{O} \end{bmatrix} \tag{14}$$

and the top block row of $\boldsymbol{M}$ as $\boldsymbol{P}$,

$$\boldsymbol{P} = \begin{bmatrix} \boldsymbol{C} & \boldsymbol{A}^\top \end{bmatrix}. \tag{15}$$

The matrix $\bar{\boldsymbol{M}}$ is guaranteed to be non-singular (see Markowitz (1987)). Therefore, Equation (11) can be solved to give

$$\begin{bmatrix} \boldsymbol{x} \\ \boldsymbol{\lambda} \end{bmatrix} = \boldsymbol{\alpha} + \boldsymbol{\beta}\lambda_{\text{E}}, \tag{16}$$

where

$$\boldsymbol{\alpha} = \bar{\boldsymbol{M}}^{-1} \begin{bmatrix} \mathbf{0} \\ \boldsymbol{b} - \boldsymbol{A}\boldsymbol{k} \end{bmatrix} \text{ and } \boldsymbol{\beta} = \bar{\boldsymbol{M}}^{-1} \begin{bmatrix} \bar{\boldsymbol{\mu}} \\ \mathbf{0} \end{bmatrix}. \tag{17}$$

Substituting Equation (17) into Equation (5) gives a closed-form expression for the derivative of the Lagrangian with respect to the portfolio weights

$$\frac{\partial \mathcal{L}}{\partial \boldsymbol{x}} = \boldsymbol{\gamma} + \boldsymbol{\delta}\lambda_{\text{E}}, \tag{18}$$

where

$$\boldsymbol{\gamma} = \boldsymbol{P}\boldsymbol{\alpha} \text{ and } \boldsymbol{\delta} = \boldsymbol{P}\boldsymbol{\beta} - \boldsymbol{\mu}. \tag{19}$$

Equations (16) through (19) provide us with the tools to trace out the efficient frontier. Equation (16) describes the straight-line segments along the efficient frontier for given IN, UP, and DN sets. As

λ_E changes, the portfolio $\boldsymbol{x}$ attains discrete critical points (i.e., corner portfolios) at which the compositions of the `IN`, `UP`, and `DN` sets change. Jacobs *et al.* (2012) provide an alternative set of equations that use compression of the dimensions of the $\boldsymbol{C}$ matrix to include entries only for securities that are `IN`. In addition, Jacobs, Levy, and Starer (2012) provide equations for benchmark-sensitive portfolios, beta-constrained portfolios, long-short portfolios, and enhanced active-equity portfolios.

The CLA is a computationally efficient method for tracing out the entire efficient frontier by finding successive critical values. The algorithm starts with λ_E effectively at infinity, at which point maximizing utility amounts to maximizing expected portfolio return subject to the required constraints. This is a linear programming problem whose solution provides the initial portfolio and the initial contents of the `IN`, `UP`, and `DN` sets. The algorithm then finds the largest value of λ_E that is smaller than its current value, and at which the contents of `IN`, `UP`, or `DN` change. This is the next critical value.

At any critical value, one of four events can take place:

L1. An `IN` security i can move to `UP`. From Equation (16), $x_i = \alpha_i + \beta_i\lambda_E$. Since x_i is attempting to increase its value as λ_E decreases, we must have $\beta_i < 0$. Also, since the security attains its upper bound, its weight must satisfy $x_i = u_i$. Combining these facts, we find that the corner portfolio occurs when $\lambda_E = \lambda_{i,\mathrm{IU}}$ with

$$\lambda_{i,\mathrm{IU}} = \frac{u_i - \alpha_i}{\beta_i}, \quad \beta_i < 0. \tag{20}$$

L2. An `IN` security i can move to `DN`. From Equation (16), $x_i = \alpha_i + \beta_i\lambda_E$. Since x_i is attempting to decrease its value as λ_E decreases, we must have $\beta_i > 0$. Also, since the security attains its lower bound, its weight must satisfy $x_i = d_i$. Combining these facts, we find that the corner portfolio occurs when $\lambda_E = \lambda_{i,\mathrm{ID}}$ with

$$\lambda_{i,\mathrm{ID}} = \frac{d_i - \alpha_i}{\beta_i}, \quad \beta_i > 0. \tag{21}$$

L3. An $\mathtt{UP}$ security i can move to $\mathtt{IN}$. From Equation (18), $\partial\mathcal{L}/\partial x_i = \gamma_i + \delta_i\lambda_{\text{E}}$. In $\mathtt{UP}$, this derivative is negative. For the security to move to $\mathtt{IN}$, the derivative must increase to zero as λ_{E} decreases. Therefore $\delta_i < 0$ and, since the derivative must attain zero, $\gamma_i + \delta_i\lambda_{\text{E}} = 0$. Combining these facts, we find that the corner portfolio occurs when $\lambda_{\text{E}} = \lambda_{i,\mathtt{UI}}$ with

$$\lambda_{i,\mathtt{UI}} = -\frac{\gamma_i}{\delta_i}, \quad \delta_i < 0. \tag{22}$$

L4. A $\mathtt{DN}$ security i can move to $\mathtt{IN}$. From Equation (18), $\partial\mathcal{L}/\partial x_i = \gamma_i + \delta_i\lambda_{\text{E}}$. In $\mathtt{DN}$, this derivative is positive. For the security to move to $\mathtt{IN}$, the derivative must decrease to zero as λ_{E} decreases. Therefore $\delta_i > 0$ and, since the derivative must attain zero, $\gamma_i + \delta_i\lambda_{\text{E}} = 0$. Combining these facts, we find that the corner portfolio occurs when $\lambda_{\text{E}} = \lambda_{i,\mathtt{DI}}$ with

$$\lambda_{i,\mathtt{DI}} = -\frac{\gamma_i}{\delta_i}, \quad \delta_i > 0. \tag{23}$$

The largest of $\lambda_{i,j}$ over all $i \in \{1,\ldots,n\}$ and $j \in \{\mathtt{IU},\mathtt{ID},\mathtt{UI},\mathtt{DI}\}$ determines the value of λ_{E} at the next corner, or if the algorithm terminates.

A convenient way to find which security is changing and the direction in which it is changing is to collect the ratios $\lambda_{i,j}$ for all $i \in \{1,\ldots,n\}$ and $j \in \{\mathtt{IU},\mathtt{ID},\mathtt{UI},\mathtt{DI}\}$ into the matrix $\boldsymbol{\Lambda}$ as follows:

$$\boldsymbol{\Lambda} = \begin{bmatrix} \lambda_{1,\mathtt{IU}} & \lambda_{1,\mathtt{ID}} & \lambda_{1,\mathtt{UI}} & \lambda_{1,\mathtt{DI}} \\ \lambda_{2,\mathtt{IU}} & \lambda_{2,\mathtt{ID}} & \lambda_{2,\mathtt{UI}} & \lambda_{2,\mathtt{DI}} \\ \vdots & & & \vdots \\ \lambda_{n,\mathtt{IU}} & \lambda_{n,\mathtt{ID}} & \lambda_{n,\mathtt{UI}} & \lambda_{n,\mathtt{DI}} \end{bmatrix}. \tag{24}$$

All entries in $\boldsymbol{\Lambda}$ that are not defined in Equations (20) through (23) are assigned a value of $-\infty$. The column of $\boldsymbol{\Lambda}$ that contains the largest value represents the type of transition made at the next corner. If the first column contains the maximum value, then the transition is for a security moving from $\mathtt{IN}$ to $\mathtt{UP}$, and so forth. The number of the row of $\boldsymbol{\Lambda}$ that contains the largest value represents the index of the security that makes the transition.

We now have all the information necessary to implement the CLA for portfolios with a constraint set that includes lower and upper bounds. In brief, the algorithm proceeds as follows:

- Read data or compute where necessary $\boldsymbol{\mu}$, $\boldsymbol{C}$, $\boldsymbol{A}$, $\boldsymbol{b}$, $\boldsymbol{d}$, and $\boldsymbol{u}$.
- Use linear programming to find the portfolio $\boldsymbol{x}$ that maximizes expected portfolio return $\boldsymbol{\mu}^\top \boldsymbol{x}$ subject to the constraints $\boldsymbol{A}\boldsymbol{x} = \boldsymbol{b}$ and $\boldsymbol{d} \leq \boldsymbol{x} \leq \boldsymbol{u}$, and initialize the `IN`, `UP`, and `DN` sets.
- Set $\lambda_{\text{E}} = \infty$.
- Repeat while $\lambda_{\text{E}} \geq 0$:
  - With the current `IN`, `UP`, and `DN` sets, calculate $\bar{\boldsymbol{C}}$, $\bar{\boldsymbol{A}}$, $\bar{\boldsymbol{M}}$, $\bar{\mu}$, and $\boldsymbol{k}$ using steps S1 through S4.
  - Calculate $\boldsymbol{\alpha}$ and $\boldsymbol{\beta}$ using Equation (17), and $\boldsymbol{\gamma}$ and $\boldsymbol{\delta}$ using Equation (19).
  - Compute the $\lambda_{i,j}$ ratios using steps L1 through L4 and form the $\boldsymbol{\Lambda}$ matrix.
  - Find the maximum value of $\boldsymbol{\Lambda}$. This is the next value of λ_{E}; the critical value at the next corner portfolio.
  - Find the row that contains the maximum value of $\boldsymbol{\Lambda}$. This is the number of the security whose state will change at the next corner.
  - Find the column that contains the maximum value of $\boldsymbol{\Lambda}$. This is an indicator of the state change that the security will undergo at the next corner portfolio.
  - With the state transition thus defined, compute the next `IN`, `UP`, and `DN` sets.
  - If $\lambda_{\text{E}} \geq 0$, compute and store the portfolio $\boldsymbol{x}$ at the next corner using the top block of Equation (16).

We describe the details of the algorithm in the following sections.

3. CLA Python Implementation

This section describes a simplified Python implementation of the CLA that maps out the efficient frontier. This simplified version omits the two-stage simplex algorithm for initializing the CLA. In addition, it omits the efficient method of updating inverse matrices, instead relying on the fast and reliable linear algebra module of Python.

Sample Python code is provided in Appendix A. Note, however, that the code is provided for illustrative purposes only and should not be used for production purposes. In particular, it contains no error checking that would be essential for production code. Further, the code is written for readability and correlation with equations presented here. Little attention is paid to the use of proper idiomatic Python.

For reference, the code is written in blocks with comments that include labels in the form `--Axx--`, where `xx` is a two-digit number. The following description refers to those labels.

The first steps necessary for the CLA are to define functions, read data, and initialize parameters. Blocks `--A01--` and `--A02--` define functions that set rows or columns of matrices or vectors to zero. These are used in the conversion of $\boldsymbol{\mu}$ to $\bar{\boldsymbol{\mu}}$ and $\boldsymbol{A}$ to $\bar{\boldsymbol{A}}$ in steps S2 and S3. Block `--A03--` is used to convert $\boldsymbol{C}$ to $\bar{\boldsymbol{C}}$ in step S1.

Block `--A04--` is a function `initport` that initializes the portfolio for λ_{E} effectively infinite. The function computes the maximum return portfolio that satisfies the constraint. In this case, the only constraints are lower bounds `lb` and upper bounds `ub`, and the budget constraint. The function uses the method described by Sharpe in `https://web.stanford.edu/~wfsharpe/mia/opt/mia_opt3.htm`. A more general initialization procedure is provided in the VBA code in Chapter 13 of Markowitz and Todd (2000), which performs initialization using a two-stage simplex algorithm.

Block `--A05--` reads the data into the returns array `ret`, and drops the first column, which is assumed to contain the date. Block `--A06--` sets the initial parameters. Specifically, it determines the number of securities from the shape of the `ret` matrix, it initializes the lower bounds `lb` and upper bounds `ub` on the portfolio weights, and it initializes the constraint matrix `A` and vector `b`. In this case, the only constraint is the budget constraint, so the number of constraints `m` is one. In this simple code, we are expecting a small number of securities, so we set the lower weight bound to 10% and the upper weight bound to 50%. These, obviously, should be modified to match the user's needs. Block `--A06--` sets a tolerance `tol` for testing whether or not variables should be considered to be zero. Block `--A07--` computes the sample mean `mu` and sample covariance `C` of the return matrix.

The first step of the CLA is performed in Block `--A08--`, which calls function `initport` to find the first portfolio on the efficient frontier. Block `--A09--` uses this first portfolio to create the first state vector `s`. The state vector contains +1, −1, and 0 in positions corresponding to securities that are in the `UP`, `DN`, and `IN` sets, respectively. Block `--A10--` sets up the `P` matrix defined in Equation (15) for calculating the derivative in Equation (18). Finally, in this set of blocks, block `--A11--` initializes storage for the quantities calculated in the CLA.

The CLA loop for stepping from corner portfolio to corner portfolio starts in block `--A12--`. Here, we use the variable `lam` to represent λ_{E}. The loop proceeds as long as λ_{E} is positive, or until it breaks when no further corner portfolios are found.

Inside the CLA loop, block `--A13--` uses the current state vector `s` to create the logical vectors `UP`, `DN`, and `IN` that represent their corresponding sets.

Block `--A14--` creates $\bar{\boldsymbol{A}}$, $\bar{\boldsymbol{C}}$, and $\bar{\boldsymbol{M}}$, represented by variables `Abar`, `Cbar`, and `Mbar`. This block first creates the vector `io` containing the indices of the weights that are not `IN`. It then creates `Abar` and `Cbar` from `A` and `C` using `io` and the functions `zerorows` and `bar`.

Block `--A15--` computes array `k` representing the vector $\boldsymbol{k}$ in Equation (12). It then calculates the right-hand side vectors $[\mathbf{0};\ \boldsymbol{b}-\boldsymbol{A}\boldsymbol{k}]$ and $[\bar{\boldsymbol{\mu}};\ \mathbf{0}]$ used in Equation (17).

Block `--A16--` computes the vectors $\boldsymbol{\alpha}$, $\boldsymbol{\beta}$, $\boldsymbol{\gamma}$, and $\boldsymbol{\delta}$ as defined in Equations (17) and (19). In this code, we merely call Numpy's function `linalg.solve()` to invert $\bar{M}$ at each corner portfolio. However, it is more efficient to keep a copy of the inverse $\bar{\boldsymbol{M}}^{-1}$ and to update this inverse as the elements of `IN`, `UP`, and `DN` change. Details of efficient updating methods are provided in Markowitz and Todd (2000).

Blocks `--A17--` through `--A24--` comprise a group that finds the maximum of $\lambda_{i,\text{IU}}$, $\lambda_{i,\text{ID}}$, $\lambda_{i,\text{UI}}$, and $\lambda_{i,\text{DI}}$ using Equations (20) through (23). To do this, the code places the ratios into the two-dimensional array `L` representing $\boldsymbol{\Lambda}$ in Equation (24).

Specifically, block `--A17--` prepares `L` and sets all of its values to $-\infty$. Blocks `--A18--` through `--A21--` fill `L` with computed values of the ratios $\lambda_{i,\text{IU}}$, $\lambda_{i,\text{ID}}$, $\lambda_{i,\text{UI}}$, and $\lambda_{i,\text{DI}}$ for all i for which the ratios are defined. Since Python uses zero-based indexing, the value of $\lambda_{i,j}$ is contained in array element `L[i-1,j-1]`.

If all entries of `L` are negative, no more corners exist. Block `--A22--` checks for this condition, and breaks the loop if it is satisfied.

Using the logic described in the paragraph following Equation (24), block `--A23--` finds which row of `L` contains the maximum value, and thus which security is about to change state. Block `--A24--` finds which column of `L` contains the maximum value, and thus what type of state change is about to occur. Block `--A25--` sets the value of `lam` to the largest value of `L`. Block `--A26--` updates the state vector `s`.

Block `--A27--` computes the portfolio vector `x` at the corner using Equation (16). It then computes the expected return and the variance of the corner portfolio.

Finally, block `--A28--` saves the portfolio vector, the state vector, the variance, the return, and the value of `lam` at the current corner. The loop then repeats with the new value of `lam` and the state vector `s`, or the program terminates if `lam` ≤ 0.

When the program terminates, the workspace contains the matrix `X` whose columns are the portfolio weights at each corner, and the vector `LAM` that contains the values of $\lambda_{\text{E}} =$ `lam` at each corner. The workspace also contains extra information in the form of the matrix `S` whose columns are the state vector at each corner, the vector `R` that contains the expected portfolio return at each corner, and the vector `V` that contains the portfolio's variance at each corner.

Recall from the top block row of Equation (16) that an efficient portfolio is a piecewise linear function of the corner portfolios that surround it. Therefore, to find the portfolio corresponding to any particular value of λ_{E} that is not a critical value, one must find the two critical values $\lambda_{(a)}$ and $\lambda_{(b)}$ immediately above and below λ_{E}, together with the corresponding corner portfolios $\boldsymbol{x}_{(a)}$ and $\boldsymbol{x}_{(b)}$. Then, the desired portfolio is the linear combination

$$\boldsymbol{x}(\lambda_{\mathrm{E}}) = \boldsymbol{x}_{(b)} + \frac{\lambda_{\mathrm{E}} - \lambda_{(b)}}{\lambda_{(a)} - \lambda_{(b)}} \left(\boldsymbol{x}_{(a)} - \boldsymbol{x}_{(b)}\right). \tag{25}$$

3.1. *Example*

For our basic example, we will use the data provided on page 195 of Markowitz (1959), repeated here in Table 1 for convenience. The table lists returns for three securities for the 18 years 1937 through 1954, together with the securities' sample mean returns $\boldsymbol{\mu}$ and sample standard deviations $\boldsymbol{\sigma}$.

Table 1. Returns of three securities.

	Security		
Year	1	2	3
1937	−0.173	−0.318	−0.319
1938	0.098	0.285	0.076
1939	0.200	−0.047	0.381
1940	0.030	0.104	-0.051
1941	−0.183	−0.171	0.087
1942	0.067	−0.039	0.262
1943	0.300	0.149	0.341
1944	0.103	0.260	0.227
1945	0.216	0.419	0.352
1946	−0.046	−0.078	0.153
1947	−0.071	0.169	−0.099
1948	0.056	−0.035	0.038
1949	0.038	0.133	0.273
1950	0.089	0.732	0.091
1951	0.090	0.021	0.054
1952	0.083	0.131	0.109
1953	0.035	0.006	0.210
1954	0.176	0.908	0.112
μ	0.062	0.146	0.128
σ	0.016	0.091	0.031

Table 2. Critical values and corner portfolios.

λ_E	Security 1	Security 2	Security 3
∞	0.1000	0.5000	0.4000
1.7567	0.1000	0.5000	0.4000
1.2203	0.1000	0.4000	0.5000
0.3142	0.1000	0.4000	0.5000
0.0973	0.3764	0.1236	0.5000
0.0853	0.4644	0.1000	0.4356
0.0770	0.5000	0.1000	0.4000
0	0.5000	0.1000	0.4000

Saving this table in the tab-separated variable file `example.tsv` and running the Python script from Appendix A, we obtain the critical values and corner portfolios (rounded to four decimal places) in Table 2. The table shows that the maximum return portfolio subject to the constraints is $\boldsymbol{x} = [0.1, 0.5, 0.4]$. This portfolio assigns the highest allowable weight to security 2 since this security has the highest sample mean return, and the lowest allowable weight to security 1 since this security has the lowest sample mean return. The remaining weight is assigned to security 3.

The algorithm finds the first corner portfolio at $\lambda_E = 1.757$, and then at successively lower values until it reaches a minimum at $\lambda_E = 0.077$, which corresponds to the lowest variance portfolio subject to the constraints. The table extrapolates this final portfolio down to $\lambda_E = 0$. At this lowest end of the efficient frontier, the algorithm has now assigned the lowest allowable weight to security 2 and the highest allowable weight to security 1, which in this case happen to have the highest and lowest standard deviations, respectively. Again, the remaining weight is assigned to security 3. Figure 1 shows the reversal of the roles of securities 1 and 2, and plots the weights of the securities as a function of λ_E. Figure 2 shows the corresponding efficient frontier in which portfolios between critical values are obtained using Equation (25).

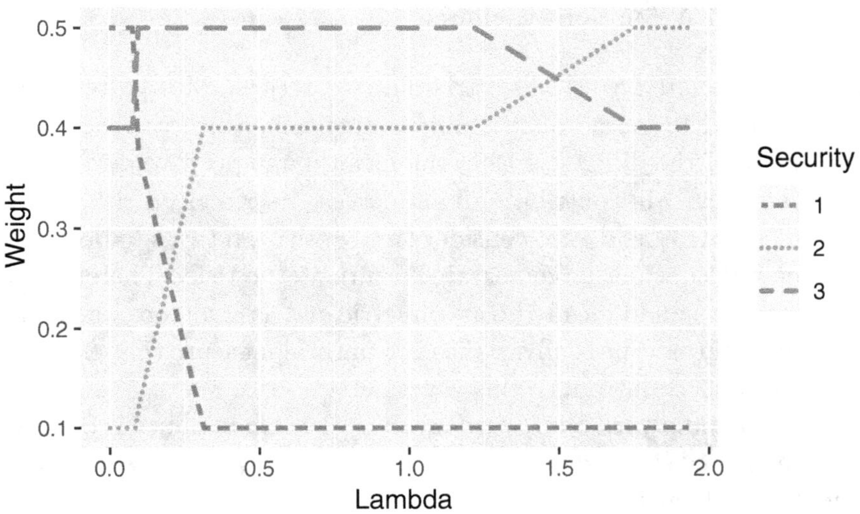

Fig. 1. Portfolio weights as a function of λ_E.

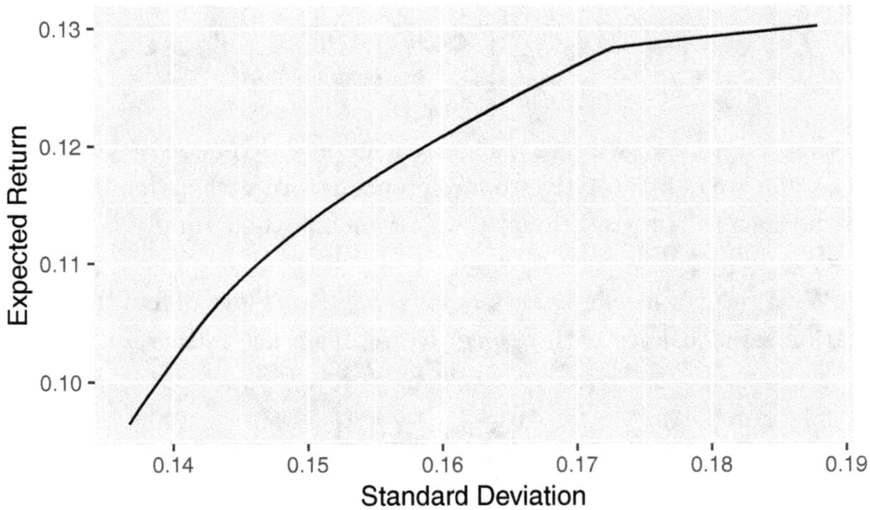

Fig. 2. Efficient frontier.

4. The CLA for Semivariance

Risk is associated with the variability of return. Most often, the statistic used to measure variability is variance. Since variance uses the square of the difference from the mean, large positive deviations from the mean will contribute to an increase in perceived risk. However, most investors do not consider large positive returns to be risky. But they do consider large negative returns to be risky. Therefore, a risk measure should ideally be asymmetric and assign more weight to negative returns. The semivariance is a natural measure that extends variance so as to introduce this asymmetry.

For a random variable R with mean μ, the semivariance is defined as the expected squared deviation from the mean when that deviation is negative. That is

$$s^2 = \mathbb{E}\left[\left\{(R-\mu)^-\right\}^2\right],$$

where the notation $(\cdot)^-$ denotes the negative part of the argument in parenthesis. That is, for any x,

$$(x)^- = \begin{cases} x & \text{if } x < 0, \\ 0 & \text{otherwise.} \end{cases}$$

In this chapter, we will use a slightly generalized version of semivariance that we define relative to a reference return rather than relative to the mean. The traditional semivariance is then simply a special case.

With return measurements r_t for $t = 1, \ldots, T$, we define the population semivariance with respect to the reference return ϱ as

$$s_\varrho^2 = \frac{1}{T}\sum_{t=1}^{T}\left\{(r_t-\varrho)^-\right\}^2. \tag{26}$$

Advantageously with semivariance, only returns below the reference return contribute to the measure of risk. Returns above the reference return are given no weight. Two particular choices of reference return interest us. If we choose the reference return to be the mean, then $s_\mu^2 \equiv s^2$ is the same as the standard definition of semivariance. If we choose the reference return to be zero, then s_0^2 is the squared downside deviation; the word 'downside' referring to any negative return.

For a symmetrical return distribution, the variance is twice the semivariance; $\sigma^2 = 2s^2$. For a left-skewed distribution, $\sigma^2 < 2s^2$, and the opposite is true for a right-skewed distribution. Therefore, the ratio $\sigma^2/(2s^2)$ is a useful indirect measure of skewness. For portfolios with the same expected return and variance, optimization based on minimizing s^2 yields the portfolio with the smallest skewness to the left.

As noted in Markowitz (1959, page 193), "Several conflicting considerations influence the choice of [variance] or [semivariance] as the measure of variability in a portfolio analysis. These considerations include cost, convenience, familiarity, and the desirability of the portfolios produced by the analysis. ... Analyses based on [semivariance] tend to produce better portfolios than those based on [variance]. Variance considers extremely high and extremely low returns equally undesirable. An analysis based on [variance] seeks to eliminate both extremes. An analysis based on s, on the other hand, concentrates on reducing losses." Importantly, with regard to familiarity, Markowitz (1959) states that "[F]amiliarity is a transient thing: use can make [semivariance] as familiar as [variance]." In this section, we hope to aid the process of familiarization.

It is straightforward to extend population variance to population semivariance. For a population of T realizations of the returns of n securities, we know that the population covariance between securities i and j is

$$\sigma_{ij} = \frac{1}{T}\sum_{t=1}^{T}(r_{t,i} - \mu_i)(r_{t,j} - \mu_j) \tag{27}$$

where $r_{t,k}$ is the return of security k over time period t, and μ_k is the average return of security k. If $\boldsymbol{R}$ is the $T \times n$ returns matrix with $r_{t,k}$ in its t-th row and k-th column, with $\boldsymbol{\iota}$ and $\boldsymbol{\mu}$ as previously defined, the elements given in Equation (27) can be written in matrix form as

$$\boldsymbol{C} = \frac{1}{T}\left(\boldsymbol{R} - \boldsymbol{\iota}\boldsymbol{\mu}^\top\right)^\top \left(\boldsymbol{R} - \boldsymbol{\iota}\boldsymbol{\mu}^\top\right).$$

Conveniently, we can write the covariance matrix in square root form as $\boldsymbol{C} = \boldsymbol{B}^\top \boldsymbol{B}$ where the square root matrix is

$$\boldsymbol{B} = \frac{1}{\sqrt{T}}\left(\boldsymbol{R} - \boldsymbol{\iota}\boldsymbol{\mu}^\top\right).$$

Note, of course, for $T > n$, that this square root matrix is not unique. That is, many different $\boldsymbol{B}$ matrices can yield the same $\boldsymbol{C}$. However, the $\boldsymbol{B}$ in our case is uniquely determined by our data. Using the square root, the variance of the return of portfolio $\boldsymbol{x}$ is

$$\sigma_{\text{P}}^2 = \boldsymbol{x}^\top \boldsymbol{B}^\top \boldsymbol{B}\boldsymbol{x} = \boldsymbol{y}^\top \boldsymbol{y}$$

where we have implicitly defined the $T \times 1$ vector of artificial variables $\boldsymbol{y} = \boldsymbol{B}\boldsymbol{x}$. More generally, in terms of the reference return $\boldsymbol{\varrho}$, we could have defined

$$\boldsymbol{B}_{\varrho} = \frac{1}{\sqrt{T}}\left(\boldsymbol{R} - \boldsymbol{\iota}\boldsymbol{\varrho}^\top\right) \tag{28}$$

and

$$\boldsymbol{y} = \boldsymbol{B}_{\varrho}\boldsymbol{x}. \tag{29}$$

In this chapter, we omit the subscript from $\boldsymbol{B}$ and infer its value from the context. Usually, we deal with $\boldsymbol{\varrho} = \boldsymbol{0}$.

The artificial variable vector $\boldsymbol{y}$ and its components y_t for $t = 1, \ldots, T$ have important interpretations. In particular, y_t is the return of the portfolio over period t that is in excess of the reference return and normalized by $\sqrt{T}$. Therefore, using the negative parts of $\boldsymbol{y}$, we can write the semivariance simply as

$$\begin{aligned} s^2 &= \sum_{t=1}^{T}((y_t)^-)^2 = \left(\boldsymbol{y}^\top\right)^- (\boldsymbol{y})^- \\ &= \left(\boldsymbol{x}^\top \boldsymbol{B}^\top\right)^- (\boldsymbol{B}\boldsymbol{x})^- . \end{aligned}$$

In general, $(\boldsymbol{B}\boldsymbol{x})^- \neq (\boldsymbol{B})^-(\boldsymbol{x})^-$. So, unlike variance, we cannot write semivariance in a simple quadratic form $s^2 = ((\boldsymbol{x})^-)^\top \boldsymbol{S}\ ((\boldsymbol{x})^-)$ for some universally applicable matrix $\boldsymbol{S}$. If this were possible, the problem could be solved with standard quadratic programming. Instead, we will find that there exist regions in which semicovariance matrices are locally applicable. In those regions, the problem *is* quadratic. To understand this, we need to examine the concept of profitability lines.

The excess portfolio return for any period is the inner product of the vector of excess returns for that period and the vector of portfolio weights. A period t is unprofitable if the excess return for all permissible values of $\boldsymbol{x}$ is negative; i.e.,

$$y_t \propto \sum_{i=1}^{n}(r_{t,i} - \varrho_i)x_i = \left(\boldsymbol{r}^t - \boldsymbol{\varrho}^\top\right)\boldsymbol{x} < 0, \tag{30}$$

where $\boldsymbol{r}^t$ is the t-th row of matrix $\boldsymbol{R}$. Since the sum of all weights must be one, this inequality defines a half-plane in $(n-1)$-dimensional portfolio space. The unprofitable region for period t is the set of all points $\boldsymbol{x}$ that satisfy Inequality (30), and the profitability line is the locus of points $\boldsymbol{x}$ that satisfy the equality $\left(\boldsymbol{r}^t - \boldsymbol{\varrho}^\top\right)\boldsymbol{x} = 0$.

We therefore have stated a criterion according to which observations should, or should not, be included in the computation of the semivariance.

The returns for period t will be included in the semivariance computation (Equation (26)) if that period is unprofitable.

In other words, if we define $\texttt{IS} \subseteq \{1, 2, \ldots, T\}$ to be the set of time periods that are included in the semicovariance computation in a region of $\boldsymbol{x}$, then period t is a member of IS if the t-th element of $\boldsymbol{y}$ is negative. That is,

$$y_t < 0 \longrightarrow t \in \texttt{IS}. \tag{31}$$

Consider a practical example with $\boldsymbol{\varrho} = \mathbf{0}$. From Table 1, we see that any long-only portfolio would be unprofitable in 1937 since all securities had negative returns in that year. In contrast, in 1938, any long-only portfolio would be profitable since all securities had positive returns in that year. Therefore, the year 1937 should always be included in calculations of the semivariance, but the year 1938 should never be included.

The case is not so trivial for years that have both positive and negative returns. Using Inequality (30) in these cases, we have the criterion that we should include period t if

$$r_{t,1}x_1 + r_{t,2}x_2 + r_{t,3}x_3 < 0.$$

Or, equivalently, since $x_3 = 1 - x_1 - x_2$, we should include period t if

$$(r_{t,1} - r_{t,3})x_1 + (r_{t,2} - r_{t,3})x_2 + r_{t,3} < 0. \tag{32}$$

This defines the unprofitable region for year t. For the year 1947, for example, we have $\boldsymbol{r}^t = [r_{t,1},\ r_{t,2},\ r_{t,3}] = [-0.071,\ +0.169,\ -0.099]$, and from Equation (32), the unprofitable region is

$$0.028x_1 + 0.268x_2 - 0.099 < 0.$$

The corresponding profitability line for 1947 is displayed in Fig. 3. The shaded region is the intersection of the unprofitable region, the non-negativity constraints ($x_1, x_2, x_3 \geq 0$), and the budget constraint ($x_1 + x_2 + x_3 = 1$). Any portfolios in this region should include 1947 in the calculation of the semivariance.

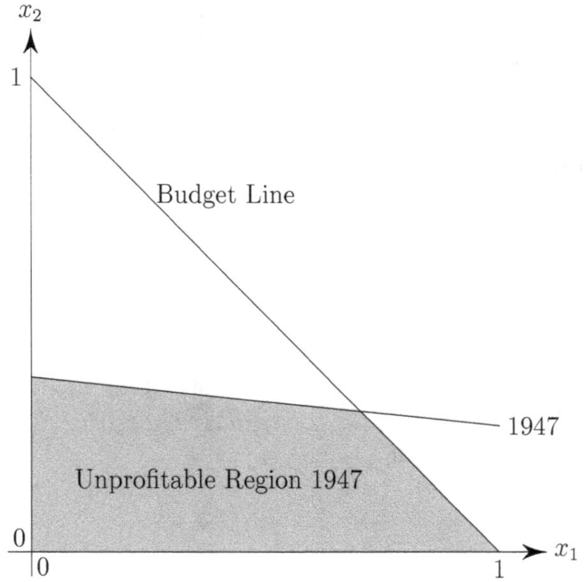

Fig. 3. Profitability line and unprofitable region for 1947.

In a region of any portfolio vector $\boldsymbol{x}$, therefore, there is a set of time periods that should be included in the computation of the semivariance. Let $\mathbb{B}$ be the matrix obtained from $\boldsymbol{B}$ by including only those rows (time periods) that lead to unprofitable portfolios in the region of $\boldsymbol{x}$. In this case, the semivariance can be written in the simple quadratic form

$$s^2 = \left(\boldsymbol{x}^\top \boldsymbol{B}^\top\right)^- \left(\boldsymbol{B}\boldsymbol{x}\right)^- = \boldsymbol{x}^\top \mathbb{B}^\top \mathbb{B}\, \boldsymbol{x} = \boldsymbol{x}^\top \boldsymbol{S}\, \boldsymbol{x}$$

where we have defined the locally applicable semicovariance matrix (LSM) as $\boldsymbol{S} = \mathbb{B}^\top \mathbb{B}$.

Given a set `IS` and a critical line for that set that contains the current portfolio $\boldsymbol{x}$, we can find the value of λ_{E} at which the constituents of `IS` change. We can thereby determine the borders of the current region. A region is locally applicable as long as portfolios within it are unprofitable for all periods.

At the border of a region, moving along the critical line as λ_{E} decreases, the current portfolio may become unprofitable for a period that was previously profitable, or vice versa. Thus, the period may need to be added to or removed from the semivariance computation. Hence, the borders are defined by lines of zero profitability.

At zero profitability, $\boldsymbol{B}_{\boldsymbol{\varrho}}\boldsymbol{x} = \boldsymbol{0}$. Using Equation (28) for the specific case $\boldsymbol{\varrho} = \boldsymbol{0}$, profitability lines are therefore defined by

$$\boldsymbol{R}\boldsymbol{x} = \boldsymbol{0}. \tag{33}$$

But, considering only the top block of Equation (16), we know that $\boldsymbol{x} = \boldsymbol{\alpha} + \boldsymbol{\beta}\lambda_{\text{E}}$. Using this in Equation (33) and defining $\boldsymbol{\xi} = \boldsymbol{R}\boldsymbol{\alpha}$ and $\boldsymbol{\zeta} = \boldsymbol{R}\boldsymbol{\beta}$, the value of λ_{E} at which the critical line crosses a profitability line for period t is

$$\lambda_{\text{E},t} = -\frac{\xi_t}{\zeta_t} \text{ for } \zeta_t \neq 0. \tag{34}$$

The particular period t entering or leaving the calculation of the LSM is the one corresponding to the maximum value of $\lambda_{\text{E},t}$ that is less than the current value of λ_{E}.

We are now ready to describe the CLA for semivariance optimization. In brief, the algorithm proceeds as follows:

1. Read data or compute where necessary $\boldsymbol{\mu}$, $\boldsymbol{C}$, $\boldsymbol{A}$, $\boldsymbol{b}$, $\boldsymbol{d}$, and $\boldsymbol{u}$.
2. Using linear programming, find the portfolio $\boldsymbol{x}$ that maximizes expected portfolio return $\boldsymbol{\mu}^\top\boldsymbol{x}$ subject to the constraints $\boldsymbol{A}\boldsymbol{x} = \boldsymbol{b}$ and $\boldsymbol{d} \leq \boldsymbol{x} \leq \boldsymbol{u}$, and initialize the `IN`, `UP`, and `DN` sets. This is independent of semivariance.
3. For the initial portfolio vector, calculate the LSM.
4. Set $\lambda_{\text{E}} = \infty$.
5. Repeat while $\lambda_{\text{E}} \geq 0$:

   a. With the current `IN`, `UP`, and `DN` sets, together with the current LSM, calculate $\bar{\boldsymbol{C}}$, $\bar{\boldsymbol{A}}$, $\bar{\boldsymbol{M}}$, and $\boldsymbol{k}$ using steps S1 through S4.
   b. Calculate $\boldsymbol{\alpha}$ and $\boldsymbol{\beta}$ using Equation (17), and $\boldsymbol{\gamma}$ and $\boldsymbol{\delta}$ using Equation (19).
   c. Compute the $\lambda_{i,j}$ ratios using steps L1 through L4 and form the $\boldsymbol{\Lambda}$ matrix.
   d. Find the maximum value of $\boldsymbol{\Lambda}$. Call this λ_{sec} to indicate that it is the λ_{E} at which a security's state changes.

e. Find the row that contains the maximum value of $\boldsymbol{\Lambda}$. This is the number of the security whose state will change at the next corner.
f. Find the column that contains the maximum value of $\boldsymbol{\Lambda}$. This is an indicator of the state change that the security will undergo at the next corner portfolio.
g. Using Equation (34), find the maximum value of $\lambda_{\mathrm{E},t}$ at which the next profitability line will be crossed. Call this λ_{obs} to indicate that it is the $\lambda_{\mathrm{E},t}$ at which the returns of the observation in period t will either be added to, or removed from, the calculation of the semivariance.
h. If $\lambda_{\mathrm{obs}} > \lambda_{\mathrm{sec}}$, then an observation is leaving or entering the semicovariance calculation. Proceed as follows:

   * Set $\lambda_{\mathrm{E}} = \lambda_{\mathrm{obs}}$. This is the critical value at the next corner portfolio.
   * Calculate the portfolio at the next corner using $\boldsymbol{x} = \boldsymbol{\alpha} + \boldsymbol{\beta}\lambda_{\mathrm{E}}$.
   * Using Equation (31), decide what observations should be included and excluded in the next segment of the critical line.
   * Calculate the LSM and the locally applicable $\boldsymbol{M}$ matrix.

i. Else, a security's state is changing at the next corner. Proceed as follows:

   * Set $\lambda_{\mathrm{E}} = \lambda_{\mathrm{sec}}$. This is the critical value at the next corner portfolio.
   * Calculate the portfolio at the next corner using $\boldsymbol{x} = \boldsymbol{\alpha} + \boldsymbol{\beta}\lambda_{\mathrm{E}}$.
   * Use the information from steps [e] and [f] to set the next state vector (and thereby the next `IN`, `UP`, and `DN` sets).

j. Store information about the current corner.

We describe the details of the algorithm in the following section.

4.1. *Semivariance CLA* R *Implementation*

We describe the CLA for mean–semivariance optimization with reference to the sample R code given in Appendix B. As in the Python code in Appendix A, the first few blocks (`--B01--` through `--B04--`) define functions for creating the matrices $\bar{\boldsymbol{A}}$, $\bar{\boldsymbol{C}}$, and $\bar{\boldsymbol{M}}$, and vector $\bar{\boldsymbol{\mu}}$, and for initializing the portfolio.

Blocks `--B05--` through `--B36--` define the `dscla` function for downside optimization using the CLA. The function's input parameters are the return matrix $\boldsymbol{R}$ represented by `R`, the constraint matrix $\boldsymbol{A} =$ `A` and vector $\boldsymbol{b} =$ `b`, the lower and upper bound vectors $\boldsymbol{d} =$ `lb` and $\boldsymbol{u} =$ `ub`, the reference return $\varrho =$ `refret`, and a tolerance scalar `tol` that is used to decide if variables are sufficiently small to be considered to be zero. The default values of `refret` and `tol` are zero and 10^{-9}, respectively.

Block `--B05--` finds basic properties of the returns data; the number of observations `no` and securities `ns`, and the securities' average return $\boldsymbol{\mu} =$ `mu`. Block `--B06--` creates the initial portfolio vector `x` that has maximum expected return and is constrained, in this example case; only by the budget constraint and the lower and upper bounds.

Block `--B07--` creates an integer vector `state` that represents the current state of the critical line. This vector contains entries of zero corresponding to securities that are `IN`, -1 for securities that are `DN`, and $+1$ for securities that are `UP`.

Block `--B08--` is the first block specific to the CLA for semivariance. It sets up the excess return matrix `Rex` that represents $\boldsymbol{R} - \boldsymbol{\iota}\varrho^{\top}$. It also computes the time series $\boldsymbol{y} =$ `y` of portfolio excess returns, and sets the logical vector `obs.in` that indicates which time periods should be included in the computation of the semicovariance matrix for the current portfolio vector.

In block `--B09--`, we use the indicator vector `obs.in` to create the local return matrix `Rloc` that contains only observations that would lead to unprofitable portfolios for the current region of $\boldsymbol{x}$. With this, we compute the LSM `Sloc`, as well as the local $\boldsymbol{M}$ matrix `Mloc` and its top block row `Ploc`.

In block `--B10--`, we allocate storage for the results of the CLA. Since we do not know *a priori* how many corners the algorithm will find, we simply allocate the first value, and then extend the result on each successful completion of the CLA loop.

Block `--B11--` starts the CLA proper. In this block, we enter the CLA loop that repeats as long as $\lambda_E > 0$. The variable `lam` represents λ_E (which has already been set to $+\infty$). Block `--B12--` converts the integer state vector `state` into logical vectors `UP`, `DN`, and `IN`. These vectors are used later in the code. The integer vector `OT` indicates the securities that are not `IN` (i.e., are either `UP` or `DN`). Block `--B13--` uses `OT` to form $\bar{\boldsymbol{S}}$, $\bar{\boldsymbol{A}}$, and $\bar{\boldsymbol{M}}$ from $\boldsymbol{S}$, $\boldsymbol{A}$, and $\boldsymbol{M}$ in accordance with steps S1 and S2, and Equation (14) above.

Block `--B14--` computes the vector $\boldsymbol{k}$ = `k` using Equation (12) and the right-hand side vectors for finding $\boldsymbol{\alpha}$ and $\boldsymbol{\beta}$ using Equation (17). With these, blocks `--B15--` and `--B16--` compute $\boldsymbol{\alpha}$, $\boldsymbol{\beta}$, $\boldsymbol{\gamma}$, and $\boldsymbol{\delta}$ using Equations (17) and (19).

At this stage, the current segment of the efficient frontier is fully defined. The portfolios on the segment satisfy $\boldsymbol{x} = \boldsymbol{\alpha} + \boldsymbol{\beta}\lambda_E$ for the current $\boldsymbol{\alpha}$ = `alf.sec` and $\boldsymbol{\beta}$ = `bet.sec`. The algorithm is therefore ready to find the value of λ_E at which either the portfolio state vector `state` changes, or the LSM `Sloc` changes. That value of λ_E is determined from the maximum of $\boldsymbol{\Lambda}$ from Equation (24) and $\lambda_{E,t}$ from Equation (34). The next steps, therefore, are to calculate $\boldsymbol{\Lambda}$ and $\lambda_{E,t}$.

Blocks `--B17--` through `--B20--` calculate the columns $\boldsymbol{\lambda}_{IU}$, $\boldsymbol{\lambda}_{ID}$, $\boldsymbol{\lambda}_{UI}$, and $\boldsymbol{\lambda}_{DI}$. Then block `--B21--` juxtaposes them to form $\boldsymbol{\Lambda}$, represented by variable `L`.

The row that contains the maximum value of `L` represents which security is changing state. The index of this security, `secchg`, is found in block `--B22--`. The column that contains the maximum value of `L` represents the direction in which the security's state is changing. The index of this change, `dirchg`, is found in block `--B23--`. Block `--B24--` stores `lam.sec`, the maximum value of λ_E for a security state change.

While blocks `--B17--` through `--B24--`, described above, focus on what security state changes might occur, blocks `--B25--` and `--B26--` focus on what changes might affect the computation of the LSM. Specifically, block `--B25--` computes $\boldsymbol{\xi} = \boldsymbol{R\alpha}$ (represented by the variable `num`) and $\boldsymbol{\zeta} = \boldsymbol{R\beta}$ (represented by the variable `den`). The maximum value of the ratio `rat = num / den`, where it is defined and less than the previous value of λ_E, is the value of λ_E at which the profitability region changes and observations in the LSM change. Block `--B26--` finds this maximum value and assigns it to the variable `lam.obs`.

Block `--B27--` decides whether the next change is a change of a security's state or a change of the profitability region. If `lam.obs` $>$ `lam.sec`, the next change is a profitability region change in which observations in the LSM change. On the other hand, if `lam.obs` $\leq$ `lam.sec`, the next change is a security state change. Blocks `--B28--` through `--B31--` handle profitability region changes, and blocks `--B32--` through `--B34--` handle security state changes.

For a change in profitability region, blocks `--B28--` and `--B29--` set the value of λ_E and compute the portfolio vector `x` at the next corner. Block `--B30--` creates the vector `obs.in` that indicates which periods are unprofitable in the region of `x` using Equation (31). With this vector, it computes the LSM, `Sloc`. Block `--B31--` sets the local matrix $\boldsymbol{M}$ in Equation (14), and its top block row $\boldsymbol{P}$.

Referring back to block `--B27--`, if the next value of λ_E had indicated a change of security state rather than a change of profitability region, the algorithm would have skipped to block `--B32--`, which sets the new value of λ_E appropriately. Block `--B33--` computes the portfolio vector at the next corner. Block `--B34--` sets the new state vector `state` appropriately, recalling that the integer `secchg` is the number of the security that changes state, `dirchg` represents the direction of the change with a value of 1 indicating a change from `IN` to `UP`, 2 indicating a change from `IN` to `DN`, and values of 3 or 4 indicating a change from `UP` or `DN` to `IN`.

We emerge from the `if else` statement to block `--B35--`, where we now have three important quantities pertaining to the current corner: the value of $\lambda_E =$ `lam`, the portfolio vector $\boldsymbol{x} =$ `x`, and the state vector `state`. Block `--B35--` stores relevant quantities together with the current expected return and semivariance.

With the new value of λ_E and state vector `state`, we can go back to block `--B11--` to reenter the CLA loop, or exit the program if $\lambda_E \leq 0$.

In Block `--B36--`, the function saves the efficient frontier in the list `ef`, and returns it to the calling program.

To find the efficient frontier, the program loads data in Block `--B37--` and defines the constraints in block `--B38--`. Finally, in block `--B39--`, it calls the downside CLA function `dscla`.

4.2. *Example*

We again use the data from Table 1, but now wish to find the mean–semivariance efficient frontier rather than the mean–variance efficient frontier. Saving this table in the tab-separated variable file `example.tsv` and running the R script from Appendix B, we obtain the critical values and corner portfolios (rounded to four decimal places) in Table 3. The table shows that the maximum return portfolio subject only to the long-only and budget constraints is $\boldsymbol{x} = [0,\ 1,\ 0]$. This portfolio assigns the highest allowable weight to security 2 since this security has the highest sample mean return.

The algorithm finds the first corner portfolio at $\lambda_{\mathrm{E}} = 0.2898$, and then at successively lower values until it reaches a minimum at λ_{E} close to zero, which corresponds to the lowest variance portfolio subject to the constraints. Figure 4 shows the weights of the securities as a function of λ_{E} and Figure 5 shows the weights of the securities

Table 3. Critical values and corner portfolios for semivariance optimization.

	Security		
λ_{E}	1	2	3
∞	0.0000	1.0000	0.0000
0.2898	0.0000	1.0000	0.0000
0.1579	0.0000	0.8902	0.1098
0.1450	0.0000	0.8704	0.1296
0.0665	0.0000	0.6623	0.3377
0.0358	0.0000	0.5205	0.4795
0.0300	0.0000	0.4919	0.5081
0.0284	0.1210	0.3567	0.5223
0.0263	0.2740	0.1858	0.5402
0.0077	0.6706	0.0000	0.3294
0	0.7688	0.0000	0.2312

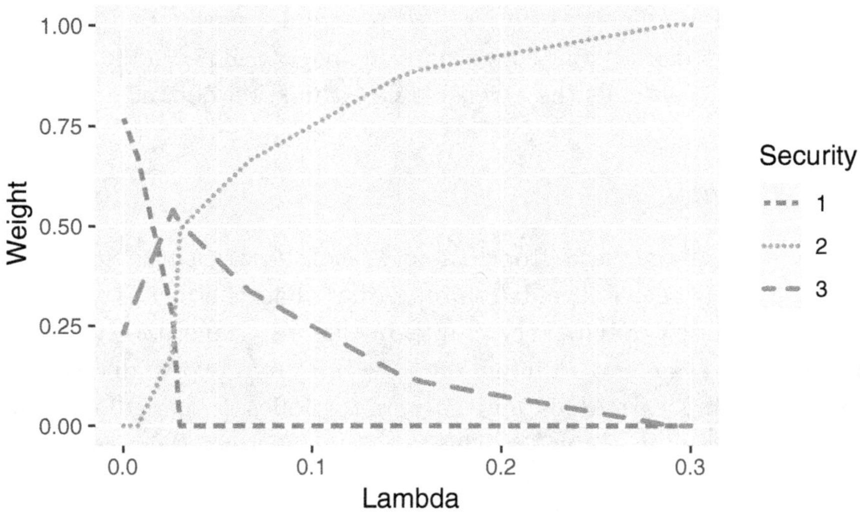

Fig. 4. Semivariance portfolio weights as a function of λ_{E}.

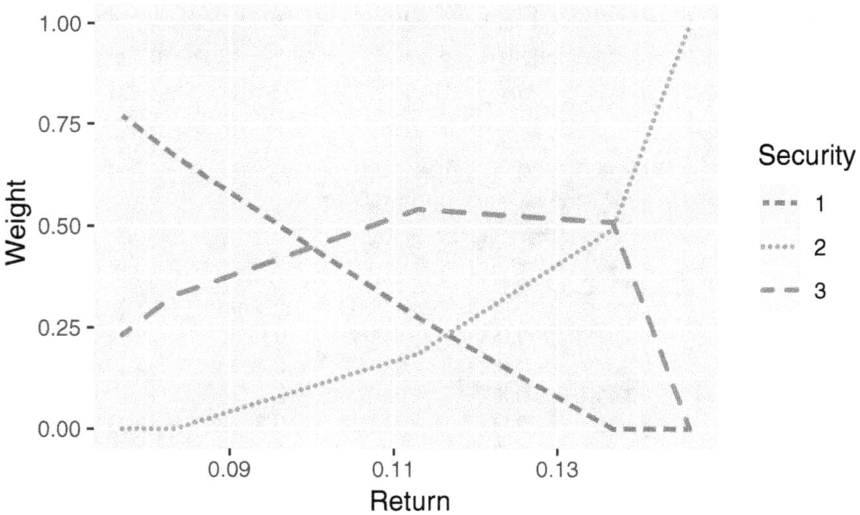

Fig. 5. Semivariance portfolio weights as a function of portfolio return.

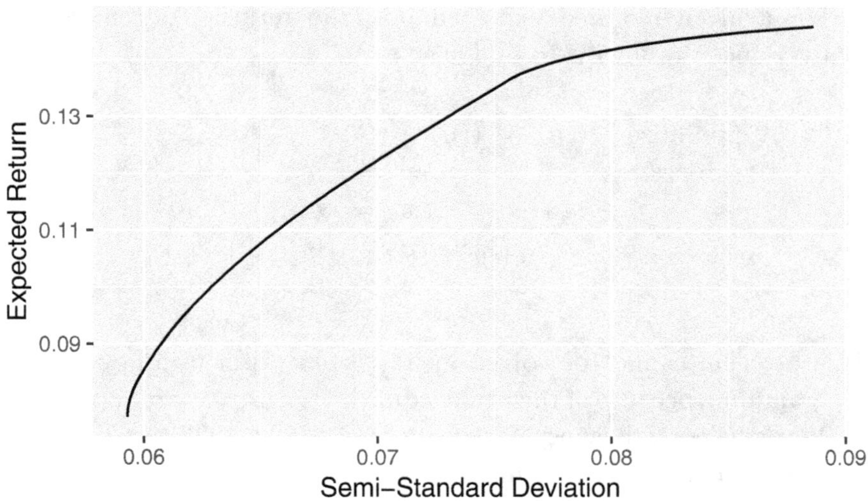

Fig. 6. Mean–semivariance efficient frontier.

as a function of portfolio return. Figure 6 shows the corresponding efficient frontier.

5. The MTXY Method

While the CLA is the most computationally economical way to find the entire efficient frontier, there exist a number of shortcuts that allow one to find individual points on the efficient frontier without mapping it out completely. For standard mean–variance optimization, one can use quadratic programming to find such points for given expected return, or for given variance, or for given λ_E.

In mean–semivariance optimization, though, shortcuts are not so readily available because of the locally applicable nature of the semicovariance matrix. However, a simple reformulation described in Markowitz *et al.* (1992, 1993) (the MTXY method) allows one to find individual efficient points if one uses historical samples to form an estimate of the semicovariance matrix.

For a given required expected portfolio return μ_{P}, the mean–semivariance problem is to find $\boldsymbol{x}$ so as to

$$\left.\begin{array}{lrcl} \text{minimize} & ((\boldsymbol{y})^-)^\top ((\boldsymbol{y})^-) & & \\ \text{subject to} & \boldsymbol{\mu}^\top \boldsymbol{x} & = & \mu_{\mathrm{P}}, \\ & \boldsymbol{A}\boldsymbol{x} & = & \boldsymbol{b}, \\ & \boldsymbol{B}_{\boldsymbol{\varrho}}\boldsymbol{x} - \boldsymbol{y} & = & \mathbf{0}, \\ & \boldsymbol{x} & \geq & \mathbf{0}. \end{array}\right\} \quad \text{(SV1)}$$

This problem cannot be solved in its current form using quadratic programming because of the presence of the "negative part" operator.

Nevertheless, following Markowitz *et al.* (1992, 1993), we can convert this into a standard form by defining new non-negative variables that separately represent the positive parts and absolute values of the negative parts of $\boldsymbol{y}$. That is, let $\boldsymbol{n} = |(\boldsymbol{y})^-|$ hold the absolute values of the negative parts of $\boldsymbol{y}$, and let $\boldsymbol{p} = (\boldsymbol{y})^+ = \boldsymbol{y} - (\boldsymbol{y})^-$ hold the positive parts. We therefore have that $\boldsymbol{y} = \boldsymbol{p} - \boldsymbol{n}$. Then, using Equation (29), we arrive at the constraint $\boldsymbol{B}_{\boldsymbol{\varrho}}\boldsymbol{x} = \boldsymbol{p} - \boldsymbol{n}$. The objective now simplifies to $\boldsymbol{n}^\top\boldsymbol{n}$. Therefore, the mean–semivariance problem (SV1) is equivalent to finding $\boldsymbol{x}$, $\boldsymbol{p}$, and $\boldsymbol{n}$ so as to

$$\left.\begin{array}{lrcl} \text{minimize} & \boldsymbol{n}^\top \boldsymbol{n} & & \\ \text{subject to} & \boldsymbol{\mu}^\top \boldsymbol{x} & = & \mu_{\mathrm{P}}, \\ & \boldsymbol{A}\boldsymbol{x} & = & \boldsymbol{b}, \\ & \boldsymbol{B}_{\boldsymbol{\varrho}}\boldsymbol{x} - \boldsymbol{p} + \boldsymbol{n} & = & \mathbf{0}, \\ & \boldsymbol{x} & \geq & \mathbf{0}, \\ & \boldsymbol{p} & \geq & \mathbf{0}, \\ & \boldsymbol{n} & \geq & \mathbf{0}. \end{array}\right\} \quad \text{(SV2)}$$

The major disadvantage of this simple approach is that it increases the number of variables from n for $\boldsymbol{x}$ to $n + 2T$ for $\boldsymbol{x}$, $\boldsymbol{p}$, and $\boldsymbol{n}$. Naturally, T can be large, and this increases the computational burden significantly. Despite this, for typical institutional portfolios, and for standard desktop computer hardware, the computational burden is not prohibitive. If minimal computational burden is absolutely essential, one can use the streamlined version described in Markowitz *et al.* (1992, 1993). Those papers describe how to reduce the dimension of the problem at the expense of slightly more tricky matrix manipulations.

The sample R function `downside.cvx` in Appendix C solves Problem (SV2) using the CVXR package of Fu *et al.* (2017). This package demonstrates the ease of using disciplined convex optimization (Grant, 2004) in this case. The input parameters to the function are the required return μ_{P} = `reqret`, the vector of expected security returns $\boldsymbol{\mu}$ = `mu`, and the matrix of centered, normalized returns $\boldsymbol{B}$ = `B`.

Block `--C01--` loads the required `CVXR` library, and block `--C02--` sets the dimensions of the problem. Block `--C03--` declares the vectors $\boldsymbol{x}$ = `x`, $\boldsymbol{p}$ = `p`, and $\boldsymbol{n}$ = `n` to be decision variables in the optimization problem. Block `--C04--` defines the objective `obj` of the optimization to be minimization of the sum of the squares of the negative parts of $\boldsymbol{y}$.

Block `--C05--` defines the constraints. `C1` through `C3` are the nonnegativity constraints on the decision variables. `C4` constrains the portfolio return to be equal to required return, and `C5` is the budget constraint. `C6` implements the constraint $\boldsymbol{B}_{\varrho}\boldsymbol{x} = \boldsymbol{p} - \boldsymbol{n}$. Finally, `C1` through `C6` are gathered together in the constraint list `con`.

Block `--C06--` defines the problem `prb` in terms of the objective `obj` and constraints `con`, and block `--C07--` solves the problem, putting the result into list `sol`. Finally, block `--C08--` extracts the values of `x`, `p`, and `n` from `sol` and returns them to the calling function.

6. Conclusions

It is often agreed that, intuitively, mean–semivariance portfolio optimization is more sensible than mean–variance optimization, but it is also often assumed that mean–semivariance optimization is too difficult. Even though the mean–semivariance problem was solved more than 60 years ago, portfolio managers are more familiar and comfortable with mean–variance optimization. Mean–semivariance optimization has, to a large extent, been forgotten. The purpose of this chapter is to serve as a reminder of the simplicity and intuitive appeal of mean–semivariance optimization, and to revive interest in it.

To accomplish this end, we provide a tutorial review of the theory of the CLA as applied to standard mean–variance portfolio optimization. Coupled with the theory, we provide sample Python code to illustrate the ease with which the CLA traces out the entire efficient frontier. The Python code contains extensive comments that link the code closely to the theory.

Following this, we show how one can reduce downside exposure using mean–semivariance optimization. In general, mean–semivariance optimization is difficult to perform. However, the problem can be simplified dramatically if one uses an estimate of the covariance matrix derived from historical asset returns. In this case, one works with a particular square root of the covariance matrix from which the portfolio's semivariance is easily computed. We provide an explanation of this theory, and follow with sample R code that is extensively cross-referenced to the theory.

Finally, we show how to use the historical square root of the covariance matrix to write the mean–semivariance problem in standard quadratic form, and we provide a simple R function to find the optimal mean–semivariance portfolio for any feasible expected portfolio return.

Appendix A: Sample Python Code for Mean–variance CLA

```
import numpy as np

# --A01--
def zerorows(x, j):
    y = x.copy()
    for k in j:
        y[k] = 0
    return y

# --A02--
def zerocols(x, j):
    y = x.copy()
    for k in j:
```

```
            y[:,k] = 0
    return y

# --A03--
def bar(x, j):
    y = x.copy()
    for k in j:
        y[k] = 0
        y[k,k] = 1
    return y

# --A04-- Portfolio Initialization.
def initport(mu, lb, ub):
   x       = lb.copy()
   ii      = np.argsort(-mu, axis=0)
   amtleft = 1 - np.sum(x)
   ix      = 0
   ns      = mu.shape[0]
   while ((amtleft > 0) and (ix < ns)):
      i       = ii[ix]
      chg     = min(ub[i]-lb[i], amtleft)
      x[i]    = x[i] + chg
      amtleft = amtleft - chg
      ix     += 1
   return(x)

# --A05-- Read the raw data.
ret = np.genfromtxt('example.tsv', delimiter="\t")
ret = np.delete(ret, 0, 1)

# --A06-- Set initial parameters.
ns  = ret.shape[1]
lb  = 0.1 * np.ones([ns, 1])
ub  = 0.5 * np.ones([ns, 1])
A   = np.ones([1, ns])
b   = 1.0
m   = 1
tol = 1E-9

# --A07-- Compute basic statistics of the data.
mu = np.mean(ret, axis=0).reshape([ns, 1])
C  = np.cov(ret.T)

# --A08-- Initialize the portfolio.
x  = initport(mu, lb, ub)

# --A09-- Set the state vector.
up = 1 * (abs(x - ub) < tol)
dn = 1 * (abs(x - lb) < tol)
s  = np.subtract(up, dn)
```

```

# --A10-- Set the P matrix.
P = np.concatenate((C, A.T), axis=1)

# --A11-- Initialize storage for quantities
# to be computed in the main loop.
LAM = float('inf')
lam = float('inf')
X   = x.copy()
V   = np.matmul(x.T, np.matmul(C, x))
R   = np.matmul(mu.T, x)
S   = s.copy()

# --A12-- The main CLA loop, which steps
# from corner portfolio to corner portfolio.
while lam > 0:

    # --A13-- Create the UP, DN, and IN
    # sets from the current state vector.
    UP = s > +0.9
    DN = s < -0.9
    IN = np.invert(np.logical_or(UP, DN))

    # --A14-- Create the Abar, Cbar, and Mbar matrices.
    io     = np.where(np.logical_not(IN))[0]
    Abar   = zerocols(A, io)
    Cbar   = bar(C, io)
    toprow = np.concatenate((Cbar, Abar.T), axis=1)
    botrow = np.concatenate((Abar, np.zeros([m, m])), axis=1)
    Mbar   = np.concatenate([toprow, botrow], axis=0)

    # --A15-- Create the right-hand sides for alpha and beta.
    up  = np.multiply(1 * UP, ub)
    dn  = np.multiply(1 * DN, lb)
    k   = np.add(up, dn)
    bot = b - np.matmul(A, k)
    top = zerorows(mu, io)
    rhsa = np.concatenate([k, bot], axis=0)
    rhsb = np.concatenate([top, np.zeros([m, m])], axis=0)

    # --A16-- Compute alpha, beta, gamma, and delta.
    alpha = np.linalg.solve(Mbar, rhsa)
    beta  = np.linalg.solve(Mbar, rhsb)
    gamma = np.matmul(P, alpha)
    delta = np.matmul(P, beta) - mu

    # --A17-- Prepare the ratio matrix.
    L = -float('inf') * np.ones([ns, 4])

    # --A18-- IN security possibly going UP.
```

```
    for i in np.where(IN & (beta[range(ns)] < -tol))[0]:
        L[i,0] = (ub[i] - alpha[i]) / beta[i]

    # --A19-- IN security possibly going DN.
    for i in np.where(IN & (beta[range(ns)] > +tol))[0]:
        L[i,1] = (lb[i] - alpha[i]) / beta[i]

    # --A20-- DN security possibly going IN.
    for i in np.where(UP & (delta < -tol))[0]:
        L[i,2] = -gamma[i] / delta[i]

    # --A21-- UP security possibly going IN.
    for i in np.where(DN & (delta > +tol))[0]:
        L[i,3] = -gamma[i] / delta[i]

    # --A22-- If all elements of ratio are negative,
    # we have reached the end of the efficient frontier.
    if np.max(L) < 0:
        lam = -float('inf')
        break

    # --A23-- Find which security is changing state.
    secmax = np.max(L, axis=1)
    secchg = np.argmax(secmax)

    # --A24-- Find in which direction it is changing.
    dirmax = np.max(L, axis=0)
    dirchg = np.argmax(dirmax)

    # --A25-- Set the new value of lambda_E.
    lam = np.max(secmax)

    # --A26-- Set the state vector for the next segment.
    s[secchg] = (+1 if dirchg == 0 else
                 -1 if dirchg == 1 else
                 0
    )

    # --A27-- Compute the portfolio at this corner.
    x = alpha[range(ns)]+ lam * beta[range(ns)]
    v = np.matmul(x.T, np.matmul(C, x))
    r = np.matmul(mu.T, x)

    # --A28-- Save the data computed at this corner.
    X = np.concatenate([X, x], axis=1)
    S = np.concatenate([S, s], axis=1)
    V = np.append(V, v)
    R = np.append(R, r)
    LAM = np.append(LAM, lam)
```

Appendix B: Sample R Code for Mean–semivariance CLA

```
#################################################################
##                      Utility functions.                    ##
#################################################################

# --B01-- Function to set rows j of matrix X to zero.
zerorows <- function(X, j) {
   Y = X; for (k in j) Y[k,] <- 0; return(Y)
}

# --B02-- Function to set columns j of matrix X to zero.
zerocols <- function(X, j) {
   Y <- X; for (k in j) Y[,k] <- 0; return(Y)
}

# --B03-- Function to set rows j of matrix X to zero,
# and diagonal elements j with 1.
overbar <- function(X, j) {
   Y <- zerorows(X, j);
   for (k in j) Y[k,k] <- 1; return(Y)
}

# --B04-- Function to initialize a long-only portfolio
# subject only to the budget constraint.
initport <- function(mu, lb, ub) {
   xinf    <- lb; amtleft <- 1 - sum(xinf)
   ii      <- order(-mu); ns <- dim(mu)[1]
   ix      <- 1
   while ((amtleft > 0) & (ix <= ns)) {
      i       <- ii[ix]
      chg     <- min(ub[i]-lb[i], amtleft)
      xinf[i] <- xinf[i] + chg
      amtleft <- amtleft - chg
      ix      <- ix + 1
   }
   return(xinf)
}

#################################################################
##   Critical Line Algorithm for Downside Optimization.        ##
#################################################################
dscla <- function(R, A, b, lb, ub, refret=0, tol=1E-9) {

   # --B05-- Basic properties of returns data.
   no    <- dim(R)[1]
   ns    <- dim(R)[2]
   mu    <- matrix(colMeans(R), ncol=1)

```

```
# --B06-- Initialize portfolio with Sharpe's method.
x  <- initport(mu, lb, ub)
x  <- matrix(x, ncol=1)

# --B07-- Set the initial state vector.
state <- matrix((x == ub) - (x == lb), ncol=1)

# --B08-- Find which securities should be included
# in the initial locally applicable semicovariance matrix.
Rex <- R - matrix(refret, no, ns, byrow=T)
y   <- Rex %*% x
obs.in <- y < -tol

# --B09-- Compute the locally applicable
# semicovariance matrix, Sloc, and set up
# the locally applicable P and M matrices.
Rloc <- Rex[obs.in,]
Sloc <- t(Rloc) %*% Rloc / no
Ploc <- cbind(Sloc, t(A))
Mloc <- rbind(Ploc, cbind(A, 0))

# --B10-- Initialize storage for quantities
# to be computed in the main loop.
portfolios <- x
semivars   <- as.numeric(t(x) %*% Sloc %*% x)
returns    <- sum(x * mu)
lambdas    <- lam <- Inf

# --B11-- Enter the main CLA loop.
while (lam > 0) {
   lam.prv <- lam

   # --B12-- Set the logical state indicators from the
   # state vector, and find securities that are OUT.
   UP <- state > +0.9; DN <- state < -0.9
   IN <- !(UP | DN);   OT <- which(!IN)

   # --B13-- Create the Abar, Sbar, and Mbar matrices.
   Sbar <- overbar(Sloc, OT); Abar <- zerocols(A, OT)
   Mbar <- rbind(cbind(Sbar, t(Abar)), cbind(Abar, 0))

   # --B14-- Create the right-hand sides for alpha and beta.
   k <- ub * UP + lb * DN
   rhsa <- rbind(matrix(0, ns, 1), b-A%*%k)
   rhsb <- rbind(zerorows(mu, OT), 0)

   # --B15-- Compute alpha, beta, gamma, and delta.
   alf <- solve(Mbar, rhsa)
   bet <- solve(Mbar, rhsb)
   gam <- Ploc %*% alf
```

```
    del <- Ploc %*% bet - mu

    # --B16-- Select alpha and beta for real securities
    # only (i.e., exclude Lagrange multipliers).
    alf.sec <- matrix(alf[1:ns], ncol=1)
    bet.sec <- matrix(bet[1:ns], ncol=1)

    # --B17-- Check for IN security possibly going UP.
    LIU <- matrix(-Inf, ns, 1)
    i   <- which(IN & (bet.sec < -tol))
    if (length(i) > 0)
       LIU[i] <- (ub[i] - alf.sec[i]) / bet.sec[i]

    # --B18-- Check for IN security possibly going DN.
    LID <- matrix(-Inf, ns, 1)
    i   <- which(IN & (bet.sec > +tol))
    if (length(i) > 0)
       LID[i] <- (lb[i] - alf.sec[i]) / bet.sec[i]

    # --B19-- Check for UP security possibly going IN.
    LUI <- matrix(-Inf, ns, 1)
    i   <- which(UP & (del < -tol))
    if (length(i) > 0) LUI[i] <- -gam[i] / del[i]

    # --B20-- Check for DN security possibly going IN.
    LDI <- matrix(-Inf, ns, 1)
    i   <- which(DN & (del > +tol))
    if (length(i) > 0) LDI[i] <- -gam[i] / del[i]

    # --B21-- Form Lambda matrix for finding lambda_E.
    L <- cbind(LIU, LID, LUI, LDI)

    # --B22-- Find which security might change state.
    secmax <- apply(L, 1, max, na.rm=T)
    secchg <- which.max(secmax)

    # --B23-- Find next possible state change.
    dirmax <- apply(L, 2, max, na.rm=T)
    dirchg <- which.max(dirmax)

    # --B24-- Set lambda_E for a changing security.
    lam.sec  <- max(secmax)

    # --B25-- Find the lambda_E ratios for possible
    # constituent changes in the semicovariance calculation.
    num <- Rex %*% alf.sec
    den <- Rex %*% bet.sec
    rat <- matrix(-Inf, no, 1)
    i   <- which(abs(den) > +tol)
    if (length(i) > 0) rat[i] <- -num[i] / den[i]
```

```

    # --B26-- Find the maximum lambda_E for
    # observations changing in the LSM.
    lam.obs <- -Inf
    i <- which(rat - lam.prv < -tol)
    if(any(i)) lam.obs <- max(rat[i])

    # --B27-- Decide if the constituents of the LSM are
    # changing or if a security's state is changing.
    if (lam.obs > lam.sec) { # crossing a profitability line.

       # --B28-- Set lambda_E.
       lam <- lam.obs

       # --B29-- Compute the portfolio at profitability line.
       x <- alf.sec + lam * bet.sec

       # --B30-- Find which securities should be
       # included in the next LSM, and compute it.
       obs.in <- Rex %*% x < -tol
       Rloc   <- Rex[obs.in,]
       Sloc   <- t(Rloc) %*% Rloc / no

       # --B31-- Form the local P and M matrices.
       Ploc   <- cbind(Sloc, t(A))
       Mloc   <- rbind(Ploc, cbind(A, 0))

    } else { # a security's state is changing.

       # --B32-- Set lambda_E.
       lam <- lam.sec

       # --B33-- Compute the portfolio at this corner.
       x <- alf.sec + lam * bet.sec

       # --B34-- Set the state vector for the next segment.
       if (dirchg == 1) {         # IN security going UP.
          state[secchg] <- +1
       } else if (dirchg == 2) { # IN security going DN.
          state[secchg] <- -1
       } else {                   # Security coming IN.
          state[secchg] <- 0
       }
    }

    # --B35-- Save the data at this value of lambda_E.
    portfolios <- cbind(portfolios, x)
    semivars   <- c(semivars, as.numeric(t(x) %*% Sloc %*% x)
  )
    returns    <- c(returns, sum(x * mu))
```

```
        lambdas     <- c(lambdas, lam)
    }

    # --B36-- Return a list representing the efficient frontier.
    ef <- list(portfolios = portfolios,
               semivars   = semivars,
               returns    = returns,
               lambdas    = lambdas)
    return(ef)
}

############################################################
##                    Main Program.                       ##
############################################################

# --B37-- Read the raw returns data.
R <- as.matrix(read.table("example.tsv",
                          row.names = 1,
                          as.is     = T))

# --B38-- Set constraints.
ns <- dim(R)[2]
A  <- matrix(1, 1, ns)   # Budget constraint matrix.
b  <- 1                  # Budget constraint constant.
lb <- matrix(0,  ns, 1)  # Long-only
ub <- matrix(10, ns, 1)  # No upper bound in practice.

# --B39-- Call the Downside CLA function.
ef <- dscla(R, A, b, lb, ub, refret=0, tol=1E-9)
```

Appendix C: MTXY Method Sample CVXR Code

```
#####################################################
## Downside portfolio optimization with CVXR
downside.cvx <- function(reqret , mu, B) {

  # --C01-- Load the CVXR package.
  suppressMessages(library(CVXR))

  # --C02-- Find the dimensions of the problem.
  NT  <- dim(B)[1]
  NS  <- dim(B)[2]

  # --C03-- Declare the variables.
  x   <- Variable(NS)
  p   <- Variable(NT)
  n   <- Variable(NT)

  # --C04-- Define the objective.
  obj <- Minimize(sum(n^2))

  # --C05-- Define the constraints.
  C1  <- x > 0
  C2  <- p > 0
  C3  <- n > 0
  C4  <- sum(x * mu) == reqret
  C5  <- sum(x) == 1
  C6  <- B %*% x - p + n == 0
  con <- list(C1, C2, C3, C4, C5, C6)

  # --C06-- Set up the problem in terms of the
  # objective and constraints.
  prb <- Problem(obj, con)

  # --C07-- Solve the problem.
  sol <- solve(prb)

  # --C08-- Create and return a list of results.
  x.o <- sol$getValue(x)
  p.o <- sol$getValue(p)
  n.o <- sol$getValue(n)
  res <- list(x=x.o, p=p.o, n=n.o)
  return(res)
}
```

Acknowledgment

The authors thank Peter Todd for his painstaking review of this chapter, and for his numerous helpful suggestions.

References

Bailey, D. H. and López de Prado, M. (2013). An open-source implementation of the critical-line algorithm for portfolio optimization. *Algorithms* **6**(1), 169–196.

Boyd, S. and Vandenberghe, L. (2004). *Convex Optimization.* Cambridge University Press.

Cumova, D. and Nawrocki, D. (2011). A symmetric LPM model for Heuristic Mean–Semivariance analysis. *Journal of Economics and Business* **63**(3), 217–236.

Cumova, D. and Nawrocki, D. (2014). Portfolio optimization in an upside potential and downside risk framework. *Journal of Economics and Business* **71**, 68–89.

Estrada, J. (2008). Mean–semivariance optimization: A Heuristic approach. *Journal of Applied Finance* Spring/Summer: 57–72.

Fu, A., Narasimhan, B., and Boyd, S. (2017). CVXR: An R Package for disciplined convex optimization. Technical report, Stanford University. https://web.stanford.edu/~boyd/papers/cvxr_paper.html

Grant, M. G. (2004). *Disciplined Convex Programming.* PhD thesis, Stanford University.

Hager, W. W. (1989). Updating the inverse of a matrix. *SIAM Review* **31**(2), 221–239.

Jacobs, B. I., Levy, K. N., and Starer, D. (2012). Practical Optimization of Enhanced Active Equity Portfolios, Chapter 3 in Bernd Scherer and Kenneth Winston (Eds.), *The Oxford Handbook of Quantitative Asset Management*, pp. 32–49. Oxford University Press, Oxford, UK.

Levy, H. and Markowitz, H. M. (1979). Approximating expected utility by a function of mean and variance. *American Economic Review* **69**(3), 308–317.

Markowitz, H. M. (1959). *Portfolio Selection: Efficient Diversification of Investments.* Basil Blackwell, Cambridge, MA.

Markowitz, H. M. (1987). *Mean-Variance Analysis in Portfolio Choice and Capital Markets.* Basil Blackwell, Cambridge, MA.

Markowitz, H. M., Todd, G. P., Xu, G., and Yamane, Y. (1992). Fast Computation of Mean-Variance Efficient Sets using Historical Covariances. *Journal of Financial Engineering* **1**(2), 117–132.

Markowitz, H. M., Todd, G. P., Xu, G., and Yamane, Y. (1993). Computation of Mean-Semivariance Efficient Sets by The Critical Line Algorithm. *Annals of Operations Research* **45**(1), 307–317.

Markowitz, H. M. and Todd, G. P. (2000). *Mean-Variance Analysis in Portfolio Choice and Capital Markets.* Frank J. Fabozzi, New Hope, PA.

Niedermayer, A. and Niedermayer, D. (2009). Applying Markowitz's Critical Line Algorithm. In John B. Guerard (Ed.), *Handbook of Portfolio Construction,* Springer, pp. 383–400.

https://doi.org/10.1142/9789811222634_0017

Chapter 17

Alternative Measures of Mutual Fund Performance: Ranking DFA, Fidelity, and Vanguard

Chong Li

Sichuan University, Chengdu, China;
Duke University, Durham, North Carolina, USA
sculichong@foxmail.com

Edward Tower

Duke University, Durham, North Carolina, USA;
Chulalongkorn University, Bangkok, Thailand
tower@econ.duke.edu

Rhona Zhang

Northwestern University, Evanston, IL 60208, USA
rhonazhang2023@u.northwestern.edu

This chapter uses four alternative ways to evaluate mutual fund performance and rank the domestic equity funds of three leading mutual fund companies: DFA, Fidelity, and Vanguard, while splitting the Fidelity and Vanguard funds into indexed and managed portfolios.

First, we use the Fama–French factors to show the extent to which various equally-weighted fund portfolios out-returned their empirically determined benchmarks, and characterize the funds according to size and book-to-market value. Our measure tweaks alpha, the extent to which a mutual fund outperforms its benchmark, and we offer a novel interpretation of alpha. Second, we use Sharpe's (1962) style analysis to explore the robustness of our analysis. Third, we ask whether funds out-return the market. Fourth, we compare the fund returns with their published benchmarks and use Fama–French factors to adjust for bias in the benchmarks.

Return relative to the stock market reflects style choice, benchmark choice, fees, transaction efficiency, and income from lending to short sellers. Fama–French and Sharpe style adjustment abstract from style choice. Comparison with style-adjusted published benchmarks further abstracts from benchmark choice. Each calculation answers a different question.

The Fama–French and Sharpe methods, recorded in Table 6, show that after style adjustment for Fidelity 2001–2018 the indexed portfolio out-returned the managed portfolio. The indexed and managed portfolios from Vanguard and the managed portfolio from Fidelity 2001–2019 out-returned the U.S. stock market as did the Fidelity indexed portfolio 2005–2018. In comparison with the style-adjusted published benchmarks, the Vanguard managed portfolio is the best and the Fidelity managed portfolio is the worst.

Keywords: DFA, Fidelity, Vanguard, active versus passive investment.

1. Introduction

Vanguard, Fidelity, and Dimensional Fund Advisors are three major American mutual fund companies. Ranked by assets under management, they are second, fourth, and 31st, respectively (*Investment News*, 2018). The retirement plan of Duke University features nine Vanguard funds and five Fidelity funds; more than those of any other company. We suspect this is true of other retirement plans as well. Each year the Vanguard Bogleheads meeting features experts, some of whom use DFA funds and some of whom do not.

"Gus" Sauter (2016, Time 1:13:47), formerly head manager of Vanguard's index funds, remarked at the 2016 Bogleheads meetings:

> I do think that Vanguard has the ability to go around the world to hire the best managers. They don't all have to live in Malvern Pennsylvania. So I think that you take the risk out of the equation by owning the total stock market and then if you want, add some more risk to hopefully enhance your return then maybe invest in some active funds.

At a subsequent meeting, he noted that he held 85% of his own assets in index funds. Here we compare the returns of both indexed and managed funds.

We explore the choice of investing in the three companies. In the process, we characterize the funds. Our calculations use Fama–French factors to show the extent to which various funds out-returned their empirically determined benchmarks, and characterize the funds according to size and book-to-market value. This allows apples-to-apples comparison of funds by different families. It also allows us to evaluate passive versus active investment, and it helps investors to pick a portfolio that balances small versus big and value versus growth. Then we check our results by asking the same question, and combining Sharpe's (1992) style analysis with Ken French's 5×5 portfolios sorted by size and the ratio of book-to-market value. We also compare fund returns with their published benchmarks after style adjustment and with the whole U.S. market.

Additional contributions of the chapter are to suggest ways to tweak the concept of alpha, the extent to which a mutual fund outperforms its benchmark, to clarify how to think about the Fama–French multifactor models, to assess two data sources: WRDS and Yahoo, and to compare performance with style-adjusted published benchmarks.

2. Setting the Stage: Previous Work

Reinker and Tower (2004) ask whether Vanguard investors earned higher returns on their managed funds or their index funds, since Vanguard's birth. RT accepted Jack Bogle's view that low cost index funds beat high cost managed funds, but they wanted to see whether index funds beat low cost managed funds as well, and Vanguard was the natural source for these. RT found that the managed portfolio out-returned the index portfolio on both a risk-adjusted and non-risk adjusted basis — a surprise since Vanguard made its name with indexing.

Here is a transcript of Paul Merriman's (2006) on-line interview with Bogle:

> **Paul Merriman:** "How does Vanguard justify with this great family of index funds also having all of these actively managed funds?"

> **John C. Bogle:** "Well I don't run Vanguard any longer, but I will take plenty of responsibility for having those active funds in all of the years I ran it. And the answer to that is really a couple of things. One, a lot of investors, no matter how persuasive the case for indexing is, and it's overpoweringly persuasive, just don't quite get it. They want a little more activity. They want something to watch. Index funds, as you all know, are roughly as exciting as watching paint dry or maybe watching the grass grow. They create great returns but they're not that exciting. So what we tried to do and what I tried to do personally was pick good managers, and that's very, very hard to do. I want to be clear on that, and I have some hits and some runs and some errors in that category, have funds with multiple managers, so you get a much broader diversification, which is not unlike an index fund. . . . [for example, take] our Windsor II fund. It's a large cap value fund, and it has five different managers. I think that's the number now. And so you are going to tend to have a value average return for that fund. And then, actually, make sure you have the other two big advantages of indexing, or three really, no sales commissions, very low expense ratios, because I negotiated with all those advisors and got those fees as low as I could possibly get them, and hire advisors with low portfolio turnover. An article was done by some professors at Duke University about a year ago and they showed that our active managers in the life of the index fund actually did a hair better than the index fund. [Reinker and Tower (2004)]. On the other hand, if we had started the comparison a little bit later, the active managers would have done a little bit worse. But I think it's a valid strategy. What can I do and tell you? I'm still 80% indexed."

Bogle's point is that a managed fund with low expenses, diversified management, and low turnover is likely to perform as well as an index fund, a point that to our knowledge he had not made previously. Reinker and Tower are grateful to Jack Bogle for penning them five hand-written notes about this paper and helping them eliminate some bugs in the early drafts.

Jared Kizer's (2005) comment on RT points out that the superior performance of Vanguard's managed portfolio was due entirely to its tendency to overweight small stocks and value stocks relative to the index portfolio during a period when stocks with these two characteristics outperformed the market. So it is style-picking skill rather than stock-picking skill that leads to the superiority of the managed portfolio in this particular instance.

Reinker and Tower (2005) in their reply find that if small and value had performed as well as the market, then the managed portfolio would have under-returned by exactly the difference in the expense ratios of the two portfolios. Jack Bogle in an email to Reinker and Tower said he "loved" our article.

Subsequently, Tower and Zheng (2008) explore the performance of the domestic equity funds of 51 mutual fund families from 1994 through 2004. They find that DFA out-returned both Vanguard and Fidelity substantially whether risk-adjusted or style-adjusted or not. The ranking of Vanguard's index funds versus its managed funds depended on the details of the calculations. Vanguard's index beat Vanguard's managed when style-adjusted, with the ranking reversed when not style-adjusted. Thus, managers were selecting the best styles, but conditional on style, index won. In each comparison, Fidelity lost to Vanguard. Tower and Zheng also found that mutual fund families that charge loads, high expenses to their most favored investors, and have high turnover tend to perform badly, even gross of these expenses. However, gross of published expenses, managed mutual fund portfolios of those families without loads, with low minimum expenses, and with low average turnover beat the corresponding indexes.

Rodriguez and Tower (2008) find that Vanguard managed funds that are closely tracked by a basket of Vanguard index funds have been beaten by their baskets, and those managed funds that are loosely tracked have beaten their index funds baskets. Also, alphas in one period did not predict subsequent alphas, and managers did not make prescient style choices.

Tower and Yang (2008) find that DFA's equity portfolio substantially outperformed Vanguard's index portfolio from the beginning of 1999 through the end of 2006. But much of that is due to DFA's emphasis on small and value stocks. Still, even after adjusting the Vanguard portfolio to achieve comparable style, DFA outperformed. They find that advisors performed a service in generating higher returns for investors than could be achieved by replicating past portfolios, but the differential does not pass a standard significance test. A major result is that over the eight-year period: 1999–2006, the

DFA domestic portfolio outperformed the Vanguard portfolio that mimicked its style by 2.17%/year averaging alternative approaches. An investor in DFA funds must purchase them through an approved advisor. In 2008, an investor with $100K could pay as little as 1.26% per year in advisor and transaction fees, which would have left him with 0.91%/year surplus from making the switch to DFA. An investor with $10 Million could pay as little as between 0.0156%/year and 0.504%/year, which would have left her with a 1.67%/year surplus. Risk-adjusting these differentials reduces them by 0.1%/year. Thus, the enhanced indexing strategy of DFA has, over the period considered, out-performed the passive indexing strategy of Vanguard.

Li *et al.* (2019) compare Vanguard and Fidelity on 21 comparable funds during 2009–2018. They find for pre-tax return, the difference between Vanguard and Fidelity is small, but Vanguard is the clear winner in after-tax return. Second, Fidelity has a lower expense ratio than Vanguard in all sample funds, while Vanguard has lower turnover. Third, Vanguard funds are more diversified, which should reduce uncompensated risk. Fourth, Fidelity funds have higher tracking precision to their benchmarks than Vanguard funds, but the difference is very small. The most important takeaways are Fidelity wins on pre-tax return by a tiny 0.01%/year and Vanguard wins on after-tax return by a surprisingly large 0.21%/year.

Tower (2009) concludes that Vanguard's index and managed equity funds are comparable. There seems to be little reason to build a portfolio solely out of one or the other if one wishes to overweight some style categories, especially since Vanguard's managed equity funds are able to overweight patches of the market not overweighted by its index funds. For example, there were no Vanguard international value, international growth, and international small index funds, although Vanguard's then new Mid-Cap Growth index and Mid-Cap Value index funds and its prospective International Small-Cap index Fund capture three more parts of the market for its index funds. However, the study does find support for the finding of Barras *et al.* (2008) that the advantage of managed funds has declined. In the first 3 years of the 10-year period (7/1998–6/2008), Vanguard's managed funds on average outperformed their tracking index fund basket. In the subsequent 7-year period, they underperformed. Similarly, in the first half most of Vanguard's managed funds out-performed, and in the second half most under-performed.

Specifically, the average alpha in the first half was 0.86% per year and in the second half it was −0.43% per year, where these alphas represent excess return over the Vanguard index basket with similar style. In the first half, 27 out of 36 alphas were positive; in the second half, 11 out of 36 alphas were positive. The study ended at a bad time, because it misses all the volatility of late 2008 and early 2009. Tower wrote, "it will be fruitful to see whether the regularities found here continue to hold." In the current chapter, we examine the excess return of the Vanguard index funds over the Vanguard managed funds from 2001 on. The excess return of the index funds over the managed funds has trended upward through 2018 for the zero, two, and three-factor models, i.e., whether returns are raw or adjusted for style (Fig. 5).

Favoring indexation, Brown *et al.* (2014) find that "fund managers may often overreact to analysts' recommendation revisions and push prices out of equilibrium." Wermers *et al.* (2012) "provide evidence consistent with the notion that fund managers' stock selection ability stems from fundamental analysis, via which fund managers may uncover information about corporate fundamentals not reflected in current stock prices." Kent *et al.* (1997) find that "mutual funds, particularly aggressive growth funds, exhibit some selectivity ability, but that funds exhibit no characteristic timing ability." Also, "the amount by which the average mutual fund beats a mechanical strategy is fairly small (under 100 basis points) and is approximately equal to the average management fee." Wermers (1999) finds that "Stocks that herds buy outperform stocks that they sell by 4 percent during the following six months; this return difference is much more pronounced among small stocks." However, Wei *et al.* (2015) find that "contrarian funds on average manage to generate superior performance than their peers," and Wei *et al.* (2017) "find that contrarian funds outperform herding funds by a significant margin."

3. Interpreting the Fama–French Three-factor Model

Kenneth French (2018) divides the U.S. stock market into six portfolios. The breakpoints are as follows:

- for small versus big companies: median capitalization
- for value: book-to-market value in top 30% of companies
- for neutral: book-to-market value in middle 40% of companies
- for growth: book-to-market value in bottom 30% of companies.

Here is our notation:

- f is the monthly yield on the one-month U.S. treasury bill (the risk-free asset),
- v is monthly return of the mutual fund,
- m is the monthly return of the U.S. stock **m**arket,
- s is the monthly return of French's **s**mall stocks,
- b is the monthly return of French's **b**ig stocks,
- h is the return of French's value stocks (standing for stocks with a **h**igh ratio of book value-to-market value),
- l is the monthly return of French's growth stocks (standing for stocks with a **l**ow ratio of book value-to-market value).

The Fama–French three-factor model is estimated by regressing $v - f$ on a constant term, which we call alpha, and $m - f$, $s - b$, and $h - l$. Thus, the Fama–French three-factor model regression is

$$\begin{aligned}[v-f] &= \text{monthly avg arithmetic } \alpha + [\beta \text{ market}][m-f] \\ &\quad + [\beta \text{ small}][s-b] + [\beta \text{ value}][h-l] + \varepsilon, \end{aligned} \tag{1}$$

where the α and the β are the regression coefficients, and ε is a random term uncorrelated with the independent variables and with mean zero.

Consider an imaginary mutual fund that invests a fraction of its portfolio, β *market*, in the domestic equity market, a fraction, $1 - \beta$ *market*, in the risk-free asset, a fraction, β *small*, long in small stocks and short in big stocks, and a fraction, β *value*, long in value stocks and short in growth stocks (high and low book-to-market). Its return is

$$\begin{aligned}\text{Imaginary fund return} \quad &= +\,[\beta\text{ market}][m-f]+[\beta\text{ small}][s-b]\\ &\quad +[\beta\text{ value}][h-l]+[1-\beta\text{ market}]f. \qquad (2)\end{aligned}$$

Consequently, the regression in Eq. (1) yields coefficients that indicate the composition of the imaginary fund that most closely mimics the return of the mutual fund in question. More precisely, the regression finds the composition of the imaginary fund that minimizes the standard deviation of the return of the mutual fund minus that of the imaginary fund. We call this mimicking imaginary fund our mutual fund's benchmark. The more positive *β small* is, the smaller are the equities in the mutual fund's portfolio on average. The more positive *β value* is, the more value focused the mutual fund's portfolio is, i.e., the higher is the ratio of book-to-market value. Finally, *β market* will be higher, the larger the share of the portfolio invested in equities. *β market* will also be higher, the greater the extent to which the firms in the mutual fund portfolio have issued short-term bonds and the lesser the extent to which these firms have invested in short-term bonds.

4. The Three and Two-factor Models and the Geometric Alpha

Table 1 describes the U.S. equity funds of Dimensional Fund Advisors, DFA. The rates of return for the funds are from the Center for Research in Security Prices at Wharton Research Data Services, WRDS (2019). We use data from January 2001 through 2018. The range incorporates the experience of the great recession. The variables in the right-hand side of the Fama–French regression are from Ken French's website. For the three-factor model, the coefficients are obtained from the regression described in Eq. (1). We calculate the arithmetic average annual alpha by multiplying the monthly alpha by 12 according to

$$\text{arithmetic avg annual } \alpha = 12 \times (\text{monthly arithmetic avg } \alpha). \qquad (3)$$

We also present the *geometric average annual alpha.* Why? Suppose our mutual fund out-returns its benchmark by 100% in month 1 and under-returns by 100% in month 2, and the return of the benchmark is zero in both months. Then the arithmetic average alpha would be zero, yet investors in the mutual fund have lost all their wealth. The average of the continuously compounded rates of return over many periods is the continuously compounded rate of return over the entire period, which is not true for arithmetic returns. In this example, the geometric average continuously compounded rate of return is 0.69%/month in month 1 and minus infinity in month 2, for an average of minus infinity. We calculate the *geometric average annual alpha cc* (for continuously compounded) as the *geometric average annual alpha cc* for the fund minus that of the benchmark. This averaging property convinces us that the geometric alpha is superior to the arithmetic alpha, yet many studies use the arithmetic alpha, Latane (1959) and Markowitz (1959) being exceptions. In all of the figures, we present the geometric alphas.

The alphas presented under the three-factor model are the excess returns of the fund over a benchmark consisting of a combination of investment in equities and in one-month U.S. Treasury bills that mimics the fund's rate of return.

For an investor who wants to invest solely in the stock market, the appropriate comparison is with an equity only benchmark. Thus, we calculate an alternative. This is what we call the two-factor model to distinguish it from the Sharpe model, which sorts portfolios according to two dimensions. The regression for the two-factor model is

$$\begin{aligned}[v-m] = \text{monthly avg arithmetic } \alpha + [\beta \text{ small}][s-b] \\ + [\beta\ \mathit{value}][h-l] + \epsilon. \end{aligned} \tag{4}$$

This regression shows how much our fund out-returns an all equity portfolio. Throughout the chapter, we use "out-returns" to mean "has a higher alpha than." Since our mutual funds are all equity funds, the information contained in this regression (4) is useful. Investors who are unconcerned with monthly riskiness will find this calculation more appealing to them than the three-factor model. Also, as Siegel (2014) points out, over long periods equities are less risky than bonds. Thus, our favorite calculation for alpha is the geometric version of (4), which is presented in the two-factor model part of Tables 1–4.

Table 1. Dimensional fund advisors.

	Fama–French three-factor model					Two-factor model				Zero-factor model (straight return differential)	
Full years	Arithmetic α %/yr	Geometric α %/yr	β market	β small	β value	Arith α %/yr	Geo α %/yr	β small	β value	Arith α %/yr	Geo α %/yr
2001–02	1.91	**1.89**	1.03	0.47	0.44	1.55	**1.43**	0.47	0.42	1.06	**1.07**
2003–04	−0.44	−0.44	1.12	0.31	0.28	0.64	**0.53**	0.38	0.33	0.58	**0.55**
2005–06	−0.52	−0.52	1.04	0.40	0.26	−0.14	−0.15	0.43	0.25	0.18	**0.16**
2007–08	−0.49	−0.52	1.06	0.33	0.25	−1.91	−2.18	0.39	0.24	−0.30	−0.35
2009–10	0.15	**0.15**	1.05	0.38	0.24	1.12	**1.01**	0.40	0.28	0.37	**0.27**
2011–12	0.30	**0.29**	1.08	0.37	0.25	1.32	**1.22**	0.48	0.28	−0.01	−0.04
2013–14	−0.57	−0.56	1.04	0.25	0.25	0.18	**0.16**	0.27	0.26	0.00	−0.01
2015–16	−0.43	−0.43	1.01	0.29	0.19	−0.36	−0.38	0.29	0.19	0.07	**0.06**
2017–18	−1.16	−1.16	1.03	0.28	0.25	−1.05	−1.09	0.28	0.24	−0.39	−0.39
2001–18	−0.14	−0.15	1.05	0.34	0.27	0.15	**0.06**	0.38	0.28	0.17	**0.15**
2003–18	−0.40	−0.40	1.05	0.33	0.25	−0.02	−0.11	0.36	0.26	0.06	**0.03**
2005–18	−0.39	−0.39	1.04	0.33	0.24	−0.12	−0.20	0.36	0.25	−0.01	−0.04
2007–18	−0.37	−0.37	1.04	0.32	0.24	−0.12	−0.21	0.35	0.25	−0.04	−0.08
2009–18	−0.34	−0.34	1.04	0.31	0.24	0.24	**0.18**	0.35	0.25	0.01	−0.02
2011–18	−0.47	−0.47	1.04	0.30	0.24	0.02	−0.02	0.33	0.24	−0.08	−0.10
2013–18	−0.72	−0.72	1.03	0.27	0.23	−0.41	−0.44	0.28	0.23	−0.10	−0.12
2015–18	−0.80	−0.80	1.02	0.28	0.22	−0.71	−0.73	0.29	0.21	−0.16	−0.17
2017–18	−1.16	−1.16	1.03	0.28	0.25	−1.05	−1.09	0.28	0.24	−0.39	−0.39

Note: Two and Zero-factor α's are positive for 2001–2018. They are negative for 2011–2018.

Table 2. Fidelity index and managed.

		Fama–French three-factor model					Two-factor model				Zero-factor	
Index or managed	Full years	Arith α %/yr	Geo α %/yr	β market	β small	β value	Arith α %/yr	Geo α %/yr	β small	β value	Arith α %/yr	Geo α %/yr
I	2005–06	1.24	**1.20**	1.20	0.15	–0.58	3.26	**3.17**	0.27	–0.65	–0.26	–0.29
I	2007–08	1.40	**1.40**	1.09	0.20	–0.13	–0.64	–0.97	0.29	–0.15	0.01	–0.03
I	2009–10	2.30	**2.18**	0.83	0.29	0.04	–1.33	–1.09	0.22	–0.12	0.11	**0.13**
I	2011–12	2.17	**2.13**	1.02	0.03	–0.15	2.47	**2.40**	0.07	–0.14	0.19	**0.19**
I	2013–14	0.57	**0.55**	1.01	0.23	–0.14	0.78	**0.76**	0.23	–0.13	0.05	**0.05**
I	2015–16	0.17	**0.16**	1.02	0.16	–0.11	0.30	**0.26**	0.16	–0.11	0.00	–0.01
I	2017–18	–0.12	–0.12	0.97	0.06	–0.02	–0.24	–0.19	0.06	0.00	–0.03	–0.03
I	2005–18	1.10	**1.07**	1.02	0.16	–0.15	0.66	**0.62**	0.19	–0.19	0.01	**0.0003**
M	2001–02	–0.14	–0.17	1.01	0.10	0.08	–0.25	–0.32	0.11	0.07	0.17	**0.17**
M	2003–04	–1.19	–1.18	0.98	0.12	0.08	–1.41	–1.38	0.11	0.07	0.02	**0.02**
M	2005–06	2.07	**2.01**	1.07	0.17	0.13	2.83	**2.75**	0.21	0.10	0.31	**0.30**
M	2007–08	1.05	**1.00**	1.14	0.17	–0.25	–1.96	–2.51	0.30	–0.27	–0.04	–0.10
M	2009–10	1.17	**1.14**	1.03	0.18	0.06	1.77	**1.68**	0.20	0.08	0.30	**0.26**
M	2011–12	–1.33	–1.34	1.08	0.08	0.03	–0.31	–0.41	0.19	0.06	–0.07	–0.09
M	2013–14	0.11	**0.11**	0.98	0.11	–0.05	–0.25	–0.24	0.10	–0.05	–0.03	–0.03
M	2015–16	–1.23	–1.24	0.98	0.08	–0.04	–1.39	–1.37	0.07	–0.04	–0.12	–0.12
M	2017–18	–1.71	–1.70	0.98	0.05	0.03	–1.77	–1.75	0.04	0.04	–0.19	–0.19
M	2001–18	–0.13	–0.15	1.03	0.12	0.01	–0.31	–0.39	0.15	0.01	0.04	**0.02**
I-M	2005–18	1.08	**1.07**	–0.02	0.04	–0.14	0.81	**0.88**	0.03	–0.17	–0.01	–0.004
I-M	2007–18	1.40	**1.39**	–0.04	0.05	–0.05	0.88	**0.96**	0.02	–0.08	0.08	**0.09**
I-M	2009–18	1.61	**1.59**	–0.04	0.06	–0.08	0.79	**0.84**	0.03	–0.12	0.09	**0.10**
I-M	2011–18	1.74	**1.72**	0.00	0.04	–0.10	1.76	**1.74**	0.03	–0.10	0.16	**0.16**
I-M	2013–18	1.15	**1.14**	0.02	0.07	–0.07	1.42	**1.39**	0.08	–0.06	0.12	**0.12**
I-M	2015–18	1.49	**1.49**	0.01	0.05	–0.06	1.61	**1.59**	0.05	–0.06	0.14	**0.14**
I-M	2017–18	1.59	**1.58**	–0.01	0.02	–0.05	1.54	**1.55**	0.01	–0.04	0.16	**0.16**

Note: All three α's for all start dates through 2018 are higher for index than for managed.

Table 3. Vanguard funds equally weighted: Index outreturns managed in 2/3 of comparisons of geo α's through 2018.

		Fama–French three-factor model					Two-factor model				Zero-factor model	
Index or managed	Full years	Arith α %/yr	Geo α %/yr	β market	β small	β value	Arith α %/yr	Geo α %/yr	β small	β value	Arith α %/yr	Geo α %/yr
I	2001–02	–3.56	–3.63	1.00	0.23	0.06	–3.57	–3.64	0.23	0.06	0.07	–0.03
I	2003–04	–1.79	–1.77	0.96	0.26	0.09	–2.16	–2.11	0.24	0.07	1.12	**1.01**
I	2005–06	0.94	**0.93**	0.97	0.33	0.01	0.64	**0.64**	0.31	0.02	0.82	**0.66**
I	2007–08	0.92	**0.93**	1.04	0.16	0.00	–0.05	–0.20	0.20	–0.01	–0.11	–0.36
I	2009–10	0.92	**0.91**	0.99	0.18	0.07	0.67	**0.68**	0.18	0.06	2.35	**2.08**
I	2011–12	0.62	**0.61**	1.00	0.17	–0.02	0.64	**0.63**	0.17	–0.02	0.17	**0.08**
I	2013–14	–0.66	–0.65	1.01	0.09	–0.04	–0.35	–0.36	0.09	–0.04	–0.40	–0.43
I	2015–16	–0.15	–0.15	0.97	0.09	–0.06	–0.36	–0.32	0.08	–0.05	–0.51	–0.50
I	2017–18	–0.81	–0.81	0.98	0.11	0.01	–0.89	–0.86	0.10	0.02	–1.41	–1.40
I	2001–18	–0.40	–0.40	0.99	0.18	0.01	–0.60	–0.62	0.18	0.01	0.23	**0.12**
M	2001–02	–0.67	–0.70	1.00	0.08	0.24	–0.62	–0.64	0.08	0.24	3.41	**3.71**
M	2003–04	0.21	**0.20**	1.01	0.17	0.10	0.31	**0.29**	0.18	0.10	3.07	**2.92**
M	2005–06	0.61	**0.60**	1.03	0.08	–0.02	0.87	**0.85**	0.10	–0.03	0.54	**0.47**
M	2007–08	–0.64	–0.67	1.02	0.16	–0.03	–1.12	–1.23	0.18	–0.03	–1.05	–1.23
M	2009–10	–0.11	–0.11	1.03	0.13	–0.04	0.58	**0.50**	0.14	–0.01	2.08	**1.90**
M	2011–12	0.31	**0.30**	1.03	0.16	0.04	0.72	**0.67**	0.20	0.05	0.15	–0.01
M	2013–14	0.56	**0.55**	1.01	0.15	0.02	0.79	**0.77**	0.15	0.02	0.70	**0.63**
M	2015–16	–1.03	–1.04	0.99	0.20	0.01	–1.08	–1.07	0.19	0.01	–0.78	–0.84
M	2017–18	–1.04	–1.04	1.00	0.19	0.07	–1.03	–1.04	0.19	0.07	–2.46	–2.50
M	2001–18	–0.20	–0.21	1.01	0.15	0.04	–0.06	–0.10	0.16	0.05	0.63	**0.56**
I-M	2001–18	–0.20	–0.19	–0.02	0.04	–0.03	–0.54	–0.52	0.02	–0.04	–0.40	–0.44
I-M	2003–18	0.14	**0.15**	–0.03	0.02	–0.01	–0.24	–0.21	0.01	–0.02	–0.03	–0.02
I-M	2005–18	0.45	**0.45**	–0.02	0.01	–0.01	0.08	**0.11**	0.00	–0.02	0.25	**0.24**
I-M	2007–18	0.47	**0.47**	–0.02	–0.03	–0.02	0.13	**0.16**	–0.04	–0.03	0.24	**0.26**
I-M	2009–18	0.25	**0.25**	–0.02	–0.03	–0.03	–0.05	–0.01	–0.05	–0.04	0.10	**0.13**
I-M	2011–18	0.05	**0.06**	–0.02	–0.06	–0.06	–0.09	–0.06	–0.07	–0.06	0.06	**0.12**
I-M	2013–18	–0.04	–0.03	–0.02	–0.08	–0.07	–0.09	–0.07	–0.08	–0.06	0.08	**0.13**
I-M	2015–18	0.56	**0.56**	–0.03	–0.09	–0.07	0.43	**0.46**	–0.10	–0.06	0.66	**0.73**
I-M	2017–18	0.23	**0.23**	–0.03	–0.08	–0.07	0.14	**0.18**	–0.08	–0.06	1.06	**1.10**

Table 4. Vanguard's broad index funds equally weighted: Total Stock Market outreturns 500 Index in 14 out of 27 comparisons of geo α's for periods through 2018. By this criterion the two funds are comparable.

		Fama–French three-factor model					Two-factor model				Zero-factor model	
Fund	Full years	Arith α %/yr	Geo α %/yr	β market	β small	β value	Arith α %/yr	Geo α %/yr	β small	β value	Arith α %/yr	Geo α %/yr
VTSAX Total Stock Market	2001–02	–0.16	–0.17	0.99	0.01	0.01	–0.06	–0.04	0.01	0.02	0.32	**0.38**
	2003–04	0.16	**0.16**	0.99	0.00	0.03	0.07	**0.07**	–0.01	0.03	0.16	**0.17**
	2005–06	–0.17	–0.17	1.02	–0.02	0.02	0.00	**0.00**	0.00	0.01	0.10	**0.10**
	2007–08	0.21	**0.21**	1.02	–0.01	0.00	–0.20	–0.27	0.01	–0.01	–0.18	–0.24
	2009–10	0.03	**0.03**	1.01	0.00	0.02	0.15	**0.14**	0.01	0.02	0.15	**0.09**
	2011–12	0.23	**0.23**	1.01	–0.01	–0.01	0.38	**0.36**	0.01	0.00	0.36	**0.34**
	2013–14	0.09	**0.09**	0.98	–0.01	0.00	–0.26	–0.25	–0.02	–0.01	–0.25	–0.23
	2015–16	0.03	**0.03**	0.99	–0.01	–0.04	–0.06	–0.05	–0.02	–0.03	–0.25	–0.22
	2017–18	–0.27	–0.27	0.98	0.01	0.01	–0.33	–0.31	0.01	0.01	–0.52	–0.50
	2001–18	0.02	**0.02**	1.00	0.00	0.00	–0.04	–0.04	0.00	0.01	–0.01	–0.01
VFIAX 500 Index Fund	2001–02	0.34	**0.34**	1.00	–0.12	0.01	0.36	**0.36**	–0.12	0.01	–1.01	–0.97
	2003–04	0.20	**0.20**	0.99	–0.16	0.01	0.15	**0.15**	–0.17	0.01	–1.80	–1.72
	2005–06	0.00	–0.49	1.02	–0.18	–0.02	0.00	–0.33	–0.17	–0.02	–0.48	–0.42
	2007–08	–0.56	–0.57	0.99	–0.14	0.01	–0.36	–0.34	–0.15	0.01	–0.35	–0.27
	2009–10	–0.46	–0.46	1.01	–0.14	0.01	–0.26	–0.28	–0.14	0.02	–1.78	–1.73
	2011–12	0.22	**0.22**	0.99	–0.15	–0.02	0.14	**0.14**	–0.15	–0.02	0.57	**0.65**
	2013–14	0.34	**0.33**	0.97	–0.14	0.03	–0.34	–0.32	–0.15	0.02	–0.25	–0.20
	2015–16	0.32	**0.31**	0.99	–0.14	–0.04	0.24	**0.25**	–0.15	–0.04	–0.12	–0.07
	2017–18	–0.04	–0.04	0.98	–0.09	0.00	–0.10	–0.08	–0.10	0.01	0.11	**0.15**
	2001–18	0.04	–0.02	0.99	–0.14	0.00	–0.02	–0.05	–0.14	0.00	–0.57	–0.51

Table 4. (*Continued*)

VTSAX-VFIAX: TSM-500	2001–18	–0.02	**0.03**	0.00	0.14	0.00	–0.02	**0.01**	0.14	0.00	0.56	**0.50**
	2003–18	0.04	**0.10**	0.01	0.14	0.00	0.03	**0.06**	0.15	0.00	0.46	**0.39**
	2005–18	0.05	**0.12**	0.01	0.14	0.00	0.05	**0.08**	0.14	0.00	0.24	**0.17**
	2007–18	0.09	**0.09**	0.01	0.13	0.00	0.06	**0.04**	0.14	0.00	0.19	**0.12**
	2009–18	–0.05	–0.05	0.01	0.13	0.00	0.04	**0.04**	0.14	0.00	0.19	**0.13**
	2011–18	–0.19	–0.19	0.01	0.13	0.00	–0.05	–0.06	0.13	0.00	–0.24	–0.29
	2013–18	–0.25	–0.25	0.00	0.12	–0.01	–0.15	–0.15	0.12	–0.01	–0.25	–0.28
	2015–18	–0.26	–0.25	0.00	0.12	0.00	–0.27	–0.26	0.12	0.00	–0.38	–0.40
	2017–18	–0.23	–0.23	0.00	0.11	0.00	–0.23	–0.23	0.11	0.00	–0.63	–0.64

Ideally, our s, b, h, and l, would have been continuously compounded, but these are not available, so we used arithmetic monthly returns.

5. DFA

Each of the tables reports returns for domestic equity funds that are extant in March 2019. The tables in the body of the chapter report returns for equally weighted portfolios of the funds that are extant in March 2019. Funds are added to the portfolio as soon as they were incepted. Thus, as new funds became available, the number of funds in the portfolio expanded. The Appendix tables report returns for the individual funds and their inception dates. We realize that this approach leaves us victims of survivorship bias, but we feel it is useful to focus on currently available funds.

Table 1 presents results for the DFA family. We have constructed Table 1 for January 1 odd year start dates. The top-half of the table shows the two-year performance of the portfolio calculated using monthly data. The bottom half aggregates the top half, with each span ending in December 2018. Thus, the alphas are the averages for the entire period. The mutual fund portfolio is the equally weighted collection of domestic DFA equity funds that are extant in March 2019, excluding the five tax managed mutual funds. The betas represent proportions of the benchmark portfolio invested in the market and the long/short equity baskets. Thus, for the three-factor 2001–2002 calculation, the benchmark portfolio invests 103% of the portfolio in the stock market, with a short position in the one-month U.S. Treasury bond of 3%, a long position in small and short in big of 47% of the portfolio, and long in value and short in growth consisting of 44% of the portfolio. The collection outperforms the benchmark by 1.89%/year continuously compounded and its excess arithmetic return is 1.91%/year. This continuously compounded geometric rate generates an annualized geometric alpha that is also 1.91%, which is slightly larger than 1.89%, due to compounding.

The two-factor model for that same year uses a benchmark of 100% of the portfolio invested in equity, and 47% and 42% in the two long short portfolios, with a geometric alpha continuously compounded of 1.43%/year.

The rightmost two columns of Table 1 are the alphas for the zero-factor model. These are the excess returns over those reported by Ken French (2019) for the U.S. equity market.

The zero-factor model shows the extent to which the fund outreturns the market, in this case 1.07%/year, continuously compounded for the two-year period 2001–2002 and 0.15% for 2001–2018 inclusive. For all of the start dates through 2018, DFA's three-factor alpha is negative. For 7/9th of the start dates through 2018, DFA's two-factor alphas are negative. All of the alphas for the zero-factor model, with start dates from 2005 on through 2018, are negative. In the tables, we have bolded the geometric alphas that are positive.

Table A1 shows the three and two-factor alphas for individual DFA funds. Most are for the start date of 2008. Some start later. All are through 3/2019. The averages and medians are negative. The table also shows expense ratios.

An investor in DFA funds must purchase them through an advisor, which adds to the cost. The *Retire Early Home Page* (2007) lists some of these financial advisors. For example, Altruist Financial Advisors LLC charges 0.235%/year for the first $10 million in an account, with a minimum of $20,000. Executive Planning LLC (https://dfaadvisors.com/) charges a fixed annual fee of 0.50%/year. We did not reckon with this cost in the chapter.

6. Fidelity

Table 2 presents similar calculations for Fidelity. The top third shows the calculations for the index funds, the middle third shows the managed funds, and the bottom third shows the index minus the managed funds. For the Fidelity funds, we selected all the domestic equity managed mutual funds (excluding the two funds incepted in 2019, FWOMX and FIFNX), all the domestic stock index mutual funds, and domestic stock ETFs (excluding sector ETFs).

We excluded the Fidelity Advisor funds from our collection. These are sold through intermediaries and some classes have relatively high expense ratios. For example, the Fidelity Advisor New Insights Fund, Class C (FNICX) has an expense ratio of 1.80%/year, and a maximum deferred sales load of 1%. The class A version of this fund has an expense ratio of 1.05%, but a whopping maximum front-end sales load of 5.75%. The class I version has an expense ratio of 0.79% and no load, but according to the prospectus is "Available only through certain eligible intermediaries." As Zheng and Tower (2008) note, many of the Advisor funds have similar Fidelity funds, with much lower expense ratios, but with different names attached, which obfuscates their similarity.

All the geometric alphas are better for the index fund aggregate than for the managed fund aggregate, except for the virtual tie in the longest zero-factor case. For the two broad Fidelity index funds (not shown), total stock market, and 500 index, the geometric two-factor and geometric zero-factor returns are higher than for the Fidelity managed aggregate over the same period.

Tables A2 and A3 present the alphas for the individual Fidelity funds. The regressions span 2008 or inception of the fund, whichever is later, through March 2019. The average and median geometric alphas for the index aggregate and the zero-expense funds (which are also index funds) are all positive except for one calculation. The median and average for the managed aggregate are all negative, and in every case, the average and median alpha is more positive for the index than for the managed aggregate. All the expense ratios for the managed funds are higher than for all of the indexed ones.

7. Vanguard

Table 3 reports the same calculations for Vanguard. We use the currently available domestic equity mutual funds and ETFs, excluding tax managed and sector funds. When Vanguard has an ETF and a mutual fund with the same portfolio, we use the asset with the earlier inception. The equally weighted index portfolio has higher geometric alphas than the equally weighted managed portfolio for 2/3 of the start dates, all ending in December 2018. For the longest investment period, 2001–2018, the index portfolio has all lower geometric alphas. For 2015–2018, the index portfolio has all higher geometric alphas. So overall, we can't rank the two portfolios.

We use monthly data in another regression to determine the gap between the performance of Vanguard's index and managed portfolio. Our Y variable is the continuously compounded geometric return of the Vanguard index portfolio minus that of the Vanguard managed portfolio. The X variables are $(s-b)$cc, $(h-l)$cc, $(s-b)\text{cc} \times t$, and $(h-l)\text{cc} \times t$, where t is time (normalized so the March 2019 value is zero) and $(s-b)$cc and $(h-l)$cc are the continuously compounded versions of $s-b$ and $h-l$. Time is introduced to recognize that the factor loads of the portfolios vary. The period is 1/2001 through 3/2019. The geometric alpha that emerged is -0.652%/year with $t = -1.44$, and the probability that we calculated the wrong sign (the one tail test) is 7.6%. This alpha is reasonably close to the corresponding alpha of -0.52 for 2001–2018 in Table 3.

Taylor Larimore (2018) recommends a portfolio using the Vanguard Total Stock Market Index fund as the domestic stock component. Warren Buffett has suggested that his wife should invest 90% of the cash left to her in the Vanguard 500 Index Fund, with the rest in short-term government bonds. Table 4 compares the two broad equity index funds, and finds that for investment periods ending in 2018, there is roughly an even split between which fund has the higher zero, two- or three-factor geometric alpha.

The same two- and three-factor calculations for Vanguard's individual funds are reported in Table A4. The average and median alphas for the index aggregate beat those of the managed aggregates.

8. Do the Small and Value Factors Outperform?

Recall the definitions of the Ken French stock categories from Section 3. Imagine an investor who buys a portfolio of Ken French small stocks, worth a dollar, uses these as collateral to borrow a dollar's worth of Ken French big stocks, and sells these big stocks short. His return on the transaction is the dividends plus appreciation of the long position minus the dividends on the short position (which he needs to pay to his lender) minus the appreciation of the short position. Thus, it is the return on the French small stocks minus the return on the French big stocks. This return arises solely from his long and short equity positions. Denote the proportional monthly return of his portfolio, by R. At the end of the month, he unwinds his investments and reinvests. Both his new long and new short portfolios are now a fraction R higher than before. He continues to reinvest month after month, and his portfolio compounds each month at that month's rate R.

The bottom curve in Fig. 1 is the natural log of cumulative returns for this investor from holding Ken French small stocks long and big stocks short. The top curve is the same from holding French value stocks long and growth stocks short. These long/short portfolio rates of return are $s-b$ and $h-l$. The slopes of the trend lines represent the two long/short geometric average continuously compounded rates of return. For the small–big portfolio, the return from mid-1926 is 2.02%/year, and for the value–growth portfolio it is 4.53%/year. Drawing on the numbers (not shown) behind Fig. 1, since the end of July 1983, the $s-b$ return has shrunk to minus 0.35%/year and from the start of 2007 $h-l$ has returned minus 3.44%/year. The cumulative value of the small–big portfolio reached its peak in July 1983, which is 16% above its April 2019 value, and the value–growth portfolio hit

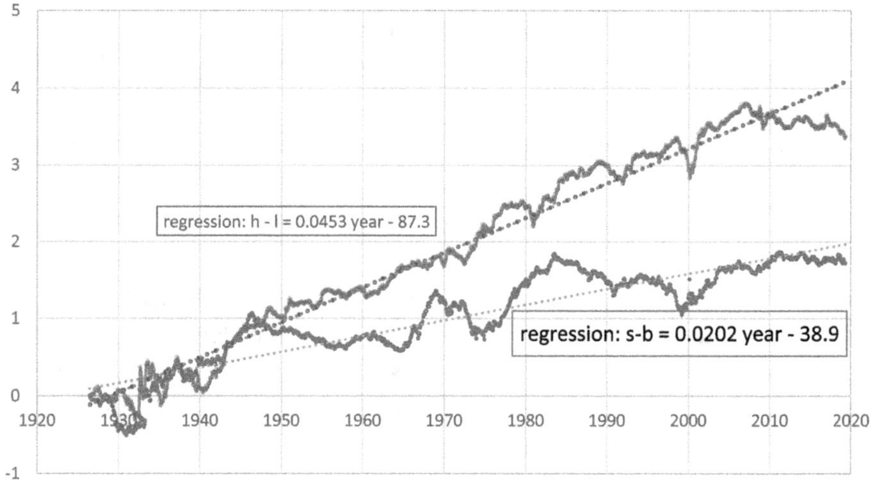

Fig. 1. Log of cumulative return of Ken French long/short portfolios. Mid 1926 through 4/2019 small/big ($s-b$) returned 1.85%/yr; value/growth ($h-l$) returned 3.63% per year. From 7/31/1983 $s-b$ returned -0.35%/yr. From peak at 12/31/2006 $h-l$ returned -3.44%.

its peak at year-end 2006, which is 53% above its April 2019 value. An investor who is uncertain whether these recent trends are likely to continue or whether returns to trends are likely will want to balance the factors of small, big, value, and growth. One might expect that, since the small and value premia are now well known, investors have piled into these asset styles, reducing their expected future returns. For a skeptical view of the future of factor-based investment, see White and Haghani (2019).

However, Blitz (2018) warns against dismissing factor-based investing. He finds "On aggregate, all factor exposures [of ETFs] turn out to be close to zero and plain market exposure is all that remains. This finding argues against the concern that factor premiums are being eroded away rapidly by investors in ETFs." The aggregate of investors can't be biased, so this finding simply says aggregate ETFs have the same factor loads as the rest of the market.

Larry Swedroe, Chief Research Officer for Buckingham Strategic Wealth, commented on an earlier draft of this chapter:

> In 1994, right after the publication of the famous Fama–French research on the value premium, the P/B of U.S. large growth stocks was 2.1 times that of large value stocks, and their price-to-earnings (P–E) spread was 1.5 (Data is from Dimensional). Using Vanguard Russell 1000 Growth ETF (VONG) and Vanguard Russell 1000 Value ETF (VONV), we find that as of January 31, 2019, the P–B spread had actually widened to 3.2, and the P–E spread was basically unchanged at 1.4. At least here, we see no evidence that cash flows have caused the value premium to narrow. The bottom line is, it appears that despite what many investors believe, a massive net inflow into value stocks relative to growth stocks has not occurred. Recently, the small and value factors have ceased to earn excess returns relative to the large and growth factors. This has not been true internationally where value, in particular, has outperformed using any value metric.

He adds that recently the raw returns, not accounting for loadings, of DFA's international funds, which load more heavily on value and size, have not deteriorated. A complementary view is Asness's (2019), which recommends overweighting value that looks like a shunned out-of-favor factor.

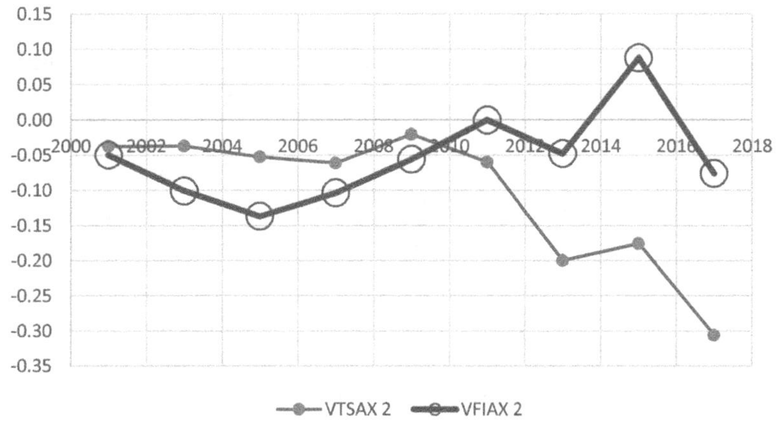

Fig. 2. Two-factor α for VTSAX (Vanguard total stock market) and VFIAX (Vgd 500 index). α's are mostly negative. In all figures α's are geometric and expressed in %/year, continuously compounded.

9. The Vanguard Broad Index Funds

Figure 2 shows the two-factor average geometric alphas for the two broad Vanguard index funds, VTSAX (Total Stock Market Index) and VFIAX (500 Index) from January 1 of the indicated date through 2018. The alphas are both mostly negative, in spite of any revenue earned by Vanguard and passed on to investors from lending shares to short sellers.

Figure 3 shows that from 2001 VTSAX has returned a hair less than the domestic market (zero-factor α of -0.012%/year). Perhaps the closeness of this alpha to zero is due to stock choice or revenue from short sales. VFIAX has under-returned the market for start dates early on. For the start date of 2011, it has beaten the market. This is consistent with small stocks outperforming large stocks early on but under-returning later on.

10. Vanguard Index Versus Managed

Figure 4 shows that the zero-factor geo alphas for Vanguard index and managed are positive for the whole period but negative recently. The two-factor geo alphas are negative throughout, except for one

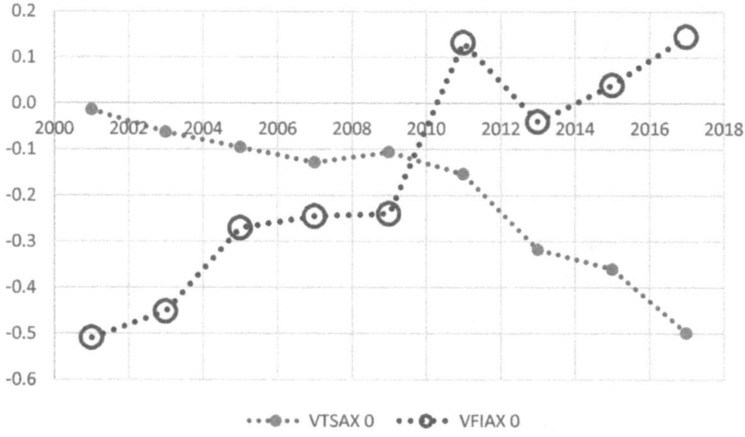

Fig. 3. Zero-factor α for VTSAX and VFIAX.

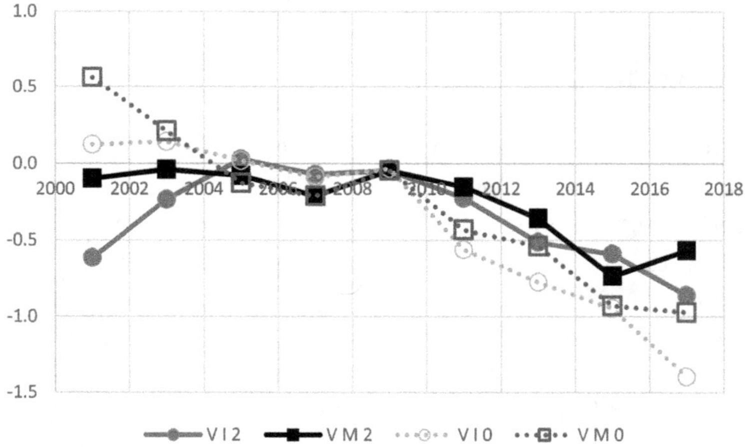

Fig. 4. Zero-factor α's for Vgd Idx & Vgd Mgd through 2018 are positive for longest spans but negative recently. Two-factor α's grow increasingly negative.

observation. Thus, revenue from short sales is not enough to balance other costs of the funds.

Figure 5 shows that Vanguard's zero-, two-, and three-factor geo alphas are lower for Vanguard's index than Vanguard's managed funds for the 2001 start date, but are higher for start dates of 2015 and 2017. Thus, on none of these grounds can we definitively rank the two portfolios.

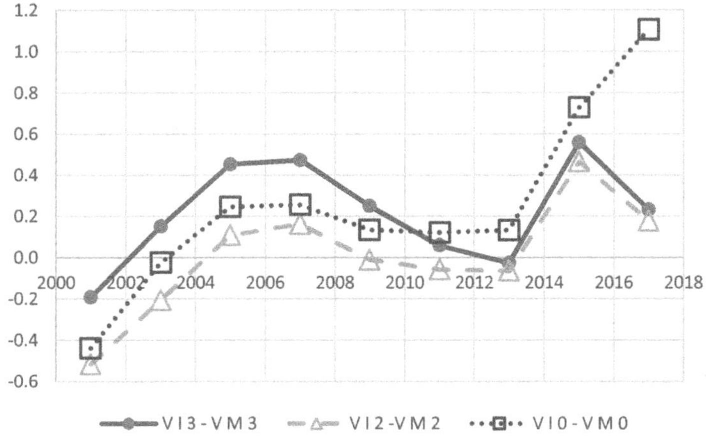

Fig. 5. α's for Vgd idx — Vgd mgd. Idx loses to mgd for earliest start date and beats mgd for latest start dates, according to all three α's.

11. Vanguard Minus DFA

Figure 6 shows the choice between Vanguard index and DFA is complex. The two-factor alpha for the 2001 start shows DFA the winner over both Vanguard index and Vanguard managed, but for start dates of 2013, 2015, and 2017, both Vanguard portfolios win.

Figure 7's zero-factor alpha tells that DFA out-returns both Vanguard portfolios through 2018 for early and late start dates. But the two Vanguard portfolios out-return for intermediate start dates. That DFA would have out-returned by more early follows from the excess return of value and small early on, the styles that DFA advocates more than Vanguard does, as indicated by the betas in Tables 1 and 3.

12. Fidelity Index Versus Fidelity Managed

From Figure 8, Fidelity index beats Fidelity managed for all 21 contests starting after 2006, whether the criterion is the three-factor, two-factor, or the zero-factor alpha. In 2005, there were only two funds in the index collection, while by October 2016 there were 15

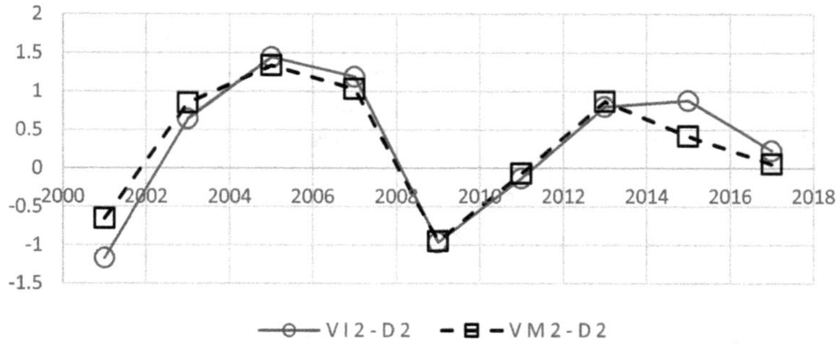

Fig. 6. Two-factor α's for Vgd idx and Vgd mgd minus DFA through 2018. For 2001 start DFA wins. For 2013 on Vgd wins.

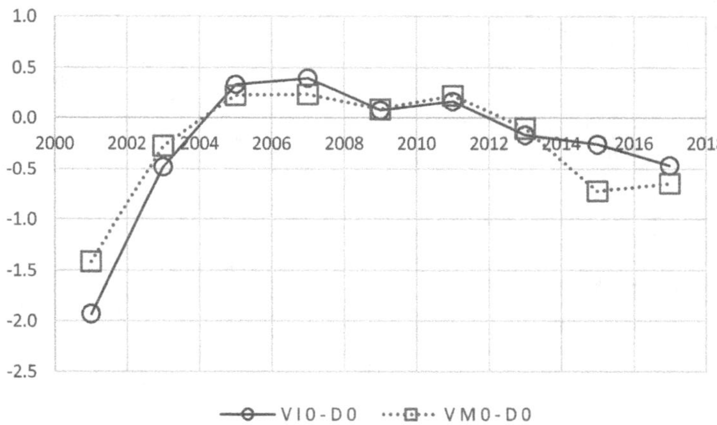

Fig. 7. Zero-factor α's for Vgd idx and mgd minus DFA through 2018. DFA wins for early and late start dates, and loses for intermediate ones.

and by October 2018, 19 funds. Thus, the slightly lower zero-factor alpha for index than managed in 2005 doesn't apply to the current selection of index funds.

13. Fidelity Versus Vanguard

Figure 9 compares managed funds by Fidelity and Vanguard for spans through 2018. Vanguard's two-factor alpha is higher for all start dates. Vanguard's zero-factor alpha beats Fidelity for early

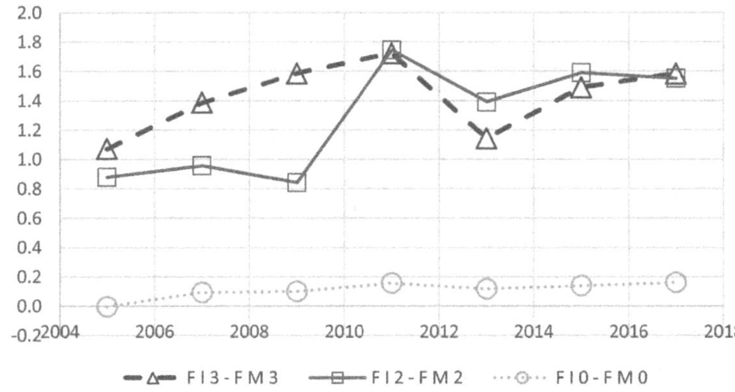

Fig. 8. α's for Fido idx minus Fido mgd through 2018. Idx loses one contest by a hair and wins all the others.

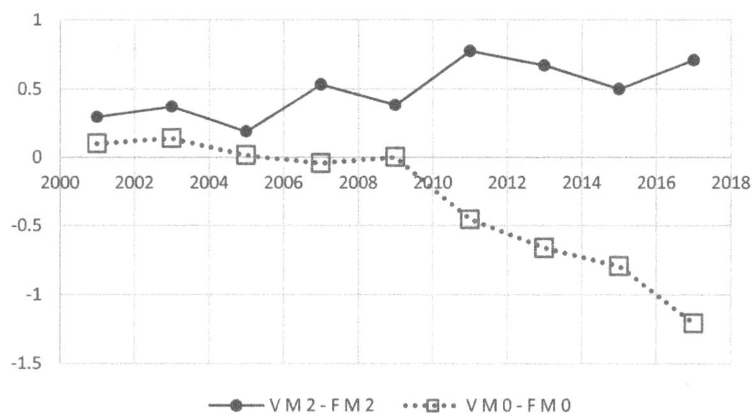

Fig. 9. Managed funds: for Two-factor α, Vgd beats Fido for all starts; for zero-factor α, Vgd beats for early starts, and loses for later starts.

starts and loses for later starts. As the relative performance of different styles varies, we would expect the zero-factor rankings to change, as it does here.

Figure 10 compares index funds. Fidelity wins all the two-factor contests, and wins all the zero-factor contests except for the 2001 start, which Vanguard wins by a hair (0.018%/year).

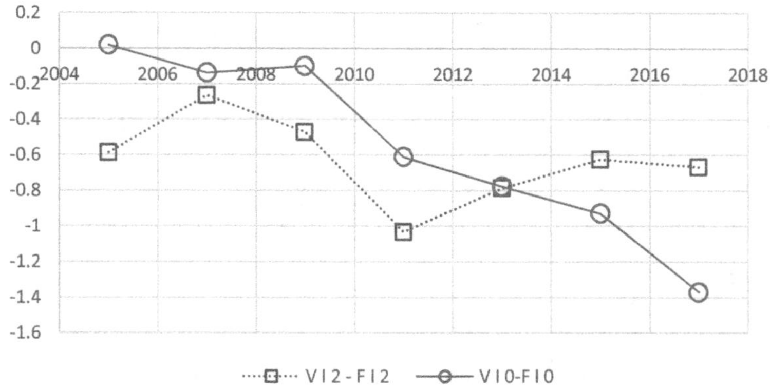

Fig. 10. Index funds. for Two-factor α Fido beats Vgd for all starts; for zero-factor α, Vgd beats by a hair for the first start & loses for later starts.

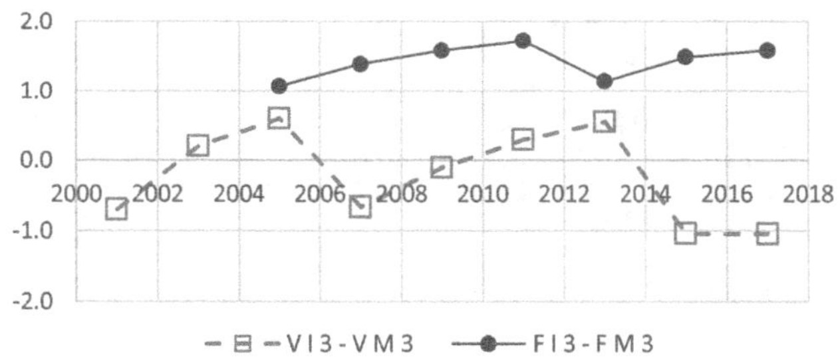

Fig. 11. Three-factor α. Fidelity: idx always beats mgd. Vanguard: mgd and idx can't be ranked consistently.

14. Index Versus Managed

Managed funds typically hold more bonds than index funds do, so comparing three-factor alphas is useful for comparison of managed versus index. That is provided in Fig. 11. For every start date, Fidelity index beats its managed. For Vanguard, the two can't be ranked consistently.

15. Comparing All the Funds

Figure 12 shows the two-factor geo alphas for 2015 through 2018 on the Y axis and for 2005 through 2018 on the X. The two managed

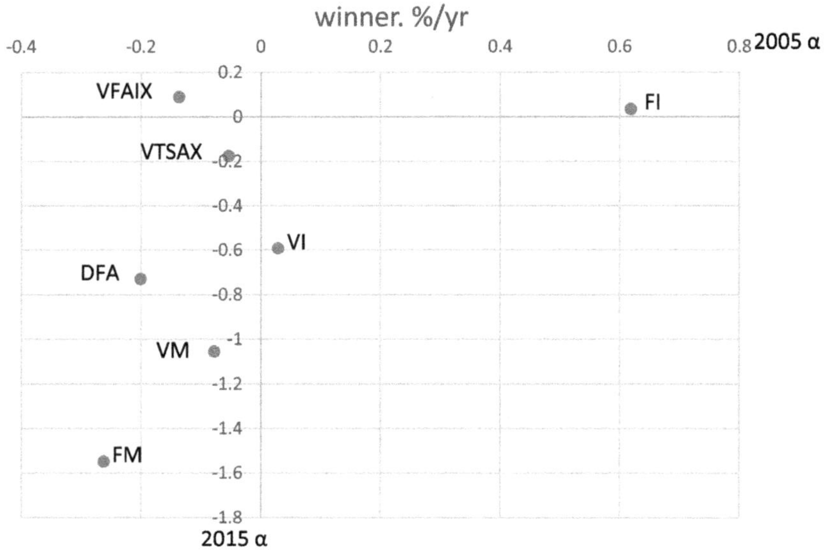

Fig. 12. α geo Two-factor for 2005–18 on X & 2015–18 on Y. Mgd funds are the 2015 losers. Fido idx is the 2005 winner. %/yr.

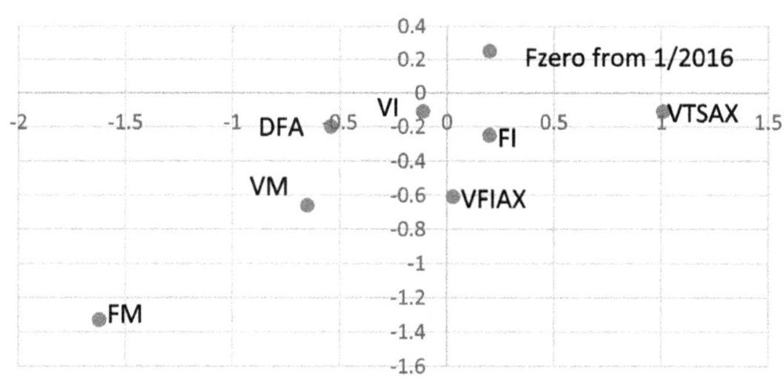

Fig. 13. Median α for individual funds, 1/2008–3/2019. Two-factor on Y axis. Three-factor on X axis. Managed lose.

fund collections are inferior to the Fidelity and Vanguard Index collections on both counts. Comparing averages of the two spans, Fidelity index is the winner followed in order by the two broad Vanguard index funds, Vanguard index, DFA, Vanguard managed, and Fidelity managed.

Figure 13 is similar, except it uses the median alpha for individual funds, with two-factor alphas on the Y and three-factor alphas on the

X, and it uses data from 2008 through 3/2019 from the Appendix tables. Again, we find that the median managed fund is inferior to the median index fund.

16. Efficient Frontiers

Figure 14 presents efficient frontiers, calculated from 2008 through 2018. For maximum return, the investor should have invested 100% in Fidelity index, and to shrink risk, he should have substituted the Vanguard 500 index until, ultimately he held 97% Fidelity index and 3% Vanguard 500. When Fidelity index is excluded, the return maximizing portfolio was 100% Vanguard index. As risk minimization becomes more important, Vanguard 500 is substituted for Vanguard index, and the risk minimizing portfolio is 100% Vanguard 500. When all the index funds from Fidelity and Vanguard are eliminated, only DFA, Fidelity managed, and Vanguard managed remain. The efficient frontier consisted only of the Fidelity and Vanguard managed collection, with no role for DFA.

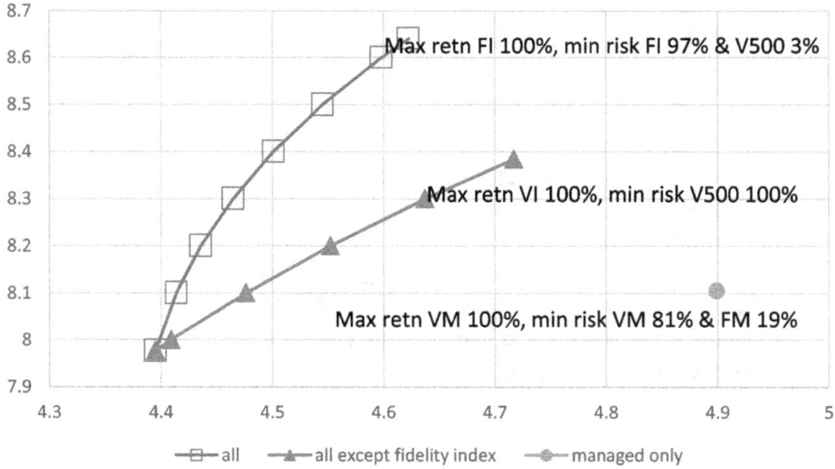

Fig. 14. Efficient frontier 1/2008–3/2019 worsens when Fidelity index is excluded and worsens further when only managed funds are included. Annual return continuously compounded %/yr on Y versus std dev %/month on X. No role for DFA or VTSAX.

Figure 15 presents the efficient frontier from 2001, so Fidelity index is excluded. DFA plays a role only for riskier portfolios.

From October 2016, Fidelity operated 15 of the 16 mutual funds that operated in March 2019. From October 2016–March 2019, the best strategies were for maximum return invest everything in the Vanguard 500 index and for minimum risk do exactly the same thing. If we exclude that fund as a possibility, for maximum return invest everything in the Vanguard index. For minimum risk, invest everything in Fidelity managed. Here DFA and Fidelity Index played no role.

In previous sections, we have run contests between various categories of funds. But ideal portfolio construction consists of combining funds to land on the best place on the efficient frontier. Our efficient frontiers are a first stab at figuring out what combinations of funds are desirable, in particular, we ask how big the shares of managed and index funds from various fund families should be. Of course, choosing monthly standard deviation of return is arbitrary. Vander Weide (2010) develops useful practical guidelines for making lifetime portfolio decisions.

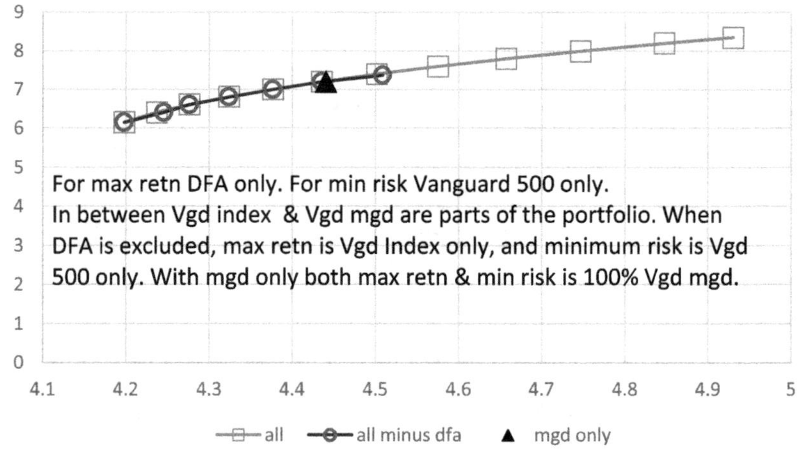

Fig. 15. Efficient frontier from 2001. The benefit of DFA exists only for higher stdev. For lower risk DFA plays no role. Index beats managed.

17. Is Jack Bogle Correct that "In Investing, You Get What You Don't Pay For"?

Figure 16 draws on the individual funds discussed in the Appendix. It regresses the two- and three-factor geometric alphas on the expense ratio. Each percentage point increase in the expense ratio cuts the two-factor alpha by 1.7 percentage points and the three-factor alpha by 2.4 percentage points, with both highly significant. The sign of this relationship is not surprising since managed funds have higher expense ratios and we have seen they have lower alphas. Figure 16 excludes funds established after 2017. This exclusion flattened the regression lines.

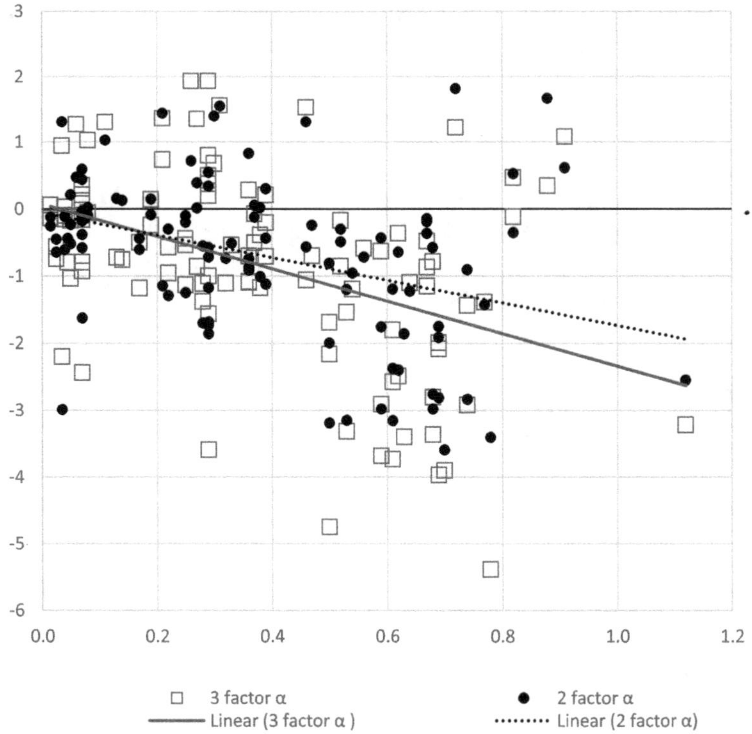

Fig. 16. Each % age point increase in the expense ratio (on X) cuts the Two-factor geo (on Y) α by 1.7% age points with $t = -4.0$, and cuts the Three-factor geo α by 2.4% age points, with $t = -4.8$. Highly significant.

18. Do Alphas Predict for Vanguard's Managed Funds?

We broke the period 2001–2018 into two-year periods, and we calculate the two-year, two-factor geometric alpha for each Vanguard managed fund for each two-year period. We ask whether the alpha for each period predicts the alpha for the subsequent period. In calculating alphas, we ran a single regression for each fund to determine the factor load. Figure 17 shows the result. The relationship is insignificant: our point estimate is a one-percentage point higher alpha in one period predicts a fall of 0.091 percentage points in the subsequent alpha.

The negative relationship is stronger for longer periods. The correlation between these same alphas for the first 5 years and the second 4 years is −0.47. Thus, chasing alpha has been value subtracting for Vanguard managed fund investors.

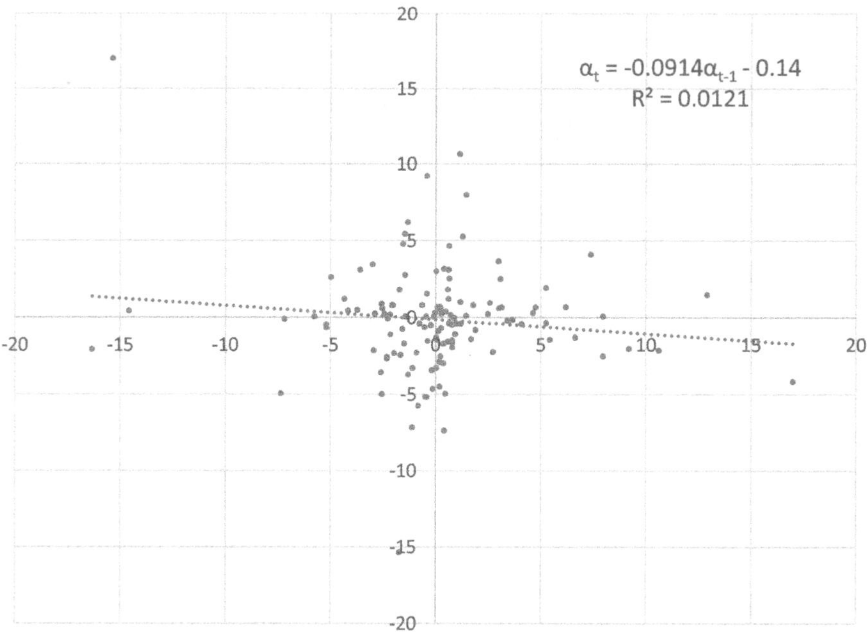

Fig. 17. 2 year two-factor geo α does not predict next 2 year two-factor geo α. The slope is −0.91.

19. Free Yahoo Versus Pricey WRDS Data

Duke subscribes to the Wharton Research Data Services for daily and monthly mutual fund returns. We could have used Yahoo instead.

For the period January 2010 through December 2018, we examined the Vanguard total stock market ETF (VTI), and Vanguard 500 index fund investor shares (VFINX). For each month in which dividends are paid (December, March, June, and September) for both funds, WRDS records a higher return than Yahoo does, and in the following month, WRDS records a lower return. So, the two series are systematically different. For both funds, WRDS has a lower monthly standard deviation of return than Yahoo does, which implies that Yahoo is recording the dividends in the wrong month. Yahoo's daily return series does record the dividends in December, March, June, and September. Thus, the Yahoo system for aggregation to monthly returns is flawed.

We also examined the Fidelity Contrafund (FCNTX). On August 1, 2015, Yahoo reported a one-month jump in its NAV from \$8.4 to \$79, and on December 9, 2016, Yahoo reported a one-month jump from \$8.4 to \$83. Thus, Yahoo suffered from misplaced decimals. On November 2, 2017, using daily data, Yahoo reported a jump in NAV from \$12.705 to \$127.05. From January 2010 through December 2018, Yahoo reported dividends paid in February and December. In both of these months, the WRDS return figure exceeds the Yahoo figure, and in each subsequent month, the Yahoo figure exceeds its WRDS counterpart. Thus, Yahoo's monthly series reports dividends one month late. Even when we expunge the data with the misplaced decimal, the standard deviation of the Yahoo monthly returns exceeds that for the WRDS return, providing further evidence that Yahoo reports dividends in the wrong month. We conclude that Yahoo monthly data are not reliable. We hope our chapter will induce Yahoo to correct these errors, so poor folks will have the same access to data that rich folks do, and make investment decisions that are informed by correct data.

However, WRDS is not perfect. For September 1985, WRDS records VWUSX as returning an improbable 46.4%, even though according to Yahoo its return including dividends that month was 2.01%. Numbers that look crazy probably are.

20. Highlights

- Recently small and value have ceased to out-return big and growth (Fig. 1).
- **2001–2018:** Vanguard's total stock market and 500 index funds have exhibited roughly the same geometric two-factor alpha. They have under-returned the stock market after style adjustment (Fig. 2).
- **2001–2018:** Vanguard's total stock market index fund has returned just a hair less than the U.S. stock market, 0.01%/year (Fig. 3).
- **2001–2018:** Vanguard's equally weighted index and managed portfolios exhibit negative two-factor alphas, but have out-returned the U.S. stock market with managed beating index both in the two- and zero-factor contests (Fig. 4).
- **2001–2018:** According to all three geometric alphas, Vanguard index loses to Vanguard managed. This is reversed for four subsequent start dates. Perhaps Vanguard managed is losing its comparative advantage (Fig 5).
- **2001–2018:** The two-factor alpha is higher for DFA than for both Vanguard portfolios for three start dates, including 2001. The reverse is true for six start dates, including the most recent three. Thus, the superiority of DFA is smaller than found in the studies referenced in Section 2 (Fig. 6).
- **2001–2018 and for four other start dates:** DFA out-returns both Vanguard portfolios. For four start dates, the reverse holds. DFA's excess return was highest from 2001, the earliest period (Fig. 7).
- **2005–2018:** All three of Fidelity index alphas match or exceed the corresponding alphas of Fidelity managed for all, except one, start dates. The outlier is a virtual tie (Fig. 8).
- **2001–2018, managed funds:** The two-factor alpha for Vanguard exceeds that of Fidelity for all starts. For zero-factor alpha,

Vanguard beats for the earliest two starts and loses for the latest four starts (Fig. 9). Thus, recently Vanguard has been winning on a style-adjusted basis but loses when unadjusted. During the span from 2011–2018, small and value under-returned and Vanguard managed is smaller and slightly of more value than Fidelity managed (Tables 2 and 3), which explains part of the result.

- **2005–2018, index funds:** Fidelity's two-factor alpha is higher than Vanguard's for all starts; for zero-factor alpha, Vanguard beats by a hair for the 2005 start and loses in later starts (Fig. 10). Thus, Fidelity is generally the winner, which is ironic given Fidelity's initial hostility toward indexing. Bogle (1997) writes:

> "But there remained a multitude of strident critics of indexing... Fidelity Chairman Edward C. Johnson III doubted Fidelity would soon follow Vanguard's lead. 'I can't believe,' he told the press, 'that the great mass of investors are [sic] going to be satisfied with just receiving average returns. The name of the game is to be the best."'

- **2001–2018 and 2005–2018, three-factor geometric alpha:** Fidelity index beats its managed; Vanguard index versus managed can't be ranked consistently (Fig. 11).
- **2005–2018 and 2015–2018, two-factor alpha:** Fidelity index has positive alpha for both spans; Fidelity managed has worst for both spans (Fig. 12).
- **1/2008–12/2018, median two-factor alpha for individual funds:** Fidelity zero expense funds have positive two- and three-factor alphas. The alphas of Fidelity managed are the most negative (Fig. 13).
- **1/2008–3/2019 efficient frontier:** 100% Fidelity index maximizes return and 97% Fidelity index minimizes risk (Fig. 14).
- **2001–3/2019:** For max return DFA only; for minimum risk Vanguard 500 index only. Fidelity index was excluded because of inception in 2008 (Fig. 15).
- Each one percentage point increase in the expense ratio cuts the two-factor geometric alpha by 1.7 percentage points and the three-factor geometric alpha by 2.4 percentage points (Fig. 16). This is similar to the result in Tower and Zheng (2008).

- Two-year alphas are negatively correlated with subsequent two-year alphas (Fig. 17). Rodriguez and Tower (2008) found the same result.
- Averaging the average and median scores, the two- and three-factor alphas for the Fidelity index funds are higher than for the Vanguard index funds, which are higher than those for the DFA and Vanguard managed funds, which are higher than those for the Fidelity managed funds (Table A5).

In summary:

- **A**. The average of zero-, two-, and three-factor alpha for Vanguard's index portfolio minus Vanguard's managed portfolio is positive for all time spans with start dates from 2005 through 2018, and negative from 2001 and from 2003 through 2018 (Fig. 5).
- **B**. DFA's two-factor style-adjusted returns through 2018 relative to Vanguard on average have fallen relative to the start date of 2001 (Fig. 6).
- **C**. DFA's recent excess returns over Vanguard through 2018 have fallen relative to the start date of 2001 and in comparison to the conclusions of earlier studies (Fig. 7).
- **D**. Fidelity's index fund portfolio has excess returns through 2018 relative to its managed funds by all three criteria in 20 out of 21 contests, and loses that one contest by only a hair (Fig. 8).
- **E**. Vanguard's two-factor style-adjusted managed portfolio out-returns Fidelity's for every start date through 2018 (Fig. 9).
- **F**. Fidelity's index portfolio out-returns Vanguard's for every start date from 2007 on through 2018 for both two-factor style-adjusted returns and unadjusted (zero factor) returns (Fig. 10).
- **G**. Useful takeaways: recently index funds have had the edge over managed funds and DFA's style-adjusted and unadjusted returns have fallen relative to Vanguard's.

21. Returns Based Style Analysis: William Sharpe's Approach

Our two-factor model does not properly account for the relationship between return and the value and growth factors if the return is a non-linear and non-additive function of these factors. We attempt to correct for this deficiency using Sharpe's (1992) style analysis.

We wish to find a benchmark portfolio for each mutual fund portfolio, such that the benchmark portfolio is that collection of stocks whose monthly return most closely tracks that of the mutual fund portfolio. Specifically, we minimize the standard deviation of the monthly return differential between the mutual fund portfolio and the benchmark portfolio.

Ken French (2019) presents monthly returns of 25 portfolios sorted according to the Fama–French $h{-}l$ and $s{-}b$ factors as well as the U.S. stock market as a whole. "The [25] portfolios ... are the intersections of 5 portfolios formed on size (market equity, ME) and 5 portfolios formed on the ratio of book equity to market equity (BE/ME). The size breakpoints are the NYSE market equity quintiles .... BE/ME is the book equity ... divided by ME .... The BE/ME breakpoints are NYSE quintiles." To implement the style analysis, for each year we minimize the standard deviation of the monthly return of the mutual fund portfolio, continuously compounded, minus the monthly return of the benchmark portfolio, continuously compounded, where the benchmark portfolio return is constructed from the 26 French monthly returns. Microsoft Excel Solver is the minimization tool. Shares of the stocks in the benchmark portfolio are all non-negative and sum to one. The constant term that emerges is the monthly alpha continuously compounded. Annual alpha is monthly alpha times 12. Table 5 and Figure 18 present these average alphas for the start of the year indicated through 2018. Positive alphas are in bold.

Now let's compare the Sharpe technique results with those in Section 20. Table 5 presents the Sharpe technique results. In each comparison, we note the average excess return over all start dates of portfolio X over portfolio Y by X-Y.

A. Vanguard index out-returns Vanguard managed for start dates of 2001 thorough 2007, and under-returns for starts thereafter.

B & C. DFA beats Vanguard index for all start dates. The trend line (not shown) for VI-DFA versus start date is flat and

Table 5. Sharpe's style analysis. Two-factor geo α through 2018. (%/year).

	DFA	FI	FM	VI	VM	VFAIX	VTSAX	VI-VM	VTSAX-VI	VFIAX-VTSAX	DFA-VI	DFA-VM	FI-FM	VI-FI	VM-FM
1975					–0.04										
1976					**0.17**										
1977					**0.43**										
1978					**0.21**										
1979					**0.01**										
1980					**0.07**										
1981					–0.02										
1982	–0.56				–0.39							–0.17			
1983	–0.44				–0.55							**0.11**			
1984	–0.42				–0.53							**0.11**			
1985	–0.33				–0.42							**0.09**			
1986	–0.25				–0.76							**0.51**			
1987	–0.16				–0.59							**0.43**			
1988	–0.23				–0.50							**0.27**			
1989	–0.19				–0.48							**0.29**			
1990	–0.08				–0.41							**0.33**			
1991	**0.08**				–0.62							**0.70**			
1992	**0.11**				–0.56							**0.66**			
1993	–0.09		–0.79		–0.43							**0.33**			**0.27**
1994	**0.02**		–0.90		–0.44							**0.46**			**0.36**
1995	**0.02**		–0.93		–0.31							**0.33**			**0.53**
1996	**0.08**		–0.95		–0.22							**0.30**			**0.62**
1997	**0.10**		–0.84		–0.03							**0.12**			**0.71**
1998	**0.04**		–0.76		**0.27**							–0.23			**0.92**
1999	–0.11		–0.61		**0.24**							–0.36			**0.74**
2000	–0.28		–0.97		**0.31**							–0.59			**1.15**

Table 5. (*Continued*)

	DFA	FI	FM	VI	VM	VFAIX	VTSAX	VI-VM	VTSAX-VI	VFIAX-VTSAX	DFA-VI	DFA-VM	FI-FM	VI-FI	VM-FM
2001	–0.06		–1.02	–0.07	–0.42	–0.45	–0.43	**0.36**	–0.36	–0.02	**0.01**	**0.36**			**0.47**
2002	**0.10**		–0.92	–0.07	–0.31	–0.45	–0.45	**0.24**	–0.38	**0.01**	**0.17**	**0.41**			**0.48**
2003	**0.37**		–0.97	–0.11	–0.30	–0.43	–0.46	**0.19**	–0.35	**0.02**	**0.48**	**0.67**			**0.56**
2004	**0.08**	–1.21	–1.13	–0.03	–0.26	–0.54	–0.50	**0.23**	–0.47	–0.05	**0.11**	**0.34**	–0.09	**1.19**	**0.74**
2005	**0.10**	–0.73	–1.01	–0.09	–0.37	–0.59	–0.56	**0.28**	–0.56	–0.03	**0.19**	**0.47**	**0.29**	**0.64**	**0.50**
2006	**0.21**	–0.84	–1.20	–0.19	–0.52	–0.58	–0.62	**0.33**	–0.62	**0.04**	**0.40**	**0.73**	**0.37**	**0.64**	**0.53**
2007	**0.24**	–0.97	–1.09	–0.21	–0.50	–0.59	–0.66	**0.30**	–0.66	**0.07**	**0.45**	**0.74**	**0.12**	**0.76**	**0.43**
2008	**0.36**	–1.28	–1.61	–0.26	–0.18	–0.56	–0.78	–0.08	–0.78	**0.22**	**0.62**	**0.54**	**0.32**	**1.02**	**1.25**
2009	**0.24**	–0.58	–0.71	–0.41	–0.08	–0.25	–0.29	–0.32	–0.29	**0.04**	**0.64**	**0.32**	**0.12**	**0.18**	**0.43**
2010	–0.09	–0.98	–0.95	–0.47	–0.09	–0.27	–0.29	–0.37	–0.29	**0.02**	**0.37**	**0.001**	–0.03	**0.52**	**0.65**
2011	–0.16	–0.23	–0.88	–0.58	–0.10	–0.07	–0.29	–0.48	–0.29	**0.22**	**0.41**	–0.07	**0.66**	–0.35	**0.55**
2012	–0.35	–0.55	–0.72	–0.65	–0.38	–0.17	–0.43	–0.27	–0.43	**0.25**	**0.30**	**0.03**	**0.18**	–0.11	**0.07**
2013	–0.72	–0.74	–1.12	–0.89	–0.44	–0.20	–0.60	–0.45	–0.60	**0.40**	**0.18**	–0.27	**0.38**	–0.15	**0.36**
2014	–0.78	–0.98	–1.17	–0.91	–0.53	0.02	–0.62	–0.39	–0.62	**0.64**	**0.13**	–0.25	**0.19**	**0.06**	**0.27**
2015	–0.90	–1.14	–1.42	–1.17	–0.71	–0.29	–1.02	–0.47	–1.02	**0.73**	**0.28**	–0.19	**0.29**	–0.04	**0.26**
2016	–1.14	–1.37	–1.61	–1.31	–0.61	–0.61	–0.98	–0.70	–0.98	**0.37**	**0.18**	–0.52	**0.24**	**0.05**	**0.39**
2017	–1.44	–2.16	–1.84	–1.95	**0.03**	–0.84	–1.37	–1.98	–1.37	**0.53**	**0.51**	–1.47	–0.32	**0.20**	**0.96**
2018	–0.36	–0.12	–3.52	–0.87	**0.07**	–0.38	–0.94	–0.94	–0.94	**0.56**	**0.52**	–0.42	**3.40**	–0.75	**3.59**

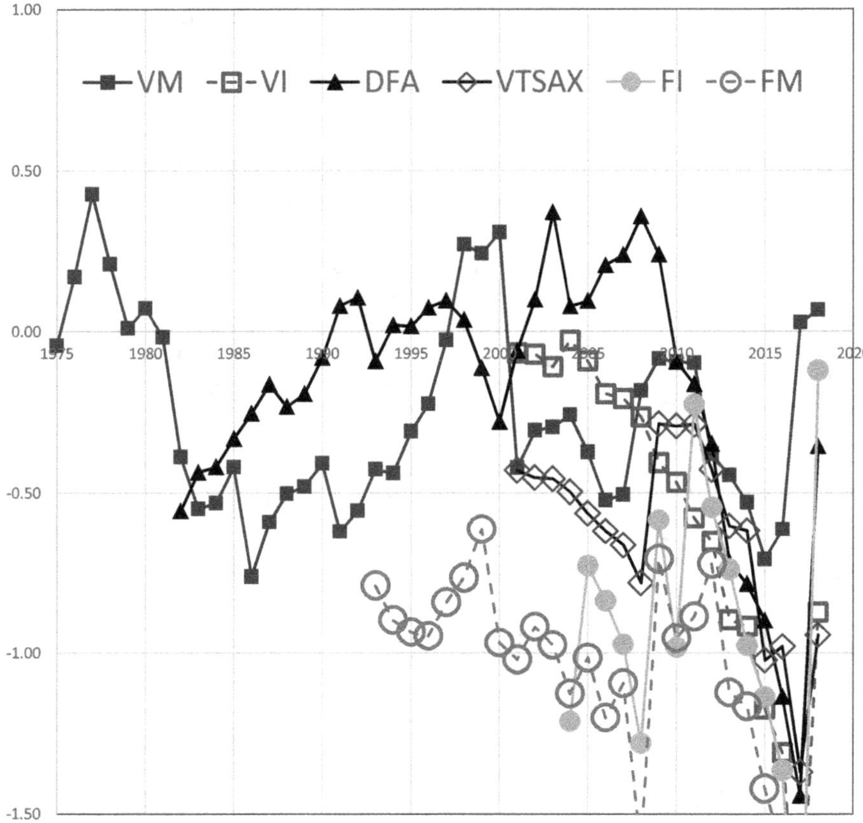

Fig. 18. Sharpe's Style Analysis: two-factor α through 2018 (%/year).

uniformly negative. DFA beats Vanguard managed for 26 start dates and loses for 11. The trend line drawn from VM-DFA (the negative of DFA-VM) in Table 5 is upward sloping, but when we eliminate the two most recent observations, it is downward sloping. However, it is uniformly negative, so based on trend lines, DFA always wins, and the margin of the win has no trend that evokes confidence.

D. FI beats FM for 12 start dates and loses for 3. One loss is for the earliest start date of 2004. The win margin of 3.40% for the start date of 2018 seems too big to be correct, but multiple checks fail to find an error.

E. VM beats FM for every start date. This is the same as the observation in E of Section 20.

F. VI beats FI for the first 7 start dates. Overall, VI beats for 10 and loses for 5. Fitting a trend line shows Vanguard wins for early start dates and loses for later start dates.

G. DFA out-returns Vanguard by 0.20%/year, when we average the differential for the start dates of the two Vanguard portfolios (0.33%/year for VI and 0.14%/year for VM). Section 5 notes that one financial advisory charges 0.235%/year and another charges 0.50%/year. Recognizing that one must invest in DFA funds through a financial advisor makes the choice between DFA and Vanguard close to a tossup for an investor who does not value advisor services. The differential for Vanguard minus Fidelity, by averaging the numbers in the VI-FI and VM-FM columns, shows Vanguard with a 0.53%/year advantage over Fidelity (0.26%/year for VI-FI and 0.68%/year for VM-FM).

Table 6 compares the two-factor alphas with the (two-dimensional) Sharpe alphas. The table averages returns from start dates over the spans. The top third uses start dates at the beginning of each year. For example, 2001, 2002, ..., 2018. The middle third uses start dates at the beginning of odd years. For example, DFA's average Sharpe alpha from the start of every odd year from 2001 through 2018 (2001, 2003, ..., 2017) is −0.28%/year. The bottom third of the table averages these figures.

Both analyses show Fidelity index beats Fidelity managed. Taking averages of the two methods: Vanguard managed beats Vanguard index, Vanguard Total Stock Market beats Vanguard index by a bit, DFA beats Vanguard index, Fidelity index beats Vanguard index, and both Vanguard index and Vanguard managed beat Fidelity managed.

22. Three Portfolios Out-returned the U.S. Stock Market

Table 7 shows the zero-factor α from the start of 4 years through 2018 for seven portfolios (except for FI which was incepted after 2001). These alphas are the extents to which the portfolios out-returned the

Table 6. Average two-factor geo α from start date through 2018.

	DFA	FI	FM	VI	VM	VFIAX	VTSAX	VI-VM	VTSAX-VI
Sharpe's style analysis with Fama–French portfolios									
earliest–2018	−0.19	−0.92	−1.14	−0.57	−0.26	−0.69	−0.63	−0.31	−0.06
2001–2018	−0.24		−1.27	−0.57	−0.32	−0.69	−0.63	−0.25	−0.06
2004–2018	−0.31	−0.92	−1.33	−0.67	−0.31	−0.78	−0.66	−0.35	**0.004**
2009–2018	−0.57	−0.88	−1.40	−0.92	−0.29	−1.01	−0.68	−0.64	**0.24**
2014–2018	−0.92	−1.15	−1.91	−1.25	−0.35	−1.27	−0.99	−0.89	**0.26**
								VM > VI	
Two-factor model with Fama–French factors									
2001–2018	−0.28		−0.39	−0.35	−0.35	−0.06	−0.11	**0.01**	**0.24**
2004–2018	−0.36	**0.62**	−0.26	−0.33	−0.44	−0.05	−0.13	**0.11**	**0.20**
2009–2018	−0.42	**0.43**	−0.42	−0.45	−0.55	−0.02	−0.16	**0.10**	**0.29**
2014–2018	−0.91	**0.04**	−1.56	−0.73	−1.05	0.00	−0.25	**0.32**	**0.48**
								VI > VM	**VTSAX > VI**
Sharpe's style analysis and two-factor model with Fama–French factors averaged									
2001–2018	−0.26		−0.83	−0.46	−0.34	−0.37	−0.37	−0.12	**0.09**
2004–2018	−0.34	−0.15	−0.80	−0.50	−0.37	−0.42	−0.40	−0.12	**0.10**
2009–2018	−0.49	−0.23	−0.91	−0.68	−0.42	−0.51	−0.42	−0.27	**0.27**
2014–2018	−0.92	−0.56	−1.74	−0.99	−0.70	−0.63	−0.62	−0.29	**0.37**
Average	−0.50	−0.31	−1.07	−0.66	−0.46	−0.48	−0.45	−0.20	**0.21**
							VM > VI	**VTSAX > VI**	**VTSAX > VI**

Note: Both analyses show that FI > FM. Averaging Sharpe & FF factors: VM > VI, VTSAX > VI, VTSAX > VFIAX, DFA > VI, FI > FM, FI > VI, VI > FM, VM > FM.

Table 6. (*Continued*)

VFIAX-VTSAX	DFA-VI	DFA-VM	FI-FM	VI-FI	VI-FM	VM-FM
−0.06	**0.38**	**0.07**	**0.22**	**0.67**	**0.57**	**0.88**
−0.06	**0.33**	**0.08**			**0.70**	**0.95**
−0.12	**0.35**	**0.00**	**0.41**	**0.61**	**0.67**	**1.02**
−0.32	**0.35**	−0.28	**0.51**	**0.60**	**0.47**	**1.11**
−0.28	**0.32**	−0.57	**0.76**	**0.80**	**0.67**	**1.56**
VTSAX > VFIAX	**DFA > VI**		**FI > FM**	**VI > FI**	**VI > FM**	**VM > FM**
0.05	**0.06**	**0.07**		−0.35	**0.05**	**0.04**
0.08	−0.03	**0.08**	**0.88**	−1.06	−0.06	−0.17
0.13	**0.03**	**0.13**	**0.85**	−0.98	−0.03	−0.13
0.25	−0.19	**0.14**	**1.60**	−1.08	**0.84**	**0.51**
VFIAX > VTSAX		**DFA > VM**	**FI > FM**	**FI > VI**		
−0.005	**0.20**	**0.07**			**0.31**	**0.50**
−0.02	**0.16**	**0.04**	**0.65**	−0.22	**0.32**	**0.42**
−0.09	**0.19**	−0.08	**0.68**	−0.19	**0.32**	**0.49**
−0.02	**0.07**	−0.22	**1.18**	−0.14	**0.65**	**1.04**
−0.03	**0.15**	−0.05	**0.83**	−0.18	**0.40**	**0.61**
VTSAX > VFIAX	**DFA > VI**		**FI > FM**	**FI > VI**	**VI > FM**	**VM > FM**

Table 7. Zero-factor geometric α from January 1 of start date through 2018 (%/year).

	DFA	FI	FM	VI	VM	VTSAX	VFIAX
2001	**0.1464**		**0.024**	**0.123**	**0.561**	−0.014	−0.509
2005	−0.0432	**0.0003**	**0.005**	**0.018**	−0.227	−0.096	−0.271
2007	−0.0779	**0.049**	−0.044	−0.088	−0.344	−0.129	−0.246
2009	−0.0240	**0.066**	−0.034	−0.034	−0.166	−0.106	−0.240
Average	**0.0003**	**0.039**	−0.012	**0.005**	−0.044	−0.086	−0.316

Notes: Three out of 7 averages are positive, and only VFIAX is more negative than a tenth of a percent per year. Thus all returns are close to that of the whole U.S. stock market.

U.S. stock market. Surprisingly, the averages for DFA, FI, and VI are positive. In every case, the excess return was between 0.039%/year and −0.316%/year, indicating that during this period the returns of all the portfolios were comparable. At the October 2019 Bogleheads meeting, Gus Sauter, as mentioned earlier, the head investment manager of Vanguard index funds from 1987 through 2003, noted with delight that in an early year of Vanguard indexing, Vanguard's 500 index fund was, through lending to short sellers and judicious use of futures markets, able to beat the U.S. market.

23. Returns Relative to Benchmarks

DFA, Fidelity, and Vanguard publish 1 year, 3 year, 5 year, and 10 year returns of their funds minus the returns of their benchmarks. From these differentials, we can determine return differentials for three intervening periods. These annualized continuously compounded return differentials are presented in Table 8. We also present the FF factors for these same periods expressed as annualized continuously compounded differentials. Vanguard's benchmarks are tailored to be closer to the investment style of the funds than are DFA's. We suspect from examining Table 8 that the DFA return net of benchmark depends positively on SMB and HML. To correct for differential returns of style, we regress the portfolio minus benchmark returns in Table 8 on the two Fama–French factors, continuously

Table 8. Annualized return: equally weighted funds minus benchmark (%/year).

Portfolio	DFA		Fido index		Fido mgd		Vgd Index		Vgd mgd		FF factors	
measure	Avg	Med	Avg	Med	Avg	Med	Avg	Med	Avg	Med	SMB	HML
1 year 10/2018–9/2019	−2.29	−2.21	0.76	0.06	−0.75	−0.83	−0.01	−0.03	−2.28	−1.98	−14.52	−5.57
3 years 10/2016–9/2019	−0.95	−0.90	0.33	0.07	−0.28	−0.49	−0.02	−0.03	−0.38	−0.30	−4.27	−4.88
5 years 10/2014–9/2019	−1.15	−0.70	0.40	0.05	−0.14	0.03	−0.03	−0.04	−0.68	−0.51	−1.48	−4.89
10 years 10/2009–9/2019	−0.01	−0.03	−0.01	−0.01	0.21	0.32	−0.04	−0.06	−0.37	−0.13	−0.85	−3.13
2 years 10/2016–9/2018	−0.28	−0.24	0.11	0.08	−0.05	−0.32	−0.02	−0.03	0.58	0.55	−0.22	−1.37
2 years 10/2014–9/2016	−1.44	−0.40	0.50	0.02	0.07	0.82	−0.03	−0.05	−1.12	−0.82	2.70	−4.91
5 years 10/2009–9/2014	−0.01	−0.03	−0.01	−0.01	0.21	0.32	−0.04	−0.06	−0.37	−0.13	0.86	−4.54
Standard deviation	0.62	0.15	0.22	0.04	0.11	0.46	0.01	0.01	0.70	0.56	1.21	1.59
α from regression	0.11	−0.08	−0.01	0.10	−0.04	−0.60	−0.02	−0.03	1.26	1.10	0	0
avg α (avg + median averaged)	0.015		0.043		−0.323		−0.022		1.179		0	
Ranking	3rd best		2nd best		5th best		4th best		best			

Notes: After adjusting for style, DFA, Fidelity index, & Vanguard index funds return close to their benchmarks, i.e. their average α's are close to zero. Also, the standard deviations of their differentials are low. The worst style adjusted return is −0.323%/year relative to benchmark. Best is 1.179%/year. After style adjustment Vanguard managed outreturns its published benchmarks. DFA and Fido Index also slightly outreturn.

compounded. Our regression uses the most recent year, the preceding two years, the two years preceding that, and the 5 years preceding that for data. We weight each observation by its duration measured in years (1, 2, 2, and 5, respectively), so our regression has 10 observations, six of which are duplicates. Consequently, each year's differential has the same weight. The standard deviations refer to the observations fed into the regression. The intercepts show what the returns would have been if SMB and HML had both been zero, i.e., if there were no bias between small and big and between high and low book-to-market ratios. These are presented as the alphas in Table 8. By this criterion, Vanguard managed is by far the best performer, and Fidelity managed is the worst, with the others hovering around zero and with slightly positive alphas for both DFA and Fidelity index. We would have preferred to compare funds with benchmarks on an annual or monthly basis, but we were not able to access annual or monthly returns of benchmarks except for DFA, which publishes both. For example, Vanguard Dividend Appreciation Index Fund, Admiral Shares (VDADX) benchmarks against the Nasdaq U.S. Dividend Achievers Select Index, and we were unable to access monthly returns for that index.

24. Conclusions

The abstract and Tables 6, 7, 8, and A5 summarize our major conclusions. Of particular interest is Section 23's Table 8 and discussion of style-adjusted returns relative to published benchmarks, with Vanguard managed the best, and Fidelity managed the worst — but still impressive with a short fall of only 0.34%/year. Here are several additional contributions.

- We have made the case for using the geometric alpha *in lieu* of the arithmetic alpha, although many of the differentials are small.
- We have offered what we believe is a novel interpretation of the Fama–French factor loads.
- We have documented the superiority of the Wharton Research Data Service to Yahoo in providing historical returns, but exposed

the fallibility of WRDS. Investigators who use WRDS need to check extreme numbers.

- One notable result is, after adjusting for style, the past performance of Fidelity's managed portfolio has been weak relative to its index funds.
- One of our favorite results is the determination of funds' performance relative to their published benchmarks after style adjustment, reported in Table 8. Vanguard managed out-returned its style-adjusted benchmarks by over 1%/year. Expense ratios do not cover all mutual fund's costs, turnover raises costs, and fund short sales boost performance. These issues make performance in excess of the style-adjusted benchmark a useful metric. Before style adjustment, on average, Vanguard managed under-returned its benchmarks, so style adjustment makes a big difference.
- We conclude once again that past alphas do not predict future alphas, and once again, high expense ratios reduce returns by even more than the excess expense, thus amending Jack Bogle's remark that "In investing, you get what you don't pay for" to "In investing, you get a multiple of what you don't pay for."

Here are some takeaways from the major questions the chapter sought to answer.

From the appendix tables, which describe individual fund expense ratios and style-adjusted returns using Fama–French factors, most of which apply from January 2008 through March 2019, averaging average and median figures for the two- and three-factor models:

- Vanguard's index funds' expense ratios are 0.26% lower than its managed expense ratios and its index return is 0.34%/year higher.
- Fidelity's index funds' expense ratios are 0.56% lower than its managed expense ratios and Fidelity's index return is 1.66%/year higher.
- Vanguard's index funds' expense ratios are 0.21% lower than DFA's and Vanguard's return is 0.25%year higher.

- Vanguard index funds' expense ratios are 0.03% lower than Fidelity's index funds' and Vanguard's return is 0.26%/year lower.
- Vanguard managed funds' expense ratios are 0.33% lower than Fidelity's managed funds' and Vanguard's return is 1.05%/year higher.
- Table 7 examines the extent to which equally weighted portfolios beat the market (zero-factor alphas) from the start of the year indicated through 2018. It tells us

  (a) Vanguard's indexed minus Vanguard's managed is –0.44%/year from 2001 and +0.24%/year from 2005.
  (b) Fidelity's index minus Fidelity's managed is –0.005%/year from 2005 and +0.093%/year from 2007.
  (c) Vanguard's index minus DFA is −0.023%/year from 2001 and +0.061%/year from 2005.
  (d) Vanguard's index minus Fidelity's index is +0.018%/year from 2005 and −0.137/year from 2007.
  (e) Vanguard's managed minus Fidelity managed is +0.054/year from 2001 and −0.23/year from 2005.

  In each of these contests, the winner's identity changes from one start date to another. This set of calculations indicates that the choice between the three companies and index versus managed is not clear-cut.

We think updating studies of this sort is important to evaluate mutual fund companies and data services and to encourage them to serve their clients well. Lessons for investors are the old saws: keep expenses low, diversify across styles, and don't chase performance.

25. Appendix

The regression periods in Table A5 begin at different times, so we attach limited significance to them, and in particular, to the high averages for Fidelity zero.

Table A1. DFA Individual funds through 3/2019. The correlation between the expense ratio and two-factor geometric α is 0.630, so a higher expense ratio does not imply lower excess return.

Fund name	Ticker	Expense ratio	Inception	Regression start	Fama–French three-factor model					Two-factor model			
					Arith α	Geo α	β market	β small	β value	Arith α	Geo α	β small	β value
Core Equity 1 (I)	DFEOX	0.19%	9/15/2005	Jan-08	–0.24	–0.24	1.02	0.13	0.07	–0.04	–0.09	0.15	0.08
Core Equity 2 (I)	DFQTX	0.22%	9/15/2005	Jan-08	–0.57	–0.58	1.04	0.21	0.17	–0.21	–0.30	0.23	0.18
High Relative Profitability	DURPX	0.25%	5/16/2017	Jun-17	–0.43	–0.44	1.06	–0.13	–0.13	0.01	–0.10	–0.10	–0.16
Large Cap Equity	DUSQX	0.17%	6/25/2013	Jul-13	–0.50	–0.50	1.01	–0.04	0.03	–0.44	–0.44	–0.04	0.03
Large Cap Growth	DUSLX	0.19%	12/20/2012	Jan-13	0.16	0.14	1.00	–0.11	–0.13	0.16	0.15	–0.11	–0.13
Large Cap Value (I)	DFLVX	0.27%	2/19/1993	Jan-08	–0.82	–0.86	1.13	–0.02	0.34	0.35	0.01	0.06	0.39
Large Cap Value (II)	DFCVX	0.14%	8/2/1994	Jan-08	–0.72	–0.76	1.13	–0.02	0.34	0.47	0.13	0.06	0.39
Large Cap Value (III)	DFUVX	0.13%	2/2/1995	Jan-08	–0.68	–0.73	1.13	–0.02	0.34	0.49	0.15	0.06	0.39
Large Company	DFUSX	0.08%	9/23/1999	Jan-08	–0.06	–0.06	0.99	–0.14	0.00	–0.11	–0.10	–0.14	0.00
Micro Cap (I)	DFSCX	0.52%	12/23/1981	Jan-08	–0.14	–0.17	0.98	0.92	0.32	–0.31	–0.30	0.91	0.31

Table A1. (*Continued*)

Fund name	Ticker	Expense ratio	Inception	Regression start	Fama-French three-factor model					Two-factor model			
					Arith α	Geo α	β market	β small	β value	Arith α	Geo α	β small	β value
Small Cap Growth	DSCGX	0.38%	12/20/2012	Jan-13	–1.15	–1.18	1.01	0.68	0.10	–0.97	–1.01	0.69	0.10
Small Cap (I)	DFSTX	0.37%	3/19/1992	Jan-08	–0.06	–0.07	1.02	0.82	0.27	0.11	0.05	0.83	0.28
Small Cap Value (I)	DFSVX	0.52%	3/2/1993	Jan-08	–0.84	–0.86	1.05	0.86	0.50	–0.35	–0.49	0.89	0.51
Social Core Equity 2	DFUEX	0.28%	10/1/2007	Sep-08	–1.11	–1.12	1.06	0.25	0.20	–0.42	–0.55	0.28	0.22
Sustainability Core 1	DFSIX	0.25%	3/12/2008	Apr-08	–0.53	–0.54	1.04	0.13	0.07	–0.10	–0.20	0.15	0.08
Targeted Value (I)	DFFVX	0.37%	2/23/2000	Jan-08	–0.49	–0.51	1.06	0.75	0.47	0.02	–0.12	0.78	0.49
Targeted Value (R1)	DFTVX	0.47%	1/31/2008	Feb-08	–0.68	–0.70	1.06	0.75	0.47	–0.09	–0.24	0.78	0.49
Vector Equity (I)	DFVEX	0.32%	12/30/2005	Jan-08	–1.10	–1.11	1.05	0.45	0.30	–0.61	–0.74	0.48	0.32
Summary. All DFA funds are indexed	Average	0.28%			–0.55	–0.57	1.05	0.30	0.21	–0.11	–0.23	0.33	0.22
	Median	0.26%			–0.55	–0.57	1.05	0.21	0.21	–0.10	–0.20	0.23	0.22

Table A2. Fidelity Individual Managed Funds through 3/2019.

Fund name	Ticker	Expense ratio	Regression start date	Fama–French three-factor model					Two-factor model			
				Arith α	Geo α	β market	β small	β value	Arith α	Geo α	β small	β value
OTC Portfolio	FOCPX	0.88%	Jan-08	0.59	0.34	1.20	0.22	–0.52	2.41	1.67	0.34	–0.45
Blue Chip Growth	FBGRX	0.72%	Jan-08	1.34	1.22	1.09	0.08	–0.28	2.15	1.82	0.14	–0.25
Growth Discovery	FDSVX	0.74%	Jan-08	–1.32	–1.44	1.08	0.04	–0.35	–0.63	–0.91	0.08	–0.32
Focused Stock	FTQGX	0.82%	Jan-08	0.60	0.47	1.01	0.05	–0.32	0.68	0.53	0.06	–0.31
Contrafund	FCNTX	0.82%	Jan-08	–0.05	–0.12	0.96	–0.07	–0.34	–0.36	–0.36	–0.09	–0.35
Trend Fund	FTRNX	0.67%	Jan-08	–0.80	–0.87	1.11	0.02	–0.36	0.16	–0.15	0.09	–0.32
Lg Cap Growth Enhanced Index	FLGEX	0.39%	Jan-08	0.23	0.21	1.01	–0.06	–0.22	0.35	0.30	–0.05	–0.21
Magellan	FMAGX	0.69%	Jan-08	–3.82	–3.98	1.18	0.02	–0.17	–2.30	–2.81	0.13	–0.10
Stock Selector All Cap	FDSSX	0.69%	Jan-08	–2.06	–2.09	1.05	0.06	–0.11	–1.63	–1.76	0.09	–0.09
Lg Cap Core Enhanced Index	FLCEX	0.39%	Jan-08	–0.19	–0.21	0.97	–0.13	0.00	–0.49	–0.44	–0.15	–0.02
Independence	FDFFX	0.50%	Jan-08	–4.36	–4.75	1.24	0.15	–0.39	–2.30	–3.19	0.29	–0.31
Fidelity® Fund	FFIDX	0.50%	Jan-08	–2.11	–2.16	1.02	–0.08	–0.11	–1.90	–2.00	–0.07	–0.10
Capital Appreciation	FDCAX	0.54%	Jan-08	–1.08	–1.20	1.04	0.15	–0.16	–0.76	–0.96	0.17	–0.15
Large Cap Stock	FLCSX	0.67%	Jan-08	–1.10	–1.15	1.15	–0.02	0.14	0.19	–0.19	0.07	0.19
Stock Selector Mid Cap	FSSMX	0.77%	Jul-12	–1.36	–1.39	1.00	0.31	0.02	–1.40	–1.43	0.31	0.02
Mega Cap Stock	FGRTX	0.68%	Jan-08	–0.77	–0.79	1.03	–0.19	0.11	–0.49	–0.58	–0.17	0.12
New Millennium	FMILX	0.67%	Jan-08	–0.41	–0.48	1.02	0.11	0.04	–0.26	–0.36	0.12	0.05
Growth & Income	FGRIX	0.61%	Jan-08	–3.60	–3.74	1.09	–0.11	0.13	–2.86	–3.16	–0.06	0.16
Growth Strategies	FDEGX	0.59%	Jan-08	–3.50	–3.69	1.11	0.16	–0.27	–2.59	–2.98	0.22	–0.23
Mid-Cap Stock	FMCSX	0.61%	Jan-08	–1.58	–1.80	1.09	0.27	–0.08	–0.78	–1.20	0.33	–0.04
Stock Selector Small Cap	FDSCX	0.68%	Jan-08	–3.25	–3.37	1.09	0.69	0.00	–2.46	–2.76	0.75	0.04
Dividend Growth	FDGFX	0.50%	Jan-08	–1.60	–1.69	1.13	–0.01	0.09	–0.43	–0.81	0.07	0.14

Table A2. (*Continued*)

Fund name	Ticker	Expense ratio	Regression start date	Fama–French three-factor model: Arith α	Geo α	β market	β small	β value	Two-factor model: Arith α	Geo α	β small	β value
Export and Multinational	FEXPX	0.74%	Jan-08	−2.82	−2.92	1.01	−0.12	−0.08	−2.71	−2.84	−0.11	−0.07
Strategic Advisers® Value	FVSAX	0.28%	Jun-09	−1.37	−1.38	0.97	−0.06	0.21	−1.72	−1.70	−0.08	0.21
Lg Cap Value Enhanced Index	FLVEX	0.39%	Jan-08	−0.69	−0.71	0.94	−0.10	0.23	−1.21	−1.12	−0.14	0.21
Mid Cap Enhanced Index	FMEIX	0.59%	Jan-08	−0.57	−0.63	1.03	0.26	−0.02	−0.31	−0.43	0.27	−0.01
Disciplined Equity	FDEQX	0.53%	Jan-08	−3.24	−3.32	1.02	−0.07	−0.07	−3.03	−3.15	−0.06	−0.06
Equity-Income	FEQIX	0.61%	Jan-08	−2.52	−2.57	1.03	−0.13	0.22	−2.26	−2.38	−0.12	0.23
Leveraged Company Stock	FLVCX	0.78%	Jan-08	−4.84	−5.39	1.31	0.34	−0.06	−2.18	−3.40	0.52	0.05
Small Cap Enhanced Index	FCPEX	0.64%	Jan-08	−1.05	−1.10	0.98	0.81	0.15	−1.22	−1.22	0.80	0.14
Equity Dividend Income	FEQTX	0.62%	Jan-08	−2.43	−2.49	1.01	−0.15	0.23	−2.32	−2.40	−0.14	0.23
Low-Priced Stock	FLPSX	0.62%	Jan-08	−0.27	−0.37	0.96	0.14	0.05	−0.63	−0.65	0.12	0.04
Value Strategies	FSLSX	0.63%	Jan-08	−3.18	−3.40	1.24	0.24	0.18	−1.11	−1.86	0.38	0.27
Stock Selector Lg Cap Value	FSLVX	0.68%	Jan-08	−2.74	−2.80	0.97	−0.06	0.23	−2.97	−2.98	−0.08	0.22
Value Discovery	FVDFX	0.69%	Jan-08	−1.94	−1.99	1.01	−0.03	0.24	−1.84	−1.91	−0.02	0.25
Value	FDVLX	0.59%	Jan-08	−2.78	−2.91	1.18	0.25	0.22	−1.25	−1.76	0.36	0.28
Blue Chip Value	FBCVX	0.70%	Jan-08	−3.78	−3.91	1.05	−0.09	0.25	−3.39	−3.60	−0.07	0.26
Small Cap Value	FCPVX	0.91%	Jan-08	1.20	1.08	0.93	0.60	0.41	0.59	0.61	0.56	0.39
Event Driven Opportunities	FARNX	1.12%	Jan-14	−2.98	−3.22	1.08	0.29	0.30	−2.22	−2.55	0.32	0.29
Mid Cap Value	FSMVX	0.53%	Jan-08	−1.43	−1.54	1.05	0.24	0.18	−0.98	−1.20	0.27	0.20

Table A3. Fidelity Individual Index Funds through 3/2019 & Summary.

				Fama–French three-factor model					Two-factor model			
Fund name	Ticker	Expense ratio	Regression start	Arith α	Geo α	β market	β small	β value	Arith α	Geo α	β small	β value
Nasdaq® Composite Index	FNCMX	0.30%	Jan-08	0.76	0.67	1.11	0.13	–0.27	1.73	1.39	0.20	–0.23
500 Index	FXAIX	0.02%	Jun-11	0.06	0.06	0.98	–0.13	–0.02	–0.14	–0.12	–0.14	–0.02
Total Market Index	FSKAX	0.02%	Oct-11	–0.14	–0.14	0.99	0.00	–0.01	–0.27	–0.25	–0.01	–0.01
Extended Market Index	FSMAX	0.05%	Oct-11	–0.79	–0.80	1.03	0.55	0.00	–0.40	–0.45	0.56	0.00
Small Cap Index	FSSNX	0.03%	Oct-11	–0.74	–0.74	1.02	0.85	0.14	–0.42	–0.45	0.86	0.14
Mid Cap Index	FSMDX	0.03%	Oct-11	–0.55	–0.57	0.99	0.20	–0.03	–0.63	–0.65	0.20	–0.03
ZEROSM Extended Market Index	FZIPX	0.00%	Oct-18	6.95	6.84	1.02	0.63	0.23	7.28	7.11	0.67	0.22
ZEROSM Large Cap Index	FNILX	0.00%	Oct-18	–0.82	–0.82	1.00	–0.17	–0.02	–0.76	–0.77	–0.16	–0.03
ZEROSM Total Mkt Index	FZROX	0.00%	Sep-18	0.19	0.20	1.00	–0.03	0.00	0.22	0.22	–0.02	0.00
Large Cap Growth Index	FSPGX	0.04%	Jul-16	0.97	0.94	1.03	–0.07	–0.33	1.38	1.30	–0.06	–0.34
Large Cap Value Index	FLCOX	0.04%	Jul-16	–2.17	–2.20	0.93	–0.05	0.26	–3.03	–3.00	–0.08	0.27
U.S. Sustainability Index	FITLX	0.11%	Jun-17	1.35	1.30	0.95	–0.09	0.08	0.98	1.02	–0.11	0.10

Table A3. (*Continued*)

Fund name	Ticker	Expense ratio	Regression start	Fama–French three-factor model: Arith α	Geo α	β market	β small	β value	Two-factor model: Arith α	Geo α	β small	β value
Nasdaq Composite Index	ONEQ	0.21%	Jan-08	0.82	0.73	1.11	0.13	−0.27	1.77	1.44	0.20	−0.23
High Dividend ETF	FDVV	0.29%	Oct-16	0.84	0.79	0.78	0.03	0.14	−1.94	−1.73	−0.09	0.17
Dividend ETF for Rising Rates	FDRR	0.29%	Oct-16	0.52	0.49	0.85	−0.08	0.09	−1.33	−1.18	−0.15	0.11
Momentum Factor ETF	FDMO	0.29%	Oct-16	−1.53	−1.57	0.99	−0.02	−0.23	−1.66	−1.68	−0.03	−0.23
Low Volatility Factor ETF	FDLO	0.29%	Oct-16	1.99	1.93	0.86	−0.11	−0.04	0.20	0.34	−0.18	−0.02
Value Factor ETF	FVAL	0.29%	Oct-16	0.21	0.20	1.03	−0.09	0.22	0.60	0.55	−0.07	0.21
Quality Factor ETF	FQAL	0.29%	Oct-16	0.39	0.37	0.92	−0.07	−0.06	−0.68	−0.58	−0.11	−0.05
Index summary	Average	0.13%		0.44	**0.40**	0.98	0.09	−0.01	0.15	**0.13**	0.08	0.00
	median	0.05%		0.21	**0.20**	0.99	−0.03	−0.01	−0.27	−0.25	−0.06	−0.01
Managed summary	average	0.64%		−1.69	−1.81	1.06	0.10	−0.01	−1.16	−1.41	0.14	0.01
	median	0.66%		−1.50	−1.62	1.03	0.04	0.01	−1.21	−1.33	0.09	0.04
Zero expense funds	average	0		2.11	**2.07**	1.01	0.14	0.07	2.25	**2.19**	0.16	0.07
	median	0		0.19	**0.20**	1.00	−0.03	0.00	0.22	**0.22**	−0.02	0.00
All Fidelity stock funds	average	0.48%		−1.00	−1.09	1.03	0.10	−0.01	−0.74	−0.91	0.12	0.01
	median	0.59%		−0.82	−0.87	1.02	0.02	0.00	−0.76	−0.91	0.07	0.00

Table A4. The individual Vanguard funds through 3/2019.

Index or managed	Fund name	Ticker	Expense ratio (%)	Inception	Fama–French three-factor model					Two-factor model			
					Arith α	Geo α	β market	β small	β value	Arith α	Geo α	β small	β value
I	500 Index A	VFIAX	0.04	Nov-00	0.05	0.03	1.35	–1.06	–0.59	0.00	–0.61	0.00	0.00
I	Dividend Appreciation ETF	VIG	0.08	Apr-06	1.10	1.03	0.85	–0.14	–0.01	–0.19	0.02	–0.23	–0.06
I	Extended Market Index A	VEXAX	0.07	Apr-00	–0.76	–0.80	1.06	0.58	0.01	–0.22	–0.39	0.61	0.03
I	Growth Index A	VIGAX	0.05	Nov-00	–0.09	–0.11	1.05	–0.02	–0.30	0.33	0.21	0.00	–0.29
I	High Dividend Yield ETF	VYM	0.06	Nov-06	1.35	1.27	0.88	–0.25	0.28	0.32	0.47	–0.32	0.24
I	Large-Cap ETF	VV	0.04	Jan-04	–0.10	–0.10	1.00	–0.11	–0.02	–0.11	–0.11	–0.11	–0.02
I	Mega Cap ETF	MGC	0.07	Dec-07	0.08	0.08	0.98	–0.17	0.00	–0.06	–0.03	–0.18	–0.01
I	Mega Cap Growth ETF	MGK	0.07	Dec-07	0.38	0.35	1.04	–0.10	–0.30	0.70	0.59	–0.07	–0.28
I	Mega Cap Value ETF	MGV	0.07	Dec-07	–0.13	–0.16	0.94	–0.25	0.27	–0.67	–0.58	–0.29	0.25
I	Mid-Cap Growth ETF	VOT	0.07	Aug-06	–2.31	–2.44	1.12	0.29	–0.33	–1.24	–1.63	0.36	–0.29
I	Mid-Cap Index A	VIMAX	0.05	Nov-01	–0.97	–1.04	1.08	0.22	–0.07	–0.29	–0.52	0.27	–0.04
I	Mid-Cap Value ETF	VOE	0.07	Aug-06	0.28	0.21	1.03	0.16	0.19	0.58	0.43	0.18	0.20

Table A4. (*Continued*)

Index or managed	Fund name	Ticker	Expense ratio (%)	Inception	Fama–French three-factor model					Two-factor model			
					Arith α	Geo α	β market	β small	β value	Arith α	Geo α	β small	β value
I	Small-Cap Growth ETF	VBK	0.07	Jan-04	–0.87	–0.93	1.11	0.72	–0.15	0.12	–0.18	0.79	–0.11
I	Small-Cap Index A	VSMAX	0.05	Nov-00	–0.13	–0.17	1.03	–0.09	–0.10	–0.13	–0.23	0.01	–0.04
I	Small-Cap Value ETF	VBR	0.07	Jan-04	–0.09	–0.10	1.04	–0.11	–0.02	–0.11	–0.11	–0.07	–0.02
I	Total Stock Mkt Index A	VTSAX	0.04	Nov-00	–0.15	–0.15	1.01	0.00	0.00	–0.10	–0.11	0.00	0.00
M	Capital Opportunity A	VHCAX	0.36	Nov-01	0.41	0.28	1.08	0.26	–0.22	1.14	0.83	0.31	–0.19
M	Capital Value	VCVLX	0.29	Dec-01	–3.34	–3.60	1.27	0.19	0.15	–1.01	–1.86	0.35	0.24
M	Diversified Equity	VDEQX	0.36	Jun-05	–1.09	–1.09	1.05	0.06	–0.08	–0.64	–0.75	0.09	–0.07
M	Dividend Growth	VDIGX	0.26	May-92	2.01	1.93	0.82	–0.21	–0.03	0.45	0.71	–0.31	–0.10
M	Equity Income	VEIPX	0.27	Mar-88	1.42	1.35	0.86	–0.22	0.21	0.18	0.39	–0.30	0.16
M	Explorer	VEXPX	0.46	Dec-67	–1.02	–1.06	1.07	0.65	–0.16	–0.38	–0.57	0.69	–0.14
M	Explorer Value	VEVFX	0.56	Mar-10	–0.56	–0.59	0.99	0.61	0.25	–0.70	–0.72	0.60	0.25
M	Growth and Income	VQNPX	0.33	Dec-86	–0.52	–0.54	1.00	–0.10	0.00	–0.49	–0.52	–0.10	0.00
M	Mid-Cap Growth	VMGRX	0.36	Dec-97	–1.01	–1.08	1.03	0.33	–0.27	–0.74	–0.87	0.35	–0.26
M	PRIMECAP A PRIMECAP	VPMAX	0.31	Nov-01	1.65	1.56	1.00	0.00	–0.11	1.64	1.55	0.00	–0.11

Table A4. (*Continued*)

M	Core	VPCCX	0.46%	Dec-04	1.61	1.53	0.97	0.05	–0.07	1.32	1.31	0.03	–0.08
M	Selected Value	VASVX	0.36%	Feb-96	–0.62	–0.70	0.97	0.20	0.15	–0.89	–0.91	0.18	0.14
M	Strategic Equity	VSEQX	0.17%	Aug-95	–1.11	–1.18	1.09	0.44	0.03	–0.35	–0.61	0.50	0.06
M	Strategic Small-Cap Eqty	VSTCX	0.29%	Apr-06	–0.95	–1.00	1.04	0.70	0.14	–0.58	–0.72	0.73	0.15
M	U.S. Growth Investor	VWUSX	0.38%	Jan-59	–0.33	–0.39	1.06	0.00	–0.36	0.21	0.02	0.04	–0.34
M	U.S. Value	VUVLX	0.22%	Jun-00	–0.91	–0.96	0.95	0.02	0.21	–1.34	–1.29	–0.01	0.19
M	Windsor A	VWNEX	0.21%	Nov-01	1.40	1.36	0.65	–0.16	0.00	–1.71	–1.15	–0.37	–0.12
M	Windsor II A	VWNAX	0.25%	May-01	–1.11	–1.13	0.98	–0.15	0.16	–1.26	–1.25	–0.16	0.16
I	summary	average	0.06%		–0.15	–0.19	1.04	–0.02	–0.07	–0.07	–0.17	0.06	–0.03
I	summary	median	0.07%		–0.09	–0.11	1.03	–0.09	–0.02	–0.10	–0.11	0.00	–0.02
M	summary	average	0.33%		–0.23	–0.30	0.99	0.15	0.00	–0.29	–0.36	0.14	0.00
M	summary	median	0.32%		–0.59	–0.65	1.00	0.05	0.00	–0.54	–0.66	0.06	–0.03

Note: Explorer Value's regression start date is 1/2011. Others start 1/2008. A means Admiral share class. α is %/yr.

Table A5. Geometric α %/yr for individual funds through 3/2019 and summary

			Fidelity			Vanguard	
Model	Criterion	DFA	Index	Mgd	Zero	Index	Mgd
Three-factor	Avg	−0.57	0.4	−1.81	2.07	−0.19	−0.3
	Median	−0.57	0.2	−1.62	0.2	−0.11	−0.65
	Average (Avg, Med)	−0.57	0.30	−1.72	1.14	−0.15	−0.48
	Avg	−0.23	0.13	−1.41	2.19	−0.17	−0.36
Two-factor	Median	−0.2	−0.25	−1.33	0.22	−0.11	−0.66
	Average (Avg, Med)	−0.22	−0.06	−1.37	1.21	−0.14	−0.51

Note: Averaging both the average and median scores the ranking is
Three-factor: FZ > FI > VI > VM > DFA > FM
Two-factor: FZ > FI > VI > DFA > VM > FM

Fidelity zero is tops, next Fidelity index, next Vanguard index, next DFA & Vanguard managed. Bottom Fidelity managed.

Acknowledgments

Thanks for suggestions, without implying approval go to Charlie Becker, Bill Bernstein, Esther Brown, Brooks Cavin III, John Guerard, Mel Lindauer, Larry Swedroe, and Steve Thorpe.

References

Asness, C. (2019). It's Time For a Venal Value-Timing Sin. Available at: https://www.AQR.com/Insights/Perspectives.

Ashworth, W. (2019). Take Buffett's Advice: 5 Vanguard Funds to Buy. Available at: https://investorplace.com/2019/06/5-vanguard-funds-warren-buffett/.

Blitz, D. (2017). Are exchange-traded funds harvesting factor premiums? *Journal of Investment Consulting* **19**(1), 24–30.

Barras, L., Scaillet, O., and Wermers, R. (2010). False discoveries in mutual fund performance: Measuring luck in estimated alphas. *The Journal of Finance* **65**(1), 179–216.

Benjamin, J. (2018). 10 largest mutual fund companies by assets. *Investment News* Available at: https://www.investmentnews.com/gallery/20180824/FREE/824009999/PH/10-largest-mutual-fund-companies-by-assets.

Bogle, J. (1997). The First Index Mutual Fund: A History of Vanguard Index Trust and the Vanguard Index Strategy. April. Available at: https://www.vanguard.com/bogle_site/lib/sp19970401.html.

Brown, N. C., Wei, K. D., and Wermers, R. (2014). Analyst recommendations, mutual fund herding, and overreaction in stock prices. *Management Science* **60**(1), 1–20.

Daniel, K., Grinblatt, M., Titman, S., and Wermers, R. (1997). Measuring mutual fund performance with characteristic-based benchmark. *Journal of Finance* **52**(3), 1035–1058.

Fama, E. F. and French, K. R. (1995). Size and book-to-market factors in earnings and returns. *Journal of Finance* **50**(1), 131–155.

French, K. (2019). *Kenneth R. French Data Library*. Available at: http://mba.tuck.dartmouth.edu/pages/faculty/ken.french/data_library.html.

Kizer, J. (2005). Index fundamentalism revisited — redux. *The Journal of Portfolio Management* **31**(2), 112–119.

Larimore, T. (2018). *The Bogleheads' Guide to the Three-Fund Portfolio: How a Simple Portfolio of Three Total Market Index Funds Outperforms Most Investors with Less Risk*. Wiley.

Li, C., Tower, E., and Zhang, R. (2019). Vanguard versus Fidelity: Multidimensional Comparison of the Index Funds and ETFs of the Two Largest Mutual Fund Families. Economic Research Initiatives at Duke (ERID) Working Paper No. 283.

Markowitz, H. M. (1959). *Portfolio Selection: Efficient Diversification of Investment*. Chapter 6: "Return in the long run." Yale.

Merriman, P. (2006). "Interview with John Bogle." on *Sound Investing*. August 4. No longer available.

Reinker, K. S. and Tower, E. (2004). Index fundamentalism revisited. *The Journal of Portfolio Management* **30**(4), 37–50.

Reinker, K. S. and Tower, E. (2005). Are Vanguard's managers good stock-pickers or style-pickers? *The Journal of Portfolio Management* **31**(3), 109–111.

Retire Early Home Page. (2007). Low-cost, fixed-fee DFA investment advisors. http://www.retireearlyhomepage.com/dfaadv.html.

Rodriguez, A. and Tower, E. (2008). Do Vanguard's managed funds beat its index funds? Looking for prescient stock and style selection. *The Journal of Indexes* **11**(2), 26–35.

Sauter, G. U. (2016). "Gus." "What Really is Smart β?", Available at: https://drive.google.com/file/d/0B9XBYifJTHBeSG05NUFQYzVKODA/view.

Seigel, J. J. (2014). *Stocks for the Long Run*. McGraw-Hill.

Sharpe, W. F. (1992). Management style and performance measurement. *Journal of Portfolio Management* **18**(2), 7–19.

Tower, E. (2009). Performance of actively managed versus index funds: The Vanguard case, In *Mutual Funds: Portfolio Structures, Analysis, Management, and Stewardship*, Chapter 12, John A. Haslem. (Ed.), Wiley, Hoboken.

Tower, E. and Yang, C.-Y. (2008). Enhanced versus passive mutual fund indexing: Has DFA outperformed Vanguard by enough to justify its advisor fees? *Journal of Investing* **17**(4), 71–81.

Tower, E. and Zheng, W. (2008). Ranking mutual fund families: Maximum loads and minimum expenses as markers for moral turpitude. *International Review of Economics* **55**(4), 315–350.

Vander Weide, J. H. (2010). Principles for lifetime portfolio selection: Lessons from portfolio theory. Chapter 7 in *Handbook of Portfolio Construction: Contemporary Applications of Markowitz techniques*, J. B. Guerard, Jr. (Ed.), Springer, Switzerland, pp. 153–178.

Wei, K. D., Wermers, R., and Yao, T. (2015). Uncommon value: The characteristics and investment performance of contrarian funds. *Management Science* **61**(10), 2394–2414.

Wei, K. D., Wermers, R., and Yao, T. (2017). Against the "Wisdom of Crowds": The investment performance of contrarian funds. Chapter 19 in *Portfolio Construction, Measurement, and Efficiency: Essays in Honor of Jack Treynor*, J. B. Guerard, Jr. (Ed.), Springer, Switzerland, pp. 431–453.

Wermers, R. (1999). Mutual fund herding and the impact on stock prices. *Journal of Finance* **54**(2), 581–622.

Wermers, R., Yao, T., and Zhao, J. (2012). Forecasting stock returns through an efficient aggregation of mutual fund holdings. *Review of Financial Studies* **25**(12), 3490–3529.

Wharton Research Data Services (2019). https://wrds-www.wharton.upenn.edu/.

White, J. and Haghani, V. (2019). Smart beta: The good, the bad and the muddy. July 17. https://papers.ssrn.com/sol3/papers.cfm?abstract_id=3417236.

Zheng, W. and Tower, E. (2005). Fidelity versus Vanguard: Comparing the performance of the two largest mutual fund families. *International Review of Economics and Business* **52**(4), 433–465.

Part IV

Asset Allocation and Non-Stock Investment Research

https://doi.org/10.1142/9789811222634_0018

Chapter 18

Wealth Management Next Frontiers — The Inevitable Need to Meet Behavioral and Quantitative Approaches

Boryana Racheva-Iotova
Senior Director, Head of Quantitative Analytics, FactSet, Norwalk, Connecticut, USA

We explain main concepts of behavioral finance within the framework of the Rational Dynamic Asset Pricing Theory (RDAPT). We discuss key modifications of the Cumulative Prospect Theory (PT) weighting function to preserve key characteristics of the price process essential for deducting derivatives pricing. We then move to value-function and provide an overview of how it relates to optimality in the framework of the Rational Finance Theory common risk and return measures such as VaR, Conditional VaR, Range-Value-at-Risk, and other related risk functions. We provide guidelines regarding how those theoretical results could be implemented and used in practice. Ultimately, the chapter bridges the gap between rational and behavioral finance by introducing both a consistent weighting function and value-function maximization criteria based on rational-finance accepted risk and return measures. Although the main motivation of the chapter has been inspired by wealth management applications, the results certainly have broader applications for both active and passive managers, such as market sentiment extraction, novel designs of quantitative strategies, as well as behavior-flavor design of ETFs and smart-beta funds.

Keywords: Behavioral finance, asset pricing, portfolio optimization.

1. Introduction

The wealth management sector witnesses a rapid growth occurring simultaneously with fundamental and disruptive changes in the wealth market of both demographic and technological nature (Global Wealth, 2018). Today's and tomorrow's clients would require their private wealth to be viewed and managed holistically, including deep level of customization to their personal preferences married to sound technology based on logical and "rational" models underlying the investment process offered in a digitalized environment.

Behavioral patterns are shaped by the socio-economic environment. Markets turmoil and evaporation of returns streaming from traditional investments turn investors into alternative investments such as hedge funds and private equity funds, direct real asset investments, as well as "passion-based" and "ethically motivated" investments, which makes behavioral consideration further important. Furthermore, certain group of profiles feel confronted by an array of social and political potential threats, that infringe on their private wealth or lifestyles and trigger severe risk aversion or strong preference toward particular asset classes. Millennials are generally shaped by bullishness and aggressive approach toward investment opportunities, but also have strong ethically driven biases. Those specific psychological elements cannot be ignored and put investment decision-making further away from the typical domain of rational finance.

Behavioral patterns related to digitalization and rising technological adeptness add further complexity. As we are already used to having our retail preferences read by apps which automatically support our decision-making, the wealth management client profile is also changing to similarly seek full use of digital infrastructure and technological capabilities. Although it starts with the presentation layer, the expectation is that the investment decisions themselves should be based on understanding personal preferences and their dynamics incorporated in sound quantitative frameworks.

The wealth management space is reshaping: this new level of flexibility in the investment approach to fit the client preferences realized in a digitally-holistic way coupled with sophisticated applications to assess and analyze the risk preference and investor profile of clients is what will differentiate the successful movers in the new wealth management era. The wealth asset management industry will continually need approaches for building "efficient" portfolios, pricing derivatives, and constructing hedges, now however, accommodating for all behavioral biases and preferences.

The trends, which on the one hand call for deep consideration of behavioral factors, and on the other, for effective automated approaches, require serious analysis in how behavioral and quantitative rational finance can be synchronized.

At present, there is a deep methodology gap between the looming requirements and quantitative investment techniques available at hand. In the theory and practice of finance, generally the accepted view is that modern rational finance has become very mathematically and computationally advanced. Meanwhile, the methods of behavioral finance (BF) are predominantly based on very sophisticated empirical studies, contributing immensely to a better understanding of important financial markets' empirical phenomena, but not allowing for a true quantitative approach to portfolio construction.

This chapter provides the ground for that synchronization. It studies several BF findings with the help of the modern methods of rational finance (RF) and translates the "language" of the first to the other. The chapter is based on the work of several authors approaching the problem from different perspectives and aims at ultimately providing a consistent and complete working framework.

The chapter is structured as follows. In Section 2, we study Kahneman and Tversky (1979) and Tversky and Kahneman's (1992) PT from the viewpoint of RDAPT. We discuss the need to modify the PT Value Function (PTVF) to make it consistent with RF and semimartingale property of the return process and then illustrate the concept under a particular case of a properly modified weighting function. In Section 3, we study the other dimension of the behavioral theory principles — the Value Function, and map it to rational finance accepted Risk and Return measures such as VaR, CVaR, Range-VaR, and Rachev's Ratio. We further provide guidelines on how CVaR and Range-VaR optimization approaches can be used to reasonably maximize broad class of value functions, with several technical aspects presented in the appendices. Section 4 provides an empirical illustration of the concepts. In Section 5, we provide our concluding remark.

2. Generalized PT Weighting Function and Modifications to Ensure RDAPT Consistency

As we aim at translating the main concepts in the PT and CPT within the rational finance and RDAPT framework and to prepare the theoretical basis for building optimal and/or hedged portfolios with behavioral components, the first step is to adapt BF so that asset return processes become semi-martingales,[1] which is not the case within current formulation of BF Theory. Semi-martingales are the most general stochastic processes used in RDAPT. Ansel and Stricker (1991) show that a suitable formulation of absence of arbitrage implies that security gains must be semi-martingales with finite conditional means. It is the cornerstone of the asset pricing theory due to Black and Scholes (1973) and Merton (1973) and follow-up extension via the Sato Theorem (Sato 1999, p. 218, Theorem 33.1.). When incorporating investors' views, the notion of no-arbitrage disappears. However, we still must be able to price a derivative through the eyes of that same investor and for that reason there should be a way to construct an equivalent risk-neutral measure that corresponds to her "mini-universe" i.e., we still do require the semi-martingale property.

We first review the original formulation of BF and then provide approaches for the required adaptation based on Rachev *et al.* (2017).

[1]A stochastic process $X(t), t \geq 0$ defined on a probability basis $(\Omega, \mathcal{F}, \mathbb{F}, \mathbb{P})$, where $\mathbb{F} = (\mathcal{F}_t, 0 \leq t \leq T)$, is a right continuous filtration with $\mathcal{F} = \mathcal{F}_T$, $T \in (0, \infty]$, $\mathcal{F}_0 = \{\emptyset, \Omega\}$ is called a **semi-martingale** if: (i) $X(\cdot)$ is $\mathbb{F}$-adapted càdlàg (right continuous with left limits) process, and (ii) $X(\cdot)$ can be decomposed as $X(t) = M(t) + A(t) - B(t)$ where $M(t)$ is càdlàg $\mathbb{F}$-adapted local martingale, and $A(t)$ and $B(t)$ are increasing càdlàg F-adapted processes. Furthermore, $M(t)\, t \geq 0$, is a local martingale if there exists a strictly increasing sequence of stopping times $\tau^{(k)} \uparrow \infty$ as $k \uparrow \infty$ on $\mathbb{F}$, such that the stopped processes $M^{\left(\tau^{(k)}\right)}(t)$, $t \geq 0$, $k = 1, 2, \ldots$ are martingales.

2.1. *The Tversky and Kahneman value function and probability weighting function*

In their seminal papers, Kahneman and Tversky (1979) and Tversky and Kahneman (1992) introduced the PT and Cumulative Prospect Theory (CPT) with a critique of the expected utility theory (EUT). They claimed that the EUT cannot be a satisfactory model for the empirically observed in market participants' decision-making under risk. Tversky and Kahneman (1992) stated: "The *most distinctive implication of prospect theory is the fourfold pattern of risk attitudes. Specifically, it is predicted that when faced with a risky prospect people will be: (1) risk-seeking over low-probability gains, (2) risk-averse over high-probability gains, (3) risk-averse over low-probability losses, and (4) risk-seeking over high-probability losses.*", see also Harbaugh *et al.* (2009), Ackert and Deaves (2010), Barberis *et al.* (2016), Abdellaoui *et al.* (2016), for some empirical studies on those basic premises of the PT and the CPT.

According to the original PT, Kahneman and Tversky (1979) suggested that preferences of subjects can best be modeled by an S-shaped Value function and a weighting function that alters small probabilities and high probabilities, i.e., the weighting function is relatively sensitive to changes in probability near the end points 0 and 1 but is relatively insensitive to changes in probability in the middle region. At the end points, the weighting function is not well behaved. The function is convex where it is well behaved.

Assuming $x = (x_1, \ldots, x_n)$ is the vector of the possible outcomes, the prospective utility function is just a weighed sum $V(x) = \sum_i \pi_i v(x_i)$, where π_i is a transformation of the probability p_i of obtaining the i-th outcome. This approach violates first-order stochastic dominance, and to overcome this "weakness", Tversky and Kahneman (1992) (T&K hereafter) introduced the CPT, where the positive return (gains) and negative returns (losses) generated by financial assets are viewed differently as a result of the general "fear" disposition of traders, but the weighing function is defined on the space of cdfs of asset returns.

T&K quantified the observation that the positive return (gains) and negative returns (losses) generated by financial assets are viewed differently as a result of the general "fear" disposition of investors by introducing the **Prospect Theory value function** (shortly, **PTVF**) of the following form:

$$\upsilon(x) = \begin{cases} v^{(+)}(x) := x^{\alpha}, \text{ for } x \geq 0 \\ v^{(-)}(x) := -\lambda(-x)^{\beta}, \text{ for } x < 0 \end{cases}, \tag{1}$$

and estimated parameters α, β, and λ as $\alpha = \beta = 0.88$ and $\lambda = 2.25$. Within the scope of BF, the PTWF $\upsilon(x)\, x \in \mathcal{R}$, should be concave for the gains, that is when $x \geq 0$, and convex for the losses, that is when $x < 0$. Hence, it is assumed that in (1), $\alpha \in (0,1)$, $\beta \in (0,1)$, and $\lambda > 1$.

Let us designate the typical investor as $\beth$. Let also $\mathfrak{R}$ denote the return of a risky asset and $F^{(\mathfrak{R})}(x) = \mathbb{P}(\mathfrak{R} \leq x), x \in R$ is the cdf of $\mathfrak{R}$. T&K further quantified their observation that $\beth$ will overweight the loss $\mathfrak{R}Ind\{\mathfrak{R} < 0\}$ and underweight the gain $\mathfrak{R}Ind\{\mathfrak{R} > 0\}$ by introducing a continuous strictly increasing *probability weighting function* (pwf) $w^{(\beth)}(u), u \in [0,1]\, w^{(\beth)}(0) = 0, w^{(\beth)}(1) = 1$, tempering the shape of $F^{(\mathfrak{R})}(x), x \in \mathcal{R}$. As a result, $\beth$ does not use $F^{(\mathfrak{R})}(x), x \in R$, but instead $\beth$ will use as the cdf for $\mathfrak{R}$ the following penalized cdf:

$$F^{(\beth,\mathfrak{R})}(x) := w^{(\beth)}\left(F^{(\mathfrak{R})}(x)\right). \tag{2}$$

In particular, T&K introduced the following pwf:[2]

$$w^{(\beth)}(u) := \omega^{(\beth,\gamma)}(u) := \frac{u^{\gamma}}{[u^{\gamma} + (1-u)^{\gamma}]^{\frac{1}{\gamma}}},\ u \in (0,1],\ \gamma \in [0,1]. \tag{3}$$

The closer parameter γ is to 0.5, the more fearful $\beth$ is. When $\gamma = 1$, $w^{(\beth,1)}(u) := u$, and $F^{(\beth,\mathfrak{R})}(x) = F^{(R)}(x), x \in R$. Indeed, $\lim_{\gamma\downarrow 0}\omega^{(\beth,\gamma)}(u) = 0$. When $\gamma >$ **1** $\beth's$ disposition is "greedy", meaning

[2]The original formulation of the weighting function of a prospect with possible outcomes $x = (x_1, \ldots, x_n)$ under CPT is defined by

$$\pi_1^- = w^-(p_1), \quad \pi_i^- = w^-(p_1 + \ldots + p_i) - w^-(p_1 + \ldots + p_{i-1}) \quad 2 \leq i \leq k$$
$$\pi_1^+ = w^+(p_n), \quad \pi_i^+ = w^+(p_i + \ldots + p_n) - w^+(p_{i+1} + \ldots + p_n) \quad k+1 \leq i \leq n-1$$

for $x_1 \leq \cdots \leq x_k \leq 0 \leq x_{k+1} \leq \cdots \leq x_n$ and w(u) defined in (3) with possibly different γ parameter for the positive and negative outcomes.

that $\beth$ will overweight the gain $\mathfrak{R}\text{Ind}\{\mathfrak{R} > 0\}$ and underweight the loss $\mathfrak{R}\text{Ind}\{\mathfrak{R} > 0\}$.

Unfortunately, according to this weighting function, we can't find a starting probability distribution $F^{(\mathfrak{R})}(x)$, such that $F^{(\beth,\mathfrak{R})}(x) := w^{(\beth)}\left(F^{(\mathfrak{R})}(x)\right)$ is a semi-martingale (Rachev *et al.*, 2017).

2.2. *Prelec probability weighting function*

Prelec (1998)[3] introduced the following weighting probability function (wpf) (designated as **Pwpf**) :

$$w^{(\beth,\delta,\rho)}(u) := \exp\left\{-\left(-\delta \ln u\right)^{\rho}\right\}, u \in [0,1], 0 < \rho < 1, \delta > 0. \quad (4)$$

(i) for $0 < \rho < 1$, and fixed $\delta > 0$, is fearful;
(ii) for fixed ρ, δ, controls the height of the wpf;
(iii) for $\rho > 1$, $\delta > 0, \beth$ becomes greedy, and the larger ρ is, the greedier become.

To define $F^{(\mathfrak{R})}(x)$, such that $F^{(\beth,\mathfrak{R})}(x) := w^{(\mathfrak{R})}\left(F^{(\mathfrak{R})}(x)\right)$ is a semi-martingale, we need to use the following minor modification of Pwpf, designated as **MPwpf**, and having the following representation (Rachev *et al.*, 2017):

$$\begin{aligned} W^{(\beth,\delta,\rho)}(u) &= 1 - w^{(\beth,\delta,\rho)}(1-u) = \\ &= 1 - \exp\left\{-\left(-\delta \ln(1-u)\right)^{\rho}\right\} u \in [0,1], \, \rho > 0, \, \delta > 0. \end{aligned} \quad (5)$$

Similar to (4), suppose $\beth$ modifies her views on the asset (strictly increasing continuous) cdf $F^{(\mathfrak{R})}(x)$, $x \in \mathcal{R}$ by applying $W^{(,\delta,\rho)}!(\cdot)$ to obtain

$$F^{(\beth,\mathfrak{R})}(x) := W^{(\beth,\delta,\rho)}\left(F^{(\mathfrak{R})}(x)\right) \quad (6)$$

a posterior cdf $F^{(\beth,\mathfrak{R})}(x)$. Then (i) (ii) and (iii) hold.

---

[3]Prelec (1998) introduced also exponential power wpf, $w^{(\beth,\gamma,\eta)}(u) := \exp\left\{-\frac{\eta}{\gamma}\left(1-u^{\gamma}\right)\right\}, 0 < u < 1, \gamma > 0, \eta > 0$, and hyperbolic-logarithmic $W^{(\beth,\gamma,\eta,\eta)}(u) = (1+\gamma \ln p)^{-\frac{\eta}{\gamma}}, 0 < u < 1, \gamma > 0, \eta > 0$.

Let $\mathcal{U} \triangleq [0,1]$ be a uniformly distributed $[0,1]$ random variable. Let $F^{(\text{inv},\mathfrak{R})}(u) := \sup\{x : F^{(\mathfrak{R})}(x) \leq u\}\, u \in [0,1]$ be the inverse of the cdf $F^{(\mathfrak{R})}(x)\, x \in R$. Then $F^{(\text{inv},\mathfrak{R})}(\mathcal{U}) \triangleq \mathfrak{R}$. Set $\mathfrak{R}^{(\beth)} := F^{(\text{inv}\beth,\mathfrak{R})}(\mathcal{U})$, where $F^{(\text{inv},\beth,\mathfrak{R})}(u), u \in [0,1]$ is the inverse of $F^{(\beth,\mathfrak{R})}(x), x \in \mathcal{R}$. Then $F^{(\beth,\mathfrak{R})}$ is the cdf for $\mathfrak{R}^{(\beth)}$. Denote by $W^{(\text{inv}\beth)}(u)$, $u \in [0,1]$, the inverse function of $W^{(\beth)}(u)\, u \in [0,1]$. Thus,

$$\mathfrak{R}^{(\beth)} \triangleq F^{(\text{inv},\mathfrak{R})}\left(W^{(\text{inv}\beth,\delta,\rho)}(F^{(\mathfrak{R})}(\mathfrak{R}))\right) \tag{7}$$

From (5), (6), and (7), it follows that a natural choice for $F^{(\mathfrak{R})}(x)$ $x \in \mathcal{R}$, is the Negative Gumbel distribution, $\mathfrak{R} \triangleq NG(\mu, \varrho)$, $\mu \in \mathcal{R}$, $\varrho > 0$, with $F^{(\mathfrak{R})}(x) = F^{(NG(\mu,\rho))}(x) = 1 - \exp(-e^{\frac{x-\mu}{\varrho}})$, $x \in \mathcal{R}$. With $\mathfrak{R} \triangleq NG(\mu, \varrho)$ it follows from (10), that $\mathfrak{R}^{(\beth)} \triangleq NG(\mu^{(\beth)}, \varrho^{(\beth)})$ where $\mu^{(\beth)} = \mu - \varrho \ln \delta$, and $\varrho^{(\beth)} = \frac{\varrho}{\rho}$ Thus, remarkably, the **MPwpf** keeps the prior cdf $F^{(\mathfrak{R})}$ and posterior cdf $F^{(\beth,\mathfrak{R})}$ at the same Negative Gumbel distributional class.

Because Negative Gumbel distribution is infinitely divisible,[4] forms a semi-martingale, is skewed to the left and heavy tailed, Gumbel Lévy process has been provided in finance literature as a useful choice to model asset returns, see Bell (2006) and Markose and Alentorn (2011). Thus, **MPwpf** is a suitable weighting function and Negative Gumbel distribution can be used as a starting distribution $F^{(\mathfrak{R})}(x)$.

Option pricing under model (5–7) can now be constructed based on Sato's Theorem[5] on equivalent martingale measure for Lévy processes. See Bell (2006) for Call and Put options derived formulas

---

[4]A random vector Y is infinitely divisible if, for each $n \in N$, there is an i.i.d. sequence $Y_{n,1} + \cdots + Y_{n,n}$ so that $Y \triangleq Y_{n,1} + \cdots + Y_{n,n}$ (See, for example, Biglova *et al.*, 2004, on equivalence between infinitely divisible distributions and increments of a Levy process (in distribution) and the proof for the semi-martingale property of *cadlag Lévy processes*).

[5]Sato (1999, p. 218), Theorem 33.1.

under Negative Gumbel returns distribution. To evaluate the fear-greedy profile of the financial market based on MPwpf, one needs to calibrate the option pricing formula (8) to market option prices, extract the fearfulness parameter, and contrast it to empirical long-term values.

2.3. *The General Form of Probability Weighting Function Consistent with the RDAPT*

We start with the following observation regarding the nature of Prelec's wpf (4). Suppose $\beth's$ prior return distribution is Gumbel distribution: $\mathfrak{R} \triangleq (G\mu, \varrho)$, $\mu \in \mathcal{R}$, $\varrho > 0$, $F^{(G(\mu,\rho))}(x) = \exp(-e^{-\frac{x-\mu}{\varrho}})$, $x \in \mathcal{R}$, and her goal is to find wpf $w^{\left(\beth,\mu,\varrho,\mu^{(\beth)},\varrho^{(\beth)}\right)}(u)$ $u \in (0,1)$ such that posterior return distribution $\mathfrak{R}^{(\beth)} \triangleq G\left(\mu^{(\beth)}, \varrho^{(\beth)}\right)$ $\mu^{(\beth)} \in \mathcal{R}$, $\varrho^{(\beth)} > 0$, with cdf $F^{\left(\mathfrak{R}^{(\beth)}\right)}(x) = w^{\left(\beth,\mu,\varrho,\mu^{(\beth)},\varrho^{(\beth)}\right)} \circ F^{(\mathfrak{R})}(x)$. Then $w^{\left(\beth,\mu,\varrho,\mu^{(\beth)},\varrho^{(\beth)}\right)}(u) = \exp(-\left(-a^{(\beth)}\ln(u)\right)^{b^{(\beth)}})$, where $a^{(\beth)} = e^{\frac{\mu-\mu^{(\beth)}}{\rho}} > 0$ and $b^{(\beth)} = \frac{\rho}{\rho^{(\beth)}} > 0$, which is Pwpf $w^{\left(\beth,a^{(\beth)},b^{(\beth)}\right)}(u)\, u \in (0,1)$ see (4).

Similarly, if the distribution is $\mathfrak{R} \triangleq NG(\mu, \varrho)$, $\mu \in \mathcal{R}, \varrho > 0$, $F^{(NG(\mu,\rho))}(x) = 1 - \exp(-e^{\frac{x-\mu}{\varrho}})$, $x \in \mathcal{R}$, and $\beth' s$ goal is to find wpf $W^{\left(\beth,\mu,\varrho,\mu^{(\beth)},\varrho^{(\beth)}\right)}(u)\, u \in (0,1)$ such that posterior return distribution $\mathfrak{R}^{(\beth)} \triangleq NG\left(\mu^{(\beth)}, \varrho^{(\beth)}\right)$, $\mu^{(\beth)} \in \mathcal{R}$, $\varrho^{(\beth)} > 0$, with cdf $F^{\left(\mathfrak{R}^{(\beth)}\right)}(x) = W^{\left(\beth,\mu,\varrho,\mu^{(\beth)},\varrho^{(\beth)}\right)} \circ F^{(\mathfrak{R})}(x)$. Then $W^{\left(\beth,\mu,\varrho,\mu^{(\beth)},\varrho^{(\beth)}\right)}(u) = 1 - \exp(-\left(-a^{(\beth)}\ln(1-u)\right)^{b^{(\beth)}})$, which is the MPwpf given by (5).

These observations lead to the following general form of wpfs consistent with the rational asset pricing theory. Let $\mathfrak{R}$ and $\mathfrak{R}^{(\beth)}$ be infinitely divisible random variables, with cdfs $F^{(\mathfrak{R})}(x)\, x \in \mathcal{R}$ and $F^{\left(\mathfrak{R}^{(\beth)}\right)}(x)$, $x \in \mathcal{R}$, and let the mgf $\mathfrak{M}^{\left(\mathfrak{R}^{(\beth)}\right)}(s) = \mathbb{E}e^{s\mathfrak{R}^{(\beth)}} < \infty$, $0 < s < s^{(0)}$ Define the *general form of wpf*, $w^{\left(\beth,\mathfrak{R},\mathfrak{R}^{(\beth)}\right)}(u)$, $u \in (0,1)$, *consistent with RDAPT* as a solution of the following equation (Rachev *et al.*, 2017):

$$F^{\left(\mathfrak{R}^{(\beth)}\right)}(x) = w^{\left(\beth,\mathfrak{R},\mathfrak{R}^{(\beth)}\right)} \circ F^{(\mathfrak{R})}(x)\, , \; x \in \mathcal{R}. \tag{8}$$

3. The Value Function and Optimization

We now aim at approaching the value function component of the Generalized Prospect Theory. As mentioned, CPT uses a value function v with the same characteristics as in PT, following (1):

$$v(x) = \begin{cases} v^{(+)}(x) := x^{\alpha}, \text{ for } x \geq 0 \\ v^{(-)}(x) := -\lambda(-x)^{\beta}, \text{ for } x < 0 \end{cases},$$

Within the scope of BF, the PTWF $v(x)\, x \in \mathcal{R}$, should be concave for the gains, that is when $x \geq 0$, and convex for the losses, that is when $x < 0$. Hence, it is assumed that in (1), $\alpha \in (0,1)$, $\beta \in (0,1)$ and $\lambda > 1$.

Due to its stylized artifacts, Reference dependence (outcomes are framed in terms of gains or losses, instead of final wealth), Diminishing sensitivity (tendency to be risk averse for large gains and risk seeking for large losses), and Loss aversion (losses are felt more intensely than gains i.e., $\lambda > 1$), the value function is often referred to as S-Shaped Value function.

It is obvious that such a value function can't be mapped into the traditional framework of Modern Portfolio Theory and Markowitz Optimization. We want to seek an alternative objective function that could incorporate such investors' preferences.

3.1. *CVaR, R-Ratio, and Range-VaR as Risk Measures in Optimization*

CVaR optimization was first introduced by Rockafellar and Uryasev (2000) assuming $F^{(\mathfrak{R})}(x)$ is described by its empirical distribution. Rachev *et al.* (2009) extend the framework to $F^{(\mathfrak{R})}(x)$ bringing within the class of infinitely divisible distributions. CVaR usage as risk measure in a portfolio optimization problem has its immediate advantages on its own as it is a coherent risk measure, penalized losses only in contrast to Mean–Variance optimization, and can be solved for any kind of returns distribution without limitations to normality. In addition, if $F^{(\mathfrak{R})}(x)$ is discretized, then CVaR becomes a liner optimization problem (Rockafellar and Uryasev, 2000). Furthermore, multiperiod optimization extensions become very natural. Appendix 1, which is based on Bilarev *et al.* (2019) provides a short overview of the CVaR optimization. Appendix 2 extends to the multiperiod case.

Biglova *et al.* (2004) introduces the concept of Rachev-Ratio defined as $RRatio_{[\alpha,\beta]}(X) = CVaR_{\alpha}(-X)/CVaR_{\beta}(X)$, as a better approach to measuring risk-adjusted performance.An alternative form to measure upside versus downside potential could be defined as $\text{CVaR}_{\alpha}(-X) - \text{CVaR}_{\beta}(X)$, which we will refer to as Upside–Downside CVaR (U-DCVaR). Optimizing Rachev-ratio makes the solution of a Non-quasi-convex optimization problem necessary. As this technical issue is very general and applies to all ratio problems which may have a negative denominator, Stein *et al.* (2009) propose genetic algorithms as a general solution method for all ratio problems being Non-quasi-convex.

Cont *et al.* (2010) introduce an alternative risk measure, called Range Value-at-Risk (RVaR), which can be seen as the average VaR over a range of returns:

$$\text{RVaR}_{[\alpha,1-\beta]}(X) = \frac{1}{1-\beta-\alpha}\int_{\alpha}^{1-\beta} \text{VaR}_{\gamma}\,(X)\,d\gamma,$$

defines RVaR at $(\alpha\beta) - \text{confidence level}\,,\ \text{for}\, 0 < \alpha < 1-\beta < 1$.

Obviously, VaR and CVaR are special cases of RVaR. RVaR can be optimized using Difference of Convex Function Algorithms (DCA) (Vitanov, 2019).

3.2. *The Value Function, Stochastic Dominance, and Risk-Measures based Optimization*

We now review the relationship between different utility and value functions and the risk measures discussed.

Levy and Wiener (1998) introduce the notion of prospect stochastic dominance (PSD) and show that the preferences toward PSD can be represented by S-shaped value functions in the EUT paradigm.

Given two cumulative distribution functions F and G, F dominates G in the sense of PSD, denoted by $F \succcurlyeq_{\text{PSD}} G$ if $\int_x^y [G(t) - F(t)]dt > 0$ for all $x \le 0 \le y$, with at least one strict inequality, which implies second-order stochastic dominance in gains and risk-seeking stochastic dominance (inverse second-order stochastic dominance) in losses. Alternatively, characterization via quantiles is also presented as

$$\int_p^q \left[F^{-1}(t) - G^{-1}(t)\right] dt \ge 0 \text{ for all } 0 \le p \le F(0) \le G(0) \le q \le 1.$$

Yang (2019) closes the loop by proving the equivalence of the PSD and $\text{RVaR}_{[\alpha,1-\beta]}(X) \le \text{RVaR}_{[\alpha,1-\beta]}(Y)$ for all $0 \le \alpha \le F(0) \le G(0) \le \beta \le 1$

Similarly, according to Pfug (2000), first-order stochastic dominance is equivalent to $\text{VaR}_\alpha(X) \le \text{VaR}_\alpha(Y)$ for all $0 < \alpha \le 1$ and second-order stochastic dominance to $\text{CVaR}_\alpha(X) \le \text{CVaR}_\alpha(Y)$ for all $0 < \alpha \le 1$.

As noted in Yang (2019), these relationships reveal the connections among VaR, CVaR, and RVaR stochastic dominance and curvature structures of utility functions (preferences), providing behavior foundations for these risk measures. The equivalence of VaR and FSD shows that a decision-maker who is rational (more to less) prefers F to G if F has smaller VaR than G at all levels of risk tolerance. The equivalence of CVaR and SSD shows that a decision-maker who is risk-averse prefers F to G if F has smaller CVaR than G at all levels of risk tolerance. The equivalence relationship between PSD and RVaR shows that decision-makers with S-shaped value functions prefer smaller RVaR at all levels of risk tolerance given equal means. Similarly, it can be shown that an inverse S-shaped investor would maximize the U-DCVaR (the linear version of the R-Ratio) over all confidence levels.

These observations are important as a whole, since we would like to account for more general profiles of the value function as the evidence of the necessary S-Shaped Value function are not always empirically proven, see, for example, Levy and Levy (2002).

3.3. *Practical implementation considerations*

We are now equipped with the necessary foundations to allow heuristic, yet practical and reliable methods for constructing optimization problems based on behavioral theory perspective and have put all the findings so far in a consistent and holistic framework of translating behavioral phenomena into the rational finance methods context.

In practice, it is hard to qualify investor's value function precisely. Thus, instead of using a value function of a particular type, one may only identify the family type of the investor's value function (Increasing, Convex, S-Shaped, or Inverse S-Shaped) and then focus on optimizing according to the respective risk measure, as suggested in Section 3.1.

The drivers for using risk-measures-based approach are two-fold: it is much easier to identify investors preferences in terms of the risk measures discussed, moreover VaR and CVaR are standard and widely employed risk measures. The method also avoids the need to choose and parametrize the value function, thus circumventing parametrization pitfalls and allowing for greater flexibility. The approach is also more natural to investment professionals used to working in the Risk–Return space.

In case of CVaR, we can use the approach described in Appendix 1. RVaR and U-DVaR would require employment of genetic algorithm or DCA approach (Optimization of Range VaR using DCA, 2019).

In order to incorporate investors sentiment and potential biases with regards to future prospect outcomes, the optimization needs to be applied over the weighted return distribution (6) $F^{(\beth,\mathfrak{R})}(x) = W^{(\beth,\delta,\rho)}\left(F^{(\beth,\mathfrak{R})}(x)\right)$ as described in Section 2.

Any of the selected optimization approaches would require discretization of the return distribution (6) $F^{(\beth,\mathfrak{R})}(x) = W^{(\beth,\delta,\rho)}\left(F^{(\beth,\mathfrak{R})}(x)\right)$ after applying a weighting function preserving its infinitely divisible property as discussed in Section 2.

In the case of a discrete distribution represented by a set of returns, we can represent stochastic dominance, subject to a selected risk measure, by requiring minimum overall possible confidence levels $\alpha\beta$ at which we have atoms of the distribution. Let's denote by $m(x; \alpha\beta)$ the selected risk measure at confidence levels α and β[6].

In reality, such a solution is hardly attainable, but a reasonable approximation can be achieved by a select set of representative confidence levels. This translates the problem into a multi-objective optimization problem of the type:

$\min\left[m\left(x; \alpha_1, \beta_1\right), \ldots, m\left(x; \alpha_k, \beta_l\right)\right]$ for all selected confidence levels $\alpha_i \beta_j \ldots i = 1, .., k,\ j = 1 \ldots l$

A thorough review of the multi-objective methods is outside the scope of the current chapter, but we provide some high-level notes and references as follows:

A multi-objective problem is often solved by combining its multiple objectives into one single-objective scalar function:

$$\min \sum_{i,j} \gamma_{i,j} m(x; \alpha_i, \beta_j)_:$$

$$\sum_{j,i} \gamma_{i,j} = 1$$

$$\gamma_{i,j} > 0,\ \text{all}\, i, j$$

This approach is in general known as the weighted-sum or scalarization method and works well for convex functions (see, for example, Boyd and Vandenberghe (2004) and Caramia and Dell'Olmo (2008)) and as such is directly employable for m(x) being CVaR(x). Alternatively, one could employ Norm Ideal Point Method as in Zhang and Zuo (2013). In particular, one first finds the "ideal point" $m^* = \left(m_1^*, \ldots, m_{i\times j}^*\right)$, which satisfies $m_k^* \leq \min_x m_k(x)$, $k = 1, .., i \times j$, after that introduces a norm and finally gets the feasible solution which is having the nearest distance with the given ideal point m* in the norm.

[6]Note that the second parameter is only needed in the case of RVaR or U-DVaR.

3.4. *Multi-period Extensions*

The final extension we need to consider is the multi-period optimization case. Long-term horizons assume both time-changing weighting function[7] and risk-aversion preferences. Fortunately, all presented methods allow for a straightforward extension. Appendix 2 provides a high-level overview of a possible approach.

4. Empirical Illustration

We now move into an empirical illustration of the presented concepts. We will study the differences in the optimal allocations within a hypothetical strategic asset-allocation mix between equity markets holdings in different regions, North America, Europe, and Asia. We will contrast the optimal asset-allocation split of the following strategies:

1. Traditional Min-Volatility Optimization.
2. Incorporation on investors sentiment through introducing a weighting function extracted from the option markets and incorporating the modified (possibly fat-tailed) distribution into the optimization problem via a min-Conditional Value-at-Risk objective function, following the principles outlined in Section 2. We use CVaR at 95% Confidence level, denoted below as CVaR (95%).
3. Incorporating a pseudo-value function via modifying the abovementioned point 2 to optimize for Range Value-at-Risk (min Range VaR – Expected Return). We run two variations for Range VaR at 5%–95% confidence levels and for Range VaR at 10%–90% confidence levels, denoted as RVaR (5%–95%) and RVaR (10%–90%).

We represent the three regions of interest via S&P 500, NIKKEI 225, and EURO STOXX 50, and allocate between them for the period from 2014-07-15 to 2017-08-15.

[7]Derivatives pricing and hedging would only be possible within the optimization steps having the same weighting function.

The weighting function fitting follows the methodology described in Section 2. In particular, we imply the Gumbel-scale parameter based on Gumbel option pricing, see Bell (2006). We use Index future data for S&P 500, NIKKEI 225, and EURO STOXX 50[8] to extract the implied dividend based on the approach presented in Bell (2006). We then solve for scale parameter sigma, keeping the shift consistent with the non-arbitrage condition. The implied sigma for each day has been fit based on raw option data from 2014-07-14 to 2017-08-14.[9] The number of data points varies across the indices and is over 2 million for each index, including illiquid options (0 volume).[10] The latter were filtered out for the experiments. The typical size of relevant points per date was a few hundred for S&P 500 and between 50 and 80 for the other indices. The distribution implied for any given date of the backtest period was then used to simulate scenarios for the CVaR and RVaR optimization problems, following the methods outlined in Section 3 and detailed in Appendix 1.

The respective allocation between the three indices are provided in Table 1 and further depicted in Figs. 1, 2, and 3a and 3b, respectively for Min Volatility, CVaR (95%) and RVaR (5%–95%) and RVaR (10%–90%).

To analyze the impact on incorporating the option markets players' sentiments via so extracted weighting function and possible behavior-based choices expressed as proxies for the value functions via CVaR and RVaR, we study the 12-month rolling correlations between the over/under-allocations into each of the indices and the following month index returns.

The respective correlations are provided in Table 2 and further depicted in Figs. 4, 5a and 5b, respectively, for CVaR (95%) and RVaR (5%–95%) and RVaR (10%–90%).

[8]Daily future quotes from 2014-07-14 to 2017-08-14 obtained from FactSet.
[9]Daily future quotes from 2014-07-14 to 2017-08-14 obtained from FactSet.
[10]Changing the liquidity threshold did not have material impact on the implied sigma parameter.

Table 1. Optimal strategies weights for min volatility, CVaR (95%) and RVaR (5–95%) and RVaR (10–90%).

	Mean variance			CVaR (95%)			RVaR (5–95%)			RVaR (10–90%)		
	Nikkei 225	STOXX 50	S&P 500	Nikkei 225	STOXX 50	S&P 500	Nikkei 225	STOXX 50	S&P 500	Nikkei 225	STOXX 50	S&P 500
7/15/2014	21.18	0.27	78.56	18.99		81.01	40.68	18.05	41.28	28.02	14.98	57.00
8/15/2014	21.53	0.92	77.56	10.60		89.40	22.87	13.82	63.31	23.83	15.12	61.05
9/15/2014	21.79	1.35	76.86	24.73		75.27	30.07	20.57	49.36	27.94	20.57	51.50
10/15/2014	22.19	3.55	74.26	30.77		69.23	31.85	22.42	45.73	31.13	22.75	46.11
11/17/2014	21.91	4.32	73.77	4.14		95.86	13.17	15.49	71.34	13.15	15.66	71.19
12/15/2014	21.06	4.00	74.94	9.36		90.64	22.58	15.53	61.89	21.62	16.35	62.03
1/15/2015	22.39	5.23	72.38	48.04	13.34	38.62	38.63	27.00	34.37	40.41	24.36	35.23
2/16/2015	23.38	6.16	70.46	12.64		87.36	24.12	17.21	58.68	23.43	20.40	56.16
3/16/2015	23.52	6.01	70.47	42.08	10.99	46.93	37.31	27.04	35.64	37.21	26.83	35.97
4/15/2015	23.76	5.95	70.28	19.79		80.21	32.73	16.18	51.09	31.21	16.67	52.12
5/15/2015	25.16	5.99	68.85	11.69		88.31	25.96	18.62	55.42	23.10	16.17	60.73
6/15/2015	26.81	5.60	67.59	34.70		65.30	35.44	13.16	51.40	37.69	17.65	44.66
7/15/2015	28.60	4.48	66.92	24.25		75.75	32.55	16.82	50.63	31.66	16.50	51.83
8/17/2015	30.01	4.13	65.86	20.87		79.13	32.76	16.43	50.81	31.73	16.18	52.09
9/15/2015	29.34	11.78	58.89	20.60		79.40	27.60	23.11	49.28	26.77	21.59	51.64
10/15/2015	29.62	11.06	59.31	19.44		80.56	26.26	24.06	49.68	24.74	24.44	50.83
11/16/2015	30.48	11.16	58.36	10.96		89.04	28.06	19.32	52.62	27.32	18.36	54.33
12/15/2015	31.25	11.94	56.81	25.11		74.89	28.01	21.12	50.87	29.97	21.32	48.71

Table 1. (*Continued*)

	Mean variance			CVaR (95%)			RVaR (5–95%)			RVaR (10–90%)		
	Nikkei 225	STOXX 50	S&P 500	Nikkei 225	STOXX 50	S&P 500	Nikkei 225	STOXX 50	S&P 500	Nikkei 225	STOXX 50	S&P 500
1/15/2016	32.38	12.90	54.72	21.57	0.82	77.61	26.00	25.22	48.78	28.14	24.49	47.37
2/15/2016	31.76	13.63	54.61	12.05		87.95	23.74	22.28	53.98	23.16	22.58	54.25
3/15/2016	29.36	14.09	56.55	37.68	5.25	57.07	33.91	28.48	37.61	32.85	28.05	39.10
4/15/2016	28.95	12.62	58.43	9.87		90.13	24.35	32.25	43.40	18.84	23.45	57.71
5/16/2016	28.43	12.43	59.14	11.81		88.19	18.24	21.36	60.40	20.40	20.40	59.21
6/15/2016	28.18	11.57	60.25	28.80	1.06	70.13	31.99	23.82	44.19	31.63	23.99	44.38
7/15/2016	28.77	5.67	65.56	12.43		87.57	18.94	30.96	50.10	20.42	30.15	49.43
8/15/2016	28.20	5.54	66.26	21.43		78.57	31.38	13.19	55.43	31.95	13.84	54.21
9/15/2016	27.75	5.63	66.63	30.51		69.49	32.22	25.18	42.60	30.00	24.83	45.17
10/17/2016	28.11	5.17	66.72	50.29		49.71	43.23	26.14	30.64	43.03	26.20	30.76
11/15/2016	27.71	5.62	66.67	22.69		77.31	32.09	32.40	35.51	28.62	25.43	45.95
12/15/2016	26.97	5.23	67.80	57.89	19.94	22.17	39.81	36.60	23.58	39.69	38.45	21.87
1/16/2017	25.93	5.47	68.59	46.02		53.98	40.01	36.68	23.31	36.15	31.20	32.65
2/15/2017	25.62	5.17	69.21	30.99		69.01	38.34	27.23	34.43	35.06	25.44	39.50
3/15/2017	25.61	5.62	68.77	39.31		60.69	38.00	27.63	34.36	38.88	26.32	34.80
4/17/2017	25.34	5.60	69.07	34.61		65.39	37.77	28.17	34.06	35.95	30.02	34.03
5/15/2017	25.12	5.54	69.34	41.11		58.89	37.45	29.16	33.39	40.52	24.81	34.67
6/15/2017	25.01	6.13	68.86	43.70	18.89	37.42	42.77	34.26	22.98	45.64	36.67	17.69
7/17/2017	24.91	6.23	68.87	50.59		49.41	50.86	20.52	28.62	53.89	18.96	27.15
8/15/2017	24.97	0.00	75.03	38.12		61.88	42.27	28.54	29.18	40.63	29.57	29.80

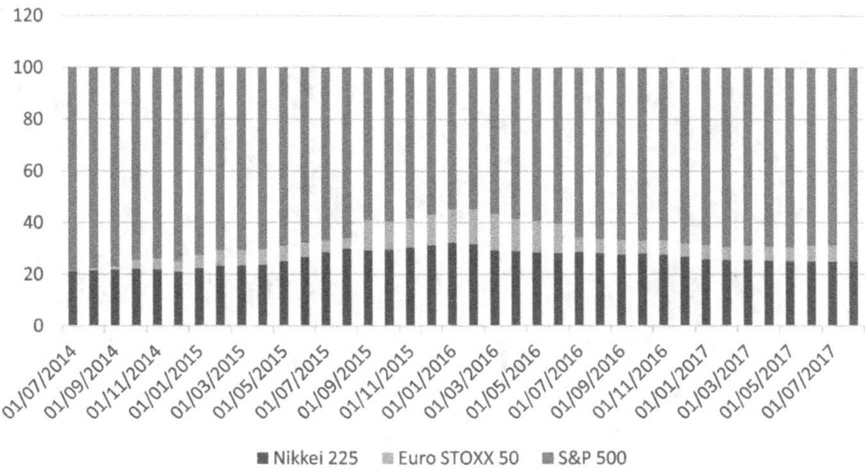

Fig. 1. Mean–variance optimal weights.

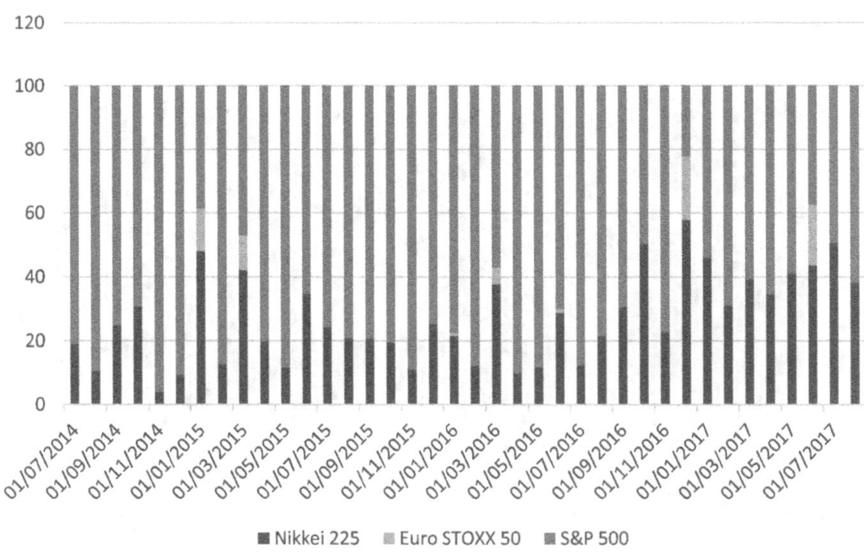

Fig. 2. CVaR (95%) optimal weights.

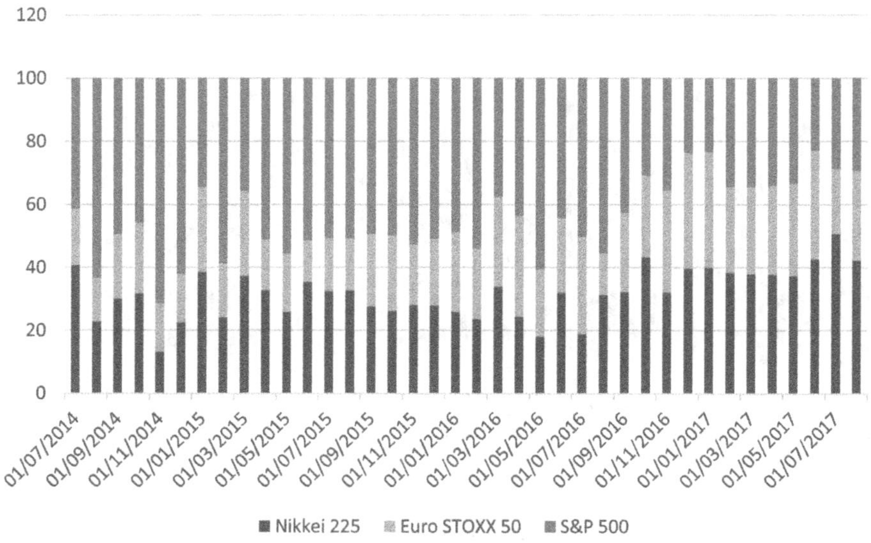

Fig. 3(a). RVaR (5–95%) optimal weights.

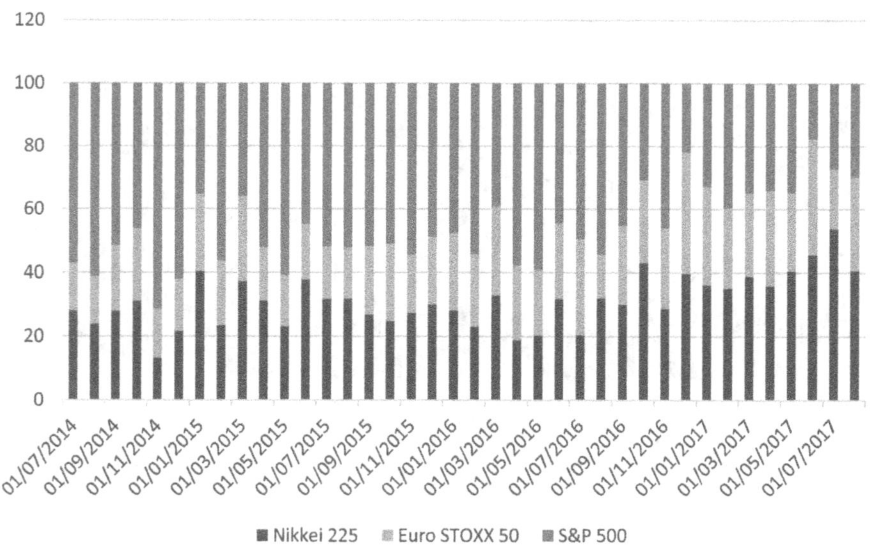

Fig. 3(b). RVaR (5–95%) optimal weights.

Table 2. Over/underweight-returns correlations. Over/underweight of CVaR and RVaR optimization objectives is estimated against mean–variance. Correlation is estimated for over/underweights as of day T against T+1-returns.

	Over–under weight CVaR (95%)			Over–under weight RVaR (5–95%)			Over–under weight RVaR (10–90%)		
12M Correl Start Date	Nikkei 225	Euro STOXX 50	S&P 500	Nikkei 225	Euro STOXX 50	S&P 500	Nikkei 225	Euro STOXX 50	S&P 500
2014-08-15	−0.1958	−0.2268	0.4627	0.0020	0.0108	0.3420	−0.1359	−0.1933	0.4877
2014-09-15	−0.2008	−0.2922	0.4706	−0.1294	−0.0711	0.4466	−0.1617	−0.2370	0.5013
2014-10-15	−0.3024	−0.2916	0.5103	−0.1994	−0.1358	0.4750	−0.2219	−0.3043	0.5276
2014-11-17	−0.3582	−0.3427	0.5580	−0.2680	−0.3669	0.6101	−0.2628	−0.5834	0.6143
2014-12-15	−0.1977	−0.2649	0.5631	−0.0437	−0.2850	0.5295	−0.0519	−0.5236	0.5413
2015-01-15	−0.2881	−0.3289	0.5203	−0.1258	−0.3210	0.4633	−0.1250	−0.5474	0.4775
2015-02-16	−0.2905	−0.4228	0.4912	−0.2412	−0.4178	0.5405	−0.1903	−0.6167	0.5018
2015-03-16	−0.1916	−0.2017	0.2231	−0.2227	−0.1609	0.3022	−0.1186	−0.4930	0.2693
2015-04-15	−0.0831	0.0367	−0.0941	−0.0487	−0.0460	−0.0679	0.0415	−0.2405	−0.0743
2015-05-15	0.1033	0.3323	−0.1345	0.1027	0.2091	−0.1251	0.2160	−0.1095	−0.1406
2015-06-15	0.0834	0.2358	−0.1229	0.1172	0.2489	−0.1692	0.1971	−0.1051	−0.1408
2015-07-15	0.0240	0.1605	−0.1280	0.0911	0.1937	−0.1397	0.1595	−0.1455	−0.1449
2015-08-17	−0.0049	0.3721	−0.1004	0.0739	0.0329	−0.0684	0.1825	−0.1562	−0.1027
2015-09-15	0.0614	0.1892	−0.0944	0.2028	−0.1683	−0.0386	0.2953	−0.2930	−0.0620

Table 2. (*Continued*)

12M Correl Start Date	Over–under weight CVaR (95%)			Over–under weight RVaR (5–95%)			Over–under weight RVaR (10–90%)		
	Nikkei 225	Euro STOXX 50	S&P 500	Nikkei 225	Euro STOXX 50	S&P 500	Nikkei 225	Euro STOXX 50	S&P 500
2015-10-15	0.0541	−0.0614	−0.0357	0.0312	−0.1948	0.0771	0.1649	−0.3488	0.0292
2015-11-16	−0.0378	−0.1195	−0.0889	−0.0567	−0.2285	−0.0029	0.0868	−0.3747	−0.0317
2015-12-15	−0.2848	−0.2000	0.0470	−0.3015	−0.2752	0.1098	−0.2258	−0.3923	0.0944
2016-01-15	−0.2014	−0.2843	0.0418	−0.3547	−0.3940	0.1811	−0.2245	−0.4379	0.1245
2016-02-15	−0.0842	−0.1012	−0.0982	−0.2491	−0.2544	−0.0591	−0.1554	−0.2820	−0.0552
2016-03-15	−0.0046	−0.0185	−0.1078	−0.1281	−0.1549	−0.0522	−0.0800	−0.2064	−0.0514
2016-04-15	−0.1752	−0.2498	0.2152	−0.2994	−0.4898	0.3613	−0.2498	−0.5061	0.3167
2016-05-16	−0.0620	−0.2350	0.1342	−0.1155	−0.4757	0.2999	−0.0275	−0.4937	0.2196
2016-06-15	−0.0062	−0.0813	0.0396	−0.1376	−0.4961	0.2760	−0.0057	−0.4493	0.1471
2016-07-15	0.2046	0.1238	−0.0407	0.1130	−0.2014	0.2233	0.2666	−0.2073	0.0591
2016-08-15	0.1886	0.1491	0.0725	0.0938	−0.3259	0.4640	0.2315	−0.2549	0.2319
2016-09-15	0.2676	0.0744	0.0785	0.2334	−0.3902	0.5178	0.3589	−0.3262	0.2271

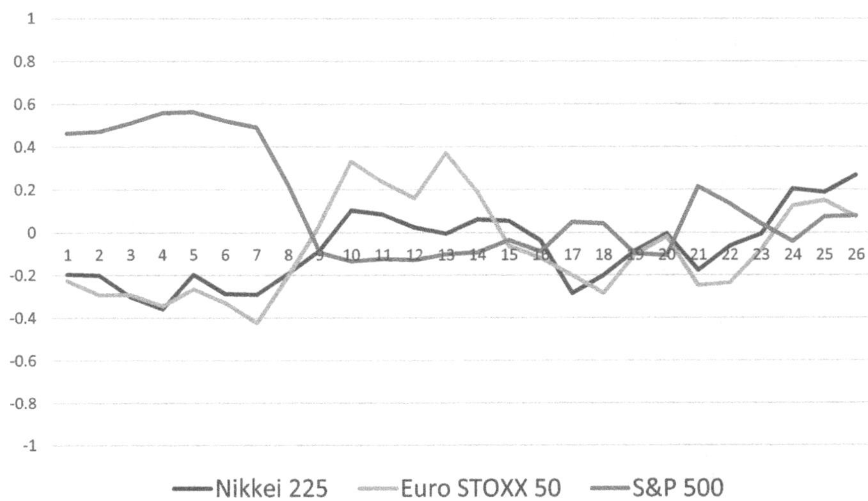

Fig. 4. Over/underweight-returns correlations CVaR (95%).

We observe that the option-market participants sentiment for S&P 500 extracted following Section 2 has some reasonable correlation with the market, which can be an indication of the skills of the investors, liquidity, and maturity of that segment. For Nikkei 225 and Euro STOXX 50, we see sentiment swings from bearish to bullish and vice versa, unjustified by the following market dynamics. Further study can focus on identifying relevant qualification criteria distinguishing between the two situations. We can further see that having a more pronounced "tail-blindness" behavior-based allocation approach via optimizing against RVaR (10–90%) contrasted to RVaR (5–95%) further amplifies the negative sentiment on Euro STOXX 50.

We can conclude that incorporating investors sentiment via weighting function based on option markets and changing the objective function to depict stylized properties of the value-function leads to significantly different asset-allocation decisions and risk-adjusted performance.

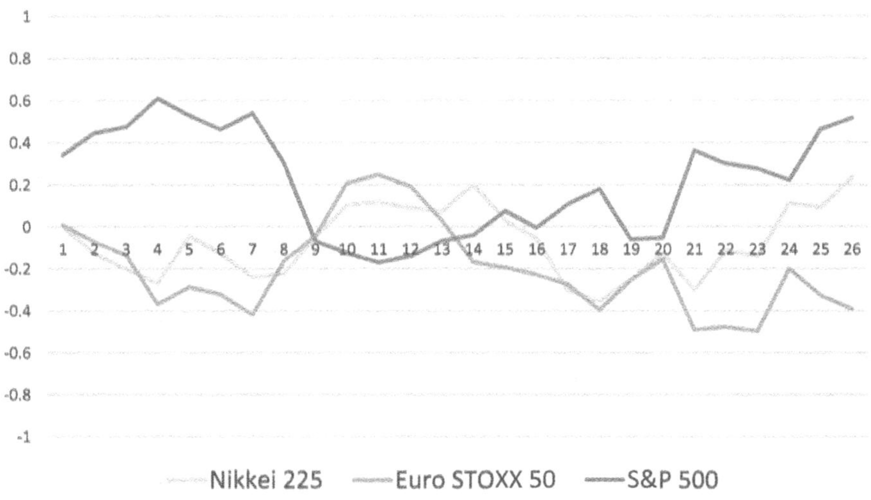

Fig. 5(a). Over/underweight-returns correlations RVaR (5–95%).

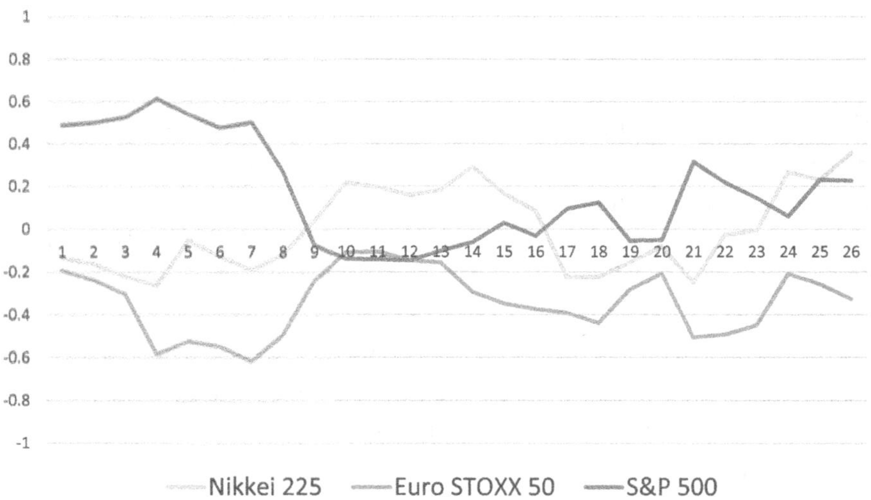

Fig. 5(b). Over/underweight returns correlations RVaR (10–90%).

5. Conclusions

We adapt the mathematical formulation of the BF principles so as to enable the use of key methods of the RF quantitative paradigm:

1. Shapes of investors' sentiments could be represented by weighting functions preserving the underlying distribution within the infinitely divisible distributions class.
2. Such chosen weighting functions further allow us to construct hedging strategies as they possess clear methods for contingent claims pricing.
3. Based on the extended notion of stochastic dominance, we propose reasonable approaches to optimize for investors value function of various shapes including the typical S-Shaped, via rational finance standard risk–return measures as CVaR, RVaR, and U-RVaR.

The chapter offers a review of the most important facts on bringing together BF and RF and illuminates key theoretical facts to build a consistent and theoretically sound unified BF–RF framework where derivatives pricing, hedging, and portfolio optimization within the behavioral paradigm are quantitatively prudent.

More importantly, the methods presented lay the grounds for a new generation practical framework for designing investment products for the wealth market.

Appendix A: CvaR Optimization (Based on Multi-Period Portfolio Optimization, 2019)

Let the investment universe consist of n assets. Denote the assets returns at time t_1 by the vector $r = (r_1, \dots, r_n)$ in which r_i stands for return of the ith asset with $i = 1, \dots, n$. The investment decision consists of choosing a set of weights $w' = (w_1, \dots, w_n)$, where for $i = 1, \dots, n$, w_i denotes the weight of the wealth invested in asset i; in this sense, we require that $\sum_{i=1}^{n} w_i = 1$, meaning that the total wealth is distributed among the risky assets. The return r_p of the portfolio at time t_1 can be expressed by $r'$and w'as

$$r_p = w^{'}r = \sum_{i=1}^{n} w_i r_i.$$

Let the vector $\mu' = (\mu_1, \ldots, \mu_n)$ collect the expected returns of the risky assets at time t_1, i.e., $\mu_i = E[r_i]$. Thus, the expected returns of the portfolio is $E[r_p] = w'r$.

The *Mean–CVaR portfolio optimization problem* is to find an optimal portfolio weight w that maximizes expected portfolio returns and minimizes the CVaR of the portfolio loss, being in this case $-r_p$. This could be achieved, for instance, by optimizing a utility function like

$$\max_w E[r_p] - \lambda \mathrm{CVaR}_\varepsilon(r_p), \tag{A.1}$$

where λ >0 is a *risk aversion* parameter and for a confidence level ε,

$$\mathrm{CVaR}_\varepsilon(r_p) := E[r_p| - r_p > \mathrm{VaR}_\varepsilon(r_p)] \tag{A.2}$$

Here for a confidence level ε, $\mathrm{VaR}_\varepsilon(r_p)$ is the lowest amount ζ_ε such that, with probability at least $1-\varepsilon$, the portfolio loss will not exceed ζ_ε. The magnitude of the risk-aversion coefficient λ represents portfolio manager risk preferences, i.e., higher λ value stipulates higher risk-averse attitude. In the general objective function (A.1), we could keep both quantities, or we could drop out either one when we build a portfolio optimization model. In this way, we arrive either at the maximum expected portfolio mean return model $E[r_p]$, or at the minimum CVaR portfolio optimization model $\mathrm{CVaR}_\varepsilon(r_p)$. All three objective functions can be optimized subject to constraints specifying different levels of CVaR and/or expected return.

Assuming that asset returns are Gaussian, it turns out that using CVaR as a risk measure is equivalent to using the variance, cf. Rockafellar and Uryasev (2000). In this case, optimization problems involving CVaR simplify to quadratic problems that could be solved efficiently and even in closed form, cf. Li and Ng (2000). This is no longer the case when more general distribution models are employed. In this case, the optimization problems involving CVaR belong to the general class of convex programming problems. However, the structure of the CVaR allows for a significant simplification of the optimization problem when we consider discretization of the underlying probability distribution via Monte Carlo *scenarios*. At the cost of introducing additional variables, the optimization problem can be formulated as a linear programming problem which, as far as the structure is concerned, is simpler than quadratic problems. In the sequel, we define the model by means of the linearization technique developed in Rockafellar and Uryasev (2002). It is crucially based on the following representation of CVaR: for a random variable X(describing for example the portfolio returns)

$$\mathrm{CVaR}_{\varepsilon}\,(X) = \min\nolimits_{\theta \in R}\left(\theta + \frac{1}{\varepsilon} E\left[(-X-\theta)_{+}\right]\right), \tag{A.3}$$

where $(x)_{+} = \max(x, 0)$

For the given number of n assets, we simulate k independent return scenarios per asset. Thus, we obtain a $k \times n$ matrix H containing those scenarios in rows (and columns per asset)

$$H = \begin{pmatrix} r_1^1 & \cdots & r_n^1 \\ \vdots & \ddots & \vdots \\ r_1^k & \cdots & r_n^k \end{pmatrix} \tag{A.4}$$

where r_j^i stands for the i-th return scenario of the j-th asset. Thus, approximating the expectation in representation (A.3) by its empirical mean and introducing auxiliary variables for each observation in the sample, we obtain the following linear programming problem that approximates the CVaR of the returns for a portfolio w:

$$\begin{aligned} \widehat{CVaR_{\varepsilon}}\,(r_p) = \min_{\theta,d} \quad & \theta + \tfrac{1}{k\varepsilon} d' e \\ \text{s.t.} \quad & -Hw - \theta\varepsilon \le d \\ & w' e = 1,\ \theta \in R,\ d \ge 0 \end{aligned} \tag{A.5}$$

where $d' = (d_1, \ldots, d_k)$ is a vector of auxiliary variables, $e = (1, \ldots, 1) \in R^k$ is the identity vector in R^k, and $\theta \in R$ is an additional variable coming from the linearization technique. The inequalities in (A.5) involving vectors should be interpreted in a component-wise manner, e.g., $-Hw - \theta\varepsilon \leq d$ is equivalent to $-r^i w - \theta \leq d_i$ for $i = 1, \ldots, k$, where r^i is the i-th row in H for i ranging from 1 to k, i.e., the vector r^i contains the i-th scenario for each asset in our portfolio. Thus, the Mean–CVaR portfolio optimization problem becomes a linear programming problem with the following objective function:

$$\max_{w,\theta,d} \; w'\mu - \lambda\left(\theta + \frac{1}{k\varepsilon} d' e\right)$$

Appendix B: Multi-period CVaR Optimization (Based on Multi-Period Portfolio Optimization, 2019)

In long-term portfolio optimization problems, the question of monitoring portfolio losses at different times naturally arises. An extension of the single-period mean–CVaR problem is to maximize a weighted sum of the mean–CVaRs for each subperiod:

$$\begin{array}{ll} \max_{td} & \sum_{i=1}^{T} E\left[r_p\left(i\right)\right] - h_i \mathrm{CVaR}_{\varepsilon_i}(r_p(i)) \\ \text{s.t.} & w_i' e = 1,\; i = 1, \ldots, T \end{array} \tag{B.1}$$

where $r_p\left(i\right)$ are the uncompounded portfolio returns at times $i = 1, \ldots, T$. In this form, solving the T-period problem is equivalent to solving a sequence of single-period problems separately. This is no longer the case when we impose *cross-period constraints* that appear naturally in many real-world problems. To exemplify this, we consider *cross-period turnover* constraints in which case the admissible portfolio allocations should satisfy

$$||w_i - w_{i-1}||_1 \leq \mathrm{TO}, \qquad \forall\, i = 1, \ldots, T,$$

where for a vector $x = (x_1, \ldots, x_n) \in R^n$, the 1-norm is defined by $||x||_1 := \sum_{i=1}^n |x_i|$; here w_0 stands for the initial portfolio allocation. In this case, the choice of allocation at time 0 affects the possibilities for the allocations at time 1, that subsequently affects the allocation at time 2, etc., and hence *wait-and-see* strategies could perform better. This shows that the multi-period optimization problems with cross-period constraints should be tackled as single optimization problems as opposed to a sequence of one-step problems that would clearly prevent wait-and-see strategies. Following the discussion in Appendix A, we re-write problem (6) with cross-period constraints as follows:

$$\begin{aligned} \max_{w,x,u} \quad & \sum_{i=1}^{T} w_i^{'}\mu(i) - h_i(x_i + \frac{1}{\varepsilon_i K}\sum_{j=1}^{K} u_i^j \\ \text{s.t.} \quad & u_i^j + w_i^{'} r_i^j + x_i \geq 0, \;\; w_i^{'} e = 1 \\ & ||w_i - w_{i-1}||_1 \leq \text{TO}, \; i = 1, \ldots, T, \; j = 1, \ldots, K. \end{aligned} \tag{B.2}$$

where $\mu = (\mu(i))_{i=1}^T$ are the (forecasted) means returns for the different periods.

References

Abdellaoui, M., Bleichrodt, H., L'Haridon, and Dennie van Dolder, O. (2016). Measuring loss aversion under ambiguity: A method to make prospect theory completely observable. *Journal of Risk and Uncertainty* **52**, 1.

Ackert, L. F. and Deaves, R. (2010). *Behavioral Finance: Psychology, Decision-Making, and Markets.* Mason, OH: South-Western Cengage Learning.

Ansel, J. P. and Stricker, C. (1991). Lois de Martingale, Densities et Dècomposition de Föllmer-Schweizer. Preprint, Universitè de Franche-Comtè, Besancon.

Barberis, N., Mukherjee, A., and Wang, B. (2016). Prospect theory and stock returns: An empirical test. *The Review of Financial Studies* **29**(11), 3068–3107.

Bell R. A. (2006). *Option Pricing with Extreme Value Distributions, Technical report, Department of Mathematics.* King's College London, September 14, 2006.

Biglova, A., Ortobelli, S., Rachev, S. T., and Stoyanov, S. (2004). Different approaches to risk estimation in portfolio theory. *Journal of Portfolio Management* **31**(1), 103–112.

Bilarev T., Mitov G., Racheva-Iotova B., and Stefanov, I. (2019). *Multi-Period Portfolio Optimization.* FactSet White Paper.

Black, F. and Scholes, M. (1973). The pricing of options and corporate liabilities. *The Journal of Political Economy* **81**, 637–654.

Boyd, S. and Vandenberghe, L. (2004). *Convex Optimization*, Chapter 4.7, Cambridge University Press, ISBN: 9780521833783.

Caramia, M. and Dell'Olmo, P. (2008). *Multi-Objective Management in Freight Logistics Increasing Capacity, Service Level and Safety with Optimization Algorithms*, Chapter 2, Springer, ISBN: 978-1-84800-382-8.

Cont, R., Deguest, R., and Scandolo, G. (2010). Robustness and sensitivity analysis of risk measurement procedures. *Quantitative Finance* **10**(6), 593–606.

Global Wealth (2018), Seizing the Analytics Advantage, The Boston Consulting Group.

Harbaugh, W.T., Krause, K., and Vesterlund, L. (2009). The fourfold pattern of risk attitudes in choice and pricing tasks. *The Economic Journal* **120**(545), 595–611.

Kahneman, D. and Tversky, A. (1979). Prospect theory: An analysis of decision under risk. *Econometrica*, **47**, 263–291.

Levy, H. and Levy, M. (2002). Experimental test of the prospect theory value function: A stochastic dominance approach. *Organizational Behavior and Human Decision Processes* **89**(2), 1058–1081.

Levy, H. and Wiener, Z. (1998). Stochastic dominance and prospect dominance with subjective weighting functions. *Journal of Risk and Uncertainty* **16**(2), 147–163.

Li, D. and Ng, W. (2000). Optimal dynamic portfolio selection: Multiperiod mean-variance formulation. *Mathematical Finance* **1**(3), 387–406.

Markose, S. M. and Alentorn, A. (2011). The generalized extreme value distribution, implied tail index, and option pricing. *The Journal of Derivatives* **18**, 35–60.

Merton, R. C. (1973). Theory of rational option pricing. *The Bell Journal of Economics and Management* **4**, 141–183.

Multi-Period Portfolio Optimization (2019). FactSet Technical Paper.

Optimization of Range VaR using DCA (2019). FactSet Technical Paper.

Pfug, G. C. (2000). Some remarks on the value-at-risk and the conditional value-at-risk. *Probabilistic Constrained Optimization*, pp. 272–281, Springer.

Prelec, D. (1998). The probability weighting function. *Econometrica* **66**, 497–527.

Qiulin, Y. (2019). *The Choice-theoretic Characterizations of Risk Changes and Risk Attitudes in Cumulative Prospect Theory: A Stochastic Dominance Approach*, Doctor of Philosophy Dissertation, Lancaster University.

Rachev, S. T., Martin, R. D., Racheva, B., and Stoyanov, S. (2009). Stable ETL optimal portfolios and extreme risk management. In Bol, G., Rachev, S.T., Würth, R. (Eds.), *Risk Assessment. Contributions to Economics.* Physica-Verlag HD.

Rachev, S., Fabozzi, F. J., and Racheva-Iotova, B. (2017). *Option Pricing with Greed and Fear Factor: The Rational Finance Approach*, arXiv:1709.08134.

Rockafellar R. T. and Uryasev, S. (2000). Optimization of conditional value-at-risk. *Journal of Risk* **2**, 21–41.

Sato, K.-I. (1999). *Lévy Processes and Infinitely Divisible Distributions.* Cambridge University Press, Cambridge: UK.

Stein, M., Rachev, S. T., and Stoyanov, S. (2009). R ratio optimization with heterogeneous assets using genetic algorithm. *Investment Management and Financial Innovations* **6**(3-1), 117–125.

Tversky, A. and Kahneman, D. (1992). Advances in prospect theory: Cumulative representation of uncertainty. *Journal of Risk and Uncertainty* **5**, 297–323.

Zhang, G. and Zuo, H. (2013). Pareto optimal solution analysis of convex multi-objective programming problem. *Journal of Networks* **8**(2), 437–444.

https://doi.org/10.1142/9789811222634_0019

Chapter 19

Foreign Exchange Rate Predictability: *Seek and Ye Shall Find It*

Foteini Kyriazi

Department of Economics, University of Peloponnese, 22 100, Tripoli, Greece
fkyriazi@uop.gr
kastaskiriazi@yahoo.gr

Dimitrios D. Thomakos

Department of Economics, University of Peloponnese, 22 100, Tripoli, Greece; Rimini Center for Economic Analysis, Rimini, Italy; ForTank, the Forecasting Think Tank and Quantf
thomakos@uop.gr
dimitrios.thomakos@gmail.com

There is ample literature on foreign exchange rate predictability and the results point out toward entirely different directions, some of it claiming that foreign exchanges are unpredictable random walks, some others that they are mean-reverting and cointegrating and yet some others insists that they can be best modeled and forecasted by nonlinear methods. In this chapter, we take a broader view for the methodology and a narrow on the application: first, we explore the predictability of the EUR/USD exchange rate, the leading currency in terms of liquidity and market attention and, second, we bring forth a number of incremental contributions. Specifically, we propose and implement two types of models that address the dual nature of exchange rates, the linear and nonlinear one, and we illustrate that on our dataset they provide possibly the best performance overall. Then, we provide strong supportive evidence on the time-varying nature of foreign exchange rate predictability and the need for forecast evaluation based on statistical and financial performance criteria. Finally, we provide several illustrations that in-sample fit and out-of-sample predictability are not necessarily separable and that increased in-sample fit can in many instances lead to improved such predictability. Practitioners that are interested in foreign exchange forecasting should consider the results of our chapter for they offer coherent suggestions to understand and exploit predictability when it decides to manifest in any currency pair.

Keywords: Delay models, euro currency, forecasting, foreign exchange rates, non-linear models, predictability, random walk, sequential elimination estimation, statistical evaluation, threshold models.

1. Introduction

The subject of exchange rate predictability is so well researched that probably the hardest part about writing another chapter on it is the introduction and the literature review, but we will not be deterred. This is a carefully constructed empirical exercise on the forecastability of the EUR/USD exchange rate at the monthly frequency that offers a number of results and confirmations to the vast literature on the topic, and we do present our mild contributions to the interested reader's toolbox.

We provide a number of interesting results on the use of explanatory variables in the context of a number of models, we examine whether model parsimony is beneficial in forecasting exchange rates, we find (for this analysis) that we can easily outperform the standard benchmarks and, in general, provide ample evidence that predictability is indeed there and that it is not so difficult to uncover it. As many other papers have claimed before, we can beat the random walk benchmark with models whose only complication is the use of data from another currency pair, the GBP/USD one. Although our analysis is specific to the euro, and the pound as the explanatory variable, the suggested models and methodology are quite general and easily applicable. We have not made an exhaustive comparison with whatever appeared in the literature before us for our aim is re-enforcing the need for model parsimony and providing an understanding between in-sample fit and out-of-sample predictability.

For our analysis, we have opted to use two types of simple models classes, one of which has never previously appeared as far we know.

The first class is a simple delay model, a simpler regression of the returns of the euro and a single lag of some explanatory variable based on the pound; here the monthly frequency becomes necessary to use variables such as realized volatilities and realized correlation, between the euro and the pound, computed for daily returns. In this way, we can assess the relative importance in uncovering predictability based on the returns or the volatilities and correlation of the variables. We suggest a simple algorithm for estimating the delay and, might we say, the changes in the estimated delay value in one of our approaches do allow for capturing some degree of nonlinearity. The second class of models is one of using threshold-based nonlinearity and interactions-based nonlinearity. Here we provide for a model where the response of the dependent variable to a change in one of the lags of the explanatory variable has a particular linear form which can potentially capture features such as breaks and sudden moves in the exchange rate. Furthermore, we show how to perform model reduction in a consistent and parsimonious way by sequential elimination that preserves the correct level of significance at the end of the elimination procedure. Both these classes of models are easily estimated by least squares. We augment our analysis with standard univariate and bivariate linear and (simple) nonlinear benchmarks and we also use the recently proposed methodology of adaptive learning forecasting of Kyriazi *et al.* (2019).

Our results indicate that our suggested model classes perform exceedingly well in forecasting the EUR/USD exchange rate returns at the monthly frequency across a number of sub-periods and the total period under examination, and under different specifications of the rolling window used in estimation. We find strong evidence of predictability and we link this predictability with the magnitude and shape of the evolution of the in-sample fit of these models. We note that, on the limited number of benchmarks and nonlinear models we used for comparison, the benchmarks appear very infrequently as top performers in the analysis. Finally, our results (particular as they may be) do support that the models that perform best in terms of statistical measures also perform best in terms of directional predictability and financial performance on a standard paper trading evaluation.

The rest of the chapter is structured as follows: in Section 2, we have a (brief) literature review on our topic of analysis; in Section 3, we present the methodology, models, and forecast evaluation that we use in the chapter; in Section 4, we discuss our dataset and the construction of explanatory variables; in Section 5, there is an extended discussion of all our empirical results, while Section 6 offers some concluding remarks.

2. Brief Literature Review

In the context of our chapter, any attempt to provide a complete literature overview will, necessarily, be incomplete. Our references are only suggestive and set the tone for the rest of our discussion. We start-off with seminal works such as those of Stein and Tower (1967), on the short-run stability of the exchange rate market, and of Dornbusch (1976), on exchange rates and expectations — the latter issue is of particular importance in the context of forming forecasts (forecasts are essentially estimated expectations). Soon after we have another seminal work of Meese and Rogoff (1983), one of the earliest models of out-of-sample exchange rate predictability. Following this, things in the literature went overboard, and the interest in many different kinds of forecasting models exploded.

Enders (1988) was one of the first to consider cointegration tests on exchange rates at the beginning of the cointegration literature, and has followed with many papers on exchange rate modeling, such as in Enders and Lee (1997) and Enders and Falk (1998). Diebold and Nason (1989) wrote one of the earliest papers on the use of nonlinear/nonparametric models on exchange rate prediction. The seminal contribution of Bollerslev (1990) on GARCH volatility modeling was written in the context of exchange rates too. The literature continued with many other papers that contested the validity of the random walk model as a suitable data generating process for exchange rates (versus a host of other models), a discussion that still holds well today.

Engel (1994) considered Markov switching models while Engel and West (2005) brought forth, again, the connection between exchange rate and economic fundamentals. MacDonald and Taylor (1994) also considered the monetary model and the interplay of long and short-run dynamics and how to beat the random walk. Crystal and MacDonald (1995) considered the properties of the British pound with the U.S. dollar, Chinn and Meese (1995) suggested that fundamental exchange rate models forecast no better than a random walk model for short-term forecasting horizons, while Newbold *et al.* (1998) considered whether the dollar/ECU (precursor to the euro) exchange rate was a random walk or not — in spirit our chapter is similar in its question; a similar analysis on the random walk issue was performed for the British pound by Smoluk *et al.* (1998). Also, Yoon (1998) considers the question as to why the random walk model is difficult to beat, as does Moose (2013), in the context of forecasting in both papers. Mark and Sul (2001), using panel regression estimates and panel-based forecasts, confirm that the ability for monetary fundamentals to forecast future exchange rate returns is probably significant.

Taylor and Peel (2000) considered nonlinear models in the context of exchange rate fundamentals, as did Boero and Marrocu (2002). Kilian and Taylor (2003) showed that despite significant rejections of the random walk based on in-sample tests, they were unable to reject significantly the random walk forecast model in a real-time recursive forecast. Abhyankar *et al.* (2005) described as a "major puzzle in international finance" the inability of models based on monetary fundamentals to outperform the random walk model. Rapach and Strauss (2008) allowed for structural breaks in the conditional volatility of the exchange rate series, while Voss and Willard (2009) provided another option to exchange rate predictability in the context, again, of comparisons with the random walk. The paper of Molodtsova and Papell (2009) suggested that there might be some degree of predictability over and above the random walk model in exchange rate forecasting by using Taylor rule-type of models, but subsequent research on their methodology by Bhattacharya and Thomakos (2018) showed that once one considers rolling window averaging of forecasts, the random walk/naíve benchmark regains its position as being one of the top performers. The results of this last paper are important because they imply that applying different information sets (rolling windows) and averaging may provide different results — this approach can be a useful extension to this chapter.

Chortareas *et al.* (2011), examining the random walk behavior of 17 OECD countries, euro exchange rate, rejected the hypothesis of random-walk behavior less often than do traditional tests while Hashimoto *et al.* (2012) in their paper suggested that a random walk hypothesis is refuted in a simple test of a run using tick-by-tick data. Butter and Jansen (2013) showed that it is hard to beat the random walk when also forecasting long-term interest rates, especially when the forecasting horizon is relatively short — where the forecast is most relevant as well, while Moose and Kelly (2014) suggested error correction modeling and dynamic specifications as an approach to try to beat the random walk. Finally, Levich and Potti (2015) provided a through analysis on the issue of exchange rate predictability, going over and above the discussion of what fits the data as a data generating process and concentrating on what and how predictability can be measured.

3. Methodology

Consider the EUR/USD foreign exchange rate at any chosen frequency of observation and denote its level by P_t and its log-return by $Y_t \stackrel{\text{def}}{=} \log(P_t/P_{t-1})$. Our analysis will be based on the log-returns and our models are geared toward the presumed properties the log-returns have. All our forecasts are one-step ahead, obtained by one of the models $m = 1, 2, \ldots M$ and are denoted as $\widehat{Y}^m_{t+1|t}$. In what follows, our notation assumes that we use the full available sample $t = 1, 2, \ldots, n$ when obtaining parameter estimates — it should be understood that when we perform our rolling window analysis, the estimates will become, by construction, time-varying.

The fundamental benchmark in the foreign exchange rate literature is the random walk, without or with drift. The naive forecast without drift is denoted $\widehat{Y}^0_{t+1|t} = 0$, and is identically zero, while the naive forecast with drift is denoted by $\widehat{Y}^1_{t+1|t} \stackrel{\text{def}}{=} \widehat{\mu}$, and is equal to the sample mean $\widehat{\mu} \stackrel{\text{def}}{=} n^{-1} \sum_{t=1}^{n} Y_t$. The next fundamental models we consider are autoregressive ones and specifically: a first-order autoregression, an autoregression with the order selected by the AIC, a bivariate first-order autoregression, and a bivariate autoregression with the order again selected by the AIC. In the bivariate models, and all other models that use an explanatory variable, we take as our explanatory variables the returns of the British pound against the U.S. dollar, GBP/USD, and various measures of volatility (of both the euro and the pound) and correlation (between the euro and the pound). We experiment with the explanatory variables entering in their defined levels and in differences. These benchmarks give us the forecasts $\widehat{Y}^m_{t+1|t}$ for $m = 2, 3, 4, 5$. We supplement these linear models and their associated forecasts with a simple linear delay model in the standard form:

$$Y_t = \alpha + \beta X_{t-\delta} + u_t \tag{1}$$

and the forecast is taken as $\widehat{Y}^m_{t+1|t} \stackrel{\text{def}}{=} \widehat{\alpha} + \widehat{\beta} X_{t-d}$ where the delay δ is estimated from the cross-correlation function between Y_t and X_{t-j} as $d \stackrel{\text{def}}{=} \underset{j}{\operatorname{argmax}} |\widehat{\rho}(Y_t, X_{t-j})|$, for $j = 1, 2, \ldots, 15$ — that is, the estimated delay is obtained as the value that maximizes the absolute value of the estimated cross-correlation function. We consider two approaches, a global one, and a local one; in the global one, the order of the delay is estimated from the whole sample and then used in the rolling window analysis, while in the local one the order of the delay is estimated (properly this time) from the data up to and including the current period. These two delay models give us forecasts $\widehat{Y}^m_{t+1|t}$ for $m = 6, 7$. These linear models complete our basic benchmarks and we consider them sufficient for comparison purposes with the rest of the models we use in the sequel.

We next turn to nonlinear models, of which we have a threefold variety. First, we consider a delay threshold autoregression as in the following:

$$\begin{aligned} Y_t &= \phi_{1,0} + \phi_{1,\delta} Y_{t-\delta} + \sigma_1 u_t, \quad \text{if } Y_{t-\delta} \leq \tau \\ Y_t &= \phi_{2,0} + \phi_{2,\delta} Y_{t-\delta} + \sigma_2 u_t, \quad \text{if } Y_{t-\delta} > \tau \end{aligned} \tag{2}$$

where δ is set to either 1 or to d as computed previously and where the threshold τ is found by in-sample search on the percentiles of the threshold variable $Y_{t-\delta}$. This model provides us with the next forecasts $\widehat{Y}^m_{t+1|t}$ for $m = 8, 9$. Then, we consider an additive autoregressive model and a simple autoregressive neural network, both of which can be expressed in standard form as follows:

$$Y_t = \alpha + f(\boldsymbol{\beta}, Y_{t-1}) + u_t, \tag{3}$$

where $\boldsymbol{\beta}$ is a vector of the underlying smoothing or network parameters and where the difference between the two models is the way the nonlinear function $f(\boldsymbol{\beta}, Y_{t-1})$ is estimated. We opt for the simplest possible models of this form for several reasons, including the relatively small dependence structure of foreign exchange returns, computational expedience, and a desire to avoid data-mining and over-fitting. These two models provide us with forecasts $\widehat{Y}^m_{t+1|t}$ for $m = 10, 11$.

On the suggestion of the editor, we have added the constant elasticity of variance (GEV) forecast, whose form in discrete time is that of an error-correcting autoregression, and is by construction mean-reverting. Our notation follows Inglesias and Phillips (2019), a recent contribution to the exact estimation of the discretized version of the corresponding differential equation. Specifically, the continuous time stochastic differential equation is given by

$$dY(t) = -\kappa [Y(t) - \mu]\, dt + \sigma Y(t)^{\rho} dW(t), \tag{4}$$

where κ is the mean-reversion coefficient, μ is the long-term mean, and σ is the constant volatility; the elasticity is given by ρ and many different models in the literature are cases where ρ takes a particular value. The discretized solution to the above is given, for a sampling interval of τ, as follows:

$$Y_t = e^{-\tau\kappa} Y_{t-1} + \left(1 - e^{-\tau\kappa}\right)\mu + \varepsilon_t, \tag{5}$$

where ε_t are uncorrelated, heteroscedastic, normally distributed errors. It is clear from the above representation that we can write the above model as follows:

$$\Delta Y_t = -\left(1 - e^{-\tau\kappa}\right)\left(Y_t - \mu\right) + \varepsilon_t, \tag{6}$$

which is in the form of a mean-reverting, error-correcting autoregression. Since τ and κ are constant, there is no need for (purposes of forecasting) to estimate κ in detail but just to estimate the composite term $(1 - e^{-\tau\kappa})$ directly. This model provides us with forecast $\widehat{Y}^m_{t+1|t}$ for $m = 12$.

Finally, we turn to a set of models and an estimation approach of our own device, an approach that is based on sign-threshold nonlinearity and interaction terms nonlinearity, where we use sequential elimination of insignificant variables. This approach offers two specific advantages: simplicity of design and coherency on reduction. For the first set of these models that include sign threshold nonlinearity, we define as our explanatory variable the indicator function $X_t \overset{\text{def}}{=} I\left(Y_{t-d} \leq 0\right)$, i.e., the indicator of negative returns; for the interaction terms nonlinearity, we simply leave X_t as was defined previously in our linear models. Suppose that we consider a maximum lag structure of d^*; then we write the full model as follows:

$$Y_t = \alpha + \sum_{j=1}^{d^*} \phi_j Y_{t-j} + \sum_{s=1}^{d^*} \beta_s X_{t-j} + \sum_{j=1}^{d^*}\sum_{s=1}^{d^*} \gamma_{j,s} Y_{t-j} X_{t-s} + u_t \tag{7}$$

and note that this model nests many useful representations, including sign-based intercept shifts at multiple lags and direct interactions between our variables. It is interesting to note that the response of the dependent variable to a change in one of the lags of the explanatory variables contains a cumulative term of the lags of the dependent variable itself, i.e.:

$$\partial \mathsf{E}\left[Y_t|\mathcal{F}_{t-1}\right]/\partial X_{t-s} = \beta_s + \sum_{j=1}^{d^*} \gamma_{j,s} Y_{t-j}, \tag{8}$$

where $\mathcal{F}_{t-1}$ is the information set, and thus different lags of the explanatory variables have their own cumulative impact on the dependent variable based on the $\gamma_{j,s}$ estimates.

The parameters of such a model can be easily estimated by least squares, but for values greater than $d^* = 2$, their number increases rapidly and the corresponding significance falls. Thus, we perform a sequential model reduction as follows: first, we define a sequence of p-values such as $\alpha_q > \alpha_{q-1} > \ldots \alpha_1$ from larger to smaller and thus the significance becomes progressively tighter; second, we estimate the model and remove all variables that have p-values less than the significance level of that particular iteration; third, we continue until there are no significant variables left (and we revert to the estimates of the last useful iteration) or until the last level of significance has been reached. This is a simple yet very robust approach for model reduction that accounts correctly for the level of significance. We consider three values for $d^* = 1, 2, d$ and therefore we have six more additional forecasts (three per the indicator explanatory variable and three for the standard explanatory variable of the linear models), these forecasts are $\widehat{Y}^m_{t+1|t}$ for $m = 13, 14, 15, 16, 17, 18$.

We add two more forecasts to our list, the adaptive learning forecasts of Kyriazi *et al.* (2019); this is a recent, novel, and powerful method of learning from past forecast errors that has shown considerable empirical success on strong theoretical foundations. In our application, we use the same parametrizations on the adaptive learning approach as in the above paper, but we use only the top forecast

Table 1. Model/Forecast abbreviations and nomenclature.

Abbreviation	Model/Forecast description
Naive	No change forecast
Naive-D	Mean forecast
AR(1)	First-order autoregressive forecast
AR(AIC)	AIC-order selected autoregressive forecast
VAR(1)	First-order bivariate autoregressive forecast
VAR(AIC)	AIC-order selected bivariate autoregressive forecast
DLM(d)	Delay linear model forecast, global delay
DLM(d-loc)	Delay linear model forecast, local delay
TAR(1)	First-order, two-regime, threshold autoregressive forecast
TAR(d)	First-order, delay, two-regime threshold autoregressive forecast
AAR	Additive autoregressive forecast
NNET	Neural network autoregressive forecast
CEV	Constant elasticity of variance forecast
SDLM(d)	Sequential elimination forecast, sign-threshold, max order is d
IDLM(d)	Sequential elimination forecasts, standard, max order is d
ADL-NS	Adaptive learning forecast, no smoothing
ADL	Adaptive learning forecast, with smoothing

of the previous 18 ones for learning. This completes our list of all model/method forecasts we used in our analysis for a sum total of 20. Table 1 has our model nomenclature.

4. Data and Forecast Evaluation

As noted in our introduction, the dataset that we use is rather limited but, to some considerable extent, also very representative. As the euro is the leading currency that is traded with the U.S. dollar, most of the major currencies, fluctuations are related to the EUR/USD exchange rate fluctuations. Thus, we considered only the EUR/USD and the GBP/USD exchange rates in conducting our empirical exercise. Our data were obtained from the Federal Reserve Bank of St. Louis FRED database, at the daily frequency, and our analysis is conducted in the monthly frequency — the data range is from the beginning of 2000 until August of 2019. There are two major reasons for limiting ourselves to the monthly frequency: first, the apparent self-similarity of exchange rates, as many financial series that exhibit the same statistical characteristics at different sampling frequencies; second, at the monthly frequency we are able to construct simple yet theory-consistent and reliable realized volatility and correlation measures for the two series that we use. In particular, we estimate the realized monthly volatility and correlation by their standard formulas, first for the realized volatility as follows:

$$\mathrm{RV}_t^2(Y) \stackrel{\text{def}}{=} \sum_{j=1}^{q} \left(Y_{j,t} - \bar{Y}_{t,q}\right)^2, \tag{9}$$

where $Y_{j,t}$ denotes the jth day of month t and $\bar{Y}_{t,q}$ is the q-day sample mean for month t, and then for the realized correlation in a similar notation:

$$\mathrm{RC}_t(Y, X) \stackrel{\text{def}}{=} \left\{\sum_{j=1}^{q} \left(Y_{j,t} - \bar{Y}_{t,q}\right)\left(X_{j,t} - \bar{X}_{t,q}\right)\right\} / \left\{\mathrm{RV}_t(Y) RV_t(X)\right\}. \tag{10}$$

We use these two measures as part of experimentation on explanatory variables — we also consider annual rolling-window versions of volatility and correlation. All in all, we have collected results on the following explanatory variables: the monthly return of the GBP/USD, the realized volatilities of the EUR/USD and the GBP/USD, the realized correlation between the EUR/USD and the GBP/USD, and then the rolling-window volatilities and the rolling-window correlation, for a sum of seven explanatory variables. We present the levels of the two series of interest and their estimated realized correlation in Fig. 1; that the two series move together is apparent from the top panel and that they maintain a consistently positive correlation above 40% all the time is clear from the bottom panel. Note also that the volatility of the correlation has clearly increased after 2010 and that there are more frequent spikes toward smaller values of the correlation (and two large spikes in highly negative territory). All these salient features of the data are useful in explaining our forecasting results later on.

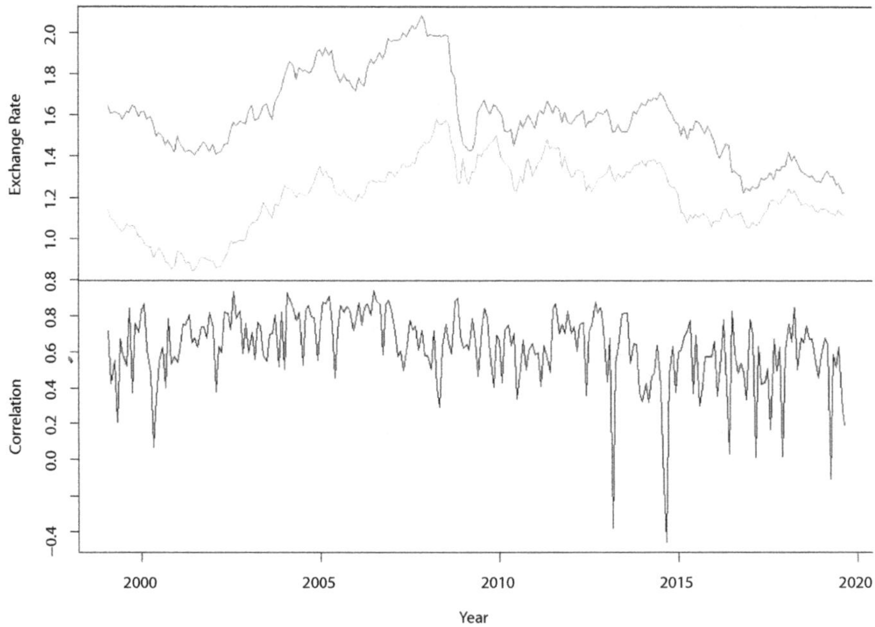

Fig. 1. EUR/USD (light gray) and GBP/USD (dark gray) monthly exchange rates and their realized correlation.

We followed a standard approach in preparing our forecasting performance results, via the generation of rolling-window forecasts on a rolling window of size n_0 and an evaluation window of size $n_1 = n - n_0$. We considered five rolling windows of $n_0 \stackrel{\text{def}}{=} \{60, 100, 120, 180, 200\}$ months with corresponding evaluation periods of $n_1 = \{176, 136, 116, 56, 36\}$ months. One additional advantage of the monthly data is that even the smaller evaluation period is long enough in economic terms, if not on observations. Our performance metrics are standard and not complicated, defined as relative to the naive forecast mean-squared and mean-absolute errors. It can be immediately seen that the mean-squared and mean-absolute errors of the naive forecast (with no drift) are, respectively:

$$\text{MSE}^0_{n_1} \stackrel{\text{def}}{=} n_1^{-1} \sum_{t=n_0+1}^{n} Y_t^2, \qquad \text{MAE}^0_{n_1} \stackrel{\text{def}}{=} n_1^{-1} \sum_{t=n_0+1}^{n} |Y_t| \tag{11}$$

and therefore our relative measures are seen to be given by

$$r\text{MSE}_{n_1}^{m,0} \stackrel{\text{def}}{=} \sum_{t=n_0}^{n} \left[\widehat{e}_{t+1|t}^{m}\right]^2 / \sum_{t=n_0+1}^{n} Y_t^2,$$

$$r\text{MAE}_{n_1}^{m,0} \stackrel{\text{def}}{=} \sum_{t=n_0}^{n} |\widehat{e}_{t+1|t}^{m}| / \sum_{t=n_0+1}^{n} |Y_t|, \tag{12}$$

where $\widehat{e}_{t+1|t}^{m}$ is the forecast error from the mth model.[1] To these global (full evaluation sample) measures, we add two rolling evaluation measures of length 12 and 24 months. Specifically, for each evaluation period, we re-compute the above relative measures over rolling windows of 12 and 24 months and then we compute the mean proportion of times that they were less than one, i.e.:

$$\text{MP}_{n_1-k}^{m,0} \stackrel{\text{def}}{=} (n_1 - k)^{-1} \sum_{t=n_0+k}^{n} \left(r\text{MSE}_k^{m,0} < 1\right) \tag{13}$$

for $k = 12, 24$ and where $r\text{MSE}_k^{m,0}$ is the k-window rolling relative MSE measure for forecast m. In this way, we can examine the time-varying predictability of our statistical measures — of considerable interest is knowing that it is very difficult to beat the naive benchmark for the kind of data that we use in our analysis.

To the above statistical evaluation measures, we add two simple economic performance measures, the sign success ratio (SSR) that measures directional accuracy of the forecasts and the total trading return (TR) obtained when one "invests" on the signs of the associated forecasts. To define these measures, consider first the variable $S_{t+1|t}^{m} \stackrel{\text{def}}{=} \mathsf{sign}\left(\widehat{Y}_{t+1|t}^{m}\right)$ which computes the sign of the forecast with respect to the current variable and then consider the variable $D_{t+1|t}^{m} \stackrel{\text{def}}{=} I\left[S_{t+1|t}^{m} = \mathsf{sign}\left(Y_{t+1}\right)\right]$ which computes whether the predicted sign was the same as the actual sign of the next

[1]The relative MSE measure is one version of Theil's Information Criterion, see the discussion in Section 5.3.

period's return. Then, we define the SSR and the TR measures as follows:

$$\begin{array}{lll} \text{SSR}^m_{n_1} & \stackrel{\text{def}}{=} & n_1^{-1} \sum_{t=n_0}^{n} D^m_{t+1|t} \\ \text{TR}^m_{n_1} & \stackrel{\text{def}}{=} & \sum_{t=n_0}^{n} S^m_{t+1|t} Y_{t+1} \end{array}. \tag{14}$$

We note that the use of financial performance measures is useful for various reasons, the least of which is a way of validating, on the one hand, the need and relevance of statistical evaluation measures and, on the other hand, the implications of sign predictability. We explore these issues at some greater depth in the discussion of our results that follow.

Finally, for part of our discussion on selected results, we estimate the following equation for the Mincer–Zarnowitz (MZ) regression:

$$\begin{array}{lll} Y_{t+1} & = & \delta_0 + \delta_1 \widehat{Y}^m_{t+1} + \eta^m_{t+1} \\ \widehat{e}^m_{t+1} & = & \delta_0 + (\delta_1 - 1)\widehat{Y}_{t+1} + \eta^m_{t+1} \end{array}, \tag{15}$$

that is, we regress the forecast error on the forecast and if forecast efficiency holds, then the joint hypothesis of $H_0^{E1} : \delta_0 = 0, \delta_1 = 1$ should hold. Note that for an unbiased forecast, we only need to look at whether $H_0^{E2} : \delta_1 = 1$ or not. We use least squares to obtain $(\widehat{\delta}_0, \widehat{\delta}_1)$, compute the standard errors from an HAC-based covariance matrix and then apply a standard F-type test on H_0^{E1} or a t-test on H_0^{E2}, the latter statistic adjusted by a suitable factor for the ratio of sample split to n_0 and n_1 observations. Standard F and normal critical values can be used for these tests. In the tables, we use t^* to indicate the p-value of the test of hypothesis H_0^{E2} and F^* to indicate the p-value of the test of hypothesis H_0^{E1}.

5. Discussion of Results

5.1. *Full-period results*

Our presentation of results will be, of necessity and in following with the title of the chapter, rather compact. We have performed all combinations of rolling windows and explanatory variables and the results are surprisingly clear: there appears to be rather strong evidence on statistical and financial (sign and total return) predictability for the EUR/USD that is both inherent in the series but also driven by the explanatory power of the returns of GBP/USD and the simplest of models, the linear delay model, across all rolling windows – the second best model usually is one of the sequential reduction models that we discussed at the end of the methodology section. We caution the reader that these are the best results available and that, especially for the larger estimation windows, other explanatory variables provide mean-squared error reductions against the naive benchmark but are nowhere as good as the results that are obtained by the use of the returns of the GBP/USD as an explanatory variable — these results are available from the authors on request.

We present our main results in five tables, one per rolling window. If any model has a mean-squared error less than one, then its performance is included in the table for all metrics; if there is a model that has a mean-squared error greater than one but is a top performer in any other of our four metrics, then it is also included in the table, again for all metrics; if a single model is best across all metrics, then we include the second best of each of the metrics as well. Each table has two panels, one for the explanatory variable in its levels and another one for the explanatory variable in its differences. We start off with an overview of our results and then we discuss each table for any particular characteristic.[2]

A casual glance at all tables shows that we have given the dominating position to the simple delay model, with global order selection — but note that as the sample size increases, the global delay and the local delay forecasts will coincide (this might be a suitable pointer to a recursive rather than a rolling exercise on the performance of the local delay model). The delay model forecasts are essentially all-around winners across most (if not all) metrics all the time, with the exception of the adaptive learning forecasts. This is a result that is,

[2]The reader should note that for Tables 2 through 4 we do not present the results from the adaptive learning forecasts because they are identical to the best model presented in terms of their characteristics; in Tables 5 and 6 where the sample is larger, we do present them; detailed results are available on request.

Table 2. Evaluation results for rolling-window of 60 months.

Model	rMSE	rMAE	MP_{12}	MP_{24}	SSR	TR
	X_t is returns of GBP/USD					
AAR	1.132	1.053	0.327	0.157	0.568	0.512
DLM(d)	0.978	1.021	0.582	0.614	0.517	0.699
IDLM(2)	1.377	1.059	0.339	0.261	0.545	0.711
	X_t is difference in returns of GBP/USD					
DLM(d)	0.961	1.010	0.628	0.671	0.606	1.060
IDLM(d)	1.596	1.145	0.372	0.178	0.583	0.628

one the one hand, particular to our series of the EUR/USD but, on the other hand, is a testimonial on the source of predictability that we find. That there is explanatory power in the use of our auxiliary series of the GBP/USD can be seen from the listings of the second best model, the sequential elimination based IDLM(d) or IDLM(d-loc) model and associated forecasts. Furthermore, we note that for this model, we frequently find sign and total return outperformance[3] with outright dismal performance in terms of statistical measures. Then, we can easily see from the tables that the presence of benchmarks is exceedingly sparse, with one appearance each for the AAR and TAR models and a double appearance of a VAR(1) model; the significance of this finding cannot be overstated (at least for practical purposes): our analysis shows that we can make good predictions with models that are as simple as the benchmarks, as computationally expedient as the benchmarks, but are better designed to capture the characteristics of the underlying series we analyze. Finally, as a general comment, we can see that there is a dichotomy when it comes to evaluating models with statistical criteria on variance and uncertainty and criteria on sign success and financial performance:

[3]The reader should note that for all model forecasts presented in the tables that follow we have the total return performance of all models always considerably greater than the total return performance of the buy & hold approach of just holding on to your euro (in fact, this excess total return ranges to levels from at least 5% to over a 100%; again, details are available on request).

the sign success ratio and the total return might be quite high even for models that have unacceptable mean-squared error performance.

Let us next look at the first table with the results of the rolling window of 60 months. Here it is not unexpected that only the global delay model can offer mean-squared error reductions; note that no model can beat the naive benchmark in terms of mean-absolute error reductions. However, it is instructive to start seeing, and noting for the discussion later, that the other models in this table provide us with either SSR performance or TR performance; for example, on the top panel of the table where the returns are used for the GBP/USD, we find that the additive autoregressive model AAR has an SSR of 57% vs that of 52% of the delay model and the sequential elimination forecast has an SSR of 54.5%. So, what makes a difference here? In this particular instance of analysis, we see that the statistical significance of the delay model provides obviously more overall performance than the other two models — it pays to "invest", so to speak, in a low mean-squared error forecast. Furthermore, note that when we take the difference in the returns of the GBP/USD as our explanatory variable, the overall performance of the delay model rises considerably: we have a marginal reduction in the mean-squared and the mean-absolute error, we have a considerable rise in the sign success ratio and a 50% improvement in total return — the use of differences in returns as explanatory variables is not common, but there is no conceptual barrier on implementing them in empirical applications, and as we will see in the following, they should definitely be considered.

Going to the second table of our results, Table 3 with the rolling window of 100 months, things start getting better. The reason is that not only do we see a re-enforcement of the results in Table 2 but now the delay model with local delay estimation appears as well. In fact, it appears only when we use the difference in returns of the GBP/USD as an explanatory variable and in this case this is a completely real-time feasible forecast along with the sequential elimination forecast of the last line in the second panel for the table. What are the things that should be noted here? First, results on overall performance appear to strengthen when differences in returns

Table 3. Evaluation results for rolling-window of 100 months.

Model	rMSE	rMAE	MP_{12}	MP_{24}	SSR	TR
			X_t is returns of GBP/USD			
DLM(d)	0.942	0.989	0.704	0.752	0.500	0.460
IDLM(2)	1.430	1.080	0.256	0.150	0.566	0.209
IDLM(d)	1.809	1.210	0.296	0.230	0.500	0.473
			X_t is difference in returns of GBP/USD			
DLM(d)	0.953	0.996	0.637	0.661	0.607	0.932
DLM(d-loc)	0.982	1.028	0.581	0.598	0.578	0.680
IDLM(d)	1.127	1.086	0.371	0.286	0.563	0.848

are used and that this explanatory variable goes well into our delay model forecasts and our sequential elimination forecast; second, note that both the SSR and the TR measures rise considerably in this case, and for the IDLM(d) model forecast, we see a reduction on the statistical measures of evaluation (that remain, however, still higher than one). It is also instructive to note that the rolling-window measures MP_k indicate that (and that was the case in our Table 1 too) about 60% of the time the delay forecasts were better (in a mean-squared error sense) than the naive benchmark — the percentage is higher in the first panel of the table. The implication for practical implementations is quite transparent: don't judge your models (or abandon them) based on full-sample performance alone; predictability is time-varying and although we cannot always beat the naive forecast, there will be stretches of time when we will certainly do so.

For the remaining three tables, our results become even more consistent and highly relevant in practical terms. In Tables 4–6, we see that the results from the global and local delay models converge and coincide in the end, we see that the differences in terms of sign success and total return performance also converge and that we now have more models with improved statistical performance, including a boost from adaptive learning on the last two rolling-windows of 180 and 200 months. In Table 4, we see the first case of increasing proximity between the global and local delay models, in essentially all their metrics, and we continue to see that the performance is

Table 4. Evaluation results for rolling window of 120 months.

Model	rMSE	rMAE	MP_{12}	MP_{24}	SSR	TR
	X_t is returns of GBP/USD					
DLM(d)	0.951	0.997	0.657	0.602	0.500	0.300
DLM(d-loc)	0.966	1.002	0.648	0.602	0.500	0.300
IDLM(d)	1.193	1.095	0.257	0.247	0.517	0.283
	X_t is difference in returns of GBP/USD					
DLM(d)	0.940	1.007	0.615	0.587	0.583	0.812
DLM(d-loc)	0.956	1.025	0.615	0.587	0.557	0.658

Table 5. Evaluation results for rolling-window of 180 months.

Model	rMSE	rMAE	MP_{12}	MP_{24}	SSR	TR
	X_t is returns of GBP/USD					
DLM(d)	0.893	0.951	0.844	0.879	0.589	0.385
DLM(d-loc)	0.893	0.951	0.844	0.879	0.589	0.385
IDLM(2)	0.958	0.985	0.578	0.909	0.589	0.349
VAR(1)	0.992	0.991	0.578	0.576	0.625	0.252
	X_t is difference in returns of GBP/USD					
DLM(d)	0.926	0.983	0.773	0.906	0.636	0.337
DLM(d-loc)	0.926	0.983	0.773	0.906	0.636	0.337
IDLM(1)	0.958	0.978	0.659	0.656	0.673	0.369
ADL	0.913	0.978	0.818	0.938	0.636	0.337
VAR(1)	0.951	0.963	0.705	0.969	0.691	0.336

higher when we consider the differences in returns of the GBP/USD as before. It is also the case, as in previous tables, that the sequential reduction model selected in the top panel of the table has comparable sign and total return performance with the delay models.

In Table 5, with the rolling-window of 180 months, we have the first appearance of the adaptive learning superior performance and also the presence of the the first-order bivariate autoregression. The performance of the global and the local delay models is identical and here we see that this performance is better for the top panel rather than the bottom one of the table, for the statistical measures and total return, but it is reversed for the sign success ratio. It is

Table 6. Evaluation results for rolling-window of 200 months.

Model	rMSE	rMAE	MP_{12}	MP_{24}	SSR	TR
			X_t is returns of GBP/USD			
DLM(d)	0.853	0.917	0.680	0.692	0.556	0.147
DLM(d-loc)	0.853	0.917	0.680	0.692	0.556	0.147
IDLM(2)	0.974	1.002	0.600	0.769	0.583	0.227
IDLM(d)	0.851	0.918	0.680	0.692	0.556	0.171
ADL-NS	0.825	0.904	0.720	0.769	0.500	0.116
			X_t is difference in returns of GBP/USD			
DLM(d)	0.960	1.005	0.625	0.750	0.629	0.190
DLM(d-loc)	0.960	1.005	0.625	0.750	0.629	0.190
IDLM(1)	0.968	0.967	0.792	1.000	0.571	0.147
TAR(d)	0.981	0.998	0.708	0.917	0.600	0.160
ADL	0.913	0.967	0.625	0.833	0.600	0.080

useful to note that the total return performance is very close across models, especially for the bottom panel of the table and although the bivariate autoregression has a higher sign success ratio than the other forecasts.

Looking at the last of our tables, Table 6 with the rolling window of 200 months, we can see that here the dominance of the delay models (again, global and local are identical) is even more pronounced. Note that the adaptive learning forecast improves in all statistical measures but not on the sign success ratio and not on total return; this is a new finding for the adaptive learning approach which we have not encountered before and deserves further investigation — it corroborates, however, our earlier claim that statistical and financial performance may not always be fully compatible. We also note that there is now close proximity between the delay models and the sequential reduction models and, in fact, for the top panel of the table the sequential reduction models give superior sign success and total return performance. This last table showcases very strong predictability and, although has the smallest evaluation window, clearly supports well all our previous results.

The issue of predictability relates to the ability of models to capture the variability of their corresponding dependent variable (for

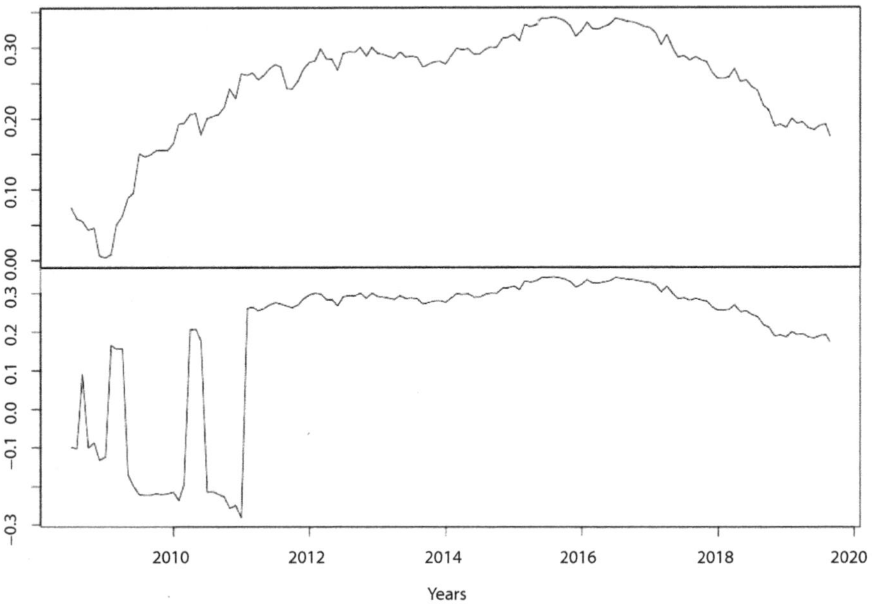

Fig. 2. Rolling estimates of slope $\widehat{\beta}$ from delay models (global on top, local at the bottom).

accurate statistical evaluation) and the sign of the forecast (for accurate financial performance evaluation). We examine more closely how these two aspects are related by presenting some visuals and casual evidence from two-rolling windows, the rolling-window of 100 months and the one for 200 months.[4] For the first rolling-window, we use only the results from the bottom panel of Table 3, while for the second rolling-window we use the results from the top panel of Table 6.

We start off with Fig. 2, which has the rolling slope estimates from the two delay models (global on top panel). We can see the differences in smoothing at the beginning of the period and up until 2011, while after that date note that the local delay model slope stabilizes at around 0.2–0.3, with a gradual decrease in both models after 2017. The associated R^2's from these predictive regressions are

[4]Similar results are available for all forecasts and rolling-windows, on request.

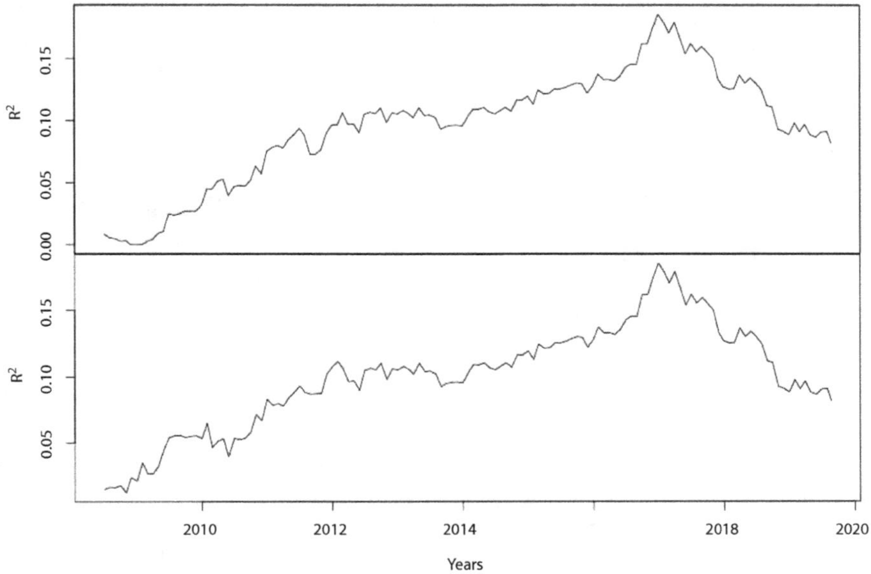

Fig. 3. Rolling estimates of R^2 from delay models (global on top, local at the bottom).

shown in Fig. 3 where it is very clear that the predictive power of the model was steadily rising up to about 2017 and steadily falling thereafter — which conforms of course to the falling estimates of Fig. 1. Compare these R^2's from the delay model to the corresponding R^2 from the sequential elimination model in the bottom panel of Table 3. We remind the reader that the model did not have good statistical evaluation measures but had good sign success ratio and total return. We see in Fig. 4 that, with much higher variability, the predictive power of that model rises steadily over all years and its value is clearly higher than that of the delay models, and note that because of the sequential elimination procedure we are assured that the coefficient estimates are indeed significant. Thus, predictability is reflected in many ways, not just with mean-squared or mean-absolute errors, and these figures are a very illustrative examples.

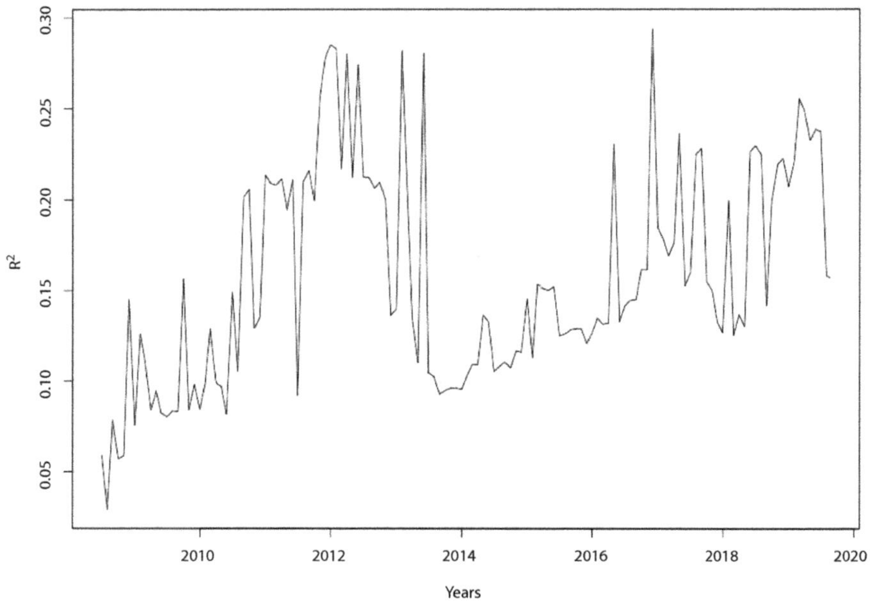

Fig. 4. Rolling estimates of R^2 from sequential elimination model.

To further investigate the issue of predictability measurement, we estimate the standard MZ regression as in for these three models, and concentrate our results on Table 7. We can easily see there that only the global delay model passes the efficiency tests of the MZ regressions, while the local model struggles at levels of significance between 1% and 10% and the sequential elimination model fails completely. However, on Table 3, we remind that this last model not only did have good sign success ratio but also had the second largest total return after the global delay model.

We can tell a similar story from the analysis of the best models in the top panel of Table 6, for the rolling-window of 200 months. Figs. 5–7 repeat the same plots as for the 100 months rolling-window and we can see, starting from Fig. 5, that the strength of association between the variables strengthens and becomes progressively more

Table 7. Mincer–Zarnowitz regressions for models of rolling-window of 100 months.

	X_t is difference in returns of GBP/USD			
	$\widehat{\delta}_0$	$\widehat{\delta}_1$	t^*	F^*
DLM(d)	−0.003	0.706	0.117	0.151
DLM(d-loc)	−0.00	0.583	0.031	0.071
IDLM(d)	−0.002	0.201	0.000	0.000

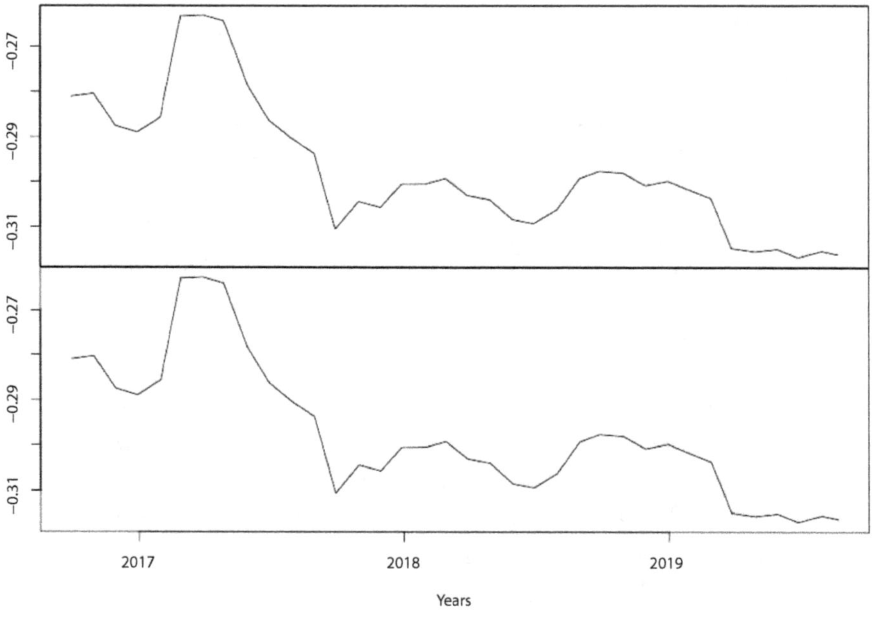

Fig. 5. Rolling estimates of slope $\widehat{\beta}$ from delay models (global on top, local at the bottom).

negative. This is in line with Fig. 2 where after 2017 the slope estimates started decreasing and now, with the larger rolling window, they actually become negative. The results should not be surprising as it is well understood that we live in a world where data exhibit frequent structural breaks and here we have one more manifestation of it.

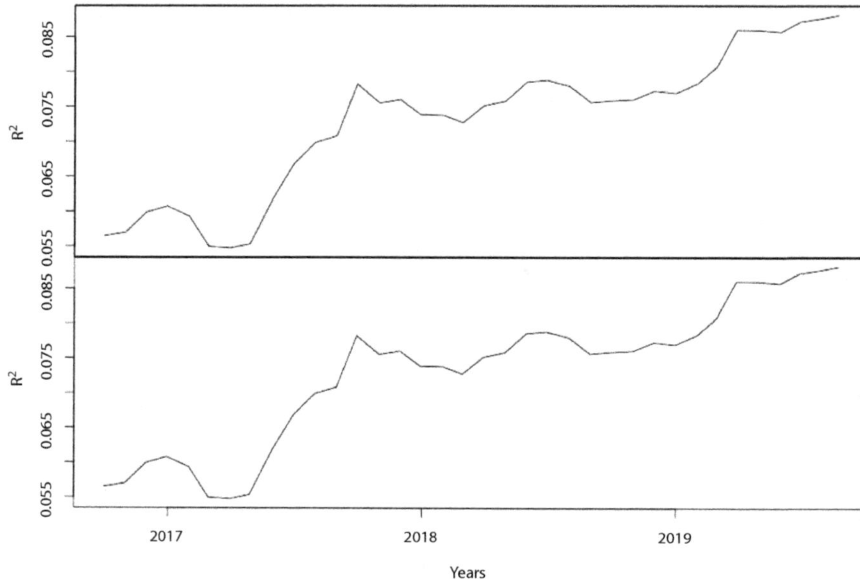

Fig. 6. Rolling estimates of R^2 from delay models (global on top, local at the bottom).

Looking next at Fig. 6, we can see the steady rise of the R^2 from the delay models — the magnitudes are small, but the implications for modeling are substantial, as in terms of statistical performance these delay models are the best for this case but are not the best in either the sign success ratio or in total return: the best model is one of the sequential elimination models, which we discuss next. Here we can only ask a question, as on the top panel of Fig. 7, we see that the best model in terms of sign success and total return in Table 6, i.e., IDLM(2), has declining (practically zero) predictability while the second best model in terms of sign success ratio and total return, i.e., IDLM(d), has increasing predictability — as this is measured by R^2.

In fact, re-doing the same analysis as in Table 7 with the estimates and tests of the MZ-regression for these four models, we can see in Table 8 that, while all of them easily pass the tests, only 3 out of 4

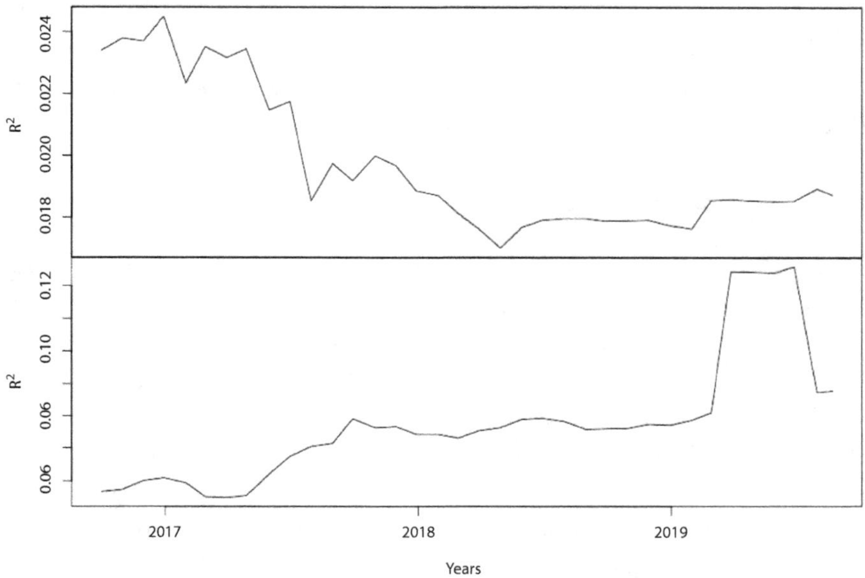

Fig. 7. Rolling estimates of R^2 from sequential elimination models, IDLM(2) on top and IDLM(d) at the bottom.

Table 8. Mincer–Zarnowitz regressions for models of rolling-window of 200 months.

	X_t is returns of GBP/USD			
	$\widehat{\delta}_0$	$\widehat{\delta}_1$	t^*	F^*
DLM(d)	−0.001	0.900	0.678	0.774
DLM(d-loc)	−0.001	0.900	0.678	0.774
IDLM(2)	0.000	1.873	0.563	0.843
IDLM(d)	−0.0005	0.890	0.652	0.852

(and not the IDLM(2) one) have slope estimates of the MZ regression that are close to one. There is clearly too much variability here to have even a slope estimate of 1.873 being statistically equal to one, but there is one more thing to note here: the intercept estimate for the IDLM(2) model is one order of magnitude (one decimal place) smaller than the estimates of the other three models; this is a sign that the forecasts produced from this model are better "centered" than the other models and possibly this leads to better sign performance and thus better total return performance.

5.2. *Sub-periods results*

The seasoned reader would, probably, not be entirely satisfied in the "ye shall find" statement of our title — yet! For one thing, one does not expect the same model(s) to generate out-performance across all time periods and sample sizes; for another, the subtleties of using volatility series as explanatory variables probably cannot be understood in the full-sample models — and it cannot be that there is strength in volatility and correlation (as we noted at the beginning of the previous section, such explanatory variables do produce performance enhancements over the naíve benchmark that are just not as large as the ones obtained by the use of the returns of the pound as explanatory variable). Thus, in this section, we perform a sub-period analysis where we split the sample in three: the 2000–2006 period, the 2007–2012 period, and the 2013–2019 period. Given that we are considering monthly forecasts, it is clear that the number of evaluation observations will not be large — even for the smallest rolling-window of 60 months — but that's not necessarily a bad thing: in real-life if you started forecasting at the beginning of these sample splits, that's what you would have available.

What is the gist of the results to be presented? First, we do continue to find strong evidence per our "ye shall find it" statement; second, DLM-type and I(S)DLM(p)-type models continue to perform very well; third, realized correlation between the euro and the pound now becomes a significant explanatory variable; and, fourth, we have the more dense appearance of the benchmark models (AR, VAR, and CEV) and in one occasion the appearance of a nonlinear model (NNET). Thus, the sub-period analysis indicates that our small army of models has considerable scope if used in unison. We turn to our detailed results next.

Table 9. Evaluation results for rolling-window of 60 months, period is 2000–2006.

Model	rMSE	rMAE	MP_{12}	MP_{24}	SSR	TR
	X_t is returns of GBP/USD					
IDLM(2)	0.961	0.981	1.000	1.000	0.583	0.189
ADL-NS	0.970	0.989	0.923	1.000	0.542	0.100
	X_t is difference in returns of GBP/USD					
VAR(1)	0.982	1.073	0.833	n.a.	0.435	0.062
SDLM(2)	0.905	1.010	1.000	n.a.	0.522	0.133
ADL-NS	0.859	0.969	1.000	n.a.	0.522	0.133

First, in Table 9, we have the collected results for the best performing models of the period 2000–2006. As before, we see that both the returns and the differences of the returns of the pound produce results that are significant vis-a-vis the benchmark. The sequential elimination models, IDLM(2) and SDLM(2), appear in both panels of the table as does the adaptive learning forecast, which is the best performer overall. We also see that the VAR(1) model enters here but has the worst performance among all of the top models that out-perform the benchmark. We also note that the more robust performance across all metrics has the IDLM(2) model on the top panel: has statistical and directional/economic metrics that essentially put it at the top of all five models (low mean-squared and mean-absolute forecast errors and the highest sign success ratio and total return). Of course, the adaptive learning forecast has considerably better performance statistically (not surprisingly, it was designed to do so) but at a cost of some reductions in the sign success ratio and the total trading return.

The results for the period 2007–2012 appear in Table 10. Since the evaluation period is now smaller, it becomes more difficult for the models to beat the benchmark, but still we can obtain performance enhancements. In this table, we have only realized volatility and realized correlation as explanatory variables — it appears that in this period the potential driving factors were not the returns of the pound but its volatility and correlation. We find again that the VAR(1)

Table 10. Evaluation results for rolling-window of 60 months, period is 2007–2012.

Model	rMSE	rMAE	MP_{12}	MP_{24}	SSR	TR
	X_t is realized volatility of GBP/USD					
DLM(d-loc)	0.971	0.968	1.000	n.a.	0.667	0.078
	X_t is realized correlation of EUR/USD and GBP/USD					
CEV	0.985	0.978	1.000	n.a.	0.667	$0.016^{b\&h}$
	X_t is difference in realized correlation of EUR/USD and GBP/USD					
VAR(1)	0.924	0.924	n.a.	n.a.	0.455	0.062
IDLM(1)	0.925	0.925	n.a.	n.a.	0.545	0.077

benchmark model enters as the top model (in fact has the best statistical performance, with the sequential elimination IDLM(1) model being the second best), while the delay DLM(d) model with local delay selection has the best sign success ratio and the highest trading return, with the IDLM(1) model being second best in trading return. For this period, we find that the CEV model enters as one that beats the naíve benchmark — albeit is the worst performer among the models in the table in all respects except its sign success ratio that matches that of the delay model.

The results for the last sub-period we examine for 2013–2019 are by far the most interesting ones for this section, all given in Table 11. Here we have for the only time the appearance of the naíve model with drift, the second nonlinear model (NNET), and also again the CEV model and the VAR(1) appear from the benchmarks. Still, the best overall performers are the delay and sequential elimination models, as before. We have three panels in the table, where we use (as in the full sample) the returns of the pound and their differences and also one additional panel where we are using the difference in realized correlation as explanatory variables.

The distinctive features of the results are as follows. First, in terms of statistical performance, the top models are the VAR(1) and the adaptive learning forecast when the explanatory variable is the

Table 11. Evaluation results for rolling-window of 60 months, period is 2013–2019.

Model	rMSE	rMAE	MP_{12}	MP_{24}	SSR	TR
	X_t is returns of GBP/USD					
Naive-D	0.967	0.999	1.000	n.a.	0.600	0.075
VAR(1)	0.899	0.918	1.000	n.a.	0.700	0.093
DLM(d)	0.934	0.976	1.000	n.a.	0.600	0.083
DLM(d-loc)	0.934	0.976	1.000	n.a.	0.600	0.083
NNET	0.981	1.013	0.333	n.a.	0.600	0.056
IDLM(d)	0.970	1.011	1.000	n.a.	0.550	0.032
CEV	0.952	0.984	1.000	n.a.	0.600	0.075
ADL-NS	0.883	0.951	1.000	n.a.	0.600	0.054
	X_t is difference in returns of GBP/USD					
Naive-D	0.931	0.992	1.000	n.a. 0.632	0.109	
AR(AIC)	0.956	0.987	1.000	n.a.	0.632	0.077
VAR(1)	0.875	0.942	0.750	n.a.	0.579	0.070
DLM(d)	0.894	0.945	1.000	n.a.	0.632	0.012
DLM(d-loc)	0.894	0.945	1.000	n.a.	0.632	0.012
IDLM(1)	0.916	0.940	0.500	n.a.	0.632	0.074
IDLM(d)	0.739	0.764	1.000	n.a.	0.632	0.072
CEV	0.897	0.969	1.000	n.a.	0.632	0.109
	X_t is difference in realized correlation of EUR/USD and GBP/USD					
DLM(d)	0.772	0.914	1.000	n.a.	0.632	0.110
DLM(d-loc)	0.842	0.997	0.625	n.a.	0.684	0.101
IDLM(d)	0.924	1.012	1.000	n.a.	0.421	0.074
SDLM(d)	0.924	1.012	1.000	n.a.	0.421	0.074

returns of the pound, the VAR(1) and the sequential elimination IDLM(d) model when the explanatory variable is the difference in returns, and the delay DLM(d) model when the explanatory variable is the difference in realized volatility. Before proceeding with our discussion, it is useful to see a "zoom-in" of the data for this period, in Fig. 8. This is a period of protracted euro and pound devaluation and is characterized by a stable downward trend — thus, many models pick this trend up and perform well.

In terms of the models' performance on their sign success ratio and the total trading returns, we see that, one the one hand, most models

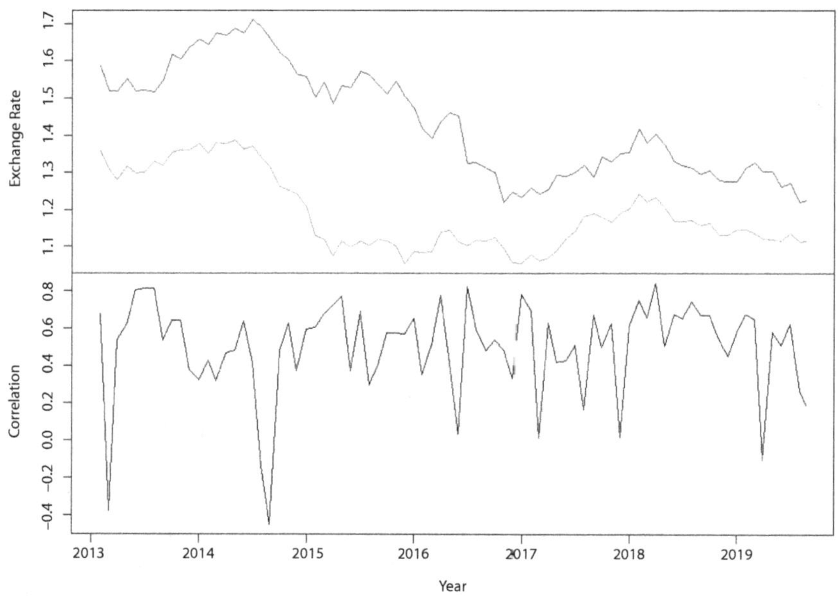

Fig. 8. EUR/USD (light gray) and GBP/USD (dark gray) monthly exchange rate and their realized correlation, 2013–2019.

have similar sign success ratios and, on the other hand, the top four performers are (in descending order) the DLM(d) and DLM(d-loc) models when the explanatory variable is the difference in realized correlation, the CEV model when the explanatory variable is the difference in returns, and the VAR(1) model when the explanatory variable is the returns of the pound. The most robust performance overall is by the sequential elimination IDLM(d) model in the second panel of the table, when the explanatory variable is the difference in returns of the pound. We took the best model for each panel of Table 11 and run the MZ-regressions as before, summarizing our results in Table 12: all models pass the test statistics with considerably high p-values, however, only the IDLM(d) model has the most reasonable (and close to 1) estimate compared to the other two top-performing models. It is important to note that there is no table where at least one of the sequential elimination models does not appear as one of the top performers.

Table 12. Mincer–Zarnowitz regressions for models of rolling-window of 60 months, 2013–2019.

	X_t is difference in returns of GBP/USD			
	$\widehat{\delta}_0$	$\widehat{\delta}_1$	t^*	F^*
VAR(1)	−0.004	0.593	0.552	0.453
IDLM(d)	−0.005	0.940	0.815	0.200
DLM(d)	−0.004	0.510	0.213	0.311

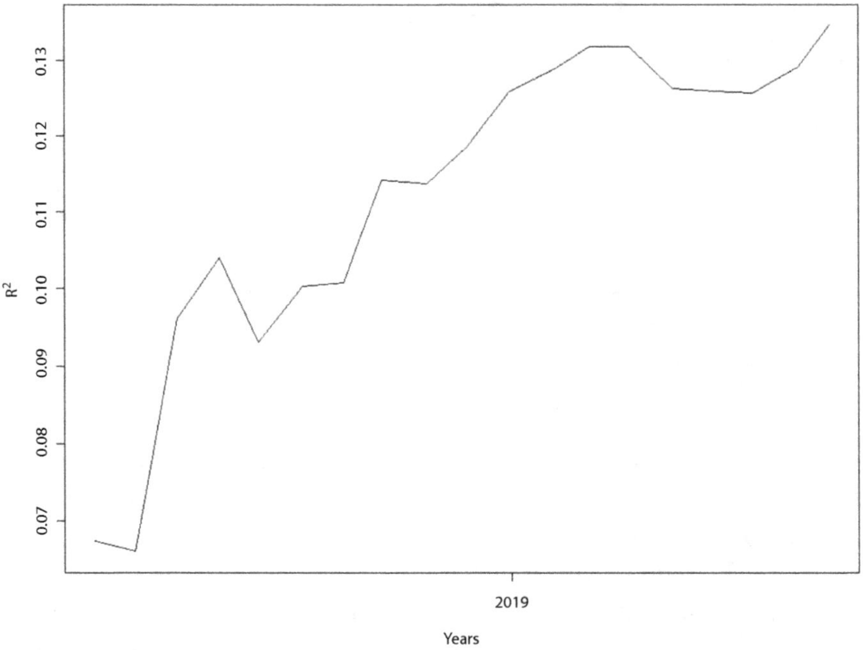

Fig. 9. Rolling estimate of R^2 from VAR(1) model.

It is interesting to see, for this last set of top performing models, and in continuation of the predictability analysis of the full-sample results, the rolling estimates of R^2's. We present them in three figures, Figs. 9–11, with the models appearing in the same order as in Table 12 that holds the MZ-regression results. There are two issues to

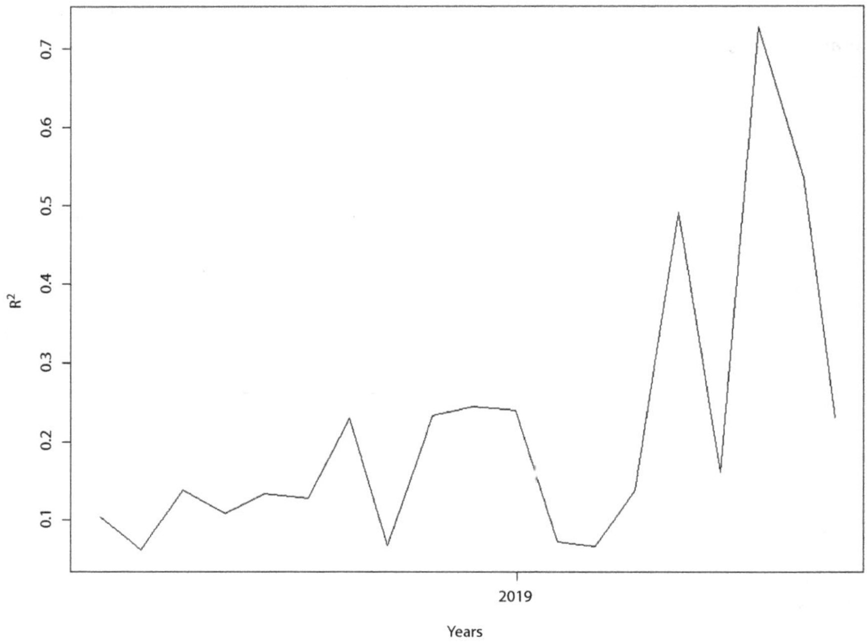

Fig. 10. Rolling estimate of R^2 from IDLM(d) model.

consider here, the magnitude of the R^2 and its direction. In Fig. 9, we have the rising R^2 of the VAR(1) model; even if its overall magnitude is small, we see that there is almost a doubling of its value from about less than 7% to almost 14% at the end of the evaluation period — and this rise is steady. For the best performing model, the IDLM(d), we have an R^2 that is between 10% and 20% up to 2019, and then the R^2 explodes with high volatility to 40% and then to 70% before dropping again to about 20%. The last model, the delay DLM(d) model, has the similar magnitude with the VAR(1) model (not surprisingly, they are essentially the same equation, but the lagged value of the explanatory variable is not on the same lag) and has also a rising trend from the whole of 2019 with some volatility as the IDLM(d) model. The VAR(1) model shows the most stable predictability, while the IDLM(d) model shows the highest predictability — and it is the

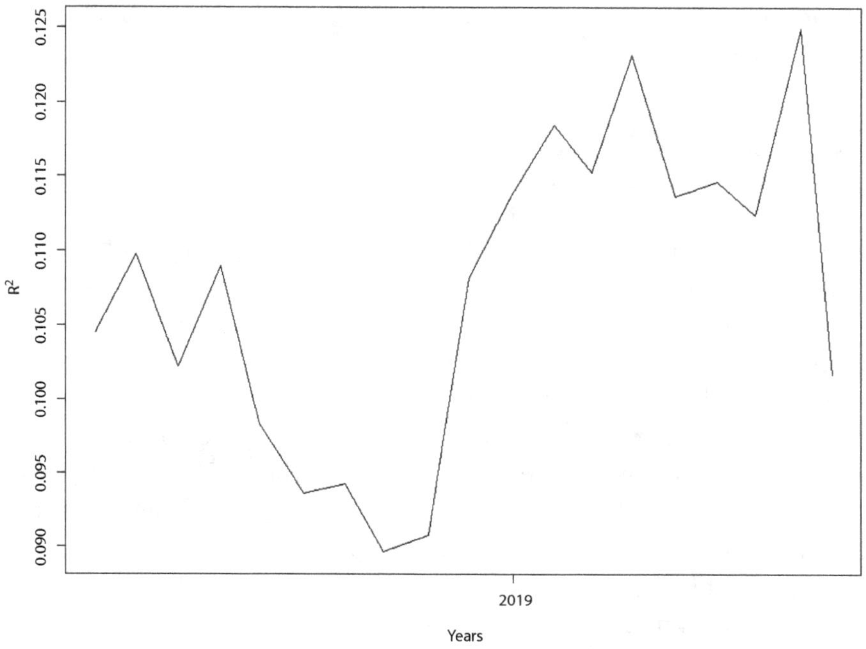

Fig. 11. Rolling estimate of R^2 from delay model.

IDLM(d) model that in terms of statistical performance dominates all else.

5.3. *Evaluation measures and scaling*

The evaluation measures of Eq. (12) are proper as they are relative to the benchmark naíve model. They do account for scaling issues, but scaling is itself a relative construct; in fact, *the relative MSE of equation (12) is one version of Theil's Information Criterion (TIC), the appropriate one based on the use of log-differences as the primary unit of measurement*; the other TIC version is that which involves a percent change evaluation of the naíve forecast — more suitable for evaluating forecasts generated in levels and not in differences.

However, there is no reason that it cannot adapt the latter version to the current context as follows:

$$r\mathrm{TIC}_{n_1}^{m,0} \stackrel{\mathrm{def}}{=} \sum_{t=n_0}^{n} \left[[\widehat{e}_{t+1|t}^{m} \big/ Y_{t-1}]^2 \Big/ \sum_{t=n_0+1}^{n} [Y_t/Y_{t-1}]^2 \right], \qquad (16)$$

which essentially evaluates the MSE relative to magnitude of the last observed value — however, the denominator of this measure has a double-differencing involved. Be that as it may, we are interested in seeing whether there are differences in model rankings by the use of the $r\mathrm{TIC}_{n_1}^{m,0}$ vs the $r\mathrm{MSE}_{n_1}^{m,0}$ that we used before, i.e., differences between the two versions of the TIC. In Tables 13 and 14, we summarize this comparison, where we include both the $r\mathrm{TIC}_{n_1}^{m,0}$ measure of Eq. (16) and the $r\mathrm{MSE}_{n_1}^{m,0}$ evaluations for all models that appeared in our tables before; in Table 13, we present the comparison with the full-sample results, while in Table 14 we present the comparison with the sub-samples results (models appearing twice in the original tables, such as DLM(d) and DLM(d-loc), with identical performance appearing only once in the following). We use a dashed line to separate the models per replicated table, with each section corresponding to a different explanatory variable.

A casual glance at both tables reveals three main results: first, the relative rankings produced by the rMSE and the rTIC, both measures of the same kind, do not change substantially; second, the models that have shown greater rMSE performance in the previous tables, such as DLM(d), and the IDLM(d), continue to dominate the rTIC rankings sometimes to a large extent, third, the values of the rTIC are mostly lower for models that use as explanatory variables differences of the corresponding X_t variable.

The full-sample results in Table 13 have some particular points of interest which we cover next. For the first three panels, corresponding to Tables 2–4, we can clearly see that the top rMSE models are also the top rTIC ones and for the panels of Tables 3 and 4, we note that the rTIC results for DLM(d-loc) are on par or better than the rTIC results for DLM(d): this is a result of practical significance as the DLM(d-loc) model is the one that obtains the more realistic

Table 13. Comparison between relative MSE and relative TIC, full-sample results.

Model	Evaluation by rMSE	Evaluation by rTIC
	Results from Table 2, all models	
AAR	1.132	0.966
DLM(d)	0.978	0.854
IDLM(2)	1.377	0.928
DLM(d)	0.961	0.884
IDLM(d)	1.596	2.277
	Results from Table 3, all models	
DLM(d)	0.942	0.801
IDLM(2)	1.430	1.043
IDLM(d)	1.809	2.884
DLM(d)	0.953	0.853
DLM(d-loc)	0.982	0.786
IDLM(d)	1.127	0.987
	Results from Table 4, all models	
DLM(d)	0.951	0.947
DLM(d-loc)	0.966	0.948
IDLM(d)	1.193	1.221
DLM(d)	0.940	0.831
DLM(d-loc)	0.956	0.823
	Results from Table 5, all models	
DLM(d)	0.893	1.008
IDLM(2)	0.958	1.358
VAR(1)	0.992	0.831
DLM(d)	0.926	0.647
IDLM(1)	0.958	0.992
IDLM(d)	0.951	0.709
	Results from Table 6, all models	
DLM(d)	0.853	1.311
IDLM(2)	0.974	1.389
IDLM(d)	0.851	1.233
DLM(d)	0.960	0.795
IDLM(1)	0.968	0.807
TAR(d)	0.981	1.777

Table 14. Comparison between relative MSE and relative TIC, sub-period results.

Model	Evaluation by rMSE	Evaluation by rTIC
	Results from Table 9, all models	
IDLM(2)	0.961	0.966
VAR(1)	0.981	0.878
SDLM(2)	0.905	0.827
	Results from Table 10, all models	
DLM(d-loc)	0.971	0.803
CEV	0.985	1.000
VAR(1)	0.924	0.872
IDLM(1)	0.925	0.818
	Results from Table 11, all models	
Naive-D	0.967	0.564
VAR(1)	0.899	0.603
DLM(d)	0.934	0.497
NNET	0.981	1.317
IDLM(d)	0.970	0.603
CEV	0.952	0.512
Naive-D	0.931	0.561
AR(AIC)	0.956	0.561
VAR(1)	0.875	0.648
DLM(d)	0.894	0.247
IDLM(1)	0.916	0.401
IDLM(d)	0.739	0.335
CEV	0.897	0.514
DLM(d)	0.772	0.495
DLM(d-loc)	0.842	0.731
IDLM(d)	0.924	1.382

value for the delay. For the last two panels that correspond to Tables 5 and 6, we see that the rTIC values for the models using plain GBP/USD returns as their explanatory variables are greater than one — these instances are in contrast to the previous three panels of the table. However, the rTIC results for the use of difference in returns of GBP/USD as explanatory variable are strikingly good and re-enforce the good results discussed just previously for the first three panels of Tables 2–4.

The results for the sub-periods in Table 14 appear even better. Here too there are some particular points of interest, especially for the DLM(d) and IDLM(d) model classes. For the first two panels, corresponding to Tables 9 and 10, the relative rankings are approximately similar for rMSE and rTIC, with two notable exceptions, the VAR(1) model (last in rMSE but second in rTIC) in the panel of Table 9, and the DLM(d-loc) model (next to last in rMSE but first in rTIC) in the panel of Table 10 — but note that the DLM(d-loc) rTIC value is very close to the corresponding rTIC value for the IDLM(1) model that ranks top with the rMSE criterion — again the result is that these models we suggested are consistently top performers in both evaluation measures. The same conclusions can be reached when we look at the last panel of the table that has the models from Table 11, among the first set of models, the top rMSE performer is the DLM(d) model, which has also the lowest, by far, value of the rTIC criterion (followed by the same ranking order of the CEV model); in the second set of models, the same qualitative result appears: here, the IDLM(d) model has the lowest rMSE value and the second lowest rTIC value, whereas the DLM(d) model has the third lowest rMSE value but the lowest, by far, value for the rTIC — note that the VAR(1) model that has the second lowest rMSE value ranks last in the rTIC criterion; finally, in the third set of models, the relative ranking of the rMSE and the rTIC criteria remains the same with the DLM(d) and DLM(d-loc), models dominating in terms of rTIC values.

The overall message from the results in Tables 13 and 14 is that, unsurprisingly, the scaling matters in evaluation of consistent model performance: many models can have competitive values on their evaluation measures (meaning considerably less than one compared to the benchmark), but not all models maintain their ranking position based on the two versions of the TIC. Our proposed set of models, of the DLM(d) and IDLM(d) variety, and the use of delay selection and sequential elimination show considerable model consistency and robustness in the use of different performance evaluation measures — and this result suggests that an honest assessment of model rankings (but also a clearer understanding of how these rankings change over time) cannot be made without the aid of both the rMSE and the rTIC measures.

5.4. *What have we learned?*

Our analysis showcases a number of interesting (old and new) features on exchange rate predictability and, could not be otherwise, comes with certain caveats. We discuss these in turn and with the understanding that they are conditional to our experimental specifications, such as rolling-window choice.

The first result refers to parsimonious modeling, as it was illustrated by the almost complete presence across rolling windows and time periods of the simple delay model. The choice of the explanatory variable in this setting is probably more important than the model itself and, furthermore, different explanatory variables and their transformations cannot possibly be dismissed on some *a priori* grounds — they need to be tested empirically. The second result, that relates to the first, is that there can be performance enhancements to predictability by the use of differences in the explanatory variable — much like the advantages that appear when we model and forecast a time series in differences vs its levels, like in the ARIMA framework. This result, possibly a bit surprising since the variables are already (log-)differenced, might be due to the fact that such additional differencing removes/reduces the natural outliers that occur in financial returns and is akin to some form of "acceleration" in the price series. In any event, and because we have found that such differencing is also useful when the explanatory variables are the realized volatility or the realized correlation, this is something that is of practical interest and should be further considered in modeling.

The third result refers to the use of the sequential elimination models that we have suggested. These models not only provide for considerable flexibility in specifying generic interaction effects, and thus capture linearity and some types of nonlinearity directly, they are also easy to estimate fast and ensure in-sample statistical significance by the process of sequential reduction of the levels of significance used for testing the individual coefficients. As is well known, this approach provides for final p-values that are meaningful to their true size. These models were of two kinds, the first where the explanatory variable enters directly and the second where the explanatory variable was an indicator function for negative returns — and see that the second kind of explanatory variable affords us (in the specification of Eq. (7)) to capture sign-based interactions for different lags. We do note that after the elimination of insignificant variables we do end up with a parsimonious model as well.

The fourth result is about the generic lack of presence of other, competing, and benchmark models as top performers. It is only on the sub-period analysis that we do find the presence of some benchmark models, notably the VAR(1), and we did explain the reasons in Section 5.3 as to why this might be so. We also did not find any considerable presence of the "pure" nonlinear models such as the AAR, TAR, and NNET, and each one appeared only once in our tables — of course, this does not mean that other nonlinear models could not provide performance enhancements, but the question is at what cost (of specification and estimation).

The fifth result is the explanation for predictability, in terms of the in-sample fit of the top performing models. There are two issues of interest here: first, the measurement of in-sample fit in our models is via the associated R^2, which is a straightforward assessor of fit in the simple delay models; it has, however, the same conceptual validity for the sequential elimination models since we ensure that insignificant variables just do not appear before computing our forecasts — this minimizes the impact of an inflated R^2 because of the inclusion of extra terms on the right-hand side. The question of predictability is linked to both the size and possibly more important, the trend of the R^2 over the evaluation period. The reader would certainly ask what is the notion of discussing R^2 values if these cannot be shown to be statistically significant — and that would be correct inasmuch we consider the issue of significant improvements in predictability. But there is more to be discussed here; first, we have to obtain reductions in the statistical evaluation measures *vis-a-vis* the naíve benchmark, which reductions are present in our results; second, we have to explain where these reductions might be coming from — from model specification, for example — and whether such reductions are associated with increased values (non-zero and possibly trending) of the associated models' R^2, which we also find in our results. Both these items being present, we then look at out-of-sample predictability, which is clearly present in terms of our statistical measures of evaluation. Now, addressing the significance of the related R^2 measures is rather straightforward for there is a test on whether the R^2 is zero or not and that test only depends on the number of explanatory variables, in addition to the R^2 itself. From the test statistic formula of $t_R \stackrel{\text{def}}{=} \sqrt{R^2(n-k-1)/(1-R^2)}$, it is easy to deduce what values of R^2 might be considered significant given our sample sizes. Let's do an illustrative example that is relevant for the 2013–2019 sub-period results, where the estimation window is 60 months and we have two simple models, the VAR(1) and the delay models. The required R^2 to obtain a test statistic value of 1.65 (a one-side, 5% level of significance) is about $R^2 = 4.5\%$, which is easily surpassed by all three models in Figs. 9–11. If we were to consider the results where the larger windows of 100 and 200 observations were used, then the required R^2 would be even lower. Thus, what we observe is that predictability is clearly linked with in-sample fit, that higher R^2 do indicate toward increased predictability, and that careful, parsimonious model construction is (as should be) always supportive of good forecasting performance.

6. Conclusions

We examined the predictability of the EUR/USD exchange rate at the monthly frequency using a variety of models, univariate and bivariate — the latter having as explanatory variables different measures of the GBP/USD returns or realized volatility or the realized correlation between the euro and the pound.

The emphasis put on this chapter is along four lines: first, on examining whether the use of simpler models — such as the delay models DLM(d) and DLM(d-loc) that we used — are up in doing a good job: we answer in the affirmative, with our results being in line with the use of simpler models of Bhattacharya and Thomakos (2018); second, on examining whether there is any merit in our proposal for the use of a class of models, IDLM(d) and SDLM(d), that can capture sign/threshold-based and interactions-based nonlinearity which are estimated by a tight, sequential elimination procedure on their insignificant variables: we also answer in the affirmative here, re-enforcing the notion of using parsimonious and appropriate specified models for forecasting; third, on attempting to explain predictability via in-sample fit, in spirit similarly to Levich and Potti (2015) but in a much simpler fashion that, however, points to the same conclusions: all our top models (which are of the variety of lines one and two above) have in-sample fit that rises over the evaluation period and is clearly linked with their predictability; finally, we have illustrated that the models that rank at the top based on statistical evaluation criteria also perform at the top using directional and financial criteria.

The summary of our results in the Section 6 cannot possibly cover the unlimited ways that the problem of exchange rate predictability can be accessed and examined. We do acknowledge this without hesitation: we have not performed any tests of assessing the statistical significance of the top models against the naíve benchmark and we have not used complicated nonlinear models or models based on economic fundamentals. These three items can be, of course, done and have been done. But our main contribution here lies in the use of a variety of different explanatory variables and in something that we have espoused in other papers as well: that models such as the DLM(d)/DLM(d-loc) or IDLM(d)/SDLM(d) or the recent ADL (adaptive learning methodology) do not have any serious computation cost to be implemented; thus, maybe we can move away from the naíve benchmark and consider other types of models as benchmarks and start comparing them with each other based on criteria of econometric parsimony, correct specification, in-sample coherence, and economic validity. For future research, we expect that we can perform at least the above (testing significance and including models of economic fundamentals mainly) but we are more interested in proceeding with a more detailed examination of the merits of the DLM(d) and IDLM(d)/SDLM(d) models and their application to other currency pairs (doing the analysis for the GBP/USD as a natural step for the anticipation of a Brexit is gnawing at those that want to see where the pound will be heading). Finally, an important issue that we could be looking at is the combination of forecasts via rolling-window averaging as in Bhattacharya and Thomakos (2018), in an attempt to see whether the above models still survive against the naíve benchmark.

The demanding reader will probably find faults in our explanations and the limitations of our work; we do hope that, on the basis of our data and results, we will not disagree that we have sought for and indeed found exchange rate predictability.

References

Abhyankar, A., Sarno, L., and Valente, G. (2005). Exchange rates and fundamentals: Evidence on the economic value of predictability. *Journal of International Economics* **66**, 325–348.

Bhattacharya, P. S. and Thomakos, D. D. (2018). Robust model rankings of forecasting performance. *Journal of Forecasting* **37**, 676–690.

Boero, G. and Marrocu, E. (2002). The performance of nonlinear exchange rate models: A forecasting comparison. *Journal of Forecasting* **21**, 513–542.

Bollerslev, T. (1990). Modelling the coherence in short-run nominal exchange rates: A multivariate generalized ARCH model. *Review of Economics and Statistics* **72**, 498–505.

Butter, F. and Jansen, P. (2013). Beating the random walk: A performance assessment of long-term interest rate forecasts. *Applied Financial Economics* **23**, 749–765.

Chinn, M. and Meese, R. (1995). Banking on currency forecasts: How predictable is change in money? *Journal of International Economics* **38**, 161–178.

Chortareas, G., Jiang, Y., and Nankervis, J. (2011). The random-walk behavior of the Euro exchange rate. *Finance Research Letters* **8**, 158–162.

Chrystal, A. and MacDonald, R. (1995). Exchange rates, financial innovation and divisia money: The sterling/dollar rate 1972–1990. *Journal of International Money and Finance* **14**, 493–513.

Diebold, F. and Nason, J. (1989). Nonparametric exchange rate prediction? *Journal of International Economics* **28**, 315–332.

Dornbusch, R. (1976). Expectations and exchange rate dynamics. *Journal of Political Economy* **84**, 1161–1176.

Enders, W. (1988). ARIMA and cointegration tests of PPP under fixed and flexible exchange rates. *Review of Economics and Statistics* **70**, 504–508.

Enders, W. and Falk, B. (1998). Threshold-autoregressive, median-unbiased, and cointegration tests of purchasing power parity. *International Journal of Forecasting* **14**, 171–186.

Enders, W. and Lee, B. S. (1997). Accounting for real and nominal exchange rate movements in the post-Bretton Woods period. *Journal of International Money and Finance* **2**, 233–254.

Engel, C. (1994). Can the Markov switching model forecast exchange rates? *Journal of International Economics* **36**, 151–165.

Engel, C. and West, K. D. (2005). Exchange rates and fundamentals. *Journal of Political Economy* **113**, 485–517.

Hashimoto, Y., Ito, T., Ohnishi, T., Takayasu, M., Takayasu, H., and Watanabe, T. (2012). Random walk or a run. Market microstructure analysis of foreign exchange rate movements based on conditional probability. *Quantitative Finance* **12**, 893–905.

Inglesias, E. and Phillips, G. (2019). Further results on the pseudo maximum-likelihood estimation and testing in the constant elasticity of variance continuous time model. *Journal of Time Series Analysis*, available online.

Kilian, L. and Taylor, M. (2003). Why is it so difficult to beat the random walk forecast of exchange rates? *Journal of International Economics* **60**, 85–107.

Kyriazi, F., Thomakos, D., and Guerard, J. B. (2019). Adaptive learning forecasting, with applications in forecasting agricultural prices. *International Journal of Forecasting* **35**, 1356–1369.

Levich, R. and Potti, V. (2015). Predictability and good deals in currency markets. *International Journal of Forecasting* **31**, 454–472.

MacDonald, R. and Taylor, M. (1994). The monetary model of the exchange rate: Long-run relationships, short-run dynamics and how to beat a random walk. *Journal of International Money and Finance* **13**, 276–290.

Mark, N. and Sul, D. (2001). Nominal exchange rates and monetary fundamentals: Evidence from a small post-Bretton woods panel. *Journal of International Economics* **53**, 29–52.

Meese, R. A. and Rogoff, K. (1983). Empirical exchange rate models of the seventies: Do they fit out of sample? *Journal of International Economics* **14**, 3–24.

Molodtsova, T. and Papell, D. H. (2009). Out-of-sample exchange rate predictability with Taylor rule fundamentals. *Journal of International Economics* **77**, 167–180.

Moosa, I. and Kelly, B. (2014). Error correction modelling and dynamic specifications as a conduit to outperforming the random walk in exchange rate forecasting. *Applied Economics* **46**, 3107–3118.

Moosa, I. (2013). Why is it so difficult to outperform the random walk in exchange rate forecasting? *Applied Economics* **45**, 3340–3346.

Newbold, P., Rayner, T., Kellard, N. and Ennew, C. (1998). Is the dollar/ECU exchange rate a random walk? *Applied Financial Economics* **8**, 553–558.

Nikolopoulos, K. and Thomakos, D. (2019). *Forecasting with the Theta Method: Theory and Applications.* John Wiley, New York.

Rapach, D. and Strauss, J. (2008). Structural breaks and GARCH models of exchange rate volatility. *Journal of Applied Econometrics* **23**, 65–90.

Smoluk, H., Vasconcellos, G., and Kramer, J. (1998). Random walks in the U.K. pound–U.S. dollar exchange rates. *International Review of Financial Analysis* **7**, 65–82.

Stein, J. and Tower, E. (1967). The short-run stability of the foreign exchange market. *Review of Economics and Statistics* **49**, 173–185.

Taylor, M. and Peel, D. (2000). Nonlinear adjustment, long-run equilibrium and exchange rate fundamentals. *Journal of International Money and Finance* **19**, 33–53.

Voss, G. and Willard, L. (2009). Monetary policy and the exchange rate: Evidence from a two-country model. *Journal of Macroeconomics* **31**, 708–720.

Yoon, G. (1998). Forecasting with structural change: Why is the random walk model so damned difficult to beat? *Applied Economics Letters* **5**, 41–42.

https://doi.org/10.1142/9789811222634_0020

Chapter 20

Tracking VIX with VIX Futures: Portfolio Construction and Performance

Tim Leung
Applied Mathematics Department, University of Washington,
Seattle WA 98195, USA
timleung@uw.edu

Brian Ward
Industrial Engineering & Operations Research (IEOR) Department,
Columbia University, New York, NY 10027, USA
bmw2150@columbia.edu

We study a series of static and dynamic portfolios of Volatility Index (VIX) futures and their effectiveness to track the VIX. We derive each portfolio using optimization methods, and evaluate its tracking performance from both empirical and theoretical perspectives. Among our results, we show that static portfolios of different VIX futures fail to track VIX closely. VIX futures simply do not react quickly enough to movements in the spot VIX. In a discrete-time model, we design and implement a dynamic trading strategy that adjusts daily to optimally track VIX. The model is calibrated to historical data and a simulation study is performed to understand the properties exhibited by the strategy. In addition, compared to the volatility ETN, VXX, we find that our dynamic strategy has a superior tracking performance.

Keywords: Futures, volatility, index tracking, portfolio construction.

1. Introduction

For all long-term investors, it is very important to be able to effectively control the risk exposure of their portfolios through

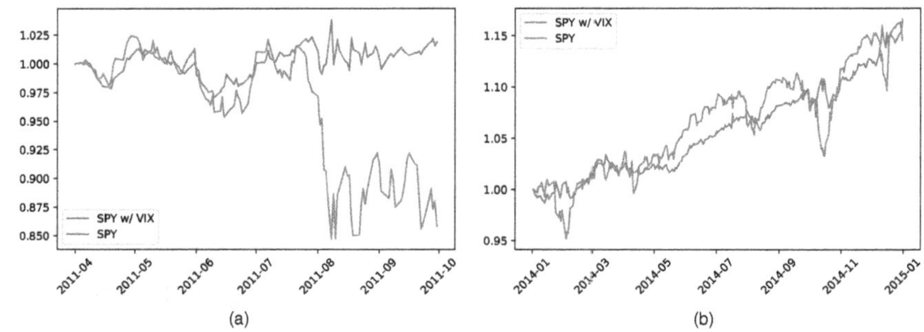

Fig. 1. Historical portfolio values during (a) April 1, 2011–September 30, 2011 and (b) January 1, 2014–December 31, 2014 for a portfolio with 100% investment in SPY, and another with 90% wealth invested in SPY and 10% in VIX.

varying market conditions. Downside risk protection is particularly crucial. This motivates investors to consider different instruments and strategies to potentially hedge against market turbulence. One of the most widely recognized measures of expected market volatility is the CBOE Volatility Index (VIX). This is a desirable asset to hold as it has been observed empirically that volatility and market returns are anti-correlated, an effect known as *asymmetric volatility*.[1] Therefore, having exposure to VIX would protect the investor by providing some gains to offset market downturns.

To illustrate this, let us consider two portfolios: a portfolio fully invested in the SPDR S&P 500 ETF (SPY), and another portfolio with 90% wealth in SPY and 10% wealth in VIX, assuming that VIX is tradable.[2] Figure 1(a) corresponds to the period of 2011 when the U.S. suffered a credit rating downgrade by Standard and Poor's. News of a negative outlook by S&P of the U.S. credit rating broke on April 18th, 2011.[3] The SPY position would go on to lose about 10% with a volatile trajectory for a few months past the official downgrade on August 5, 2011.[4] In contrast, a hypothetical portfolio with a 90/10

[1]See Black (1976) for the first use of this term.
[2]Also discussed in the authors' companion paper, Leung and Ward (2018).
[3]See New York Times article: http://www.nytimes.com/2011/04/19/business/19markets.html.
[4]See http://www.nytimes.com/2011/08/06/business/us-debt-downgraded-by-sp.html.

mix of SPY and VIX would be stable through the downgrade and end up with a positive return. In Fig. 1(b), we observe that the same pair of portfolios earned roughly the same 15% return in 2014. However, with SPY alone, the portfolio is visibly more volatile than the portfolio with SPY and VIX. The reason is that large drawdowns (for example, on October 15, 2014) were met by rises in VIX, creating a stabilizing effect on the portfolio's value.

Such a strategy is also beneficial for longer-term investment. If one invests 10% of wealth in VIX and the remaining fraction in SPY on January 30, 2009, then the realized Sharpe ratio of holding this portfolio till December 27, 2017 is 1.16. By comparison, the SPY-only portfolio attains a Sharpe ratio of 1. The improvement is due mostly to a strong reduction in volatility from 16.07% to 12.55% and our calculations show further that investing up to 26% of wealth in VIX, with remainder in SPY, would yield an even higher Sharpe ratio of 1.45.

The benefits of having VIX exposure are obvious, but in reality VIX is not directly tradable. Instead, volatility exposure is achieved through the use of VIX futures or options, and a number of exchange-traded funds/notes (ETF/Ns). The most traded VIX-based ETN is the iPath S&P 500 VIX Short-Term Futures ETN (ticker: VXX). However, as we will discuss, VXX fails to track VIX well and more generally, VIX ETF/Ns bring persistent negative returns. In the literature, a number of studies (Deng *et al.*, 2012; Eraker and Wu, 2013; Whaley, 2013) have also illustrated the negative returns associated with VIX futures and ETNs such as VXX. Nevertheless, VIX futures are also widely used for speculative trading and managed futures portfolios (Leung *et al.*, 2016; Jiao, 2016; Leung and Yan, 2018, 2019). As summarized by Bloomberg on January 29, 2019, "due to a structural quirk, the note lost 99 percent of its value over its life — but it also democratized investor access to implied U.S. equity volatility."

In this chapter, we discuss the price dynamics of VIX futures and the underlying index, and construct static and dynamic portfolios of VIX futures for the purpose of tracking the index. In addition to deriving and implementing the optimal tracking strategies, our main objective is to examine closely the effectiveness of the tracking portfolios. For a thorough related study by the authors on discrete-time and continuous-time tracking of VIX and other indices involving futures/other derivatives, we refer to Leung and Ward (2015, 2018) and Ward (2017).

Our study is structured as follows. In Section 2, we analyze the empirically observed return dependency of the VIX and VIX futures. In Section 3, we construct static portfolios of VIX futures for tracking VIX and investigate their tracking effectiveness over a long period of time. Our study illustrates a number of pitfalls in using static futures portfolios to attempt to track VIX, which motivates us to consider a dynamic approach as discussed in Section 4. Assuming a model that captures the mean-reverting dynamics of VIX, we derive the optimal dynamic replicating strategy that is adaptive to the daily fluctuations of VIX. The replicating strategy is implemented in Section 5. Concluding remarks are provided in Section 6.

2. VIX Spot & Futures

We begin by analyzing the price dynamics of the VIX Futures with respect to spot VIX. The historical price data for VIX futures are obtained from Quandl.[5] We have validated the Quandl data against that directly received from the CBOE.[6] For the spot VIX data as well as the related ETNs, we use Yahoo! Finance.[7]

After compiling, our dataset consists of the entire closing price history from March 26, 2004 (the first day VIX futures began trading) through January 27, 2017. However, we chose to analyze only the period from January 3, 2011 (first trading date of 2011) through December 30, 2016, which is a 6-year period from 2011 to 2016.

---

[5]Refer to https://www.quandl.com/collections/futures/cboe for documentation on the available CBOE data. One can search for specific contracts at https://www.quandl.com/data/CBOE-Chicago-Board-Options-Exchange.

[6]CBOE publishes the historical data as well here: http://cfe.cboe.com/data/historicaldata.aspx.

[7]Quandl also has spot VIX data available, but it is sourced from *Yahoo! Finance* and we have validated the two datasets against each other.

In our opinion, this amount of data is sufficient to avoid overfitting and recent enough to understand the current dynamics among VIX, futures, and VXX. The entire sample period from 2011 to 2016 contains 1,510 total trading days of data. Moreover, on any given day of the sample set, there are between 7 and 9 futures contracts available. In particular, there are 15 days with only 7 futures contracts available, 278 days with only 8 futures contracts available, and 1,217 days with a full 9 months of contracts available. These contracts are always consecutive months (starting with the 1-month contract) over this time period. In other words, when there are N futures contracts available for trading, they always consist of the N front months. As an example, if the current trading date were sometime early in January (before the January futures expiry), and 7 futures contracts were available for trading, then the maturities of the futures contracts would be the months of January through July, consecutively. These features of the dataset are consistent with CBOE protocol. They state they will currently list up to 9 near-term months for trading.[8] However, in our analysis, we eliminate the eighth and ninth month contract as it is not always the case that one can trade the eighth or ninth month contract. This allows us to use the full 1,510 days of data and avoid the need to eliminate the $15 + 278 = 293$ days with only 7 or 8 futures for trading.

2.1. *Return dependency*

We begin with a regression of the 1-day returns of VIX futures against the corresponding 1-day returns of VIX. The results are summarized in Table 1.

In Table 1, we observe the high R^2 values for all futures, suggesting that they are highly correlated with the spot. The futures with shorter maturities have higher R^2 values. This can be explained by (i) the fact that futures prices tend to approach the spot price toward maturity, and (ii) that long dated contracts are less liquid than the

[8]See http://cfe.cboe.com/products/spec_vix.aspx.

Table 1. A summary of the regression coefficients and measures of goodness-of-fit for regressing one-day returns of 1-month through 7-month futures on 1-day returns of spot VIX from January 3, 2011 to December 30, 2016.

Futures	Slope β	Intercept α	R^2	RMSE
1-month	0.604	$-3.54{\cdot}10^{-3}$	0.792	0.0242
2-month	0.428	$-3.33{\cdot}10^{-3}$	0.759	0.0189
3-month	0.321	$-2.45{\cdot}10^{-3}$	0.718	0.0158
4-month	0.267	$-1.98{\cdot}10^{-3}$	0.688	0.0141
5-month	0.226	$-1.79{\cdot}10^{-3}$	0.645	0.0131
6-month	0.200	$-1.62{\cdot}10^{-3}$	0.615	0.0124
7-month	0.184	$-1.35{\cdot}10^{-3}$	0.597	0.0118

Note: The root mean-squared error is defined by RMSE:= $\sqrt{\sum_{i=1}^{n}(r_i^{(V)} - \alpha - \beta r_i^{(j)})^2/n}$, where $r_i^{(j)}$ is the 1-day return of the jth futures contract on trading day i, $r_i^{(V)}$ is the corresponding return of spot VIX, and n is the number of trading days. The front 7-month contracts are indexed by $j \in \{1, \ldots, 7\}$.

short-term contracts. The slope coefficients are all statistically significant and less than 1, which is intuitive as futures returns tend to be less volatile than spot returns. The negative intercepts, which are statistically significant, indicate that futures prices tend to fall even if the spot price does not move. The reason lies in the term structure of VIX futures, which as we will see is typically increasing in time-to-maturity. Even if the spot price does not move, the futures prices tend to decrease to match the spot price toward maturity, contributing to a negative intercept.

In Fig. 2, we plot the time series of spot VIX, the 1-month futures price (May-16 contract), and the 7-month futures price (Nov-16 contract) over the period from April 22, 2016 (1 day after the expiration of the April-16 contract) to May 18, 2016 (the expiration date of the May-16 contract). Notice that the spot, 1-month futures price, and 7-month futures price all tend to move together. However, the moves in the spot are larger than moves in the futures prices. We also observe that the spot and futures prices often move in the same direction, but the futures prices do not move 1 for 1 with the spot. As one might expect, this effect is more pronounced for the 7-month contract, which barely moves over the period. For example, from

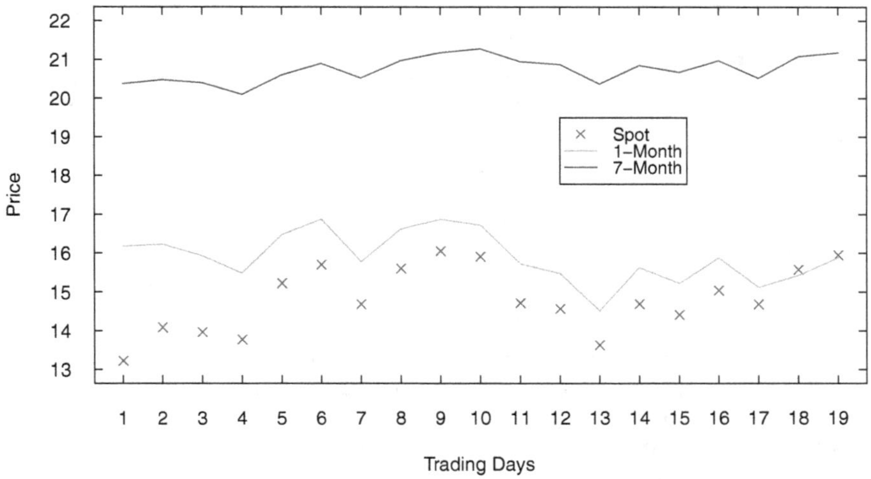

Fig. 2. Time series of VIX, 1-month futures price (May-16 contract) and 7-month futures price (Nov-16 contract) over the period from April 22, 2016 to May 18, 2016. The x-axis marks the trading day number, while the y-axis marks the price.

trading day 4 to 5, we have a large up move in VIX of \$1.45, which is only met by an increase of \$1.00 by the 1-month contract and an increase of \$0.50 by the 7-month contract.

Notice also that there is a slight discrepancy between the 1-month futures price at maturity and spot price. In theory, futures prices should converge to the spot price. However, market frictions, settlement rules[9] and non-tradability of the spot can substantially limit this convergence, as is seen in other futures markets, e.g., agricultural futures (Guo and Leung, 2017). For the non-convergence phenomenon of VIX futures, we refer to Pavlova and Daigler (2008) for an empirical study.

We plot the term structure of VIX futures as observed at several different time points throughout the first 6 months of 2016 (left) and 2009 (right) in Fig. 3. The typical case for the VIX market is an increasing and concave futures curve (see left panel). However, in

[9]See https://cfe.cboe.com/products/settlement_vix.aspx for VIX derivatives' settlement procedures.

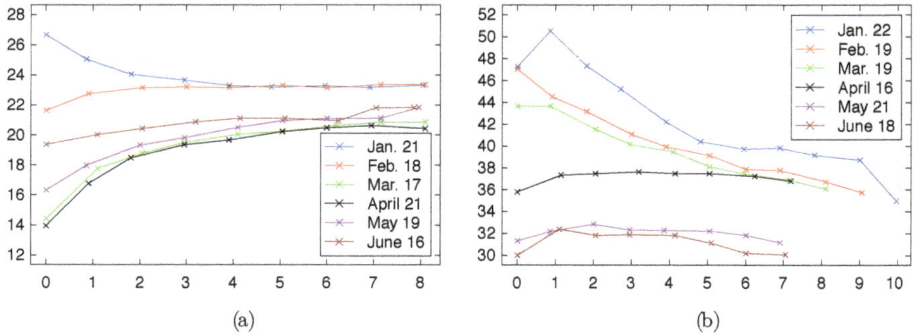

Fig. 3. Term structures from January–June in (a) 2016 and (b) 2009. The legend shows the dates upon which the term structures are constructed. Each date is the day after that month's futures contract expires. The x-axis marks the time-to-maturity (in months) assuming each month is exactly 21 (= 252/12) days, while the y-axis marks the price.

January 2016, VIX spiked as did expectations of futures volatility.[10] Spikes like this can cause the term structure of VIX futures to invert, yielding a decreasing and convex futures curve. On the right panel of Fig. 3, we plot the term structures in early 2009 where futures prices are at very high levels and the term structure shows different shape properties. In the literature, there exist several models for VIX dynamics that yield the observed term structures (e.g., increasing concave or decreasing convex). These include the Cox–Ingersoll–Ross (CIR) model (see Grübichler and Longstaff, 1996 and Zhang and Zhu, 2006), Ornstein–Uhlenbeck (OU) model and exponential OU model (see Leung and Li, 2016), and models with multiple stochastic factors and regimes (see Mencia and Sentana, 2013; Jiao, 2016).

2.2. *Long-term dependency*

When we conduct regressions of futures returns against spot returns over longer holding periods, new patterns emerge. We use *disjoint* intervals of various lengths when we compute the returns, meaning

[10]One can find a discussion of trends in volatility in late January 2016 in the following article: https://tickertape.tdameritrade.com/options/2016/01/volatility-high-early-2016-42727.

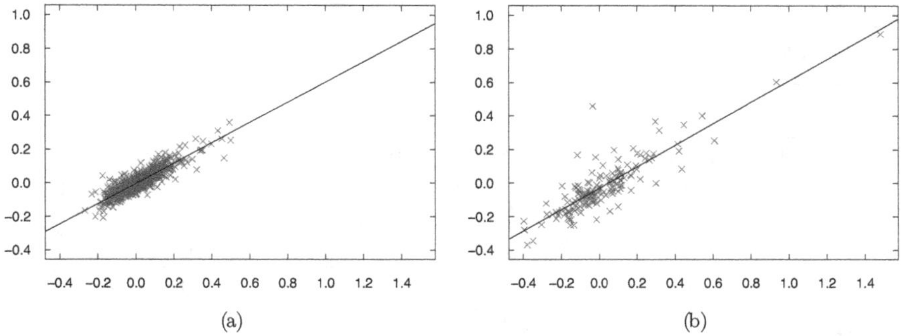

Fig. 4. Linear regressions of 1-month futures returns vs. spot VIX returns based on (a) 1-day returns and (b) 10-day returns. The x-axis marks the returns (in decimals) of spot VIX and the y-axis marks the returns (in decimals) of the 1-month futures.

that for the longer horizons we have fewer data points, but even for the 30-day horizon we have approximately 50 data points.

In Fig. 4, we plot the regressions of 1-month futures returns versus VIX returns for both 1-day returns (left) and 10-day returns (right), plotted on the same $x - y$ axis scale. The dark x's mark pairs of returns, while the black line is the best fit line. One observes that the 10-day returns are much larger and consequently more volatile than the 1-day returns. However, for both holding periods, the futures returns are less volatile than the corresponding spot returns. To be precise, we find that the 1-day returns of the spot vary between -26.96% and 50%, while for the 10-day returns they vary between -39.76% and 148.06% (i.e., the longer holding period has more volatile returns). On the other hand, for the 1-month futures, the 1-day returns vary between -20.81% and 35.83%, while the 10-day returns vary between -36.91% and 88.89% (i.e., futures returns are less volatile than the respective spot returns).

In the plot, the slope is slightly higher for the 10-day returns as compared to the 1-day returns. Moreover, for the 1-day returns, the scatter plot is more tightly bound to the best fit line indicating a better fit than observed for the 10-day returns. However, this pattern does not hold in general. There is no discernible pattern in either the R^2 values or slope coefficients as the holding period is lengthened.

Table 2. A summary of the slopes and R^2s from the regressions of futures returns versus VIX returns over different holding periods.

	Days	1-Mon	2-Mon	3-Mon	4-Mon	5-Mon	6-Mon	7-Mon
Slope	1	0.604	0.428	0.321	0.267	0.226	0.200	0.184
	5	0.668	0.471	0.358	0.291	0.244	0.219	0.199
	10	0.641	0.424	0.320	0.254	0.206	0.185	0.167
	15	0.622	0.373	0.283	0.218	0.171	0.153	0.139
R^2	1	0.792	0.759	0.718	0.688	0.645	0.615	0.597
	5	0.832	0.825	0.779	0.738	0.697	0.673	0.649
	10	0.750	0.750	0.691	0.630	0.562	0.540	0.519
	15	0.663	0.639	0.574	0.488	0.395	0.376	0.352

This can be demonstrated by looking at a plot of R^2 or slope vs. holding period. We omit such a plot here as there is no clear pattern of increasing or decreasing predictive power (as measured by R^2) or leverage necessary to replicate the spot returns in the plot for any maturity contract. (Leverage can be measured by the reciprocal of the slope.)

On the other hand, if we fix the holding period and increase the maturity of the contract, we see a decrease in predictive power and a decrease in slope. (Thus, an increase in leverage necessary to replicate the spot.) We demonstrate this for a number of different holding periods (1, 5, 10, and 15 days) in Table 2. In the top half, we give the slope coefficients for the regressions of futures returns against spot returns and in the bottom half, we display the R^2 values. By looking across the rows in either half, one notices a decrease in the reported statistic. This reaffirms our earlier observation that the spot is more closely tracked by short-term futures than long-term futures. Indeed, over a 15-day period, the results indicate that about 1.6× leverage is required to track the spot with 1-month futures vs. 7.2× leverage for the 7-month futures. These implied leverage values are obtained by computing the reciprocals of the slopes (0.622 and 0.139, respectively). The leverage for the 7-month futures is quite substantial and is likely not feasible in the marketplace due to trading costs or exchange limits.

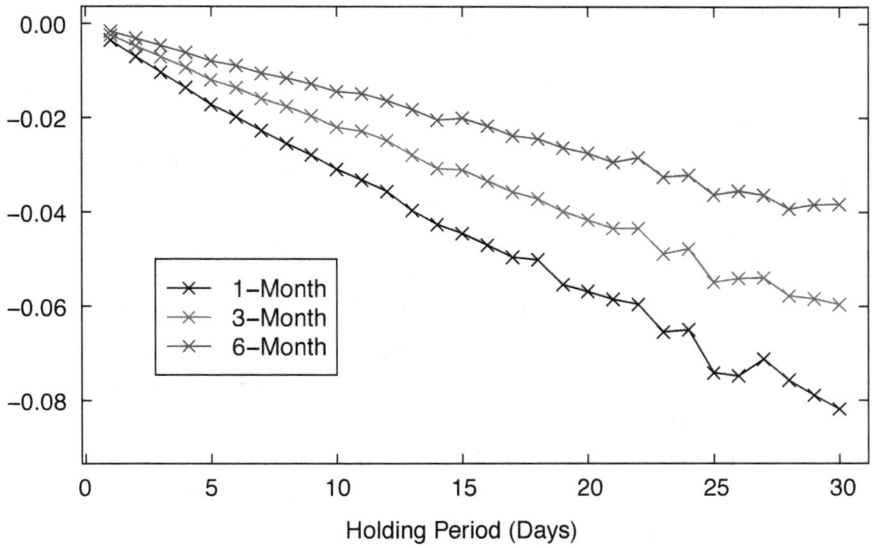

Fig. 5. The intercepts from regressions of returns from a rolling futures position against spot returns, plotted against the holding period measured in trading days. From top to bottom: 6-month, 3-month, and 1-month futures.

Although not immediately discernible, in Fig. 4, the intercept is more negative for the 10-day returns as compared to the 1-day returns. This confirms a property we have already discussed: futures tend to underperform and lose money relative to the spot returns. The more negative intercept indicates that this underperformance worsens over longer horizons. To see this more generally, in Fig. 5, we plot the intercepts for the regressions of returns of 1-month futures, 3-month futures, and 6-month futures across many different holding periods (from 1 day up to 30 days). It is quite clear that as the holding period is lengthened, the intercept becomes increasingly more negative. All intercepts (as well as the slopes from before) reported here are statistically significant at the 1% significance level. Thus, a statistically significant discrepancy exists and continues to worsen as the holding period is lengthened.

3. Static Replication Strategies

In this section, we investigate the static replication of VIX using futures. Portfolios based on two different optimization criteria are considered. In Section 3.1, we consider replication by optimizing the weights of the portfolio to match the physical dollar price of VIX over the training period. Due to the mean-reverting nature of VIX, the optimal portfolio is effectively all cash as this will keep the portfolio roughly near the mean level of VIX through the in-sample period. This motivates optimizing the portfolio to match the returns as closely as possible. The performance is improved upon with this change of criterion, but we demonstrate that it simply is difficult to track VIX with a static portfolio of futures. Unless otherwise noted, the training or in-sample period is the 5-year period from 2011 to 2015, and the test or out-of-sample period is the year 2016.

3.1. *Physical replication by static futures portfolios*

In this section, we consider static positions including 1 or more futures contracts. By a static position in the futures contract, we mean a position that is constantly rolled over into the next futures contract. For example, a static investment of $\$P_0$ in 1-month futures would proceed as follows. First, purchase P_0/F_0 units of the current 1-month contract and hold it until maturity. The position's value at that time can be denoted by P_1. Then, one uses this final value to purchase what was previously (e.g., at time 0) the 2-month futures, but is now the 1-month futures. If this futures price is denoted F_1, then one purchases P_1/F_1 units of the new 1-month contract and holds *that* contract until maturity. This process is continued indefinitely at each maturity date.

There will be no cash withdrawals/injections at the roll periods (e.g., to keep the number of units of futures constant.) This makes the position completely self-financing, though the number of achievable units of futures will vary over time (i.e., it is completely possible that $P_0/F_0 \neq P_1/F_1$). The static position described here, starting on January 3, 2011, with \$100 will be called the value of the 1-month futures contract. One can analogously define the 2-month, 3-month, etc. values as positions that always maintain all money in 2-month, 3-month, etc. contracts.

The portfolio value on day j is denoted by P_j and consists of various VIX futures contracts. The value of spot VIX on day j is denoted by V_j. The precise weightings among the futures will be chosen so as to minimize the sum of squared errors:

$$\mathrm{SSE} = \sum_{j=1}^{n} (V_j - G_j)^2, \tag{1}$$

where n is the number of trading days in the in-sample period.

Let k be the number of futures contracts being considered and $\mathbf{w} := (w_0, \ldots, w_k)$ be the real-valued vector of portfolio weights. In particular, w_0 represents the weight given to the money market account.[11] Next, denote by $\mathbf{C} \in \mathbb{R}^{n \times k+1}$ a matrix containing as columns the historical values of the money market account and the various futures contracts. Finally, denote by $\mathbf{d} \in \mathbb{R}^n$ a vector containing the historical values of VIX. All prices come from the in-sample set and are normalized to start at \$100 on day $j = 1$. With this notation and optimization criterion (1), we derive the following constrained least squares optimization problem:

$$\begin{aligned} \min_{\mathbf{w} \in \mathbb{R}^{k+1}} \quad & \|\mathbf{C}\mathbf{w} - \mathbf{d}\|^2 \\ \text{s.t.} \quad & \sum_{j=0}^{k} w_j = 1. \end{aligned} \tag{2}$$

The normalization implies that an investor starting with \$100 will invest $\$100 \cdot w_j$ into the jth futures contract and $\$\ 100 \cdot w_0$ into the money market account. For simplicity of the subsequent analysis,

[11]The money market account yields overnight LIBOR. The data were obtained from the Federal Reserve Bank of St. Louis (FRED); see https://fred.stlouisfed.org/series/USDONTD156N.

Table 3. Optimal portfolio weights/performance measures for portfolios of VIX futures for tracking the dollar value of VIX. Portfolios utilize any subset of the 1-month, 2-month, 6-month, and 7-month contracts.

Futures	w_0	w_1	w_2	w_3	w_4	in-RMSE	out-RMSE
1-m	0.848	0.152	—	—	—	30.724	23.345
2-m	0.857	0.143	—	—	—	31.153	26.074
6-m	0.811	0.189	—	—	—	31.026	28.840
7-m	0.777	0.223	—	—	—	30.835	28.616
1-m, 2-m	0.932	2.114	−2.046	—	—	27.741	19.521
1-m, 6-m	0.917	0.345	−0.262	—	—	30.576	17.197
1-m, 7-m	0.840	0.137	0.022	—	—	30.722	23.819
2-m, 6-m	0.757	−0.203	0.446	—	—	30.960	32.971
2-m, 7-m	0.669	−0.252	0.582	—	—	30.627	33.518
6-m, 7-m	0.492	−2.146	2.654	—	—	29.801	27.021
1-m, 2-m, 6-m	0.453	3.770	−5.615	2.392	—	23.404	22.174
1-m, 2-m, 7-m	0.341	3.745	−5.095	2.009	—	22.414	24.742
1-m, 6-m, 7-m	0.229	1.979	−11.066	9.858	—	22.960	61.713
2-m, 6-m, 7-m	0.359	2.449	−11.032	9.224	—	27.437	37.218
1-m, 2-m, 6-m, 7-m	0.225	3.292	−3.151	−5.548	6.183	21.492	44.222

we consider portfolios containing any of the four of the following contracts: 1-month, 2-month, 6-month, and 7-month. Allowing for any number of futures in the portfolio, this naturally yields $2^4 - 1 = 15$ (subtract 1 because we do not look at the portfolio using no futures as that is trivial) different potential portfolios. Using all 7 available futures and their $2^7 - 1 = 127$ subsets would be untenable and obscure the analysis. The four contracts selected here represent the shortest and longest dated maturities that are available in the VIX futures market on every day of both the in-sample and out-of-sample period.

The results of the optimization are given in Table 3. As above, w_0 always represents the weight on the money market account. All other w_i are ordered so that if $i < j$, w_i represents the weight on a nearer term contract than w_j. For example, in row 6, we are considering a portfolio of 1-month and 6-month futures. Thus, w_1 is the weight on 1-month futures, while w_2 represents the weight on 6-month futures.

The RMSE has a standard definition in terms of the SSE defined in Equation (1). Precisely,

$$\text{RMSE} := \sqrt{\frac{\text{SSE}}{n}}, \tag{3}$$

where $n = 1,258$ for the in-sample period and $n = 252$ for the out-of-sample period. Our choice of initial capital of \$100 allows us to interpret RMSE as the average percentage deviation of the portfolio value from the spot price during the in-sample or out-of-sample period.

The RMSE values are quite large, indicating poor in-sample and out-of-sample tracking performance. To benchmark the performance, we can compare the RMSE values to those achieved by VXX. The in-sample RMSE for VXX is 72.05%, while the out-of-sample value is 21.97%. The values indicate the futures-based portfolios perform significantly better in-sample than do VXX. Out-of-sample, the futures-based portfolios perform only slightly better in a few cases.

Remark 3.1 *The difference in performance in-sample vs. out-of-sample for VXX is driven mostly by the difference in length of the two datasets. Recall that VXX is an unlevered portfolio of VIX futures, which we have demonstrated in Section 2 does not react quickly to spot VIX price movements. Thus, once VXX has fallen away from VIX, it cannot return to the dollar value of VIX and additions to SSE continue to accumulate.*

Though the performance is somewhat better than VXX, the resulting strategies break with intuition. All portfolios are barely net long in the various futures contracts employed. This is seen prominently in those with one or two futures only. For example, the 1-month only portfolio invests only 15.2% of wealth in the value of the 1-month futures contract and the remaining 84.8% is held in cash. This is due to the choice of SSE as an optimization criterion and that we measure SSE on the physical dollar price. This combination makes the optimization somewhat forward looking. It considers all at once the values VIX will take over the in-sample period. In

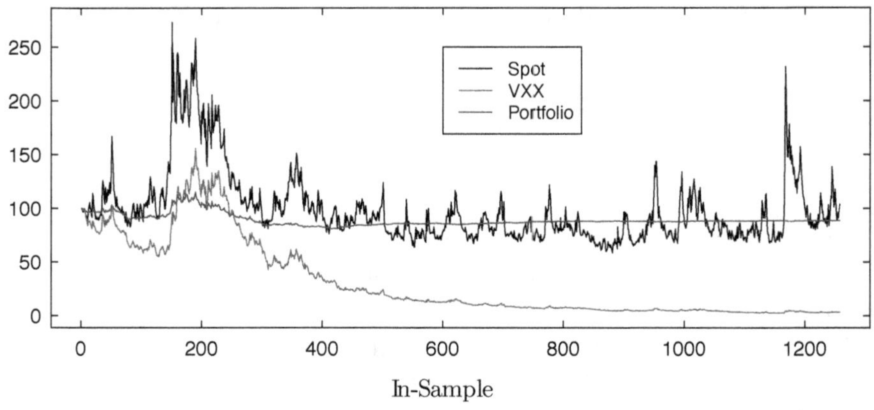

Fig. 6. Time series of spot VIX, the ETF VXX, and the optimal VIX dollar value tracking portfolio. The x-axis marks the trading day number, while the y-axis marks the price. All prices are normalized to start at \$100.

particular, VIX is highly mean-reverting and thus, holding the portfolio value at the average level of VIX over the period is the best choice. Futures simply do not track the spot well, so it is best to ignore any spikes and remain constant over time.

Finally, in Fig. 6, we plot the time series of spot VIX, the ETF VXX, and the optimal (across all combinations of portfolio components) out-of-sample portfolio. As discussed above, the optimal portfolio is relatively flat holding most of its value (91.7%) and is barely net long in 1-month and 6-month futures (8.3%). On the other hand, VXX is more reactive to the spot price movements, but quickly diverges from spot VIX. Thereafter, it is unable to recover and continues to fall away from spot VIX. By the end of the in-sample period, VXX has fallen to \$3.44, and for the out-of-sample period, it has fallen to \$29.89. In neither samples does the optimal portfolio diverge in this manner. It instead stays roughly constant at VIX's average level over both periods. Neither portfolio appears a perfect surrogate for trading VIX and therefore we consider alternative methods to constructing portfolios of futures to track VIX in Section 3.2.

3.2. *Returns replication with static portfolios*

The results of Section 3.1 motivate considering a different tracking criterion. In particular, the tracking portfolios were all roughly constant and were barely net long VIX futures. Moreover, VXX had substantial discrepancies that were unrecoverable over a long trading period, but it was at least somewhat reactive to VIX price movements. Our calculations show that VXX does well in tracking the returns of VIX relative to our portfolios. If we instead compute the RMSE value on the returns (rather than the physical price), we find in-sample VXX has a return RMSE of 4.63% as compared to 7.51% for our best (the 1-month, 6-month pair from before) portfolio. Those values are 4.55% and 7.21%, respectively, for the out-of-sample period. Since VXX tracks the returns well, it suggests building portfolios of VIX futures that also track the returns.

In the previous section, our target for the tracking portfolios was the dollar value of VIX. If that were achievable at all points in time, the portfolios necessarily would have matched the VIX returns on each day as well. The converse need not be true: it is possible for the returns to be close to VIX returns while the physical values still diverge over time. This is clearly evidenced in the above paragraph whence VXX more closely matches the returns than our portfolio does, but more poorly tracks the physical price of VIX than the tracking portfolio does. In spite of this, we will consider return matching as the criterion for building portfolios in this section.

The optimization problem remains mathematically the same as stated in Section 3.1:

$$\begin{aligned} \min_{\mathbf{w}\in\mathbb{R}^{k+1}} \quad & \|\mathbf{Bw}-\mathbf{y}\|^2 \\ \text{s.t.} \quad & \sum_{j=0}^{k} w_j = 1. \end{aligned} \tag{4}$$

The matrix $\mathbf{B}$ contains as columns the returns of the money market account and the various futures contracts under consideration. The vector, $\mathbf{y}$, contains the historical returns of spot VIX. Final in-sample and out-of-sample performance is based on RMSE as defined in (3), but this is done on the returns of the portfolio vs. the spot.

The results of the optimization are reported in Table 4. By considering this new criterion, we obtain portfolios that are net long and are leveraged. The regression analysis of Section 2 suggested this would be the case. In fact, for all 15 portfolios, the weight on the money market account, w_0, is negative, indicating that borrowing is required. For example, the 6-month/7-month portfolio requires a leverage of about 3 to track the VIX returns (it borrows about 2x its value from the bank). This is also seen in the 6-month only portfolio and the 7-month only portfolios.

For this tracking criterion, almost all portfolios outperform VXX in-sample (RMSE = 4.63%) as well as out-of-sample (RMSE = 4.55%). The exceptions are the 6-month only, 7-month only, and 6-month/7-month portfolios. These two observations (extreme leverage and poor tracking performance) echo our previous discussion regarding the fact that the longer dated contracts are not as reactive to spot movements as the shorter dated contracts.

In terms of physical price replication, both VXX and the optimized portfolio continue to underperform, but that is not the goal of this section. Rather, we are concerned with return replication. Indeed, the optimized portfolio is more reactive to spot movements and is no longer constant over the time period, and the RMSE calculations demonstrate that the portfolio is tracking VIX returns well. However, with the leveraging, the portfolio has eroded so far in value that both in-sample and out-of-sample it has gone negative! The leveraging in combination with the fact that VIX futures tend to lose money even when the spot is unchanged causes the substantial loss in value. Interestingly, this portfolio is not overly leveraged (only about 1.24×).

Negative portfolio values are uncommon, but can occur when there is leveraging. As a simple example, suppose an investor begins with \$100 and constructs a 3× leveraged investment in an asset currently priced at \$30. Therefore, she borrows \$200 from the bank

Table 4. Optimal portfolio weights/performance measures for portfolios of VIX futures for tracking VIX returns. Portfolios utilize any subset of the 1-month, 2-month, 6-month, and 7-month contracts. The reported RMSE values are for the returns of the portfolio.

Futures	w_0	w_1	w_2	w_3	w_4	in-RMSE	out-RMSE
1-m	−0.317	1.317	—	—	—	3.620	3.491
2-m	−0.751	1.751	—	—	—	3.929	3.685
6-m	−2.018	3.018	—	—	—	4.926	4.659
7-m	−2.178	3.178	—	—	—	5.020	4.832
1-m, 2-m	−0.499	0.921	0.578	—	—	3.532	3.430
1-m, 6-m	−0.542	1.210	0.333	—	—	3.603	3.492
1-m, 7-m	−0.503	1.237	0.265	—	—	3.610	3.491
2-m, 6-m	−0.445	2.033	−0.588	—	—	3.903	3.607
2-m, 7-m	−0.380	2.050	−0.669	—	—	3.896	3.598
6-m, 7-m	−1.989	3.391	−0.401	—	—	4.925	4.645
1-m, 2-m, 6-m	−0.319	0.905	0.769	−0.355	—	3.522	3.400
1-m, 2-m, 7-m	−0.244	0.904	0.810	−0.470	—	3.515	3.396
1-m, 6-m, 7-m	−0.463	1.215	1.269	−1.021	—	3.592	3.494
2-m, 6-m, 7-m	−0.379	2.040	0.193	−0.854	—	3.896	3.600
1-m, 2-m, 6-m, 7-m	−0.237	0.910	0.770	0.594	−1.036	3.511	3.405

at, e.g., a constant (and annually compounded) interest rate of 5% and purchases 10 units of the asset. Suppose that after 1 year's time, the asset's value has plummeted to \$20. The investor's 10 units are worth a total of \$200, but she owes $200 \cdot 1.05 = 210$ to the bank. The net value of her portfolio is therefore, −10, meaning a cash injection of \$10 is necessary just to liquidate the portfolio. A similar situation (though not as extreme) has occurred for the tracking portfolios here. The combination of leveraging along with the poor returns of VIX futures drove the portfolio to a negative value (Fig. 7).

From this section and the previous one, it is quite evident that dynamic strategies are needed if one is to track the VIX with a portfolio of futures. Directly optimizing for the price trajectory yielded portfolios that did not react to VIX movements, and directly optimizing for return trajectory yielded portfolios with negative

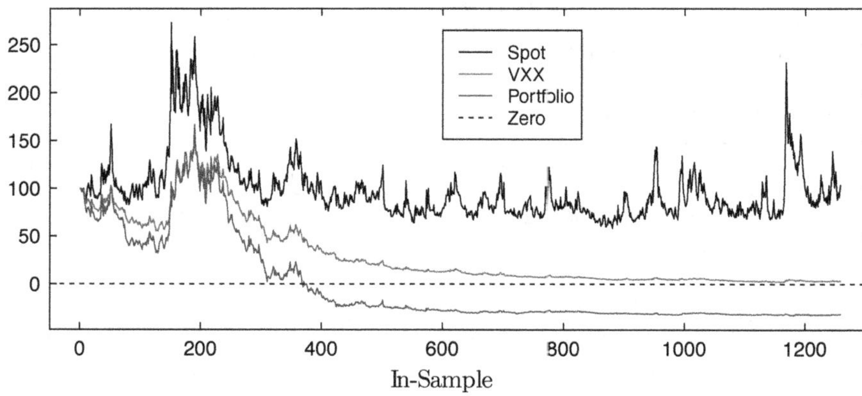

Fig. 7. Time series of spot VIX, the ETF VXX, and the optimal VIX return portfolio. The x-axis marks the trading day number, while the y-axis marks the price. All prices are normalized to start at \$100.

values due to overleveraging. In the Section 4, we see a model-driven and dynamic strategy which appears to combat both pitfalls.

4. Optimal Dynamic Replication

In this section, we develop an optimal strategy for replicating the returns of an index. The model is built on discrete-time dynamics for the index, futures on the index, and the tracking portfolio. By working in discrete time, we will be able to capture the daily mark-to-market feature that is present in futures markets. We will then find the optimal dynamic weights to allocate capital among two futures contracts so as to replicate the daily returns of the index.

4.1. *Futures portfolio and price dynamics*

To maintain a futures position, the investor places a certain fraction of the exposure, e.g., 20% of the dollar value, on margin with the clearing agency. This amount is called the *initial margin*, while the account held with the clearing agency is called the *margin account.* The margin account is *marked-to-market*, which means that if we denote the futures price for maturity T_i, as observed on day j by $f_j^{(i)}$, the margin account receives a cash flow equal to $f_j^{(i)} - f_{j-1}^{(i)}$ for each unit of futures the investor is long at the end of day j.

The investor is assumed to have no position limits when trading futures. Therefore, it is possible for any portfolio weight (fraction of the portfolio wealth) to be of any positive or negative value. The magnitude of the portfolio weight indicates the degree of leverage in the exposure. Moreover, if these cash flows accumulate to a substantially negative value, the margin account will fall below a level called the *maintenance margin*. In that case, the investor receives a *margin call* and must replenish the account's funds back up to the initial margin. The account will otherwise be paid the risk-free rate in exchange for the collateral. In our discrete-time model, we assume for simplicity that the full amount of the exposure is held on margin. This simplifies matters as there is no need to incorporate margin calls or maintenance margins in the model.

Each time step will be one day, which we denote by Δt. Here, $\Delta t = 1/252$ as there are $n = 252$ trading days per year. Thus, the futures contracts are marked-to-market in accordance with the time step. Consequently, the investor must make all decisions for the next day's holdings based on information generated by the previous day's prices, and intraday positions are held constant. The value of the investor's holdings is denoted by the discrete-time process, $\{X_j\}_{j=0}^{\infty}$, where X_0 is the initial wealth.

Further, suppose there are N futures contracts available for trading with maturities $T_1 < \cdots < T_N$. Then a portfolio holding a fraction of wealth, $w_j^{(i)}$, in the ith maturity, $(i = 1, \ldots, N)$ will have $\frac{w_j^{(i)} X_j}{f_j^{(i)}}$ many units of futures contract of maturity T_i on day j. Let the continuously compounded risk-free rate be r so that 1 dollar grows to $e^{r\Delta t}$ dollars the next day. From the above, it follows that if the portfolio of futures contracts is worth X_j on day j, then it is worth

$$X_{j+1} = X_j e^{r\Delta t} + \sum_{i=1}^{N} \frac{w_j^{(i)} X_j}{f_j^{(i)}} \left[f_{j+1}^{(i)} - f_j^{(i)} \right], \qquad \forall j \geq 0 \qquad (5)$$

on day $j+1$. It follows that the daily return of the portfolio is given by

$$\frac{X_{j+1}}{X_j} - 1 = e^{r\Delta t} - 1 + \sum_{i=1}^{N} w_j^{(i)} \left[\frac{f_{j+1}^{(i)}}{f_j^{(i)}} - 1 \right], \qquad \forall j \geq 0. \tag{6}$$

This is the sum of the risk-free return for placing collateral with the exchange and the weighted average daily returns of the various futures contracts the investor holds.

The value of the index the investor tracks is denoted by the discrete-time stochastic process, $\{S_j\}_{j=0}^{\infty}$. Suppose the index satisfies the following equation (see below for motivation and discussion):

$$S_{j+1} - S_j = \mu(\theta - S_j)\Delta t + g(j\Delta t, S_j)\sqrt{\Delta t} Z_{j+1}, \qquad \forall j \geq 0, \tag{7}$$

where $\{Z_j\}_{j=1}^{\infty}$ are independent and identically distributed standard normal random variables under the historical measure $\mathbb{P}$. It follows that the daily return of the index is equal to

$$\frac{S_{j+1}}{S_j} - 1 = \frac{\mu\theta\Delta t}{S_j} - \mu\Delta t + \frac{g(j\Delta t, S_j)}{S_j}\sqrt{\Delta t} Z_{j+1}, \qquad \forall j \geq 0. \tag{8}$$

This is motivated by the continuous-time mean-reverting model

$$dS_t = \mu(\theta - S_t)dt + g(t, S_t)dZ_t, \tag{9}$$

where μ, θ are positive parameters, $g(\cdot,\cdot)$ is a generic local volatility function, and Z_t is a standard Brownian motion (SBM) under the historical measure $\mathbb{P}$. The drift $\mu(\theta - S_t)$ is positive (resp. negative) when $S_t < \theta$ (resp. $S_t > \theta$) and thus S_t tends to rise (resp. fall). That implies that S_t mean-reverts to θ.

By instantiating $g(\cdot,\cdot)$ with a particular function, one obtains many well-known mean-reverting models. For example, when $g(t, S_t) = \sigma$, the model is called the Ornstein–Uhlenbeck (OU) Model (Uhlenbeck and Ornstein, 1930) and when $g(t, S_t) = \sigma\sqrt{S_t}$, the model is called the Cox–Ingersoll–Ross (CIR) Model (Cox *et al.*, 1985). For volatility futures as an example, Grübichler and Longstaff (1996) and Zhang and Zhu (2006) model the S&P 500 VIX by the CIR process and provide a formula for the futures price. Futures prices are computed under the risk-neutral measure, but for tracking and trading we also need to consider their dynamics under the historical measure. As a result, the investor's optimal trading strategy depends on parameters from both measures.

We further assume that under the risk-neutral measure, $\mathbb{Q}$, the index maintains the same mean-reverting property, but with different parameters. Namely,

$$dS_t = \widetilde{\mu}(\widetilde{\theta} - S_t)dt + g(t, S_t)d\widetilde{Z}_t, \tag{10}$$

where $\widetilde{\mu}, \widetilde{\theta} > 0$, $g(\cdot,\cdot)$ is the same local volatility function as above[12] and $\widetilde{Z}_t$ is a SBM under the risk-neutral measure. We denote by $\lambda(t, S_t)$ the market price of risk that satisfies $dZ_t = d\widetilde{Z}_t - \lambda(t, S_t)dt$ so that

$$\lambda(t, S_t) = \frac{\mu(\theta - S_t) - \widetilde{\mu}(\widetilde{\theta} - S_t)}{g(t, S_t)}. \tag{11}$$

This form of risk premium preserves the mean-reverting property of the index under two measures.

Under this model, the price of a futures contract written on S with maturity T is

$$f_t^T := f(t, S; T) = \mathbb{E}^{\mathbb{Q}}\left[S_T | S_t = S\right] = (S - \widetilde{\theta})e^{-\widetilde{\mu}(T-t)} + \widetilde{\theta}, \tag{12}$$

as long as the function $g(\cdot,\cdot)$ satisfies the integrability condition

$$\mathbb{E}^{\mathbb{Q}}\left[\int_0^T e^{2\widetilde{\mu}\xi} g^2(\xi, S_\xi)d\xi\right] < \infty, \quad \forall\ T. \tag{13}$$

[12]This is a standard property when we change measures: the drift changes, but the volatility remains the same.

It follow from Ito's Formula that the dynamics of f_t^T are given by

$$\begin{aligned} df_t^T &= dS_t e^{-\widetilde{\mu}(T-t)} + \widetilde{\mu} e^{-\widetilde{\mu}(T-t)}(S_t - \widetilde{\theta})dt & (14) \\ &= e^{-\widetilde{\mu}(T-t)} g(t, S_t) d\widetilde{Z}_t & (15) \\ &= e^{-\widetilde{\mu}(T-t)} g(t, S_t)(\lambda(t, S_t)dt + dZ_t). & (16) \end{aligned}$$

Equation (15) indicates the dynamics under $\mathbb{Q}$, while (16) reflects the dynamics under $\mathbb{P}$.

Following (12), we write the futures price with the discrete-time index, j, as

$$f_j^{(i)} = \widetilde{\theta} + (S_j - \widetilde{\theta})e^{-\widetilde{\mu}(T_i - j\Delta t)}, \quad \forall\, j \leq \frac{T_i}{\Delta t}. \tag{17}$$

Here, T_i is the maturity (measured in years) of the ith futures contract and is a multiple of Δt. The above is defined as $\forall\, j \leq \frac{T_i}{\Delta t}$. To simplify notation, we have assumed that all contracts being considered have incepted at or before time $j = 0$. For VIX futures, this assumption is valid if $N \leq 7$ and the trading horizon is less than or equal 6 months. In the general case, one can simply update the set of available futures as well and still maintain the above equations for all $j \leq \frac{T_i}{\Delta t}$.

To write down the return of each futures contract, we discretize (16) to get

$$f_{j+1}^{(i)} - f_j^{(i)} = e^{-\widetilde{\mu}(T_i - j\Delta t)} g(j\Delta t, S_j) \left(\lambda_j \Delta t + \sqrt{\Delta t} Z_{j+1}\right), \quad \forall\, j \geq 0, \tag{18}$$

where

$$\lambda_j := \lambda(j, S_j) = \frac{\mu(\theta - S_j) - \widetilde{\mu}(\widetilde{\theta} - S_j)}{g(j\Delta t, S_j)}, \qquad \forall\, j \geq 0 \tag{19}$$

is the discrete-time market price of risk. Let the time-to-maturity (in years) of the ith futures contract on day j be denoted by $D_j^{(i)} := T_i - j\Delta t$. It follows that the daily return of the ith futures contract is

$$
\begin{aligned}
\frac{f_{j+1}^{(i)}}{f_j^{(i)}} - 1 &= \frac{e^{-\widetilde{\mu}D_j^{(i)}} g(j\Delta t, S_j)}{\widetilde{\theta} + \left(S_j - \widetilde{\theta}\right) e^{-\widetilde{\mu}D_j^{(i)}}} \left(\lambda_j \Delta t + \sqrt{\Delta t} Z_{j+1}\right) \\
&= \frac{g(j\Delta t, S_j)}{\widetilde{\theta} e^{\widetilde{\mu}D_j^{(i)}} + S_j - \widetilde{\theta}} \left(\lambda_j \Delta t + \sqrt{\Delta t} Z_{j+1}\right) \\
&= B_j^{(i)} \left(\lambda_j \Delta t + \sqrt{\Delta t} Z_{j+1}\right), \forall j \geq 0,
\end{aligned} \tag{20}
$$

where we have defined

$$
B_j^{(i)} := \frac{g(j\Delta t, S_j)}{\widetilde{\theta} e^{\widetilde{\mu}D_j^{(i)}} + S_j - \widetilde{\theta}}, \qquad \forall j \geq 0. \tag{21}
$$

Putting (20) into (6), we now obtain the equation for the portfolio's return at each time step j:

$$
\begin{aligned}
\frac{X_{j+1}}{X_j} - 1 = e^{r\Delta t} - 1 &+ \Delta t \sum_{i=1}^{N} w_j^{(i)} B_j^{(i)} \lambda_j \\
&+ \sqrt{\Delta t} \sum_{i=1}^{N} w_j^{(i)} B_j^{(i)} Z_{j+1}, \quad \forall j \geq 0.
\end{aligned} \tag{22}
$$

4.2. *Optimal tracking problem*

We now discuss a dynamic portfolio of VIX futures designed to track the daily returns of VIX. On each day j, the investor seeks to minimize the conditional expected squared deviation of the portfolio's return from a multiple $\beta \in \mathbb{R}$ of the index's return.

$$
\min_{w_j^{(i)}, i=1,\ldots,N} \mathbb{E}^{\mathbb{P}} \left[\left(\frac{X_{j+1}}{X_j} - \beta \frac{S_{j+1}}{S_j} + \beta - 1 \right)^2 \middle| \mathcal{F}_j \right], \tag{23}
$$

where $\{\mathcal{F}_j\}_{j=0}^{\infty}$ is the discrete-time filtration representing information generated by prices observed as of day j. The leverage factor allows us to consider more general targets, though the value of $\beta = 1$ was of particular interest in Sections 2 and 3. The quantity $\beta - 1$ comes from the fact that the objective criterion in Optimization Problem (23) is a squared *return* difference. That is,

$$\frac{X_{j+1}}{X_j} - 1 - \beta\left(\frac{S_{j+1}}{S_j} - 1\right) = \frac{X_{j+1}}{X_j} - \beta\frac{S_{j+1}}{S_j} + \beta - 1.$$

Moreover, expectation is measured w.r.t. the historical measure, $\mathbb{P}$. We make this choice because the investor realizes cash flows in accordance with the historical (rather than risk-neutral) measure. The risk-neutral measure was only necessary to write down the discrete-time futures, price equation.

The ETN, VXX, is an exchange traded product that dynamically allocates wealth to two futures contracts. The rebalancing is based on the roll cycle of VIX futures and repeats itself during each cycle. In particular, at the beginning of the cycle, VXX holds 100% of its wealth in the 1-month futures, and via daily rebalancing, reduces its holdings in 1-month futures and purchases 2-month futures. By maturity of the 1-month futures, VXX has sold off its entire position in 1-month futures and holds 100% of its wealth in 2-month futures (which, at maturity is the 1-month futures). The reduction in 1-month holdings by VXX is linear and deterministic.

To reduce the complexity of Optimization Problem (23) and facilitate comparison to VXX, we consider a particular case where $N = 2$ with the added constraint that on each day j, we must have $w_j^{(i_1)} + w_j^{(i_2)} = 1$. We do not require any other restrictions on the weights. Specifically, we do not set any constraints on the sign or size of the weights and in general we will find that leveraging the position in one futures contract is required to optimally track the VIX according to Optimization Problem (23). Note that i_1 and i_2 are parameters for the optimization problem and are not optimization variables themselves. They are left generic and we will consider several different pairs in the numerical implementation.

The following proposition gives the complete solution to (23) in our particular case:

Proposition 4.1 *Under the discrete-time model* (7) *for the index* S *with a portfolio of* $N = 2$ *futures contracts on* S *with maturities* $T_{i_1} \neq T_{i_2}$ *given by* (5)*, the optimal strategy* $(w_j^{(i_1)*}, w_j^{(i_2)*})$ *associated with Optimization Problem* (23) *is given by*

$$w_j^{(i_1)*} = -\frac{\alpha_0\alpha_1 + \nu_0\nu_1}{\alpha_1^2 + \nu_1^2}, \quad w_j^{(i_2)} = 1 - w_j^{(i_1)*},$$

with the optimal objective function value

$$\frac{(\nu_1\alpha_0 - \nu_0\alpha_1)^2}{\alpha_1^2 + \nu_1^2},$$

where

$$\alpha_0 := e^{r\Delta t} - 1 + \Delta t B_j^{(i_2)}\lambda_j - \beta\mu\Delta t\left(\frac{\theta}{S_j} - 1\right), \tag{24}$$

$$\alpha_1 := \Delta t\lambda_j\left(B_j^{(i_1)} - B_j^{(i_2)}\right), \tag{25}$$

$$\nu_0 := \sqrt{\Delta t}\left(B_j^{(i_2)} - \frac{\beta g(j\Delta t, S_j)}{S_j}\right), \tag{26}$$

$$\nu_1 := \sqrt{\Delta t}\left(B_j^{(i_1)} - B_j^{(i_2)}\right). \tag{27}$$

Proof. Combining (8) and (22), we compute the difference between the portfolio's return and targeted multiple of the index's return:

$$\begin{aligned}
&\frac{X_{j+1}}{X_j} - 1 - \beta\left(\frac{S_{j+1}}{S_j} - 1\right) \\
&\quad = e^{r\Delta t} - 1 + \Delta t\sum_{i=1}^{N} w_j^{(i)} B_j^{(i)}\lambda_j + \sqrt{\Delta t}\sum_{i=1}^{N} w_j^{(i)} B_j^{(i)} Z_{j+1} \\
&\qquad - \beta\mu\Delta t\left(\frac{\theta}{S_j} - 1\right) - \frac{\beta g(j\Delta t, S_j)}{S_j}\sqrt{\Delta t} Z_{j+1}.
\end{aligned}$$

This can be expressed in the affine form $\phi_0 + \phi_1 Z_{j+1}$, where

$$\phi_0 := e^{r\Delta t} - 1 + \Delta t \sum_{i=1}^{N} w_j^{(i)} B_j^{(i)} \lambda_j - \beta\mu\Delta t \left(\frac{\theta}{S_j} - 1\right),$$

and

$$\phi_1 := \sqrt{\Delta t} \sum_{i=1}^{N} w_j^{(i)} B_j^{(i)} - \frac{\beta g(j\Delta t, S_j)}{S_j}\sqrt{\Delta t}.$$

Both ϕ_0 and ϕ_1 are stochastic and depend on j, S_j, along with other model parameters. However, they are both measurable with respect to $\mathcal{F}_j$. Using this with the fact that Z_{j+1} is independent of $\mathcal{F}_j$, we conclude that, conditional on $\mathcal{F}_j$, the return difference is *normally* distributed mean ϕ_0 and variance ϕ_1^2, and its conditional second moment is given by

$$\left(e^{r\Delta t} - 1 + \Delta t \sum_{i=1}^{N} w_j^{(i)} B_j^{(i)} \lambda_j + \beta\mu\Delta t \left(1 - \frac{\theta}{S_j}\right)\right)^2 + \left(\sqrt{\Delta t} \sum_{i=1}^{N} w_j^{(i)} B_j^{(i)} - \frac{\beta g(j\Delta t, S_j)}{S_j}\sqrt{\Delta t}\right)^2.$$

Now, we set $N = 2$ and $w \equiv w_j^{(i_1)}$ so that $w_j^{(i_2)} = 1 - w$. Then Optimization Problem (23) is equivalent to

$$\min_{w\in\mathbb{R}} (\alpha_0 + \alpha_1 w)^2 + (\nu_0 + \nu_1 w)^2, \tag{28}$$

where α_1, α_0, ν_1, and ν_0 are defined in (24)–(27). As with ϕ_0 and ϕ_1, all four of these coefficients are stochastic and depend on j, S_j as well as the parameters of the model and futures contracts, but we suppress the dependence here.

The square of a linear function is always convex and since the sum of convex function is convex, the overall optimization problem is convex. Therefore, the first-order condition, which is necessary and sufficient for global optimality when solvable, is given by

$$2\left(\alpha_0+\alpha_1 w\right)\alpha_1+2\left(\nu_0+\nu_1 w\right)\nu_1=0,$$

which gives the optimal strategy

$$w^*=-\frac{\alpha_0\alpha_1+\nu_0\nu_1}{\alpha_1^2+\nu_1^2}.$$

In order for this critical point to exist, we require $\alpha_1\neq 0$ or $\nu_1\neq 0$. Both are the case so long as $B_j^{(i_1)}\neq B_j^{(i_2)}$, which is equivalent to

$$\frac{g(j\Delta t,S_j)}{\widetilde{\theta}e^{\widetilde{\mu}D_j^{(i_1)}}+S_j-\widetilde{\theta}}\neq\frac{g(j\Delta t,S_j)}{\widetilde{\theta}e^{\widetilde{\mu}D_j^{(i_1)}}+S_j-\widetilde{\theta}}\iff e^{\widetilde{\mu}D_j^{(i_1)}}\neq e^{\widetilde{\mu}D_j^{(i_2)}}$$

$$\iff D_j^{(i_1)}\neq D_j^{(i_2)}.$$

This final condition is equivalent to futures contracts i_1 and i_2 having different times to maturity, which is assumed here. Finally, direct substitution of w^* into the objective function, $\left(\alpha_0+\alpha_1 w\right)^2+\left(\nu_0+\nu_1 w\right)^2$ yields the optimal objective function value. □

As a corollary to the above proposition, we can derive an index value S_j such that there is zero expected squared error.

Corollary 4.1 *Under the discrete-time model* (7) *for the index S with a portfolio of $N=2$ futures contracts on S with maturities $T_{i_1}\neq T_{i_2}$ given by* (5), *the objective function of Optimization Problem* (23) *has an optimal value of 0 if and only if*

$$S_j=\frac{\beta\widetilde{\mu}\widetilde{\theta}}{\beta\widetilde{\mu}+\bar{r}},\tag{29}$$

where $\bar{r}:=(e^{r\Delta t}-1)/\Delta t$.

Proof. With the notation from Proposition 4.1, the optimal objective function value is 0 for Optimization Problem (23) if and only if $\frac{\alpha_0}{\alpha_1} = \frac{\nu_0}{\nu_1}$. This is equivalent to

$$\frac{e^{r\Delta t} - 1 + \Delta t B_j^{(i_2)}\lambda_j + \beta\mu\Delta t\left(1 - \frac{\theta}{S_j}\right)}{\Delta t\lambda_j(B_j^{(i_1)} - B_j^{(i_2)})} = \frac{\sqrt{\Delta t}\left(B_j^{(i_2)} - \frac{\beta g(j\Delta t, S_j)}{S_j}\right)}{\sqrt{\Delta t}(B_j^{(i_1)} - B_j^{(i_2)})}.$$

After rearranging terms and using $\bar{r} = (e^{r\Delta t} - 1)/\Delta t$, we get

$$\bar{r}S_j + \beta\mu(S_j - \theta) = -\beta g(j\Delta t, S_j)\lambda_j\,.$$

Now applying equation (19) for the market price of risk λ_j, the last equation reduces to

$$\begin{aligned}\bar{r}S_j + \beta\mu(S_j - \theta) &= -\beta\left[\mu(\theta - S_j) - \widetilde{\mu}(\widetilde{\theta} - S_j)\right]\\ \iff \bar{r}S_j &= \beta\widetilde{\mu}(\widetilde{\theta} - S_j),\end{aligned}$$

which leads us to (29) as desired. □

Remark 4.1 *Interestingly, the critical value is independent of both the trading day j and maturities of the contracts. Leung and Ward (2018) provide the continuous-time analogue of this result with $\bar{r}$ being replaced by the continuously compounded interest rate. This is an intuitive correspondence between the trading frequency and compounding frequency of the interest rate that arises in dynamic replication.*

5. Implementation and Discussion

In this section, we implement the optimal strategy described in Section 4.2. In particular, we will set the function $g(\cdot,\cdot)$ as $g(t, S_t) = \sigma\sqrt{S_t}$, corresponding to the discrete-time version of the well-known CIR Model (see e.g. Cox *et al.*, 1985). We begin in Section 5.1, by discussing the calibration of this model under the historical and risk neutral measures. In Section 5.2, we simulate the strategy and discuss its properties, comparing and contrasting to VXX.

5.1. *Empirical estimation*

The optimal strategy derived in Proposition 4.1 requires two sets of parameters: those under the historical measure and those under the risk-neutral measure. We begin with the historical measure, where we utilize the Maximum Likelihood Estimation (MLE) framework to derive the parameters μ, θ, and σ. Suppose that the index S follows the CIR model

$$dS_t = \mu(\theta - S_t)dt + \sigma\sqrt{S_t}dZ_t,$$

where $\mu, \theta, \sigma > 0$ and Z_t is an SBM. Further, suppose we have observed a discrete sampling of S_t as $\{S_{t_1}, ..., S_{t_n}\}$. Then, the conditional probability density of S_{t_j} at time t_j given $S_{t_{j-1}} = s_{j-1}$ with (equally spaced) time increment $\Delta t := t_j - t_{j-1}$ is given by

$$f^{\text{CIR}}(s_j|s_{j-1};\theta,\mu,\sigma) = \frac{1}{\tilde{\sigma}^2}\exp\left(-\frac{s_j + s_{j-1}e^{-\mu\Delta t}}{\tilde{\sigma}^2}\right)\left(\frac{s_j}{s_{j-1}e^{-\mu\Delta t}}\right)^{\frac{\mathfrak{q}}{2}} \times I_{\mathfrak{q}}\left(\frac{2}{\tilde{\sigma}^2}\sqrt{s_j s_{j-1}e^{-\mu\Delta t}}\right),$$

with the constants

$$\tilde{\sigma}^2 = \sigma^2\frac{1 - e^{-\mu\Delta t}}{2\mu}, \quad \mathfrak{q} = \frac{2\mu\theta}{\sigma^2} - 1,$$

and $I_{\mathfrak{q}}(z)$ is modified Bessel function of the first kind and of order $\mathfrak{q}$.

Using the observed values $\{s_j\}_{j=1}^n$, the CIR model parameters can be estimated by maximizing the average log-likelihood as follows:

$$\begin{aligned}\ell(\theta,\mu,\sigma|s_1,\ldots,s_n) &:= \frac{1}{n-1}\sum_{j=2}^{n}\ln f^{\mathrm{CIR}}(s_j|s_{j-1};\theta,\mu,\sigma)\\ &= -2\ln(\tilde{\sigma}) - \frac{1}{(n-1)\tilde{\sigma}^2}\sum_{j=2}^{n}(s_j + s_{j-1}e^{-\mu\Delta t})\\ &\quad + \frac{1}{n-1}\sum_{j=2}^{n}\left(\frac{\mathfrak{q}}{2}\ln\left(\frac{s_j}{s_{j-1}e^{-\mu\Delta t}}\right)\right.\\ &\quad \left. + \ln I_{\mathfrak{q}}\left(\frac{2}{\tilde{\sigma}^2}\sqrt{s_j s_{j-1}e^{-\mu\Delta t}}\right)\right).\end{aligned}$$

After calibrating the model to in-sample data, we obtain $(\mu,\theta,\sigma) = (10.86, 18.81, 6.37)$.

Next, we turn to the risk-neutral measure. Recalling that the volatility will not change under this measure, we need only calibrate the parameters of the mean reversion: $\widetilde{\mu}$ and $\widetilde{\theta}$. To do so, we employ the Method of Moments (MOM) framework, which is the industry standard. In particular, we will match the conditional expectations $\mathbb{E}^{\mathbb{Q}}\left[S_{T_i}|S_t\right]$, both across time and across contract maturity. In particular, the futures price on S, with maturity T_i, as observed at time t_j is given by

$$f_t^{T_i} = (S_{t_j} - \widetilde{\theta})e^{-\widetilde{\mu}(T_i - t_j)} + \widetilde{\theta}.$$

On any particular trade date, we observe the spot price as well as the entire term structure. Therefore, the dataset for calibration of the risk-neutral parameters is the set of triples

$$\left\{\left(S_{t_j}, T_i, f_{t_j}^{T_i}\right) : j = 1, ..., n, i = 1, ..., N_j\right\},$$

where N_j is the number of futures contracts available for trading on day j. We utilize all available price data from all traded VIX futures contracts. Let us denote $s_j := S_{t_j}$ and $f_j^{(i)} := f_{t_j}^{T_i}$. To implement the MOM for a particular trade date, we consider the loss function

$$L\left(\widetilde{\mu}, \widetilde{\theta} \middle| s_j\right) := \frac{1}{2N_j} \sum_{i=1}^{N_j} \left((s_j - \widetilde{\theta})e^{-\widetilde{\mu}T_i} + \widetilde{\theta} - f_j^{(i)}\right)^2.$$

To obtain a single set of parameters across all days, we average the loss function over the entire sample and minimize

$$\begin{aligned} L_{\mathrm{RN}}\left(\widetilde{\mu}, \widetilde{\theta} \middle| s_1, \ldots, s_n\right) &:= \frac{1}{n} \sum_{j=1}^{n} L\left(\widetilde{\mu}, \widetilde{\theta} \middle| s_j\right) \\ &= \frac{1}{n} \sum_{j=1}^{n} \frac{1}{2N_j} \sum_{i=1}^{N_j} \left((s_j - \widetilde{\theta})e^{-\widetilde{\mu}T_i} + \widetilde{\theta} - f_j^{(i)}\right)^2, \end{aligned} \tag{30}$$

by choosing $\widetilde{\mu}$ and $\widetilde{\theta}$. After calibrating to the in-sample data, the estimators for $\widetilde{\mu}$ and $\widetilde{\theta}$ are given as 1.39 and 26.03, respectively.

5.2. *Performance and properties of tracking strategy*

In this section, we discuss the properties of the optimal dynamic strategy derived in Section 4. Specifically, we use the parameters computed in Section 5.1, and simulate the index and its corresponding futures prices via (7) and (17). In turn, the dynamic portfolio values and VXX prices are generated by their corresponding strategies. For both, 1-month and 2-month futures are used in the portfolios. Recall that VXX has a linear strategy that starts from 100% invested in the first-month futures and linearly decreases the holding in the first-month contract while increasing the holding of the second-month contract day by day until the first-month futures expires.

Three different scenarios are simulated in Fig. 8. We consider a 3-contract cycle (63 total days) period and separate the analysis into three cases. In panel (a), S starts at its historical long-run level of θ. In panel (b), S starts at a low value of $\theta/3$, and in panel (c),

S starts at a high value of $3 \cdot \theta$. In these scenarios, the index itself exhibits (a) non-directional, (b) upward trending, or (c) downward trending movements. In all cases, we see that the dynamic portfolio is clearly co-moving with the index though the magnitude of movements differ. The same is true for VXX. Recall that the strategy is designed to track the index returns, rather than the physical price. In other words, the tracking strategy does not account for current or past price deviations, and only seeks to optimize tracking of the index return for the next period. As a result, the tracking portfolio tends to move in the same direction as the index regardless of their dollar values relative to each other. Over time, price deviations may even accumulate. Nevertheless, as we can see in Fig. 8, the dynamic tracking strategy tend to stay closer to the index in all three scenarios.

To see that the dynamic portfolio tracks the returns of VIX better than VXX, we display a simulated return scatterplot in Fig. 10 over 6 contract cycles. Panel (a) shows the scatterplot of the returns of the dynamic portfolio vs. the returns of VIX, while panel (b) gives the scatterplot of the returns of VXX vs. the returns of VIX. Both plots have the same $x-y$ axis scale for easy comparison. We also superimpose (in black) the line $y = x$. One notices that for the dynamic portfolio, the return pairs are closer to the line $y = x$ indicating that the portfolio returns closely match the returns of VIX. On the other hand, for VXX the returns are further from this line and the slope appears to be less than 1 in value. In fact, both statements are statistically significant.

Our linear regressions to the two scatterplots yield the following results: In (a), the slope is 1.0030 with a standard error of $1.6408 \cdot 10^{-3}$, the intercept is $-8.5514 \cdot 10^{-4}$ with a standard error of $1.2979 \cdot 10^{-4}$, and $R^2 = 99.97\%$. In (b), the slope is 0.8734 with a standard error of $2.9477 \cdot 10^{-3}$, the intercept is $-10.1524 \cdot 10^{-4}$ with a standard error of $2.3318 \cdot 10^{-4}$, and $R^2 = 99.86\%$. We obtain a p-value of 0.078 for testing the null hypothesis $H_0 : \{\text{slope} = 1\}$ for the regression of the dynamic portfolio returns vs. VIX returns in panel (a), which is greater than many standard significance levels. The corresponding test for VXX has a p-value of $6.521 \cdot 10^{-76}$. Finally, we caution that

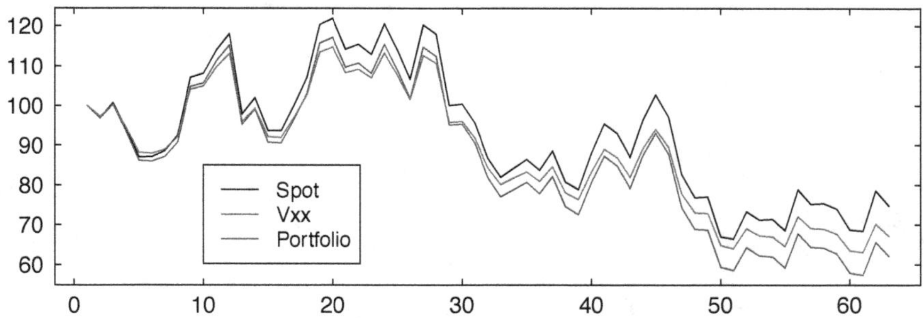

(a) $S_0 = \Theta$

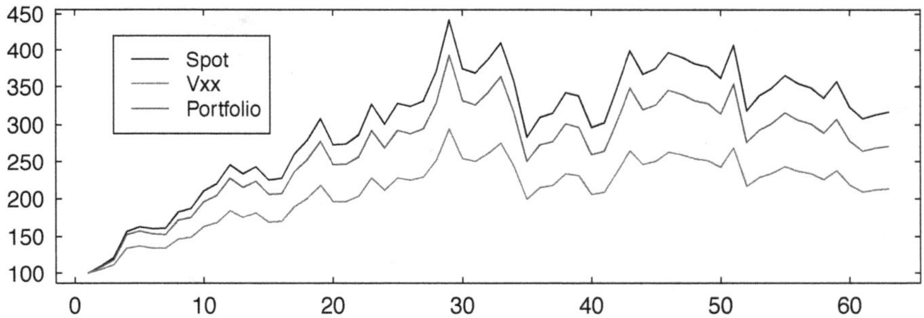

(b) $S_0 = \frac{1}{3} \cdot \Theta$

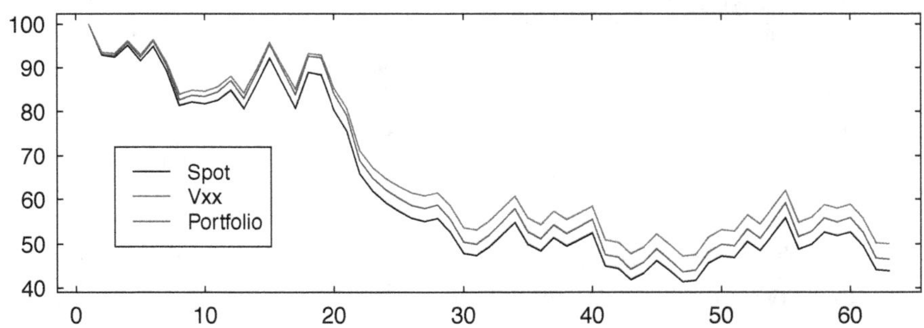

(c) $S_0 = 3 \cdot \Theta$

Fig. 8. Sample paths of the index, VXX, and dynamic portfolio under three different scenarios: (a) when VIX starts at its historical long-run mean θ, (b) when VIX starts at a lower value $\theta/3$, and (c) when VIX starts at a higher value 3θ. All portfolios are normalized to start at \$100 and their time series are plotted over 3 contract cycles. The parameters are $\mu = 10.86$, $\theta = 18.81$, $\sigma = 6.38$, $\widetilde{\mu} = 1.39$, and $\widetilde{\theta} = 26.03$. The x-axis marks the trading day, while the y-axis marks the price.

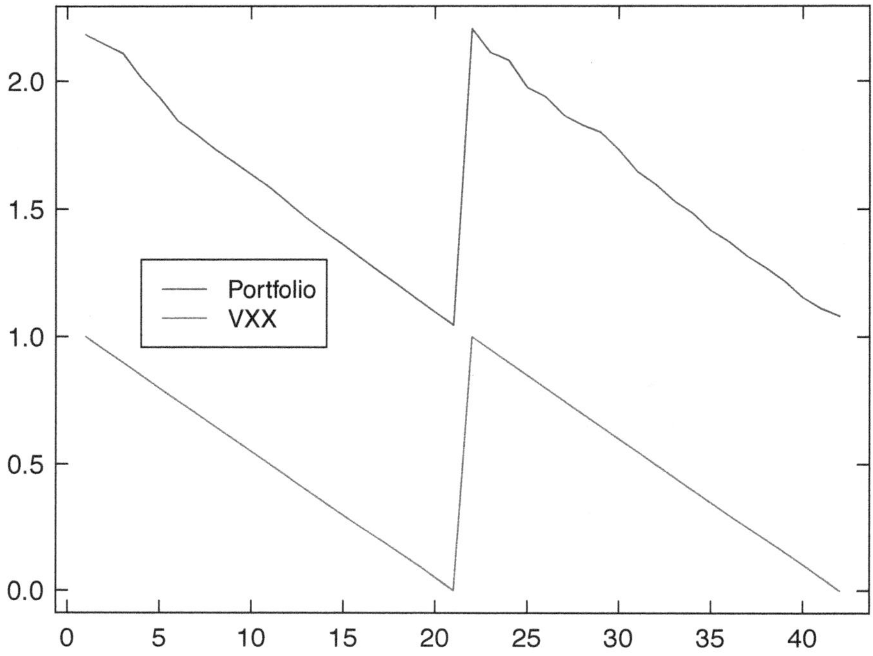

Fig. 9. Sample paths of the portfolio weight, expressed in terms of the fraction of wealth invested in the 1-month futures, associated with the dynamic portfolio and VXX over 42 trading days (i.e., 2 contract cycles). The rest of the portfolio is invested in the 2-month futures. The parameters are $\mu = 10.86$, $\theta = 18.81$, $\sigma = 6.38$, $\widetilde{\mu} = 1.39$, $\widetilde{\theta} = 26.03$, and $S_0 = \theta$. The x-axis marks the trading day, while the y-axis marks the weight on 1-month futures.

the high R^2 value (over 99%) implies that the dynamic portfolio can generate very similar returns to the VIX on a daily basis, but does not mean that it can perfectly replicate the physical dollar value of VIX over a long period of time.

As for the strategy, we give an example in Fig. 9 over two contract cycles. Interestingly, the dynamic strategy is quite linear falling from a little over 2 in value to 1 by maturity. This indicates that the strategy is also short 100% of its value in 2-month futures rising to 0% by maturity of the 1-month futures. For comparison, we also plot the strategy of VXX, which is linear from 1 to 0 over each contract cycle.

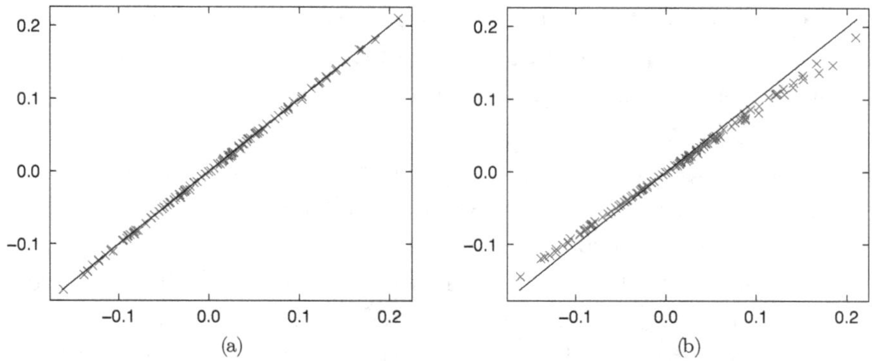

Fig. 10. Scatterplots of returns for (a) dynamic portfolio vs. VIX and (b) VXX vs. VIX. We also plot a solid straight line with zero intercept to illustrate the deviations of the dynamic portfolio or VXX returns from the VIX returns. The parameters are $\mu = 10.86$, $\theta = 18.81$, $\sigma = 6.38$, $\widetilde{\mu} = 1.39$, $\widetilde{\theta} = 26.03$, and $S_0 = \theta$. Trading is over 126 trading days (6 contract cycles). The x-axis marks the index returns (in decimals), while the y-axis marks the dynamic portfolio/VXX returns (in decimals).

6. Conclusions

In this chapter, we have presented the construction of static and dynamic portfolios of VIX futures that are optimized for VIX tracking. As discussed from both empirical and theoretical perspectives, futures prices tend not to react quickly enough to movements in the spot VIX. They also bring persistent negative returns and thus make tracking VIX difficult. In view of the pitfalls of static portfolios, we design and implement a dynamic trading strategy that adjusts futures positions daily to optimally replicate VIX's returns. The model is calibrated to historical data and a simulation study is performed to understand the properties exhibited by the strategy. In addition, compared to the volatility ETN, VXX, we find that our dynamic strategy has a superior tracking performance.

In practice, both static and dynamic futures portfolios will involve trading costs. Nevertheless, in recent years, commission fees for futures trading have decreased significantly to around or less than \$1/contract for long and short futures positions on major brokerages.

Moreover, our static futures portfolios (see Table 3) involve only 1–4 contracts and require no rebalancing once initialized, while our dynamic portfolio (see Fig. 9) only needs an incremental adjustment once a day. For all our portfolios, we have used futures with the shortest terms, which are typically most liquid with smaller bid–ask spreads. Hence, trading costs are unlikely to have a prohibitive impact on performance.

There are a number of directions for future research. The question of how well ETFs or ETNs track their reference index is not limited to VIX-based products. It is relevant and important for all other asset classes, ranging from equities to commodities.[13] In our static replicating portfolios, we have chosen to include futures only for comparison to VXX. Alternatively, one can also construct a static portfolio of options and optimize to minimize tracking errors with respect to an index or its leveraged exposure (see Leung and Lorig, 2016). It would be interesting to compare the tracking performance of portfolios with different derivatives. Strategies and instruments aside, a major challenge in all tracking problems is to properly model the evolution of the index. Hence, accurate predictions of the index movements can potentially enhance tracking performance. To that end, one future research direction is to apply machine learning techniques to incorporate predictive analytics into the tracking problem.

Acknowledgment

The authors are grateful to the editor and two anonymous referees for their helpful remarks and suggestions.

References

Black, F. (1976). Studies of stock price volatility changes. In *Proceedings of the 1976 Meetings of the American Statistical Association, Business and Economics Statistics Section*, pp. 177–181.

[13]See Guo and Leung (2015) for a study on the tracking performance of commodity ETFs.

Cox, J. C., Ingersoll, J. E., and Ross, S. A. (1985). A theory of the term structure of interest rates. *Econometrica* **53**(2), 385–408.

Deng, G., McCann, C., and Wang, O. (2012). Are VIX futures ETPs effective hedges? *The Journal of Index Investing* **3**(3), 35–48.

Eraker, B. and Wu, Y. (2013). Explaining the negative returns to VIX futures and ETNs: An equilibrium approach. Working Paper.

Grübichler, A. and Longstaff, F. (1996). Valuing futures and options on volatility. *Journal of Banking and Finance* **20**(6), 985–1001.

Guo, K. and Leung, T. (2015). Understanding the tracking errors of commodity leveraged ETFs. In Aid, R., Ludkovski, M., and Sircar, R. (Eds.). *Commodities, Energy and Environmental Finance, Fields Institute Communications.* Springer.

Guo, K. and Leung, T. (2017). Understanding the non-convergence of agricultural futures via stochastic storage costs and timing options. *Journal of Commodity Markets* **6**, 32–49.

Jiao, L. (2016). Trading vix futures under mean reversion with regime switching. *International Journal of Financial Engineering* **3**(3), 1650021 (2016) https://www.worldscientific.com/doi/abs/10.1142/S2424786316500213

Leung, T., Li, J., Li, X., and Wang, Z. (2016). Speculative futures trading under mean reversion. *Asia-Pacific Financial Markets* **23**(4), 281–304.

Leung, T. and Li, X. (2016). *Optimal Mean Reversion Trading: Mathematical Analysis and Practical Applications.* Modern Trends in Financial Engineering. World Scientific Publishing Company.

Leung, T. and Lorig, M. (2016). Optimal quadratic static hedging. *Quantitative Finance* **9**(16), 1341–1355.

Leung, T. and Ward, B. (2015). The golden target: Analyzing the tracking performance of leveraged gold ETFs. *Studies in Economics and Finance* **32**(3), 278–297.

Leung, T. and Ward, B. (2018). Dynamic index tracking and risk exposure control using derivatives. *Applied Mathematical Finance* **25**(2), 180–212.

Leung, T. and Yan, R. (2018). Optimal dynamic pairs trading of futures under a two-factor mean-reverting model. *International Journal of Financial Engineering* **5**(3), 1850027.

Leung, T. and Yan, R. (2019). A stochastic control approach to managed futures portfolios. *International Journal of Financial Engineering* **6**(1), 1950005.

Mencia, J. and Sentana, E. (2013). Valuation of VIX derivatives. *Journal of Financial Economics* **108**, 367–391.

Pavlova, I. and Daigler, R. T. (2008). The non-convergence of VIX futures at expiration. *Review of Futures Markets* **17**(2), 201–223.

Uhlenbeck, G. E. and Ornstein, L. S. (1930). On the theory of the Brownian motion. *Physical Review* **36**(5), 823–841.

Ward, B. (2017). *Optimal Dynamic Strategies for Index Tracking and Algorithmic Trading*. PhD thesis, Columbia University.

Whaley, R. E. (2013). Trading volatility: At what cost? *The Journal of Portfolio Management* **40**(1), 95–108.

Zhang, J. E. and Zhu, Y. (2006). VIX futures. *Journal of Futures Markets* **26**(6), 521–531.

https://doi.org/10.1142/9789811222634_0021

Chapter 21

Long-Memory Processes in High-Frequency Foreign Exchange and U.S. Equity Market

Barret Pengyuan Shao

Evince Asset Management, Arlington, VA, USA

Long-memory processes in the financial time series is an important research topic in derivative pricing and risk management. Most of the past empirical research about the long-memory processes have been conducted based on a lower frequency sampling, such as daily or monthly data. Very few works have been done with high-frequency financial data.

In this study, we apply some widely used statistical tests (R/S, modified R/S, correlogram, and GPH tests) to investigate the existence of long-memory processes in the high-frequency Foreign Exchange (FX) and U.S. equity market returns and its realized volatility. In these financial markets, we find that the existence of long-memory processes in the high-frequency returns is insignificant; but the existence of long-memory processes is significant in the high-frequency realized volatility. For the realized volatility of U.S. equity market, we also report that the presence of long-memory processes is more significant with higher Hurst exponent when sampling at a higher frequency.

Keywords: Long-memory process, high-frequency financial data, modified R/S, correlogram, GPH test.

1. Introduction

1.1. *Long-memory processes*

The memory of a stochastic process is usually defined based on its autocovariance functions. Short-memory stationary processes refer to the stochastic process whose autocovariance functions decay fast and whose spectral density is bounded everywhere. One of the most widely applied time series models with short memory is the stationary autoregressive moving average model (ARMA). Compared to short-memory processes, long-memory processes are stochastic processes with a slowly decaying autocovariance function, which is not integrable or summable (see McLeod and Hipel, 1978). Equivalently, the spectrum density of long-memory processes is unbounded. The definition of the long-memory process is as follows:

Definition 1. A time series x_t, whose $E(x_t) = \mu$ and $\mathrm{Cov}(x_t, x_{t+j}) = \gamma_j$ do not depend on time t, is said to be a covariance stationary time series (Robinson, 2003). Given the autocovariance function γ_k, autocorrelation function ρ_k is defined as $\rho_k = \gamma_k/\gamma_0$. Then the time series x_t is a long-memory process when the autocorrelations are not absolutely summable:

$$\lim_{T\to\infty} \sum_{k=0}^{T} |\rho_k| = \infty. \tag{1}$$

1.2. *Hurst exponent*

Hurst exponent is a widely used measure of the long-memory in observable time series, and it is also related to the fractional differencing parameter in FARIMA model, which will be described in Section 1.3. The classical rescaled range statistic (R/S) was developed by Hurst (1951):

$$\begin{aligned} R/S(n) = \frac{1}{S(n)} \Bigg[&\max_{0\le t\le n} \left(Y(t) - \frac{t}{n} Y(n) \right) \\ &- \min_{0\le t\le n} \left(Y(t) - \frac{t}{n} Y(n) \right) \Bigg], n \ge 1, \end{aligned} \tag{2}$$

where $S(n)$ is the standard deviation estimator and $Y(n)$ is the sample returns.

$$S(n) = \sqrt{\frac{1}{n} \sum_{0 \leq t \leq n} \left(Y(t) - \bar{Y}_n\right)^2}. \tag{3}$$

The relationship between Hurst exponent and the R/S statistic is

$$Q(n) = R/S(n) = an^H, \tag{4}$$

where H is the estimated Hurst exponent. Traditionally, processes with long-memory are identified with Hurst exponents $\frac{1}{2} < H < 1$.

Also the well-known fractional Brownian motion(fBm) is defined based on the Hurst exponent by Mandelbrot and Van Ness (1968):

$$B_H(t) = \frac{1}{\Gamma\left(H + \frac{1}{2}\right)} \int_{-\infty}^{t} (t - \tau)^{H - \frac{1}{2}} \, dB(\tau), \tag{5}$$

where $\Gamma(\cdot)$ is the gamma function and H is the Hurst parameter, $0 < H < 1$.

From the definition, we can also obtain the covariance function for fractional Brownian motion described by Hurst exponent H:

$$R_H(t, s) = E\left[B_H(t) B_H(s)\right] = \frac{1}{2}\left(t^{2H} + s^{2H} - |t - s|^{2H}\right) \tag{6}$$

$$B_H(t) = \frac{1}{\Gamma\left(H + \frac{1}{2}\right)} \int_{0}^{t} (t - s)^{H - \frac{1}{2}} \, dB(s). \tag{7}$$

1.3. *Long-memory processes in financial time series*

The existence of long-memory phenomenon in financial time series has been discussed by numerous researches for a long time. We briefly review some of the pioneering works and important literatures here. The main discussions regarding the long-memory processes can be classified by financial asset returns and financial asset volatility.

One of the most widely used detections of long-memory processes is rescaled range analysis, R/S, which is proposed by Mandelbrot

(1972). The reason we mention R/S first is that many pioneering researches were based on R/S or the modified R/S in the following years. Lo (1989) proposed the modified R/S analysis and found little evidence of long-memory in the U.S. stock market returns by this measurement. Nawrocki (1995) claimed that there existed the long-memory from the view of R/S statistic and suggest that the dependence raised from general economic cycle. Chow (1996) did the research on 22 international equity market indexes based on modified R/S test and rescaled variance ratio test. They found evidence against the random walk hypothesis is very weak, in agreement with Lo's result (1989). Mandelbrott (1997) claimed that the long-memory phenomenon existed in stock prices. Lobato and Savin (1998) analyzed the subperiods of returns and individual stocks in U.S. stock market and found no long-memory in these returns. Willinger *et al.* (1999) argued that Lo (1989) had a bias to accept the null hypothesis and they used the CRSP[1] daily data to show empirical evidence of long-memory, but with low Hurst exponent (around 0.6). Sadique and Silvapulle (2001) found long-memory, suggesting that some countries are not efficient markets. In currency markets, Cheung and Lai (2001) gave an alternative explanation to puzzling behavior of yen exchange rate based on long-memory. In the S&P 500 Index options, one of the most actively traded derivatives, Kim (2016) captured the long-memory property in the S&P 500 Index options through the calibration of a fractional normal tempered stable process. Kim *et al.* (2019) also discovered the Hurst index was typically larger than 0.5 when the same market was not volatile while below 0.5 when the market was turbulent, such as the U.S. credit rating downgrade in August 2011.

Compared to the debate on the existence of long-memory processes in financial returns, financial volatility has been shown to have more pronounced long-memory phenomenon by many studies in the literature. Ding *et al.* (1993) did the research on the absolute returns $|r_t|^d$, and claimed that this power transformation had very

[1]CRSP: Center for Research in Security Prices is one of the major providers of historical stock market data. CRSP covers the U.S. traded stock data back to 1926. For more information, readers are referred to: http://www.crsp.chicagobooth.edu/index.html.

high autocorrelation for long lags. Bollerslev and Mikkelsen (1996) show the existence of long-memory processes in U.S. stock market volatility and proposed to use fractionally integrated EGARCH model for characterizing the long-memory. Breidt (1998) show the empirical evidence of the long-memory existence in an extensive set of U.S. stock return indexes and proposed the long-memory stochastic volatility (LMSV) model, which incorporates FARIMA processes in a standard stochastic scheme, to model the value-weighted CRSP market index. In 1998, Lobato and Savin (1998) show that squared returns have strong long-memory in individual stock returns.

Besides the financial returns and volatility series, the existence and property of long-memory processes have also been investigated in other parts of financial markets. For example, Gatheral *et al.* (2004) reported the long-memory effect in market order flow in the Paris Stock Exchange in 2004. Baillie and Bollerslev (1994) show that in foreign exchange market, the forward premium had long-memory. From the perspective of classical financial theory, one of the main reasons that we want to know whether a financial time series belongs to long-memory or short-memory processes is related to the efficient market hypothesis (EMH). The EMH has a long history in finance and the existence of long-memory processes means that the information from the distant past can still affect current value significantly, which would cast doubt on EMH.

Also, in the Black–Scholes option pricing model, one important assumption is that stock returns follow the exponential Brownian motion. Pricing financial derivatives using martingales does not deal with the long-memory property easily. CAPM, or arbitrage pricing theory, also has problems with long-memory process.

1.4. *Long-memory process and other stochastic processes*

There are many theoretical literatures discussing about whether non-long-memory processes can present the properties of long-memory processes, which they call spurious long-memory processes. Klemeš (1974) show that the infinite memory of a process could be caused by the nonstationarity. Granger and Joyeux (1980) proved that some specific aggregation of AR models could have long-memory properties. Taqqu *et al.* (1997) found that the aggregation of stationary processes with superposition of many ON/OFF converged to fractional Brownian motion with long-memory property. Diebold and Inoue (2001) show that various structural break models could be confused with the long-memory process. Barndorff-Nielsen *et al.* (2011) show that the superpositions of Ornstein–Uhlenbeck processes, supOU, can exhibit long-memory property under certain conditions. However, most of these "analytical connections" have very strong assumptions and we can construct the spurious long-memory processes with these assumptions as many times as we want.

In reality, when we have finite samples instead of infinite length, the analytical difference between the spurious and real ones might not be too important. For example, Diebold and Inoue (2001) did the statistical tests on simulation from short-memory processes and conclude that it is hard to clear the confusion between real long-memory processes and spurious ones given the small number of samples. Specifically in their empirical part, they show the GPH result with a static markov-switching model, which is a short-memory process. He said that when sample size was not large (5,000 in this case), the test would reject the null hypothesis that the process is a short-memory process. But when sample size is large, this kind of fake process eventually will not be rejected as a short-memory process. If the null hypothesis is $d = 0$ for $I(d)$ process, finding the relation between the rate of rejection and sample size is important for identifying long-memory process with finite sample size. This is worth mentioning when we discuss whether long-memory processes exist in the financial data.

2. Statistical Tests on The Long-Memory Process

In this section, we briefly describe three statistical tests that are used to investigate the existence of long-memory processes in the high-frequency FX and U.S. equity market data here: Modified R/S test, Correlogram test, and GPH tests.

2.1. *Modified R/S test*

Lo (1989) shows that the normalized R/S statistic, $V_c = \frac{1}{\sqrt{n}} Q(n)$, has the asymptotic distribution as follows:

$$F_V(v) \sim 1 + 2\sum_{k=1}^{\infty} \left(1 - 4k^2\nu\right) e^{-2(kv)^2}. \tag{8}$$

Also Lo (1989) states that the classic R/S statistic could be biased caused by the short-term memory and he proposes the modified R/S statistic $\tilde{Q}(n,q)$ in the following form:

$$\tilde{Q}(n,q) = R(n) / \tilde{S}(n,q), \tag{9}$$

where

$$\tilde{S}(n,q) = S(n) + 2\sum_{i=1}^{q} \omega_i(q)\,\hat{\gamma}_i, \omega_i(q) = 1 - \frac{i}{q+1}, q < n, \tag{10}$$

where $\hat{\gamma}_i$ are the sample estimated autocorrelations and we denote the normalized modified rescaled range statistic as

$$V(q) = \frac{1}{\sqrt{n}} \tilde{Q}(n,q), \tag{11}$$

Modified rescaled range statistic excludes part of long-term dependence implied by short-term dependence. However, the shortcoming of modified R/S statistic is the need to choose parameter lag q, which is difficult to do robustly (see Lo, 1989). Lo (1989) gives the fractiles of the distribution $F_V(v)$, which will be used to implement the statistical tests in Section 3.

2.2. *Correlogram test*

Recall that the definition of long-memory process is based on the decay speed of the autocorrelation function of the underlying processes. Let ρ_k be the autocorrelation function of a time series r_t and the long-memory processes have the absolute value of autocorrelation not summable: $\lim_{n\to\infty} \sum_{k=1}^{n} |\rho_k| = \infty$.

Therefore, another way to examine long-memory is through the limiting decay rate of the autocorrelation function (see Beran, 1992; Hiemstra and Jones, 1997). Many previous works compare the estimated autocorrelation at lag k to the 95% confidence interval, which is $\pm 2/\sqrt{k}$ in this case, and argue whether there exists long-memory in the time series observed.

Beran (1994) shows that for stationary long-memory processes, there exists a real number $\alpha \in (0,1)$ and a constant $c_\rho > 0$ such that

$$\lim_{k \to \infty} \frac{\rho_k}{c_\rho k^{-\alpha}} = 1. \tag{12}$$

So one alternative way to test for long-memory processes is to see how the $\log |\rho_k|$ for the process decays asymptotically. A linear relation can be obtained by taking logarithm of the asymptotic relationship as $k \to \infty$:

$$\log(|\rho(k)|) \sim \log c_\rho - \alpha \log(k). \tag{13}$$

Given the estimated $\hat{\alpha}$ from the sampled autocorrelation, we can also estimate the Hurst exponent H by $\hat{H} = 1 - \frac{1}{2}\hat{\alpha}$.

2.3. *GPH test*

Before introducing the GPH test, here is a brief description of the fractional autoregressive integrated moving average model (FARIMA process), which is a commonly used stochastic process to model long-memory processes.

The fractional differencing operator is one of the fundamental parts in the FARIMA model and it is also the part that adds the long-memory property to the short-memory ARMA process. The definition of the fractional difference operator is defined as follows (see Hosking, 1981):

Fractional differencing operator ∇^d can be defined by a binomial series of backward-shift operators:

$$\nabla^d = (1-L)^d = \sum_{k=0}^{\infty} \binom{d}{k} (-L)^k = \sum_{k=0}^{\infty} \frac{\prod_{a=0}^{k-1}(d-a)}{k!} (-L)^k, \tag{14}$$

where L is the backward-shift operator, such that $Lx_t = x_{t-1}$, and we also have the following expression: $\nabla^{-d} = \sum_{k=0}^{\infty} \binom{d}{k} L^k$.

FARIMA(p,d,q) process is then defined to have the following form (see Hoskin, 1981; Granger and Joyeux, 1980, for more details):

$$\phi(L) \nabla^d x_t = \theta(L) \varepsilon_t, \tag{15}$$

where ∇^d is the fractional differencing operator; $\phi(L)$ and $\theta(L)$ are polynomials of the backward-shift operator L:

$$\begin{aligned} \phi(L) &= 1 - \phi_1 L - \phi_2 L^2 - \cdots - \phi_p L^p \\ \theta(L) &= 1 - \theta_1 L - \theta_2 L^2 - \cdots - \theta_q L^q, \end{aligned}$$

p and q define the order of Autoregressive (AR) and Moving Average (MA) parts, respectively, and they are integers. d represents the order of fractional difference and it can take fractional value. The relationship between the d and the Hurst exponent H is $d = H - \frac{1}{2}$.

An alternative way to examine whether a selected time series is a long-memory process is to examine the fractional differencing parameter d in FARIMA(0,d,0) process. There are different methodologies to estimate the fractional differencing parameter d and we use the GPH test here.

Without the ARMA part in FARIMA(p,d,q) processes, x_t is said to follow FARIMA(0,d,0) process when $x_t = (1-z)^{-d} \varepsilon_t$. So its autocovariance-generating function is

$$g_x(z) = \sigma^2 (1-z)^{-d} \left(1 - z^{-1}\right)^{-d} = \left[(1-z)\left(1-z^{-1}\right)\right]^{-d} \tag{16}$$

as $\sigma^2 = 1$ for standard Gaussian innovations. The spectral density function of FARIMA(0,d,0) is as follows:

$$f(\omega) = \frac{1}{2\pi} \left[\left(1 - e^{i\omega}\right)\left(1 - e^{-i\omega}\right)\right]^{-d} = \frac{1}{2\pi} \left(4 \sin^2 \frac{\omega}{2}\right)^{-d}. \tag{17}$$

To estimate the fractional differencing parameter d, Geweke and Porter-Hudak (1983) proposed to use the periodogram estimator to estimate the spectrum density function $f(\omega)$ and estimate the d through the linear regression of $\log f(\omega)$:

$$\log f(\omega) = -\log 2\pi - 2d \log\left(2 \sin \frac{\omega}{2}\right). \tag{18}$$

In Section 3, we apply this method to estimate the fractional differencing parameter d, which then gives us the estimated Hurst exponent H, to investigate whether long-memory processes exist in the high-frequency financial time series.

3. Empirical Results

In this section, we apply the above-mentioned statistical tests of the long-memory processes to the high frequency financial returns and volatility time series. We examine the long-memory phenomena on spot foreign exchange (FX) markets and U.S. equity markets.

3.1. *FX market*

Data in this empirical analysis are from the tick-by-tick quote database, recorded in Hotspot trading venue. The dataset are the seven most liquid currencies in the world, which are called G7 currencies in the following sections. The G7 currencies are Australian Dollar (AUD), Canadian Dollar (CAD), Swiss Franc (CHF), Euro (EUR), British Pound (GBP), Japanese Yen (JPY), and U.S. Dollar (USD). The main reason that we only use G7 currencies here is the liquidity.

Compared to other trading instruments, FX trading is more liquid and multi-venues traded. Instead of a single electronic exchange, various trading venues exist, such as Reuters, Hotspot, FXCM, and a lot of single-bank e-commerce platforms (Shao and Frank, 2012). For this reason, it is almost impossible to get a completely aggregate FX order book among the entire existing trading venues. In this empirical study, we apply the tick-by-tick data from Hotspot, which are dense and have higher trading volumes than most of the other trading venues. The following graph is the FX volume trend in some major trading venues.[2]

[2] *Source*: Hotspot Monthly Statistics.

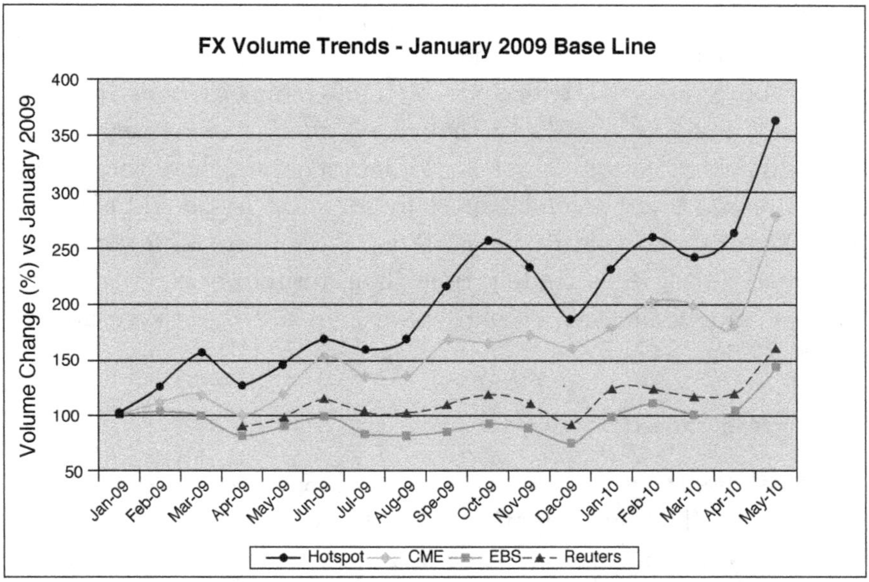

Fig. 1. FX volume trends — December 2008 base line.

This graph (Fig. 1) shows us that it is reasonable to use Hotspot quote data for our purpose to examine the existence of long-memory processes in the FX markets. The top five currency pairs by volume in Hotspot are EUR/USD(47.33%), AUD/USD(10.74%), USD/JPY(9.52%), GBP/USD(8.92%), and USD/CAD(5.05%).[3] G7 currencies contribute the majority of trading volumes in FX trading and that is why only G7 currencies are under consideration in this empirical study.

There are few published research studies concerning the long-memory processes in high-frequency financial data, especially in the FX market. We extract the last mid-price of ask price and bid price for every second. The data range from 2008-01-01 00:00:01 to 2011-12-31-23:59:59, which include 4 years of data. 20 currency pairs from the G7 currencies are examined here, such as USD/CHF, AUD/CAD, AUD/NZD, etc.

[3]Hotspot Monthly Statistics, January 2012.

FX market is a 24×5 trading asset class and generally trading events do not occur during the weekends (trading typically starts 2100GMT Sunday). We exclude all non-trading periods, such as weekends, holidays, etc. Even though FX market is actively traded almost 24 hours per day, there is no guarantee that there will be new quotes placed every second, especially for some less liquid currency pairs. For example, considering EUR/CHF, there are far fewer quotes generated during Asia trading time than during the New York and London trading times. A second was excluded if there were no new quotes in that second.

3.1.1. *R/S statistic*

Table 1 shows the classical and modified R/S statistic of selected FX pair returns. The null hypothesis for the test is long-memory does not exist in the return series. The null hypothesis cannot be rejected based on the results and there is no strong evidence to say that there exists long-memory processes in high frequency (second) FX returns series.

Because it is hard to decide the lag parameter q in the modified R/S statistic, we apply some short-memory processes to remove the short range dependence from the raw time series. Then we use normalized classical range scaled statistic V_c to test the existence of long-memory in the residuals. AR (1), MA (1), ARMA (1, 1) and ARMA (1, 1) − GARCH (1, 1) processes are fitted to the data to remove the short-range dependence components.

The critical values of the modified R/S statistic are given by Lo (1989): 90% confidence interval is $(0.861, 1.747)$; 95% confidence interval is $(0.809, 1.862)$, and 99% confidence interval is $(0.721, 2.098)$. Table 1 shows the results of the test and we find that none of the tested currency pairs can reject the null hypothesis. After removing the short-range dependence part by filtering through these short-memory processes, we still find little evidence that there exists long-memory in returns series of FX rate at high frequency.

Table 2 shows the results for the same test but based on absolute returns of the FX rates. The results show that strong long-memory exists in the absolute return series.

Table 1. Classic and modified R/S statistic of FX return series (second).

r_t	V_c	$V_c^{(1)}$	$V_c^{(2)}$	$V_c^{(3)}$	$V_c^{(4)}$	$V_{(5)}$	$V_{(10)}$	$V_{(20)}$	$V_{(40)}$	$V_{(80)}$
AUD/CAD	0.65	0.73	0.75	0.85	0.89	0.88	0.80	0.84	0.87	0.90
AUD/CHF	0.65	0.79	0.86	0.94	0.93	0.97	0.89	0.94	0.97	0.99
AUD/JPY	1.23	1.26	1.26	1.26	1.22	1.22	1.26	1.24	1.23	1.21
AUD/USD	1.22	1.25	1.26	1.29	1.19	1.28	1.29	1.29	1.28	1.28
CAD/JPY	1.09	1.15	1.09	1.17	1.09	1.18	1.17	1.18	1.18	1.18
CHF/JPY	1.03	1.18	1.23	1.33	1.20	1.35	1.28	1.32	1.34	1.37
EUR/AUD	0.77	0.86	0.89	1.00	1.08	1.05	0.95	1.00	1.04	1.07
EUR/CAD	0.77	0.86	0.89	0.99	1.01	1.05	0.94	0.99	1.03	1.08
EUR/CHF	1.04	1.13	1.15	1.24	1.29	1.27	1.21	1.24	1.26	1.28
EUR/GBP	0.86	1.00	0.86	1.04	0.98	1.09	1.03	1.06	1.08	1.11
EUR/JPY	0.97	0.99	0.99	1.02	0.97	0.99	1.00	1.00	0.99	1.00
EUR/USD	0.88	0.94	0.94	0.99	0.83	0.98	0.97	0.97	0.98	0.99
GBP/AUD	0.77	0.86	0.88	0.95	0.97	0.98	0.92	0.95	0.98	1.00
GBP/CAD	0.58	0.64	0.66	0.73	0.74	0.77	0.70	0.73	0.76	0.79
GBP/CHF	0.73	0.83	0.86	0.91	0.90	0.96	0.89	0.92	0.95	0.97
GBP/JPY	1.21	1.28	1.29	1.33	1.20	1.31	1.31	1.32	1.31	1.31
GBP/USD	1.34	1.37	1.38	1.37	1.27	1.37	1.38	1.38	1.37	1.37
USD/CAD	1.12	1.17	1.17	1.25	1.11	1.24	1.22	1.23	1.24	1.25
USD/CHF	1.47	1.48	1.48	1.56	1.44	1.55	1.53	1.54	1.55	1.56
USD/JPY	0.63	0.69	0.71	0.74	0.62	0.73	0.71	0.72	0.73	0.73

Notes: V_c: classic R/S statistic; $V_c^{(1)}$: classic R/S statistic after filtering by AR(1); $V_c^{(2)}$: classic R/S statistic after filtering by MA(1); $V_c^{(3)}$: classic R/S statistic after filtering by ARMA(1,1); $V_c^{(4)}$: classic R/S statistic after filtering by ARMA(1,1)-GARCH(1,1); $V_{(q)}$: modified R/S statistic with lag parameter q; (**) and (*) denote the statistic is significant at 99% and 95% level, respectively.

3.1.2. *Correlogram estimations*

Correlogram estimation is much less accurate when the long-memory effect is less significant. So we only apply the correlogram estimation to the absolute returns to see whether the evidence of long-memory in the absolute return series still exists. To see whether the result is robust, or the tail of autocorrelation decays stably, we estimate it by different number of lags N. Tables 3 and 4 show the estimated Hurst exponents when $N = 100$ and $N = 10,000$, respectively. These results also show that very strong long-memory phenomenon

Table 2. Classic and modified R/S statistic of absolute values of FX return series (second).

$\lvert r_t \rvert$	V_c	$V_{(5)}$	$V_{(10)}$	$V_{(20)}$	$V_{(40)}$	$V_{(80)}$
AUD/CAD	631.52**	195.88**	353.84**	279.86**	214.46**	160.88**
AUD/CHF	486.14**	150.10**	272.33**	215.33**	164.58**	122.79**
AUD/JPY	658.89**	210.69**	374.09**	297.38**	230.01**	173.98**
AUD/USD	778.26**	226.29**	414.67**	325.05**	247.92**	185.66**
CAD/JPY	500.25**	158.98**	281.40**	224.45**	173.57**	131.32**
CHF/JPY	330.55**	102.42**	181.42**	143.79**	111.38**	85.56**
EUR/AUD	616.96**	203.31**	353.25**	283.54**	221.22**	169.17**
EUR/CAD	522.89**	180.47**	308.49**	249.45**	195.90**	151.08**
EUR/CHF	292.86**	98.86**	168.90**	136.25**	107.14**	83.11**
EUR/GBP	505.59**	148.47**	263.18**	206.26**	160.39**	127.23**
EUR/JPY	470.75**	164.86**	281.53**	227.19**	178.52**	139.15**
EUR/USD	385.32**	134.52**	219.96**	177.82**	143.78**	116.94**
GBP/AUD	646.62**	211.03**	369.53**	296.24**	230.08**	174.77**
GBP/CAD	516.26**	178.96**	307.40**	248.49**	194.65**	148.80**
GBP/CHF	423.04**	136.55**	237.09**	189.96**	148.36**	114.20**
GBP/JPY	432.19**	152.55**	256.01**	207.66**	164.70**	129.33**
GBP/USD	522.40**	179.73**	304.41**	245.98**	194.44**	151.32**
USD/CAD	662.87**	205.53**	366.00**	290.54**	224.27**	170.11**
USD/CHF	271.76**	102.81**	167.64**	138.37**	110.84**	87.32**
USD/JPY	393.40**	128.53**	214.05**	171.54**	137.48**	111.69**

Note: $V_{(q)}$: modified R/S statistic with lag parameter q; (**) and (*) denote the statistic is significant at 99% and 95% level, respectively.

exists in the absolute return of FX rates at the frequency of second, which stands the same as modified R/S results. All of the selected currency pairs have strong long-memory and most of the estimated Hurst exponents are even larger than 0.9. AUD/USD has the highest Hurst exponent estimation, which is 0.97. This level of long-memory has not been reported in published research previously.

3.1.3. *GPH estimation*

We implement the GPH estimation on the high frequency FX returns and absolute returns. To see whether our data are sensitive to the choice of sample length n in estimating the fractional

Table 3. Correlogram estimations of FX absolute returns (second) with the number of lags equal to 100.

$N = 100$	$\hat{H}$	95% CI	99% CI
AUD/CAD	0.952310	[0.952270, 0.952350]	[0.952302, 0.952318]
AUD/CHF	0.961603	[0.961537, 0.961669]	[0.961590, 0.961616]
AUD/JPY	0.943674	[0.943594, 0.943753]	[0.943658, 0.943689]
AUD/USD	0.950410	[0.950359, 0.950460]	[0.950399, 0.950420]
CAD/JPY	0.940665	[0.940607, 0.940722]	[0.940653, 0.940676]
CHF/JPY	0.908390	[0.908293, 0.908488]	[0.908371, 0.908410]
EUR/AUD	0.925992	[0.925948, 0.926037]	[0.925983, 0.926001]
EUR/CAD	0.912354	[0.912326, 0.912383]	[0.912349, 0.912360]
EUR/CHF	0.900993	[0.900909, 0.901077]	[0.900976, 0.901010]
EUR/GBP	0.816872	[0.816493, 0.817252]	[0.816797, 0.816948]
EUR/JPY	0.894664	[0.894516, 0.894812]	[0.894634, 0.894694]
EUR/USD	0.828689	[0.828376, 0.829002]	[0.828626, 0.828752]
GBP/AUD	0.936937	[0.936873, 0.937001]	[0.936924, 0.936950]
GBP/CAD	0.932685	[0.932622, 0.932748]	[0.932672, 0.932698]
GBP/CHF	0.909436	[0.909398, 0.909473]	[0.909428, 0.909443]
GBP/JPY	0.892867	[0.892708, 0.893026]	[0.892835, 0.892899]
GBP/USD	0.905427	[0.905304, 0.905550]	[0.905403, 0.905452]
USD/CAD	0.935134	[0.935081, 0.935187]	[0.935123, 0.935145]
USD/CHF	0.886113	[0.886010, 0.886216]	[0.886092, 0.886133]
USD/JPY	0.818747	[0.818466, 0.819029]	[0.818691, 0.818803]

differencing parameters, we try different n in this empirical study: $n = T^{0.45}, T^{0.5}, T^{0.55}$. Recalling the relationship between Hurst exponent H and fractional differencing parameter d, $H = \frac{1}{2} + d$, Tables 5 and 6 show the estimated Hurst exponents of return series and absolute return series in GPH estimations, respectively. The null hypothesis in this test is $d = 0$ (or $H = 1/2$ equivalently).

In Table 5, only EUR/CHF and EUR/GBP have a statistically significant H that is above 0.5, but the nulls are only marginally rejected for some specified choice of n. The results seem to be consistent with previous long-memory tests: there is no strong evidence to show long-memory processes exist in FX return series at the second frequency.

Table 4. Correlogram estimations of FX absolute returns (second) with the number of lags equal to 1000.

$N = 10000$	$\hat{H}$	95% CI	99% CI
AUD/CAD	0.968843	[0.968840, 0.968846]	[0.968842, 0.968844]
AUD/CHF	0.929510	[0.929498, 0.929521]	[0.929507, 0.929512]
AUD/JPY	0.961892	[0.961890, 0.961894]	[0.961892, 0.961893]
AUD/USD	0.974766	[0.974764, 0.974768]	[0.974766, 0.974766]
CAD/JPY	0.929779	[0.929777, 0.929782]	[0.929779, 0.929780]
CHF/JPY	0.853738	[0.853724, 0.853751]	[0.853735, 0.853740]
EUR/AUD	0.956222	[0.956219, 0.956225]	[0.956221, 0.956222]
EUR/CAD	0.925398	[0.925391, 0.925405]	[0.925397, 0.925400]
EUR/CHF	0.900955	[0.900950, 0.900960]	[0.900954, 0.900956]
EUR/GBP	0.939420	[0.939408, 0.939431]	[0.939417, 0.939422]
EUR/JPY	0.919640	[0.919636, 0.919643]	[0.919639, 0.919640]
EUR/USD	0.922862	[0.922852, 0.922871]	[0.922860, 0.922864]
GBP/AUD	0.954527	[0.954525, 0.954529]	[0.954527, 0.954527]
GBP/CAD	0.939754	[0.939751, 0.939757]	[0.939753, 0.939754]
GBP/CHF	0.901365	[0.901360, 0.901369]	[0.901364, 0.901366]
GBP/JPY	0.924787	[0.924784, 0.924791]	[0.924787, 0.924788]
GBP/USD	0.952395	[0.952391, 0.952399]	[0.952394, 0.952396]
USD/CAD	0.963177	[0.963173, 0.963180]	[0.963176, 0.963177]
USD/CHF	0.881305	[0.881301, 0.881309]	[0.881304, 0.881306]
USD/JPY	0.929824	[0.929815, 0.929833]	[0.929822, 0.929826]

In Table 6, all of the currency pairs show a very strong long-memory in the absolute return series and they are statistically significant at 99.99% level. The results agree with the empirical results of modified R/S statistic and the correlogram results show that there exist very strong long-memory processes in absolute returns of FX rates at second frequency.

3.2. *Long-memory in equity market*

Compared to the FX market, there have been more literatures regarding the existence of the long-memory processes in the equity market, such as Lo (1989), Chow (1996), Mandelbrott (1997), Lobato and Savin (1998), and Willinger *et al.* (1999). However, there have

Table 5. GPH estimations of FX returns (second).

r_t	$T^{0.45}$	$T^{0.5}$	$T^{0.55}$		$T^{0.45}$	$T^{0.5}$	$T^{0.55}$
AUD/CAD	0.4348**	0.4477**	0.4433**	EUR/JPY	0.4803	0.4926	0.4935
	(0.0000)	(0.0000)	(0.0000)		(0.0953)	(0.3370)	(0.1876)
AUD/CHF	0.5122	0.4973	0.5011	EUR/USD	0.5138	0.4999	0.4969
	(0.3626)	(0.7503)	(0.8464)		(0.2706)	(0.9891)	(0.5373)
AUD/JPY	0.4782	0.4885	0.4981	GBP/AUD	0.4778	0.4759**	0.4844**
	(0.0895)	(0.1615)	(0.7239)		(0.0631)	(0.0019)	(0.0026)
AUD/USD	0.4946	0.4840	0.4865*	GBP/CAD	0.4656**	0.4791*	0.4793**
	(0.6703)	(0.0563)	(0.0117)		(0.0089)	(0.0121)	(0.0001)
CAD/JPY	0.4764	0.4856	0.5058	GBP/CHF	0.5090	0.5166*	0.5014
	(0.0859)	(0.1078)	(0.3191)		(0.4632)	(0.0352)	(0.7749)
CHF/JPY	0.4971	0.4926	0.4814**	GBP/JPY	0.0491	0.4839*	0.4898*
	(0.8179)	(0.3492)	(0.0002)		(0.4682)	(0.0368)	(0.0375)
EUR/AUD	0.4998	0.4898	0.4905	GBP/USD	0.4911	0.4956	0.4889*
	(0.9856)	(0.1919)	(0.0582)		(0.4873)	(0.5947)	(0.0357)
EUR/CAD	0.4916	0.4959	0.4947	USD/CAD	0.5111	0.5056	0.4994
	(0.4973)	(0.6064)	(0.3007)		(0.4043)	(0.5277)	(0.9242)
EUR/CHF	0.5276*	0.5051	0.4990	USD/CHF	0.5246	0.5074	0.4979
	(0.0371)	(0.5487)	(0.8580)		(0.0643)	(0.3774)	(0.6937)
EUR/GBP	0.5102	0.5186**	0.5061	USD/JPY	0.4707*	0.4777**	0.4852**
	(0.4108)	(0.0192)	(0.2367)		(0.0305)	(0.0099)	(0.0073)

Table 6. GPH estimations of absolute values of FX returns (second).

$\|r_t\|$	$T^{0.45}$	$T^{0.5}$	$T^{0.55}$		$T^{0.45}$	$T^{0.5}$	$T^{0.55}$
AUD/CAD	0.8863** (0.0000)	0.8698** (0.0000)	0.8859** (0.0000)	EUR/JPY	0.8163** (0.0000)	0.8545** (0.0000)	0.8939** (0.0000)
AUD/CHF	0.9116** (0.0000)	0.9922** (0.0000)	1.0638** (0.0000)	EUR/USD	0.7802** (0.0000)	0.8242** (0.0000)	0.8058** (0.0000)
AUD/JPY	0.8639** (0.0000)	0.9001** (0.0000)	0.9355** (0.0000)	GBP/AUD	0.8129** (0.0000)	0.8620** (0.0000)	0.8820** (0.0000)
AUD/USD	0.8327** (0.0000)	0.8917** (0.0000)	0.9429** (0.0000)	GBP/CAD	0.7716** (0.0000)	0.8242** (0.0000)	0.8771** (0.0000)
CAD/JPY	0.7898** (0.0000)	0.8376** (0.0000)	0.8637** (0.0000)	GBP/CHF	0.8229** (0.0000)	0.8252** (0.0000)	0.8508** (0.0000)
CHF/JPY	0.7761** (0.0000)	0.7711** (0.0000)	0.8398** (0.0000)	GBP/JPY	0.8340** (0.0000)	0.8406** (0.0000)	0.8758** (0.0000)
EUR/AUD	0.8619** (0.0000)	0.8774** (0.0000)	0.8875** (0.0000)	GBP/USD	0.7741** (0.0000)	0.8490** (0.0000)	0.8931** (0.0000)
EUR/CAD	0.7546** (0.0000)	0.7671** (0.0000)	0.8067*ast (0.0000)	USD/CAD	0.7216** (0.0000)	0.8418** (0.0000)	0.8672** (0.0000)
EUR/CHF	0.7936** (0.0000)	0.8349** (0.0000)	0.8287** (0.0000)	USD/CHF	0.7700** (0.0000)	0.8112** (0.0000)	0.8530** (0.0000)
EUR/GBP	0.7936** (0.0000)	0.8349** (0.0000)	0.8287** (0.0000)	USD/JPY	0.8221** (0.0000)	0.8512** (0.0000)	0.8675** (0.0000)

been much fewer works that examine the long-memory phenomenon at a frequency higher than daily returns. Kim (2015) modeled the 1-min U.S. stock returns with a ARMA–GARCH model with fractional Normal Tempered Stable innovations to capture the long-memory property.

To examine the long-memory effects in high frequency equity market, we use S&P 500 listed stocks data from the Trade and Quote, TAQ, database.[4] We use 465 stocks out of S&P 500 listed stocks and estimated the Hurst exponent at different frequencies varying from 1 minute to 390 minutes. There are numerous outliers in high-frequency data, which are usually caused by the misplacement of quotes or incorrectly recorded quotes. Thompson's τ method (Thompson, 1985) here is used to remove the statistically significant outliers.

After removing the ARMA–GARCH effect by filtering through ARMA(1,1)–GARCH(1,1) model, the Hurst exponents are estimated based on the innovations series. Figure 2 shows the estimated Hurst exponents by R/S statistic quantiles of the return series across 465 stocks. Based on the classic R/S estimation, more than 25% of the selected stocks show long-memory existence in their intraday return series. Also some of the stocks' Hurst estimation increases when the frequency is lower.

Compared to the debates on the existence of long-memory in stock return series, realized volatility of the stock returns has been examined to demonstrate long-memory property as shown in many published works. Similar to the analysis on the intraday equity returns series, we examine the Hurst exponents estimation of stocks realized volatility ranging from 1 minute to 390 minutes. Figures 3 and 4 show the estimated Hurst exponents quantiles of the realized volatility across 465 stocks based on classic R/S and correlogram estimations, respectively. Realized volatility series of most stocks are estimated to have long-memory property in both studies and they show

[4]TAQ: Trade and Quote database is a high-frequency database at Stony Brook University. The data are originally collected from NYSE, extracted and maintained by Quantitative Finance Program at Stony Brook University.

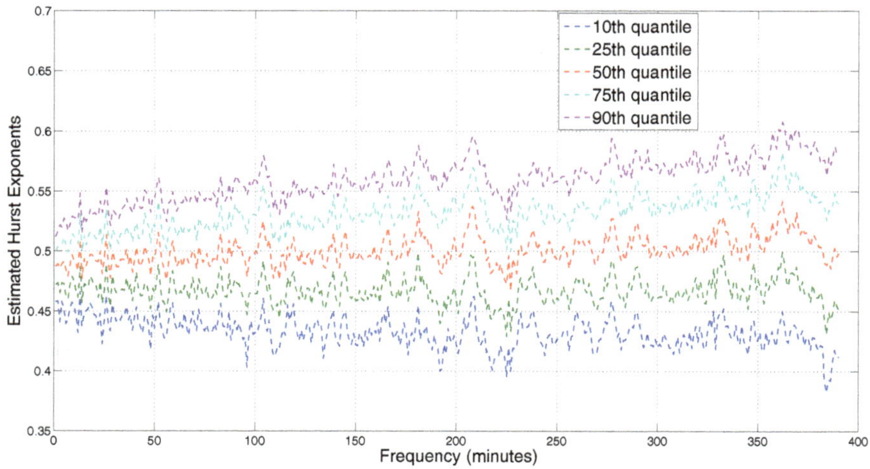

Fig. 2. Hurst exponents estimation (R/S) of S&P 500 stocks r_t at different frequencies.

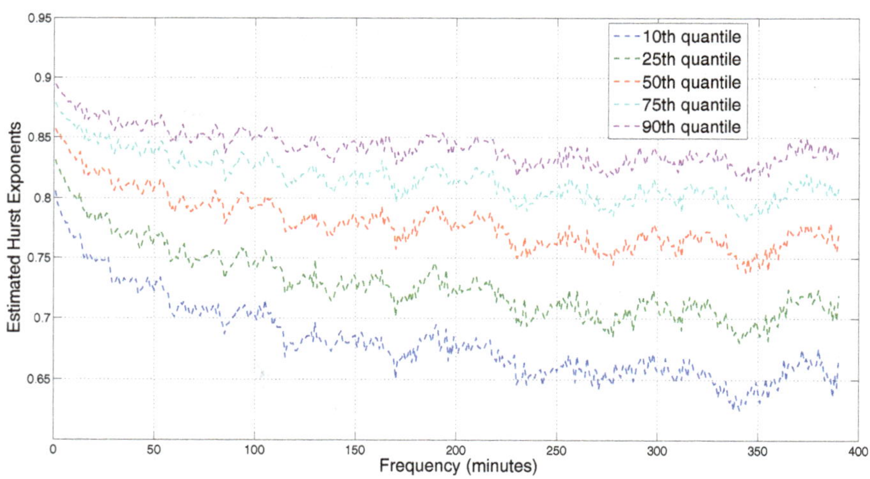

Fig. 3. Hurst exponents estimation (R/S) of S&P 500 stocks $|r_t|$ at different frequencies.

similar decaying pattern with lower frequency. The estimated Hurst exponents of realized volatility series decay with lower sampling frequencies, which is different from the pattern in return series.

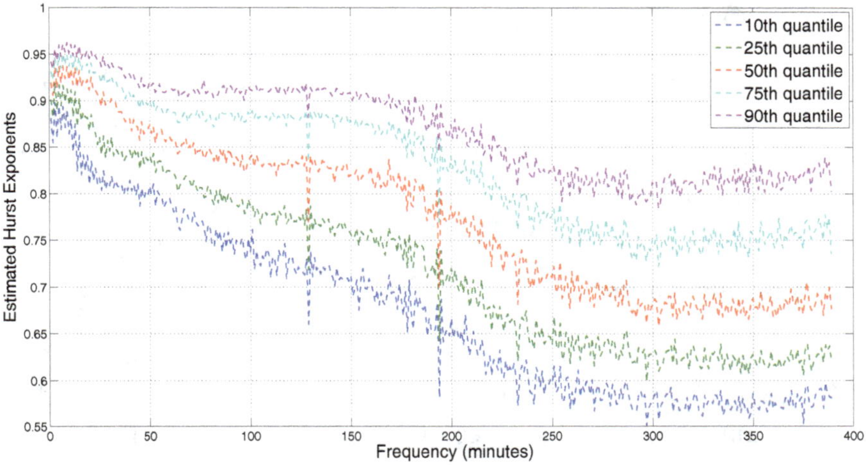

Fig. 4. Hurst exponents estimation (Correlogram) of S&P500 stocks $|r_t|$ at different frequencies.

4. Conclusions

In this chapter, we examine whether there is evidence to support the existence of long-memory processes in high-frequency FX and U.S. equity returns and volatility. We investigate the FX returns and volatility at the sampling frequency of second and U.S. equity returns and volatility at sampling frequency of minute. Three statistical tests are applied here: modified R/S, correlogram, and GPH tests.

We find that (1) for the FX and U.S. equity market, the existence of long-memory processes in the returns series is insignificant at the tested frequencies; (2) for the FX and U.S. equity market, the existence of long-memory processes in the realized volatility series is significant at the tested frequencies; and (3) for the U.S equity market the significance of long-memory processes in the realized volatility series decays with lower sampling frequencies, which is different from the pattern observed in the high-frequency FX and U.S. equity returns.

Statement

Author Barret Pengyuan Shao is employed by Evince Asset Management LP. The views and opinions expressed in this chapter are those of the author and do not represent or reflect those of Evince Asset Management LP.

Acknowledgments

The author gratefully acknowledges helpful comments and suggestions from by Dr. Andrew Mullhaupt, Dr. Svetlozar Rachev, and Dr. Young Shin Kim. Any errors remaining are the responsibility of the author.

References

Baillie, R. T. and Bollerslev, T. (1994). The long memory of the forward premium. *Journal of International Money and Finance* **13**(5), 565–571. doi:10.1016/0261-5606(94)90005-1.

Barndorff-Nielsen, O. E. and Stelzer, R., *et al.* (2011). Multivariate supou processes. *The Annals of Applied Probability* **21**(1), 140–182.

Beran, J. (1992). Statistical methods for data with long-range dependence. *Statistical Science* **7**(4), 404–416. doi:10.1214/ss/1177011122.

Beran, J. (1994). *Statistics for Long-Memory Processes.* Vol. 61, Chapman & Hall.

Bollerslev, T. and Mikkelsen, H. O. (1996). Modeling and pricing long memory in stock market volatility. *Journal of Econometrics* **73**(1), 151–184. arXiv:arXiv:1011.1669v3, doi:10.1016/0304-4076(95)01736-4.

Breidt, J. F., Crato, N., and Lima, P. D. (1998). On the detection and estimation of long memory in stochastic volatility. *Journal of Econometrics* **83**(1–2), 325–348. doi:10.1016/S0304-4076(97)00072-9.

Cheung, Y. W. and Lai, K. S. (2001). Long memory and nonlinear mean reversion in Japanese yen-based real exchange rates. *Journal of International Money and Finance* **20**(1), 115–132. doi:10.1016/S0261-5606(00)00037-1.

Chow, K., Pan, M.-S., and Sakano, R. (1996). On the long-term or short-term dependence in stock prices: Evidence from international stock markets. *Review of Quantitative Finance and Accounting* **6**(2), 181–194.

Diebold, F. X. and Inoue, A. (2001). Long memory and regime switching. *Journal of Econometrics* **105**(1), 131–159. doi:10.1016/S0304-4076(01)00073-2.

Ding, Z., Granger, C. W. J., and Engle, R. F. (1993). A long memory property of stock market returns and a new model. *Journal of Empirical Finance* **1**(1), 83–106. doi:10.1016/0927-5398(93)90006-D.

Gatheral, J., Oomen, R. C. A., Bouchaud, J. J.-P., Gefen, Y., Potters, M., and Wyart, M. (2004). Fluctuations and response in financial markets: The subtle nature of "random" price changes. *Quantitative Finance* **4**(2), 1–26. arXiv:0307332, doi:10.1007/s00780-009-0120-1.

Geweke, J. and Porter-Hudak, S. (1983). The estimation and application of long-memory time series models. *Journal of Time Series Analysis* **4**(4), 221–238. doi:10.1111/j.1467-9892.1983.tb00371.x.

Granger, C. W. J. and Joyeux, R. (1980). An introduction to long-memory time series models and fractional differencing. *Journal of Time Series Analysis* **1**(1), 15–29. doi:10.1111/j.1467-9892.1980.tb00297.x.

Hiemstra, C. and Jones, J. D. (1997). Another look at long memory in common stock returns. *Journal of Empirical Finance* **4**(4), 373–401. doi:10.1016/S0927-5398(96)00016-3.

Hosking, J. R. M. (1981). Fractional differencing. *Biometrika* **68**(1), 165–176. doi:10.1093/biomet/68.1.165.

Hurst, H. E. (1951). Long-term storage capacity of reservoirs. *Transactions of the American Society of Civil Engineers* **116**(1), 770–799.

Kim, Y. S. (2015). Multivariate tempered stable model with long-range dependence and time-varying volatility. *Frontiers in Applied Mathematics and Statistics* **1**.

Kim, Y. S. (2016). Long-range dependence in the risk-neutral measure for the market on Lehman brothers collapse. *Applied Mathematical Finance* **23**(4), 309–322.

Kim, Y. S., Jiang, D., and Stoyanov, S. (2019). Long and short memory in the risk-neutral pricing process. *The Journal of Derivatives* **26**(4), 71–88.

Klemeš, V. (1974). The Hurst phenomenon: A puzzle? *Water Resources Research* **10**(4), 675–688. doi:10.1029/WR010i004p00675.

Lo, A. W. (1989). *Long-Term Memory in Stock Market Prices*, Tech. Rep., National Bureau of Economic Research, Cambridge, MA.

Lobato, I. N. and Savin, N. (1998). Real and spurious long-memory properties of stock-market data. *Journal of Business and Economic Statistics* **16**(3), 261–268. doi:10.1080/07350015.1998.10524760.

Mandelbrot, B. B. (1972). Statistical methodology for nonperiodic cycles: From the covariance to R/S analysis. *Annals of Economic and Social Measurement* **1**(3), 259–290.

Mandelbrott, B. B. (1997). Three fractal models in finance: discontinuity, concentration, risk. ECONOMIC NOTES-SIENA, 171–212.

Mandelbrot, B. B. and Van Ness, J. W. (1968). Fractional Brownian Motions. *Fractional Noises and Applications*: *SIAM Review* **10**(4), 422–437.

McLeod, A. I. and Hipel, K. W. (1978). Preservation of the rescaled adjusted range: A reassessment of the Hurst phenomenon. *Water Resources Research* **3**, 491–508.

Nawrocki, D. (1995). R/S analysis and long-term dependence in stock market indices. *Managerial Finance* **21**(7), 78–91.

Robinson, P. M. (2003). *Time Series with Long Memory.* Oxford University Press.

Sadique, S. and Silvapulle, P. (2001). Long-term memory in stock market returns: International evidence. *International Journal of Finance and Economics* **6**(1), 59–67. doi:10.1002/ijfe.143.

Shao, B. P. and Frank, G. (2012). Aggregation of an Fx order book based on complex event processing. *Investment Management and Financial Innovation* **9**(1), 88–92.

Taqqu, M. S., Willinger, W., and R. Sherman (1997). Proof of a fundamental result in self-similar traffic modeling. *ACM SIGCOMM Computer Communication Review* **27**(2), 5–23. doi:10.1145/263876.263879.

Thompson, R. (1985). A note on restricted maximum-likelihood estimation with an alternative outlier model. *Journal of the Royal Statistical Society: Series B (Methodological)* **47**(1), 53–55.

Willinger, W., Taqqu, M. S., and Teverovsky, V. (1999). Stock market prices and long-range dependence. *Finance and Stochastics* **3**(1), 1–13. doi:10.1007/s007800050049.

https://doi.org/10.1142/9789811222634_0022

Chapter 22

Arbitrage and Risk Arbitrage in the Nikkei Put Warrant Market

William T. Ziemba

Sauder School of Business (Emeritus), University of British Columbia, Vancouver, Canada Distinguished Visiting Research Associate, Systemic Risk Center, London School of Economics, London, United Kingdom

This paper describes a risk arbitrage set of trades using the Nikkei put warrants traded in Toronto and New York around the time of the great 1990 crash in Japanese stock and land prices.

Keywords: Arbitrage, risk arbitrage, Nikkei put warrants quantos, land and stock prices in Japan, fair price of warrant options.

Arbitrage is when you construct a sure bet so that no matter the outcome, you either break even or turn a profit. Most observers say that arbitrage does not exist, but actually it does in many instances because there are different financial markets for the same sports betting or financial security situation. This is because different people have different sets of information and beliefs. In the simplest case, either A or B wins. Let O_{ah} be the British odds given on the event that A wins from betting source h and O_{bi} that B wins from betting source i. With these UK odds, the odds are the total return per 1 unit bet. In comparison, U.S. odds are UK odds -1 and their payoffs are U.S. odds $+1 =$ UK odds.

Arbitrage exists when $(O_{ah} - 1)(O_{bi} - 1) \geqslant 1$. This holds for all utility functions. Arbitrage involves two bets made at the same time at different prices so you cannot lose. You might have different prices for the same event at different places or can construct an arbitrage. Risk arbitrage is when one attempts to create both sides of a betting situation at different times so the equation holds. But the match might never exist or there could be a sequence of risk arbitrages. Betfair odds and U.S. track odds in racing frequently are sufficiently different to create risk arbitrages and, sometimes, arbitrages.[1]

I do a lot of betting on Betfair in London where they use British odds. Betfair is blocked in the U.S. and some other countries. It had been legal in Canada, but unfortunately Canadian accounts, even in pounds, were shutdown in January 2016 even though I was writing for their website. On Betfair, you could wager on NFL games, NCAA and NBA basketball, major league baseball, U.S. and UK politics including the U.S. presidency, Fed interest rate announcements — these are all ones I trade. There are also a myriad of other situations that are on Betfair.[2] As an example of political events, I shorted Howard Dean at 4–5 U.S. odds and covered at 16 to 1 once he had his rant on TV that ruined his changes of getting the Democratic presidential nomination in 2004. In 2014, I went long Mitt Romney to get the 2016 Republican nomination at 38 to 1, then, when it looked like he was going to run again, I hedged him at much lower prices, around 8 to 1. Thus, I have a sequence of bets so that I win no matter who wins the nomination. Later in 2015, I went long Donald Trump at 36-1 then reduced the bet when he was 6-1 to lock in some gains. The Republican nomination was very interesting with about 15 candidates with many long shots to short. Scott Walker and Rick Perry had already dropped out guaranteeing a win on their short bets. On the Democratic side, Hillary Clinton was a 1-2 odds

[1]Hausch and Ziemba (1990a) discusses arbitrage across different venues. Hausch and Ziemba (1990b) discuss construction of arbitrages. Ziemba (2015) has examples of arbitrages using Betfair odds versus track odds.

[2]The last 10 NFL season games, playoffs, and Superbowl wagers are in *Wilmott* columns with three of them in the book Ziemba and Ziemba (2013). The NFL guidebook by Ziemba and MacLean (2018) discusses all these seasons, prediction models, optimized strategies for coaches, and many other topics. Many strategies used based on *ad hoc* coaches, feelings are in fact not optimal. There is mean reversion (risk arbitrage heaven) in NFL games. In some cases, there are up to four lead changes in 3–4 minutes. Each leads to a mean reversion risk arbitrage. See Ziemba and MacLean (2018) for many of them in recent seasons.

on favorite. Before her email and Benaghi troubles (trumped up by unfair Republicans), she was 1-5. Joe Biden, who then was most likely not to run, was an attractive short at 6-1. Bernie Sanders, at 8-1, was leading Hillary in some states but the odds still favored her. The actual scoring of the money happened after the event was settled. So the wager stake is tied up till then. In my own betting, I try to use rebate shops for racing and Betfair and other betting shops for other wagers.

Two advantages of Betfair are that you can go long or short and the odds are changing as the game or other situation evolves. I regularly do this in NFL football games where the prices, namely the odds, are going up and down as the scores go up and down. This movement is what we call *mean reversion*, which originated in the 1983 Poterba and Summers paper on the U.S. stock market. I take advantage of this in the S&P 500 futures markets. A classic example of mean reversion risk arbitrage was an NFL playoff game between New Orleans and San Francisco in 2012 when there were four lead changes in the last three minutes. It was mean reversion heaven.[3] In my money management of client and personal accounts and a futures fund, I use various strategies based on anomalies, institutional practices, and investor behavior and mean reversion trades in the S&P 500 and Russell 2000 small cap index. See Ziemba (2016) for a tutorial on this.

1. A Risk Arbitrage Convergence Trade: The Nikkei Put Warrant Market of 1989–1990

Ed Thorp and I, with assistance from Julian Shaw (then of Gordon Capital, Toronto, now the risk control manager for Barclays trading in London), did a convergence trade based on differing put warrant prices on the Toronto and American stock exchanges. The trade was successful and Thorp won the over $1 million risk-adjusted hedge fund contest run by Barron's in 1990. There were risks involved and careful risk management was needed. This hedge was based on the

[3]See Ziemba and Ziemba (2013), Ziemba (2017) and Ziemba and MacLean (2008) for discussions of the mean reversion heaven.

fact that the Japanese stock and land prices were astronomical and very intertwined.[4]

Here is the historical development leading up to the NSA put warrants.

- The Tsukamoto Sozan Building in Ginza 2-Chome in central Tokyo was the most expensive land in the country with one square meter priced at ¥37.7 million or about U.S. $279,000 at the (December 1990) exchange rate of about ¥135 per U.S. dollar.
- Downtown Tokyo land values are the highest in the world, about $800 million an acre.
- Office rents in Tokyo are twice those in London yet land costs 40 times as much.
- The Japanese stock market, as measured by the Nikkei stock average (NSA), was up 221 times in yen and 553 in dollars from 1949 to the end of 1989.
- Despite this huge rise, there were 20 declines of 10% or more in the NSA from 1949 to 1989. The market was particularly volatile with two more in 1990 and two more in 1991. Stocks, bonds, and land were highly levered with debt.
- There was a tremendous feeling in the West that the Japanese stock market was overpriced as was the land market. For example, the Emperor's palace was reputed to be worth all of California or Canada. Japanese land was about 23% of world's non-human capital. Japanese PE ratios were 60+.
- Various studies by academics and brokerage researchers argued that the high prices of stocks and land were justified by higher long run growth rates and lower interest rates in Japan versus the U.S. However, similar models predicted a large fall in prices once interest rates rose from late 1998 to August 1990.[5]
- Hence, both must crash!

[4]Additional discussion and technical details of the trade appears in Shaw *et al.* (1995). See Stone and Ziemba (1993) for more on the relationship between the Japanese stock and land prices.

[5]The relationship between interest rates and growth is discussed in Ziemba and Schwartz (1991), French and Poterba (1991), and Ziemba *et al.* (2017).

- There was a tremendous feeling in Japan that their economy and products were the best in the world.
- There was a natural trade in 1989 and early 1990:
  - Westerners bet Japanese market will fall
  - Japanese bet Japanese market will not fall

Various Nikkei put warrants, which were three year American options, were offered to the market to fill the demand by speculators who wanted to bet that the NSA would fall.

2. NSA Puts and Calls on the Toronto and American Stock Exchanges, 1989–1992

The various NSA puts and calls were of three basic types: I's were ordinary puts traded in yen. II's were currency protected puts (often called quantos). III's were the Nikkei in Canadian or U.S. dollars. The latter were marketed with comments like: you can win if the Nikkei falls, the yen falls or both fall. The payoffs were in yen, U.S. or Canadian dollars. A simulation showed us that for similar parameter values, I's were worth more than II's, which were worth more than III's. But investors preferred the currency protected aspect of the II's and overpaid (relative to hedging that risk separately in the currency futures markets) for them relative to the I's. Table 1 and Fig. 1 have details.

At the peak, the puts were selling for more than three times their fair price.

Our convergence trades in late 1989 to early 1990 involved:

1. selling expensive Canadian currency Bankers Trust I's and II's and buying cheaper U.S. currency BT's on the American Stock Exchange; and
2. selling expensive Kingdom of Denmark and Salomon I puts on the ASE and buying the same BT I's also on the ASE both in U.S. dollars. This convergence trade was especially interesting because the price discrepancy was based mainly on the unit size and used instruments on the same exchange.

Table 1. The types of puts on the NSA.

The various puts are of three basic types. Let NSA_0 be the strike price and NSA_e the expiry price of the Nikkei stock average. Let E_0 be today's exchange rate and E_e be the exchange rate on expiry for Canadian or US dollars into yen. The symbol (X)+ means the greater of X or zero. Then we have

	US/Cdn Dollars	Puts	Calls	Terminology
I.	$a\left(\frac{NSA_0 - NSA_e}{E_e}\right) +$	BT-I, SEK, BTB, London OTC	PW	Ordinary
II.	$b\left(\frac{NSA_0 - NSA_e}{E_0}\right) +$	BT-III, BT-IV, TFC, DXA, EXW, SXA, SXO, PXB	Sal	Product
III.	$c\left(\frac{NSA_0}{E_0} - \frac{NSA_e}{E_e}\right) +$	BT-II		Option to Exchange

	Puts
Canadian \$, Toronto	BT-I, NK; BT-II, NKA; BT-III, NKB; BT-IV, NKC; TFC, SEK
US \$, New York	BTB, DXA, SXA, SXO, EXW

	In Yen		US/Cdn Person
I.	$a\,(NSA_0 - NSA_e) +$	I.	Takes currency risk
II.	$b\,(NSA_0 - NSA_e) + \frac{E_e}{E_0}$	II.	No currency risk
III.	$c\left(\frac{NSA_0}{E_0} - \frac{NSA_e}{E_e}\right) + E_e$	III.	Currency risk in final conversion in strike price

We shorted expensive puts, bought cheap puts that were very similar, waited for the prices to converge, and then we exited the trades. We preformed a complex pricing of all the warrants, which was useful in the optimization of the position sizes. However, comparing options premiums simply provides the trades that were good to make. For example, 9.8% premium year means that if you buy the option, the NSA must fall 9.8% each year to breakeven. So selling these at 9.8% and BT-II's at 6.9%, and buying BT-US at 2.6%, looks like a good trade, which is what we did (see Table 2).

Some of the reasons for the different prices were:

- Large price discrepancy across the Canada/U.S. border.
- Canadians trade in Canada, Americans trade in the U.S.
- Different credit risk.
- Different currency risk.

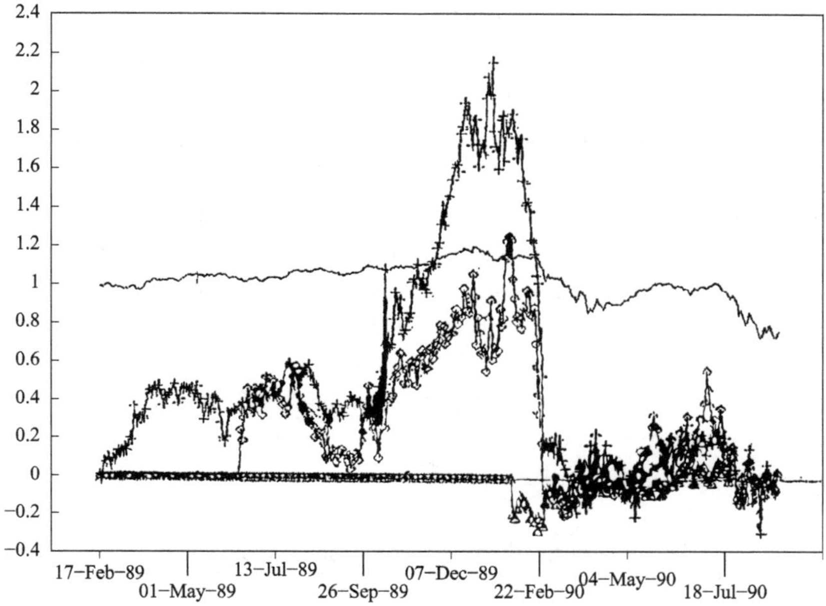

Fig. 1. Relative cost of BT-I, BT-II, and BTB NSA put warrants with NSA volatility of 20% and exchange rate volatility of 10%, 17 February 1989–21 September 1990. Relative deviation from model price = (actual cost − theoretical value)/(theoretical value).

Note: BT-1 Canadian Type I is the +; BT-II Canadian Type III is the diamond; and BTB U.S. Type I is the triangle; the top line is normalized NSA.

Source: Shaw *et al.* (1995).

Table 2. Comparison of prices and premium values for four Canadian and three U.S. NSA put warrants on February 1, 1990.

		% of NSA	Expiry Date	Premium		Hedge Action	
Warrant	Price	Unit	(yrs to ex)	%	% pa	A	B
BT-I	C$2.70	11.68%	2/17/92(2.05)	20.1	9.8	Sell	
BT-II	C$1.93	10.31%	6/15/92(2.37)	16.4	6.9	Sell	
BT-III	C$2.50n	14.29%	2/16/93(3.05)	7.0	2.3		
Trilon Finl	C$2.75	13.7%	2/22/93(3.05)	7.25	2.4		
K of Denmark	US$5.63	20%	1/3/93(2.93)	10.1	3.4		Sell
Salomon-I	US$4.63	20%	1/19/93(2.97)	10.1	3.4		Sell
BT-US	US$9.17	50%	1/16/93(3.00)	8.0	2.6	Buy	Buy

- Difficulties with borrowing for short sales.
- Blind emotions vs. reality.
- An inability of speculators to properly price the warrants.

I's were ordinary puts traded in yen. II's were currency protected puts (often called quantos). III's were the Nikkei in Canadian or U.S. dollars. The latter were marketed with comments like: you can win if the Nikkei falls, the yen falls or both fall The payoffs in yen and in U.S./Cdn are shown in Table 2. A simulation in Shaw *et al.* (1995) showed that for similar parameter values, I's were worth more than II's, which were worth more than III's. But investors preferred the currency protected aspect of the II's and overpaid (relative to hedging that risk separately in the currency futures markets) for them relative to the I's. Figures 1 and 2 show the two convergence trades.

$$\text{Relative Cost} = \frac{\text{Actual Cost} - \text{Theoretical Cost}}{\text{Theoretical Cost}} \quad \text{when } \sigma = 20\%$$

is plotted rather than implied volatility since the latter did not exist when they were deep in the money options trading for less than intrinsic as in this market. Fair value at 20% NSA volatility and 10% exchange rate volatility is zero on the graph. At one, the puts are trading for double their fair price. At the peak, the puts were selling for more than three times their fair price.

Fair value at 20% NSA volatility and 10% exchange rate volatility is zero on the graph. At one, the puts are trading for double their fair price. At the peak, the puts were selling for more than three times their fair price.

The BT-I's did not trade until January 1990 and in about a month the Canadian BT-I's and BT-II's collapsed to fair value and then the trade was unwound. See Fig. 2. The Toronto newspapers inadvertently helped the trade by pointing out that the Canadian puts were overpriced relative to the U.S. puts so eventually there was selling of the Canadians, which led to the convergence to efficiency. To hedge before January 1990, one needed to buy over-the-counter puts from a brokerage firm such as Salomon in London who made a market in these puts. Additional risks of such trades is being bought in and

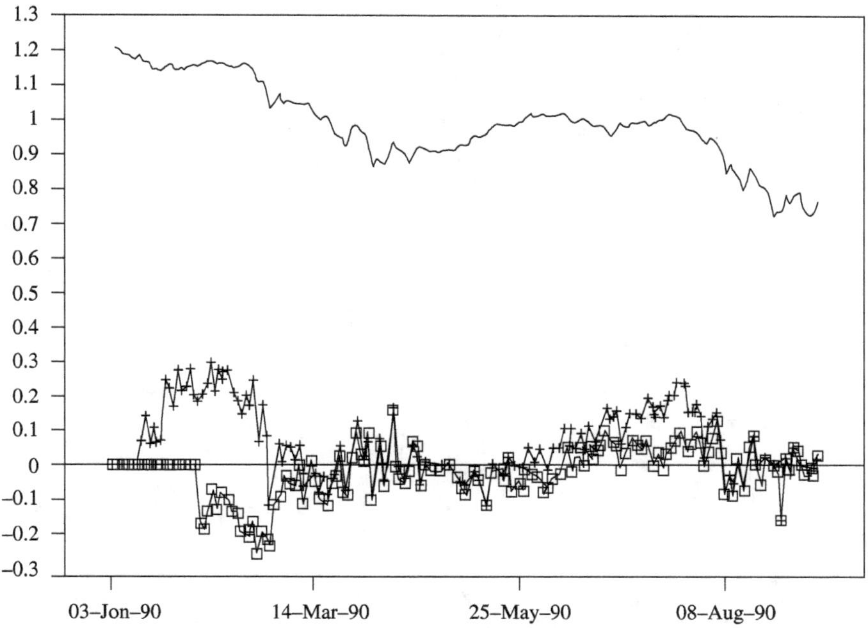

Fig. 2. Relative cost of U.S. Type I versus U.S. Type II NSA put warrants with NSA volatility of 20% versus the NSA, January–December 1990.

Note: U.S. Type I (BTB, 0.5 NSA shown as square) versus U.S. Type II (average of DXA+SXA+SXO), 0.2 NSA shown as +, top line is normalized NSA.

shorting the puts too soon, and having the market price of them go higher. We had only minor problems with these risks.

For the second trade, the price discrepancy lasted about a month. The market prices were about \$18 and \$9 where they theoretically should have had a 5 to 2 ratio since one put was worth 20% of the Nikkei and the other 50% of the Nikkei, and trade at \$20 and \$8. These puts were not identical so this is risk arbitrage not arbitrage. The discrepancy here is similar to the small firm, low price effect (see Ziemba, 2012a). Both puts were trading on the American stock exchange (see Fig. 3).

The brokerage firms in the U.S. which made a lot of money in Japan on the way down wanted to cash in on the expected rebound. There was a similar inefficiency in the call market where the currency protected options traded for higher than fair prices. There was

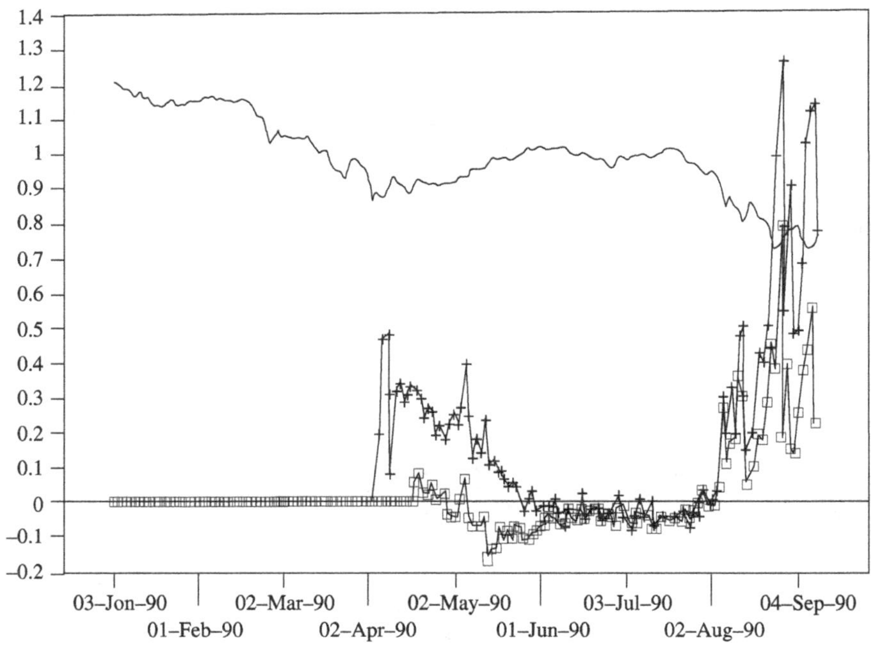

Fig. 3. Relative cost of Paine Webber (PXA) and Saloman (SXZ) NSA call warrants with NSA historical volatility of 20%, April–October 1990. Relative deviation from model price = (actual cost − theoretical value)/(theoretical value).

Note: The PXA is a +; SXZ is a square, the top line is the normalized NSA.

a successful trade here but this was a low volume market. This market never took off as investors lost interest when the NSA did not rally. U.S. traders preferred Type II (Salomon's SXZ) denominated in dollars rather than the Paine Webber (PXA) which were in yen.

The Canadian speculators, who had little knowledge of options pricing and *overpaid* for the put warrants that our trade was based on, made \$500 million Canadian since the NSA's fall was so great. This is a great example of the mean dominating, see Chopra and Ziemba (1993). That's a lot more than we scientists made but we did ok. The issuers of the puts also did well and hedged their positions with futures in Osaka and Singapore. The losers were the holders of Japanese stocks. We did a similar trade with Canadian dollar puts traded in Canada and hedged in the U.S. The difference in price (measured by implied volatility) between the Canadian and U.S. puts stayed relatively constant over an entire year (a gross violation of efficient markets). The trade was also successful, but again like the Nikkei calls, the volume was low.

3. Conclusion and Final Remarks

The reader might ask "how did we decide to do this trade?" and "how did we implement it?" Ed Thorp was a well-known hedge fund trader. I had a long relationship with him providing papers in my books. He wrote the forward to our book Ziemba and Hausch (1984) *Beat the Racetrack.* That year I took him to the first Breeders' Cup in Los Angeles to discuss and try out the system. That was a big success and the story about it is written up in Ziemba and Hausch (1986) *Betting at the Racetrack* and my memoirs, Ziemba (2017) *Adventures of a Modern Renaissance Academic in Investing and Gambling.*

In 1988–1989, I was the first Yamaichi professor of finance at the University of Tsukuba, 60 miles above Toyko. I taught at the university from Monday to Wednesday and consulted on Thursday and Friday in Tokyo for the Yamaichi Research Institute. There I had two projects: (1) stock market anomalies and (2) stock market crashes. Part of #2 was to discover the BSEYD model, see Ziemba *et al.* (2017). After we returned to Vancouver, I discovered that the Nikkei puts in Toronto, Canada, were trading 3–4 times the fair price. I called Thorp and suggested that we try to do a risk arbitrage. I had wanted to do a good trade with him of the type he is well known for. He was interested in doing this but he said you have the sell but where is the buy side of the risk arbitrage?

Soon after, I went to the Wharton School at the University of Pennsylvania and spoke at a conference organized by Stavros Zenios, with whom I would later co-edit the ALM Handbook for North Holland and where Thorp would have a paper which I considered to be the best theoretical Kelly criterion paper ever written. There I met Julian Shaw, who was at Gordon Capital in Toronto (later Gordon Capital asked me to be their Japan expert and I wrote reports for their clients). He wanted to meet me as he really liked *Beat the*

Racetrack. In our conversation, I mentioned these Nikkei puts. Shaw replied I know about these and have already shorted 3 million contracts, which is about a $9 million position. Wow!

He then told me I could get the other side by calling Salomon London and they would sell us a private over-the-counter Nikkei put at fair value, but we needed to have a $500,000 investment. I informed Thorp and we agreed to do it. I established accounts in Vancouver for him and me. We then started establishing the shorts in Toronto. Then we had the good fortune that Nikkei puts for retail investors began trading in NY on the American stock exchange. We could then buy exactly the quantity we wanted and did not need to work with Salomon London.

The rest is in the text. I made a nice gain for myself and Thorp gave me a small fee for his part and he won the over $1 million hedge fund contest that year organized by Barrons. I then gave talks on this and wrote the paper Shaw *et al.* (1995). It was a good experience for me as well as for Shaw and Thorp. Shaw is now a risk manager for Barclays in London. My Japanese experience helped me to better trade markets and for a large period in 2013–2018 I was the top performing trader in the U.S. futures markets in my category. See Ziemba (2016) for a tutorial.

Acknowledgment

Thanks to Julian Shaw and Edward O. Thorp who worked on this with me.

References

Boone, P. (1989). High land values in Japan: Is the archipelago worth eleven trillion dollars? Technical Report, Department of Economics, Harvard University, Tokyo.

Canaway, H. (1990). *Land Prices in Japan: No Cause for Alarm*. Baring Securities.

Chopra, V. and Ziemba, W. T. (1993). The Effect of errors in mean and co-variance estimates on optimal portfolio choice. *Journal of Portfolio Management* 6–11.

Comolli, L. R. and Ziemba, W. T. (2000). Japanese security market regularities, 1990–1994. In D. B. Keim and W. T. Ziemba (Eds.), *Security Market Imperfections in World Wide Equity Markets*, Cambridge University Press, Cambridge, UK, pp. 458–491.

French, K. R. and Poterba, J. (1991). Were Japanese stock prices too high? *Journal of Financial Economics* **29**(2), 337–363.

Hausch, D. B. and Ziemba, W. T. (1990). Arbitrage strategies for cross-track betting on major horseraces. *Journal of Business*, **LXIII**, 61–78.

Hausch, D. B. and Ziemba, W. T. (1990). Locks at the Racetrack. *Interfaces* 41–48.

Schwartz, S. L. and Ziemba, W. T. (2000). Predicting returns on the Tokyo stock exchange. In D. B. Keim, and W. T. Ziemba (Eds.), *Security Market Imperfections in World Wide Equity Markets*, Cambridge University Press, Cambridge, UK, pp. 492–511.

Shaw, J., Thorp, E. O., and Ziemba, W. T. (1995). Risk arbitrage in the Nikkei put warrant market, 1989–1990. *Applied Mathematical Finance* **2**, 243–271.

Stone, D. and Ziemba, W. T. (1993). Land and stock prices in Japan. *Journal of Economic Perspectives* **7**(3), 149–165.

Ziemba, W. T. (1991). The chicken or the egg: Land and stock prices in Japan. In W. T. Ziemba, W. Bailey, and Y. Hamao (Eds.), *Japanese Financial Market Research*, North Holland, pp. 45–68.

Ziemba, W. T. and Hausch, D. B. (1986). *Betting at the Racetrack*, 2nd Edition, Norris Strauss, New York.

Ziemba, R. E. S. and Ziemba, W. T. (2013). Investing in the Modern Age, Wilmott columns revised and expanded, 2007–2012. World Scientific (hardback and paperback), Singapore.

Ziemba, W. T. (2016). Understanding the U.S. index futures stock market using research. In A. Gupta and A. Capponi (Eds.), *Tutorials in Operations Research, INFORMS*, Catonsville, Maryland, pp. 250–268.

Ziemba, W. T. (2017). *Adventures of a Modern Renaissance Academic in Investing and Gambling.* World Scientific, Singapore.

Ziemba, W. T. (2015). Portfolio optimization: Theory and practice, In K. Zopoundis (Ed.), *Quantitative Financial Risk Management: Theory and Practice*, The Frank–Fabozzi Series, Wiley.

Ziemba, W. T., Lleo, S., and Zhitlukhin, M. (2017). *Stock Market Crashes: Predictable and Unpredictable and What To Do About Them.* World Scientific, Singapore.

Ziemba, W. T. and MacLean, L. C. (2018). *Dr. Z's NFL Guidebook*, in press.

Ziemba, W. T. and Schwartz, S. L. (1991). *Invest Japan.* Probus, Chicago.

https://doi.org/10.1142/9789811222634_0023

Chapter 23

A Stopping Rule Model for Exiting Bubble-like Markets with Applications*

William T. Ziemba, S. Lleo, and M. Zhitlukhin

We present applications of a stochastic changepoint detection model in the context of bubble-like financial markets. The aim is to detect a direction change in a sequence of stock market or other asset index values as soon as it happens. A detection rule thus models an exit strategy in a possible market crash. We describe theoretical results in Sections 9.2 and apply them to several bubbles including markets in the US, China, Japan and Iceland in Sections 9.3–9.5.

9.1. Introduction

In this chapter, we study bubble-like markets, which are ones that are going up just because they are going up and often result eventually in a crash. We study strategies to optimally exit such markets.[1]

Trading bubbles is difficult and even the best traders sometimes lose a lot of money by shorting too soon. The finance and economics literature has little on timing bubbles. There is, however, some interest by inefficient market researchers, see for example, Stiglitz (1990) and Evanoff *et al.* (2012). In this chapter, we present a model that seems to work well, timing when to exit a long position. The basic idea is that there is a fast rate of growth in prices, then a peak and then a fast decline. The model tries to exit near the peak in prices. The mathematics of the model is sketched in Section 9.2 and is an application of the *changepoint detection* theory for random processes. For readers interested in how the model works, Appendix B should

---

*This article originally appeared in *Stock Market Crashes: Predictable, Unpredictable and What to Do About Them,* Chapter 9, by W. T. Ziemba, M. Zhitlukhin, and S. Lleo (2018), World Scientific Series in Finance: Volume 13, pp. 209–233.

[1]This chapter relies heavily on our three papers concerning this model, namely, Shiryaev, Zhitlukhin and Ziemba (2014, 2015) and Zhitlukhin and Ziemba (2016).

be helpful, but it is not important to read it to understand the results of the model which are in tables and figures showing entries and exits.

Changepoint detection methods have been successfully applied in production quality control, radiolocation, information security, and have shown their usefulness. Their history goes back to the pioneering works of Shewhart of 1920s, and the first results by Page, Roberts, Shiryaev and others of 1950–1960s. Surveys of the history and the recent developments in this field can be found in e.g. the introduction to the book by Poor and Hadjiliadis (2009).

In the financial context, a changepoint may represent a moment when the market starts to decline. It can be identified with a moment of time when the trend of the sequence of the market's index value becomes negative. The objective of the model is to detect this change after it occurs and to close a long position maximizing the gain.

We emphasize that the changepoint model does not *predict* a decline of price, but considers the problem to detect it *after* it has started, taking into account that temporal declines may be caused by the volatility of the price rather than a real change of the trend. In particular, such a decline need not necessarily be caused by a crash of a bubble, but can be due to e.g. a structural change in an economy or bad news for a company. Thus we do not need the price process to be a bubble in terms of one definition or another.

This chapter contains applications of the changepoint model to various stock market situations where there was a crash, with the view to test how the model can find exit points in markets that appeared to be bubbles. We apply the method to the three crashes in the US markets in 1929, 1987 and 2008, to the crash in the Iceland market in 2008, and to the crash in the Chinese market in 2015 plus Apple Computer stock in 2012, the NASDAQ in 2000 and the circa 1990 Japanese stock and land markets.

In part, the choice of the data was motivated by the fact that these various crashes had somewhat different characteristics, if judged by the pattern of underlying market indices or stock prices. The 1929 and 1987 crashes were similar in the behavior before the crash, showing a steady growth and then a sharp decline; the recovery patterns were much different though: it took about 2 years for the S&P500 to reach the value its pre-crash peak in 1987, while the Dow Jones Industrial of Average (DJIA) needed almost 25 years to recover only in 1954 (there were of course different macroeconomic environments, but our model is unaware of those because it uses only historical time series of index values). The crash of 2008 was

A Stopping Rule Model for Exiting Bubble-like Markets with Applications 211

characterized by a slow growth preceding the crash, and then a slow decline. In contrast, the Chinese market in 2014–2015 showed the fastest growth and the decline was comparable to the 1929 and 1929 US crashes. The Japanese stock and land markets crashed and ushered in a 20+ year depression-like atmosphere in the country. Even now in 2016, the Nikkei stock average is well below its 1989 value. We refer to Consigli *et al.* (2009), Lleo and Ziemba (2012, 2016a,b) and the references already cited, all of which discuss crashes in various markets and possible methods of how to predict them.

9.2. A brief overview of the mathematics of the model

Broadly speaking, a *changepoint* is a random time when a random sequence (or a random process) changes the structure of its probability distribution. The basic example is a sequence of independent random variables with one value of the mean before a changepoint and another value of the mean after the changepoint, with all other parameters being the same before and after. The general theory of changepoint detection, of course, is not limited to detection of changes in means only; but the model we will use is of this basic type. This model is derived from one of the pioneering papers, Shiryaev (1963), but adapted to our investigation of bubble-like markets. The reader is referred to specialized literature for the state of the art changepoint detection methods; e.g. the monograph Tartakovsky *et al.* (2014) provides a detailed exposition of the theory.

The problem of detecting a changepoint consists in that an observer does not know when a change occurs and she can make a conclusion about it based only on the observed random sequence. We will consider *online* changepoint detection problems, which are characterized by the fact that new observations in a random sequence arrive one by one, and a decision about a possible change of the probability distribution should be made based on the data available up to the current moment of time. The goal is to recognize the change as soon as possible after it happens, but not earlier. (*Offline* changepoint problems, on the other hand, assume the whole realization of a random sequence is available.)

In the context of bubble-like markets, a changepoint is a moment when the price trend reverses and the observer wants to detect the reversion soon after it happens. The quantitative side of the problem is to distinguish between temporal declines in prices caused by volatility and a real structural change.

We will model bubble-like prices of stock or index values by a random sequence S_t, where time t runs through $t = 0, 1, \dots, T$; the moment $t = 0$ is the start of observations, $t = T$ is the terminal moment specifying the time horizon of the model. The sequence of prices S is assumed to follow a geometric random walk with mean μ_1 and volatility σ_1 before a changepoint, and mean μ_2 and volatility σ_2 after a changepoint. Both pairs (μ_1, σ_1) and (μ_2, σ_2) are assumed to be known or can be estimated (see the remark below how to estimate them). It is assumed there is no more than one changepoint between $t = 0$ and $t = T$, occurring at some time $t = \theta$. Thus, the sequence S can be described by its log-returns X_t as follows:

$$X_t := \log \frac{S_t}{S_{t-1}} = \begin{cases} \mu_1 + \sigma_1 \xi_t, & t < \theta, \\ \mu_2 + \sigma_2 \xi_t, & t \geq \theta, \end{cases} \qquad \text{for } t = 1, 2, \dots, T,$$

where ξ_t are independent standard normal random variables.

We will work in the Bayesian setting, assuming that θ is a random variable taking values in the set $\{1, 2, \dots, T+1\}$ with known prior probabilities $p_t = P(\theta = t)$. It is assumed θ is independent of the sequence ξ_t. The value p_1 is the probability that from the beginning of observation the sequence S follows parameters (μ_2, σ_2) (e.g. the bubble burst before the beginning of observation), and p_{T+1} is the probability that S_t follows (μ_1, σ_1) until the end of the time horizon of the model (e.g. the bubble continues at least until T).

Under an appropriate criterion of the optimality of a detection rule (see Appendix B, which contains all the mathematical details) we show that the optimal detection rule can be expressed through the *Shiryaev–Roberts statistic* ψ_t, which is a sequence constructed recursively as follows:

$$\psi_0 = 0, \ \psi_t = (p_t + \psi_{t-1}) \cdot \frac{\sigma^1}{\sigma^2} \exp\left(\frac{(X_t - \mu_1)^2}{2\sigma_1^2} - \frac{(X_t - \mu_2)^2}{2\sigma_2^2} \right), \quad t = 1, \dots, T.$$

The main theorem that we prove in Appendix B states that it is optimal to declare a changepoint when the value of ψ_t exceeds a certain time-dependent threshold $b(t)$:

$$\text{the first time } t \text{ when } \psi_t \geq b(t).$$

The threshold $b(t)$ depends on the parameters of the problem, such as μ, σ, p_t, etc., and it is shown in the Appendix how one can compute it.

The parameters $\mu_1, \mu_2, \sigma_1, \sigma_2$ are required to be estimated. This is not a restrictive assumption for μ_1, σ_1 since they can be estimated from past data.

A Stopping Rule Model for Exiting Bubble-like Markets with Applications 213

On the other hand, μ_2 and σ_2 cannot be estimated before a changepoint. So their values should be chosen in advance, and it might be a difficult problem to predict appropriate values for them. We will not study this question, however, all our applications that even a simple choice $\mu_2 = -\mu_1$, $\sigma_2 = \sigma_1$ gives acceptable results in many cases.

The same applies to the prior distribution of θ. In all the cases where we apply the model it is simply assumed to be uniform over $t = 1, \ldots, T$ with a reasonable choice of probability 0.25 that there is no changepoint before T. We tried several other choices, which however does not give much difference, see our papers mentioned in the introduction to this chapter for details.

9.3. Stock market crashes in the US

9.3.1. *The great crash in 1929*

The substantial economic advance of the later half of the 1920s led to the significant growth of the US stock market. That growth was further increased by a speculative bubble, which attracted more people to the stock market in a hope that the prices would continue to increase. The market measured by the DJIA index peaked on September 3, 1929 but then declined by 10% by the end of the month. There was a short stabilization during the first half of October, which was followed by the crash on Black Thursday, October 24 and Black Tuesday, October 29, when the market was down almost 40% from its peak.

We applied the changepoint model to the values of the DJIA index with several choices of the parameters: five starting dates throughout 1928–1929, five combinations of the post-changepoint parameters (depending on the values of the pre-changepoint parameters estimated from the data), and two possible terminal dates corresponding to the time horizon T in the model (see the mathematical description). The parameters of drift and volatility μ_1, σ_1 of the model were estimated from 1 year of past data before each entry point; based on them, the post-changepoint parameters were chosen as shown in Table 9.1. In all the combinations of parameters, we took the changepoint probability to be 75% that a change in the drift happens in the given time horizon.

The results are presented in Table 9.1 and Fig. 9.1. The table shows the exit dates corresponding to the different choices of parameters and the percent ratio of the price on the exit date and the peak value (in brackets).

Table 9.1. The DJIA 1929 crash exit points.

Entry	Exit date (% of max. value)				
	$\mu_2 = -\mu$ $\sigma_1 = \sigma_2$	$\mu_2 = -2\mu$ $\sigma_1 = \sigma_2$	$\mu_2 = -2\mu$ $\sigma_1 = 2\sigma_2$	$\mu_2 = -3\mu$ $\sigma_1 = \sigma_2$	$\mu_2 = -3\mu$ $\sigma_1 = 3\sigma_2$
	T = end of 1929				
1927-07-01	29-10-21 (84)	29-10-03 (87)	27-10-10 (50)	29-05-27 (77)	27-10-10 (50)
1928-01-01	29-10-03 (87)	29-05-27 (77)	28-06-11 (54)	28-12-10 (69)	28-06-12 (53)
1928-07-01	29-10-03 (87)	29-09-27 (90)	28-12-06 (73)	29-05-27 (77)	28-12-06 (73)
1929-01-01	29-10-03 (87)	29-09-27 (90)	29-02-11 (81)	29-05-27 (77)	29-03-25 (78)
1929-07-01	29-10-01 (90)	29-09-27 (90)	29-08-12 (92)	29-09-27 (90)	29-08-12 (92)
	T = end of 1930				
1927-07-01	29-10-28 (68)	29-10-23 (80)	27-10-10 (50)	29-10-04 (85)	27-10-10 (50)
1928-01-01	29-10-21 (84)	29-10-03 (87)	28-06-11 (54)	29-10-03 (87)	28-06-13 (55)
1928-07-01	29-10-23 (80)	29-10-21 (84)	28-12-06 (73)	29-10-03 (87)	28-12-07 (71)
1929-01-01	29-10-23 (80)	29-10-04 (85)	29-04-01 (79)	29-10-03 (87)	29-05-22 (79)
1929-07-01	29-10-23 (80)	29-10-23 (80)	29-10-07 (91)	29-10-23 (80)	29-10-07 (91)

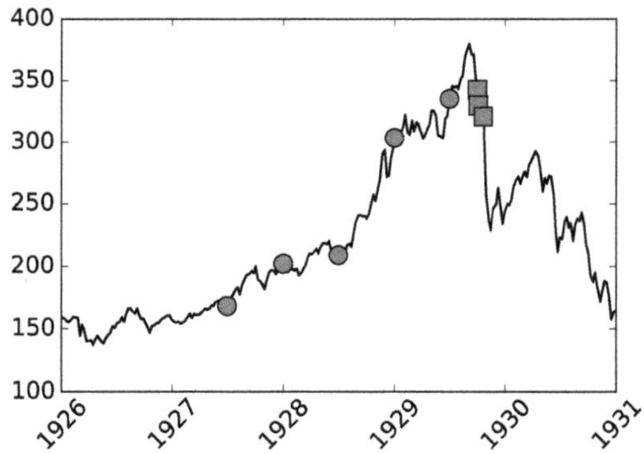

Fig. 9.1. The DJIA index in 1926–1930 and the exit points for $\mu_2 = -\mu_1$, $\sigma_2 = \sigma_1$.

The shaded cells mark the dates after the peak on September 3 and before the Black Monday.

Although the model had some false detections before the crash (caused by short-time declines), and acted too late for particular choices of the parameters after the crash, in most of the cases it was able to provide an exit point well before the local market trough. It follows that with respect to the post-crash volatility, the choice $\sigma_1 = \sigma_2$ gave results better than the other choices. With respect to the drift μ, the choices $\mu_2 = -\mu_1$ and

$\mu_2 = -2\mu_1$ are preferable to $\mu_2 = -3\mu_1$, as the latter detected false exit points in May 1929. The exit points for the parameters $\mu_2 = -\mu_1$, $\sigma_2 = \sigma_1$ are shown by the red marks on the graph in Fig. 9.1.

9.3.2. *The 1987 crash of S&P500*

On Monday October 19, 1987 the S&P500 futures fell 29% and the S&P500 cash index fell 22%. It was the greatest one-day decline ever in US history. Portfolio insurance which sold futures when they were falling was part of the cause. The BSEYD model based on high interest rates relative to stock earnings discussed in Chapters 2–4 did predict the crash. So did the T-model based on high call prices relative to put prices discussed in Chapter 5. The pre-crash and the crash price patterns resemble those of the 1929 crash. However, while the 1987 crash was very severe in a short term, it did not lead to a depression as in 1929 or even a recession. The market bounced back, and in about 2 years the S&P500 reached its pre-crash values.

The results of the application of the changepoint model to the crash are in Table 9.2 and Fig. 9.2. We use the same notation and estimate the parameters in the same way as in the previous section. The shaded cells in the table shows the exit points after the market peak on August 25 and before the Black Monday October 19.

Table 9.2. Exit points for S&P500 during the crash of 1987.

	Exit date (% of max. value)				
Entry	$\mu_2 = -\mu$, $\sigma_1 = \sigma_2$	$\mu_2 = -2\mu$, $\sigma_1 = \sigma_2$	$\mu_2 = -2\mu$, $\sigma_1 = 2\sigma_2$	$\mu_2 = -3\mu$, $\sigma_1 = \sigma_2$	$\mu_2 = -3\mu$, $\sigma_1 = 3\sigma_2$
	T = end of 1987				
1985-07-01	87-10-15 (89)	87-10-12 (92)	86-07-08 (72)	86-09-12 (68)	86-07-07 (72)
1986-01-01	87-10-12 (92)	86-09-12 (68)	86-01-08 (62)	86-09-11 (70)	86-01-08 (62)
1986-07-01	87-10-14 (91)	87-09-21 (92)	86-07-15 (69)	86-09-12 (68)	86-09-11 (70)
1987-01-01	87-10-14 (91)	87-09-21 (92)	87-04-14 (83)	87-09-08 (93)	87-04-15 (84)
1987-07-01	87-10-12 (92)	87-09-21 (92)	87-10-14 (91)	87-09-08 (93)	87-10-14 (91)
	T = end of 1988				
1985-07-01	87-10-16 (84)	87-10-16 (84)	86-07-15 (69)	87-10-15 (89)	86-07-15 (69)
1986-01-01	87-10-15 (89)	87-10-15 (89)	86-04-08 (69)	86-09-12 (68)	86-01-08 (62)
1986-07-01	87-10-16 (84)	87-10-15 (89)	86-07-15 (69)	87-10-15 (89)	86-09-11 (70)
1987-01-01	87-10-19 (67)	87-10-16 (84)	87-04-15 (84)	87-10-16 (84)	87-10-15 (89)
1987-07-01	87-10-19 (67)	87-10-16 (84)	87-10-15 (89)	87-10-16 (84)	87-10-16 (84)

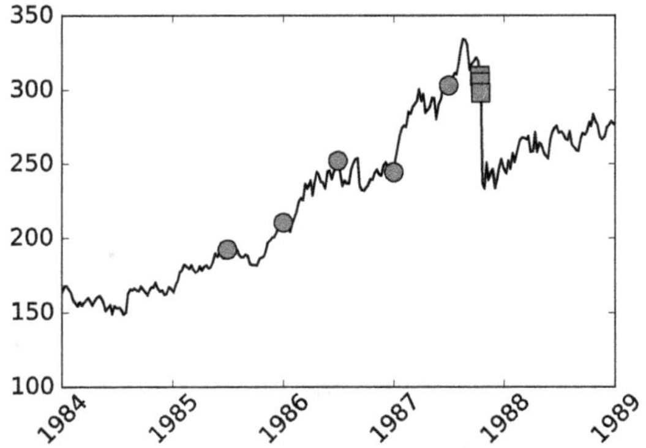

Fig. 9.2. The S&P500 index in 1984–1988 and the exit points for $\mu_2 = -\mu_1$, $\sigma_2 = \sigma_1$.

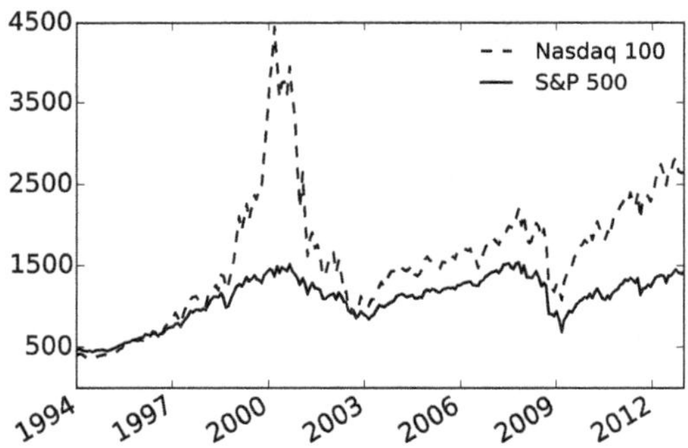

Fig. 9.3. The Internet crash in the US in 2000–2002.

Again, the choice of $\sigma_1 = \sigma_2$ seems to work the best of the settings considered, while both the choices of $\mu_2 = -\mu_1$ and $\mu_2 = -2\mu_1$ still provide good results (however, the latter reacted exactly on the day of the crash under the assumption that the time horizon of the model is chosen as the end of 1988), and $\mu_2 = -3\mu_1$ works well in that case too.

9.3.3. *The internet bubble crash during 2000–2002*

Alan Greenspan, the chairman of the US Federal Reserve System (Fed), began in 1994 a low interest rate policy that reduced short-term rates continuously over a multiyear period. This led to an increase in the S&P500 stock index from 470.42 in January 1995 to 1469.25 at the end of 1999, as shown in Fig. 9.3. The price earnings (P/E) ratios were high and Shiller

A Stopping Rule Model for Exiting Bubble-like Markets with Applications 217

used these to predict the crash starting in 1996, see Campbell and Shiller (1998) and Shiller (1996, 2000, 2009). It is known that stock price rises usually start with low P/E ratios and end with high P/E ratios, see Bertocchi, Schwartz and Ziemba (2010). But predicting when the market will crash using just P/E ratios is problematic.

However, as discussed in Chapters 2–4, it has been found in many markets over many years the BSEYD model predicts crashes better than just high P/E ratios, see Ziemba and Schwartz (1991), Ziemba (2003) and Lleo and Ziemba (2012) and our summary in Chapters 2–4. The model signaled a crash in the S&P500 in April 1999. It was in the danger zone all of 1999 starting in April and it got deeper in the danger zone as the year progressed, see Table 9.2. The signal did work but the real decline was not until September 2000 with a temporary fall from the March 24, 2000 high of 1552.87 and a recovery into the September 1, 2000 peak of 1530.09. By October 10, 2002 S&P500 fell to 768.63 having two temporary recoveries from the local lows of 1091.99 on April 4, 2001 and 944.75 on September 21, 2001. There were other signals:

> History shows that a period of shrinking breadth is usually followed by a sharp decline in stock values of the small group of leaders. Then broader market takes a more modest tumble.
> Paul Bagnell in late November 1999 in the *Globe and Mail.*

Ziemba (2003, Chapter 2) describes this episode in stock market history. There was considerable mean-reversion in the eventual crash in 2000, the September 11, 2001 attack and in the subsequent 2002 decline of 22%. This decline was similar to previous crashes.

The concentration of stock market gains into very few stocks with momentum and size being the key variables predicting performance was increasing before 1997 in Europe and North America. Table 2.6 in Ziemba (2003) shows that in 1998, the largest cap stocks had the highest return in North America and Europe but small cap stocks outperformed in Asia and Japan. The situation was similar from 1995 to 1999 with 1998 and 1999 the most exaggerated.

Fully 41% of the stocks in the S&P500 did not fall or actually rose during this period and an additional 19% declined by 10% or less annualized. These were small cap stocks with market values of $10 billion of less. The fall in the S&P500 was mainly in three areas: information technology, telecommunications and large cap stocks. Information technology stocks in the S&P500 fell 64% and telecom stocks fell 60% from January 1 to October 31, 2002. The largest cap stocks (with market caps of $50 billion plus) lost 37%. But most other stocks either lost only a little or actually gained. Materials fell 10% but consumer discretionary gained 4.5%, consumer staples gained 21%, energy gained 12%, financial services gained 19%, health care gained 29%, industrials gained 7% and utilities gained 2%. Equally weighted, the S&P500 index lost only 3%. So there was a strong small cap effect. The stocks that gained were the very small cap stocks with market caps below $10 billion. Some 138 companies with market caps between $5–10 billion gained 4% on average and 157 companies with market caps below $5 billion gained on average 23%.

While the BSEYD model has been shown to be useful in predicting S&P500 declines, it is silent on the NASDAQ technology index of the largest 100 stocks by market capitalization, the NDX100. This index with a major Internet component had a spectacular increase during a period where many thought the Internet companies would prosper despite P/E ratios of 100 plus and many with no earnings at all (see Fig. 9.3). Valuation attempts were made to justify these high prices; see Schwartz and Moon (2000) for one such example. Predicting the top of this bubble was not easy as the Internet index (not shown) fell 17% one day and then proceeded to reach new highs. For example, the noted investor George Soros lost some $5 billion of the $12 billion in the Quantum hedge fund during this crash.

The Nasdaq 100 peaked at 4816.35 on March 24, 2000 starting from 398.26 in 1994. In the decline, it fell to 795.25 on October 8, 2002. Below we apply the changepoint model to the questions when to close a long–short positions on NDX100 for various entering dates. The results appear in Table 9.3 and Fig. 9.4. Depending upon the long position entry, the exit yielded about 65–75% of the maximum price. Here the parameters $\mu_2 = -\mu_1$, $\sigma_2 = \sigma_1$ seem to show better performance than the other choices, however, all the three values of μ_2 with $\sigma_2 = \sigma_1$ give quite close results.

9.3.4. *The 2008 crash*

The roots of the 2008 crash can be found in the mortgage market problems. US real estate prices peaked in 2005–2006 and included loans to many unqualified buyers who were only safe if the real estate prices continued

Table 9.3. Exit points for NDX100 during the Internet crash.

Entry	Exit date (% of max. value) $\mu_2 = -\mu$, $\sigma_1 = \sigma_2$	$\mu_2 = -2\mu$, $\sigma_1 = \sigma_2$	$\mu_2 = -2\mu$, $\sigma_1 = 2\sigma_2$	$\mu_2 = -3\mu$, $\sigma_1 = \sigma_2$	$\mu_2 = -3\mu$, $\sigma_1 = 3\sigma_2$
T = end of 2000					
1997-07-01	00-05-23 (64)	00-04-14 (68)	97-10-27 (21)	00-04-12 (77)	97-10-27 (21)
1998-01-01	00-10-10 (68)	00-05-23 (64)	98-08-31 (24)	00-04-14 (68)	98-08-31 (24)
1998-07-01	00-04-14 (68)	00-04-13 (76)	98-08-31 (24)	00-04-12 (77)	98-08-31 (24)
1999-01-01	00-04-14 (68)	00-04-12 (77)	00-01-07 (75)	00-04-12 (77)	00-01-07 (75)
1999-07-01	00-04-14 (68)	00-04-12 (77)	00-01-10 (79)	00-04-12 (77)	00-01-11 (75)
T = end of 2001					
1997-07-01	00-10-12 (64)	00-04-14 (68)	97-10-27 (21)	00-04-14 (68)	97-10-27 (21)
1998-01-01	00-11-30 (53)	00-11-20 (59)	98-08-31 (24)	00-11-10 (61)	98-08-31 (24)
1998-07-01	00-10-11 (66)	00-04-14 (68)	98-08-31 (24)	00-04-14 (68)	98-08-31 (24)
1999-01-01	00-05-23 (64)	00-04-14 (68)	00-01-07 (75)	00-04-13 (76)	00-01-10 (79)
1999-07-01	00-10-10 (68)	00-04-14 (68)	00-01-11 (75)	00-04-14 (68)	00-04-12 (77)

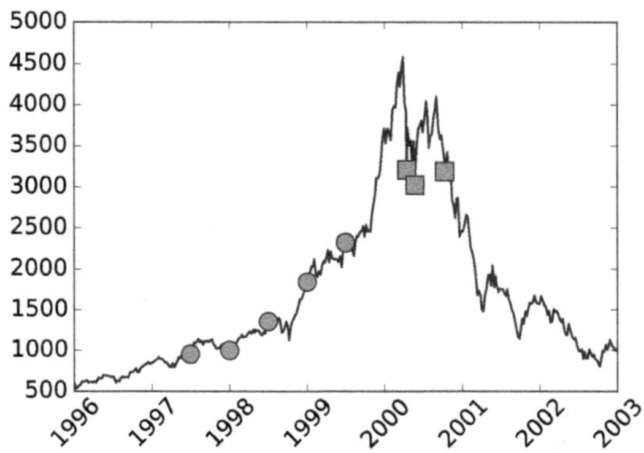

Fig. 9.4. The Nasdaq 100 index in 1996–2002 and the exit points for $\mu_2 = -\mu_1$, $\sigma_2 = \sigma_1$.

to rise. Unlike the two crashes considered above, this one had a different pattern: the crash was followed for about a year of slowly decreasing equity index prices (which peaked in October 2007) and a decline overall slower than those in 1929 and 1987. The total fall was huge with the index losing more than 57% of its value by March 2009. We refer to Chapter 3 and Lleo and Ziemba (2012) for a discussion of this crash and the application of the BSEYD model to predict it on June 14, 2007.

Table 9.4. Exit points for S&P500 around the 2008 crash.

	Exit date (% of max. value)				
Entry	$\mu_2 = -\mu$ $\sigma_1 = \sigma_2$	$\mu_2 = -2\mu$ $\sigma_1 = \sigma_2$	$\mu_2 = -2\mu$ $\sigma_1 = 2\sigma_2$	$\mu_2 = -3\mu$ $\sigma_1 = \sigma_2$	$\mu_2 = -3\mu$ $\sigma_1 = 3\sigma_2$
	T = end of 2008				
2005-07-01	08-01-15 (88)	07-11-21 (91)	07-02-27 (89)	07-11-19 (92)	07-02-27 (89)
2006-01-01	08-01-08 (89)	07-11-09 (93)	06-06-15 (80)	07-08-14 (91)	07-02-27 (89)
2006-07-01	08-01-08 (89)	07-11-21 (91)	07-02-27 (89)	07-08-15 (90)	07-02-27 (89)
2007-01-01	08-01-08 (89)	07-11-21 (91)	07-02-27 (89)	07-08-15 (90)	07-02-27 (89)
2007-07-01	08-01-08 (89)	07-11-21 (91)	07-07-26 (95)	07-08-15 (90)	07-07-26 (95)
	T = end of 2009				
2005-07-01	08-03-06 (83)	08-01-17 (85)	07-02-27 (89)	08-01-15 (88)	07-02-27 (89)
2006-01-01	08-03-06 (83)	08-01-08 (89)	06-06-15 (80)	07-11-26 (90)	07-02-27 (89)
2006-07-01	08-03-06 (83)	08-01-16 (88)	07-02-27 (89)	08-01-08 (89)	07-02-27 (89)
2007-01-01	08-01-17 (85)	08-01-15 (88)	07-02-27 (89)	08-01-15 (88)	07-02-27 (89)
2007-07-01	08-01-17 (85)	08-01-15 (88)	07-07-26 (95)	08-01-15 (88)	07-07-26 (95)

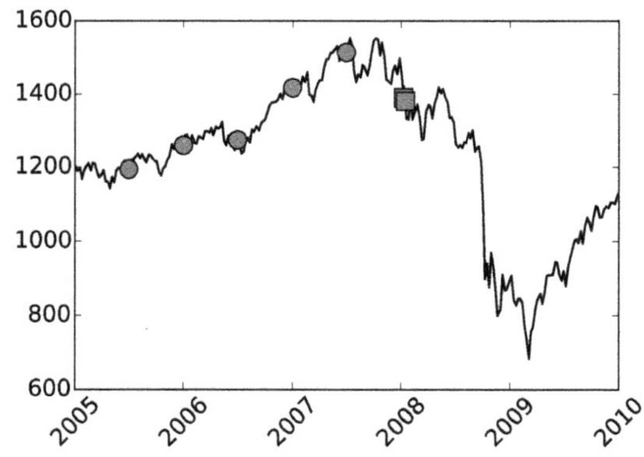

Fig. 9.5. The S&P500 index in 2005–2010 and the exit points for $\mu_2 = -\mu_1$, $\sigma_2 = \sigma_1$.

The changepoint model for any choice of the parameters detected the changepoint well before the actual crash in September 2008 though there were several too early detections (see Table 9.4). The results shown in Table 9.4 and Fig. 9.5 again support the choice of the post-crash volatility $\sigma_2 = \sigma_1$ and the post-crash drift $\mu_2 = -\mu_1$ or $\mu_2 = -2\mu_1$ (the shaded cells show exit points after the market peak).

A Stopping Rule Model for Exiting Bubble-like Markets with Applications 221

9.4. Crashes in the Japanese stock and land markets

9.4.1. *The crash in the Nikkei stock average index*

The Japanese stock market was closed after World War II ended in 1945 until its reopening in 1948. From 1948 to 1988, there was a huge rise in the stock market measured by the Nikkei price weighted index of 225 stocks as well as the Topix value weighted index of more than 1000 stocks. A steady increase in quality and quantity of equipment and automobiles of various kinds led to an enormous inflow of financial assets. These in turn were invested primarily in Japanese stocks and land.

Low interest rates in the mid to late 1980s fueled the stock and land, and the Nikkei rose 220 times in yen and 550 times in US dollars from 1948 to 1988. There were however 20 corrections/declines of 10% or more from 1949 to 1988 as shown in Table 9.5.

Table 9.5. The 20 Corrections of 10% or more on the NSA from 1949 to 1988.

	Index Value			Date		
	Peak	Valley	% decrease	Peak	Valley	# Months
1	176.89	85.25	−51.8	01-Sep-49	06-Jul-50	11
2	474.43	295.18	−37.8	4-Feb-53	1-Apr-53	2
3	366.69	321.79	−12.2	6-May-53	3-Jun-53	1
4	595.46	471.53	−20.8	4-May-57	27-Dec-57	8
5	1,829.74	1,258.00	−31.2	18-Jul-61	19-Dec-61	5
6	1,589.76	1,216.04	−23.5	14-Feb-62	29-Oct-62	9
7	1,634.37	1201.26	−26.5	5-Apr-63	18-Dec-63	9
8	1,369.00	1,020.49	−25.5	3-Jul-64	12-Jul-65	13
9	1,588.73	1,364.34	−14.1	1-Apr-66	15-Dec-66	8
10	1,506.27	1,250.40	−17.0	1-Mar-67	11-Dec-67	9
11	2,534.45	1,929.64	−23.9	6-Apr-70	27-May-70	2
12	2,740.98	2,227.25	−18.7	13-Aug-71	20-Oct-71	3
13	5,359.74	3,355.13	−37.4	24-Jan-73	9-Oct-74	21
14	4,564.52	3,814.02	−16.4	12-May-75	29-Sep-75	5
15	5,287.65	4,597.26	−13.1	5-Sep-77	24-Nov-77	3
16	8,019.14	6,849.78	−14.6	17-Aug-81	1-Oct-82	14
17	11,190.17	9,703.35	−13.3	4-May-84	23-Jul-84	3
18	18,936.24	15,819.58	−16.5	20-Aug-86	22-Oct-86	2
19	25,929.42	22,702.74	−12.4	17-Jun-87	22-Jul-87	1
20	26,646.43	21,036.76	−21.1	14-Oct-87	11-Nov-87	1
Average			−0.224			6.5

Source: Yamaichi Research Institute.

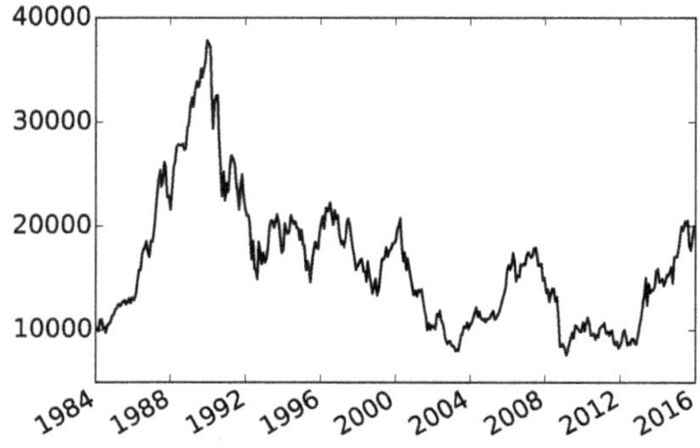

Fig. 9.6. The Nikkei stock average index, 1984–2016.

The Nikkei peaked at the end of December 1989 at 39,816. In Chapter 2, the bond–stock earnings yield model was shown to go into the danger zone in April 1989, based on too high interest rates relative to earnings yield. That model suggested that a large decline or crash was coming. The stock market started to fall on the first trading day of 1990. When the index bottomed, the market had fallen 48% from 38,916 at the end of December 1989 to 20,222 on October 1, 1990. Figure 9.6 shows the Nikkei stock average index from 1984 to 2014.

Interest rates increased 8 full months till August 1990. It took years and years to recover from this despite dropping interest rates after August 1990 for many years and in 2016, they were still low. Overall, the crash ushered in more than two decades of deflation, weak economic markets and a lost generation of young people. Various Japanese policies and regulatory constraints exacerbated the poor economic situation and never resolved the basic problem of overleveraging and excessive debt that was a major part of the 1980s buildup.

We tested the changepoint model on the Japanese crash of 1990 applying it to the Nikkei index with the results shown in Table 9.6 and Fig. 9.7. The meaning of the parameters is the same as in the previous section. For all the choices of the parameters, the model stopped well near the peak.

9.4.2. *The crash in the land market*

While the Nikkei stock average in the late 1980s and its −48% crash in 1990 are generally recognized as a financial market bubble, a bigger bubble and crash were in the land market which started to fall in 1990. The land and stock markets were greatly intertwined as discussed by Ziemba (1991)

Table 9.6. Exit points for the Nikkei stock average.

	Exit date (% of max. value)				
Entry	$\mu_2 = -\mu$ $\sigma_1 = \sigma_2$	$\mu_2 = -2\mu$ $\sigma_1 = \sigma_2$	$\mu_2 = -2\mu$ $\sigma_1 = 2\sigma_2$	$\mu_2 = -3\mu$ $\sigma_1 = \sigma_2$	$\mu_2 = -3\mu$ $\sigma_1 = 3\sigma_2$
	T = end of 1990				
1987-07-01	90-03-14 (83)	87-11-11 (54)	87-10-20 (56)	87-10-20 (56)	87-10-20 (56)
1988-01-01	90-02-26 (86)	90-02-23 (90)	90-04-02 (72)	90-02-23 (90)	90-04-02 (72)
1988-07-01	90-02-26 (86)	90-02-21 (92)	90-04-02 (72)	90-02-21 (92)	90-04-02 (72)
1989-01-01	90-02-23 (90)	90-02-23 (90)	90-02-21 (92)	90-02-23 (90)	90-02-21 (92)
1989-07-01	90-02-23 (90)	90-02-23 (90)	90-01-16 (95)	90-02-21 (92)	90-01-16 (95)
	T = end of 1991				
1987-07-01	90-03-20 (79)	90-03-19 (80)	87-10-20 (56)	87-10-20 (56)	87-10-20 (56)
1988-01-01	90-04-02 (72)	90-03-20 (79)	90-04-02 (72)	90-03-19 (80)	90-04-02 (72)
1988-07-01	90-04-02 (72)	90-03-19 (80)	90-04-02 (72)	90-03-19 (80)	90-04-02 (72)
1989-01-01	90-02-26 (86)	90-02-26 (86)	90-02-23 (90)	90-02-26 (86)	90-02-23 (90)
1989-07-01	90-02-26 (86)	90-02-26 (86)	90-02-21 (92)	90-02-23 (90)	90-02-21 (92)

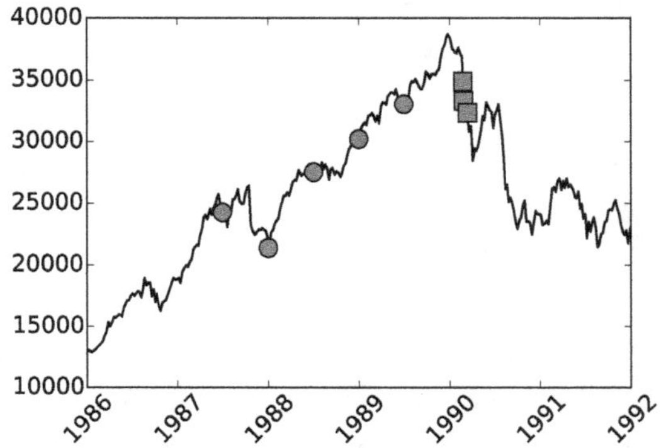

Fig. 9.7. The Nikkei stock average in 1986–1991 and the exit points for $\mu_2 = -\mu_1$, $\sigma_2 = \sigma_1$.

and Stone and Ziemba (1993) and the discussion below. To get an idea of the price pressure on Japanese land prices, consider that in the late 1980s:

- some 120 million people lived in Japan in an area the size of Montana,
- only 5% of the land was used to house the people, buildings and factories because most of the land is mountainous,
- most of the land was owned by large corporations but 60% of Japanese families and 55% of those in Tokyo owned their own home,

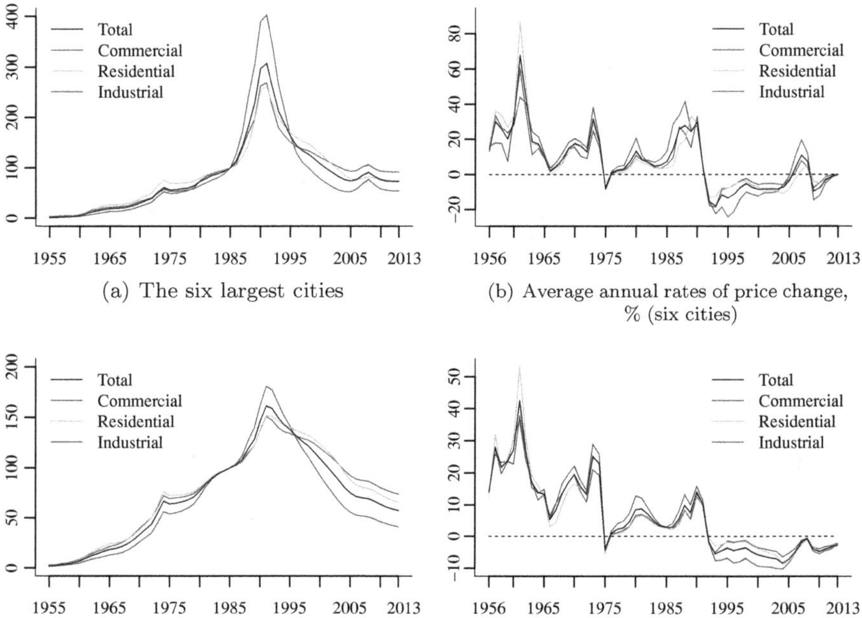

(a) The six largest cities

(b) Average annual rates of price change, % (six cities)

(c) All of Japan

(d) Average annual rates of price change, % (all of Japan)

Fig. 9.8. Land price indices for industrial, residential, commercial and all land and annual rates of price change, 1955–2013.

Source: Japan Real Estate Institute.

- there was massive savings by households,
- only some 3% of Japanese assets were invested abroad despite great fear in the west and some very public purchases at inflated prices of expensive property such as the Pebble Beach golf course.

Figure 9.8 gives the Japan Real Estate Institute's land indices for the six largest cities, and for all of Japan for commercial, housing, industrial and total land for each 6-month period from 1955 to 2013. The graphs also give the yearly rate of changes. The six largest cities are Tokyo, Yokohama, Osaka, Nagoya, Kobe and Kyoto.

The countrywide indices are based on 140 cities. The data are appraisal based which tends to smooth the price levels and lag the market. Simple averages of samples of 10 lots in each city form the indices which were normalized at 100 as of 1985. The sampling procedure separates land into high, medium and low grades reflecting location, social circumstances, yield, etc.

A Stopping Rule Model for Exiting Bubble-like Markets with Applications 225

Table 9.7. Increase of land prices, 1955–1990, %.

	Nationwide				6 largest cities			
	Total	Com	Res	Ind	Total	Com	Res	Ind
1955 to 1990	65.5	59.6	81.2	56.7	178.8	127.7	219.1	150.8
1955 to 1970	15.1	14.5	15.5	15.8	18.7	11.0	20.2	23.6
1970 to 1990	4.3	4.1	5.2	3.6	9.6	11.6	10.8	6.4

Source: Japan Real Estate Institute.

The sampling procedure selects lots randomly and equally from each of these three classes.

Figure 9.8 and Table 9.7 indicate that the price increase has been largest in the six largest cities. Despite large rises in the 1980s, the relative gain in the period 1955–1970 was much larger than from 1970 to the circa 1990 peak. For land in the whole country, the 1955–1970 period produced gains of about 15 times the 1955 values. These prices then increased only about four-fold in the ensuing 20 years. In the six largest cities, the increase was also much larger in the 1955–1970 period versus the next two decades.

Land values in the six largest cities outpaced the Consumer Prices Index (CPI) by 20 times from 1955 to 1990. In the Ginza district of Tokyo each square meter of land was worth well over US$200,000 with some plots approaching $300,000. Choice downtown land in Tokyo sold for the equivalent of nearly a billion dollars an acre. At neighboring land prices, the value of land under the Emperor's palace and garden in Tokyo equaled that of all California or of Canada. The total land value in Japan in 1990 was about 4.1 times that of the whole US. The average acre of land in Japan was worth fully 100 times the average acre in the US. So even though the US has about 25 times more land than Japan, its 1990 total value was less than a fourth as much. Essentially half the world's land value at 1987–1990 prices was accounted for by Japanese land!

The price was kept up and bid higher because of the excess of demand over supply. Land turnover was very small as the Japanese believe in holding land whenever possible. This was reinforced by the tax system which encourages the purchase of more land and discourages land sales. High interest rates which led to a sharp fall in stock prices in 1990 did not lead to any decline in land prices until 1991 as shown in Fig. 9.8. However, there was a sharp decline in speculative land such as golf course membership and condos, see Stone and Ziemba (1993). As interest rates rise, land demand fell but in Tokyo, with virtually no new supply, demand still greatly exceeded supply. At the same time, supply declines with higher interest rates as development costs are curtailed. All the incentives favored holding land and not even developing it. As Canaway (1990) pointed out, land held for less than 5 years was taxed at fully 52% of its sale value. Meanwhile, yearly taxes paid to hold land were about 0.05 to 0.10% of its current value. Even upon death, it paid to borrow money which was deductible at full value while land was valued at about half its market value. Hence inheritance taxes are minimized. Canaway argued that in a major crash the stock market will go first, then the economy and finally the land markets. Our results confirm this.

9.4.3. *The golf course membership index as a proxy for the land market*

Japanese land prices are difficult for a direct analysis since only low frequency time series are available. In part, this makes difficult to apply the changepoint model. Nevertheless, the overall land market can be well proxied by speculative land prices. In this section as such a proxy we use data on membership prices in Japanese golf courses.

In 1989 there were more than 400 golf courses in Japan with a total value of more than US$300 billion, a value larger than the Australian stock exchange capitalization of A$250 billion. Memberships, which cost as much as US$8 million, allowed play at a reduced cost plus the right to bring guests to play for a higher fee. However, their main value was not the ability to play golf but their share of the land occupied by the course and as an instrument to play the land market for relatively low stake with liquidity. These memberships were actively traded as speculative investments whose market was maintained by six market makers in Tokyo and Osaka. Weekly data were available in various areas of Japan since the beginning of 1982. These data were the best widely available data series on land prices in Japan and forms an ideal source for many types of analyses.

Rachev and Ziemba (1992) modeled the price changes as stable variants. The tails had considerable mass and the distributions were considered to have fat tails with a characteristic exponent about 1.4. This is consistent with the hypothesis that there was a speculative bubble in the late 1980s and the subsequent crash in 1990–1992.

Figure 9.9 shows the golf course membership (GCM) prices in various regions of the country: the western and the eastern parts of Japan, the

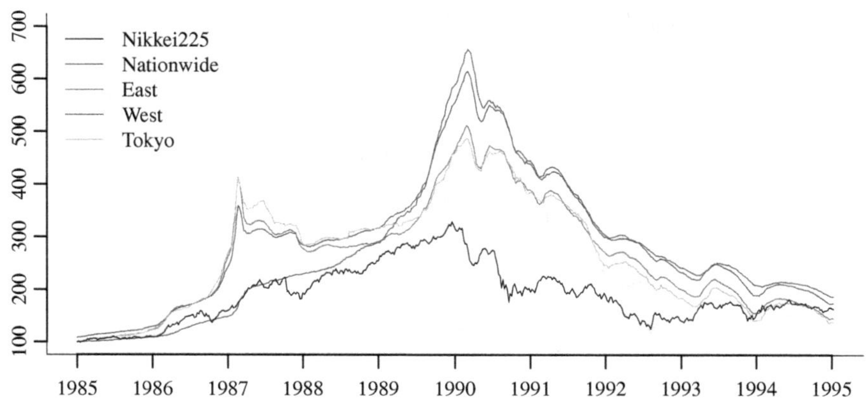

Fig. 9.9. Graphs of the golf course membership prices in various areas of Japan and the Nikkei stock average, 1985–1995, with the 1985 values as 100%.

Table 9.8. Exit points for the Golf Course Index crash.

	Exit date (% of max. value)				
Entry	$\mu_2 = -\mu$ $\sigma_1 = \sigma_2$	$\mu_2 = -2\mu$ $\sigma_1 = \sigma_2$	$\mu_2 = -2\mu$ $\sigma_1 = 2\sigma_2$	$\mu_2 = -3\mu$ $\sigma_1 = \sigma_2$	$\mu_2 = -3\mu$ $\sigma_1 = 3\sigma_2$
			T = end of 1991		
1988-07-01	90-04-01 (95)	90-03-25 (98)	89-07-09 (62)	90-03-25 (98)	89-02-12 (54)
1989-01-01	90-03-18 (99)	90-03-18 (99)	89-07-09 (62)	90-03-18 (99)	89-02-05 (53)
1989-07-01	90-03-18 (99)	90-03-18 (99)	90-03-18 (99)	90-03-25 (98)	89-09-17 (72)
1989-10-01	90-04-01 (95)	90-04-01 (95)	90-04-01 (95)	90-04-01 (95)	90-04-01 (95)
			T = end of 1992		
1988-07-01	90-04-01 (95)	90-04-01 (95)	89-07-09 (62)	90-03-25 (98)	89-02-26 (55)
1989-01-01	90-03-18 (99)	90-03-18 (99)	89-07-09 (62)	90-03-18 (99)	89-02-05 (53)
1989-07-01	90-03-25 (98)	90-03-18 (99)	90-03-18 (99)	90-03-25 (98)	89-09-17 (72)
1989-10-01	90-04-01 (95)	90-04-01 (95)	90-04-01 (95)	90-04-01 (95)	90-04-01 (95)

Tokyo area and the nationwide average. The golf course memberships market was a much bigger bubble than the stock market.

The results of applying the changepoint model are displayed in Table 9.8 with the same notation as the previous sections. We show only the nationwide index, although similar results and exit dates were obtained for the three other indices (the results can be found in Shiryaev, *et al.* 2015). In all the cases, the model exits well above 90% of the global maximum price, see Fig. 9.10. Compared with the stock market bubble, the changepoint model

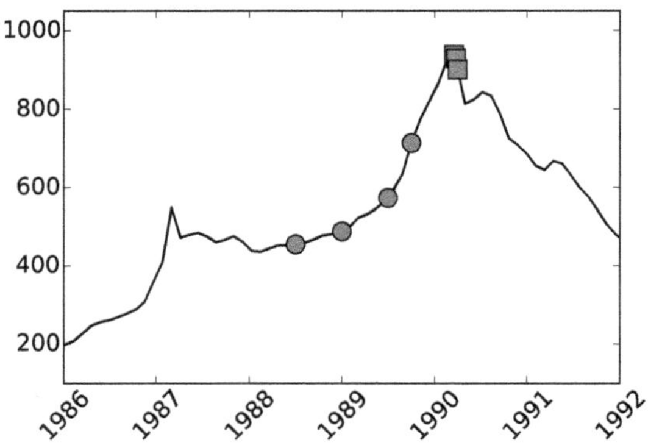

Fig. 9.10. The Japan GCM index and the exit points for $\mu_2 = -\mu_1$, $\sigma_2 = \sigma_1$.

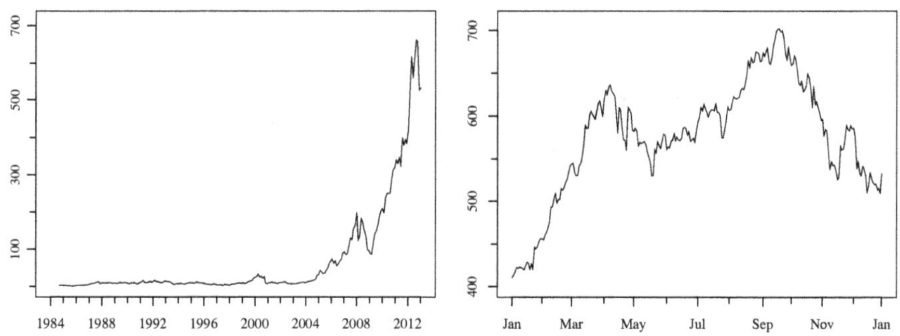

(a) (b)

Fig. 9.11. The history of AAPL stock price (adjusted for dividends and splits). (a) From September 1984 to the end of 2012. (b) In 2009–2012.

applied to the golf course membership index exits almost immediately after the peak. One reason for that is much higher ratio μ_1/σ of the drift to volatility, which governs the statistic ψ_t from the model.

9.5. Other crashes: Apple stock, China and Iceland

9.5.1. *The crash in Apple computer stock in 2012*

AAPL stock had a spectacular run from the bottom of the 2007–2009 crash in March 2009, see Fig. 9.11 which shows the price history from September 1984 to the end of 2012; and the more recent period, from the beginning of 2009 to the end of 2012.

A Stopping Rule Model for Exiting Bubble-like Markets with Applications 229

A sequence of valuable and easy to use products inspired by legendary visionary Steve Jobs created huge interest and sales around the world. All of these products had high margins which accumulated large cash levels. In November 2012 they had $121 billion in cash or $128 per share of the 941 million shares outstanding. The company has generated cash faster than any corporation in history. The stock was never at a high P/E ratio and was a favorite of hedge funds, open and closed mutual funds, ETFs and various small and large investors. It was traded as a proxy for the market with high liquidity. Its forward P/E ratio in November 2012 was 10.17 with estimated earnings per share of $49.28. The company had a quarterly dividend of $2.65 per share and a buy back of about $10 million in stock.

Steve Jobs left Apple in 1985 because of a power struggle with John Sculley who he brought over from Pepsi asking "do you want to sell sugared water all your life or change the world". Sculley came to Apple but he and Jobs had a disagreement on strategy and marketing which stagnated the company. The board favored the marketer over the genius. Jobs sold all but one of his AAPL shares. The company languished while he continued developing his ideas at NeXT and Pixar. When Jobs returned to Apple in 1996, he brought the new NeXT platform and ideas for user friendly products that had not yet been imagined by the market. He transformed the company into a winner. He held a lot of AAPL stock but more of Pixar which merged with Disney.

After his death on October 5, 2011, many feared that the sequence of great products would cease and that the pace of innovation could not be maintained and that the market cap of about $500 billion, various lawsuits for patent infringement, competition and labor and supply chain issues might slow it down. Some thought it was a bubble and others thought it would continue rallying because it was not expensive, not feeding on itself as in a typical bubble. The stock peaked at 705.07 on September 21, 2012 and then fell dramatically to the local low of 505.75 on November 16, 2012. Later, in pre-market trading on December 17, 2012, it fell to 499. On December 31, 2012, AAPL closed the year at 532; see Fig. 9.11.

The concentration of ownership by mutual funds (see Fig. 9.12) creates conundrum for Apple as regulations prohibit ownership to exceed a percentage of a fund's assets, so as AAPL rises relative to other stocks, funds often must sell shares. Some of the selling was tax loss selling in 2012 before expected higher capital gains and dividend rates in 2013 since more gains

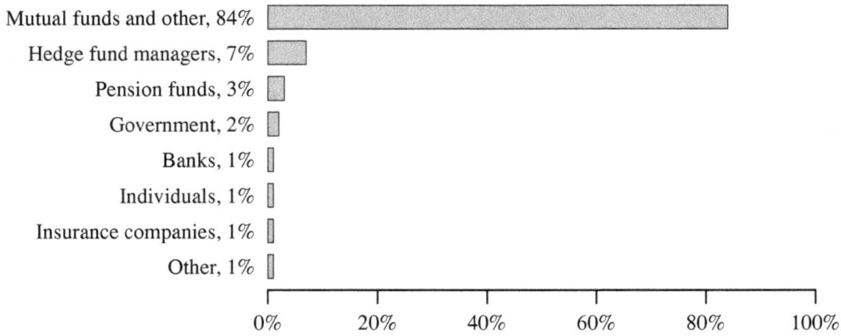

Fig. 9.12. Holders of Apple, April 17, 2012.
Source: Bloomberg via Eric Jackson.

are in AAPL than in any other stock. Despite the large decline in the latter part of 2012 the stock increased 30% in 2012.

Shiryaev, *et al.* (2014) applied the model to the Apple price bubble starting at the local low of 82.33 on March 6, 2009 and considering various entering dates for opening a long position in 2009–2012. It was assumed that the trend reversal will happen before the end of 2012. Higher tax rates on dividends and capital gains were expected in 2013, thus a sale in 2012 is suggested.

Table 9.9 and Fig. 9.13 present the result of the changepoint model application. Tests indicate that the choice $\mu_2 = -\mu_1$ is the optimal one, and for the 2012 time horizon works equally well both for early and late entering dates giving nearly 90% of the maximum price.

9.5.2. *The crash in Iceland in 2007–2009*

Iceland is a small country with only about 300 000 people. From 2002 to 2007, the economy and asset prices rose dramatically, with much leveraging of investments, especially by the banks. This led to high interest rates of about 10% long term and 16% short term. Eventually, it all collapsed in the wake of the 2007–2009 worldwide financial crisis. The decline was a massive crash of −95% in the equity index and a currency collapse.

The crash in Iceland is discussed in Section 3.2 with the BSEYD model prediction, the decline which occurred around the time of the Lehman Brothers collapse in the fall of 2008.

In Table 9.10 and Fig. 9.14, we show entries and exits using the changepoint model. We consider two entry points in April and June 2007,

A Stopping Rule Model for Exiting Bubble-like Markets with Applications 231

Table 9.9. Exit points for the Apple stock around the 2012 crash.

Entry	Exit date (% of max. value) $\mu_2 = -\mu$, $\sigma_1 = \sigma_2$	$\mu_2 = -2\mu$, $\sigma_1 = \sigma_2$	$\mu_2 = -2\mu$, $\sigma_1 = 2\sigma_2$	$\mu_2 = -3\mu$, $\sigma_1 = \sigma_2$	$\mu_2 = -3\mu$, $\sigma_1 = 3\sigma_2$
			T = end of 2012		
2012-07-01	12-10-19 (87)	12-10-11 (89)	12-11-08 (77)	12-10-09 (91)	12-11-19 (81)
2012-01-01	12-10-11 (89)	12-10-05 (93)	12-04-17 (87)	12-05-17 (76)	12-01-25 (64)
2011-07-01	12-10-25 (87)	12-05-17 (76)	11-08-08 (50)	12-05-17 (76)	11-08-08 (50)
2011-01-01	12-11-02 (82)	12-10-26 (86)	11-08-09 (53)	12-10-26 (86)	11-08-09 (53)
2010-07-01	12-11-02 (82)	12-11-02 (82)	11-08-09 (53)	12-11-02 (82)	11-08-09 (53)
			T = end of 2013		
2012-07-01	12-12-14 (73)	12-11-08 (77)	13-01-24 (64)	12-11-08 (77)	13-01-24 (64)
2012-01-01	12-12-14 (73)	12-11-08 (77)	12-04-19 (84)	12-11-07 (79)	12-04-25 (87)
2011-07-01	12-11-08 (77)	12-11-07 (79)	11-08-08 (50)	12-11-07 (79)	11-08-08 (50)
2011-01-01	12-12-14 (73)	12-11-08 (77)	11-08-09 (53)	12-11-08 (77)	11-08-09 (53)
2010-07-01	12-12-14 (73)	12-11-15 (75)	11-08-10 (52)	12-11-08 (77)	12-04-25 (87)

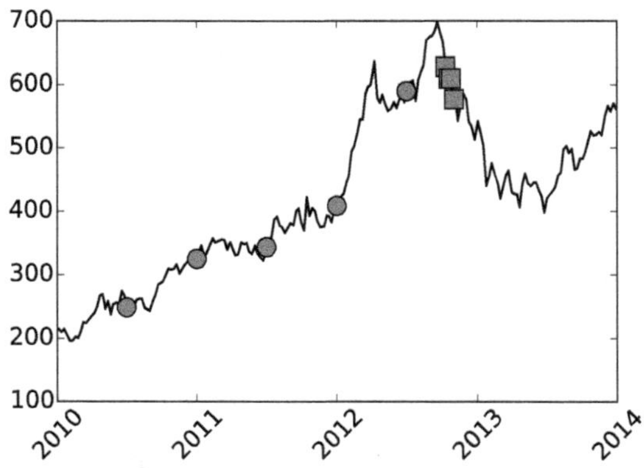

Fig. 9.13. The Apple stock price in 2010–2014 and the exit points.

Table 9.10. Exit points for the Iceland stock market crash in 2007.

Entry	Exit date (% of max. value) $\mu_2 = -\mu$, $\sigma_1 = \sigma_2$	$\mu_2 = -2\mu$, $\sigma_1 = \sigma_2$	$\mu_2 = -2\mu$, $\sigma_1 = 2\sigma_2$	$\mu_2 = -3\mu$, $\sigma_1 = \sigma_2$	$\mu_2 = -3\mu$, $\sigma_1 = 3\sigma_2$
2007-04-01	07-08-10 (89)	07-08-09 (92)	07-08-10 (89)	07-08-09 (92)	07-08-10 (89)
2007-06-01	07-08-09 (92)	07-08-03 (93)	07-08-01 (94)	07-07-30 (94)	07-08-10 (89)

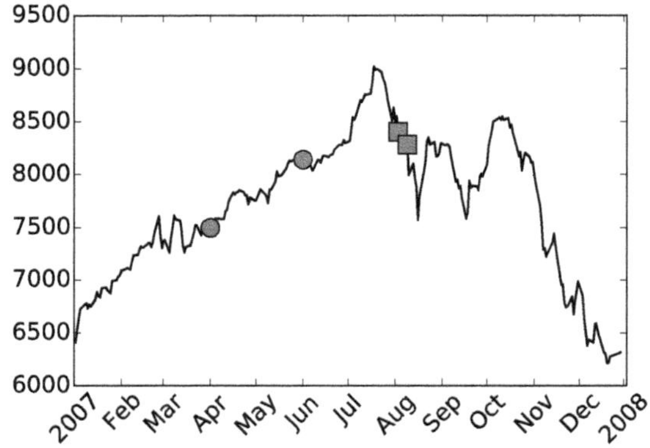

Fig. 9.14. OMX Iceland 15 Index in 2007 and the exit points.

Table 9.11. Exit points for the Chinese stock market crash in 2015.

	Exit date (% of max. value)				
Entry	$\mu_2 = -\mu$ $\sigma_1 = \sigma_2$	$\mu_2 = -2\mu$ $\sigma_1 = \sigma_2$	$\mu_2 = -2\mu$ $\sigma_1 = 2\sigma_2$	$\mu_2 = -3\mu$ $\sigma_1 = \sigma_2$	$\mu_2 = -3\mu$ $\sigma_1 = 3\sigma_2$
2015-04-01	15-06-26 (81)	15-06-19 (87)	15-05-11 (84)	15-06-19 (87)	15-05-28 (89)
2015-01-01	15-06-26 (81)	15-06-19 (87)	15-01-19 (60)	15-06-19 (87)	15-01-19 (60)
2014-08-01	15-07-03 (71)	15-06-26 (81)	14-12-02 (53)	15-06-19 (87)	14-12-04 (56)

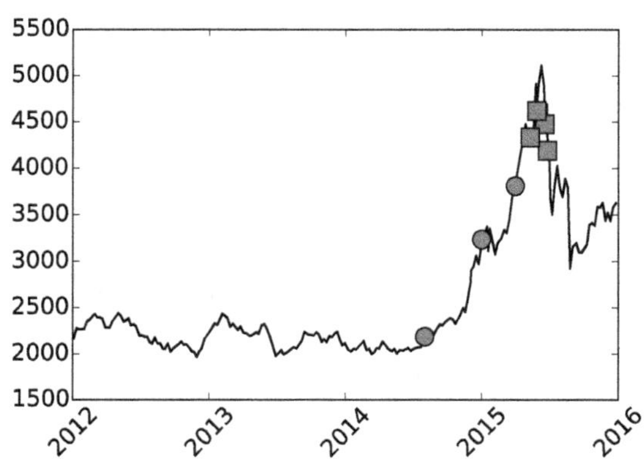

Fig. 9.15. The SSEC Index in 2012–2015 and the exit point.

with the time horizon taken as the end of 2007. The model exits at about 90% of the index's maximum value.

9.5.3. *The crash in China in 2015*

The growing Chinese economy has recently attracted many individual investors, whose actions are believed to fuel the bubble in the stock market. They borrowed heavily to buy equities, which resulted in stocks priced beyond their fundamental values. Thus a little decrease could potentially lead to a large sell-off due to investors facing margin calls, which is believed what has happened starting from the summer of 2015.

The Shanghai Stock Exchange Composite Index (SSEC) peaked in the middle of June 2015 showing about a 70% increase from the beginning of the year — of the bubbles considered in this chapter, the Chinese one is the sharpest. By the end of August, the index lost almost a half of its peak value. A local trough was also on July 2, with a loss of about 40% of the maximum value. In Chapter 3, we applied the BSEYD model to predict this Chinese stock market crash and the results are discussed there.

The changepoint detection model for all the parameters we consider signaled the changepoint before the July decline, in most cases being able to exit at more than 80% of the maximum value. There were, however, several false detections triggered by the temporary decline in the beginning of 2015. Table 9.11 and Fig. 9.15 illustrate the results. The shaded cells in the table mark the four highest exit points shown on the graph, all above 80% of the peak value.

https://doi.org/10.1142/9789811222634_0024

Chapter 24

Econometric Tools for Stress Testing Using Time Heterogeneity and Maximum Entropy

H. D. Vinod

Professor of Economics, Fordham University, Bronx, New York, USA 10458
vinod@fordham.edu

Stress testing of economic policies, regulations, financial risk evaluations, and statistical inference have lately become a "requirement." This chapter highlights extant econometric tools for stress testing with an emphasis on: (a) maximum entropy bootstraps, recently implemented in a new version of the R software package called "meboot," and (b) creation of stress scenarios by considering time heterogeneous nonstationary time series. We use published simulation designs of other authors to report the superiority of meboot over the moving block bootstrap (mbb) and the blocking external bootstrap (BEB) in the context of many types of time-heterogeneity. For illustration, we apply meboot tools to stress test inference regarding Granger-causality between asset prices and world savings rates, and also to the "Value at Risk" used in finance. We indicate potential uses in stress testing of banks.

Keywords: Maximum entropy, bootstrap, simulation, causality tests, convergence, FDIC, Value at Risk.

1. Introduction

Responding to the great recession of 2008, Dodd–Frank Act of 2010 mandated the stress testing of banks, which began in early 2011,

FDIC (2011). It asks all large banks, to prepare a forward-looking assessment of their risks. Kapinos and Mitnik (2016) discuss two key quantities available in bank income statements: pre-provision net revenue (PPNR) and net charge-offs (NCO). They study macroeconomic predictors of these quantities by using least absolute shrinkage selection operator (LASSO) and the first factor from a standard principal component analysis of a large number of macroeconomic variables. The quantile regression approach of Covas *et al.* (2014) simulates densities estimated from quantile regressions. This chapter argues that researchers in this field should consider the maximum entropy bootstrap tools for simulating non-stationary time series subject to structural breaks.

We claim that structural breaks can arise from a phenomenon known as "Lucas critique," whereby human agents adjust their behavior in response to changing regulations. A major new regulation can influence agent behavior near its starting date enough to create a new structure. Rajan *et al.* (2010) show that default risk assessments of securitized subprime mortgages failed, partly because of a failure to allow for the Lucas critique.

Since Efron's traditional bootstrap merely reshuffles available series x_t, it is not generally known that the maximum entropy bootstraps[1] can create a large number $J = 1000$, say, of scenarios of short-time heterogeneous nonstationary series for statistical inference and stress testing. A brief description of flexMeboot is given in Section 2.1. It provides a new option to randomly shrink, expand, or change the original trend direction by a flat, up, or down direction. Unlike some *ad hoc* scenario analyses, the meboot satisfies the ergodic theorem and the maximum entropy principle.

How well does the meboot work with small samples? This chapter uses published simulation designs of other authors to report superiority of meboot over moving block bootstrap (mbb) and blocking external bootstrap (BEB) in the context of many types of time-heterogeneity.

[1] Freely available in an R package, Vinod and López-de-Lacalle (2009), having functions named "meboot" and "flexMeboot".

In this chapter, we report two more examples of success of the meboot. The first involves stress testing the reliability of Granager causality tests. Due to globalization, the US macroeconomy is increasingly sensitive to heterogeneous global trends. For example, Fair (2011) highlights huge fluctuations in recent years in world private sector savings as a proportion of world GDP (SPS) and the S&P index of 500 stock prices as a proportion of US GDP (SP500). He explains why the latter is a good proxy for world asset prices and focuses on a somewhat puzzling and little noticed fact that SPS and SP500 are statistically significantly negatively correlated with each other, seen as dashed lines in Fig. 1. However, Prof. Fair does

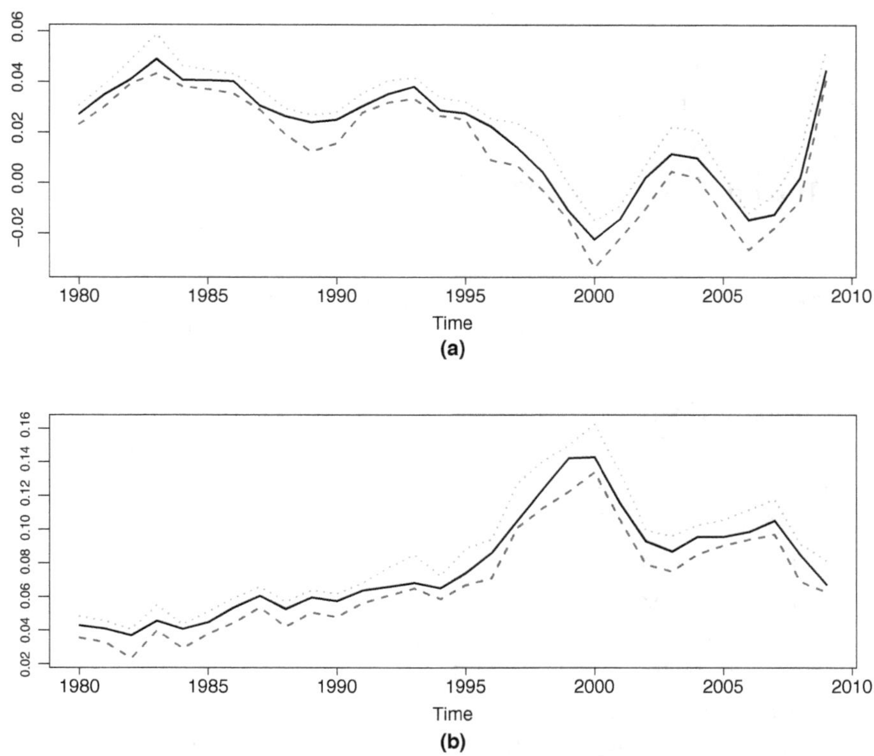

Fig. 1. Fluctuating SPS and SP500 data and meboot depicted at the lower 5 percentile and upper 95 percentiles among J resamples. (a) World Private Savings/ World GDP meboot. Actual (solid), 90% range: Lo (dashed) and Up (dotted). (b) meboot (S&P 500 price/US GDP) Ratio. Actual (solid), 90% range: Lo (dashed) and Up (dotted).

not report Granger causality tests among the two series, perhaps because the annual 1980–2009 data series are time heterogeneous, possibly non-stationary and short ($T = 30$). Our second application shows how to use meboot to assess "Value at Risk" [VaR is defined in Section 5.1].

The outline of the remainder of the chapter is as follows. Section 2 provides a quick introduction to meboot resampling. Section 3 describes our simulation with subsections for t-heterogeneity in mean and variance. Section 4 describes a comparison of closeness to true values of regression coefficients arising from t-heterogeneity in mean models for meboot versus the moving blocks bootstrap (mbb) and one of its extensions called BEB. Section 5 discusses two real-world applications of meboot for inference regarding causality testing and to stress testing of estimated Value at Risk (VaR). Section 6 concludes with a short summary.

2. Introduction to the Meboot Algorithm

Normal theory inference for cross-section data assumes that the observed statistic such as a sample mean $\bar{x}$ or a regression coefficient is *invariant* to reordering of x_t. Hence, the observed data can be viewed as one realization from an infinitely large Normal population. By analogy, time series inference developed in 1930s by Wiener, Kolmogorov, and Khintchine (WKK), among others, imagined an infinite ensemble Ω as a population of stationary ($I(0)$) time series with the observed series in a generic notation x_t as its element. The observed time series x_t is also denoted as $\omega_0 \in \Omega$, viewed as an element of the ensemble.

Efron's traditional independent and identically distributed (iid) bootstrap directly shuffles individual data points *with replacement* to create a large number J, say, of resamples. Since the iid bootstrap fails for m-dependent time series data, one must use the moving block bootstrap (mbb) explained by various authors including Davison and Hinkley (1997), Liu (1988), and Lahiri (2003). Since m-dependent means that roughly speaking blocks of size m are independent, mbb shuffles blocks of data. Spanos and Kourtellos (2002) have found that mbb performs poorly. Vinod (2010a) shows that "meboot" estimates are closer to true values than the mbb in the context of spurious regression, such as when the coefficient of determination (R^2) exceeds the Durbin Watson statistic. The focus in this chapter is on t-heterogeneous data and we compare the performance of meboot-type bootstraps with the mbb in Section 4.

Vinod (2010b) views the meboot algorithm with a slightly new angle, in terms of two-way mappings based on simultaneous sorting of two columns of a matrix from the time domain (t-dom) to numerical magnitudes or "values" domain (v-dom) and back. The first step of the algorithm sorts a matrix with the first column containing $t = 1, \ldots, T$ and second column containing x_t to obtain the usual order statistics $x_{(t)}$ in the second column, while remembering the first column of sorted t subscripts. This is a one-one onto bijection mapping: (t-dom)$\rightarrow$ (v-dom). Lemma 2 in Vinod (2010b) shows that the map is linear, being represented by a matrix multiplication.

Unlike iid or mbb, meboot admits resamples values from a small neighborhood of $x_{(t)}$ in the (v-dom). Vinod and López-de-Lacalle (2009) use a simple example of five observations: $x_t = (4, 12, 36, 20, 8)$, to illustrate these neighborhoods using averages of adjacent order statistics: $x_{(t)} = (4, 8, 12, 20, 36)$. Since the limits are finite and known, the maximum entropy (ME) principle implies that the ME density is "uniform." For the simple example, the ME density is shown to consist of five half open uniform density intervals: $U(-11, 6] * U(6, 10] * U(10, 16] * U(16, 28] * U(28, 51]$, illustrated in Fig. 2.

The meboot algorithm further requires the ME density to satisfy two constraints: (1) Mass-preserving: On average, a fraction $1/T$ of the mass of the probability distribution must lie in each small interval. (2) Mean-preserving: This constraint numerically ensures that the time average equals the ensemble average. Hence, meboot resamples are designed to satisfy the **ergodic theorem**.

The algorithm goes on to construct a *cumulative* ME density implied by the ME density illustrated in Fig. 2 residing in the (v-dom). Now, one independently selects a large number (J, say) of

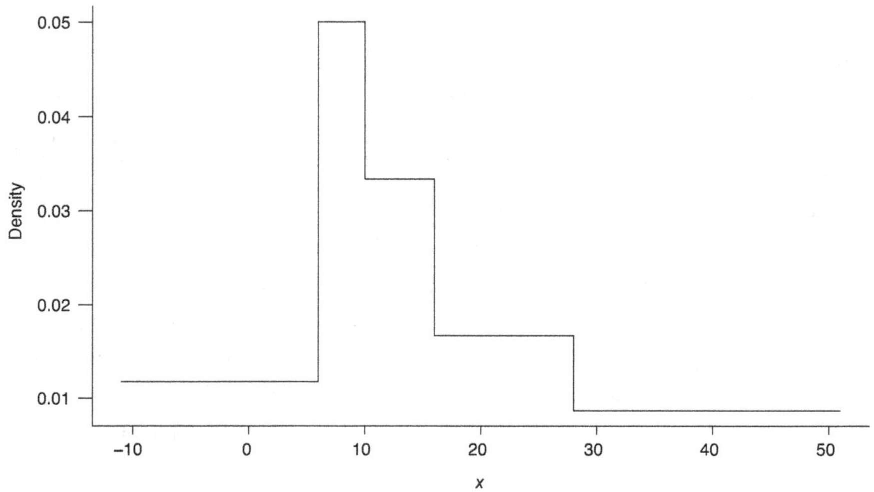

Fig. 2. Toy ME density for $x_t = (4, 12, 36, 20, 8)$.

resamples from the ME density, just like the iid bootstrap selecting a large number of resamples from the empirical cumulative density function (ECDF) defined from x_t residing in the (t-dom). Further theoretical discussion with examples is found in Vinod (2006).

Finally, the algorithm maps all iid resamples from (v-dom) to (t-dom) by using the *sorted t* subscripts of the first step in the first column and iid resamples from the ME density in the second column. This is a simultaneous sort of matrix with a focus on the first column, which recovers the time subscript, as it were.

An important property of all resampled series: $x_{t,j}, j = 1, \ldots, J$ is that Spearman's rank correlation coefficient between the original data x_t and $x_{t,j}$ is always near unity, that is, all resampled series are strongly dependent on the original x_t. Since strong dependence tends to retain in $x_{t,j}$, the (upward or downward) trend of original series x_t, it may not be appropriate for some purposes. Combining the idea of blocks with the need to admit flexible directions of the trends within these blocks leads to an extension of the meboot algorithm discussed in the next subsection.

2.1. *Random trends within blocks using a new "flexMeboot" algorithm*

This chapter suggests a mild extension of the R function "meboot" from the R package "meboot." The extension called "flexMeboot" uses non-overlapping blocks, each having only m observations. It avoids excessive reliance on historical trends by allowing for the possibility of random trend reversals.

The R function "flexMeboot" is described in the new version of meboot package. Its steps are as follows:

1. Choose the block size m (default $m = 5$) and divide the original time series x_t of length T into $k = \text{floor}(T/m)$ blocks or subsets. Note that when T/m is not an integer, the k-th block will have a few more than m items. Hence, let us denote the number of observations in each block as m', which equals m for most blocks, except the last, or k-th block.
2. Regress each block having m' observations as subsets of x_t on the set $\tau = 1, 2, \ldots, m'$, and store the intercept b_0, the slope b_1 of τ, and the residuals r.
3. Note that the positive (negative) sign of the slope b_1 in this regression determines the up (down) direction of the time series in that block. Hence, the next step of the algorithm replaces b_1 by $B_1 = b_1 * w$, defined by a randomly chosen weight, $w \in \{-1, 0, 1\}$. Thus, in about 1/3 realizations the random choice yields $w = -1$ and the sign of b_1 is reversed, converting an upward trend into a downward trend. Also, about 1/3 realizations have $w = 0$, which flattens the trend. The randomized change of directions is limited to the current block.
4. Reconstruct all time series blocks as: $b_0 + b_1 * w * \tau + r$, by adding back the residual vector r of the regression on τ.
5. The next step applies the meboot function of the R package to each block of time series — now having a modified trend — and create a large number $= J$ of resampled time series for each of the k blocks.

6. The final step sequentially joins the J meboot replicates of all k blocks or subsets together to generate a matrix of J rows so that each row represents a resample.

3. Simulation of t-heterogeneous Series

It is quite clear from the graphs of "meboot" resamples given in various papers that resamples are quite close but not too close to the original series. Koutris *et al.* (2008) call series exhibiting time dependence in the mean and /or variance "t-heterogeneity," and propose a general test for stationarity. They show that such time-dependence or t-heterogeneity is more general than nonstationarity discussed in unit root models. In particular, some unit root tests consider only the following kind of t-heterogeneity:

$$E(x_t) = \mu_0 + \mu_1 t, \text{ and } \mathrm{Cov}(\mathrm{x_t}, \mathrm{x_{t-k}}) = \sigma(0)\,(\mathrm{t} - \mathrm{k}), \tag{1}$$

where $k = 0, 1, \ldots, t \in \mathcal{T}$.

Let the error term be as follows:

$$u_t,\ t = 1, 2, \ldots, T, \tag{2}$$

where each vector u_t is created from T pseudo-random numbers from $N(0, 1)$, the standard Normal density. Next, we substitute u_t in a general form of Eq. (1) given as follows:

$$x_t = \mu(t) + \sigma(t)\, u_t, \tag{3}$$

where one chooses various functional forms of $\mu(t), \sigma(t)$ allowing for t-heterogeneity in mean and variance, respectively. This then creates one sample realization of a t-heterogeneous stochastic process, which can be repeated as many times as needed.

Note that the "meboot" function of the "meboot" package creates an ensemble of a large number $j = 1, \ldots, J$ of resampled time series $x_{t,j}$ for each x_t defined by Eq. (3). We are mainly interested in checking whether the J artificial series reproduce the t-heterogeneity of the original x_t.

How close are the resampled series $x_{t,j}$ to the original x_t? One way to see closeness is to plot them as in Figure 3. Engineers including hydrologists use a distance measure of closeness developed by Willmott (1981) implemented in the R package called "hydroGOF" by Zambrano-Bigiarini (2011).

$$d_j = 1 - \frac{[(\sum_t((x_t - x_{t,j})^2)]}{\sum_t((abs(x_{t,j} - (\bar{x}_t)) + abs(x_t - (\bar{x}_t)))^2)}, \tag{4}$$

where x_t are the observed series and $x_{t,j}$ is the j-th meboot resampled series and where $abs()$ denotes the absolute value. The Index of Agreement (d_j) is a standardized measure of the degree of model prediction error and varies between 0 (no match) and 1 (perfect match).

3.1. *Simulation of smooth trends in the mean*

The simulation design for our experiments uses exactly the same t-heterogeneous specifications as in Koutris *et al.* (2008). In particular, we generate data with four different time "trends in the mean" of the series with the following functional forms:

1. Linear: $\mu(t) = \mu + 0.02\,t,\ \sigma^2(t) = 1;$
2. Quadratic: $\mu(t) = \mu + 10^{-3}t + 5(10)^{-4}t^2,\ \sigma^2(t) = 1;$
3. Exponential: $\mu(t) = exp(10^{-2}t) + \mu,\ \sigma^2(t) = 1;$
4. Logistic: $\mu(t) = \frac{5}{1+exp(\frac{-t}{4})} + \mu,\ \sigma^2(t) = 1.$

where the quadratic specification has rather small coefficients: $0.001, 0.0005$.

Figure 3 shows the closeness of a few time series generated by the meboot. Since it is not practical to plot J series, Table 1 reports the descriptive statistics associated with values of the index of agreement d_j defined in Eq. (4).

Table 1 is a standard table of descriptive statistics. "NAs" refers to number of missing values. The column titles have a suffix "M" for mean. For example, "Linear.M" refers to a linear trend in mean.

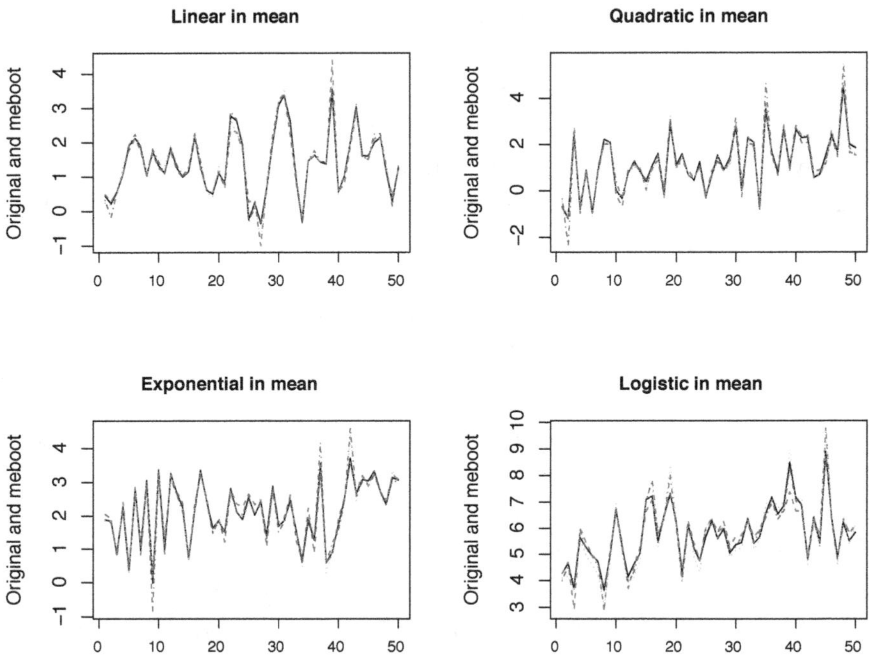

Fig. 3. Time series plots of two series $x_{t,j}$ with original x_t when smooth trends in mean are considered.

Table 1. Descriptive statistics for the index of agreement d_j of the J **meboot** series to x_t with specified t-heterogeneity in **mean**.

	Linear.M	Quadratic.M	Exponential.M	Logistic.M
J	1000.00	1000.00	1000.00	1000.00
NAs	0.00	0.00	0.00	0.00
Minimum	0.96	0.95	0.96	0.96
Maximum	1.00	1.00	1.00	1.00
1. Quartile	0.99	0.98	0.99	0.98
3. Quartile	0.99	0.99	0.99	0.99
Mean	0.99	0.99	0.99	0.99
Median	0.99	0.99	0.99	0.99
Sum	990.45	987.64	989.69	987.13
SE Mean	0.00	0.00	0.00	0.00
Stdev	0.00	0.01	0.01	0.01
Skewness	−1.53	−1.58	−1.42	−1.19
Kurtosis	4.79	4.15	2.81	1.80

If a number shown is 0.00, it means that is the value rounded to two digits, not that the actual value is zero. The values of d_j in this column show that the indexes of agreement are on both the mean and median equal to 0.99 — very close to unity — showing high agreement, with near zero standard deviation. The distribution of d_j values over 1000 meboot resamples in Table 1 have high kurtosis and slight negative skewness. Almost the same results hold for the three other types of t-heterogeneity in mean.

3.1.1. *Flexible meboot mean trends*

The results for the R function meboot seem too close from Table 1 and Fig. 3, perhaps because meboot resamples $x_{t,j}$ have perfect rank correlation of unity with x_t. Recall that our new and flexible R function "flexMeboot" discussed in Section 2.1 allows random shifts in the directions of local trends. We shall now turn to the performance of the flexible function. As expected, the flexible version creates $x_{t,j}$ series exhibiting distinct trending patterns compared to the x_t seen in Fig. 4.

Table 2 reports descriptive statistics associated with values of the index of agreement d_j defined in Eq. (4) for the flexible version of meboot. As before, the column entitled "Linear.M" refers to a linear trend in the mean. The values in this column show that the indexes of agreement d_j have their mean and median equal to 0.54. Since these are not close to unity, they imply only a modest agreement among $x_{t,j}$, with a low standard deviation 0.01. The distribution of d_j values over 1000 meboot resamples in Table 2 have modest kurtosis and negative skewness. Similar results hold for two other types of t-heterogeneity in the mean, suggesting that the flexMeboot may be more appropriate when the focus is on counter factual scenarios for stress testing.

3.2. *Simulation of smooth trends in variance*

Since this section is similar to Section 3.1, we omit some details for brevity. We generate data with three different time "trends in

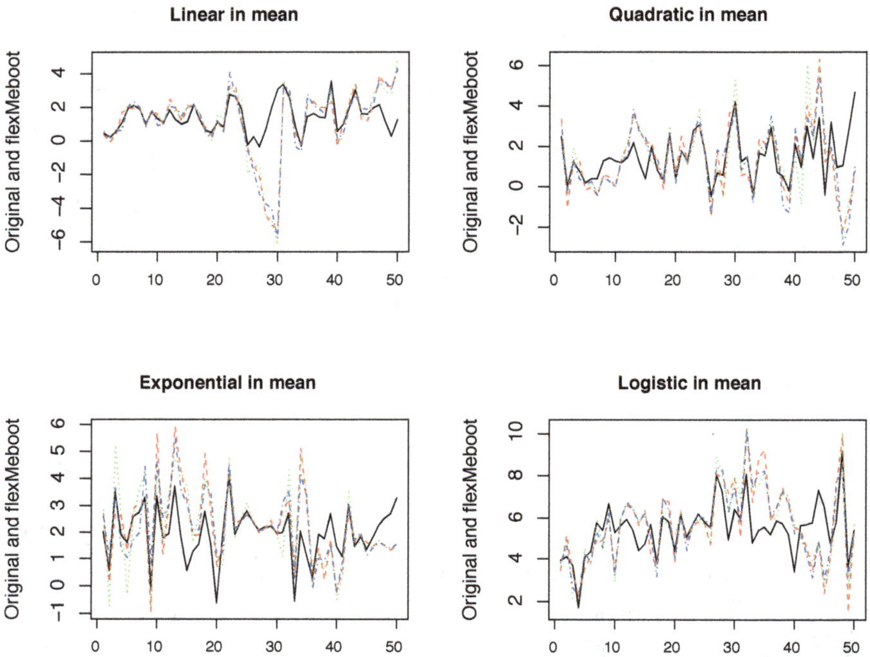

Fig. 4. Time series plots of two flexible meboot series $x_{t,j}$ with original x_t when smooth trends in mean are considered.

Table 2. Descriptive statistics for the index of agreement d_j of the J **flexible meboot** series to x_t with specified t-heterogeneity in **mean**.

	Linear.M	Quadratic.M	Exponential.M	Logistic.M
J	1000.00	1000.00	1000.00	1000.00
NAs	0.00	0.00	0.00	0.00
Minimum	0.48	0.69	0.66	0.72
Maximum	0.58	0.78	0.80	0.82
1. Quartile	0.53	0.73	0.73	0.77
3. Quartile	0.55	0.75	0.76	0.79
Mean	0.54	0.74	0.75	0.78
Median	0.54	0.74	0.75	0.78
Sum	536.22	740.60	745.25	780.59
SE Mean	0.00	0.00	0.00	0.00
Stdev	0.01	0.01	0.02	0.02
Skewness	−0.11	−0.29	−0.43	−0.37
Kurtosis	0.43	0.03	0.36	−0.07

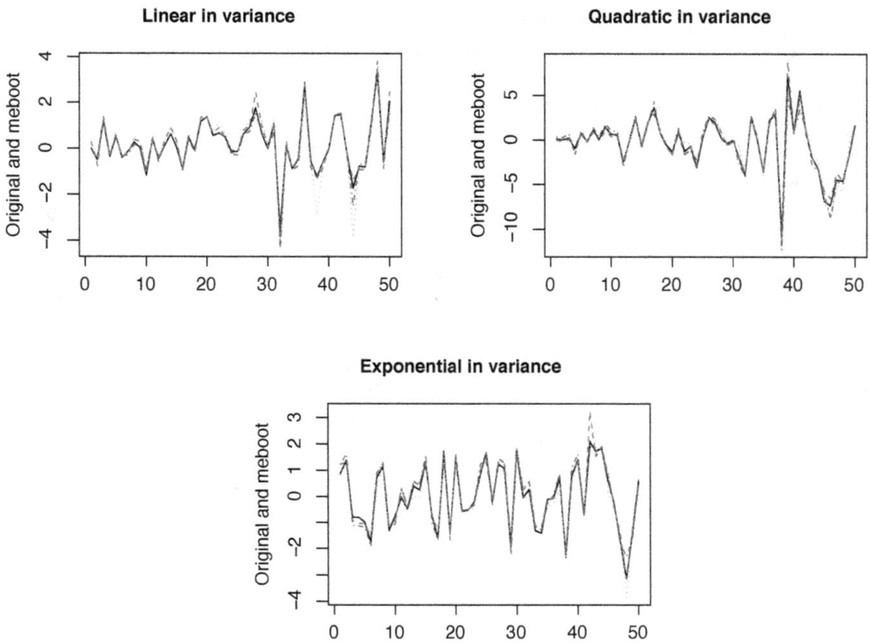

Fig. 5. Time series plots of few series $x_{t,j}$ with original x_t when smooth trends in variance are considered.

variance" of the series with following functional forms, exactly as in Koutris *et al.* (2008):

1. Linear: $\mu(t) = 0, \sigma^2(t) = \sigma^2 + 0.05\,t$;
2. Quadratic: $\mu(t) = 0, \sigma^2(t) = \sigma^2 + 0.03\,t + 0.01\,t^2$;
3. Exponential: $\mu(t) = 0, \sigma^2(t) = \sigma^2 + exp(0.02t)$.

Figure 5 shows the closeness of a $x_{t,j}, j = 1, 2, 3$ series generated by the meboot function. The plots for variance are visually somewhat less close than those in Fig. 3 for the mean t-heterogeneity. Again, Table 3 reports the descriptive statistics associated with values of the index of agreement d_j defined in Eq. (4). The column titles have a suffix "V" for variance. For example, the column entitled "Linear.V" refers to a linear trend in variance. It reports both the mean and median of 0.98, implying high agreement. The negative skewness of -1.30 in the "Linear.V" column is more negative than that in the

Table 3. Descriptive statistics for the index of agreement d_j of the J **meboot** series to x_t with specified t-heterogeneity in **variance**.

	Linear.V	Quadratic.V	Exponential.V
J	1000.00	1000.00	1000.00
NAs	0.00	0.00	0.00
Minimum	0.92	0.94	0.96
Maximum	1.00	1.00	1.00
1. Quartile	0.97	0.98	0.99
3. Quartile	0.99	0.99	0.99
Mean	0.98	0.98	0.99
Median	0.98	0.99	0.99
Sum	980.66	984.92	989.83
SE Mean	0.00	0.00	0.00
Stdev	0.01	0.01	0.01
Skewness	−1.30	−1.42	−1.49
Kurtosis	2.57	2.82	3.31

"Linear.M" column of Table 1 implies that when we consider three or more digits, mean and median would differ. The results are similar for columns entitled "Quadratic.V" and "Exponential.V" in Table 3.

3.2.1. *Flexible meboot variance trends*

This subsection reports the results upon using the "flexMeboot" function.

Figure 6 shows the closeness of a few time series generated by the flexible meboot function admitting counter factual series. Table 4 reports the descriptive statistics associated with values of the index of agreement d_j defined in Eq. (4) for the flexible version of meboot. The column entitled "Linear.V" refers to a linear trend in variance. The values of d_j in this column show that the indexes of agreement are on both the mean and median equal to 0.46 – not close to unity – showing modest agreement, with a low standard deviation 0.01. The distribution of d_j values in Table 4 over 1000 flexible meboot resamples have modest kurtosis and negative skewness. Similar results hold for the two other types of t-heterogeneity in variance. Again, the flexible version of meboot may be more appropriate for some simulation

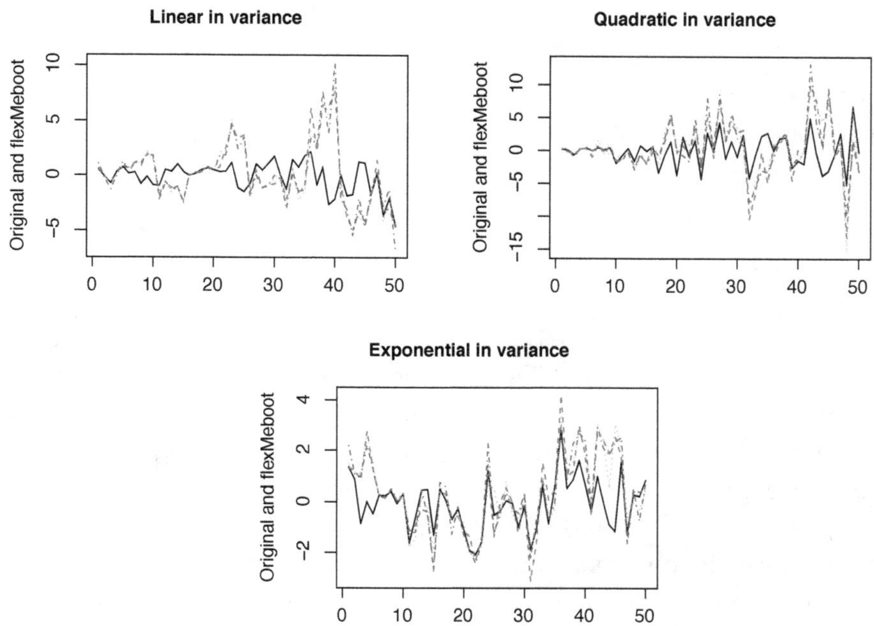

Fig. 6. Time series plots of two series $x_{t,j}$ from flexible meboot with original x_t when smooth trends in variance are considered.

Table 4. Descriptive statistics for the index of agreement d_j of the J **flexMeboot** series to x_t with specified t-heterogeneity in **variance**.

	Linear.V	Quadratic.V	Exponential.V
J	1000.00	1000.00	1000.00
NAs	0.00	0.00	0.00
Minimum	0.41	0.62	0.79
Maximum	0.50	0.72	0.85
1. Quartile	0.45	0.67	0.82
3. Quartile	0.47	0.69	0.83
Mean	0.46	0.68	0.83
Median	0.46	0.68	0.83
Sum	459.49	678.52	825.59
SE Mean	0.00	0.00	0.00
Stdev	0.01	0.02	0.01
Skewness	−0.19	−0.10	−0.44
Kurtosis	0.33	−0.07	0.33

studies with a focus on stress testing and admitting counter factual series. This section has demonstrated that meboot and flexMeboot provide effective tools for mimicking linear, quadratic, exponential, and logistic t-heterogeneous series.

4. Comparison of Estimated Coefficients with Moving Block Bootstrap

Vinod (2010a) compares the closeness to true values of estimated coefficients from "meboot" with those from the moving block bootstrap (mbb) in the context of spurious regression. This section makes a similar comparison in the present context of t-heterogeneity. The data are generated assuming Linear, Quadratic, Exponential, and Logistic functions stated earlier in Section 3.1. Although each functional form involves two or more pre-specified regression parameters, our simulation focuses on only one coefficient of interest. Both meboot and mbb bootstraps yield $J = 1000$ resamples of the data series x_t denoted as $x_{t,j}$. Denote a generic regression coefficient of a t-heterogeneous model using T observations as $b_T(x_{t,j})$ computed for each resample. Denote the corresponding true values used to create the data by β. Let the error in estimating of $j-$th resample during an l-th experiment be defined as follows:

$$\mathcal{E}_{j,l} = (b_T(x_{t,j}) - \beta), \; (j = 1, \ldots, J), \; (l = 1, \ldots, L). \tag{5}$$

Let the mean and standard deviation of these errors for the l-th experiment over J resamples be denoted by $(\bar{\mathcal{E}})_l$ and $\sigma(\mathcal{E})_l$, respectively.

Since one realization denoted by the subscript l might be susceptible to randomness, we estimate the t-heterogeneous models $L = 100$ times for each functional form, separately for meboot and mbb, assuming that the researcher knows the functional form. Nonlinear estimation for exponential and logistic forms poses some challenges including a need to give starting values. For both meboot and mbb, we gave the true values as starting values.

Table 5. Average error and average standard deviation of 1000 estimates further averaged over 100 experiments for Linear and Quadratic t-heterogeneous functions in mean.

	Linear		Quadratic	
T	meboot	mbb	meboot	mbb
50	0.00074	−0.02001	0.02861	−0.00105
50.sd	0.00231	0.01051	0.00265	0.01206
100	0.00044	−0.02000	0.05202	−0.00098
100.sd	0.00095	0.00506	0.00194	0.01069
150	0.00076	−0.01998	0.07760	−0.00094
150.sd	0.00066	0.00368	0.00193	0.01258
200	0.00054	−0.02001	0.10310	−0.00107
200.sd	0.00052	0.00301	0.00219	0.01458

Table 6. Average error and average standard deviation of 1000 estimates further averaged over 100 experiments for Exponential and Logistic t-heterogeneous functions in mean.

	Exponential		Logistic	
T	meboot	mbb	meboot	mbb
50	−0.00088	−0.01723	0.0007356	−0.0200082
50.sd	0.00197	0.02840	0.002314	0.010513
100	−0.00000	−0.01325	0.0004405	−0.0199997
100.sd	0.00032	0.01397	0.0009478	0.0050628
150	0.00020	−0.01383	0.0007583	−0.0199833
150.sd	0.00017	0.01360	0.0006557	0.0036822
200	0.00011	−0.01441	0.0005361	−0.0200149
200.sd	0.00011	0.01341	0.0005154	0.0030102

Tables 5 and 6 report a summary of our results. We report the simple average of averages $\bar{\mathcal{E}_l}$ and simple average of standard deviations from $\sigma(\mathcal{E})_l$, where the error is defined in Eq. (5). The tables have two rows for each of the sample sizes $T = 50, 100, 150, 200$ with the first row for the average of $\bar{\mathcal{E}_l}$ over L and second for the average of $\sigma(\mathcal{E})_l$ identified by the row label ($T.sd$), with the appropriate T.

It is clear from the side-by-side columns for meboot and mbb in Tables 5 and 6 that the average errors for meboot are generally much smaller than those for the mbb in all, except the quadratic case. This exception may be related to the fact that our quadratic specification has rather small coefficients: 0.001, 0.0005. The signs of $\bar{\mathcal{E}}_l$ over L trials may indicate the potential bias of an estimator. We note that mbb always has a negative sign suggesting a persistent negative bias, whereas meboot has mostly positive values with some negatives, suggesting less bias persistence.

The averages of standard deviations are always smaller for the meboot than mbb, including for the quadratic case. That is, meboot regression coefficients are less volatile. Tables 5 and 6 suggest that meboot resamples are closer than mbb in the following sense. The meboot estimated regression coefficients are closer to the known parametric values used to generate the data than the block bootstrap in columns titled mbb.

Let us denote the true unknown cumulative distribution function (cdf) of our generic regression coefficient b_T as $G(z)$ having the following Edgeworth expansion:

$$G(z) = Pr(b_T \leq z) = \Phi(z) + (1/\sqrt{T})q(z)\phi(z) + O(1/T), \tag{6}$$

where $q(z)$ is an even quadratic polynomial, and Φ, ϕ respectively denote the cdf and probability density function (pdf) of the standard Normal density $N(0, 1)$, and where $O()$ denotes the order of the error in approximation. The Edgeworth expansions converge only if Cramer's condition is fulfilled (Hall, 1992, p. 45). Hall notes that this is a "very severe restriction" which fails for exponentially distributed random variables with infinite support.

Hall (1992, p. 83) shows that the cdf of a typical bootstrap also has a similar Edgeworth expansion:

$$\begin{aligned} G_{\text{boot}}(z) = Pr(b_{j,T} \leq z|\omega_0) = \Phi(z) + (1/\sqrt{T})\hat{q}(z)\phi(z) \\ + O_p(1/T), \end{aligned} \tag{7}$$

where $\hat{q}(z)$ denotes the bootstrap counterpart of $q(z)$ in Eq. (6) and where $O_p()$ denotes the order of the error in probability. Using these expansions, the bootstrap literature proves that for pivotal statistics similar to regression coefficients, the difference in two cdfs is written as follows:

LEMMA 1 (Consistency of Bootstrap)

$$G_{\text{boot}}(z) - G(z) = Pr(b_{j,T} \leq z|\omega_0) - Pr(b_T \leq z) = O_p(1/T), \quad (8)$$

where the bootstrap is not only consistent, but its approximation error rate in Eq. (8) is smaller than the Normal theory approximation error rate of $(1/\sqrt{T})$, Hall (1992, Theorem 5.1, pp. 238–259). Our simulation experiments reported in Tables 5 and 6 assume known functional forms and do not consider misspecification errors. Our tables do make the asymptotic consistency of meboot suggested by the Lemma plausible, even at relatively small sample sizes.

4.1. *BEB comparison*

In this subsection, we carry forward the theme of using published simulation designs to check the performance of meboot. Yeh (1998) uses nonstationary residuals to claim that BEB is superior to mbb. Table 7 shows that meboot has smaller mean squared error (averaged over 1000 samples) than the BEB for this range of sample sizes and

Table 7. Table comparing MSEs of Yeh's BEB with meboot for his range of sample sizes (T), block sizes (b), and number of blocks (k) and his simulation design.

Row No.	T	b	k	MSE-BEB	MSE-meboot	MSE-Ratio
1	30	3	10	0.0866	0.0047	18.5282
2	30	5	6	0.0915	0.0045	20.4005
3	30	10	3	0.0914	0.0090	10.2044
4	50	2	25	0.0584	0.0050	11.5811
5	50	5	10	0.0514	0.0054	9.4941
6	50	10	5	0.0558	0.0031	18.1027
7	60	3	20	0.0510	0.0050	10.1898
8	60	5	12	0.0505	0.0058	8.6618
9	60	10	6	0.0534	0.0054	9.9150
10	100	4	25	0.0352	0.0056	6.2835
11	100	5	20	0.0297	0.0052	5.6762
12	100	10	10	0.0271	0.0048	5.6862

block sizes. The MSE-Ratio in the last column shows superiority of meboot declining somewhat as the sample size T increases from 30 to 100.

Let us conclude this section by stating that the superiority of meboot over mbb and its extensions is fairly robust.

5. Applications of Meboot and FlexMeboot in Macroeconomics and Finance

Having seen the simulation results that meboot-type bootstraps are reliable in t-heterogeneous models, we turn to real-world examples from macroeconomics and Finance. We begin with a macroeconomics example dealing with testing for Granger causality from two short time series. Our introduction mentions Fair (2011) result showing that world private sector savings (SPS) and asset prices (SP500) are negatively correlated.

In this section, we apply "meboot" and "flexMeboot" functions in R to create a large number J of resamples of these SPS and SP500. Recall our Fig. 1 for the plots of the 5 percentile "Lo" and 95 percentile "Up" among the J resamples. A correlation matrix (omitted for brevity) among the SPS, its "Lo" and "Up" and also the SP500 along with its "Lo" and "Up" show high negative correlations, with all p-values near zero, suggesting that reported correlations are significantly different from zero.

The plot for "flexMeboot" seen in Fig. 7 has a wider range between the new 5 percentile and new 95 percentile, exhibiting greater flexibility among the resamples. We chose "myseq" argument to the R function "flexMeboot" as (0.8, 0.9, and 1), which shrinks the slope but does not change the direction of local trends.

A correlation matrix among the SPS, its "Lo" and "Up" and also the SP500 along with its own "Lo" and "Up" based on "flexMeboot" also show equally high negative correlations with all near zero p-values, suggesting that all correlations are significantly different from zero. Note from the first row (or column) of Table 8 that SPS, Lo-SPS, and Up-SPS are positively correlated, whereas SPS, Lo-SP500, and Up-SP500 are negatively correlated.

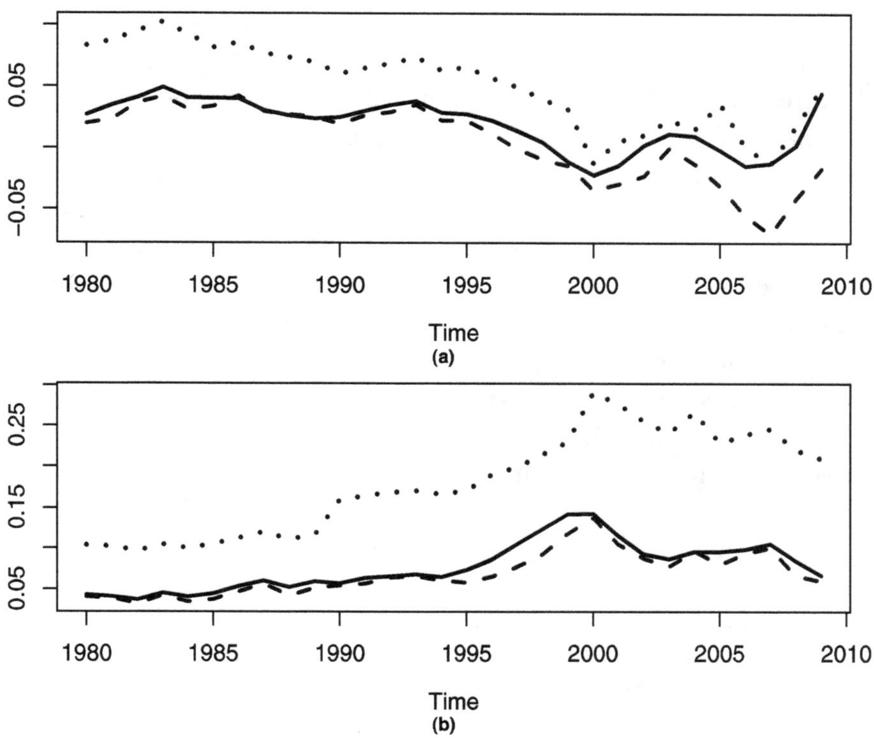

Fig. 7. Fluctuating SPS and SP500 data and "flexMeboot" depicted at the lower 5 percentile and upper 95 percentiles among J resamples. (a) World Private Savings/World GDP, Ratio. Actual (solid), 90% range: Lo (dashed) and Up (dotted) (b) S&P 500 price/US GDP, Ratio. Actual (solid), 90% range: Lo (dashed) and Up (dotted)

Table 8. Correlation matrix for SPS, SP500, and their 5 and 95 percentiles.

	SPS	Lo-SPS	Up-SPS	SP500	Lo-SP500	Up-SP500
SPS	1.0000	0.8836	0.8983	−0.8793	−0.8896	−0.8262
Lo	0.8836	1.0000	0.9276	−0.7392	−0.7889	−0.7899
Up	0.8983	0.9276	1.0000	−0.7738	−0.8505	−0.8693
SP500	−0.8793	−0.7392	−0.7738	1.0000	0.9682	0.8967
Lo2	−0.8896	−0.7889	−0.8505	0.9682	1.0000	0.9092
Up2	−0.8262	−0.7899	−0.8693	0.8967	0.9092	1.0000

Now we turn to the standard Granger non-causality testing as implemented in an R package called "vars" by Pfaff (2008). Since the direct use of these tests based on only 30 observations might not be convincing, we use meboot and "flexMeboot" to repeat these tests J times and save the p-values of the tests for the two null hypotheses. The median of the p-values over our large number J of resamples by meboot (respectively, flexMeboot) is 0.477 (resp., 0.467) for the null hypothesis that SPS does *not* Granger-cause SP500, implying non-rejection of the null. Conversely, the median p-values over J resamples by meboot is only 0.014 (resp., 0.015) for the null hypothesis that SP500 does *not* Granger-cause SPS, implying rejection of the null at the usual 5% level.

We plot the kernel density of the J estimates of p-values for the two hypotheses for meboot in Fig. 8. One limitation of these plots is that even though the p-values never go below zero or exceed unity,

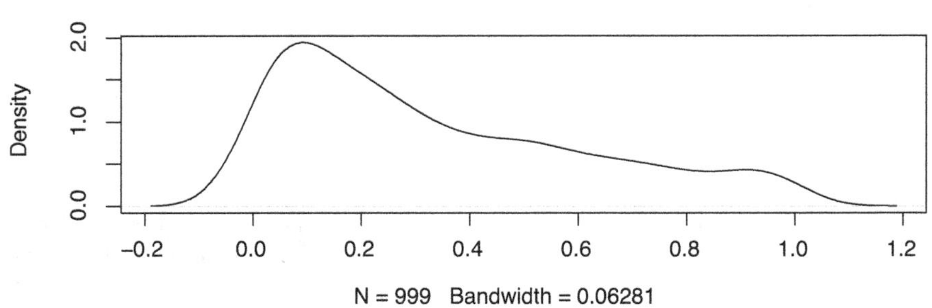

(a)

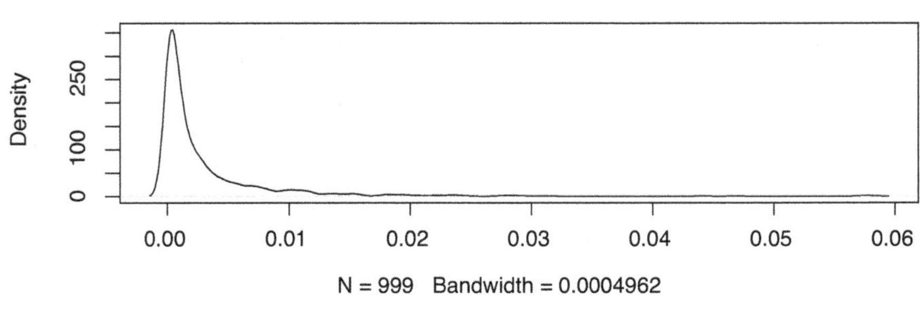

(b)

Fig. 8. Smoothed kernel densities of J **meboot** estimates of p-values in Granger causality tests. (a) Null: SPS does not Gr-cause SP500, p-values meboot. (b) Null: SP500 does not Gr-cause SPS, p-values meboot.

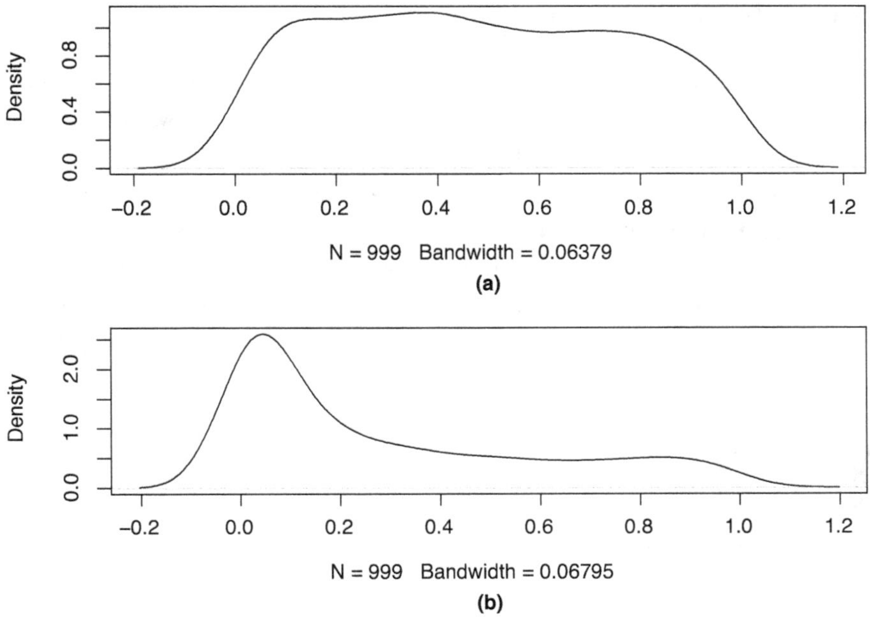

Fig. 9. Kernel densities of J **flexMeboot** estimates of p-values in Granger causality tests. (a) Null: SPS does not Gr-cause SP500, p-values flexMeboot. (b) Null: SP500 does not Gr-cause SPS, p-values flexMeboot.

the kernel smoothing near boundary values do extend beyond these limits. However, the figure does give a good view of the entire distribution of J p-values from the large number of distinct causality tests. In any case, Fig. 8 shows that the inference suggested by the median of p-values is supported.

A similar figure for "flexMeboot" is Fig. 9. As expected, it shows a stronger rejection of the null in the upper half of the figure in this flexible meboot case. Both figures support Prof. Fair's overall assessment that "... variation in the world private saving rate can be explained by forces that affect world asset prices." We are using the bootstrap as a new stress testing tool to formally check the robustness of a corresponding Granger causality result. The conclusion does not change even if we do Granger causality test on a 1000 reincarnations of the two series.

5.1. *Stress testing the value at risk*

Value at Risk (VaR, Note: middle "a" is lower case) is a Finance industry standard for measuring downside risk. See Vinod and Reagle (2005, Chapter 5) and the R package called "PerformanceAnalytics" by Carl and Peterson (2010). We refer the reader to the package reference manual available on the Internet for several references to the literature. Roughly speaking, given a time series of returns, VaR is defined as the high quantile (e.g., a 95% or 99% quantile) of the *negative* value of the returns.

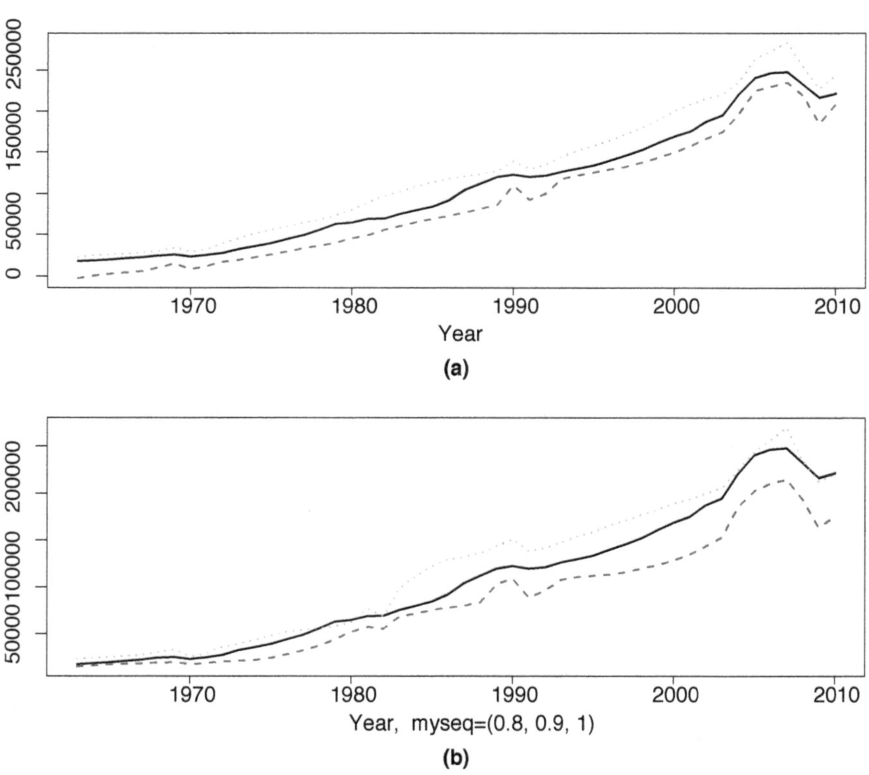

Fig. 10. Trending Median Housing Prices data with meboot and flexMeboot at the lower 5 percentile and upper 95 percentiles among J resamples. (a) U.S. Median House Prices Meboot Scenarios Actual (solid), 90% range: Lo (dashed) and Up (dotted). (b) U.S. Median House Prices flexMeboot Scenarios Actual (solid), 90% range: Lo (dashed) and Up (dotted).

The U.S. median housing prices have consistently edged up and have been blamed for the recent housing bubble. Their 90% range among meboot and flexMeboot resamples is depicted in Fig. 10. It shows the power of flexMeboot in bringing attention to possible bubbles by showing the potentially lower price ranges.

One may argue that Fig. 10 may not be useful, since sophisticated investors do not invest in the median house. Hence, we consider explicit "returns" data for the Fixed Income Arbitrage (FixInc) monthly series (January 1997 to August 2009) as a proxy for housing market investor (using EDHEC composite hedge fund style index returns data available in the above-mentioned R package). These data readily permit calculation of the Value at Risk for FixInc as: VaR(FixInc) $= -0.00929$.

Figure 11 plots the kernel densities for original FixInc returns (dashed line) as well as kernel densities for the J resampled meboot

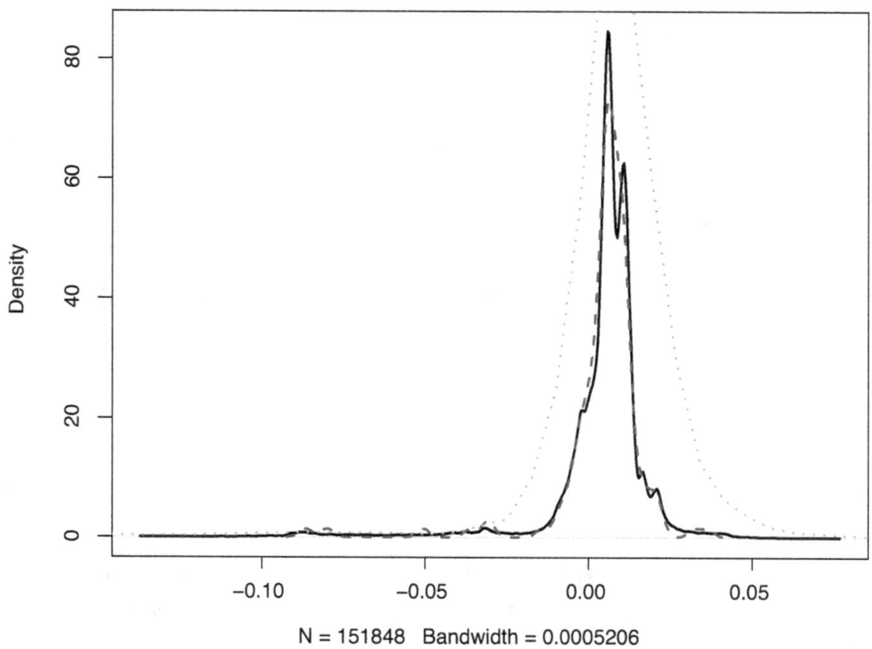

Fig. 11. Kernel densities of FixInc, and their J meboot and flexMeboot resamples showing fatter tails for meboot types, implying a greater VaR.

Note: Density of FixInc (dashed), meboot (solid) and flexMeboot (dotted)

Table 9. Descriptive statistics for value at risk computed for all J series from meboot and flexMeboot resamples.

	meboot	flexMeboot
Min.	−0.0569	−0.0989
1st Qu.	−0.0193	−0.0324
Median	−0.0121	−0.0240
Mean	−0.0152	−0.0273
3rd Qu.	−0.0093	−0.0185
Max.	−0.0034	−0.0110

(solid line) and flexMeboot (dotted line) values. The meboot and flexMeboot densities have visually fatter tails.

Table 9 reports the descriptive statistics of VaR values for all J series computed from meboot and flexMeboot resamples. Note that the minimum VaR from both meboot and flexMeboot is more negative than the VaR $= -0.00929$ for the original series.

It is therefore plausible that if the bankers had used meboot or flexMeboot to stress test their default risk forecasting models for securitized subprime mortgages, they could have seen larger potential losses. Moreover, if (a big if?) the bank lending officials' incentives were properly aligned with the interests of bank stock owners, the U.S. housing market bubble might have been visible sooner. FDIC (2011) has recommended stress tests to avoid excess risk taking by big banks.

6. Conclusions

There is a long standing need in econometrics for simulation cum inference tools for short t-heterogeneous time series subject to structural shifts. Lucas critique has shown that regulatory changes can create such shifts and for simulating them this chapter highlights the use of the maximum entropy bootstrap implemented in an R software package called "meboot".

There are many reasons why a time series x_t might switch directions and behave in a counter-factual manner. Government and business decision makers, regulators (e.g. FDIC, 2011), and risk professionals have long been aware of direction switchings and of the need for stress testing. Hence, we consider a flexible extension (flexMeboot function) of the meboot available in a newer version of the meboot package described in the on-line manual. It generates a large number $J = 1000$ of plausible scenarios $x_{t,j}$ as follows. It divides the data x_t series into blocks of few (=5, say) points. An argument "myseq" to the flexMeboot function allows the user to randomly choose the weight of the slope of the trend within each block. A negative weight reverses the direction of the trend, while a zero weight deletes the trend. Finally, flexMeboot joins the blocks to create $x_{t,j}$.

How well do meboot and flexMeboot perform in artificial situations where answers are known? The chapter reports a simulation study using an objective study design from Koutris *et al.* (2008) to create a large number of t-heterogeneous models, distinguishing between heterogeneity in mean and variance. Our graphs and tables show that our $x_{t,j}$ based on the original meboot stay close to the factual series x_t useful for constructing baseline scenarios whereas flexMeboot is useful for counter-factual scenarios. In addition to graphics, we use a standardized popular measure of the degree of model prediction d_j from Willmott (1981) for assessing closeness. We demonstrate that meboot and flexMeboot are capable of mimicking linear, quadratic, exponential, and logistic t-heterogeneity in mean and variance.

The moving block bootstrap (mbb) and some extensions have been used in the literature for nonstationary time series. This chapter reports additional simulations showing that parameter estimates using the meboot and flexMeboot are closer to the (known) true values than the mbb (and the BEB). The closeness result is seen to be robust, with lesser variability within the J meboot-type estimates compared the the variability within mbb estimates.

What about real-world examples of stress testing in macro economics and Finance? Consider the traditional inference involving Granger causality tests between world private saving rate (SPS) and asset prices (SP500) mentioned above in the introduction. We find

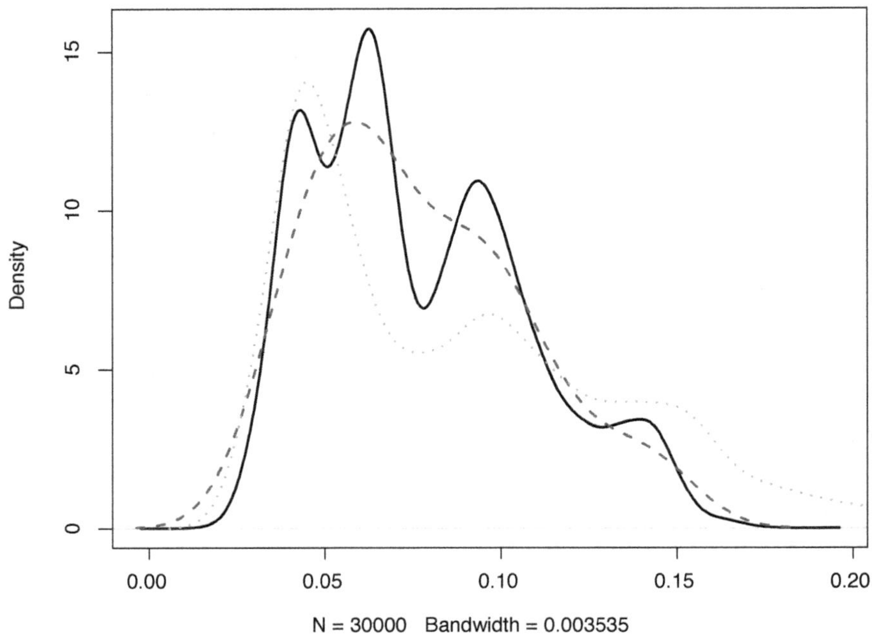

Fig. 12. Kernel densities of SP500, and their J meboot and flexMeboot resamples showing fatter tails for meboot types implying a greater VaR.

Note: Density of SP500 (dashed), meboot (solid) and flexMeboot (dotted).

that both meboot and flexMeboot behave predictably and formally support the robustness of Prof. Fair's result that vagaries of asset price fluctuations do seem to influence important world-wide macro economic variables.

Our finance example considers stress testing of the Value at Risk. Spectacular failures of default risk forecasting models for securitized subprime mortgages in recent years have made us all the more aware of the importance of sensitivity analysis or stress testing of models by using at least some counter-factual data. We use hedge fund style monthly index for Fixed Income Arbitrage (FixInc) leading to J computations of VaRs by both meboot and flexMeboot. The kernel approximations to their densities are non-normal with fatter tails than the densities based on the observed data leading to more extreme VaRs implying a greater risk in such investments.

FDIC (2011) asks large banks to stress test by using stock prices as one of the variables. The kernel densities based on stress testing of our SP500 series in Figure 12 also exhibits fatter tails for the flexMeboot. Thus, we have shown that our tools can inexpensively reveal potential risk from investing in fixed income arbitrage and stock market. It would be interesting to apply these tools in predicting PPNR and NCO variables along with their macro drivers mentioned by Kapinos and Mitnik (2016) for stress testing of banks.

Since we have demonstrated with simulations and examples that meboot type functions can provide J appropriately counter factual series for quantitative stress testing and inference, meboot deserves further study and attention.

Acknowledgment

I thank Professor Ray Fair for providing his data. An earlier version was presented at the London School of Economics on March 16, 2012.

References

Carl, P. and Peterson, B. G. (2010). Performance Analytics: Econometric tools for performance and risk analysis, http://CRAN.R-project.org/package=PerformanceAnalytics.

Covas, F., Rump, B., and Zakrajsek, E. (2014). Stress-testing US bank holding companies: A dynamic panel quantile regression approach. *International Journal of Forecasting* **30**(3), 691–713.

Davison, A. C. and Hinkley, D. V. (1997). *Bootstrap Methods and Their Application.* Cambridge University Press, Cambridge.

Fair, R. C. (2011). A World Macro Saving Fact and an Explanation, Cowles Foundation Discussion Paper No. 1776, Yale University, New Haven, CT, http://cowles.econ.yale.edu/P/cd/d17b/d1776.pdf.

FDIC (2011). Proposed Guidance on Stress Testing for Banking Organizations with more than $10 Billion in Total Consolidated Assets, Federal Deposit Insurance Corporation (FDIC). Docket No. OCC-2011-0011, http://www.fdic.gov/news/news/press/2011/pr11102a.pdf.

Hall, P. (1992). *The Bootstrap and Edgeworth Expansion.* Springer Verlag, New York.

Kapinos, P. S. and Mitnik, O. A. (2016). A top-down approach to stress-testing banks. *Journal of Financial Services Research* **49**(1–2), 229–264.

Koutris, A., Heracleous, M. S., and Spanos, A. (2008). Testing for non-stationarity using maximum entropy resampling: A misspecification testing perspective. *Econometric Reviews* **27**, 363–384.

Lahiri, S. N. (2003). *Resampling Methods for Dependent Data*. Springer Verlag, New York.

Liu, R. Y. (1988). Bootstrap procedures under some non-iid models. *The Annals of Statistics* **16**, 1696–1708.

Pfaff, B. (2008). VAR, SVAR and SVEC models: Implementation within R package vars. *Journal of Statistical Software* **27**, http://www.jstatsoft.org/v27/i04/.

Rajan, U., Seru, A., and Vig, V. (2010). The Failure of Models that Predict Failure: Distance, Incentives and Defaults, SSRN eLibrary, http://ssrn.com/paper=1296982.

Spanos, A. and Kourtellos, A. (2002). Model Validation and Resampling, Working Paper, Economics Department, Virginia Tech.

Vinod, H. D. (2006). Maximum entropy ensembles for time series inference in economics. *Journal of Asian Economics* **17**(6), 955–978.

Vinod, H. D. (2010a). New Solution to Time Series Inference in Spurious Regression Problems. SSRN eLibrary, http://ssrn.com/paper=1560074.

Vinod, H. D. (2010b). Superior Estimation and Inference Avoiding Heteroscedasticity and Flawed Pivots: R-example of Ination Unemployment Trade-Off, in *Advances in Social Science Research Using R*, Vinod, H. D. (Ed.). Springer, New York, pp. 39–63.

Vinod, H. D. and Lopez-de-Lacalle, J. (2009). Maximum entropy bootstrap for time series: The meboot R package. *Journal of Statistical Software* **29**, 1–19, http://www.jstatsoft.org/v29/i05/.

Vinod, H. D. and Reagle, D. (2005). *Preparing for the Worst: Incorporating Downside Risk in Stock Market Investments* (Monograph). Wiley, New York.

Willmott, C. J. (1981). On the validation of models, *Physical Geography* **2**, 184–194.

Yeh, A. B. (1998). A bootstrap procedure in linear regression with non-stationary errors. *The Canadian Journal of Statistics* **26**, 149–160.

Zambrano-Bigiarini, M. (2011). *hydroGOF: Goodness-of-fit functions for comparison of simulated and observed hydrological time series*, r package version 0.3-2, http://CRAN.R-project.org/package=hydroGOF.

https://doi.org/10.1142/9789811222634_0025

Chapter 25

Causality Studies of Real GDP, Unemployment, and Leading Indicators

H. D. Vinod

Professor of Economics, Fordham University Bronx, NY 10458, USA
Director, Institute for Ethics and Economic Policy (IEEP)
vinod@fordham.edu

John B. Guerard, Jr.

McKinley Capital Management, LLC
Anchorage, AK 99503, USA
jguerard@mckinleycapital.com

Conference Board's leading economic index (LEI) is constructed to reveal common turning point patterns in economic data, indirectly guiding fiscal and monetary policy aimed at the dual objectives of increasing the real GDP and reducing the unemployment rate. We study new econometric tools to help identify the exogenous macroeconomic time series "causally" driving the dual objectives. We study components of LEI including oil prices, building permits, stock prices, leading credit index, interest-rate spreads, productivity, among others. Such identification allows policymakers to focus on providing incentives for guiding the actionable variables to achieve dual objectives.

Keywords: Time Series Modeling, Forecasting, Causality Analysis
JEL classifications: C32; C50; C51; C53

1. Introduction

Scholars in various fields including investors are interested in obtaining good forecasts of fundamental macroeconomic variables: U.S. real

GDP and unemployment rate which often drive U.S. government fiscal and monetary policy.

Economists have constructed a leading economic indicator, LEI, time series to serve as a business barometer of the changing U.S. economy since the time of Wesley C. Mitchell (1913). Burns and Mitchell (1946), Mitchell (1951), Moore (1961), and Zarnowitz (1992) created impressive volume to update and extend LEI modeling. To celebrate the life of Moore at his passing, Dua (2001, 2004) edited a Special Issue of *The Indian Economic Review* and a subsequent Oxford University Press volume. The Dua research outlets provided substantial evidence on the continued effectiveness of LEI modeling. Guerard (2001, 2004) and Thomakos and Guerard (2004) reported that the leading indicators can be used as an input to a transfer function model of real Gross Domestic Product, GDP. Chapter 24 employed four quarterly lags of the LEI series to estimate regression models of association between current rates of growth of real U.S. GDP and the composite index of LEI. This chapter asks the question as to whether changes in forecasted economic indexes help forecast changes in real economic growth. The transfer function model forecasts are compared to several naïve models in terms of testing which model produces the most accurate forecast of real GDP. No-change forecasts of real GDP and random walk with drift models may be useful for forecasting benchmarks (Mincer and Zarnowitz, 1969 and Granger and Newbold, 1977). Guerard, Thomakos, and Kyriazi (2020) recently re-confirmed the statistically significant relationship among the Leading Economic Indicators , LEI, and read GDP, 1959-2018. Moreover, Guerard et al., re-confirmed the relationship between the LEI and weekly unemployment claims,for the 1959-2018 time period, and for the post-publication time period of Montgomery, Zarnowitz, Tsay, and Tiao (1998). The purpose of this chapter is to examine the time series forecasts of composite economic indexes produced by The Conference Board (TCB), and test the hypothesis that the leading indicators are useful as an input to a time series model to forecast real output in the United States.

Economic indicators are descriptive and anticipatory time series data used to analyze and forecast changing business conditions. Cyclical indicators are comprehensive series that are systemically related to the business cycle. Business cycles are recurrent sequences of expansions and contractions in aggregate economic activity. Coincident indicators have cyclical movements that approximately correspond with the overall business cycle expansions and contractions. Leading indicators reach their turning points before the corresponding business cycle turns. The lagging indicators reach their turning points after the corresponding turns in the business cycle. This chapter is inspired by Guerard (2001, 2004, 2013).

Koopmans (1950) was the first to propose that the right-hand side (RHS) variables in an econometric regression be "exogenous" in the sense of having independent or self-dependent data generating process (DGP) being "approximately causal" for the left-hand side (LHS) variable.

Granger causality in Econometrics texts, Vinod (2008), refer to Granger (1969) who proposed tools for the detection of causal paths between two or more economic time series. Roughly speaking, we say that the Granger's causal path $X_i \xrightarrow{Gr} X_j$ holds if variable X_i helps to predict variable X_j. The idea can be formulated in terms of mean square error (MSE) of forecasting h steps ahead based on the information set $I_{nf,t}$, at time t. For example, we say that X_i Granger-causes X_j if the MSEs satisfy the following inequality:

$$\text{MSE}_h\,(I_{nf,t,\text{with}}\ x_i) < \text{MSE}_h(I_{nf,t,\text{without}}\ x_i) \qquad (1)$$

where we have spelled out the condition on the information set that forecasting MSE should be smaller when X_i is included compared to the MSE based on information without the benefit of related X_i variable.

Any statistical test based on lags and leads of effects is subject to the famous fallacy called "post hoc ergo propter hoc." The ancients were aware that a rooster crowing at sunrise before the sun rises was not the cause of the sunrise. Since Granger causality focuses on time precedence, it remains subject to the fallacy, although it obviously remains useful when used with care.

1.1. *Causal analysis for economic policy*

Assume we have $t = 1,2,...T$observations. Consider a model having X_j on the left-hand side (LHS) and X_i plus a set of variable(s) combined into generic X_k on the RHS:

$$X_{jt} = f(X_{it}\,,\, X_{kt}) + \in_{j|ik,} \tag{2}$$

where we use a generic symbols f to denote a possibly nonlinear function and unobserved shocks or errors. We use nonlinear non-parametric kernel regressions to estimate the conditional expectation functions. The specification (2) implies the causal path (RHS→LHS) or (X_i→X_j).

We also consider a model for the opposite causal path, (X_j→X_i) obtained by flipping X_j with X_i:

$$X_{it} = f(X_{jt},\, X_{kt}) + \in_{i|jk,}. \tag{3}$$

By analogy with Granger causality, but avoiding the time-precedence requirement, the data support the causal path ($X_i \to X_j$), provided the model (2) has a superior fit (smaller forecasting MSE) compared to the model (3). Theorem 1 in Vinod (2019) extends Granger's intuition to develop computational methods for assessing causal paths and their strength indices. There are at least three coequal empirical criteria, denoted by Cr1, Cr2, and Cr3, which quantify the empirical support for the causal path ($X_i \to X_j$).

The criterion Cr1 evaluates finite sample implications of consistency of conditional expectation functions of flipped kernel regressions. The true unknown errors $\in_{j|ik}$ should be orthogonal to the regressors with probability limit satisfying

$$\text{plim}_{T\to\infty}\left(\in_{j|ik,}\, X_{it}\right)/T = 0 \tag{4}$$

Koopmans (1950) formulated the consistency requirement of Eq. (4) as exogeneity of X_i, and went on to require that each RHS variable should "approximately cause" the LHS variable. We plug observable residuals into the (consistency) exogeneity condition (4), yielding two sets of T multiplications $\in_{j|ik,}\ X_{it}$ and $\in_{i|jk,}\ X_{jt}$, where we replace the true unknown errors $\in .|..$ by corresponding residuals $e_{.|..}$.

Our Cr1 assumes that closeness to zero of these observable expressions reveals relative speeds of convergence. The criterion Cr2 checks which flip has "lower" absolute values of residuals. We use asymmetric generalized partial correlation coefficients from Vinod (2014) as our third criterion.

Since it is not possible to prove why one criterion should dominate others, we use the "preponderance of evidence" standard by constructing a unanimity index using a weighted sum of the three criteria denoted by $ui \in [-100, 000]$. Given a 5% threshold, say, (or $\tau = 5$), the index allows us to propose the following decision rules:

Rule 1: If $(ui < -\tau)$, the causal path is: $X_i \to X_j$.

Rule 2: If $(ui > -\tau)$, the causal path is: $X_j \to X_i$.

Rule 3: If $(|ui| \leq -\tau)$, we obtain bidirectional causality: $X_i \leftrightarrow X_j$, that is, the variables are jointly dependent.

Complete computational details for using these decision rules on any given dataset are a part of an open source and free software package called "generalCorr", Vinod (2017), in computer language called R. It is readily available in open forum for further checking and development. The R package comes with three vignettes which provide theoretical details about the algorithms used, as well as examples.

2. Abbreviated Data Names and Sources

Monthly Data are obtained from Conference Board website: http://www.conference-board.org/data/bci.cfm. Notation LEI refers to Conference Board's leading economic index code named = GOM910 with base year 2010 = 100. https://www.conference-board.org/pdf_free/press/US%20LEI%20-%20Tech%20Notes%20May%202019.pdf lists the following 10 components of LEI. We now list a self-explanatory abbreviation, up to five characters long, along with a code name in the source dataset, as well as its relative weight as ("wt.=") in the LEI and the units of measurement as "unit=". These weights of 10 components of LEI do add up to unity.

1. WkHr = AOMOOI – Average weekly hours, manufacturing (wt. = 0.2795), unit = (hours).
2. WkUn = AOM005 – Average weekly initial claims for unemployment insurance (wt. = 0.0324), unit = (thous.).
3. MfNuC = AOM008 – Manufacturers' new orders, consumer goods and materials (wt. = 0.0832), unit = (mil. 1982$).
4. ISM new orders index (wt. = 0.1586).
5. MfNuK = AOM033 – Manufacturers' new orders, nondefense capital goods excl. aircraft (wt. = 0.0405), unit = (mil. chain 1982$).
6. BldP = AOM029 – Building permits for new private housing units (wt. = 0.0290), unit = (thous.).
7. S500 = UOM019 – Stock prices, 500 common stocks (wt. = 0.0395), unit = (1941–43 = 10).
8. LeCrd = UOM107 – Leading Credit Index, (wt. = 0.0813), unit = (std. dev.).
9. InSpr = UOM129 – Interest rate spread, 10-year Treasury bonds less federal funds rate (wt. = 0.1132).
10. ConBU = AOM125 – Avg. consumer expectations for business conditions, (wt. = 0.1428), unit = (std. dev.).

We also have data on Univ. of Michigan's survey index of consumer expectations, which was a component of LEI until December 1977. It is abbreviated as ConEx with code name UOM083.

1. GDP = AOQ055 – Gross domestic product (AR bil. Chain 2012$).
2. GNP = AOQ050 – Gross national product (AR bil. Chain 2012$).
3. CProf = AOQ018 – Corporate profits after tax (AR bil. 2012$).
4. CCash = AOQ035 – Corporate net cash flow (AR bil. chain 2012$).
5. OilPr = A0M339 – The Producer Price Index of Petroleum Products.
6. BalMe = A0Q622 – Balance of merchandise trade (bil. $).
7. Cprof = A0Q018 – Corporate profits after tax (bil. 2012$).
8. YhrBu = A0Q370 – Output per hour in business sector.

3. Causal Paths in Monthly Data for LEI

Inflation rate, unemployment rate, and percapita GDP are policy objectives. As noted in the data section, some of our variables are components of LEI, some are policy instruments, some are policy outcomes determined by markets, and some are mixtures of policy outcomes and instruments. For example, the interest spread (InSpr) between 10-year Treasury bill rate (determined by markets) and federal funds rate (determined by the federal reserve bank) is a mixture. We study whether the 10 components of Conference Board's LEI are exogenous with independent DGPs using methods reviewed above for influencing policy objectives.

Table 1 uses our entire (January 1959–March 2019) monthly dataset and explicitly reports for each flipped pair the "cause" and "response" such that policy objective on the left-hand side is present in all pairs as it is paired with a component of LEI. The column entitled "strength" reports the absolute value $|ui|$. The names of variables to go in the "cause" and "response" columns are dictated by the sign of ui. The column entitled "corr" reports Pearson correlation coefficient with LEI, while the column entitled "p-value" reports the p-value for testing the null of zero correlation. Of course, Kernel causality and exogeneity need not agree with traditional correlation inference, since the latter assumes linearity and Normal distributions.

Table 1. Causal paths paired with LEI and related variables using entire data.

Cause	Response	Strength	Corr.	p-value
1 LEI	WkHr	31.496	0.6419	0
2 LEI	WkUn	100	−0.0054	0.88409
3 LEI	MfNuC	31.496	0.9503	0
4 LEI	MfNuK	100	0.9313	0
5 LEI	BldP	100	−0.0602	0.10582
6 LEI	S500	37.008	0.8946	0
7 LeCrd	LEI	31.496	−0.1088	0.04309
8 LEI	InSpr	31.496	0.2106	0
9 LEI	ConEx	100	−0.1325	0.00036
10 LEI	ConBu	31.496	0.154	0.00059
11 OilP	LEI	100	0.679	0
12 OilP	S500	31.496	0.7256	0

Table 2 is similar to Table 1, except that it uses pre-1999 subset of the data (January 1959–December 1999). Table 3 uses post-1999 subset of the data (January 1999–March 2019). An extra line numbered 12 is added to these three tables where we pair oil prices (OilP) with S&P 500 stock price index (S500).

Further comments on the interpretation of our "cause" and "response" classification follow. Since our cause avoids any reference

Table 2. Causal paths paired with LEI and related variables using pre-1999 data.

Cause	Response	Strength	Corr.	p-value
1 LEI	WkHr	100	0.5743	0
2 LEI	WkUn	100	0.1194	0.00803
3 LEI	MfNuC	37.008	0.9904	0
4 LEI	MfNuK	100	0.9399	0
5 LEI	BldP	100	0.0774	0.08614
6 LEI	S500	100	0.8429	0
7 LEI	LeCrd	31.496	−0.0536	0.56765
8 LEI	InSpr	31.496	0.0948	0.03551
9 LEI	ConEx	100	−0.0894	0.04756
10 LEI	ConBu	31.496	0.4908	0
11 OilP	LEI	100	0.2946	0
12 OilP	S500	37.008	0.2248	1e-05

Table 3. Causal paths paired with LEI and related variables using post-1999 data.

Cause	Response	Strength	Corr.	p-value
1 LEI	WkHr	100	0.5743	0
2 LEI	WkUn	100	0.1194	0.00803
3 LEI	MfNuC	37.008	0.9904	0
4 LEI	MfNuK	100	0.9399	0
5 LEI	BldP	100	0.0774	0.08614
6 LEI	S500	100	0.8429	0
7 LEI	LeCrd	31.496	−0.0536	0.56765
8 LEI	InSpr	31.496	0.0948	0.03551
9 LEI	ConEx	100	−0.0894	0.04756
10 LEI	ConBu	31.496	0.4908	0
11 OilP	LEI	100	0.2946	0
12 OilP	S500	37.008	0.2248	1e-05

to timing of events, it avoids the "post hoc ergo propter hoc" fallacy affecting the Granger causality. We are comparing flipped models involving two data generating processes (DGPs) to check which DGP has more independent variation. The LEI is a weighted sum of 10 components. When we observe a causal path *LEI component*, it simply means that the weighted sum has greater independent variation than the named component, without any requirement that the cause should precede the response in time. For example, line 12 in all three tables support the path OilP $\rightarrow S500$ implying that prices of petroleum products have greater independent variability than a weighted average of 500 stocks or the S&P-500 index.

Let us discuss the causal paths from Tables 1 to 3 together, since the results are similar in the three datasets. Lines 1 and 2 in all three tables suggest the path LEI → WkHr for weekly hours and LEI → WkUn and weekly unemployment claims, respectively. The path LEI → S500 stock prices is plausible.

The path between leading credit index LeCrd and LEI is not the same in the three tables. When the entire dataset is used, we have the path.

LeCrd → LEI, suggesting that the credit index has considerable exogenous information. Line 11 in all three tables for petroleum prices suggest the same path OilP → LEI.

4. Causal Paths in Quarterly Data for GDP

Since GDP data are available only on a quarterly basis, if we want to consider policy variables influencing GDP, we must consider quarterly data. Our results are presented in Tables 4 and 5.

Table 4. Causal paths from quarterly data paired with GDP.

Cause	Response	Strength	Corr.	p-value
1 GDP	LEIq	31.496	0.9621	0
2 GDP	A0Q043	31.496	0.028	0.66581
3 GDP	Cprof	31.496	0.9286	0
4 YhrBu	GDP	100	0.9944	0
5 GDP	BalMe	31.496	−0.9476	0

Table 5. Causal paths from quarterly data paired with GNP.

Cause	Response	Strength	Corr.	p-value
1 GNP	LEIq	31.496	0.9604	0
2 GNP	A0Q043	31.496	0.0312	0.63041
3 GNP	Cprof	31.496	0.9311	0
4 YhrBu	GNP	100	0.995	0
5 GNP	BalMe	31.496	−0.9486	0

Since these results support the causal paths GDP → LEIq, we find that the quarterly index of leading indicators LEIq is not exogenous but driven by changes in GDP level. On the other hand, output per hour in business sector (YhrBu) has considerable independent influence on GDP and GNP. See Tables 4 and 5, respectively. This suggests that output growth is driven by productivity growth. But balance of merchandise trade and corporate profits do not have independent innovations, as they are a response to innovations in GDP or GNP.

5. Causal Paths in Quarterly Data for the U.S. Employment Rate: A Second Causality Approach

This section develops traditional time series forecasting models of the U.S. unemployment rate using primarily the outlier-adjusted past history of the series and transfer function models using Weekly Unemployment Claims and LEI data. Montgomery, Zarnowitz, Tsay, and Tiao (MZTT, 1998) modeled the U.S. unemployment rate as a function of the weekly unemployment claims time series, 1948–1993. A similar conclusion is found for the impact of the LEI and weekly unemployment claims series leading to the unemployment rate series. The time series modeling approach of Box and Jenkins involves the identification, estimation, and forecasting of stationary (or series transformed to stationarity) series through the analysis of the series autocorrelation function (see Appendix). An autocorrelation estimate is considered statistically different from zero if it exceeds approximately twice its standard error.

5.1. *The autoregressive and moving average processes*

A stochastic process, or time series, can be repeated as the output resulting from a white noise input, α_t.[1]

$$\begin{aligned}\widetilde{Z}_t &= \alpha_t + \Psi_1\alpha_{t-1} + \Psi_2\alpha_{t-2} + \dots \\ &= \alpha_t + \sum_{j=1}^{\infty} \Psi_j a_{t-j}.\end{aligned} \tag{5}$$

The filter weight, ψ_j, transforms input into the output series. One normally expresses the output, $\widetilde{Z}_t$, as a deviation of the time series from its mean, μ, or origin

$$\widetilde{Z}_t = Z_t - \mu.$$

The general linear process leads one to represent the output of a time series, $\widetilde{Z}_t$, as a function of the current and previous value of the white noise process, α_t which may be represented as a series of shocks. The white noise process, α_t, is a series of random variables characterized by

$$\begin{aligned} E[\alpha_t] &\cong 0 \\ Var[\alpha_{kk}] &= \sigma_\alpha^2 \\ \gamma_k = E[\alpha_t\alpha_{t+k}] &= \alpha_\alpha^2 \quad k \neq 0; \text{ else} \\ &\ 0 \qquad k = 0. \end{aligned}$$

The autocorrelation function of a linear process may be given by

$$\gamma_k = \sigma_\alpha^2 \sum_{j=1}^{\infty} \Psi_j \Psi_{j+k}.$$

[1]Please see Box and Jenkins, *Time Series Analysis*, Chapter 3, for the most complete discussion of the ARMA (p,q) models.

The backward shift operator, B, is defined as $BZ_t = Z_{t-1}$ and $B^j Z_t = Z_{t-j}$. The autocorrelation generating function may be written as follows:

$$\gamma(B) = \sum_{j=\infty}^{\infty} \gamma_k B^k$$

For stationarity, the Ψ weights of a linear process must satisfy that Ψ (6) converges on or lies within the unit circle.

In an autoregressive (AR) model, the current value of the time series may be expressed as a linear combination of the previous values of the series and a random shock, α_t.

$$\widetilde{Z}_{\mathrm{t}} = \phi_1 \quad \widetilde{Z}_{\mathrm{t}-1} + \phi_2 \quad \widetilde{Z}_{\mathrm{t}-2} + \quad \cdots \quad + \phi_{\mathrm{p}} \quad \widetilde{Z}_{\mathrm{t}-\mathrm{p}} + \alpha_t$$

The autoregressive operator of order P is given by

$$\phi B) = 1 - \phi_1(B)^1 - \phi_2(B)^2 \cdots - \phi_{\mathrm{p}}(B)^{\mathrm{P}}$$

or

$$\phi(\mathrm{B})\widetilde{\mathrm{Z}}_{\mathrm{t}} = \alpha_t \qquad (6)$$

In an autoregressive model, the current value of the time series, $\widetilde{Z}_t$, is a function of previous values of the time series, $\widetilde{Z}_{\mathrm{t}-1}, \widetilde{Z}_{\mathrm{t}-2}, \ldots$ and is similar to a multiple regression model. An autoregressive model of order p implies that only the first p order weights are non-zero. In many economic time series, the relevant autoregressive order is one and the autoregressive process of order p, AR(p), is written as follows:

$$\widetilde{Z}_t = \phi_1 \widetilde{Z}_{t-1} + \alpha_t$$

or

$$(1 - \phi_1 B)\widetilde{Z}_t = \alpha_t$$
$$\widetilde{Z}_t = \phi_1^{-1}(B)\alpha_t.$$

The relevant stationarity condition is |B|<1 implying that $|\phi_1|<1$.

The autocorrelation function of a stationary autoregressive process,

$$\widetilde{Z}_t = \phi_1 \widetilde{Z}_{t-1} + \phi_2 \widetilde{Z}_{t-2} + \ldots + \phi_p \widetilde{Z}_{t-p} + \alpha_t$$

may be expressed by the difference equation

$$\mathrm{P_k} = \phi_1 \rho_{k-1} + \phi_2 \rho_{k-2} + \cdots + \phi_k \rho_{k-p} \; k > 0.$$

Or expressed in terms of the Yule–Walker equation as

$$\begin{aligned} \rho_1 &= \phi_1 + \phi_2 \; \rho_1 + \cdots + \phi_p \rho_{\mathrm{p}-1} \\ \rho_2 &= \phi_1 \; \rho_1 + \phi_2 + \cdots + \phi_p \rho_{\mathrm{p}-2} \\ \rho_{\overline{\overline{p}}} &= \phi_1 \rho_{p-1} + \phi_2 \; \rho_{p-2} + \cdots + \phi_{\overline{\overline{\mathrm{p}}}}. \end{aligned}$$

For the first-order AR process, AR(1)

$$\rho_k = \phi_1 \rho_{k-1} = \phi_{\mathrm{p}}^{\wedge}. \tag{7}$$

The autocorrelation function decays exponentially to zero when ϕ_1 is positive and oscillates in sign and decays exponentially to zero when ϕ_1 is negative.

$$\mathrm{P}_1 = \phi_1$$

and

$$\sigma_2 = \frac{\sigma_\alpha^2}{1 - \phi_1^2}.$$

We employ an AR(1) process in the forthcoming empirical section.

An integrated stochastic progress generates a time series if the series is made stationary by differencing (applying a time-invariant filter to) the data. In an integrated process, the general form of the time series model is

$$\phi(B)(1-B)^d X_t = \theta(B)\varepsilon_t, \tag{8}$$

where $\phi(B)$ and $\theta(B)$ are the autoregressive and moving average polynomials in B of orders p and q, ε_t is a white noise error term, and d is an integer representing the order of the data differencing. In economic time series, a first-difference of the data is normally performed.[2] The application of the differencing operator, d, produces a stationary ARMA(p,q) process. The autoregressive integrated moving average ARMA model is characterized by orders p, d, and q [ARIMA (p,d.q)]. Many economics series follow a random walk with drift. An ARMA (1,1) may be written as follows:

$$\bar{V}^{\mathrm{d}} X_{\mathrm{t}} = X_t - X_{t-1} = \varepsilon_t + \mathrm{b}\varepsilon_{t-l}. \tag{9}$$

An examination of the autocorrelation function estimates may lead one to investigate using a first-difference model when the autocorrelation function estimates decay slowly. In an integrated process, the $\mathrm{corr}(X_t, X_{t-\tau})$ is approximately unity for small values of time, τ.

Granger and Newbold (1977) and McCracken (2002) use several criteria to evaluate the effectiveness of the forecasts with respect to the forecast errors. In this chapter, we use the root mean square error (RMSE) criteria. One seeks to minimize the square root of the sum of the forecast errors squared. That is, we calculate the absolute value of the forecast error, square the error, sum the squared errors, divided by the number of forecast periods, and take the square root of the resulting calculation. Intuitively, one seeks to minimize the forecast errors. The absolute value of the forecast errors is important because if one calculated only a mean error, a

[2] Box and Jenkins, *Time Series Analysis*. Chapter 6; Granger, C. W. J. and Newbold, P. (1986). *Forecasting Economic Time Series*. 2nd Edition (New York: Academic Press), pp. 109–110, 115–117, 206.

5% positive error could "cancel out" a 5% negative error. Thus, we minimize the out-of-sample forecast errors. We need a benchmark for forecast error evaluation. An accepted benchmark (Mincer and Zarnowitz, 1969) for forecast evaluation is a no-change, NoCH. A forecasting model should produce a lower RMSE than the no-change model. If several models are tested, the lowest RMSE model is preferred.

In the world of business and statistics, one often speaks of autoregressive, moving average, and random walk with drift models, or processes, as we have just introduced. It is well known that the majority of economic series, including real Gross National Product (GDP) in the U.S., follow a random walk with drift, and are represented with autoregressive integrated moving average (ARIMA) model with a first-order moving average operator applied to the first-difference of the data. The data are differenced to produce stationary, where a process has a (finite) mean and variance that do not change over time and the covariance between data points of two series depends upon the distance between the data points, not on the time itself. The RWD process, estimated with an ARIMA (0,1,1) model, is approximately equal to a first-order exponential smoothing model (Cogger, 1974). The random walk with drift model has been supported by the work of Nelson and Plosser (1982).

6. LEI and the U.S. Employment Rate: The Statistical Evidence of the Initial Period, 1959–2018

We introduce the time series modeling process in this study because we will use the Conference Board U.S. composite LEI as an input to a transfer function model of U.S. real GDP, both series being first-differenced and log-transformed. The authors test the null hypothesis that there is no statistical association between changes in the logged LEI and changes in logged real GDP in the U.S. A positive and statistically significant coefficient indicates that when the leading indicator composite series is associated with rising real output, and leads to the rejection of the null hypothesis.

Zarnowitz (1992) examined the determinants of Real GDP, 1953–1982, using VAR models. In this analysis, we test the statistical significance of the Conference Board LEI by adding the lags of the variable to an AR(1) model. Does the knowledge of the LEI help forecast future changes in GDP, and can past values of the GDP data predict the future growth of GDP? In a recent study of univariate and time series model post-sample forecasting, Thomakos and Guerard (2001) compared Random Walk with Drift (RWD) and transfer-function models with no-change forecasts using rolling one-period-ahead post-sample periods. Guerard (2001) found that the AR (1) and random walk with drift processes are adequate representations of the time series process of real GDP, given the lags of the autocorrelation and partial autocorrelation functions. Guerard (2001) reported the estimated cross-correlation functions between the G7 respective LEI and real GDP for the 1970–2000 period and found that the resulting transfer function models were statistically significant in forecasting real GDP in the G7 nations.

A rational transfer function model, TF, can be estimated as an extension to a multiple regression model

$$y_t = \beta_0 + \beta_1 x_{1t} + \beta_2 x_{2t} + \cdots + \beta_m x_{mt} + \varepsilon_t. \tag{10}$$

If, $x_t = \phi x_{t-1} + a_t$, an AR(1) model previously discussed, then a simple transfer function can be estimated as

$$y_t = \beta_0 + \beta_1 x_{1t} + \beta_2 x_{2t} + \cdots + \beta_m x_{mt} + \frac{1}{1-\phi_1 B} a_t. \tag{11}$$

A simple input transfer function may be written as follows:

$$y_t = \frac{w(B)}{z(B)} X_t + N_t, \tag{12}$$

where $w(B) = \left(w_o + w_1 B + \cdots + w_{h-1} B^{h-1}\right) B^b$

$$\delta(B) = 1 - \delta_1 B - \cdots - \delta_r B^r,$$
$$\phi(B) = 1 - \phi B - \cdots - \phi_p B^p,$$

and $$\theta(B) = 1 - \theta_1 B - \cdots - \theta_q B^q.$$

The polynomial $w(B)$ is the delay of the input function in the transfer.

Outliers have long been recognized in economic time series. A very useful outlier analysis and software application can be found in Tsay (1988, 2010) and the SCA software. An additive outlier (AO) is an event that affects a time series for one period only,

$$y_t = z_t + w_A P_t^{(T)} \tag{13}$$

where $P_t^{(T)}$ is a pulse function.

An innovative outlier (IO) is an event that effects the ARIMA model

$$y_t = z_t + \frac{\phi(B)}{\phi(B)} w_I P_t^{(T)},$$

$$y_t = z_t + \frac{\phi(B)}{\phi(B)} (a_z + w_I P_t^{(T)}). \tag{14}$$

The IO event affects all Y according to the Ψ weights of the model.

A level shift, LS, is an event that permanently effects the time series,

$$y_t = z_t + w_L S_t^{(T)}, \tag{15}$$

where $S_t^{(T)}$ is a step function.

A temporary change event, TC, has an initial impact and an effect that decays exponentially by δ

$$y_t = z_t + \frac{1}{1 - \delta(B)} w_c P_t^{(T)}. \tag{16}$$

We report AR(1) and transfer function models of the U.S. unemployment rate in Tables 6–9. The unemployment rate transfer function models use weekly unemployment claims and the full set of LEI. We report five sets of modeling results in each of the Tables 6–8. Tables 6 and 8 report five transfer function models using an AR(1) and weekly unemployment claims input for the 1959–1993 and 1959–2013 time periods, respectively. First, lags of 3 months and 12 months of the weekly unemployment claims time series input are

Table 6. The U.S. unemployment rate and weekly unemployment claims, 1959–1993.

Weekly unemployment claims			
Variable name	Order	Value	T-stat
Equation 1			
DWKUCL	1	0.0027	6.16
DWKUCL	2	0.002	4.69
DWKUCL	3	0.0014	3.31
DUE	1	−0.1361	−2.65
R^2 0.175			
Residual standard error 0.176192e+00			
AIC −0.253312e+03			
Equation 2			
DWKUCL	1	0.0021	5.98
DWKUCL	2	0.0014	3.84
DWKUCL	3	0.0011	3.18
DUE	1	−0.1919	−0.97
DUE	1	−0.4228	−2.34
Residual standard error (without outlier adjustment) 0.178210e+00			
Residual standard error (with outlier adjustment) 0.148377e+00			
Equation 3			
DWKUCL	1	0.0021	5.98
DWKUCL	2	0.0014	3.84
DWKUCL	3	0.0011	3.18
DUE	1	−0.1919	−0.97
DUE	1	−0.4228	−2.34
Residual standard error (without outlier adjustment) 0.178210e+00			
Residual standard error (with outlier adjustment) 0.119688e+00			
Equation 4			
DWKUCL	1	0.0023	6.5
DWKUCL	2	0.0014	3.53
DWKUCL	3	0.0007	1.95
DWKUCL	4	0.0005	1.22
DWKUCL	5	0.0009	2.57
DWKUCL	7	0.0017	5.22
DWKUCL	9	0.0018	5.64
DUE	1	−0.3364	−6.92
R^2 0.244			
Residual standard error 0.168691e+00			
AIC −0.264929e+03			

Table 6. (*Continued*)

Equation 5

Parameter number	Parameter description	Final estimate	Estimated std. error
1	Constant (1)	−0.002853	0.045483
2	Constant (2)	0.042311	0.681504
3	Autoregressive (1,1,1)	0.753550	.0221117
4	Autoregressive (1,1,2)	0.048005	0.046047
5	Autoregressive (1,2,2)	1.912724	3.342386
6	Autoregressive (1,1,1)	0.318802	0.203694
7	Moving Average (1,1,2)	1.068396	0.212032
8	Moving Average (1,1,2)	0.044522	0.045986
9	Moving Average (1,2,1)	−2.141790	3.767034
10	Moving Average (1,2,2)	0.334928	0.192629

Result based on the backward procedure (Y: Due, X: Dwkucl)
Due $\Longleftrightarrow$ Dwkucl (Y and X have feedback relation)
Result based on the forward procedure (Y: Due, X: Dwkucl)
Due $\Longleftrightarrow$ Dwkucl (Y And X have feedback relation)

Table 7. The U.S. unemployment rate and LEI, 1959–1993.

Variable name	Order	Value	T-stat
Equation 1			
DLEI	1	−0.1037	−3.12
DLEI	2	−0.1083	−2.92
DLEI	3	−0.0354	−1.08
DUE	1	−0.0906	−1.84
R^2 0.179			
Residual standard error 0.175740E+00			
AIC −0.255442E+03			
Equation 2			
DLEI	1	−0.0729	−2.75
DLEI	2	−0.11	−4.14
DLUE	1	0.3879	3.28
DLUE	1	0.1291	0.28
Residual standard error (without outlier adjustment) ... 0.190863e+00			
Residual standard error (with outlier adjustment) ... 0.140982e+00			
Equation 3			
DLEI	1	−0.0729	−2.75
DLEI	2	−0.11	−4.14

Table 7. (*Continued*)

Variable name	Order	Value	T-stat
DLUE	1	0.3879	3.28
DLUE	1	0.0363	0.28
Residual standard error (without outlier adjustment) ... 0.190863e+00			
Residual standard error (with outlier adjustment) ... 0.113836e+00			
Equation 4			
DLEI	1	−0.0841	−2.94
DLEI	2	−0.0836	−2.72
DLEI	4	−0.0599	−2.16
DLEI	9	−0.0895	−3.82
Residual standard error (without outlier adjustment) ... 0.172779e+00			
Residual standard error (with outlier adjustment) ... 0.156499e+00			
Variable name order value T-stat			

Equation 5

Parameter number	Parameter description	Final estimate	Estimated std. error
1	Constant (1)	0.007181	0.003101
2	Constant (2)	−0.010655	0.007280
3	Autoregressive (1,1,1)	0.781951	0.055383
4	Autoregressive (1,1,2)	−0.064217	0.022034
5	Autoregressive (1,2,2)	0.510876	0.129085
6	Autoregressive (1,1,1)	1.095485	0.051517
7	Moving Average (1,1,2)	0.804953	0.063443
8	Moving Average (1,1,2)	0.061788	0.031849
9	Moving Average (1,2,1)	0.293963	0.150721
10	Moving Average (1,2,2)	0.732353	0.068170
Result based on the backward procedure (Y: Due, X: Dlei)			
Due $\Longleftrightarrow$ Dlei (Y and X have feedback relation)			
Result based on the forward procedure (Y: Due, X: Dlei)			
Due $\Longleftrightarrow$ Dlei (Y and X have feedback relation)			

Table 8. The U.S. unemployment rate and weekly unemployment claims, 1959–2018.

Weekly unemployment claims			
Variable name	Order	Value	T-stat
Equation 1			
DWKUCL	1	0.0025	7.45
DWKUCL	2	0.0023	7.18
DWKUCL	3	0.0017	5.33
DUE	1	−0.1062	−2.75
R^2 . . . . 0.179			
Residual standard error. . . . . . . 0.162237e+00			
AIC. . . . . −0.558458e+03			
Equation 2			
DWKUCL	1	0.0018	6.24
DWKUCL	2	0.0019	6.81
DWKUCL	3	0.0013	4.69
Residual standard error (without outlier adjustment) 0.178210e+00			
Residual standard error (with outlier adjustment) 0.119688e+00			
Equation 3			
DWKUCL	1	0.0018	6.24
DWKUCL	2	0.0019	6.81
DWKUCL	3	0.0013	4.69
Residual standard error (without outlier adjustment) . . . 0.163581e+00			
Residual standard error (with outlier adjustment) . . . 0.115401e+00			
Equation 4			
DWKUCL	1	0.0029	9.52
DWKUCL	2	0.0023	7.66
DWKUCL	3	0.0017	5.56
DWKUCL	4	0.0008	2.63
DWKUCL	5	0.0009	3.01
DWKUCL	6	0.0013	4.16
DWKUCL	7	0.001	3.23
DWKUCL	8	0.0003	0.92
DWKUCL	9	0.0015	4.88
DWKUCL	10	0.0002	0.82
DWKUCL	11	0.0008	2.74
DWKUCL	12	2.31E-05	0.08
DWKUCL	13	0.0008	2.77
DWKUCL	14	0.0005	1.79
DWKUCL	15	−8.94E-05	−0.3
DWKUCL	16	0.0002	0.76
DWKUCL	17	0.0004	1.43
DWKUCL	18	0.0008	2.95
DUE	1	0.2506	6.44

Table 8. (*Continued*)

Variable name	Order	Value	T-stat
R^2 . . . . 0.361			
Residual standard error. . . . . . . 0.143176e+00			
AIC. . . . . −0.691487e+03			
DWKUCL	1	0.0025	9.71
DWKUCL	2	0.0023	8.42
DWKUCL	3	0.0015	5.43
DWKUCL	4	0.0005	1.96
DWKUCL	5	0.0007	2.69
DWKUCL	6	0.0013	4.73
DWKUCL	7	0.001	3.85
DWKUCL	8	0.0005	1.81
DWKUCL	9	0.0015	5.77
DWKUCL	10	0.0004	1.51
DWKUCL	11	0.0012	4.46
DWKUCL	12	0.0001	0.39
DWKUCL	13	0.0012	4.37
DWKUCL	14	0.001	3.83
DWKUCL	15	−0.0002	−0.62
DWKUCL	16	6.32E−05	0.24
DWKUCL	17	0.0003	0.96
DWKUCL	18	0.001	3.91
DUE	1	0.3789	10.45
Residual standard error (without outlier adjustment) ... 0.147850e+00			
Residual standard error (with outlier adjustment) ... 0.121937e+00			

Equation 5

Parameter number	Parameter description	Final estimate	Estimated std. error
1	Constant (1)	0.005287	0.031948
2	Constant (2)	−0.071517	0.431469
3	Autoregressive (1,1,1)	0.801816	0.135546
4	Autoregressive (1,1,2)	0.048194	0.024176
5	Autoregressive (1,2,2)	1.384773	1.646831
6	Autoregressive (1,1,1)	0.378608	0.110662
7	Moving average (1,1,2)	1.115580	0.127634
8	Moving average (1,1,2)	0.044682	0.024126
9	Moving average (1,2,1)	−2.491080	2.243462
10	Moving average (1,2,2)	0.397171	0.102255
Result based on the backward procedure (Y: Due, X: Dwkucl)			
Due $\Longleftrightarrow$ Dwkucl (Y and X have feedback relation)			
Result based on the forward procedure (Y: Due, X: Dwkucl)			
Due $\Longleftrightarrow$ Dwkucl (Y and X have feedback relation)			

Table 9. The U.S. unemployment rate and LEI, 1959–2018.

Variable name	Order	Value	T-stat
Equation 1			
DLEI	1	−0.0452	−2.67
DLEI	2	−0.0709	−3.99
DLUE	3	−0.0598	−3.55
DUE	1	−0.0789	−2.1
R^2 . . . . 0.185			
Residual standard error. . . . . . . 0.161612e+00			
AIC. . . . . −0.563949e+03			
DLEI	1	−0.0429	−2.55
DLEI	2	−0.0725	−4.31
DLEI	3	−0.0584	−3.47
R^2 . . . . 0.181			
Residual standard error. . . . . . . 0.162013e+00			
AIC. . . . . −0.563222e+03			
Equation 2			
DLEI	1	−0.026	−1.78
DLEI	2	−0.0673	−4.55
DLEI	3	−0.0542	−3.71
Residual standard error (without outlier adjustment) . . . 0.162458e+00			
Residual standard error (with outlier adjustment) . . . 0.140456e+00			
Equation 3			
DLEI	1	−0.026	−1.78
DLEI	2	−0.0673	−4.55
DLEI	3	−0.0542	−3.71
Residual standard error (without outlier adjustment) . . . 0.162458e+00			
Residual standard error (with outlier adjustment) . . . 0.140456e+00			
DLEI	1	−0.425	−2.56
DLEI	2	−0.0553	−3.07
DLEI	3	−0.0399	−2.16
DLEI	4	−0.0067	−0.36
DLEI	5	0.0124	0.66
DLEI	6	−0.0327	−1.75
DLEI	7	0.0027	0.15
DLEI	8	−0.0019	−0.1
DLEI	9	−0.0391	−2.1

Table 9. (*Continued*)

Variable name	Order	Value	T-stat
DLEI	10	−0.0004	−0.02
DLEI	11	−0.0233	−1.25
DLEI	12	0.0277	1.48
DLEI	13	−0.0204	−1.08
DLEI	14	−0.0077	−0.41
DLEI	15	0.0269	1.43
DLEI	16	0.0079	0.42
DLEI	17	−0.0222	−1.22
DLEI	18	−0.0079	−0.47
DUE	1	−0.0948	−2.51
R^2 . . . . 0.256			
Residual standard error. . . . . . . 0.154484e+00			
AIC. . . . . −0.584629e+03			
Equation 4			
DLEI	1	−0.0397	−2.39
DLEI	2	−0.0563	−3.21
DLEI	3	−0.0405	−2.23
DLEI	4	−0.0071	−0.39
DLEI	5	0.012	0.65
DLEI	6	−0.0328	−1.77
DLEI	7	0.0027	0.14
DLEI	8	−0.0009	−0.05
DLEI	9	−0.0394	−2.14
DLEI	10	−0.0009	−0.05
DLEI	11	−0.0233	−1.26
DLEI	12	0.0274	1.48
DLEI	13	−0.02	−1.08
DLEI	14	−0.0077	−0.42
DLEI	15	0.0273	1.47
DLEI	16	0.0081	0.44
DLEI	17	−0.0216	−1.22
DLEI	18	−0.0089	−0.53
R^2 . . . . 0.249			
Residual standard error. . . . . . . 0.155125e+00			
AIC. . . . . −0.581754E+03			
DLEI	1	−0.195	−1.32
DLEI	2	−0.0497	−3.19

Table 9. (*Continued*)

Variable name	Order	Value	T-stat
DLEI	3	−0.0445	−2.76
DLEI	4	−0.0054	−0.33
DLEI	5	0.026	1.58
DLEI	6	−0.0275	−1.67
DLEI	7	0.0008	0.05
DLEI	8	−0.0158	−0.97
DLEI	9	−0.0282	−1.72
DLEI	10	0.0039	0.24
DLEI	11	−0.0308	−1.88
DLEI	12	0.0261	1.58
DLEI	13	−0.0212	−1.28
DLEI	14	−0.0169	−1.02
DLEI	15	0.0264	1.6
DLEI	16	−0.0043	−0.27
DLEI	17	−0.0134	−0.85
DLEI	18	−0.0036	−0.24
Residual standard error (without outlier adjustment) ... 0.156092e+00			
Residual standard error (with outlier adjustment) ... 0.137999e+00			
DLEI	1	−0.195	−1.32
DLEI	2	−0.0497	−3.19
DLEI	3	−0.0445	−2.76
DLEI	4	−0.0054	−0.33
DLEI	5	0.026	1.58
DLEI	6	−0.0275	−1.67
DLEI	7	0.0008	0.05
DLEI	8	−0.0158	−0.97
DLEI	9	−0.0282	−1.72
DLEI	10	0.0039	0.24
DLEI	11	−0.0308	−1.88
DLEI	12	0.0261	1.58
DLEI	13	−0.0212	−1.28
DLEI	14	−0.0169	−1.02
DLEI	15	0.0264	1.6
DLEI	16	−0.0043	−0.27
DLEI	17	−0.0134	−0.85
DLEI	18	−0.0036	−0.24
Residual standard error (without outlier adjustment) ... 0.156092e+00			
Residual standard error (with outlier adjustment) ... 0.110108e+00			

Table 9. (*Continued*)

Summary of final parameter estimates and their standard errors

Parameter number	Parameter description	Final estimate	Estimated std. error
Equation 5			
1	Constant (1)	0.052124	0.016013
2	Constant (2)	−0.138469	0.044296
3	Autoregressive (1,1,1)	−1.377163	0.263322
4	Autoregressive (1,1,2)	−0.530786	0.064085
5	Autoregressive (1,2,1)	6.484085	0.782178
6	Autoregressive (1,2,2)	2.413705	0.204443
7	Moving average (1,1,1)	−1.322794	0.263844
8	Moving average (1,1,2)	−0.475195	0.065672
9	Moving average (1,2,1)	6.300207	0.780190
10	Moving average (1,2,2)	2.111769	0.209422
Result based on the backward procedure (Y: DUE , X: DLEI)			
DUE $\Lleftarrow$ DLEI (Y is strongly caused by X)			
Result based on the forward procedure (Y: DUE , X: DLEI)			
DUE $\Lleftarrow$ DLEI (Y is strongly caused by X)			

(positively) statistically associated with the U.S. unemployment rate, as was reported in the seminal MZTT (1998) analysis. Second, SCA-estimated outliers are statistically significant and reduce the mean square error of the time series models. Third, there is a feedback relationship between the weekly unemployment claims and the U.S. unemployment rate time series reported in 1959–1993 and 1959–2019 time periods. Tables 7 and 9 report five transfer function models using an AR(1) and the LEI time series input for the 1959–1993 and 1959–2013 time periods, respectively. First, lags of 3 months and 12 months of weekly unemployment claims input are (negatively; as LEI rises, the unemployment rate should fall) statistically associated with the U.S. unemployment rate, as was reported in Thomakos and Guerard (2004) analysis. Third, there is a feedback relationship between the LEI time series and the U.S. unemployment rate time series reported in 1959–1993 and a Granger-causal 1959–2019 time period, in which LEI leads the U.S. unemployment rate.

7. Summary and Conclusions

In our replication study of the MZTT (1998), U.S. unemployment rate, weekly unemployment claims, and LEI time series, we applied traditional Granger-causality modeling which substantially reduces regression sum of squares measures relative to a traditional variation on the random walk with drift model. We replicate the seminal study and extend the analysis to 2018. The modeling process of including the LEI in forecasting the U.S. unemployment rate has been addressed before, but our results are more statistically significant. The transfer function models estimated using the SCA software system were the software used in the original MZTT analysis. We establish Granger causality between the LEI time series and the unemployment rate for 1959–2018 time period. We establish feedback between the LEI time series and the unemployment rate for 1959–1993 time period, and for weekly unemployment claims and the unemployment rate for both 1959–1993 and 1959–2019 time series.

We report that the variables studied in a seminal study of the unemployment rate continue to be highly statistically significant. Increases in LEI and one of its components, the unemployment claims time series, precede a reduction in the unemployment rate. Why are these results important? The unemployment rate was at a 50-year low in the U.S when the pandemic occurred. What reduces unemployment? Increasing economic activity drives down unemployment. The LEI were created by Mitchell (1913) to be a barometer of economic activity. The LEI time series and its underlying methodology have evolved through the research of Burns and Mitchell (1946), Moore (1961), and Zarnowitz (1992). The LEI time series, and one of its components, weekly employment claims, are statistically significant in forecasting the unemployment rate. The LEI time series passes the Chen–Lee test for Granger causality.

In summary, we report on the statistically significant impact of the LEI and weekly unemployment claims time series on the unemployment rate series. The MZTT variable relationships are confirmed, in-sample, and post-publication.

Appendix: Review of Box-Jenkins ARMA(p,q) models

This section draws heavily from Box and Jenkins, *Time Series Analysis*, Chapters 2 and 3. The autocorrelation function examines the correlations of the current value of the economic times series and its previous k-lags. That is, one can measure the correlation of an economic time series, x, by calculating:

$$x_{jt} = a + b\ x_{jt-1}$$

where x_{jt} = today's value of time series x;
x_{jt-1} = last period's value of time series x; and
b is the correlation coefficient.

In a daily time series, b is quite large, often approaching a value of 1.00. As the number of lags, or previous number of periods increase, the correlation tend to fall. The decrease is usually very gradual.

The partial autocorrelation function examines the correlation between p_{jt} and p_{jt-2}, holding constant the association between x_{jt} and x_{jt-1}. If a series follows a random walk, the correlation between x_{jt} and x_{jt-1} is one, and the correlation between x_j and x_{jt-2}, holding constant the correlation of x_{jt} and x_{jt-1} is zero. Random walk series are characterized with decaying autocorrelation functions and a partial autocorrelation function with a "spike" at lag one, and zeros thereafter. Stationarity implies that the joint probability $[p(Z)]$ distribution $\mathrm{P}(Z_{t1}, Z_{t2})$ is the same for all times t, t_1, and t_2 where the observations are separated by a constant time interval. The autocovariance of a time series at some lag or interval, k, is defined to be the covariance between Z_t and $Z_{t+k.}$

$$\gamma_k = \mathrm{cov}[Z_t,\ Z_{t+k}] = E[(Z_t - \mu)(Z_{t+k} - \mu)].$$

One must standardize the autocovariance, as one standardizes the covariance in traditional regression analysis before one can quantify the statistically significant association between Z_t and Z_{t+k}. The autocorrelation of a time series is the standardization of the autocovariance of a time series relative to the variance of the time series, and the autocorrelation at lag k, ρ_k, is bounded between $+1$ and -1.

The statistical estimates of the autocorrelation function are calculated from a finite series of N observations, Z_1, Z_2, Z_3, $\ldots$, Z_n. The statistical estimate of the autocorrelation function at lag k, r_k, is found by

$$r_k = \frac{C_k}{C_0},$$

where

$$C_k = \frac{1}{N}\sum_{t=1}^{N-k}(Z_t - \overline{Z})(Z_{t+k} - \overline{Z}),\ k = 0, 1, 2, ..., K.$$

C_k is, of course, the sample estimate of the autocovariance function at lag k. In identifying and estimating parameters in a time series model, one seeks to identify orders (lags) of the time series that are statistically different from zero. The implication of testing whether an autocorrelation estimate is statistically different from zero leads one back to the t-tests used in regression analysis to examine the statistically significant association between variables. One must develop a standard error of the autocorrelation estimate such that a formal t-test can be performed to measure the statistical significance of the autocorrelation estimate. Such a standard error, S_e, estimate was found by Bartlett and, in large samples, is approximated by

$$Var[r_k] \cong \frac{1}{N}, \quad \text{and} \quad \mathrm{S}_e[r_k] \cong \frac{1}{\sqrt{N}}.$$

A second statistical estimate useful in time series analysis is the partial autocorrelation estimate of coefficient j at lag k, ϕ_{kj} of time series x. The partial autocorrelations are found in the following manner:

$$\rho_j = \phi_{kl}x_{j-1} + \phi_{k2}\rho x_{j-2} + \cdots + \phi_{k(k-1)}\ x_{jk-1} + \phi_{kk}x_{j-k}$$
$$j = 1, 2, \ldots, k$$

$$\text{or} \quad \begin{bmatrix} 1 & \rho_1 & \rho_2 & \cdots & \rho_{k-1} \\ \rho_1 & 1 & \rho_2 & \cdots & \rho_{k-2} \\ \vdots & \vdots & \vdots & \cdots & \vdots \\ \rho_{k-1} & \rho_{k-2} & \rho_{k-3} & \cdots & 1 \end{bmatrix} \begin{bmatrix} \phi_{k1} \\ \phi_{k2} \\ \vdots \\ \phi_{kk} \end{bmatrix} \begin{bmatrix} \rho_1 \\ \rho_2 \\ \vdots \\ \rho_k \end{bmatrix}$$

The partial autocorrelation estimates may be found by solving the above equation systems for $k = 1, 2, 3, \ldots, k$.

$$\phi_{11} = \rho_1$$

$$\phi_{22} = \frac{\rho_2 - \rho_1^2}{1 - \rho_1^2} = \frac{\begin{vmatrix} 1 & \rho_1 \\ \rho_2 & \rho_2 \end{vmatrix}}{\begin{vmatrix} 1 & \rho_1 \\ \rho_1 & 1 \end{vmatrix}}$$

$$\phi_{33} = \frac{\begin{vmatrix} 1 & \rho_1 & \rho_1 \\ \rho_1 & 1 & \rho_2 \\ \rho_2 & \rho_1 & \rho_3 \end{vmatrix}}{\begin{vmatrix} 1 & \rho_1 & \rho_2 \\ \rho_1 & 1 & \rho_1 \\ \rho_2 & \rho_1 & 1 \end{vmatrix}}$$

The partial autocorrelation function is estimated by expressing the current autocorrelation function estimates as a linear combination of previous orders of autocorrelation estimates.

The standard error of the partial autocorrelation function is approximately

$$\mathrm{Var}[\hat{\phi}_{kk}] \cong \frac{1}{N}, \text{ and}$$

$$S_e[\phi_{kk}] \cong \frac{1}{\sqrt{N}}.$$

References

Ashley, R. A. (2003). Statistically significant forecasting improvements: How much out-of-sample data is likely necessary? *International Journal of Forecasting* **19**, 229–240.

Ashley, R. (1998). A new technique for post-sample model selection and validation. *Journal of Economic Dynamics and Control* **22**, 647–665.

Ashley, R., Granger, C. W. J., and Schmalensee, R. (1980). Advertising and aggregate consumption: An analysis of causality. *Econometrica* **48**, 149–1167.

Batchelor, R. (2001). Confidence indexes and the probability of recession: A Markov switching model. *Indian Economic Review* **36**, 107–124.

Box, G. E. P. and Jenkins, G. M. (1970). *Time Series Analysis: Forecasting and Control.* San Francisco: Holden-Day.

Burns, A. F. and Mitchell, W. C. (1946). *Measuring Business Cycles.* New York, NBER.

Chen, C. and Lee, C. J. (1990). A VARMA test on the Gibson paradox. *Review of Economics and Statistics* **72**, 96–107.

Chen, C. and Liu, L.-M. (1993a). Joint estimation of model parameters and outliers in time series. *Journal of the American Statistical Association* **88**, 284–297.

Chen, C. and Liu, L.-M. (1993a). Forecasting time series with outliers. *Journal of Forecasting*, **12**, 13–35.

Clemen, R. T. and Guerard, J. B. (1989). Econometric GNP forecasts: Incremental information relative to naive extrapolation. *International Journal of Forecasting* **5**, 417–426.

Clements, M. P. and Hendry, D. F. (1998). *Forecasting Economic Time Series.* Cambridge: Cambridge University Press.

Dhrymes, P. J. (2017). *Introductory Econometrics.* New York: Springer.

Diebold, F. and Rudebusch, G. D. (1999). *Business Cycles.* Princeton: Princeton University Press.

Diebold, F. X. and Rudebusch, G. D. (1999). *Business Cycles: Durations, Dynamics and Forecasting.* Princeton: Princeton University Press.

Diebold, F. X. and Mariano, R. S. (1995). Comparing predictive accuracy. *Journal of Business and Economic Statistics* **13**, 253–263.

Friedman, M. and A. Schwartz (1963). Money and business cycles. *Review of Economics and Statistics* **45**, 32–64.

Gordon, R. J. (1986). *The American Business Cycle.* Chicago: University of Chicago Press.

Granger, C. W. J. and Newbold, P. (1977). *Forecasting Economic Time Series.* Academic Press, New York.

Granger, C. W. J. (1969). Investigating casual relations by economic models and cross-spectral methods. *Econometrica* **37**, 424–438.

Granger, C. W. J. (1980). Testing for causality: A personal viewpoint. *Journal of Economic Dynamics and Control* **2**, 329–352.

Granger, C. W. J. (1986). Developments in the study of cointegrated economic variables. *Oxford Bulletin of Economics and Statistics* **48**, 213–228.

Granger, C. W. J. (1989). *Forecasting in Business and Economics.* Academic Press, New York.

Granger, C. W. J. (2001). *Essays in Econometrics.* Two Volumes (eds.). E. Ghysels, N. R. Swanson, and M. W. Watson Cambridge University Press, Cambridge, UK.

Granger, C. W. J. (1980). Testing for causality: A personal viewpoint. *Journal of Economic Dynamics and Control* **2**, 329–352.

Granger, C. W. J. and Newbold, P. (1977). *Forecasting Economic Time Series.* New York Academic Press.

Guerard, J. B., Jr. (2004). The forecasting effectiveness of the U.S. leading economic indicators: Further evidence and initial G7 results." In P. Dua (Ed.)., *Business Cycles and Economic Growth: An Analysis Using Leading Indicators.* New York: Oxford University Press, pp. 174–187.

Guerard, J. B., Jr. (2001). A note on the forecasting effectiveness of the U.S. leading economic indicators. *Indian Economic Review* **36**, pp. 251–268.

Guerard, Thomakos, and Kyriazi (2020). Automatic time series modeling and forecasting: A replication case study of forecasting real GDP, the unemployment rate and the impact of leading economic indicators. *Cogent Economics & Finance* **8**, 1759483 https://doi.org/10.1080/23322039.2020.1759483.

Hamilton, J. D. (1994). *Time Series Analysis.* Princeton University Press, Princeton.

Hamilton, J. D. (2011). Calling recessions in real time. *International Journal of Forecasting* **27**, 1006–1026.

Koopmans, T. C. (1947). Measure without theory. *The Review of Economic Statistics*, reprinted in R. Gordon and L. Klein, *Readings in Business Cycles*, Homewood, Illinois, R. A. Irwin, Inc.

Koopmans, T. C. (1950). When is an equation system complete for statistical purposes. Tech. rep., Yale University. http://cowles.econ.yale.edu/P/cm/m10/m10-17.pdf.

Krolzig, Hans-Martin. (2001). Business cycle measurement in the presence of structural change: International evidence. *International Journal of Forecasting* **17**, 349–368.

Lahiri, K. and Moore, G. H. (1991). *Leading Economic Indicators.* Cambridge University Press, Cambridge.

Makridakis, S. and Hibon, M. (2000). The M3-competition: Results, conclusions and implications. *International Journal of Forecasting* **16**, 451–476.

McCracken, M. (2000). Robust out-of-sample inference. *Journal of Econometrics* **39**, 195–223.

Mincer, J. and Zarnowitz, V. (1969). The evaluation of economic forecasts, (ed.)., J. Mincer, *Economic Forecasts and Expectations.* Columbia University Press, New York.

Mitchell, W. C. (1913). *Business Cycles.* Burt Franklin reprint, New York.

Mitchell, W. C. (1951). *What Happens During Business Cycles: A Progress Report.* NBER: New York.

Montgomery, A. L., Zarnowitz, V., Tsay, R. S., and Tiao, G. C. (1998). Forecasting the U.S. unemployment rate. *Journal of the American Statistical Association* **93**, 478–493.

Moore, G. H. (1961). *Business Cycle Indicators.* 2 volumes, Princeton University Press, Princeton.

Nelson, C. R. and Plosser, C. I. (1982). Trends and random walks in macroeconomic time series. *Journal of Monetary Economics* **10**, 139–162.

Theil, H. (1966). *Applied Economic Forecasting.* Amsterdam, North-Holland.

Tsay, R. S. (1988). Outliers, level shifts, and variance changes in time series. *Journal of Forecasting* **7**, 1–20.

Tsay. R. S. (1989). Testing and modeling threshold autoregressive processes. *Journal of the American Statistical Association* **84**, 231–249.

Tsay, R. S. (2010). *Analysis of Financial Time Series.* New York, NY: Wiley, Third Edition.

Tsay, R. S. and Chen, R. (2019). *Nonlinear Time Series Analysis.* New York, NY: Wiley.

Thomakos, D. and Guerard, J. (2004). Naïve, ARIMA, transfer function, and VAR models: A comparison of forecasting performance. *The International Journal of Forecasting* **20**, 53–67.

Vinod, H. D. (2008). *Hands-on Intermediate Econometrics Using R: Templates for Extending Dozens of Practical Examples.* World Scientific, Hackensack, NJ, ISBN 10-981-281-885-5. http://www.worldscibooks.com/economics/6895.html.

Vinod, H. D. (2014). Matrix algebra topics in statistics and economics using R, (eds.). Rao, M. B., Rao, C. R., *Handbook of Statistics: Computational Statistics with R.* Volume 34. North Holland, Elsevier Science, New York, Chapter 4, pp. 143–176.

Vinod, H. D. (2017). Causal paths and exogeneity tests in general Corr package for air pollution and monetary policy. A vignette accompanying the package "generalCorr" of R. https://cloud.r-project.org/web/packages/generalCorr/vignettes/generalCorr-vignette3.pdf.

Vinod, H. D. (2019). New exogeneity tests and causal paths. In Vinod, H. D., Rao, C. R. (Eds.). *Handbook of Statistics: Conceptual Econometrics Using*

R. Volume 41. North Holland, Elsevier, New York, Chapter 2, pp. 33–64. https://doi.org/10.1016/bs.host.2018.11.011.

Vining, R. (1949). Koopmans on the choice of variables to be studied and on methods of measurement. *The Review of Economics and Statistics*, reprinted in R. Gorgon and L. Klein, *Readings in Business Cycles.* Homewood, Illinois: Richard A. Irwin, Inc, 1965.

West, K. and McCracken, M. (1998). Regression-based tests of predictive ability. *International Economic Review* **39**, 817–840.

Zarnowitz, V. (2004). The autonomy of recent U.S. growth and business cycles. In P. Dua, (Ed.), *Business Cycles and Economic Growth: An Analysis Using Leading Indicators.* Oxford University Press, New York, pp. 44–82.

Zarnowitz, V. (2001). The Old and the New in the U.S. Economic Expansion. The Conference Board. EPWP #01-01.

Zarnowitz, V. and Ozyildirim, A. (2001). On the measurement of business cycles and growth cycles. *Indian Economic Review* **36**, 34–54.

Zarnowitz, V. (1992). *Business Cycles*: *Theory, History, Indicators, and Forecasting.* University of Chicago Press, Chicago.

https://doi.org/10.1142/9789811222634_0026

Chapter 26

Investing on the "Far Side of the Moon": Capturing Capital Market Inclusion Opportunity across MEASA (Middle East–Africa–South Asia)

Robert A. Gillam

Chief Executive Officer and Chief Investment Officer of McKinley Capital Management, LLC, USA

Russell Read

Chief Investment Officer of the Alaska Permanent Fund Corporation (APFC), USA

The MEASA region forms a crescent of countries beginning with Bangladesh and India in the East, continuing through the Middle East and West Africa, and terminating with the South African nations. This grouping of countries has a long history of cultural, economic, and political advantages and achievements. One need only consider the energy riches of the Middle East, the mineral, agricultural, and fishery resources of Africa, or the large and educated population of India to understand the potential for the region. The MEASA region covers 45% of the worlds population and is expected to be one of the most rapidly growing regions. Moreover, the MEASA region is approximately 18% of global GDP and is likely to grow at much faster than developed countries in the coming decade. Our study reports that the MEASA region stocks have produced exceptional returns and returns relative to risk compared to MSCI Emerging Markets stocks, Frontier Market stocks, and World Index stocks during the January 2003 to September 2017 time period. The situation today in the MEASA region countries seems like the situation in the BRICs countries in the early 2000s. As happened with the BRICs countries, the barriers to investing in the MEASA region are being removed as we write. Innovative investment advisors are set to offer mechanisms to access these markets. The rewards will go to those visionary investors who are able to first see the possibilities.

Keywords: MEASA, Middle East, Africa, South Asia, Emerging Markets, Investing, Alaska, Quant.

The MEASA Region:

- 45% of the world's population; median age below 23 years (leading future growth).
- 18% of the world's GDP; likely to have achieved triple the developed world economic growth rate in 2017 and home to 7 out of the 10 fastest-growing economies in the world.
- 6% share of MSCI combined global market capitalization.
- 2% weighting in the MSCI ACW Index.
- A unique capital markets development opportunity as population and economic growth lead capital markets to grow, with likely market upgrades to emerging or frontier status and subsequent increase in market-cap weighted indexes.
- A simulated market-cap weighted MEASA index would have generated a 13.6% annualized return from January 2003 through September 2017 (versus 9.2% for the MSCI World Index).
- Efficient access to MEASA stock investments is difficult, but investors should seek opportunities to purchase stocks in the region as opportunities arise.

1. Introduction and Executive Summary

The MEASA region forms a crescent of countries beginning with Bangladesh and India in the East, continuing through the Middle East and West Africa, and terminating with the South African nations. This grouping of countries has a long history of cultural, economic, and political advantages and achievements. One need only consider the energy riches of the Middle East, the mineral, agricultural, and fishery resources of Africa, or the large and educated population of India to understand the potential for the region (see Fig. 1).

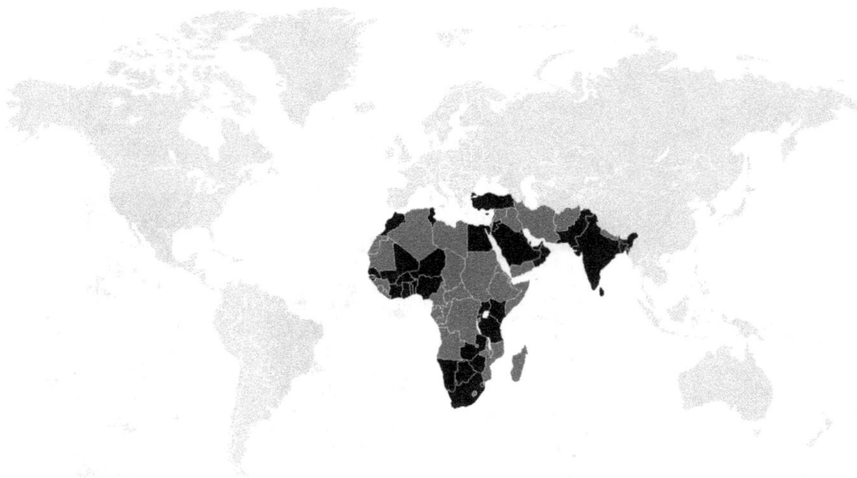

Fig. 1. The MSCI MEASA region is shown in darkest shade.

The MEASA region covers 45% of the world's population, and, with an average age of 23 years, is expected to be the most rapidly growing. This growth, combined with increased labor and resource productivity, will drive explosive economic growth. Already at 18% of global GDP, the MEASA GDP likely grew at triple the developed world economic growth rate in 2017, with 7 of the 10 fastest growing economies being in the region (see Fig. 2).

At the same time, and despite the economic potential for the region, the regional capital markets are grossly under-represented in the major MSCI world equity indexes. Out of the total 83 countries in the region, only 7 are part of the MSCI Emerging Market ("EM") Index, 15 in the MSCI Frontier Market ("FM") Index, and 5 in the MSCI Standalone Market Indexes. Despite that the MEASA markets account for 6% of total global market capitalization and 18% of global GDP, the weighting in the MSCI ACW Index is only 2%. As its countries are upgraded to frontier or emerging status, we believe that interest in the region will explode, that the index weights of its stocks will multiply, and that significant excess returns will be available.

While a breathtaking economic potential exists, institutional investors do face significant barriers to effectively purchasing stock

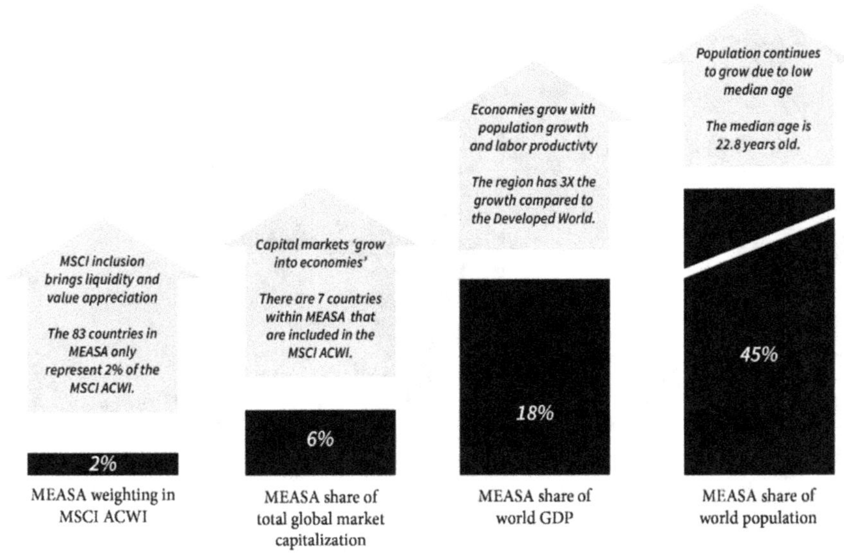

Fig. 2. The MASCI MEASA region expectations of GDP and Population Growth Far Exceed MSCI Relative Market Capitalization.

Source: UN, Population Division, 6/1/2017, International Monetary Fund, 6/1/2017. The World Bank, 5/22/2018, MSCI 6/1/2017, FactSet Database. GDP is based on Purchasing Power Parity (PPP) and is measured in international dollars. Percentages are approximated. Information is believed to be accurate, but may change without notice.

at scale and in diversity from the region. Liquidity appears limited, and registration and custody arrangements are formidable. We describe this essentially as investing on the "far side of the moon," in that despite its conceptual appeal, it has remained difficult or impossible for many institutional investors from around the world to gain effective access to this region's opportunities. Yet, savvy investment managers are now developing innovative approaches to access MEASA region stocks. As these managers introduce broad-based fund products, the riches of the region will open to those institutions with a vision for what can be. Already, the performance of stocks in the region has exceeded broad global benchmarks by hundreds of basis points over the last 15 years.

In summary, we believe that in many ways, the situation of the MEASA region today looks very much like the BRICs in the early 2000s.

2. Population

At their core, people represent the potential for any region, and the MEASA region in particular is loaded with both a large number of people and vast high-quality human resources. These countries currently account for 45% of the world's population, which is expected to grow to 54% by 2050 (see Fig. 3). While the populations of the developed countries (such as the U.S., Japan, and Western Europe) are aging rapidly, the MEASA region population is relatively young and consists of a high and rising share of the working-age group. Figure 4 shows the median age in the MEASA region as 22.8 years, compared to 27.8 years for the traditional emerging countries, and 41.2 years for the developed countries.

The situation in India is a prime example (see Fig. 5). Two thirds of India's population is under the age of 35; giving the country a significant competitive edge with low labor costs. Many Indian people speak English, and have benefited from one of the most developed higher education systems in the world. This highly skilled workforce makes India an attractive haven for multinational corporations

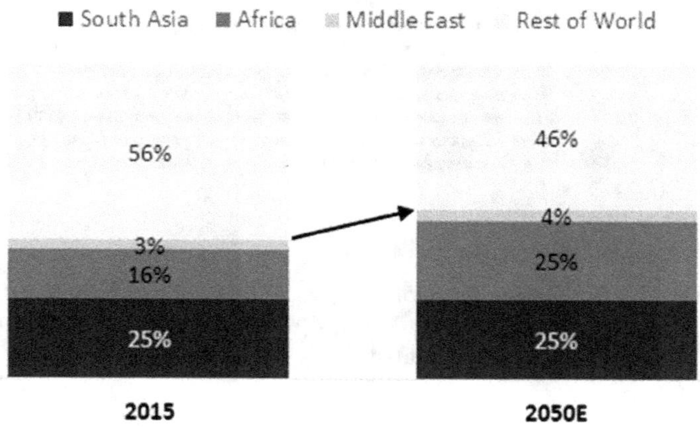

Fig. 3. Share of global population (from 44% of global population in 2015 to 56% in 2050 - percentage of global population).
Source: UN, Population Division, 6/1/2017.

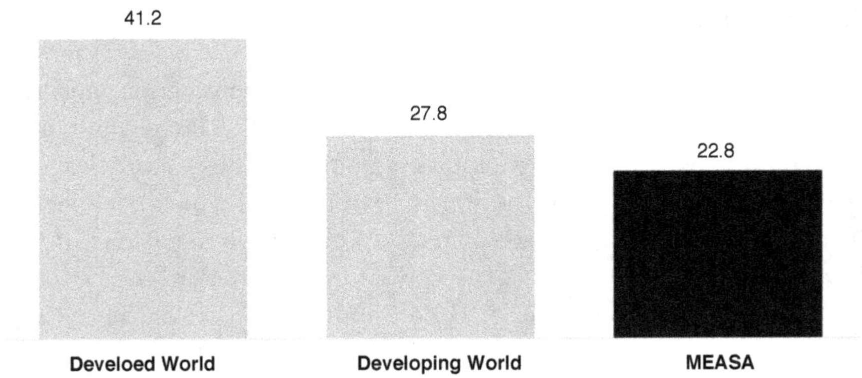

Fig. 4. Median age (median population age below 23 years - median age, years).
Source: UN, Population Division, 6/1/2017.

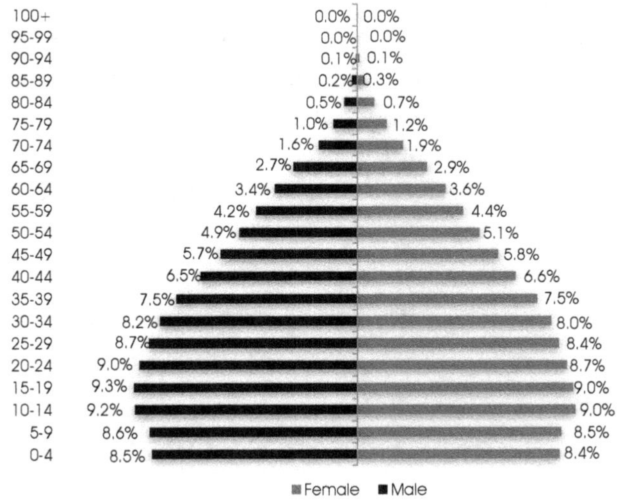

Fig. 5. 2015 India's population by age group.
Sources: UN, Population Division, 6/1/2017; 2016 World Economic Forum, Science, Technology, Engineering, Math; Queen Elizabeth Prize for engineering, 2005; UNESCO Institute for Statistics.

looking to expand overseas. India's young population drives strong growth in consumer spending; having increased from \$478 billion in 2010 to \$957 billion in 2015. India is on the path to becoming one of the world's largest consumer markets by 2025.

3. Economic Position and Growth

The MEASA region currently accounts for 18% of the world's GDP and is expected to be one of the fastest growing regions over the next several years. Combined MEASA region GDP is likely to have grown by 5.9% in 2017, compared to 1.8% for developed market (see Fig. 6). 7 out of the 10 fastest-growing economies in the world come from this region (see Fig. 7).

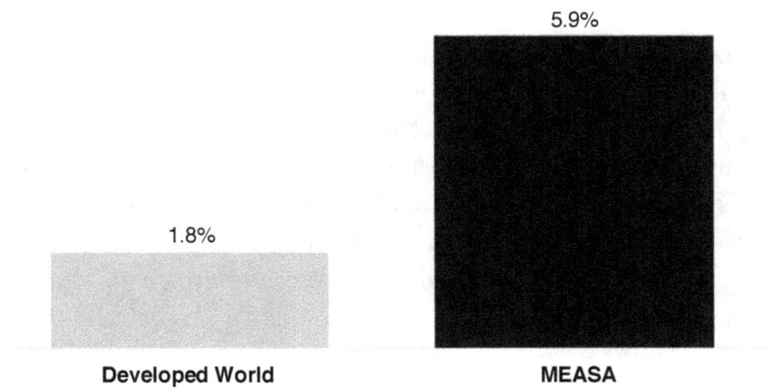

Fig. 6. 2017 likely economic growth.
Source: International Monetary Fund, 6/1/2017.

Country	2016F	2017F	2018F	2016 - 2018 GDP CAGR
Libya*	11.4%	64.1%	33.2%	34.5%
Sudan*	15.9%	22.7%	19.2%	19.2%
Iceland	19.4%	14.6%	12.0%	15.3%
Eritrea*	14.7%	13.1%	13.3%	13.7%
Central African Republic*	11.7%	11.9%	12.1%	11.9%
Myanmar	11.4%	9.1%	10.6%	10.4%
Djibouti*	9.7%	10.2%	10.2%	10.0%
Bangladesh*	10.3%	9.2%	9.4%	9.6%
Turkmenistan	0.4%	17.1%	11.4%	9.4%
Angola*	-6.9%	27.7%	9.8%	9.3%

* Countries within MEASA region

Fig. 7. Top 10 fastest growing economies (nominal annualized growth).
Note: * Countries within MEASA region
Source: International Monetary Fund, 6/1/2017.

Not content to rest on their laurels, many MEASA countries are initiating economic reforms in an attempt to further boost their economies. For example, in the Middle East, the 2014–2015 slump in oil prices further compelled the GCC countries to adopt and/or accelerate reforms to diversify their economies away from hydrocarbon dependence. The recent IPO of a portion of the Abu Dhabi National Oil Company and the upcoming massive Saudi Aramco IPO are two illustrations. These actions will not only provide funds for economic diversification, but will provide a liquid supply of Mideast equity securities. As another example, in India, Prime Minister Modi has liberalized and simplified the process for foreign investment in India. These kinds of actions show the possibilities.

We believe the situation for the MEASA region today is similar to the situation for the BRICS in the early 2000s (noting of course that India is included in both groups). For example, in 2001, the BRICS countries accounted for about 8% of the world's GDP on a current basis (O' Neill, 2001). By 2015, the share had grown to almost 22% (World Bank, 2017). While it is impossible to predict the degree to which the MEASA region will reflect the performance of the BRICS economies, these numbers illustrate the potential.

4. Capital Markets Development: Index Representation

Despite the economic position and potential for the MEASA region, the index companies have yet to catch on. Though representing 18% of the world's GDP, the MEASA region companies only account for 6% of the market cap of the total for the MSCI ACWI Index constituents, and significantly only account for 2% of the index weight. As these anomalies are corrected, we believe that investor interest in the region will explode, with subsequent positive effects on the region's equity returns. The difference in percentages (2% versus 11%) thus represents a significant 9% potential gap that is expected to narrow for the benefit of investors in these markets over time.

A similar situation existed for the BRICS stocks in the early 2000s. By what mechanism was the situation rectified and index weight increased, and what was the investment result? As the BRIC's countries gained in stature due to growth and economic reform, they were upgraded to "frontier and emerging" status by MSCI. Superior investment returns followed.

An MSCI index upgrade is typically a significant positive catalyst for a country's market. Upgrades tend to boost liquidity and portfolio inflows into the country as index-oriented investors seek to rebalance. Also, some institutional investors are restricted to traditional developed and emerging markets. Market reclassification means that a new group of investors enter a market. MSCI classifies countries based on dozens of criteria including: openness to foreign ownership, ease of capital flow, and efficiency and stability of the market's operational framework. When conditions change, MSCI reclassifies markets (see Fig. 8). Typically, when a country's market approaches the criteria for a reclassification, MSCI places it on a watchlist, gathers feedback from institutional investors, and finally announces a decision to reclassify the market. When the market is selected, MSCI specifies a date at which the reclassification will become effective, usually in about a year.

For most investors, the relevant dates are the announcement and effective dates for reclassification. Several MEASA region countries have already been "upgraded." As Figs. 9 and 10 show, the UAE returned 99%, and trading volume increased by 473% between the time MSCI announced the UAE upgrade to emerging market status (May 31, 2013) until the time the upgrade was implemented (May 30, 2014). Similarly, Pakistan saw a 26% return and a 337% increase in trading volume between the MSCI upgrade announcement (June 14, 2016) and effective date (June 1, 2017) — Figs. 11 and 12.

Active investors start including key names in their portfolios right after the announcement; even ahead of the effective date. Passive investors typically wait until the effective date to adjust their positions. We expect similar results from future MEASA region upgrades.

5. Recent MEASA Equity Returns

The exceptional returns that we believe will be available in MEASA region investments have already been demonstrated to some degree.

All MEASA Countries by GDP							
Africa					Middle East		South Asia
Nigeria	Cote d'Ivorire	Mozambique	Niger	Guinea-Bissau	Turkey	Jordon	India
Algeria	Uganda	Zimbabwe	Mauritania	Seychelles	Saudi Arabia	Bahrain	Pakistan
South Africa	Zambia	Burkina Faso	Swaziland	Comoros	Egypt	Cyprus	Bangladesh
Morocco	Democratic Republic of the Congo	Chad	Togo	Sao Tome and Principe	United Arab Emirates	Syria	Sri Lanka
Angola	Senegal	Republic of Congo	Sierra Leone	Eritrea	Iraq	Georgia	Nepal
Ethiopia	Botswana	Namibia	Burundi	Libya	Qatar	Palestine	Afghanistan
Kenya	Mali	Mauritius	Lesotho	Mayotte	Kuwait	Armenia	Maldives
Tanzania	Madagascar	South Sudan	Liberia	Reunion	Oman		Bhutan
Tunisia	Gabon	Guinea	Cape Verde	Saint Helena	Azerbaijan		
Ghana	Equatorial Guinea	Benin	Gambia	Somalia	Lebanon		
Sudan		Rwanda	Djibouti	Western Sahara	Yemen		
Cameroon		Malawi	Central African Rep.				

MEASA Investible Universe							
MSCI EM INDEX			MSCI FM INDEX			Other MEASA Countries	
Middle East	Africa	South Asia	Middle East	Africa	South Asia	Middle East	Africa
Egypt*	South Africa*	India*	Bahrain*	Kenya*	Bangladesh*	Cyprus*	Botswana*
Qatar		Pakistan*	Jordan*	Mauritius*	Sri Lanka*	Saudi Arabia*	Ghana*
Turkey*			Kuwait*	Morocco*			Malawi
United Arab Emirates*			Lebanon*	Nigeria*			Namibia*
			Oman*	Tunisia*			Rwanda
				WAEMU[1]			Swaziland
							Tanzania*
							Uganda
							Zambia
							Zimbabwe

Fig. 8. The MSCI Classification of the MSCI MEASA Countries.

Notes: *Represents countries the MEASA Strategy is registered in or for which registration on is pending as of 05/31/2018.

[1]The West African Economic and Monetary Union (WAEMU) consists of the following countries: Benin, Burkina Faso, Cote d'Ivoire, Guinea-Bissau, Mali, Nigar, Senegal, and Togo Currently, the MSCI WAEMU Indices include securities classified in Burkina Faso, Cote d'Ivorie, and Senegal.

Source: MSCI, and McKinley Capital, retrieved May, 2018. Information is believed to be accurate, but may change without notice.

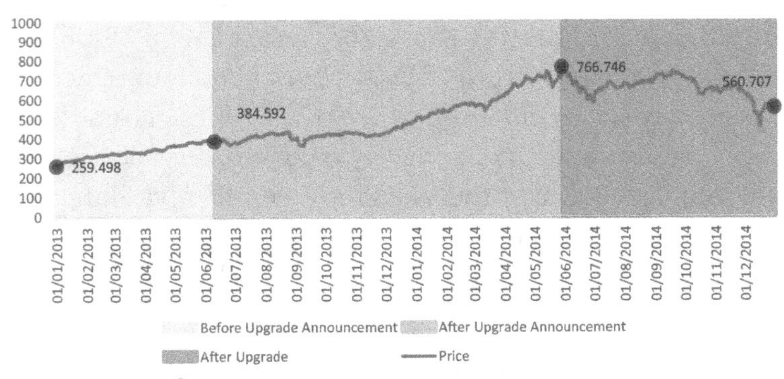

Fig. 9. MSCI UAE index inclusion - Index price.

Source: MSCI, FactSet, 12/1/2017.

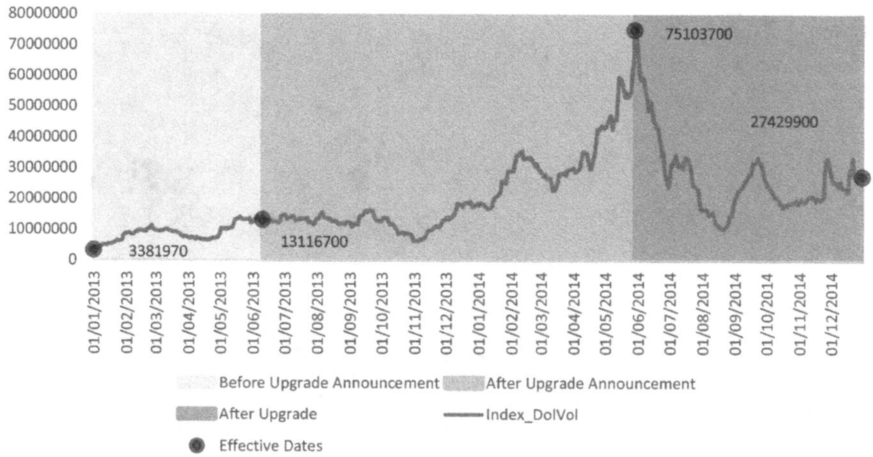

Fig. 10. MSCI UAE index inclusion - Index dollar volume.
Source: MSCI, FactSet, 12/1/2017.

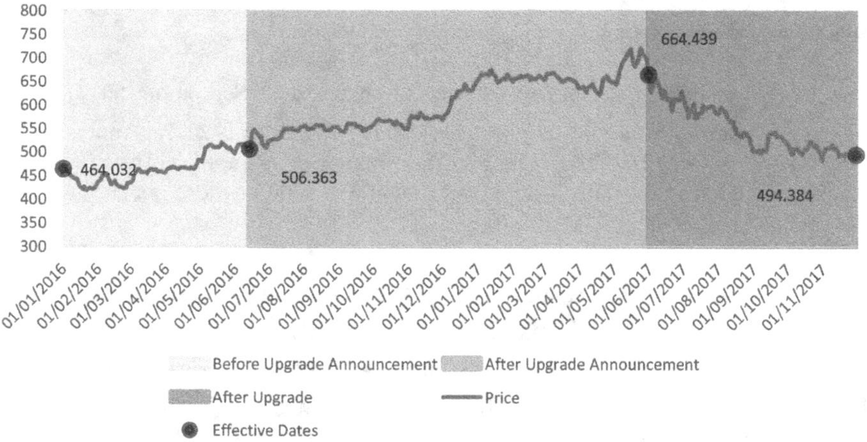

Fig. 11. MSCI Pakistan index inclusion - price (USD).
Source: MSCI, FactSet, 12/1/2017.

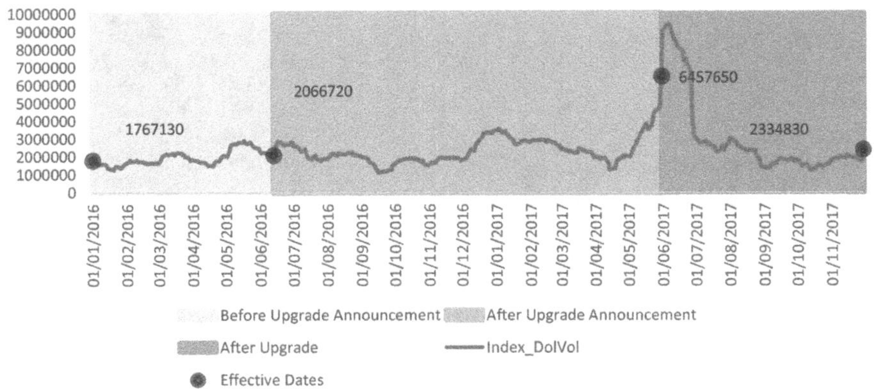

Fig. 12. MSCI Pakistan index inclusion - index dollar volume (USD).
Source: MSCI, FactSet, 12/1/2017.

Index	Annualized Return (%)	Annualized Risk (%)	Sharpe Ratio
MEASA Simulated - Market Cap Weighted	13.64	24.59	0.51
MSCI Frontier Markets Index	8.57	23.57	0.31
MSCI Emerging Markets Index	12.36	23.16	0.48
MSCI World Index	9.22	16.06	0.50

Fig. 13. Simulation risk–return statistics (January 2003–September 2017).
Sources: FactSet, Axioma, Zephyr StyleADVISOR, 12/1/2017. Analysis by McKinley Capital, 12/1/2017. The MEASA simulation is based on the returns of stocks with an average daily trading volume of $100,000 or more per day.

Figure 13 shows the returns of a simulated market-cap weighted MEASA equity index. This simulated MEASA index outperformed the MSCI World Index, the MSCI Emerging Index, and the MSCI Frontier Market indices from January 2003 through September 2017. The simulated MEASA index generated a 13.6% annualized return over that time period, compared with 9.2% for the MSCI World Index. Figure 13 shows that it also produced better Sharpe ratios, than the comparison MSCI indexes. We are firmly convinced that similar results are possible in the years ahead.

6. Conclusions

The rapidly growing MEASA region countries and their companies would seem to be burgeoning with attractive investment opportunities. Yet, we think of investing in this region as investing on the "far side of the moon!" This opinion is based on the perception of illiquidity and institutional barriers to investment. The situation today in the MEASA region countries seems similar to the situation in the BRICS countries in the early 2000s. As happened with the BRICS countries, the barriers to investing in the MEASA region are being removed as we write. Innovative investment advisors are set to offer mechanisms to access these markets. The rewards will go to those visionary investors who are able to first see the possibilities.

Acknowledgments

We thank Gregory Samorajski and Shierley Widjaja of McKinley Capital Management, LLC and Peter Lejre, Senior Executive Officer of McKinley Middle East, LTD, for their research, technical and editorial assistance.

Disclosure

McKinley Capital Management, LLC ("McKinley Capital") is a registered investment adviser under the U.S. Investment Advisers Act of 1940. McKinley Capital is not registered with, approved by, regulated by, or associated with the Financial Conduct Authority ("FCA"), the Prudential Regulation Authority ("PRA"), the Securities & Futures Commission of Hong Kong, or the China Securities Regulatory Commission. Additionally, none of the authorities or commissions listed in the previous sentence has commented on the firm, the content of any marketing material, or any individual suitability assessments.

The material provided herein has been prepared for a one-on-one institutional presentation to a qualified purchaser, may contain confidential and/or proprietary information, and should not be further disseminated without written approval from McKinley Capital's Compliance Department. This is not an offer to purchase or sell a product or security. This chapter contains simulated returns and may not be relied upon for investment decisions. Strategy returns were generated using McKinley Capital's proprietary growth investment methodology as described in McKinley Capital's Form ADV Part 2A, are unaudited, and do not replicate actual returns for any client. McKinley Capital's investment methodology has not materially changed since its inception, but it has undergone various enhancements.

The model presented here is not currently an investable strategy. Simulated returns may differ materially from the indexes due to the data and content of the investable universe represented. No security or strategy is profitable all of the time and there is always the possibility of selling at a loss. The MEASA Custom Benchmark includes all active securities as defined in the MEASA countries universe. Active is defined by the availability of the Daily Volume, Market Cap, and Price. All securities are Market Cap weighted. Non-traded shares are excluded when calculating Market Cap. The benchmark is rebalanced semi-annually at the end of May and November each year to coordinate with MSCI index rebalancing. Investments and commentary are subject to immediate change without notice. Comments and general market-related perspectives are for informational purposes only and were based on data available at the time of writing and may not be relied upon for individual investing purposes.

No fees or expenses of any kind have been deducted, all of which will negatively impact actual returns. Trading activity, asset allocation, and portfolio decisions are based on the management style that McKinley Capital may have followed had it been actively managing a discretionary account for that period. Returns are calculated using the internal rate of return and reflect the reinvestment of hypothetical gains, dividends, interest, and other income. Returns are gross of all investment management fees and other costs and expenses. Returns do not include any transactional or brokerage fees, custodial fees, or adjust for other external cash flows. Individual tax considerations are not included in any analysis and will negatively impact total returns. Detailed account inclusion/exclusion policies are available upon request.

The currency used to calculate theoretical performance is the USD, and the benchmark presented is believed to be the most appropriate for this client portfolio, but it may also be used in unrelated strategies. McKinley Capital portfolios and allocation comparisons to the specified benchmark may or may not outperform an index at any point in time depending on multiple hurdles including but not limited to currency exchange fluctuations, material economic events, variable weightings, or other market factors. Investors should realize that the application of other currencies or benchmarks to this simulation may provide materially different results. Decisions and information provided were based on the McKinley Capital quantitative approach. No composite or representative account currently exists. Although trading records are illustrative of the proposed strategy, absolute security timing, liquidity, and execution are not actual and may not have been available during the periods presented.

Global market investing, including developed, emerging, and frontier markets, also carries additional risks and/or costs including but not limited to: political, economic, financial market, currency exchange, liquidity, accounting, and trading capability risks. Derivatives trading and short selling may materially increase investment risk and potential returns. These risks may include, but are not limited to, margin/mark-to-market cash calls, currency exchange, liquidity, unlimited asset exposure, and counter-party risk. Future investments may be made under different economic conditions, in different global growth-based securities and related strategies. McKinley Capital's proprietary investment process considers factors such as additional guidelines, restrictions, weightings, allocations, market conditions, and other investment characteristics. Thus, returns may at times materially differ from the stated benchmark and/or other disciplines and funds provided for comparison.

Charts, graphs, and other visual presentations and text information were derived from internal, proprietary, and/or service vendor technology sources and/or may have been extracted from other firm data-bases. As a result, the tabulation of certain reports may not precisely match other published data.

Data may have originated from various sources including, but not limited to, Bloomberg, TQA, APT, Zephyr, and/or other similar systems and programs. "FTSE®", "Russell®", "MTS®", "FTSE TMX®", and "FTSE Russell" and other service marks and trademarks related to the FTSE or Russell indexes are trademarks of the London Stock Exchange Group companies. All rights in these indices vest in FTSE and/or its licensors. Neither FTSE nor its licensors accept any liability for any errors or omissions in the FTSE Indices or underlying data.

With regards to materials, if any, accredited to MSCI®: Neither MSCI nor any other party involved in or related to compiling, computing, or creating the MSCI data makes any express or implied warranties or representations with respect to such data (or the results to be obtained by the use thereof), and all such parties hereby expressly disclaim all warranties of originality, accuracy, completeness, merchantability, or fitness for a particular purpose with respect to any of such data. Without limiting any of the foregoing, in no event shall MSCI, any of its affiliates, or any third party involved in or related to compiling, computing, or creating the data have any liability for any direct, indirect, special, punitive, consequential, or any other damages (including lost profits) even if notified of the possibility of such damages. No further distribution or dissemination of the MSCI data is permitted without MSCI's express written consent. Please refer to the specific service provider's website for complete details on all indices. McKinley Capital makes no representation or endorsement concerning the accuracy or propriety of information received from any third party. All information is believed to be correct, but accuracy cannot be guaranteed. Clients should rely on their custodial statements for the official investment activity records. Clients should contact their custodian with any questions regarding monthly/quarterly receipt of those statements.

Fees are billed monthly or quarterly, which produces a compounding effect on the total rate of return net of management fees. As an example, the quarterly effect of investment management fees on the total value of a client's portfolio assuming (a) $1,000,000 investment, (b) portfolio return of 5% a year, and (c) 1.00% annual investment advisory fee would be $10,038 in the first year, and cumulative effects of $51,210 over 5 years and $110,503 over 10 years. Actual client fees vary. A fee schedule, available upon request, is described in the firm's Form ADV part 2A. To receive a copy of the firm's Form ADV Part 2A or a description of all McKinley Capital's composites, please contact McKinley Capital at 3301 C Street, Suite 500, Anchorage AK 99503 or 1.907.563.4488.

All information is believed to be correct, but accuracy cannot be guaranteed.

https://doi.org/10.1142/9789811222634_bmatter

Index

B

D

G

K

P

Q

R

S

W

Y

Z

www.ingramcontent.com/pod-product-compliance
Lightning Source LLC
LaVergne TN
LVHW010321220926
848484LV00004BB/820

9789811216725